CONTRACT: CASES AND MATERIALS

THIRD EDITION

CONTRACT: CASES AND MATERIALS

THIRD EDITION

by

John AK Huntley

Published in 2015 by W.Green, 21 Alva Street,
Edinburgh EH2 4PS
Part of Thomson Reuters (Professional) UK Limited
(Registered in England & Wales, Company No 1679046. Registered Office and address for service:
2nd Floor, 1 Mark Square, Leonard Street, London EC2A 4EG)

Typeset by YHT Ltd, London
Printed and bound in the UK by CPI Group (UK) Ltd, Croydon, CR0 4YY

No natural forests were destroyed to make this product; only
farmed timber was used and replanted.

A CIP catalogue record for this title is available from the British Library

ISBN 978-0-414-03113-5

ACKNOWLEDGEMENTS

I wish to express my thanks to Dr Gillian Black, Professor John Blackie and Professor Hector MacQueen. Their help and advice was extremely helpful and gratefully received.

I must especially thank Janet Campbell at Greens, without whom this book would never have reached the shelves. With just the right blend of help, encouragement and forbearance she got me there. My sincere thanks also to Ciara Daly for her excellent editing and the imaginative changes she helped make to presentation and layout. I am also very grateful to Thomson Reuters for so generously giving me access to Westlaw, without which the writing of this edition would have been a much slower process.

Finally, my thanks to my wife, Christine, for her gentle encouragement and support.

PREFACE TO THE THIRD EDITION

More than a decade has passed since the last edition. It was written in difficult personal circumstances and I remain grateful to Professor John Blackie and Craig Cathcart for their help. Since then I had retired with a question mark over my health and few links with academic life. I was surprised when Janet Campbell asked me to write a new edition. I agreed to do it for two reasons: I believed I could improve on previous editions; and I hope to leave something useful for a new generation of law students in Scotland.

So much has changed since 2005. The case law has developed and expanded apace, with new emphases, such as the interpretation of contracts, the law of error and the role of intention in the creation of contracts. The Scottish Law Commission has issued several important Discussion Papers and Reports under its Review of the Law of Contract in the Light of the DCFR, some of which have already resulted in legislation by the Scottish Parliament. The UK Parliament has also been active, most notably in the Consumer Rights Act 2015, which came very late in the writing of this edition. That Act was a consolidation of European Union legislation and this, together with the development of the DCFR, has introduced many changes, actual and potential.

This edition has been substantially rewritten to accommodate these developments. Also, 10 years of reflection has led me to revise, sometimes fundamentally most of the content.

There are also changes in presentation. This book remains a sourcebook of cases and other materials. It is not a textbook. It is an edited version of cases and other materials and for that I take full responsibility. The editing is intended to introduce the student to the material as a readable and cohesive whole. It is not a substitute for the primary sources, which diligent students will read for themselves. Even when most source material is accessible at the touch of a keyboard button, there is still room for presentation of such material in a single book in hard copy.

The text between extracts is intended not only as a commentary and guide to the material, but also to provide continuity between extracts. The stress remains on the cases and materials and for that reason it is now presented in shaded format. Author's comments are not shaded. This innovation will also hopefully help the text as a whole to flow better. The introduction of paragraph numbering should help greatly with referencing and searching the text.

John AK Huntley
November 2015

CONTENTS

TABLE OF CASES

TABLE OF STATUTES

TABLE OF SCOTTISH STATUTES

TABLE OF STATUTORY INSTRUMENTS

TABLE OF SCOTTISH STATUTORY INSTRUMENTS

TABLE OF EU AND INTERNATIONAL MATERIAL

PART 1

INTRODUCTION

CHAPTER 1

GENERAL PRINCIPLES

Contracts are just one category of obligations recognised and given legal effect by the law of Scotland. It is necessary at the outset to distinguish contracts from other legal obligations. **1–01**

For the time being, it is enough to note that the primary distinguishing feature of a contractual obligation is that it is based on agreement, objectively established between at least two parties.

A contract is a voluntary obligation based on agreement

An obligation is contractual only if it is voluntarily undertaken. Thus an obligation imposed by statute could never form the basis of a contract, nor give rise to contractual remedies if breached. That obligation would arise from the authority of the statute itself, which normally will also stipulate the consequences of failing to comply. Similarly, obligations imposed by the law of delict, such as that imposed on a driver of a vehicle not to drive negligently, are not voluntarily assumed. A person may owe to another an obligation, voluntarily assumed; but it will only be a contractual obligation if it is based on the consent of *both* parties. Contracts are therefore *voluntary* obligations which are based on agreement. The essentially consensual nature of contract was emphasised by the Institutional writers. According to Stair, "Conventional [contractual] obligations do arise from our will and consent".[1] For the purposes of legal analysis, this means that evidence of agreement between the parties, or *consensus in idem*, is an essential element of a contract; although agreement is not the only essential of a contract.[2] **1–02**

The basis for this view is the so-called "will theory" of contract: a contract can only exist if it is the free expression of the will of the parties. This is, from one perspective, a highly subjective matter: a contract would only arise if both parties clearly willed it. Could a party refuse to perform by claiming that it was never that party's intention to perform, or that the agreement was made under the influence of alcohol, or at a time when, due to age or mental or economic distress, that party was vulnerable to undue pressure by the other party?[3]

Who can enter into voluntary obligations?

Capacity to make contracts is an aspect of the law of persons. Thus, Title II of Book I of Erskine's *Institute* begins: **1–03**

> "The objects of law, or the matters of which it treats, are three: *First*, Persons; *2dly* Things, or rights ...; *3dly* Actions ... "[4]

He devotes four Titles to the status of judges and the clergy and then:

> "After having treated of the several ranks of persons as they are distinguished by their public characters, they may be considered in their more private capacities, as husband and wife, father and child, tutor and pupil, master and servant."[5]

---

[1] Erskine, *Institute*, I.x.1.
[2] This aspect is considered in the next chapter.
[3] These matters are considered separately in Ch.5, "The Exertion of Pressure or Influence".
[4] Erskine, *Institute*, 1.2.1.
[5] Erskine, *Institute*, 1.4.1.

In that context, he also deals with the limited capacity of "idiots, furious and imbecilic persons".[6] He does not deal with capacity when considering contracts.[7]

It can be difficult for a 21st century reader to understand that, even in Erskine's day, a person's capacity to contract (among other things) was determined by status—whether the status of a spouse, a child, a servant, an idiot, etc. It was still a society with feudal overtones, where dominion and patronage by one person over another was accepted as normal. The laissez faire environment of the 19th century replaced status with contract. People's relationships with each other were increasingly based on contract, not status. At its most extreme, this led to the exploitation of workers, including children and increasingly of consumers through contracts that took much from them, but gave less in return. From the early 19th century to the present day much employment, safety and consumer legislation has tried to redress the balance.

There has always been in the law an underlying purpose to protect certain categories of people from exploitation, including exploitation by contracts. Courts have in the past insisted that certain categories of persons are incapable of consenting. The guiding principle is whether the agreement or the party in question falls into a category where it is unsafe to assume that consent was freely given. These rules, not unnaturally, tend to reflect the social realities of the day and have changed over the years. Until 1920,[8] for example, it was presumed that a woman, upon marriage, lost her power to contract. Her husband, upon the marriage, became her curator and she could no longer contract without her husband's consent. The presumption was that she came under the total dominion of her husband. Any vestiges of this view of marriage were swept away by the Law Reform (Husband and Wife) (Scotland) Act 1984.

Children and young persons form the only category of any significance that does not have power to contract. Since the Age of Legal Capacity (Scotland) Act 1991, only children below the age of 16 lack the capacity to contract, with limited exceptions. Young persons aged 16 and 17 have full capacity to contract, with certain protective provisions. The matter of contractual capacity—even the contractual capacity of children—thus no longer requires extensive treatment in a casebook on contract. In particular, the Children (Scotland) Act 1995 instituted major reforms in the law relating to children, establishing a statutory regime of which the Age of Legal Capacity (Scotland) Act 1991 and the capacity of children and young persons to make contracts is a part. The subject is now so extensive and detailed that it better constitutes part of family law and is best studied in relevant family law texts.[9]

1–04 Contracts made by, or on behalf of adults with incapacity are now largely regulated by statute.[10] Detailed discussion of the limits on the capacity of corporate and unincorporated bodies is beyond the scope of this book[11] and there are many other limitations on contractual capacity that are best treated elsewhere.[12]

Age of Legal Capacity (Scotland) Act 1991

"1.—(1) As from the commencement of this Act—

---

[6] Erskine, *Institute*, 1.4.48 onwards.

[7] Erskine, *Institute*, 3.1.

[8] By a series of statutes, beginning with the Conjugal Rights (Scotland) Amendment Act 1861 and culminating in the Married Women's Property (Scotland) Act 1920, the common law limitations on a married woman's powers to contract were abolished.

[9] See particularly J Thomson, *Family Law in Scotland*, 7th edn (London: Bloomsbury, 2014), particularly Ch.10.

[10] Adults with Incapacity (Scotland) Act 2000. For the effect of mental illness and intoxication on the capacity to make or perform contracts see WW McBryde, *The Law of Contract in Scotland*, 3rd edn (Edinburgh: W. Green, 2007) paras 3–40—3–55.

[11] WW McBryde, *The Law of Contract in Scotland*, 3rd edn (Edinburgh: W. Green, 2007) paras 3–60—3–117 deals at length with contractual capacity of such bodies.

[12] See generally WW McBryde, *The Law of Contract in Scotland*, 3rd edn (Edinburgh: W. Green, 2007), Ch.4.

(a) a person under the age of 16 years shall, subject to section 2 below, have no legal capacity to enter into any transaction;
(b) a person of or over the age of 16 years shall have legal capacity to enter into any transaction.

(2) Subject to section 8 below, any reference in any enactment to a pupil (other than in the context of education or training) or to a person under legal disability or incapacity by reason of nonage shall, insofar as it relates to any time after the commencement of this Act, be construed as a reference to a person under the age of 16 years.

(3) Nothing in this Act shall—

(a) apply to any transaction entered into before the commencement of this Act;
(b) confer any legal capacity on any person who is under legal disability or incapacity other than by reason of nonage;
(c) affect the delictual or criminal responsibility of any person;
(d) affect any enactment which lays down an age limit expressed in years for any particular purpose;
(e) prevent any person under the age of 16 years from receiving or holding any right, title or interest;
(f) affect any existing rule of law or practice whereby—

(i) any civil proceedings may be brought or defended, or any step in civil proceedings may be taken, in the name of a person under the age of 16 years [in relation to whom there is no person entitled to act as his legal representative (within the meaning of Part I of the Children (Scotland) Act 1995), or where there is such a person] is unable (whether by reason of conflict of interest or otherwise) or refuses to bring or defend such proceedings or take such step;
(ii) the court may, in any civil proceedings, appoint a curator ad litem to a person under the age of 16 years;
(iii) the court may, in relation to the approval of an arrangement under section 1 of the Trusts (Scotland) Act 1961, appoint a curator ad litem to a person of or over the age of 16 years but under the age of 18 years;
(iv) the court may appoint a curator bonis to any person;

(g) prevent any person under the age of 16 years from [exercising parental responsibilities and parental rights (within the meaning of sections 1(3) and 2(4) respectively of the Children (Scotland) Act 1995) in relation to any child of his.]

(4) Any existing rule of law relating to the legal capacity of minors and pupils which is inconsistent with the provisions of this Act shall cease to have effect.

(5) Any existing rule of law relating to reduction of a transaction on the ground of minority and lesion shall cease to have effect.

2.—(1) A person under the age of 16 years shall have legal capacity to enter into a transaction—

(a) of a kind commonly entered into by persons of his age and circumstances, and
(b) on terms which are not unreasonable.

(2) A person of or over the age of 12 years shall have testamentary capacity, including legal capacity to exercise by testamentary writing any power of appointment.

. . .

(5) Any transaction—

(a) which a person under the age of 16 years purports to enter into after the commencement of this Act, and

(b) in relation to which that person does not have legal capacity by virtue of this section, shall be void.

3.—(1) A person under the age of 21 years ("the applicant") may make application to the court to set aside a transaction which he entered into while he was of or over the age of 16 years but under the age of 18 years and which is a prejudicial transaction.

(2) In this section "prejudicial transaction" means a transaction which—

(a) an adult, exercising reasonable prudence, would not have entered into in the circumstances of the applicant at the time of entering into the transaction, and
(b) has caused or is likely to cause substantial prejudice to the applicant.

(3) Subsection (1) above shall not apply to—

. . .

(d) the bringing or defending of, or the taking of any step in, civil proceedings;

. . .

(f) a transaction in the course of the applicant's trade, business or profession;
(g) a transaction into which any other party was induced to enter by virtue of any fraudulent misrepresentation by the applicant as to age or other material fact;
(h) a transaction ratified by the applicant after he attained the age of 18 years and in the knowledge that it could be the subject of an application to the court under this section to set it aside; or
(j) a transaction ratified by the court under section 4 below.

(4) Where an application to set aside a transaction can be made or could have been made under this section by the person referred to in subsection (1) above, such application may instead be made by that person's executor, trustee in bankruptcy, trustee acting under a trust deed for creditors or curator bonis at any time prior to the date on which that person attains or would have attained the age of 21 years.

(5) An application under this section to set aside a transaction may be made—

(a) by an action in the Court of Session or the sheriff court, or
(b) by an incidental application in other proceedings in such court, and the court may make an order setting aside the transaction and such further order, if any, as seems appropriate to the court in order to give effect to the rights of the parties.

4.—(1) Where a person of or over the age of 16 years but under the age of 18 years proposes to enter into a transaction which, if completed, could be the subject of an application to the court under section 3 above to set aside, all parties to the proposed transaction may make a joint application to have it ratified by the court.

(2) The court shall not grant an application under this section if it appears to the court that an adult, exercising reasonable prudence and in the circumstances of the person referred to in subsection (1) above, would not enter into the transaction.

(3) An application under this section shall be made by means of a summary application—

(a) to the sheriff of the sheriffdom in which any of the parties to the proposed transaction resides, or
(b) where none of the said parties resides in Scotland, to the sheriff at Edinburgh, and the decision of the sheriff on such application shall be final."

Formalities in contracting

1–05 The common law of Scotland had complex and elaborate rules to determine the formalities required for some obligations. Those rules had developed accretions so complex and so numerous that they had become an impediment. It is an achievement of the Scottish Law

Commission that those rules have now been simplified into a simple yet effective scheme of formalities that preserves the balance between the need to protect the parties and the need to protect the public. The original scheme in the Requirements of Writing (Scotland) Act 1995 was updated by the Land Registration etc. (Scotland) Act 2012 to include a scheme for electronic documents—probably one of the most advanced and comprehensive schemes on the subject. The following annotation by Professor Reid more than meets the needs of the student of general principles of contract law.

Requirements of Writing (Scotland) Act 1995 (1995 c.7)[13]

"INTRODUCTION AND GENERAL NOTE **1–06**

This Act implements most of the recommendations of the Scottish Law Commission's Report on Requirements of Writing, which was published in July 1988 (Scot. Law Com. No. 112). A previous Requirements of Writing Bill was introduced to the House of Commons on April 26, 1989 by a Private Member but did not proceed beyond its first reading. The Act substantially follows the text of this earlier Bill and, less directly, of the draft Bill attached to the Scottish Law Commission's Report. It has since been amended on a number of occasions, most notably by the Land Registration etc. (Scotland Act 2012 (asp 5) ss.96–98 and Sch.3 (and coming largely into force on either May 11, 2014 or December 8, 2014) to the effect of allowing the written documents required by the Act to be made in electronic form. This implements Pt 34 of the Scottish Law Commission's Report on Land Registration (The Stationery Office, 2010), Scot. Law Com. No.222.

The Act sweeps away a great deal of archaic and obscure law, much of it based on statutes of the pre-Union Scots Parliament, and presents in its place a coherent and systematic scheme for the execution of deeds and other documents under the law of Scotland. The Act deals with six [*sic*] main topics.

(1) *The requirement for writing.* Section 1 of the Act simplifies and re-states in modern language the rule of the common law that formally executed writing is required (a) for the constitution of certain types of contracts and other obligations (the so-called *obligationes literis*), (b) for the performance of certain juristic acts in relation to land, and (c) for the making of a will or other testamentary disposition. At the same time s.11(l) (now repealed) abolishes the rule whereby certain other obligations, although capable of constitution without writing, could only be proved by writ or oath. Homologation is also abolished, and the principles of rei interventus are restated in modern language.

(2) *Traditional documents and electronic documents.* As originally enacted, the 1995 Act made provision only for what are now called, after amendment, "traditional" documents, that is to say, documents written on paper, parchment or other similar tangible surface. In 2006, limited provision for "electronic" documents was added but restricted to documents used within the e-registration system known as automated registration of title to land ("ARTL"). After further amendment to the Act which took effect in 2014, electronic documents can now be used instead of traditional documents in all cases, although this facility has not yet been brought into force in respect of wills and other testamentary deeds.

(3) *Execution of deeds: the minimum formalities.* Before the 1995 Act there were three methods by which a deed or other document could be formally executed: (a) the deed was subscribed by the granter and attested by two witnesses

[13] Annotations by Kenneth GC Reid, MA, LLB, Solicitor, Professor of Property Law at the University of Edinburgh, see Kenneth GC Reid, *Requirements of Writing (Scotland) Act*, 2nd edn (Edinburgh: W. Green, 2015).

(attested writing); (b) it was in the handwriting of and subscribed by the granter (holograph writing); or (c) it was subscribed by the granter with the addition of the holograph docquet (adopted as holograph). The 1995 Act abolishes all three methods. In their place there is now only one method of formal execution: s.2 provides that a deed is formally valid if it is subscribed by the granter. Witnesses are not required. This new method of execution is mandatory in all cases where s.1(2) requires writing and it is optional in the case of any other obligation or juridical act.

For traditional deeds, the Act also contains provisions defining the meaning of signature (s.7), and allowing for "notarial" execution on behalf of a person who is blind or unable to write (s.9). By contrast, the definition of electronic signature is left to regulations (s.9(B)(2)(c)), thus providing the flexibility needed to accommodate future changes in technology.

(4) *Execution of deeds: presumption of valid execution.* A deed which is merely subscribed under s.2 or authenticated by an electronic signature under s.9B is not self-evidencing (or "probative", in traditional vocabulary). This means that the onus of proving that such a deed truly was subscribed by the granter would rest on any person who wished to rely on its terms. However, a deed may be made self-evidencing by attestation by a single witness (in the case of traditional deeds) or by third-party certification (in the case of electronic deeds). For traditional deeds, s.3(1) provides that a deed which bears to be subscribed by the granter and attested by the signature of one witness is presumed to have been subscribed by the granter. Similarly if the deed or testing clause contains information as to date and place of execution, the deed is presumed to have been executed on that date and at that place (s.3(8)). There is continuity here with the previous law which conferred similar presumptions in relation to attested writings (although under that law two witnesses were required for attestation). There are equivalent provisions for electronic deeds in ss.9C and 9E.

A deed which has not been attested can nevertheless be made self-evidencing by application to the sheriff court (ss.4 and 9D). If the court is satisfied, usually by affidavit evidence, that the deed was subscribed (or, for electronic deeds, authenticated) by the granter, it will grant a decree to that effect and, in the case of a traditional document, cause a docquet to be endorsed on the deed.

In practice, most documents used in normal conveyancing practice are attested or certified, not least because they cannot otherwise be registered (see ss.6 and 9G).

(5) *Annexations and alterations.* For traditional documents, special provision is made for the authentication, both of annexations (such as schedules or plans) attached to deeds (s.8), and also of alterations ("vitiations" in traditional terminology) made to deeds (s.5). In both cases separate provision is made depending upon whether the deed is subscribed only or attested. The Scottish Ministers are empowered to make equivalent provision for electronic documents by regulations (s.9E), and the power has been exercised in resect of annexations (but not, so far, alterations): see the Electronic Documents (Scotland) Regulations 2014 (SSI 2014/83) reg.4.

(6) *Companies and other special categories of granter.* Schedule 2 makes provision for the execution of deeds by (a) partnerships; (b) companies; (c) limited liability partnerships; (d) local authorities; (e) other bodies corporate; and (f) Ministers of the Crown and other office-holders. In all cases there are dual provisions depending on whether the deed is subscribed only or is self-evidencing ("probative"). In the case of some of the categories dealt with in Sch.2, attestation is

not the only method by which a deed can be made self-evidencing. Equivalent provision for electronic documents is made by the Electronic Documents (Scotland) Regulations 2014 reg.5.

Since a juristic person cannot sign personally, a question arises as to the authority of the person who signs on their behalf. Schedule 2 approaches this issue differently in respect of different granters. In some cases (e.g. local authorities) the presumption arising from attestation (or equivalent) is a double presumption, namely (i) that the deed is presumed to have been subscribed by the signatory, and (ii) that the signatory is presumed to have had authority to sign on behalf of the granter. In other cases (e.g. companies) the presumption stops with (i), and the deed is not self-evidencing in relation to authority to sign.

(7) *Wills and other testamentary dispositions.* In general the Act treats wills in the same way as other traditional documents. However, two special rules deserve mention.

First, even where a will is attested by a witness, it is not self-evidencing unless it has been signed by the granter on every sheet (s.3(2)). This simply re-enacts the previous law. By contrast, a will which is subscribed only and not witnessed need not be signed on every sheet.

Secondly, the date and place of execution given in a will are presumed to be correct in all cases, even where the will is not attested (s.3(10)).

The provisions in Pt 3 on electronic documents have not so far been brought into force in respect of wills and other testamentary dispositions. Until such time as they are, wills can only be made in paper-form, in traditional documents.

PART 1

WHEN WRITING IS REQUIRED

Writing required for certain contracts, obligations, trusts, conveyances and wills

[1]1.—(1) Subject to subsection (2) below and any other enactment, writing shall not be required for the constitution of a contract, unilateral obligation or trust. **1–07**

[2,4](2) Subject to subsection (3) below, a written document which is a traditional document complying with section 2 or an electronic document complying with section 9B of this Act shall be required for—

(a) the constitution of—

  (i) a contract or unilateral obligation for the creation, transfer, variation or extinction of a real in land;
  (ii) a gratuitous unilateral obligation except an obligation undertaken in the course of business; and
  (iii) a trust whereby a person declares himself to be sole trustee of his own property or any property which he may acquire;

(b) the creation, transfer, variation or extinction of a real right in land otherwise than by the operation of a court decree, enactment or rule of law;

[5](ba) the constitution of an agreement under section 66(1) of the Land Registration etc. (Scotland) Act 2012 (asp 5), and

(c) the making of any will, testamentary trust disposition and settlement or codicil.

. . .

[3,4](3) Where a contract, obligation or trust mentioned in subsection (2)(a) above is not constituted in a written document complying with section 2 or, as the case may be, section 9B, of this Act, but one of the parties to the contract, a creditor in the obligation or a beneficiary under the trust ("the first person") has acted or refrained from acting in reliance on the contract, obligation or trust with the knowledge and acquiescence of the other party to the contract, the debtor in the obligation or the truster ("the second person")—

(a) the second person shall not be entitled to withdraw from the contract, obligation or trust; and
(b) the contract, obligation or trust shall not be regarded as invalid,

on the ground that it is not so constituted, if the condition set out in subsection (4) below is satisfied.

(4) The condition referred to in subsection (3) above is that the position of the first person—

(a) as a result of acting or refraining from acting as mentioned in that subsection has been affected to a material extent; and
(b) as a result of such a withdrawal as is mentioned in that subsection would be adversely affected to a material extent.

[2,5](5) In relation to the constitution of any contract, obligation or trust mentioned in subsection (2)(a) above, subsections (3) and (4) above replace the rules of law known as *rei interventus* and homologation.

(6) This section shall apply to the variation of a contract, obligation or trust as it applies to the constitution thereof but as if in subsections (3) and (4) for the references to acting or refraining from acting in reliance on the contract, obligation or trust and withdrawing therefrom there were substituted respectively references to acting or refraining from acting in reliance on the variation of the contract, obligation or trust and withdrawing from the variation.

(7) In this section "real right in land" means any real right in or over land, including any right to occupy or to use land or to restrict the occupation or use of land, but does not include—

(a) a tenancy;
(b) a right to occupy or use land; or
(c) a right to restrict the occupation or use of land,

if the tenancy or right is not granted for more than one year, unless the tenancy or right is for a recurring period or recurring periods and there is a gap of more than one year between the beginning of the first, and the end of the last, such period.

(8) For the purposes of subsection (7) above "land" does not include—

(a) growing crops; or
(b) a moveable building or other moveable structure.

NOTES

[1] As amended by the Abolition of Feudal Tenure (Scotland) Act 2000 (asp 5) Sch.12 Pt 1 (effective November 28, 2004).

[2] As amended by the Automated Registration of Title to Land (Electronic Communications) (Scotland) Order 2006 (SSI 2006/491) art.3 (effective October 5, 2006).

[3] Inserted by the Automated Registration of Title to Land (Electronic Communications) (Scotland) Order 2006 (SSI 2006/491) art.3 (effective October 5, 2006).

[4] As amended by the Land Registration etc. (Scotland) Act 2012 (asp 5) Pt 10 s.96 (effective May 11, 2014 as per SSSI 2014/41 Sch.1(2); December 8, 2014 otherwise).

[5] Inserted by the Land Registration etc. (Scotland) Act 2012 (asp 5) Pt 10 s.96 (effective December 8, 2014).

GENERAL NOTE 1–08

This section makes far-reaching alterations to the law relating to the use of writing in the constitution and variation of contracts and other voluntary obligations. It also makes provision for the use of writing for conveyances and other dealings in relation to land, and for the making of wills. The section should be read together with s.11 (now repealed) which abolished the rule by which certain voluntary obligations, though capable of oral constitution, might only be proved by writ or oath.

Subs.(1) 1–09

This reaffirms the basic rule of the common law that voluntary obligations may be constituted without writing. The common law exceptions to that rule—known collectively as the *obligationes literis*—are abolished by s.11(3)(a) (now repealed) and are replaced by the new statutory list set out in subs.(2)(a).

Any other enactment. For example, the Consumer Credit Act 1974 (c.39), s.60, provides that regulated consumer credit agreements and consumer hire agreements shall be constituted in a prescribed written form and with a prescribed content.

Unilateral obligation. Section 1 distinguishes unilateral obligations from contracts. The only unilateral obligation recognised in Scots law is a promise.

See *Pesimmon Homes Ltd v Bellway Homes Ltd* [2011] CSOH 149.

Subs.(2) 1–10

Where subs.(2) applies, not only must there be writing but the writing must be in a form which complies with s.2 (traditional documents) or s.9B (electronic documents). A written document complies with s.2 if it is subscribed by the granter; it complies with s.9B if it is authenticated by an advanced electronic signature.

Para.(a). Under the previous law certain voluntary obligations, known collectively as 1–11
obligationes literis, could be constituted only in formal writing (that is to say, in writing which was attested, holograph of the granter, or adopted as holograph). These included obligations relating to land, contracts of service for more than a year, submissions to arbitration, and possibly (although the law was open to doubt) contracts of insurance and cautionary obligations. The previous law is abolished by s.11(3)(a) (since repealed), and this paragraph provides in replacement a much abbreviated list of obligations which must continue to be constituted in (formal) writing. The list is exhaustive: obligations which do not appear on the list fall within subs.(1) and do not require written constitution (except in the rare cases where some other statute or statutory instrument provides otherwise). Where writing is required for initial constitution it is also, by subs.(6), required for any subsequent variation of the obligation. The requirement of writing may be displaced in certain circumstances where there have been appropriate actings: see subs.(3).

Subparagraph (i) is narrower than the common law rule it replaces, which required formal writing for *all* obligations relating to heritable property. Paragraph (b) of subs.(2) (see below) provides for writing in the case of the creation, transfer, variation or extinction of a real right in land, and para.(a)(i) simply extends the same rule to any preliminary contract or promise. Common examples of such preliminary obligations are missives for the sale of land, missives of let, and undertakings to grant servitudes. While an offer forming part of a contract requires to be in writing (see also s.2(2)), no corresponding provision is made about the withdrawal of such an offer before it has been accepted and the common law rule that a withdrawal may be made orally continues to apply. See *McMillan v Caldwell*, 1991 S.L.T. 325.

Under the previous law a gratuitous promise could be constituted orally but could be proved only by writ or oath. Proof by writ or oath is abolished by s.11(1) (now repealed), but it is provided by subpara.(ii) that gratuitous unilateral obligations (i.e. promises) must be constituted in writing subscribed by the obligant. This includes (gratuitous) cautionary obligations, so replacing the former, and unclear, rule contained in s.6 of the Mercantile Law Amendment Act 1856 (c.97) (which is repealed by Sch.5). It appears that the rule is not extended to gratuitous contracts (see e.g. *Morton's Tr. v Aged Christian Friend Society of Scotland* (1899) 2 F. 82), and such contracts may therefore be constituted without writing. In practice the majority of unilateral obligations are likely to be gratuitous (see e.g *Gibson v Gibson*, 2010 G.W.D. 30-614). Two which may be argued not to be so are (a) where the obligant enters into the obligation only in virtue of payment by the obligee or by some third party (e.g. a personal bond to repay a loan), and (b) where the obligation is entered into gratuitously but the obligee, while not bound to make payment, cannot enforce the obligation without such payment being made (e.g. an option to buy property). On (b) see further Thomson, "Promises and the Requirement of Writing", 1997 S.L.T. (News) 284, and Hogg, "A Few Tricky Problems Surrounding Unilateral Promises", 1998 S.L.T. (News) 25. The exception for obligations undertaken in the course of business is because businessmen are regarded as less prone to rash and impulsive promises. It is also a shadowy survival of the former privilege (abolished by s.11(3)(b)(ii)) which was accorded to writs in *re mercatoria*. For the arguments in favour of this exception see H.L. MacQueen, "Constitution and Proof of Gratuitous Obligations", 1986 S.L.T. (News) 1. It is thought that only the obligant need act in the course of business.

Subparagraph (iii) is in effect confined to inter vivos trusts.

...

1–12 *Subss.(3)–(5)*

These three subsections apply only to the rights set out in para.(a) of subs.(2) (i.e. certain contracts, promises and trusts). In relation to these rights the personal bar doctrines of *rei interventus* and homologation are abolished by subs.(5) and replaced by a statutory version of *rei interventus*, set out in subss.(3) and (4). There is no statutory counterpart of homologation, which thus disappears as a legal doctrine. In general the need for personal bar will be lessened by the reduction in the formalities in execution effected by s.2 of the Act.

Subsections (3) and (4) re-enact the common law rules of *rei interventus*, but in a simplified form. For a detailed analysis see E. Reid and J. Blackie, *Personal Bar* (2006), Ch.7. Under the new rules a contract, promise or trust will not fail for lack of formal validity where it has been followed by significant actings. More specifically, a party is personally barred from withdrawing from an informal contract (or promise or trust) if (i) the other party has acted or refrained from acting in reliance on the contract, (ii) to the knowledge of and with the acquiescence of the party now seeking to withdraw, and (iii) the actings (or absence of actings) have been material such that the other party would be prejudiced by such withdrawal. The new wording follows quite closely the personal bar provisions in relation to rectification of defectively expressed documents contained in s.9(2) of the Law Reform (Miscellaneous Provisions) (Scotland) Act 1985 (c.73). The most important change in the law is the removal, by s.11(1) (now repealed), of the need to prove the informal contract by writ or oath. Now there is no restriction as to proof and in many cases the actings which evidence personal bar are likely to be used to evidence also the fact of agreement. Under the new law the oral promise in *Smith v Oliver*, 1911 S.C. 103 (to make a will bequeathing money to pay for improvements to a church, which was then followed by actings) would have been perfectly enforceable.

The new personal bar provisions are confined to the rights listed in para. (a) of subs. (2), and so do not apply to para.(b) and para.(c) rights. At common law personal bar was also available in respect of para.(b) rights, i.e. real rights in land. See e.g. *Clark's Exr. v. Cameron*

1982 S.L.T. 68. An important change is that personal bat is no longer available for leases (as opposed to contracts for the grant of a lease): see *The Advice Centre for Mortgages v McNicoll*, 2006 S.L.T. 591.

The Act's silence on this subject may give rise to the argument that the common law of *rei interventus* and homologation is preserved in relation to para.(b) rights, so that for example a lease could continue to be set up by homologation. In support of this argument it might be pointed out that the abolition of *rei interventus* and homologation in subs.(5) is expressly confined to para.(a) rights. The alternative and, it is submitted, the better view is that the bald and unqualified statement in subs.(2) that writing is required for para.(b) rights has the effect of excluding the common law of personal bar. See *The Advice Centre for Mortgages v McNicoll*, 2006 S.L.T. 591 per Lord Drummond Young at para.22. That was certainly the intention of the Scottish Law Commission: see Scot. Law Com. No. 112, para.2.50. Assuming this to be correct, it is possible to question the policy assumptions on which the change in the law is based. The Commission argued that if a deed intended to create a real right failed for lack of formality, the grantee would be able to rely on the antecedent contract, which could itself, if necessary, be set up by personal bar. There are two difficulties with this argument. One is that in some cases where real rights are being created there is no such antecedent contract (as in the case of a lease constituted only by missives of let and without a preliminary contract). The other is that there may have been supervening insolvency of the granter which would prevent the enforcement of any contract.

Subs.(6) **1–13**

Writing formally executed under s.2 or s.9B of the Act is required for the variation of the contracts, obligations and trusts listed in para.(a) of subs.(2). Writing is not required for their extinction.

...

PART 2 **1–14**

TRADITIONAL DOCUMENTS

Application of Part 2

[1]**1A.** This Part of this Act applies to documents written on paper, parchment or some similar tangible surface ("traditional documents").

NOTE

[1] Inserted by the Land Registration etc. (Scotland) Act 2012 (asp 5) Sch.3 para.2 (effective December 8, 2014).

GENERAL NOTE **1–15**

... Tangible surfaces which are not "similar"—sand on a beach, for example or a bar of soap—do not qualify. Th rules for the other type of permitted document, "electronic documents", are set out in Pt 3.

Type of writing required for formal validity of certain documents

2.—[1](1) No traditional document required by section 1(2) of this Act shall be valid in respect of the formalities of execution unless it is subscribed by the granter of it or, if there is more than one granter, by each granter, but nothing apart from such subscription shall be required for the document to be valid as aforesaid.

(2) A contract mentioned in section 1(2)(a)(i) of this Act may be regarded as constituted or varied (as the case may be) if the offer is contained in one or more traditional documents and the acceptance is contained in another traditional document or other traditional documents, and each such document is subscribed by the granter or granters thereof.

(3) Nothing in this section shall prevent a traditional document which has not been subscribed by the granter or granters of it from being used as evidence in relation to any right or obligation to which the document relates.

(4) This section is without prejudice to any other enactment which makes different provision in respect of the formalities of execution of a document to which this section applies.

NOTE

[1] As amended by the Land Registration etc. (Scotland) Act 2012 (asp 5) Sch.3 paras3 and 4 (effective May 11, 2014).

1–16 GENERAL NOTE

This provision effects a radical change in, and simplification of, the previous law. Under that law a "traditional" (i.e. paper or equivalent) document was formally valid if it was either (i) subscribed by the granter and by two witnesses, or (ii) holograph of and subscribed by the granter, or (iii) subscribed by the granter who was also required to write the words "adopted as holograph". In addition, writs in re mercatoria, an obscure and uncertain category, were formally valid if they were subscribed by the granter (only).

This whole complicated structure is swept away by the 1995 Act. Section 11(3)(b) abolishes the special status attached to documents which are holograph or adopted as holograph or in *re mercatoria*; and s.3 re-casts the rules for attestation by witnesses. Section 2 introduces a single type of formally valid document to replace the three types of document mentioned above. Under s.2 a document is formally valid if it is subscribed by the granter. No further steps are required. However, the addition of a witness, although not improving on the formal validity of a document, will confer the benefit of a presumption under s.3 that the document was indeed subscribed by the granter. The equivalent provisions for electronic documents are s.9B (formal validity) and s.9C (presumption of authentication).

1–17 *Subs.(1)*

This sets out a universal rule for formal validity of a traditional document. The rule is mandatory only in relation to the documents required to be in writing by s.1(2), but even in other cases parties may elect—or be taken to have elected—that their agreement should be reduced to a document subscribed in accordance with this subsection. The rule in subs.(1) makes no distinction between cases where the granter is a natural person and cases where the granter is a juristic person, although the actual mechanics of subscription (see s.7) are necessarily different in the two cases. The previous law is preserved by which a granter who is blind or unable to write may subscribe through the agency of a solicitor or certain other categories of authorised person (see s.9), while s.12(2) continues the common law rule by which an agent acting under a power of attorney may subscribe on behalf of his principal.

It has been held that a provision to the effect that documentation must be probative or self-proving writing will not preclude effect being given to a subscribed writing which is not probative or self-proving (*Gibson v Royal Bank of Scotland Plc*, 2009 S.L.T. 444).

1–18 *Subs.(2)*

Subsection (1) takes as its model a single document, for example a will or a declaration of trust. However, in practice contracts often comprise a series of letters or documents; an offer, a qualified acceptance, a further qualified acceptance, and so on until the final acceptance is given. Subsection (2) makes clear that such a contract is formally valid provided that each constituent letter or document is subscribed by the "granter", i.e. by the person issuing that letter or document. This does no more than re-state the existing law. The equivalent provisions for electronic documents is s.9B(3).

. . .

Subs.(3) 1–19

This provision is inserted for the avoidance of doubt. In practice an unsubscribed document might be useful evidence of the terms of an agreement or other juristic act conferring rights. In the small number of cases where the right fell within s.1(2) and required subscribed writing, the absence of the proper formalities might then be cured by actings under s.1(3). The equivalent provisions for electronic documents is s.9B(5).

Subs.(4) 1–20

In particular cases statute may make more, or less, onerous the rules of formal validity. An example of the former is the general provision in para.1(1) of Sch.4 in terms of which any reference in any enactment to a probative document is to be construed as a reference to a document in conformity with s.6(2) or s.9G(2). A document is not in conformity with s.6(2) where it has merely been subscribed, or authenticated with an electronic signature, by the granter.

Presumption as to granter's subscription or date or place of subscription

3.—(1) Subject to subsections (2) to (7) below, where—

[1](a) a traditional document bears to have been subscribed by a granter of it;
(b) the document bears to have been signed by a person as a witness of that granter's subscription and the document, or the testing clause or its equivalent, bears to state the name and address of the witness; and
(c) nothing in the document, or in the testing clause or its equivalent, indicates—
  (i) that it was not subscribed by that granter as it bears to have been so subscribed; or
  (ii) that it was not validly witnessed for any reason specified in paragraphs (a) to (e) of subsection (4) below, the document shall be presumed to have been subscribed by that granter.

. . .

(3) For the purposes of subsection (1)(b) above—

. . .

(b) the name and address of a witness need not be written by the witness himself.

. . .

NOTE

[1] As amended by the Land Registration etc. (Scotland) Act 2012 (asp 5) Sch.3 para.6 (effective May 11, 2014).

GENERAL NOTE 1–21

This section provides for the attestation of "traditional" (i.e. paper or equivalent) documents by witnesses. By contrast to the previous law (where two witnesses were necessary) only a single witness is required, thus bringing the rules for instrumentary witnesses into line with the Civil Evidence (Scotland) Act 1988 (c. 32), s.l, which abolished the requirement of corroboration in civil proceedings. In most other respects the rules of attestation are unchanged, and much of s.3 is a statutory restatement of rules originally introduced by the Subscription of Deeds Act 1681 and later developed by the common law.

The main difference between the new law and the old law lies in function rather than in form. Under the old law attestation by witnesses had two distinct functions. In the first place it made the document formally valid. In the second place it made the deed self-evidencing or "probative", that is to say, it gave rise to an evidential presumption of formal validity such that a person founding on a deed which appeared to have been validly attested was relieved of having to lead evidence as to that validity. Under the new law only the second function remains. By s.2 a traditional document is already formally valid from the moment that it is subscribed by the granter. Attestation adds nothing to formal validity. However, once a document has been attested by a witness it carries an evidential presumption under s.3(l) that it was subscribed by the granter.

A significant advantage of the new law is that a defect in attestation does not affect the formal validity of the deed. As long as the granter has subscribed, the deed is valid. By contrast, the old law was obliged to grade defects in execution as either "informalities of execution" (which could be cured by s.39 of the Conveyancing (Scotland) Act 1874 (c.94)) or as more serious defects (which could not be cured and which therefore rendered the deed invalid). Section 39 of the 1874 Act is now repealed and there is no direct equivalent in the new law.

At first sight, s.3 may seem to be set out in a strange and unhelpful way. The key to understanding the section is the realisation that it is concerned exclusively with matters evidential. The question of whether a deed has in fact been properly executed is a question for s.2. The question of whether a traditional document has in fact been properly executed is a question for s.2. The question of whether a document is presumed to have been properly executed is a question for s.3. The presumption is activated (as under the former law) if the deed appears to have been validly attested. The requirements as to appearance which have to be satisfied are set out in subss.(1)–(3). Once activated, the presumption is rebuttable by establishing in court proceedings that the deed was not validly attested due to some latent factor not apparent on the face of the deed. An exhaustive list of possible latent factors is given in subss.(4)–(7). As already noted, invalid attestation does not of itself mean invalid execution. A deed is invalid only if it was not in fact subscribed by the granter. The effect of establishing that the attestation was invalid is simply to alter the onus of proof by extinguishing the presumption of valid execution. Thereafter the onus of showing formal validity rests on the person seeking to found on the deed.

The final three subsections (subss.(8)–(10)) are concerned with ancillary presumptions in relation to date and place of execution . . .

Subscription and signing

7.—[2](1) Except where an enactment expressly provides otherwise, a traditional document is subscribed by a granter of it if it is signed by him at the end of the last page (excluding any annexation, whether or not incorporated in the document as provided for in section 8 of this Act).

[2](2) Subject to paragraph 2(2) of Schedule 2 to this Act, a traditional document, or an alteration to such a document, is signed by an individual natural person as a granter or on behalf of a granter of it if it is signed by him—

(a) with the full name by which he is identified in the document or in any testing clause or its equivalent; or
(b) with his surname, preceded by at least one forename (or an initial or abbreviation or familiar form of a forename); or

(c) except for the purposes of section 3(1) to (7) of this Act, with a name (not in accordance with paragraph (a) or
(b) above) or description or an initial or mark if it is established that the name, description, initial or mark—

(i) was his usual method of signing, or his usual method of signing documents or alterations of the type in question; or
(ii) was intended by him as his signature of the document or alteration.

(3) Where there is more than one granter, the requirement under subsection (1) above of signing at the end of the last page of a document shall be regarded as complied with if at least one granter signs at the end of the last page and any other granter signs on an additional page.

[2](4) Where a person grants a traditional document in more than one capacity, one subscription of the document by him shall be sufficient to bind him in all such capacities.

[2](5) A traditional document, or an alteration to such a document, is signed by a witness if it is signed by him—

(a) with the full name by which he is identified in the document or in any testing clause or its equivalent; or
(b) with his surname, preceded by at least one forename (or an initial or abbreviation or familiar form of a forename), and if the witness is witnessing the signature of more than one granter, it shall be unnecessary for him to sign the document or alteration more than once.

(6) This section is without prejudice to any rule of law relating to the subscription or signing of documents by members of the Royal Family, by peers or by the wives or the eldest sons of peers.

[1,2](7) Schedule 2 to this Act (special rules relating to subscription and signing of traditional documents etc by partnerships, companies, local authorities, other bodies corporate and Ministers) shall have effect.

NOTE

[1] As amended by Limited Liability Partnerships (Scotland) Regulations 2001 (SSI 2001/128), Sch. 1 para.4 (effective April 6, 2001).

[2] As amended by the Land Registration etc. (Scotland) Act 2012 (asp 5) Sch.3 para.14 (effective December 8, 2014).

GENERAL NOTE 1–22

Section 7 begins by defining subscription as the signature of a traditional document at the end of the last page. Thereafter the section is mainly concerned with prescribing the methods by which a natural person may sign. Parallel provision for signatures by juristic persons and by Ministers of the Crown is made in Sch.2. The new rules as to signature are welcome as introducing relative certainty into an area of law where the existing rules were very far from clear.

Section 7 applies to all "traditional" (i.e. paper or equivalent) documents and not merely to those which are "required" by s.l(2). It is thought that the rules as to signature are intended to be exhaustive and that a signature made in some other way would not be legally effective. If that were not so there would have been no need for the saving provision in subs. (6) for peers and members of the Royal Family. However, the methods of signature permitted by subs. (2) are so wide that this result is unlikely to cause hardship in practice ...

1–23 [1]PART 3

ELECTRONIC DOCUMENTS

NOTE
[1] Inserted by the Land Registration etc. (Scotland) Act 2012 (asp 5) Pt 10 s.97(2) (effective March 22, 2014 for the purpose of making regulations; May 11, 2014 except for purposes specified in SSI 2014/41 Sch.1 Pt 2 subject to transitional provision specified in SSI 2014/41 art.3(2)).

Application of Part 3

9A. This Part applies to documents which, rather than being written on paper, parchment or some similar tangible surface are created in electronic form ("electronic documents").

1–24 GENERAL NOTE
This is the opening provision of the new Pt 3 of the Act, which was added by s.97 of the Land Registration etc. (Scotland) Act 2012 (asp 5). Part 3 is not yet in force in respect of wills, testamentary trust dispositions and settlements, or codicils (i.e. the matters in respect of which writing is required by s.l(2)(c) above); otherwise it has been fully in force since May 11,2014: see SSI 2014/41. The purpose of Pt 3 is to allow the written documents required by s.1 (2) to take electronic form. Thus, except (for the time being at least) in respect of testamentary writings, there is an open choice between paper (or equivalent) documents (now renamed as "traditional" documents, and the subject of Pt 2 of the Act) and the "electronic" documents which are the subject of Pt 3. There are, however, restrictions on the registration of electronic documents in the Land Register, Register of Sasines, and Books of Council and Session: see s.9G.

Validity of electronic documents

9B.—(l) No electronic document required by section 1(2) is valid in respect of the formalities of execution unless—

(a) it is authenticated by the granter, or if there is more than one granter by each granter, in accordance with subsection (2), and
(b) it meets such other requirements (if any) as may be prescribed by the Scottish Ministers in regulations.

(2) An electronic document is authenticated by a person if the electronic signature of that person—

(a) is incorporated into, or logically associated with, the electronic document,
(b) was created by the person by whom it purports to have been created, and
(c) is of such type, and satisfies such requirements (if any), as may be prescribed by the Scottish Ministers in regulations.

(3) A contract mentioned in section 1(2)(a) may be regarded as constituted or varied (as the case may be) if—

(a) the offer is contained in one or more electronic documents,
(b) the acceptance is contained in another electronic document or in other such documents, and
(c) each of the documents is authenticated by its granter or granters.

(4) Where a person grants an electronic document in more than one capacity, authentication by the person of the document, in accordance with subsection (3), is sufficient to bind the person in all such capacities.

(5) Nothing in this section prevents an electronic document which has not been authenticated by the granter or granters of it from being used as evidence in relation to any right or obligation to which the document relates.

(6) Regulations under subsection (l)(b) or (2)(c) are subject to the negative procedure.

GENERAL NOTE 1–25

As with "traditional" (i.e. paper or equivalent) documents, so with electronic documents, a distinction is made between the requirements for formal validity and those for "probativity" or self-proving status. Section 9B sets out the requirements for formal validity, and is thus the equivalent for electronic documents of s.2 for traditional documents. The next section (s.9C) sets out the requirements for probativity, and is thus the equivalent for electronic documents of s.3 for traditional documents. A document which is authenticated by electronic signature in accordance with s.9B satisfies the requirements of form stipulated by s.1(2). At least in the early years of the new provisions, however, it seems likely that the types of electronic signature available will usually comply with s.9C as well as with s.9B, with the result that electronic documents will generally be probative as well as formally valid.

Subs.(1) 1–26

Of the two requirements set out for formal validity, the first (authentication by the granter) is concerned with the granter's signature while the second (such other requirements as may be prescribed in regulations) is concerned with the form of the document itself. The origins of the latter lie in the view of the Scottish Law Commission that an electronic document should be neither too informal and ephemeral (as with, e.g. an SMS text message) nor vulnerable to becoming unreadable in the future as technology moves on: see *Report on Land Registration* (The Stationery Office, 2010), Scot. Law Com. No.222, paras 34.36–34.38. In the event, the Scottish Ministers have not, so far at least, chosen to make any regulations. As a result, the only requirement for formal validity is that the document be "authenticated" by the granter or granters. Authentication is thus the equivalent of subscription in the case of traditional documents. The meaning of "authentication" is given in subs.(2).

Subs.(2) 1–27

Broadly speaking, an electronic document is authenticated by being signed by means of an electronic signature. Paragraphs (a)–(c) give further details. In practice, granters of documents will not usually have an electronic signature of the type which is needed, with the result that they will typically sign through an agent (generally a solicitor). Section 12(3) makes clear that an agent can carry out authentication on behalf of a granter. Where the granter is a juristic person such as a company or local authority, the electronic signature is applied by one of the signatories listed in reg.5 of the Electronic Documents (Scotland) Regulations 2014 (SSI 2014/83) (inserted by reg.9(3) of the Land Register of Scotland (Automated Registration) etc. Regulations 2014 (SS1 2014/347)). This is substantially the same as the list given in Sch.2 of the Act in the context of traditional documents. So, e.g. an electronic document granted by a company must be signed by a director, secretary, or authorised person; a document granted by a limited liability partnership must be signed by a member of the partnership.

Para.(a). This uses what has become standard terminology for the connection between electronic signature and electronic document: see Directive 1999/93/EC of the European Parliament and of the Council on a Community framework for electronic signatures (the "E-Signatures Directive") art.2 (definition of "electronic signature") and the Electronic Communications Act 2000 s.7(2)(a). "Incorporated" speaks for itself. A signature is "logically associated" with an electronic document if there is a link or connection between the data 1–28 which comprises the document and the data which comprises the signature (in the same way as, to take a familiar example, between an email and one of its attachments).

1–29 *Para.(b)*. In the same way that a conventional, handwritten signature might be forged, so an electronic signature might be stolen and used by someone else. Hence the requirement in para.(b). Although the provision does not say so, the presupposition appears to be that "the person by whom it purports to have been created" is necessarily the person whose signature it is (and not some other person who happens, with or without permission, to be using the signature).

1–30 *Para.(c)*. "Electronic signature" is defined, rather generally, in s.12(1) as "so much of anything electronic form as (a) is incorporated into, or logically associated with, an electronic document, and (b) purports to be so incorporated or associated for the purpose of being used in establishing the authenticity of the electronic document, its integrity or both its authenticity and its integrity". By 5.12(4), "authenticity" means whether a document has been electronically signed by a particular person, and "integrity" whether there has been any tampering with, or other modification of, the document. At its simplest an electronic signature might be no more than a name typed on an electronic document. That, however, would lack the distinctive features which any signature must have if it is to be of evidential value. For the purposes of s.9B (and s.9C), a much higher-level type of signature is needed. In the interests of future-proofing, however, the definition is left to regulations, which can more easily be changed in order to take account of changing technology.

The first (and current) regulations to be made, the Electronic Documents Regulations 2014 (SSI 2014/83) regs 1 and 2, require the use of an "advanced electronic signature", as defined in reg.2 of the Electronic Signatures Regulations 2002 (S1 2002/318). That definition, which is taken in turn from the E-Signatures Directive (which the Regulations implement in part), is "an electronic signature (a) which is uniquely related to the signatory, (b) which is capable of identifying the signatory, (c) which is created using means that the signatory can maintain under his sole control, and (d) which is linked to the data to which it relates in such a manner that any subsequent change of data is detectable".

Unlike with handwritten signatures (see s.7(2)), there is no requirement that the signature includes the person's name, and in practice it is much more likely to comprise a number. The final criterion brings out a key advantage of such a signature over one which is merely handwritten: an advanced electronic signature evidences not merely the assent of the granter at the time of signing ("authenticity") but also that the document has not been altered after execution ("integrity").

1–31 *Subs.(3)*

This corresponds to s.2(2) for traditional documents and deals with where a contract consists of an offer and one or more acceptances. For further discussion, see the note to s.2(2).

1–32 *Subs.(4)*

This corresponds to s.7(4) for traditional documents. Its effect is that a person who grants an electronic document in two different capacities, e.g. as an executor and as an individual, need only complete the authentication process once.

1–33 *Subs.(5)*

This corresponds to s.2(3) for traditional documents. In practice an unauthenticated document might be useful evidence of the terms of an agreement or other juridical act. If the agreement was one requiring formal writing under s.l(2), the absence of the proper formalities might be cured by actings under s.1(3).

Presumption as to authentication of electronic documents

9C.—(1) Where—

(a) an electronic document bears to have been authenticated by the granter,
(b) nothing in the document or in the authentication indicates that it was not so authenticated, and
(c) the conditions set out in subsection (2) are satisfied,

the document is to be presumed to have been authenticated by the granter.

(2) The conditions are that the electronic signature incorporated into, or logically associated with, the document—

(a) is of such type and satisfies such requirements as may be prescribed by the Scottish Ministers in regulations, and
(b) (either or both)—
    (i) is used in such circumstances as may be so prescribed,
    (ii) bears to be certified,

and that if the electronic signature bears to be certified (and does not conform with paragraph (b) the certification is of such type and satisfies such requirements as may be so prescribed.

(3) Regulations under subsection (2) are subject to the negative procedure.

GENERAL NOTE **1–34**

Introduction

As with "traditional" (i.e. paper or equivalent) documents so with electronic documents, a distinction is made between the requirements for formal validity and those for "probativity" or self-proving status. The previous section (s.9B) set out the requirements for formal validity, and is thus the equivalent for electronic documents of s.2 for traditional documents. The current section (s.9C) sets out the requirements for probativity, and is thus the equivalent for electronic documents of s.3 for traditional documents. An electronic document is formally valid if it is authenticated by an advanced electronic signature; it is probative if it appears to be so authenticated, and in addition the signature appears to have been certified by a "qualified certificate". Certification fulfils the same function as attestation in the case of traditional documents.

Three requirements of probativity **1–35**

The details can be found in subss.(1) and (2) as amplified by art.3 of the Electronic Documents Regulations 2014 (SSI 2014/83), made under these subsections. There are three requirements. An electronic document is probative (self-proving) where (i) it bears to have been authenticated by the granter by means of an advanced electronic signature, (ii) nothing in the document or the authentication indicates that it was not so authenticated, and (iii) it bears to be certified by a "qualified certificate". As with s.3, s.9C is concerned solely with the appearance of the document. If an electronic document bears to have been properly authenticated and certified, then proper authentication, and hence formal validity-under s.9B, is presumed. But the presumption can be overcome by contrary evidence, and it is possible (though it will be rare in practice) for a document to comply with s.9C but be nonetheless invalid under s.9B (e.g. because the electronic signature was applied by someone-other than the person whose signature it is). For reasons which are not clear, there is no equivalent in s.9C to s.3(4) (by which a document is stripped of its probative status if an irregularity in the attestation can be proved).

For the purposes of requirement (i), the meaning of "advanced-electronic signature" is given in reg.2 of the Electronic Signatures Regulations 2002 (SI 2002/318) (see SSI 2014/83 regs 1(2) and 3(a)). Further information on such signatures can be found in the notes to s.9B(2)(c) above.

Requirement (ii) corresponds to s.3(1)(c) in the case of traditional deeds.

The certification in requirement (iii) is the equivalent of attestation in traditional deeds, a third-party verification of the authenticity of the granter's signature. "Certification" is defined in s.12(1), and the words "authenticity" and "integrity" which appear in that definition are defined in turn in s.12(4). Certification must be by "qualified certificate" (see the Electronic Documents Regulations 2014 (SSI 2014/83) reg.3(b)), an expression which is defined in SI 2002/318 reg.2 in terms which are taken from the E-Signatures Directive (Directive 1999/93/EC). The definition is: "a certificate which meets the requirements in Schedule I and is provided by a certification-service-provider who fulfils the requirements in Schedule 2". Schedule I stipulates that qualified certificates must contain:

> '(a) an indication that the certificate is issued as a qualified certificate; (b) the identification of the certification-service-provider and the State in which it is established; (c) the name of the signatory or a pseudonym, which shall be identified as such; (d) provision 'for a specific attribute of the signatory to be included if relevant, depending on the purpose for which the certificate is intended; (e) signature-verification data which correspond to signature-creation data under the control of the signatory; (f) an indication of the beginning and end of the period of validity of the certificate; (g) the identity code of the certificate; (h) the advanced electronic signature of the certification-service-provider issuing it; (i) limitations on the scope of use of the certificate, if applicable; and (j) limits on the value of transactions for which the certificate can be used, if applicable.'

1–36 *Signature and certification in practice*

At the time when s.9C came into force, in 2014, the only certification-service-providers ("CSP"s) active in the Scottish legal market were the Keeper of the Registers of Scotland and the Law Society of Scotland. The Keeper had been issuing electronic signatures and certification to Scottish solicitors since 2006 in connection with deeds used within the e-registration system known as automated registration of title to land ("ARTL"). Originally, the use of electronic deeds within the ARTL system (only) was authorised by a series of provisions added to the Act in 2006 (most notably ss.2A, 2B, 2C and 3A) and repealed in 2014; the new provisions in Pt 3 of the Act are sufficient to encompass ARTL deeds as well as other electronic documents, although some further provision for ARTL deeds is made by the Land Register of Scotland (Automated Registration) etc. Regulations 2014 (SSI 2014/347). The entry of the Law Society of Scotland into the market as a CSP, in 2014, was so as to enable Scottish solicitors to execute the much wider range of electronic documents which are permitted by Pt 3.

As the Scottish Law Commission points out (*Report on Land Registration* (The Stationery Office, 2010), Scot. Law Com. No.222, para.34.20), the E-Signatures Directive seems to have been predicated on the use of a form of asymmetric key-pair public-key infrastructure ("PKI"). The Law Commission continues (para.34.20, note 21):

> 'In the Directive Scheme, where a party seeks to obtain an electronic signature, the CSP carries out identity checks and, once satisfied that the party is who they claim to be, creates a 'key pair' which are two extremely large numbers which bear a complex mathematical relationship. Someone with access to the public key can know to an exceptionally high degree of probability that data has been operated on by the related private key without however finding out the actual value of the private key. The private key is given to the signatory, who keeps it secure and uses it to create electronic

signatures. The CSP makes the public key publicly available in the form of a certificate, which confirms that signatures created by the private key were created by the identified individual.'

The signatory, of course, is spared the need to understand this complex technology. Under the system operated by both the Keeper of the Registers and the Law Society of Scotland, each solicitor who is to be a signatory is issued with a PIN-protected smartcard containing an electronic signature which incorporates a unique digital certificate. An electronic signature is made by using the smartcard in association with a smartcard reader, which provides the interface from smartcard to computer via a USB cable. The signature can then be read by anyone to whom the document is sent.

An alternative to certification 1–37

A possible alternative to certification, in subs.(2)(b)(i), is that the electronic signature "is used in circumstances as may be so prescribed". No such circumstances have so far been prescribed. The provision derives from the following passage by the Scottish Law Commission (*Report on Land Registration* (The Stationery Office, 2010), Scot. Law Com. No.222, para.34.49):

> 'There are other approaches to electronic signature which do not involvel a trusted third party but which can be effective to authenticate communications between parties who already know each other. The Scottish conveyancing profession is small and to a considerable extent practitioners at least know of each other if not actually knowing each other. Accordingly, at least for authenticating missives, there seems some scope for a simpler approach to electronic signature to be adopted. We therefore consider that it should be possible for an electronic signature which is not certified to nevertheless achieve a presumption as to authentication if it is used in such circumstances and if it satisfies such requirements as may be laid down by Regulations.'

An alternative to certification which is already available is to demonstrate the authenticity of the signature by means of an application to the sheriff court under s.9D(1).

Final matters 1–38

Two minor departures from s.3 may be noted. First, s.9C(1)(a) requires the appearance of proper authentication from "the" granter and not merely from "a" granter, suggesting that it is not possible for an electronic document to be probative in respect of one granter but not in respect of another. Yet this seems not to be what was intended because s.9G(2)(b) expressly contemplates the possibility that a document might be probative in respect of only "one of the granters". Secondly, the presumption is confined to validity of authentication and does not extend to statements as to the date and place of execution. Such further presumptions can be added in the form of regulations (see s.9E(l)) but no regulations have so far been made. It remains open to parties to seek a court decree in respect of time, date and place under s.9D(2).

Presumptions as to granter's authentication etc. when established in court proceedings

9D.—(1) Where—

(a) an electronic document bears to have been authenticated by a granter of it, and
(b) there is no presumption under section 9C that the document has been authenticated by that granter,

the court must, on an application being made to it by any person who has an interest in the document, if satisfied that the document was authenticated by that granter, grant decree to that effect.

(2) Where—

(a) an electronic document bears to have been authenticated by a granter of it, and
(b) there is no presumption by virtue of section 9E(1) as to the time, date or place of authentication,

the court must, on an application being made to it by any person who has an interest in the document, if satisfied as to that time, date or place, grant decree to that effect.

(3) On an application under subsection (1) or (2), evidence is, unless the court otherwise directs, to be given by affidavit.

(4) An application under subsection (1) or (2) may be made either as a summary application or as incidental to, and in the course of, other proceedings.

(5) The effect of a decree—

(a) under subsection (1), is to establish a presumption that the document has been authenticated by the granter concerned, or

(b) under subsection (2), is to establish a presumption that the statement in the decree as to time, date or place is correct.

(6) In this section, "the court" means—

(a) in the case of a summary application—
  (i) the sheriff in whose sheriffdom the applicant resides, or
  (ii) if the applicant does not reside in Scotland, the sheriff at Edinburgh, or
(b) in the case of an application made in the course of other proceedings, the court before which those proceedings are pending.

1–39 GENERAL NOTE

An electronic document which has been authenticated by the granter's (advanced) electronic signature is formally valid but not probative (self-proving). The normal way of achieving probativity is for the signature to be certified by a certification-service-provider under s.9C; and indeed current technology is usually for certification to be embedded in the actual signature. If, however, a document turns out to be formally valid without being probative, there are two ways in which probativity can be achieved. One is by certification (assuming that to be available, and possible from the point of view of technology). The other is by an application to the court in terms of s.9D, the provision under review. That provision corresponds to s.4 for "traditional" (i.e. paper or equivalent) deeds.

Section 9D provides a procedure for the court (usually the sheriff court, see subs.(6)) to grant a decree that it is satisfied that a document was authenticated (i.e. with an advanced electronic signature) by the granter. The court will usually be satisfied by affidavit evidence alone (subs.(3)). The effect of the decree is to establish a presumption-no more-that the document has indeed been authenticated by the granter (subs.(5)). A s.9D document is thus of equivalent weight to a s.9C document and, as with the former, remains vulnerable to challenge through contrary evidence. There is a parallel provision (subs.(2) in relation to the time, date and place of execution.

1–40 *Subs.(1)*

This is the judicial counterpart of s.9C. A court application is only possible where "there is no presumption under section 9C", i.e. where the electronic signature lacks certification.

Subs.(2) 1–41

As compared to the corresponding provision for traditional documents (s.4(2)), this allows the court to pronounce in respect of time of authentication and not merely of date and place. There can be two reasons why there is not already a presumption by virtue of s.9E(1). One is that the conditions set by the regulations made under that section have not been met. The other-which is the position at present-is that no regulations have been made, with the result that no presumption can arise.

Subs.(3) 1–42

The court is entitled, but not bound, to be satisfied on the basis of a single affidavit: see the Civil Evidence (Scotland) Act 1988 (c.32) s.l(1).

Subs.(5) 1–43

In view of the role played by uncorroborated affidavit evidence, there is no reason to suppose that the (judicial) presumption established under s.9D is stronger than the (extra-judicial) presumption established under s.9C.

Further provision by Scottish Ministers about electronic documents

9E.—(1) Th6 Scottish Ministers may, in regulations, make provision as to the effectiveness or formal validity of, or presumptions to be made with regard to—

(a) any alteration made, whether before or after authentication, to an electronic document,
(b) the authentication, by or on behalf of the granter, of such a document,
(c) the authentication, by or on behalf of a person with a disability, of such a document, or
(d) any annexation to such a document,

(including, without prejudice to the generality of this subsection, presumptions to be made with regard to the time, date and place of authentication of such a document).

(2) Regulations under subsection (1) may make such incidental, supplemental, consequential, transitional, transitory or saving provision as the Scottish Ministers consider necessary or expedient for the purposes of, or in consequence of the regulations.

(3) Subject to subsection (4), regulations under subsection (1) are subject to the negative procedure.

(4) Regulations which—

(a) make provision of the kind mentioned in subsection (l)(b), or
(b) add to, replace or omit any part of an Act (including this Act),

are subject to the affirmative procedure.

GENERAL NOTE 1–44

A number of matters which are provided for in the case of "traditional" (i.e. paper or equivalent) documents lack a corresponding provision in the Act in the case of electronic documents. These are: presumptions as to date and place of execution (s.3(8)–(10); alterations to the document (s.5 and Sch.1); execution by juristic persons (s.7(7) and Sch.2); annexations (s.8); and execution by a granter who is blind or unable to write (s.9 and Sch.3). The reason for the omission, according to the Scottish Law Commission (*Report on Land Registration* (The Stationery Office, 2010), Scot. Law Com. No.222, para.34.54), is the impossibility of predicting what provisions would be appropriate to meet future developments in technology and in conveyancing practice. The Law Commission's solution, now taken up by s.9E, is to empower the Scottish Ministers to make provision by regulation. So far this power has been exercised in respect of juristic persons and annexations. The first of these was discussed at p.32 above; the second is discussed below.

1–45 *Annexations*

Regulation 4 of the Electronic Communications (Scotland) Regulations 2014 (SSI 2014/83), is in the following terms:

> 'For an annexation to an electronic document to be regarded as incorporated in that document it must be (a) referred to in the document; (b) identified on its face as being the annexation referred to in the document; and (c) annexed to the document before the electronic signature under regulation 2 is incorporated into or logically associated with the document and the annexation.'

This is modelled on the equivalent provision for traditional documents (s.8(1)).

Undefined in the Regulations, "annexation" is defined in s.12(1) of the Act as including any inventory, appendix, schedule, other writing, plan, drawing, photograph or other representation annexed to a document. Although reg.4 does not say so expressly, the fact that, under para.(c), the electronic signature is apparently to be "incorporated into or logically associated with the document and the annexation" implies that the annexation too must be in electronic form. It need not, however, form part of the same electronic document; indeed if it did, it might be questioned whether it is an annexation at all.

The provision requires that the fact of incorporation should be manifest both from the document itself and from the annexation. Thus (i) the document must refer to the annexation (e.g. "the Schedule annexed as relative hereto"); and (ii) the annexation must in turn be identified on its face as the thing which has been incorporated. It is probably enough to satisfy (ii) if the annexation is simply headed with the appropriate name (e.g. "Schedule"), but it is preferable to add some kind of identifying docquet (e.g. "this is the Schedule referred to in the foregoing Disposition by Donald Ramsay Macdonald in favour of Lucy Anne Robertson").

Delivery of electronic documents

9F.—(l) An electronic document may be delivered electronically or by such other means as are reasonably practicable.

(2) But such a document must be in a form, and such delivery must be by a means—

(a) the intended recipient has agreed to accept, or
(b) which it is reasonable in all the circumstances for the intended recipient to accept.

1–46 GENERAL NOTE

Unilateral documents do not take effect until delivery. For a "traditional" (i.e. paper or equivalent) document, delivery is typically achieved simply by handing over the piece of paper on which the document is written. Section 9F provides a parallel set of rules for electronic deeds. The default method, as might be expected, is electronic delivery, for example as an e-mail attachment, by fax, or by delivery within an electronic system such as ARTL. The reference in subs.(2) to the use of a method which is reasonable or to which the recipient has agreed seems aimed particularly at the alternative method allowed by subs.(l) ("such other means as are reasonably practicable"). Possible examples might include physical delivery of a DVD or USB memory stick containing the document.

A similar but more prescriptive provision for the delivery of an electronic copy of a traditional deed can be found in s.4 of the Legal Writings (Counterparts and Delivery) (Scotland) Bill, currently before the Scottish Parliament.

Registration and recording of electronic documents

9G.—(l) Subject to subsection (6), it is not competent—

(a) to record an electronic document in the Register of Sasines,
(b) to register such a document in the Land Register of Scotland,
(c) to register such a document for execution or preservation in the Books of Council and Session, or
(d) to record or register such a document in any other register under the management and control of the Keeper of the Registers of Scotland, unless both subsection (2) and subsection (3) apply in relation to the document.

(2) This subsection applies where—

(a) the document is presumed under section 9C or 9D or by virtue of section 9E(1) to have been authenticated by the granter, or
(b) if there is more than one granter, the document is presumed by virtue of any of those provisions to have been authenticated by at least one of the granters.

(3) This subsection applies where—

(a) the document,
(b) the electronic signature authenticating it, and
(c) if the document bears to be certified, the certification,

are in such form and of such type as are prescribed by the Scottish Ministers in regulations.

(4) Before making regulations under subsection (3), the Scottish Ministers must consult with—

(a) the Keeper of the Registers of Scotland,
(b) the Keeper of the Records of Scotland, and
(c) the Lord President of the Court of Session.

(5) Regulations under subsection (3)—

(a) may make different provision for different cases or classes of case, and
(b) are subject to the negative procedure.

(6) Subsection (1) above does not apply in relation to

(a) a document's—

(i) being recorded in the Register of Sasines,
(ii) being registered in the Land Register of Scotland or in the Books of Council and Session, or
(iii) being recorded or registered in any other register under the management and control of the Keeper of the Registers of Scotland,

if an enactment requires or expressly permits such recording or registration notwithstanding that the document is not presumed to have been authenticated by the granter or by at least one of the granters,

(b) the recording of a court decree in the Register of Sasines or the registering of such a decree in the Land Register of Scotland,
(c) the registering in the Books of Council and Session of—

(i) a document registration of which is directed by the Court of Session,

(ii) a document the formal validity of which is governed by a law other than Scots law, provided that the Keeper of the Registers of Scotland is satisfied that the document is formally valid according to that other law,

(iii) a court decree granted under section 9D, or by virtue of section 9E(l), of this Act in relation to a document already registered in the Books of Council and Session, or

(d) the registration of a court decree in a separate register maintained for that purpose.

(7) An electronic document may be registered for preservation in the Books of Council and Session without a clause of consent to registration.

1–47 GENERAL NOTE

Subject to the exceptions listed in subs.(6), an electronic document will not be accepted for registration in the Land Register, Register of Sasines or in the Books of Council and Session unless it is probative (typically by being certified under s.9C) and also the subject of regulations made under subs.(3). A parallel provision for "traditional" (i.e. paper or equivalent) deeds can be found in s.6.

1–48 *Subs.(1)*

The list of registers is not identical to the comparable list in s.6(1) for traditional deeds.

1–49 *Subs.(2)*

As no relevant regulations have yet been made under s.9E(1), the current position is that a document, to be registrable, must be presumed to have been authenticated, in respect of at least one granter, under either s.9C or s.9D.

1–50

PART 4

GENERAL PROVISIONS

Forms of testing clause

10.—(1) Without prejudice to the effectiveness of any other means of providing information relating to the execution of a document, this information may be provided in such form of testing clause as may be prescribed in regulations made by the Secretary of State.

(2) Regulations under subsection (1) above shall be made by statutory instrument which shall be subject to annulment in pursuance of a resolution of either House of Parliament and may prescribe different forms for different cases or classes of case.

1–51 GENERAL NOTE

This empowers the Secretary of State to prescribe model testing clauses. Any testing clauses so prescribed would be purely permissive. No firm decision has been reached as to whether this power will be exercised, but it is understood that if regulations are to be made they will come into force at the same time as the Act. Any regulations are likely to prescribe testing clauses along the lines of those proposed by the Scottish Law Commission: see Scot. Law Com. No. 112, pp.192–196. The Commission's styles are designed to be typed on the document in advance, thus preventing the testing clause from being used to alter the deed after execution, notably by a false declaration that an alteration to the deed was in place prior to subscription: see s.5(5)(b). There is of course no reason why the Commission's styles should not be used without regulations having been made under this section.

Abolition of proof by writ or oath, reference to oath and other common law rules

11.—*[Repealed by the Land Registration etc. (Scotland) Act 2012 (asp 5) Sch.3 para.18 (effective May 11, 2014)*]"

Execution in counterpart

This is the practice whereby each party to a document, instead of meeting together with the other party or parties to sign the document, executes a copy of the document. That copy is then transmitted to the other parties, or collated with their executed copies of the document, so that each party ends up with copies of the document executed by all parties. Although this a long-established practice in English law,[14] especially the "exchange of contracts" in English conveyancing practice, it has never been part of the law of Scotland.[15] This has been seen as a difficulty and a disadvantage by Scottish practitioners for some time,[16] and has been highlighted by modern electronic communications. In 2012 the Scottish Law Commission raised and extensively reviewed the issues in its Discussion Paper on Contract Formation[17] and the following year issued a Report[18] proposing legislative reform. This was implemented by the Legal Writings (Counterparts and Delivery) (Scotland) Act 2015 (the 2015 Act), which came into force in July 2015.[19] **1–52**

Legal Writings (Counterparts and Delivery) (Scotland) Act 2015

Execution of documents in counterpart

"1 Execution of documents in counterpart

(1) A document may be executed in counterpart.
(2) A document is executed in counterpart if—

(a) it is executed in two or more duplicate, interchangeable, parts, and
(b) no part is subscribed by both or all parties.

(3) On such execution, the counterparts are to be treated as a single document.
(4) That single document may be made up of—

---

[14] The English law on the subject was extensively reviewed by the Scottish Law Commission, *Report on Formation of Contract: Execution in Counterpart*, April 2013, paras 1.11–1.17. See *http://www.scotlawcom.gov.uk/files/9513/3241/0632/dp154.pdf* [Accessed 4 November 2015].

[15] See Scottish Law Commission, *Discussion Paper on the Formation of Contract*, March 2012, paras 6.22–6.29 and Ch.7. See *http://www.scotlawcom.gov.uk/files/8214/1710/1226/Report_No_231_-_Review_of_Contract_Law.pdf* [Accessed 4 November 2015].

[16] See Scottish Law Commission, *Report on Formation of Contract: Execution in Counterpart*, April 2013, paras 1.1–1.7. See *http://www.scotlawcom.gov.uk/files/9513/3241/0632/dp154.pdf* [Accessed 4 November 2015]; and Scottish Law Commission, *Discussion Paper on the Formation of Contract*, March 2012, paras 6.5–6.20. See *http://www.scotlawcom.gov.uk/files/8214/1710/1226/Report_No_231_-_Review_of_Contract_Law.pdf* [Accessed 4 November 2015].

[17] Scottish Law Commission, *Discussion Paper on the Formation of Contract*, March 2012, Chs 6 and 7. See *http://www.scotlawcom.gov.uk/files/8214/1710/1226/Report_No_231_-_Review_of_Contract_Law.pdf* [Accessed 4 November 2015].

[18] Scottish Law Commission, *Report on Formation of Contract: Execution in Counterpart*, April 2013, *http://www.scotlawcom.gov.uk/files/9513/3241/0632/dp154.pdf* [Accessed 4 November 2015].

[19] The Legal Writings (Counterparts and Delivery) (Scotland) Act 2015 (Commencement) Order 2015 (SSI 2015/242 (c.33)).

(a) both or all the counterparts in their entirety, or
(b) one of the counterparts in its entirety, collated with the page or pages on which the other counterpart has, or other counterparts have, been subscribed.

(5) A document executed in counterpart becomes effective when—

(a) both or all the counterparts have been delivered in accordance with subsection (6) or (7), and
(b) any other step required by an enactment or rule of law for the document to become effective has been taken.

(6) Each counterpart is to be delivered to the party or parties who did not subscribe the counterpart in question unless it is a counterpart which falls to be delivered under subsection (7).

(7) If a party has, under section 2(1), nominated a person to take delivery of one or more counterparts, the counterpart in question is (or counterparts in question are) to be delivered to that person.

(8) Subsection (5) is subject to subsection (9).

(9) Where a counterpart is to be held by the recipient as undelivered, the counterpart is not to be treated as delivered for the purposes of subsection (5)(a) until—

(a) the person from whom the counterpart is received indicates to the recipient that it is to be so treated, or
(b) if a specified condition is to be satisfied before the counterpart may be so treated, the condition has been satisfied.

2 Nomination of person to take delivery of counterparts

(1) Parties to a document executed in counterpart may nominate a person to take delivery of one or more of the counterparts.

(2) Subsection (1) does not prevent one of the parties, or an agent of one or more of the parties, being so nominated.

(3) A person so nominated must, after taking delivery of a counterpart by virtue of subsection (1), hold and preserve it for the benefit of the parties.

(4) Subsection (3) does not apply in so far as the parties may agree, or be taken to have agreed, otherwise (whether before or after the document has effect).

(5) A document's having effect is not dependent on compliance with subsection (3) or (4).

3 Use of counterparts: electronic documents

(1) Sections 1 and 2 apply to traditional documents and electronic documents.

(2) In section 1 any reference to subscription is to be read, in the case of an electronic document to which section 1(2) of the Requirements of Writing (Scotland) Act 1995 ("the 1995 Act") applies, as a reference to authentication of the electronic document within the meaning of section 9B of the 1995 Act.

(3) In this section—

"electronic document" has the meaning given by section 9A of the 1995 Act, "traditional document" has the meaning given by section 1A of the 1995 Act.

Delivery of traditional documents by electronic means

4 Delivery of traditional documents by electronic means

(a) This section applies where there is a requirement for delivery of a traditional document (whether or not a document executed in counterpart).

(2) The requirement may be satisfied by delivery by electronic means of—

(a) a copy of the document, or
(b) a part of such a copy.

(3) But the requirement may be satisfied by delivery of a part of such a copy only if the part—

(a) is sufficient in all the circumstances to show that it is part of the document, and
(b) is, or includes, the page on which the sender (or the person on whose behalf the sender has effected the delivery) has subscribed the document.

(4) Delivery under subsection (2) must be by a means (and what is delivered must be in a form) which the intended recipient has agreed to accept (the "accepted method"), unless subsection (5) applies.

(5) If—

(a) no accepted method has been agreed,
(b) there is uncertainty about the accepted method, or
(c) the accepted method is impracticable,

delivery may be by such means (and in such form) as is reasonable in all the circumstances.

(6) Although delivery by electronic means constitutes effective delivery in relation to a traditional document, what is received by that means is not to be treated as being the traditional document itself.

(7) A traditional document, in relation to which delivery by electronic means has been effected, is to be held by the sender in accordance with whatever arrangements have been made by the sender and the recipient (or, if there is a number of recipients, have been made by the sender and the recipients as a group).

(8) Any reference in subsection (7) to a recipient is to be construed, in a case where a person takes delivery by virtue of section 2(1), as a reference to the parties who nominated that person.

(9) In this section, references to delivery by electronic means are to delivery—

(a) by means of an electronic communications network (for example as an attachment to an e-mail),
(b) by fax,
(c) by means of a device on which the thing delivered is stored electronically (such as a disc, a memory stick or other removable or portable media), or
(d) by other means but in a form which requires the use of electronic apparatus by the recipient to render the thing delivered intelligible.

(10) In this section—

"electronic communications network" has the meaning given by section 32 of the Communications Act 2003,

"traditional document" has the meaning given by section 1A of the 1995 Act.

. . ."

The scheme established by the 2015 Act is relatively simple: all counterparts are treated as a single document: s.1(2). Electronic documents and traditional documents delivered electronically are similarly treated: ss.3 and 4. Following the Scottish Law Commission's recommendation, that single document may comprise all those counterparts in their entirety (s.1(4)(b)); or one counterpart in its entirety and the parts, or pages, of the document on which the other parties subscribed. This covers the vast majority of documents encountered in contracting, especially in commercial contracts. To widen the range of documents covered, the 2015 Act also allows transmission of counterparts (more likely the subscribed page of the counterpart) to a person nominated to receive it (s.1(7) and 1(9)). This means, for example, that a solicitor so nominated could collate the subscribed pages sent by all the parties and collate it with the full document, thereby constituting them as a single document under the 2015 Act. This would greatly expedite the entire process, making the new Scottish procedures one of the most expeditious in general commerce.

The crucial factor, however, is delivery and s.4 is designed to facilitate the use of electronic communications even with traditional documents, where their use is either the "accepted method" (s.4(4)), or where it is ""reasonable in the circumstances" (s.4(5)).

Voluntary undertakings and the intention to contract

1–53 Clearly not every agreement creates contractual obligations. The difficulty lies in establishing logical and fair rules for differentiating those which do from those which do not. As we have seen in the preceding pages, some agreements are so serious in their consequences—contracts to sell land, for example—that the law generally requires that they be in the appropriate form if they are to be legally binding. Similarly, when a person voluntarily undertakes to give something for nothing—a gratuitous, rather than an onerous undertaking—the law may require formal evidence of the intention to do so. This is considered more fully below.

Another technique is to establish a presumption that parties to certain types of agreement intend to enter into legally binding relations. The corollary would be that other categories of agreement are presumed not to be legally binding. English law, for example, generally presumes that parties to a commercial agreement intend to enter into legally binding relations, whereas parties to a "domestic" agreement do not.

There is no evidence that Scots law operates such a series of presumptions, nor is there any compelling reason why it should. English law requires consideration to establish a contract. Gratuitous obligations, or agreements in a domestic environment, are situations where proof of consideration is difficult, if not impossible to establish and English courts may be unwilling to find a contract arising in such circumstances. In *Balfour v Balfour*,[20] the parties entered into an oral agreement that the husband would pay the wife £30 maintenance per month while they were temporarily living apart. The payments were not made and the wife claimed what was due under the agreement. On appeal to the Court of Appeal, all the judges (Warrington, Dukes and Atkin LJJ) agreed that there was no obligation to pay. Atkin LJ found (at 589) that such arrangements

> "are not contracts because the parties did not intend that they should be attended by legal consequences ... They are not sued upon, not because the parties are reluctant to enforce their legal rights when the agreement is broken, but because the parties, in the inception of the arrangement, never intended that they should be sued upon. Agreements such as these are outside the realm of contracts altogether".[21]

The position in Scots law was expounded by Stair when he said: "In the act of contracting, it must be of purpose to oblige, either really or presumptively, and so must be serious, so that what is expressed in jest or scorn makes no contract".[22]

There is no indication in this, or any subsequent statements, institutional or judicial, that a presumption such as that in *Balfour v Balfour* is part of the law of Scotland. If a similar situation arose in Scotland, the court would probably determine that the husband's promise was either

---

[20] *Balfour v Balfour* [1919] 2 K.B. 591.

[21] This line of reasoning was subsequently adopted by the Court of Appeal in *Gould v Gould* [1970] 1 Q.B. 275 and *Pettitt v Pettitt* [1970] A.C. 777 to cover all agreements between husband and wife and was extended to cover other analogous relationships by the House of Lords in *Jones v Padavatton* [1969] 3 W.L.R. 328.

[22] Stair, *Institutions of the Law of Scotland,* I. x. 13.

unilateral or that such agreement as there was, was gratuitous. In either case, that would have been enough to dispose of the matter. At the very least it can be said that a Scottish court would look at the facts of the case as a whole and determine whether the parties had, objectively on the facts, entered into an agreement, rather than merely exchanged informal promises. Similarly, if one of the parties agrees to make an "ex gratia payment" the indication is that the payment is voluntary, and not intended to be legally binding.

Wick Harbour Trustees v The Admiralty 1–54

1921 2 S.L.T. 109

Court of Session, Outer House: Lord Sands

Under s.28 of the Harbours, Docks, and Piers Clauses Act 1847, vessels in His Majesty's service were exempt from harbour and similar rates and dues.

In 1916, an agreement was reached through an exchange of letters between representatives of the Admiralty and of a committee representing the Dock and Harbour Authorities throughout the UK, under which the Admiralty would make "ex gratia" payments for use of the Authorities' facilities in accordance with a specified scheme of rates and charges.

The Wick Harbour Trustees now claimed £6,169 17s. under the terms of the agreement. The admiralty offered £1,400 in full settlement, which the trustees rejected as wholly inadequate.

Lord Sands found that the obligation was binding upon the admiralty.

"LORD SANDS: . . . I appreciate that it is possible for a person to give an undertaking under an express stipulation that it shall not be legally enforceable. In certain circumstances, which it is not difficult to figure, such an arrangement may not be unreasonable. But such a peculiar qualification of anything in the form of an undertaking would require to be very clear and explicit.

But for the use of the words 'ex gratia' I do not think that there would be any difficulty in reaching the conclusion that the correspondence constituted a binding agreement. The construction which the defenders seek to put upon the correspondence with special reference to these words is that it amounted to this: 'I am not bound to pay anything, but I am willing to come to a general understanding that I will make certain payments, each, however, only as a voluntary donation and not as in implement of any binding undertaking now given.' The pursuers, on the other hand, construe the attitude of the Minister as embodied in the correspondence as importing this: 'I am not bound to pay you anything, and if I agree to pay anything I do so ex gratia, but I do agree to pay you so and so'. The question, therefore, comes to be whether the words 'ex gratia' are a quality of an agreement or are they resolutive of any binding agreement? To put it otherwise, are the words properly descriptive of each individual payment after the offer has been accepted, or are they descriptive of the original category of the payments which the Minister has now agreed to make? 'I agree to make a voluntary payment' is a self-contradictory statement if 'voluntary' is construed as still adhering to the payment which is agreed to, and not as descriptive of its original character. No doubt cases may be figured where, in view of the relationship of the parties, 'agree' may be construed as not meaning more than 'intend'. For example, if a father says to his son who is going to Oxford: 'I agree to allow you £300 for three years,' it may very well be that this does not constitute a continuous and binding obligation. On the other hand, if a brother were to write to his widowed sister: 'I agree to allow your boy £300 for three years at Oxford,' that, I think, might very well be construed as an absolute undertaking.

I was referred to the case of *Morton's Trs. v. Aged Christian Friend Society of Scotland* (1899 2 F. 82) as the leading authority ... in relation to an obligation to make a payment which is purely voluntary. That is not perhaps an altogether satisfactory authority upon the pure question, as there was an element of *rei interventus*. But I take it to be in accordance with the general principle of our law that if a person voluntarily offers to make a payment which he is under no legal obligation to make, and the offer is accepted, that forms a binding contract. Now suppose that a person who has hitherto been in the way of contributing to a charity were to write to the secretary: 'In lieu of the donation which I have recently been making I agree this year to make a payment of £100,' it appears to me that this would constitute a binding obligation, for the law of Scotland does not discriminate between onerous and gratuitous obligations. But, on the other hand, if the contributor wrote: 'Instead of the donation I have recently been making I agree this year to make ... a donation of £100,' would the use of the word 'donation' in the undertaking make any difference? I do not think so. The word 'donation' is descriptive of the original character of the payment and not a qualification of the obligation. If he has agreed to a payment it does not matter what he calls it. I have some recollection of a somewhat cognate question, though I cannot find any report of the case. A person who repudiated fault and consequent liability for some accident agreed to make an ex gratia payment. In a question with his executors it was found that the obligatory character of the obligation was not avoided by the use of the words ex gratia. It just came to this: 'I do not admit any antecedent liability, but I agree to pay.'

I have come to the conclusion that the words 'ex gratia' in Mr McKinnon-Wood's letter must be similarly regarded. All payments, whether of local rates or harbour dues, by a Government Department are ex gratia, and may be properly so described. But when the Department agrees to make certain payments, although in the eye of public law they are still ex gratia payments, as a matter of particular undertaking the obligation is binding."

1–55 The opening remarks in this judgment indicate a general acceptance of the view that a Scottish court would not hold the parties to an agreement where they had expressly stated that they were not entering into a contract, for example by stating that "this agreement is binding in honour only". Such an "honour" clause or "gentlemen's agreement" does not have the force of law: it permits the parties to behave neither honourably nor as gentlemen. A particularly elaborate form of such a clause is to be found in the English case of *Rose & Frank Co v JR Crompton & Brothers Ltd*,[23] a decision of the House of Lords. There, the written agreement included the following provision:

> "This arrangement is not entered into, nor is this memorandum written, as a formal or written agreement, and shall not be subject to legal jurisdiction in the Law Courts either of the United States or England, but it is only a definite expression and record of the purpose and intention of the three parties concerned, to which they each honourably pledge themselves, with the fullest confidence—based on past business with each other—that it will be carried through by each of the three parties with mutual loyalty and co-operation. This is hereinafter referred to as the 'honourable pledge' clause."

Not surprisingly, the undue moral strain placed upon the parties by such a stentorian agreement eventually proved too much, although it was, apparently, operated for at least six years!

Such "honour" clauses are surprisingly common but, by their very nature, rarely come before the courts. They are a common feature, for example, of the recent phenomenon of "partnering"

[23] *Rose & Frank Co v JR Crompton & Brothers Ltd* [1925] A.C. 445.

agreements in the construction industry.[24] They are historically common in football pools coupons (although they do not seem to be considered necessary in more contemporary gaming competitions) and there is English authority to the effect that such an "honour clause" is effective to preclude the existence of a contractual obligation to pay winnings.[25]

Ferguson v Littlewoods Pools Ltd 1–56
1997 S.L.T. 307
Court of Session, Outer House: Lord Coulsfield

The pursuers were members of a football pools syndicate. Every week they completed Littlewoods coupons, which they gave, together with the stake money to a pools agent, Baxter. Baxter kept the money and did not pass on the coupons to Littlewoods. He was subsequently convicted of theft. One of the coupons handed to Baxter contained a winning line that would have entitled the pursuers to about £2.3 million.

Littlewoods, who had received neither the completed coupons nor the stake money, refused to pay, arguing, inter alia, that an honour clause in the coupon relieved them of any liability. The clause provided:

> "I have read and agreed to Littlewoods' current football pool rules which govern this entry and agree that this transaction (apart from the provisions about the Foundation referred to in Rule 7) is binding in honour only (copies of the Rules can be had on request). I acknowledge that any collector, main collector or concessionaire through whom my coupon is submitted is my agent and I agree with all such collectors, main collectors and concessionaires that any transaction between me and them (apart from that in relation to the Foundation referred to in Rule 7) is likewise binding in honour only. I am not under 18 years of age."

In dismissing the action, Lord Coulsfield decided to allow proof before answer on the question of the validity of the honour clause since, while it was difficult to point to anything other than the document containing the clause as evidence that a contract existed, it was unlikely that there was a general answer to the problem raised and accordingly each situation had to be considered on its own facts and circumstances.

"LORD COULSFIELD: . . . [I]t is not necessary for me to reach a concluded view on the . . . argument before me, but I shall make some comment upon it. The defenders referred to *Rose & Frank Co v Crompton*. That case dealt with a situation in which a clause, to the effect that the arrangement should be held binding in honour only, had been included in an arrangement which, otherwise, would have formed a legally binding contract. The effect of the decision was that the clause prevented legal force being given to the arrangement. The defenders further pointed out that effect had been given to that decision in the particular case of football pools, and in relation to clauses very similar to that involved in the present case, in *Jones v Vernons Pools Ltd* and *Appleby v Littlewoods Pools Ltd*. The pursuers did not dispute that such a clause might have the effect of preventing the emergence of a legally binding arrangement. Their submission was that in the present case the Unfair Contract Terms Act 1977 applies so as to prevent the defenders from escaping liability upon the arrangement . . . In reply, the defenders submitted that in the present case the effect of the honour clause was that there was no contract at all between the parties and so nothing to which the Act could apply. Senior

[24] Paul Begg, "The legal content of partnering arrangements in the Construction Industry", S.L.P.Q. 2003, 8(3), 179–196.

[25] *Jones v Vernon's Pools* [1938] 2 All E.R. 626.

> counsel for the defenders accepted that the question whether a clause of this kind could have the effect of enabling a party to avoid the effect of the Act in an ordinary consumer contract was difficult and observed that it was one which had been the subject of much inconclusive academic discussion. Nevertheless, he submitted that, at least in the circumstances of the present case, it was clear that the honour clause could not be denied effect and consequently the pursuers could not succeed.
>
> It seems to me that, if it is assumed that participation in a pool betting transaction is capable of constituting a legally binding contract, the activities of the promoter of the pool might well be described as the provision of services, and therefore come within the scope of the 1977 Act. It can, I think, also be said, with some force, that if the inclusion of an honour clause in an ordinary consumer contract, for example a contract of sale and purchase or a contract of insurance, could prevent liability arising, in accordance with the ordinary effect of such a contract, there would be a possibility that the 1977 Act could be evaded. On the other hand, however, there is a serious logical difficulty in holding that any contract has been made when the documents on which reliance is placed include an honour clause of the kind here in issue. I am inclined to think that there is unlikely to be any general answer to this problem, and that decisions will have to turn on the particular circumstances of each case. For example, if there is, in fact, a transfer of goods in exchange for a payment, it may be possible to say that, notwithstanding the presence of any honour clause, some contract must be inferred to exist between the parties and that the 1977 Act can therefore be applied. In the present case, it is difficult to point to any facts which could be held to evidence a contract other than the submission of the document containing the honour clause. I do not find it easy to approach this problem on the assumption indicated earlier in this paragraph, because it seems to be, to some extent, artificial to do so. I have reached the view, however, that this is a case in which the proper approach would be to look at everything contained in the communications between the parties in order to see whether or not there might be a binding contract with legal effect."

It is important at this stage to distinguish between the intention to enter into legal relations (the subject being considered here) and the intention to agree. This latter question, which has greatly preoccupied the courts in recent years, is an aspect of contract formation, which will be considered in the next chapter.

Gratuitous and onerous obligations: patrimonial interest

1–57 It is noticeable that some of the institutional writers refer to the requirement of "consideration". This suggests that there must be an element of bargain before a contract can arise; that each party to the contract must contribute something of economic value to the contract. This is undoubtedly an essential requirement of a contract under English law, but not under Scots law. If there is such consideration, or quid pro quo, then the contract will be regarded as an onerous obligation, but in Scots law, even a gratuitous obligation may be binding. Indeed, some contracts, such as mandate, deposit and loan, are in essence gratuitous.

As a rule, contracts in the commercial world will tend to be onerous rather than gratuitous, in that both parties undertake obligations under such agreements, whether to provide goods for a price, work for a wage, carry for freight and so on. In any case, Scottish courts will only enforce obligations where some patrimonial interest is involved. Such interest includes a right to property, or a right to the use of property, but may also extend to an opportunity for gain, or for attaining status, such as an office or position.[26]

[26] On whether a promise conditional on performance or acts by the promisee ceases to be gratuitous, see J Thomson and H MacQueen, *Contract Law in Scotland*, 3rd edn (London: Butterworths, 2012) para.2.55 and fn.2 thereto. The inclination is to agree with Professor MacQueen: it does not.

Bilateral and unilateral obligations: contracts and promises distinguished

If contractual obligations are consensual, they are therefore essentially bilateral: in other words, there are at least two parties to a contract. At least one person voluntarily undertakes an obligation on condition that the other parties to the contract consent to them so doing. This distinguishes a contract from a variety of unilateral obligations that are enforceable in Scots law. In particular, a contract must be distinguished from a promise, which is a unilateral obligation. In such a case, one person only voluntarily undertakes an obligation to do or give something for the benefit of another. Scots law[27] does not require that a promise must be accepted to become a binding obligation. The unilateral expression of will is binding, although it can be rejected by any person to whom its benefit is conferred. It is a principle common to several European civil law systems. The *Principles of European Contract Law*[28] (PECL) provide in art.2:107: Promises binding without acceptance: "A promise which is intended to be legally binding without acceptance is binding". The unilateral promise is unknown to English common law. **1–58**

The following extract places in a modern context the relationship between *promise* and contract.

[29]*Promises in Scots Law* **1–59**

WW McBryde (1993) I.C.L.Q. 48

A. THE RELUCTANCE TO CONSTRUE A STATEMENT AS A PROMISE

It would be a mistake to imagine that promises were or are frequently enforced in Scottish courts. The reality is probably that few practitioners and judges have acquired a familiarity with this area of law. In the last 25 years there has been only one reported case with a clear unilateral promise (leaving aside *jus quaesitum tertio* and guarantees or cautionary obligations which are referred to frequently). The case is *Bathgate v Rosie*, in which a mother promised to pay for the repair of a shop window damaged by her son.[30] Reasons for this lack of authority may include the dominance of the 'offer and acceptance' model, the limited circumstances in which it may be possible to prove a promise ... and a lack of knowledge of the law on unilateral obligations. Experience in other areas of law suggests that knowledge of concepts leads to increased use and so it may be that one factor which will promote the growth of the jurisprudence of the unilateral promise is more academic writing. The problem is not confined to Scotland ...

B. PROBLEMS OF PROOF

The history of Scots law has some very unattractive rules on the constitution and proof of obligations which remain the law. It was decided in *Millar v Tremamondo* (1771 Mor. 12395.)[31] by a bare majority of a court of 13 judges, that a promise was not proveable by witnesses. The early law might have been different particularly because the canon law looked to substance rather than form ...

---

[27] For a full discussion of the historical development of promise in Scots law see WDH Sellar, "Promise", in R Zimmerman and K Reid (eds), *A History of Scottish Private Law* (Oxford: OUP, 2000).

[28] O Lando and H Beale (eds), *Principles of European Contract Law* (The Hague: Kluwer Law International, 1999).

[29] WW McBryde, *Promises in Scots Law*, (1993) I.C.L.Q 48 (© British Institute of International and Comparative Law: Cambridge University Press, reproduced with permission).

[30] *Bathgate v Rosie*, 1976 S.L.T. (Sh. Ct.) 16: it seems that the mother admitted the promise in the witness box and no attempt was made to insist on a proof by writ or a formal reference to oath.

[31] *Millar v Tremamondo*, 1771 Mor. 12395.

The reason for the limitation on the mode of proof can be gleaned from imperfect law reports. Hailes' *Decisions* reveals that Lord Pitfour thought that the Court of Session 'has been always narrowing a proof by witnesses: hence perjury is prevented more with us than in some countries'.[32] A modern commentator might suggest that this argument leads to the conclusion that excluding the evidence of all witnesses would be the best way to avoid perjury and, perhaps, of avoiding the damnation of souls . . .

The amount of literacy in the population may have encouraged the Scottish courts to make writing a requirement for at least some obligations. The period from 1700 to 1760 had seen an expansion of parish schools in Lowland rural areas and in these areas instruction for children in reading and writing would have been available. That does not mean that all children, including girls, were taught to read and write. But Smout[33] has concluded that the combination of parish schools and private schools was 'able to maintain a rural society in which almost everyone seems to have been able to read and write from at least as early as the mid eighteenth century . . . That was a remarkable achievement, certainly not paralleled in England, and probably paralleled in very few societies anywhere in the world, except for Prussia, parts of Switzerland and a few Puritan areas in the United States.'

In the Highland regions, on the other hand, where Gaelic was the main language, there were fewer schools, virtually no Gaelic books, and an indifferent attendance at schools. What the Court of Session judges might not have foreseen was that the shift of population from rural to urban areas from 1780 onwards may have resulted in a decrease in the percentage of the population which could write, given the difficulties of educating large numbers in the towns.

In any event the requirement that writing was necessary for an enforceable promise was bound to reduce the frequency of cases before the courts, although, as later history demonstrated, writing does not always remove a doubt about whether any obligation was intended and, if so, what the promisor was obliged to do.

A promise had to be proved by the writ or oath of the promisor. The 'writ' and the 'oath' acquired very technical definitions. In broad practical terms it meant that unless a promise was in writing it probably could not be enforced. Few pursuers would peril their case on a reference to the defender's oath when, as a consequence of the special procedure, challenge or contradiction of the answer was incompetent. Indeed the pursuer in *Millar v Tremamondo* refused to 'put his father-in-law on oath, lest he should perjure himself' . . .

1–60 D. THE DISTINCTION BETWEEN PROMISE AND OFFER

An offer or a completed contract is not subject to the limitations of proof which apply to a promise. This has emphasised the distinction between offer and promise. At the same time if there was anything which might be construed as acceptance there was, and is, a tendency to apply the offer and acceptance model to the end result. An offer followed by an acceptance is a familiar and relatively easily proved method of entering into a voluntary obligation. A promise followed by actions is another matter. If something has followed upon the promise it may be treated as the more familiar contract, even although this might not be the theoretically correct result. A promise is enforceable even although nothing has followed on it; conversely, actions following on a promise do not always convert into a contract, e.g. when there was an oral promise to pay for work on

[32] *Millar v Tremamondo*, 1771 Mor. 12395.
[33] T.C. Smout, *A History of the Scottish People*, 1560–1830.

church buildings followed by the building work, that did not result in an enforceable obligation against the promisor.[34]

The attraction of the offer/acceptance model can be illustrated by so-called offers of reward. In *Hunter v Hunter*, 1904 7F. 136, weekly publications known as *Answers* and *Titbits* offered to pay sums to next of kin if the deceased should have on him or her a current copy of the publication at the time of the accident. This morbid enquiry into the possessions of an accident victim yielded unexpected results when a painter, William Hunter, was killed in a train crash at St Enoch station, Glasgow, in 1903. An excursion express full of holiday-makers crashed into the buffers. It was the worst railway disaster in Scotland since the Tay Bridge collapse in 1879. Mr. Hunter, perhaps in holiday mood, had in his possession copies of the current editions of both *Answers* and *Titbits*. The subsequent litigation was about which relatives were entitled to the payments which had been made. For present purposes, the more interesting question is whether the relatives, or any of them, could have sued the proprietors of the magazines if there had been no payment.

Lord Young had doubts about whether there was a right to payment, as possibly did Lords Trayner and Hunter. The problem may be solved by following the offer/acceptance model and looking for evidence of acceptance including either communication of the acceptance or, more likely, waiver of the need for acceptance. An alternative approach in Scots law is to treat the 'offers' as promises'. Acceptance is then irrelevant; and the promises being in writing, proof may not be a difficulty.

In *Carlill v Carbolic Smoke Ball Co* [1893] 1 Q.B. 256 it was observed that there were circumstances in which notification of acceptance of an offer was not necessary to constitute a binding contract. This was applied to the promise to pay money to someone who used a smoke ball in certain circumstances. A parallel was drawn with the reward to the person who found a lost dog. When notification of acceptance is not required, until what stage may the offer be withdrawn? The questions raise many difficulties and the answers contrast markedly with the very strict rules which otherwise exist on communication of an acceptance. If the offer of a reward is treated as an enforceable promise, which it could be in Scots law, the problems posed by the *Carlill* analysis disappear. Another difficulty arises, however, because it is necessary to decide whether or not the promise can be revoked. Normally a promise cannot be revoked; but there is no theoretical objection to a promise which is expressly revocable or to a promise in variable terms, e.g. 'we will pay a pension to relatives of members of the association on terms which may be altered from time to time'[35]; or 'we will pay £10,000 to anyone who finds the Loch Ness Monster, but this reward may be withdrawn or varied by a notice in the Inverness Courier'. The problem, unresolved, and rarely discussed in Scotland, is the extent to which it may be implied that a promise can be revoked. As terms may be implied into a contract, so it should be possible to imply terms into a promise (whose express terms are typically brief). But an implication that there is a power of revocation of a promise may be unusual because one of the main features of a promise is that it is an obligation and thus different from a revocable offer ...

---

[34] *Smith v Oliver*, 1911 S.C. 103.

[35] *Love v Amalgamated Society of Lithographic Printers of Great Britain and Ireland*, 1912 S.C. 1078; *Cadoux v Central RC*, 1986 S.L.T. 117.

1–61

VIII. THE ACCEPTED PROMISE[36]

A promise need not be accepted; but what if it is accepted? It appears that in Scots law the result might be to create an agreement which can be proved by witnesses (while a promise needs proof by writ or oath). Of more general interest is the effect on the promisee. A promisee may reject a promise. As Stair said, 'It is true, if he in whose favour they are made, accept not, they become void, not by the negative non-acceptance, but by the contrary rejection. For as the will of the promisor constitutes a right in the other, so the other's will, by renouncing and rejecting that right, voids it, and makes it return.'[37] But once a promisee has accepted a promise it would appear that the ability to reject the promise disappears. There is an agreement binding on both promisor and promisee.

There is a question as to when a promise lapses by the passage of time. The correct view appears to be that a promise does not lapse after a reasonable time, because that would be to introduce 'reasonable time' as a period of prescription or limitation of obligations.[38] As a general rule a promise will prescribe in five years, unless it is constituted or evidenced in probative writing or it is a banknote, in which case a 20-year rule applies (although the periods of prescription can be interrupted by certain events)."[39]

It should not be assumed that the unilateral promise is restricted to family arrangements and rewards. There are many instances where the promise plays an important role in commercial transactions.

1–62

Constitution and Proof of Gratuitous Obligations: A comment on Scottish Law Commission Memorandum No.66

Hector MacQueen

1986 S.L.T. (News) 1

"Although the [Scottish Law] commission does not make this point in its [Memorandum No. 66], its proposals here are to some extent in line with the law of other major western legal systems. In England gratuitous transactions have no effect except when constituted in deeds under seal. The French Code Civil (art.931) and the German Bürgerliches Gesetzbuch (art.518) both provide that promises to make gifts must be notarially attested. But these rules have often been narrowly interpreted. Thus in one French case, comparable in some respects to *Smith v Oliver*, a promise to pay for a church bell if made to the promisor's specifications was found enforceable despite lack of notarisation, because the transaction was held to be onerous and not one of donation (Nicholas, *French Law of Contract*, pp.141–143). Equally in England manipulation of the concepts of contract and consideration has enabled the courts to make conditional promises legally enforceable although not written. If a person makes a statement undertaking to do X if someone else does Y, then that is an offer capable of acceptance by the act of doing Y, which is also the consideration for the obligation to do X. This is known as a 'unilateral contract' because only one party, the offeror, comes under any obligation by it. The classic example is the advertisement of a reward in certain circumstances, the

---

[36] WW McBryde discusses the issue of the accepted promise more fully in *The Law of Contract in Scotland*, 3rd edn (Edinburgh: W. Green, 2007), paras 2.31–2.34.

[37] Stair, *Institutions*, I.x.4.

[38] *Sichi v Biagi*, 1946 S.N. 66, per Lord Keith at 68.

[39] Prescription and Limitation (Scotland) Act 1973 ss.6 and 7, Sch.1.

best-known instance in the case law being *Carlill v Carbolic Smoke Ball Co* [1893] 1 Q.B. 256:

What all this shows is a recognition of the factual onerosity of these conditional undertakings, which has led the courts to seek escape routes from the rules on gratuitous obligations and gifts. But there are analytical difficulties with these routes which can have important practical effects. In particular there is the problem of the legal status of the initial statement while the acts for which it calls remain unperformed or incomplete. If, for example, it is only an offer, then no matter how promissory or obligatory it may appear to be, it is freely revocable by its maker, even though an offeree may have proceeded far with the acts constituting acceptance. In England ways of resolving this dilemma—for instance, that the offeror may not prevent acceptance being completed or has waived the need for communication to him of the acceptance—have been proposed but seem to lack any solid basis in principle (see *Daulia Ltd v Four Millbank Nominees* [1978] Ch. 231, per Goff LJ at p.239). But each attempt of this kind reinforces the view that the original statement ought to be regarded as creating an obligation from which the maker cannot withdraw.

In Scotland the concept of promise seems to permit avoidance of the difficulties which have so troubled the English courts and textbook writers. But it has yet to be fully recognised how useful the concept might be in the commercial context. Indeed the whole discussion of gratuitous obligations has been bedevilled by the consideration of trivial examples such as the promise of a reward for walking to York, and by the belief that: 'The commonest purpose of a unilateral promise is probably to make a gift, benefit a person or a charity, or to reward services performed not under contract or to an extent not contractually exigible' (Walker, Contracts (2nd edn), para.2.13). But in fact many unilateral undertakings are given in the business world and are normally treated there as binding. The courts have dealt with grants of options for the purchase of heritage and promises to hold offers open for acceptance for a stated period as obligatory (see *Littlejohn v Hadwen* (1882) 20 S.L.R. 5; *Stone v Macdonald*, 1979 S.L.T. 288), so fulfilling the reasonable expectations of those making and receiving such statements. Another example may be found in the letter of credit issued by a banker where the parties to an international sale of goods arrange for payment through a bank by means of a documentary credit transaction. The letter of credit is an undertaking by the buyer's banker to pay the seller upon presentation of the documents which represent the goods. It is fundamental to such an arrangement that the banker cannot withdraw the credit; the legal basis for this has never been clear in England, but in Scotland can clearly be found in the binding conditional promise (Gow, *Mercantile Law*, p.471, fn.98) . . .

The Scottish concept of gratuitous obligations and in particular the promise seems usefully and naturally applicable to all these situations, always provided that there is appropriate writing . . .

All this depends . . . on there being some appropriate writing to hand: under the present law, to prove the obligation; under the Scottish Law Commission scheme, to constitute it. Each of the undertakings mentioned in the last few paragraphs is gratuitous . . . In its memorandum the commission states quite correctly that the present law on requirements of writing 'is not, to put it at its lowest, likely to impress the international business world as being designed for the needs of the present day' (para.3.9). It is submitted that the business world would remain unimpressed with a law which required subscribed writing to be used in the constitution of gratuitous obligations such as those we have been considering. Of course it is true that many of these are already customarily framed in writing, but that writing does not necessarily meet even such a simple formality as subscription by the grantor. Thus for example a firm offer may be made by telex (see, e.g. *Wolf and Wolf v Forfar Potato Co*, 1984 S.L.T. 100), as may a promise to sell to the highest bidder (Harvela)."

1–63 The courts, as Professor McBryde suggests,[40] are reluctant to construe a statement as a promise. They will be particularly reluctant to do so if the transaction is essentially commercial. Such a statement is more likely to be interpreted as an offer, which will require acceptance. There is also the unfortunate tendency to think of promises in terms of domestic, rather than commercial arrangements. There is a similar preference on the part of judges to regard transactions as contracts, rather than promises. Thus, in a borderline case, where it is difficult to establish whether an obligation is founded on contract or promise, the courts will prefer to look for evidence of contract. Consider and contrast the cases of *Littlejohn v Hadwen* and *Paterson v Highland Railway*.[41] Written evidence is still required to establish a promise in a non-business transaction.[42] It is likely that it will continue to be important to establish whether such a transaction is on the facts a promise, or a contract. The two cases that follow illustrate just how difficult that distinction might be.

1–64

Smith v Oliver

1911 S.C. 103

Court of Session, First Division: Lord President (Dunedin), Lords Kinnear, Salvesen and Johnston

Mrs Oliver had allegedly promised to leave £7,000 in her will to a church in Edinburgh to be used for completing alterations to the church. The work was completed on the strength of Mrs Oliver's promise. Mrs Oliver failed to provide in her will for the £7,000. The trustees of the church claimed the £7,000 from Mrs Oliver's executor, claiming that they had relied on Mrs Oliver's assurances.

The court rejected the church's claim.

"LORD PRESIDENT (DUNEDIN): . . . The Lord Ordinary has held that the outcome of the pursuers' averments is, that Mrs. Oliver made a promise to leave a certain sum of money in her will; and that such a promise can be proved only by writ. A reclaiming note has been taken to your Lordships, and the argument before us was that such a promise could be proved by parole. The argument of the reclaimers was strenuously directed to attempting to make out that there was a contract here; and it was said that although there is a rule that innominate contracts of an unusual character can only be proved by writ, yet this was not a contract of such an unusual character as to exclude parole proof. Now I think that the first objection to that argument is this, that, look at the averments with all the indulgence that you like, the outcome will always be that there is in truth no contract at all averred here, but merely a promise to pay. And if that is so, I suppose that it is very well settled law that a gratuitous promise to pay can be proved only by writ. It is vain to try and make out that this was a mutual contract or that it was a contract of agency. The simple answer to all that is this, that, so far as agency is concerned, no one supposes that a tradesman could have had an action against the lady; that, so far as mandate is concerned, there was no mandate to do anything for the mandant; and that so far as mutual contract is concerned, the lady was getting no benefit except in the sense in which anybody may be said to get something when anything is done in which he is interested. Now it is quite well settled by a series of cases that a party cannot turn what is, in its nature, a mere promise into a contract, so as to be allowed to prove it by parole, by simply averring that on the faith of the promise certain things were done by him; that is to say, he cannot turn a promise into a contract by *rei interventus*, so to speak . . . I

[40] WW McBryde, *The Law of Contract in Scotland*, 3rd edn (Edinburgh: W. Green, 2007).

[41] See below, paras 4–44—4–47.

[42] Requirements of Writing (Scotland) Act, s.1(2)(a)(ii); see above, paras 1–07—1–11.

> have no doubt, of course, that it is perfectly possible for one to bind himself in his lifetime to leave something in his will ... But although it is quite possible for one so to bind himself, I do not think it has ever been suggested that proof of his doing so could be by anything except writ, and—although this is not perhaps entirely conclusive—it would certainly be a most extraordinary result if at one and the same moment the law was that a nuncupative will for more than one hundred pounds Scots was not good, but that nevertheless it was possible to prove by parole a promise to make a will. The rule may in individual cases cause hardship, but it is a salutary rule on the whole, because if it was allowable to prove by parole that a person had promised to leave a sum by will, there might be no end to the imposture which might be practised on the Court."

If Mrs Oliver's promise were part of a contract, would that contract have been a gratuitous contract, or might it be classified as onerous? The question of whether or not a contract is gratuitous is largely irrelevant.[43] **1–65**

The feature which distinguishes a contract from a "bare" promise is that a contract comprises an offer which is conditional upon acceptance by the person to whom it is made. What differentiates the bare promise is that the language or conduct of the person making the promise must clearly indicate that his or her obligations are not conditional upon acceptance by the intended beneficiary, although they may be subject to other conditions.[44]

Petrie v Earl of Airlie **1–66**
(1834) 13 S. 68
Court of Session, First Division: Lord Corehouse

Airlie had presided at a meeting to discuss the Great Reform Bill. Airlie was in the minority which voted against the Bill. Shortly afterwards, anonymous placards appeared in burghs throughout Forfarshire, naming those who voted in favour of the Bill and those who voted against. Airlie issued a proclamation, offering 100 guineas reward "to any person who will give such information as may lead to the detection of the author & printer. The reward will be paid on conviction". Alexander Petrie, an Arbroath weaver, gave the names of his brother, David Petrie, and James Lindsay. The Lord Advocate decided not to prosecute, and, although it was open to Airlie to prosecute, there was no prosecution. Petrie claimed the reward. Airlie contended that the reward was not payable, as there had been no conviction.

The First Division of the Inner House of the Court of Session upheld the decision of the Lord Ordinary (Corehouse) in the Outer House that Airlie was bound to pay the reward.

What follows is an extract of Lord Corehouse's note of the case to the First Division.

> "LORD COREHOUSE: ... In the notice issued by the respondent, it is stated that a false and scandalous placard had been put up without the printer's name or date being attached to it, and a reward of one hundred guineas is offered to any person who will give such information as may lead to the detection of the author or printer. So far the offer is unconditional; but it is added, that the reward will be paid on conviction. The advocator says that he gave the information required; his declaration was taken in writing by the clerk of the lieutenancy employed by the respondent for that purpose, and it is not disputed that it led to the detection of the author and printer of the placard.

[43] See above, para.1–56.

[44] See WW McBryde, *The Law of Contract in Scotland*, 3rd edn (Edinburgh: W. Green, 2007), paras 2–25—2–27.

> The advocator claims the reward, but he is met with the defence, that conviction has not taken place . . . [I]f the respondent had chosen to prosecute, he might unquestionably have convicted the printer . . . But assuming that [a conviction] could not [be obtained], if the respondent offered a reward for detecting the author, under a mistaken idea that the offence was indictable when it was not so, it is he and not the informer who is responsible for that mistake. If the time specified for payment of the reward, namely, the date of the conviction, is held to involve a condition, that condition cannot import more, than that the information given should be sufficient to satisfy the Court or Jury, as in a question of proof, to which alone it refers, and not as in a question of relevancy, with which it has no connexion. The respondent having obtained from the advocator all that he stipulated for, he is not entitled to evade payment of the price which he offered for it, because it does not answer the purpose which he had in view."

This does not mean that a promise automatically becomes a contract merely because it is conditional upon the occurrence of some event unless that required event can truly be considered an acceptance. The distinction, important though it is, is difficult to draw, especially where the language is that of a gratuitous contract. The following case, albeit tangentially, raises important issues on the relationship between contract and promise.

1–67 **Morton's Trustees v The Aged Christian Friend Society of Scotland**

(1899) 2 F. 82

Court of Session, First Division: Lord Kinnear, Lords McLaren and Adam

Morton wrote to a potential director of the Society, a charity not yet constituted, undertaking to pay £1,000 by 10 annual instalments for the provision of pensions by the Society. The undertaking was accepted by the Society once it had been constituted, but Morton died before he had paid the last two instalments. Lord Kinnear found a contractual obligation to make the payments.

> "LORD KINNEAR: The questions in this case are of some novelty, but they depend upon principles which are perfectly simple in themselves and are well established. The late Mr Morton of Rosemount, who appears to have been a generous and benevolent person, undertook to pay certain sums of money to a charitable society called the Aged Christian Friend Society of Scotland, and duly performed his promises so long as he lived. But he died before they had been completely performed, and the question is whether his representatives are now under obligation to do what he would certainly have done himself if he had been still in life. That appears to me to be a mere question of construction of the documents in which the promises of the deceased are embodied. If a promise is intended, as Mr Bell puts it, as a final engagement it is binding, but it is not binding if it is a mere expression of a probable intention which the promisor might or might not fulfil. It is a familiar doctrine in the law of Scotland, differing in that respect from the law of England, that an obligation is binding although it may not proceed on a valuable consideration, or may not be expressed in a solemn form, such as a deed under seal. What is necessary is that the promisor should intend to bind himself by an enforceable obligation and should express that intention in clear words. Now, in applying this doctrine to the documents before us, I do not see that there can be much doubt as to the meaning and legal effect of the letters which we are required to consider.
>
> In the first of these letters, that of the 27th November 1888, Mr Morton explains the nature of a benevolent scheme which he is desirous to see established, and says to the person to whom he is writing:—'If you saw your way to constitute' such a society as is

described 'for Scotland, you would do a good work, and I would have much pleasure in assisting the finding of funds to start the Society.' So far, I think, there is no obligation at all; but then he goes on to describe in some specific detail the nature of the charitable society which he desires to see founded, and then, after inviting his correspondent to form a committee for the purpose of establishing the Society, he says: 'I will be happy to subscribe £100 towards commencing the work when you can get another £100 subscribed and a committee formed'. This letter is addressed to the Rev. Mr Lowe, who was a member of the provisional committee by whom the Society was afterwards established, and who was ultimately a director of the Society. In the second letter, Mr Morton observes upon the character of a society which it would appear had been described to him by his correspondent, Mr Lowe, and says that the society so described 'would be a valuable addition to the Scottish societies, but it is not the kind of society which I am desirous of helping the formation of,' and therefore it is quite clear he had a specific and definite idea in his mind of the kind of society which he wished his correspondent to form; and after explaining the character of the society, which he himself approves of, he goes on to say:—'It is a society which, if properly established and conducted, would stand at the very head and top of all Scotch benevolent societies, and I am willing to increase my offer of help to the establishment of such a society to a subscription of £1,000 (one thousand pounds), to be payable in ten annual subscriptions of £100 each, provided a properly constituted committee can be found and a fair amount subscribed in proportion to the above subscription offered by myself.' In the last letter of the three, the letter of 16th May 1889, he expresses a quite sufficiently specific opinion as to what would be necessary in order to satisfy his condition that a fair amount should be subscribed in proportion to the amount subscribed by himself.

Now, these two first letters appear to me to contain a clear offer which invites acceptance, because the offer is made on certain conditions. The writer says—If you will do certain things involving the expenditure of time and trouble as well as money, then I, on my part, promise to give you a definite sum of money within a definite time. That offer was accepted. It is one of the facts on which the parties are agreed and which we are bound to take as facts established in this case, that the offer was duly accepted by the provisional committee of this society, which was formed and established under the countenance and advice and to the satisfaction of Mr Morton, the offerer. Accordingly Mr Morton, during his life, paid regularly to the said Society eight annual subscriptions of £100 each, the last payment being made on 5th January 1897, and the case states that two annual subscriptions of £100 each due on 1st January 1898 and 1st January 1899 are still unpaid, and are required to make up the £1,000 promised.

The result of these facts, taken in connection with the letters is, that we have in the letters a definite offer determined by acceptance. I do not know that anything more is required in order to make a contract according to the law of Scotland."

The last two paragraphs in the above extract clearly show that Lord Kinnear regarded the exchange between the parties as a contract. Why, then, in the preceding paragraphs did he dwell on whether or not Mr Morton had made a promise to pay?

Clearly the gratuitous contract—the "promise" or "offer" that requires acceptance—will be difficult to differentiate from the unilateral promise. Because of changes in the law relating to the requirements of writing necessary to establish a promise,[45] the difference may become less important in practice. The following more recent illustration, in a commercial context, clearly suggests that the matter is by no means irrelevant.

[45] See above, para.1–06 onwards.

1–68 **Dawson International Plc v Coats Paton Plc**

1993 S.L.T. 80

Court of Session, Outer House: Lord Prosser

Coats Paton, a major Scottish textile company, was vulnerable to takeover bids. Its board of directors received an offer from Dawson, another large Scottish textile company, and the formal offer document was due to go out to shareholders on 10 February 1986. In the interim, Vantona, another potential bidder, made an offer which put a higher value on Coats Paton than Dawson's offer had done. The Coats Paton board withdrew support for the Dawson offer and accepted the merger with Vantona.

Dawson claimed the costs that they had incurred in designing and underwriting their proposed offer as damages or reimbursement based either on breach of contract by Coats Paton, or on their reliance on representations made fraudulently, or negligently, by Coats Paton.

Lord Prosser found that there was nothing in the actions of Dawson and Coats Paton to indicate that they were entering into a binding contract.

"LORD PROSSER: ... Speaking generally, I would accept that when two parties are talking to one another about a matter which has commercial significance to both, a statement by one party that he will do some particular thing will normally be construed as obligatory, or as an offer, rather than as a mere statement of intention, if the words and deeds of the other party indicate that the statement was so understood, and the obligation confirmed or the offer accepted so that parties appeared to regard the commercial "deal" as concluded. But in considering whether there is indeed a contract between the parties, in any particular case, it will always be essential to look at the particular facts, with a view to discovering whether these facts, rather than some general rule of thumb, can be said to reveal consensus and an intention to conclude a contract.

In the present case, I am not persuaded that it was the intention of the parties to form a contract whereby they became reciprocally obliged to make and recommend the proposed offer to the defenders' shareholders. It is not merely that the use of the future tense is found in a statement to third parties, rather than in a statement made by one party to another. Indeed, it is not difficult to imagine circumstances in which a public statement to third parties, incorporating an indication of acceptance or agreement, might be evidence of prior agreement, or might itself constitute the contract between the parties. But in the present case, the language of the press announcement appears to me, when taken along with the language in which the two sides describe the decisions they were taking, to reflect agreement (whether contractual or not) as to various things that will be done in the event of a merger, without any prior contractual obligation on the pursuers to make the offer, and (in the absence of that obligation upon the pursuers) with no reciprocal obligation upon the defenders. Moreover, one must look at the subject matter. Where the subject matter is a simple commercial act, such as the delivery of goods, it seems to me to be a quite simple step to an inference of concluded contractual intent. But in the present case, with the two sides discussing changes which would be effected by contracts between the pursuers and the defenders' shareholders, the suggestion of a prior contract, with obligations to make the offer and recommend it, strikes me as much less natural. The unlikelihood of a preliminary contract of that kind is increased by the fact that the wish of each party, to be able to rely upon the other fulfilling his stated intentions, could be met without contractual ties, by relying on the code being followed, and by each side's commitment only being expressed in the one joint statement by both. Whether there was any contract as to what would be done after

> merger is another matter. I am not satisfied by the language used that there was any contract in relation to the steps of offer and recommendation which would precede any eventual merger.
>
> I have concentrated thus far upon the use of the future tense, and the language of agreement, in the press announcement. But there is a second aspect of that statement which may be important in considering whether the parties had contracted to make and recommend the proposed offer. The subject matter of the alleged contract is the making and 'recommending' of an offer. I see no real problem in the concept of one party binding himself, in a contract with another party, to make an offer to third parties. But the position in relation to recommendation is perhaps more complicated. What is in issue is not a *de praesenti* recommendation; what is in issue is a binding obligation, undertaken at one point in time, to make a recommendation at a subsequent point in time—presumably the time when the offer is open for acceptance. Counsel for the pursuers acknowledged that the nature of recommendation was what gave rise to some of the problems or complexities in regard to the supposed contract. I do not think it necessary or appropriate to embark on any attempt at a definition of 'recommendation', but whether as an integral part of its meaning, or as a prerequisite of any bona fide recommendation, it appears to me (and was not I think disputed) that recommendation entails or implies that the person making the recommendation believes that what he is recommending is good and appropriate. If a future recommendation is contemplated, this belief must also be in the future.
>
> To bind oneself to do something which is dependent on one's future beliefs, or even to bind oneself to believe something in the future, is no doubt possible in law. But where it is suggested that someone has done this, I would be inclined to be slow in putting such a construction upon their words and deeds. And more specifically, if someone has thus bound themselves, I think it is clear that any such contract, or the rules regulating its enforcement, would have to allow for the possibility that the person who has bound himself to make the recommendation quite simply cannot do so in good faith, for want of the necessary belief in it. In some circumstances, it might be that this 'let out' might legitimately be read into the contract as an implied term. It might also be a question of construction, in relation to a particular contract, whether the person undertaking the obligation to recommend was warranting his belief at the time of that undertaking."

This case brings us back to the beginning of this chapter. The question Lord Prosser had to answer was whether this "undertaking" to put the offer to the board was binding. He only considered whether it was binding as an offer in a contract, not whether it was binding as a promise. In any case, the stumbling block for Dawson was to establish that, as a matter of future conduct, the directors intended to bind Coats Paton.[46]

Regus (Maxim) Ltd v Bank of Scotland Plc 1–69
[2013] CSIH 12; 2013 S.C. 331
Court of Session, Inner House, First Division: Lord President (Gill), Lord Bonomy, Lord Wheatley

A scheme of investment was established to develop a site that became "Eurocentral" in what was the North Lanarkshire Enterprise Zone, encouraged by tax incentives and a simplified planning regime. A developer would construct a building or buildings and find the tenants. A headline rent was agreed between the landlord and the developer, which was payable whether or not the premises were let. The headline rent was payable by the

[46] These are matters explored more fully in Ch.2.

developer from a rent guarantee fund, set up by the developer with Bank of Scotland (BoS), representing a certain number of years' rental income, thus securing the landlord's position.

Maxim Office Park at Eurocentral was bought by Tritax from the original developer, partly with funds provided by BoS, although they employed TAL CPT to manage and implement the development.

A facility agreement was created by Tritax with BoS and money was deposited by Tritax with BoS representing rent and project cost guarantees. No payments could be made from the accounts without BoS's permission. The facility agreement specified that insolvency or a failure to make payment when due would amount to a default, on the occurrence of which on the part of Tritax, BoS was entitled, inter alia, to apply the funds in the guarantee account to payment of the sums owed to it by Tritax (cl.24.2.5).

Regus took a sublease of premises at Maxim Office Park. As an inducement, Tritax agreed to meet Regus's fitting out costs through what was called a "capital contribution", payable from the facility agreement with BoS.

When Regus claimed £913,172 from BoS as the fit-out costs, BoS refused payment because Tritax had defaulted. Regus claimed, inter alia, that the money was nevertheless payable, because a letter from BoS to Tritax, issued after the facility agreement was created, was a binding undertaking by BoS, separate from the facility agreement, to make the payment to Regus and that moneys representing the fit-out costs were held by BoS solely for that purpose. That letter stated:

> "On behalf of the landlord (Tritax Eurocentral EZ Unit Trust) and TAL CPT, we hold the sum of £913,172 to meet the landlord's commitment to fit-out costs. These funds will be released in accordance with the drawdown procedure agreed between the parties, whereby the proposed tenant's contractors will issue monthly certificates."

1–70 "Lord President (Gill)

Conclusions

Promise issue

Nature of promissory liability

[31] Counsel for both parties took as the starting point the opinion of Lord Kinnear in *Morton's Trs v Aged Christian Friend Society of Scotland*. That case is often cited for the proposition that a promise is binding in Scots law. Lord Kinnear's statement of the principle is as follows (p.85):

'If a promise is intended, as Mr Bell puts it, as a final engagement it is binding, but it is not binding if it is a mere expression of a probable intention which the promissor might or might not fulfil ... What is necessary is that the promissor should intend to bind himself by an enforceable obligation and should express that intention in clear words.'

[32] The unreferenced quotation from Bell is to be found in the Principles (i, 8). Lord Kinnear then professes to apply that principle to the letters of the late Mr Morton on which the case turned. He treats the first and second of the three 'charity letters' as being offers that were accepted. He then turns to the 'pension letters'. He considers that the first of them constitutes a promise, but nevertheless concludes that it is a 'distinct offer of personal responsibility, and an offer that invites acceptance or rejection as an offer on conditions' that was in the event accepted. Later he refers to the pension letters in terms of agency and mandate (*Morton's Trs*, p.88). In these respects Lord Kinnear's analysis is confused and confusing. The difficulties that it causes in these respects are readily explained by the fact that counsel for the Society in that case argued, inter alia, that the

relevant correspondence constituted a series of binding contracts, and that there had been actings in reliance on the deceased's offers constituting *rei interventus* (*Morton's Trs*, p.85).

[33] In my opinion, a promise in the law of Scotland is a unilateral juristic act. It acquires its binding force by reason of the declarant's expression of his will to be bound. Stair tells us that a promise is obligatory per se (*Institutions*, I, x, 4). He says that 'the will of the promiser constitutes a right in the other' (ibid). In this respect, as Erskine observes, Stair differs from Grotius and von Pufendorf , who adhered to the view that an absolute promise required acceptance because no obligation could be formed without the joint consent or concurrence of both parties (Erskine, *Institute*, II, iii, 88; cf Swain, "Contract as Promise", p.13). Erskine considered Stair's view to be 'agreeable to our practice' (loc cit).

[34] It follows, therefore, that because in Scots law a promise acquires its obligatory nature at the moment at which it is made, questions of acceptance and of actings in reliance on it are irrelevant (*Smith v Oliver (No.1)*, Lord President Dunedin, p.111). A valid promise has serious consequences. It is irrevocable, unlike an offer, which may be withdrawn at any time before acceptance. It is binding even though it is not known to the promisee. If it is conditional, it will become binding if the condition is fulfilled, even though the promisee did not know of the original promise. Moreover, a promise places an obligation on the promisor and on no one else. It may result in the promisor's being given something in return, typically where the promise is made subject to a condition; but the promise does not oblige the promisee to fulfil the condition.

[35] Furthermore, in my view, where the promise is made subject to a condition requiring action by the promisee, the fulfilment of the condition does not convert the promise into a contract ex post facto. The late Sir Thomas Smith pointed out that the distinction between a conditional promise and a conditional offer may be narrow ('Pollicitatio—Promise and Offer', pp.148–150); but in my view it is a material and significant distinction nonetheless.

Clear words **1–71**

[36] Counsel for the pursuer submitted that there was no special rule that a promissory obligation could be created only by clear words. If Lord Kinnear's dictum was understood in context, it became apparent that the words used in the instrument were only one consideration. He pointed out that on the charity issue, Lord Kinnear relied, inter alia, on the fact that the deceased had begun payment of the sums referred to. From the terms of the letters, together with the background circumstances, he inferred an intention to make a definite offer (*Morton's Trs*, p.86). On the pension issue, Lord Kinnear started with the explicit language of the first pension letter that in his view was 'perfectly conclusive'. He considered that it was a fair construction, in light of the first letter, that the subsequent letters which were not in such strong terms disclosed an intention to incur a legal obligation (*Morton's Tr*, pp.87, 88).

[37] I do not accept this submission. In my opinion, an obligation of this kind can be created only by clear words. Since any promissory obligation is intention-based, the court's task is to consider whether the evidence, objectively assessed, discloses an intention on the part of the alleged promisor to incur a legally binding engagement (Stair, *Institutions*, I, x, 2; cf. *Cawdor v Cawdor*). That question, in my view, is to be decided on a consideration of the alleged promisor's own words. Bearing in mind the stringent consequences of a valid promise that I have described, I consider that a promise is binding only if the promisor's own words are clear and unambiguous.

[38] Erskine sets a demanding standard. He indicates that a promise may be proved provided that it is made 'in words proper to express a present act of the will, such as, "I promise", or, "I oblige myself to give," or "make over in a present" (*Institute*, III, iii,

88). I doubt whether clarity always requires such a specific expression. It may be that the meaning of the promisor's words will be clear if they derive their meaning from the relevant factual background known to both parties. I agree with the view of Lady Paton in *Ballast Plc v Laurieston Properties Ltd* that in a commercial context, the words of an alleged promise should be interpreted in the same way as any other alleged commercial obligation would be. Lady Paton accepted that the question of construction should be approached objectively on the basis of what a reasonable recipient with knowledge of the background would have understood by the documents in question (para.143). I understood counsel for the defender to be content with that approach.

[39] Counsel for the pursuer submitted that if there was a requirement of clear words, it applied only when the promise was gratuitous. He submitted that the bank letter was not gratuitous. It was issued in the defender's own self-interest. The defender was closely involved in the lease negotiations. The bank letter helped to secure the rental income of the pursuer from which the defender's lending could be repaid. Therefore any requirement for clear words did not apply.

[40] I do not agree. The expression 'gratuitous unilateral obligation' is used in sec 1(2)(a)(ii) of the Requirements of Writing (Scotland) Act 1995 (cap 7); but the interpretation of it in that context is not free from difficulty. In *Van Klaveren v Servisair (UK) Ltd* (para.9), an Extra Division said that the requirement for clear words existed because 'a unilateral obligation [i.e. promise] is normally gratuitous and a clear intention must be shown if a gratuitous obligation is to be undertaken'. But the court did not explain what was required where a unilateral obligation was onerous. That is surprising since the alleged unilateral obligation in that case was an undertaking by an insurer to admit liability in an action of damages for personal injury. Other references in the case law to a gratuitous promise (e.g. *Smith v Oliver (No.1)*, Lord President Dunedin, p.110) do not assist us in a search for the definition of that concept.

[41] In my view, it is unnecessary to pursue the meaning of gratuitous in the context of this action, even if one assumes that there is a meaningful distinction between a gratuitous and an onerous unilateral obligation. The consequences that I have described apply to every promise, regardless of the reason for which, or the motive with which, the promise is made. In view of those consequences, I am of the opinion that the distinction for which counsel for the pursuer has contended, if it is meaningful, is irrelevant. Clear words are required to constitute a promissory obligation in every case.

1–72 *Construction of the bank letter*

[42] I am unable to construe the bank letter as constituting a binding promise by the defender to pay to the pursuer any sum in respect of its fit-out costs. On the contrary, like the Lord Ordinary, I consider that it is clear that the defender expressed no such promise. There is an initial improbability in the idea that a bank, whose normal obligations are owed to its customer, should choose to make a binding promise in favour of a third party.

[43] The unlikelihood that the bank letter constituted a promise to the pursuer is confirmed by the fact that the letter is not addressed to the pursuer. The defender contemplated that it would be shown to the pursuer; but that does not of itself have the consequence that, in a question with the pursuer, the document had promissory effect (cf. Gloag, pp.16, 17).

[44] The letter makes clear that the defender holds the money on behalf of Tritax and TAL CPT and not in its own right. It follows therefore that the defender's freedom to pay out any of the money to a third party will be regulated by the terms and conditions on which the defender holds the fund. That, in my view, excludes the possibility that the defender was undertaking to pay the money to the pursuer even if, when the pursuer came to demand payment, it no longer held any funds on behalf of Tritax and TAL CPT.

[45] That view is consistent with the email of 18 August 2009 sent on behalf of Tritax and HUB to the pursuer's property agents which suggested that 'blocked accounts' were available to meet costs other than tenant incentives.

[46] Furthermore, the bank letter spells out that the release of the money is governed by an agreed procedure. That, in my view, is at odds with the submission for the pursuer that the defender was promising to pay it to the pursuer on demand as its own debt. In these circumstances the use of the words 'will be released in accordance with the drawdown procedure' cannot, as counsel for the pursuer accepts, necessarily create a promissory obligation (*Ballast Plc v Laurieston Properties Ltd*, para.147; *Kleinwort Benson Ltd v Malaysia Mining Corporation Bhd*). In my view, those words are not in any sense a guarantee by the defender. They simply presuppose that the funds will still be available when the time comes.

[47] Moreover, the letter refers only to funds actually held by the defender at the date of the letter. As counsel for the pursuer accepted, circumstances could arise, such as an arrestment or a liquidation, that could prevent the defender from releasing the funds to the pursuer. Counsel for the pursuer submitted that notwithstanding that the occurrence of an event of default, as defined in the facility agreement, gave the defender the right to transfer the funds to another account (cf. facility agreement, cl.24.2.5), the defender effectively renounced that right in the bank letter. I do not agree. In my opinion, that submission overlooks the fact that in a question with Tritax, the defender had the right at common law to balance accounts. There is nothing in the letter to suggest that the defender was renouncing its rights under the facility agreement or at common law.

[48] All of these considerations point strongly against the pursuer's proposed interpretation of the letter.

[49] It is also significant that in a question with the pursuer, the obligation to meet the capital contribution lay with HUB as head-tenant, yet HUB is not mentioned in the letter at all.

[50] Finally, I agree with the Lord Ordinary that the last sentence of the letter is fatal to the pursuer's case. It makes plain that the defender's 'confirmation' is not unconditional.

[51] In reaching these conclusions I have looked only at the wording of the letter. If counsel for the pursuer is right in submitting that the court should interpret the letter in the context of the surrounding circumstances, then that approach would lead me to the same conclusion. The key to this whole dispute is that the defender refused the pursuer's request that funds to cover the capital contribution should be placed in escrow or in joint names. That is the only reason why the defender issued the bank letter at all. Since the defender had refused the pursuer's proposal, I fail to see why the defender could be thought to have accepted the direct liability to the pursuer that is now contended for. Furthermore, since the email of 18 August 2009 disclosed to the pursuer that the release of money from the defender's accounts was subject to Tritax's consent; and since in the exchange of emails on 21 August 2009 the pursuer expressly acknowledged its willingness to accept that the capital contribution was not to be held on joint deposit, I fail to see how the pursuer could reasonably have construed the bank letter in the sense for which it now contends.

[52] I should add that I am not convinced that the bank letter can properly be described, as the Lord Ordinary thought, as a comfort letter. The essence of a comfort letter, in my view, is that the party issuing it, while disclaiming a legal liability to act as the letter describes, nonetheless makes an assertion in good faith of its present intention so to act (cf. *Kleinwort Benson Ltd v Malaysia Mining Corporation Bhd*). In my view, the better interpretation of the bank letter is that, in consequence of the defender's refusal to

place the funds in escrow or in joint names, it gives clear and precise notice that an acknowledgment that it holds the funds to meet the capital contribution, subject to the qualifications that it sets out, is the only assurance of payment that the pursuer is to get."

Good faith

1–73 Towards the end of the 19th century the development of the law of contract in Scotland suffered a tragic setback, in a well-meaning attempt to approximate the laws of Scotland and England through statutory intervention (most notably the Sale of Goods Act 1893) and judicial creativity (most notably Lord Watson's importation of the English principle of misrepresentation into the nascent law of induced error[47]). By introducing English common law principles, without the leavening principles of English equity, Scots law appears to have stunted the development of an overriding principle of good faith. The Draft Common Frame of Reference (DCFR) contains such an overriding principle: "(3) In [the] interpretation and development [of these rules] regard should be had to the need to promote . . . (b) good faith and fair dealing . . . "[48] and, more specifically in relation to contracts: "(1) Parties are free to make a contract or other juridical act and to determine in contents, subject to the rules of good faith and fair dealing . . .".[49] PECL, in s.2, "General Duties", art.1.201(1) also introduces a compulsory overriding duty of "Good faith and fair dealing": "Each party must act in accordance with good faith". Nevertheless, good faith in Scots law does at least operate in a piecemeal fashion to remedy instances of bad faith.[50]

In recent years there has been increasing academic focus on the concept of good faith. This has been brought about not only by some developments in the case law and the influence of European and international attempts at codification of contract law, but also by recent judicial pronouncements, notably that of Lord Clyde in *Smith v Bank of Scotland*[51] (the case is considered at para.5–17 onwards.). The following extracts consider whether there is such a general concept in Scots law and what the doctrine entails.

1–74 [52]*Good Faith in the Scots Law of contract: An undisclosed principle?*

HL MacQueen

ADM Forte (ed), *Good Faith in Contract and Property* (Oxford: Hart Publishing, 1999), pp.5–37

"The Utility of Recognising a Good Faith Principle

It is, however, relatively easy to proceed through a system of rules like Scots contract law, as I have just done, and to pick out those parts of it which seem to reflect the requirements and values of good faith as it has been understood in Europe in modern times. It would be surprising to find rules which encouraged or allowed bad faith; but not so for rules embodying requirements of good faith. The real question is, what difference does it make to the system to declare now that there is a general principle of good faith holding it all together? Given that the rules are expressions of good faith, why do they need to be reinforced by a generalisation? What function that is not currently

---

[47] On which see below, paras 6–03—6–10.

[48] Draft Common Frame of Reference I.–1:102: Interpretation and Development.

[49] Draft Common Frame of Reference II.–1:102: Party Autonomy.

[50] See in particular recent developments in uninduced error, below, para.6–33 onwards.

[51] *Smith v Bank of Scotland*, 1997 S.C. (HL) 111.

[52] © ADM Forte (ed), *Good Faith in Contract and Property* (Oxford: Hart Publishing (an imprint of Bloombury Publishing Plc), 1999).

performed by the system would such a generalisation bring about? The answer would seem to be that the articulation of the general principle enables the identification and solution of problems which the existing rules do not, or seem unable to reach. The history of the good faith doctrine in Germany illustrates this very well. The celebrated Article 242 of the BGB enabled the German courts to develop doctrines of *culpa in contrahendo*, change in circumstances, contracts with protective effects vis-a-vis third parties, positive breach of contract, abuse of contractual rights and termination of long-term contracts, without any other support from the code. Problems arose for which no direct codal provision appeared to exist, or which existed as the result of what the code said; Article 242 enabled the court to overcome these obstacles without incurring the reproach of pure judicial law-making.[53] *Smith v Bank* of Scotland may be a domestic example of the same phenomenon. The general principle of good faith enabled the House of Lords to deal with a problem for which there was thought to be no satisfactory answer in the existing specific rules of Scots law. An apparent gap was filled, and a new rule came into being.[54] It is exactly the same as recognising a general duty of care in negligence,[55] or a principle against unjustified enrichment[56]; the law can move on, and new rules develop. As a result, the principle may remain relatively latent, or continue to be stated in extremely general terms, without doing too much damage to the important values of certainty and predictability in the law, since it is constantly in the process of being refined by the formulation of more concrete rules in particular cases.[57] The principle also provides a basis upon which existing rules inconsistent with it can be criticised and reformed, whether judicially or by legislation ... [58]

Conclusion 1–75

This essay has argued that good faith does play a substantial role in the Scottish law of contract, but that on the whole this has been expressed by way of particular rules rather than through broad general statements of the principle. As a result its role in the law has been submerged, or subterranean, and the effects have not been so far-reaching as in the Continental systems. The overall result is rather typical of the mixed system that is Scots law. A particularly good example is provided by the authorities on pre-contractual liability discussed in the final section of this essay. These authorities do recognise a form

---

[53] See WF Ebke and BM Steinhauer, "The Doctrine of Good Faith in German Contract Law" in J Beatson and D Friedmann (eds), *Good Faith and Fault in Contract Law* (Oxford: Clarendon Press, 1995), above, p.171; BS Markesinis, W Lorenz and G Dannemann, *The German Law of Obligations Volume I: The Law of Contracts and Restitution: A Comparative Introduction* (Oxford: Clarendon Press, 1997), Ch.7.

[54] Commentators are at one in seeing *Smith* as judicial innovation: GL Gretton, "Sexually Transmitted Debt", 1997 S.L.T. (News) 195; JM Thomson, "Misplaced Concern?" (1997) 65 S.L.G. 124; R Dunlop, "Spouses, Caution and the Banks" (1997) 42 J.L.S.S. 446; LJ MacGregor, "The House of Lords Applies *O'Brien* North of the Border" (1998) 2 Edin. L.R. 90; SF Dickson, "Good Faith in Contract: Spousal Guarantees and *Smith v Bank of Scotland*", 1998 S.L.T. (News) 39.

[55] As in *Donoghue v Stevenson*, 1932 S.C. (H.L.) 31.

[56] As may have happened in *Shilliday v Smith*, 1998 S.C. 725 and *Dollar Land (Cumbernauld) Ltd v CIN Properties Ltd*, 1998 S.C. (H.L.) 90.

[57] See also Hesselink's "Good Faith" in A. Hartkamp,et al (eds), *Towards a European Civil Code*, 2nd edn (Nijmegen: Kluwer, 1998), p.309 conclusion that "if the role of the judge as a creator of rules is fully recognised, there is no need for a general good faith clause in a code or restatement of European private law. It may even do harm because it gives the courts an excuse for not formulating the rule that they apply. If however there is still some doubt as to the power of the courts, a good faith clause could be useful in order to assure that the judge may create new rules".

[58] An example here might be *While and Carler (Councils) Ltd v McGregor*, 1962 S.C. (H.L.) 1; [1962] A.C. 413.

of such liability which appears to go beyond anything established in the Anglo-American common law but which is not nearly as extensive as that recognised in Germany, France or the Netherlands.

The comparison of Scots law with the *Principles of European Contract Law* is also of interest. The Principles begin with the proposition that parties are free to negotiate and are, in general, not liable for failure to conclude a contract. This is the Scottish position too. For over a hundred years, courts and text writers have said that *Walker v Milne* does not give rise to a general principle, but is rather an equitable exception to the general rule; by implication, that general rule is one of no pre-contractual liability. This is perhaps most explicit in Lord Cullen's observation in *Dawson International Plc v Coats Paton Plc*, that "the law does not favour the recovery of expenditure made merely in the hope or expectation of agreement being entered into or of a stated intention being fulfilled".[59] Such a starting point seems entirely consistent with the values and policies which underlie a market economy: each person must look after its own interests and if risks are taken on the basis of hopes or expectations not resting upon a contractual base, then the loss must lie where it falls in the absence of wrongdoing by the other party.

Having freedom to negotiate and to break off negotiations unless there is some special factor explains why, for example, a party inviting bids or tenders from a number of other parties is not liable for the expenses of the unsuccessful tenderers or bidders. Unless the invitor's conduct has reasonably induced other expectations, the competing offerors assume the risk of failure and there is no breach of good faith in leaving the losses where they fall. It is important to remember Finn's point that good faith does not involve the complete protection of the other party's interests at the expense of one's own, and that in this it is to be distinguished from a fiduciary obligation.

However, Article 2:301 of the European Principles states the exception to the general rule of freedom to give up negotiations in much wider terms than have so far emerged in Scots law. The exception rests squarely on the principle of good faith and is exemplified (although not exhausted) by entry into or continuation of negotiations without any real intention of concluding a contract thereby. In contrast, Lord Cullen's theory of pre-contractual liability depends upon there being an "implied assurance" that an *agreement* already reached is a binding contract. If we recognise, as it is submitted we must, that this rests upon the principle of good faith in contracting, is it possible to take that principle as a basis for further extensions of Scots law in this field?

1–76 We may begin with the specific example of bad faith given in Article 2:301 of the European Principles, the problem of negotiations which amount to no more than "stringing along"; that is, unknown to one of the negotiating parties, A, the other, B, has no intention of ever forming a contract. B's reason for appearing to enter into negotiations is an effort to force a third party, C, with whom B does intend to contract to make a better offer than C would otherwise have been prepared to do. When an acceptable offer is made to B by C, negotiations with A are dropped. In a number of jurisdictions, A will have a claim against B in such circumstances by which at least reliance losses will be recoverable;[60] but in Scotland, under the current understanding of *Walker v Milne*, A would have no recovery, since there is no implied assurance that there is a binding agreement.

---

[59] *Dawson International Plc v Coats Paton Plc*, 1988 S.L.T. at 866D–866E.

[60] For example, see the French decision of 1972 discussed in B Nicholas, *The French Law of Contract*, 2nd edn (Oxford: OUP, 1992), pp.70–71; *Hoffmann v Red Owl Stores* (1965) 133 N.W. (2d) 267 (USA); *Walton Stores (Interstate) Ltd v Maher* (1988) 164 C.L.R. 387 (Australia).

A variety of cases from around the world raise further questions about the limitations which have so far been placed upon the Scots law of pre-contractual liability. The denial of recovery in the *Regalian* case may be contrasted with the Australian decision, *Sabemo Pty Ltd v North Sydney Municipal Council*.[61] Sabemo tendered to carry out a commercial development of land owned by the Council. The parties negotiated for three years and Sabemo spent large sums on preparatory works before the Council finally decided to abandon the development. The Supreme Court of New South Wales held that Sabemo could recover their wasted expenditure, on the basis that the termination was a unilateral decision of the Council rather than the result of an inability to agree upon terms, and that the Council's decision took account only of its own interests, not those of Sabemo. The court spoke of "fault" in relation to the Council's behaviour, and certainly there is much in the judgment to conjure up thoughts of *culpa in contrahendo*. However, the case was both distinguished and doubted by Rattee J in *Regalian*. The distinction lay first in the use of the "subject to contract" formula in *Regalian*, and in the fact that there was also genuine dissensus about price in that case: the doubt concerned the existence in English law of any principle that unilateral termination of negotiations without taking into account the interests of the other party inferred liability for that other's consequently wasted expenditure. What of Scots law? Do the facts of *Sabemo* suggest that there was an agreement between the parties and that there was also an implied assurance that this agreement was a binding contract? If not, is this another case where there nevertheless ought to be liability?

There are other cases where it is reasonably clear that there was no agreement and no implied assurance that there was a contract, yet there was enough to suggest that there would be a contractual agreement in the reasonably near future after some further negotiation. The best example is the "letter of intent" by which a party will signal to one of a group of tenderers or bidders for a contract that he now intends to enter a contract with that party although the tender/bid is not to be accepted without further negotiation. The purpose of the letter of intent is to allow the chosen party to commence preparation for the contract, and it is not unusual for preparation to pass on to performance before the contract is concluded. Typically the letter of intent will provide that such work will be paid for at the contract price once agreed.[62] But suppose the contract is never concluded because the negotiations are unsuccessful. What, if any, claims may be made by the recipient of the letter of intent? Now where the performance involves a transfer of value to the party who has issued the letter of intent, the solution may well lie in unjustified enrichment.[63] If, however, there is no transfer of value but only reliance expenditure by the recipient of the letter, enrichment solutions may not be available or appropriate to cover the loss. As I have argued elsewhere, Scots law could here call upon its doctrine of unilateral promise, giving the letter obligatory effect and implying some sort of reasonable payment for the recipient's wasted work.[64] But given that letters of intent are often expressly not intended to have obligatory effect, the promise analysis may be rather forced. An approach based on good faith, allowing recovery of justified reliance or the "negative interest", is perhaps more attractive and avoids the need for strained construction and the implication of terms based, however artificially, upon the intention of the party issuing the letter of intent.

---

[61] *Sabemo Pty Ltd v North Sydney Municipal Council* [1977] N.S.W.L.R. 880, N.S.W.S.C.

[62] On letters of intent and the legal difficulties to which they give rise see SN Ball, "Work Carried Out in Pursuance of Letters of Intent-Contract or Restitution?" (1983) 99 L.Q.R. 572; MP Furmston, J Poole, T Norisada, *Contract Formation and Letters of Intent* (Chichester: John Wiley & Sons, 1998).

[63] As in *British Steel Corporation v Cleveland Bridge and Engineering Co Ltd* [1984] 1 All E.R. 504. See further E McKendrick, "The Battle of the Forms and the Law of Restitution" (1988) 8 O.J.L.S. 197.

[64] HL MacQueen, "Constitution and Proof of Gratuitous Obligations", 1986 S.L.T. (News) 1, pp.3–4.

1–77 Another interesting situation can be illustrated from the English case of *Blackpool & Fylde Aero Club Ltd v Blackpool Borough Council*.[65] The Council invited tenders for a contract in a document which set out the procedure which it would follow in considering the tenders received. The Court of Appeal held that the Council was liable in damages to an unsuccessful tenderer for having failed to follow this procedure, but left unclear whether this was a matter of tort or of contract. The decision seems unquestionably right, but the judgments reveal the relative conceptual limits of the English law of obligations. A Scots lawyer might approach this case, not through a contractual or delictual, but rather through a promissory route.[66] But if this is thought artificial or to involve strained construction of the invitation to tender, then a wider concept of good faith might provide a better solution. This would undoubtedly go further than anything found in Lord Cullen's opinion in *Dawson International Plc v Coats Paton Plc*. Again there is no real question of agreements and implied assurances that a binding contract exists. The contract, if it is going to come into existence at all, is not assured to any particular party.[67]

In the final analysis, therefore, Scots law appears to have a number of specific tools or concepts with which to address liability issues in pre-contractual negotiations that is, not just contract, misrepresentation and enrichment, but also promise and *Walker v Milne* reimbursement of expenditure. While these tools can be turned to a good number of different jobs, not all the potential issues of pre-contractual liability have yet been addressed or could be handled with them alone. Good faith appears to permeate the existing law in this area. If this principle is allowed the role suggested for it earlier in this essay—that is, the identification and solution through the creation of new rules of problems which the existing rules do not, or seem unable to reach—Scots law can still respond creatively, yet consistently with what has already been decided, when these as yet unanswered questions arise for decision in the future. If so, equity, in its proper Scottish sense as the basis of the whole law, will not after all turn out to be past the age of child-bearing."

The issue of liability for pre-contractual negotiations (and Professor MacQueen's views on the matter) is considered more fully below.[68] What follows is a more sceptical view about the existence and desirability of a general duty of good faith.

1–78

[69]Good Faith in Contracting: A Sceptical View

Joseph M. Thomson

ADM Forte (ed), *Good Faith in Contract and Property* (Oxford: Hart Publishing, 1999, pp.63–76

"It has been argued that there is no general principle of good faith in contracting in Scots law. While there are various doctrines which achieve similar objectives as some of the meanings of good faith, Scots law allows a party to a contract a large degree of freedom to use economic power, knowledge and skill to conclude a bargain or flake a

---

[65] *Blackpool & Fylde Aero Club Ltd v Blackpool Borough Council* [1990] 1 W.L.R. 1995. The case has recently been followed by Finn J of the Federal Court of Australia in *Hughes Aircraft Systems International v Air Services Australia* (1997) 146 A.L.R. 1; noted by MP Furmston (1998) 114 L.Q.R. 362.

[66] The concept of promise might also be the way in which Scots law would solve such famous "difficult" cases as *Hoffman v Red Owl Stores*; and *Walton Stores (Interstate) Ltd v Maher*.

[67] Note that it is common for such invitations to tender to provide that the invitor is not bound to accept the highest or lowest (as the case may be) or indeed any offer that may be made.

[68] See paras 3–40—3–49.

[69]

profit. Where there is economic imbalance between the parties, particularly in consumer contracts, legislative regimes exist to protect consumers from unfair terms, but even here the substantive fairness of the actual exchange is not subject to scrutiny. Again, this seems to me to be consonant with the economic demands of a western capitalist society. In short, there is no need for the adoption of such an amorphous concept as good faith in contracting, the meanings and parameters of which are controversial, resulting in an enormous volume of doctrine and jurisprudence in those modern civilian legal systems which adopt it.

That said, there are stirrings afoot at the highest judicial levels that the concept of good faith in contracting not only should be but, indeed, is already part of Scots private law. I am, of course, referring to *Smith v Bank of Scotland* (1997 S.C. (H.L.) 111). There, in a blatant example of judicial legislation, the House of Lords held that a lender, who sought security from the debtor's wife, was obliged to ensure that she received independent advice before signing a standard security. While, in my view, the policy considerations advanced by the House of Lords display a misplaced concern for the social and economic position of wives in contemporary Scottish society, the ratio of the case, in so far as there is one, was clearly based on the 'element of good faith which is required of a creditor on the constitution of a contract' (at p.121 per Lord Clyde). It is not surprising that authority for such a principle was scant, but his Lordship did refer to cases relating to cautionary obligations. As is well known, cautionary obligations, like contracts of insurance, form a particular (and peculiar) area of the law of contract. Moreover, the potential scope of *Smith* has been severely restricted by the decision of the Lord Ordinary (Hamilton) in *Braithwaite v Bank of Scotland* (1999 S.L.T. 25). There Lord Hamilton insisted that before the creditor's obligation arose to ensure that a wife obtained independent advice, it must be averred that she was in fact under the undue influence of her husband or had been a victim of a misrepresentation made by him as to the legal effects of the transaction he was asking her to enter. In these circumstances, it is unlikely that the concept of good faith relied upon by Lord Clyde in Smith, will percolate beyond the confines of inter spousal/cohabitant security transactions. No doubt this will be to the chagrin of those academic commentators who have treated Lord Clyde's speech as if it were a statute in order to find authority for a general principle of good faith in contracting in Scots law.

It will be clear that the debate on the value of a principle of good faith in contracting has not been won by either side: indeed, in Scots law, the debate has only begun. As this paper has argued, proponents of the doctrine can find little support for its existence in Scots law before *Smith*.

More importantly, perhaps, great care should be given to transplanting the doctrine into Scots law. It is amorphous, complex and at variance with the cultural values which have moulded the current law. In particular, the Scottish Parliament should be cautious before embarking on such a task—and so should the Scottish judiciary. In the present writer's view, it is not the function of a system of private law to compel persons to act in an altruistic manner nor, indeed, is it its function to ensure that they do not act in a morally reprehensible way. To do so, would be to remove the edge of competition and self interest which are also human values and which have created the wealth upon which our society currently depends."

More recently, the issue of good faith arose indirectly in the Outer House in the case of *WS Karoulias SA v The Drambuie Liqueur Company Ltd*[70] and, as the following extract suggests, the role of good faith in Scots law of contract remains unclear.

1–79 [71]*WS Karoulias SA v The Drambuie Liqueur Company Ltd*

Gillian Black, (2006) Edin. L.R. 10, 132–140

"...

(2) Good faith

Despite the legal rationalisation of the judgment, the facts of the case arouse sympathy for the pursuers. Lord Clarke commented on Drambuie's 'somewhat cynical' actions and noted that Drambuie 'could be seen to have exploited the longstanding, amicable and successful commercial relationship between the parties'[28] for its own ends. Given these observations regarding Drambuie's conduct, it is disappointing that issues about good faith were not raised by either counsel or judge in this case, and the opportunity to consider what role, if any, it has in Scots law was lost.

Perhaps this reluctance to introduce a good faith argument reflects the limited role it has played to date in Scots law[29]—a situation which enabled Lord Clarke to comment that his quest to decide the legal issue "cannot be driven by any view about the moral behaviour or the commercial manners of the parties."[30] However, although McBryde states that 'there is no single principle of good faith'[31] in Scots law, both he and MacQueen provide examples of the use of good faith as a latent concept in Scots law, operating, for example, in actions for undue influence, the requirement to perform a contract within a reasonable time, and the requirement not to prevent performance by the other contract party.[32] In this way, it can be seen that good faith does enjoy recognition in Scots law, but this role 'has been expressed by way of particular rules rather than through broad general statements of the principle'.[33]

Despite these examples, good faith at the stage of contract negotiations has been rejected by the courts in the past.[34] Liability for pre-contractual expenditure was considered in *Dawson International Plc v Coats Paton Plc*[35] by Lord Cullen who, following analysis of the case-law in this area, concluded that such reimbursement was only available where the pursuer had acted 'in reliance on the implied assurance by [the defender] that there was a binding contract between them when in fact there was no more than an agreement which fell short of being a binding contract'.[36] Where there was no such assurance from the defender then the pursuer had no remedy, unless there was evidence of mala fides or misrepresentation to enable a claim in delict.[37] Lord Cullen also maintained that 'any tendency to extend the scope of the remedy is to be discouraged'.[38] Accordingly, only where the pursuer could show that the defender had acted in such a way to give an implied assurance of a concluded contract, would an action for pre-contractual liability succeed.

Further, even where a claim for pre-contractual liability is successful, the pursuer's remedy is reimbursement of expenditure, rather than damages,[39] and in any event such a claim would certainly not operate to conclude a contract where substantive principles of contract law would otherwise deny one. This can be compared with a more developed principle of good faith in Europe: for example Dutch law awards expectation damages, intended to place the pursuer in the position in which it would have been had the contract been performed, where one party breaks off negotiations in breach of the good faith requirement.[40] Admittedly this is only operative where the negotiations are

[70] *WS Karoulias SA v The Drambuie Liqueur Company Ltd* [2005] CSOH 112, the facts of which are given below, see para.3–02.

[71] © Gillian Black, "WS Karoulias SA v The Drambuie Liqeur Company Ltd" (2006) Edinburgh Law Review 10.

far-advanced, but Karoulias would arguably meet this requirement on the facts of the case. Perhaps then the issue is whether Scotland is out of step with the rest of Europe?

It is therefore instructive to consider the European approach—particularly in a case involving cross-border negotiations and a Greek pursuer. Article 1:201 of the *Principles of European Contract Law* requires both parties to a contract to 'act in accordance with good faith and fair dealing'.[41] Further, Article 2:301 requires parties to *negotiate* in good faith and any party which breaks off negotiations contrary to the requirement of good faith will be liable for losses caused. This European standard of good faith might well be regarded as onerous and uncommercial by practitioners in Scotland, accustomed to notions of freedom of contract, but would almost certainly have defeated Drambuie's attempts to keep Karoulias waiting while its negotiations with a third party distributor were ongoing. The influence of civilian legal systems and European contract codes, such as the *Principles of European Contract Law* or the *Common Frame of Reference* currently being developed, may therefore have a significant impact on Scots law in the future.

There is, however, a difference between the continental doctrine of good faith, which places contracting parties under a positive obligation, and a lesser duty which requires only the absence of bad faith. This lesser standard would not necessitate compliance with duties of disclosure, co-operation or loyalty, but would prevent unreasonable or cynical conduct capable of creating false or misleading impressions. Seen in this way, the principle of good faith would operate as an 'excluder principle', that is, by 'merely excluding the unreasonable rather than imposing positive standards of conduct'.[42] And this standard of 'good faith' would arguably still be sufficient to encompass Drambuie's unreasonable actions in this case.

The question remains whether or not an attempt to invoke this excluder principle in *Karoulias* would have been successful. If any case could prove an appropriate test case for such a principle, then *Karoulias* is (or was) it. It would be possible to argue that Drambuie's actions amounted to 'an implied assurance' that there was a contract between the parties.[43] The existence of a final draft agreement, acknowledgement from both sides that negotiations had concluded, their long-term amicable relationship, and Drambuie's conduct in continuing to make positive overtures[44] right up until four weeks before termination, all amounted to 'cynical' and 'misleading' conduct[45] and would certainly present strong facts on which to argue for such a remedy.

Karoulias did not in fact make any judicial claim for pre-contractual expenditure, although evidence brought suggests that it did incur such expenses. It may be therefore that Drambuie had already reimbursed it for this or, alternatively, that the amount was so low as to be insignificant compared to the value of the five-year contract for which it was suing. However, the fact that Karoulias did not include pre-contractual expenditure in its claim may also explain why it did not raise any argument as to good faith: from a practical point of view it would have seemed a challenging prospect which, even if successful, would have no direct benefit for their contract claim.

Consequently, the issues of morality and bad faith in commercial dealings entitled Karoulias to a sympathy vote from Lord Clarke but, absent a plea of an overarching principle of good faith in Scots contract law, they did not translate into a commercial remedy.

. . .

---

[28] At para 52.

[29] For a general discussion of good faith in contract law see McBryde, *Contract* ch 17.

[30] At para 52. In light of Lord Clarke's other comments in this paragraph, it is to be presumed that his reference to moral behaviour and commercial manners was directed at Drambuie. However, as noted at note 9 above, Karoulias' commercial tactics were also questioned, so a wider reading of this quotation could potentially encompass both parties.

[31] McBryde, *Contract* para 17-25

[32] See H L MacQueen, "Good faith", in H L MacQueen and R Zimmermann (eds), *European Contract Law: Scots and South African Perspectives* (2006, forthcoming)
[33] H L MacQueen, "Good faith in the Scots law of contract: an undisclosed principle?", in A D M Forte (ed), *Good Faith in Contract and Property Law* (1999) 5 at 33.
[34] See McBryde, *Contract* para 5-60, who makes reference to the House of Lords decision in *Walford v Miles* [1992] 2 AC 128, and MacQueen's summary of good faith in Scots contract law, "Good Faith in the Scots Law of Contract", note 33 above, particularly note 4 thereof.
[35] *Dawson International plc v Coats Paton plc* 1988 SLT 854.
[36] *Dawson* at 866.
[37] *Dawson* at 865.
[38] *Dawson* at 865.
[39] Known as "Melville Monument liability": see *Walker v Milne* (1825) 2 S 379 (2nd ed, 338) and McBryde, *Contract* para 5-63
[40] See H Beale, A Hartkamp, H Kötz and D Tallon, *Cases Materials and Text on Contract Law* (2002) 262- 264, although they observe that this remedy has not so far been awarded by the Dutch courts; see also MacQueen, "Good Faith in the Scots Law of Contract", note 33 above, at 21.
[41] See H Beale, A Hartkamp, H Kötz and D Tallon, *Cases Materials and Text on Contract Law* (2002) 262- 264, although they observe that this remedy has not so far been awarded by the Dutch courts; see also MacQueen, "Good Faith in the Scots Law of Contract", note 33 above, at 21.
[42] MacQueen, "Good faith", note 32 above.
[43] As per the test in *Dawson*, note 35 above.
[44] The email of 2 June emphasising Drambuie's commitment to Karoulias being the most obvious of these.
[45] The descriptions applied by Lord Clarke at para 52."

The "Europeanisation" of contract law

1–80 Contracting does not happen only within the jurisdictional confines of Scotland. The development of Scottish contract law is, as any chapter of this book indicates, a perpetual interchange of ideas between Scotland and the rest of the UK. Although the Act of Union 1707 established a "common market" in these islands, it established no common rules for contracts, the most common mechanism for commercial intercourse. Over the centuries, our laws have been adapted to deal with commercial needs, while at the same time—not always successfully—maintaining the integrity of the Scottish law of contract.

In 1973 we became part of a much bigger common market—one that now encompasses most of the states of the continent of Europe. The very purpose of the common market created in 1956 has been to increase commerce across state barriers. Such trade would inevitably create conflicts and misunderstandings between people divided not only by language and culture, but also by laws. The laws of all those states differ, sometimes fundamentally. The differences between the common law jurisdictions of the European Union (England, Wales and the whole of Ireland) and the civilian systems of most European countries are notorious and often fundamental. Even within the civilian world of Europe, despite a common Roman heritage, legal systems differ fundamentally and many others, such as our own, bear features common to both and different from all others.

In such an environment the pressures to create some commonality are great. As early as 1968 the Brussels Convention created a common jurisdictional framework for contracting, embodied for the UK in the Civil Jurisdiction and Judgments Act 1982. Common rules for establishing the law that will govern any particular contract were established by the Rome convention on the Law Applicable to Contractual Obligations 1980, embodied for the UK in the Contracts (Applicable Law) Act 1990.[72] Throughout this book other elements of European legislation impacting on our law of contract are considered. As Professor McBryde states:

[72] The Rome Convention was replaced by Regulation (EC) 593/2008 on the law applicable to Contractual Obligations (Rome I), available at: *http://www.eur-lex.europa.eu/LexUriServ/LexUriServ.do?uri=OJ:L:2008:177:0006:0016:en:PDF* [Accessed 2 October 2015].

"It is no longer possible for a Scottish lawyer to be content with a Scottish description of contract or contractual obligations. It may be necessary to consider the law of other States of the European Union and decisions of the European court of Justice. European legislation has influenced, in particular, rules on jurisdiction, choice of law, consumer contracts and contracts of employment."[73]

To the list we might now readily add rules on electronic contracting.[74] As the Scottish Law Commission observed, in the context of its review of contract formation rules in 1993,

"emails were then used by only a limited number, mostly in universities and other research institutions, and the internet had scarcely begun to develop as a means of publishing information, never mind as a way of doing business, whether between businesses, between businesses and consumers, or between private individuals who might or might not be acting in the course of a business. The situation has thus been transformed in the last 20 years. In our own observation, email is now the normal method of distance communication between businesspeople and e-commerce involving consumers is growing much faster than retail sales in high street stores. None of these developments was anticipated in [1993] but the application of traditional formation rules in these new contexts has been the subject of much discussion and some case law, in Scotland and elsewhere".[75]

Some have argued that such diversity in contracting principles amongst the Member States is wasteful and confusing. A Commission on European Contract Law under the chairmanship of Professor Ole Lando was established as

"a response to a need for a Union-wide infrastructure of contract law to consolidate the rapidly expanding volume of Community law regulating specific types of contract".[76]

The Commission has included lawyers (almost entirely academics) from every Member State.[77] **1–81**
The outcome of the commission's work is PECL (1995) revised 1998 and 2002.[78] In their introduction to PECL, Professors Lando and Beale suggest several benefits to be derived from the formulation of the principles: facilitation of cross-border trade within Europe; strengthening the Single European Market; provision of guidelines for national courts and legislatures; construction of a bridge between the civil law and the common law.[79] In their words:

---

[73] WW McBryde, *The Law of Contract in Scotland*, 3rd edn (Edinburgh: W. Green, 2007), para.1–09.

[74] For a comprehensive review, WW McBryde, *The Law of Contract in Scotland*, 3rd edn (Edinburgh: W. Green, 2007), paras 5–80—5–85. The most thorough examination of the potential impact of electronic contracting on contract law in Scotland is in Pt 3, "Execution in Counterpart: of the Scottish Law Commission's *Discussion Paper on the Formation of Contract* (Scot Law Com. No.154, 2012) (see next footnote).

[75] Scottish Law Commission, *Review of Contract Law: Discussion Paper on the Formation of Contract* (Scot Law Com. No.154, March 2012), available at: *http://www.scotlawcom.gov.uk/files/9513/3241/0632/dp154.pdf* [Accessed 12 July 2015].

[76] O Lando and H Beale (eds), *Principles of European Contract Law (Parts II and III)* (The Hague: Kluwer Law International, 2000), "Introduction".

[77] The UK Members are Professor Hugh Beale (and formerly Professor Roy Goode) and Professor Hector MacQueen (and formerly the late Professor Bill Wilson).

[78] The full text of *Principles* can be found at: *http://www.jus.uio.no/lm/eu.contract.principles.parts.1.to.3.2002/* [Accessed 12 July 2015].

[79] O Lando and H Beale (eds), *Principles of European Contract Law (Parts II and III)* (The Hague: Kluwer Law International, 2000).

> "They are available for immediate use by parties making contracts, by courts and arbitrators deciding contract disputes and by legislators in drafting contract rules whether at the European of the national level. Their longer-term objective is to help bring about the harmonization of general contract law within the European Union."[80]

These "principles" do not have the status of law. They could be described as "soft law" but even that might be overstating their legal status. They are, however, highly influential. In 2003, the European Commission, founding on PECL, initiated an *Action Plan on a More Coherent European Contract Law*[81] to develop a "Common Frame of Reference" (CFR) that it could use in reviewing the *acquis communautaire* and in drafting new legislation. The Commission went further in 2004 and suggested that the CFR should provide "fundamental principles, definitions and model rules" the "main goal" of which would be to "serve as a tool box for the Commission when preparing proposals, both for reviewing the existing acquis and for new instruments," but also "would be likely to serve as the basis for the development of a possible optional instrument".[82] The result of that process is the DCFR, or *Principles, Definitions and Model Rules of European private law*.[83] Wider in its scope than PECL, the DCFR contains a comprehensive statement of contract rules founded on extensive comparative research. "The greatest part of the DCFR", according to the Introduction to the DCFR (para.24)

> "consists of 'model rules'. The adjective 'model' indicates that the rules are not put forward as having any normative force but are soft law rules of the kind contained in the Principles of European Contract Law and similar publications. Whether particular rules might be used as a model for legislation, for example, for the improvement of the internal coherence of the *acquis communautaire* is for others to decide".

The Scottish Law Commission has decided that contract law in the light of the DCFR[84] is one of four elements of its Ninth Programme of Law Reform. Under the auspices of Commissioner Professor Hector MacQueen, the Commission has already published several Consultations and Reports, most of which are referred to extensively throughout this book.[85]

---

[80] O Lando and H Beale (eds), *Principles of European Contract Law (Parts II and III)* (The Hague: Kluwer Law International, 2000).

[81] Commission of the European Communities, Communication from the Commission to the European Parliament and the Council: A More Coherent European Contract Law, COM(2003) 68 final.

[82] *The Way Forward*, Commission Communication COM (2004) 651 final. The Communication was not published in the Official Journal, but is available here: *http://eur-lex.europa.eu/legal-content/EN/TXT/?uri=celex:52004DC0651* [Accessed 12 July 2015].

[83] The *Draft* DCFR, published as an "Outline Edition", by Professors von Barr, Clive and Schulte-Noelke (eds) (Munich: Sellier, 2009) is available at: *http://ec.europa.eu/justice/policies/civil/docs/dcfr_outline_edition_en.pdf* [Accessed 12 July 2015]. The work on DCFR was entrusted to the Study Group on a European Civil Code (SGECC) (*http://www.sgecc.net* [Accessed 12 July 2015]) and the Research Group on EC Private Law (Acquis Group) (*http://www.acquis-group.jura.uni-osnabrueck.de* [Accessed 12 July 2015])

[84] See: *http://www.scotlawcom.gov.uk/law-reform/law-reform-projects/contract-law-light-draft-common-frame-reference-dcf/* [Accessed 12 July 2015].

[85] Most notably, Scottish Law Commission, *Review of Contract Law: Discussion Paper on the Formation of Contract* (Scot Law Com. No.154, March 2012) and *Discussion Paper on Third Party Rights in Contract* (Scot Law Com. No.157, 2014).

Review of Contract Law: Formation of Contract **1–82**

Scottish Law Commission Discussion Paper No.154 (March 2012)

"Chapter 1: Introduction

. . .

1.5 Why are the DCFR and the ensuing developments in the European Union of interest for this Commission, with regard to the law of contract in particular?[11] First, the DCFR purports to be a modern or contemporary statement of the best rules of contract law for use in the European Union, and is based upon extensive comparative research and intensive collaboration by an international team of contract law experts. Seeing how Scots law measures up against this standard is thus an exercise of some interest. But it has a greater significance than that. As suggested in the Eighth Programme,[12] contract law is clearly a critical element in economic activity of all kinds, whether B2B, B2C, or between parties transacting with each other privately. It is thus very important that an area of law of such significance for the Scottish economy, including the attraction of foreign business into Scotland, should be of the highest international quality. Scottish Ministers' interest in the contract law review proposed in our Eighth Programme was based primarily upon this consideration.

1.6 A second point is that if the DCFR is used in the European Union as a basis of any kind for harmonizing contract law or if an optional instrument such as the proposed CESL comes into existence for use by contracting parties as an alternative to domestic contract law, it will be necessary to ensure that Scots law at least compares favourably or keeps pace with such emerging European norms. In our Discussion Paper on Interpretation of Contract we noted similar thinking occurring in other major European jurisdictions.[13] Our joint project on Insurance with the Law Commission of England & Wales has also helped to make us aware of the need to keep domestic law in good repair if it is to have any influence as a model in European or even wider international developments.

1.7 A third point is that the comparative information in the DCFR facilitates our statutory task of keeping the law under review and obtaining information about the law of other countries in pursuit of that function.[14] Finally, the DCFR is descended from a number of instruments—notably the United Nations Convention on Contracts for the International Sale of Goods (CISG), the UNIDROIT Principles of International Commercial Contracts (PICC) and the Principles of European Contract Law (PECL)—which were used by this Commission in some of the contract law projects in the 1990s.[15] Since, as will be explained further below, we have set about our review by returning to the subject matter of these projects, it is appropriate to consider how far these models have themselves been developed in more recent texts.

1.8 The existence of the proposed CESL does not mean, however, that the DCFR has been superseded as the basis for our review of the law of contract. The former is limited to the contract of sale of goods while our review is directed towards the general law of contract, including but by no means limited to sales contracts. The DCFR text starts on the general law of contract (its Books I–III), supplemented by subsequent provisions on several specific contracts including not only sale but also lease of goods, services, mandate, commercial agency, franchise, distributorship, loan, personal security, and donation (Book IV.A–H).[16] The full version includes extensive commentary on each of the model rules as well as comparative notes on the laws of each of the jurisdictions to be found in the European Union Member States (including Scotland). In contrast, neither the proposed CESL nor the preceding Feasibility Study contain any commentary or comparative notes. The DCFR is therefore not only more directly relevant than the proposed CESL to a review of general contract law but also considerably clearer about the reasoning and comparative observations underpinning its provisions, giving it significantly greater value as a law reform tool. This will be so whether or not the European Commission makes use of it as a 'toolbox' for its own legislative purposes.

1.9 Having said all this, the proposed CESL does draw directly upon many of the general contract law provisions of the DCFR, especially with regard to the formation of contract, the subject of our present Paper. It is clearly relevant to our project to know whether the proposed CESL has copied, modified or not used DCFR material, and we accordingly include and, where appropriate, discuss its relevant provisions within this Discussion Paper.

1.10 It should be emphasised that the objective of this review of contract law is not necessarily to adopt the rules in the DCFR or the proposed CESL as a legislative statement for Scots law. First and foremost review in light of the DCFR will, as the Eighth Programme says,[17] operate as a health check for the existing Scots law of contract. The results will determine whether legislative intervention is required in pursuit of the general objectives of simplification and modernisation, and to ensure that contract law provides an appropriate framework for economic activity in Scotland, be that entirely domestic, involving cross-border transactions or originating outside of Scotland. The check may also throw up issues that are not directly considered in the DCFR or the proposed CESL. In this Paper, for example, questions will be asked about the practice known as 'execution in counterpart'. The conclusion of our inquiry may be that the present law is satisfactory; or that it requires some patching; or that a full legislative statement would be useful (whether or not the DCFR or the proposed CESL is taken as the model for such a statement, and whether or not that statement changes the law as it presently stands). In this Paper we also suggest the possible development of a facility to be managed by Registers of Scotland (RoS) intended to ease the process of electronic contracting.

---

[11] The DCFR is also relevant to the current SLC projects on Prescription and Title to Moveable Property (DP No 144, 2010), Trusts (DP No 148, 2011), and Moveable Transactions (DP No 151, 2011).
[12] See para 1.1 above.
[13] DP No 147, 2011, para 1.5. Since then there have been further developments, eg a conference in Spain, with German input, at the University of Santiago de Compostela in February 2011 to discuss the Spanish and French reforms.
[14] Law Commissions Act 1965, s 3.
[15] See further Nils Jansen and Reinhard Zimmermann, "Contract formation and mistake in European contract law: a genetic comparison of transnational model rules" (2011) 31(4) Oxford Journal of Legal Studies, 625.
[16] There are further Books on "benevolent intervention in another's affairs" (V), delict (VI), unjustified enrichment (VII), acquisition and loss of ownership of goods (VIII), proprietary security in movable assets (IX) and trusts (X). There is also an introductory statement and discussion of the principles underlying the DCFR, namely, freedom, security, justice and efficiency, and an annex of definitions of key words and phrases.
[17] See para 1.1 above."

Transnational contract law

1–83 It is noticeable from the above extract that the Scottish Law Commission is concerned with "soft law" that emanates not only from within the European Union, but also those drafted in international bodies and organisations. In an increasingly globalised trading environment, the complexities of international contracting are multiplied. Attempts to develop uniform rules that can be adopted by parties to a contract have been many and varied. The most successful to date are rules on formation of contract in the United Nations Convention on Contracts for the

International Sale of Goods 1980. Although the Convention is limited in scope, Pt II attempts to lay down internationally agreed and simplified rules on the formation of contracts. The Convention itself has been ratified by and is in force in many states, including the USA and several Member States of the European Union. The UK has not, at the time of writing, ratified the Convention. Nevertheless, the Scottish Law Commission was so impressed by Pt II of the Convention that in 1993, in its *Report on formation of contract: Scottish law and the United Nations Convention on Contracts for the International Sale of Goods*[86] it recommended the adoption of those rules in the form of a Schedule to a draft Bill. It should also be noted that the Convention from which the proposed rules were extracted might be applicable to a Scottish contract, either where the parties agree that it shall, or where the contract has a connection with a state that has adopted the Convention.[87]

A further attempt to establish standard rules for transnational contracts, the UNIDROIT Principles for International Contracts 1994 would also apply where the parties agree that they should. The intention is to provide a framework for international contracting. The aims are stated in the preamble:

> "These Principles set forth general rules for international commercial contracts. They shall be applied when the parties have agreed that their contract be governed by them. They may be applied when the parties have agreed that their contract be governed by 'general principles of law', the 'lex mercatoria' or the like. They may provide a solution to an issue raised when it proves impossible to establish the relevant rule of the applicable law. They may be used to interpret or supplement international uniform law instruments. They may serve as a model for national and international legislators."

Regrettably the Principles and the very extensive commentary that accompanies them are beyond the scope of this text, but are available at the UNIDROIT website.[88]

---

[86] Scottish Law Commission, *Report on Formation of Contract: Scottish Law and the United Nations Convention on Contracts for the International Sale of Goods* (Scottish Law Com. No.144, 1993). Events (notably the PECL and the DCFR, have since intervened, but the Scottish Law Commission Discussion Paper, *Review of Contract Law: Discussion Paper on Formation of Contract* (Scot. Law Com. No.154, 2012) goes to great lengths to incorporate and expand on its recommendations in 1993.

[87] The case law that the Convention has generated internationally can be accessed at the UNCITRAL web site (*http://www.uncitral.org* [Accessed 12 August 2015]) by following the links to the Case Law on UNCITRAL Texts (CLOUT).

[88] *http://www.unidroit.org/english/principles/pr-main.htm* [Accessed 12 August 2015].

PART 2

CONTRACT FORMATION

Chapter 2

AGREEMENT AS THE BASIS OF CONTRACTUAL OBLIGATIONS

Introduction

The parties to a contract must do more than show an intention or willingness to enter into a contractual relationship; they must show that they have firmly committed themselves to the agreement that they have themselves established. If the parties are still at the stage of negotiations then no such commitment exists. **2–01**

If one party has decided on what they want from the other, but has not yet persuaded the other to commit, again there is no agreement: there is no *consensus in idem,* i.e. no meeting of minds.

The terminology of agreement: offer and acceptance

Such a commitment to the agreement is conveniently expressed in the concept that there must be an offer made by one party and full acceptance of that particular offer by the other party. **2–02**

The sometimes highly formalised rules for establishing offer and acceptance are a relatively recent development, dating from the 19th century. They were developed primarily in English courts, and Scottish authorities have tended to adopt them. It must be stressed, however, that the development of contract law in England was fundamentally different from, and more recent than, that of Scotland. The idea of a consensual contract, based upon promises by the parties to do something in the future, emerged piecemeal in English cases towards the beginning of the 19th century[1]; whereas in Scotland it can be traced to the general principles enunciated by the earliest institutional writers. Since English law adopts "a rather technical and schematic doctrine of contract",[2] English authorities must be handled with extreme caution.

Agreement objectively established

Whatever the theoretical foundations of the "offer and acceptance" approach, the underlying principle is that *consensus in idem* will be established objectively from what the parties said and did, and not on their subjective view, which are often irreconcilable. As McBryde states[3]: **2–03**

> "It is probable that in the early history of the law of contract the subjective sense was dominant, but this was replaced in the nineteenth century with an appreciation that in business dealings the objective sense was more realistic."

The intention of the parties to contract will be objectively determined on the basis of all the evidence presented to the court, not on the subjective declarations or assumptions of the parties.

---

[1] PS Atiyah, *The Rise and Fall of Freedom of Contract* (Oxford: OUP, 1979), pp.446–448.

[2] Per Lord Wilberforce, *New Zealand Shipping Co v AM Satterthwaite & Co* [1975] A.C. 154 at 167.

[3] WW McBryde, *The Law of Contract in Scotland*, 3rd edn (Edinburgh: W. Green, 2007), para.6–10.

Muirhead & Turnbull v Dickson
(1905) 13 S.L.T. 151
Court of Session, First Division: The Lord President (Dunedin), Lords Adam, McLaren, Kinnear

M & T supplied a piano to D. The price was £26. Instalments were payable at 15s. per month. When D fell behind with instalment payments, M & T sought recovery of the piano. They did so on the basis that either there was no contract between the parties or that the contract was one of hire-purchase, so that in either case ownership of the goods remained with M & T. D claimed that the contract was one of sale by instalments, so that ownership had passed to D and the remedy of recovery was not available.

The First Division found, and the House of Lords upheld, that the piano had been sold for £26 and that therefore M & T's remedy was not recovery, but an action for payment of the outstanding instalments.

2–04 "LORD PRESIDENT (DUNEDIN): . . . Now, the description of the bargain is given by three witnesses. It is given by the pursuer, or the person who is the manager of the pursuing firm, and it is given by the defender and by the defender's wife. The crucial part of it is contained in a very few sentences, and here I find the justification for the other observation I made, as to the way in which the witnesses have been examined. The one thing that is not asked, either on the one side or the other, is what the people said; and yet, of course, it is on what the people said that the whole question depends. But your Lordships must take the evidence and see what it comes to. Mr Grant, the pursuer's manager, says that there were present at the interview the defender, his wife and himself, and then he goes on—turning his evidence into *oratio directa*—as follows:—'We sell pianos for cash, the full sum being paid in cash, and we sell on the hire-purchase system, and also let out on hire. I offered defender an instrument at the value of £26, payable 15s. per month.' Now, I agree that, if that evidence is taken fairly to Mr. Grant, it means that he had in his mind to let out this instrument upon his own hire-purchase system. Your Lordships see that he details three methods, in which he conducts his business: selling pianos for cash, the whole sum being paid down; hire purchase; and mere hire.

Now, the offer which he details is an offer of the piano for £26, payable 15s. per month.

This cannot be the first of his methods of business, because it is not a sum in cash; and it cannot be the third, because it is not a mere hire; and therefore it is the middle kind, according to his views.

At the same time Mr. Grant—and I think it right, in fairness to Mr. Grant, to say that I see no reason to suppose that he was anything but perfectly honest and upright in the evidence he has given—says, in cross-examination, 'I cannot say that I made it clear to the defender that it was a trial hire.' Now, the defender says that Grant called and stated he would 'be pleased to let me have a piano. I left it with himself, because I was no judge. After discussing terms, I agreed to purchase the piano in dispute at the price of £26. I told him I was unable, in the meantime, to pay the full value, and that he would require to take it by the instalment principle. He said that was all right.' The defender's wife's view is substantially the same. She says, 'He, Grant, said we would get the piano by paying 15s. every month, and if it was paid in three years there would be a good discount. My husband and I were present on that occasion. Nothing was said about a hire contract.' Now, my Lords, of course, if the matter really was as to what in their inmost hearts people thought, I think that, taking these people as honest people on both one side and the other, what they thought would lead me to the conclusion ... that Grant [one of the partners in the pursuers' firm] thought he was selling on the hire-purchase system, and the other person thought he was buying upon some instalment plan. But commercial contracts cannot be arranged by what people think in their inmost minds. Commercial contracts are made according to what people say, and, accordingly, I come to the conclusion that what was said here was, in the words of Mr Grant himself, that he offered the defender an instrument of the value of £26, payable 15s. per month, and that the defender accepted that offer, namely, to buy the piano at £26, but payable on the instalment principle at the rate of 15s. a month ... When you have a word like instalment principle, you can only give it a meaning by one of two methods. It has either the ordinary meaning of the English language, or you can shew, by appropriate evidence, that instalment principle means a certain sort of arrangement. I think you can only do that by shewing that a certain custom is so well known that it has become part of the general law merchant—and nobody suggests that that is the case here—or you can shew that a particular custom has been so generally accepted in a particular trade, that it has become an implied part of every bargain made in the ordinary course of that trade. But in order to do that you must have appropriate averments and appropriate proof. [Counsel for the pursuer] said that everybody in Glasgow knew about it. But I should say that the knowledge of it in Glasgow is of a fluctuating character ... by merely using the word 'principle', you cannot bring in the very peculiar and very particular stipulations of the [hire purchase] agreement ...

The plain lesson to be derived, I hope, from the judgment is this, that when parties wish to bind persons to a contract with unusual stipulations, they must bring that contract clearly to their knowledge, and that, on the other hand, if they use words which are capable of ordinary interpretation, they must expect the persons who hear them to take them up in their ordinary significance."

Hire-purchase became a very popular credit transaction throughout most of the 20th century. Is hire-purchase still so common that it would be implied into the contract in similar circumstances?[4]

What constitutes an offer?

An offer is a statement, or course of conduct, which clearly shows that the offerer intends to be bound by the terms that the offer lays down, on condition that the person or persons to whom it is directed (the offeree) accepts the same terms. It follows that a person who specifies in adequate detail (and in a form that is capable of acceptance)[5] the terms under which they are willing to contract, thereby makes an offer. **2–05**

The Draft Common Frame of Reference (DCFR) II–4:201(1) puts it more succinctly:

> "A proposal amounts to an offer if: (a) it is intended to result in a contract if the other party accepts it; and (b) it contains sufficiently definite terms to be a contract."[6]

---

[4] For very different consequences resulting from misunderstandings about the nature of the contract, see the discussion of *Mathieson Gee v Quigley*, 1952 S.L.T. 239; 1952 S.C. (H.L.) 38 below, paras 6–25—6–27.

[5] Below, paras 2–41—2–45.

[6] A different and novel definition was given by Lord Clarke in *William Lippe Architects Ltd v Innes* [2006] CSOH 182A: "[A] statement of terms which the offeror proposes to the offeree as the basis of an agreement, coupled with a promise, express or implied, to adhere to these terms if the offer is accepted". Although the Inner House affirmed Lord Clarke's finding that there was no offer capable of acceptance, they did not expressly adopt Lord Clarke's definition of offer. There seems no justification for introducing the concept of a promise as an essential part of the definition of an offer.

This definition, (and similar provisions in other international restatements) was recently considered by the Scottish Law Commission.

2–06 *Review of Contract Law: Discussion Paper on Formation of Contract*

Scottish Law Commission Discussion Paper No.154 (March 2012)

Chapter 3: The Offer

(i) Offer

DCFR: II.–4:201 Offer

. . .

3.5 . . . In essence, in [DCFR II.-4:201, CISG art.14, CESL art.31 and PICC 2.1.2] an offer is defined as a proposal from one party which is sufficiently definite in its terms to form a contract and also manifests an intention to be legally binding on the offeror should it be accepted by the party to whom it is addressed. We think, as did our predecessors in the RFC,[3] that this definition of 'offer' is consistent with the existing law of Scotland. It is, however, quite difficult to find an authoritative definition in either textbooks or judicial statements.[4] The recent case of *William Lippe Architects Ltd v Innes*[5] provides a useful illustration of a situation in which a detailed business proposal is deemed insufficiently definite in its terms to constitute an offer because it leaves open alternative methods for determining price. The manifestation of an intention to be legally bound is also, ultimately, a question of the construction of the proposal, even in the context of particular situations where there was once thought to be a presumption in the opposite direction, as in social and domestic arrangements or the relationship between a church and its ministers.[6] There is much case law in which the courts have decided whether or not particular forms of wording amount to an offer on this ground.[7]

3.6 With regard to 'general offers', or proposals made to the public rather than to a specific person—for example, advertisements, shop window displays, the circulation of catalogues of goods for sale, and consumer-oriented e-commerce websites—THE CISG states that these are invitations to treat unless the contrary is clearly indicated whereas the DCFR simply says that they are offers if they otherwise meet the requirements of the general definition of an offer. The proposed CESL reverts to something like the CISG formula, however, in providing that proposals made to the public rather than to one or more specific persons are not offers unless the contrary is clearly indicated. The CISG and the proposed CESL are here more consistent with the way in which Scots law tends to analyse such proposals.[8] Proposals to the public at large, or to a group of persons, which are not offers would include such communications as advertisements merely indicating the existence of a product on the marketplace (for instance, a brand of perfume), requests for the submission of tenders or estimates for the supply of goods or services, and the circular or website indicating the availability of a product or a service to customers making orders.[9] There are, however, several cases in which proposals made to the public have been held to be offers, the key features of such proposals being sufficient certainty about their content and the manifestation of an intention to be legally bound in the event of acceptance.[10] The classic example is provided by the English case of *Carlill v Carbolic Smoke Ball Co Ltd* (followed many times in Scotland) where a commitment in a newspaper advertisement of a product supposed to ward off influenza to pay key features of such proposals being sufficient certainty about their content and the manif, a question of the construction of the prisement included a statement that the defendant had deposited £1000 in a bank to meet its potential liabilities, showing the 'sincerity of [the defendant's] promise to pay this £100', i.e. a clear intention to be bound by the terms of the advertisement.[11]

3.7 We think that the definition of an offer stated in the international texts is in general consistent with Scots law. We therefore propose:

9. In any statutory restatement of the law on formation of contract, an offer should be defined as a proposal made to one or more specific persons containing sufficiently definite terms to form a contract and indicating the intention of the offeror to be bound if the offer is accepted by the other party or parties.

. . .

---

[3] RFC, para 3.2.

[4] Neither Gloag, *Contract* or McBryde, *Contract*, actually defines an offer. There is a definition in *SME*, vol 15, para 620 ("a statement of terms which the offeror proposes to the offeree as the basis of an agreement, coupled with a promise, express or implied, to adhere to these terms if the offer is accepted"), which is also deployed in MacQueen & Thomson, *Contract*, para 2.10. This is very close to the DCFR/CISG texts, with the use of the concept of "promise" being equivalent to the latters' "intention to be bound". Walker, *Contracts*, para 7.6, says that "an offer is a conditional promise, an expression by one party to another or others of willingness to become legally bound by contract to that other, or one or more of the others on certain terms, conditionally on the other party being willing to become bound to the counterpart performance." He cites Stair, *Institutions* I, 3, 9, which, however, simply distinguishes an offer from a promise in that it needs acceptance to become obligatory. See further Martin Hogg, *Promises and Contract Law* (2011), pp 210-219. For English law, *Chitty on Contracts*, para 2-003 and Furmston and Tolhurst, *Contract Formation*, para 2.14 (the latter quoting J Beatson, *Anson's Law of Contract* (28th edn, 2002), p 32, and W E Peel, *Treitel: The Law of Contract* (12th edn, 2007), p 9), provide definitions of "offer" which are also similar to the DCFR/CISG texts.

[5] [2006] CSOH 182, 2007 GWD 2-22 (Lord Clarke), affirmed on this point [2007] CSIH 84, paras 24-26.

[6] See *Percy v Board of National Mission of the Church of Scotland* 2006 SC (HL) 1; *MacDonald v Free Presbyterian Church of Scotland* [2010] UKEATS/0034/09/BI (10 February 2010); *President of the Methodist Church v Preston (formerly Moore)* [2011] EWCA Civ 1581.

[7] See Gloag, *Contract*, pp 17-24; McBryde, *Contract*, paras 6.14-6.25. See also Furmston and Tolhurst, *Contract Formation*, paras 2.22-2.29, discussing "weak words of commitment" and "words expressly denying a commitment". In the context of distinguishing an offer from an invitation to treat under English law, *Chitty on Contracts*, para 2-009, discusses inconclusive wording and the fact that use of the word "offer" is not determinative of the existence of an intention to be bound.

[8] Gloag, *Contract*, pp 21-24; McBryde, *Contract*, paras 6.14-6.17 and 6.22-6.23. This parallel can also be drawn with English law: *Chitty on Contracts*, paras 2-010-2-021, describes a number of public proposals and explains that most are considered in law to be invitations to treat unless, in some instances, contrary intention is shown.

[9] English law is generally to the same effect: *Chitty on Contracts*, paras 2.017 and 2.022.

[10] Gloag, *Contract*, p 22; McBryde, *Contract*, paras 6.25-6.27.

[11] *Carlill v Carbolic Smoke Ball Co Ltd* [1893] 1 QB 256 (CA) at 261-2 (Lindley LJ). For Scottish cases following *Carlill* see *Hunter v General Accident Fire & Life Assurance Corp* 1909 SC (HL) 30; *Law v Newnes* (1894) 21 R 1027; *A & G Paterson v Highland Railway Co* 1927 SC (HL) 32. See also *Petrie v Earl of Airlie* (1834) 13 S 68.

Communication of the offer

2–07 It goes without saying that an offer must be communicated to the offeree.[7] In the words of Lord President McNeill:

> "An offer is nothing until it is communicated to the party to whom it is made, and who is to decide whether he will or will not accept the offer."[8]

By implication, an offer cannot be accepted by an offeree who is unaware of its existence[9]; and an offer made to one person or group of persons only, cannot be accepted by anyone else. In *Fleming Buildings Ltd v Forrest*,[10] a letter from KWF, a company owned by Mr and Mrs Fleming purporting to accept an offer made by Forrest to Mr and Mrs Fleming, but not to KWF, was characterised by Lady Paton as "a mistaken attempt to accept [Forrest's] offer, and as such . . . it did not call for any acknowledgment".[11] As the following extract suggests, whether the offer has been communicated must be objectively established on the evidence.

2–08 *Review of Contract Law: Discussion Paper on Formation of Contract*

Scottish Law Commission Discussion Paper No.154 (March 2012)

> "**(ii) When offer effective**
>
> . . .
>
> **DCFR and proposed CESL: I.–1:109 Notice and Article 10: Notice**
>
> (3) The [offer] becomes effective when it reaches the [offeree], unless it provides for a delayed effect.
>
> 3.14 The effect of the general rule on when 'notices' (which include offers) become effective under the DCFR and the proposed CESL is that their rule on when offers become effective is the same as that of the CISG and is thus, as the RFC also stated, in line with present Scots law: that is, an offer becomes effective, in the sense of being available for acceptance, when it 'reaches' the offeree. As discussed above in Chapter 2, the DCFR's 'notices' rule also provides an objective definition of 'reaching' for these purposes (i.e. delivery or making accessible to the offeree), rather than the subjective rule, which would require the offeree to have read the offer or at least be aware of its existence as such.[19] This objective approach is again consistent with Scots law. The best example is *Burnley v Alford*.[20]
>
> 3.15 While the DCFR and the proposed CESL do not need a specific rule on when offers take effect like that in the CISG and the PICC, thanks to their general rule on 'notices', a Scots law enactment on formation of contract would require statements like those in the CISG and the PICC, as well as a definition of 'reaching'. The 'notices' rule

---

[7] The suggestion made by Walker that an offer by post is effective "possibly [from] the time it was posted" (DM Walker, *The Law of Contracts and Related Obligations in Scotland*, 3rd edn (Edinburgh: W. Green, 1995), para.7.24), or that "It has been held that an offer sent by post is made where it was posted" (DM Walker, *The Law of Contracts and Related Obligations in Scotland*, 3rd edn (Edinburgh: W. Green, 1995), para.7.23), is neither practical nor supported by the authorities cited (*Dunlop v Higgins* (1848) 6 Bell's App. 195, also reported at 1 H.L.C. 857; *Taylor v Jones* (1875) 1 C.P.D. 87).

[8] *Thomson v James*, (1855) 18 D 1. considered below, para.4–41.

[9] There is no authority in Scots law; and English authorities show a degree of inconsistency: see P Mitchell and J Phillips, "The Contractual Nexus: Is Reliance Essential?" (2002) 22(1) OJLS, 155.

[10] *Fleming Buildings Ltd v Forrest* [2010] CSIH 8; 2010 GWD 13–234.

[11] *Fleming Buildings Ltd v Forrest* [2010] CSIH 8; 2010 GWD 13–234 [21]. A unilateral promise, similarly, is binding on the promiser only when the intention to benefit another has been communicated to the party to be benefited: DM Walker, *Contracts*, para.2.8.

could, we think, be adapted for this purpose as well as for the determination of when an acceptance becomes effective ...

[19] See paras 2.15-2.29, and also PICC Art 2.1.3(1): Vogenauer and Kleinheisterkamp, *PICC Commentary*, p 242.
[20] 1919 2 SLT 123 (OH) Alf."

How specific must an offer be?

An offer need not be addressed to specific persons, so long as the persons in fact accepting are within the class contemplated by the offer. Thus an offer may be made to subscribers to a magazine or even to the world at large, as in the case of an advertisement.[12] 2–09

Carlill v Carbolic Smoke Ball Co
[1893] 1 Q.B. 256
English Court of Appeal, Civil Division: Bowen, Lindley and L.A. Smith LJJ

The defendants placed advertisements in several newspapers that their product, the Carbolic Smoke Ball, "will positively cure", amongst other ailments and diseases, "influenza ... in 24 hours". The advertisements stated that a £100 reward would be paid to anyone who, after using the smoke ball in accordance with the instructions provided, contracted influenza (there was, at that time, a virulent epidemic of the disease); and that £1,000 had been deposited with a bank "showing our sincerity in the matter".

Mrs Carlill purchased a smoke ball and used it in accordance with the instructions for almost eight weeks, when she contracted influenza. She successfully claimed her reward.

"LINDLEY LJ: ... [I]t is contended that [the advertisement] is not binding. In the first place, it is said that it is not made with anybody in particular. Now that point is common to the words of this advertisement and to the words of all other advertisements offering rewards. They are offers to anybody who performs the conditions named in the advertisement, and anybody who does perform the condition accepts the offer. In point of law this advertisement is an offer to pay £100 to anybody who will perform these conditions, and the performance of these conditions is the acceptance of the offer ... 2–10

We, therefore, find here all the elements which are necessary to form a binding contract enforceable in point of law ... the true construction of this advertisement is that £100 will be paid to anybody who uses this smoke ball three times daily for two weeks according to the printed directions, and who gets the influenza or cold or other diseases caused by taking cold within a reasonable time after so using it; and if that is the true construction, it is enough for the plaintiff ...

BOWEN LJ: The first observation which arises is that the document itself is not a contract at all, it is only an offer made to the public. The defendants contend next, that it is an offer the terms of which are too vague to be treated as a definite offer, inasmuch as there is no limit of time fixed for the catching of the influenza ... It seems to me that in order to arrive at a right conclusion we must read this advertisement in its plain meaning, as the public would understand it. It was intended to be issued to the public and to be read by the public. How would an ordinary person reading this document construe it? It was intended unquestionably to have some effect, and I think the effect 2–11

[12] See DCFR II–4:201(2): "An offer may be made to one or more specific persons or to the public".

which it was intended to have, was to make people use the smoke ball, because the suggestions and allegations which it contains are directed immediately to the use of the smoke ball as distinct from the purchase of it. It did not follow that the smoke ball was to be purchased from the defendants directly, or even from agents of theirs directly. The intention was that the circulation of the smoke ball should be promoted, and that the use of it should be increased. The advertisement ... is written in colloquial and popular language, and I think that it is equivalent to this: '£100 will be paid to any person who shall contract the increasing epidemic after having used the carbolic smoke ball three times daily for two weeks.' ... Then again it was said: 'How long is this protection to endure? Is it to go on for ever, or for what limit of time?' ... I think the immunity is to last during the use of the ball. That is the way in which I should naturally read it, and it seems to me that the subsequent language of the advertisement supports that construction ...

Was it intended that the £100 should, if the conditions were fulfilled, be paid? The advertisement says that £1000 is lodged at the bank for the purpose. Therefore, it cannot be said that the statement that £100 would be paid was intended to be a mere puff. I think it was intended to be understood by the public as an offer which was to be acted upon.

But it was said that there was no check on the part of the persons who issued the advertisement, and that it would be an insensate thing to promise £100 to a person who used the smoke ball unless you could check or superintend his manner of using it. The answer to that argument seems to me to be that if a person chooses to make extravagant promises of this kind he probably does so because it pays him to make them, and, if he has made them, the extravagance of the promises is no reason in law why he should not be bound by them.

It was also said that the contract is made with all the world—that is, with everybody, and that you cannot contract with everybody. It is not a contract made with all the world. There is the fallacy of the argument. It is an offer made to all the world; and why should not an offer be made to all the world which is to ripen into a contract with anybody who comes forward and performs the condition? It is an offer to become liable to anyone who, before it is retracted, performs the condition, and, although the offer is made to the world, the contract is made with that limited portion of the public who come forward and perform the condition on the faith of the advertisement. It is not like cases in which you offer to negotiate, or you issue advertisements that you have got a stock of books to sell, or houses to let, in which case there is no offer to be bound by any contract. Such advertisements are offers to negotiate—offers to receive offers—offers to chaffer, as, I think, some learned judge in one of the cases has said."

When did Mrs Carlill "perform the condition and accept the offer"?

In general practice, especially in the course of business, contracts are the result of a process of negotiation. An offer would arise in the course of such negotiations. For example, a manufacturer may want supplies of a component or raw material. The manufacturer would normally put out enquiries to possible suppliers, asking for prices, dates of delivery, specifications and so on. Only when the manufacturer is satisfied as to the relevant particulars will the manufacturer offer to purchase goods by placing an order with a particular supplier.

A specific, isolated and initial statement or act will, however, in certain circumstances, be interpreted as an offer. The crucial factor in every instance is whether the acts or statements in question clearly establish the essential features of the proposed contract. Although it is impossible to generalise, certain categories of such specific acts or statements can be classified, so that with a reasonable degree of certainty, they will be seen either as offers, or as invitations for offers.

Specific instances of offer

Advertisements and shop displays—offers or "offers to receive offers"?

Bowen LJ in *Carlill* differentiated advertisements that are "offers to negotiate—offers to receive offers—offers to chaffer". **2–12**

Merely to display goods for sale on a market stall, or even in a shop window is not an offer to sell to the first person who wishes to buy; it is an inducement for prospective purchasers to make offers, or an invitation to treat. In England, it has been held that such a display, even with a specific price attached, is not an offer to sell, but an invitation of offers to buy.

Fisher v Bell

[1961] 1 Q.B. 394

English Court of Criminal Appeal: Lord Parker CJ, Ashworth & Elwes JJ

The "flick knife", a particularly vicious weapon, had become a favourite of the "teddy boy" street gangs of the 1950s. The weapon was "outlawed" by the Restriction of Offensive Weapons Act 1959. Section 1(1) of that Act stated:

> "Any person who manufactures, sells or hires or offers for sale or hire, or lends or gives to any other person-(a)any knife which has a blade which opens automatically by hand pressure applied to a button, spring or other device in or attached to the handle of the knife, sometimes known as a 'flick knife' or 'flick gun'; ... shall be guilty of an offence".

Bell displayed a "flick knife" in his shop window. A label behind it stated: "Ejector knife-4s." He was prosecuted for offering the knife for sale contrary to s.1(1) of the Offensive Weapons Act 1959.

The court upheld Bell's acquittal.

"LORD PARKER C.J.: ... The sole question is whether the exhibition of that knife in the window with the ticket constituted an offer for sale within the statute. I confess that I think that most lay people and, indeed, I myself when I first read the papers, would be inclined to the view that to say that if a knife was displayed in a window like that with a price attached to it was not offering it for sale was just nonsense. In ordinary language it is there inviting people to buy it, and it is for sale; but any statute must of course be looked at in the light of the general law of the country. Parliament in its wisdom ... must be taken to know the general law. It is perfectly clear that according to the ordinary law of contract, the display of an article with a price on it in a shop window is merely an invitation to treat. It is in no sense an offer for sale the acceptance of which constitutes a contract. That is clearly the general law of the country. Not only is that so, but it is to be observed that in many statutes and orders which prohibit selling and offering for sale of goods it is very common when it is so desired to insert the words 'offering or exposing for sale', 'exposing for sale' being clearly words which would cover the display of goods in a shop window. Not only that, but it appears that under several statutes—we have been referred in particular to the Prices of Goods Act 1939, and the Goods and Services (Price Control) Act 1941—Parliament, when it desires to enlarge the ordinary meaning of those words, includes a definition section enlarging the ordinary meaning of 'offer for sale' to cover other matters including, be it observed, exposure of goods for sale with the price attached. **2–13**

In those circumstances I am driven to the conclusion, though I confess reluctantly, that no offence was here committed. At first sight it sounds absurd that knives of this sort cannot be manufactured, sold, hired, lent, or given, but apparently they can be displayed in shop windows; but even if this—and I am by no means saying it is—is a casus omissus it is not for this court to supply the omission. I am mindful of the strong words of Lord Simonds in *Magor & St. Mellons Rural District Council v Newport Corporation*.[13] In that case one of the Lords Justices in the Court of Appeal had, in effect, said[14] that the court having discovered the supposed intention of Parliament must proceed to fill in the gaps—what the Legislature has not written the court must write—and in answer to that contention Lord Simonds in his speech said[15]: 'It appears to me to be a naked usurpation of the legislative function under the thin disguise of interpretation.' "

Similarly, an advertisement of goods for sale in a newspaper,[16] circular[17] or catalogue[18] is—in English law at least—an invitation to treat not capable of acceptance. "The reason for this" according to Lord Russell of Killowen

> "is the eminently sound one that the vendor might otherwise find himself bound to a series of contracts that he would be quite unable to fulfil: since it is a mere invitation to treat he reserves to himself the ability to refuse an offer from a would-be purchaser".[19]

This makes sense, for example, where unspecified or unmeasured quantities or descriptions of goods are being "offered" for sale, because such are, in the words of Bowen LJ in the *Carlill* case above,

> "cases in which you offer to negotiate, or you issue advertisements that you have got a stock of books to sell, or houses to let, in which case there is no offer to be bound by any contract".

Shop displays

2–14 Can this line of reasoning be extended by analogy to the advertisement or display of specific items, at specified prices and where there is no expectation of "haggling" between the parties? It has been extended, in England at least, to cover the display of specific goods on supermarket shelves.

2–15 **Pharmaceutical Society of Great Britain v Boots Cash Chemists (Southern) Ltd**
[1953] 1 Q.B. 401
English Court of Criminal Appeal: Somervell, Birkett and Romer LJJ

Medicines were displayed on the shelves of Boots, a sell-service store in Edgware. They were individually wrapped and price-marked.

Under s.18(1) of the Pharmacy & Poisons Act 1933, it would be a criminal offence to "sell" such preparations unless "[t]he sale is effected by, or under the supervision of a registered pharmacist".

---

[13] *Magor & St. Mellons Rural District Council v Newport Corporation* [1952] A.C. 189; [1951] 2 T.L.R 935; [1951] 2 All E.R 839 H.L

[14] *Magor & St. Mellons Rural District Council v Newport Corporation* [1950] 2 All E.R. 1226, 1236, C.A.

[15] *Magor & St. Mellons Rural District Council v Newport Corporation* [1952] A.C. 189, at 191.

[16] *Partridge v Crittenden* [1968] 1 W.L.R 1204; [1968] 2 All E.R 421.

[17] *Spencer v Harding* (1870) L.R 5 C.P. 561.

[18] *Grainger & Son v Gough* [1896] A.C. 325.

[19] *Esso Petroleum Co Ltd v Customs & Excise Commissioners* [1976] 1 All E.R. 117; [1976] 1 W.L.R. 1, 11. See, however, wording of DCFR II–4:201(3).

Two customers took such medicines from the shelves, placed them in the wire basket provided and took them to the check-out. The cashier, in the presence of a registered pharmacist, marked the items on the till and took payment. The Pharmaceutical Society prosecuted Boots, claiming that an offence had been committed. It was argued that the sale was complete when the customers accepted the offer made by displaying the goods, by placing them in the basket.

The court refused to convict.

"SOMERVELL LJ: ... Whether the view contended for by the plaintiffs is a right view depends on what are the legal implications of this layout—the invitation to the customer. Is a contract to be regarded as being completed ... when the article is put into the receptacle, or is this to be regarded as a more organized way of doing what is done already in many types of shops—and a bookseller is perhaps the best example—namely, enabling customers to have free access to what is in the shop, to look at the different articles, and then, ultimately, having got the ones which they wish to buy, to come to the assistant saying 'I want this'? The assistant in 999 times out of 1,000 says 'That is all right,' and the money passes and the transaction is completed. I agree entirely with what the Lord Chief Justice has said, and with the reasons which he has given for his conclusion, that in the case of the ordinary shop, although goods are displayed and it is intended that customers should go and choose what they want, the contract is not completed until, the customer having indicated the article which he needs, the shopkeeper, or someone on his behalf, accepts that offer. Then the contract is completed. I can see no reason at all, that being clearly the normal position, for drawing any different implication as a result of this layout. 2–16

The Lord Chief Justice, I think, expressed one of the most formidable difficulties in the way of the plaintiffs' contention when he pointed out that, if the plaintiffs are right, once an article has been placed in the receptacle the customer himself is bound and he would have no right, without paying for the first article, to substitute an article which he saw later of the similar kind and which he perhaps preferred. I can see no reason for implying from this self-service arrangement any implication other than that which the Lord Chief Justice found in it, namely, that it is a convenient method of enabling customers to see what there is and choose, and possibly put back and substitute, articles which they wish to have, and then go up to the cashier and offer to buy what they have so far chosen. On that conclusion the case fails, because it is admitted that [in those circumstances] there was supervision in the sense required by the Act and at the appropriate moment of time. For these reasons, in my opinion, the appeal should be dismissed."

This, it can be argued, does not conform with the principle outlined at the beginning of this section that an offer arises where the words or conduct in question (e.g. displaying goods on a supermarket shelf) establish the essential features of the proposed contract. Where goods are displayed in this way, little remains for the parties to "chaffer" about. The only choice left to the customer is to take particular items at specific prices. It may be more accurate to regard such displays as offers, so that the real issue is what constitutes the act of acceptance; and it would be unlikely to be the mere placing of the goods in the basket provided: it would much more likely be the act of presenting the goods at the check-out.

Lord Somervell appears in no doubt that the display was an invitation to offer. Why so? Is the analogy with the bookshop accurate? Is the display of a wrapped, sealed product on the supermarket shelf an offer? If the display is the offer, what is the acceptance?

2–17 Although there seems to be a consistently expressed view that such advertisements and displays, even of specific items at specific prices, are not offers there has been no pronouncement on the matter by the Inner House or the Supreme Court. Furthermore, all the cases involved the interpretation of words like "sale" or "offer" in criminal statutes.[20] The general view must remain that of Gloag:

> "These and analogous questions do not admit of any general answer; much must depend on the circumstances of a particular case."[21]

Consider the following facts. Pat saw a bottle of "Bruaichladdich" single malt whisky on a shelf in his local supermarket. The bottle had a bar code label on it. It was one of several bottles of the same brand in the same section of the shelf. Below the bottles, on the shelf, was a label which stated: "Bruaichladdich: £25.00."

Pat placed the bottle in his trolley, with other groceries and went to the check-out. He noticed when the assistant ran the bottle over the bar code sensor that the price "£29.50" showed on the till. He immediately drew the assistant's attention to the difference between that price and the price on the shelf.

Has Pat bought the bottle, and if so, at which price?

It is arguable that, should such an issue arise in the Court of Session, it would be free to adopt the principles set out in DCFR II–4:201(3):

> "A proposal to supply goods or services at stated prices made by a business in a public advertisement or catalogue, or by a display of goods, is treated, unless the circumstances indicate otherwise, as an offer to sell or supply at that price until the stock of goods, or the business's capacity to supply the service, is exhausted."

Advertisements of reward

2–18 Advertisements of reward, if they are not unilateral promises, would normally be regarded as offers (see above, Ch.1).

Law v George Newnes Ltd[22] and *Hunter v Hunter*[23] both concerned advertisements that appeared in Newnes's newspapers to the effect that a specified sum of money would be paid to any person adjudged by the proprietors to be the next-of-kin of a person killed in a railway accident. The only proviso was that the person killed had in their possession at the time of the accident a copy of the current issue of the relevant publication. In both cases, relatives challenged the proprietors' selection of the next-of-kin.

In both cases, a similarly composed Court of Session rejected the claims on the apparent basis that there was a contractual obligation to pay the money to the person whom the proprietors adjudged to be the next-of-kin, although this finding was not essential to either decision. (Lord Young, however, in both cases doubted whether there was any contractual obligation, seeing the advertisement as a mere inducement to purchase the newspaper.[24])

---

[20] See *Lacis v Cashmarts* [1969] 2 Q.B 400.

[21] Gloag, *The Law of Contract*, 2nd edn (Edinburgh: W. Green, 1929), p.21.

[22] *Law v George Newnes Ltd* (1894) 21 R. 1027.

[23] *Hunter v Hunter* (1904) 7 F. 136.

[24] *Law v George Newnes Ltd* (1594) 21 R. 1027, 1032–1033; *Hunter v Hunter* (1904) 7 F. 136, 139–140. See also *Petrie v Earl of Airlie*, discussed above, para.1–65 and *Carlill v Carbolic Smoke Ball Co*, above, para.2–09.

General offers of services

It has long been the law in Scotland that persons who hold themselves out as providing certain services must provide such services upon request to members of the general public. Common carriers, by land or sea, and common innkeepers and stable keepers fell into this category. Such services, like similar services today, were normally provided under contract. However, as a residual effect of their position at common law, persons providing analogous services today would be regarded as making a contractual offer by the mere provision of such service. For example, running a bus on a particular route constitutes an offer of carriage to the general public[25]; and an hotel makes an offer of accommodation by opening its doors to the general public, this offer being accepted when the guest "books in".[26] By analogy, because they provide a service to the general public, a car park is regarded as making an offer to the general public to park their cars[27]; and even a local authority makes an offer when it places a pile of deck-chairs on a beach and invites the general public to use them for a small charge.[28] **2–19**

Such an analysis cannot be taken much further in a modern context. The mere provision of a railway service, or the scheduling of an air route, cannot amount to an offer. A great many preliminaries must be carried out—such as checking the availability of seats—before the issue of the ticket completes the contract. Booking a holiday through a travel agent similarly involves the completion of an application form which constitutes the offer to the tour operator.[29]

Orders

Much confusion surrounds this subject. When a prospective purchaser places an order, does that constitute an offer to buy goods in accordance with the order? What if the order is placed with a dealer who, in the normal course of trade or business, undertakes to procure goods ordered? Bell[30] suggests that such an "order in trade" does not require acceptance to become binding on the trader. If he does not wish to fulfil the order, the trader is under an obligation to notify the person placing the order to that effect. **2–20**

Barry, Ostlere and Shepherd Ltd v Edinburgh Cork Importing Co **2–21**

1909 S.C. 1113

Court of Session, Extra Division: Lords Pearson, Dundas and McLaren

After negotiations at the pursuers' premises, the pursuers handed to the defenders' representative a written order for a specific quantity of cork shavings, at a specified price and to be delivered at specified times.

No deliveries were made; prices rose and the pursuers brought this action for damages for breach of contract. The defenders claimed that the order was but an offer to purchase and that no contract had arisen with the pursuers because there had been no acceptance of their offer.

The court found that there was a contract between the parties.

---

25 *Wilkie v London Public Transport Board* [1947] 1 All E.R. 258, where the Court of Appeal in England found that a contract would arise when the passenger boards the bus: presumably, with modern driver-operated vehicles, the contract is completed at the point where the ticket is issued by the driver.

26 *Olley v Marlborough Court Hotel Ltd* [1949] 1 K.B. 532.

27 *Thornton v Shoe Lane Parking Ltd* [1971] 2 QB 163, considered below, 9–38.

28 *Chapelton v Barry Urban District Council* [1940] 1 K.B. 532, considered below, 9–36.

29 For a comment on DCFR II–4:201(3) in this context, see below para.2–26.

30 *Principles*, ss.80–82.

2–22 "LORD PEARSON: ... I have assumed down to this point that the terms of the document ... are such as, when taken in connection with the surrounding circumstances, amount to a contract of sale. The defenders maintain that they do not. Their contention is, that although the document is in form an order, it was not intended as an order, but was merely an offer on the part of the pursuers to purchase cork shavings, which required the defenders' acceptance to make it a binding contract. I cannot so read the document. It bears to be not an offer but an order, and in my opinion it assumes the existence of a contract, and is the expression of an order in pursuance of that contract. The defenders themselves certainly did not treat it as an offer, nor had the pursuers any notice that they meant to do so. On the contrary, the defenders, having the document in their hands, allowed six weeks to elapse before making any communication to the pursuers on the subject; and when they did, it was not to accept or reject it as an offer but to ask for delay in the fulfilment of the 'conditional order.' To this the pursuers promptly replied, claiming delivery of the cork shavings 'as per terms of contract'; and a correspondence ensued, in which the defenders notably abstained from answering or repudiating the reiterated demands of the pursuers for fulfilment of the contract sale."

Why did Lord Pearson say: "the document bears not to be an offer but an order?" Is the case support for the view that an "order in trade" is normally an acceptance of an offer? When was this contract made?

If, however, the trader makes an unequivocal offer to sell a specific quantity of specified goods at a stated price and on stated terms, that will be regarded as an offer and the placing of an order will be an acceptance, as the following case indicates.

2–23 **Philp & Co v Knoblauch**

907 S.C. 994

Court of Session, Second Division: The Lord Justice Clerk (Macdonald), Lords Stormonth-Darling, Low and Ardwall

The defender, a Leith trader, wrote to the pursuer in Lower Largo:

> "I am offering today Plate Linseed for January/February shipment to Leith, and have pleasure in quoting you 100 tons at 41/3, usual Plate terms. I shall be glad to hear if you are buyers, and await your esteemed reply."

The pursuer telegraphed an acceptance upon receipt of the letter on the following day.

The court found that a contract had arisen between the parties.

2–24 "LORD JUSTICE-CLERK (MacDonald): ... The first letter ... is not a letter merely indicating that the defender had certain goods at his disposal and would be glad to enter into negotiations with regard to them, but ... was clearly an offer of the 100 tons at a named price. Now, that letter was replied to by a telegram in these terms—'Accept hundred January/February Plate 41s. 3d., Leith, per steamer Leith.' That was a shorthand way of stating their reply to be followed by a letter. I think the telegram was a very plain acceptance of the 100 tons which the defender had quoted. I think it must be read along with the letter which followed ... The pursuers' telegram read with their letter is a very plain acceptance of what I consider is the plain offer contained in the defender's letter of 28th December. Without going nicely into the phraseology used I am distinctly of that opinion. The only difficulty is the question of whether the words used by the pursuers involved an acceptance of the usual Plate terms as a condition of the contract. I think they did when we read the telegram and the letter together. The telegram 'accepts'

> without any reservation on this point, and the letter contains the words 'usual contract,' which plainly mean the same thing as the words 'usual Plate terms' in the offer.
> The case of *Harvey v Facey*[31] which was quoted to us has no bearing. That was a case regarding an alleged purchase and sale of heritable property, not a transaction like this in *re mercatoria*. Further there was never really an offer. The telegram founded on as an offer was not an offer. It was merely an opening of negotiations. It offered nothing. It was merely an intimation of the lowest price which would be considered if anyone came forward offering it. I have no doubt that decision was right, but it has no bearing here."

Similarly, if a trader issues order forms, with only the quantity left blank, that constitutes an offer which is accepted on the return of the order form so that all orders received must be fulfilled.[32]

Orders in trade

Could a trader, merchant or manufacturer of a particular commodity or in a particular line of business, be considered to make a general offer to sell to the public at large, so that a contract arises whenever an order is placed or, because of the posting rule, posted? Gloag[33] states unequivocally that such so-called "orders in trade" are merely offers, but the only institutional writer on the matter, Bell, states that such an order is not "a mere offer"; that it "may be rejected but does not require acceptance to bind the person who gives the order. It will also bind the person to whom it is addressed, if strictly in his line of trade, unless refused in course of post"; and that **2–25**

> "acceptance is presumed from the undertaking which one in trade is held to profess, that he will answer any orders in the line of his trade, or immediately intimate his refusal".[34]

Analysis suggests[35] that there is no support for the view that a trader is bound to supply an order in the general course of trade. Indeed, the traditional analysis of offer and acceptance was applied to this wider concept of orders in trade in *Barry, Ostlere and Shepherd Ltd v Edinburgh Cork Importing Co*[36] (see para.2–21). The contract had been concluded in the course of negotiations which were subsequently reduced to writing in the form of the order. There is no need, however, to regard this as something special by calling it an "order in trade" or by invoking mandate. There was simply an established agreement between the parties, prior to the placing of the order.

The DCFR, however, suggests an alternative approach. DCFR II.–4:201(3) provides:

> "A proposal to supply goods from stock, or a service, at a stated price made by a business in a public advertisement or a catalogue, or by a display of goods, is treated, unless the circumstances indicate otherwise, as an offer to supply at that price until the stock of goods, or the business's capacity to supply the service, is exhausted."

This provision was considered favourably by the Scottish Law Commission.

---

31 [1893] A.C. 552.
32 *Chisholm v Robertson* (1883) 10 R. 760.
33 Gloag, *The Law of Contract*, 2nd edn (Edinburgh: W. Green, 1929), p.27.
34 Bell, *Principles*, ss.80–81.
35 See generally John AK Huntley, "The Status of Purchase Orders in Modern Commercial Practice", 1989 S.L.T. (News) 221.
36 *Barry, Ostdere and Shepard Ltd v Edinburgh Cork Importing Co*, 1909 S.C. 1113.

2–26 *Review of Contract Law: Discussion Paper on Formation of Contract*

Scottish Law Commission Discussion Paper No 154, March 2012

Chapter 3: The Offer

<u>(i) Offer</u>

DCFR: II.–4:201 Offer

. . .

3.8 Also consistent with Scots law, we think, is the proposition that a proposal made to the general public rather than to one or more specified persons is not an offer unless it otherwise meets the general criteria defining an offer, that is to say, it contains sufficiently definite terms to form a contract and indicates the intention of the party making the proposal to be bound by it if it is accepted by another party or parties. We say nothing here of the further possibility that such proposals to the public may be unilateral promises in Scots law (which may, however, be matter for discussion on another occasion).[12]

3.9 An innovation in the DCFR by comparison with the CISG or the PICC, is a rule that advertisements, catalogues and displays of goods or services for sale by a business at a stated price are offers to supply until the stock is exhausted or the business becomes incapable of supplying the service. Present Scots (and English) law would tend to see these as invitations to treat, so that it is the customer responding to the statement who makes the offer and the business whose stock or capacity is potentially affected which may then accept or decline that offer.[13] But the current law also in effect enables the business which has stock never the less to refuse the customer's offer, for example because the former harbours doubts about the latter's creditworthiness. Again, however, the view that advertisements are generally invitations to treat and not offers seems to apply even in cases where the business contracts only on cash terms and does not give credit to its customers.[14] The DCFR approach is thus more protective of the customer's interest in securing a contract and holding a business to a stated price than the present law.[15] It may well therefore be attractive to consumers.

3.10 It is worth noting that, despite the existing rules already discussed making proposals to the public generally invitations to treat rather than offers, the approach of the DCFR to advertisements announcing the availability of a stock of goods or services each at a stated price is not necessarily inconsistent with retail practice in Scotland or the wider United Kingdom. In self-service stores, once the shelf is empty of stock, no offer is being made under the DCFR rule.[16] It is common for advertisements announcing the availability of goods or services to consumers to indicate that they subsist only while stocks remain or capacity is not exhausted. Consumer-oriented websites use this technique too, not infrequently stating exactly in advance of any transaction how many goods remain available in the supplier's warehouse or at a particular branch, or how many seats remain unfilled on the airline flight.

3.11 On the other hand, although the DCFR rule was included in the Feasibility Study, it was dropped for the proposed CESL. This may suggest that, despite the rule's attractiveness from a consumer point of view, it was seen as containing potential problems. In particular, such a rule could create real difficulties for internet traders, who not uncommonly, but through administrative error rather than with intent, misprice goods or services advertised as available on their websites. Such traders could therefore, under the proposed rule, find themselves bound to supply an indefinite number of customers placing orders at the stated price, with orders far outnumbering the available stock. The DCFR rule also gives rise to other, more general uncertainties: for example, what constitutes the stock of a trader with multiple outlets? Is it only the stock at the outlet where the customer seeks to make the purchase, or is it the stock available across the whole chain? The problem may become still greater where the trader's business is international, with outlets in jurisdictions beyond the United Kingdom.

3.12 In our view, while there are some attractions in a basic rule like that found in the DCFR, in particular from the point of view of consumer protection, these are offset by some of the uncertainties mentioned above. Its introduction would have to be balanced at least by being subject to party autonomy (as indeed it is in the DCFR). This would enable traders, for example, to define what constituted stock for the purposes of the rule, or to go further and declare that a statement on a website about the availability of goods or services at a certain price was not an offer, or lay down a procedure for the conclusion of a contract for the supply of goods or services. Well-advised traders would doubtless do this,[17] with the possibilities for abuse of this autonomy by rogue traders being picked up by consumer protection law; but the smaller-scale trader unable to afford legal advice might be exposed to undue risk by a default rule that its exposure of goods and services at a stated price is an offer.

---

[12] Note that, again like Scots law, the DCFR recognises the enforceability of what it calls a 'unilateral undertaking' even without acceptance by the party to whom it is made (DCFR I.–1:103(2), II.–4:301–303). See further Martin Hogg, *Promises and Contract Law* (2011), pp.228–230.

[13] See the cases cited in McBryde, *Contract*, para 6.15; SME, vol 15, paras 621-624; Walker, *Contracts*, paras 7.2 and 7.6-7.12; and discussion in MacQueen & Thomson, *Contract*, paras 2.13-2.15.

[14] McBryde, *Contract*, para 6.15, fn 46; see eg *Partridge v Crittenden* [1968] 2 All ER 421 (newspaper advertisement of "Cage and Aviary birds" for sale at 25 shillings each held to be an invitation to treat and not an offer, although only cash transactions appear to have been contemplated).

[15] DCFR, vol 1, p 294 (Comment D). There may be an issue here with obvious mispricing by a business, a situation which has quite frequently occurred with consumer-oriented websites. The correct approach to this subject appears to us to be through the law of error rather than the law of formation. See, eg, the Singaporean case *Chwee Kin Keong v Digilandmail.com Pte Ltd* [2004] 2 SLR 594, [2004] SGHC 71.

[16] Furmston and Tolhurst, *Contract Formation*, para 2.39. The display of goods on the supermarket shelf being an offer need not mean that when customers put goods in a basket or trolley there is then and there acceptance and a contract concluded so that they cannot subsequently change their minds without being in breach of contract. Acceptance would take place, it is suggested, when an indication of assent reaches the offeror, i.e. when customers pass their goods over the screen that activates the bar codes or allow the cashier to do so, placing them on the list of goods purchased and to be paid for by the customer.

[17] E.g. *Amazon.co.uk* uses the following clause on its website: 'When you place an order to purchase a product from Amazon.co.uk, we will send you an email confirming receipt of your order and confirming the details of your order. Your order represents an offer to us to purchase a product which is accepted by us when we send email confirmation to you that we've dispatched that product to you (the "Dispatch Confirmation E-mail"). That acceptance will be complete at the time we send the Dispatch Confirmation E-mail to you.' We understand that clauses of this kind are in widespread use by commercial internet sellers of goods. Consumers are presumably protected against any unfairness by the application of the Unfair Contract Terms Act 1977 to non-contractual notices as well as to standard form contract terms."

Quotations and specifications

The quotation of prices in commercial transactions is usually a response to an inquiry from a **2–27**
prospective purchaser. It is not normally intended to be or regarded as an offer. In Scots law, the promise to hold the rate for a specific period might be regarded as a unilateral promise.[37] A

---

[37] See below, paras 4–43—4–47.

quotation may nevertheless be specific enough to amount to an offer. A mere quotation of a price, or the transmission of information in a price list in unlikely to be regarded as an offer; but each case will depend on its facts. The more specific the quotation, the more likely it is to be an offer.

2–28 **Jaeger Bros Ltd v J &A McMorland**

(1902) 10 S.L.T. 63

Court of Session, First Division: Lords Adam, Kinnear and Pearson

The pursuers wanted to buy iron for shipment to Australia. They wrote to the defenders on 2 May in the following terms, asking for specific prices of five to 600 tons of certain specifications of iron, and stating:

"Please wire us to-morrow the following prices for a cargo of five to 600 tons 1/2 No. 1, 1/2 No. 3 G.M.B. Scotch, naming brand, shipment next Monday, the 7th. inst. ... We require your offer here at 12.30 at latest, as we have to cable out to Australia."

The defenders sent a telegram which stated: "Offer 600 tons half one, half three, Govan, Leith, 75s. 9d.; c.i.f. Hamburg, 80s. 9d". The pursuers wrote the same day to "accept your offer of 500 tons Govan 1/2 No.1, 1/2 No. 3, at 80s. 9d. c.i.f. Hamburg". The court found that a contract had arisen between the parties.

2–29 "LORD KINNEAR: ... Reading the letter of 2nd May, I agree ... that it means an invitation to Messrs McMorland to make an offer on certain conditions and not otherwise. Now, Messrs McMorland reply in a very short telegram, and express their offer, as the Lord Ordinary says, with a remarkable and perhaps unfortunate economy of words which is common to people who conduct their affairs by telegram. But if people will put their bargains into such an exceedingly elliptical form as that of a telegram, they must run the risk of its being held against them that they have left the ellipsis to be supplied by the receiver of the telegram, who is quite entitled to do so, because if he does not, he cannot put any meaning upon it at all. And therefore it appears to me that when one comes to construe such a telegram as that referred to, with reference to the preceding letter of the 2nd May, the writer of the telegram must be held to intend the meaning which the original offerer, he being a reasonable person, might naturally be expected to put upon it, and so reading it, I agree with your lordship that the right view is that maintained by the respondent.

I think it is an offer to supply 500 to 600 tons by ship from Leith to Hamburg at a price of 75s. 9d. f.o.b. at Leith, or 80s 9d. c.i.f. at Hamburg. That seems to me to be the fair meaning of the telegram which was sent by the defenders. And that being so, I do not think that there is any material question which could be raised between the parties. I have said that I think the offer in the telegram must be taken to refer to the proposal made under the conditions specified in the letter of 2nd May, and, if the telegram is, as has been said, elliptical, there is no very violent effort of construction required to read 'offer 600 tons' as meaning 'in accordance with the conditions you mention in your letter, we offer you 600 tons.' And therefore I cannot see sufficient ground for holding that the defenders rejected the explicit terms of pursuers' letter that shipment must be made on 7th May.

I think it is ... a proposal to make an offer, not of a definite number of tons but of a cargo of 500 to 600 tons. And I read the telegram, in the most reasonable way, as an offer of these terms. And I further think the letter of 3rd May, written the same day as the telegram, may be referred to for the purpose of seeing what was the meaning put by the writer himself on the words he used in his telegram".

For an English example of a quotation regarded by the Court of Appeal as an offer without discussion of the issue, see *Butler Machine Tool Co Ltd v Ex-Cell-O Corp*.[38] In *Uniroyal Ltd v Miller & Co*,[39] two separate quotations were involved, one made in 1974 and the other in 1977. Lord Allanbridge found that only the 1977 quotation was an offer. There is no clear statement in the judgment why this is so, but it is perhaps significant that he refers to the statement attached to the 1976 quotation that "this quotation remains open for acceptance within 30 days from to-day's date", and that he found the order sent by the pursuers in reply to the quotation as a counter-offer.[40]

Tenders

An invitation for tenders, whether for the supply of goods or work, is not an offer, but an invitation to offer. The tender is an offer so that a contract is made when the inviter accepts one of the tenders submitted.[41] There is no obligation to accept the lowest tender or indeed any tender at all, unless there was a unilateral promise to that effect. If a tender is accepted, the accepter is bound to take supplies of goods or services covered by the tender exclusively from the tenderer and the tenderer is similarly bound to supply the goods as and when requested by the accepter. **2–30**

Tenders are sometimes in the form of "requirements contracts", whereby the tenderer offers to supply goods or services as and when required by the contractor. The difficulty encountered in the English case of *Great Northern Railway v Whitham*[42] in finding consideration for the tenderer's promise to supply as and when required, where the acceptor was under no obligation to make such a request, does not arise in Scots law. There is therefore no need in Scots law to regard the tender as a "standing offer" which blossoms into a series of independent contracts every time an order is placed, unless this was clearly the intention of the parties. In England, such a "standing offer" would be revocable once any individual order had been fulfilled; whereas in Scots law, there would be an enforceable unilateral promise not to revoke the standing offer while it subsisted. Even in England, however, as the following case shows, courts are now willing to find a separate contractual obligation to consider a tender which is submitted in accordance with the requirements of the call for tenders.

Blackpool and Fylde Aero Club Ltd v Blackpool Borough Council **2–31**
[1990] 1 W.L.R. 1195
English Court of Appeal, Civil Division: Stocker, Bingham and Farquharson LJJ

The council, which owned and managed an airport, raised revenue by granting a concession to an air operator to operate pleasure flights from the airport. The club was granted the concession in 1975, 1978 and 1980. In 1983 the council sent invitations to tender to the club and six other parties, all of whom were connected with the airport. The invitations to tender stated that tenders were to be submitted in the envelope provided and were not to bear any name or mark that would identify the sender, and that tenders received after the date and time specified namely 12:00 noon on 17 March 1983 would not be considered. Only the club and two other tenderers responded to the council's invitation. The club's tender was put in the town hall letter box at 11:00 on 17 March, but the letter box was not cleared by council staff at noon that day as it was supposed to be.

---

[38] Below paras 2–61—2–63.
[39] Below, paras 3–27—3–28.
[40] For a discussion of the status of quotations, see Huntley, "Quotations, Business Practice and the Law", 1989 S.L.T. (News) 12L.
[41] *Spencer v Harding* (1870) L.R. 5 C P. 561; and see *Wylie & Lochhead v McElroy* (1873) 1 R. 41, considered below, paras 4–30—4–31; 4–49.
[42] *Great Northern Railway v Whitham* (1873) L.R. 9 C.P. 16.

The club's tender was recorded as being received late and was not considered. The club successfully brought an action against the council claiming damages for breach of contract.

2–32 "BINGHAM L.J.: ...A tendering procedure of this kind is, in many respects, heavily weighted in favour of the invitor. He can invite tenders from as many or as few parties as he chooses. He need not tell any of them who else, or how many others, he has invited. The invitee may often, although not here, be put to considerable labour and expense in preparing a tender, ordinarily without recompense if he is unsuccessful. The invitation to tender may itself, in a complex case, although again not here, involve time and expense to prepare, but the invitor does not commit himself to proceed with the project, whatever it is; he need not accept the highest tender; he need not accept any tender; he need not give reasons to justify his acceptance or rejection of any tender received. The risk to which the tenderer is exposed does not end with the risk that his tender may not be the highest or, as the case may be, lowest. But where, as here, tenders are solicited from selected parties all of them known to the invitor, and where a local authority's invitation prescribes a clear, orderly and familiar procedure—draft contract conditions available for inspection and plainly not open to negotiation, a prescribed common form of tender, the supply of envelopes designed to preserve the absolute anonymity of tenderers and clearly to identify the tender in question, and an absolute deadline—the invitee is in my judgment protected at least to this extent: if he submits a conforming tender before the deadline he is entitled, not as a matter of mere expectation but of contractual right, to be sure that his tender will after the deadline be opened and considered in conjunction with all other conforming tenders or at least that his tender will be considered if others are. Had the club, before tendering, inquired of the council whether it could rely on any timely and conforming tender being considered along with others, I feel quite sure that the answer would have been 'of course'. The law would, I think, be defective if it did not give effect to that.

It is of course true that the invitation to tender does not explicitly state that the council will consider timely and conforming tenders. That is why one is concerned with implication. But the council do not either say that they do not bind themselves to do so, and in the context a reasonable invitee would understand the invitation to be saying, quite clearly, that if he submitted a timely and conforming tender it would be considered, at least if any other such tender were considered.

I readily accept that contracts are not to be lightly implied. Having examined what the parties said and did, the court must be able to conclude with confidence both that the parties intended to create contractual relations and that the agreement was to the effect contended for. It must also, in most cases, be able to answer the question posed by Mustill LJ in *Hispanica de Petroleos SA v Vencedora Oceanica Navegacion SA* [*The Kapetan Markos* NL] (No.2) (Note) [1987] 2 Lloyd's Rep. 321, 331: 'What was the mechanism for offer and acceptance?' In all the circumstances of this case, and I say nothing about any other, I have no doubt that the parties did intend to create contractual relations to the limited extent contended for. Since it has never been the law that a person is only entitled to enforce his contractual rights in a reasonable way (*White and Carter (Councils) Ltd v McGregor* [1962] A.C. 413, 430A per Lord Reid), [counsel for the club] was in my view right to contend for no more than a contractual duty to consider. I think it plain that the council's invitation to tender was, to this limited extent, an offer, and the club's submission of a timely and conforming tender an acceptance."

English law does not recognise unilateral promises; the court, here, implied a separate contract to consider each tender submitted.

Would a Scottish court regard the obligations above as arising out of contract; or are they more likely to look at the council's obligation as arising out of a unilateral promise to consider every timously submitted tender? Alternatively, might there be a duty to recompense such pre-contractual losses?[43]

Auction sales

Auctions may take many forms. Most people are familiar with the *public*, or *open* auction of goods, usually held at the auction house, in which goods are displayed for sale. The same process is used in the sale of cattle and fish. Even houses and land are often sold by public auction—or, to use the Scottish term, public *roup*. **2–33**

Auctions may also be *closed*. The sale of land in Scotland is normally a closed auction. The seller's solicitor will notify prospective buyers of a closing date on the property (usually midday on a Friday). All interested in bidding must submit their bids in writing and in a sealed envelope in accordance with the instructions of the seller. The bids are opened on closing of the auction and usually the house or property is sold to the highest bidder. Any other property (for example, shares in a private company) could also be sold in this way.

The *tender* is a similar process used commonly in procuring contracts for major (usually public) works or services, such as the construction of public buildings or the provision of facility management services. A local authority wishing to construct a new school, for example, will "put out to tender" the contract, specifying the works and a closing date for the submission of tenders. Prospective contractors will submit tenders, specifying how they would build the works and for what price. The tender is, therefore, like a sealed bid in a closed auction.

A slightly different situation is the exercise of an *option*. A good illustration of an option is the option to purchase the goods which a person has hired under a hire purchase contract. For the duration of the hire, the goods belong to the hire purchase company (usually both seller and owner); but the contract of hire gives the hirer an option to buy the goods at the end of the hire purchase term. A seller of land, a service provider, or a company issuing shares may give existing customers, shareholders, etc. the option to make further purchases at favourable terms. These are not, of course, auctions in any sense, but they bear similar features and are therefore dealt with in this section.

In a sale by public auction, the holding of the auction is not an offer. In the English case of *Harris v Nickerson*,[44] Nickerson, an auctioneer, advertised a sale over three days in Bury St Edmunds in London newspapers. Harris, a commission broker in London, went to the sale, but the furniture that he hoped to purchase on the third day was withdrawn. Harris sought to recover for his loss of time and expenses, on the basis of a contract to hold the sale. In dismissing this claim, Blackburn J thought it

> "a startling proposition, and would be excessively inconvenient if carried out. It amounts to saying that anyone who advertises a sale by publishing an advertisement becomes responsible to everyone who attends the sale for his cab hire or travelling expenses".

Would the position be the same in Scotland, or might the courts find a unilateral promise to hold the auction? What would be the remedies? In particular, might there be any right to recover pre-contractual costs?[45]

---

[43] On which see below, paras 3–40—3–49.
[44] *Harris v Nickerson* (1873) L.R. 8 (Q.B.) 286.
[45] On which see below, paras 3–40—3–49.

Under s.57(2) of the Sale of Goods Act 1979:

> "A sale by auction is complete when the auctioneer announces its completion by the fall of the hammer, or in other customary manner; and until the announcement is made any bidder may retract his bid."

Each bid therefore constitutes an offer. By implication this provision imposes no obligation on the seller to accept any bid or offer. This provision alters the common law position in Scotland, at least in the sale of goods, whereby, in a sale by auction, the owner of any particular lot of items could not withdraw that lot after the bidding had commenced and the highest bidder was entitled to be declared the buyer.[46] This may still be the position in a sale by auction of, for example, land or stocks and shares, where the Sale of Goods Act does not apply. Furthermore, the view that the contract is concluded by the highest bid could be applied forcefully, even in a sale of goods, where the goods were offered for sale by auction "without reserve", i.e. where it is indicated, usually in the auction catalogue, that there is no "reserve" price below which the owner is unwilling to sell. This was the view adopted obiter by the English court in *Warlow v Harrison*.[47] The position in Scotland is less clear.

2–34 **Fenwick v Macdonald, Fraser & Co Ltd**

(1904) 6 F. 850

Court of Session, Second Division: The Lord Justice-Clerk (Macdonald), Lords Young and Trayner

The defenders, a firm of auctioneers, offered cattle for sale. The catalogue stated that the herd was being "offered for unreserved sale". No reserve price was intimated in the catalogue. The pursuer, as he was entitled to do under the conditions of sale, made the last bid of 42 guineas for lot 50, a bull elegantly named "Margrave of Ballindalloch". The defenders, who stated that the owner, Hamilton, had a reserve price of 150 guineas on it, then withdrew it from sale. No intimation of a reserve was made by either of the defenders before lot 50 was exposed for sale. The conditions of sale stated that this was an "unreserved sale", but also that "the exposers [Hamilton] reserve the usual power to make one offer for each animal". The court unanimously rejected Fenwick's claim that he had bought the animal when he made the highest bid.

2–35 "LORD JUSTICE-CLERK (MACDONALD): ...Whatever might have been the law formerly, the law of Scotland is now that 'a sale by auction is complete when the auctioneer announces its completion by the fall of the hammer, or in other customary manner. Until such announcement is made any bidder may retract his bid'. In this case the question is, whether a party who puts up an article for sale is entitled to the same privilege—that is to say, whether there is no sale till the fall of the hammer, and whether he is equally entitled to withdraw before the fall of the hammer takes place? I think there is a simple answer to that question ... when this question was raised with regard to the conditions of sale, stress was laid upon the note of the conditions of sale, which say that it is to be an unreserved sale. I do not think that that is inconsistent with anything contained in the other condition that it is an express condition of sale that the owner is entitled to one bid ... we do not require to decide that.

---

[46] *Cree v Durie*, Dec. 1, 1810 F.C.; *Fenwick v Macdonald, Fraser & Co Ltd* (1904) 6 F. 850, per Lord Trayner at 854.

[47] *Warlow v Harrison* (1859) 1 E. & E. 309.

...

LORD YOUNG: ... I think there is no sale until the fall of the hammer, and that until then any competitor is entitled to withdraw his bid. Of course, it follows that any proprietor is entitled to withdraw the article he is selling. One party is not bound while the other is free. I think, further, that there is no good ground of action against the auctioneer. He was employed by Mr Hamilton, the owner of this stud animal, to sell the animal with others or separately as seemed to him fit, and if his employer told him not to sell he was entitled to act upon that order which the seller was entitled to give him. I think it perfectly clear that the pursuer of this action was not the purchaser, and that there was no acceptance of his offer, no knockdown of the hammer, and he never was under any obligation and was due nobody anything because he had made the offer. I think, further, as your Lordship has said, although it is not necessary for the decision of this case to say, that, in my opinion, it was the intention of the seller, that is, of the owner, and that intention was sufficiently intimated to all who followed the catalogue, that there should be a reservation in his favour,—in short, that he was at liberty to fix a sum at any period of the sale below which the subject could not be sold. ... I have never seen a reservation of a right to make one bid. But the plain object of that and the meaning of it to everybody who read it was that it was in his power to determine the amount below which the animal should not be sold. I think that everybody with this catalogue in his hand would see that that was the intention, and it was acted upon in the ordinary way. He intimated to the auctioneer in the course of the sale, 'You are not to let this go at the price which has been offered', and he named £150 as the amount below which it was not to go... **2–36**

...

LORD TRAYNER: I think it was the law of Scotland prior to 1893 that a subject exposed for sale by public auction and for which a single bid had been made could not be withdrawn from the sale, and the person who had made the offer was entitled to call upon the auctioneer to knock it down to him at the amount he had offered. I think that is the import of the case of *Cree v Durie*.[48] But that case proceeded upon a view which is to be found stated in the successful argument in the report, to the effect that 'in the circumstances an offerer was bound when he gave his offer, and could not withdraw it,' and it bound the exposer, because there was thus a contract made between them. But that is not the law now". **2–37**

The matter becomes even more complex where the auction is by closed or fixed bidding rather than by open bidding, as in a public auction. In the buying and selling of land in Scotland, as we have seen, such closed bidding is normal practice. The seller would normally accept the highest bid, but since the bids are offers, no contract arises unless and until one of the bids is accepted. The seller is under no obligation to accept the highest, or indeed any other bid.

What if, in a closed auction, the seller has indicated that they will sell to the highest bidder? To complicate matters further, what if the highest bid is "topped" by a "referential" bid from another bidder, who offers to buy at £1,000 more than the highest bid? The following case is persuasive authority for the view that, if the true intention of the seller is to establish closed bidding, rather than an open auction, then referential bids cannot be accepted.

---

[48] *Cree v Durie*, Dec. 1, 1810, F.C.

2–38

Harvela Investments v Royal Trust Company of Canada (CI)
[1986] 1 A.C. 207
House of Lords: Lords Fraser, Diplock, Edmund-Davies, Bridge and Templeman

The Royal Trust Company of Canada (RTCC) was a registered shareholder of shares in Harvey & Co Ltd (Harvey), which it held as trustee of a settlement. Sir Leonard Outerbridge (L) and Harvela were also shareholders in Harvey. Either could gain control of Harvey by acquiring RTCC's shares.

RTCC, by telex, invited both Harvela and L each to submit a single offer for all RTCC's shares by sealed tender or confidential telex. The contents would not be disclosed until both were opened after the deadline for receipt of bids. RTCC bound itself to accept the highest offer that complied with their telex.

Harvela made an offer of C$2,175,000. L made an offer of "C$2,100,000, or C$101,000 in excess of any other offer ... expressed as a fixed monetary amount, whichever is higher". By telex communicated to both bidders, RTCC accepted L's offer.

Harvela claimed the shares, on the basis that RTCC was, by the terms of its first telex, bound to sell to Harvela as it had made the highest offer.

The House found that a contract had arisen between RTCC and Harvela.

2–39 "LORD TEMPLEMAN: ... Where a vendor undertakes to sell to the highest bidder, the vendor may conduct the sale by auction or by fixed bidding. In an auction sale each bidder may adjust his bid by reference to rival bids. In an auction sale the purchaser pays more than any other bidder is prepared to pay to secure the property. The purchaser does not necessarily pay as much as the purchaser was prepared to pay to secure the property. In an auction a purchaser who is prepared to pay $2.5m. to secure a property will be able to purchase for $2.2m. if no other bidder is prepared to offer as much as $2.2m.

In a fixed bidding sale a bidder may not adjust his bid. Each bidder specifies a fixed amount which he hopes will be sufficient, but not more than sufficient, to exceed any other bid. The purchaser in a fixed bidding sale does not necessarily pay as much as the purchaser was prepared to pay to secure the property. But any bidder who specifies less than his best price knowingly takes a risk of being outbid. In a fixed bidding sale a purchaser who is prepared to pay $2.5m. to secure the property may be able to purchase for $2.2m. if the purchaser offers $2.2m. and no other bidder offers as much as $2.2m. But if a bidder prepared to pay $2.5m. only offers $2.2m. he will run the risk of losing the property and will be mortified to lose the property if another bidder offers $2.3m. Where there are two bidders with ample resources, each determined to secure the property and to prevent the other bidder from acquiring the property, the stronger will prevail in the fixed bidding sale and may pay more than in an auction which is decided not by the strength of the stronger but by the weakness of the weaker of the two bidders. On the other hand, an open auction provides the stimulus of perceived bidding and compels each bidder, except the purchaser, to bid up to his maximum.

Thus auction sales and fixed bidding sales are liable to affect vendors and purchasers in different ways to produce different results. The first question raised by this appeal, therefore, is whether Harvela and Sir Leonard were invited to participate in a fixed bidding sale, which only invited fixed bids, or were invited to participate in an auction sale, which enabled the bid of each bidder to be adjusted by reference to the other bid. A vendor chooses between a fixed bidding sale and an auction sale. A bidder can only choose to participate in the sale or to abstain from the sale. The ascertainment of the choice of the vendors in the present case between a fixed bidding sale and an auction sale by means of referential bids depends on the presumed intention of the vendors. That presumed intention must be deduced from the terms of the invitation read as a whole. The invitation contains three provisions which are only consistent with the presumed intention to create a fixed bidding sale and which are inconsistent with any presumed intention to create an auction sale by means of referential bids.

By the first significant provision, the vendors undertook to accept the highest offer; this shows that the vendors were anxious to ensure that a sale should result from the invitation. By the second provision, the vendors extended the same invitation to Harvela and Sir Leonard; this shows that the vendors were desirous that each of them, Harvela and Sir Leonard, and nobody else, should be given an equal opportunity to purchase the shares. By the third provision, the vendors insisted that offers must be confidential and must remain confidential until the time specified by the vendors for the submission of offers had elapsed; this shows that the vendors were desirous of provoking from Sir Leonard an offer of the best price he was prepared to pay in ignorance of the bid made by Harvela and equally provoking from Harvela the best price they were prepared to pay in ignorance of the bid made by Sir Leonard.

A fixed bidding sale met all the requirements of the vendors deducible from the terms of the invitation. A fixed bidding sale was bound to result in a sale of shares save in the unlikely event of both Harvela and Sir Leonard failing to respond to the invitation. A fixed bidding sale gave an equal opportunity to Harvela and Sir Leonard to acquire the shares. A fixed bidding sale provoked the best price, or at any rate something approximate to the best price, which the purchaser was prepared to pay to secure the shares and to ensure that the rival bidder did not acquire the shares. On the other hand, if the invitation is construed so as to create an auction sale by means of referential bids, the requirements of the vendors deducible from the terms of the invitation could not be met.

First, if referential bids were permissible, there was a danger, far from negligible, that the sale might be abortive and the shares remain unsold. The shares would only be sold if at least one bidder submitted a fixed bid and the other bidder based his referential offer on that fixed bid. In the events which happened, Harvela put forward a fixed bid of $2,175,000 and Sir Leonard made a referential bid of $101,000 more than Harvela's fixed bid, thus enabling Sir Leonard's referential bid to be quantified at $2,276,000. But if Sir Leonard's referential bid had not been expressed to be based on Harvela's fixed bid, or if Harvela had not made a fixed bid but only a referential bid, then Sir Leonard's bid could not have been quantified. Similarly, if Harvela had made a referential bid not expressed to be tied to Sir Leonard's fixed bid, or if Sir Leonard had not made a fixed bid but only a referential bid, then Harvela's bid could not have been quantified. The sale would have been abortive although both bidders were anxious to purchase and submitted offers.

Secondly, if referential bids were permissible, there was also a possibility, which in fact occurred, that one bidder would never have an opportunity to buy. In the present case Harvela, by putting forward a fixed bid, could never succeed in buying the shares although the invitation had been extended to them. Harvela's only part in the sale was unwittingly to determine the price at which Sir Leonard was entitled and bound to purchase the shares. Harvela could not win and Sir Leonard could not lose. There was nothing in the invitation to warn Harvela that they must submit a referential bid if they wished to make sure of being able to compete with Sir Leonard. There was nothing in the invitation which indicated to Sir Leonard that he was entitled to submit a referential bid. But no one has argued that the invitation did not invite fixed bids; indeed, Sir Leonard submitted a fixed bid albeit as an unsuccessful alternative to his referential bid.

Thirdly, if referential bids were permissible, the vendors' object of provoking the best price that Harvela and Sir Leonard were each prepared to offer in ignorance of the rival bid was frustrated. Harvela put forward the fixed bid of $2,175,000 which represented the amount which Harvela hoped would exceed Sir Leonard's bid and which, because Harvela were bidding in ignorance of Sir Leonard's bid, must be or approximate to the best price which Harvela were prepared to pay to secure the shares and to ensure that Sir Leonard did not acquire the shares. Sir Leonard did not put forward his best price; Sir Leonard put forward his worst price, $2,100,000, but declared that he would pay $101,000 more than Harvela. Sir Leonard could have achieved the same purpose by offering five dollars or one dollar more than Harvela. If Sir Leonard had appreciated that he was taking part in a fixed bidding sale, then, judging by his minimum fixed bid of $2,100,000 and his unlimited referential bid, he might have been prepared to offer as his best price more than the sum of $2,276,000 which he now claims to be the purchase price of the shares. We shall never know because Sir Leonard did not reveal his best price.

Finally, if referential bids were permissible by implication, without express provision in the invitation for that purpose, and without any indication in the invitation of the nature of the referential bids which would be acceptable, the results could have been bizarre. In the present case, Sir Leonard bid $2,100,000 or $101,000 in excess of Harvela's fixed bid. If Harvela had bid $2,000,000 or one dollar more than Sir Leonard's fixed bid, then Sir Leonard would have become the purchaser with his referential bid of $2,101,000 as against Harvela's referential bid of $2,100,001. But if Harvela had offered $1,900,000 or one dollar more than Sir Leonard's fixed bid, then Harvela would have been the purchaser at their referential bid of $2,100,001 as against Sir Leonard's referential bid of $2,001,000. Sir Leonard's bid in the second example is the same as his bid in the first example but he loses. Harvela's bid in the second example is lower than Harvela's bid in the first example but Harvela wins. The vendors are worse off by $999 in the second example.

It would have been possible for the vendors to conduct an auction sale through the medium of confidential referential bids but only by making express provision in the invitation for the purpose. It would not have been sufficient for the invitation expressly to authorise 'referential bids' without more. For such an authorisation would have rendered the result of the sale uncertain and random in view of the illustrations and examples I have already given. It would have been necessary for the invitation to require each bidder who made a referential bid to specify a maximum sum he was prepared to bid. That requirement would ensure that the sale was not abortive and that both bidders had a genuine chance of winning. A maximum bid requirement would ensure a sale at a price in excess of the maximum bid of the unsuccessful bidder, but it would not necessarily procure a sale at the maximum price of the successful bidder. The sale would in effect be an auction sale and produce the consequences of an auction sale because the vendors would have made express provision for bids to be adjusted and finalised by reference to the maximum bid of the unsuccessful bidder. But without such express provisions the invitation is not consistent with an auction sale.

To constitute a fixed bidding sale all that was necessary was that the vendors should invite confidential offers and should undertake to accept the highest offer. Such was the form of the invitation. It follows that the invitation on its true construction created a fixed bidding sale and that Sir Leonard was not entitled to submit and the vendors were not entitled to accept a referential bid."

The legal basis of Lord Templeman's speech is that RTCC's invitation was a "fixed bidding sale", which precluded the use of referential bids, rather than an "auction sale", which would have permitted referential bids. In other words, the practice adopted was that normally adopted in the sale of land in Scotland. Nevertheless, such a contractual analysis may be unnecessary in Scots law, where the promise to accept the highest bid can be seen as a binding unilateral promise.

Offers, Promises and Options 2–40

Hector MacQueen 1985 S.L.T. (News) 187

"The observation that a gap in English law could be filled more satisfactorily than at present if unilateral promises unsupported by consideration were binding is not a new one. Professor Sir Thomas Smith devoted much attention to the theme some 20 years ago, building his discussion from the case of *Carlill v Carbolic Smoke Ball Co* [1893] 1 Q.B. 256, and suggesting that some of the difficulties of the analysis of a 'unilateral' or 'if' contract which flow from that case could be avoided in Scotland by the use of the concept of promise. In particular the problem of how and when an offer to all the world is accepted does not arise since the promise is enforceable without acceptance. If it requires the performance of some act by a would-be beneficiary, there is nonetheless an obligation, albeit one that is suspended until a condition is fulfilled. Thus although technically gratuitous (since the character of an obligation is determined at the moment of its formation), the benefit of the promise may only be acquired through some onerous performance by the promisee (*Studies Critical and Comparative*, pp.168 182) . . .

There are indeed essentially two stages in the formation of the obligations of the parties. But these do not occur within the framework of a single chameleon-like contract. Only the grantor is bound to begin with and this is truly a unilateral promise. But the promise is not, as the Scottish courts have had it, to sell if there is payment of the price because, as we have seen, it must be the case that at some stage in the transaction the beneficiary of the option comes under an enforceable obligation to pay. Rather the option is a promise by the grantor to enter a contract on certain terms if the promisee so desires within a given period of time. For that period the grantor may not withdraw. This analysis seems entirely consistent with the usual terms of such options. The second stage of the transaction is the formation of the actual contract of sale, triggered by the notice of the intention to exercise the option. The notice may be regarded as an offer to enter a contract which the promisor is bound to accept (comparable with the Harvela type of case discussed earlier) or as an acceptance of a firm offer of a contract constituted by the option. Only in this way can the basic difficulty of analysing options be satisfactorily resolved in Scotland.

What then of the practical problem with which the Scottish courts have been faced, the informality of the notice of intention to exercise the option [to purchase heritage or enter into a lease for a term longer than a year]? If it is necessarily either an offer or an acceptance of a contract, then as the transaction relates to land, informality may be fatal to its enforceability. The solution may be to say that, regardless of the informality of the notice, the grantor of the option is, by virtue of his initial promise to enter a contract, bound to conclude it with the necessary formalities. In the alternative situation where it is the beneficiary who seeks to resile after having given his notice, he may still be held to the bargain on the basis of the informal agreement if it is perfected by actings constituting *rei interventus* or homologation. It seems therefore that, properly understood and applied, the concept of a unilateral promise enforceable despite lack of consideration does offer a more flexible approach to options which for the most part ensures that the reasonable expectations of those granting and holding options are not frustrated by mere technicalities of the law relating to formation of contract."

Acceptance: creating a contractual agreement

2–41 The offeree must indicate acceptance of the precise terms of the offer. In the language of the DCFR, the offer must contain "sufficiently definite terms to be a contract".[49] If the offeree does not accept those terms in their entirety, or qualifies them in any way, then no contract arises. Misunderstandings and errors as to the terms of the offer are possible[50]; but if those essential terms are accepted by the offeree, the validity of the contract is not affected by lack of express agreement on specific details.

2–42 *Review of Contract Law: Discussion Paper on Formation of Contract*

Scottish Law Commission Discussion Paper No.154 (March 2012)

"<u>(i) Acceptance</u>

. . .

DCFR: II.–4:204 Acceptance

(1) Any form of statement or conduct by the offeree is an acceptance if it indicates assent to the offer.

(2) Silence or inactivity does not in itself amount to acceptance.

4.2 The definition of acceptance in the DCFR and the proposed CESL is much as in the CISG and the PICC. It is consistent with present Scots law.[1] The rule would, if adopted in Scots law, remove any doubt there may be as to whether a third party who is not a named offeree's agent can accept an offer—as for example when a party purchases the business of an offeree during the currency of an offer and then attempts to accept it.[2] The rule's application is also illustrated in the recent case of *Fleming Buildings Ltd v Forrest*,[3] where the defenders attempted to accept in the name of their company a building tender made to them personally and it was held that there was no contract. It would also seem that if an offer is made to two or more persons jointly a contract is only formed when all accept.[4]

4.3 The rule would also mean that conduct ostensibly fulfilling the requirements of acceptance of a general offer, i.e. an offer to the public, but which was carried out in ignorance of the offer, would not conclude a contract.[5] Furthermore, the rule would confirm the position that where parties make each other offers whose terms are identical in substance and which then cross each other en route to their respective recipients, no contract is formed.[6]

4.4 The rule on silence or inactivity as not being acceptance is not stated absolutely, and this leaves room for the exceptional case where there may be a course of dealing or usage between parties such that silence or inactivity in response to an offer is treated by them as concluding a contract.[7] The RFC also noted that the over-arching party autonomy principle means that an offeror may stipulate what will constitute acceptance, either going further than the rule in adding to its requirements—for example, that an acceptance be in writing or through a particular form of conduct; or in subtracting from them—for example by providing that no statement of assent is needed to bind the offeror.[8] The rule continues to appear to us a sensible and concisely stated one which, while consistent with Scots law, could also clarify some currently doubtful or uncertain points on which there is no direct Scottish precedent. It would therefore form a useful part of any statutory restatement of the law on formation of contract.

4.5 In the event of a statutory restatement of the Scots law on formation of contract, a definition of acceptance would be needed, probably going along with a sub-rule explaining that generally silence or inactivity cannot amount to acceptance. Such rules

---

[49] DCFR: II–4: 201(1). See above, para.2–05.

[50] Below, Ch.6 "Error".

would of course be subject to party autonomy in determining what constitutes acceptance of an offer.

---

[1] McBryde, *Contract*, paras 6.71–6.91. For recent examples of acceptance of a written offer by the offeree's conduct see *Langstane Housing Association Ltd v Riverside Construction (Aberdeen) Ltd*, 2009 S.C.L.R. 639 (OH) and *Prosper Properties v Bell* unreported Dumfries Sheriff Court 26 March 2008.

[2] The example is drawn from the English case of *Boulton v Jones* (1857) 2 Hurl & N 564, discussed in McBryde, *Contract*, para.6.107. McBryde suggests that an offer to a named person cannot be assigned by the offeree without the offeror's consent (para.6.106). The problem does not arise with general offers where anyone may accept.

[3] [2010] CSIH 8; 2010 GWD 13-234.

[4] See *Glasgow City Council v Peart* 1999 Hous. L.R. 117; 1999 G.W.D. 29–1390 (OH).

[5] See our Memorandum No.36, *Constitution and Proof of Voluntary Obligations: Formation of Contract* (1977), para.27, available at *http://www.scotlawcom.gov.uk/publications/discussion-papers-and-consultative memoranda/1970-1979/*; see also McBryde, *Contract*, paras 6.33 and 6.75. The position is different if the statement is a unilateral promise.

[6] See our Memorandum No.36 (cited in fn above), para.28. And see *Tinn v Hoffmann & Co* (1873) 29 L.T. 271.

[7] McBryde, *Contract*, para.6.81, citing the English case *Rust v Abbey Life Insurance Co Ltd* [1979] 2 Lloyd's Rep. 334, which was approved in the repudiation case *Vitol SA v Norelf Ltd (The Santa Clara)* [1996] A.C. 800 at 812 (Lord Steyn).

[8] RFC, para.4.3."

Statements made during protracted negotiations

Where, as is often the case, the parties to a transaction are involved in protracted negotiations, no contract will arise unless and until the negotiations crystallise into an offer and an acceptance of that offer. 2–43

Harvey v Facey 2–44

[1893] A.C. 552

Privy Council. The judgment was delivered by Lord Morris

Harvey asked Facey to telegraph the price for his farm, Bumper Hall Pen. Facey replied: "Lowest price Bumper Hall Pen £900". Harvey telegraphed in response:

"We agree to buy Bumper Hall Pen for £900 asked by you. Please send us your title deeds in order that we may get early possession."

Facey did not reply, but Harvey claimed a contract for the sale of the farm and arisen. The court found that no contract had arisen between the parties.

"LORD MORRIS: ... The third telegram from the appellants treats the answer from LM Facey stating his lowest price as an unconditional offer to sell to them at the price named. Their Lordships cannot treat the telegram from LM Facey as binding him in any respect, except to the extent it does by its terms, viz, the lowest price. Everything else is left open, and the reply telegram from the appellant cannot be treated as an acceptance of an offer to sell to them; it is an offer that required to be accepted by LM Facey. The contract could only be completed if L.M. Facey had accepted the appellant's last telegram ... Their Lordships are of the opinion that the mere statement of the lowest price at which the vendor would sell contains no implied contract to sell at the price to the persons making the inquiry." 2–45

It is possible to offer to sell land in a single letter; but normally, where there are protracted negotiations, such as in the sale of land, and especially where the negotiations are by the exchange of letters, the law will tend to look for the first clear statement of the terms of an agreement to which one of the parties is willing to commit. Such a statement will be treated as an offer. Consider, for example, the facts of the case of *Burnley v Alford*.[51]

Statements made subsequent to the offer: the effect of a counter-offer

2–46 Not every word or action by the offeree following an offer is tantamount to acceptance.[52] In practice, the response to an offer is unlikely to be a curt "yes" or "no." If the parties are involved in negotiations, each response will try to elucidate what the other party is willing to accept, and indicate how far the party making the response is willing to compromise. The response may, for example, attempt to reduce the price, or facilitate credit terms; or it may define more specifically the time for delivery. In each case, the crucial issue will be whether the offeree's response was so radically different from the terms of the offer, that it must be considered a new, or counter-offer.[53]

The effect of such a counter-offer would be to destroy the original offer, so that, as with an express rejection of the offer, it is no longer capable of acceptance by that particular offeree, unless it is revived by the offerer.[54] The origin of this rule seems to be the English case of *Hyde v Wrench*.

2–47 **Hyde v Wrench**
(1840) 3 Beav. 334
Lord Langdale MR

Wrench offered to sell his farm to Hyde for £1,000. Hyde replied, offering £950. Wrench declined and Hyde purported to accept Wrench's original offer of £1,000.

The court found that no contract had arisen between the parties.

"LORD LANGDALE M.R.: . . . I think there exists no valid binding contract between the parties for the purchase of the property. The defendant offered to sell it for £1,000, and if that had been at once unconditionally accepted, there would undoubtedly have been a perfect binding contract; instead of that, the plaintiff made an offer of his own, to purchase the property for £950, and he thereby rejected the offer previously made by the defendant. I think that it was not afterwards competent for him to revive the proposal of the defendant, by tendering an acceptance of it; and that, therefore, there exists no obligation of any sort between the parties".

Gloag also refers to the earlier Scottish case of *Hunter v Hunters*,[55] but the case is irrelevant to the issue. He states the rule as follows:

---

[51] Above, paras 4–09—4–10.

[52] Gloag, *The Law of Contract*, 2nd edn (Edinburgh: W. Green, 1929), p.39.

[53] Draft Common Frame of Reference, II–4:208 provides: "(1) A reply by the offeree which states or implies additional or different terms which materially alter the terms of the offer is a rejections and a new offer".

[54] Whether an offer declared to be open for acceptance during a specified period may be accepted within the time-limit by an offeree who has previously indicated rejection is considered below, para.4–50 onwards.

[55] *Hunter v Hunters* (1745) Mor. 9169.

> "If the refusal is not peremptory, but combined with a request for better terms, the general construction is that the offer is gone, and that the party to whom it was made, on failure to obtain the terms be requests, cannot fall back on an acceptance of the original offer."[56]

The House of Lords has approved of the rule in *Hyde v Wrench*,[57] and the rule was also clearly adopted by the Inner House in the next case.

Wolf and Wolf v Forfar Potato Co 2–48
1984 S.L.T. 100
Court of Session, Second Division: The Lord Justice-Clerk (Wheatley), Lords Robertson and McDonald

The defenders, potato merchants in Forfar, sent a telex (telex message 6/1), dated 29 November 1977, to the pursuers, potato merchants in Amsterdam. In the telex, the defenders offered for sale on specific terms a specific quantity and grade of potatoes and added: "this offer is valid till 17.00 hours on Wednesday 30th November 1977 and thereafter subject to availability".

The pursuers replied by telex (telex message 6/2) dated 30 November 1977, stating "we accept the offer", and then continued by varying the terms of the defenders' offer.

On 30 November 1977, following a telephone conversation between the parties the pursuers sent a further telex (telex 6/3), before the expiry of the defenders' offer, stating: "we confirm that we have accepted your offer" and adding: "we would highly appreciate if you could take into consideration the points we have raised".

The defenders did not supply the potatoes and were being sued for damages. The question arose whether any contractual agreement had ever been made by the parties.

The court found that no contract had arisen between the parties.

"LORD JUSTICE-CLERK (LORD WHEATLEY): . . . The first argument advanced by defenders' counsel is a simple and straightforward one, and turns on a proposition in law. In my opinion it is well-founded. The sheriff took the view that 6/2 was a counter-offer. He made a finding (no. 12) to that effect. Counsel for the pursuers did not dispute this. Gloag supra, under reference to *Hunter v Hunters* and *Hyde v Wrench*, says at p.37: 'An offer falls if it is refused. If the refusal is not peremptory, but combined with a request for better terms, the general consideration is that the offer is gone, and that the party to whom it was made, on failure to obtain the terms he requests, cannot fall back on the original offer'. Whether or not the cases referred to by Gloag in themselves vouch that legal proposition, I am satisfied that it is sound, and, as previously noted, senior counsel for the pursuers did not dispute it as a general proposition. Moreover, he maintained that consideration stopped with the issue of 6/3 and that nothing subsequent thereto was relevant. The question of bar was neither pled nor mooted. The case for the pursuers rested on the validity of 6/3 as a timeous acceptance of 6/1. I do not consider that the fact that the original offer had a terminal date within which it could be accepted takes it out of the category to which Gloag refers. According to Gloag, when the counter-offer is made the general construction is that the offer is gone. Once the offer is gone it cannot be accepted. It is not suggested that the counter-offer in 6/2 was accepted by the defenders, and on that short basis it seems to me that the defenders' case must succeed. 2–49

---

[56] Gloag, *The Law of Contract*, 2nd edn (Edinburgh: W. Green, 1929), p.37.
[57] *Gibson v Manchester County Council* [1979] 1 W.L.R. 294; [1979] 1 All E.R. 972.

Even if that were wrong, there still falls to be considered the second of the defenders' submissions on 'no concluded contract'. This has to proceed on the basis that after 6/2 was sent it was still open to the pursuers to accept the offer in 6/1, and the question is whether 6/3 constituted a valid acceptance. Senior counsel for the pursuers accepted that if 6/3 did not do so that was the end of the pursuers' case. The sheriff took the view that, against the background of 6/2 and the telephone conversation which revealed no. consensus, 6/3 did not advance the position. 6/3 was in these terms: 'Following our telex no. 906 [i.e. 6/2] and telephone conversation with Mr McKay we confirm that we have accepted your offer. In order to facilitate matters for us we would highly appreciate if you can take into consideration the points we have raised. Telephone number of Mr Sam Wolf is Amsterdam (20) 908259 where you can call after 18.30 hours your time.' Counsel for the pursuers argued that this was a simple and direct acceptance of the defenders' offer in 6/1, that the material conditions on which there had been no consensus previously had been accepted, and that these had been replaced by a request to see whether the points which they (i.e. the pursuers) had raised in relation to these matters could be given consideration.

This interpretation has to be considered against the background of what had happened. The pursuers considered at the time that 6/2 was sent that it constituted a valid acceptance of 6/1. That was their initial case on the pleadings. Nonetheless, Dr Schoonderwoerd had expressed doubts whether the word 'but' in 6/2 did not import new conditions, and so the telephone conversation took place between Mr Wolf and Mr McKay. These two were unable to reach any agreement regarding the disputed conditions and certainly no acceptance of 6/1 was achieved either by 6/2 or the telephone conversation or both. 6/3 was then despatched, and under reference to these two events it says 'we confirm that we have accepted your offer' (the emphasis is mine). Plainly they had not accepted or offered to accept the terms of 6/1 before the despatch of that communication. Was the wording then just a matter of bad grammar when the present tense was intended? This could be a dangerous line to follow in re mercatoria, unless it was clear that the present tense was meant. Why then the use of the word 'confirm' in relation to an acceptance when no previous acceptance had been tendered? The subsequent words—'if you can take into consideration the points we have raised'—and the information supplied as to how Mr Hollywood of the defenders could contact Mr Wolf by telephone when only he could negotiate conditions on behalf of the defenders seem to confirm that the negotiations were still pending and that no legally binding contract had been concluded. It is perhaps not without significance that Mr Wolf thought that he was accepting the offer when he sent 6/2, and the phrase 'accept your offer' is used there as well. 6/3 begins by the words 'following our telex no. 906 [6/2] and the telephone conversation', and while different meanings were attributed to that phrase, the plain meaning is not just the temporal one but is 'consequential upon' or 'as a result of. Once it is established and conceded that these two factors, either alone or in combination, did not conclude a contract, the interpretation which the pursuers seek to place on 6/3 as a whole disappears. According to Mr McKay's version of the telephone conversation, not only did he not agree to Mr Wolf's counter-proposals, but he informed Mr Wolf that only Mr Hollywood could agree terms. In that situation the information in 6/3 as to how Mr Hollywood could contact Mr Wolf is not without significance. Nor is it without significance that communings continued after 6/3 had been received. For all these reasons I am satisfied that the sheriff was right in holding that 6/3 did not conclude a contract. That being so, then *ex concessu* the pursuers' case fails."

Does this mean that every response to an offer which is in any way qualified amounts to a counter-offer which prevents agreement on the terms of the original offer?

If the response from the offeree is merely seeking further information or particulars about the terms of the offer, the offer must subsist. This seems to be the reasoning of the following English case.

Stevenson, Jaques & Co v McLean 2–50
[1880] 5 Q.B.D. 346
English High Court, Queen's Bench: Lush J

After some correspondence, McLean wrote to Stevenson offering iron which he wished Stevenson to sell on his behalf at 40s. per ton, the offer to be held open until the following Monday. At 9:42 on Monday, Stevenson telegraphed McLean, stating: "Please wire whether you would accept forty for delivery over two months, or if not, longest limit you could give". McLean received the telegram, sold the iron to another buyer and at 13:25 the same day telegraphed Stevenson, telling him that he had done so. Stevenson had by this time himself found a purchaser for the iron and at 13:34 before the arrival of the telegram sent by McLean at 13:25, sent a telegram to McLean stating that he had secured his price. McLean refused to deliver the iron to Stevenson, claiming that no contract had arisen between them. The jury found that the relationship between McLean and Stevenson was that of seller and buyer and that a contract existed between them.

"LUSH J: . . . All parties knew that the market was in an unsettled state, and that no one could predict at the early hour when the telegram was sent how the prices would range during the day. It was reasonable that, under these circumstances, [the plaintiffs] should desire to know before business began whether they were to be at liberty in case of need to make any and what concessions as to the time or times of delivery, which would be the time or times of payment, or whether the defendant was determined to adhere to the terms of his letter; and it was highly unreasonable that the plaintiffs should have intended to close the negotiation while it was uncertain whether they could find a buyer or not, having the whole of the business hours of the day to look for one. Then again, the form of the telegram is one of inquiry. It is not 'I offer forty for delivery over two months', which would have likened the case to *Hyde v Wrench* . . . here there is no counter proposal . . . There is nothing specific by way of offer or rejection, but a mere inquiry, which should have been answered and not treated as a rejection of the offer. The ground of objection therefore fails." 2–51

This decision suggests that a mere request for information is not a counter-offer, thus leaving the original offer open for acceptance. Note that the revocation of offer by telegram was ineffectual until communicated; and that before that point, acceptance by telegram (which was effected upon the sending of the telegram by the post office) had already been made.[58]

Similarly, the reaction of a person negotiating a contract who receives an offer might be to pick up the telephone and attempt to clarify the details. It would be disruptive of the process of negotiation if counter-suggestions or proposals from the offeree precluded conclusion of the contract on the terms of that original offer.

In particular, what if the offeree seeks to negotiate better terms in his response; will that constitute a counteroffer? Gloag suggests the need,

---

[58] On communications by post, see below, paras 4–19—4–26. For a variety of exceptions to the counter-offer rule, see ADM Forte and HL MacQueen, "Contract Procedure, Contract Formation and the Battle of Forms" (1986) 31 J.L.S. 224.

"to distinguish between an actual, though perhaps hesitating and reluctant, acceptance, and an offer to accept if the offerer is prepared to alter his terms. In the former case the contract is complete; in the latter the reply is in effect a new offer, and there is no contract unless the original offerer accedes to it. There is another possibility. What is put forward as an acceptance may be read as a mere expression of willingness to contract and of expectation that terms will be arranged".[59]

This passage from Gloag was extensively considered by Lord Allanbridge in *Uniroyal v Miller*. Although paying lip-service to Gloag's view that not every response to an offer can be seen simply as either an acceptance or a counter-offer, he applied the standard view that a purported acceptance which includes conditions is a counter-offer.[60]

Gloag's distinction between a counter-offer and an expression of willingness to contract on expectation that terms will be arranged nevertheless finds support (although not expressly considered) in the (partly dissenting) judgment of Lord McDonald in *Wolf v Forfar Potato*.

2–52 **Wolf and Wolf v Forfar Potato Co**

1984 S.L.T. 100

Court of Session, Second Division: The Lord Justice-Clerk (Wheatley), Lords Robertson and McDonald

The facts are as stated above, paras 2–48—2–49.

2–53 "LORD MCDONALD: ... If 6/3 had fallen to be construed as an unequivocal withdrawal of the qualifications contained in 6/2, I would have felt some reservation in applying the general proposition stated by Gloag at p.37 to the circumstances of the present case. That proposition is tated thus: 'An offer falls if it is refused. If the refusal is not peremptory, but combined with a request for better terms, the general construction is that the offer is gone, and that the party to whom it was made, on failure to obtain the terms he requests cannot fall back on an acceptance of the original offer'. Two authorities are cited for this proposition. The first is *Hunter v Hunters* [(1745) Mor. 91629. I have read the report in this old case with care and have difficulty in finding in it support for such a general proposition as is stated by Gloag. The other is the English case of *Hyde v Wrench* [(1840) 3 Beav. 334]. I read that case as one in which an offer was peremptorily refused and therefore not one which supports Gloag's proposition. It is moreover a case relating to heritable property in England and based upon the Statute of Frauds. Neither case bears much relationship to the present mercantile transaction.

I accept that a qualified acceptance can properly be regarded as a counter-offer which in turn requires acceptance by the original offeror before the bargain is complete. I also accept that if the qualifications are unacceptable to the original offeror he is entitled to regard his original offer, including any time limit contained therein, as having fallen. If, however, he continues to negotiate with the offeree and the latter, within the period of the original time-limit, unreservedly accepts the original offer, I feel that the offeror may well be barred from maintaining at a later date that no bargain had been concluded. In the present case the parties did continue to negotiate during the period of the time limit and indeed beyond it as the sheriff's finding no. 17 reveals. Had they reached a concluded bargain within that period, albeit by a withdrawal by the pursuers of the conditions contained in their qualified acceptance or counter-offer, and had the defenders

[59] Gloag, *The Law of Contract*, 2nd edn (Edinburgh: W. Green, 1929), p.39.

[60] For a full and comparative debate of the issues raised by the case, see ADM Forte and HL MacQueen, "Contract Procedure, Contract Formation and the Battle of Forms" (1986) 31 J.L.S. 224.

subsequently discovered that they could not supply the potatoes, I do not consider that they could then be heard to say that there was no contract because their original offer had fallen in toto as soon as the qualified acceptance or counteroffer was received. As, however, I agree that 6/3 did not withdraw the earlier qualifications which the pursuers sought to insist upon, this matter does not arise."

The above cases raise important questions about the application of the traditional "offer/acceptance/counter-offer" analysis to protracted contractual negotiations. Although the extent of application of this approach has been questioned in recent years,[61] the following cases suggest that the courts are unwilling to depart from it.

Rutterford Ltd v Allied Breweries Ltd 2–54
1990 S.L.T. 249; 1990 S.C.L.R. 186
Court of Session, Outer House: Lord Caplan

Allied owned a shop in Greenock. Between 5 May 1988 and 11 January 1989 formal letters were exchanged between the parties' solicitors with a view to concluding a contract for the pursuers to purchase the shop. The original offer by Rutterford was followed in turn by a qualified acceptance by Allied, a counter-offer by Rutterford and a further counter-offer by Allied. Rutterford sent a qualified acceptance of Allied's counter-offer. Three months later, following further negotiations, Rutterford sent an unqualified acceptance of that counter-offer. Allied's informal reply thanked Rutterford for concluding missives, and various draft conveyancing documents were prepared and exchanged.

Allied now denied that a contract had been concluded. Lord Caplan found that it had.

"LORD CAPLAN: ... The law on the matter may not be supported by voluminous authority but the authority which exists is clear and has remained uncontradicted over a long period of time. Professor Gloag sets out in his textbook on contract at p. 37 of the second edition the position as he understood it. Certainly the effect of *Hunter v Hunter* (one of the two cases he relies on) is somewhat obscure but *Hyde v Wrench* is a clear enough case and appears to proceed upon principles which would be common to both Scots and English law. That *Hyde v Wrench* is still the cornerstone of English law on the relevant topic was made clear by the judicial observations in *Butler Machine Tool Co Ltd v Ex-Cell-O Corporation (England) Ltd*. The position in Scotland has been made no less clear in the recent case of *Wolf & Wolf v Forfar Potato Co*. As Lord Robertson observes at p.106 the rule spoken to by Gloag accords with common sense. In the case of an offer with no time-limit attached, the offer by implication remains open for a reasonable time and that would include such time as in all the particular circumstances of the case may reasonably be required to allow the offeree to reply. However, when the offeree replies by way of a qualified acceptance he is in effect saying that this is my response to your offer. The focus then shifts to the original offeror who has to consider whether or not he will accept the counterproposals. He does not require to consider whether or not specifically to withdraw his original offer for he already has had the offeree's response to it. If the position were otherwise, there would effectively be two offers affecting the same subjects on the table at the same time. If the original offeror were to accept the qualified acceptance simultaneously with the offeree withdrawing his qualified acceptance and accepting the original offer, then considerable practical difficulties could emerge. The 2–55

[61] See, e.g. JAK Huntley, "Commercial Practice and the Formation of Contracts", 1988 S.L.T. (News) 221.

great advantage of the law as I understand it to be is that it is clear and certain. The arguments advanced on behalf of the pursuers may be imaginative but they find no support in the authorities. It may be that in the course of protracted negotiation an acceptor who tries to obtain improved terms does not want to reject the original offer outright. However, he can only be judged by what he states formally not by unexpressed reservations and the clear import of a qualified acceptance is to the effect that these are the terms upon which I am now prepared to conclude to contract. If, as the pursuers contend, negotiation is an evolutionary process, negotiations have evolved to the point where it is the acceptor's counter offer which is under active consideration, not the earlier offer. Moreover, I do not find the attempt by pursuers' counsel to draw a distinction between essential and inessential conditions of the contract helpful. If the effect of a qualified acceptance has to be weighed by assessing the degree by which the qualifications may be regarded as essential to the contract, this could only lead to confusion and uncertainty for the contracting parties. I cannot see that the law as it presently stands presents any particular difficulty. A party who receives an offer, knows that he must accept it, refuse it outright, or replace it with a counterproposal. The pursuers relied to a large extent on the obiter observations of Lord McDonald in *Wolf & Wolf*. However, Lord McDonald did not disagree with the view of the majority that if a qualified acceptance is unacceptable to the original offeror he is entitled to regard his original offer as fallen. It follows that his Lordship's reference to the effect of further negotiation must apply to a situation where the offeror through such negotiations effectively represents that he is prepared to keep the original offer alive—that is to say, to restore it. No doubt the inference would be available in particular circumstances. However, Lord McDonald's observations must not be taken as applying to negotiations in the abstract but rather to particular negotiations from which the requisite inference can be drawn. In the present case the pursuers merely offer to prove that between September 1988 and 11th January 1989 the parties' solicitors corresponded 'on certain matters' relating to the contract of sale. I do not see how it would be possible to infer from these bland facts, if proved, that the defenders were representing that they were prepared to regard their original offer as being restored. It follows from the foregoing that the pursuers are not able to prove that their letter of 11th January 1989 concluded formal missives.

I have decided therefore that the letter from the pursuers' solicitors dated 11th January 1989 does not do what it purports to do, namely to conclude a formal contract."

Wolf and Wolf v Forfar Potato Co was again considered and subjected to a novel analysis by the Inner House in the following case.

2–56

Findlater v Maan

1990 S.L.T. 465

Court of Session, Second Division: The Lord Justice-Clerk (Ross), Lords Murray and Morton of Shuna

A series of formal solicitors' letters between the agents of Mr Maan and the agents of Mr and Mrs Findlater related to the sale of a house by Mr Maan to the Findlaters. On 25 March 1988, the Findlaters offered to buy Mr Maan's house. On 28 March 1988 Mr Maan accepted the offer subject to a number of qualifications. On 29 March 1988 the Findlaters accepted the qualifications contained in the letter of 28 March 1988, but added a further qualification. In a letter dated 30 March 1988 Mr Maan added a further qualification. In a formal letter from their agents dated 6 April 1988 the Findlaters "accept[ed] the terms of [Mr Maan's] formal letter of amendment dated 30 March 1988 . . . and . . . [withdrew] the qualification contained in [their] letter of 29 March 1988 thereby holding a bargain concluded".

Mr Maan changed his mind about the sale and claimed that no contract had arisen. The Findlaters sought declarator that the letters comprised a binding contract. The sheriff dismissed the action on the basis that the circumstances were indistinguishable from those in *Wolf and Wolf v Forfar Potato Co.*[62] The Findlaters appealed to the sheriff principal, who allowed the appeal, holding that the correspondence should not be construed as a series of offers and counter offers but as a series of letters continuing negotiations and reflecting both parties' willingness to contract and both parties' expectation that consensus would be achieved. Mr Maan appealed to the Court of Session, submitting, inter alia, that it was not open to the Findlaters to withdraw the offer in the letter of 29 March, in order to conclude a bargain without his consent; that the letter of 6 April 1988 did not make it clear what the bargain was between the parties, and that the Findlaters were not entitled to waive the provisions in the letter of 26 March 1988 although conceived solely in their favour, a distinction falling to be drawn between the terms of a contract and the terms of an offer.

The court found that a contract had been concluded.

"LORD JUSTICE-CLERK (ROSS): . . . I have reached the clear conclusion that this case can readily be distinguished from *Wolf and Wolf v Forfar Potato Co.* What was critical in that case was that the qualified acceptance constituted a counteroffer; the result of sending the counter-offer was that the original offer had fallen and could not thereafter be accepted. What the pursuers did in the present case by their letter of 6 April 1988 was to accept the terms of the letter of 30 March 1988. They did not purport to accept the original offer, and accordingly the present case is different to *Wolf and Wolf v Forfar Potato Co.* It is true that the letter of 30 March 1988 refers to the letter of 25 March which was the original offer, but it is plain from the terms of the letter of 6 April 1988 that what is being accepted is the letter of 30 March 1988. That letter no doubt incorporated the earlier letters of 25 March and 28 March. In a sense it revived the original offer which had been superseded by the qualified acceptance, but there was no question of the pursuers seeking to disregard the intervening correspondence and to go back to the original offer. **2–57**

In my opinion the true approach to be made in the present case is as follows. The letter of 29 March and the letter of 30 March were two offers which existed at the same time, one at the instance of the seller and one at the instance of the purchaser. They were not written under reference to one another and neither of them superseded the other; they both coexisted. In that situation I am of opinion that it was open to the pursuer to accept the offer contained in the letter of 30 March 1988. It was not disputed that that letter fell to be regarded as an offer, and it was an offer which was open for acceptance. The pursuer did accept that offer by their letter of 6 April 1988. Of course so long as the other offer of 29 March 1988 remained in existence there could be no final consensus in idem. However, there was no reason why the pursuers should not withdraw the letter of 29 March 1988. 'Except in cases where there is an undertaking to hold the offer open for a definite time, it may be withdrawn at any time before acceptance' (Gloag on *Contract*, p. 37).

---

[62] *Wolf and Wolf v Forfar Potato Co*, 1984 S.L.T. 100.

By their letter of 6 April 1988 the pursuers did withdraw the letter of 29 March 1988, and, in my opinion, the consequence was that consensus was reached and a bargain was concluded for the purchase by them of the subjects from the defender. I am not persuaded that the defender required to consent to the withdrawal of the letter of 29 March 1988. I know of no principle of law which would require the consent of the defender to the withdrawal of such a letter. The argument for the defender was that the consent of the defender was required to the withdrawal of the letter of 29 March because if the pursuers withdrew the letter of 29 March that would revive the letter of 28 March and that, it was said, could not be done without the consent of the defender. In my opinion this submission is not well founded. By the time the pursuers withdrew the letter of 29 March they were aware that the defender had also superseded his own letter of 28 March by his later letter of 30 March which varied its terms by adding to them. Accordingly, when they withdrew their letter of 29 March that would not have the effect of reviving the letter of 28 March, because the defender himself had departed from the position taken up on 28 March and had stated a new position on 30 March 1988. The fact was that on 6 April 1988 there were two outstanding offers. Before there could be consensus in idem both these offers had to be dealt with. What the pursuers did was to accept one of these offers and withdraw the other. That having been done, there were no longer any matters at issue between the parties and in my opinion consensus in idem was achieved. A question was raised as to whether the letter of 6 April 1988 made it clear what the bargain was between the parties. With some hesitation, I have come to the conclusion that it does define the agreement with sufficient precision. I agree with counsel for the defender that it would have accorded with what I understood to be good practice if it had been expressly stated in the letter that the bargain being concluded was that constituted by the letters of 25, 28 and 30 March and 6 April. The letter of 6 April did, however, refer expressly to the letter of 30 March which in turn referred expressly to the letters of 25 and 28 March, and these references thus defined the letters which constituted the bargain between the parties."

Lord Ross, on the facts, decided that there was a series of counter-offers resulting in two offers. How could this be?

Note that art.II.–4:208(1) (on modified acceptance) of the DCFR adopts the view that a counter-offer is a rejection of the offer and constitutes a new offer, but art.II.–4.208(2) and (3) provide that, with certain exceptions, additional or different terms that do not materially alter the terms of the offer become part of the contract and the reply to the offer that contains them operates as an acceptance.

2–58 *Review of Contract Law: Discussion Paper on Formation of Contract*

Scottish Law Commission Discussion Paper No.154 (March 2012)

"(vi) Modified acceptance

...

DCFR: II.–4:208 Modified acceptance

(1) A reply by the offeree which states or implies additional or different terms which materially alter the terms of the offer is a rejection and a new offer.

(2) A reply which gives a definite assent to an offer operates as an acceptance even if it states or implies additional or different terms, provided these do not materially alter the terms of the offer. The additional or different terms then become part of the contract.

(3) However, such a reply is treated as a rejection of the offer if:

(a) the offer expressly limits acceptance to the terms of the offer;

(b) the offeror objects to the additional or different terms without undue delay; or
(c) the offeree makes the acceptance conditional upon the offeror's assent to the additional or different terms, and the assent does not reach the offeree within a reasonable time.

...

4.21 The DCFR re-jigs the wording of the CISG and the PICC into a form accepted for the proposed CESL. The basic effect of the texts is, however, identical.[40]

4.22 First, if an offeree replies to an offer with what purports to be an acceptance but which contains terms materially different from those in the offer, the reply is not an acceptance but a rejection of the offer and a new (or in the language of the CISG and the PICC, a counter) offer ... It has also been held that although an offer falls as such when met with a qualified acceptance, those parts of the offer with which the qualified acceptance is consistent can be carried forward as part of the counter-offer which is also constituted by the qualified acceptance.[41]

4.23 It is less certain how far the second proposition to emerge, those parts of the offer with which the qualified acceptance is consistent can be carried forward as part of a contract taken as concluded by that acceptance, is also good Scots law. This was not discussed in the RFC, which instead concentrated on the extent to which the rule could provide a solution to the problem of the 'battle of the forms'.[42] We deal with that problem in the next chapter. Here we focus simply on the position where a purported acceptance in fact introduces new but 'non-material' elements compared to the offer. Can there ever be such a purported acceptance, and could it ever form a contract in Scots law?

4.24 Professor McBryde points to some case law which may suggest that there can be a contract in at least some such situations.[43] In *Wight v Newton*,[44] where there was agreement between parties on the essentials of a lease, a contract was found to exist despite discrepancies between them on other non-essential matters. But this is not quite like the outcome envisaged in the CISG, the PICC, the DCFR and the proposed CESL, where the non-material additions or alterations made by the acceptance, far from failing to prevent a contract coming into existence, form part of that contract rather than, as in Wight, simply being disregarded.

4.25 More significant is a body of Scottish cases showing, in Professor McBryde's words, that 'conditions can be added to the acceptance which do not prevent consensus'.[45] By conditions, he means, not terms of the contract, but rather facts or circumstances upon which the enforcement or enforceability of the contract will depend. If the condition proposed in the acceptance is one which does not require the consent of the offeror, for example because it is about the inevitable mechanics of the transaction, then its statement does not prevent there being a contract, and the condition will be part of the contract. McBryde cites as instances of this, statements in acceptances that the offeror would need to execute a disposition[46] or a formal lease[47] or a stock transfer[48] or to complete a form.[49] Again, if the offeree's statement is something the law would imply anyway—for example, that goods to be sold will be of satisfactory quality—there is no need for the to consent before a contract is formed. In all these instances the additional element stipulated in the acceptance not only fails to prevent a contract being formed but is in fact part of the contract, on the basis that it would have been so anyway.

4.26 If on the other hand the condition stated by the offeree is suspensive, deferring the contract's enforceability (for example, it says that acceptance is "subject to contract"),[50] or if it is contrary to what the law would imply,[51] the offeror's agreement to that condition is required before a contract can be formed. McBryde also doubts whether the introduction by the offeree of a resolutive condition upon the occurrence of which the contract would come to an end—for example, if a trial of the goods supplied is failed, or if an event does not take place would come to an end—for example, if a trial of the goods supplied is failed, or if an event does not take place—is possible without acceptance by the original offeror: "[t]he existence of a sword of Damocles should require the assent of both parties."[52]

4.27 If then there is anything in Scots law like the CISG/PICC/DCFR/proposed CESL rule about non-material alterations and additions in a purported acceptance not blocking the formation of a contract, its scope is very limited, probably covering only the situations where the extra stipulation would have been part of the contract regardless, either as an implied term or as a necessary action to give effect to the contract. The adoption of a rule like that in the international instruments would therefore be quite a significant development of the present law. It might create uncertainty in an area where certainty of outcome is highly desirable, by forcing parties to consider whether alterations or additions to an offer made in a purported acceptance were material or not.

4.28 On the other hand, such a rule could prevent a party escaping what was very substantially an agreement because of some relatively trivial difference between the offer and acceptance. We note that when the basic rule on qualified acceptances was first applied to exchanges of missives in the 1990s, there was some surprise about it in the conveyancing world.[53] It can certainly be argued that the legal effects of a qualified acceptance should not necessarily be the same as that of an outright rejection or refusal of an offer.[54]

4.29 The element of uncertainty is considerably mitigated in the CISG, the PICC, the DCFR and the proposed CESL texts by allowing the offeror to stipulate in the offer that only complete acceptance will be binding, or to prevent the acceptance forming a contract by objecting to the new terms without undue delay. The offeree can also reduce uncertainty by making the acceptance conditional upon the offeror's assent within a reasonable time to the additional or different terms.

---

[40] On the PICC version see Vogenauer and Kleinheisterkamp, *PICC Commentary*, pp 278-284.

[41] *Howgate Shopping Centre Ltd v GLS* 164 Ltd 2002 SLT 820 (OH) at 826 (Lord Macfadyen).

[42] RFC, paras 4.17-4.19.

[43] McBryde, *Contract*, paras 6.86-6.88.

[44] *Wight v Newton* 1911 SC 762 (IH). This case is usually contrasted with *Buchanan v Duke of Hamilton* (1878) 5 R (HL) 69. See also *Avintair Ltd v Ryder Airline Services Ltd* 1994 SC 270 (IH), where a contract of services was held to exist, despite dissensus upon the price, because the court could fix a reasonable price.

[45] McBryde, *Contract*, para 6.87.

[46] *Thomson v James* (1855) 18 D 1.

[47] *Erskine v Glendinning* (1871) 9 M 656.

[48] *Tait & Crichton v Mitchell* (1889) 26 SLR 573.

[49] *Seaton Brick and Tile Co v Mitchell* (1900) 7 SLT 384 (IH).

[50] As in *Stobo Ltd v Morrisons (Gowns) Ltd* 1949 SC 184 (IH); *Chisholm v Wardrope* 2005 SCLR 530 (OH).

[51] See *Towill & Co v British Agricultural Association* (1875) 3 R 117 (IH), where a seller of goods had stipulated that payment of the price must be by cash on delivery but the buyer's confirmation provided for payment by cash 14 days later. With regard to sale of goods, the default rule is that delivery and payment are concurrent conditions.

[52] McBryde, *Contract*, para 6.88. But see *Hardy v Sime* 1938 SLT 18 (OH) at 20 (Lord Keith).

[53] David A Brand, Andrew J M Steven and Scott Wortley, *Professor McDonald's Conveyancing Manual* (7th edn, 2004), para 28.8, as cited by McBryde, *Contract*, para 6.94, fn 295.

[54] See the discussion in McBryde, *Contract*, para 6.94."

"Standard form" contracts and the "battle of the forms"

It is common business practice to negotiate contracts in standard form. Order forms often contain printed conditions on the reverse, as do printed quotation forms and receipts. **2–59**

In practice, an offer made on such a printed order form may be "accepted" by the offeree, usually in an "acknowledgment of order" form, even though the terms of the order form are different from those on the quotation form. The quotation form is, as we have seen (above, paras 2–27—2–29), the document on which the supplier states the details of what is to be supplied and is the document on which the prospective purchaser will base the drafting of their quotation.

Two issues arise from such negotiations: first, whether the parties have made a contract and, if so, on what terms that contract has been made. If only the offer is made subject to such standard terms then, as long as the existence of the standard terms is brought to the offeree's notice before he or she purports to accept, the contract would be made subject to those terms.

This analysis was not applied by the Court of Session in *Star Fire & Burglary Insurance Co Ltd v Davidson & Sons Ltd.*[63] The pursuers offered to insure the defenders' premises against risk of fire for £5,000. The defenders accepted, through their agent, but when the policy was sent together with the demand for the premium, it included terms which purported to make the defenders a member of the insurance company (the company was, unknown to the defenders, a mutual company). The Second Division unanimously found that no contract had arisen because there was no consensus between the parties as to membership. It is clear from the judgments that the parties were regarded as still at the stage of negotiations, but it is difficult to see why this was so. If the pursuers' original quotation is regarded as an offer, then it would have been accepted by the defenders' response. A valid contract would have arisen, but the stipulation in the policy as to membership would not form part of that contract, since it was not notified prior to acceptance.

It sometimes happens that both parties to an agreement use conflicting standard forms of contractual conditions. Standard forms of offer frequently contain conditions that would form part of the offer. If the standard form of acceptance contains contradictory conditions, does the acceptance form thereby become a counter-offer, which destroys the original offer, but is itself capable of acceptance? If the offerer accepts performance by the offeree, do the offeree's own conditions apply, or those of the offerer? Which form of conditions wins the "battle of the forms"? **2–60**

In practice, when parties deal in standard forms, they do not necessarily see themselves as being involved in a process of negotiation over their contents. This is what distinguishes a "battle of the forms" from, e.g. the amendments introduced by the defender in *Roofcare v Gillies* (below, para.2–66), or by both parties in *Uniroyal v Miller* (below, para.3–27) as to price and description. As the standard clauses those cases show, standard forms of contracting may be drafted so as to preclude any further negotiation or alteration of the terms of contracting. Such "overriding" clauses are increasingly common in standard forms of contract. They mark the battle lines when dispute arises between the parties as to whose form should prevail.

An additional problem is whether the authority of the employees or agents negotiating the transaction extends to accepting the other party's terms when their own contract terms are the only terms on which their employers are prepared to contract.

If the rules on offer, acceptance and counter-offer govern such battles, the terms of that contract will tend to be those of the party who managed to get in the last shot (or form).

In *British Road Services v Arthur V Crutchley & Co Ltd*,[64] British Road Services (BRS) delivered whisky worth £9,126 to Arthur V Crutchley's (AVC) warehouse for storage. The BRS driver handed over a delivery note which included BRS conditions of carriage. The note was stamped by AVC with the words: "Received on A.V.C. conditions". One such condition limited

---

[63] *Star Fire & Burglary Insurance Co Ltd v Davidson & Sons Ltd* (1902) 5 F. 83.

[64] *British Road Services v Arthur V Crutchley & Co Ltd* [1968] 1 All E.R. 811.

AVC's liability for loss or damage to £800 per ton. The goods were stolen as a result of AVC's negligence.

It was expressly pleaded by BRS in the Court of Appeal that the parties were "never *ad idem* as to any special terms of contract between them" and that they were therefore entitled to the full value of the whisky. The court, however, held that AVC's conditions formed part of the contract, although it is by no means clear on what grounds.

2–61

Butler Machine Tool Co Ltd v Ex-Cell-O Corporation (England) Ltd
[1979] 1 W.L.R. 401
English Court of Appeal, Civil Division: Lord Denning MR, Lawton & Bridge LJJ

On 23 May 1969 Ex-Cell-O received from Butler a quotation for the supply of a Butler planing machine for £75,535. The quotation stated that delivery was "10 months (subject to confirmation at time of ordering)", and that "other terms and conditions are on the reverse of this quotation". On the back of the form were printed 16 conditions, including the following:

> "All orders are accepted only upon and subject to the terms set out in our quotation and the following conditions. These terms and conditions shall prevail over any terms and conditions in the Buyer's order"; "prices are based on present day costs of manufacture and design and having regard to the delivery quoted and uncertainty as to the cost of labour, materials etc. during the period of manufacture, we regret that we have no alternative but to make it a condition of acceptance of order that goods will be charged at prices ruling upon date of delivery."

On 27 May 1969 Ex-Cell-O placed an order for a planing machine. The terms and conditions attached to the order differed from those on the quotation in several particulars. They extended the delivery period to "10 to 11 months"; stated the installation cost as £3,100; included transport costs in the price whereas the quotation price did not include transport costs; reserved the buyer's right to cancel for late delivery, whereas the quotation stated that cancellation for late delivery would not be accepted; and had attached to it a tear-off slip which stated:

> "ACKNOWLEDGMENT: Please sign and return to [Ex-Cell-O], We accept your order on the terms & conditions stated thereon—and undertake to deliver by [date]."

On 5 June 1969, Butler wrote to Ex-Cell-O, acknowledging receipt of their order and, in accordance with their quotation, agreed to delivery in 10/11 months, i.e. March/April 1970. They also signed and returned Ex-Cell-O's Acknowledgment slip, having inserted March/April 1970 as the delivery date.

The machine was not ready for delivery until September 1970, but Ex-Cell-O would no longer accept delivery before November 1970. Butler also sought to recover an additional £2,892 under the price variation clause in their quotation as the increase in costs between May 1969 and April 1970.

The court found that a contract had been concluded on Ex-Cell-O's terms and conditions.

"LORD DENNING MR: ... If those documents are analysed in our traditional method, the result would seem to me to be this: the quotation of May 23, 1969 was an offer by the sellers to the buyers containing the terms and conditions on the back. The order of May 27, 1969 purported to be an acceptance of that offer in that it was for the same machine at the same price, but it contained such additions as to cost of installation, date of delivery and so forth that it was in law a rejection of the offer and constituted a counter-offer. That is clear from *Hyde v Wrench*.[65] As Megaw J said in *Trollope & Colls Ltd v Atomic Power Constructions Ltd*[66]: '... the counter-offer kills the original offer'. The letter of the sellers of June 5th 1969 was an acceptance of that counter-offer, as is shown by the acknowledgment which the sellers signed and returned to the buyers. The reference to the quotation of May 23, 1969 referred only to the price and identity of the machine. **2–62**

I have much sympathy with the judge's approach to this case. In many of these cases our traditional analysis of offer, counter-offer, rejection, acceptance and so forth is out of date. This was observed by Lord Wilberforce in *New Zealand Shipping Co Ltd v AM Satterthwaite & Co Ltd*.[67] The better way is to look at all the documents passing between the parties—and glean from them, or from the conduct of the parties, whether they have reached agreement on all material points—even though there may be differences between the forms and conditions printed on the back of them. As Lord Cairns said in *Brogden v Metropolitan Railway Co*[68]: '... there may be a *consensus* between the parties far short of a complete mode of expressing it and that *consensus* may be discovered from letters or from other documents of an imperfect and incomplete description'. Applying this guide, it will be found that in most cases when there is a 'battle of forms' there is a contract as soon as the last of the forms is sent and received without objection being taken to it. That is well observed in *Benjamin's Sale of Goods*.[69] The difficulty is to decide which form, or which part of which form, is a term or condition of the contract. In some case the battle is won by the man who fires the last shot. He is the man who puts forward the latest terms and conditions: and, if they are not objected to by the other party, he may be taken to have agreed to them. Such was *British Road Services Ltd v Arthur V Crutchley & Co Ltd*[70] per Lord Pearson; and the illustration given by Professor Guest in *Anson's Law of Contract*[71] when he says that 'the terms of the contract consist of the terms of the offer subject to the modifications contained in the acceptance'. (That may however go too far.) In some cases, the battle is won by the man who gets the blow in first. If he offers to sell at a named price on the terms and conditions stated on the back: and the buyer orders the goods purporting to accept the offer—on an order form with his own different terms and conditions on the back—then if the difference is so material that it would affect the price, the buyer ought not to be allowed to take advantage of the difference unless he draws it specifically to the attention of the seller. There are yet other cases where the battle depends on the shots fired on both sides. There is a concluded contract but the forms vary. The terms and conditions of both parties are to be construed together. If they can be reconciled so as to give a harmonious result, all well and good. If differences are irreconcilable—so that they are mutually contradictory—then the conflicting terms may have to be scrapped and replaced by a reasonable implication.

---

[65] (1840) 3 Beav. 334.
[66] [1962] 3 All E.R. 1035 at 1038; [1963] 1 W.L.R. 333 at 337.
[67] [1974] 1 All E.R. 1015 at 1019–1020; [1975] A.C.154 at 167.
[68] (1877) 2 App. Cas. 666 at 672.
[69] *Benjamin's Sale of Goods* (9th ed., 1974), pp.84–85.
[70] [1968] 1 All E.R. 811 at 816–817; [1968] 1 Lloyd's Rep. 271 at 281–282.
[71] (24th ed., 1975), pp.37–38.

In the present case the judge thought that the sellers in their original quotation got their blow in first: especially by the provision that these terms and conditions shall prevail over any terms and conditions in the buyer s order. It was so emphatic that the price variation clause continued through all the subsequent dealings and that the buyer must be taken to have agreed to it. I can understand that point of view. But I think that the documents have to be considered as a whole And, as a matter of construction, I think the acknowledgment of June 5, 1969 is the decisive document. It makes it clear that the contract was on the buyers' terms and not on the sellers' terms: and the buyers' terms did not include a price variation clause.

I would therefore allow the appeal and enter judgment for the defendants [the buyers].

...

2–63 BRIDGE LJ: ... This is a case which on its facts is plainly governed by what I may call the classical doctrine that a counter-offer amounts to a rejection of an offer and puts an end to the effect of the offer.

The first offer between the parties here was the sellers' quotation dated May 23, 1969. The conditions of sale m the small print on the back of that document, as well as embodying the price variation clause, to which reference has been made in the judgments already delivered, embodied a number of other important conditions. There was a condition providing that orders should in no circumstances be cancelled without the written consent of the sellers and should only be cancelled on terms which indemnified the sellers against loss. There was a condition that the sellers should not be liable for any loss or damage from delay however caused. There was a condition purporting to limit the sellers' liability for damage due to defective workmanship or materials in the goods sold. And there was a condition providing that the buyers should be responsible for the cost of delivery.

When one turns from that document to the buyers' order of May 27, 1969, it is perfectly clear not only that the order was a counter-offer but that it did not purport in any way to be an acceptance of the terms of the sellers' offer dated May

23. In addition, when one compares the terms and conditions of the buyers' offer, it is clear that they are in fact contrary in a number of vitally important respects to the conditions of sale in the sellers' offer. Amongst the buyers' proposed conditions are conditions that the price of the goods shall include the cost of delivery to the buyers' premises; that the buyers shall be entitled to cancel for any delay in delivery; and a condition giving the buyers a tight to reject if on inspection the goods are found to be faulty in any respect.

The position then was, when the sellers received the buyers' offer of May 27, that was an offer open to them to accept or reject. They replied in two letters dated June 4 and 5 respectively. The letter of June 4 was an informal acknowledgment of the order, and the letter of June 5 enclosed the formal acknowledgment, as Lord Denning MR and Lawton LJ have said, embodied in the printed tear-off slip taken from the order itself and including the perfectly clear and unambiguous sentence: 'We accept your order on the terms and conditions stated thereon.' On the face of it, at that moment of time, there was a complete contract in existence, and the parties were ad idem as to the terms of the contract embodied in the buyers' order.

[Counsel for the sellers,] Mr. Scott has struggled manfully to say that the contract concluded on those terms and conditions was in some way overruled or varied by the references in the two letters dated June 4 and 5 to the quotation of May 23, 1969. The first refers to the machinery being as quoted on May 23. The second letter says that the order has been entered in accordance with the quotation of May 23. I agree with Lord Denning MR and Lawton LJ that that language has no other effect than to identify the machinery and to refer to the prices quoted on May 23. But on any view, at its highest, the language is equivocal and wholly ineffective to override the plain and unequivocal terms of the printed acknowledgment of order which was enclosed with the letter of June 5. Even if that were not so and if Mr. Scott [counsel for the sellers] could show that the sellers' acknowledgment of the order was itself a further counter-offer, I suspect that he would be in considerable difficulties in showing that any later circumstance amounted to an acceptance of that counter-offer in the terms of the original quotation of May 23 by the buyers. But I do not consider that question further because I am content to rest on the view that there is nothing in the letter of June 5 which overrides the plain effect of the acceptance of the order on the terms and conditions stated thereon.

I too would allow the appeal and enter judgment for the defendants.

LAWTON LJ concurred with BRIDGE LJ."

Price variation clauses were common in the 1960s and 1970s. They attempted to counteract the effects of high rates of inflation upon prices. **2–64**

The majority on the bench applied a standard "offer/counter-offer" analysis. Lord Denning came to the same conclusion under such an analysis, but offered the alternative solution that a contract was concluded where the documents passing between the parties showed, on construction, that they had agreed "on all material points". This would be so even where there are differences between the terms and conditions in those documents. See the discussion on materiality, paras 3–01—3–13. The approach is not dissimilar to that adopted by the United Nations Convention on the International Sale of Goods 1980 and by the Scottish Law Commission and the DCFR. It would appear that DCFR II.–4:209(1) adopts an approach similar to that adopted by Lord Denning: a contract is formed and the conflicting "general conditions" (defined in II.–4.209(3)) "form part of the contract to the extent that they are common in substance".

Lord Denning also suggested that, even where those terms were "irreconcilable ... the conflicting terms may have to be scrapped and replaced by a reasonable implication". On what basis would such terms be implied?[72]

Why was the original quotation regarded as an offer?[73]

The effect of overriding clauses

It is common, as with Condition 16 of the quotation in *Butler*, for standard forms to indicate that the party inserting them is prepared to contract on such terms and conditions only and that any attempt to alter them is subject to express consent. A mechanistic application of the "offer/counter-offer" approach would make it difficult for the parties to avoid a "battle of the forms" by clearly stating in their terms and conditions that they will contract only on their terms and conditions and no others. Butler had clearly tried to do this by inserting such an "overriding clause" in their terms and conditions, but found it impossible to make it stick. A person who believes he is making an offer exclusively on his standard terms may find that he has contracted on terms which are totally different. Lord Denning was clearly aware of this in *Butler* when he stated: **2–65**

> "The better way is to look at all the documents passing between the parties and glean from them, or from the conduct of the parties, whether they have reached agreement on all material points, even though there may be differences between the forms and conditions printed on the back of them."

---

[72] Implied terms are considered more fully below, paras 8–04—8–39.

[73] See the consideration of quotations and specifications above, paras 2–27—2–29.

This statement was quoted with approval by Lord Allanbridge in the *Uniroyal* case,[74] although he found that this was not a simple battle of forms, since the parties had entered into negotiation on price and deliver. The suggestion is that if there was agreement on all the material terms of the contract, the attempt by the offeree to insert a term apparently altering the pursuers' liabilities, contrary to the overriding clause in the offer, is invalid and could not invalidate that offer. Alternatively, there is no good reason why one party to the negotiations should preclude the other from negotiating by deploying an overriding clause. Contracts are, in essence, freely negotiated bargains. Such an overriding clause prevailed in the following case.

2–66 **Roofcare Ltd v Gillies**

1984 S.L.T. (Sh. Ct.) 8

Sheriff Court of North Strathclyde at Dumbarton: Sheriff Principal RA Bennett QC

Roofcare submitted a quotation to the defender to repair the roofs of extensions to his home. The quotation included an "overriding clause" which stated:

> "This quotation is made subject to the undernoted terms and conditions and no alterations, exclusions, additions, or qualifications to the quotation and specification will be made unless confirmed in writing by Roofcare."

Gillies accepted the quotation by letter, stating:

> "Further to your quotation ... I confirm that you should proceed with the work ... making the same wind and watertight, for the price of £574."

Roofcare did not reply to the letter, but carried out the work. The roof continued to leak, although there was no evidence of bad workmanship. Gillies refused to pay, relying on the "condition" that the roof would be made "wind or watertight" which, he claimed, had been incorporated into the contract; or, alternatively, that there was no consensus in idem between the parties.

The sheriff principal found that Roofcare were entitled to payment.

2–67 "SHERIFF PRINCIPAL (RA BENNETT QC): ... The solicitor for the defender and appellant then proceeded to submit in the first place, that there was no consensus ad idem between the parties and he referred to *Mathieson Gee (Ayrshire) Ltd v Quigley*, 1952 S.L.T. 239; 1952 S.C. (H.L.) 38 ... I do not regard *Mathieson Gee* as having any application to the circumstances here. This is not a case, like *Mathieson Gee*, where the parties were at cross-purposes and their minds had not met. This is a case where an offer was accepted subject to a condition—a familiar everyday situation—and the sole question is whether that condition was eventually imported into the contract. The solicitor for the defender and appellant then adopted the sheriff's obiter view on the applicability of *Butler Machine Tool Co Ltd* ...

In the first place, I would respectfully disagree with the sheriff's view that the qualification was imported into the contract. I do not find the case of *Butler Machine Tool Co Ltd* of assistance since the facts were very different from those in the present case. The pursuers and respondents here presented an offer which was the only basis upon which they were prepared to carry out the contract unless they otherwise agreed in writing. The defender and appellant who must be presumed to have known of this condition, added his qualification in the knowledge that if it was to be accepted the pursuers and respondents would do so in writing. Although they did not do so, the defender and appellant ordered the work to proceed, and this in my opinion was on the basis that the

[74] See below, paras 3–27—3–28.

> unaccepted qualification or condition did not apply. It follows that the pursuers and respondents were not in breach of their contract in failing to make the roof of the kitchen extension wind and watertight."

There is clearly no solution which has been uniformly applied to the battle of forms. The tendency in England to apply mechanistically the counter-offer approach is not evident in Scotland, but the problem remains that of finding when a contract has arisen. Since the standard forms used by the parties conflict as to what that contract comprises, the time at which the agreement was completed will determine which terms were incorporated into the contract.[75] **2–68**

Consider the following facts. X advertised an industrial press for sale in a trade magazine at £10,000. Y wrote that they would buy if their existing equipment were compatible with the press. X did not respond to the letter, so Y wrote again, accepting the original offer. X replied by sending a letter which included standard terms and conditions. Is there a contract between X and Y and if so, on what terms?

Scottish Law Commission Discussion Paper No.154 devotes an entire chapter to the problems raised by the battle of the forms, the lack of clarity in the case law and the potential solutions posited by the DCFR and other instruments.

Review of Contract Law: Discussion Paper on Formation of Contract **2–69**

Scottish Law Commission Discussion Paper No.154 (March 2012)

> **"Chapter 5: The Battle of the Forms**
>
> **Introduction**
>
> 5.1 . . . a problem raised which has been considered by the Commission on a number of previous occasions: the 'battle of the forms' . . . where both sides make a large number of similar transactions, probably with third parties in both cases as well as with each other. The buyer will use what are often known as 'purchase order' forms, while the supplier will respond with an 'acknowledgement of order'. The requirements of the particular transaction . . . Each party is aiming to keep to the essential minimum the amount of negotiation preceding the formation of a contract, and often there is also significant interest in speedy performance. Each party's forms are often processed by specialist departments or staff members whose job is not negotiation but keeping and processing records and then ensuring that performance is initiated once the documentation process is complete . . .
>
> **The problem and how it is currently resolved** **2–70**
>
> 5.2 It is of common occurrence that the two sets of terms exchanged by the parties conflict with each other on crucial matters such as delivery obligations, price calculations, and liability for defective, late or complete non-performance of the contract. Thus according to the ordinary rules of offer and acceptance, the failure of the parties' exchange to produce consensus on the terms can mean that there is no contract. Yet very often the parties will proceed to performance and the supply of goods, services and even payment, at least in part. Only if dispute breaks out does it become critical to know whether there is a contract and what its terms may be. The general assumption is that, at least where there has been actual performance, the solution must lie in contract law rather than the obvious alternative, unjustified enrichment, especially as it may be

[75] For a discussion of the problems raised by the battle of forms and various solutions suggested, see ADM Forte and HL MacQueen, "Contract Procedure, Contract Formation and the Battle of Forms" (1986) 31 J.L.S. 224.

problematic for the latter to deal adequately with the commonest kinds of problem such as liability for defective goods, delayed performance and disputes about price.[1] A contract solution also avoids the danger of enabling one of the parties to an on-going transaction to pull out with relative impunity if the bargain starts to go badly for that person.[2]

5.3 In resolving such disputes, the Scottish courts have tended to utilise a traditional offer and acceptance analysis of the exchange of forms to determine whether or not there is a contract, and if so, what its terms are.[3] This has generally meant that the 'battle of the forms' is won by the party which is the last to send out its terms. The other party's previous sending of its form is an offer which is however met, not with unqualified acceptance but with a different set of terms, i.e. a counter-offer. If the first party then does no more than commence performance, that falls to be treated as acceptance by conduct of the second party's terms of business. Under this analysis, then, the 'last shot fired' wins the battle because a contract is found to exist upon the firer's terms alone. In the simple situation where a buyer sends a purchase order to which the supplier responds with an acknowledgement of order (possibly sending the goods at the same time or shortly thereafter), the buyer's acceptance will be constituted by taking delivery of the goods without immediate objection or, perhaps, by paying the price or part of it ahead of delivery.[4]

2–71 **Difficulties with the current solution**

5.4 The apparently inevitable victory of the 'last shot fired' may tend to encourage inappropriate attempts to be the firer of that shot, defeating the general policy goal of enabling business parties (which the participants in a battle of the forms will invariably be) to conclude their contracts with the minimum necessary legal complication and formality. In our simple example above, the alert buyer might respond to the supplier's acknowledgement of order with a further form reinstating its own terms, so that the supplier's subsequent performance could become an acceptance of those terms. But this, it has been said by an experienced English commercial lawyer, 'does not work well in practice', at least for the buyer seeking to ensure that its terms prevail:

'In many cases, it does not fit into the administrative systems of the parties, nor is it a usual way of doing business. Not only is this burdensome and difficult to administer, but it becomes very noticeable to the seller. The seller is then likely specifically to reject the buyer's acknowledgement, and a detailed negotiation as to whose conditions are to govern the contract will probably ensue. This defeats the purpose of doing business on standard conditions (speed and efficiency in dealing with a large number of transactions), and the purchasing departments of both the buyer and the seller will probably be unable to cope with the work load imposed if there are many such special negotiations.'[5]

5.5 Parties may also send with their standard terms documents for the other side to sign and return, purporting to accept the terms proposed. The same English commercial lawyer has said of one situation where this approach was used by a business over a number of years, 'it was found to operate successfully in more than 50 per cent of the cases'.[6] This, however, carries the implication that the procedure did not work in a large number of cases, amounting to perhaps more than 40 per cent of them. The reason for these failures emerges in a further passage from the same author:

'The only practical problem encountered (apart from cases where the proffered acknowledgement form was ignored, and the seller returned his own acknowledgement form or called for a special negotiation) was that some sellers' administrative systems required the issue of their own acknowledgement form before an order could be logged. They therefore issued their own form and sent back both the buyer's form and their own form. Under these circumstances, unless the seller's own acknowledgement was poorly drafted . . . without a special negotiation it was almost impossible to decide in individual cases which set of conditions prevailed.'[7]

5.6 Another technique designed to prevent victory going to the last shot fired is the use of so-called over-riding or paramount clauses in standard forms. Such a clause declares in effect that the set of terms in which it appears prevails over any other terms which may be included in the other side's response. The courts have, however, tended to hold that such clauses fail to prevent any response being a counter-offer with a knock-out effect on the over-riding clause along with the rest of the terms in which it appeared.[8] Professor Angelo Forte of the Aberdeen Law School has argued strongly for many years that the courts should give greater recognition to such over-riding clauses.[9] The basis in principle for this argument is that an offeror may provide in the offer what is needed for acceptance; so that if the offer states that it will be accepted by the return of the offeree's standard form, even if that form contains different terms, then that will be enough to form a contract. It may be thought, however, that this approach might simply mean that the first shot would always win the battle rather than the last, which may be no more satisfactory an outcome to the problem. Nor does it really explain why the offeror's form should be the sole basis for the terms of the resultant contract. Further, the effect where each side uses an over-riding clause in its standard terms, which has not yet been discussed in either the Scottish or English courts, is problematic.[10] Just because a party happens to be the offeror does not seem to be a good reason for preferring that party's over-riding clause to the offeree's.

5.7 It can of course be suggested that the best way for business parties to avoid a battle of the forms is to negotiate about the differences between their respective standard forms. But the whole point of such forms and their use is to reduce as much as possible the time spent bargaining in advance about eventualities which the parties do not actually expect to arise and which, if they do arise, the parties expect to bargain about then rather than now. Lawyers in many jurisdictions have long argued, therefore, that the application of offer and acceptance rules in this way to the battle of the forms leads to an inappropriate result, at least in so far as it declares that there is no contract in an exchange of forms alone. Further, the approach of treating the last shot fired as an offer which is then accepted by the other party's conduct makes the conclusion and the terms of the contract a matter of chance rather than agreement. In the supply of goods cases, the odds are probably stacked in favour of the supplier responding to the purchaser's order with its acknowledgement form, the usual sequence of the exchange of documents. But where there are more than two documents in a case nt form, theample, where the seller produces a 'quotation' in response to a prospective buyer's inquiry, followed by that buyer's purchase order and then by the seller's acknowledgement of order, all with the respective parties' standard terms of business appended to them two documents in a case nt form, theample, where tffer and which of the latter two, therefore, is the acceptance and the 'last shot' winner of the battle.

A solution by way of a special regime?

5.8 Hence, the argument runs, the law should provide a regime to deal specifically with the battle of the forms, holding the balance between the parties a little better, and, to achieve this, take the analysis of the situation outside the law of offer and acceptance. What matters is agreement, not offer and acceptance . . .

[Following an analysis of ss.2–207 of the Uniform Commercial Code of the USA and the solutions provided in the DCFR and other texts, the Commission continued.] **2–72**

5.18 ... The gist of the solutions is very similar. Provided that the parties can be shown to be in sufficient agreement on the substance of the contract (which will generally be by way of performance on each side such as delivery of goods and payment or part-payment of a price, but might also be, for example, by way of a telephone call ahead of sending off a purchase or acknowledgement of order form[16]), an exchange of standard terms produces a contract despite the differences between the forms. The terms of the contract are those that have actually been agreed plus any common ground that there may be between the standard terms. This does not preclude the inclusion of terms from other sources such as the implied terms regimes found in all three documents. It is, however, possible for a party to declare in advance that it does not intend to contract under this regime, i.e. to insist upon contracting only under its own standard terms. It is also possible for a party who has made no such advance declaration to advise the other party that it does not intend to contract under the special regime once the standard forms have been exchanged, provided it does so without undue delay. Maximum scope is therefore given to party autonomy; but where the parties do not exercise this privilege but simply exchange forms and commence performance, any subsequent dispute will be decided in accordance with these rules.

5.19 In our RFC in 1993 we discussed a solution to the problem of the battle of the forms which we had first put forward in a consultation paper ten years earlier.[17] That solution bore some resemblance to the ones now being put forward in the PICC, the DCFR and the proposed CESL. It read: 'Where there are differences between the terms of an offer and those of a purported acceptance of it, but it is reasonable to infer from the conduct of the parties that they share an assumption that a contract between them has been concluded, a contract should be deemed to have come into existence'. The terms of the contract would be those on which the parties had agreed with either (a) 'such other terms as may be necessary to give the contract proper effect' or (b) 'such other terms as may be reasonable'.

...

5.21 The approach bears some resemblance to that found in a few recent English decisions in battle of the forms cases. Richard Christou summarises the effect of these cases as follows:

'The parties will have agreed express terms which represent the basis for the transaction and are sufficiently certain to bring a legally binding contract into existence, but since neither of them is willing that the other's standard conditions should apply, the proper inference is that neither set of terms was applicable, and the remaining terms of the contract will be governed by statute and common law.'[19]

Christou suggested in 2009 that this approach 'is likely to be applied more often in the future ... [T]he courts are increasingly likely to adopt this ... approach'.[20] His prediction has, however, not been borne out in the subsequent decision of the Court of Appeal in *Tekdata Interconnections v Amphenol Ltd*,[21] where the 'last shot' approach was unanimously reaffirmed, and Dyson LJ (now a Justice of the UK Supreme Court) said:

'[I]t seems to me that the general rule should be that the traditional offer and acceptance analysis is to be applied in battle of the forms cases. That has the great merit of providing a degree of certainty which is both desirable and necessary in order to promote effective commercial relationships.'[22]

5.22 A recent Scottish example along lines similar to those in the English cases discussed by Christou may, however, be provided by the decision of Lady Clark of Calton in *CR Smith Glaziers (Dunfermline) Ltd v Toolcom Supplies Ltd*.[23] In this case the parties exchanged, respectively, 'purchase requisition order' and 'despatch note' forms, the terms of neither of which, Lady Clark found, were incorporated into the contracts. It was not disputed, however, that many different contracts had come into existence between the parties from 1996 on and these had been successively performed over a period of several years. Following a preliminary proof, Lady Clark concluded that the contracts included the terms implied under section 14(2) (general fitness of the goods for their purpose) and 14(3) (reasonable fitness of the goods for the buyer's particular purpose) of the Sale of Goods Act 1979 as well as a further implied term that the goods were to be the products of one particular manufacturer. It was not necessary for the purposes of the case for her conclusions to go any wider than this, and Lady Clark's opinion makes no reference to the jurisprudence on the battle of the forms. But the background facts clearly did involve an element of battle of the forms, and it is clear that the failure of each side to ensure that its form was the basis for the contract terms did not prevent the court reaching a method of resolving the dispute between them on a contractual basis.

5.23 We sense, however, that despite the English cases discussed by Richard Christou and the *CR Smith* decision in Scotland, consultees may still have concerns about commercial uncertainty if a solution to the battle of the forms problem is adopted following the lines suggested by the PICC, the DCFR and the proposed CESL ...

A solution for long term relationships only? **2–73**

5.24 A narrower approach to the problem of the battle of the forms may be raised by other comments in the *Tekdata* case.[24] Here the parties to a battle of forms were part of a production chain involving the manufacturing of aircraft components. Longmore LJ in obiter remarks suggested that 'the context of a long term relationship and the conduct of the parties' could in certain circumstances dislodge the application of a 'last shot wins' conceptual analysis of a battle of the forms.[25] His suggestion seems to be that, in certain types of case where the parties have dealt with each other many times before, it may be open to them to argue that their previous course of dealing shows an intention to contract under terms and conditions other than those contained in what happens to be in the final counter-offer in the particular transaction under scrutiny.

5.25 Such an approach might be consistent with the rules on 'usages and practices' in the DCFR and the proposed CESL,[26] and would also be possible, it is thought, under Scots law as it stands at present in relation to the concept of incorporation of a set of terms by a course of dealing between the parties.[27] We have, however, already indicated some hesitancy about proposing the introduction of a legislative rule on usages, practice, custom or course of dealing in the context of an exercise limited to questions about formation of contract[28]; and we feel even greater hesitancy about proposing a rule based on such matters as a solution to the problem of the battle of the forms limited to long-term business relationships (however these might be defined).

---

[1] In England, Professor Ewan McKendrick has offered a detailed argument about how the law of restitution might apply in a battle of the forms case if there was held to be no contract: Ewan McKendrick, "The battle of the forms and the law of restitution" (1988) 8 Oxford Journal of Legal Studies 197. No equivalent analysis exists as yet for Scots law, although the law of unjustified enrichment might now be thought sufficiently mature for the attempt to be made. We think, however, that this is not the place for such an exercise.

[2] Furmston and Tolhurst, *Contract Formation*, para 4.134.

[3] McBryde, *Contract*, paras 6.97-6.105; *Chitton Bros Ltd v S Eker Ltd* (OH, Lord Grieve), 8 July 1980, unreported; *Uniroyal Ltd v Miller & Co Ltd* 1985 SLT 101 (OH); *Continental Tyre & Rubber Co Ltd v Trunk Trailer Co Ltd* 1985 SC 163 (IH). For a recent case in which each party to a commercial contract for the supply of goods used its own standard terms but it was held that neither set of terms was incorporated into the contract, see *C R Smith Glaziers (Dunfermline) Ltd v Toolcom Supplies Ltd* [2010] CSOH 7; 2010 GWD 13-236, discussed at para 5.22.

[4] The English courts also tend to follow this approach: see most recently *Tekdata Interconnections Ltd v Amphenol Ltd* [2009] EWCA Civ 1209, [2010] 2 All ER (Comm) 302. The approach stems

from the classic cases of *British Road Services v Arthur V Crutchley & Co Ltd* [1968] 1 All ER 811 (CA) and *Butler Machine Tool Co v Ex-cell-o Corp (England)* [1979] 1 WLR 401 (CA). See generally *Chitty on Contracts*, paras 2.034-2.037.
[5] Christou, *Drafting Commercial Agreements*, p 115.
[6] Ibid.
[7] Ibid. Examples of the problem can be seen in *Butler Machine Tool Co Ltd* [1979] 1 WLR 401 and *Chitton Bros Ltd v S Eker Ltd* (OH, Lord Grieve), 8 July 1980, unreported.
[8] See *Butler Machine Tool Co Ltd* [1979] 1 WLR 401; *Uniroyal Ltd v Miller & Co Ltd* 1985 SLT 101 (OH). Note, however, *Roofcare v Gillies* 1984 SLT (Sh Ct) 8.
[9] The most recent statement of Professor Forte's arguments is in his article, "The battle of forms" in Hector MacQueen and Reinhard Zimmermann (eds), *European Contract Law: Scots and South African Perspectives* (2006), pp 98-122.
[10] Ibid at p 119 suggests that Uniroyal (cited in fn 8 above) was such a case, but this does not emerge clearly from the report and the matter was not discussed by the judge.
8
[16] This was the situation in Uniroyal Ltd v Miller & Co Ltd 1985 SLT 101 (OH).
[17] See Consultation Paper on Contract Law: Exchange of Standard Term Forms in Contract Formation (1982), available at http://www.scotlawcom.gov.uk/download_file/view/523/410/. tt
[19] Christou, *Drafting Commercial Agreements*, p 116, citing and discussing *Lidl UK GmbH v Hertford Foods Ltd* [2001] EWCA Civ 938; *J Murphy & Sons Ltd v Johnston Precast Ltd (formerly Johnston Pipes Ltd)* [2008] EWHC 3104 (TCC); *Tesco Stores Ltd v Costain Constructions Ltd* [2003] EWHC 1487 (TCC).
[20] Ibid.
[21] [2009] EWCA Civ 1209, [2010] 2 All ER (Comm) 302. 22 Ibid at para 25.
[23] [2010] CSOH 7, 2010 GWD 13-236.
[24] [2009] EWCA Civ 1209, [2010] 2 All ER (Comm) 302.
[25] Ibid at para 21.
[26] See paras 2.32-2.35 above. It may also be that the long-term practice of the parties could in a particular transaction within that relationship amount to an explicit advance indication that one party did not intend to be bound by the other's standard terms.
[27] See McBryde, *Contract*, paras 7.21-7.32.
[28] See paras 2.32-2.35 above."

Chapter 3
PROTRACTED NEGOTIATIONS

The basic rule: intention to agree

Lord Dunedin in *May & Butcher Ltd v The King*,[1] stated the basic rule: **3–01**

> "To be a good contract, there must be a concluded bargain, and a concluded contract is one which settles everything that is necessary to be settled and leaves nothing to be settled by agreement between the parties. Of course it may leave something which still has to be determined, but then that determination must be a determination which does not depend upon the agreement between the parties. In the system of law in which I was brought up, that was expressed by one of those brocards of which perhaps we have been too fond, but which often express very neatly what is wanted: '*certum est quod certum reddi potest* [If something is capable of being made certain, it should be treated as certain].' Therefore, you may very well agree that a certain part of the contract of sale, such as price, may be settled by someone else. As a matter of the general law of contract all the essentials have to be settled. What are the essentials may vary according to the particular contract under consideration."

More recently, in *RTS Flexible Systems Ltd v Molkerei Alois Müller Gmbh*[2] Lord Clarke restated the rule in slightly different terms:

> "Lord Clarke restated the rule in slightly different terms:he contract of sale, such as price, may be settled by someone else. As a matter of the general law of contract all the essentials have to be settled. What are the essentia them by words or conduct, and whether that leads objectively to a conclusion that they intended to create legal relations and had agreed upon all the terms which they regarded or the law requires as essential for the formation of legally binding relations. Even if certain terms of economic or other significance to the parties have not been finalised, an objective appraisal of their words and conduct may lead to the conclusion that they did not intend agreement of such terms to be a pre-condition to a concluded and legally binding agreement."

Transactions that fail to agree those essentials are occasionally referred to as "inchoate" or incomplete contracts; although the effect of this failure is that there is no contract at all. The modern tendency is to regard such failures as failures to show objectively that a contract was intended. The parties themselves may decide what is or is not essential. Even something as essential as the price in a contract of sale may be left to be determined by some agreed formula at a future time,[3] or by a third party.[4] For example, in negotiating complex transactions, it is common for the parties to agree that, even where the essentials are agreed, no contract will arise until a formal contract is drawn up. The effects of such a clause, or device are considered more fully elsewhere[5]; but for present purposes such a device could be seen objectively as an essential element that, if not fulfilled, prevents a contract from arising. In an earlier decision, Lord Clarke

---

1 *May & Butcher Ltd v The King* [1934] 2 K.B. 17, HL at 21.

2 *RTS Flexible Systems Ltd v Molkerei Alois Müller Gmbh* [2010] UKSC 14 at [45].

3 *R&J Dempster v Motherwell Bridge and Engineering Co*, 1964 S.C. 308.

4 Sale of Goods Act 1979 s.8.

5 Below, paras 3–30—3–34.

had emphasised this relationship between the essentials of a contact and the intention to enter into a binding agreement in the context of such a clause.

3–02 **WS Karoulias SA v The Drambuie Liqueur Co Ltd**
[2005] CSOH 112; 2005 S.L.T. 813
Outer House, Lord Clarke

Karoulias had been the highly successful exclusive distributor of Drambuie's products in Greece since at least 1977. The parties operated under a series of written distibutorship agreements, the latest of which was dated May 1998 and was due to expire in July 2003. All these documents had been formally attested by the parties.

In June 2002, protracted discussions began between the parties for a new distributorship agreement. On 30 January 2003 J, a director of Drambuie, sent an email to A, Karoulias's managing director, in which he stated:

> "I am attaching for your approval the final draft of the Agreement which incorporates all the changes requested in your email of 30 December subject to a small amendment in 10.3. Once you have confirmed that it is in order I shall send two copies for signature."

The attached draft contained a testing clause. A replied by email on 5 February in the following terms:

> "Contract
> Many thanks for the above final draft which is ok with thanks from us. So pls. send us two copies for signing."

Despite intermittent emailed requests from Karoulias, the documents were never sent.

Karoulias continued to operate as distributors of Drambuie products. In May 2003, Karoulias became aware that Drambuie were considering another possible distributor in Greece. Discussions continued between the parties and J proposed some changes to the "contract" in an email that stated: "Our commitment to Karoulias ... is absolute". A agreed to most, but not all the changes and, in an email to E (managing director of Drambuie's parent company) dated 2 June 2003 stated:

> "Pls find their resposne [*sic*] after our meeting and my reply. We are almost there."

In a letter dated 11 July 2003, J sent a letter to A terminating the distributorship agreement of May 1998, with effect from 31 December 2003.

A continued to negotiate with J, but at a meeting in Paris on 2 December 2003, J informed A that the distributorship would be transferred to another company, Bacardi.

Karoulias sought specific implement of an exclusive distributor agreement against Drambuie.

3–03 LORD CLARKE:

[50] In my previous Opinion, in this case, I said at pages 25 to 26: 'The law of contract is concerned with concluded agreements between parties, which are given legal effect. There is no requirement, in the law, that a concluded agreement, of the sort upon which the pursuer relies in the present case, should be in writing, far less that any such writing should be signed, or executed in some other prescribed way. Absent any such requirement by the law, what the Court is looking for is whether or not the parties have reached finality in their agreement. The question is whether or not the parties have passed beyond negotiation and have a concluded agreement. They may, of course, themselves, legislate that, whatever the appearance may be as to the finality, neither party will be

bound, in law, until a certain condition is fulfilled, such as that their agreement should be embodied in a particular form, and/or that it should be formalised by signature and/or witnessed, but as, in most questions in the law of contract, the primary focus is on the parties' intentions'.

I have no reason to depart from that statement of the law having regard to the evidence led at the proof, and the subsequent submissions made to me. In the present case . . . there was nothing further to negotiate between the parties as to the terms of a new five year distributorship agreement commencing on 1 July 2003. The document . . . contained a complete agreement between the parties. There were no outstanding points to be discussed and agreed. To that extent, I am entirely satisfied that the pursuer has met the requirements set out in the first part of the statement of the law I endeavoured to formulate in the passage just cited. But the remaining question is whether, nevertheless, there was no agreement, binding in law, because the document was never executed by the parties, they having intended that neither would be bound by the terms of the document until it was signed by both of them. It is important, in my view, to recognise that while there may be complete agreement between parties, in the sense of negotiations being over, there may not yet necessarily be a binding agreement. That distinction is, I think, what Lord Mackay of Clashfern was alluding to at page 102 of the *Comex Houlder Diving Limited* case when he said 'final mutual assent as spoken of by Lord Blackburn in *Rossiter* v *Miller* . . . means mutual assent to be bound in law'. In many situations, in the law of contract, a person's words are deemed to be his bond but the law of contract provides that, in certain situations, it is a person's signature or equivalent that is his bond. The question, in a case like the present, is whether or not it was the parties' intentions, as objectively discerned from the relevant facts and circumstances that, notwithstanding that they had agreed the terms of the deal, they had postponed its coming into legal effect until they acknowledged its terms formally by executing the document in which the terms were set out. In the present case, the evidence before the Court, as to how the parties had conducted themselves prior to February 2003, as regards their contractual arrangements, was consistent and compelling. The Court had before it three previous written agreements between the parties dating from 1990 (although, of course, the evidence was that the parties had a commercial relationship with each other since the late 1970s) . . . It is, therefore, clear to me that since 1990, at least, these parties chose to regulate their contractual arrangements with a significant degree of formality and did so on a consistent basis . . . I am entirely satisfied that up until January 2003 the parties did intend to enter into a fresh distribution agreement to replace the 1998 Agreement and were negotiating, in good faith, to that end. The correspondence to which I was referred covering that period all confirms that as being the position. By early December 2002, indeed, most, if not all, matters of substance had been agreed between the parties . . . The negotiation stage, however, did continue until late January 2003 . . . But the process of negotiation, I am satisfied, came to a conclusion by the exchange of emails of 30 January 2003 and 5 February 2003 . . . As matters then stood, Mr Arghyrou was entitled to believe that a final agreement had been reached as to the terms of a new distributorship contract. There had been *consensus in idem*. Did he, however, consider, and more importantly was he entitled, in law, to consider that the parties now, that is at 5 February 2003, had a *binding* legal agreement even though the document had not been signed and he himself was recognising that it was the parties' intentions that it should be signed?—I consider these questions fall to be answered in the negative. There was certainly nothing in the way that the parties had dealt with each other, in the past, to lead him to believe that they would consider themselves bound before formal execution of the relevant agreement. Nor was there anything in the evidence of what was done and said in the negotiation of the terms of the 2003 document that this would be so on that occasion. Whenever one has these factors in mind, an explanation emerges for the somewhat remarkable feature of the evidence that, at no time, did anyone from the pursuer, after 5 February 2003, up until the raising of the present proceedings, assert, in any shape or form, that a binding legal agreement had come into force on 5 February 2003, notwithstanding that the 2003 document was never executed by either of the parties. The evidence, of course, of Mr Arghyrou was that the explanation for the lack of reference by him or anyone else from the pursuer to the existence of a binding agreement arose from a desire not to upset the relationship of the parties and, in particular, to diminish or remove the possibility of the defender affirming its commitment to the pursuer. These considerations, it was said, were coupled to a deep and longstanding reluctance on the part of the pursuer and its parent company to indulge in litigation. I have considered those explanations carefully but have come to the view that they do not provide a plausible explanation for the *complete* lack of reference by Mr Arghyrou or anyone from the pursuer from 5 February onwards and, in particular, from 11 June onwards to the existence of an established binding agreement. As senior counsel for the defender observed the pursuer could have alluded to its belief that there was in place a binding agreement without threatening legal proceedings. It could have done so, in my view, in a measured way which any commercial party might have done in the situation, in discussion with another commercial party, with whom it had had a longstanding and amicable commercial relationship. Mr Arghyrou struck me, in giving his evidence, as a shrewd, astute and very intelligent businessman. I found it difficult to believe that, in the situation that had developed from 5 February until December 2003 between the parties he chose never once to refer to the existence of a binding agreement simply for the reasons he put forward at the proof. I am not necessarily suggesting that he was setting out to mislead the Court in that respect. It may be that his hopes and expectations regarding a continuing relationship with the defender having been dashed, and having taken legal advice on the matter, he, *ex post facto*, sought to provide an explanation for his conduct which he, himself, began to convince himself about ... This is not a case where the Court is concerned with the construction of the terms of an agreement which the parties accept is binding, but where their dispute is as to its effect. It is a case where the question is whether parties had concluded a *binding* agreement. The matter, I accept, ultimately has to be tested, primarily as to what the parties' intentions were as at 5 February 2003. The question, however, being whether there was a binding agreement at all at that date, it is legitimate, in my opinion, where the parties have not expressly provided as to what the purpose and effect of formal execution is to be, to look at what occurred from that date and how the parties conducted themselves thereafter. That exercise is for the purpose of seeing whether there was consistent actings of the party which do not contradict, if not support, the position being advanced by one or other of them as to what those intentions were. In that respect, for the reasons given, I have reached the conclusion that the evidence of the parties' conduct since 5 February 2003 was consistent with the position being that the parties' intentions as at 5 February were that there was to be no binding agreement between them until the document was formally executed.

[51] I ... agree with the submission made on behalf of the defender that, adopting the language of Viscount Haldane in *Gordon's Executors*, the evidence, in this case, established that, as at 5 February they had not negotiated with a view of stopping there, but intended to suspend the coming into force of a binding agreement between them until the document was formally executed by them. Just as Lord Mackay of Clashfern, in the *Comex Houlder Diving* case at page 101 considered that, in that case, the parties' agents 'were proceeding upon the understanding that the binding legal obligation would be consented to in the *form of execution of the formal release*, in the terms satisfactory to both parties' (my emphasis), I consider that, in the present case, the parties were proceeding upon the understanding that binding legal rights and obligations, in accordance

with the document, would be consented to in the form of the execution of the deed, that is, by it being signed on behalf of both parties.

[52] I have no difficulty in feeling some sympathy for the pursuer in the situation that emerged as between the parties. The defender, no doubt, strung the pursuer along from 5 February and relied on the fact that the agreement had not been executed to explore the possibility of replacing the pursuer with Bacardi as the distributor in Greece. The defender could be seen to have exploited the longstanding, amicable and successful commercial relationship between the parties for its own ends. The terms of Mr Jeffray's email of 2 June 2003 to the effect that 'our commitment to Karoulias and more particular to you is absolute' were somewhat cynical, if not downright misleading and it was not surprising that Mr Jeffray displayed considerable discomfort in the witness box when asked about them. Nevertheless the task of the Court, in this case, is to answer a legal question according to the law, and the answer to that question cannot be driven by any view about the moral behaviour or the commercial manners of the parties. Ultimately, I have little hesitation in answering the legal question in the way already indicated, namely that the defender never became bound by the term of the document 44/1/46 of process because it was the parties' intention that neither side should be bound by it until it was formally executed ... "

A key issue in the case was whether the parties had formulated an intention to enter into a contract; whether the parties intended the testing clause as an essential element and, if so, whether it was a suspensive condition.[6] This seems to be in complete contrast with Lord Clarke's later decision in *RTS*, in that virtually no regard was paid to the fact that the contract was executed and acted upon for almost a year. None of the relevant case law seems to have been referred to in argument. Perhaps what was fatal to the case was that the action was for specific implement only. It is worth arguing that if an action were brought in the alternative for damages based on breach of good faith, there may have been grounds for success.[7]

[8]*WS Karoulias SA v The Drambuie Liqueur Company Ltd* 3–04

G Black, (2006) Edin. L.R. 10, 132

(1) Contractual intention

Contractual intention—the requirement that both parties to an agreement intend their arrangement to be legally binding[14]—is generally recognised as being one aspect required for the formation of a contract,[15] along with consensus and capacity. Scots law has tended to give priority to the need for *consensus in idem* and to presume that such an intention will be present in commercial contracts, unless the parties take steps to agree objectively otherwise.[16] Conversely, 'social' agreements carry a presumption that the parties do *not* have the requisite contractual intention, unless it can be established objectively.[17] As this was a commercial contract between two companies which had a history of trading together, a cautious legal advisor would certainly have had justification for pointing to the completed negotiations and the final draft contract as objective evidence of *consensus*, together with section (1) of the Requirements of Writing (Scotland) Act 1995,[18] and concluded that the written but unsigned contract was all that was required to form an enforceable contract, in a situation where intention could safely be presumed.

---

[6] On which see below, paras 3–30—3–34.

[7] See below, para.3–40 onwards.

[8] © Gillian Black, "WS Karoulias SA v The Drambuie Liqeur Company Ltd" (2006) Edinburgh Law Review 10.

This approach was rejected by Lord Clarke however, who stated, 'it is important, in my view, to recognise that while there may be complete agreement between parties, in the sense of negotiations being over, there may not necessarily be a binding agreement'.[19] To this extent, intention was used to imply a condition delaying conclusion until execution. As the parties were not yet contractually bound, nor was there any obligation on either to take 'the further necessary steps to complete the contract',[20] there was *locus poenitentiae* as recognised by Gloag, albeit not explicitly referred to in court. This modern application of *locus poenitentiae* can be interpreted in three possible ways.

Firstly, it can be seen as a straightforward application of the standard presumption as to contractual intention. As noted above, this presumption can be rebutted, allowing parties in commercial situations to prove that they did *not* possess the necessary contractual intention. Applying this interpretation, Drambuie's evidence was sufficient to rebut the presumption and to show that it did not intend to be bound by the contract at the moment of conclusion of negotiation, on 5 February, but only once authorised representatives of both parties had signed on the line. As this element was not fulfilled, there was agreement as to contract terms between the party but no enforceable contract.

A second, more progressive, interpretation is that the decision can be seen as an explicit declaration by the court that the role of intention is developing and that it should no longer be seen merely as a rebuttable presumption. Instead, intention now plays a crucial role in regulating the relationship between parties. For example, the requirement for intention could be used to confer upon contracting parties the freedom to introduce their own contractual rules governing formation, such as a requirement for a written document where one would not otherwise be required, as in this case. This would allow parties to regulate their relationship in accordance with their own preferences, by creating a final hurdle prior to conclusion: the need for evidence of intention to enter into a binding legal relationship. Until that moment, there is *locus poenitentiae,* and either party can walk away. Support for this approach comes from Lord Clarke's judgment, where he states that the question at issue is whether or not it was the parties' intentions, as objectively discerned from the relevant facts and circumstances that, notwithstanding that they had agreed the terms of the deal, they had *postponed its coming into legal effect* until they acknowledged its terms formally by executing the document in which the terms were set out.[21]

Until the necessary contractual intention was objectively demonstrated, the only agreement reached by the parties on 5 February was an agreement to sign a contract at an unspecified future date, or perhaps an agreement as to the terms of the future contract to be signed, rather than agreement as to the contract itself. This interpretation also recognises the complex layers of intention and future intention present in every contract.[22] Thus, the intention to enter into negotiations, the intention to provide goods or services of a specific type, the intention to draft a contract or conclude negotiations are usually present in all contracts, but the focus remains with the final agreement reached between the parties: the contract itself, which will only come into existence once there is a concluded intention to enter into a legally binding relationship.[23]

This line of argument can in fact be seen as a development of the rebuttable presumption argument noted above: intention will be presumed unless it can be demonstrated that it was the intention of both parties to impose an additional hurdle to the conclusion of their contract. It is nonetheless an important development of the law, and perhaps reflects the desire of many commercial parties to retain control over contract formation, by disapplying the traditional rules of offer and acceptance and by stipulating their own prerequisite for conclusion. This trend can frequently be seen in practice where, for example, standard disclaimers on email messages might read: 'Unless specifically stated otherwise, this email (or any attachments to it) is not an offer capable of acceptance or acceptance of an offer and it does not form part of a binding contractual agreement'.[24]

A third possible interpretation of the judgment does not rely on intention, but on the terms of the contract itself. Arguably, the contract was formed *but for* the presence of an express (but unwritten) contract term. The express term in this case required proper execution of the contract document to finalise the deal, and was derived from the past dealings between the parties. This argument is simply an application of the classic rule in *McCutcheon v David MacBrayne Ltd*[25] as to the implication of terms by a course of dealing: in the current case Drambuie was able to show that previous contracts between the parties had been formally executed and their dealings had consistently been regulated with 'a significant degree of formality'.[26] Accordingly, the agreement reached between the parties was not elevated to a legally enforceable contract because the final draft had not been signed, in contravention of the implicit term as to execution.

Which of these three interpretations, if any, is to be preferred? It is likely that Lord Clarke's decision was influenced by all these factors. There is certainly judicial support (considered above) for the second option, which indicates a development of the role of contractual intention. Whether or not the role of intention will continue to be developed in this vein by the courts remains to be seen. An increase in the role of contractual intention should be welcomed, since this allows parties to take control of the moment of formation and thereby avoid the disputes as to formation which arise from application of the simplistic, and arguably out-dated, principles of offer and acceptance to the complex world of commercial negotiations and business practices.[27] Although a full discussion as to the applicability of the rules of offer and acceptance to contracts in the twenty-first century is beyond the scope of this case-note, there is a considerable divergence between commercial reality and the theory of contract formation. An expanded doctrine of intention as suggested in the second option could therefore allow parties to determine their own moment of contract formation, in accordance with their intentions, and create greater certainty as to their legal liabilities.

---

[14] For example, see W M Gloag, *The Law of Contract*, 2nd edn (1929), 7, where he refers to applicability of the rules of offer and acceptance; W McBryde, *The Law of Contract in Scotland*, 2nd edn (2001), para 5-02; H L MacQueen and J Thomson, *Contract Law in Scotland* (2000) para 2.64; and, regarding English law, G Treitel, *The Law of Contract*, 11th edn (2003), 162.

[15] For one particular debate on this issue, see McBryde, *Contract* para 5-06, note 25 and the authorities referred to therein.

[16] See Gloag at 9; McBryde, para 5-06; Treitel at 171. MacQueen and Thomson suggest that this presumption can be explained on grounds of practicality, whereby it would be inefficient for the court to enquire into the parties' intentions in every commercial situation (para 2.64). (All reference to texts at note 14 above.)

[17] E.g. *Robertson v Anderson* 2003 SLT 235.

[18] Which states that "writing shall not be required for the constitution of a contract". The exceptions to this rule, provided in section 1(2), do not encompass a distribution agreement.

[19] At para 50.

[20] Gloag, *Contract* at 46.

[21] At para 50, emphasis added.

[22] The layers of intention in every contract are set out and discussed in G MacCormack, "Some Problems of Contractual Theory" 1976 JR 70.

[23] Stair refers to the three stages of contracting as "desire, resolution and engagement". The first two of these are insufficient to conclude a contract, so that "the only act of the will, which is efficacious, is that whereby the will ... becomes engaged to that other to perform" (Stair, *Institutions*, 1.10.2).

[24] With thanks to an anonymous practitioner who provided a number of such examples from her own experience.

[25] 1964 SC (HL) 28.

[26] At para 50.
[27] It is interesting to note that offer and acceptance, as a mechanism for determining formation of contract, was not advanced by *either* party in this case, nor raised judicially.

This analysis conflates two issues: the possibility that the parties lack the necessary intention to reach agreement, with the lack of an intention to enter into legal relations, even where agreement has been reached. The latter remains a matter of controversy in Scots law and is considered elsewhere[9]; but the point is well made: no agreement, and therefore no contract arises if the parties have expressly, or objectively stated that it will not until a specific event.[10] The interpretation outlined by Gillian Black resonates with the approach of the Draft Common Frame of Reference (DCFR), which was closely analysed in the Scottish Law Commission resonates with the approach.

3–05 *Review of Contract Law: Discussion Paper on Formation of Contract*

Scottish Law Commission Discussion Paper No.154 (March 2012)

[2.1] The major focus of the Report of Formation of Contract ("RFC") was the formation of contract by way of an offer from one party met by an acceptance from the offeree. In this chapter we consider a number of other important issues relating to the formation of contract which … we have become convinced warrant consideration. In particular, discussion of the general principle that contracts are agreements between two or more parties which they intend to take legal effect between them seems important. Offer and acceptance is one way of showing the agreement that is necessary for a contract. But it is not necessary to force the question of formation in every case to fit this model: for example, contracts may be created by parties' performances, or by complex oral negotiations resolved at some decisive meeting of the parties. The most significant practical example of formation without offer and acceptance is the formal written document which the parties intend to be their contract only after they have each signed it. … The principle also has important implications for the so-called 'battle of the forms', discussed in Chapter 5. Here the problem is that while the documents exchanged by the parties can be analysed in offer-acceptance terms, the end result will often be the appearance of no contract despite a real underlying agreement between the parties. The question is whether that underlying agreement should be given precedence over the apparent outcome of the offer-acceptance analysis.

DCFR

II.–1:101 Meaning of 'contract' and 'juridical act'

(1) A contract is an agreement which is intended to give rise to a binding legal relationship or to have some other legal effect. It is a bilateral or multilateral juridical act.

(2) A juridical act is any statement or agreement, whether express or implied from conduct, which is intended to have legal effect as such. It may be unilateral, bilateral or multilateral.

II.–4:101: Requirements for the conclusion of a contract

A contract is concluded, without any further requirement, if the parties: (a) intend to enter into a binding legal relationship or bring about some other legal effect; and (b) reach a sufficient agreement.

[9] See paras 1–52—1–55.
[10] See paras 3–30—3–34.

II:–4:102: How intention is determined

The intention of a party to enter into a binding legal relationship or bring about some other legal effect is to be determined from the party's statements or conduct as they were reasonably understood by the other party.

II.–4:103: Sufficient agreement

(1) Agreement is sufficient if: (a) the terms of the contract have been sufficiently defined by the parties for the contract to be given effect; or (b) the terms of the contract, or the rights and obligations of the parties under it, can be otherwise sufficiently determined for the contract to be given effect.

(2) If one of the parties refuses to conclude a contract unless the parties have agreed on some specific matter, there is no contract unless agreement on that matter has been reached.

II.–4:211: Contracts not concluded through offer and acceptance

The rules in this Section [Section 2: Offer and acceptance] apply with appropriate adaptations even though the process of conclusion of a contract cannot be analysed into offer and acceptance.

[2.9] McBryde has observed, '[o]ffer and acceptance ... should not be regarded as the necessary form of every contract'.[10] The master concept of contract to which McBryde elsewhere refers is that of an 'agreement between two or more parties ... intended to establish, regulate, alter or extinguish a legal relationship and which gives rise to obligations and has other effects, even in respect of one party only'.[11] Offer and acceptance is but one means of showing that the parties have reached agreement; there are other possibilities, some of which we have already mentioned.[12] McBryde also instances many everyday situations such as the purchase of a ticket to travel on a local bus.[13] Another example may be multi-party contracts to which the several parties agree at different times without necessarily going through a series of exchanges of offer and acceptance.[14] McBryde's chapter on offer and acceptance is preceded by one entitled 'The Formation of a Contract', and in this he explores requirements for enforceable agreements in general—notably for present purposes an intention to create legal relations, agreement on the 'essentials' of the contract, and certainty of terms.[15] These are precisely equivalent to the requirements set out in the DCFR and confirmed by the proposed CESL.

[2.10] In his chapter on formation, McBryde also discusses the situation where the parties agree to put their contract into a single document or set of documents.[16] While the general rule of Scots law is that writing is not required for the constitution of a contract save in the case of contracts for the creation, transfer, variation or extinction of a real right in land,[17] nothing prevents parties from putting their contracts into writing if they so wish.[18] The main focus of McBryde's discussion of this topic is the relationship between the written agreement and the parties' preceding agreement;[19] but implicit throughout is that the former is a contract, formed by virtue of its having been executed by the parties with the intention that it should be the basis of the legal relationship between them thenceforth. Gloag possibly puts the matter more plainly when he states: 'Parties may, indeed, put their agreement into writing ... '.[20] This situation is then another example of a contract formed without offer and acceptance. The parties' mutual consent is shown by the terms of the document itself and, where it has been signed by the parties, by those signatures.

[2.11] A question for analysis in many cases may be whether the parties' unwritten or informal agreement prior to the drawing up of a formal document embodying the agreement is itself a contract. A range of possibilities exists and here we need only address three.[21] It is possible for the parties to make explicitly clear that they have no intention to be legally bound until the completion and execution of a formal document. If so, there will be no contract between them, however much their informal agreement may meet contract law's general requirements of consensus on the essentials of the agreement in question.[22] An alternative possibility is that the parties' informal agreement is a contract, but that its enforceability as such is subject to a suspensive condition of being put in more or less formal writing.[23] Thus the contract only becomes enforceable as such when the suspensive condition is fulfilled, although meantime the parties are obliged not to impede the condition's purification, for example by refusing to draw up a formal document of the kind required, or declining to sign it once it has been drawn up. A third possibility is for the parties to agree that an informal agreement amounting to a contract is enforceable as such but that it will be or is superseded by a subsequent formal document embodying the same agreement. It does not appear that the informal agreement will necessarily be void from uncertainty as a mere 'agreement to agree'.[24]

[2.12] The rules in the DCFR and the other texts are consistent with present Scots law and, moreover, as we will show elsewhere in this Discussion Paper, of considerable practical importance. A statutory restatement of the Scots law of contract formation should therefore include similar rules. The most appropriate model to adopt for these purposes from those surveyed in the table above would, we suggest, be that provided by the Expert Group revision of the DCFR, which appears to cover all the points in a succinct and intellectually lucid fashion. ...

---

[10] McBryde, *Contract*, para 6.05. See also *SME*, vol 15, para 655.

[11] McBryde, *Contract*, para 1.03 (quoting H McGregor). Gloag, *Contract*, p 6, also defines contract in terms of agreement: 'the consent of two or more parties to form some engagement or to rescind or modify an engagement already made'; the agreement may be 'expressed in words, writing or conduct'. See also MacQueen & Thomson, *Contract*, paras 1.9-1.14 and 2.2-2.8; *SME*, vol 15, paras 611 and 619; Walker, *Contracts*, paras 1.19-1.20; Gloag & Henderson, paras 5.03-5.08. Martin Hogg, *Promises and Contract Law: Comparative Perspectives* (2011), pp 50-52, argues that agreement becomes contractually binding only when it contains promises.

[12] See para 2.1.

[13] McBryde, *Contract*, paras 6.04-6.05. See also *SME*, vol 15, para 655.

[14] The classic example in the books is *Clarke v Earl of Dunraven (The Satanita)* [1897] AC 59 (yacht race competitors bound by competition rules as contract to which all had at various points subscribed). Other examples might be partnerships, unincorporated associations and the rules of tender competitions which bind all tenderers.

[15] McBryde, *Contract*, chapter 5. See also Gloag, *Contract*, pp 8-12; Walker, Contracts, paras 3.13 and 7.1, and chs 8 and 9; *SME*, vol 15, paras 656-658; MacQueen & Thomson, *Contract*, paras 2.4 and 2.64. On the increasing significance attached to intention to be legally bound in recent Scottish case law, see Gillian Black, "Formation of contract: the role of contractual intention and email disclaimers" 2011 *Juridical Review* 97.

[16] McBryde, *Contract*, paras 5.41-5.44, and also para 5.79.

[17] RoW(S)A, s 1(1). See further McBryde, *Contract*, paras 5.71-5.78.

[18] McBryde, *Contract*, para 5.79.

[19] Ibid, paras 5.41-5.44.

[20] Gloag, *Contract*, p 161.

[21] Consider further Gillian Black, "Formation of contract: the role of contractual intention and email disclaimers", 2011 *Juridical Review* 97, and *Aisling Developments Ltd v Persimmon Homes Ltd* 2009 SLT 494 (OH) (court found no intention to create legal relations in parties' informal arrangements).

[22] *Karoulias (WS) SA v The Drambuie Liqueur Co Ltd* (No 2) 2005 SLT 813 (OH). We think that this case is not so much about 'an implied agreement between the parties that each has the power to withdraw until formal signature of the written contract' (Ross Gilbert Anderson, "Fax and email in corporate completions" 2010 *SLT (News)* 73 at 73), as an express agreement that the parties do not intend legal relations or legal effect until the formal document is executed. For another recent example of an express exclusion of an intention to be legally bound in a pre-contractual document see *McDougall v Heritage Hotels Ltd* 2008 SLT 494 (OH). Note also the recent Supreme Court decision, *RTS Flexible Systems Limited v Molkerei Alois MMois GmbH &*

Company KG (UK Production) [2010] 1 WLR 753 (UKSC), in which the parties were held to have impliedly waived their previous agreement that there would be no contract until the agreement was formally executed.

[23] E.g. where parties agree 'subject to contract'; see *Stobo Ltd v Morrisons (Gowns) Ltd* 1949 SC 184 (IH) per Lord President Cooper at 192.

[24] Parties wishing to ensure that their earlier informal agreement is indeed superseded by the more formal written contract may find the conclusive effect of an 'entire agreement' clause under the Contract (Scotland) Act 1997 of assistance. This, we think, answers the question raised in Ross Gilbert Anderson, "Fax and email in corporate completions" 2010 *SLT (News)* 73 at 73 ('how the Karoulias interpretation squares with boiler plate "entire agreement" clauses is not free from difficulty'.) See also fn 22 to para 2.11 above."

Agreement on the essentials of the contract

There are, therefore, two distinct questions: have the parties reached agreement; and what does that agreement comprise? The parties must demonstrate by their words or acts a commitment to the essentials of the agreement, even though they might not have not resolved every minor issue or contingency. **3–06**

Those essentials will in each case depend on the class or type of contract being transacted. In a lease, for example, there are "four cardinal elements" or "incidents" which must be adequately defined before any contract arises: the parties; the subjects; the rent; and the duration. In a contract for the sale of heritage there must consensus as to the parties, the subjects and the price to establish agreement. Whether such consensus has arisen is a matter of construction.

Grant v Peter G Gauld & Co **3–07**

1985 S.L.T. 545; 1985 S.C. 251

Court of Session, Second Division: The Lord Justice-Clerk (Lord Wheatley), Lords Hunter and Brand

Gauld offered to purchase land from Grant in a letter which stated:

> "[We] hereby offer to purchase from you the ground at present being quarried by our client and the surrounding thereto extending to twelve acres at a price of Fifteen Thousand Pounds (£15,000) per acre and that on the following terms and conditions, namely: 1. The actual boundaries will be agreed between you and our client. 2. Entry and actual possession will be given on the completion of the missives when the purchase price will be payable. 3. It is understood that our clients will have the sole quarrying rights on and for the farm and lands of Bogend and any planning consent for such quarrying in existence will be assigned to him. 4. In addition to the ground under offer our client will have an option to acquire other land adjacent to the quarry at a price to be agreed between you and our client and that to reflect the agricultural value of the land with an addition of £600 per acre. Failing agreement then the matter of the price would be referred to an arbiter."

Grant purported to accept the offer by holograph letter. He now sought to enforce the contract, but the Second Division found no contract to enforce.

"JUSTICE-CLERK (LORD WHEATLEY): ... There is no doubt that a definite description of the heritage which is being offered for sale is essential to a valid contract, and must be contained in the missives of offer ... On a purely grammatical construction of the words in issue I would attribute the qualification imposed by the words 'extending to twelve acres' to the words immediately preceding that qualification, namely 'and the surroundings thereto'. That interpretation leads, in my view, to the further construction that what was being offered were two distinct parcels of heritage, namely the ground at present being quarried and the surroundings thereto extending to 12 acres. The first condition attached to the offer was in these terms: 'The actual boundaries will be agreed between you and our client'. Counsel for the defenders laid great stress on this as demonstrating that the actual limits of the ground offered had not been defined, and required an agreement that they should be defined by some future agreement between the parties. That could not constitute the precision required for such an essential factor in a contract of heritage, and acceptance of such an indefinite offer could not constitute a concluded contract of heritage. I agree with that submission, which is determinative of the whole issue ...

LORD HUNTER: It is agreed on both sides of the bar that one of the essentials of a contract for the sale of heritage is that the parties should be in agreement as to the subjects of the sale. If not, there is no completed contract. Moreover, as was pointed out by Viscount Dunedin in a passage from his speech in *May and Butcher Ltd v R*, quoted in a note to *Foley v Classique Coaches Ltd*. The question as to what may be the result of the application of this principle to the circumstances of a particular case may sometimes be a matter of difficulty. See, e.g. *R & J Dempster v Motherwell Bridge and Engineering Co*. However, I am satisfied that in the present case the application of the principle demonstrates that there was no completed contract."

Had the parties failed to agree what was being sold, or had they merely been imprecise in expressing this? Was this lack of precision merely an indication that the parties were still negotiating, or was the fact that "the actual boundaries will be agreed" fatal to this argument? Was the court merely applying an objective view of what the parties had agreed?

What must the parties have agreed? Does every "i" have to be dotted and every "t" crossed? The preceding case suggests that there can be no contract unless and at least the essentials or incidents of the contract have been agreed. Does a contract arise when the incidents are agreed; or must there be evidence that every element of the offer has been accepted?

In *Bogie (trading as Oakbank Services) v Forestry Commission*,[11] a case concerning an option to purchase land for landfill, the failure to identify the land in question with sufficient clarity meant that there was no agreement on the essentials and therefore no contract.

3–08

Andert Ltd v J & J Johnston
1987 S.L.T. 268
Court of Session, Outer House: Lord McDonald

Andert claimed that they had leased farmlands belonging to Johnston on the basis of a document which was couched in the following terms:

> "We the undersigned of J. & J. Johnston, Herdshill Farm, New Mains, hereby agree to lease the lands of Herdshill Farm to Andert Ltd., 266 High Street, Newarthill, for the extraction of coal and minerals (subject to planning permission being granted). Payment being £2.50 (two pounds fifty pence) per ton of coal extracted. This payment covers the damage and loss of crops, etc."

Agreement was subsequently reached with the planning authority on the conditions regulating the development, at least in relation to 8.9 acres of the land in question.

Johnston now claimed that there was no lease between the parties, because:

[11] *Bogie (trading as Oakbank Services) v Forestry Commission*, 2002 S.C.L.R. 278.

(a) the subjects were uncertain;
(b) no "ish", or duration, for the lease was stipulated; and
(c) there was no provision for rent.

The Lord Ordinary allowed the possibility of a contract between the parties to go to proof.

"LORD MCDONALD: 3–09

(a) Uncertainty of the subjects

The basic proposition was that the subject of a lease must be described so as to be fully identified (Bell, *Prin.*, s. 1206). It was accepted, however, that a general description by reference to the occupancy of the grantor will suffice, even if this involves extrinsic proof as to the extent of the occupancy. In the present case the document of 10 November 1981 purports to lease 'the lands of Herdshill Farm, and this description is substantially echoed in the pursuers' second conclusion. On the face of this would be a description sufficient to cover the farm lands owned by the defendant even if this involved proof as to their extent. I was referred, however, to the case of *Grant v Peter G Gauld & Co.*

In my opinion the description in the present case contained in the document of 10 November 1981, viz. grantor will Herdshill Farm; is comparable to what the description in the *Grant* case would have been had it consisted only of the words 'the ground at present being quarried by our client'. It is, in my view, a sufficiently precise description capable of exact definition by reference to the defender's title deeds and extends to the whole lands of Herdshill farm belonging to the defenders. It is not qualified by ambiguous words as was the case in Grant.

It was argued, however, that the extent of the subjects involved was still uncertain because the area involved in the minute of agreement was only 8.9 acres, which was a small part of the lands of Herdshill farm. It was also pointed out that in the related action [for reduction of the document] the pursuers have an averment that it was the intention of the parties that the lease would extend to the area from which minerals would be extracted, and that this contradicted the proposition that the lease covered the whole lands of Herdshill farm. I do not consider that it is proper to seek to construe the wording of the document of 10 November 1981 by reference to subsequent negotiations between the parties and the planning authority. The document bears to grant a lease of the whole lands of Herdshill farm, but for the limited purpose of the extraction of coal and minerals, and that subject to planning permission being granted. It is not difficult to envisage circumstances under which a planning authority would restrict these activities to part only of the farm lands, but this cannot, in my opinion, affect the description in the document of 10 November 1981 which is a pure matter of construction. The pursuers' averments in the related action, on the other hand, do raise the suggestion that the parties had in mind some area of ground less than the whole lands of Herdshill farm. If this be the case it may still be that the document of 10 November 1981 is not a valid lease because the extent of the subjects is uncertain, but I consider that this is a matter which can only be satisfactorily ascertained after proof. I am therefore not prepared, at this stage, to uphold this aspect of the defenders' argument.

(b) No ish or duration 3–10

The argument under this heading was that the document of 10 November 1981 which the pursuers found upon as a lease contains no sufficiently specific provisions as to its ish. The date of commencement may be open to inference as being either the date of the document or the date when planning permission was obtained. There was, however, no provision from which the duration of the tenure could be inferred, and this was fatal to the pursuers' proposition that the document was a lease . . . Counsel for the defenders in the present case argued that there had been no possession and that therefore no inference as to duration could arise: One of the cardinal elements of a lease, viz. duration, was missing and there was no valid lease. As he crisply put it: "no ish, no lease".

While this is an attractive argument, I am not prepared to sustain it at this stage. I note that in *Gray v Edinburgh University* the Lord Justice-Clerk (Thomson) said:[1] in the absence of possession as showing consensus there must have been consensus in the negotiations not only to the parties, subjects and rent but to the acceptance of the mutual relationship of landlord and tenant on the footing that there was to be possession whether its duration was explicitly defined or not. In that way there can be said to be a "lease" although the precise length of time for which it is to last is not explicitly agreed to (1962 S.L.T. at p.176). In the case of *Grey* the averments showed that that stage had never been reached. In my opinion the pursuers' averments in the present case and in the related action are sufficient to merit inquiry as to whether there was consensus as to the duration of the purported lease. There are positive averments as to considerable discussion leading to consensus as to the rate of royalty. As was pointed out by Lord Patrick in *Gray v Edinburgh University*, rent and duration are interlinked, the amount of rent being influenced by the duration. If it can be proved that there was considerable discussion leading to consensus as to rent, it would seem that this may also involve consensus as to duration.

3–11 **(c) No definite rent**

It was accepted that the use of the word 'royalty' could include rent. In the document of 10 November 1981 the words used are: 'Payment being £2.50 (two pounds fifty pence) per ton of coal extracted. This payment covers the damage and loss of crops, etc.' It was argued on behalf of the defenders that this provision was imprecise, as it did not specify what proportion was rent and what compensation for damage. I do not read the provision in this way. I regard it as a fixed sum representing rent or royalty with an exclusion of liability on the part of the tenant for damage caused by his operations. On that basis the rent stipulated is specific and sufficient to satisfy the requirements of a valid lease. For the reasons above stated I shall allow parties proof before answer of their respective averments, leaving all pleas standing."

There are two issues in this case. The first is a matter of construction: what did the parties actually say, and what did they mean by it? The court must examine what the parties have said and done. Did Lord MacDonald apply an objective test?

The second issue is whether what the parties agreed amounts to a lease. This depends on whether the cardinal elements of a lease are satisfied. Looking at the facts as outlined in the judgment, would you say that the parties had entered into a contract; that they were still at the stage of negotiation; or that the contract which they were negotiating was inchoate?

Why did his Lordship distinguish *Gauld*?

A similar approach was adopted by Lord Macfadyen in *Small v Fleming*.[12] Having decided that after lengthy negotiations nothing that the defender had said committed him to a joint venture to purchase land from a third party, he added[13]:

---

[12] *Small v Fleming*, 2003 S.C.L.R. (OH), 647.

[13] *Small v Fleming*, 2003 S.C.L.R. (OH), 647 at [60].

"Had I held otherwise, I would have taken the view that what was agreed at that stage fell far short of all that would have had to be agreed to constitute an enforceable joint venture."

Just as it is possible for the parties, through their words and actions to indicate the essentials of the contract, so it is possible for them to indicate that what might otherwise be considered essential—even matters relating to price.

Neilson v Stewart 3–12

1991 S.L.T. 523

House of Lords: Lords Keith, Brandon, Ackner, Oliver of Aylmerton and Jauncey

Neilson sold to Stewart a 50 per cent shareholding in a company which ran a disco in Dundee called "Maxims". The parties had verbally agreed the sale and confirmed it in a typewritten agreement subsequently signed by the two of them and by a third party, Reilly, who was to assist Stewart in running the business. The agreement recorded that Neilson would transfer his holding to Stewart, who would also take over Neilson's liabilities, for a payment of £50,000, which Neilson would then lend back to Stewart and Reilly. The loan would be secured on the company's premises. Repayment of the loan was to be deferred for one year, "after which time, payment shall be negotiated to our mutual agreement and satisfaction".

The purchaser argued, inter alia, that the phrase quoted, which was admittedly too uncertain to be enforced, rendered the entire agreement to be no more than an agreement to agree.

"LORD JAUNCEY OF TULLICHETTLE: ... My Lords, it is trite law that an agreement which leaves a part, essential, to its implementation, to be determined by later negotiation does not constitute a concluded and enforceable contact. In *May & Butcher Ltd v The King*, Viscount Dunedin at p. 21 said: 'This case arises upon a question of sale, but in my view the principles which we are applying are not confined to sale, but are the general principles of the law of contract. To be a good contract there must be a concluded bargain, and a concluded contract is one which settles everything that is necessary to be settled and leaves nothing to be settled by agreement between the parties. Of course it may leave something which still has to be determined, but then that determination must be a determination which does not depend upon the agreement between the parties. In the system of law in which I was brought up, that was expressed by one of those brocards of which perhaps we have been too fond, but which often express very neatly what is wanted: "certum est quod certum reddi potest." Therefore, you may very well agree that a certain part of the contract of sale, such as price, may be settled by someone else. As a matter of the general law of contract all the essentials have to be settled. What are the essentials may vary according to the particular contract under consideration.' 3–13

Observations to a similar effect are to be found in *G Scammell & Nephew Ltd v HC & JG Ouston*, per Lord Russell of Killowen at p. 261, *Nicolene Ltd v Simmonds* per Denning L.J. at p. 551, and *Courtney & Fairbairn Ltd v Tolaini Brothers (Hotels) Ltd* per Lord Denning M.R. at p. 301. However that principle does not necessarily determine the issue in favour of the appellant. The fact that in the usual case a particular term will be considered essential to the existence of a concluded agreement does not prevent parties from contracting in a particular case that it shall not be essential. In *R & J Dempster Ltd v Motherwell Bridge and Engineering Co*, a contract for the sale of steel over a period of three years contained this provision: 'The prices to be mutually settled at a later and appropriate date.' It was held that this did not prevent there being a concluded contract between the parties. Lord Guthrie at 1964 S.L.T., p. 367 said: 'The object of our law of contract is to facilitate the transactions of commercial men, and not to create obstacles in the way of solving practical problems arising out of the circumstances confronting them, or to expose them to unnecessary pitfalls. I know of no rule of law which prevents men from entering into special agreements to meet the requirements of special circumstances.'

Later on the same page he said: The matter for decision must always be whether parties have not got beyond the stage of negotiation, or whether there is a concluded bargain. In the usual case, the price to be paid is one of the essential matters on which agreement is necessary before either party is bound. If they have not agreed upon the actual sum or on a method of deciding that sum, there is not the *consensus in idem* requisite before a contract can be completed. But if they agree that the question of price shall be deferred, and agree on the things to be done to meet the immediate needs of the situation, there is *consensus in idem*, and each can require the other to do what he has undertaken to do before the price is settled. In such circumstances, the matter of price is not "vital to the arrangement between them," to use the words of Lord Buckmaster in *May and Butcher v. The King*.'

The question here is whether the time and manner of repayment of the loan were essential to the taking effect of the contract as a whole. On analysis the document contains provisions for six matters: (1) transfer of shares by the respondent to the appellant in exchange for a payment of £50,000; (2) assumption by the appellant of the respondent's liabilities; (3) the lending back of £50,000 by the respondent to the two directors, the appellant and Reilly; (4) the securing of the loan on Maxims; (5) payment of the loan to be deferred for one year; and (6) thereafter payment to be negotiated. The document also refers to the transfer of shares being concluded quickly. It is quite clear that the parties intended that the transfer of shares and the subsequent loan back should take place as soon as possible. It is equally clear that they contemplated that this would take place long before the time and manner of repayment of the loan fell to be considered by them. Indeed until payment for the shares had been made there would be no loan and the one year period would not start running. As the Lord President said (1990 S.L.T. at p. 349J), repayment of the loan was 'deliberately being left over until a future date.'

My Lords, on no view was agreement as to the time and manner of repayment of the loan necessary to the completion of the sale and transfer of the shares. Was it then essential to that part of the agreement dealing with the loan? In *Thomson v Geekie*, Lord Justice-Clerk Inglis at p. 701 said: 'It admits of no doubt, that an acknowledgment for money generally presumes that the money was advanced in loan, and it follows that there is, first, an obligation to the party granting it instantly to repay the sum; and secondly, another obligation that, so long as the sum remains unpaid, the party shall pay legal interest. The acknowledgment itself does not express these obligations; but these are the obligations which result in law from the loan. This is the general case.'

In Bell's *Principles of the Law of Scotland* (10th ed.), s. 201, it is stated in relation to mutuum: 'And so action will lie for the thing or its value as at the time and place stipulated for restoration, or otherwise at the time when a legitimate demand for restitution of the thing lent may be made.'

I take from these passages that every loan carries with it an obligation of the borrower to repay. If the contract contains provisions for repayment those provisions will prevail. If, however, the contract contains no provisions or if for some reason the provisions turn out to be ineffectual then the obligation to repay on demand revives. I entirely agree with the observations of the Lord President at p. 350C that: 'It is not essential that the parties should agree about the period of the loan because, in the absence of agreement to the contrary, a loan is repayable at any time on demand.' Furthermore, payment of interest is not an essential condition of a contract of loan. An interest free loan is perfectly valid and parties can contract to that end. If nothing is said about interest it becomes a question of construction whether the parties intended that none should be payable or that the rule of law referred to by the Lord Justice-Clerk in *Thomson v Geekie* should apply.

For the foregoing reasons I have no doubt that the parties never intended that agreement as to the time and manner of repayment of the loan was a condition essential to the implementation of the agreement to sell the shares. It follows that the First Division reached the correct conclusion and that the appeal should therefore be dismissed."

Acceptance by conduct

As a rule, no contract arises unless a specific offer has been unequivocally accepted: "[a]ny form of statement or conduct by the offeree is an acceptance if it indicates assent to the offer": DCFR II–4:204(1). In most instances, all that the offerer requires from the offeree as acceptance is an indication of assent: a simple "yes". However, just as it is possible to infer an offer from conduct it is also possible to imply acceptance from the offeree's conduct. Thus, the act of supplying goods in response to an offer to purchase them constitutes acceptance.[14] Similarly, the sending of unsolicited goods through the post would normally be a specific offer to sell those goods to the recipient. The recipient who uses the unsolicited goods, or in any other way indicates acceptance of them, would be contractually bound.[15] In general, any acts which show a clear intention to accept a valid offer will create an agreement. The court will determine that by an objective review of the parties' conduct. **3–14**

Avintair Ltd v Ryder Airline Services Ltd **3–15**

1994 S.L.T. 613

First Division: Lord President (Hope), Lords Allanbridge and Clyde

Avintair, a firm of aviation consultants, entered into negotiations for a contract with Ryder, an aircraft engineering company, under which Avintair would be paid commission in return for acting as Ryder's consultants in obtaining engineering contracts for Ryder. During the negotiating period Avintair acted as aviation consultants for the defenders in relation to the obtaining of contracts for engine overhaul and similar work from Pakistan International Airways. Work proceeded under that contract although Ryder had still not yet agreed the rate of commission which Avintair were to be paid. Avintair were still pressing for agreement on this matter when Ryder faxed them that they declined Avintair's offer to work on their behalf. Avintair claimed remuneration under contract, even although commission had not been agreed.

The Lord Ordinary dismissed the action, holding that negotiations as to price not having resulted in agreement, there was no consensus in idem on what was in the circumstances an essential term of the contract; and that there could be no implied term where the matter had been in active dispute.

On appeal the Inner House found that there was a contract and that a reasonable remuneration must be paid.

---

[14] Bell, *Commentaries*, I, 343.

[15] By s.1 of the Unsolicited Goods & Services Act 1971, the recipient of unsolicited goods may, in circumstances stipulated by the Act, treat the goods as an unconditional gift.

3–16 "LORD HOPE: ... There is no doubt that parties must achieve *consensus in idem* upon all the essential matters before there can be said to be a contract between them. As Lord Dunedin said in *May & Butcher Ltd v The King* at p 21, for there to be a good contract there must be a concluded bargain, and a concluded contract is one which settles everything which is necessary to be settled between the parties. But it does not always follow that there is no contract where something which affects the parties' contractual relationship has not yet been agreed. It may be clear from the terms of the bargain that the parties were content that agreement on this matter should be deferred for the time being, because they have agreed upon all that was necessary for there to be a binding contract between them. *R & J Dempster v Motherwell Bridge & Engineering Co* is an example of such a case where, although the parties had not agreed on the price which was to be mutually settled at a later date, it was held that there was a concluded contract by which the defenders were obliged to place orders with the pursuers for the steel which the pursuers had agreed to supply. The law on this matter was reviewed recently in *Neilson v Stewart* and was summarised by Lord Jauncey of Tullichettle at 1991 SLT, p 526G where he said: 'The fact that in the usual case a particular term will be considered essential to the existence of a concluded agreement does not prevent parties from contracting in a particular case that it shall not be essential.'

The question whether the parties have so contracted must be answered by reference to what they agreed, and it will be for the party who seeks to show that this was the basis of the contract to set out in his averments the stipulations or actings from which this can be inferred.

But there is an important difference between cases where nothing has been done by either party to implement the alleged contract and cases where a party to the alleged contract has already provided the goods or services for which he seeks payment. It is likely to be more difficult in the former case to enforce the contract if there is no agreement about the remuneration which is to be paid, because in the ordinary case the price is one of the essential matters upon which agreement is required. Where goods or services have been provided, however, the usual rule is that there is an obligation to pay for them unless they have been provided gratuitously. So it is easier in these cases, if there is no agreement about the price or remuneration, for an obligation to pay a reasonable sum to be implied.

Gloag on *Contract* (2nd ed), at p 291 states: 'There can be no doubt of the general rule that the receipt of goods or services under a contract implies an obligation to pay for them.' In a later passage at p 328 he states that when goods have been supplied, or services rendered, without any express provision as to the terms, it may often be unnecessary to decide whether a claim for payment should be rested on implied contract or on the principle of recompense. With regard to an action on implied contract, which is the alternative which the pursuer has selected in this case, he states that this involves a claim for payment *quantum meruit*, measured by the ordinary rate of payment for the particular goods and services. McBryde on *Contract*, para 6-45 is to the same effect. He states that when there is a contract for services but no agreement on the amount of remuneration, the entitlement is to payment *quantum meruit*, and that if there is no customary rate which can be established the court will fix a reasonable rate.

In our opinion these observations are consistent with the authorities. In *Kennedy v Glassat* p 1087 Lord Adam said that it is a well known principle that if one man uses another for the purpose and with the effect of doing business, the ordinary rule is that the person employed is entitled to some remuneration. ... In *Wilkie v Scottish Aviation Ltd* a chartered surveyor claimed payment of a fee calculated according to a scale of professional charges, remuneration on the basis of which he averred was customary and was accordingly an implied condition of the contract. ... Lord President Clyde said at 1956 SC, p 203 that it was well settled that, in the absence of express agreement as to the basis of remuneration for his services, there is no presumption that a professional man does his work for nothing. The same principle can be applied to any case where a person provides services to another in the course of a business.

The distinction between a case where the alleged contract has yet to be performed to any extent by either party on the one hand and the case where goods or services have been rendered under the contract was noted in *British Bank for Foreign Trade Ltd v Novinex Ltd*. In that case, to which the Lord Ordinary was not referred, it was held that, since the contract was executed on one side by reason of the fact that the plaintiffs had put the defendants in direct touch with a company from whom they obtained business, there was necessarily implied from the conduct of the parties a contract that, in default of agreement, a reasonable sum was to be paid for commission. It was argued for the defendants, under reference to Lord Dunedin's observations in *May & Butcher Ltd v The King*, that the parties never reached agreement on the remuneration which was to be paid and accordingly that there was no contract. They submitted that there was no difference on this issue between an executory and an executed contract, that is, between a contract which has yet to be and one which has been performed. In the Court of Appeal, however, the following passage in the opinion of Denning J, as he then was, was cited with approval by Cohen LJ at pp 629-630: "The principle to be deduced from the cases is that, if there is an essential term which has yet to be agreed and there is no express or implied provision for its solution, the result in point of law is that there is no binding contract. In seeing whether there is an implied provision for its solution, however, there is a difference between an arrangement which is wholly executory on both sides, and one which has been executed on one side or the other. In the ordinary way, if there is an arrangement to supply goods at a price 'to be agreed', or to perform services on terms 'to be agreed', then although, while the matter is still executory, there may be no binding contract, nevertheless, if it is executed on one side, that is, if the one does his part without having come to an agreement as to the price or the terms, then the law will say that there is necessarily implied, from the conduct of the parties, a contract that, in default of agreement, a reasonable sum is to be paid."

These comments are consistent with the Scottish authorities and in our opinion they are in point in the present case.

. . .

The Lord Ordinary rejected the pursuers' argument that, in the absence of an agreement to fix the rate of remuneration, they were entitled to rely upon an implied term as the basis for their claim. He did so because it appears from the pursuers' averments that the parties were from the start actively negotiating as to what was a reasonable rate of remuneration. In his view there would have been no need for the proposals and counter proposals during the course of these negotiations if they were intending to enter into a contract with an implied term to this effect. Thus the parties' attempts to reach agreement on the point excluded the possibility of a term to that effect being implied into the contract and, as there was no concluded agreement on the point, there was no contract in reliance upon which the pursuers could enforce a right to payment.

In our opinion, however, this approach does not take sufficient account of the fact that the pursuers' case is that they have already rendered the services for which they claim payment. They seek to rely on the implied term because there was no agreed rate of commission for these services in circumstances in which it cannot be presumed that they were provided gratuitously. The fact that the parties were in negotiation about this matter is not inconsistent with the pursuers' reliance upon the implied term as there was no agreement. The purpose of the implied term is to provide a basis for payment where there is no agreed rate for this in circumstances where, according to the ordinary rule, the person who has provided goods or services is entitled to be paid something for what he has done. The reason why the contract made no express provision for payment is not important. What matters is that goods or services were provided which ought to be paid for. In such circumstances a claim may be based either on recompense or implied contract, and where the work was done under a contract as is averred in this case, the appropriate claim is on implied contract on the principle of quantum meruit".

It is important to note in this case that there was a question whether the case should be brought in recompense or implied contract, but that the pursuer in this case chose to bring the action in implied contract only.

The case is a clear statement that the formal analysis of negotiations in terms of offer and acceptance is not always appropriate. This is a matter that will be considered more fully in the following chapter. For the present, the importance of *Avintair* lies in its confirmation that actings are as much evidence of a contract as the exchange of formal documents or verbal assurances. The matter seems to be confirmed by the following English decision of the House of Lords.

3–17 **G Percy Trentham Ltd v Archital Luxfer Ltd**
[1993] 1 Lloyd's Rep. 25
Court of Appeal: Neill, Ralph Gibson and Steyn LJJ

Trentham were engaged as main contractors by Municipal Mutual Insurance Ltd (MM) to design and build industrial units in two phases in Farnborough, Hampshire. The main contract dated 2 February 1984 governed phase 1 and a supplemental agreement dated 18 December 1984 governed phase 2. Both phases included the design, supply and installation of aluminium window walling and similar works.

Archital made and installed aluminium window walling, doors, screens and windows and undertook the window works in phases 1 and 2 for Trentham. Archital was paid by Trentham for carrying out the window works, so that the transactions between Trentham and Archital were fully executed.

MM made claims against Trentham for alleged delays and defects and two interim awards were made against Trentham amounting to almost £1m. Trentham instituted proceedings against seven subcontractors, including Archital, for an indemnity in respect of such liability to MM. Trentham alleged that there were defects in the window works in both phase 1 and phase 2, and therefore breach of two separate subcontracts, one covering phase 1 window works and the other phase 2 window works. Archital did not admit the alleged defects and disputed that any subcontracts ever came into existence, but the court found that they had.

3–18 STEYN LJ . . . It is necessary to consider the basis of the Judge's decision that Trentham proved the formation of two valid sub-contracts. It is common ground that as between Trentham and Archital no integrated written sub-contracts ever came into existence. There was no orderly negotiation of terms. Rather the picture is one of the parties, jockeying for advantage, inching towards finalisation of the transaction. The case bears some superficial resemblance to cases that have become known as "battle of the forms" cases where each party seeks to impose his standard conditions on the other in correspondence without there ever being any express resolution of that issue. In such cases it is usually common ground that there is a contract but the issue is what set of standard conditions, if any, is applicable. Here the issue is one of contract formation. Moreover, the present case is different in the sense that Trentham's case was that the subcontracts came into existence not simply by an exchange of correspondence but partly by reason of written exchanges, partly by oral discussions and partly by performance of the transactions.

. . .

Before I turn to the facts it is important to consider briefly the approach to be adopted to the issue of contract formation in this case. It seems to me that four matters are of importance. The first is the fact that English law generally adopts an objective theory of contract formation. That means that in practice our law generally ignores the subjective expectations and the unexpressed mental reservations of the parties. Instead the governing criterion is the reasonable expectations of honest men. And in the present case that means that the yardstick is the reasonable expectations of sensible businessmen. Secondly, it is true that the coincidence of offer and acceptance will in the vast majority of cases represent the mechanism of contract formation. It is so in the case of a contract alleged to have been made by an exchange of correspondence. But it is not necessarily so in the case of a contract alleged to have come into existence during and as a result of performance. See *Brogden v. Metropolitan Railway*, (1877) 2 A.C. 666; *New Zealand Shipping Co. Ltd. v. A.M. Satterthwaite & Co. Ltd.* [1974] 1 Lloyd's Rep. 534 at p. 539, col. 1; [1975] A.C. 154 at p. 167 D-E; *Gibson v. Manchester City Council*, [1979] 1 W.L.R. 294. The third matter is the impact of the fact that the transaction is executed rather than executory. It is a consideration of the first importance on a number of levels. See *British Bank for Foreign Trade Ltd. v. Novinex*, [1949] 1 K.B. 628, at p. 630. The fact that the transaction was performed on both sides will often make it unrealistic to argue that there was no intention to enter into legal relations. It will often make it difficult to submit that the contract is void for vagueness or uncertainty. Specifically, the fact that the transaction is executed makes it easier to imply a term resolving any uncertainty, or, alternatively, it may make it possible to treat a matter not finalised in negotiations as inessential. In this case fully executed transactions are under consideration. Clearly, similar considerations may sometimes be relevant in partly executed transactions. Fourthly, if a contract only comes into existence during and as a result of performance of the transaction it will frequently be possible to hold that the contract impliedly and retrospectively covers pre-contractual performance. See *Trollope & Colls Ltd. v. Atomic Power Construction Ltd.*, [1963] 1 W.L.R. 333.

. . .

Conclusions on phase 1 3–19

. . .In a case where the transaction was fully performed the argument that there was no evidence upon which the Judge could find that a contract was proved is implausible. A contract can be concluded by conduct. Thus in *Brogden v. Metropolitan Railway*, sup., decided in 1877, the House of Lords concluded in a case where the parties had acted in accordance with an unsigned draft agreement for the delivery of consignments of coal that there was a contract on the basis of the draft. That inference was drawn from the performance in accordance with the terms of the draft agreement. In 1992 we ought not to yield to Victorian times in realism about the practical application of rules of contract formation. The argument that there was insufficient evidence to support a finding that a contract was concluded is wrong. But, in deference to Counsel's submissions, I would go further.

One must not lose sight of the commercial character of the transaction. It involved the carrying out of work on one side in return for payment by the other side, the performance by both sides being subject to agreed qualifying stipulations. In the negotiations and during the performance of phase 1 of the work all obstacles to the formation of a contract were removed. It is not a case where there was a continuing stipulation that a contract would only come into existence if a written agreement was concluded. Plainly the parties intended to enter into binding contractual relations. The only question is whether they succeeded in doing so. The contemporary exchanges, and the carrying out of what was agreed in those exchanges, support the view that there was a course of dealing which on Trentham's side created a right to performance of the work by Archital, and on Archital's side it created a right to be paid on an agreed basis. What the parties did in respect of phase 1 is only explicable on the basis of what they had agreed in respect of phase 1. The Judge analysed the matter in terms of offer and acceptance. I agree with his conclusion. But I am, in any event, satisfied that in this fully executed transaction a contract came into existence during performance even if it cannot be precisely analysed in terms of offer and acceptance. And it does not matter that a contract came into existence after part of the work had been carried out and paid for. The conclusion must be that when the contract came into existence it impliedly governed pre-contractual performance. I would therefore hold that a binding contract was concluded in respect of phase 1.

3–20 *Phase 2*

It is possible to deal with the issues on phase 2 quite briefly . . .

The starting point of the challenge of the Judge's conclusion in respect of phase 2 is that the parties had not concluded a contract in respect of phase 1. The appellants submit that during negotiations for phase 2 the parties were mistakenly of the view that a contract had been made in respect of phase 1. I have already concluded that a contract was made in respect of phase 1. In my view the springboard of the argument in respect of phase 2 therefore collapses.

The exchanges regarding phase 2, and what was done in respect of this transaction, leave me in no doubt that the Judge came to the right conclusion.

3–21 *Conclusion*

I would dismiss the appeal."

Note particularly the emphasis that Steyn LJ placed on the need to establish agreement on the objective evidence, rather than the subjective notions of the parties.

If an objective test is to be applied, there is no reason why multiple contracts should not arise between several associate individuals, for example, the members of a club.

3–22 **Clarke v The Earl of Dunraven and Mount Earl The Satanita**

[1897] A.C. 59

House of Lords: Lord Halsbury LC, Lords Herschell, Macnaghten, Shand, Davey

The Mudhook Yacht Club advertised a regatta to be held on the Clyde. Clarke entered his yacht, the *Satanita*, and Dunraven his, the *Valkyrie*. Each signed a letter to the club secretary undertaking to obey and be bound by the sailing rules of the Yacht Club Association. The rules were to the effect that the owner of any yacht disobeying any of the rules was to be liable for "all damages arising therefrom". Section 54 of the Merchant Shipping Act Amendment Act 1862 was to the effect that the owner of any ship which, through improper navigation caused any loss or damage to another ship, would be liable in damages to an aggregate sum not exceeding £8 per ton of the registered tonnage of the ship at fault.

The *Satanita* broke one of the rules and through negligent navigation ran into and sank the *Valkyrie*.

When Dunraven sued for "all damages" arising from the breach of the rules, Clarke claimed that the amount should be limited in accordance with the 1862 Act, suggesting that no contract had arisen into which the club rules had been incorporated and thereby replaced the provisions of the Act.

The House found that a contract existed between the parties.

"LORD HERSCHELL: ... I cannot entertain any doubt that there was a contractual relation between the parties to this litigation. The effect of their entering for the race, and undertaking to be bound by these rules to the knowledge of each other, is sufficient, I think, where those rules indicate a liability on the part of the one to the other, to create a contractual obligation to discharge that liability. That being so, the parties must be taken to have contracted that a breach of any of these rules would render the party guilty of that breach liable ... to 'pay all damages,' ... It is admitted that the appellant broke one of those rules, and having broken or disobeyed that rule, it is quite clear, on the assumption of a contract such as I have described that there arose the liability to 'pay all damages'." **3–23**

This is perhaps an extreme illustration of a contract arising objectively from the evidence. The **3–24** above cases do not mean that courts pay no regard to how the parties themselves classified their particular statements and conduct. Each case will depend on its facts and the expressions used by the parties may prove decisive. In *Muirhead v Gribben*,[16] the parties were two firms of solicitors acting for the two parties to the sale of a house. The defenders wrote to the pursuers:

> "On the understanding that we shall remit the sums [in respect of unpaid fees] due to yourself immediately on receipt of the settlement cheque from the purchaser's solicitors, we should be obliged if you could arrange to deliver the papers to ourselves."

The pursuers then wrote to the defenders: "We acknowledge your letter of 8 January and in view of your undertaking enclose the papers". Instead of remitting the unpaid fees to the pursuers, the defenders paid the money to their client and wrote to the pursuers:

> "We refer to our conversation and regret to advise you that despite our advice [our client] is not prepared to pay your accounts. We have released all funds held by us on his behalf. You will therefore require to contact [our client] direct concerning payment."

The pursuers unsuccessfully claimed that the letter evidenced a contract between themselves and the defenders which the defenders had broken by failing to make payment. Here, the court was able to attach ordinary meanings to common words like "undertaking" and "understanding". It may be, however, that the terminology used by the parties is too uncertain, or so inchoate that no agreement can be discerned. Again, however, the underlying approach is to find the sense of the agreement so that, as the following case shows, it will be difficult to establish that the uncertainty was such that no contract arose.

Conditions for acceptance attached to the offer

Sometimes the offer may stipulate what the offeree must do in order to accept. Only by **3–25** performing those stipulations will the offeree be deemed to accept. Specific conditions for acceptance may be attached to the offer. The conditions may, for example, require the offeree to accept on a specified form; or by signature to a written agreement; or stipulate a time limit for

[16] *Muirhead v Gribben*, 1983 S.L.T. (Sh. Ct.) 102.

acceptance, or state the duration of the offer; or insist on the use of a specified mode of communication: "by return of post", for example.

Frequently, the condition for acceptance attached to the offer is full performance of their contractual obligations by the offeree. Normally, no contract would arise until those acts are completed. In the *Carlill* case, as is common with offers of rewards, it was Mrs Carlill's acts which constituted the acceptance. The question is: which of those acts completed acceptance? Was it the purchase of the smoke ball, or its use, or the actual contracting of influenza? Or was acceptance constituted when all those conditions were fulfilled?

In Scots law such an offer might be regarded as a unilateral promise. If so, the promise is binding upon the promiser as soon as it is communicated to the person to be benefited.

This matter is addressed more fully below, in the next chapter. The general issue is: where an offer calls for acceptance by some form of conduct, does the offerer have to keep the offer open until the offeree has an opportunity to accept, or can the offer be withdrawn?

As a matter of construction courts tend to regard rewards and the like as offers, rather than promises, especially in commercial transactions,

> "while every case must present an independent question of construction, it is conceived that a proposal to give will usually be read as a promise, a proposal to enter into business relations merely as an offer".[17]

The effect of express and implied terms

3–26 The law will imply many of the detailed obligations of a contract, whether by statute or by custom and practice, or at common law.[18] In commercial documents connected with dealings in a trade with which the parties are perfectly familiar, the court is very willing, if satisfied that the parties thought that they made a binding contract, to imply terms, and in particular terms as to the method of carrying out the contract, which it would be impossible to imply in other kinds of contract.[19] In the sale of goods, for example, where the parties have not agreed a price, a reasonable price must be paid[20]; and if a wage or salary is not fixed in a contract of employment, a reasonable remuneration will be implied.[21]

If the parties are in negotiation about a particular aspect of the transaction, such as price, this would indicate that they consider it an essential element on which agreement must be reached before a contract will arise. This is so even though the parties may have reached agreement on what might otherwise be regarded as the essentials of the contract. This was one of the complicated issues of fact and law which arose in the following case. You are advised to read the facts very carefully, both as summarised and as stated by Lord Allanbridge in his judgment.

---

[17] Gloag, *The Law of Contract*, 2nd edn (Edinburgh: W. Green, 1929), p.25.

[18] This is considered more fully in Ch.8.

[19] Per Viscount Maugham in *Scammell Brothers v Ouston* [1941] A.C. 251 at 255.

[20] Sale of Goods Act 1979 s.8(2).

[21] "Where offer and acceptance, taken together, do not fix the amount of the return to be paid—price, rent, wage, etc.—the inference in ordinary contracts of everyday life, such as the purchase of goods on credit, taking a room at a hotel, will be that the parties regard the contact as complete, and the amount of the return, in the event of dispute, is to be fixed by the Court on a consideration of what is reasonable", Gloag, *The Law of Contract*, 2nd edn (Edinburgh: W. Green, 1929), p.40.

Uniroyal Ltd v Miller & Co Ltd 3–27
1985 S.L.T. 101
Court of Session, Outer House: Lord Allanbridge

In 1974, Miller sent to Uniroyal a quotation of prices for the supply of specified items. Uniroyal sent an order for a specific quantity of those items at the prices quoted. The printed "conditions of purchase" of the order stated,

> "any provisions in the form of acceptance used which modify, conflict with or contradict any provision of the contract or order shall be deemed to be waived unless expressly agreed in writing by [Uniroyal], and signed by an authorised representative ... these conditions contain the entire agreement between the Purchaser and the Vendor and there are no prior or current, oral or written understanding or agreements binding on the purchaser affecting the subject matter of the within contract or order other than those expressly referred to therein. No agreement or other understanding in any way modifying the conditions ... will be binding upon the Purchaser unless made in writing and signed by its authorised representatives".

Miller sent an acknowledgment of the order, but increased the prices previously quoted and specified a delivery date. The acknowledgment also included conditions which, unlike the conditions in Uniroyal's order form, excluded Miller's liability in respect of defects in their products in the following terms:

> "We shall not be liable in respect of defects ... and we shall not ... be liable for loss of profits, detention or other consequential damages or expenses whatsoever."

Uniroyal sued for damages in relation to the goods supplied under both contracts. The issue was whether the measure of damages should be in accordance with Uniroyal's or Miller's conditions.

"LORD ALLANBRIDGE: ... Turning first to the 1974 contract the final position of the pursuers was to argue that their purchase order dated 23 May 1974, was an offer which was accepted by the defenders by their acknowledgment of order dated 7 June 1974. The question is thus whether the acknowledgment is an actual, though perhaps hesitating and reluctant, acceptance or an offer to accept if the offerer is prepared to alter his terms. Having studied both documents with care I have come to the conclusion that the acknowledgment of order is not an acceptance but a counter offer or offer to accept if the pursuers were prepared to alter his terms ... My main reason for coming to that conclusion is because this was a contract between the pursuers, as purchasers, and the defenders, as suppliers, of what are described as 'hollow rolls.' It was a contract to purchase specific and carefully described items at a particular price. The actual price of the items ordered is a fundamental and essential part of the contract. If the parties are not agreed about price, apart altogether about agreement as to what are the conditions of the contract, then there cannot be consensus ad idem between them as regards such a contract. Consensus ad idem means there is agreement between the parties in the essentials of the contract. The price, in my opinion, is one of the essentials of the contract. 3–28

On the process copy of the purchase order the price is typed as £888 each for four hollow rolls and £1,244 each for six different hollow rolls. It is true that a pencil has been used to strike out these prices and insert new prices but it seems clear that this was done by the defenders themselves after receipt of the document from the pursuers, as the process copy seems to have been the actual copy received by them and stamped for 'attention' on 27 May. The pursuers' counsel did not suggest that the typed price was amended before it was sent out to the defenders. The defenders in their acknowledgment of price did not accept the pursuers' prices (which in fact are those originally quoted by the defenders in their quotation). What the defenders did was to quote substantially higher prices, namely, £1,066 and £1,493. This they did quite clearly by stating 'Price Please Note Revised Price—EI2465/8—£1,066 each. E2469I74—£1,493 each.'

Faced with this difficulty as regards the prices, the pursuers tried to argue that their conditions, and in particular conditions 1 and 2 printed on reverse of the purchase order, were so strongly and clearly worded that any qualifications at all in the defenders' acceptance were waived unless the pursuers otherwise agreed in writing. Thus the contract prices were the lower prices contained in pursuers' purchase order. I am not prepared to accept that these conditions 1 and 2 can have this remarkable effect. It seems to me, and as in fact was argued by counsel for the pursuers, that the ratio behind condition 1 was that it was appreciated that some vendors might prefer to use their own form of acknowledgment rather than the acceptance slip referred to at the foot of the front page of the purchase order in 'Instruction to Suppliers.' If that happened then condition 1 was intended to ensure that the pursuers' conditions rather than the vendors' conditions applied to the contract. But these are the 'conditions' and not such fundamental and different matters such as the price or the number of articles to be supplied. I appreciate also that condition 2 states the 'purchase order and these conditions contain the entire agreement between the Purchaser and Vendor.' It cannot, however, in my view, be assumed that the defenders were agreeing to the prices quoted in the purchase order because they accepted that conditions 1 and 2 of that purchase order meant the pursuers' price ruled whatever the defenders might say in their acceptance. It is quite clear the defenders did not accept such an interpretation of the conditions. The fact that they quoted quite clearly revised prices makes it clear there was no consensus about price and that is fatal, in my opinion, to the pursuers' argument that the defenders accepted their purchase order. I consider that the defenders' acknowledgment of order contained a counteroffer as regards price which effectively killed the pursuers' offer in their purchase order. That is sufficient to decide the argument in the defenders' favour on the 1974 contract and is my reason for doing so."

Was Lord Allanbridge saying that price is an essential of every contract; or of contracts of this "type"; or of this particular contract? On what did he base his view that agreement as to price was essential and had not been achieved in this case? It is notable that Lord Allanbridge did not regard the "overriding" clauses as decisive.[22]

Contracts subject to conditions

3–29 Although a conditional acceptance is no acceptance, this does not mean that the parties cannot agree that the contract will be subject to conditions. If so, when would that agreement become enforceable? It is not uncommon, for example for parties involved in lengthy or complex negotiations to arrive at an agreement on condition that it should be put into writing. The issue in such cases is whether a contract arises unless and until the condition is fulfilled. As a rule, if a term like "agreement to be reduced to writing" is used, the parties are merely stipulating in the agreement that what has already been agreed must be put into written form. Ultimately, it is a matter of timing. If the requirement of writing was there from the beginning and the objective intention of the parties was that no agreement would arise until it was met, then no contract arises until such event.

[22] See below, paras 2–65—2–68 and see JAK Huntley, "Commercial Practice and the Formation of Contracts: A Consensual Analysis" 1988 S.L.T. (News) 221.

In *Erskine v Glendinning*,[23] the defender offered by letter to lease certain corn and flour mills from the pursuer. The pursuer wrote, accepting "subject to lease drawn out in due form". The defender subsequently withdrew his offer and proposed new terms which the pursuer found unacceptable. The pursuer claimed that a contract had arisen from the letter.

The First Division found for the pursuer. The parties were, on the facts, agreed on the essentials and the effect of the term "subject to lease drawn out in due form" was not to import a condition into the acceptance. The phrase

> "did not require the offerer to consent to that, or the acceptor to stipulate for it. The landlord was entitled to require that his tenant should enter into formal lease whenever asked, embodying the terms of their contract".[24]

The effect of suspensive conditions on contract formation[25]

Erskine v Glendinning is very much a case that depends on its facts. In all other instances **3–30** where acceptance is conditional, the effect may be either that the parties are still at the stage of negotiation, or that the parties have entered into a contract subject to a suspensive condition. "Under a suspensive condition there is no debt until the event exists ... and yet the engagement cannot be defeated otherwise than by failure of the condition": Bell, *Principles*, s.47; "the granter of even (conditional obligations) has no right to resile": Erskine, *Principles*, III, I, 3).

The distinction between negotiations and a suspensive condition may be difficult to draw, but if the parties are still at the stage of negotiation, then neither party is contractually bound; whereas if they have reached agreement subject to a suspensive condition, a contract arises, although the obligation is suspended and contingent upon the condition being fulfilled, or purified. The parties to an agreement subject to a suspensive condition cannot resile from that agreement, although it is not enforceable unless and until the condition is fulfilled. Clearly, if the facts indicate that any understanding is subject to agreement on the essentials of the contract, no contract will have arisen.

In *Heiton v Waverley Hydropathic Co*,[26] the parties had been involved in lengthy negotiations over the proposed purchase by the pursuer of lands belonging to the defenders. Eventually, the defenders suggested that the pursuer draft the necessary documents for the sale, but added: "Of course until there be a *written acceptance* (of our terms) there cannot be a concluded sale" [emphasis added]. At all times, the issue of the buyer's rights over adjoining land belonging to the defenders remained unsettled. In due course, the defenders received, revised and returned to the pursuer his draft conveyance, with a letter stipulating that the defenders should have the opportunity of further reviewing the draft, "in case we have overlooked conditions which should be inserted in it". Although the pursuer had taken possession of the land, the shareholders of the seller company resolved that negotiations for the sale must cease.

The First Division rejected the pursuer's claim that a contract had arisen for the sale of the land. The parties' failure to agree upon the servitudes relating to the adjoining land prevented consensus from arising; but only Lord Shand expressed the view that since the pursuer had failed to accept in the method stipulated by the defenders, i.e. in writing, the offer to sell could be withdrawn.[27] There is no indication that the court placed any significance on the stipulation that the defenders should have a further opportunity to consider the draft conveyance.

An agreement may be subject to a suspensive condition where for example, it states that "this **3–31** agreement is to come into effect on January 1, 2016"; or that "this agreement will not come into

---

23 *Erskine v Glendinning* (1871) 9 M. 656.

24 *Erskine v Glendinning* (1871) 9 M. 656, per Lord President Inglis at 659.

25 See consideration of conditions generally below, paras 8–02, 8–03.

26 *Heiton v Waverley Hydropathic Co* (1877) 4 R. 830.

27 *Heiton v Waverley Hydropathic Co* (1877) 4 R. 830, at 842–843.

force unless the company is formed." In both cases, an agreement has come into being, but not into force.

In *Van Laun & Co v Neilson Reid & Co*,[28] the pursuer was instructed to arrange the amalgamation between the defenders and two other locomotive builders in Glasgow on the basis that the defenders would "enter into a proper legal contract when prepared with" the pursuer "for the purpose of placing in their hands the conduct of the amalgamation". The rate of remuneration was agreed.

No formal contract was ever executed, but the defenders nevertheless executed the amalgamation on lines suggested by the pursuer. The pursuer claimed his remuneration.

The First Division decided that no contract had arisen upon which the pursuer could base his claim, because no formal contract was executed. The court did not clearly state either that the parties had not reached a final agreement, or that the agreement was subject to a suspensive condition. The words used by Lord Kinnear suggest that he at least did not regard the condition as suspensive.[29] This merely restates the rule that a contract must be in writing where the parties so agree.

It is normal practice in England that offers to purchase land are accepted "subject to contract" that is subject to a formal contract for the sale of land in accordance with statutory requirements being duly executed. This and similar expressions in an acceptance mean that

> "the nature of that agreement was inchoate ... until a proper contract had been prepared concluded and executed there was no agreement at all".[30]

This device is less common in Scottish conveyancing practice, but it did arise in the following case.

3–32 **Stobo Ltd v Morrisons (Gowns) Ltd**

1949 S.C. 184

Court of Session, First Division: Lord President (Cooper), Lords Carmont, Keith and Russell

A landlord wished to sell two shops, one occupied by the defender and the other, 66 Renfield Street, Glasgow, by the pursuer. The arrangement was that the defender would purchase both shops and resell to the pursuer the shop which it occupied. The pursuer's offer to buy from the defender was accepted by the defender "subject to contract".

Having purchased both shops from the landlord, the defender now refused to implement the resale to the pursuer. The pursuer unsuccessfully brought an action for specific implement.

---

[28] *Van Laun & Co v Neilson Reid & Co* (1904) 6 F. 644.

[29] "Now the general rule of law is beyond question—that when parties see that their arrangements are to be embodied in a formal written contract to be executed there is a *locus poenitentiae* until the execution of that written document is completed, and either party may resile until the written document is completed, and either party may resile until the written instrument is executed": *Van Laun & Co v Neilson Reid & Co* (1904) 6 F. 644, at 652.

[30] *Chillingworth v Esche* [1924] 1 Ch. 97 per Pollock, MR.

"LORD PRESIDENT (COOPER): ... The real issue, and it is not an easy one, is whether the letters disclose a concluded agreement, and what effect is to be given to the words 'subject to contract'. 3–33

We were referred to a large number of English decisions dealing with sales and other contracts expressed to have been made 'subject to contract', 'subject to formal contract', or in other equivalent terms, and our attention was directed to the difficulty which Professor Gloag seemingly felt—*Contract* (2nd ed.), p.44—in reconciling these decisions with *Erskine v Glendinning*.[31] I have not derived much assistance from this line of approach. Many of the English decisions belong to the law and practice of vendor and purchaser with which we have no concern. It appears that according to that law and practice the phrases in question have acquired by long usage a technical meaning, approaching in definiteness the meaning attached in mercantile parlance to 'c.i.f.' or 'f.o.b.'—*Chillingworth v Esche*, at p.114[32]; *Keppel v Wheeler*, at p. 592.[33] That is certainly not true of Scots law and practice; for it is nearly eighty years since such an expression was judicially considered in this Court, and there is no evidence in our conveyancing works or style books to suggest that these formulas are normally employed in Scotland or that they have acquired with us any special meaning or efficacy ... Even if it be the case ... that in England it would now be held that the introduction of the phrase 'subject to contract' or one of its variants automatically excludes concluded agreement, I know of no such rule in Scots law. Further, I see no necessary conflict between the trend of the recent English cases and *Erskine v Glendinning* ... an acceptance cannot be read as subject to a suspensive condition merely because the acceptor puts into words what the law would imply as the method in which an agreement, *ex hypothesi* complete, would be carried into legal effect. It follows from that ratio not only that *Erskine v Glendinning* was, in my humble opinion, rightly decided, but that it is distinguishable ...

The only rules of Scots law which it appears to me to be possible to extract from past decisions and general principles are that it is perfectly possible for the parties to an apparent contract to provide that there shall be *locus poenitentiae* until the terms of their agreement have been reduced to a formal contract; but that the bare fact that the parties to a completed agreement stipulate that it shall be embodied in a formal contract does not necessarily import that they are still in the stage of negotiation. In each instance it is a matter of the construction of the correspondence in the light of the facts, proved or averred, on which side of the border line the case lies ...

When ... we examine the acceptance ... we find (a) that, though it covers adequately the cardinal points of the intended bargain, it is not exhaustive of details; (b) that, though it is sent in reply to a binding holograph offer, it is not itself probative; and (c) that it expressly bears to be conditional—the words 'subject to' being suggestive of suspense of commitment ... unless the words are to be given no meaning or effect whatever, I can only read them as a qualification of the acceptance ...

LORD KEITH: But for the words 'subject to contract' there is no doubt that the letters of 14th and 15th February 1947 would have formed complete, although improbative, missives of sale constituting an agreement on which *rei interventus* could be founded. The offer contains all the essentials necessary, if accepted, to instruct a sale of heritable property. The subjects are identified. The price and term of entry are stated. A basis is fixed for the allocation of the ground burdens ... These particulars of offer were accepted in terms, and ordinarily, if the letters were probative, or had been followed by *rei inteventus*, this would have been enough to have concluded the bargain. An 3–34

[31] 9 Macph. 656.
[32] [1924] 1 Ch. 97.
[33] [1927] 1 K.B. 557.

obligation on the seller to give a valid title and convey the subjects free of encumbrances would have been implied. In cases where circumstances required it, it would, no doubt, be proper to introduce into the missives other stipulations to meet the special circumstances ...

The present case seems to be such a case in which there were such special circumstances as might well have induced the seller to introduce special stipulations into the missives for consideration and acceptance by a prospective purchaser, and this consideration gives special force to the argument that the words 'subject to contract' were intended to suspend concluded agreement until some subsequent minute or agreement of sale was adjusted. I should hesitate to say that such words must in all cases be suspensive of agreement. If everything that was normally required by the circumstances had been agreed, I should be slow to hold that a loophole could thus be given to either party to escape from the conclusion that a completed bargain had been made. But in the present case an opposite conclusion can, in my opinion, be supported. These very words are discussed by so eminent an authority as the late Mr. Burns, in connexion with missives of sale of heritage (Greens Encyclopaedia, vol. xii, par. 368), and under reference to Scots authority, in terms that show that in the eye of a Scots conveyancer such words cannot safely be regarded as mere surplusage except possibly where the parties take the trouble to adopt the missives as holograph. In the present case only one of the missives has been adopted as holograph, and the one which has not been so adopted is the one that contains the words 'subject to contract.' This, in my opinion, gives added force to the contention that the words were suspensive of obligation, and, if so, there was no basis on which *rei interventus* could operate."

There is no clear indication in any of the judgments whether the phrase "subject to contract" was to be regarded as "a qualification of the acceptance" which prevented an agreement from arising or regarded as a suspensive condition (although in distinguishing *Erskine v Glendinning* Lord Cooper did state that "an agreement cannot be read subject to a suspensive condition merely because the acceptor puts into words what the law would imply as the method in which an agreement, *ex hypothesi* complete, would be carried into legal effect").[34] Lord Cooper's judgment permits both interpretations and although Lord Keith regarded the words as "suspensive of the obligation",[35] his judgment does not make it clear that this meant subject to a suspensive condition. It is suggested that since the court found *locus poenitentiae* as in the *Van Laun* case, and permitted the parties to resile, the case is inconsistent with the view that the contract was subject to a suspensive condition—no contract at all had in fact arisen.

Letter of intent

3–35 Similar problems arise when an offer is accepted subject to a "letter of intent". In certain trades, such as the construction industry, the purchaser or employer indicates to the supplier or subcontractor that work should commence, even though the details or specifications of the contract have not yet been worked out. The subcontractor may therefore be asked to begin work through such a letter, on the basis that a formal contract will subsequently be executed. As with an acceptance "subject to contract", the use of a letter of intent may render acceptance conditional upon the execution of a formal contract. Since such commercial communications are often on the basis of standard forms, it may be particularly difficult to establish the terms of such a putative contract.

---

[34] *Stobo Ltd v Morrisons (Gowns) Ltd*, 1949 S.C. 184, at 191.
[35] *Stobo Ltd v Morrisons (Gowns) Ltd*, 1949 S.C. 184, at 195.

British Steel Corporation v Cleveland Bridge and Engineering Co Ltd 3–36
[1984] 1 All E.R. 504
English High Court, Queen's Bench (Commercial Court): Robert Goff J

CBE had contracted to construct a building in Saudi Arabia. The design required steel beams to be joined to a steel frame by means of steel nodes. BSC, who were approached by CBE to produce a variety of cast-steel nodes for the project, drafted a price estimate based on incomplete information and sent it to CBE by telex on 9 February 1979. After further discussions on specifications and technical requirements, CBE sent a letter of intent to BSC on 21 February which: (1) recorded CBE's intention to enter into a contract with BSC for the supply of cast-steel nodes at the prices itemised in the telex of 9 February; (2) proposed that the contract be on CBE's standard form, which provided for unlimited liability on the part of BSC in the event of consequential loss due to late delivery; and (3) requested BSC to commence work immediately "[p]ending the preparation and issuing to you of the official form of sub-contract". BSC would not have agreed to CBE's standard form of contract and intended to submit a formal quotation once they had the requisite information.

BSC did not reply to the letter of intent since they expected a formal order to follow shortly and instead they went ahead with the manufacture of the nodes. CBE then indicated for the BSC first time that they required delivery in a particular sequence. There were further discussions on specifications but no final agreement was reached. The specifications were then changed extensively by CBE after the first castings proved to be unsatisfactory. On 16 May BSC sent CBE a formal quotation on their standard form, quoting a significantly higher price with delivery dates to be agreed. CBE rejected the quotation and again changed the specifications.

BSC went ahead with the manufacture and delivery of the nodes and eventually, at a meeting between the parties on 1 August, the parties reached provisional agreement on the basis of the quotation given on 16 May but they were unable to agree on other contract terms such as progress payments and liability for loss arising from late delivery. By 28 December all but one of the nodes had been delivered, delivery of the remaining node being held up until 11 April 1980 due to an industrial dispute at BSC's plant. CBE refused to make any interim or final payment for the nodes and instead sent a written claim for damages for late delivery or delivery of the nodes out of sequence. The amount claimed far exceeded the quoted price. BSC sued for the value of the nodes on a quantum meruit basis, contending, inter alia, that no binding contract had been entered into. CBE counterclaimed for damages for breach of contract for late delivery and delivery out of sequence and claimed a right of set-off, contending, inter alia, that a binding contract had been created by the various documents, especially the letter of intent, and by BSC's conduct in proceeding with the manufacture of the nodes and that BSC were entitled to a quantum meruit.

The judge found that no contract had arisen between the parties.

"ROBERT GOFF J: ... Now the question whether in a case such as the present any contract has come into existence must depend on a true construction of the relevant communications which have passed between the parties and the effect (if any) of their actions pursuant to those communications. There can be no hard and fast answer to the question whether a letter of intent will give rise to a binding agreement: everything must depend on the circumstances of the particular case ... 3–37

In my judgment, the true analysis of the situation is simply this. Both parties confidently expected a formal contract to eventuate. In these circumstances, to expedite performance under that anticipated contract, one requested the other to commence the contract work, and the other complied with that request. If thereafter, as anticipated, a contract was entered into, the work done as requested will be treated as having been performed under that contract; if, contrary to their expectation, no contract was entered into, then the performance of the work is not referable to any contract the terms of which can be ascertained, and the law simply imposes an obligation on the party who made the request to pay a reasonable sum for such work as has been done pursuant to that request, such an obligation sounding in quasi contract or, as we now say, in restitution. Consistently with that solution, the party making the request may find himself liable to pay for work which he would not have had to pay for as such if the anticipated contract had come into existence, e.g. preparatory work which will, if the contract is made, be allowed for in the price of the finished work (cf. *William Lacey (Hounslow) Ltd v Davis* ... [1957] 1 WLR 932). This solution moreover accords with authority: see the decision in *Lacey v Davis*, the decision of the Court of Appeal in *Sanders & Forster Ltd v A Monk & Co Ltd* [1980] CA Transcript 35, though that decision rested in part on a concession, and the crisp dictum of Parker J in *OTM Ltd v Hydranautics* [1981] 2 Lloyd's Rep 211 at 214, when he said of a letter of intent that 'its only effect would be to enable the defendants to recover on a quantum meruit for work done pursuant to the direction' contained in the letter. I only wish to add to this part of my judgment the footnote that, even if I had concluded that in the circumstances of the present case there was a contract between the parties and that that contract was of the kind I have described as an 'if' contract, then I would still have concluded that there was no obligation under that contract on the part of BSC to continue with or complete the contract work, and therefore no obligation on their part to complete the work within a reasonable time. However, my conclusion in the present case is that the parties never entered into any contract at all.

In the course of his argument counsel for BSC submitted that, in a contract of this kind, the price is always an essential term in the sense that, if it is not agreed, no contract can come into existence. In support of his contention counsel relied on a dictum of Lord Denning MR in *Courtney & Fairbairn Ltd v Tolaini Bros (Hotels) Ltd* [1975] 1 WLR 297 at 301 to the effect that the price in a building contract is of fundamental importance. I do not however read Lord Denning MR's dictum as stating that in every building contract the price is invariably an essential term, particularly as he expressly referred to the substantial size of the contract then before the court. No doubt in the vast majority of business transactions, particularly those of substantial size, the price will indeed be an essential term, but in the final analysis it must be a question of construction of the particular transaction whether it is so. This is plain from the familiar trilogy of cases which show that no hard and fast rule can be laid down but that the question in each case is whether, on a true construction of the relevant transaction, it was consistent with the intention of the parties that even though no price had been agreed a reasonable price should be paid (*May & Butcher Ltd v R* [1934] 2 KB 17 ... ; *Hillas & Co Ltd v Arcos Ltd*... [1932] All E.R. Rep. 494 and *Foley v Classique Coaches Ltd* [1934] 2 KB 1 ...). In the present case, however, I have no doubt whatsoever that, consistently with the view expressed by Lord Denning MR in *Courtney & Fairbairn Ltd v Tolaini Bros (Hotels) Ltd*, the price was indeed an essential term, on which (among other essential terms) no final agreement was ever reached."

After referring to the judgment of Robert Goff J, Lord Allanbridge in *Uniroyal v Miller* found that the use of the term "letter of intent follows" by the pursuers in their telephoned counter-offer was of no significance. Had it been, no contract would have arisen at least until the "letter of intent" had been sent, thereby providing the pursuers with the opportunity of inserting their terms into the contract.

Uniroyal Ltd v Miller & Co Ltd 3–38
1985 S.L.T. 101
Court of Session, Outer House: Lord Allanbridge

The facts are as stated on paras 3–27—3–28.

"LORD ALLANBRIDGE: ... I consider first what effect should be given to the words 'letter of intent follows'. In my view they must be regarded in their context. On 11 March 1976 the defenders had sent a quotation which, according to the parties' agreement by joint minute, quite clearly indicated that the quotation was subject to the conditions printed on the back of the form. The pursuers' telephoned order on 23 March 1976 was equally clearly based on that quotation. It refers to certain of its terms and in the pursuers' own pleadings it is stated that following on this quotation the pursuers telephoned an order. I consider it very significant that the pursuers' telephoned order made no reference to any conditions, or in particular, conditions of their own being imposed in this contract. The only way in which their order does not meet the quotation is in respect of a 'request' (the actual word used) for 'hardness to be near 484 DPN'. Therefore if the defenders met that request or counteroffer on this matter alone with all other matters such as price, specification and the like remaining the same, it could be said that consensus had then occurred on all essential matters. Put another way the pursuers were silent in their offer about the defenders' conditions attached to their quotation and must be presumed to have accepted them in the absence of any contrary expression of intention. Having considered the matter as best I can, I am not persuaded that the insertion of the words 'letter of intent follows' can be said to indicate that the pursuers did not accept the defenders' conditions or at least reserved the right to reject them and possibly impose their own conditions on the contract, or at the very least indicated that no contract at all would be completed until at earliest the 'letter of intent' was sent. I can well appreciate that if the pursuers had used clear words to indicate no contract could be agreed or completed until, for example, they had sent their standard and printed purchase order, the situation would be entirely different. But that is not what the pursuers said. They simply indicated that what they describe as a 'letter of intent' would follow. It may be of some limited assistance to consider the legal effect of what is described as a 'letter of intent'. If a 'letter of intent' can be rescinded at any time, as suggested by junior counsel for the pursuers with reference to the case of *A & G Paterson Ltd*, then the use of such words suggests that a letter will follow which cannot and would not create a contract at all. The pursuers, of course, accept that approach and argue that in fact the letter of intent had no effect when it did arrive but merely postponed negotiations until the purchase order was issued. My own view on the effect of a 'letter of intent' would be to agree with Goff J.'s observations in the very recent case of *British Steel Corporation* that there can be no hard and fast answer to the question whether a letter of intent would give rise to a binding agreement; everything depends on the circumstances of the particular case. If that is correct then at best for the pursuers what they were in effect saying was that a letter will follow which may or may not affect this telephoned order for supply of the defenders' rolls. That in my view is not a very clear way of indicating that a contract was still being 'negotiated'. I stress the word 'negotiated' because that word was repeatedly and understandably used by counsel for the pursuers. In essence what they are saying is that inter alia the conditions of contract remained to be negotiated and had not been accepted by the pursuers. It may not be without significance that if that be the case the only form these negotiations were to take was that the pursuers would eventually send their purchase order and if the defenders did nothing further (as in fact happened) the pursuers would then argue (as they do) that the contract is to be found only in that purchase order followed by performance by the defenders which indicated acceptance of the purchase order. Such one-sided actions do not seem apt to be described as 'negotiations'."

3–39 In certain trades, such as the construction industry, the purchaser or employer indicates to the supplier that work should commence, even though the details, or specifications, of the contract have not yet been worked out. They may therefore be asked to begin work through such a letter, on the basis that a formal contract will subsequently be executed. As with an acceptance "subject to contract", the use of a letter of intent may render acceptance conditional upon the execution of a formal contract. Since, as has been stated, such commercial communications are often on the basis of standard forms, it may be particularly difficult to establish the terms of such a putative contract.

A vital issue in such cases will be whether the letter of intent operates as a suspensive condition (rather like the term "subject to contract") so that a contract arises between the parties, or whether the letter indicates that the parties are still in the process of negotiation. For example, on the facts in *Uniroyal Ltd v Miller & Co Ltd*, considered above, at para.3–27, it is at least arguable that the effect of the phrase was to operate as a suspensive condition. This would mean that, although the contract had been finally settled by the time of the defenders' acknowledgment of 23 March 1976, its operation was suspended until the suspensive condition was purified by the pursuers' letter of 26 March, which confirmed the telephone order and which stated "please accept in the meantime this correspondence as our letter of intent to purchase the items previously specified herein". The effect of this letter would have been to bring the contract into operation at a time when no reference had been made by either party to the pursuers' terms and conditions. The result for the parties in the case should not have been different; but in other cases it may be vital to establish the point at which the contract comes into operation, so that the terms of the contract can be established. The ultimate issue is whether the use of such a device indicates that the parties are still negotiating, or whether they have suspended the operation of their obligations until the contract documentation is finalised. It is not enough simply to say that the letter is or is not a counteroffer.[36] Alternatively, the letter of intent may be a unilateral promise to enter into a contract.[37]

The costs of pre-contractual negotiations

3–40 As we have seen, contractual negotiations, especially in commercial contracts are often protracted and therefore costly. We have also seen that it may be possible, under the terms of an implied contract or a promise, for the parties to allocate the costs of negotiations (see above, Ch.1). These costs, as the cases illustrate, can be significant. The question is whether, absent such contractual or promise liability there is a general obligation on the party who wrongly breaks off negotiations to recompense the other party for the losses incurred. Such liability is common in other civilian jurisdictions as a matter of good faith. Such liability is recognised by DCFR, II.–3:301. Whether Scots law incorporates such a principle came under judicial comment in *Dawson*. What follows is a comment that attempts to rationalise the basis for such liability in Scots law.

---

[36] See generally JAK Huntley, "Conditional Acceptance and Letters of Intent", 1990 S.L.T. (News) 121.

[37] See above, see para.1–97 onwards.

[38]*Good Faith in the Scots Law of Contract: an Undisclosed Principle?* 3–41

HL MacQueen

ADM Forte (ed), *Good Faith in Contract and Property* (1999), pp.5–37

"The following sections of this essay seek to elucidate another area of Scots law in which the recognition of the underlying principle of good faith might assist in the development from a rather incoherent and difficult body of cases of a set of rules dealing with a hitherto unrecognised problem, namely the legal effect of pre-contractual negotiations not involving any of the traditional bases of invalidity and liability such as misrepresentation, fraud or force. In other words, can Scots law, like German law before it, use the doctrine of good faith to develop rules on *culpa in contrahendo*?

That there is a problem in this field needing to be addressed is suggested by stories in the Scottish press concerned with failed negotiations in the domestic housing market. Under Scots law, contracts for the sale of heritable property must be in formal writing: a requirement which in normal practice is met by the prospective purchaser submitting a written offer and receiving the seller's written acceptance. Usually the seller has several offers from which to choose. The seller's formal acceptance of the preferred bid is often preceded by a verbal intimation of success to the selected bidder. However, this may be followed by a game of 'missives tennis' in which the buyer's offer is formally met with a qualified, not a full, acceptance, thereby initiating what can be a protracted exchange of counter-offers between the parties, during which there is no concluded contract unless one or other side gives an unqualified acceptance of an offer open for the purpose.[39] In the recently reported stories, a seller who had made a verbal intimation of acceptance to one buyer then received another, higher offer from a third party, with whom a formal contract was subsequently concluded. The general understanding was that in these circumstances the disappointed offeror had no legal remedy, since no contract had been concluded by the purely verbal statement of the seller. However, the Law Society of Scotland declared that the seller's advisers had acted unprofessionally in countenancing his behaviour, and adverse comment was also made in the media.[40] Is it really the case that Scots law tolerates conduct of this kind in the name of freedom to negotiate and freedom to withdraw from negotiations which have not yet reached the stage of contract? Can an obligation to negotiate in good faith provide a solution to the problem?

Culpa in Contrahendo 3–42

In the English House of Lords decision *Walford v Miles*,[41] Lord Ackner remarked:

'The concept of a duty to carryon negotiations in good faith is inherently repugnant to the adversarial position of the parties when involved in negotiations. Each party to the negotiations is entitled to pursue his (or her) own interest, so long as he avoids making misrepresentations. To advance that interest he must be entitled, if he thinks it appropriate, to threaten to withdraw from further negotiations or to withdraw in fact in the hope that the opposite party may seek to reopen the negotiations by offering him improved terms … [H]ow is a vendor ever to know that he is entitled to withdraw from further negotiations? How is the court to police such an "agreement"? A duty to negotiate in good faith is as unworkable in practice as it is inherently inconsistent with the position of a negotiating party … In my judgment, while negotiations are in

---

[39] See, for example, *Rutterford Ltd v Allied Breweries*, 1990 S.L.T. 249; *Findlater v Maan*, 1990 S.C. 150.

[40] *The Scotsman*, August 27, 1998 ("Couple Threaten to Sue over Gazumping").

[41] [1992] 2 A.C. 128.

existence either party is entitled to withdraw from these negotiations, at any time and for any reason. There can be thus no obligation to continue to negotiate until there is a "proper reason" to withdraw.'[42]

These remarks were greeted with horror on the Continent, as a classic example of how irreconcilably different English law is from the codified systems.[43] Continental lawyers, especially those in the Germanic tradition, regard the obligation to negotiate in good faith as a fundamental instance of the general principle of good faith.[44] In Germany the concept of *culpa in contrahendo*, first developed by Rudolf von Ihering in the nineteenth century,[45] is now said to mean that: 'a party who negligently nourishes in the other party the hope that a contract will come about, although this is unfounded from an objective viewpoint, must make compensation for any outlay which the opposite party could have regarded as necessary under the circumstances'.[46]

...

It is thus not surprising to find the following in the forthcoming text of the Principles of European Contract Law [Art.2.301: negotiations contrary to good faith].[47]

3–43 **Scots Law on Pre-contractual Liability**

A Scots law student asked about liability for pre-contractual negotiations would most likely agree with Lord Ackner and say that, some basic points apart, there is none.[48] The general rules are that parties negotiating a contract are at arms' length in the sense that each has to look after its own interests, and there are no obligations to the other party short of not telling lies (misrepresentation), practising deception (fraud), coercing the other party into entering the contract (force and fear), or exploiting a special relationship one has with the other party quite separately from the contract under negotiation (undue influence). If any of these factors is present in negotiations which lead to an apparent contract, then that contract may be either void or voidable, with obligations of unjustified enrichment or restitution arising in respect of any performance which may have been rendered prior to the discovery of the flaw in the lead-up to the contract.[49] Insofar as the perpetration of the flaw in the negotiations may also have been a civil wrong, there can be delictual liability, of which the most important examples in practice are negligent misrepresentation under section 10 of the Law Reform (Miscellaneous Provisions)

---

[42] *Ibid.* at 138.

[43] See in particular the comparative commentaries in (1994) 2 *European Review of Private Law* 267–327.

[44] See generally, F. Kessler, E. Fine, "Culpa In Contrahendo, Bargaining in Good Faith, and Freedom of Contract: a Comparative Study" (1964) 7 *Harvard Law Review* 401; E.H. Hondius (ed.), *Precontractual Liability: Reports to the XIIIth Congress International Academy of Comparative Law* (Deventer, Boston, 1991); N. Cohen, "Pre-contractual Duties: Two Freedoms and the Contract to Negotiate" in Beatson and Friedmann (eds), [above, note 55], pp.25–56; Kotz, ["Towards a European Civil code: The Duty of Good Faith" in P. Cane, J. Stapleton (eds.), *The Law of Obligations: Essays in Celebration of John Fleming* (Oxford, 1998)], pp.34–41; S. Van Erp, "The Pre-contractual Stage" in Hartkamp *et al.*

[45] In a famous article entitled "Culpa in contrahendo oder Schadensersatz bei nichtigen oder nicht zu perfektionen gelangten Vertragen", *Jahrbücher für die Dogmatik des heutigen römischen und deutschen Privatrechts* (1861) Vol. iv, 1–113. As far as I know this article has never been translated into English.

[46] Markesinis *et al*, [*The German Law of Obligations* Vol.I: The Law of Contract and Restitution: A Comparative Introduction (Oxford, 1997)].

[47] The wording here is virtually identical to that of the UNIDROIT *Principles of International Commercial Contracts* (1994), Art.2.15.

[48] Note, however, T.B. Smith's undeveloped suggestion, ..., that although "this doctrine of *culpa in contrahendo* ... has yet to be considered fully by the Scottish courts ... there are, however, straws to be clutched at".

[49] See McBryde, *Contract*, Chs 9–12; *Stair Memorial Encyclopaedia*, vol. 15, paras 670–94.

(Scotland) Act 1985 and fraud at common law.[50] Again, where negotiations break down, but there has been some preceding transfer of value between the parties, then an obligation to restore any benefits received may arise under the rules of unjustified enrichment. ...

These basic rules, and the way in which they operate in practice, seem consistent with the ideals and values of a market economy in which each participant looks after the advancement of its own interests and does not have to be concerned with the position and interests of the other party. Yet what I have found over the years is that these basic rules are not necessarily consistent with how the players in the market place actually conduct the game of negotiating and concluding contracts. ...

What is ... clear ... from ... the reported cases, is that the real world does not quite fit into a legal model in which negotiations take place, a contract is formed, and then and only then do the parties commence the performance which the contract requires. In many commercial situations time does not allow for such dalliance: negotiations and performance go together, perhaps with an expectation that the formal contract to be concluded in due course will have retrospective effect. It may even be that the parties never make use of formal written contracts and pursue an entirely informal relationship in which negotiations, performance and contract are almost indistinguishable. Cases of these kinds have often come before the Scottish courts and, in at least some, the outcome has not been consistent with the legal model so far discussed of parties at arms' length, entitled to look after their own interests only and to ignore those of the other party without incurring liability as a result. In some the court has found that a contract has come into existence despite the continuation of negotiations.[51] Equally, where there has been a transfer of value between the parties but there is no contract, the party suffering loss in the transfer, for example, through payment or performance ahead of conclusion of the contract may well have a claim in unjustified enrichment.[52]

But some other cases, involving successful claims for wasted pre-contractual expenditure without either delictual wrong by or enrichment of the other party, have caused great difficulties of analysis for commentators, since they do not fit easily into the traditional categories of the law of obligations.[53] However, an analysis of these difficult **3–44**

[50] See *Stair Memorial Encyclopaedia*, vol. 11, paras 701–89.

[51] A recent example is *Avintair Ltd v Ryder Airline Services Ltd*, 1994 S.C. 270. See H.L. MacQueen, "Contract, Unjustified Enrichment and Concurrent Liability" (1997) *Acta Juridica* 176, pp.188–189.

[52] For two modern examples of (unsuccessful) enrichment claims in respect of pre-contractual activity, see *Microwave Systems (Scotland) Ltd v Electro-Physiological Instruments Ltd*, 1971 S.C. 140; *Site Preparations Ltd v Secretary of State for Scotland*, 1975 S.L.T. (Notes) 41.

[53] See Gloag, *Contract*, pp.19–20, 176–177 (favouring a basically contractual explanation); D.I. Ashton-Cross, "The Scots Law Regarding Actions of Reparation Based on False Statements", 1951 J.R. 199 (favouring a reparation explanation); and W.J. Stewart, *The Law of Restitution in Scotland* (Edinburgh, 1992), paras 10.1–10.9 (Melville Monument liability: "doubtfully restitutionary but sufficiently 'quasi-contractual' to appear in any examination of restitutionary obligations" (para.10.1).) Stewart also suggests (para.10.8) that these cases may be examples of restitution for wrongs. With respect, it is difficult in many of them to see either restitution or wrongs. I have discussed the cases as a possible application of a concept of "unjust sacrifice" or "unjustified impoverishment" in an unpublished section of a paper on unjustified enrichment and contract delivered at a seminar mounted jointly by the Scottish Law Commission and the Universities of Edinburgh and Strathclyde on October 21, 1993. For "unjust sacrifice" see S.J. Stoljar, "Unjust Enrichment and Unjust Sacrifice" (1987) 50 M.L.R. 603; G. Muir, "Unjust Sacrifice and the Officious Intervener" in P. Finn (ed.), *Essays in Restitution* (Sydney, 1990). For criticism see P. Birks, *Restitution: The Future* (Sydney, 1992), pp.100–105; A. Burrows, *The Law of Restitution* (London, 1993), pp.4–6, 299.

cases as the application of the concept of good faith to pre-contractual negotiations yields interesting results.

The foundation authority is the Melville Monument case, *Walker v Milne*.[54] Walker owned the estate of Coates and he and his father developed the New Town in the West End of Edinburgh in the area which now embraces St Mary's Cathedral, Coates Crescent, Walker Street and Melville Street (the last two having a particularly striking intersection designed by Gillespie Graham). In this intersection (I suspect) there was to be located a monument to Viscount Melville, paid for by subscribers led by Milne. With Walker's permission, the subscribers entered the lands of Coates, broke it up and carried out operations which disrupted Walker's feuing plans on his estate. The subscribers then took their monument off to St Andrews Square, where it stands to this day. Walker sued for breach of contract. Milne defended on the basis that, as the alleged agreement related to heritage and was not in writing, he enjoyed *locus poenitentiae* and could not be liable. The Lord Ordinary upheld this argument. But the Inner House, although they agreed with the judge that no effectual contract had been concluded, held, *inter alia*, that the pursuer was entitled to be indemnified for any loss and damage he might have sustained and for the expenses incurred in consequence of the alteration of the site of the monument.

The court plainly did not see this as either a contractual or an enrichment case; but it is also not clear that it was one of reparation for wrongdoing. It seems rather to fit quite nicely into the concept of *culpa in contrahendo*, inasmuch as the subscribers took their decision unilaterally rather than as a result of disagreement about terms; the bargain being substantially settled, their abandonment of Coates in favour of St Andrews Square was contrary to good faith. Moreover, the court's award of damages was based upon what in Continental systems is known as the 'negative interest', that is to say, what the pursuer had expended upon the faith of the bargain, rather than upon his 'positive interest', namely the position he would have been in had the arrangement been carried through to contractual completion.

3–45 There is, of course, a link with contract in *Walker*, inasmuch as the reason why the contract 'failed to materialise' was a result of the rules about writing in contracts relating to land, rather than because the parties were not agreed in substance. These rules have played an important part in the development of the Scots law relating to anticipated but nonmaterialising contracts, because, as will be seen below, in many of the cases where recovery has been allowed, all that has stood between the facts and the conclusion that a contract exists is the requirement of writing. The key point in *Walker*, thinking about when it is contrary to good faith to break off a pre-contractual relationship, is that negotiations were essentially complete, making it reasonable to assume that the formalities would be carried through.

Walker v Milne was used in a number of subsequent cases in the nineteenth century . . .

. . . To summarise the principles to be drawn from these cases is far from easy. In most of them it could be said that the parties had reached (or at least averred) an agreement, which was not contractual only because some other legal rule about the constitution and proof of contracts stood in the way.[55] At one level, then, these cases are not about anticipated contracts so much as about agreements which are only non-contractual for technical reasons. Further, the cases are not about the recovery of enrichment (although in some there was undoubtedly an enrichment element). Instead the pursuer is reimbursed or indemnified against expenditure incurred on the faith of the non-contractual agreement, although in none of the cases had this expenditure been made to the defender. In some of them—*Walker v Milne* is the prime example—a claim for other loss

[54] (1823) 2 S. 379.

[55] See also Gloag, *Contract*, p.19.

is also allowed. The injustice of the situation of the pursuer seems to arise from the other side's unilateral withdrawal from arrangements which could reasonably have been regarded as settled.

Restriction of the scope of *Walker v Milne* began in 1875, with the decision of *Allan* v. *Gilchrist*[56] in which the court declared that it did not give rise to a principle of general application ...

Gloag regarded *Gilchrist v Whyte* as the leading case on the whole subject, and commented that it had disapproved earlier decisions, as well as noting that 'it is not easy to see any legal principle on which liability can be imposed when nothing is averred beyond an expression of intention'.[57] He explained *Bell v Bell* on the ground of fraud and recompense.[58] He accepted that starting with *Walker v Milne*: **3–46**

> '[T]here is a good deal of authority for the contention that [where A, in circumstances where it is impossible to suggest fraud, has resiled from a verbal agreement after B has been led to incur expenditure, but expenditure in no wise beneficial to A], A is bound to meet the expenditure B has incurred.'[59]

Gloag went on to note, however, that this was not a general principle. The latest cases confirm the narrow approach to *Walker v Milne*. In *Dawson International plc v Coats Paton plc*[60] two companies were negotiating a merger whereby Dawson would purchase Coats Paton's shares. This also included a 'lock-out' arrangement under which Coats Paton would not encourage third party bids.[61] Dawson incurred expense in preparing offer documentation. A third party bid materialised, with which Coats Paton co-operated, and which was ultimately successful. Dawson claimed unwarrantable and reckless misrepresentations by Coats and sought reimbursement of their expenditure. The claim failed. In an impressive opinion later approved by the First Division, Lord Cullen gave detailed consideration to all the authorities from *Walker* v. *Milne* onward.[62] He held that this was an exceptional branch of the law and that any tendency to expand its scope should be discouraged. It was equitable in nature and not dependent upon contract, recompense or delict for its concepts. He continued:

> 'Having reviewed the cases in this field to which I was referred I am not satisfied that they provide authority for reimbursement of expenditure by one party occasioned by the representations of another beyond *the case where the former acted in reliance on the implied assurance by the latter that there was a binding contract between them when in fact there was no more than an agreement which fell short of being a binding contract* ... I should add that I consider that there are sound reasons for not extending the remedy to the case where the parties did not reach an agreement. It is clear that *the law does not favour the recovery of expenditure made merely in the hope or expectation of agreement being entered into or of a stated intention being fulfilled* [emphasis added].'[63]

---

[56] See above.
[57] See [Gloag, *Contract*], p.19.
[58] *ibid*, 176–177.
[59] See [Gloag, *Contract*], p.177.
[60] 1988 S.L.T. 854. Lord Cullen's opinion was affirmed in the Inner House: see 1989 S.L.T. 655. At a later stage it was held by Lord Prosser that the negotiations had not given rise to a contract between the parties (1993 S.L.T. 80).
[61] *Cf. Walford v Miles* [1992] 2 A.C. 128.
[62] See 862K ff.
[63] 1988 S.L.T. 854, at 866.

A key concept here is that of the "implied assurance" of the binding contract when there was no more than an agreement falling short of being a contract. In other words, claims did not depend upon misrepresentation, at least in the conventional sense of a positive statement.

3–47 Lord Cullen's analysis was applied in *Bank of Scotland v 3i PLC*.[64] The bank made a loan to a company which subsequently went into receivership. The bank sued 3i in respect of a representation that it had provided financial accommodation to the company. The claims were for (1) damages for negligent misrepresentation and (2) reimbursement of expenditure. Both claims failed. Lord Cameron of Lochbroom said of the reimbursement claim: 'There is no suggestion that the pursuers acted in reliance on an implied assurance by the defenders that there was a binding contract between them when, in fact, there was no more than an agreement which fell short of being a binding agreement ... In addition, there is a second and, in my opinion, equally conclusive answer to the pursuers' case on this head. The remedy given by the court is an equitable one and is only available in limited circumstances ... I agree with Lord Cullen where he says (1988 SLT at p. 865K–L), "I should also add that in the present state of the law I see no need for a court to resort to an equitable remedy to deal with a case in which one party has by means of a representation which is in *mala fides* or fraudulent misled another into incurring expenditure or suffering other loss. The law of delict provides a remedy for fraudulent misrepresentation. It also covers negligent misrepresentation, including where the latter has given rise to the making of a contract. See s 10 of the Law Reform (Miscellaneous Provisions) (Scotland) Act 1985".[65] The claim for reimbursement proceeding upon exactly the same facts as that for delictual misrepresentation, it should be rejected.'

With the opinions of both Lord Cullen and Lord Cameron of Lochbroom, therefore, quite clear limits are drawn upon the remedy of reimbursement in Scots law, including the notion that it is excluded by facts (i.e., fraudulent or negligent misrepresentation) giving rise to the alternative of a delictual remedy. However, while each opinion is in the negative for the *application* of the remedy in the particular circumstances, neither denies its *existence*, and the analysis by Lord Cullen in particular clearly shows its separation from the established concepts of contract, delict and enrichment. The idea of an expenditure-based liability arising from an 'implied assurance' that an agreement was a binding contract seems perfectly consistent with an overall basis in good faith, while at the same time manifesting the tendency of Scots law to concretise that concept in carefully defined rules. In this connection, however, the emphasis on the 'equitable' nature of the liability carries with it the risk of a perception, perhaps not wholly avoided in Lord Cameron's opinion, that it can be used only when there is no other remedy 'at law': i.e., instead of understanding that the principles of the law are suffused with, and based upon, equity; the position, it is submitted, of Stair and of Scots law in general.[66]

---

[64] 1990 S.C. 215.

[65] *ibid.* at 225.

[66] I find attractive and helpful the recent analysis of this subject in E. Örücü, "Equity in the Scottish Legal System" in Rabello (ed.), [*Aequitas and Equity: Equity in Civil Law and Mixed Jurisdictions* (Jerusalem, 1997)], pp.383–394. For other recent views, see J.M. Thomson, "The Role of Equity in Scots law" in S. Goldstein (ed.), *Equity and Contemporary Legal Development* (Jerusalem, 1992); *Stair Memorial Encyclopaedia* (1987), vol.22, paras 394–432.

These authorities nevertheless support an argument that, in the type of case which provided our point of departure for a discussion of *culpa in contrahendo* in Scots law, the seller of heritable property who verbally accepts a formal offer and then withdraws from the arrangement could at least be liable for the wasted expenditure of the disappointed offeror. There is an agreement which, however, falls short of a binding contract, and an assurance that there is a contract can surely be readily implied in the circumstances, given most people's ignorance of the law's requirements for contracts for the sale of land. The only question is how much of the offeror's wasted expenditure might be recoverable? Would it extend to the surveyor's fees, for example? Or would it cover only expenditure incurred after the conclusion of the informal agreement? Would there be an element for foregone opportunities to purchase another property?

On the basis stated by Lord Cullen, however, a Scottish court would probably have reached the same result as Rattee J in the recent English case, *Regalian Properties plc v London Dockland Development Corporation.*[67] An agreement to build a residential development in London Docklands was 'subject to contract' while the parties negotiated about details for over two years between 1986 and 1988. Regalian, who were the contractors, spent three million pounds on the project, although none of this went directly to LDDC. By the end of the period the housing market had collapsed and LDDC, realising that the original arrangement had ceased to be commercially viable, withdrew after attempts to renegotiate. Rattee J held that parties making arrangements "subject to contract" took the risk that if no contract was ultimately concluded any losses would lie where they fell. Regalian had undertaken the expenditure for their own benefit and LDDC had not been enriched thereby. 3–48

The failure of the negotiations was due to genuine disagreement about price. Now the phrase 'subject to contract' has no special magic in Scots law, unlike English law, but where, as here, its use manifests an intention of the parties that their agreement should not have contractual force, the Scottish courts will give effect to that intention.[68] Thus there is no question on *Regalian-type* facts of any implied assurance that the agreement was a binding contract, and so no possibility that the expenditure of the contractors could be recouped by way of *Walker v Milne.*[69]

Conclusion ... 3–49

The comparison of Scots law with the *Principles of European Contract Law* is also of interest. The *Principles* begin with the proposition that parties are free to negotiate and are, in general, not liable for failure to conclude a contract. This is the Scottish position too. For over a hundred years, courts and text writers have said that *Walker* v. *Milne* does not give rise to a general principle, but is rather an equitable exception to the general rule; by implication, that general rule is one of no pre-contractual liability. This is perhaps most explicit in Lord Cullen's observation in *Dawson International plc v Coats Paton plc,* that 'the law does not favour the recovery of expenditure made merely in the hope or expectation of agreement being entered into or of a stated intention being fulfilled'.[70] Such a starting point seems entirely consistent with the values and policies which underlie a market economy: each person must look after its own interests and if

[67] [1995] 1 All E.R. 1005 (Rattee J). The result but not the reasoning is approved by E. McKendrick, "Negotiations Subject to Contract and the Law of Restitution" [1995] 3 Restitution Law Review 100.
[68] *Erskine v Glendinning* (1871) 9 M. 656; *Stobo Ltd v Morrisons (Gowns) Ltd*, 1949 S.C. 184.
[69] A similar conclusion would probably arise in *Walford v Miles* where the agreement to sell the business was likewise "subject to contract".
[70] 1988 S.L.T. 854 at 866D–E.

risks are taken on the basis of hopes or expectations not resting upon a contractual base, then the loss must lie where it falls in the absence of wrongdoing by the other party.

Having freedom to negotiate and to break off negotiations unless there is some special factor explains why, for example, a party inviting bids or tenders from a number of other parties is not liable for the expenses of the unsuccessful tenderers or bidders. Unless the invitor's conduct has reasonably induced other expectations, the competing offerors assume the risk of failure and there is no breach of good faith in leaving the losses where they fall. It is important to remember Finn's point that good faith does not involve the complete protection of the other party's interests at the expense of one's own, and that in this it is to be distinguished from a fiduciary obligation.

However, Article 2:301 of the European Principles states the exception to the general rule of freedom to give up negotiations in much wider terms than have so far emerged in Scots law. The exception rests squarely on the principle of good faith and is exemplified (although not exhausted) by entry into or continuation of negotiations without any real intention of concluding a contract thereby. In contrast, Lord Cullen's theory of pre-contractual liability depends upon there being an 'implied assurance' that an *agreement* already reached is a binding contract. If we recognise, as it is submitted we must, that this rests upon the principle of good faith in contracting, is it possible to take that principle as a basis for further extensions of Scots law in this field?

We may begin with the specific example of bad faith given in Article 2:301 of the European Principles, the problem of negotiations which amount to no more than 'stringing along'; that is, unknown to one of the negotiating parties, A, the other, B, has no intention of ever forming a contract. B's reason for appearing to enter into negotiations is an effort to force a third party, C, with whom B does intend to contract to make a better offer than C would otherwise have been prepared to do. When an acceptable offer is made to B by C, negotiations with A are dropped. In a number of jurisdictions, A will have a claim against B in such circumstances by which at least reliance losses will be recoverable[71]; but in Scotland, under the current understanding of *Walker* v. *Milne*, A would have no recovery, since there is no implied assurance that there is a binding agreement.

A variety of cases from around the world raise further questions about the limitations which have so far been placed upon the Scots law of pre-contractual liability . . .

There are other cases where it is reasonably clear that there was no agreement and no implied assurance that there was a contract, yet there was enough to suggest that there would be a contractual agreement in the reasonably near future after some further negotiation. The best example is the 'letter of intent' by which a party will signal to one of a group of tenderers or bidders for a contract that he now intends to enter a contract with that party although the tender/bid is not to be accepted without further negotiation. The purpose of the letter of intent is to allow the chosen party to commence preparation for the contract, and it is not unusual for preparation to pass on to performance before the contract is concluded. Typically the letter of intent will provide that such work will be paid for at the contract price once agreed.[72] But suppose the contract is never concluded because the negotiations are unsuccessful. What, if any, claims may be made by the recipient of the letter of intent? Now where the performance involves a transfer of value to the party who has issued the letter of intent, the solution may well lie in

---

[71] For example, see the French decision of 1972 discussed in *Nicholas*, n.[52] above, pp.70–71; *Hoffmann v Red Owl Stores* (1965) 133 N.W. (2d) 267 (USA); *Walton Stores (Interstate) Ltd v Maher* (1988) 164 C.L.R. 387 (Australia).

[72] On letters of intent and the legal difficulties to which they give rise see S.N. Ball, "Work Carried Out in Pursuance of Letters of Intent-Contract or Restitution?" (1983) 99 L.Q.R. 572; M.P. Furmston, J. Poole, T. Norisada, *Contract Formation and Letters of Intent* (Chichester, 1998).

unjustified enrichment.[73] If, however, there is no transfer of value but only reliance expenditure by the recipient of the letter, enrichment solutions may not be available or appropriate to cover the loss. As I have argued elsewhere, Scots law could here call upon its doctrine of unilateral promise, giving the letter obligatory effect and implying some sort of reasonable payment for the recipient's wasted work.[74] But given that letters of intent are often expressly not intended to have obligatory effect, the promise analysis may be rather forced. An approach based on good faith, allowing recovery of justified reliance or the 'negative interest', is perhaps more attractive and avoids the need for strained construction and the implication of terms based, however artificially, upon the intention of the party issuing the letter of intent.

Another interesting situation can be illustrated from the English case of *Blackpool & Fylde Aero Club Ltd v Blackpool Borough Council*.[75] The Council invited tenders for a contract in a document which set out the procedure which it would follow in considering the tenders received. The Court of Appeal held that the Council was liable in damages to an unsuccessful tenderer for having failed to follow this procedure, but left unclear whether this was a matter of tort or of contract. The decision seems unquestionably right, but the judgments reveal the relative conceptual limits of the English law of obligations. A Scots lawyer might approach this case, not through a contractual or delictual, but rather through a promissory route.[76] But if this is thought artificial or to involve strained construction of the invitation to tender, then a wider concept of good faith might provide a better solution. This would undoubtedly go further than anything found in Lord Cullen's opinion in *Dawson International plc v Coats Paton plc*. Again there is no real question of agreements and implied assurances that a binding contract exists. The contract, if it is going to come into existence at all, is not assured to any particular party."[77]

---

[73] As in *British Steel Corporation v Cleveland Bridge and Engineering Co Ltd* [1984] 1 All E.R. 504. See further E. McKendrick, "The Battle of the Forms and the Law of Restitution" (1988) 8 O.J.L.S. 197.

[74] H.L. MacQueen, "Constitution and Proof of Gratuitous Obligations", 1986 S.L.T. (News) 1, 3–4.

[75] [1990] 1 W.L.R. 1995. The case has recently been followed by Finn J of the Federal Court of Australia in *Hughes Aircraft Systems International v Air Services Australia* (1997) 146 A.L.R. 1; noted by M.P. Furmston (1998) 114 L.Q.R. 362.

[76] The concept of promise might also be the way in which Scots law would solve such famous "difficult" cases as *Hoffman v Red Owl Stores* and *Walton Stores (Interstate) Ltd v Maher*.

[77] Note that it is common for invitations to tender of the kind under consideration here to provide that the invitor is not bound to accept the highest or lowest (as the case may be) or indeed any offer that may be made.

CHAPTER 4

THE NEED FOR COMMUNICATION

In the previous two chapters we considered what is necessary to establish an agreement between the parties. Implicit in this is that the parties have actually communicated. The offerer will have communicated the offer to the offeree, and the offeree will have responded with an acceptance of that offer. In practice, communications between the parties can raise many problems. When, for example, must acceptance be communicated to be effective? What degree of communication is necessary? What method of communication must be used, or are the parties free to choose? Is every form of communication equally effective? If the offerer wishes to withdraw an offer, is the offerer free to do so and when should such withdrawal be effective? As Professor McBryde suggests: **4–01**

> "Instead of saying that acceptance must be communicated, it may be more accurate to state that the offeree must go beyond the deliberative stage. What is required is (1) intention to accept, followed by (2) actions showing the intention to be irrevocable."[1]

Acceptance must be communicated while the offer subsists

For a contract to arise, each party must know that the other knows and accepts the terms of the agreement. A court will not enforce some abstract "meeting of minds"; it demands evidence that the parties had struck a bargain. In practical terms, this means evidence that the offeree communicated acceptance of the offer to the offerer. **4–02**

To show communication, three things are essential:

(a) a sufficient degree of communication of the acceptance;
(b) communication in the appropriate mode; and
(c) communication while the offer subsists.

Sufficiency of communication: notice

The crucial factor is knowledge in the offerer. Although special considerations apply to the communication of acceptance through the post, the general rule, whether the parties are dealing face to face or at a distance, is that the contract is made when the acceptance is received by the offerer and thereby has notice of it. The position, in English law at least, was expressed in the following case. **4–03**

4–04

Entores v Miles Far East Corporation
[1955] 2 Q.B. 327
English Court of Appeal: Denning, Birkett and Parker, LJJ

Entores in London made an offer by telex to the defendants' agents in Amsterdam, which the agents accepted by telex. To establish the jurisdiction of the English courts, the place where the contract was made had to be in England. If the offer from Entores had been accepted when the agents' telex was sent, the contract would have been made in Amsterdam and there would be no jurisdiction. If the offer had been accepted when the agents' telex was received on Entores's telex machine in London, there would be jurisdiction.

The court found that the offer was accepted in London.

---

[1] WW McBryde, *The Law of Contract in Scotland*, 3rd edn (Edinburgh: W. Green, 2007), para.6–110.

4–05 "DENNING LJ: ... When a contract is made by post it is clear law throughout the common law countries that the acceptance is complete as soon as the letter of acceptance is put into the post box, and that is the place where the contract is made. But there is no clear rule about contracts made by telephone or by telex. Communications by these means are virtually instantaneous and stand on a different footing.

The problem can only by solved by going in stages. Let me first consider a case where two people make a contract by word of mouth in the presence of one another. Suppose, for instance, that I shout an offer to a man across a river or a courtyard but I do not hear his reply because it is drowned by an aircraft flying overhead. There is no contract at that moment. If he wishes to make a contract, he must wait until the aircraft is gone and then shout back his acceptance so that I can hear what he says. Not until I have his answer am I bound ...

Now take a case where two people make a contract by telephone. Suppose, for instance, that I make an offer to a man by telephone and, in the middle of his reply, the line goes 'dead' so that I do not hear his words of acceptance. There is no contract at that moment. The other man may not know the precise moment when the line failed. But he will know that the telephone conversation was abruptly broken off: because, people usually say something to signify the end of the conversation. If he wishes to make a contract, he must therefore get through again so as to make sure that I heard. Suppose next that the line does not go dead, but it is nevertheless so indistinct that I do not catch what he says and I ask him to repeat it. He then repeats it and I hear his acceptance. The contract is made, not on the first time when I do not hear, but only the second time when I do hear. If he does not repeat it, there is no contract. The contract is only complete when I have his answer accepting the offer.

Lastly take the telex. Suppose a clerk in a London office taps out on the teleprinter an offer which is immediately recorded on a teleprinter in a Manchester office, and a clerk at that end taps out an acceptance. If the line goes dead in the middle of the sentence of acceptance, the teleprinter motor will stop. There is then obviously no contract. The clerk at Manchester must get through again and send his complete sentence. But it may happen that the line does not go dead, yet the message does not get through to London. Thus the clerk at Manchester may tap out his message of acceptance and it will not be recorded in London because the ink at the London end fails or something of that kind. In that case the Manchester clerk will not know of the failure but the London clerk will know of it and will immediately send back a message 'not receiving'. Then, when the fault is rectified the Manchester clerk will repeat his message. Only then is there a contract. If he does not repeat it, there is no contract. It is not until his message is received that the contract is complete.

In all the instances I have taken so far, the man who sends the message of acceptance knows that it has not been received or he has reason to know it. So he must repeat it. But suppose that he does not know that his message did not get home. He thinks it has. This may happen if the listener on the telephone does not catch the words of acceptance, but nevertheless does not trouble to ask for them to be repeated: or if the ink on the teleprinter fails at the receiving end, but the clerk does not ask for the message to be repeated: so that the man who sends an acceptance reasonably believes that his message has been received. The offeror in such circumstances is clearly bound, because he will be estopped from saying that he did not receive the message of acceptance. It is his own fault that he did not get it. But if there should be a case where the offeror without any fault on his part does not receive the message of acceptance—yet the sender of it reasonably believes it has got home when it has not—then I think there is no contract.

My conclusion is that the rule about instantaneous communication between the parties is different from the rule about the post. The contract is only complete when the acceptance is received by the offeror: and the contract is made at the place where the acceptance is received."

Lord Denning's analysis is generally accepted and is equally applicable to other forms of telecommunicated acceptance, which are of increasing commercial significance. To the telephone and telex can be added the fax, electronic mail, systems which can transmit both voice and digital information, communications directly from one computerised system to another, and the use of satellites in international telecommunications. The use of such instantaneous, long-distance communications raises several legal issues.

What if the telephone goes dead; or the fax machine breaks down; or the computer terminal malfunctions? Does a contract nevertheless arise? What if the fax machine on the offeror's premises is left on after normal working hours to receive messages; or the message is received, but nobody looks at the machine for some time. Is an acceptance valid as soon as it appears on the fax machine, or must it first be read and understood by the offerer at the other end?

Brinkibon v Stahag Stahl und Stahlwarenhandels GmbH 4–06

[1983] 2 A.C. 34

House of Lords: Lords Wilberforce, Fraser, Russell, Bridge and Brandon

Brinkibon, in England, acting for a Swiss company offered by telex to buy steel bars from Stahag in Austria. Stahag sent a counter-offer by telex from their premises in Vienna to Brinkibon's premises in London. Briakibon purported to accept that counter-offer by a telex sent from London to Vienna.

A dispute arose between the parties. For the purposes of establishing whether English courts had jurisdiction, the House of Lords had to determine whether any contract had arisen between the parties either when Brinkibon's acceptance telex was transmitted in London, or when it was received on Stahag's telex machine in Vienna.

The court found that acceptance was complete when it was received.

"LORD WILBERFORCE: ... [H]ow should communications by telex be categorised? 4–07
In *Entores Ltd v Far East Corp* [1955] 2 Q.B. 327 the Court of Appeal classified them with instantaneous communications. Their ruling, which has passed into the textbooks, including *Williston on Contracts*, 3rd ed. (1957), appears not to have caused either adverse comment, or any difficulty to businessmen. I would accept it as a general rule. Where the condition of simultaneity is met, and where it appears to be within the mutual intention of the parties that contractual exchanges should take place in this way, I think it a sound rule, but not necessarily a universal rule.

Since 1955 the use of telex communication has been greatly expanded, and there are many variants on it. The senders and recipients may not be the principals to the contemplated contract. They may be servants or agents with limited authority. The message may not reach, or be intended to reach, the designated recipient immediately: messages may be sent out of office hours, or at night, with the intention, or on the assumption, that they will be read at a later time. There may be some error or default at the recipient's end which prevents receipt at the time contemplated and believed in by the sender. The message may have been sent and/or received through machines operated by third persons. And many other variations may occur. No universal rule can cover all such cases; they must be resolved by reference to the intentions of the parties, by sound business practice and in some cases by a judgment where the risks should lie: see *Household Fire and Carriage Accident Insurance Co Ltd v Grant* (1879) 4 Ex. D. 216 at

227 per Baggallay L.J. and *Henthorn v Fraser* (1892] 2 Ch. 27; [1891] All E.R. Rep. 908 per Lord Herschell.

4–08 LORD FRASER OF TULLYBELTON: ... I have reached the opinion that, on balance, an acceptance sent by telex directly from the acceptor's office to the offeror's office should be treated as if it were an instantaneous communication between principals, like a telephone conversation. One reason is that the decision to that effect in *Entores Ltd v Miles Far East Corp.* [1955] 2 All E.R. 493; [1955] 2 Q.B. 327 seems to have worked without leading to serious difficulty or complaint from the business community. Secondly, once the message has been received on the offeror's telex machine, it is not unreasonable to treat it as delivered to the principal offeror, because it is his responsibility to arrange for prompt handling of messages within his own office. Thirdly, a party (the acceptor) who tries to send a message by telex can generally tell if his message has not been received on the other party's (the offeror's) machine, whereas the offeror, of course, will not know if an unsuccessful attempt has been made to send an acceptance to him. It is therefore convenient that the acceptor, being in the better position, should have the responsibility of ensuring that his message is received. For these reasons I think it is right that in the ordinary simple case, such as I take this to, be, the general rule and not the postal rule should apply. But I agree with both my noble and learned friends that the general rule will not cover all the many variations that may occur with telex messages."

The most interesting aspect of the decision is their Lordships' comments on the steps necessary to establish communication of the acceptance. The issue is really the same as that which arose in *Burnley v Alford* in relation to revocation of an offer by letter, namely: would it be enough that the communication reached its destination in the normal course of business, or would it be necessary to show that the recipient had actual notice of it?

4–09

Burnley v Alford

1919 2 S.L.T. 123

Court of Session, Outer House: Lord Ormidale

Burnley, a Yorkshire worsted manufacturer, hoped to retire and sought the purchase of a Scottish estate. To that end, he visited Dalcross Castle. On 9 August 1918, he offered £4,500 for the purchase, from Colonel Alford, of the lease of Dalcross Castle, the "shootings and fishings" and "all the furniture and effects contained therein, with the exception of the moose head and such family pictures and plate as Colonel Alford may wish to remove."

Colonel Alford replied in writing that he was disappointed at the low sum, but would accept £4,400 for the leasehold. He also sent a list of effects which he was unwilling to sell and which should be removed from the original inventory and added: "subject to this I am willing to sell for £100—making the £4,500—everything in the inventory and no more". After several exchanges, the colonel posted a letter on 4th September to Burnley's agent apparently reverting "to the exact terms and conditions of the offer of August 9".

On 11 September, having changed his mind again, the colonel sent telegrams to Burnley and his agent, breaking off all negotiations for the sale.

Burnley sent a telegram purporting to accept the offer in the colonel's letter of 4 September. That telegram was sent at 12:59pm on 12 September. At the time, neither Burnley nor his agent had seen the colonel's telegrams of 11 September, because neither had been at their respective normal addresses at the time when the telegrams arrived. The issue was whether Burnley had accepted the colonel's offer in the letter of 4 September before the colonel had revoked it by the telegrams of 11 September.

The court found that he had not.

"LORD ORMIDALE: . . . Now the general rule of law is that in ordinary circumstances where parties are contracting by letter and an offer is received by post if acceptance of that offer is made by letter the contract is completed as soon as the letter of acceptance is posted. On the other hand, if a retractation of an offer is sent by post the mere posting of the retractation does not make the withdrawal effectual. To become operative it must be brought to the knowledge or mind of the party holding the offer (*Thomson v James*, 1855, 18 D. 1; *Byrne v Vantienhoven*, 5 C.P.D. 345; *Hewthorn v Fraser* [1892] 2 Ch. 27; *Stevenson v M'Lean*, 5 Q.B.D. 346) . . . 4–10

It is proved that the cancellation telegrams of 11th September were properly addressed and were duly delivered in ordinary course prior to the hour, viz. 12.59, at which the telegram of acceptance was despatched to Colonel Alford. They would in ordinary course have been received and seen by both the pursuer and Mr Feather [his agent] if these gentlemen had been present to receive them. But they happened to be absent from the addresses which they had duly furnished to the defender and they had not left anyone on the spot to represent and act for them. This was not business, and the matter in hand was essentially a matter of business. The rule of law in question appears to me to be applicable only when business rules and practices are observed. In my opinion therefore the pursuer is not entitled to plead that he accepted the offer of 4th September before he knew of the cancellation of the offer of sale. He ought to have known and would have known in the normal course of dealing. In none of the cases which were cited to me is there any indication that the bringing of the cancellation or recall of an offer home to the knowledge of the party holding the offer is of rigid application. In all of them the posting and the receipt of the letters of acceptance and recall were in the ordinary course of business transactions. It is one thing for the addressee to be absent from his office after business hours so that the delivery of the letter is delayed until his office opens the following day. It is a totally different thing for him to be absent from his office during business hours, with the result that the letter may lie on his desk unopened for a considerable length of time. In the present case the telegrams are said to have been left unopened or unread from the morning of the 12th September to the evening of the 14th. They ought to have been read on receipt, and, if they had been, the cancellation of the sale would have been known at the appropriate addresses long before the telegram was despatched from Bradford at 12.59."

The issue of what amounts to sufficient communication, or notice (of all contractual communications, rather than just communication of acceptance) was recently reviewed by the Scottish Law Commission.

Review of Contract Law: Formation of Contract 4–11

Scottish Law Commission Discussion Paper No.154 (March 2012)

(iii) When does a communication take effect?

DCFR I.–1:109 Notice

(1) . . . 'Notice' includes the communication of information or of a juridical act.

(2) The notice may be given by any means appropriate to the circumstances.

(3) The notice becomes effective when it reaches the addressee, unless it provides for a delayed effect.

(4) The notice reaches the addressee:

(a) when it is delivered to the addressee;
(b) when it is delivered to the addressee's place of business or, where there is no such place of business or the notice does not relate to a business matter, to the addressee's habitual residence;
(c) in the case of a notice transmitted by electronic means, when it can be accessed by the addressee; or
(d) when it is otherwise made available to the addressee at such a place and in such a way that the addressee could reasonably be expected to obtain access to it without undue delay.

(5) The notice has no effect if a revocation of it reaches the addressee before or at the same time as the notice ...

...

[2.18] By emphasising accessibility to the addressee as the test of legal effectiveness in this way, the DCFR ... avoid[s] some of the technical difficulties that may arise from the nature of the infrastructure through which an online communication makes its way from sender to addressee, described as follows by Eliza Mik:

'Most online communications ... rely on the client-server architecture. In the case of email, there are at least two originating devices (the sender's mail-client and the outgoing mail-server) and two terminating devices (the addressee's incoming mail-server and the mail-client). Is it the mail-client or the mail-server that should be taken into account? ... [T]here may be substantial delays between the moment a message arrives at the server and the moment it is transferred to the client ... [O]nline communications are characterized by a number of novel risks. The Internet is not like the post or the telephone. Despite its ubiquity, it does not (yet) have the uniformity of one global system. The Internet is heterogeneous—each of its component networks retains some individual characteristics. Routing from one network to another may involve a conversion between the 'idiosyncrasies of the two original networks' and require the trans-coding, translation or reformatting of messages. Each of these operations aims to adapt the message to the requirements of the next step in the transmission. Such conversions are, however, not always successful. As a result, there are many reasons an email may not be delivered or be delivered in unreadable form.'[34]

[2.19] It has been suggested that the default rule as to when an email communication is received by its addressee should be arrival on the server that manages that party's email.[35] This is in line with the UNCITRAL Model Law on Electronic Commerce.[36]

[2.20] Arrival at the recipient's server will generally make the communication accessible to the addressee and so satisfy the DCFR test, even if the addressee does not in fact access it. The objective requirement of 'accessibility' probably also means that the email which the addressee cannot access as a result of the operation of the network, or firewalls, or anti virus filters is an effective notice; likewise if the communication fails because a recipient's inbox is full or is consigned by security systems to a 'suspected spam' folder. In all these cases the email is an effective notice because the obstacles to accessing the email are within the addressee's control: the addressee has selected the system by which it wishes to receive communications of the type in question. The position may be different if the sender is alerted by the system to the fate that has befallen its attempted communication, in which case the sender should know that the communication has failed and make another attempt.[37] Automatic 'out of office' or 'vacation' messages set up by an absent addressee may also postpone the effectiveness of an email notice but much might depend on the specificity and reliability of the absentee's message.

Scots law: communication generally required 4–12

2.21 The Scots law on when offers, acceptances and their withdrawal or revocation have legal effect is clear, at least in terms of general principle. With two exceptions—the postal acceptance rule and the acceptance of general offers (to be discussed further below)[38] communication to the other party is required.[39] But an objective approach is taken in determining whether or not communication has occurred, and this may make effective a communication about the existence and content of which the recipient is subjectively unaware.

[2.22] The most striking example of this objective approach to communication in the Scottish books is *Burnley v Alford*,[40] ... [The Discussion Paper gives the facts of the case and quotes extensively from Lord Ormidale's judgment and continues.]

[2.23] Although Lord Ormidale said that the facts of the case were special, the underlying principle of the decision appears to be reasonable, consistent with the approach found in the CISG, the PICC and the DCFR, and also supported by more recent House of Lords and Court of Appeal authority in England.[42]

[2.24] A similarly objective approach is also apparent in the more recent Outer House decision of *Carmarthen Developments Ltd v Pennington*.[43] [The Discussion Paper gives the facts of the case, quotes extensively from Lord Hodge's judgment and continues.]

[2.26] There appear to have been no Scottish decisions on forms of communication other than the mail service, but textbooks generally accept the decisions in English cases about telexes,[46] which also take an objective approach to the question of when communication is effected by such means, and show that in general this means upon receipt at the point where in the ordinary course of business the recipient ought to have been aware that a communication had been made.

[2.27] The generally objective approach of Scots law to when a communication is made is consistent with the approach found in the international texts forming the basis for our review, and we would not suggest any change to that position ...

[2.28] Scots law generally has a flexible approach as to when a communication of one party's intention should have become known to its addressee, and there are no rules specifying, for example, delivery to the addressee or the latter's place of business or habitual residence as in the international texts. The words of Lord Wilberforce in one of the leading modern English cases were cited and applied in the Carmarthen case: 'No universal rule can cover all such cases: they must be resolved by reference to the intentions of the parties, by sound business practice and in some cases by a judgment where the risks should lie'.[47] While this is attractive in the context of what may often be complex fact situations, it may be open to the criticism that only by going to court will it be possible to get an answer to the question in any given case.

2.29 The Scottish courts have so far had no opportunity to consider the question of when an electronic communication of a party's intention takes effect. We note that the international texts, here including the UNCITRAL Model Law on Electronic Commerce,[48] favour a broadly similar default rule, namely that the communication takes effect when it becomes accessible to its intended addressee, which is generally taken to be when the message enters the addressee's communications system and becomes accessible to that person. We think that this appears to be a workable rule and one which fairly apportions the risks of mis- or non-communication between the parties involved.

---

[34] Eliza Mik, "Formation Online" in Furmston and Tolhurst, *Contract Formation*, paras 6.59-6.60. An example of when there may be more than two devices on each side of a transaction is when parties are using mobile devices such as blackberries, tablets, netbooks and laptops "which rely on the classic architecture but interpose an additional server between the incoming mail-server and the end-user. The message is pushed to the terminating device because the addressee previously configured a server or device to do so" (ibid, para 6.47, fn 131). The use of the concept of

"accessibility" to determine whether or not an electronic communication has reached its recipient should mean that it does not matter which machine the latter uses to gain access. It also suggests, however, that automatic "out of office" response messages should make clear if a party is also not using any other means of access to incoming email communications.

[35] Donal Nolan, "Offer and acceptance in the electronic age" in Burrows and Peel, *Contract Formation*, p 76; Vogenauer and Kleinheisterkamp, *PICC Commentary*, p 206; Eliza Mik, "Formation Online", in Furmston and Tolhurst, *Contract Formation*, paras 6.55-6.67.

[36] Adopted in 1996; available at *http://www.cnudmi.org/pdf/english/texts/electcom/05-89450_Ebook.pdf*.

[37] Donal Nolan, "Offer and acceptance in the electronic age" in Burrows and Peel, *Contract Formation*, pp 76-79; the argument is founded on the principles stated by Denning LJ in *Entores Ltd v Miles Far East Corp* [1955] 2 QB 327 at 333-4. See also Furmston and Tolhurst, *Contract Formation*, at para 6.57.

[38] See, respectively, paras 4.8-4.14 and 4.15.

[39] The key case settling the general approach is *Thomson v James* (1855) 18 D 1. See also Gloag, *Contract*, pp 16-17; McBryde, *Contract*, paras 6.31-6.35, 6.53-6.55 and 6.109-6.113; SME, vol 15, para 6.28.

[40] 1919 2 SLT 123 (OH) 19.

[42] *Eaglehill Ltd v J Needham (Builders) Ltd* [1973] AC 992 at 1011; *Tenax Steamship Co v Owners of the Motor Vessel Brimnes* [1975] QB 929.

[43] [2008] CSOH 139, 2008 GWD 33-494. For commentary on other aspects of the case see para 2.34 below and Martin Hogg, "Contract Formation in the Electronic Age" 2009 13 Edin LR 121.

...

[46] *Entores Ltd v Miles Far East Corp* [1955] 2 QB 327 and *Brinkibon Ltd v Stahag Stahl und Stahlwarenhandels GmbH* [1983] 2 AC 34. See further McBryde, *Contract*, para 6.118; SME, vol 15, paras 629, 641 and 643; MacQueen & Thomson, *Contract*, para 2.35.

[47] *Brinkibon Ltd v Stahag Stahl und Stahlwarenhandels GmbH* [1983] 2 AC 34 at 42, and see *Carmarthen Developments Ltd v Pennington* [2008] CSOH 139, 2008 GWD 33-494 at para 33 (Lord Hodge), (iii) Withdrawal of offer.

Digitised electronic communications

4–13 Communications through the internet, via the world wide web, by email or even by simple mobile phone "texting" raise even more complex problems. When is an emailed acceptance, for example, "received"? Is it when the message is received by the offeror's Internet Service Provider (ISP); when the message enters the offeror's network or server; is it when the message is actually retrieved by the offeree? Some jurisdictions, such as Singapore, quickly dealt with such novel matters expressly by statute (Electronic Transactions Act 1998 (the 1998 Act). That 1998 Act, in common with those of other jurisdictions is closely based on the provisions of the UNCITRAL Model Law on Electronic Commerce 1994 (amended 1998). At the time of writing, UNCITRAL is considering a Preliminary Draft Convention on Electronic Contracting. The draft is itself influenced by some of the provisions of Directive 2000/31/EC of the European Parliament and of the Council of 8 June 2000 on certain legal aspects of information society services, in particular electronic commerce, in the Internal Market ("Directive on electronic commerce").[2] This Directive is the legal framework for contracts to which it applies. The Directive, in general terms, applies to advertising on the internet or by email; to the sale of goods or services to businesses or consumers on the internet or by email; and to the conveying or storage of electronic content or access to communications networks. There are some exceptions.

The Directive requires that the recipients of such "electronic society services" (effectively online services) are given clear information about the trader, the nature of any commercial

---

[2] Directive 2000/31/EC of the European Parliament and of the Council of 8 June 2000 on certain legal aspects of information society services, in particular electronic commerce, in the Internal Market ("Directive on electronic commerce"), O.J. (L) 178, 17/07/2000 pp.0001–0016.

communications and on how to complete an online transaction. More importantly, regs 8–11 establish information obligations for online service providers, especially in relation to the taking of online orders and, although these do not in any sense replace the rules on offer and acceptance, they do have an impact on their operation.

The Directive has been implemented into the law of the UK by the Electronic Commerce (EC Directive) Regulations 2002,[3] which came into force on 21 August 2002 (with the exception of reg.16, which comes into force on 23 October 2002). The key provisions of the Regulations relating to contracts concluded by electronic means are reproduced below.

The Electronic Commerce (EC Directive) Regulations 2002 **4–14**

(SI 2002/2013)

"Information to be provided where contracts are concluded by electronic means

9.(1) Unless parties who are not consumers have agreed otherwise, a service provider shall, prior to an order being placed by the recipient of a service, provide to that recipient in a clear, comprehensible and unambiguous manner the information set out in (a) to (d) below:
The different technical steps to follow to conclude the contract; whether or not the concluded contract will be filed by the service provider and whether it will be accessible; the technical means for identifying and correcting input errors prior to the placing of the order; the languages offered for the conclusion of the contract.

(2) Unless parties who are not consumers have agreed otherwise, a service provider shall indicate which relevant codes of conduct he subscribes to and give information on how those codes can be consulted electronically.

(3) Where the service provider provides terms and conditions applicable to the contract to the recipient, the service provider shall make them available to him in a way that allows him to store and reproduce them.

(4) The requirements of paragraphs (1) and (2) above shall not apply to contracts concluded exclusively by exchange of electronic mail or by equivalent individual communications.

...

Placing of the order

11.(1) Unless parties who are not consumers have agreed otherwise, where the recipient of the service places his order through technological means, a service provider shall:

(a) acknowledge receipt of the order to the recipient of the service without undue delay and by electronic means; and
(b) make available to the recipient of the service appropriate, effective and accessible technical means allowing him to identify and correct input errors prior to the placing of the order.

(2) For the purposes of paragraph (1) (a) above:

(a) the order and the acknowledgment of receipt will be deemed to be received when the parties to whom they are addressed are able to access them; and

[3] Electronic Commerce (EC Directive) Regulations 2002 (SI 2002/2013). The full text of the Directive can be found online at *http://eur-lex.europa.eu/legal-content/EN/TXT/HTML/?uri=CELEX:32000L0031&from=EN* and of the Regulations at *http://www.hmso.gov.uk/si/si2002/20022013.htm*.

(b) the acknowledgment of receipt may take the form of the provision of the service paid for where that service is an information society service.

(3) The requirements of paragraph (1) above shall not apply to contracts concluded exclusively by exchange of electronic mail or by equivalent individual communications.

Meaning of the term "order"

12. Except in relation to regulation 9(1)(c) and regulation 11(1)(b) where "order" shall be the contractual offer,
"order" may be but need not be the contractual offer for the purposes of regulations 9 and 11.

Liability of the service provider

13. The duties imposed by regulations 6,7,8,9(1) and 11(1)(a) shall be enforceable, at the suit of any recipient of a service, by an action against the service provider for damages for breach of statutory duty.

Compliance with regulation 9(3)

14. Where on request a service provider has failed to comply with the requirement in regulation 9(3), the recipient may seek an order from any court having jurisdiction in relation to the contract requiring that service provider to comply with that requirement.

Right to rescind contract

15. Where a person:

(a) has entered into a contract to which these Regulations apply, and
(b) the service provider has not made available means of allowing him to identify and correct input errors in compliance with regulation 11(1)(b),

he shall be entitled to rescind the contract unless any court having jurisdiction in relation to the contract in question orders otherwise on the application of the service provider."

4–15 The Regulation (and the Directive) make exceptions for "consumers". This is because consumers are also protected by the Consumer Protection (Distance Selling) Regulations 2000,[4] which implement Directive 97/7/EC of the European Parliament and of the Council of 20 May 1997 on the protection of consumers in relation to distance contracts.[5] The Regulations do not apply simply to electronic communications, but apply also to other distance communications, such as newspapers, mail shots, broadcast media, etc. The Regulations impose an obligation to provide the consumer (a person who is not acting in a business capacity) with a defined minimum of written information; give the consumer a right to cancel the contract; and impose a duty on the supplier to perform within 30 days from when the contract was made.

On the general position in Scots law, see *Beta Computers (Europe) Ltd v Adobe Systems (Europe) Ltd*.[6]

[4] Consumer Protection (Distance Selling) Regulations 2000 (SI 2000/2334).

[5] Directive 97/7/EC of the European Parliament and of the Council of 20 May 1997 on the protection of consumers in relation to distance contracts, O.J. (L) 144/19.

[6] *Beta Computers (Europe) Ltd v Adobe Systems (Europe) Ltd*, 1996 S.L.T. 604.

Acceptance may be communicated by conduct

If the offerer must have knowledge of the acceptance, does a contract arise where the offerer becomes aware of conduct by the offeree which indicates acceptance; or must there be actual communication by the offeree? In *Carlill*, for example, the contract arose when Mrs Carlill did what was expected of her—she did not actually have to communicate her acceptance to the Smoke Ball Company. Her conduct was the acceptance. Sometimes, as in *Carlill*, the courts are willing to infer that the offeree's acts are consistent only with acceptance of the offer, so that the offerer has by implication waived the need for the acceptance to be communicated. Indeed, it is possible that both the offer and the acceptance—the entire agreement, in fact—might be constituted by conduct. **4–16**

But how far can this be taken? Does conduct that is consistent only with acceptance of the offer create the contract, or is there still a need to communicate this to the offerer? The following case suggests that there is no such requirement.

Chapman v Sulphite Pulp Co Ltd **4–17**

1892 19 R. 837

Court of Session, First Division: Lord President (Robertson), Lords Adam, Kinnear and McLaren

On 26 November 1890, Mr Chapman applied for 12 shares in Sulphite. The paid-up value of each share was £10. Mr Chapman deposited £60 with his application, or 50 per cent of the paid-up value of the shares. On 12 January 1891, Mr Chapman applied for another 12 shares with a similar deposit. Both of Mr Chapman's applications contained a request that the applicant's name be placed on the register of shareholders. Both applications had been taken to Sulphite's office by Mr Chapman's wife. On a separate occasion when Mrs Chapman visited Sulphite's office, she had been told that Mr Chapman's name was on the register of shareholders for 24 shares.

Having received no indication that the shares had been allotted to him, Mr Chapman wrote on 7 August 1981, withdrawing "unconditionally" his applications for the shares. He petitioned the court, unsuccessfully requesting that his name be deleted from the register of shareholders.

"LORD PRESIDENT (ROBERTSON): ... On two occasions in spring 1891, after he had been put on the register, Mr Chapman was in communication with the officials of the company regarding those shares, and I think the result of the evidence is that, apart altogether from the disputed letters, he was then sufficiently apprised that the company had accepted him as a shareholder in terms of his applications. On one of those occasions the petitioner's wife went, as arranged with the petitioner, to see the secretary of the company, and unquestionably was in law his agent. Now, [the secretary] says that he told her that Mr Chapman was on the register ... I hold, therefore, that on this occasion Mr Chapman's agent was informed that his name was on the register. **4–18**

The other fact to which I refer is that, he being on the register, the company sent to the petitioner a circular calling him to a meeting of shareholders. This was, unless explained away, an intimation that the company treated him as a shareholder ...

In my opinion, therefore, it is proved that in March 1891 the company had adequately informed the petitioner that he had been accepted as a member, and from that time, therefore, he was not entitled to resile."

Communication to the agent of the offerer is apparently enough, but simply to communicate acceptance through a third party would not be adequate. A similar situation would arise where the offeree is sent unsolicited goods, but deals with the goods in such a way as to show that they adopted the transaction. If, for example, they use the goods, or if they resell them or otherwise show that they have accepted them, they are bound in contract. What if, however, the recipient merely keeps the goods? In the English case of *Weatherby v Banham*,[7] Weatherby published the Racing Calendar and had for some years supplied issues as they appeared to X. When X died, Banham took over X's premises and continued to receive the copies of the periodical. He refused to pay for two years' issues that he had received. In finding that Banham was contractually bound to pay, Tenterden LCJ stated:

> "If the defendant receives the books, and uses them, I think that the action is maintainable. These books come addressed to the deceased gentleman, whose estate has come to the defendant, and he keeps the books. I think that the defendant is clearly liable in this form of action."

This case, although briefly reported, suggests that the offerer has waived the need for the offeree to communicate acceptance of the calendar every time it was sent; it sufficed that the calendar was not returned. It is for such reasons that the Unsolicited Goods and Services Act 1971 was enacted.[8]

Postal acceptance

4–19 An acceptance by post takes effect as soon as the letter is posted; that is as soon as the letter is placed in the post box or handed over to a postal employee authorised to receive it.[9] This is the established rule[10] in Scotland.[11] This "postal rule" derogates from the general rule that acceptance must be communicated. It was developed in the early 19th century[12] at a time of unprecedented industrial expansion, when great reliance had to be placed by commerce on fledgling postal services over which they had no control.[13] The rule was therefore based on practical convenience,[14] but its theoretical basis is less secure. It has been suggested[15] that the post office (and by implication any other carrier of mail in today's deregulated environment) is acting as an agent for the parties so that delivery to the agent constitutes delivery to the principal; but it is artificial to speak of an agent being notified of a communication which they are not legally entitled to open. Elsewhere[16] it is suggested that the most coherent theory is that the offerer by implication stipulates that the act of posting the letter will constitute acceptance and waives the need for actual communication. This must be the case particularly where the offer states, for

---

[7] *Weatherby v Banham* (1832) 5 Car. & P. 227.

[8] That provision was replaced by the Consumer Protection (Distance Selling) Regulations 2000 (SI 2000/2334) and was in turn replaced by the Consumer Contracts (Information, Cancellation and Additional Charges) Regulations 2013 (SI 2013/2134). The details are beyond the scope of this book and are best pursued in the major work on the subject, WCH Ervine, *Consumer Law in Scotland*, 5th edn (Edinburgh: W. Green, 2015).

[9] "It is the act of acceptance that binds the bargain and in the common case it is not necessary that the acceptance should have reached the person who makes the offer": Bell, *Commentaries*, i, 327. The reference to this passage in Walker, *Contracts*, para.7.37, in relation to acceptance generally must therefore be read as being limited to acceptance by post.

[10] The rule was approved by the House of Lords in the *Brinkibon* case (see above), but the court refused to extend its application beyond the traditional categories of letters and the now defunct telegrams—per Lord Wilberforce [1983] 2 A.C. 34 at 41.

[11] Bell, *Commentaries*, i, 334; *Dunlop v Higgins* (1848) 6 Bell's App. 195, also reported at 1 H.L.C. 857; *Thomson v James* (1855) 18 D.1.

[12] The earliest authority is *Adams v Lindsell* (1818) 1 B. & Ald. 621.

[13] See, e.g. Lord Cottenham's comments in *Dunlop v Higgins*, below.

[14] Thesiger LJ, in *Household Fire & Carriage Accident Insurance Co Ltd v Grant* (1879) 4 Ex. D. 216 at 223.

[15] See Walker, *Contract*, para.7.53, and cases referred at fn.3 therein.

[16] For example Gloag, *The Law of Contract* (Edinburgh: W. Green) p.34.

example, "acceptance to be by return of post",[17] but again there is an element of artificiality in this approach. Whatever the theoretical difficulties, the practical reality (and after all, the law of contract should be based on practical reality) is that the rule places the burden upon the offerer to stipulate in the offer that postal acceptance must be communicated.

Brinkibon v Stahag Stahl und Stahlwarenhandels GmbH[18] is the only House of Lords decision since *Dunlop v Higgins* that considered the postal rule and the scope of its application. Their Lordships were clearly unwilling to extend the postal rule to modem methods of telecommunications.

Dunlop, Wilson & Co v Higgins & Son 4–20
(1848) 6 Bell's App. 195
House of Lords: Lord Chancellor (Lord Cottenham)

Following lengthy negotiation over terms, Dunlop, in a letter dated 28 January and posted in Glasgow, had offered to sell pig iron to Higgins in Liverpool. A reply posted by Higgins in Liverpool and addressed to Dunlop in Glasgow stated: "Gentlemen, we will take the 2000 tons pigs, you offer us."

That letter was posted on 30 January, but mistakenly dated 31 January. Because of a severe frost, the letter arrived in Glasgow on 1 February, rather than 31 January, when it should have arrived in the ordinary course. On 1 February Dunlop wrote to Higgins: "We have your letter of yesterday, but we are sorry that we cannot now enter the 2000 tons pig iron, our offer of the 28th not having been accepted in course."

Higgins successfully claimed that a contract for the supply of the pig iron had arisen on the basis of the letters.

"LORD CHANCELLOR (LORD COTTENHAM): . . . If there be a usage of trade to accept such an offer, and to return an answer to such an offer, and to forward it by means of the post, and if the party accepting the offer puts his letter into the post on the correct day, has he not done everything that he was bound to do? How can he be responsible for that over which he has no control? Is it not the same as if the date of the party's accepting the offer had been the subject of a special contract, as if the contract had been, 'I make you this offer but you must return me an answer on the 30th'? If he puts his letter into the post office on the 30th, that is undoubtedly what the usage of trade would require. He, therefore, did on the 30th, in proper time, return an answer by the right conveyance, the post office . . . 4–21

There is also . . . the case of *Adams and Lindsell* . . . That is a case where the letter went, by the error of the party sending it, to the wrong place, but the party receiving it answered it in proper time. The party, however, who originally sent the offer, not receiving the answer in proper time, thought he was discharged, and entered into a contract and sold the goods to somebody else. The question was, whether the party making the offer had a right to withdraw after notice of acceptance. He sold the goods after the party had written the letter of acceptance, but before it arrived he said, 'I withdraw my offer,' therefore he said, 'before I received your acceptance of my offer I had withdrawn it'. And that raised the question when the acceptance took place, and what constituted the acceptance. It was argued that 'till the Plaintiff's answer was actually received there could be no binding contract between the parties, and that before then the Defendants had retracted their offer by selling the wool to other persons'. But

---

[17] This is certainly the theme underlying decisions like *Adams v Lindsell* and *Dunlop v Higgins*.

[18] *Brinkibon v Stahag Stahl und Stahlwarenhandels GmbH* [1983] 2 A.C. 34; [1982] 1 All E.R. 293; [1982] 2 W.L.R. 264.

> the Court said, 'If that were so, no contract could ever be completed by the post. For if the Defendants were not bound by their offer when accepted by the Plaintiffs till the answer was received, then the Plaintiffs ought not to be bound till after they had received the notification that the Defendants had received their answer and assented to it. And so it might go on *ad infinitum*. The Defendants must be considered in law as making, during every instant of the time their letter was travelling, the same identical offer to the Plaintiffs, and then the contract is completed by the acceptance of it by letter.' ...
>
> Mr Bell's commentary appears to lay down the same rule in Scotland, and the contrary to that does not appear to exist."

4–22 This case introduced the postal rule into Scots law. The references to Bell suggest that he relied upon English decisions.

Would the court have decided differently had the letter actually been posted on 31 January, i.e. not in the ordinary course, but still arrived on 1 February? In England, the rule appears to be that a contract arises even if the letter of acceptance never arrives, as long as it has been properly posted.[19] In a dissenting judgment, Bramwell LJ (dissenting) stated:

> "I am of opinion that this judgment should be reversed. I am of opinion that there was no bargain between these parties to allot and take shares, that to make such bargain there should have been an acceptance of the defendant's offer and a communication to him of that acceptance. That there was no such communication. That posting a letter does not differ from other attempts at communication in any of its consequences, save that it is irrevocable as between the poster and the post office ... a communication to affect a man must be a communication, i.e., must reach him."

This case has never been approved in Scotland. Echoing Bramwell LJ's view, Lord Shand in *Mason v Benhar Coal Co*,[20] expressly refused to follow that decision. At the very least, it is submitted, if the letter is delayed or does not reach the offerer, because of some act or omission by the offeree, then the offeree will not have performed the acts which by implication are necessary to indicate acceptance. The only sure way in which the offerer may avoid the vagaries of the postal service is to stipulate that acceptance will be complete when it is received: a practice that is increasingly common in business negotiations.[21]

The rule in *Dunlop* has been strictly limited to letters of acceptance, but even there the rule can be displaced by express provision in the offer to the contrary.

4–23 **Holwell Securities Ltd v Hughes**

(1974) 1 W.L.R. 155

English Court of Appeal: Russell, Buckley and Lawton LJJ

The defendant quoted the plaintiff an option to purchase a house. The option was to be exercised "by notice in writing to the intending vendor". The plaintiff sought to exercise his option by sending a notice in writing to the defendant by ordinary post, but the letter was never received.

The court found that the sending of the letter did not constitute the exercise of the option.

---

[19] *Household Fire and Carriage Accident Insurance Co Ltd v Grant* (1879) 4 Ex. D. 216.

[20] *Mason v Benhar Coal Co* (1992) 9 R. 883, 890.

[21] For a thoughtful analysis of the position in Scotland arising from this complex case law, see Blackie, "Lost in the Post", 1975 J.L.S. 134.)

"LAWTON LJ: ... [T]he plaintiffs submitted that the option was exercised when the letter was posted, as the rule relating to the acceptance of offers by post did apply. The foundation of [t]his argument was that the parties to this agreement must have contemplated that the option might be, and probably would be, exercised by means of a letter sent through the post. I agree. This ... was enough to bring the rule into operation. I do not agree ... 4–24

Does the rule apply in all cases where one party makes an offer which both he and the person with whom he was dealing must have expected the post to be used as a means of accepting it? In my judgment, it does not. First, it does not apply when the express terms of the offer specify that the acceptance must reach the offeror. The public nowadays are familiar with this exception to the general rule through their handling of football pool coupons. Secondly, it probably does not operate if its application would produce manifest inconvenience and absurdity ... Is a stockbroker who is holding shares to the orders of his client liable in damages because he did not sell in a falling market in accordance with the instructions in a letter which was posted but never received? ... In my judgment, the factors of inconvenience and absurdity are but illustrations of a wider principle, namely, that the rule does not apply if, having regard to all the circumstances, including the nature of the subject-matter under consideration, the negotiating parties cannot have intended that there should be a binding agreement until the party accepting an offer or exercising an option had in fact communicated the acceptance or exercise to the other. In my judgment, when this principle is applied to the facts of this case it becomes clear that the parties cannot have intended that the posting of a letter should constitute the exercise of the option."

Acceptance must be posted within any time limit specified in the offer; but what if it arrives later than expected because it has been wrongly addressed by the accepter?

Jacobsen, Sons & Co v E Underwood & Son Ltd 4–25

(1894) 21 R. 654

Court of Session, Second Division: The Lord Justice-Clerk (Macdonald), Lords Young, Rutherford Clark, Trayner

The defenders offered to buy from the pursuers a quantity of straw and required "reply by Monday, 6th inst.". On the evening of the 6 March, the pursuers wrote a letter of acceptance, but the street name and number had been omitted from the defenders' address. As a result, the letter was not received until the midday post on the following day, whereas if the letter had been properly addressed, it should have arrived in the morning post. The defenders returned the letter stating that, as they had not received a reply on the 6th as required, the contract was off. Subsequently, they refused to take delivery of the straw when it arrived. The pursuers now claimed the difference between the contract price and the price which the straw realised when it was eventually sold.

The court found that the defenders' offer had been accepted and a contract had arisen.

"LORD JUSTICE-CLERK (MACDONALD): ... When a letter of acceptance is posted, it is out of the power of the accepting party. He has committed it to a medium of communication which is bound to hold it and safely deliver it to the other party in due course. The dispatcher of the letter has effectually bound himself the moment he has committed his acceptance to the mail. He has done that act of acceptance which, in the language of Mr Bell in his commentaries, 'binds the bargain.' If Mr Bell be correct in his statement of the law,—and there is nothing to be found to the contrary, so far as I can 4–26

> see,—viz., that an offer to sell goods is a consent provisionally to a bargain, if it shall be accepted within a certain time fixed by the offerer or by the law, then I feel compelled to hold that when the offerer names a time such as a certain day of the month, there is given to the person to whom the offer is made the whole of that day to make his decision, and that if within that day he accepts, in a manner to bind himself, the bargain is closed. Up to the end of the time named, the consent of the offerer must be held to subsist, so that it may be taken advantage of by the other party. Now, it has been made a matter of distinct decision that acceptance by post, that is by posting a letter of acceptance, completes the contract. It is in this case undoubted that acceptance by post was a suitable mode, and indeed was contemplated, and that the defenders' representative expected that the acceptance would so come …
>
> A point was raised on the fact that the acceptance did not reach the defender … till noon on the Tuesday, and this was said to have arisen from the pursuers' fault in using an insufficient address. No such point is raised in the pleading, but even if it had been, I should have no difficulty in denying any effect to it. The address upon the letter was the same as was regularly used by the pursuers in their communications to the defenders, and appears not to have led to any delay on other occasions. It probably arose from some defect of acquaintance with the district on the part of some less informed official than the one who usually took charge of letters for the district. It is certain that the defender … never informed the pursuers that their letters were unsatisfactorily addressed, and it is not proved that they were delayed in consequence of the address."

Here the letter was delayed, rather than never arriving. The posting of the letter was within the requirements of the offer and that appears to have been decisive.

There are, however, limits to the rule. The letter must be "posted" so that it is within the control of the postal service or its authorised collectors; but it is not clear whether in Scotland acceptance takes effect on posting, even though it fails to reach the offerer, due to fault or misdirection by the offerer, the offeree or the postal service.

International sales

4–27 The postal rule may also be excluded if the contract is a contract for the sale of goods under the Uniform Law on the Formation of Contracts for the International Sale of Goods 1964, as enacted in the Uniform Laws on International Sales Act 1967 (the 1967 Act). Article 6(1) of that Convention states: "Acceptance of an offer consists of a declaration communicated by any means whatsoever by the offeree". Since this provision apples only where the parties expressly agree that it shall, and since few states have adopted the convention, it has had virtually no impact. In any case, the terminology is not particularly clear. Since there is also a perceived need for an international convention in this field, it is likely that the 1967 Act will eventually be replaced, as recommended by the Scottish Law Commission, Memorandum No.144, by the provisions of the United Nations Convention on Contracts for the International Sale of Goods 1980. Article 18 of that Convention is of much wider scope and contains clearer provisions which, inter alia, preclude the operation of the postal rule in international sale of goods.[22] It must be stressed that these provisions are not yet law, and would only apply to international sales as defined by the convention. Despite their limited scope, they will, when operational, further limit the application of the posting rule.

---

[22] The Article is reproduced in Ch.6.

Mode of communication and the objective intentions of the parties

Although agreement must be established on the objective evidence rather than the subjective intentions of the parties (above, Ch.2) and a person's conduct might be enough to establish objectively that they have accepted, the general rule is that acceptance must be communicated to the offerer through the positive words or acts of the offeree. If such words or acts objectively show acceptance, a contract arises eve if that were not the subjective intention of the person accepting. As professor McBryde points out[23]: **4–28**

> "Because an objective theory of formation is followed a person may act in such a way as to accept an offer, even though that was not the person's intention. This proposition is not as clearly supported by authority as one could wish but it is consistent with principle."

The offerer may also stipulate the positive acts or words which will constitute acceptance: for example, "by return of post" or "on the form provided". If the offeree wishes to accept, the offerss must comply with the conditions stipulated. However, to quote Professor McBryde again[24]:

> "All the consequences of an offeror trying to impose a method of acceptance on the offeree have yet to be worked out in Scotland. This is particularly so in two circumstances: where the offerer has stipulated the offeree's silence as indication of acceptance; and where the mode of acceptance indicated by the offerer is apparently exclusive."

The offeree's silence

Since the mode of acceptance may require some positive act, a stipulation by the offerer that silence will be deemed acceptance will not be a valid stipulation of the mode of acceptance. **4–29**

Wylie & Lochhead v McElroy & Sons **4–30**

(1873) 1 R. 41

Court of Session, Second Division: The Lord Justice-Clerk (Moncreiff), Lords Cowan and Neaves

Wylie & Lochhead (W & L) sought tenders to execute the iron-work in the construction of their new premises. On 23 April, McElroy wrote offering to do the work for £1,253 13s. 4d. They added: "our offer to you of this date is not open for acceptance after tomorrow". On 27 May, W & L wrote accepting the offer, but on new terms. Months later, W & L pressed for performance claiming that an acceptance could be inferred from McElroy's failure to reply to W & L's "letter of acceptance" of 27 May.

The court found that McElroy and Sons were not contractually bound.

> "LORD NEAVES: ... The offer was originally made by the defenders in their letter to the pursuers of 23d April 1872. On the day after this letter was written a discrepancy was found between the defenders' calculations and their offer, and another letter was written making a correction on the offer and reducing it slightly. This probably arose from the fact of the defenders having come in contact with the pursuers' manager, and having been given to understand that they were not the lowest offerers. At any rate the amended offer was intended to be the true offer. It was forwarded to the pursuers during business hours, and the defenders were entitled to have an answer in due course. It was received **4–31**

[23] WW McBryde, *The Law of Contract in Scotland*, 3rd edn (Edinburgh: W. Green, 2007) para.6–79.
[24] WW McBryde, *The Law of Contract in Scotland*, 3rd edn (Edinburgh: W. Green, 2007) para.6–80.

by the pursuers but there is no evidence of the time it was so received. Now, on the one hand, I am not prepared to hold that the sending of the letter on the 24th in no way affected the condition as to acceptance contained in the letter of the 23d. But, on the other, I cannot understand that the writing of the letter of 24th imported an indefinite extension of the time for acceptance, nor do I think that the pursuers ever for a moment so understood it. It may have extended the time for acceptance from the 24th to the 25th ...

There remains, then, the question whether, after such delay in the matter of such a fluctuating commodity, and with a new stipulation of this kind, which would effectually have prevented any mutuality of contract, clogging their acceptance, Messrs Wylie and Lochhead were entitled to think that the mere silence of the defenders inferred a concluded bargain. They had no right whatever to think so. Their letter of 27th May placed the contract on a new basis altogether, and the defenders were entitled to take no notice of it at all if they chose. I do not say that that was a prudent course. It would have been both more courteous and more safe had they sent a reply declining the new terms proposed. But that their mere silence inferred acceptance is a most unreasonable contention. After such delay, and with that new condition attached to make the contract binding, their positive acceptance was required, or such plain acts of adoption and acquiescence as conclusively shewed that they meant to accept. Now, there is no evidence of this. On the contrary, their actings shewed that they considered Messrs Wylie and Lochhead's proposal so preposterous and out of the question as to require no answer. There is nothing in their subsequent actings and correspondence to alter the position of matters. They consistently repudiated throughout the idea of any contract having been entered into. And the case just came to this, that the original offer not having been accepted in due time, and the intended acceptance when sent having been clogged with such a condition, an express acceptance on the part of the defenders, or such mutual actings as conclusively shewed they intended to dispense with that, were required before the contract became binding. Of this there is no proof, and therefore the defenders must be assoilzied."

4–32 This was not always the position in Scots law.[25] Before the firm establishment of the objective test in defining the creation of a contractual agreement, a dominant view was that, in business dealings at least, silence inferred acceptance. We have also seen that, as a general rule, silence cannot be deemed acceptance. Yet, as the *Carlill* case illustrates, the need for communication may be waived. As Bowen LJ said in that decision:

> "One cannot doubt that, as an ordinary rule of law, an acceptance of an offer made ought to be notified to the person who makes the offer, in order that the two minds may come together ... But there is this clear gloss to be made upon that doctrine, that as notification of acceptance is required for the benefit of the person who makes the offer, the person who makes the offer may dispense with notice to himself if he thinks it desirable to do so, and I suppose there can be no doubt that where a person in an offer made by him to another person, expressly or impliedly intimates a particular mode of acceptance as sufficient to make the bargain binding, it is only necessary for the other person to whom such offer is made to follow the indicated method of acceptance; and if the person making the offer, expressly or impliedly intimates in his offer that it will be sufficient to act on the proposal without communicating acceptance of it to himself, performance of the condition is a sufficient acceptance without notification."[26]

[25] WW McBryde, *The Law of Contract in Scotland*, 3rd edn (Edinburgh: W. Green, 2007) paras 6–81—6–83.

[26] *Carlill* [1893] 1 Q.B. 256, 269–70.

Although the case and the statement is no authority in Scots law, the suggestion is that the parties may waive the need for communication of acceptance. Similarly, if A offers to sell their car to B and B replies "I'm not sure; let me think it over and if I don't telephone you by midday tomorrow, you can assume that I've bought it", B is agreeing to be bound by their own silence. It may also be that the parties impliedly waive the need to communicate acceptance under a course of dealings,[27] or where it is a custom of trade for suppliers to send their products to customers on the mutual understanding that they will be paid for in due course unless they are rejected. Such circumstances are, in commercial dealings at least, likely to be rare.[28]

Whether exclusive mode of acceptance required

If the offerer stipulates a particular form of acceptance and clearly indicates that such form of acceptance is exclusive, no other mode of acceptance will suffice. In hire or hire-purchase, the consumer normally makes the offer to hire the goods on a form provided by the hire-purchase or finance company. Such forms normally stipulate that the offer will be accepted when signed by or on behalf of the offeree. If this is stipulated as the only form of acceptance, there is no contract until that form is signed. What if, as in the next case, the goods are damaged before the form is signed by the finance company: is acceptance no longer possible? **4–33**

Financings Ltd v Stimson **4–34**
[1962] 1 W.L.R. 1184
English Court of Appeal: Lord Denning MR, Donovan and Pearson LJJ

On 16 March 1961, the defendant saw a motor car on the premises of a dealer and signed a hire-purchase form provided by the plaintiff finance company and produced by the dealer. The form contained, amongst others, clauses that the agreement should be binding on the finance company only on acceptance by their signature, that the hirer acknowledged that before he signed the agreement he had examined the goods and satisfied himself that they were in good order and condition, and that the goods should be at the risk of the hirer from the time of purchase by the owner. On 18 March the defendant paid the first instalment due and was allowed to take possession of the motor car, but, on 20 March being dissatisfied with it, he returned it to the dealer, saying that he did not want it and offering to forfeit the instalment which he had paid. Neither the defendant nor the dealer informed the finance company of the return of the car. On the night of 24/25 March the car was stolen from the dealer's premises and recovered severely damaged. On 25 March the finance company signed the agreement. Subsequently the finance company sold the damaged car and claimed, inter alia, damages from the defendant for breach of the hire-purchase agreement.

The court found that no contract had arisen.

"LORD DENNING MR: ... [I]t seems to me that the crucial matter in the case is whether there was ever a binding agreement between the hirer [defendant] and the finance company [plaintiffs]. The document which he the [defendant] signed on March 16 was only an offer. Before it was accepted, he returned the car to the dealer and made it clear that he did not want it any more ... **4–35**

---

[27] In *Weatherby v Banham*, 1832 5 Car. & P. 227, e.g. because of the previous course of dealings between the parties, the offeree's inactivity could justifiably be considered an acceptance.

[28] See the opening comments in the judgment of Buckley J in the *Manchester Diocesan* case, below, para.4–38.

It seems to me that, on the facts of this ease, the offer made by the hirer [defendant] was a conditional offer. It was conditional on the car remaining in substantially the same condition until the moment of acceptance. Take the case put by ... Donovan [LJ] in the course of the argument: suppose an offer is made to buy a Rolls Royce car at a high price on one day and before it is accepted, it suffers the next day severe damage. Can it be accepted and the offeror bound? My answer to that is: no, because the offer is conditional on the goods at the moment of acceptance remaining in substantially the same condition as at the time of the offer.

Mr. Rowley [Counsel for the plaintiffs] argued ... that there was an express clause here saying that the goods were to be 'at the risk of the hirer from the time of purchase by the owner.' The time of purchase by the owner, he said, was March 18, when the finance company [the plaintiffs] told the dealer orally that they accepted the transaction. Thenceforward, he said, the goods were at the risk of the hirer [defendant]. This shows, says [counsel], that the condition which I have suggested is inconsistent with the express terms, or, at all events, is not to be implied. In my judgment, however, this clause on which [counsel] relies only comes into operation when a contract is concluded and accepted. Meanwhile the offer is made on the understanding that, so long as it remains an offer, it is conditional on the goods being in substantially the same condition as at the time when the offer was made.

I agree, therefore, with the county court judge in thinking that, in view of the damage which occurred to this car before the acceptance was given, the [plaintiffs] were not in a position to accept the offer, because the condition on which it was made had not been fulfilled. So on that ground also there was no contract."

DONOVAN and PEARSON LJJ concurred with Lord Denning.

This decision should be contrasted with the following dissenting judgment of Lord Denning MR.

4–36 **Robophone Facilities Ltd v Blank**
[1966] 1 W.L.R. 1428
English Court of Appeal: Diplock and Harman LJJ, Lord Denning MR, dissenting

A seven-year lease of a telephone answering machine was to "become binding on the company only upon acceptance thereof by signature on their behalf". The Court of Appeal (Lord Denning dissenting) held that an agreement arose, even though there was no clear evidence as to whether or when the company had signed the agreement, and whether such acceptance had been communicated to the offerer expressly or by conduct before he revoked his offer. The court seemed influenced by the fact that steps had already been taken to install the machine. Lord Denning's views are given below.

4–37 "LORD DENNING MR (dissenting): ... It is clear that the document, although called an agreement, was only an offer. It could be revoked by [the defendant] at any time before it was accepted by the plaintiffs: see *Financings Ltd v Stimson*.[29] In order to become binding, someone duly authorised would have to sign it as accepted on behalf of the plaintiffs: and, moreover, their acceptance would have to be communicated to [the defendant]. The general rule undoubtedly is that, when an offer is made, it is necessary, in order to make a binding contract, not only that it should be accepted, but that the

[29] [1962] 3 All E.R. 386.

acceptance should be notified: see *Carlill v Carbolic Smoke Ball Co*,[30] per Lindley LJ; *Entores Ltd v Miles Far East Corporation*,[31] per Parker LJ. Clause 14 does not dispense with the necessity of notification. Signing without notification is not enough. It would be deplorable if it were. The plaintiffs would be able to keep the form in their office unsigned, and then play fast and loose as they pleased. [The defendant][32] would not know whether or not there was a contract binding them to supply or him to take. Just as mental acceptance is not enough: *Felthouse v Bindley*: nor is internal acceptance within the [plaintiffs'] office. In this very case we know that the plaintiffs signed it sometime or other (for it was produced at the trial complete with signature), but we do not know when the plaintiffs signed it. No evidence was given on the point. In the circumstances I think that until the plaintiffs notified [the defendant] of their acceptance, the agreement was not complete. It was, in the words of [the defendant] himself, provisional ...

The salesman seems to have regarded [the defendant] as bound when he signed the document on June 4, 1965. That was not correct. He was not bound until the [plaintiffs] had signed the acceptance and notified him of it. So far as I can see, they never did so. On June 29, 1965, [the defendant] replied, saying he had nothing further to add. He also cancelled his instructions to the telephone manager of the G.P.O. for the installation in connection with Robophones. On June 29, 1965, the plaintiffs wrote to [the defendant]: 'We now understand that you have firmly refused to instal the Robophone, and thereby cause yourself to be in breach of our rental agreement. We therefore give you notice that the agreement is terminated forthwith, and call upon you pursuant to clause 11 to pay the sum of £245 14s., being 50 per cent. of total rental which would have been due for the agreed period of hiring.'

On July 8, 1965, the plaintiffs issued a writ against [the defendant] claiming £245 14s. under clause 11, and applied for summary judgment ... The plaintiffs never notified him of their acceptance: and, before they did so, he cancelled. I would allow the appeal on this ground alone."

Consider this case in the light of the discussion on unconditional acceptance in Ch.3, above.

The offerer may, alternatively, expressly stipulate a mode of acceptance, e.g. "by completing and posting the enclosed form" without stating that it is exclusive. Must the offeree regard the form stipulated as exclusive? If they use an alternative method, do they risk making an invalid acceptance? These are questions which have neither been considered by the Scottish courts,[33] nor commented upon by the institutional writers. Such issues were, however, raised by the facts in the next case. Although the case involved the sale of land in England, the judge's observations on agreement are equally relevant to Scots law.

Manchester Diocesan Council for Education v Commercial & General Investments Ltd 4–38

(1970) 1 W.L.R. 241

English High Court, Chancery: Buckley J

The defendant tendered to buy old school buildings from the plaintiff. The plaintiff's conditions stated that tenders were to be submitted to the plaintiff's surveyor by a specified date, and that the tenderer selected would be told by letter "sent to him" at "the

[30] [1890-94] All E.R. 127 at 130; [1893] 1 Q.B. 256 at 262.
[31] [1955] 2 All E.R. 493 at 497; [1955] 2 Q.B. 327 at 336.
[32] (1862) 11 C.B.N.S. 869.
[33] In *Jaeger Bros v McMorland* (1902) 10 S.L.T. 63, above, para.2–28, an acceptance by letter of an offer made by telegram did not raise comment.

address given in the tender" (condition 4 of the offer). The conditions also stated that the sale was subject to the approval of the purchase price by the Secretary of State for Education and Science.

A letter of acceptance was sent on 15 September 1964 by the plaintiff's surveyor to the defendant's surveyor at an address different from that stated in the tender. Ministerial approval was obtained on 18 November 1964. The defendant's solicitor subsequently was unable to confirm that there was a binding contract and on 7 January the plaintiff's solicitor sent a formal letter of acceptance to the defendant at the address given in the tender. On the same day, the defendant wrote purporting to withdraw the offer.

The plaintiff successfully sought a declaration that a contract had arisen either on 15 September 1964, or on 7 January 1965.

4–39 "BUCKLEY J: ... An offeror may by the terms of his offer indicate that it may be accepted in a particular manner ... If an offeror stipulates by the terms of his offer it may, or that it shall, be accepted in a particular manner a contract results as soon as the offeree does the stipulated act, whether it has come to the notice of the offeror or not. In such a case the offeror conditionally waives either expressly or by implication the normal requirement that acceptance must be communicated to the offeror to conclude a contract. There can be no doubt that in the present case, if the plaintiff or its authorised agent had posted a letter addressed to the defendant company at No. 15, Berkeley Street on or about 15th September informing the defendant of the acceptance of its tender, the contract would have been complete at the moment when such letter was posted, but that course was not taken.

Condition 4, however, does not say that that shall be the sole permitted method of communicating an acceptance. It may be that an offeror, who by the terms of his offer insists upon acceptance in a particular manner, is entitled to insist that he is not bound unless acceptance is effected or communicated in that precise way, although it seems probable that, even so, if the other party communicates his acceptance in some other way, the offeror may by conduct or otherwise waive his right to insist upon the prescribed method of acceptance. Where, however, the offeror has prescribed a particular method of acceptance, but not in terms insisting that only acceptance in that mode shall be binding, I am of opinion that acceptance communicated to the offeror by any other mode which is no less advantageous to him will conclude the contract. Thus in *Tinn v Hoffman & Co.* (1873) 29 L.T. 271, where acceptance was requested by return of post, Honeyman J. said, at p. 274: 'That does not mean exclusively a reply by letter by return of post, but you may reply by telegram or by verbal message or by any means not later than a letter written [and sent] by return of post.' If an offeror intends that he shall be bound only if his offer is accepted in some particular manner, it must be for him to make this clear. Condition 4 in the present case has not, in my judgment, this effect."

An important feature of the case is that the mode of acceptance was stipulated by the offeree presumably for their benefit. This is quite normal in business transactions, where standard forms of contract, such as tenders, are frequently used. If, as in this case, neither the offerer nor the offeree is adversely affected when another mode is used, a contract will arise.[34] By contrast, in

[34] The stipulation of a signed acceptance should not "be regarded as a condition or stipulation imposed by the defendant company as offeror upon the plaintiff as offeree, but as a term introduced into the bargain by the plaintiff and presumably considered by the plaintiff in some way for the protection or the benefit of the plaintiff. It would consequently be a term, strict compliance with which the plaintiff could waive, provided the defendant company was not adversely affected": [1970] 1 W.L.R. 241, 246, per Buckley J.

Financings v Stimson, if the signed acceptance was not expressly exclusive, there would still be no contract because both parties would have been adversely affected by the substituted form of acceptance. The defendant would have been left with the burnt-out shell of a motor car that he did not want, and the plaintiff with a contract that did not expressly include the terms in the unsigned HP form which it regarded as so important that it expressly stated them in writing. Again, reference should be made to the section on conditional acceptance in the preceding chapter. In particular, the case of *Jaeger Bros Ltd v J&A McMorland*[35] should be carefully considered.

Time of communication: duration of the offer

The offeree must accept while the offer still subsists. The subsistence of the offer depends on the length of time for which it has been left open for acceptance and on the words or actions of the parties. **4–40**

An offer cannot be accepted once it has been withdrawn. An offer may be withdrawn, or revoked, at any time before acceptance, unless it is combined with a promise that it is to remain open for a specified time. Such revocation must be communicated to the offeree prior to acceptance:

> "A state of mind not notified cannot be regarded in dealings between man and man; . . . an uncommunicated revocation is for all practical purposes and in point of law no revocation at all."[36]

Thus, the mere fact that the offerer subjectively no longer intends to be bound does not preclude consent. To do so, the intention must be communicated to the offeree before they accept.

Thomson v James **4–41**

(1855) 18 D. 1

Court of Session, First Division: Lord President (McNeill), Lords Ivory, Curriehill, Deas

J, on 21 November, sent a letter in which he offered to buy an estate from T for £6,400. On 24 November, T wrote to J, recommending that he should increase his offer by £50. J replied by letter on 26 November, again offering £6,400.

T replied by letter dated 28 November, but posted on 1 December, accepting J's offer. That same day, J posted a letter to P, withdrawing his offer. Both letters were delivered on 2 December.

The court found that a contract had arisen between the parties.

> "LORD PRESIDENT (McNEILL): . . . I have formed the opinion, that the offer of purchase made by the defender in his letter of 26th November was effectually accepted by the pursuers' letter of 1st December, and that the contract was thereby completed . . . **4–42**
>
> I hold that a simple unconditional offer may be recalled at any time before acceptance, and that it may be so recalled by a letter transmitted by post; but I hold that the mere posting of a letter of recall does not make that letter effectual as a recall, so as from the moment of posting to prevent the completion of the contract by acceptance. An offer is nothing until it is communicated to the party to whom it is made, and who is to decide whether he will or will not accept the offer. In like manner, I think the recall or withdrawal of an offer that has been communicated can have no effect until the recall or

---

[35] Above, paras 2–28—2–29.

[36] *Byrne v Tienhoven* (1840) 5 C.P.D. 344, per Lindley J.

withdrawal has been communicated, or may be assumed to have been communicated, to the party holding the offer. An offer, pure and unconditional, puts it in the power of the party to whom it is addressed to accept the offer, until by the lapse of a reasonable time he has lost the right, or until the party who has made the offer gives notice that is, makes known that he withdraws it. The purpose of the recall is to prevent the party to whom the offer was made from acting upon the offer by accepting it. This necessarily implies precommunication to the party who is to be so prevented ... Revocation or recall is an act of the offerer, by which he communicates his change of purpose, and withdraws from the offeree the right he had given him to complete the contract by acceptance. Having communicated his purpose to purchase, the offeree is entitled to regard that purpose as unchanged until ... it is withdrawn from him by a communication from the party who conferred it. If he exercises the right by a completed act of acceptance of the offer before notice has reached him, or ought in ordinary course to have reached him, the contract will be binding, although a change of mind on the part of the offerer had taken place, and although he had taken a step towards communicating that change of mind by writing a letter, or even putting it into the post-office ... Mere change of mind, on the part of the offerer, will not prevent an effectual acceptance—not even although that change of mind should be evinced by having been communicated to a third party, or recorded in a formal writing, as for instance in a notarial instrument. In all these cases a binding contract may be made between the parties without that consensus or concursus which a rigidly literal reading of the maxim or rule would require."

If communication of the revocation is necessary, the question arises: what acts amount to a sufficient degree of communication? As with an acceptance, the crucial factor is knowledge in the other party: in this case, the offeree. As with acceptance, the communication must be by the offerer or their authorised agent. Despite English authority to the contrary,[37] it is unlikely that hearing of a revocation from an unauthorised source, however reliable, would be a valid communication. In determining whether a revocation has been adequately communicated, courts apply an objective test. It is not necessary that the offeree should have actually read and understood the revocation, but that it was received in the normal course of business.[38]

An offer stated to be open for a specified time cannot be revoked

4–43 It is not uncommon for an offer to be stated as open for a specified time, or until the happening of a specified event: for example "Offer closes on 31 December", or "Offer open while stocks last". Such an offer cannot validly be accepted once the stated limit has elapsed. An issue which may arise with such offers, however, is whether the offer may be revoked by the offerer before the stated limit has elapsed.

Merely to state that the offer is open for a specified time does not of itself preclude revocation.

---

[37] *Dickinson v Dodds* (1876) 2 Ch.D. 463, C.A.

[38] In discussing the degree of communication necessary to notify a banker that a cheque has been countermanded Lord Cross, in *Eaglehill Ltd v J Neddham (Builders)* [1973] A.C. 922, 1011, stated: "such notice is received when it is opened in the ordinary course of business or would be so opened if the ordinary coarse of business was followed."

A & G Paterson Ltd v Highland Railway Co 4–44
1927 S.C. (H.L.) 32
House of Lords: Viscount Dunedin, Lord Shaw of Dunfermline, Lords Sumner, Wrenbury and Blanesburgh

To help meet the demand for timber during the war, the railway companies introduced "exceptional rates" of l0s. per ton. The Railway Executive Committee, which represented the defenders and all the other railway companies, wrote to the Board of Trade stating that they were prepared to continue the special rates "for so long after the war as the present arrangement entered into between the government and the railway companies remains in force".

The companies withdrew the rates before the war officially ended and before the government surrendered control of the railway companies. The pursuers claimed they had been overcharged in that interim period, in breach of an allegedly binding contract to carry at the exclusive rate.

The House (Lord Shaw dissenting), in reversing the decision of the Second Division, held that the defenders were not bound by the letter. Its terms never became a matter of contract between them and the pursuers, because the offer contained in the letter had never been accepted by, or on behalf of, the pursuers.

"LORD DUNEDIN: . . . Great stress was laid on the distinction between Scottish and English law in respect of the doctrine of consideration. I have on more than one occasion had to deal with this topic, and I do not think I have ever shown any desire to introduce the doctrine of consideration into the law of Scotland. Nay, more, I am prepared to say that the opinion of Lord Ordinary Fraser, expressed in the now old case of *Littlejohn v Hadwen*[39] in which I was counsel many years ago, is right, i.e., if I offer my property to a certain person at a certain price, and go on to say: 'This offer is to be open up to a certain date,' I cannot withdraw that offer before that date, if the person to whom I made the offer chooses to accept it. It would be different in England, for in the case supposed there would be no consideration for the promise to keep the offer open. But what is the reason of this? It is because the offer as made contained two distinct promises: (1) to sell at a certain price, and (2) to keep the offer open. It seems to me that (2) is completely wanting in the present case. It is just as if a tradesman put up a notice: 'My price for such-and-such goods during November will be so-and-so'. That offer may at any time be converted into a contract by a person tendering the price for the goods, but there is no contract that the tradesman may not change his mind and withdraw his offer. Therefore, upon the simple question of contract, I think the argument for the respondents breaks down, and that in my mind disposes of the case. 4–45

The consequences of the other view would be very remarkable. An offer is made to do a certain thing at a certain price during a certain time. It is not specially addressed to some person, but is proclaimed, so to speak, *urbi et orbi*, so that anyone may come forward and say: 'I will now take advantage of the price, and though you have withdrawn it, I say you were bound not to withdraw it'."

It is clear from this that if the offer is combined with a specific, unilateral promise that the offer will not be revoked for a specific period of time, that unilateral promise is itself binding, so that the offer cannot be revoked before that time elapses.

---

[39] *Littlejohn v Hadwen* (1882) 24 S.L.R. 5.

4–46

Littlejohn v Hadwen
(1882) 20 S.L.R. 5
Court of Session, Outer House: Lord Fraser

H, through his agent, Black, informed L that he was willing to sell his estate for £12,000. L wrote asking for further particulars, which were supplied by letter. A postscript, written by Black in his own hand but only initialled by him, stated:

> "P.S. it is understood that Mr Littlejohn has the offer of Rielonny at the above price of £12,000 for ten days from this date."

Four days later, H wrote withdrawing the estate from the market. L immediately responded that the offer was binding and could not be withdrawn and, two days later, sent a formal acceptance.

The Lord Ordinary (Fraser) found for the defender, on the basis that the letter and its postscript were not holograph and therefore binding upon the defender, because Black's signature rather than his mere initials were required. In the course of his judgment the Lord Ordinary added:

4–47 "LORD FRASER: . . . The question now is, whether this letter and postscript constitute a binding obligation against the defender to sell his estate of Rielonny at the sum specified . . . The Lord Ordinary is of opinion that the defender was not entitled to withdraw his offer before the expiry of the ten days; that it was an obligation, no doubt unilateral, but still binding upon the offerer during the appointed period. According to the law of England, such an offer as this was revocable before acceptance; and that law was pressed upon the Lord Ordinary as one which should be followed here. In a recent case the point was expressly determined. [His Lordship then referred to the Case of *Dickinson v Dodds* L.R. 2 Ch. Div. 463 and continued:] . . . The defender contended that those principles [that a promise unsupported by consideration from the other party is unenforceable as a *nudum pactum*] ought to be recognised in a Scottish Court, as being consistent with good sense, and as giving effect to the rule of law that both parties must be bound or neither. But the reason for the English rule is not in accordance with the law of Scotland. The English law as to *nudum pactum* is, that an offer being without consideration, is not binding either in law or equity, and therefore a statement that the offer is open until a particular date means merely, that if not accepted on or before that date it will be at an end without further notice of withdrawal.

The same rule that *ex nudo pacto non oritur actio* was recognised by the civil law, but the ground of it in that system was not the want of consideration but the want of solemnities. A mere gratuitous promise or offer had no legal efficacy by the civil law, unless it was entered into in the solemn and formal mode of *stipulatio*, which was held to indicate that the parties really intended and meant that it should constitute a binding obligation.

The question has been dealt with by Professor Bell in two of his works—1st, *The principles*, sec. 79; and 2ndly, in the last work he published—his *Treatise on the Law of Sale*. In his *Principles* he says—'If a time be limited for acceptance, the offer is held to subsist, and not to be revocable during that time; and to be withdrawn by the expiration of that time without acceptance; and the return of post is in mercantile cases *presumed* to be the time limited.' In his *Treatise on Sale* he deals with the matter more at large, and holds that a contrary doctrine rests upon 'the subtleties of lawyers,' and is contrary to 'the common sense and understanding of mankind.' Whether a rule which constitutes a part of the law of all countries where English jurisprudence prevails, and which was recognised in the civil law, can be fitly so designated, may be fairly questioned. But

> undoubtedly the learned author is correct in stating that a gratuitous unilateral obligation, or promise, or offer, if written in the appropriate manner, will be enforced according to the law of Scotland. In short, the rule *ex nudo pacto non oritur actio* constitutes no part of that law.[40]
>
> Professor Bell deals with the case as if the point had never occurred for decision; but this is not so. Elchies reports the decision in *Marshall v. Blackwood*, 12th November 1747 ... This decision was affirmed in the House of Lords, as noted by Elchies ... The affirmance of the judgment of the Court of Session (which, however, was only carried, as Elchies states, by the casting vote of the President) must be taken as conclusive upon the question, and so it has been regarded by Professor More, who refers to it in his notes to Stair (p. 58) in the following terms: 'Though it be a general rule in regard to all mutual contracts that both parties must be bound, or both free, a person may nevertheless bind himself by an offer to sell an article, provided it shall be accepted of by the other party within a certain time'."

If a counter-offer destroys the original offer, does it thereby also destroy a promise to keep an offer open for a specified time? Gloag suggests this is so:

> "If the refusal (of the offer) is not peremptory, but combined with a request for better terms, the general construction is that the offer is gone, and the party to whom it was made, on failure to obtain the terms he requests, cannot fall back on an acceptance of the original offer."

This statement was considered in *Wolf and Wolf v Forfar Potato Co*, above at para.2–53. The view of the majority of the Court of Session in this case is based on a very strict view of the effects of counter-offer. The dissenting judgment of Lord McDonald, however, raises some interesting issues when one considers the battle of the forms.[41]

An offer which has lapsed is no longer capable of acceptance

Offers are not indefinite. An offer must be accepted while it subsists. If a time for acceptance is stipulated, or if the offer is of a specified duration, the offer can be accepted only at the time stipulated or within the specified duration. Defining duration may be difficult[42] and if this cannot be done, or if no duration is stipulated, the offer remains open for acceptance within a reasonable time. What is reasonable depends on the circumstances of the particular case. If it can be implied from the offer, or the way it was communicated, that an immediate or early response was required, but the offeree delays in communicating their acceptance, the offer may have lapsed. The acceptance would therefore be ineffective. In *Quenerduaine v Cole*,[43] where a telegraphed counter-offer was purportedly accepted by letter, Grove J held that **4–48**

> "the fact of receiving the offer by telegram imposing a new condition implied the expectation of a prompt reply, and the acceptance by letter was not, therefore, made in reasonable time".

---

[40] Erskine, iii. 2. 1.

[41] See above, para.2–53.

[42] In *A&G Paterson v Highland Ry Co*, 1919 2 S.L.T.123, for example, the duration of the offer as stated depended on the duration of the war. Although the matter was not essential to the decision of the majority of the House of Lords, Lord Sumner interpreted this as meaning the cessation of hostilities in November 1918, rather than the official termination under statutory instrument of 31 August 1921.

[43] *Quenerduaine v Cole* (1883) 32 W.R. 185.

Similarly, an offer to purchase shares in a company could not be open for acceptance for almost six months.[44] In negotiations over the purchase of extensive and expensive buildings, five months was a reasonable length of time for the offer to purchase to remain open, especially as continuing negotiations between the parties indicated a mutual willingness to proceed.[45]

4–49 **Wylie & Lochhead v McElroy & Sons**

(1873) 1 R. 41

Court of Session, Second Division: Lord Neaves

The facts are as stated above, paras 4–30—4–31.

"LORD NEAVES: ... [D]elay until 27th May was utterly unreasonable and unwarrantable. Supposing the offer still open, they were in a position, at least by the beginning of May, to close with it. But there is evidence, I think to shew that the pursuers were, during this lapse of time, trying to play one offerer against another, and by the use of ambiguous terms to induce them to bid one another down. The propriety and necessity of an early decision on a matter of this kind renders such a course of dealing most questionable. Where such a fluctuating commodity as iron is concerned hours must suffice for decision, not weeks or months. Here, however, we have nothing done till the end of May, when a letter is written which is founded on as an acceptance of the offer of the 23d and 24th April. If it was intended to be so it should have contained nothing but an acceptance. But instead of this a most important condition is attached, which, if agreed to, would have put the parties in a most anomalous position. Had it been agreed to, the defenders would have found themselves liable in the event of any failure to fulfil the contract, while the pursuers might have drawn back in the middle of the execution of the work, and been liable for no breach of contract. They would have had to pay for actual work done. But as for any general claim for non-implement of the bargain, that would have been barred."

An offer may lapse on the occurrence or non-occurrence of an event stipulated in the offer. An offer may for example, be open "while stocks last", so that it lapses when stocks are depleted. Similarly, an offer to purchase a car from a hire-purchase company may lapse if the vehicle is no longer in a reasonable condition by the time the company purports to accept the offer.[46]

An offer lapses when it is rejected

4–50 The rejection is effective from the time that it is communicated. This raises particular problems where the communications between the parties are through the post. The following example illustrates the problem.

The offeree posts an acceptance. They subsequently decides to reject and posts a letter to that effect. That rejection reaches the offerer before the acceptance. The offerer, having received the rejection, resells to a third party, before they receive the acceptance. Since the posting rule applies to the acceptance, but not to the rejection, the offer subsisted at the time of acceptance and a binding contract would arise upon posting of the acceptance. The seller would be bound to sell to a person who does not wish to buy, and could not sell to the third party who wishes to buy. This was not the view adopted by the Court of Session in the case which follows.

---

[44] *Ramsgate Victoria Hotel Co v Montefiore* (1866) L.R. 1 Ex. 109.

[45] *Manchester Diocesan Council for Education v Commercial & General Investments Ltd* [1970] 1 W.L.R. 241; [1969] 3 All E.R. 1593.

[46] *Financings Ltd v Stimson* [1622] 1 W.L.R. 11944; [1962] 3 All E.R. 386 (see above, para.4–34).

Countess of Dunmore v Alexander 4–51
(1830) 9 S. 190
Court of Session, First Division: The Lord President (Hope), Lords Craigie, Balgray and Gillies

The Countess had accepted Betty Alexander's offer of service in a letter sent through Alexander's former employer, Lady Agnew. She subsequently revoked that acceptance in a letter, sent through Lady Agnew, which was delivered to Alexander at the same time as the letter of acceptance.

Alexander unsuccessfully sued for loss of wages, contending that the contract was complete either by the writing or putting of the letter of acceptance into the post office, or at least by it being received by Lady Agnew.

"LORD BALGRAY: The admission that the two letters were simultaneously received, puts an end to the case. Had the one arrived in the morning, and the other in the evening of the same day, it would have been different. Lady Dunmore conveys a request to Lady Agnew to engage Alexander, which request she recal[l]s by a subsequent letter that arrives in time to be forwarded to Alexander as soon as the first. This, therefore, is just the same as if a man had put an order into the post-office, desiring his agent to buy stock for him. He afterwards changes his mind, but cannot recover his letter from the post-office. He therefore writes a second letter countermanding the first. They both arrive together, and the result is, that no purchase can be made to bind the principal. 4–52

LORD CRAIGIE: I take a different view. Lady Agnew, acting for the servant, writes to Lady Dunmore, stating Alexander's readiness to accept the proposed wages, recommending her on account of her character, and concluding thus:—'If Lady Dunmore decides on taking Betty Alexander, perhaps she will have the goodness to mention whether she expects her at the new or the old term.' Now, what is the answer of the Countess?—a request to Lady Agnew to engage the servant at the wages mentioned, accompanied with a notice that 'she wishes to have her at the new term,' &c. Lady Agnew was thus the mandatory for both parties, the mistress and the servant; she was on the same footing as a person in the well-known situation of broker for both buyer and seller. Every letter between the principals, relative to an offer or an acceptance respectively was, as soon as it reached Lady Agnew, the same as delivered for behoof of the party on whose account it was written. I hold, therefore, that when Lady Dunmore's letter reached Lady Agnew, the contract of hiring Alexander was complete; the offer on the part of Alexander being met by an intimated acceptance on the part of the Countess. No subsequent letter from the Countess to Lady Agnew could annul what had passed by the mere circumstance of its being delivered, at the same time with the first, into the hands of Alexander. I do not think the servant could have retracted after the first letter reached Lady Agnew; and if she was bound, it seems clear that the Countess could not be free. 4–53

LORD GILLIES: I am decidedly of the opinion first expressed. Lady Agnew received a letter desiring her to engage a servant for Lady Dunmore. She proceeds to take steps towards this by putting a letter into the post-office for the purpose of making the engagement. But, before this letter reaches its destination her authority to hire the servant is recalled, and, by the help of an express, she forwards the recal [sic], so that it is eventually delivered through the same post with the former letter, and both reach the servant at once. They thus neutralize each other, precisely as in the case put by Lord Balgray of an order and a countermand being sent through one post to an agent. I am therefore for adhering. 4–54

4–55 LORD PRESIDENT (HOPE): I concur with the majority. There was no completed contract here, and Lady Dunmore was at liberty to resile as she did."

The First Division made no reference to the posting rule, which was not established in Scotland at the time. The majority found that no contract had arisen. Although argument in the courts below centred on whether Lady Agnew could make the contract under mandate, the judgments in the Court of Session give no consistent or clear reason for finding no contract. The general view was that the two letters had "neutralised" each other. The better view is that the case is "an exception, conceived in the interests of common sense, to the general rule that the posting of an acceptance concludes the contract".[47]

Consider the following situations: B rejects by letter an offer received from A. They subsequently send a letter of acceptance. The letter of rejection reaches A first. Upon receiving the rejection, A sells to a third party. Does it make legal or commercial sense to allow an offeree to change their mind in these circumstances? Is it perhaps better to regard such a subsequent acceptance as a new offer, which the other party is free to accept or reject? Suppose that B rejects the offer by letter. They subsequently sends a letter of acceptance, which reaches A first. Is B in a different position from the offeree who makes up their mind to reject, tells nobody, changes their mind and then communicates acceptance?

The DCFR provides in detail for the withdrawal and revocation of an offer. The issues surrounding withdrawal and revocation, withdrawal and lapse were recently considered by the Scottish Law Commission in the context of, amongst other instruments, the DCFR.

4–56 *Review of Contract Law: Discussion on Formation of Contract*

Scottish Law Commission Discussion Paper No.154 (March 2012)

[3.17] " . . . and the proposed CESL do not mention the possibility of the offer being stated to be irrevocable but it would follow from the overall system of 'notice' that an irrevocability provision in an offer would not take effect until it reached the addressee. Thus such an offer could be withdrawn up to and including that point in time.

3.18 Scots law has not addressed this question directly but it would, in principle, reach the same answer. It is established that offers can be terminated without liability unless either declared to be irrevocable in some way (a firm offer) or effectively accepted by the offeree.[25] But even the declaration of irrevocability probably requires objective communication to the offeree to be effective, so if the offeror communicates withdrawal before or at the same time as the declaration it is thought that the courts would find the offeror not bound.

4–57 **(iv) Revocation of offer**

DCFR II.–4:202 Revocation of offer

CFR An offer may be revoked if the revocation reaches the offeree before the offeree has dispatched an acceptance or, in cases of acceptance by conduct, before the contract has been concluded.

(2) An offer made to the public can be revoked by the same means as were used to make the offer.

(3) However, a revocation of an offer is ineffective if:

(a) the offer indicates that it is irrevocable;
(b) the offer states a fixed time for its acceptance; or

[47] AD Gibb, *Select Cases in the Law of Scotland* 2nd edn (Edinburgh: W. Green, 1951), p.12.

(c) it was reasonable for the offeree to rely on the offer as being irrevocable and the offeree has acted in reliance on the offer.

[3.20] The basic rules stated in the CISG Article 16(1) and (2)(a) (that an offer may be revoked at any time until the completion of acceptance by the offeree unless the offeror has declared it to be irrevocable) are, as the RFC pointed out, consistent with existing Scots law.[26] It is to be noted, however, that under the CISG scheme dispatching an acceptance by post does not immediately conclude the contract, rather, the contract is concluded when the acceptance reaches the offeror.[27] In Scots law, dispatching the acceptance not only precludes any subsequently arriving revocation of the offer from having effect but also concludes the contract.[28] It is, however, another question whether an offeree who has done everything reasonably possible to effect an acceptance should be protected from the offeror's subsequently arriving revocation. The CISG view, a further affirmed by ... the DCFR is that the offeree should indeed be protected in this way.

[3.21] ... The DCFR deals explicitly with acceptance by conduct and makes it clear that the revocation of an offer prior to such acceptance will also be effective. This was what the RFC thought would be "the appropriate result",[32] and we agree.

[3.22] ... Since ... the DCFR regards general offers as normally offers, it has to provide an explicit rule ... which enables offerors to revoke using the same method of communication as was deployed in making the offer in the first place. ... That rule appears to be a sensible and practical solution to the problem. It is of course a default rule, and it remains open to a party making a general offer to specify time limits or methods of recall.

[3.23] We note that there appears to be still no authority on this matter in Scots law.[34] Professor McBryde has argued that revoking a general offer in the same way that it was made may not be any more practicable than notifying all possible offerees.[35] We would nevertheless regard this default rule as a useful addition, if only to encourage those making general offers to consider whether or not to include in them express statements about their revocation. Professor McBryde's concern for the offeree who acts in reasonable reliance upon a general offer not having been revoked[36] may be met if, as the DCFR ... provide[s], such an offeree can prevent the offer being revoked.[37]

3.24 A final point of difficulty ... concerns the provisions on when an offer cannot be revoked. ... The DCFR ... may be thought to offer a slightly different, harder-edged rule: an offer may indicate that it is irrevocable, or state a fixed time for its acceptance, in which case it is irrevocable. It is, however, still a question of construction ultimately whether or not an offer has indicated its irrevocability, or stated a fixed time for its acceptance.

3.25 The DCFR ... rule would therefore not necessarily change the outcome of ... two Scottish cases ... In the first of these, it was held that an offer 'made on condition of acceptance within three days' was one which could not be accepted after three days rather than one which was irrevocable within the same period.[40] Likewise in the second case an offer in which it was stated that the contract must be concluded by a particular date and time was held not to be irrevocable.[41] We think that, subject always to whether an offer on its proper construction meets the requirements of irrevocability, the DCFR ... formulation of the rule is ... more readily understood by the reader. We would therefore suggest that, if there is to be a statutory restatement of the law of formation of contract, on this topic the DCFR ... rule provides the better model to be followed ...

3.26 Finally on irrevocability ... the DCFR ... differs from present Scots law in allowing for the possibility of an offer being irrevocable where it was reasonable for the offeree to rely on the offer being irrevocable and the offeree has acted in reliance upon it. The RFC suggested that a typical case for the application of this rule would be 'where the offer itself did not indicate irrevocability but where there was a collateral assurance on which it was reasonable for the offeree to rely'.[42] There would have been difficulty under the law as it stood in 1993 ... was reasonable for the offeree would be "where the offer itself did not indicate irrevocability because such a promise then required proof by the promisor's writ or oath. However, in 1995 RoW(S)A implemented our recommendation for the abolition of the writ or oath rule, replacing it with a rule requiring the constitution of a promise by writing signed by the promisor.[43] There is moreover an exception from the requirement of writing where the promise is made in the course of a business. Thus the only difficulty that would now stand in the way of using the concept of promise in the case figured in the RFC is the question of whether or not the assurance amounted to a promise.[44]

3.27 It might therefore be thought that there was no need in Scots law for a reliance rule like that in ... the DCFR ... However, there is one further scenario upon which we have already touched: that of the general offer. If the DCFR provision on this was followed in any statutory restatement of the law of contract formation, then as a default rule such an offer would generally be revocable in the same way as it was made in the first place. We have already noted Professor McBryde's concern that this could work unfairly in a case where a party had acted in reliance upon the general offer without having any reasonable opportunity to become aware of the offeror's revocation.[45] The reliance rule might give some protection to such a party by making a revocation ineffective so far as that party was concerned. Equally the offeror could make clear in the offer that a right to revoke was retained, thus making offeree reliance on its irrevocability not reasonable. The example makes it clear that in thinking about this specific issue one should consider it in the context of the system of rules as a whole, including their default character ...

4–58 **DCFR: II.–4:203 Rejection of offer**

CFR: II.–4:203 Rejection of offert reasonofferor, the offer lapses.

3.30 The DCFR and the proposed CESL are the same as the CISG on the subject of the rejection of an offer except that, like the PICC, they omit the latter's phrase, 'even if it is irrevocable'. This is presumably on the grounds of redundancy. Scots law is to the same effect: and even the irrevocable offer falls when it is rejected.[53]

3.31 We continue to hold that view.

...

4–59 **Delayed offer**

3.43 A final question not mentioned in the RFC or in any of the instruments surveyed for the purposes of this Discussion Paper is the offer that is delayed in its transmission to the offeree. The scenario is one where the offer states a time limit within which an acceptance must be completed but does not reach the offeree until after the time limit expires. A typical case might be one where the offer is posted but held up in the mail; another might be the emailed offer which suffers from network delays. In these cases the delay is generally not the offeror's fault, unless the communication is sent at a time when the system is generally known to be likely to suffer problems—for example, when a postal workers' strike is imminent. But delay may also be caused by the offeror having misaddressed the offer, for example by sending a letter to a previous address of the offeree's, or by putting the wrong house/flat number or street name (for example, 'Acacia Way' for 'Acacia Avenue'). Emails can also be misaddressed, and while frequently that will lead to the sender receiving immediate notification of a failed transmission, it can also be that the address used is one that, although still technically available, the recipient has given notice is no longer in regular use. But the offeror may remain unaware of the difficulty because, for example, the address used was pulled from an electronic address book or the email address field was populated automatically when the email was being composed.

3.44 The US Restatement (2d) Contracts provides that the offeree 'who knows or has reason to know of the delay'[88] cannot accept, even if the delay is due to the fault of the offeror. Furmston & Tolhurst suggest that '[s]ince a delay is normally apparent from the date of the letter or its postmark, in these circumstances the offeree will know or have reason to know of the delay and cannot accept the offer'.[89] The same holds true for emails. But, the Restatement continues, 'if the delay is due to the fault of the offeror or to the means of transmission adopted by him, and the offeree neither knows nor has reason to know that there has been delay', the time within which the offeree can accept is extended by the delay. It is difficult to figure a case for the application of this rule other than one where the time-limit is stated in very imprecise terms (for example, 'by the end of today/this week/this month') but the offeror's communication itself remains completely undateable: for instance, an undated letter which is either hand-delivered at a point in time unknown to the offeree or posted but with a postmark on its envelope too faint or blurred to be legible.

3.45 We are uncertain as to the regularity with which this potential problem occurs, and we would welcome information from any consultees who may have had relevant experience about whether any difficulties have arisen in consequence. We think that the first leg of Section 49 of the Restatement is undoubtedly the rule which the Scottish courts would develop should a relevant case come before them, and we have no hesitation in recommending the enactment of such a rule should it be thought useful to have it. We are less clear whether there really is a need for a rule like that in the second leg of Section 49, since the number of cases in which it might be applied must, we think, be very few . . .

---

[21] This text is in the table above para 2.15 and has been adapted here by replacing "The notice" and "addressee" with "An offer" and "offeree".

[22] For which see paras 3.20-3.27 below.

[23] See Vogenauer and Kleinheisterkamp, *PICC Commentary*, pp 241 and 245; DCFR, vol 1, pp 114 (Comment F) and 301 (Comment A).

[25] Walker, *Contracts*, para 7.37; *SME*, vol 15, para 617; McBryde, *Contract*, paras 6.45-6.46 and 6.57; Gloag, *Contract*, pp 35-36. This is the general rule under English law also: *Chitty on Contracts*, para 2-088.

[26] RFC, paras 3.11 and 3.13.

[27] See further at paras 4.6-4.14 below.

[28] See in particular *Thomson v James* (1855) 18 D 1.

[32] Ibid.

[34] McBryde, Contract, paras 6.58-6.61.[35] Ibid, para 6.60.[36] Ibid, para 6.61: "Logic and equity suggest that the offeror should pay for the consequences of actions known to and relied upon by the offeree".

[37] See further paras 3.20-3.21.

[40] *Heys v Kimball and Morton* (1890) 17 R 381 at 384-385.

[41] *Effold Properties Ltd v Sprot* 1979 SLT (Notes) 85 (OH).

[42] RFC, para 3.15.

[43] RoW(S)A, ss 1 and 11; and see fn 18 to para 1.11 above.

[44] For an example of difficulties of this kind, see the recent case of *Wylie v Grosset* 2011 SLT 609 (OH).

[45] See para 3.23.

[53] *Wolf & Wolf v Forfar Potato Co* 1984 SLT 100 (IH); *Rutterford Ltd v Allied Breweries Ltd* 1990 SLT 249 (OH). It should be noted that both these cases concerned "qualified acceptances" rather than outright rejections of offers, but there can be no doubt that the same principle would apply to an outright rejection: McBryde, *Contract*, para 6.37, citing *Lawrence v Knight* 1972 SC 26 (OH) and *Tenbey v Stolt Comex Seaway Ltd* 2001 SC 638 (OH); also Walker, *Contracts*, para 7.37; *SME*, vol 15, para 655. Gloag does not appear to discuss the point.

[88] At Section 49.

[89] Furmston and Tolhurst, *Contract Formation*, para 3.13 (citing, at fn 28, the case of *Chesebrough v Western Union Telegraph Co* 76 Misc 516, 135 NY Supp 583 (1912) affirmed 157 App Div 914, 142 NY Supp 1112 (1913), which, however, is about an acceptance telegram, rather than an offer, being delayed in transmission but held nonetheless, in an application of the postal acceptance rule, to be effective).

PART 3

VALIDITY

CHAPTER 5

THE EXERTION OF PRESSURE OR INFLUENCE

In many cases where fraud, error and misrepresentation are pled, there are often accompanying averments that the contract was otherwise affected by influences brought to bear by the defender on the pursuer. For example, a pursuer challenging the validity of a contract signed by them might argue that they signed under pressure brought by the defender, in addition to arguing that they signed in error or were misled by the other party. **5–01**

The following chapter will consider how error and misrepresentation may affect an otherwise valid contract and, in particular, how fraud plays an important role in deciding whether a contract is voidable. This chapter considers cases where pressure has been exerted by one party to a contract on another. The validity of a contract might be challenged on the grounds of: facility and circumvention; undue influence; and force and fear[1] or extortion. As a general rule, the contract is rendered voidable, although it is not clear whether force and fear makes the contract void or voidable.

It is difficult to separate the grounds in many of the cases because they are so often pled jointly or as alternatives. The following extracts must be read in that light. The extracts that follow have been selected to illustrate and highlight the more contentious and complex aspects of this topic.

Facility and circumvention

Facility and circumvention is a rare plea, but, even today, it is important in circumstances which do not amount to fraud, but where there is an element of disingenuousness in one party coupled with relative weakness in the other. **5–02**

Defective Consent and Consequential Matters **5–03**

Scottish Law Commission Memo. No.42 (1 June 1978)

"Volume 1, Part 1

1.44 *Facility and circumvention.* As a ground for annulment of obligations, facility and circumvention developed out of the law of fraud. Initially, even in the case of a facile person, fraud, in the sense of a machination or contrivance to deceive, had to be established before annulment was possible. But the courts were very ready in such cases to infer fraud, especially where a person of weak intellect, albeit not incapax, entered into a grossly unequal bargain. However, around the middle of the 19th century, it was decided that facility and circumvention was not simply a species of fraud or a way in which fraud could be established. They were separate pleas, and separate issues raising these pleas could be sent to the jury for trial. Since that time most discussion of facility and circumvention has been centred around the form of issue which has come to be accepted as appropriate in such cases, namely: 'Whether on or about . . . the pursuer was weak and facile in mind and easily imposed on; on whether the defender, taking advantage of the pursuer's said facility and weakness did, by fraud or circumvention, procure [the obligation in question] to the lesion of the pursuer?' *McCulloch v McCracken* (1857) 20 D. 206. It is clear from the decided cases, in spite of an isolated expression to the contrary, that it is not necessary that both fraud and circumvention be

---

[1] As Professor McBryde points out, it is probably more accurate to speak of "force or fear": WW McBryde, *The Law of Contract*, 3rd edn (Edinburgh: W. Green, 2007), para.16–02.

established. However, it has quite recently been indicated by the House of Lords that, at least where the grantor of a deed is still alive, dishonesty or deceit must be shown before circumvention can be held to exist (*Mackay v Campbell*, 1967 S.C. (H.L.) 53). Our view ... is that it would be preferable if facility and circumvention (and also undue influence; and one form of extortion) were replaced by a more general and comprehensive ground of annulment. But if facility and circumvention is to be preserved as a separate ground upon which annulment can be sought, we think that the reference to 'fraud' in the issue is misleading and should be eliminated. And while we regard as valuable the recent stressing by the House of Lords of the requirement that *dishonest* advantage must be shown to have been taken of the obligor's weakness, we also think that it should be made clear that dishonesty can, in appropriate cases, be inferred from the circumstances in which an obligation was concluded, without the necessity of proving actual concrete instances of dishonest or deceitful conduct. Thus, repeated and ultimately successful solicitation from a weak and facile person of an agreement highly favourable to the other party might in certain situations give rise to an inference of dishonesty."

The Scottish Law Commission would replace facility and circumvention with a general ground of lesion; for the present, two key issues remain contentious: the degree of "facility" that is required; and the extent and nature of the "circumvention" necessary to establish the plea, bearing in mind that it developed out of fraud.

5–04

Gray v Binny
(1879) 7 R. 332
Court of Session, First Division: The Lord President (Inglis), Lords Shand, Deas

Gray, then 24 and heir-apparent under a deed of entail, executed a deed whereby he consented to a disentail. The estimated value of the estate was £125,000. Once the estate was vested in him, he could have legally converted it into a fee simple.

The heiress of the entail in possession, Gray's mother, was extensively in debt to Binny, her legal adviser and also wished to provide for her children by her second marriage. She and Binny negotiated with Gray the disentailment, but, instead of £41,000, the value of his reversionary interest, he signed away his entitlements for £6,277 17s. The difference went to his mother and she transferred the moneys into a trust of which Binny was a trustee to pay off her debt to Binny and to provide for her other children. The mother died shortly afterwards and Gray now brought an action against his mother's trustees to reduce the disentail and his mother's trust-disposition. The Lord Ordinary found for Gray on the basis that undue influence had been exerted over him by his mother. Binny reclaimed, basing his claim on undue influence. The court found for Binny, but in the course of their judgments, their Lordships considered the possibility of facility and circumvention.

"LORD SHAND: ... It appears to me to be very clear that a deed so prejudicial to the granter, and obtained in such circumstances, cannot, when challenged, be allowed to stand.

The defenders have maintained that the deed can only be set aside by a judgment which shall expressly affirm that it was obtained by fraud. They plead that there are two forms of issues, and two only, in the law of this country, applicable to such a case, in both of which fraud must be established, the first being the ordinary issue of whether the deed was obtained through fraudulent representations or fraudulent concealment; and the second, whether the pursuer was weak and facile in his mind and easily imposed on, and whether the pursuer's mother, taking advantage of his weakness and facility, did by fraud or circumvention procure the deed to his lesion ...

The case is one in which confidence was invited and given, and parental influence unduly used by the pursuer's mother, with the assistance of her agent, in procuring a deed to her own great advantage, and to the corresponding disadvantage of her son; and a deed so obtained is, I think, liable to be set aside without affirming that it was procured through fraud ... I am not satisfied that either Mrs Gray or Mr Binny realised at all to its full extent the value of the concession which the pursuer was making, for there had been no calculation made by an actuary or otherwise, such as we have in evidence now, as to the value of the pursuer's interest in the estate, while all the parties seem to have thought that at least it was questionable whether Mrs Gray's prospects of life were not even better than those of her son. And while it is impossible to regard Mr Binny's conduct except with much disapproval—for he ought certainly to have taken care that the pursuer had independent advice and assistance—yet the considerations I have now mentioned are of no small weight against the view that the transaction is to be traced to a corrupt motive, or to deceit or fraudulent conduct on the part of those who procured the deed.

Again, I am unable to affirm that the pursuer was weak and facile in mind, and that advantage was taken of such weakness and facility. I cannot regard it as weakness and facility on the part of a son that he should be induced by filial affection to help his mother out of pecuniary difficulties, and to place so much trust and confidence in her as to execute a deed dealing with rights of his own, which he knows to be of value, in terms of her request, and in a form approved of by her agent, and that without thinking it necessary to resort to independent professional advice as a means of protection for himself. Indeed, I believe that the great majority of young men—certainly the majority of young men who had been brought up without business training, as the pursuer had been—would have acted precisely as he did, and in so doing would have exhibited only natural affection and trust—not mental weakness or facility ...

[I]t is a question of circumstances in every case in which circumvention is alleged whether circumvention has been employed. I know of no fixed criterion or definite standard to which an appeal can be made as to what amounts to circumvention used in the case of a person who labours under weakness of facility of mind.

...

LORD DEAS: ... [This case] might have been quite well tried under our ordinary and well established issue of facility coupled with fraud or circumvention to the lesion of the granter of the deed. A verdict affirmative of that issue has always been regarded as importing an imputation on character somewhat short of a verdict on our equally well-known issue of fraud, because circumvention of a person easily persuaded is considered a less daring species of fraud than a verdict on the direct issue of fraud imports.

Weakness or facility of mind in the sense in which we use the words in the first of these forms of issue may arise from many different causes, temporary or permanent—for instance, from old age, excitability, timidity, sickness, or, as in this case, from affection. The cases ... illustrate how great the variation may be in that which in practice we hold may constitute weakness or facility of mind.

It seems to me, in short, that the two classes of issues under which cases of reduction similar to the present have been tried in our practice sufficiently comprehend the various cases of undue influence, [*etc.*], which Lord Shand has spoken of as good grounds of action in England."

The case on appeal appears to have been argued solely on the issue of undue influence. The comments of the judges on facility and circumvention are therefore obiter.

It is clear from these extracts that fraud and circumvention differ in degree and that either will suffice to reduce a contract entered into by a facile person.

Note the categories of facility suggested by Lord Deas. How, as he suggests, could they "comprehend the cases of undue influence" considered below? Furthermore, Lord Deas appears to disagree with Lord Shand, who clearly did not equate "affection" with facility or "weakness of mind".

Despite the pronouncements of Lord Shand above, as suggested in the Law Commission's Memorandum No.42, the definition and degree of "circumvention" necessary to establish the plea remains an issue. The following decision of the House of Lords seems to establish a high standard of proof.

5–05 **Mackay v Campbell**

1967 S.C. (H.L.) 53

House of Lords: Lords Reid, Guest, Upjohn, Wilberforce and Pearson

Campbell claimed that his signature on missives to sell a farm to Mackay had been obtained while he was in a state of facility. At the age of 64, he suffered an accident that resulted in an operation and made him believe that he might die or be unable to walk and look after the farm. While in hospital, he signed a paper in which the price of the farm was put at £10,250 and he alleged that Mackay and his solicitor led him to believe that he was bound to sell. Believing he had no option, Campbell then completed the missives.

The court found for Mackay.

"LORD GUEST: ... In assessing the relevancy of the appellant's averments three matters have to be considered: (1) weakness and facility, (2) circumvention, and (3) lesion. These three factors are all interrelated and they must be looked at as a whole and not in separate compartments. The strength of averments on one matter may compensate for the weakness of averments upon the other matters ...

There are no specific averments of the respects in which his mind was weak and facile. It is not said that his false belief in the severity of his illness and the consequences of his accident were so irrational as to lead to the conclusion that his sense of judgment was impaired. It is not suggested that he was suffering from any form of senile or other mental decay. A mere averment that he was in a weak and facile state of mind, without further specification, is not, in my view, sufficient. I am very doubtful whether there are relevant averments of facility; they are certainly not so strong as to relieve the appellant of the necessity of averring and proving circumvention.

'Circumvention signifieth the act of fraud, whereby a person is induced to a deed or obligation by deceit'—Stair, I, ix, 9. Bell's Dictionary [(7th ed., p.181)] put the matter thus: 'Circumvention; deceit or fraud.' This is not a case where the person upon whom the circumvention has been practised is dead or incapax, as may be in the case of the reduction of a testamentary document. In such a case if facility or weakness of mind is satisfactorily averred and the deed is impetrated in favour of the impetrator or his relatives, there is probably no need to aver or prove any specific act of circumvention. Indeed, it may not be possible to do so, because the act would be in secret. Circumvention would in such circumstances be assumed

But this is a different case. The injured party is alive and a party to the action. To succeed he must aver some facts and circumstances from which circumvention can be inferred. There is a notable lack of anything suggestive of deceit or dishonesty on the part of the respondent or his solicitor. In particular, there is no averment that the respondent or his solicitor knew that the appellant was not bound by the document of 18th November 1963 but none the less deliberately misled him into thinking that he was bound. Upon the pleadings as they stand, all the facts are quite consistent with honesty on the part of the respondent and his solicitor. None of the averments are, in my view, facts from which circumvention or fraud can be inferred. In the present state of the pleadings the appellant would not be allowed to prove fraud or dishonesty on the part of the respondent or his solicitor and it would be quite unfair, if a proof was allowed, that the appellant should be permitted without notice to cross-examine the respondent or his solicitor in order to show some form of dishonesty or deceit."

The case is important in that it indicates that facility, circumvention and lesion are all elements of the plea and that, although all must be established, the severity of one will affect the degree of proof for the others.

The case also confirms that there must be facts which establish circumvention. The suggestion that there must be "dishonesty" seems to go further than the judgments in *Gray v Binny*, but there must be some evidence that the other party, by words or actions, took advantage of such facility.

What degree of evidence is necessary and is evidence necessary in every case? Note that the evidence of facility must also be clearly and specifically averred.

The two cases that follow are modern examples where facility and circumvention has been successfully pled.

McGilvary v Gilmartin 5–06

1986 S.L.T. 89

Court of Session, Outer House: Lord McDonald

Mrs McGilvary disponed to her daughter, Mrs Gilmartin, the defender, a property in Luing which she, Mrs McGilvary, had inherited from her father. Her intention had always been to give the property to her son, John, in accordance with her father's wishes.

In the summer of 1980 Mrs Gilmartin came to stay with Mrs McGilvary and her husband, who died shortly afterwards. The death left Mrs McGilvary "in a weak physical and mental state," and "she relied heavily upon the defender for support, advice and guidance". Mrs McGilvary's contention was that while she was in this state, her daughter persuaded her to accompany her to a solicitor's office in Oban and there to sign a piece of paper which was the disposition of the property. Alternatively, she contended that she was persuaded to sign the disposition afterwards while living with her daughter at her home in Ayr.

Mrs McGilvary sought to have the disposition reduced, on the grounds of facility and circumvention and/or undue influence, although she provided no averments of any specific means or circumvention.

The court found that Mrs McGilvary's averments opened an inference of circumvention.

"LORD MCDONALD: ... We are not concerned with fraud, but with the alleged circumvention of a facile lady who bears to have signed a disposition gratuitously conveying her property to the defender, to her lesion. Counsel for the defender argued that even so there should be a positive averment specifying the means of the deceit adopted. I do not consider that this is necessary in every case. In *Clunie v Stirling* the opinion was expressed that, where there is evidence of lesion and facility, it is not necessary that anything amounting to moral fraud should be proved, or that any specific acts of circumvention should be established. It was pointed out that in such cases what passes between the impetrator and the facile person is often unknown, and may properly be a matter of inference from the whole circumstances of the case. Similar comments 5–07 were made in *Horsburgh v Thomson's Trs.* There is sufficient background in the present case, in my opinion, to leave open the inference of circumvention. For the defender it was argued that in both these cases the allegedly facile person was deceased and evidence as to the means of circumvention adopted could not be expected. I was not, however, referred to any authority for the proposition that different considerations should apply where the individual is still alive.

It is clear from the pleadings that the pursuer may be unable to give a clear account of what she understood to have happened in the solicitor's office and what paper, if any, she signed there. The defender avers that the pursuer gave positive instructions to the solicitor on that occasion to prepare the disposition; and that he did so and sent it on to Ayr where it was signed by the pursuer on 12 August 1980. No doubt with the intention of countering this, the pursuer has a further averment that, *esto* the paper she signed in the Oban office was not the disposition, she was persuaded by the defender to sign the disposition a few days later while still in a facile condition. She avers that she has no recollection of signing any documents while staying in Ayr. While in Ayr she alleges that the defender represented to her that the subjects still belonged to her and that everything was alright. She says that the disposition was subsequently witnessed at Ayr although the testing clause was completed at Oban. At no time did she intend to dispose of the subjects to the defender.

These averments were criticised by counsel for the defender in much the same way as the averments as to the alleged happenings in the solicitor's office in Oban. Again I consider that there is sufficient background in the pursuer's whole averments to leave open an inference of circumvention, and I am not prepared to sustain the argument".

5–08

Anderson v The Beacon Fellowship
1992 S.L.T. 111
Court of Session, Outer House: Lord McCluskey

The Fellowship, a religious voluntary association, rented a hall from Anderson and in 1985 entered into missives for its purchase. Representatives of the Fellowship visited Anderson and allegedly pressed their religious practice upon him. Anderson gave certain donations to representatives of the Fellowship. He now sought repayment of the donations, which he averred were impetrated by fraud and circumvention while he was in a condition of weakness and facility and, in any event, procured from him by undue influence. He averred that at that time he was seriously ill and depressed, had suffered from a manic depressive illness since 1981 and was weak of mind, emotionally vulnerable, scared and upset, as well as noticeably confused, frequently in a trance-like condition and being treated from time to time with drugs prescribed for hypomania and depression. The representatives of the association had paid him frequent visits, engaged in religious practices with him, purported to heal him, preached to him that money was valueless and exhorted him to renounce all of his possessions.

The court allowed proof before answer on the basis of Anderson's averments.

5–09 "LORD MCCLUSKEY: ... Substantial lesion is averred. There are many averments from which the court might infer weakness and facility in the pursuer at all material times. The averments of repeated pressure in relation to financial matters coupled with religious observances and exhortation, all at a time when the pursuer was in fact owed money by the defenders, appear to me to be sufficient to warrant an inference of circumvention capable of supporting a case of undue influence. ... [T]here is clear authority to support the view that the concept of fraud, in this context, is not 'necessarily confined to the use of deliberate deceit by the use of false pretences in order to trick a person into doing that which he would not otherwise do. I refer particularly to *Mackay v Campbell* and to *MacGilvary* . . . "

Undue influence

The doctrine of undue influence is a creature of English equity. As such, it is a flexible concept that has been successfully employed in countless cases where, regardless of the issue of fraud or dishonesty, there was clear evidence that one party was in a position unduly to influence the decision of the other party in entering into the contract. It is not surprising that it influenced Scottish decisions from the 19th century onwards. **5–10**

Defective Consent and Consequential Matters **5–11**

Scottish Law Commission, Memo. No.42 (1 June 1978)

"Volume 1, Part 1

1.45. *Undue Influence*. The English equitable doctrine of undue influence has been accepted, to a somewhat uncertain extent, as a ground of annulment of obligations in Scots law. What is meant by undue influence in England varies according to whether it is a testamentary writing or an *inter vivos* transaction that is being challenged. In the former case an element of coercion must be established. But this is not a necessary requirement as far as *inter vivos* transactions are concerned. There it is sufficient to show the abuse by the party against whom annulment is sought of a personal influence over the mind of the obligant such that, in conscience, he should not be allowed to retain the benefit conferred upon him. The development of the concept of undue influence was rendered necessary in English law largely because of its very narrow definition of duress, which is in effect restricted to cases of extortion by physical violence or imprisonment. In continental systems, by contrast, many situations which English law would classify as involving undue influence would fall within the general category of force and fear (*vis ac metus*), or within the category of exploitation.

1.46. It was not until quite late in the 19th century that undue influence as a separate category of vitiation of consent made its appearance in Scotland, and even then it was often combined with facility and circumvention. The factors necessary for the operation of the doctrine have been stated to be (a) the existence in one of the parties of a dominant and ascendant influence over the other; (b) confidence and trust reposed in him by the other; and (c) the granting of a material benefit to the ascendant party by the other in circumstances giving rise to an inference that the ascendant party had betrayed the confidence reposed in him. Clearly the doctrine is, in the present law of Scotland, a somewhat vague and amorphous one. It has, however, been recognised as operative in Scotland in respect of the relationship between parent and child, and lawyer and client; and it has been suggested that it might also extend to other relationships. As we have already stated, we think that undue influence (and certain other grounds of annulment) should be replaced by a more comprehensive category. However, if undue influence is to be retained as ground upon which a court may be asked to annul, it may well be thought that the existing authorities leave its scope and precise area of application somewhat undefined and lacking in clarity".

Is it likely that a doctrine which, by its very nature and purpose is flexible, will ever have a "precise area of application"? The cases which follow illustrate the range of its scope.

5–12 **Gray v Binny**

(1879) 7 R. 332

Court of Session, First Division: The Lord President (Inglis), Lords Shand, Deas

The facts are as stated above, para.5–04.

"LORD PRESIDENT (INGLIS): ... It is not enough, however, for the pursuer of such an action as this is to prove that he has given away valuable rights for a grossly inadequate consideration, and that he has been betrayed into the transaction by his own ignorance of his rights, without proving deceit or unfair dealing on the part of those who take benefit by his loss. But in order to determine what kind and amount of deceit or unfair practices will be sufficient to entitle the injured party to redress regard must always be had to the relation in which the transacting parties stand to one another. If they are strangers to each other, and dealing at arm's length, each is not only entitled to make the best bargain he can, but to assume that the other fully understands and is the best judge of his own interests. If, on the other hand, the relation of the parties is such as to beget mutual trust and confidence, each owes to the other a duty which has no place as between strangers. But if the trust and confidence, instead of being mutual, are all given on one side and not reciprocated, the party trusted and confided in is bound, by the most obvious principles of fair dealing and honesty, not to abuse the power thus put into his hands.

LORD SHAND: ... It is said that the exercise of parental influence is quite legitimate and most frequently salutary and beneficial to the person who yields to it. The observation is undoubtedly just. The same thing may be truly said of the influence which arises from the relations of agent and client, physician and patient, and clergyman and parishioner or penitent—these being the most common of the more intimate relations in life from which a dominant or ascendant influence is known to arise, although not necessarily an exhaustive enumeration of such relations. But the law looks with great jealousy on all gratuitous benefits obtained by the exercise of influence arising from these relations ... I am not moved by the consideration that there is no fixed criterion or defined standard to which an appeal can be made in ascertaining whether undue influence has been used. That is a question of circumstances in each case, just as it is a question of circumstances in every case in which circumvention is alleged whether circumvention has been employed ...

The circumstances which establish a case of undue influence are, in the first place, the existence of a relation between the granter and grantee of the deed which creates a dominant or ascendant influence, the fact that confidence and trust arose from that relation, the fact that a material and gratuitous benefit was given to the prejudice of the granter, and the circumstance that the granter entered into the transaction without the benefit of independent advice or assistance. In such circumstances the Court is warranted in holding that undue influence has been exercised; but cases will often occur—and I think the present is clearly one of that class—in which over and above all this, and beyond what I hold to be necessary, it is proved that pressure was actually used, and that the granter of the deed was in ignorance of facts, the knowledge of which was material with reference to the act he performed. In such a case the right to be restored against the act is of course made all the more clear ...

The absence of information or knowledge as to the value of the right he was renouncing is, in my opinion, in the circumstances fatal to the transaction. But I must add that even if it had been shewn that information had been given on that point it would not have altered my judgment in the case, for even with such information, in the absence of any protection by independent advice, I should still have held that the deed was in the circumstances the result of influence unduly used . . . It is against all ordinary experience to suppose that if a business man or any independent adviser had presented the transaction to the pursuer in the light of what was reasonable from his point of view, allowing for the fullest desire on his part to relieve his mother from present difficulties and help her for the future, that a transaction so prejudicial to himself would have followed. It would have been pointed out to him that such a sacrifice as it was proposed he should make was quite unnecessary to secure all he had in view, and that the assistance he desired to give and to get could easily be obtained consistently with his preserving substantially his right of succession to the estate."

Was Lord Shand attempting to establish a definitive range of relationships that raise undue influence; or did he establish a more general test for determining whether any particular relationship raises a presumption of undue influence?

Note the emphasis which Lord Shand placed on taking independent advice.

McGilvary v Gilmartin 5–13

1986 S.L.T. 89

Court of Session, Outer House: Lord McDonald

The facts are as stated above, para.5–06.

"LORD MCDONALD: . . . So far as undue influence is concerned, it was conceded that the relationship between the parties was such as to admit of this doctrine in an appropriate case. No separate argument on this aspect of the case was advanced. It was simply argued that, as in the case based upon circumvention, there was insufficient specification of the method by which undue influence had been exerted. In *Gray v Binny* it was observed by Lord Shand at p. 347 that where there is a relationship between the grantor and the grantee of a deed which creates a dominant or ascendant influence where confidence and trust arises from that relationship, where a material and gratuitous benefit is given to the prejudice of the grantor and where the grantor does not have independent advice or assistance, undue influence may be inferred. In my opinion the pursuer's averments in the present case are sufficient to meet these requirements." 5–14

Note that in this case, as in *Gray v Binny*, undue influence was pleaded in the alternative with facility and circumvention.

The next case is a modern illustration of the flexibility of the doctrine. Lord Maxwell's opinion is also perhaps the most thorough review of the relevant authorities and clearest restatement of the modern law on the subject.

Honeyman's Executors v Sharp 5–15

1978 S.C. 223

Court of Session, Outer House: Lord Maxwell

Sharp was a dealer with a firm of fine art dealers which had valued the contents of houses which belonged to Mrs Honeyman's late husband. The contents included several valuable paintings by the French artist Boudin. Sharp visited Mrs Honeyman from time to time and organised the transfer of her possessions when she moved house.

When Mrs Honeyman became seriously ill with cancer, she discussed the terms of her will with Sharp and on her instructions he prepared a codicil. When Mrs Honeyman died,

Sharp produced a document, signed by Mrs Honeyman and apparently gifting four Boudin paintings to him. The executor sought declarator that the gift should be reduced for undue influence exerted by Sharp over Mrs Honeyman.

The court allowed proof before answer.

5–16 "LORD MAXWELL: … Counsel for the defender attacked the relevancy of the pursuers' averments on two grounds. First he said that the relationship between the defender and deceased was not of the class in respect of which our law admits the application of the principle of undue influence. Second, he said that the averments did not disclose any influence exercised by the defender on the deceased, still less any influence of a kind which the defender had a duty not to exert, and in any event they did not disclose ground for holding that the gifts resulted from the exercise of any such influence.

I shall consider each of these contentions in turn.

On the first question, the category of relationships, counsel for the defender conceded that, leaving aside natural relationships, the class cannot be a closed class confined to lawyers, doctors and clergymen. In my opinion this is plainly correct. Though reference is made to lawyers, doctors and clergymen from time to time in the authorities, I find it nowhere said that they are the only relationships to which the principle applies and there are dicta which imply that they are not. Thus in *Ross v Gosselin's Executors*, 1926 S.C. 325, a case relating to a law agent, Lord President Clyde said: 'So far as averment goes, the pursuer accordingly makes out a good case for attributing to the defender a position of influence over his aunt which, like all similar positions, might easily be abused'. Gloag on *Contract* (2nd ed.), at p. 526 refers to 'persons such as doctors and clergymen who are m a position to exercise influence'. It would in my opinion be quite out of keeping with the general approach of our law to confine the principle to some artificial list of relationships and I see no reason why, nowadays, when so much work, which was in former times done by law agents as general 'men of business,' has been taken over by specialist advisers such as accountants, the principle should not be applied to them.

Having conceded that the class of relationship to which the principle applies is not closed, counsel for the defender was not unnaturally in some difficulty in defining the essential characteristics of the class.

An examination of *M'Kechnie v M'Kechnie's Trustees*, sup. cit., and *Ross v Gosselin's Executor*, *sup. cit.*, persuades me that the facts of the present case as ascertained after proof may well reveal a relationship of a kind to which our law would in any event apply the principle. M'Kechnie was a case in which the Court refused to recognise the relationship between a man and his mistress as one to which the principle applies, although there was strong evidence that the mistress in fact exerted a dominant influence over the man. The Lord Justice-Clerk said, referring to earlier cases, 'These are cases of persons who having from an official position towards another person some capacity for influence over him, misuse at position for the purposes of inducing him to do or to abstain from doing something that he has a right to do or abstain from doing in the exercise of his rights as regards his own property. The essence of the matter is that persons in that official position, such as a clergyman, or doctor or lawyer, are persons who have not only a duty but a right to advise and urge those with whom they deal to act in certain directions and it is natural and right that a person who is so dealt with should give effect to or at least be greatly influenced by the advice of those persons and what is urged upon them by those persons. Therefore the person who has that influence and ought to have it, in dealing with a person who ought to be influenced by it, must take the greatest possible care that he does not outstep the bounds of his official position and endeavour to get other things done under the influence which he has, with which he has no right whatever to interfere'. In *Ross v Gosselin's Executors*, a law agent case, Lord President Clyde analysed the matter as follows:—'The essence of undue influence is that a person, who has assumed or undertaken a position of quasi fiduciary responsibility in relation to the affairs of another, allows his own self interest to deflect the advice of guidance he gives in his own favour'. I think it can at least be taken from these *dicta* and from a passage in Gloag on Contract, (2nd ed.), p. 528 that where a person, in pursuance of his profession or calling, undertakes the giving of advice to another and where, as a result, there develops a relationship between the adviser and the advised in which, as matter of fact, the latter places trust and confidence in the former then the law recognises a moral duty on the adviser not to take advantage of the advised at least in relation to matters connected with the area to which the advice relates, and gives legal effect to that moral duty by applying the principle of 'undue influence' in appropriate cases. I see no reason why this principle should not apply when the 'professional' adviser is a fine art dealer rather than, say, a solicitor though I accept that grounds of public policy may have made the rules of its application stricter in the case of solicitors than in the case of others professing special skill or knowledge. It may be, as counsel for the pursuers contends, that the principle applies to a wider class of relationship than that which I have mentioned. It is enough, however, for present purposes that, in my opinion, the averments in this case are wide enough to enable the pursuers to prove if they can that the relationship here in question fell within the class which I have endeavoured to describe.

Turning to the second branch of the case, the lack of averment of the use of any act or conduct amounting to undue influence, I find this more difficult especially as the pursuers' pleadings do not in terms appear to go even as far as saying that the use of 'undue' influence is to be inferred from the facts averred.

There are two related questions here. First what kind of conduct amounts to 'undue influence' and second, how is it proved and where does the *onus* lie? As to the first, counsel founded strongly on the opinion of Lord President Inglis in *Gray v Binny* where he says that a pursuer must prove 'deceit or unfair dealings' and the well-known passage in the speech of the Lord Chancellor in *Weir v Grace*, sup. cit., where, quoting from Lord Cranworth in an earlier case, he appears to say that, to. make a case of undue influence, it is necessary to prove 'coercion or fraud.' It is to be noted that in *Gray v Binny* Lord Shand expressly rejected, for reasons which seem to me convincing, the notion that undue influence necessarily involves fraud. *Weir v Grace* was decided in the Inner House on the ground that the defender's solicitor had discharged the onus on him of showing no improper dealings and Lord Robertson in the House of Lords appears to adopt the same approach. I find it difficult to reconcile numerous *dicta* in both earlier and later authorities (e.g. *Johnson v Goodlet, Munro v. Strain, M'Kechnie v M Kechnie's Trustees, Ross v Gosselin's Executors*, Gloag, op. cit., p. 526) with the idea that proof of 'fraud', 'coercion' or 'deceit' are essential unless those words are given a strained and unnatural meaning. In *Forbes v Forbes' Trustees* Lord Guthrie referring to the judgment of Lindley L.J. in *Allcard v Skinner* (1887) 36 Ch. D. 145, said: 'I do not think that it is desirable or indeed possible to frame a comprehensive statement of what does and what does not amount to undue influence'. I respectfully agree. What is involved is some kind of abuse of the position of trust for the benefit of the person in whom the trust is confided and it seems to me that whether there had been such an abuse to an extent which would justify the Court's interference is a matter which cannot readily be confined within stated rules or ascertained on the basis of written pleadings without enquiry into the facts.

This brings me to the question of presumptions and *onus*. ... [T]here must be cases where the facts as proved raise a *prima facie* inference that a gift has been acquired by abuse of a position of trust and which at least cry out for an explanation even though the precise mode of abuse is not known and might indeed be too subtle to be readily capable of precise expression. In my opinion the averments in this case, if proved, in the light of the appearance these facts take on when developed in evidence, may (I put it no higher) raise such an inference. We have here averred not merely the relationship and the gift of large amount. There is a number of other allegations. There is, for example, the deceased's ill health, which may be relevant even though 'facility' is not founded on (*Munro v Strain, sup. cit.*, per the Lord Justice-Clerk at 525, *M'Callum v Graham* (1894) 21 R. 824). There is the fact that the defender apparently took a hand in the deceased's testamentary arrangements in relation to the matter of the codicil and perhaps more important the admitted fact that he himself drafted the letter of gift with the provisions apparently intended to have a bearing on the incidence of capital transfer tax. It might appear after proof that these actings suggest that the defender outstepped 'the bounds of his official position and endeavoured to get other things done with which he had no right to interfere,' to quote from the words of the Lord Justice-Clerk in *M'Kechnie v M'Kechnie's Trustees, sup. cit.* There is on averment a suspicion of secrecy and concealment on the part of the defender in relation to the gift both before and after the death of the deceased. There is apparently an absence of any independent advice or assistance or any suggestion that such advice or assistance should be obtained. I do not say that these facts, if proved, along with the whole other facts will establish undue influence or will even necessarily raise a rebuttable presumption of undue influence, but looking at the averments as a whole I am of the opinion that this is not a case which I could safely decide against the pursuer without enquiry. I shall accordingly allow a proof before answer."

Note that in this case, as in the cases referred to by Lord Maxwell, the person influenced had not sought or obtained independent advice.

Undue influence, third parties and good faith

5–17 Although there is no evidence that a general concept of "abuse of economic power" or "unconscionability" has made inroads in Scotland (indeed, it is unlikely that, after *National Westminster Bank Plc v Morgan*[2] it will have much influence in England), it has found much favour with academics. That it is a theorem with the potential to wreak general injustice in the pursuit of individual fairness is shown by its unequivocal rejection in the House of Lords in *Morgan* (especially the speech of Lord Scarman, which rejected Lord Denning's attempt to redefine undue influence in such terms in *Lloyds Bank Ltd v Bundy*[3]).

Most of the reported cases since 1985 have been brought by the wife of a customer of the bank who has issued a guarantee in the bank's favour, secured by a charge against her home. In return, the bank has agreed to advance a loan to the husband, usually to pay off the debts of the husband's business, with which the wife is not involved. The cases often involve misrepresentation to the wife by the husband about the effect of the guarantee on the home should the loan not be repaid. The key issue in the cases is whether undue influence has been exercised by the husband over the wife and the extent to which the bank, even though not party to any misrepresentation, should take action to ensure that such influence is negatived, especially by ensuring that the wife takes appropriate independent advice. The decision of the House of Lords in *Barclays Bank Plc v O'Brien*,[4] where Mrs O'Brien successfully claimed that the mortgage agreement should be set aside on the grounds of her husband's exertion of undue influence and his misrepresentations, established that, *in English law*, misrepresentation or undue influence by one spouse will entitle the other spouse to avoid the contract, provided the first spouse was

[2] *National Westminster Bank Plc v Morgan* [1985] 1 A.C. 686.
[3] *Lloyds Bank Ltd v Bundy* [1975] Q.B. 326.
[4] *Barclays Bank Plc v O'Brien* [1994] 1 A.C. 180.

acting as agent for the Bank, or the Bank had actual or *constructive* notice of those actings. The potential outcome was that the protection afforded to a wife or partner in similar circumstances in Scotland might be weaker than that in England and Wales.

In *CIBC Mortgages Plc v Pitt*,[5] Lord Browne-Wilkinson distinguished the decision in *O'Brien* on the grounds that there was no evidence that Mr Pitt has either acted as agent for CIBC, nor that CIBC had notice, actual or constructive, of Mr Pitt's exertion of undue influence upon Mrs Pitt (there was no evidence of misrepresentation).

The major problem with both the *O'Brien* and *Pitt* decisions is that they countenance the possibility that the contract might be set aside because the bank had *constructive* notice of undue influence. Such a concept has no place in Scots law and this was made clear by Lord Johnston in *Mumford v Bank of Scotland*.[6] That case went on appeal to the House of Lords as *Smith v Bank of Scotland*.

Smith v Bank of Scotland 5–18

1997 S.C. (H.L.) 111

House of Lords: Lords Goff, Jauncey, Lloyd, Hoffmann Clyde

Mrs Smith executed, along with her husband and at his request, a standard security, or "mortgage" over their house in favour of the bank, thereby becoming a cautioner, or guarantor for her husband's business debts to the bank. She averred that she had been induced to sign the document by her husband who had made representations that were false or misleading and but for which she would not have signed the document. She had obtained no independent advice, nor had she been given any warning as to the consequences of the document she was signing. She was given no opportunity to peruse the document. The granting of the security was essential to procuring additional finance from the bank for Mr Smith's business in which she had no financial interest. She sought partial reduction of the standard security insofar as it affected her. It was not alleged that the bank had any actual knowledge of Mr Smith's misrepresentation.

The Lord Ordinary dismissed the action, holding that the law of Scotland did not, outwith the context of agency, infer constructive notice and that in the absence of actual knowledge of undue influence or misrepresentation the bank was under no duty either to explain to the Mrs Smith the nature and consequences of the transaction or to require her to take independent advice.

On appeal, the First Division held that Scots law did not recognise any presumption of undue influence arising merely from the nature of the transaction and the fact that the parties were related by marriage; and that it was necessary to establish knowledge by the creditor of facts and circumstances indicating that undue influence was in fact exercised by a husband in order to obtain the wife's consent to a transaction, in order to justify constructive knowledge by a creditor.

The House of Lords allowed the appeal and extended *Barclays Bank v O'Brien* to Scotland on the grounds that the requirement for good faith on behalf of the creditor had always required disclosure to a potential cautioner in certain circumstances, and which now included the duty to advise the potential cautioner in circumstances where the creditor should reasonably suspect that as a result of her intimate relationship with the debtor, the cautioner's participation might be flawed.

The court also decided that the duty of the creditor to advise a potential cautioner was restricted to circumstances which would lead a reasonable man to believe that owing to the personal relationship between the debtor and the proposed cautioner, the latter's consent might not be fully informed or freely given; and that it would be sufficient for a

[5] *CIBC Mortgages Plc v Pitt* [1994] 1 A.C. 200.

[6] *Mumford v Bank of Scotland*, 1994 S.L.T. 1288.

creditor to remain in good faith for him to warn a potential cautioner of the consequences of entering into such a contract and to advise him or her to take independent advice.

5–19 "LORD JAUNCEY OF TULLICHETTLE: My Lords, the decision in *Barclays Bank plc v O'Brien* undoubtedly extended the law of England in favour of sureties cohabiting with a principal debtor. It did so by fixing the creditor with constructive notice of the risk of undue influence or misrepresentation by the debtor. The difficult question in this appeal is whether a similar extension should be made to the law of Scotland. By clothing the creditor with constructive knowledge English law appears to accept that there is a presumption that a husband in circumstances such as the present is likely to exercise undue influence over or misrepresent to his wife. No such presumption as to undue influence presently exists in Scotland although there will be cases in which an inference may without difficulty be drawn from the particular facts (Professor Walker's *Law of Contracts and Related Obligations in Scotland* (2nd ed), p 306, para 15.26). Misrepresentation seems to me to be even less likely to lead to a presumption although it is treated in the same way as undue influence in *O'Brien*. On one view a non-cohabiting principal debtor might be thought to have even more incentive to misrepresent than a cohabiting one who would sooner or later have to face the music at close quarters, and perhaps for a prolonged period, when the truth was out.

My Lords, while I can follow the policy reasons for clothing a creditor with constructive knowledge of the risk of undue influence by a husband in the special circumstances of a cautionary obligation, I have the greatest difficulty in seeing why such constructive knowledge should extend to misrepresentation. There has so far as I am aware never been any suggestion in the law of Scotland that any particular class of persons is more likely to misrepresent in relation to a contract than any other class. Applying the principles of Scots law alone I would therefore have been disposed to dismiss this appeal. Nevertheless I am conscious that your Lordships do not share my difficulties and I appreciate the practical advantages of applying the same law to identical transactions in both jurisdictions. In these circumstances I do not feel able to dissent from your Lordships' view that the appeal should be allowed.

I would however make two further points. In the first place, it is not difficult to conceive of other situations in which a wife enters into a contract with a third party which is to her financial disadvantage but is to the apparent advantage of her husband. ... I would resist any attempt to extend the concept of constructive knowledge embodied in *O'Brien* to other types of contracts between a wife and a third party. In the second place, when it is apparent from the terms of the transaction that the cautioner and principal debtor are, as here, husband and wife or that they are cohabiting as for example by living at the same address, the creditor should take the steps suggested by my noble and learned friend, Lord Clyde. However if the creditor has no information to suggest that cautioner and principal debtor are cohabiting I do not consider that he is under any obligation to make inquiries thereanent. Furthermore the degree of non-marital cohabitation which can give rise to constructive notice must be a matter for decision in each individual case.

5–20 LORD CLYDE: The general rule in the law of Scotland is that misrepresentations by a debtor which induce another person to enter into a cautionary obligation have no effect on the contract of caution. Indeed, the proposition may be stated more generally that a voluntary obligation is not rendered open to challenge simply on the ground that it has been entered into as the result of a misrepresentation made by a third party. To the generality of the rule there are apparent exceptions ...

Lying behind these examples of situations where the creditor is obliged to take steps in the interest of the cautioner is the basic element of good faith. As was recognised by Gloag and Irvine (p 706), there must be perfect fairness of representation on the part of the creditor in the constitution of the contract. Thus if the creditor misleads the cautioner either by his silence or by some positive representation he will be acting in bad faith and may thereby lose the right to enforce the contract.

It is apparent that the law of Scotland has broadly developed in harmony with the law of England. Historically no doubt their respective roots have been distinct but the general principles which are applied are nearly the same (Bell's Commentaries, i, 364). It was observed in *Aitken's Trs v Bank of Scotland*, 1944 SC at p 279; 1945 SLT at p 90, that the decisions on the English cases on matters of general principle may have persuasive authority in Scotland, and in *Royal Bank of Scotland v Brown*, 1982 SC at p 100; 1983 SLT at p 128, it was observed that such decisions are entitled to be treated with great respect. On the other hand due regard has to be paid to the differences in the specialties of the two systems.

In the present case the pursuer seeks to extend to Scotland the decision in the recent case in this House of *Barclays Bank plc v O'Brien*. In that case a bank was seeking to enforce a mortgage over the matrimonial home granted by a husband and wife ... This House held that the mortgage was not enforceable against the wife who had signed the deed without reading it, in reliance on her husband's misrepresentation as to the effect of it. It was held that in the circumstances the bank had constructive notice of the wrongful representation made by the husband and that the wife was entitled to have the legal charge set aside. This House went further and decided that the principle should apply not only to cases of husband and wife but to all cases where the creditor is aware that the relationship between the surety and the debtor is such that the former will be reposing trust and confidence in the latter in relation to the financial affairs of the debtor. The view was expressed that in all such cases the creditor should be put on his inquiry. The First Division of the Court of Session in Scotland correctly recognised that the decision goes beyond the present situation of the law in Scotland, and, applying the existing Scottish law, declined to follow it. In *O'Brien* this House consciously sought to extend the law of England. The question for your Lordships is whether a corresponding extension should be made to the law of Scotland.

My Lords, it is not easy to identify any major distinction between the law in England in this matter as it stood before the decision in *O'Brien* and the corresponding law of Scotland. ... It was also recognised that at least on a broad basis the policy considerations which lay behind the decision in *O'Brien* were applicable north of the border. The use of the matrimonial home as a security for the business debts of one of the spouses must be a matter of practical experience on both sides of the border. The only area in which issue was seriously joined was in relation to the proposition put forward by the pursuer to the effect that the law in relation to undue influence was in essence the same in each jurisdiction. The only substantial ground on which counsel for the bank argued that there was a difference between the two systems which could justify a decision not to apply the decision in *O'Brien* to Scotland related to the law regarding undue influence. While the decision in *O'Brien* touches on what was referred to in English law as the 'invalidating tendency' or the law's 'tender treatment' of married women, that does not seem to be at the heart of the decision and was not prominent in the argument before the House in the present case.

...

The reception from England of the concept of undue influence as a ground of action distinct from fraud was clearly established in *Gray v Binny*, but in relation to contracts between close relations the necessity for fairness and avoidance of undue pressure had already been recognised. In *Fraser v Fraser's Trs* (1834) 13 S at p 710, the Lord

President, Lord Hope, observed: 'where bargains and contracts are entered into between persons standing in the relationship to each other, such as that of husband and wife, parent and child, everything ought to be done as fairly, equally, openly, and candidly as possible'.

It is unnecessary to explore all the kinds of relationships in which the possibility of undue influence may now be admitted. ... And so far as the recognition of any presumption is concerned, even if it be the case that Scotland has never accepted that there is a presumption of undue influence in the formation of contracts between husband and wife, it is evident that despite the so called "invalidating tendency" England did not recognise any such a presumption in the case of a husband and wife (*Bank of Montreal v Stuart* [1911] AC at p 137), so that in that respect at least the position seems to have been the same. In any event the existence of any such presumption in the context of undue influence is primarily of evidential significance and does not seem to be of such general materiality as to prevent development of the Scottish law on the substantial issue which is now before the House.

Counsel for the bank cautioned against the imposition of a change in the law of Scotland where, as was recognised in *Invercargill City Council v Hamlin*, a monolithic uniformity might be destructive of the individual development of a distinct common law system. But in the present case we are dealing with an area of the law whose development has for a long time been influenced by decisions on the other side of the border. I am not persuaded that there are any social or economic considerations which would justify a difference in the law between the two jurisdictions in the particular point here under consideration.

...

I have not been persuaded that there are sufficiently cogent grounds for refusing the extension to Scotland of the development which has been achieved in England by the decision there in *Barclays Bank plc v O'Brien*. On the contrary I take the view that it is desirable to recognise a corresponding extension of the law in Scotland. But the basis on which that might be done requires consideration. The route which this House took in developing the law in *O'Brien* related substantially to the concept of notice. It was pointed out that such a concept is not unknown in Scotland and reference was made in particular to *Rodger (Builders) Ltd v Fawdry*. But the basis on which the court proceeded in that case was not in terms the doctrine of notice, which is properly a development of the English principles of equity, but rather a recognition of the requirement of good faith on the part of the second purchaser. As was noticed in *Trade Development Bank v David W Haig (Bellshill) Ltd*, 1983 SLT at p 517, the decision in *Rodger (Builders) Ltd v Fawdry* rested upon the broad principle in the field of contract law of fair dealing in good faith. The point can, as the Lord President observed in the present case, be expressed in Scotland in terms of personal bar. That approach may serve as a defence to enforcement against the cautioner by the creditor.

But in the present case the cautioner is seeking reduction of the contract against the creditor. This could be expressed in terms of a legal fiction that the bank should be treated as a party to the misrepresentation. But that may only be describing the effect and not explaining the principle.

It was not disputed that effect could be given in Scotland to the decision in *O'Brien* by the use of the concept of constructive notice. Reference was made to a footnote in para 13A of Bell's *Principles* (10th ed), where it is indicated that notice of fraud which may prevent a third party from taking benefit from a fraudulent transaction includes knowledge of facts and circumstances which ought to have put them on their inquiry. But it seems to me preferable to recognise the element of good faith which is required of the creditor on the constitution of a contract of cautionry and find there a proper basis for decision. The law already recognises, as I have sought to explain, that there may arise a duty of disclosure to a potential cautioner in certain circumstances. As a part of that same good faith which lies behind that duty it seems to me reasonable to accept that there should also be a duty in particular circumstances to give the potential cautioner certain advice. Thus in circumstances where the creditor should reasonably suspect that there may be factors bearing on the participation of the cautioner which might undermine the validity of the contract through his or her intimate relationship with the debtor, the duty would arise and would have to be fulfilled if the creditor is not to be prevented from later enforcing the contract. Such a duty does not alter the existing law regarding the duty, or the absence of a duty, to make representations. Nor does it carry with it a duty of investigation. This is simply a duty arising out of the good faith of the contract to give advice. It is unnecessary on the approach which I have suggested to deem the creditor a potential participant in any misrepresentation by the debtor.

In extending to Scotland the development of the law which was achieved in *Barclays Bank plc v O'Brien* it is desirable to say something more about what the effect of it should be. In the first place, the duty which arises on the creditor at the stage of the negotiation of the contract should only arise on the creditor if the circumstances of the case are such as to lead a reasonable man to believe that owing to the personal relationship between the debtor and the proposed cautioner the latter's consent may not be fully informed or freely given. Of course if the creditor, acting honestly and in good faith, has no reason to believe that there is any particularly close relationship between the debtor and the proposed cautioner the duty will not arise. It is unnecessary to attempt any further classification or analysis of the range of personal relationships. Given the range of circumstances in which persons may be prepared or prevailed upon to act as cautioners it seems to me unwise to endeavour to make any more precise formulation but to leave the matter to the application of common sense to the circumstances.

Secondly, if the duty arises, then it requires that the creditor should take certain steps to secure that he remains in good faith so far as the proposed transaction is concerned. Whether there has in fact been or may yet be any conduct by the debtor directed at the cautioner which might vitiate the contract is not a matter necessarily to be explored by the creditor. All that is required of him is that he should take reasonable steps to secure that in relation to the proposed contract he acts throughout in good faith. So far as the substance of those steps is concerned it seems to me that it would be sufficient for the creditor to warn the potential cautioner of the consequences of entering into the proposed cautionary obligation and to advise him or her to take independent advice. Of course, in accordance with the existing law, he will still have the duty to make a full and honest disclosure if occasion arises for that to be done. But apart from that it seems to me that the giving of the warning and the advice should be sufficient so far as Scots law is concerned to fulfil the duty on the creditor and secure that he remains in good faith in relation to the proposed transaction. As was recorded by the Lord President a practice has been recognised by banks and building societies of advising private individuals proposing to act as guarantors or cautioners for the liabilities of another to issue a warning regarding the consequences and to point out the importance of receiving independent advice. This practice may extend more widely than is required by the duty which I have described insofar as it may not be limited to cases where a close personal relationship exists, but adoption of the wider practice would clearly help to obviate any practical problem in deciding whether or not the duty arises in any given case.

In my view the appeal should be allowed so that the case may proceed to a proof before answer."

5–21 The decision in *Smith* incorporated *O'Brien* into Scots law, but the grounds on which it did so are opaque, as are the consequences of doing so. As Professor Gretton has hinted,[7] the impact of *O'Brien* and *Smith* on banking practice has been extensive. In *Royal Bank of Scotland Plc v Etridge (No.2)*,[8] in an English action, the House of Commons went even further in prescribing the extent of the burden placed upon the advising solicitor in such circumstances:

> "The responsibility of a solicitor giving such advice will be to: explain the nature of the documents and the practical consequences of signing them; point out the seriousness of the risks involved; explain that the decision as to signing the documents is for the wife alone to make; check if the wife is willing to proceed; and ensure that all explanations are given in non-technical language."[9]

Although it has clarified the burden on the legal adviser in England, the status of *Ettridge (No.2)* in Scotland was considered in the following decision of the Inner house.

5–22

Clydesdale Bank Plc v Black
2002 S.L.T. 764
Inner House, Extra Division: Lords Coulsfield, Marnoch and Sutherland

Clydesdale sought to enforce a standard security granted by Mrs Black supporting a guarantee in respect of Mr Black's business debts. Her defence was that the guarantee should be set aside because although she had taken independent legal advice, she signed it without being aware of its true nature and under the undue influence of Mr Black, on whom she relied to take all financial decisions. The bank argued that the guarantee document emphasised the nature of the obligations being undertaken by Mrs Black and that she should seek independent legal advice; and that Mrs Black had put her signature below that warning on the document, outwith her home and in the presence of two witnesses. Mrs Black disputed these facts and argued that *Royal Bank of Scotland Plc v Etridge (No.2)* should be applied in Scotland to require a creditor to take certain particular steps before it could be held to have acted in good faith in terms of *Smith v Bank of Scotland.*

The court found that *Etridge* did not affect the creditor's duties in Scots law, that the bank had acted in good faith in terms of the law as understood at the time of the transaction and refused Mrs Smith's appeal.

5–23 "LORD COULSFIELD: . . .

[12] On the pleadings, therefore, it is clear that this is a case of a class which is now familiar and that it raises questions of the kind discussed in *Barclays Bank plc v O'Brien*, *Smith v Bank of Scotland* and *Royal Bank of Scotland plc v Etridge (No 2).*

. . .

[14] The essence of the pursuers' argument which the sheriff and sheriff principal accepted, is that whatever may be the requirements which, under English law, are imposed upon the person in whose favour a gratuitous guarantee is granted in circumstances in which the possibility of undue influence arises, the issue in Scotland is whether the creditor acted in good faith. The pursuers maintain that they can show that they acted in good faith by showing that they took reasonable steps to warn the defender

[7] GL Gretton, "Sexually Transmitted Debt," 1997 S.L.T. (Articles) 195–197.
[8] *Royal Bank of Scotland Plc v Etridge (No.2)* [2002] 2 A. C. 773.
[9] R Russell, "Royal Bank of Scotland v Etridge (No.2). The End of a Sorry Tale?", 2002 S.L.T. (News) 55–58.

that she was entering into a contract of guarantee, which might have consequences for the family home. They further argue that the more onerous requirements explained in *Barclays Bank plc v O'Brien* and in *Etridge (No 2)*, which, in short, require that the nature of the deed in question be "brought home" to the person signing it, are derived from English rules of equity and are not applicable or necessary in Scotland. For the present purpose, it is not necessary, in my view, to discuss what those more onerous requirements are. The pursuers' argument does, however, require consideration of two issues. The first is what is the principle on which the requirements discussed in *O'Brien* and, more fully, in *Etridge* are based. The second is what is the basis on which the authority of *O'Brien* was accepted in regard to Scotland in *Smith*.

[15] Much of the discussion in *O'Brien* was directed towards English rules of equity, and with the circumstances in which a presumption of undue influence might be held to arise: these are matters on which I am not qualified to comment. What does, nevertheless, seem to me to stand out in the speech of Lord Browne-Wilkinson, is that his Lordship recognised a need to guard against an injustice, or potential injustice, to wives (and also, in some circumstances at least, to cohabitees). That is reflected at [1994] 1 AC, p 196 where his Lordship referred to the law's 'tender treatment' of married women and continued: 'As I have said above in dealing with undue influence, this tenderness of the law towards married women is due to the fact that, even today, many wives repose confidence and trust in their husbands, in relation to their financial affairs.'

...

[22] As I have said, it is only with great diffidence that I can comment on any aspect of the English law of equity. It does, however, respectfully appear to me that, in reading the decisions in *O'Brien* and *Etridge (No 2)*, it is possible to distinguish between the terminology of equity, in the technical sense, in which the reasoning is expressed, and an underlying determination that social and economic justice requires certain positive steps to be taken by a creditor bank when dealing with a gratuitous obligation granted by a wife. The practical upshot seems to me to be clear, namely that the cases require the creditor to take positive steps to satisfy itself that the wife understands the transaction. The necessary positive steps are discussed at very considerable length, but there seems to me to be no doubt that in both cases their Lordships were suggesting that the creditor should not merely rely on some written communication to the wife drawing attention to the nature of the transaction, but should satisfy itself that steps had been taken to protect the wife by giving her proper advice by itself or by others. It is, I think, also of interest that in some of the speeches their Lordships were fortified by the practice already adopted by many banks which recognised that some such positive steps should be taken.

[23] The extension of the law approved in *O'Brien* was accepted as applying to Scotland in *Smith*. Before looking at the House of Lords decision in *Smith*, however, it is, I think, helpful to mention the Inner House decision, which was reversed by the House of Lords. The decision is reported under the name *Mumford v Bank of Scotland; Smith v Bank of Scotland*. In giving the opinion of the court, Lord President Hope first of all pointed out that the apparent basis of the cases for the two wives involved was one of bad faith, but went on to demonstrate that there was no existing authority in Scots law which could justify the application of such a principle in favour of the wives in these circumstances. He discussed the reception of the concept of undue influence into Scots law in *Gray v Binny* and quoted from the opinion of Lord Shand in that case and went on to say: 'There is no indication in this passage that a presumption of undue influence can arise merely from the nature of the transaction and the fact of the relationship. What is important is the effect of that relationship in the particular case, with the result that each case must be examined upon its own facts' (1996 SLT at p 397K–L).

[24] On the following page he said: 'It is significant that we were not referred to any Scottish case—and we are not aware of any—where the law of Scotland has recognised

that a presumption of undue influence can arise in a question with a third party, where the transaction is not on its face to the wife's advantage, merely because it may be expected that the wife has reposed in her husband trust and confidence in relation to their financial affairs. The Scottish cases indicate that something more is needed to justify constructive knowledge by the third party that consent to the wife's transaction has been obtained by the husband's undue influence. What is needed, according to the law of Scotland, is proof of knowledge by the third party of facts and circumstances indicating that undue influence was in fact exercised. This requires knowledge of the assumption by the husband of a position of quasi-fiduciary responsibility over his wife's affairs, such as to deprive her of her own power of decision making. In our opinion the tendency in English law to invalidate such transactions between husband and wife in a question with a third party merely on the ground of the wife's vulnerability to undue influence goes well beyond the limits of the law of undue influence as hitherto recognised in this country' (1996 SLT at p 398C-F).

[25] The decision in *O'Brien* was, of course, relied on before the Inner House and it is, in my opinion, clear that the Inner House considered the issue on the basis of principles of good faith as recognised in Scotland up to that point and declined to accept that the policy considerations underlying the decision in *O'Brien* justified any alteration in the law of Scotland, at least at the hand of the court. The Lord President did suggest that if there was any perceived injustice, the matter might be one for legislation.

[26] When the case came to the House of Lords, the only two substantial speeches were given by Lord Jauncey and Lord Clyde. Lord Jauncey's speech shows that he had considerable reservations about the decision which was adopted, although he did not dissent from it. The grounds on which the extension of *O'Brien* to Scotland proceeded, have to be found in the speech of Lord Clyde. Three passages in his Lordship's speech have to be particularly examined. [Lord Coulsfield then proceeded to quote the relevant passages from Lord Clyde's speech and continued:]

...

[29] In his speech in *Etridge (No 2)*, Lord Clyde also made observations which are relevant in considering the position in Scotland. Lord Clyde expressed reservations about attempting to categorise instances of undue influence and in particular about attempting to categorise presumed undue influence. He emphasised that cases of undue influence may be very varied and that the question whether undue influence has been exercised is one primarily for evidence and proof. When he came to deal with the steps to be taken by a creditor, his Lordship quoted what Lord Browne-Wilkinson had said in *O'Brien* to the effect that the creditor could reasonably be expected to take steps to bring home to the wife the risk she was running and referred to his own suggestion in *Smith*, which I have already quoted. He then observed that what he had said echoed what was understood to be the existing practice recognised by banks and building societies and that it seemed to him that steps of that kind should be enough to counter allegations of bad faith. [Lord Coulsfield quoted the relevant passages from Lord Clyde's speech and continued:]

...

[31] I think that it is reasonably clear from the passages which I have quoted that Lord Clyde had reservations about any attempts, whether in Scotland or in England, to set out in too much detail the steps which a creditor can be regarded as obliged to take. I think that it can also be said that Lord Clyde does not regard it as required by, or even consistent with, the basis upon which he approved the extension of the *O'Brien* requirements into Scotland that any definite requirements should be prescribed to satisfy the demands of good faith. To lay down any such detailed and prescribed requirements would, in any event, be difficult to reconcile with the normal approach of Scots law to questions of good faith. There is, therefore, nothing in Lord Clyde's opinion and, I

would respectfully suggest, nothing in the speeches of the other members of the House in any of the cases to which I have referred which need be construed as requiring this court to hold that the specific requirements discussed in *Etridge (No 2)* form part of the law of Scotland.

[32] The more difficult question is whether the extension of the *O'Brien* decision to Scotland requires the Scottish courts to apply the same underlying test in determining whether the creditor has acted in good faith as the English courts apparently require to do in determining whether the creditor is or is not affected by constructive notice. In other words, the question is whether, as a result of *Smith*, the Scottish courts require to ask whether the creditor has taken reasonable steps to satisfy itself that the wife understands the nature and effect of the transaction. This is a question which I have found very difficult. On the one hand, I do not detect any significant reservations on the part of Lord Clyde in regard to the underlying reasons which motivated the decision in *O'Brien*. As I have explained above, it seems to me that these reasons were the need that the law should extend protection to granters of securities, such as wives, who may be exposed to undue influence and the need to make some extension to the law in order to cope with that problem. In any event, it seems to me to be difficult to envisage that there should be any material difference in principle between the obligations incumbent on a lender in Scotland and England respectively, given that it was recognised in *Smith* that the same problems existed in both jurisdictions and that it was expressly stated that consistency between the jurisdictions was to be desired. On the other hand, when Lord Clyde discussed the steps which a creditor should take he spoke in terms of 'advising' or 'warning' the potential cautioner, rather than in terms of 'bringing home' to her the nature of the transaction or 'satisfying itself' that she had been properly advised. Lord Clyde also apparently approved the decision in *Forsyth v Royal Bank of Scotland*. That was a case in which the bank had asked solicitors to see that the wife was given separate advice and to confirm that that had been done, but had proceeded without receiving such confirmation: it may be questionable whether what the bank had done would meet the requirements explained in *Etridge (No 2)*. More generally, for the reasons given by the Lord President in *Smith* and by Lord Marnoch and Lord Sutherland in this case, it is very hard indeed to see how any requirement of the kind called for in *Etridge (No 2)* could be derived from the preexisting law in Scotland as to the requirements of good faith. The force of that point is perhaps reduced by the argument that *O'Brien* represented a conscious extension of the law of England and that *Smith* similarly represented a conscious extension of the law of Scotland. Nevertheless, the basis on which the extension was made in *Smith* was good faith, and one would hope that the consequences could be logically related to that concept.

[33] In view of these difficulties, as I have said, I am extremely reluctant to attempt to set out any general conclusion, and I would prefer to deal with the problems on a case by case basis and on established facts. As regards the present case, however, there is an additional consideration, to which Lord Sutherland has drawn attention. That is that at the time of the transaction in the present case, the law was understood to be as it was stated by the Inner House in *Smith*, and that the House of Lords decision was expressly an 'extension' of the law. What the pursuers did in this case complied exactly with the requirements of good faith and proper banking practice, as understood in Scotland at the time. The distinction between the tests to be applied to past actings and future actings is clearly recognised in the cases. It is true, as Lord Marnoch points out, that normally a court decision on a question of common law is regarded as stating the law as it always has been. In this case, however, we are dealing with the effects of decisions which expressly extended the law and expressly distinguished between consequences for past transactions and consequences for future transactions. Accordingly, I agree with Lord Sutherland that in the particular circumstances of this case, it has not been

relevantly averred that the pursuers failed in their duty of good faith. It follows that this appeal should be refused.

5–24 LORD MARNOCH: . . . Although the speeches delivered in [*Etridge (No. 2)*] were in some instances both lengthy and complex, it seems to me that for present purposes the relevant ratio is conveniently encapsulated by the following passage from the speech of Lord Nicholls of Birkenhead at [2001] 3 WLR, p 1046: 'In respect of past transactions, the bank would ordinarily be regarded as having discharged its obligations if a solicitor who was acting for the wife in the transaction gave the bank confirmation to the effect that he had brought home to the wife the risks she was running by standing as surety.'

Counsel for the defender and appellant submitted that this should be regarded as the law, both in Scotland and England, and it had not been complied with in the present case. The policy considerations in favour of uniformity had been made clear in *Smith* and there was no reason, said counsel for the defender and appellant, why satisfaction of this requirement should not now be deemed to have been embraced by the wider duty to evince 'good faith' referred to by Lord Clyde in *Smith*.

[8] I have given anxious consideration to this submission but, in the end, I reject it. Unlike your Lordships, I do not attach much importance to the consideration that the events with which this case is concerned predated the decision in *Etridge (No 2)*. Court decisions which affect the common law are of their nature retrospective in character, even if they touch on what appear to be subjective matters such as the presence or absence of good faith. In such cases the real question remains what, in the eyes of the law at its present stage of development, is treated as satisfying the requirement in question. The passage from the speech of Lord Nicholls of Birkenhead which is quoted above was, for example, both recognised and intended to have retrospective effect although there are, of course, other passages in both *O'Brien* and *Etridge (No 2)* which, rather unusually, bear to relate only to the future. In any event, I am satisfied that the submission in question should in general be rejected.

[9] In this connection, the first point to notice, in my opinion, is that in *Smith* there was, as I see it, no intention to achieve exact uniformity as between the laws of Scotland and England. In particular, and as stated above, I see no indication of any intention to import into Scots law the more precise requirements set out for England in the earlier case of *Barclays Bank plc v O'Brien*. As it happens, I do not, myself, see why policy considerations in favour of broadly similar results in this area of the law should extend to even a desire for precise assimilation. If, however, I am wrong about that, the best course might be to resort to legislation.

[10] The second point to notice is that in England this whole area of the law has been developed by an extension of the equitable concept of constructive notice—see generally *Royal Bank of Scotland plc v Etridge (No 2)* per Lord Nicholls of Birkenhead at [2001] 3 WLR, pp 1036 et seq. This means that the question, as it presents in England, is whether the bank or other creditor has done enough to 'shed the constructive notice imputed to it'—per Lord Scott of Foscote at p 1096. In relation to Scotland, however, this jurisprudential route was expressly disavowed in *Smith*—perhaps, not least, because of what had been said on that matter in the courts below—and instead, and in accordance with existing principle, the route chosen by the House of Lords was to develop the concept of 'good faith' which could already be detected in Scottish authority. This concept was explored in some detail by Lord Clyde in *Smith* at 1997 SC (HL), pp 117I–118C; 1997 SLT, pp 1065L-1066B, where, after dealing with cases of knowledge or imputed knowledge of actual fraud, Lord Clyde goes on to deal with another category of case which, he says, forms an exception to the general rule that a cautioner is expected to look to his own interests. [Lord Marnoch quoted the relevant passages from Lord Clyde's speech and continued:]

. . .

[12] According to that statement of the law, therefore, there is, in my opinion, no place for the sort of investigation envisaged by their Lordships' House in *Royal Bank of Scotland plc v Etridge (No 2)*. Nor, indeed, is the emphasis necessarily on "bringing home" to the wife the risks she was running by standing as surety. Unlike England, there is no requirement for the creditor to 'shed' the constructive notice which might otherwise be imputed to him. On the contrary, as Lord Clyde puts the matter in *Smith* (at 1997 SC (HL), p 122B; 1997 SLT, p 1068G): 'Whether there has in fact been or may yet be any conduct by the debtor directed at the cautioner which might vitiate the contract is not a matter necessarily to be explored by the creditor. All that is required of him is that *he* should take reasonable steps to secure that in relation to the proposed contract *he* acts throughout in good faith' (my italics).

In short, as I see it, all that is requisite in Scotland is that, in the course of his communings with the cautioner, in addition to compliance with the duties already incumbent upon him under the earlier law, the creditor should now 'warn the potential cautioner of the consequences of entering into the proposed cautionary obligation and ... advise him or her to take independent advice'—at 1997 SC (HL), p 122; 1997 SLT, p 1068. As it happens, these same steps are again referred to by Lord Clyde in *Royal Bank of Scotland plc v Etridge* (No 2), at [2001] 3 WLR, p 1051, and I see no suggestion there that, for Scotland, the position should be regarded as having in any way altered. In particular, there is no suggestion that the duty which Lord Clyde identified in *Smith* should now be seen, contrary to what was said in *Smith*, 'to carry with it a duty of investigation'.

[13] There is one final point I wish to make, and that relates to what was said by Lord Nicholls of Birkenhead in *Royal Bank of Scotland v Etridge (No 2)* regarding what, *for the future*, would be necessary if creditors in England were successfully to 'shed' the constructive notice imputed to them. The relevant passage is again to be found at p 1046 of the report (para 79) and is to the effect that the creditor should volunteer to the wife's solicitor 'the necessary financial information' including, inter alia, 'the current amount of the husband's indebtedness'. So far, at least, as Scotland is concerned, this would traverse a strong and clear line of authority which is referred to by Lord Clyde in *Smith*, at 1997 SC (HL), p 117; 1997 SLT, p 1065. Accordingly, in my opinion, this is a further reason why their Lordships' decision in *Royal Bank of Scotland v Etridge (No 2)* should not—and, indeed, cannot—be regarded as touching on Scots law.

[14] For all the foregoing reasons I am of opinion that in the present case there are no relevant averments that the pursuers have breached their duty of good faith, even assuming that undue influence on the part of Mr Black were to be established. It follows that this appeal should be refused.

LORD SUTHERLAND: ... [3] It only remains to consider the effect of *Etridge*. The 5–25
decision in that case was to add yet further steps to be taken for the future by lenders in England to avoid being held to have constructive notice of the risk of undue influence being exerted against the guarantor. Lord Clyde took part in that case. [Lord Sutherland quoted the relevant extracts from Lord Clyde's speech and continued:]

...

[4]... Obviously it has to be borne in mind that Lord Clyde's decision to agree in the result was taken in the context of English law. Furthermore, the comments which he makes as to the steps which have to be taken by a lender are also to be seen in the context of English law. I have quoted this passage in full to ascertain if there can be discerned any departure referable to Scots law from what he said in *Smith*. Having considered the matter carefully I am satisfied not only that he did not seek to extend (or further "develop") the law of Scotland but that he confirms what he said in *Smith*. I am therefore satisfied that *Etridge* makes no practical difference to the law of Scotland. In any event, again, it is difficult to see how it could have any bearing on whether or not the

respondents acted in good faith in 1996. I do not consider that any inference can be drawn from what Lord Clyde said either in *Smith* or in *Etridge* that he was of opinion that in Scotland there was or should be a duty to investigate how far the written warnings and advice had been seen, understood and followed up by a guarantor and thereby "satisfy" themselves that all was well. To achieve such satisfaction would in my view require a lender to indulge in investigation of the type which it is agreed he has no duty to carry out. It follows that I am of opinion that the defender and appellant has failed to aver any relevant basis for saying that the pursuers and respondents failed in any duty owed by them to her, and that accordingly this appeal should be refused.

[5] I would only add that what I have said so far has been on the assumption that the defender has averred sufficient to show that she was unduly influenced by her husband. I agree with your Lordships that her pleadings are seriously defective in this regard. For my own part I would have been inclined to agree with the courts below that she has not averred a relevant case of undue influence. In particular I find it totally unsatisfactory that a person who is imputing a failure to act in good faith on the part of another party should produce pleadings which, on one view, may be thought to be totally lacking in frankness. It is not necessary however to investigate this matter further as the appeal has been refused on another ground."

Force and fear

5–26 As a basis for annulment of a contract, force and fear can be traced to Roman law. A preliminary question, however, is whether force and fear renders the contract void, or merely voidable.

5–27 *Defective Consent and Consequential Matters*
Scottish Law Commission Memo. No.42 (1 June 1978)

"**Volume 1, Part 1**

Enforced simulation of consent

1.1. ... In most cases in which coercion or threats (usually referred to as 'force and fear') have been used the law, we think, at present takes the view that consent, though improperly extracted, has been given; that an obligation consequently comes into existence; but that the victim may subsequently be entitled to annul it ... But it is recognised—at least in the United States and in most continental European systems—that there are some very rare situations in which the coercive measures are so extreme that no consent at all has been given and no obligation created, the ostensible obligation being from the outset absolutely null.

1.2. We find it difficult to think of examples which are not far-fetched of cases in which it might reasonably be held, not that a party gave his consent under pressure, but that he did not exercise his will at all. However, such cases might include seizing a person's hand and using it as an instrument for signing a document; the use of hypnosis or of hypnotic drugs; and, perhaps, the use of torture. In those highly exceptional instances in which the effect of the coercion on the mind of the obligor is of such severity that there was merely a simulacrum or appearance of consent, we think that the obligation or transaction should be absolutely null. The problem is how to determine the circumstances in which coercion should be regarded as totally excluding consent and so rendering the obligation void *ab initio* ...

1.47. *Force and fear* (or coercion, or threats, or extortion). Roman law, and modern systems derived therefrom, distinguish between situations in which the result of the exercise of coercion is that a party's will is so completely overborne that no consent at all has been given and situations in which the effect of coercion is to induce a party to

> consent, albeit unwillingly. With situations of the first type, which are in any event of the utmost rarity, in our view, we are not at present concerned ... Where coercion of the second type has been resorted to, the result in civil law systems is that the obligation is not absolutely null but is open to annulment. In Roman law, at least as reflected in the Digest, it was necessary before relief could be obtained that the threats or coercion should have been such as would have intimidated a man of robust character, and that the threats employed should have been of actual physical harm.
>
> 1.48. Of the Scottish institutional writers only Bankton clearly and expressly distinguishes between force and fear which is so extreme as to preclude consent, and so renders an ostensible obligation absolutely null, and force and fear which induces consent (albeit unwillingly) but renders the resulting obligation annullable ...
>
> 1.49. There is little modern judicial discussion of force and fear to be found. Such authority as there is supports the view that threats normally render an obligation annullable, not absolutely null. Apart from threats of violence and threats of the use of diligence by a creditor to extort more than the amount actually due to him, it has been held to be a relevant ground of reduction that an obligant was threatened with loss of employment. And if a party's goods are unwarrantably seized, an obligation entered into to secure their release is reducible. But there has been no exhaustive or clear definition of just what types of coercion or duress or threats render an obligation annullable, and certainly no real development in Scotland of anything comparable to what American lawyers call 'economic duress' (or taking advantage of a party's weak economic position, as for example by threatening to place him on a credit black list) as a ground for annulment of obligations."

The assumption made by the Scottish Law Commission that a contract is rendered only annullable by force and fear is not borne out by modern decisions. At the very least, there is an element of doubt.

As Lord Deas pointed out in the following case, it is more accurate to speak of the ground of "extortion" in Scots law, rather than force and fear.

Priestnell v Hutcheson 5–28

(1857) 19 D. 495

Court of Session, First Division: Lord President (McNeill), Lords Deas and Curriehill

The pursuer's husband, "having been unfortunate in business", persuaded her to sign a deed granting security over her property in favour of the bank to which her husband was indebted. In seeking reduction of the deed on grounds of force and fear, the pursuer

> "averred that her husband came hurriedly into her bedroom, when she was unwell, and told her that the bank threatened him with diligence and ruin unless she consented to grant the deed; and, on her refusal, peremptorily repeated that she must sign it without anybody knowing of it, otherwise, to avoid imprisonment, he would flee the country, and leave her and her family to do as best they might: that, at this juncture, the bank agent came with the deed prepared: that, without reading it, or having it explained to her, she was compelled to sign it, and without time given for deliberation or reflection".

The Court repelled her claim that the contract be set aside.

> "LORD DEAS: ... Although, translating the language of the Roman Law, we couple together force and fear as one ground of reduction, the act of force is truly, as Lord Stair 5–29

observes (i. 9, 8), only one means of inducing fear, the true ground of reduction being *extortion*, through the influence of fear, induced in the various ways, of which he gives instances, partly from the civil law and partly from our own law, such as the fear of torture, fear of infamy, fear of danger to life, and so on. It would be very difficult... to point out all the means by which, and which alone, such fear may be induced, on the part of a married woman, as the law will recognise as sufficient to void her solemn deed. Certain it is, on the one hand, that it is not every sort of fear—or rather it is not the fear of consequences of every sort, which will void such a deed; and, on the other hand, that fear of particular consequences may be sufficient in the case of a married woman, though of full capacity, which would not be sufficient in the case of a man of full capacity, and that these consequences need not necessarily be injury to herself, either in her person or character, but may be injury to her husband or to her children, the fear for whose safety may be stronger even than the fear for her own ...

[T]he grounds of fear must be such as the law recognizes as relevant to void a solemn written deed; and here the only fear alleged is fear of consequences, which it was quite lawful for the bank to hold out, and equally lawful for the husband to communicate to his wife, as well as to tell her what he himself might thereupon feel constrained to do, in order to avoid imprisonment and gain a livelihood; and when the wife, to avoid the consequences thus impending, agreed to sign the deed, it would be more correct to say that she acted from affection than that she acted from fear; and although affection may no doubt induce fear for the person who is its object, yet if the fear so induced be merely the fear of (or in other words, the desire to avoid) such consequences as are stated here, all which might have ensued without illegality on the part of anybody, this is not the sort of fear which we can hold relevant to void a formal and delivered deed. The bank threatened nothing which was unlawful, and the husband held out nothing which was unlawful, for he only said he would be constrained to leave the country, which might be a very natural course for him to take to avoid imprisonment, and seek a livelihood, and was very different from the case put (upon which I give no opinion) of a threat by the husband to commit suicide, or some other violent and unlawful act. In a reduction on the ground of force and fear, I hold it necessary to specify the things said and done in such a way as to enable the Court to judge whether they really amount to force and fear in the eye of the law, very much as in the case of fraud it must be specifically stated in what the alleged fraud consists."

What do you think "unlawful" means in this context? Would a threat, for example, to drive a person out of business by means of a restrictive trade practice be enough?

Although only a sheriff court decision, the following case is an illustration of how restrictively the category of "threats" is interpreted in practice.

5–30 **Wolfson v Edelman**

1952 S.L.T. (Sh. Ct.) 97

Sheriff Court of Lanark at Glasgow: Sheriff-Substitute William Jardine Dobie

Wolfson sued Edelman for repetition of certain sums paid by him to Edelman in cash for delivery of certain bills of exchange granted by him. Wolfson averred that he had paid the sums and accepted the bills under threats: (1) that the transactions of Wolfson's company which was in financial difficulties would be investigated; (2) that Edelman would use all his influence to bring Wolfson's company into bankruptcy; and (3) that Edelman would hold Wolfson's company and directors liable for personal payments to Wolfson and for other payments which Edelman claimed were illegal.

He failed in his submissions to the court.

"SHERIFF-SUBSTITUTE (DOBIE): ... It seems to me that these averments fall far short of what is needed to make out a case of force and fear. It was suggested for the pursuer that the threats used referred to criminal actions which would have involved prosecution, but the averments made seem to me to be carefully framed to avoid any such suggestion. The fact that the company's accounts included personal debts due by the pursuer does not of itself involve anything criminal, and the threat of the individual responsibility of the directors for repayment seems to confirm that civil liability was alone in view. The suggested investigation of the company's transactions is quite unspecific and, in my view, almost meaningless, while its bankruptcy at the instance of a creditor is clearly a lawful and legitimate threat. It is significant that the averments remain in that state despite an express, and insistent, call for further specification. **5–31**

So far as the law is concerned it is clear that to justify an attack in respect of force and fear the threats must be such as to affect the mind of a reasonable person (Gloag, *Contract*, 2nd edition, 488). Empty or futile threats are of no avail (*McIntosh v Chalmers*, (1883), 11 R. 8, per Lord Kinnear at p. 10, see also Bell's *Commentaries* I, 315) and in this case [the] pursuer specifically avers that the basis on which the threats were made had no foundation in fact. Nor can such a ground of action succeed if the threats were lawful threats of diligence, or even of imprisonment if that is a competent remedy (*Priestnell v Hutcheson* (1857), 19 D. 495; *Education Authority of Dumfriesshire v Wright*, 1926 S.L.T. 217; Gloag, *Contract*, 2nd edition 489). Finally, it has been laid down that in cases of this kind-proper specification of the averments is necessary (*Priestnell v Hutcheson* (supra), Lord Deas at p. 500) and in a very recent case (*Sinclair v M'Laren & Co Ltd*, First Division, 3rd June 1952 (not reported)) the Lord President said that such cases ought to be specifically averred and clearly proved. By these tests the averments obviously fail to reach the required standard and this ground of action must, in my view, fail."

Since the sheriff-substitute did not find the threats established, he did not need to consider whether the threats were such as to negative consent. The issue arose directly in the following case, where the question of threats of legal action was again raised. The opinion of Lord Maxwell introduces the notion that the "threat" in such instances might be the attempt by the other party to be "bought off" by agreeing not to pursue legal action.

Hislop v Dickson Motors (Forres) Ltd **5–32**
1978 S.L.T. (Notes) 73
Court of Session, Outer House: Lord Maxwell

Hislop (H) was employed as cashier by Dickson Motors (DM). In one month, less money was apparently banked than was received and there were false entries in DM's books. H admitted the false entries.

When the directors of DM visited her at her home, H gave them a pass book to her savings account and transferred to them possession of a car she was buying on hire-purchase. The directors withdrew £381 from that account the same day. When they discovered that H also had a current account they immediately returned to her house and, after some hectoring, she gave them a blank cheque which they used to withdraw a further £195. H sought recovery of the money and the motorcar on the grounds that she was compelled to part with them by force and fear. She was tried for embezzlement but was acquitted on a "not proven" verdict.

5–33 "LORD MAXWELL: ... As regards threats, the pursuer on record relies on alleged threats to report her to the police, with consequent fear of prosecution and damage to reputation ... [T]he only thing proved which might be construed as a threat was the statement by Mr Thomas Dickson ... that, rather than accept the pursuer's position of admission of liability for false entries in the books while denying actual receipt of the money, he would report the matter to the police. I do not consider however that that was a 'threat' at all in the sense in which this word is used in extortion cases. The characteristic of such a threat is the expression or implication of intention to do something, as for example to report to the police, unless the victim gives way to the extortioner's demand. No doubt there may be cases where the extortionate nature of the transaction is implied rather than expressed in plain terms ... but I think that extortion by threats involves some contemplation on the part of the extortioner and the victim of the 'buying off' of the thing threatened. In this case there is no evidence that Mr Thomas Dickson ever suggested that he would not report the matter to the police, if the pursuer admitted having taken the money or agreed to make repayment and I do not think that this can be implied into what he said. It may be that the pursuer hoped that admission and repayment would in fact save her from police enquiries and the consequent risk of prosecution and of injury to reputation and also perhaps to save her job, but, as was pointed out in *Ferrier v Mackenzie* (1889) 6 S.L.T. 597; 1 F. 597, there is an important distinction between a hope that, if payment is made, prosecution will be averted and an agreement to that effect. In *Ferrier v Mackenzie* the plea was *pactum illicitum*, not extortion, but the distinction in my opinion is equally important in cases of alleged extortion. I can see nothing wrong or unreasonable in ... Dickson's suggestion ... that he would report the matter to the police and since in my opinion he never said or implied that he would refrain from doing so if repayment was effected, I also reject counsel for the pursuer's argument that the defenders acted wrongfully in reporting after repayment was effected ...

In some cases, payment to 'buy off' a threat of procedure in itself legal, such as a report of a crime to police, will be recoverable on the grounds of extortion. This ... will not apply where the money paid is no more than is in fact due and where the legal procedure threatened is for the purpose of private recovery of that money or the public prosecution of a criminal act giving rise to the debt. If the threatened action is not itself illegal or unwarrantable ... then it does not found a plea of extortion, if it is only used in good faith to get back that which is due in respect of the matter with regard to which the threat is made ... I was referred to some English cases ... which suggest an approach more favourable to the pursuer, but I do not consider that English authority is a safe guide in this field. Equity in England appears to have moved further in favour of the party seeking reduction of the payment than has the common law in Scotland and the different basis of prosecution in England may also lead to different results ... In my opinion when the threat of proceedings is legal and warrantable the onus is on the party seeking repayment to show that the payment was excessive or related to a matter extraneous to the proceedings threatened (Bankton (I.x.5]). In the present case the pursuer has not discharged that onus ...

While the writers and cases on this branch of the law deal largely with threats, there is a broader underlying principle that deeds will be reducible and payments recoverable when they have been extracted by pressure of a certain degree. In general the pressure must be such as would overpower the mind of a person of ordinary firmness so that there is no true consent. In considering that it is necessary to take into account factors special to the case, such as the sex of the victim and her position relative to the person applying pressure ... It is I think arguable that when dealing with the particular type of pressure involved in threats and also perhaps when there is actual imprisonment ... the requirement of the overpowering of the mind of reasonable firmness has been somewhat departed from ... but in other cases in my opinion it is still the law ... our law cannot allow a person to extract a payment from another by pressure which the payer could not reasonably be expected to resist and then throw upon the payer the onus of proving that the payment made was not in fact due."

Why should the gender of the pursuer be relevant? Contrast Lord Maxwell's views with those of the Inner House in *Clydesdale Bank Plc v Black* (above, paras 5–23—5–25).

In the following case, the central issue was whether threats exerted by a person who was not a party to the contract could establish the plea.

Trustee Savings Bank v Balloch 5–34
1983 S.L.T. 240
Court of Session, Outer House: Lord Cowie

The bank raised an action against Mr and Mrs Balloch for repayment of a sum outstanding under a loan. Mrs Balloch maintained that she was not liable under the agreement, having been forced to enter into it by her husband who had, she averred, threatened her and put her into an extreme state of fear for her life. The bank averred inter alia that even if the averments of force and fear were sufficient, there were no averments that the pursuers were implicated in such actings or cognisant of them, and thus, in a question with them, it was immaterial whether the agreement had been induced by fear of a third party or had been entered into by Mrs Balloch of her own free will.

The court allowed proof.

"LORD COWIE: ... There is undoubtedly judicial support for the view that in a question as to the validity of an agreement between two parties, if one of them has been forced into the agreement by force and fear applied by a third party, that is irrelevant unless the other party was implicated in the force and fear or was cognisant of it. This view was expressed by Lord Trayner in the rather unsatisfactorily reported case of *Stewart Brothers v Kiddie* (1899) 7 S.L.T. 92, and must be given due weight by me. It is fair to point out however that the decision was a majority one and that there is no indication that a case which appears to be to the contrary effect was ever cited to the court. That case is *Cassie v Fleming* (1632) Mor. 10279, which, while not easy to follow, supports counsel for the second defender's submission. 5–35

Professor Gloag in his textbook on *Contract* (2nd ed.) at p. 492, while setting out the two sides of the argument with reference to the above cases does not seem to venture a firm view of his own, but he does state that: 'On the theory that a contract induced by force and fear is void and not merely voidable, it ought to be ineffectual even in a question with a party who is not responsible for, nor cognisant of, the force which has been used.' He then refers to the case of *Cassie v Fleming*.

In my opinion, notwithstanding the case of *Stewart Brothers v Keddie* [*sic*], the correct view in principle is that if one party to a contract has been forced to enter into it by fear, whether induced by the other party to the contract or by a third party, the former has not freely and voluntarily given his or her consent and the contract is void. In these circumstances it matters not that the other party to the contract was not implicated in the force and fear not that he was not aware of its use. This seems to me to be the ratio decidendi in *Cassie v Fleming* and I see no reason to dissent from it. The case of *Stewart Brothers v Keddie* [*sic*] was a majority decision and while prima facie binding on me, the

> point which I have decided was given scant attention by Lord Trayner and was based on very different facts."

Note that, in addition to admitting as evidence of extortion the acts of a third party, Lord Cowie was clearly of the view that the effect of force and fear is to render the contract void.

Force and fear and "economic duress"

5–36 It is clear from the above cases that "threat" is not restricted to threats of violence or imprisonment. There are no Scottish cases, however, on whether threats of economic injury—such as a threat to indulge in restrictive trade practices to the economic detriment of the other party—would be enough.

The following case is an English House of Lords decision which admits the possibility in English law, but which has not been applied in any Scottish case.

5–37 **Pao On v Lau Yiu Long**

[1980] A.C. 614

Privy Council: Viscount Dilhorne, Lords Wilberforce, Simon of Glaisdale, Salmon and Scarman

The plaintiffs owned the issued share capital of a private company (Shing On) incorporated in Hong Kong. The defendants were the majority shareholders in a public investment company (Fu Chip) in Hong Kong. Shing On's principal asset was a building. In February 1973 the plaintiffs agreed to sell to Fu Chip their shares in Shing On in return for shares in Fu Chip. To avoid depressing the share price of Fu Chip, the plaintiffs agreed to retain 60 per cent of their newly-acquired shares until after 30 April 1974. The plaintiffs realised that by giving an undertaking to postpone sale of the Fu Chip shares they exposed themselves to the risk that the price of the shares might fall. Accordingly, by a subsidiary agreement dated 27 February the defendants agreed to buy back from the plaintiffs, on or before 30 April 1974, 2.5 million of the allotted Fu Chip shares at the price of $2.50 a share.

By April, the plaintiffs realised their mistake: under the subsidiary agreement, they would have to sell 60 per cent of their shares back to the defendants at $2.50 a share even if, as was expected, the value of the shares would greatly exceed that amount.

The plaintiffs indicated to the defendants that they would not complete the main agreement with Fu Chip unless the subsidiary agreement was cancelled and replaced by a true guarantee by way of indemnity, guaranteeing the price of 2.5 million of the allotted shares at $2.50 a share. The defendants were anxious to complete the transaction for otherwise public confidence in Fu Chip (which had only recently gone public) might be impaired. They chose to avoid litigation and to accede to the cancellation of the subsidiary agreement and its replacement by a guarantee by way of indemnity.

Between 4 May1973 and 30 April 1974 share prices slumped and by 30 April Fu Chip shares had fallen to 36 cents a share. The defendants failed to fulfil their promise of indemnity under the guarantee of 4 May 1973. The plaintiffs brought an action against them claiming $5,392,800 due under the guarantee, or alternatively specific performance of the guarantee.

The defendants asserted, inter alia, that the guarantee was void on the ground that it was induced by economic duress on the plaintiffs' part.

The Privy Council rejected the defence.

"LORD SCARMAN: ... Duress, whatever form it takes, is a coercion of the will so as to negative consent. Their Lordships agree with the observation of Kerr J. in *Occidental Worldwide Investment Corporation v Skibs A/S Avanti* [1976] 1 Lloyd's Rep. 293, 336 that in a contractual situation commercial pressure is not enough. There must be present some factor 'which could in law be regarded as a coercion of his will so as to vitiate his consent.' This conception is in line with what was said in this Board's decision in *Barton v Armstrong* [1976] A.C. 104, 121 by Lord Wilberforce and Lord Simon of Glaisdale—observations with which the majority judgment appears to be in agreement. In determining whether there was a coercion of will such that there was no true consent, it is material to inquire whether the person alleged to have been coerced did or did not protest; whether, at the time he was allegedly coerced into making the contract, he did or did not have an alternative course open to him such as an adequate legal remedy; whether he was independently advised; and whether after entering the contract he took steps to avoid it. All these matters are, as was recognised in *Maskell v Horner* [1915] 3 K.B.106, relevant in determining whether he acted voluntarily or not. **5–38**

In the present case there is unanimity amongst the judges below that there was no coercion of the first defendant's will. In the Court of Appeal the trial judge's finding ... that the first defendant considered the matter thoroughly, chose to avoid litigation, and formed the opinion that the risk in giving the guarantee was more apparent than real was upheld. In short, there was commercial pressure, but no coercion. Even if this Board was disposed, which it is not, to take a different view, it would not substitute its opinion for that of the judges below on this question of fact.

It is, therefore, unnecessary for the Board to embark on an enquiry into the question whether English law recognises a category of duress known as 'economic duress.' But, since the question has been fully argued in this appeal, their Lordships will indicate very briefly the view which they have formed. At common law money paid under economic compulsion could be recovered in an action for money had and received: see *Astley v Reynolds* (1731) 2 Str. 915. The compulsion had to be such that the party was deprived of 'his freedom of exercising his will' (at p. 916). It is doubtful, however, whether at common law any duress other than duress to the person sufficed to render a contract voidable: see Blackstone's *Commentaries*, Book 1, l2th ed. pp. 134–131 and *Skeate v Beale* (1841) I1 Ad. 8c E. 983. American law (*Williston on Contracts*, 3rd ed.) now recognises that a contract may be avoided on the ground of economic duress. The commercial pressure alleged to constitute such duress must, however, be such that the victim must have entered the contract against his will, must have had no alternative course open to him, and must have been confronted with coercive acts by the party exerting the pressure: *Williston on Contracts*, 3rd ed., vol. 13 (1970), s.1603. American judges pay great attention to such evidential matters as the effectiveness of the alternative remedy available, the fact or absence of protest, the availability of independent advice, the benefit received, and the speed with which the victim has sought to avoid the contract. Recently two English judges have recognised that commercial pressure may constitute duress the pressure of which can render a contract voidable: see Kerr J. in *Occidental Worldwide Investment Corporation v Skibs A/S Avanti* [1976] 1 Lloyd's Rep. 293 and Mocatta J. in *North Ocean Shipping Co Ltd v Hyundai Construction Co. Ltd.* [1979] Q.B. 705. Both stressed that the pressure must be such that the victim's consent to the contract was not a voluntary act on his part. In their Lordships' view, there is nothing contrary to principle in recognising economic duress as a factor which may render a contract voidable, provided always that the basis of such recognition is that it must amount to a coercion of will, which vitiates consent. It must be shown that the payment made or the contract entered into was not a voluntary act."

It appears that Lord Scarman laid down severe strictures on the development of the doctrine—"it must amount to a coercion of will, which vitiates consent". It is difficult to conceive of situations where this might arise, yet, as Lord Scarman acknowledged, the doctrine has been applied by English courts, most recently by Tucker J in *Atlas Express Ltd v Kafko (Importers and Distributors) Ltd*,[10] on the basis of Lord Scarman's speech.

It has been suggested that the doctrine can and ought to be incorporated into Scots law. There is much to be said for the view that matters purportedly amounting to "economic duress" are often practices with far wider implications than the interests of the parties. There is a public interest element whenever undue economic pressure is deployed in the economy, especially where it results from market power or collusion. Such matters are the stuff of competition law. It is perhaps better that remedies are sought and developed in that context, rather than yet another vague quasi-legal theorem which attempts to balance the economic interests of the parties.

5–39 *Defective Consent and Consequential Matters*

Scottish Law Commission Memo. No.42 (1 June 1978)

> "Volume 1, Part 1
> 1.50. *Our general approach.* There have, of course, been substantial social and commercial changes since the heyday in the 19th century of 'sanctity of contract'. The time has come for a re-examination and redefinition of those aspects of Scots law at present grouped under the headings of force and fear, extortion, facility and circumvention, and undue influence. In particular, the limits of legitimate economic pressure need to be considered. Our provisional conclusion is that the category of threats, suitably clarified and redefined, should be recognised as a ground for annulment; and that the ideas which lie behind facility and circumvention, undue influence and extortion (in Erskine's sense of taking undue advantage of a neighbour's necessities) should be drawn together in the formulation of a comprehensive and generalised new category of vitiation of consent, which we refer to as 'lesion'."

Another possible "formulation of a comprehensive and generalised new category" is that provided by the DCFR.

5–40 II. I. 206: Coercion or threats

> (1) A party may avoid a contract when the other party has induced the conclusion of the contract by coercion or by the threat of an imminent and serious harm which it is wrongful to inflict, or wrongful to use as a means to obtain the conclusion of the contract.
>
> (2) A threat is not regarded as inducing the contract if in the circumstances the threatened party had a reasonable alternative.

5–41 II. I7:207: Unfair exploitation

> (1) A party may avoid a contract if, at the time of the conclusion of the contract:
>
> (a) the party was dependent on or had a relationship of trust with the other party, was in economic distress or had urgent needs, was improvident, ignorant, inexperienced or lacking in bargaining skill; and

---

[10] *Atlas Express Ltd v Kafko (Importers and Distributors) Ltd* [1989] 1 All E.R. 641.

(b) the other party knew or could reasonably be expected to have known this and, given the circumstances and purpose of the contract, exploited the first party's situation by taking an excessive benefit or grossly unfair advantage.

(2) Upon the request of the party entitled to avoidance, a court may if it is appropriate adapt the contract in order to bring it into accordance with what might have been agreed had the requirements of good faith and fair dealing been observed.

(3) A court may similarly adapt the contract upon the request of a party receiving notice of avoidance for unfair exploitation, provided that this party informs the party who gave the notice without undue delay after receiving it and before that party has acted in reliance on it."

CHAPTER 6
ERROR

Introduction: errors, mistakes, misunderstandings and lies

6–01 The preceding chapters explored the question: have the parties agreed? This chapter begins the exploration of the next major question: *what* have the parties agreed? More specifically, it explores the effect upon the contract of misunderstandings or *error* about what has been agreed.[1] Such errors can arise from the simplest misunderstandings, to downright lies and fraud. Such matters come under the generic heading of "error".

This chapter concerns errors made leading up to the point where the parties have reached agreement, usually when an offer has been accepted. Errors that arise, or operate after the contract is made are generally matters of construction[2] and performance[3] respectively.

For several reasons the law on error is relatively complicated.[4] First, it necessarily involves the making of fine distinctions of fact and intention, so that it is often difficult for the reader to discern the reasoning in the case law. This should be borne in mind when reading the case extracts below. Secondly, it is an area on which Roman law and the institutional writers are frequently vague, so that it is difficult to find clearly stated underlying principle; and again, the reader should be carefully critical of the statements of principle given below. Thirdly, much of the case law is itself opaque, primarily because no clear and unambiguous classification of error is used by the judges. Fourthly, for such a complex area, there has, until recent years, been relatively little Scottish academic comment[5] and what there is does not constitute a consensus. Fifthly, it is an area where much confusion has been created by reference to English authority.[6] Finally, error poses theoretical questions such as: Is the law of contract based upon mutual promises or upon mutual reliance?[7] How does the law balance subjective considerations with the need for objectivity?

---

[1] See WW McBryde, *The Law of Contract in Scotland*, 3rd edn (Edinburgh: W. Green, 2007), Ch.15. McBryde deals separately with fraud in Ch.14. Although the term "error" is invariably used in Scots law, *mistake* is more generally used, for example in common law systems and in the *Principles of European Contract Law* (Ch.4:103 onwards.).

[2] Considered below, Ch.8. Errors of *expression*, however, are considered in this chapter at paras 6–71—6–82.

[3] Considered below, Ch.11. *Pre-contractual frustration*, however, is considered in this chapter at paras 6–31—6–32.

[4] The complex and confused development of the Scots law of error is most thoroughly exposed by WW McBryde, "Error" in Reid and Zimmerman (eds), *History of Scottish Private Law* (Oxford: Oxford University Press, 2000), Vol.2, pp.72–100.

[5] The major contributions by academic writers on error in recent years are: JJ Gow, "Mistake and Error" (1952) 1 I.C.L.Q. pp.472–483; JJ Gow, "Some Observations on Error" (1953) 7 R. 221; JJ Gow, "*Culpa in docendo*", 1954 J.R. 253; TB Smith, "Error in the Scottish Law of Contract" (1955) 71 L.Q.R. 507; WW McBryde, "A History of Error", 1977 J.R. 1; S Woolman, "Error Revisited", 1986 S.L.T. (News) 317; WW McBryde, "A Note on *Sword v Sinclair* and the Law of Error", 1997 J.R. 281; WW McBryde, "Error" in Reid and Zimmermann (eds), *History of Scottish Private Law* (Oxford: Oxford University Press, 2000), Vol.2, pp.72–100.

[6] A notable failure to wed English concepts of mistake and the Scots law of error is H Burn Murdoch, "English Law in Scots Practice" (1909) 20 J.R. 59–66. The most notable analysis of the differences between the English and Scottish positions is the series of articles by JJ Gow, referred to in fn.2, above. See also *Constitution and Proof of Voluntary Obligations: Abortive Constitution*, Scot. Law Com. Memo. 37 (March 1977), paras 6–9; and *Defective Consent and Consequential Matters*, Scot. Law Com. Memo. 42 (Vol. II, June 1978), paras 3.33–3.40.

[7] For a full consideration of this topic, see S. Woolman, "Error Revisited", 1986 S.L.T. (News) 317.

Terminology is a major and persistent problem. The same term is often used to describe more than one kind of error; and one kind of error is often described by several different terms. For simplicity, this chapter will approach the various categories of error and their consequences in the structured sequence suggested here.

6–02 Mistakes do happen, but it has never been the law of Scotland that a party may escape from an otherwise valid contract, merely because of a mistake, however insignificant. Once a contractual agreement has been established, courts are very unwilling to interfere with that agreement, even where there has been error. There must be something about the error and its effects that undermines the free and voluntary nature of the contract.

The first important distinction is between errors of *intention* and errors of *expression*. There is an important difference between an agreement reached on the basis of an error, and an agreement that is not based on a mistake, but which has been mistakenly expressed, for example, when it is put into writing. This chapter is concerned primarily with the first category, errors of intention.

Around such errors a major distinction can be drawn: that between *unilateral* error, where the misunderstanding arises from a mistake made by only one of the parties; and *bilateral* error, where the misunderstanding arises from both parties making a mistake. Where both parties have made the same mistake—for example, where A agrees to buy a car from B, but unknown to both parties the car had already been destroyed in a fire—that is often referred to as a *common* bilateral error. Where each party makes a different mistake—for example, where A believes that they are buying car X, but Y believes that they are selling car Y—that is often referred to as a *mutual* bilateral error.

In bilateral error, the law has developed around the question of whether the error concerned a matter so serious, so *essential* or *substantial*, that it precluded *consensus*, or agreement between the parties.

If the error is unilateral, the general rule is that the party in error must suffer the consequences: the contact is valid. This is particularly true of onerous and especially commercial contracts, where it would be economically disruptive if parties could resile from contractual obligations merely by declaring that the contract is not the contract they thought they were making.[8] Nevertheless, there are exceptions to this general rule and here the law has focused on two circumstances:

- where the error is not induced by A, but only B is aware of the error; and
- where the error is *induced* by a *representation* made by B which is *relied upon* by A and *but for which* A should not have entered into the contract.

Errors of intention: when is an error substantial, or essential?

6–03 What degree of error must there be before the contract is affected? Must there be a misunderstanding about the "really important" or "substantial" or "essential" issues in the agreement and, if so, how will these be identified?

Error in the substantials

6–04 An error in the substantials of the contract will normally render the contract void, although it must be stressed at the outset that the courts will, in practice, rarely find that an error was so fundamental as to have such a destructive effect upon the contract. Stair's statement that

[8] Recent cases concerning the effect of good faith on unilateral error have highlighted this general principle: see paras 6–33—6–54, below. Thre are dicta that suggest there may be exceptional circumstances where a unilateral error might be operative, but it is difficult to see where therse might arise without negligence on the party in error or bad faith by the other party. See generally WW McBryde *The Law of Contract in Scotland*, 3rd edn (Edinburgh: W. Green, 2007), paras 15–40—15–41.

"[t]hose who err in the substantials of what is done, contract not"[9] is too broad to be of guidance today. Thus simple misunderstandings like the quality of goods bought, or the extent of liability under a signed document, would not amount to error such that, despite appearances, there is no contract, that the contract is void. There would still be a valid contract, although if, for example, the quality of the goods is inferior, there may be an action for breach of contract on the ground that they were not in conformity with what was impliedly agreed as to quality. Such a mistake, not being essential and therefore not operative on the contract, is often termed *concomitant* or *collateral* error.[10]

One possible approach, like that taken by Professor Bell in his *Principles of the Laws of Scotland* (1829) is to list or catalogue the key matters on which there must be no misunderstanding for a contract to arise. Professor Bell's comments are generally taken as the foundation of the modern law of error. They are a reworking of various elements of the law on error as developed in Europe before he wrote, and building on the Roman law.

Bell, *Principles of the Law of Scotland* 6–05

10th edn (Edinburgh: T&T Clarke, 1899)

> "Chapter 1: Of Conventional Obligations
> 11. (1.) *Error* ... Error in substantials, whether in fact or in law, invalidates consent, ... where reliance is placed on the thing mistaken. Such error in substantials may be—1. In relation to the *subject* of the contract or obligation; ... 2. In relation to the *person* who undertakes the engagement, or to whom it is supposed to be undertaken, wherever personal identity is essential; 3. In relation to the *price* or consideration for the undertaking; 4. In relation to the *quality* ... of the thing engaged for, if expressly or tacitly essential to the bargain; or 5. In relation to the *nature* of the contract itself supposed to be entered into ... Although error in *law* as well as error in *fact* will invalidate a contract, it will not always entitle to restitution after the contract is fulfilled or money paid."

Note that Bell uses both the word "substantial" and the word "essential". He was dealing with a problem that has plagued philosophers since the time of Aristotle: what are the elements without which the thing being described cannot be properly defined?[11] What are the essences, the essentials? Does the definition of a chair, for example, require that it should have legs? If so, how many? We have already come across this problem in looking at contract formation and have seen that failure to agree on the incidents (or essential elements) of certain types of contract, or on elements that the parties negotiating have made essential of the contract, means there is no consent and therefore no contract.[12] Bell, however, uses the expression "essential" only in relation to two of his categories. In speaking of quality, for example, Bell appears not to mean how good something is, but rather to refer to the qualities or attributes of the object "essential to the bargain". Yet his overarching definition of operative error is error "in the substantials", suggesting that it is wide enough to cover aspects of the contract beyond its essentials. Was Bell using the words interchangeably, or to indicate a qualitative difference?[13]

Bell states that there must be *reliance* on the mistake, suggesting that, if the error is to be "in essentials", reliance is a further requirement before such an error vitiates consent. Contracts

---

[9] Stair, *Institutions*, I x 13.

[10] In the older cases and textbooks, you will find references to the Latin equivalents: error *in substantialibus* and error *concomitans*.

[11] For the general influence of Aristotelian philosophy on contract law see J Gordley, *The Philosophical Doctrine of Modern Contract Law* (Oxford: Clarendon Press, 1993).

[12] See above, para.3–06—3–13.

[13] See the discussion in WW McBryde *The Law of Contract in Scotland*, 3rd edn (Edinburgh: W. Green, 2007), para.15–04.

cannot be set aside merely because parties say that they were mistaken. There must be "reliance placed on the thing mistaken" and this will be established by objective consideration of the evidence.[14]

Bell's classification has been described as "of limited assistance, unnecessary and potentially misleading".[15] On their own, Professor Bell's categories cannot indicate whether the error was essential, or in the substantials, in a way which would vitiate consent. Bell's statement of principle raises, but does not answer, the qualitative issue: what are the "essential elements" of a contract, or of a contract or particular type, such as one of sale, or one of hire, or one of loan and so on? Nor does Bell explain what degree of misunderstanding between the parties is necessary to preclude consent; or whether an error by one of the parties only (a unilateral error) "invalidates consent"; or the effect of an error *induced* by the other party.

The degree of error necessary to affect the contract

6–06 Professor Bell's approach to the problem of what constitutes an operative error was refined by the House of Lords in the following cases.

6–07

Stewart v Kennedy
(1890) 17 R. (H.L.) 25
House of Lords: Lords Herschell, Watson and Macnaughten

Stewart owned land in the form of an "entail" or "tailzie".[16]

Stewart sent a letter to Kennedy offering to sell to him the land at a specified price. It also contained a provision that "in the event of your acceptance the sale is made subject to the ratification of the Court". Kennedy accepted the offer in writing. Stewart, now wishing to escape from the transaction, brought this action for reduction, averring that throughout the negotiations for the sale he believed that the sale was conditional upon the court determining that the sale was for a reasonable price. He maintained that his error stemmed partly from his personal experience of buying and selling an entailed estate when earlier statutes applied and had required court approval,[17] and partly from being misled by Kennedy's agent into believing that Kennedy's acceptance would be conditional on a court considering the terms of the bargain fair and reasonable.

The court rejected Stewart's plea.

---

[14] See generally S Woolman, "Error Revisited", 1986 S.L.T. (News) 317.

[15] WW McBryde, "Error" in Reid and Zimmerman (eds), *History of Scottish Private Law* (Oxford: Oxford University Press, 2000), Vol.2, pp.72–100, 76 and WW McBryde, *The Law of Contract in Scotland*, 3rd edn (Edinburgh: W. Green, 2007) para.15–07.

[16] Old Scots, pronounced "tailie". He is described in the case by the technical term, "heir of entail in possession". As such, unlike an ordinary owner, Stewart could not freely sell the entailed land nor could he pass it to whomsoever he chose on death. This was because there was a valid term in the title deeds restricting him, and determining to whom it would next pass.

[17] Entails were intended to prevent landed estates from being split up by their owners, and so to keep them in the hands of the current head of the family down the generations. However, the law by this time had been progressively changed by a series of statutes to permit such owners, if they followed certain procedures, to sell just like an ordinary owner, and in the process the buyer would also accordingly acquire an ordinary right of ownership. The most recent statute had been held already by the House of Lords to provide that the terms of a contract to sell would be valid so long as an application was made to and approved by the Court of Session. This was an action by Kennedy (where the question of error was not raised by Stewart) to require Stewart to carry through the sale (*Stewart v Kennedy* (1890) 17 R. (HL) 1). The court would award sums of money to a range of people who might turn out to have been otherwise entitled in terms of the entail to succeed when the current owner died. The previous statutes in certain circumstances had further required the court to determine that the sale was for a reasonable price, but that was no longer the law.

> "LORD WATSON: ... I concur with all their Lordships as to the accuracy of the general doctrine laid down by Professor Bell (Bell's Prin. sec.11) to the effect that error in substantials such as will invalidate consent given to a contract or obligation must be in relation to either (1) its subject matter; (2) the persons undertaking or to whom it is undertaken; (3) the price or consideration; (4) the quality of the thing engaged for ... ; or (5) the nature of the contract or engagement supposed to be entered into. I believe that these five categories will be found to embrace all the forms of essential error which, either *per se* or when induced by the other party to the contract, give the person labouring under such error a right to rescind it ...
>
> Lord Shand held, I think rightly, that the error averred by the appellant is 'error in substantials' within the meaning of that phrase as used by Bell. I cannot read the words 'nature of the contract itself' in the limited sense which the Lord President appears to have attached to them. The nature of the contract involves in my opinion far wider considerations than that of the legal category to which the contract is assigned by lawyers. One contract of sale may differ as essentially from another (apart from all considerations of subject, persons, price, or quality of subject) as a contract of sale does from a contract of pledge or lease. And I venture to think that an absolute contract to execute a conveyance of an entailed estate, and then to obtain its approval by the Court, is in its very nature different from a conditional contract to sell the same estate for a fixed price if in an application for an order of sale under the Act of 1882 the Court shall sanction a private sale at that price, and the next heir of entail does not exercise his power of forbidding the bargain ...
>
> I am of opinion that the alleged error of the appellant is by itself insufficient to invalidate his consent, but that it will be sufficient for that purpose if it can be shewn to have been induced by the representations of the respondent, or of anyone for whose conduct he is responsible. Whether the appellant is entitled to an issue raising the matter of representation chiefly depends upon the relevancy of his averments ... I have come to the conclusion that an issue of essential error induced by [Kennedy's agent] ought to be allowed."

Although accepting Professor Bell's classification of error, it is clear that in *Stewart v Kennedy* the House of Lords stressed that for the error to be essential/substantial (Bell uses both terms), it is not enough that it should fall within one of Bell's categories. **6–08**

In his reference to Bell's categories, Lord Watson refers both to error "per se" and error "induced by the other party to the contract". Is Lord Watson saying that no error affects the contract unless it has been induced?

He also suggests that in *both* cases the erring party is entitled to "rescind" the contract. Can this be correct?[18]

This case is generally recognised as the case which introduced the concept of misrepresentation to Scots law. In particular, note the notion of "induced", "essential" error. The House of Lords were therefore treating this case as one where entry into the contract by one party was induced by the representations of the other party. Why do you think the House of Lords stressed this requirement?

In holding that the case could proceed to a hearing on the facts with regard to the alleged misrepresentation, does Lord Watson imply that, if misrepresentation were proved, there was only an apparent contract, a "void contract" or does he imply that there was only a "voidable contract," or did he have no views on this one way or the other?

In the next case, the House of Lords took the opportunity to elaborate what constituted an "essential" error for the purposes of misrepresentation.

---

[18] See the discussion of induced error/misrepresentation, below, para.6–83.

6–09

Menzies v Menzies

(1893) 20 R. (H.L.) 108

House of Lords: Lord Chancellor (Herschell), Lords Watson, Ashborne, Field and Hannen

An heir to an entailed estate agreed by deed with his only son, the next heir to the estate, that he would disentail the estate. The estate would be transferred to trustees, who would hold it for the benefit of the father during his lifetime, then, on the father's death, for the son during his lifetime and then, on the son's death, to convey the estate to the son's heir. Under the agreement, the son's debts (amounting to £6,000) would be paid off and the son would receive an annuity of £900 per annum during the father's lifetime.

The son, as pursuer, brought an action against the trustees and his father, claiming that the agreement be set aside because he was induced to enter into the agreement by representations made to him by his father's law agent, to the effect that it would otherwise be difficult, if not impossible, for the son to raise the necessary money to pay off his debts.

"LORD WATSON: ... Although the appellant did thereby surrender rights in expectancy which were of considerable value, and also submitted to restrictions which might deprive him of his right to possess the estates after his father's death, I find it impossible to say that in the circumstances the terms of the arrangement were unreasonable or unfair. On the contrary, I think they are such as a friendly adviser, having full knowledge of these circumstances and of his legal rights and powers present and prospective, might with perfect propriety have urged the appellant to accept. I should certainly hesitate to disturb the transaction were I satisfied that in becoming a party to it the appellant either knew his own rights or had the benefit of independent legal advice.

The case presented by the appellant, in the argument addressed to the House, shortly stated, was this: (1) that he would not have consented to the arrangement had he not believed that it was difficult, if not impossible for him to raise money upon his *spes successionis* [future potential inheritance]; (2) that his belief was induced by representations made to him by Mr Jamieson, in communications passing between them with reference to the arrangement; and (3) that at the time he understood and believed that Mr Jamieson was acting as his agent as well as his father's, although he subsequently learned that such was not the case. That these allegations, if established, are sufficient in law to infer the appellant's right to rescind, does not appear to me to admit of serious question. Error becomes essential whenever it is shewn that but for it one of the parties would have declined to contract. He cannot rescind unless his error was induced by the representations of the other contracting party, or of his agent, made in the course of negotiation, and with reference to the subject matter of the contract. If his error is proved to have been so induced, the fact that the misleading representations were made in good faith affords no defence against the remedy of rescission. That principle had been recently affirmed by the House in *Adam v Newbigging*, 1888, L.R., 13 App. Cas. 308; *Stewart v Kennedy*, 1890, L.R., 15 App. Cas. 108, 17 R. (H.L.) 25—a Scotch case; and in *Evans v Newfoundland Bank*, decided this week."

6–10 Why did Lord Watson used the expression "unreasonable or unfair" in the context of the arrangement? Does "reasonableness" or "fairness" have a role to play in the law of error? Should it?

Compare Lord Watson's definition of essential error with that which he developed in *Stewart v Kennedy* (above). Did Lord Watson extend that definition? Compare Lord Watson's definition with that given by Bell—in particular, the opening words. How different are these?

The case establishes the principle that, for the purposes of misrepresentation, an error is essential if, "but for" that error, the party in error would not have entered into the contract. In his book on *Contract*, Professor McBryde[19] gives the following illustration of the effect of Lord Watson's redefinition of essential error in *Menzies*:

> "Assume that X buys a farm because he thinks that the ground contains oil reserves. X intends to exploit these reserves. X is the only person who believes in the existence of the oil and he keeps his belief secret. There is no oil. According to the theory of Stair and Bell, there is no essential error on X's part. X's error did not exclude consensus. According to Lord Watson's standard, X is in essential error. But for the error, X would not have contracted."

Effects of error

If it is established that an error is operative on a contract, what *effect* will the error have upon the contract? Even this apparently straightforward question poses problems, as the case *of Menzies v Menzies* itself illustrates. **6–11**

An error may affect a contract in various ways. The error may *vitiate* an agreement in such a way that no contract arises; in other words, the so-called contract is only an apparent contract. It does not and never has existed. In legal language it is *void*, or a *nullity*, so that no rights or obligations arise under it. There may be remedies in circumstances of "unjustified enrichment", given by the rules of that area of law, but not in contract. Alternatively, the error may render the contract "voidable" or "annullable" at the option of the erring party. The contract exists, but will now cease to exist and so have no further effect if the party affected by the error now brings it to an end on this ground. To bring it to an end is to "avoid" it or to "annul" it.

Scots law contains rules which provide in different contexts for each of these three logically possible effects.

A Short Commentary on the Law of Scotland **6–12**

TB Smith (Edinburgh: W. Green, 1962)
Ch.35, p.789

> "A 'contract' is ineffective if, despite the fact that there has been offer and acceptance, there is lacking some element which the law regards as essential for validity, or if any essential element is vitiated in some way ... When considering problems of nullity or reduction, it is particularly desirable to avoid the citation of English authorities in Scottish cases. When such citation has been resorted to, confusion of principle has almost inevitably resulted. Nullity in Scots law, as in other systems derived from the Roman law, may affect the efficacy of an ostensible contract in two ways. The ostensible agreement may be absolutely null or relatively null—that is, subsisting until reduced by judicial decision. The terms absolute and relative nullity seem preferable to 'void' and 'voidable,' which have overtones of English law. Moreover, the Scottish institutional writers occasionally use the term 'void' as implying 'null', but without distinguishing between the two forms of nullity. It would be justifiable to subdivide the category of absolute nullity into a sub-category covering cases where no legal agreement had ever existed and a subcategory covering cases where, for reasons of public policy, the law refuses recognition to agreement."

---

[19] WW McBryde *The Law of Contract in Scotland*, 3rd edn (Edinburgh: W. Green, 2007), para.15–15.

Would all cases of error come under Professor Smith's first subcategory of "absolute nullity"? It may be historically neat and jurisprudentially correct to speak of "null" and "relatively null" (or "annullable") contracts; the reality is that the terminology consistently used, especially in the modern case law and in modern formulations of the subject, is that of "void" and "voidable".

That a significant degree of disagreement over the effects of error continues is illustrated by the following extracts.

6–13 *Defective Consent and Consequential Matters*

Scottish Law Commission Memo. No.42 (June 1978), Vol.I

"Defective consent or vitiation of consent

1.8 **General**. Vitiation of the will or consent upon which voluntary obligations are founded may result from misapprehension, either self-induced or induced (whether deliberately, negligently or entirely innocently) by another; it may also . . . be the result of coercion. In legal systems the three legal grounds of vitiation of consent which are recognised as justifying the annulment of obligations (or other voluntary legal acts) are force and fear, fraud, and error . . .

1.9 The effect of defective consent (or vitiation of consent or 'vice of consent') is, in general, to render an obligation annullable. This must be contrasted with the real vice (**vitium reale**) which attaches to stolen property and bars even a third party in good faith who has given value from acquiring title to it. Vitiated or defective consent is also something quite different from complete absence of consent . . . Under the existing law annulment for error, fraud, force and fear, etc. is possible only if the parties to the obligation are still in a position to restore to each other any benefits received under it . . .

1.10 **Error**. It would, we think, be generally agreed that the present law of Scotland regarding the effect of error on obligations stands in need of clarification. The authorities on this branch of the law are confusing and difficult, if not impossible, to reconcile. The institutional writers did not always distinguish between the various different classes of error, such as dissensus (failure of offer and acceptance to correspond), common (or shared) error and unilateral error. Perhaps as a consequence of this, it is not always clear whether these writers regarded the effect of error (or of a particular type of error) as being to render an obligation absolutely null or merely annullable at the instance of the party in error. However, all accepted that what was legally relevant was 'essential error' or 'error **in essentialibus**' as distinct from error in motive . . . The institutional writers concerned themselves, to a greater extent than would be thought justifiable today, with the actual subjective state of mind of the contracting parties rather than with whether the error was objectively reasonable and probable."

Effect of error on the passing of property rights

6–14 The Scottish Law Commission (in para.1.9) suggests that where an error is such as to prevent an apparent contract from ever having existed, and so a "void contract", ownership does not pass to the other party to the apparent contract. If there is no contract, no property rights can pass from one party to another. The following suggests there may be some situations where the contract may be "void" because of error, yet there is "consent to transfer" the property right. The "error" as to consent may be such that there is no consensus and no contract, but it might not go so far as to take away consent to transfer ownership in some item of property.

The Law of Property in Scotland 6–15

KGC Reid (Edinburgh: Butterworths/Law Society of Scotland, 1996)

> "**614. Vices of consent and real vices.** Where a transaction is accompanied by error ... difficult questions may arise as to whether consent to the transfer [of the right of ownership in something] has been truly given. The answer depends upon whether the error ... is a 'real' vice (*vitium reale* or *labes realis*) or merely a 'vice of consent', the distinction being that a real vice absolutely prevents the giving of consent [to the transfer of the right of ownership]. Where there is a real vice and hence no consent there can, of course, be no transfer. Conversely, where there is consent, albeit wrongfully induced, the ownership passes but the title of the transferee is voidable at the instance of the transferor. A vice of consent, therefore, makes a title voidable, whereas a real vice makes it void.
>
> The difficulty lies in classifying the different vices. It appears that usually error ... [is a] vice of consent only, and so [does] not prevent the passing of ownership ...
>
> **617. Error.** In the transfer of property, error may qualify as a vice of consent, or more rarely, as a real vice."

Note that the terminology: "real" as used here has a technical meaning in Scots law. It is from 6–16 the Latin word "res", which means "thing", or as we might say "item of property". "Title" refers to the right of ownership, not the contract or apparent contract. On this view, ownership as a rule does pass even though the contract is void. Professor Reid instances two relatively common situations where it does not:

(a) Where a party signs a written deed of transfer in the mistaken belief that he is signing some other document entirely (as opposed to where the party is mistaken not about the deed but about its content).
(b) Theft, including situations where the party not in error was dishonest in a way that amounted to theft of the item of property as opposed to a situation where there was an error regarding the qualities of a person (such as his creditworthiness).[20]

What general principle, if any, links these together? For other possible, although more controversial, situations where ownership does not pass on the ground of "real vice" see KGC Reid's *The Law of Property in Scotland*.[21]

Bilateral errors that render the contract null

We have already seen that it is not enough merely that an error, even if bilateral, falls into one 6–17 of Professor Bell's five categories. In what circumstances will such an error become operative and render the contract a nullity?

Dissensus

We have also seen that there can be no contract unless there is consensus in idem between 6–18 the parties. We must carefully differentiate errors which result in complete absence of consent and thereby prevent *consensus* and the creation of a contract (so the apparent contract is

---

[20] See *Morrison v Robertson*, 1908 S.C. 332.

[21] KGC Reid, *The Law of Property in Scotland* (Edinburgh: Butterworths/Law Society of Scotland, 1996), p.617, paras (2)–(5).

"void") and those errors which affect consent less extensively, so that the contract is only "voidable".

In reality, errors that prevent *consensus* are examples of *dissensus*—of failure to agree the substantials of the contract.[22] Such errors are often referred to as *errors of intention* or as *mutual errors*. There are many ways of categorising error. Much confusion in the subject arises from the often conflicting definitions and terminology. The definitions used are not legal definitions; they are rather working definitions or categories of error.[23]

6–19 *Scottish Law Commission*
Constitution and Proof of Voluntary Obligations: Abortive Constitution

Memo. No.37 (10 March 1977)

"A. *INTRODUCTION*

. . .

4. *Scots Law*

[10.] It is impossible to harmonise in a convincing manner the institutional and judicial pronouncements on error in the broadest sense, and it is only in the past thirty or so years that Scottish legal writers[18] have tended to distinguish between what they call (1) 'mutual error' (i.e., *dissensus*) (2) 'common error' i.e. a fundamental misapprehension shared by both (or all) contracting parties and (3) other cases of error which may occasion nullity or reduction of obligation. . .

. . .

B. *DISSENSUS*

[12.] Stair, Erskine and Bankton[19] state a very broad theory that where there is error in the substantials, there is not true consent. In the 18th century typically no clear distinction was drawn between unilateral error and bilateral error or between *dissensus* and common error, though these two types of bilateral error are essentially different in nature. When Bell[20] discusses error, however, he seemingly is considering it in the context of an *ex facie* regular and valid contract which subsists until it is reduced. His classification of error which has often been approved judicially—in particular by Lord Watson in *Stewart v Kennedy*[21]—was seemingly related, as Gloag appreciated, to annulment rather than nullity of contract[22] and therefore presumably was concerned with error as a vice of consent rather than as an impediment to constitution of obligation. As Professors Gloag and Walker have pointed out an application which is a nullity need not, and cannot, be reduced.[23] In a legal system which accepts an entirely subjective theory of *consensus*, clearly if one contracting party thinks, however unreasonably, that the actual terms of a contract should be construed in one way and the other party assumes that they are to be construed otherwise there is no *consensus*—but *dissensus*. This may possibly have been the generalised view of some earlier Scottish authority, but in a system

[22] See discussion below, para.6–21 onwards on what the parties must agree.

[23] There are three main types of error of intention—(1) common bilateral error: both parties make the same mistake. Each knows the intention of the other and accepts it, but each is mistaken about some fact relating to the agreement, e.g. that the subject matter of the agreement has already perished, or that the painting being sold is by a particular artist; (2) mutual bilateral error or dissensus: both parties misunderstand each other and are at cross-purposes; for example where X intends to sell his 1300 Escort but Y believes that the offer relates to the 1600 Escort also owned by X; (3) unilateral error: only one of the parties is mistaken and the other knows, or must be taken to know of his error. For example, A agrees to buy from B a specific painting which A believes to be by Raeburn, but which it is not. If B is ignorant of A's erroneous belief, the case is one of mutual error, but if B knows of it, the error is unilateral on A's part. The vital issue in all cases is agreement.

where written obligations were the normal expression of agreement in matters of importance an objective construction of the writ itself ultimately tended to prevail.[24] Eventually *consensus* and *dissensus* have come to be tested by objective construction of an obligation by reference to writing, oral communication and other conduct whereby the obligation was allegedly constituted.[25] However, in some cases, not even objective construction can overcome latent *dissensus*—where apparently clear words conceal ambiguity. Moreover, much as in construing a will, the Court has to put itself in the place of the parties, taking account of their knowledge and the meanings which they attach to words.[26]

---

[18] Gow, *The Mercantile and Industrial Law of Scotland*, pp. 52 58; Smith, *A Short Commentary on the Law of Scotland*, pp.808-828; Walker, *Principles of Scottish Private Law*, 2nd ed., pp.577–8, 581–3.

[19] Stair I.9.9., IV.40.24; Erskine III.1.16; Bankton I.23.63, I.19.6.

[20] Principles, 4th. ed., pp. 442 footnote 3.

[21] (1890) 17R. (H.L.) 25 qt p. 27.

[22] Contract 2nd. ed., pp. 442 footnote 3.

[23] Gloag *op. cit* pp. 441-2; Walker *Civil Remedies* pp. 139. It may, however, be expedient even in cases of nullity to reduce a writ e.g. a disposition recorded in the Register of Sasines - *Stobie v Smith* 1921 S.C. 894. A consensual contract which is not constituted or evidenced by writ cannot be reduced.

[24] The conflict between the subjective and objective tests of *consensus* is possibly best illustrated by the division of opinion in the Court of Session in the case of *Stewart v. Kennedy*...

[25] See, e.g., *Muirhead & Turnbull v. Dickson* 1905 7F. 606 esp. *per* Lord President Dunedin at p. 694.

[26] See e.g. *Sutton & Co v Ciceri & Co.* (1890) 17R. (H.L.) 40, esp. *per* Lord Herschell at p. 40 and Lord Watson at p. 43; *Charrington & Co. v Wooder* [1914] A.C 71 es. *per* Lord Kinnear at p. 80 and Lord Dunedin at p. 82; *Reardon Smith Line v Hansen Tangen* [1976] 3 All E.R. 570 (H.L.)."

What kinds of error do you think might fall under the third category of "other cases of error"? **6–20**
In the light of the above comments on "objective tests of *consensus*", consider the facts of *Muirhead & Turnbull v Dickson*.[24] Had the parties failed to arrive at an agreement? If so, would it be because there was dissensus as defined in the above extract; or because each party had thought they were agreeing to something other than that to which the other party thought they were agreeing? Does the above extract suggest that cases of dissensus are examples of an "impediment to the constitution of obligation", whereas other forms of error merely permit the reduction of an otherwise valid and subsisting contract?

Today, the effect of error is largely dependent not only on the type of error but also on the quality of the error involved.

Dissensus objectively established

If the very existence of agreement is being denied, then instead of consensus, there is dissensus **6–21**
and equally therefore no enforceable agreement. The approach here must be objective, to assess whether the parties have reached agreement. The court must therefore consider primarily what the parties have written, then what they have said and done, in order to make whatever sense of their agreement that is possible.

It must be stressed that the essential terms of the agreement must be certain and settled; if not, the court will interpret what the parties have written or said so as to give it legal effect, if at all possible. If, however, the terms of the agreement are too vague or uncertain, it cannot be given

---

[24] Above, para.2–04.

effect and is therefore null. Meaningless words or expressions may be disregarded by the court. To establish dissensus, the court must discover the intention of each party from the terms of the agreement. If no agreement can be ascertained, because each party reasonably took a differing interpretation, there is no contract. If only one party's interpretation is reasonable or can be preferred over that of the other party, the element of mutuality is lost and dissensus becomes difficult to establish. Only one of the parties appears to be in error and it will be more difficult to establish that the "contract" is a nullity.[25]

The error may, for example, fall under any one of the categories listed by Professor Bell; but whether the agreement is null will depend on whether the error prevents the court from making any sense of the agreement. If no agreement can be ascertained, because each party reasonably took a differing interpretation, there is no agreement. As the following case illustrates, courts will not readily put aside a contract merely because there is disagreement as to price; and the same could be said about qualitative errors that fall under any of the other categories listed by Professor Bell.

6–22 **Wilson v Marquis of Breadalbane**

(1859) 21 D. 957

Court of Session, Second Division: Lord Justice-Clerk (Inglis), Lords Cowan and Benholme

W supplied B with cattle and in a letter stated that the price was £15 per head. B took delivery, but stated that he believed he was buying at £13 per head and sent payment at that price. No sense could be made of any agreement as to price, because B had supposed the price to be fixed at £13 per head, whereas W believed that the price had been left unfixed and would depend on the quality of the cattle that would be supplied from a particular lot.

The court found that a contract had arisen.

6–23 "LORD JUSTICE-CLERK (INGLIS): ... In order to the constitution [*sic*] of a contract of sale, there must be *consensus in idem placitum*. If one party thought that the price was fixed, and the other not, and each believed a different thing to be the contract, there could be no *consensus in idem placitum*. Looking to the whole circumstances ... there was no contract as to the price. Then what is the legal result? If the question had arisen *rebus integris*,[26] there would have been no contract. The cattle would have belonged to the pursuer, the vendor; and the price to the defender, the vendee. But, *res non sunt integrae*.[27] Both parties went on with the sale. The cattle have been taken, and have been appropriated by the defender... There is no contract price. I think there is nothing for it, but that the defender must pay the value. That is satisfactorily proved to be £15 per head."

The facts of one or two of the English authorities are illustrative of the qualitative issues involved.

---

[25] See *McIntyre v McIntyre*, 1996 S.C.L.R. 175.

[26] *Rebus integris* is a situation where neither party has acted or refrained from acting adversely following the purported agreement. In such situations, it is easier for the court to allow the party to resile from the agreement. Literally, it means "a complete thing".

[27] This is the opposite of *rebus integris* and means that the parties have now changed their positions. Literally, it means "the things are no longer complete".

In *Scriven v Hindley*,[28] the buyer at auction thought he was buying bales of hemp, whereas the seller believed he was selling bales of tow. The price bid by the buyer was extravagant for tow. Since there was no consensus as to the essence of the subject matter, no binding contract was created.

In *Raffles v Wichelhaus*,[29] a sale was agreed of goods to be shipped "ex *Peerless* from Bombay". The seller meant a *Peerless* sailing in December, whereas the buyer had in mind another *Peerless*, sailing in October. Again, no sense could be made of the agreement.

Relationship between dissensus and formation of contracts

If error must be in the substantials/essential, in the sense that there is no *consensus in idem*, is it not more accurate to say that no contract has arisen between the parties, rather than to say that the contract has been rendered a nullity by the error? In other words, does the error merely show that the parties have not agreed on the essential terms of the agreement? **6–24**

Mathieson Gee (Ayrshire) Ltd v Quigley **6–25**
1952 S.C. (H.L.) 38
House of Lords: Lords Normand, Reid, Tucker and Cohen

Mathieson Gee offered to supply plant and equipment for the purpose of dredging a pond on Dr Quigley's land. The offer was stated to be subject to standard terms and conditions which provided a scale of charges. Dr Quigley purported to accept by a letter that referred to Mathieson Gee's "offer to remove the silt and deposit from the pond", but which made no reference to price.

"LORD NORMAND: ... The respondents' letter of 2nd March appears to me to be free from all ambiguity. It is an offer to supply the necessary mechanical plant, with an undertaking that the plant would consist initially of specified machines. Then there is the important stipulation that all charges will be in accordance with normal S.R. & O. rules and conditions.[30] When the S.R. & O. (No.1277 of 1941, as amended by No. 915 of 1947) was referred to, it was found that it provided a schedule of charges for the hire of various items of plant and that one of the conditions is that these charges do not cover charges for drivers or operators. The second paragraph of the letter intimates that the plant would be available for the appellant's use within the week. So far there is nothing but the offer of plant on hire for use by the appellant, a *locatio rei* in the older terminology, to be paid for in accordance with charges which apply only to the hire of machines or plant, with an undertaking as to the time when the *res* will be available for use.[31] The final assurance that 'you will have every co-operation from ourselves to ensure a speedy and satisfactory conclusion of the work involved' is an additional obligation, but it must surely be read as an assurance relative to the contract whose nature has been already expressed and not as having the effect of setting up a different kind of contract. It can and ought naturally to be read as assuring the appellant that the respondents will co-operate in selecting the right kind of plant for the work on which it was to be used from time to time and supplying it in good order and fit for the work to be done. Now, the letter of 3rd March is, when it is studied, equally unambiguous and it is a purported **6–26**

---

[28] *Scriven v Hindley* (1913) 3 K.B. 564.
[29] *Raffles v Wichelhaus* (1864) 2 H. & C. 906.
[30] This is a reference to "Statutory Regulations and Orders" wartime regulations restricting activity to maintain the war effort, but maintained for some years after the Second World War had ended.
[31] *Locatio rei* is a contract for the hire of goods.

acceptance of a contract to remove the silt, a *locatio operis*,[32] a different kind of contract from that in the offer, and with different incidents. I agree with Lord Carmont that no contract existed between the parties. The respondents offered one sort of contract and the appellant accepted another kind of contract. I am unable to read into the letters the implications which the majority of the First Division read into them, or by a benignant construction to read the letter of 3rd March as an acceptance of the offer made in the letter of 2nd March. Drivers were sent by the respondents with the machines to operate them. But I can find in the letter of 2nd March no offer of an undertaking to supply drivers and there is no provision in the alleged contract for payment by the appellant for the services of drivers. I think this is an instance of conduct by the parties inconsistent with the contract alleged by them.

I have no doubt that, when the parties to a litigation put forward what they say is a concluded contract and ask the Court to construe it, it is competent for the Court to find that there was in fact no contract and nothing to be construed ...

6–27 LORD REID: This case turns on the construction of two letters: the offer of the respondents of 2nd March 1948, and the appellant's reply of 3rd March. Certain averments of earlier verbal negotiations were held by the Lord Ordinary to be irrelevant, and I do not find anything which would require or justify a departure from the ordinary rule that the subsequent actings of parties cannot be used to determine the true construction of what the parties have written. So the meaning of the letters must be determined from a consideration of their terms, read in light of the circumstances known to both parties at the time. Both parties have throughout contended that these letters constitute a contract between them. No other case is made by either party on record. The main issue between the parties has been what are the terms of this contract. But in the Inner House Lord Carmont, who dissented, held that no contract could be found to have existed between the parties, and before the House counsel for the appellant supported this view as an alternative to his main argument.

It is necessary, therefore, to consider whether it is open to a Court to decide that there was no *consensus in idem* and therefore no contract when neither party has any plea to that effect. In my opinion, it must be open to a Court so to decide. No doubt, if an agreement could be spelled out from the documents, the Court in such circumstances would be inclined to do that and proceed to determine what were its terms. But, if it clearly appears to the Court that the true construction of the documents is such as to show that there was no agreement, then it is plainly an impossible task for the Court to find the terms of an agreement which never existed. If authority be necessary for this I find it in the speech of Lord Loreburn, L.C., in *Houldsworth v. Gordon Cumming* [1910 S.C. (H.L.) 49, at p. 52, [1910] A.C. 537, at p. 543], where he said: 'It is not enough for the parties to agree in saying there was a concluded contract if there was none, and then to ask a judicial decision as to what the contract in fact was. That would be the same thing as asking us to make the bargain, whereas our sole function is to interpret it'."

Their Lordships in the above extract made no reference to error. Was this a case of error in the substantials, with reference to the nature of the contract? What were the substantials of this contract? Does the case suggest that no contract can arise if the parties are mistaken on the essentials of the contract?

The following case raises more clearly the issue of what might constitute the essentials of a contract for the sale of goods and deals in more detail with the relationship between the law of error and the law of offer and acceptance.

---

[32] *Locatio operis* is a contract for the hire of labour.

Glynwed Distribution Ltd v S Koronka & Co 6–28
1977 S.C. I; 1977 S.L.T. 65
Court of Session, Second Division: Lords Kissen, Leechman and Thomson

The pursuers, steel distributors, sold and delivered a quantity of hot rolled steel to the defenders, manufacturers of agricultural implements. The defenders accepted the steel.

A dispute arose as to the price of the steel. The pursuers claimed that the price was £149 per tonne, whereas the defenders claimed that the price was £103.50 per tonne.

The steel supplied was of mixed foreign and British origin. In the original negotiation between the parties, the defenders said they wanted to buy British steel. The defenders entered the purchase in their purchase book at £103.50 per tonne, the price at which they believed they had bought. The pursuers entered the sale in their day sales book at £149 per tonne. At the time, the selling price for British steel (which was controlled), was about £100 per tonne, whereas that of foreign steel was £140 to £150 per tonne. It was not the pursuers' practice to sell British steel separately. Prices were averaged regardless of origin. At the time, they were selling steel at £148 to £150 per tonne.

The defenders' intention in buying the steel was to build stocks before an anticipated price rise. When they were invoiced at £149 per tonne, they refused to pay.

The court found that a contract had arisen and that a reasonable price must be paid.

"LORD KISSEN: ... The basis of the decision of the sheriff principal on this aspect was the case of *Mathieson Gee (Ayrshire) Ltd v Quigley*, which he considered to be inconsistent with *Wilson v Marquis of Breadalbane*. Senior counsel for the defenders agreed that there was no inconsistency between these two cases. He was perfectly justified in so agreeing. The facts in the former case are very different from the facts in the present case ... The offer and the purported acceptance in that case differed in that the former was for *locatio rei* and the latter for *locatio operis*: different kinds of contracts with different incidents. In *Wilson* and in the later case of *Stuart & Co. v Kennedy*, which followed *Wilson*, the position was that there was a contract of sale but the misunderstanding was in relation to the price. 6–29

Following the cases of *Wilson* and *Stuart*, it was agreed by defenders' counsel that if there was agreement on the subjects of sale and the goods in question had been accepted, there would have been consensus in idem. The submission, which at one stage appeared to have been abandoned, was, however, that there was no agreement on the subjects of sale. I cannot see how, on the pleadings and on the findings, it could be said that there was no agreement on the subjects of sale. These were clearly quantities of hot rolled steel. The origin of that steel, on the defenders' own averments and on the findings, was immaterial. I cannot find any basis, in the findings, especially 2, 3 and 5, for the view expressed by the sheriff principal that the pursuers thought that they had sold 'foreign steel' or that the defenders thought they had bought 'British steel'. The fact that Mr Koronka said that he 'wanted to buy British steel' cannot affect the position. There was, in this case, as in *Wilson* and *Stuart* agreement on the subjects of sale but not on the price. This submission must fail ...

Finally, I would again stress an unusual feature about the subjects of this sale in that it is only the origin of the steel which affects the price. For all practical purposes, according to the findings, although not expressly stated but clearly implicit in them, there is no other difference between British-made steel and foreign-imported steel."

Why did Lord Kissen decide that the disagreement between the parties as to price did not affect consensus, whereas Lords Normand and Reid in *Mathieson Gee* regarded as fatal to the contract the failure to agree whether the contract was to carry out work (*locatio operis*) or to supply equipment (*locatio rei*)? Was the court right to avoid a futile argument about what degree of error as to price would vitiate the contract?

Error arising from a common misunderstanding

6–30 Where both parties had the same misconception when entering into the contract, in common error, there is clearly agreement. The only issue is whether the agreement is stillborn, or robbed of efficacy as a result of this common misconception. As there is an agreement, by definition the contract cannot be void on the ground of error; yet the contract cannot be brought into existence because the parties' joint expectations were frustrated by this common misconception. In *Dawson v Muir*,[33] both parties believed that the sunken vats being sold by M to D were empty. When they were later discovered to contain valuable quantities of white lead, the contract nevertheless subsisted and the seller was not entitled to the return of the vats—nor, of course, the lead. Scots textbook writers generally concede the view that common error may be in the substantials and may vitiate the contract,[34] but the case law is slender. The only clear authority is *Hamilton v Western Bank of Scotland*.[35] The bank sold to Hamilton a piece of ground in Maryhill together with "the whole buildings and houses erected thereon". Both parties had wrongly assumed that the buildings sold were all built on the piece of land owned by the bank: in fact, "one-fourth or one-8th part of the whole building" was not. In cursory judgments,[36] the First Division reduced the sale, the Lord President stating that there was a "material error, particularly considering the nature of the subject" and Lord Deas declaring that "[t]his is the clearest case of essential error that I have ever seen". This was held, despite the facts that the land had been sold at auction and the written considerations of this "public roup" clearly stated that

> "the purchaser should be understood to have satisfied himself with the regularity and sufficiency of the said title-deeds ... and it shall not be competent for the purchaser, after the sale to object to the sufficiency or regularity of title".[37]

It is difficult to see why in such a case, the court did not merely construe the agreement. If X agrees to sell something to Y and subsequently discovers that they are not in a position to do so, why, bearing in mind that contractual liabilities are strict, should X not be liable to Y? Why should X not be allowed to cover that eventuality by means of a contractual term, as the bank clearly had done in *Hamilton*? In an Australian case,[38] for example, the defendant had sold to the plaintiff a wreck which was stated to be lying on a reef. The plaintiff subsequently discovered that there was no reef and no wreck at the co-ordinates given. The Supreme Court of Australia refused to accept the defendant's plea of common error and, instead, found them in breach of contract.

6–31 The only major exception to the general rule that common errors will not affect the contract appears to be that an error as to the existence of the subject matter of the contract will render it void. There is little reliable authority for the proposition in Scots law. Even the English case of

---

[33] *Dawson v Muir* (1851) 13 D. 843.

[34] Gloag, *Contract Law in Scotland*, 2nd edn (Edinburgh: W. Green, 1929), pp.453–455 (under the heading "mutual error"); WW McBryde *The Law of Contract in Scotland*, 3rd edn (Edinburgh: W. Green, 2007), paras 15–36—15–39; Walker, *Contract*, paras 14.33–4.39.

[35] *Hamilton v Western Bank of Scotland* (1861) 23 D. 1033.

[36] *Hamilton v Western Bank of Scotland* (1861) 23 D. 1033 at 1038. The case arose following the spectacular collapse of the Western Bank of Scotland during one of Scotland's greatest banking crises: see R Saville, *Bank of Scotland: A History; 1695–1995* (Edinburgh: Edinburgh University Press, 1996), pp.392–400.

[37] *Hamilton v Western Bank of Scotland* (1861) 23 D. 1033 at 1035.

[38] *McRae v Commonwealth Disposals Commission* (1950) 84 C.L.R. 377.

Couturier v Hastie[39] is doubtful authority that the contract is thereby rendered void. In that case the parties entered into a contract for the sale of corn from the Crimea which unknown to either party, had fermented and been sold by the master in Tunis. The House of Lords found that the contract was void because of the non-existence of its subject matter.

This principle has been codified, in relation to a proposed sale of specific goods, by s.6 of the Sale of Goods Act 1979, which states:

"Where there is a contract for the sale of specific goods, and the goods without the knowledge of the seller have perished at the time when the contract is made, the contract is void."

Note that this provision is not founded on error based on a common misconception, as it requires that only the seller need be suffering under a misconception as to the existence of the subject matter. Such situations would, it appears, cover cases of common misconception and are sometimes referred to as instances of "pre-contractual frustration".[40] The following extract illustrates that beyond contracts covered by the Sale of Goods Act, there is little evidence in Scots law to support a doctrine of "pre-contractual frustration".

Scottish Law Commission Constitution and Proof of Voluntary Obligations **6–32**

Abortive Constitution
Memo. No.37 (10 March 1977)

"E. *PRE-CONTRACTUAL FRUSTRATION* 30 . . . It is also our view that, unless in exceptional circumstances, no contract should come into being where, unknown to either party, the illegality or impossibility already exists at the time the offer is made, or where the event, which could have resulted in the discharge by frustration of a concluded contract, has before then already occurred. Thus, in a case of a contract for the sale of specific goods, the contract is void if, at the time it is made, the goods have, unknown to the seller, already perished; if a ship is chartered which at the time of conclusion of the charterparty has already been lost, no contract comes into being; if goods are sold which in fact already belong to the purchaser, there is no contract; if a lease is concluded of a house which has already been burned down, the contract is void. Although there appears to be no Scottish authority on the point, we think it likely that a court would reach the same conclusion in a case where parties have made an agreement of a type, the conclusion or performance of which is prohibited or impossible under the law as it stands. It is clearly the case that an existing contract is discharged by a change in the law which renders it, or the performance illegal; it would therefore seem reasonable to conclude that an already existing prohibition on transactions of the kind in question should prevent the formation of a contract. Indeed, it may be difficult to determine in some cases whether the prohibition should be classified as a supervening one or as one which already existed when the parties made their agreement, as where the court, after the agreement has been concluded, interprets a statutory provision, which had previously not been thought to have that effect, as rendering such contracts or their performance, illegal."

Where the contract is precluded by reason of illegality, the contract is unenforceable.[41] It really makes no difference whether the frustrating event, being one of which the Commission does not

---

[39] *Couturier v Hastie* (1856) 5 H.L. Cas. 673.

[40] Frustration proper arises where an external event over which the parties have no control renders performance of an existing contract impossible. The effects of frustration are complex and significantly different from the effects of nullity founded on error (see below, para.11–27 onwards).

[41] See below, para.11–40 onwards.

go so far as to suggest that the contract is "frustrated" where the subject matter has ceased to exist.

Uninduced unilateral error

6–33 The general rule is that a person must look out for their own bargains. If, for example, X buys a second-rate painting for £75 mistakenly believing it to be an old master, X has only X to blame when subsequently disillusioned. So far as the law of error is concerned, particularly buying and selling goods, the general rule is still caveat emptor ("buyer beware").

There will be instances where unilateral error may drastically alter the erring party's perception of the contract. A unilateral error may be essential, in the sense that it falls within Bell's definition and that of Lord Watson in *Stewart v Kennedy* and *Menzies v Menzies*; but can such an error ever vitiate consent?

6–34 **Stewart v Kennedy**

(1890) 17 R. (H.L.) 25

House of Lords: Lords Herschell, Watson and Macnaughten

The facts are as stated above, para.6–07.

6–35 "LORD WATSON: ... Professor Bell does not in his useful treatise deal with the important question, how far in the case of contracts and onerous unilateral obligations an erroneous belief entertained by one party only will give him a right to rescind. Without venturing to affirm that there can be no exceptions to the rule, I think it may be safely said that in the case of onerous contracts reduced to writing the erroneous belief of one of the contracting parties in regard to the nature of the obligations which he has undertaken will not be sufficient to give him the right, unless such belief has been induced by the representations, fraudulent or not, of the other party to the contract."

The effect of this formulation is that a unilateral error does not affect the contract, unless the error was induced by the other party: in other words, unless the other party has misrepresented the facts.

Nevertheless, Lord Watson admits that there can be exceptions to the rule.

Uninduced unilateral error and good faith

6–36 Consider the following: A is elderly, has no financial expertise, but has a large shareholding in X Plc. B, A's neighbour and a financial adviser, offers to buy A's shares. B has information that the share price will rise steeply in the next week because of a likely takeover, but she does not discuss this with A.[42] A agrees to sell the shares, only to find three days later that the shares are worth five times the price which B has agreed to pay.

A, the seller of the shares was clearly mistaken about their value. That, according to Bell is an error as to price. We have already seen that such an error, unless it vitiates consent, is unlikely to affect the contract.[43] What if, however, B knew, or ought reasonably to have known, that A was mistaken as to the value of the shares, but did nothing to enlighten him? Although she has not induced A's error, would B's silence make A's error essential? Lord Watson's unequivocal

[42] The use of such information by B might also be a criminal offence under the insider dealing provisions of the Criminal Justice Act 1993.

[43] Above, paras 6–04—6–24.

answer would be "no". If, indeed, the test is one of reliance,[44] then the answer must be "no". A's expectations will not have been raised by B's words or actions.[45]

Yet the fact that Lord Watson's formulation contemplates exceptions suggests that B, who is clearly acting in bad faith, would not be allowed to "snatch at a bargain" by enforcing the contract with A. There is authority which suggests that, in Scots law, even where the error was uninduced and not otherwise in the substantials, the erring party may resile if it can be shown that the other party failed to disclose facts in circumstances which would indicate bad faith. There has recently been a resurgence in the role of good faith in contract law generally and it is at least arguable that some of the older error cases can be reinterpreted as involving considerations of good faith. In particular, "the snatching at a bargain" doctrine can quite easily be seen as an example of a "bad faith" qualification. This seems to have been the reasoning of the Inner House in *Steuart's Trustees v Hart*.

Steuart's Trustees v Hart 6–37

(1875) 3 R. 192

Court of Session, First Division: The Lord President (Inglis), Lords Deas, Ardmillan, Mure

John Steuart, a Glasgow solicitor, died leaving property that included a plot on Cogan Street, Pollokshaws. The plot, which was part of a much larger parcel of land owned by Steuart, was advertised for sale by Steuart's trustees. The larger plot was subject to a feuduty; that is a fixed payment made annually by the owner of the land (in this case, Steuart's trustees) to the original owner of the land (in this case, Lord Maxwell who had originally owned most of the land around Pollokshaws). The feuduty on the plot being sold was stated by the trustees to be £9. 15s. Hart, through his agent, Brown knew that the portion of that duty attaching to the plot for sale was only 3s. and was aware of the trustees' mistake. A disposition of the land was made by the trustees to Hart and he took possession. The disposition referred to the smaller sum. The trustees now sought from the Inner House either reduction of the disposition, or alternatively decree that the feuduty of £9. 15s. be now attached to the plot sold, and that the Register of Sasines be amended accordingly. The Lord Ordinary (Lord Shand) granted the decree, but did not reduce the disposition.

The Inner House refused to amend the Register and reduced the disposition.

"LORD PRESIDENT (INGLIS): . . . It appears to me that the property was advertised as being burdened with a feu-duty of £9, 15s., and that it was very distinctly announced in various other ways that it was to be so burdened. The defender's attention and that of his agent were called to that condition of the sale very precisely. It is also apparent that the pursuers were acting in the belief that, by some means or other, they had secured this object. It is not very clear how they could imagine that they had done so by this disposition, but that is not of much consequence. It is abundantly evident that they were acting under this error, and as clear that the defender and his agent, while they knew of the pursuers' intention to impose the burden, and belief that it had been imposed, were aware that it had not really been done . . . 6–38

I am not prepared to say that this is a wrong without a remedy. But it is very clear that the remedy given by the Lord Ordinary is not the right one, and indeed, is not a competent remedy at all. What he does is this. He does not reduce the sale, but alters its conditions, and not only so, but alters the defender's title and inserts new clauses constituting real burdens, which are all apparently to enter the Register of Sasines. This is a

[44] For a full consideration of this topic, see S Woolman, "Error Revisited", 1986 S.L.T. (News) 317.

[45] Should your answer be different if A were a young and successful stockbroker? See Ch.5 above.

startling proceeding. I never saw anything like it. I am humbly of the opinion that it is not competent to reform the contract of parties in the way which has been done by the Lord Ordinary. It is not in the power of any Court to alter the contract of the parties, or the terms of a conveyance in implement of a contract of sale . . . the pursuers are entitled to reduce the [contract] on the ground of essential error known to the purchaser and taken advantage of by him, and therefore the remedy I propose is under the reductive conclusion of the summons."

The court clearly regarded the case as one of essential error. His Lordship's final statement quoted in the extract suggests that the Lord President saw it as a case where the parties were at odds—that is as a case of dissensus. The reason for allowing the trustees to reduce the contract was clearly the defender's bad faith in "snatching at a bargain". Furthermore, it is yet another case where the contract had been reduced to writing and bearing in mind that no remedy of rectification of the document would be generally available in Scots law (a position now changed by the Law Reform (Miscellaneous Provisions) (Scotland) Act 1985 so far as errors of expression are concerned), the temptation for the court to annul the contract on the basis of error was great. This is a major recurring theme throughout the case law on uninduced unilateral error and is one of the complicating issues. As a result this has been the most litigated aspect of the law of error (other than misrepresentation) in recent decades. It is therefore important to consider the case law in some detail.

6–39 **Steel v Bradley Homes (Scotland) Ltd**

1972 S.C. 48; 1974 S.L.T. 133

Court of Session, Outer House: Lord Dunpark

The defenders agreed to buy land from Mrs Steel, but later backed out. After Mrs Steel's death the pursuer, her executor, brought an action against the defenders, but both parties sought a settlement. In a letter offering terms of settlement the defenders said they would pay interest, backdated to 16 March 1971. The pursuer's reply, accepting those terms, also referred to payment of interest backdated to 16 March 1971. The pursuer now claimed that, at the time of writing the letter of acceptance, he had never contemplated an agreement from the date stated in both letters, namely 16 March 1971, but that the date which he had always had in mind was 16 March 1969.

The court found that the agreement was valid and irreducible.

6–40 "LORD DUNPARK: ... In theory, unilateral error in substantials should, by excluding consent of the party in error, render an agreement void whether or not that error has been induced by misrepresentations of the other party; but the authorities on this matter seem to me to be so confused that any statement of my opinion would be worthless without a detailed examination of this topic. I make no such examination because in this case I am satisfied that the settlement agreement is valid and irreducible. *Esto* the unilateral error of one party may be of such a nature and occur in such circumstances that the purported agreement is void, this is not such a case ...

I do not agree with the suggestion ... that *Stewart's Trustees v Hart (cit. sup.)* [*sic*] and *Robertson v Rutherford* (1841) 4 D. 121, were wrongly decided. In neither of these cases did the Court reduce the contract on the ground of 'pure' uninduced unilateral error. The former may reasonably be regarded as an application of the doctrine of personal bar; but in any event the fact that the purchaser's knowledge of the sellers' mistake formed the basis of the *ratio decidendi* takes it out of the 'pure' category. The latter, in my opinion, is a case in which the Court construed the contract to the effect that the seller was unable to deliver the agreed subject matter.

The rule stated by Lord Watson in *Stewart v Kennedy* p. 29 (see also Lord Herschell at p. 27), that unilateral error in regard to the nature of obligations undertaken in an onerous contract reduced to writing will not normally give the party in error a right to rescind, seems to me to be equally applicable to unilateral error in relation to a price plainly stated in a written contract. Counsel for the pursuer referred me to the passage in Bell's Principles, section 11, upon which Lord Watson is there commenting, as authority for the proposition that this contract was void because Mr M'Millan's misreading of the date from which interest was to run was tantamount to an error as to price which excluded real consent on his part. While I accept Mr M'Millan's mistake as equivalent to an error as to price, Lord Watson did not construe the passage in the sense for which the pursuer contends. Indeed his interpretation of that section is that Bell was not dealing with the important question 'how far in the case of contracts ... an erroneous belief entertained by one party only will give him a right to rescind'. Lord Watson opines that this right may exist only in exceptional cases; and reference to Lord Watson's qualification of Bell's statement was included by Guthrie in his 10th edition of the Principles.

In my opinion, it is essential in the interests of business efficacy that the ordinary rule should be that an onerous contract reduced to writing in plain terms should bind the parties thereto. In *Hunter and Another v Bradford Property Trust Limited*, 1970 S.L.T. 173, Lord Reid said (at p.184): 'Of course, unilateral error would not be a ground for reduction if the contract were not gratuitous', and Lord President Clyde said (at p. 176): 'It is now well settled in the law of Scotland that a person who enters into a gratuitous obligation can reduce the contract if he can establish that he entered into it under essential error. In this respect gratuitous obligations stand in a quite special position. For no such right of reduction would operate in the case of an onerous contract'. These obiter dicta reiterate the general rule that uninduced unilateral error will not per se found reduction of an onerous contract but, unlike Lord Watson, neither Lord Reid nor Lord President Clyde concede exceptions to this general rule ... I do not regard *Steuart's Trustees v Hart* as a case of 'pure' uninduced unilateral error, but the ratio decidendi of *Wemyss v Campbell* (1858) 20 D. 1090 is an example of such an exception. In that case the Second Division allowed an issue in inter alia the following terms: 'Whether the pursuer entered into the said sub-contract under essential error as to the true nature of the said subject, the said tract of ground not being a deer forest in which such sport could be enjoyed?' The fact that the defender had advertised the ground to let as a deer-forest when the pursuer averred that there were never any stags on it during the stalking season suggests that the pursuer might have sought reduction on the ground of error induced by the defender's misrepresentation but there is not a word in the opinions about the advertisement or about the misrepresentation. Nevertheless, notwithstanding the ratio decidendi, the facts are not solely consistent with the proposition that 'pure' uninduced unilateral error in substantials will found the reduction of an onerous contract reduced to writing because, if the defender let the ground in the honest belief that it was a deer forest and the pursuer proved that it was not, then there would have been common error in substantials, namely, either as to the subject matter of the contract or at least as to the quality thereof, which both parties obviously regarded as material.

I am not to be taken as saying that no case can ever occur in which equitable considerations require the reduction of a contract by application of the principle suggested by Professor T.B. Smith (see *Short Commentary on the Law of Scotland*, pp.819–820; also *The British Commonwealth*, Vol. I, pp.100–1011), that uninduced unilateral error in substantials may found reduction of an onerous contract provided that the error is justus et probabilis. The fact that no such case has yet found its way into our law reports, while not precluding that possibility, may reasonably be thought to render the prospect less probable, particularly when regard is had to the need for certainty in the commercial world".

6–41 *Justus et probabilis* means excusable error. The decision confirms that, if there are circumstances where a unilateral uninduced error will affect a contract, it will only do so if, in accordance with Lord Watson's test in *Menzies v Menzies* that, but for the error, one of the parties would not have entered into it.

Here, as in *Steuart's Trustees v Hart* and virtually all cases where uninduced unilateral error was raised, the agreement had been reduced to writing. Because there was then no remedy of rectification available in Scots law[46] it would be difficult to persuade the court to alter the writing. If uninduced unilateral error had been successfully pleaded, the entire agreement could have been annulled. The focus of the case, therefore, was on whether the original agreement was in any way defective. The evidence clearly suggested that it was not. How does this tie in with the more relaxed approach taken to unilateral errors involving gratuitous contracts?[47]

Nevertheless, although Lord Dunpark's analysis of *Steuart's Trustees* and *Sword v Sinclair* is obiter. It supports the view that "equitable considerations" may, in certain cases, lead to the reduction of a contract due to unilateral uninduced error, despite the general restatement of error in *Stewart v Kennedy*. What are these equitable considerations and do they indicate the importance of good faith?

The issue of bad faith more directly came before Lord Marnoch in the following case.

6–42

Spook Erection (Northern) Ltd v Kaye
1990 S.L.T. 676
Court of Session, Outer House: Lord Marnoch

Spook agreed to buy land from Kaye and entered into missives for a 99-year lease. The purchasers sought implement of the lease and the seller counterclaimed for reduction on the ground of essential error, namely that he entered into the contract under the mistaken belief that the lease was for 990 years. Kaye claimed that, although the contract was a formal one and the error was unilateral and not in any way induced by Spook, the contract was void through lack of consensus, because the purchasers were aware of the seller's mistaken belief at the time of entering the contract, and had taken advantage of it.

The court upheld the contract.

6–43 "LORD MARNOCH: ... [C]ounsel for the defenders ... maintained... that the error in question was known to the pursuers at the time the contract was entered into and was taken advantage of by them. In such circumstances, so it was claimed, it remained the law of Scotland that a unilateral 'essential' error was of itself sufficient to avoid the contract.

In advancing this proposition counsel cited Stair, Inst., I.ix.9 and I.x.13, Erskine, *Inst.*, III.i.16, Bell, *Prin.*, s. 11, and the early case of *Sword v Sinclairs* as authority for the view that at least in its early stages Scots law adopted what counsel termed the 'consensual' approach to error, with the result that error in substantialibus of itself vitiated consent. However, as the Scottish economy developed, this approach in its pure form became impracticable and came to be modified by the line of authority exemplified by the cases cited earlier in this opinion to the effect, as Lord Dunpark put it in *Steel*, 1974 S.L.T. at

[46] See below, paras 6–71—6–82.

[47] The position of gratuitous contracts, highlighted by Lord Dunpark, is considered in more detail below, paras 6–65—6–70.

p.136: 'it is essential in the interests of business efficacy that the ordinary rule should be that an onerous contract... in plain terms should bind the parties thereto'. According to counsel for the defenders the important point was that where, as here, it was averred that the error was known to the other party there was no reason why the original 'consensual' principle should not remain operative.

I found this line of argument not unattractive and counsel's rationalisation of how, in general, the law had developed seemed to me to carry conviction. However, despite its attractions, I have reached the view that, at least in so far as it is said to rest on principle, the proposition in question is unsound.

In the first place, whatever else may be said of the case, it seems to me that in *Stewart v Kennedy* the House of Lords departed once and for all from the notion that error in substantialibus of itself excluded the consensual foundation of contract. It is clear from the speeches, and in particular the celebrated speech of Lord Watson, that thenceforth a written contract might or might not be invalid depending on what additional circumstances attended the error in question. In my view this leaves no room for any remnant fundamentalist doctrine such as that for which counsel for the defenders contended. Quite apart from this, and even if the argument were restricted to the five categories of error in substantialibus identified by Bell, I can see great difficulty in deciding just where what might otherwise be termed 'a good bargain' would fall foul of the proposition in question. As it was, counsel felt constrained to adopt as the definition of error in substantialibus or 'essential error' for this purpose Lord Watson's dictum in the later case of *Menzies v Menzies* at p.142, viz.: 'Error becomes essential whenever it is shewn that but for it one of the parties would have declined to contract.' This, of course, opens the door still wider with the result that, if counsel for the defenders is correct, anyone who thought himself fortunate enough to have discovered a rare book, valuable painting or antique could find his bargain reduced at the instance of the unwitting seller. There seems to be little equity in all this and the proposition in question is in conflict with what is stated by Gloag on *Contract* (2nd ed.), at p. 440: 'It is not a sufficient ground for the reduction of a contract that one party gave his assent to it under a mistake. Parties are supposed to inform themselves on points material to their contracts, or to take the consequences if they do not. As it is put by an editor of Bell's *Principles*, if a man "buys too dear or sells too cheap, he is not by reason of his mistake protected from loss".'

Even more to the point, so far as the present case is concerned, it seems to me very arguable that the proprietor of heritable subjects must always be deemed to know the burdens or limitations on his own title. In any event, parties were agreed that in the case of the defenders' title not only was the lease in question a registered one, but there was attached to the disposition in favour of the defenders a schedule which specifically made reference to the duration of that lease as being one of 99 years. For all these reasons I have to say that, in the end, counsel for the defenders failed to persuade me that the principle for which he contended was either a practicable or beneficial one.

However the matter does not end there because it was contended that there was Inner House authority in the shape of *Steuart's Trs v Hart* which was binding on me and which vouchsafed the proposition in question. It may be said at the outset that the case is mentioned with little enthusiasm by Gloag at pp. 437–138 and with even less enthusiasm by Lord President Clyde in *Brooker-Simpson Ltd v Duncan Logan (Builders) Ltd* at p. 305, and it is instructive that, although the decision has in the past been interpreted as having depended upon unilateral essential error known to and taken advantage of by the other party, Gloag at footnote 1 on p. 438 doubts whether this was in fact the true ground of judgment. I accordingly propose to address that matter but I should note, for the record, that the above interpretation has found expression in *Welsh v Cousin*, per Lord Kyllachy at p. 281 and, more recently, in *Steel v Bradley Homes (Scotland) Ltd*, per Lord Dunpark at 1974 S.L.T., p.135. It is fair to add, also, that in *Seaton Brick &*

Tile Co Ltd v Mitchell, the following dictum of Lord Moncrieff appears at (1900) 7 S.L.T., p. 385: 'Now, I understand the law to be that a party who enters into a contract under a mistake must be held to it unless the mistake was induced by the other party or was brought under the other party's notice before acceptance.' So far as Lord Kyllachy and Lord Moncrieff are concerned, all I propose to say is that on the facts of the cases cited neither of these learned judges required to explore the proposition in any depth and their remarks are entirely obiter. So far as Lord Dunpark is concerned I shall require to revert to the case of Steel and to study in some detail the opinion there delivered.

But first I turn to deal with the case of *Steuart's Trs v Hart* . . . [T]he matters which were principally the subject of discussion in the Inner House were the competency or otherwise of the Lord Ordinary's 'rewriting the contract' and the soundness or otherwise of the defenders' contention (recorded at p.198 of the report) that restitution in integrum was impossible. Accordingly it is important to analyse with some care the reasoning of the Lord Ordinary, Lord Shand, on the more fundamental question as to the initial validity of the contract in question. In my opinion, and in agreement with the footnote in Gloag referred to above, it is quite clear that the reasoning is based on the belief that there was error in substantialibus as to the price and that that error would itself have been a sufficient basis for setting aside the missives . . . I am satisfied that the ratio of this decision in both the Outer House and Inner House depended on a view and understanding as to the effect of error in substantialibus which 15 years later was disapproved by the House of Lords in the case of *Stewart v Kennedy*. In particular, I do not consider that the references to the knowledge by the defender of the pursuers' error were intended to have any jurisprudential significance beyond negating a possible argument based on 'estoppel' or personal bar. Moreover, it is, I think, possible that the further references in the Inner House to the defender 'taking advantage' of the error in question have in mind the misleading letters referred to by the Lord Ordinary in support of his alternative ground of decision. If this is so, the case is not truly an example of uninduced essential error. For all these reasons and even assuming, without necessarily accepting, that the case is indistinguishable on its facts from the present one, I do not consider that the decision is binding on me to the effect contended for by counsel for the defenders.

That leaves me to deal with the case of *Steel v Bradley Homes (Scotland) Ltd.* where, at 1974 S.L.T., p.135, Lord Dunpark refers with apparent approval to 'the equitable principle that, where an offer price is so low as to afford reasonable grounds for suspicion that it has been erroneously and substantially understated, the court may refuse to allow the offeree to take advantage of the offeror's mistake'. My first observation is that this passage is undoubtedly obiter. Secondly, it appears that the context is that of Lord Dunpark seeking to explain the early case of *Sword v Sinclairs* as being other than a pure case of error in substantialibus and, on the contrary, as being one falling within the 'equitable principle' in question. In the present case, as I have already mentioned, counsel for the defenders was content to regard the case of *Sword* as being, indeed, a pure case of error in substantialibus but, whatever else, it is, I think, clear that in *Steel* Lord Dunpark did not require to consider to the same extent or with the benefit of a contradictor the issue which now arises sharply for my own decision. In the result, albeit with diffidence and respect, I take leave to disagree with the obiter remarks founded upon."

6–44 Why was this case not regarded as one of common error?

Lord Marnoch seems to identify a shift in commercial attitudes as heralding a shift in the law's approach to error.[48] In criticising *Steuart's Trustees v Hart*, he argues that *Stewart v*

[48] See S Woolman, "Error Revisited", 1986 S.L.T. (News) 317.

Kennedy once and for all departed from its ratio. Consider whether there are any ways in which the decisions can be reconciled. In particular, why if *Steuart's Trustees v Hart* is a case involving "snatching at a bargain" or bad faith, can it not simply be one of the exceptions which Lord Watson spoke of in *Stewart v Kennedy*? With good faith being in resurgence, is Lord Marnoch correct to say that *Steuart's Trustees v Hart* was based on an old fashioned view of the law of error?

With commercial certainty being so important, is it satisfactory to say that the law after *Stewart v Kennedy* was that "a written contract might or might not be invalid depending on what additional circumstances attended the error in question"? What other factors might Lord Marnoch be thinking of?

Was the fact that the sellers erred as to their own rights over their own property decisive in this case? Was this a factor that pointed to the buyer being in "good faith"? To what extent can this decision be reconciled with an overarching concept of good faith? Consider, in particular, Lord Marnoch's statement that there seems to be "little equity" in the bookseller example.

The comments regarding *Sword v Sinclair* should be read with care. In *Spook*, Counsel accepted that the case was an example of "pure" unilateral error—that is, unilateral error where the party not in error has not acted in bad faith, i.e. snatched at a bargain. Many commentators, including TB Smith and JJ Gow, advanced that very position. Gloag, however, found the decision more difficult and could not reconcile it with the decision in *Seaton Brick and Tile Co v Mitchell*.[49] Following the discovery of the Session Papers for *Sword* (the papers prepared by both sides and lodged with the court), it appears as if Gloag's analysis was correct. As the following extract shows, *Sword v Sinclair* appears to have been yet another example of snatching at a bargain.

A Note on Sword v Sinclair and the Law of Error **6–45**

WW McBryde, 1997 J.R. 281

"**The facts in *Sword v Sinclair***

The facts can be gathered from the petition by the Sinclairs and Campbell. Many of these facts were not obviously disputed by Sword. In any event, it was on the basis of the papers that the judges made their decision.

Robert and Alexander Sinclair were merchants in Greenock and dealers in tea and other goods. In the summer of 1770 they ordered from their correspondent in London, David Mitchell, three chests of Bohea tea. The tea cost in London 2s. 10d. per pound. When excise duties and a variety of other charges were added the total cost was 3s. 7½d. per pound. The Sinclairs wrote to Archibald Campbell, 'apprentice in Glasgow', asking him to sell various teas at as high a price as he could, but not under listed prices. Eight lots of tea were specified, with prices up to 9s. per pound for Suchong. In addition 'green teas' were available from 7s. to 14s. per pound. By far the largest quantity available was the Bohea tea, which seems to have been a fairly ordinary tea.[50] It was the cheapest on the list. Two chests, amounting to 660 lb. were for sale.

In affixing the note of price in the letter to Campbell the writer by mistake wrote 2s. 8d. for Bohea instead of 3s. 8d. Bell in his *Illustrations* was wrong to describe the case as based on 'manifest error on the part of the agent, who, having been empowered to sell the tea at 3s. 8d., erroneously, in writing out the note of prices, set down 2s. 8d. instead

---

[49] *Seaton Brick and Tile Co v Mitchell* (1900) 2 F. 550.

[50] Sword averred in his petition of 9 August 1771 that: "He will prove by the sample that is still in his custody, that it is as coarse as any smuggled tea that ever was brought into country, or, at least, as coarse as any tea that ever he, the petitioner, had in his shop". This *is*, no doubt, a claim made for its particular purpose, but the list of teas in the Sinclairs' petition suggests that Bohea was not the best quality tea.

of 3s. 8d., and so there was not *consensus in idem placitum,* and no sale'.[51] The mistake was not made by Campbell. There is a critical averment worth quoting: 'Mr Campbell, a young man, ignorant of these matters, and who did not . . . know there was any mistake, was so unlucky as to apply to John Sword shop-keeper in Glasgow, an old experienced dealer in this commodity. who, upon considering the letter, and note subjoined, with the samples exhibited to him, very soon perceived where the pennyworth lay; and so unconscionable was he, as to grasp at no less than 600 pound of the 660 contained in article 1. Accordingly the bargain was concluded in a hurry . . . for fear of explanations, and the following missives were exchanged.'

There was a written contract between Sword and Campbell, with delivery to be within eight days. When Campbell told the Sinclairs they immediately replied that there was a mistake. The source of the mistake was not at first sight obvious to the Sinclairs, who had not kept a copy of the letter written *to* Campbell. Matters were entire. The tea had not been delivered, nor the price paid. Sword wanted to stick to the bargain. He offered an extra 2d. in the pound, provided that the whole quantity of the tea was sold to him. This offer was not well received. The Sinclairs sold the tea to others at 3s. 8d and 3s. 9d,—'the then current price of such tea at the time'.

6–46 **The litigation**

The case started with an action of damages brought by Sword against Campbell before Glasgow magistrates. The magistrates found Sword entitled to a proof of damages. The case is really *Sword v Campbell.*[52] Campbell brought an advocation to the Court of Session and at some stage[53] the Sinclairs were added as parties. The Lord Ordinary, Lord Barjarg,[54] found the defenders conjunctly and severally liable to Sword in damages for non-implementation of the bargain. The petition in *Session Papers* is the petition review of the earlier interlocutors.

The arguments for the petitioners were, in summary: (1) Sale is a contract *bona fide* and if there is deceit or error, which may affect the essentials of the transaction the law will rectify. (2) Sale is founded on consent. Without consent there is no sale. If error in price shows no agreement on price the contract is void. If there is error in substantials there is no consent. Reference was made to Ulpian, Voet and Stair. This is largely the argument reported in Morison's *Dictionary.*[55] (3) There was an error in calculo which might be rectified. Stair was again referred to. There was much said about the prices of tea to demonstrate that 2s. 8d. must have been wrong. (4) The difference between the prices was £33 in total. The claim for damages of £50 was excessive. (5) There had been no delivery. Reference was made to *Aiton v Fairie*[56] and *Wallwood v Gray.*[57] (6) Sword had admitted that there had been a mistake. The conclusion was that 'Upon the whole, the petitioners confide your Lordships' justice, that you will not allow the undue catch to be taken of them which the pursuer is here aiming at.'

---

[51] GJ Bell, *Illustrations from Adjudged Cases of the Principles of the Law of Scotland* (Edinburgh: T Clarke, 1838), Vol.1.

[52] Hume described it as such in his *Lectures*, which suggests some knowledge of the case.

[53] In the absence of the process the details are obscure.

[54] Who changed his title to Lord Alva soon thereafter. See Act of Sederunt of 10 March 1772.

[55] Although a careful reading of Morison's *Dictionary* will show traces of the bona fide and error *in calculo* arguments.

[56] (1668) Mor. 14230 Stair's *Decisions*, Vol.1, p.517. In texts and indices there are variations in the spellings of the names of parties in this and the next case referred to. For example, in the petition the cases are named as "Lord Aiton contra Fairy" and "Wellwood contra Gray" Discrepancies in case names, and dates, exist in abundance in our early reports.

[57] (1681) Mor. 14235.

Sword's answers are difficult to summarise accurately. He, deliberately or not, altered the designation of Campbell in the instance to that of 'Merchant in Glasgow'. The points made were: (1) The bargain was clearly established by mutual missives. (2) The mistake was made by the petitioners. (3) There was no evidence that the tea sold to Sword was the same tea as that which came from London; the petitioners dealt extensively in tea. (4) There was no fraud The tea was a 'good enough bargain' and such bargains would be very precarious if this sale was reduced. (5) The price had been agreed in this case and Ulpian and Voet were authorities which supported this sale. (6) It was not a good reason for vitiating a sale that the seller had sold the thing cheaper than he ought to have done or that the buyer agreed to pay too high a price. (7) There was no error in calculation in the missives. (8) Decisions dealing with hull in the thing sold were not relevant. (9) The question of damages depended on proof.

On August 8, 1771 their Lordships sustained the defence for the petitioners, assoilzied them from the process and found Sword liable in expenses.[58] The following day, Sword petitioned to have extract superseded until November 14 for a further review of the case at greater length. He acted with speed because of the late hour of the session.[59] He said much about the price of tea and the sale of the tea to his correspondents. His petition was refused.[60]

The reasons for the decision **6–47**

In the absence of judicial reasons it is a matter for speculation as to why the case was decided as it was. Some of Sword's arguments seem cogent. Cases on defects in horses were not relevant, nor was there a patent error in calculation in the missives. There was a blunder by a draftsman but it is arguable, as Lord Dunpark shrewdly guessed, that this was an obvious error. The cheapest price for any other type of tea for sale by Campbell was 6s. 6d. Even at 3s. 8d. the profit to be made by the Sinclairs was one halfpenny per pound. The seller Campbell was an 'apprentice'—in what trade is unknown. The buyer was an experienced shopkeeper[61] who snatched at the bargain.

The case is probably an early example of an error known to and taken advantage of by the other party. It is the same type of case as the much-discussed *Steuart's Trustees v Hart*.[62] It is not a case of 'pure' unilateral error. It might appear so because of the way in which the arguments have been reported, but there is much discussion in the petitions and answers on what was the true price of tea in Glasgow. The petitioners' case did not rest only on the fact that there had been mistake as to price.

---

[58] See Sword's petition of August 9, 1771.

[59] The sittings of the court varied considerably over the centuries, being altered originally by Acts of the Parliament of Scotland recorded in the Sederunt Books of the Court, November 1 was a very common start to the winter session; and obviously in 1771 the court was sitting at beginning of August. There were traditional holidays in September and October. The details for 1771 are elusive.

[60] According to a manuscript note which is consistent with the report in Morison's Dictionary and Faculty Collection.

[61] Even Sword in his answers averred that he dealt '"pretty extensively in groceries, teas, wine, rum, etc".

[62] On which see *Brooker-Simpson Ltd v Duncan Logan (Builders) Ltd*, 1969 S.L.T. 304 at 305, *per* L.P. Clyde; *Spook Erection (Northern) Ltd v Kaye*, above; *Angus v Bryden*, above. L.P. Clyde suggested that *Steuart's Trs* had never been followed but this is wrong: see *Inglis'sTrs v Inglis* (1887) 14 R. 740 at 760, *per* Lord Shand; affirmed (1890) 17 R. (HL) 76; and *Moncrieff v Lawrie* (1896) 23 R. 577 (opinion of the Lord Ordinary, Lord Kyllachy).

The Session Papers demonstrate the dangers of using the existing reports of the case; a factor which may be relevant in other instances of early reports of cases.[63] At the least, whatever the ground for decision, and whatever corrections or additions further research may suggest, reliance on incomplete version of the facts and arguments can no longer be justified. So far as *Sword v Sinclair* is concerned, it is submitted that it should not be cited as a case of pure unilateral error."

6–48 If, as appears to be the case, *Sword v Sinclair* is not a "pure unilateral error" case, one must pose the question whether there are any "pure unilateral error" cases reported or unreported. If there is not, then one has to question whether unilateral uninduced error where the party not in error is in good faith is or ever has been a ground for reduction.

One consistent feature of the cases, whether before or after *Stewart v Kennedy,* is that, even where the one party knows that the other is in error, but in bad faith remains silent, not every unilateral error will affect the contract. The party in error must be able to show that, but for the error, they would not have entered into the contract.

The status of *Steuart's Trustees v Hart* and the overriding effect of good faith came up for consideration, albeit obiter in the next case. Unlike the cases considered so far, at issue was not only whether a unilateral error had been made at the time the contract was concluded; at issue was also whether the contract, once concluded, had been wrongly expressed in writing (i.e. the disposition, rather than the missives). This should be borne in mind when looking at Lord Cameron's judgment.

6–49

Angus v Bryden
1992 S.L.T. 884
Court of Session, Outer House: Lord Cameron of Lochbroom

Angus owned river fishing rights and sea fishing rights on and at the mouth of the River Ayr. The Annbank Angling Club, of which the defenders were the officers, were tenants of those fishing rights. After lengthy discussions, the parties agreed that Angus would sell the river fishings to the club for £30,000. A formal offer from the club to purchase the river fishings at a price of £30,000 followed. The offer included the following:

> "We hereby offer to purchase from your client . . . all and whole sole and exclusive right to fish for salmon, sea trout and brown trout over the lands and water presently enjoyed by your client, together with the whole other fishings."

The club maintained that this was intended to include all the fishings owned by Angus, including the sea fishings.

Angus sent a qualified acceptance which, Angus averred, was intended to be an acceptance of the club's offer to purchase the river fishings. The acceptance included the following:

> "We hereby accept your offer . . . to purchase all the whole certain fishings rights in the River Ayr and that at the price of £30,000 and on the terms and conditions set forth in your said offer."

The missives were concluded by a formal acceptance by the club's solicitors dated 3 November 1986. Thereafter a disposition dated 8 December 1986 was executed by the

[63] See the discussion of the accuracy of reporting in Morison's Dictionary and the Faculty Collection in the Notes to W. Tait, *Index of Decisions* (1823) Nor can it be assumed that the printed papers are always accurate. An Act of Sederunt of July 15, 1768 provided for agents to be fined if they put printed papers into court with "imperfect quotations or typographical errors".

pursuer and recorded in the General Register of Sasines for the county of Ayr on 17 December 1986. The disposition specifically disponed the sea fishing as well as the river fishings.

In this action, the Lord Ordinary concluded that, on construction, only the river fishings had been conveyed. Angus had further argued that, if this were not the case, the club knew that the sea fishings were included by mistake and had taken advantage of it.

"LORD CAMERON OF LOCHBROOM: ... Counsel for the defenders [argued that this was] ... a case of uninduced unilateral error which gave no ground for reduction (*Stewart v Kennedy*; *Bennie's Trs v Couper*). In my opinion the short answer to this point is that the court is entitled in certain circumstances to go behind a disposition and consider the circumstances in which the missives came to be concluded (*Anderson v Lambie*). The question therefore which properly falls to be considered is whether the pursuer is well founded in asserting that he is entitled to a remedy where there is no inducement to error on the part of the pursuer by the defenders but rather bad faith on the part of the defenders in the sense of taking advantage of that which they know to be an unintended error by the pursuer or, as here, on the part of the pursuer's agents. **6–50**

In the end of the day the issue resolved itself into two questions. The first was whether the error here averred was of the nature of the error illustrated in *Steuart's Trs v Hart* and the second was whether *Steuart's Trs v Hart* was still sound law and thus whether a remedy was available in the circumstances averred. It is appropriate to consider the second question first. Counsel for the defenders contended that the decision in *Steuart's Trs v Hart* should not be followed in the light of the line of authority which begins with *Stewart v Kennedy*. In particular he founded upon the case of *Spook Erection v Kaye*. In that case the Lord Ordinary declined to accept the decision of *Steuart's Trs v Hart* as binding upon him after a consideration of the ratio in that case in the light of later authority, including House of Lords authority in *Stewart v Kennedy*. In my opinion, the ratio of *Steuart's Trs v Hart* is that an unintentional error being an error of expression by one party to a contract known to and taken advantage of by the other party is a wrong for which our law provides a remedy, the error being of the nature of essential error, that is, one but for which the party making the error would not have contracted (*Menzies v Menzies*). In my opinion that ground of judgment clearly appears from the opinion of Lord President Inglis. At p.199 he said: 'But the pursuers allege that during the whole of the communings they had it in view to impose on this subject a feu-duty of £9, 15s, then payable to them, not in respect of this subject only, but of another also. Their object was to relieve the other subject altogether, and they say that they believed that that would be the effect of the transaction, and that the disposition was granted on that footing. They allege, farther, that the defender and his agent were aware of their intention and belief. In short, the allegation is, that the sellers were acting under essential error and that the purchaser knew that and took advantage of it. That case certainly presents an appearance of relevancy, and I think it is fairly established by the evidence.'

Subsequently he makes clear his opinion that such was a wrong which the court was entitled to right. The other opinions also appear to me to proceed upon that same ground. I refer in particular to the opinion of Lord Deas. Furthermore, as the Lord Ordinary in *Spook Erection v Kaye* pointed out, the case has been referred to with approval either explicitly or by implication in judicial opinion since the case of *Stewart v Kennedy*. More particularly that ground of judgment is specifically referred to in the speech of Lord Keith of Avonholm in *Anderson v Lambie*. The law makes a distinction between error of expression and error of intention. The latter error is that with which the cases of *Stewart v Kennedy* and *Menzies v Menzies* were concerned. See also Gloag on

Contract (2nd ed.), pp. 440 and following. It is now clearly determined that error in intention, even if essential, but not induced by the other party, cannot ground an action of reduction. Such error affecting intention arises where it is present in the contract and the party founding on the error is ignorant of the true facts. (See Gloag on *Contract*, p. 440.) It is perhaps pertinent to observe that such would be the error which would exist in the case where a rare and valuable book was bought from a bookstall by a knowledgeable and eagle eyed book collector at its stated price, one far below what it would otherwise fetch at auction or be priced by an antiquarian book seller. In such a case the book seller intends to sell the book and has fixed the price accordingly. In such an event if he sells too cheap, he is not by reason of his mistake protected from his loss. In that context the error arises because he did not know the true facts and on the general principle stated in *Stewart v Kennedy* he cannot recover. On the other hand if one party offers to sell A and the other party in accepting the offer makes clear that he intends to do so but by mistake appears to accept B, so that the error is made in transmitting the acceptance of A, then the offeror knowing that the purpose of the acceptance is related to A, cannot deliberately proceed to acceptance as though it was an offer of B.

Such an approach seems to me to fall within the dictum of Lord Reid in *Anderson v Lambie*, 1954 S.L.T. where at p. 78 he said this: 'In my judgment, if the two parties both intend their contract to deal with one thing and by mistake the contract or conveyance is so written out that it deals with another, then as a general rule the written document cannot stand if either party attacks it. That appears to me to be supported both by authority and by principle.'

I observe that Lord Reid then goes on to express his agreement with the speech of Lord Keith of Avonholm in which explicit reference is made to the case of *Steuart's Trs v Hart* and to the ground of decision in that case. It is not without note that in the same speech Lord Reid without any disapproval examined *Krupp v Menzies*. There the defenders averred that the pursuer and her husband well knew of the clerical error as to the rate of bonus arranged for between the parties. *Steuart's Trs v Hart* was cited in argument and appears consistent with the decision that the court reached. As Lord McLaren observed, 'It is a condition of the pursuer's case that neither party was under error as to the terms of the contract intended'.

In the present case the pursuer seeks to prove that neither party was under error as to the terms of the contract intended to be constituted by the offer and qualified acceptance. The formal acceptance of the defenders did not suggest that they were extending their original offer or regarding the qualified acceptance as one which included subjects not originally included within the offer by the defenders. Differing from the Lord Ordinary in *Spook Erection v Kaye*, and in agreement with the opinion of Lord Dunpark in *Steel v Bradley Homes*, I consider that *Steuart's Trs v Hart* is still good law and is therefore binding upon me. I would only add that counsel for the pursuer also referred me to *Rodger (Builders) Ltd v Fawdry* for the proposition that good faith was a necessary concomitant to a binding contract and as a decision providing an elegant rationalisation of the nature of the wrong which was the basis of the decision in *Steuart's Trs v Hart*. This proposition would appear to be consistent with what was said by Lord Dunpark in *Steel v Bradley Homes*, 1974 S.L.T. at p.136. There he demurs to a suggestion that *Steuart's Trs. v Hart* and another case were wrongly decided. He continues: 'In neither of these cases did the court reduce the contract on the ground of "pure" uninduced unilateral error. The former may reasonably be regarded as an application of the doctrine of personal bar.' In the whole circumstances, I would have been against the defenders' argument on this branch of the case and would have allowed a proof before answer in the matter."

The following extract from Professor Thomson's article is an attempt to rationalise the law on unilateral error following the decision in *Angus v Bryden.*

Error Revised 6–51

JM Thomson, 1992 S.L.T. 215

"I think it is now clear that an uninduced unilateral error as to either the corpus of a contract or the legal effect of such a contract is no longer a ground of reduction where an onerous contract has been reduced to writing. We can confirm that there are no exceptions to Lord Watson's general rule that in order to be operative an error in relation to the legal effect of obligations where an onerous contract has been reduced to writing is only operative if the error has been induced by the misrepresentation of the party to the contract or his agent: *Menzies v Menzies* . . .

However this only applies to an error as to the legal effect of a contract: can an uninduced, unilateral error in relation to another matter which is in substantialibus operate as a ground of reduction or defence to an action of specific implement? In other words, is *Steuart's Trs v Hart* still good law and, if it is, what is its precise scope?

These questions have been explored in two recent Outer House decisions. The first is *Spook Erection (Northern) Ltd v Kaye*, 1990 S.L.T 676 . . .

The Lord Ordinary (Marnoch) nevertheless held that the defender's plea of 'unilateral error' was irrelevant. He maintained that *Steuart's Trs v Hart* was no longer binding on him as it had been overtaken by *Stewart v Kennedy* which had 'for once and for all' departed from the notion that error in substantialibus per se could vitiate the consensual foundation of the contract.

With respect, that is not the effect of *Stewart v Kennedy*. As we have seen, that case was only concerned with a unilateral error as to the legal effect of the obligations entered into under a prima facie valid, written, onerous contract: in this context, a party's unilateral error as to the legal effect of the contract is not operative unless the error was induced. Moreover, *Steuart's Trs v Hart* was cited without disapproval in *Anderson v Lambie*, supra. It is therefore contended that as a decision of the Inner House, Lord Marnoch was not entitled to dismiss *Steuart's Trs v Hart* as a precedent binding upon him.

A different attitude towards *Steuart's Trs v Hart* can be discerned in the judgment of the Lord Ordinary (Lord Cameron of Lochbroom) in *Angus v Bryden*, 1992 S.L.T. 884.

[F]or our purpose, the interesting point is the esto case. If the missives had included the sea fishings, could the pursuer plead uninduced unilateral error if that was known to the defender, i.e. that throughout the negotiations leading to the informal agreement the defender knew that the pursuer had only intended to sell the river fishings. Lord Cameron held that *Anderson v Lambie*, supra, was authority for the proposition that the court could go behind the disposition and consider the circumstances in which the missives had been concluded. Moreover, he felt that *Steuart's Trs v Hart* remained a binding authority for the proposition that 'an unintentional error being an error of expression by one party to a contract known to and taken advantage of by the other party is a wrong for which our law provides a remedy'. By an error of expression, the Lord Ordinary has in mind a case where, from the evidence of the negotiations including any informal agreement, it is clear to both parties that the seller is intending to sell A but when a formal offer to sell is made there is an error in expression in the offer and the offer stipulates that B is being sold. In these circumstances, the purchaser, who knows that the seller was intending to sell A, cannot take advantage of the error and purport to accept the offer to sell B: and because the buyer is aware of the seller's error, the seller is not personally barred from relying on his unilateral, uninduced error of expression in the offer. Thus in this case, the defender made an offer for the river fishings only: if the pursuer's qualified acceptance had by his own error included both the river and sea fishings, because the defender knew throughout the negotiations that only the river fishings were intended to be sold, the defender cannot purport to accept the counter offer. If he did so, the pursuer could seek reduction of the disposition and missives on the ground of his unilateral uninduced error because it was known to the defender at the time the counter offer was made. But it must always be remembered that since consensus is objectively determined, the contract for the sale of both the river and sea fishings is valid until it is reduced: accordingly, a bona fide purchaser relying on the recorded disposition would obtain good title to both the river and sea fishings if he bought the fishings before the disposition and missives were reduced.

It is thought that the approach of Lord Cameron in *Angus v Bryden* is to be preferred to the approach of Lord Marnoch in *Spook Erections*. However, it must be emphasised that the scope of unilateral error in this context remains narrow. We are only concerned with the situation where it is clear from the negotiations that a party is only prepared to contract on particular terms: as a result of a unilateral error known to the other party the offer is made on different terms which the offeree then purports to accept. Since consensus is tested objectively, a contract is formed in spite of the error, but because he knows the offeror's intentions, the offeree is not prejudiced by relying on the terms as stipulated in the offer, with the result that the offeror is not personally barred from relying on his own unilateral, uninduced error. In practice, this will usually arise in contracts for the sale of heritage when the parties have reached an informed agreement on terms A but owing to the uninduced unilateral error in the formal offer, which is known to the offeree, the missives and disposition are conducted on terms B.

The doctrine of uninduced unilateral error—even if known to the other party does not enable an offeror to escape from a bad bargain. If A offers a book for sale at £500 which B accepts knowing it is worth £50,000, not only will there be objective consensus for the sale of the book at £500 but A will not be able to rely on his uninduced, unilateral error in respect of the value of the book because in the context of that particular contract there is no error going to the root of the contract: A's error would only be operative if it had been induced by B's misrepresentation. This is an example of an error in intention or motive which is not operative unless induced. The principle in *Steuart's Trs v Hart* would only give relief if B knew from negotiations that A was only prepared to sell the book for £50,000 but when A offered B the book A erroneously cited the price as £500.

Then B is not allowed to take advantage of A's error in expression of his offer, even though because consensus is tested objectively, a contract will subsist until reduced or rescinded if B purports to accept A's offer. It is only in such very limited circumstances that unilateral, uninduced error continues to be operative."

Professor Thomson's comments, and those of Professor McBryde in his article on *Sword v Sinclair*,[64] recently found favour in the following decision. Although an Outer House decision, Lord Malcolm's review of the law is such a detailed and thorough exposition of the subject that it is reproduced here almost in full.

6–52 **Wills v Strategic Procurement (UK) Limited**

[2013] CSOH 26

Court of Session; Outer House: Lord Malcolm

The facts are summarised at para.6–56.

[64] Above, paras 6–45—6–48.

"LORD MALCOLM

[1] The effect of error on the validity of a contract is one of the most uncertain areas in our private law. This is the result of a tension between two fundamental principles. Firstly, a contract is constituted by the agreement of the parties to it. It is based on mutual consent. Secondly, however, one party is entitled to hold the other to what he has said, even if he did not mean it. 'When all the external *indicia* of agreement are present the fact of agreement will, as a general rule, be assumed' (*Gloag on Contract*, 2nd ed. page 7). So long as a clear and enforceable bargain emerges, the subjective intention, or lack of consent of one party, is defeated by an objective interpretation of what was said or done. From time to time this is explained in terms of personal bar. The mistaken party is barred from relying upon his real intention.

[2] Nonetheless, there are circumstances when error on the part of one or both parties to a mutual onerous contract will bear upon its validity. As the case law has developed, the conventional view is that if one party can say no more than—'I did not mean that'—the objective approach will hold sway. If, however, some additional factor can be prayed in aid, the absence of real agreement may prevail; for example, if one party has caused the contract by misleading the other on an important matter. (Professor McBryde describes this as –'error plus': '*The Law of Contract in Scotland*' 3rd ed. paragraph 15–23.) The present case is a good example of how difficult questions can arise when, on the face of it, a party has bound himself to unintended obligations. In particular, can the other party's knowledge of an uninduced error justify reduction of the apparent bargain, and, if so, what kind of error is sufficient for this purpose?

. . .

Discussion and decision 6–53

[9] The key issue focussed in the debate was—is *Steuart's Trustees v Hart* still good law? I am satisfied that the decision in *Stewart v Kennedy* did not overrule *Steuart's Trustees*, so I answer this question in the affirmative. The outcome in *Steuart's Trustees* depended upon the knowledge of one party that the other was in error. *Stewart v Kennedy* did not proceed upon the basis of an uninduced, but known error. Lord Herschell rejected any contention that a contract could be set aside simply because one party understood and intended it to be other than it really was. There was reference to an exception in respect of induced essential errors, but there is nothing to suggest that his Lordship intended to reject the reasoning of the Inner House in *Steuart's Trustees v Hart*. That case is not mentioned in any of the speeches. Lord Watson adopted a relatively expansive approach as to when an error as to the nature of a contract might be regarded as an error *in substantialibus* in terms of Professor Bell's classification. He rejected the proposition that the mere existence of such an error in the mind of one party allows the court to annul the contract.

'The result of admitting any other principle would be that no contract in writing could be obligatory if the parties honestly attached in their own minds different meanings to any mentioned stipulation' (page 30).

Lord Watson was of the opinion that

'the alleged error of the appellant is by itself insufficient to invalidate his consent, but it will be sufficient for that purpose if it can be shewn to have been induced by the representations of the respondent, or of anyone for whose conduct he is responsible' (page 30).

As a result, their Lordships allowed an issue to go to a jury as to whether the error was induced by the defender's representative.

[10] I attach importance to the words 'by itself' in the above passage. This is consistent with principle. If nothing suggests otherwise, a contracting party is deemed to be agreeable to what he says or does. If I speak or act in such a way as to indicate to

another that I am content to contract on the basis of X, and the other party proceeds on that reasonable assumption, I cannot thereafter say that my real intention was Y. It would be wholly unfair and destructive of the necessary certainty of contractual obligation, and of commerce in general, if apparent agreements could be challenged in that manner. But what is the position if it is proved that the person seeking to enforce a contract was aware that there was no true agreement on a key element? In such circumstances, and if matters remain entire, for example, no third party interests are involved, why should the law insist on the objective interpretation, thereby allowing one party to take advantage of the other's mistake? Gloag says (at page 7):

'If, however, the words or acts of one party are calculated to convey to a reasonable and neutral person the impression that he agreed to a proposal, *and did convey that impression to the other party*, agreement for all legal purposes, is established, irrespective of the possibility that the apparent was not the real intention' (emphasis added).

The underlined passage suggests that where the party seeking to enforce the contract is aware of the other's mistake as to the bargain, there will be no presumption that the parties were in agreement. This seems fair, in that he knew that there was no true meeting of minds. The discussion in *Chitty on Contracts*, 31st ed. at volume I para 5–075 indicates that, in the law of England and Wales, a mistake as to the terms of a contract 'if known to the other party', may affect its validity. Reference is made to *Hartog v Colin and Shields* [1939] 3 All ER 566. In *Bell v Lever Bros Ltd* [1932] AC 161, when Lord Aitken stressed that it is of 'the paramount importance that contracts should be observed', this was in the express context of the parties 'honestly' complying with the essentials of the formation of contracts (p 227). It is of interest to note that the 'Principles, Definitions and Model Rules of European Private Law: Draft Common Frame of Reference' provide that a contract can be avoided in respect of a mistake of fact or law existing in the mind of one party, if the other party 'caused the contract to be concluded in mistake by leaving the mistaken party in error, contrary to good faith and fair dealing, when the other party knew or could reasonably be expected to have known of the mistake' (section II–7.201(1)(b)).

[11] In the above discussion, I referred to a mistake concerning 'a key element of the agreement'. This is to distinguish another type of erroneous belief, namely one which provides a reason or motive for entering into a bargain. Such errors can co-exist with a full understanding and agreement on the part of everyone as to the nature, meaning and effect of the contract. In other words, despite the error, there was a true consensus as to the essential elements of the bargain. This distinction, though important, can be difficult to make. The present case may well be one where much can be said on both sides, and in particular as to whether the error, if proved, is, to use Mr Dunlop's preferred terminology, an 'error in transaction' or an 'error in motive'.

[12] It is well established that bad, yet fully valid bargains can be made and enforced, and this despite the fact that one or both of the parties misunderstood the true state of affairs. The expert who spots a rare first edition for sale in a bookshop at a low price is an often quoted example. In such a case the seller's error has no impact on the validity of the contract. It relates to a collateral matter, namely the value of the item, not to the subject matter, meaning or effect of the bargain. If both were ignorant as to the true value of the book, again that shared error has no effect. Professor McBryde has pointed out that often both parties will have, or must be deemed to have, understood the risks inherent in their transaction; see his contribution on the law of error in 'A History of Private Law in Scotland', edited by Reid and Zimmerman, at pages 95/6. (He contrasts a case such as the purchase of a cabinet, which, unknown to the seller, contains a valuable jewel in a secret drawer.) In some respects, commerce thrives on uncertainties. It is no part of our law to undermine the validity of commercial agreements because risks taken

have turned out badly for one party. It may well be possible to analyse some of the cases in terms of implied conditions, for example, as to acceptance of risk, warranties, etc.

[13] The question raised by Mr Lake in the present case is whether there can be circumstances when one party's knowledge of an error on the part of the other, prevents the enforcement of an apparently concluded bargain? This is not a straightforward matter. On the one side are issues of simple fairness or justice, not to mention the consensual basis of contractual obligations; on the other, the need to promote certainty and personal responsibility. The interests of third parties may require to be taken into account. In the present case one might ask, why should the pursuer escape the consequences of his solicitor's mistake? Surely his remedy is against his lawyer in negligence. On the other hand, is it right that the defender be allowed to escape a potential liability in damages, if its representative knew that this was never the intention of Mr Wills' agent.

[14] For present purposes I require to proceed upon the basis that it will be proved that, at the time of the settlement of the Scottish proceedings, Mr Wills' solicitor did not appreciate that a decree of absolvitor would prevent pursuit of the shares claim in England—as opposed to clearing the way for such proceedings—and that it was understood by all involved that an action was to be raised in London. The debate also proceeded upon the assumption that the defender's solicitor laboured under no such error, but was aware of his counterpart's mistake, kept quiet about it, and completed the agreement, thereafter obtaining a court decree consistent with its terms. This is a different type of case from *Anderson v Lambie* 1954 SC(HL) 43, where both parties were under the same error as to the extent of the heritable subjects being disponed. It is also important to appreciate that there is no suggestion that the error was caused or induced by the defender or its agents: but nor is it a case of pure uninduced unilateral error—it is 'error plus', in that the allegation is that the defender's agent knew and took advantage of the other's mistake.

[15] Reverting to Lord Marnoch's decision in *Spook Erection*, Mr Dunlop QC submitted that his Lordship failed to appreciate that *Stewart v Kennedy* was a case of pure error, involving no additional factor which might justify reduction of the contract. Given that it raised a very different question, *Stewart v Kennedy* does not cast doubt on the earlier case.

[16] I now consider the Lord Ordinary's reasoning in *Spook Erection*. His Lordship observed that in *Stewart v Kennedy* the House of Lords departed from the notion that, of itself, error *in substantialibus* excludes the consensual foundation of contract. That left 'no room for any fundamentalist doctrine such as that for which counsel for the defenders contended'. As to *Steuart's Trustees v Hart*, Lord Marnoch said that the main issue in the Inner House was the competency of the Lord Ordinary 'rewriting the contract' and the soundness of the defender's contention that restitution in integrum was impossible.

'Accordingly it is important to analyse with some care the reasoning of the Lord Ordinary, Lord Shand, on the more fundamental question as to the initial validity of the contract in question. In my opinion . . . it is quite clear that that reasoning is based on the belief that there was error *in substantialibus* as to the price and that that error would itself have been a sufficient basis for setting aside the missives.' (page 678 I–J)

Lord Marnoch considered that Lord Shand placed reliance on the defender's knowledge of the mistake only in the context that a man will be estopped from relying on his subjective intention, as opposed to the apparent meaning of his words or conduct (page 678 k–l). His Lordship continued:

'As a separate matter, Lord Shand then goes on to hold that the defender in that case was unable to rely on his own subsequent actings and expenditure, saying that "he was not entitled to demand and take implement of a contract which he knew had no real existence, because the parties had never agreed as to the price".'

(Reference was then made to an alternative ground of Lord Shand's decision, namely fraud on the part of the defender's agent.)

[17] Lord Marnoch drew a dividing line between, on the one hand, the impact of error on the validity of a contract, and, on the other, the effect of estoppel or personal bar in preventing the party in error from relying upon it when challenging the agreement. For my part, I would be reluctant to make such a clear demarcation. It is the operation of personal bar—or, as it might otherwise be put, the objective approach to the formation of contract—which means that, despite the absence of true consensus, the apparent bargain can be enforced. If the objective approach is suspended by the other party's awareness of the mistake, this does not require any assumption as to an underlying pure doctrine of error of the kind discussed in *Stewart v Kennedy*. Lord Shand was entitled to require knowledge of an error in the substantials of the bargain as a necessary minimum to any challenge, but that is a different matter altogether from reliance on a purely consensual approach.

[18] Lord Marnoch continued:

'It is in the light of the above reasoning that one must interpret the bare statements in the Inner House by Lord President Inglis, Lord Deas, Lord Ardmillan and Lord Mure to the effect that the pursuers were, in the words of the Lord President (at page 200), "entitled to reduce the sale on the ground of essential error known to the purchaser and taken advantage of by him". In the result, I am satisfied that the ratio of this decision in both the Outer House and Inner House depended on a view and understanding as to the effect of error *in substantialibus* which 15 years later was disapproved by the House of Lords in the case of *Stewart v Kennedy*. In particular I do not consider that the references to the knowledge by the defender of the pursuers' error were intended to have any jurisprudential significance beyond negating a possible argument based on "estoppel" or personal bar.'

For myself, I am not persuaded that the knowledge of the other party's error played only a secondary role in the decision of Lord Shand in *Steuart's Trustees v Hart*. I would not separate or compartmentalise the issues of error and personal bar. In my opinion, and for the reasons explained earlier, in this area of the law these concepts are linked.

[19] For Lord Shand, the knowledge of the error was directly relevant to the invalidity of the purported agreement. His Note begins with a reference to the defender seeking 'unfair advantage' from the pursuers' agent's 'serious error', of which both the defender and his agent were aware. It was proved beyond question that the case was not one of mutual error. The defender thought that 'it was no duty of his to enlighten them as to their mistake'. For present purposes, it is important to note that, in such circumstances, Lord Shand considered that the sellers could have resisted implement of the missives of sale and purchase of the land in question. His comments as to the essential error and its effect were expressly couched in the context of the facts of the case before him. Importantly, he said:

'It is unnecessary to consider whether such an error would have been sufficient to render the contract void if the defender had been entirely in ignorance of the pursuers' real intention and state of mind' (page 197).

The reason why the defender could not rely on the objective construction of the pursuers' words and conduct was his own knowledge of the pursuers' mistake. None of this involved any reliance upon the pure consensual doctrine subsequently discredited in *Stewart v Kennedy*.

[20] In *Angus v Bryden* 1992 SLT 884, in *obiter* remarks, Lord Cameron of Lochbroom expressly differed from Lord Marnoch and offered the view that *Steuart's Trustees v Hart* is 'still good law', and is binding on an Outer House judge. These observations

have been supported by Professor Joe Thompson in an article entitled 'Error Revised', 1992 SLT (News) 215. I acknowledge the assistance which I have received from it, and from chapter 15 in Professor McBryde's treatise on the law of contract. In his article, Professor Thompson said (page 219):

'Since consensus is tested objectively, a contract is formed in spite of the error, but because he knows the offeror's intentions, the offeree is not prejudiced by relying on the terms as stipulated in the offer, with the result that the offeror is not personally barred from relying on his own unilateral, uninduced error.'

This is consistent with the Outer House and Inner House decisions in *Steuart's Trustees v Hart*. It is also in tune with the approach adopted in the leading English case of *Smith v Hughes* (1871) LR 6QB 597, in which Blackburn J said:

'If, whatever a man's real intention may be, he so conducts himself that a reasonable man would believe that he was assenting to the terms proposed by the other party, *and that other party upon that belief enters into the contract with him*, the man thus conducting himself would be equally bound as if he had intended to agree to the other side's terms' (emphasis added).

[21] The view which I have reached is in line with the careful discussion of many of these issues provided by Lord Dunpark in *Steel's Trustee* (cited earlier). His Lordship disagreed with the proposition that *Steuart's Trustees* was wrongly decided. The case

'may reasonably be regarded as an application of the doctrine of personal bar; but in any event the fact that the purchaser's knowledge of the mistake formed the basis of the *ratio decidendi* takes it out of the "pure" category' (page 57).

Lord Dunpark considered the elderly case of *Sword v Sinclair* (1771) M 14,241. As is often the case, the report in Morrison's Dictionary is not particularly enlightening, but Lord Dunpark 'speculated' that the decision was based on one party knowingly taking advantage of the other's mistake. Subsequently Professor McBryde researched the Session Papers in the case and, as a result, has supported his Lordship's views (1997 JR 281). In *Parvaiz v Thresher Wines Acquistions Ltd* 2008 SC 151, Lord Brodie allowed a similar issue to go to proof (paragraph 20).

[22] For the above reasons, I reject the primary proposition presented by Mr Lake, namely that the ratio of *Steuart's Trustees* has been overruled. It may be that Gloag's concerns about *Steuart's Trustees* (pages 437/8) arose from an anxiety that the Inner House judgments might open the way for a known, though uninduced error, on a collateral, but highly influential matter, to disturb the enforceability of a bargain, perhaps by analogy with the law on contracts induced by a misrepresentation of one party. Unfortunately, this area of the law is bedevilled by the frequent use of inexact terminology. Hence, in this opinion I have tried to avoid the phrase "essential error", which can be interpreted in a variety of senses, for example, as a mistaken understanding which causes a party to make a contract, or as one which goes to 'the essentials' of the proposed bargain. Nothing in this opinion will prevent discussion at the proof as to whether an uninduced error of the former type, if known to the other side, can prevent enforcement of an agreement, though my provisional conclusion is that the current state of the authorities does not support that proposition (albeit something may depend on the specific context of the transaction).

Mr Lake's alternative argument **6–54**

[23] Mr Lake's secondary submission was that the pursuer's case is nonetheless irrelevant, in that the solicitor's mistaken belief does not fall into the category of the kind of error which, if known, will allow reduction. Assuming that *Steuart's Trustees* is good law, it is not every error which, even if appreciated by the other party, will justify a challenge to a contract. In general terms, I regard that proposition as sound. The difficulty is in identifying on which side of the line any particular case falls. The point is

> discussed in Professor Thompson's article, again at page 219: 'The doctrine of uninduced unilateral error—even if known to the other party—does not enable an offeror to escape from a bad bargain.' The author discriminates between errors 'going to the root of the contract' and errors 'in intention or motive', the latter being operative only if material to the bargain and induced by the other party. Much could be said upon this topic, but I am of the view that, in the present case, this issue should be resolved after proof, when the full facts and circumstances have been explored in evidence. Then, to use the language of Stair (I.10, 13), the court will be better placed to judge whether Mr Wills' agent erred 'in the substantials of what (was) done'. There are plenty of decisions in the books where a judge or a jury has upheld a case based on a mistake as to the meaning or effect of an agreement, but much can depend on the full circumstances."

Shortly after this decision, Lord Burns in *Edgar v Edgar*[65] set aside a gratuitous disposition on the grounds of uninduced unilateral error. Both cases were the subject of a useful case note in the Edinburgh Law Review.

6–55 [66]*Error reduced*

Gillian Black, Edin. L.R. 2015, 140

> "Professor McBryde has observed that '[a]t no point in the history of the Scots law of error has it been easy to explain what the law is'.[1] Indeed, such is the uncertainty that one judge has stated: 'The effect of error on the validity of a contract is one of the most uncertain areas in our private law'.[2] Lord Brodie has reached further back in time, to observe 'We have the authority of Grotius for the proposition that the law of error in relation to contract is difficult'.[3]
>
> Two recent Outer House cases have addressed the thorny question of when a contract can be set aside as a result of the pursuer's unilateral and uninduced error wo recent Outer House cases have addressed the thorny question of when a contract can be set aside aitous deed. Critically, how do these fit into Professor McBryde's analysis of 'error plus'?

6–56 A. ***WILLS V STRATEGIC PROCUREMENT (UK) LTD***

> The most important recent case is *Wills v Strategic Procurement (UK) Limited*.[8] Here the pursuer had initially raised an action against the defender in relation to an alleged failure to provide him with shares worth £3.5 million. The parties agreed to end the Scottish proceedings and litigate in England instead. Accordingly, they entered into an agreement that a decree of absolvitor should be granted in respect of the Scottish proceedings to allow the pursuer to continue the action in England. However, he (and his solicitors) were unaware that a decree of absolvitor would actually bar the claim in England. The correct order sought in the Scottish courts should have been a decree of dismissal, which would have allowed the claim to proceed in England. Mr Wills alleged that the defender knew of this error and took advantage of it. It was, however, clear that the defender had not induced the error:[9] the claim was simply that, by allowing Mr Wills to enter into the agreement without pointing out his mistake, the defender was taking advantage of the situation.
>
> It might be thought that in a commercial transaction at arm's length there could be no objection to the defender proceeding with the transaction, with no duty incumbent upon it to correct the pursuer's unilateral, uninduced error. However, when the situation was

---

[65] *Edgar v Edgar* [2014] CSOH 60.

[66] © Gillian Black, "Error Reduced" (2015) Edinburgh Law Review 140.

framed in terms of consent, a different picture emerged. For Lord Malcolm the relevant question was 'what is the position if it is proved that the person seeking to enforce a contract was aware that there was no true agreement on a key element?'[10] The fact that the defender knew about the pursuer's mistake as to the effect of the agreement—a key element—meant that the objective approach to contract formation was suspended.[11] Lord Malcolm was careful to emphasise that the objective approach to contract formation remained paramount:[12]

'it would be wholly unfair and destructive of the necessary certainty of contractual obligation, and of commerce in general, if apparent agreements could be challenged [on the basis of an undisclosed subjective intention].'

Nevertheless, where one party *does* know of the other's error, there is no true agreement: 'why should the law insist on the objective interpretation, thereby allowing one party to take advantage of the other's mistake?'. In reaching this conclusion, he adopted an argument advanced by Professor Thomson, regarding personal bar[13];

'Since consensus is tested objectively, a contract is formed in spite of the error, but because he knows the offeror's intentions, the offeree is not prejudiced by relying on the terms as stipulated in the offer, with the result that the offeror is not personally barred from relying on his own unilateral, uninduced error.'

The pursuer was therefore able to plead his own unilateral, uninduced error, as relevant.

Three points can be drawn from *Wills* for future application. The first concerns precedent. In reaching his decision, Lord Malcolm helpfully clarified a point of some debate: could the pursuer rely on the nineteenth-century decision in *Steuart's Trustees v Hart*?[14] Here a seller sold land believing it to be burdened with a feu duty of ecision[15] The purchaser knew that the feu duty was only three shillings and also knew of the seller's mistake, although again had not been responsible for the mistake. The seller was held entitled to reduce the contract since the mistake was essential and his error had been taken advantage of by the purchaser. The defender in *Wills*, however, argued that *Steuart's Trustees* had been overruled by the House of Lords in *Stewart v Kennedy*.[16] Lord Malcolm declared that he was satisfied that *Stewart v Kennedy* did not overrule *Steuart's Trustees*. We therefore have a clear statement from the Outer House that *Steuart's Trustees* is good law.[17]

Lord Malcolm also addressed the oft-raised concern that a buyer who picks up an antique 'for a song' risks being challenged by the mistaken seller, on the basis that the buyer took advantage of the seller's error. He laid this fear to rest[18]:

'The expert who spots a rare first edition for sale in a bookshop at a low price is an often quoted example. In such a case the seller's error has no impact on the validity of the contract. It relates to a collateral matter, namely the value of the item, not the subject matter, meaning or effect of the bargain. If both were ignorant as to the true value of the book, again that shared error has no effect.'

The third point of significance in this case concerns the doctrine of 'error plus', as described by Professor McBryde.[19] Under this approach, a unilateral error alone will not be sufficient to challenge the contract: there must be some additional factor. In *Wills*, the additional factor was the defender's knowledge of the pursuer's error, which he then took advantage of. Judicial approval has been given to the 'error plus' analysis: 'If a rule of thumb were required it would be difficult to improve on Professor McBryde's suggestion that for error to be relevant there must be some other factor in addition'.[20]

However, there is some debate as to the scope of 'error plus'. McBryde identifies four circumstances where an error 'in the substantials'[21] will be relevant: (i) where the error is mutual; (ii) where the defender took advantage of the pursuer's error, or snatched at a bargain; (iii) where the contract is gratuitous; and (iv) where the error was induced through misrepresentation. The problem is that he does not link these two parts: he does not expressly state that these four factors are the 'error plus' factors. On the other hand, nor does he expressly state that these factors are *not* 'error plus' factors but instead separate bases for challenge. This has led to confusion. While there is broad agreement in the judicial decisions and amongst academics with the 'error plus' analysis, there is a divergence between (i) those who think that the four factors listed constitute the requisite 'plus' element,[22] and (ii) those who think that they are four separate bases for challenging a contract, in addition to a general ground of 'error plus'.[23] Lord Malcolm apparently belongs to the former school[24]:

'[*Wills* is not] a case of pure uninduced unilateral error—it is "error plus", in that the allegation is that the defender's agent knew and took advantage of the other's mistake.'

6–57 C. ***EDGAR V EDGAR***

Our next case also illustrates the complexities of 'error plus'. *Edgar v Edgar*[25] concerned an action for reduction of a disposition on the grounds of error. The pursuer, Mrs Edgar had disponed a one-half share in her house to her son, and both parties had then granted a standard security to secure a loan of just over £25,000.[26] She claimed that she was in error as to the nature of the disposition[27] and Lord Burns agreed[28]:

'I have concluded that when she signed that disposition, she did not appreciate that she was transferring one half ownership of the property to the defender but thought she was signing a document related only to a loan. She did so, therefore, under a material and substantial error. Had she realised the true import of what she was being asked to sign, she would not have done so.'

However, her error as to the nature of the deed alone would not be sufficient to reduce it. Thus, Mrs Edgar also claimed that the deed was gratuitous, as it had been granted for love, favour and affection. In response, her son argued that the disposition was preliminary to the loan, which was to benefit both of them. The evidence, however, demonstrated that Mrs Edgar had no need of a loan and that in fact none of the loan amount had been spent on improving her flat. Rather the son had spent the whole of the amount paying off his own debts and buying a new car.[29] She, therefore, gained no benefit from conveying half her house to her son in order to enter into the loan. Accordingly, Lord Burns held that the disposition was a gratuitous deed,[30] and reduced it on the basis of Mrs Edgar's unilateral, uninduced error.

The fact the deed was gratuitous was an issue of 'some consequence'.[31] Lord Burns stated that *Hunter v Bradford Property Trust Ltd*[32] is 'high authority for the proposition that a gratuitous obligation granted under unilateral material error can be reduced although that error was un-induced. *As McBryde sets out at paragraph 15-39, there need be no "error plus"*'.[33] Thus, where the transaction is gratuitous, a unilateral uninduced error is sufficient to challenge the contract.

However, Lord Burns' assertion there need not be 'error plus' when the contract is gratuitous is troubling. He reaches this conclusion with reference to paragraph 15-39 of McBryde, which simply states: 'In *Stewart v Kennedy,* Lord Watson referred to itous is troubling'. The result has been to enable the Scottish courts to apply a rule that unilateral error can be relevant when the obligation is gratuitous.'[34] There is nothing here which specifically discounts 'error plus' in such cases. It is equally possible to argue that the gratuitous nature of the contract *is* the extra factor required for error plus. This case therefore illustrates the divergence highlighted above: what is the precise scope of 'error plus'?

D. A SUGGESTED RESOLUTION OF THE ERROR PROBLEM 6–58

It is suggested that the four situations outlined by McBryde should be seen as instances of 'error plus', and not separate categories of contracts which are open to challenge. Thus, 'error plus' can be constituted by an error which is mutual, or induced; or which is unilateral and uninduced but either the other party took advantage of it or the deed was gratuitous. The mutuality, misrepresentation, taking advantage, and gratuitous elements are the 'plus' elements. However, there is nothing in McBryde's analysis or in the judicial decisions which would limit the scope of 'error plus' to these four situations. It is, therefore, theoretically possible that a pursuer could advance a further 'plus' situation which would justify the reduction of the contract. Hence, it is necessary to add a caveat that these four instances are not necessarily exhaustive.

If this approach is adopted, Lord Burns' analysis in *Edgar* could be reframed: instead of stating that, where the contract is gratuitous, 'error plus' is not required, it would acknowledge that where the contract is gratuitous *that* is the necessary 'plus' element. The end result remains the same, but the case then falls within a coherent scheme of 'error plus'.

It is therefore proposed that questions on error can be addressed by asking five sequential questions[35]:

1. Is the error so serious that it prevents *consensus in idem* and there is, therefore, no contract at all?[36]
2. Is the error 'in the substantials', as per Bell's classification?[37]
3. Is the error unilateral or bilateral? I.e. is only one party mistaken, or are both parties labouring under an error, either in the same way (common error[38]) or at cross purposes (mutual error[39])?
4. Is there an error, plus some additional factor which would justify the contract not being enforced, i.e. is there 'error plus'?
5. Has the error been induced by the other party to the contract or his agent?

---

[1] McBryde, "Error", in K Reid and R Zimmermann (eds), *A History of Private Law in Scotland* vol II (2000) 88.
[2] *Wills v Strategic Procurement (UK) Limited* [2013] CSOH 26 at para 1 per Lord Malcolm.
[3] *Parvaiz v Thresher Wines Acquisitions Ltd* [2008] CSOH 160 at para 10 per Lord Brodie.
[8] [2013] CSOH 26.
[9] *Wills* para 14 per Lord Malcolm.
[10] Para 10.
[11] Para 17.
[12] Para 10.
[13] J Thomson, "Error revised", 1992 S.L.T. (News) 215 at 219, cited in *Wills* at para 20.
[14] (1875) 3R 192. This case had also been affirmed in *Angus v Bryden* 1992 SLT 884, but remained the subject of discussion.
[15] *Steuart's Trustees v Hart* (1875) 3 R 192.
[16] (1890) 17 R (HL) 25.
[17] *Wills* para 9.
[18] *Wills* para 12.
[19] McBryde, *Contract* paras 15-23-15-39.
[20] *Parvaiz* para 11 per Lord Brodie.
[21] That is, according to Bell's criteria, being an error as to subject matter, identity, price, quality, or the nature of the contract: Bell, *Princ* ri11. These classes are apparently not exhaustive: see *Stewart v Kennedy* (1890) 17 R (HL) 25 at 28 per Lord Watson.
[22] Reid and MacQueen (n 7) 344; Lord Brodie, at least to the extent of mutual error and possibly also bad faith on the part of the defender: *Parvaiz* at paras 18 and 20 per Lord Brodie.
[23] M Hogg, "The continuing confused saga of contract and error" (2009) 13 EdinLR 286 at 289.

[24] *Wills* para 14.
[25] *Edgar v Edgar* [2014] CSOH 60.
[26] The action was to reduce the disposition conveying half her property to her son: the subsequent loan agreement was not challenged by Mrs Edgar.
[27] She also advanced arguments that there had been bad faith on the part of her son, or alternatively that the deed was procured through facility and circumvention, in light of her age (74) and ill health. She succeeded on her primary claim, although Lord Burns noted that he would also have found for her if the deed had been onerous, in light of the bad faith on the part of the defender, and also on the basis of facility and circumvention: *Edgar* paras 51 and 59 per Lord Burns.
[28] *Edgar* para 49 per Lord Burns.
[29] Mr Edgar apparently managed to spend all but £203 in the first 6 weeks after the loan was drawn down: para 33.
[30] Para 46.
[31] Para 47.
[32] 1970 SLT 173.
[33] *Edgar* para 48, emphasis added.
[34] McBryde, *Contract* para.15–39, references omitted.
[35] It should be noted that not all of these points have been addressed in this note.
[36] *Raffles v Wichelhaus* (1864) 2 H & C 906; *Mathieson Gee (Ayrshire) Ltd v Quigley* 1952 SC (HL) 38; Gloag, *Contract* 442–444.
[37] Bell, *Principles*, 11; adopted by Lord Watson in *Stewart v Kennedy* (1890) 17 R (HL) 25 at 28.
[38] In one recent case involving common error, the Sheriff Principal described the error as "mutual". Nonetheless, he was clear that both parties had made the same mistake and he therefore held the contract was void: *McLaughlin* v *Thenew Housing Association Ltd* 2008 SLT (Sh Ct) 137.
[39] It is important to note that the terminology in this area is not fixed, and some judges and commentators use the terms "mutual" and "common" interchangeably: see McBryde, *Contract*, para.15–36.

Uninduced unilateral error and mistaken identity

6–59 Another form of uninduced unilateral error is that which might arise where the identity of the other party was such an essential element in the contract that the erring party would not have contemplated making the contract with anyone other than the party they had in mind.

Here, the courts are faced with a different, but equally serious, dilemma as in the cases where the contract has been reduced to writing. If a thief should steal goods belonging to A and sell them to B, no title will pass from the thief to B. Title in the goods remains with A. If a crook should obtain goods from A by deception and transmit them to a bona fide purchaser, B, title thereby passes to B, if the contract between A and the crook is valid. In either case, the court is faced with Solomon's dilemma: the goods must go to A or B, but cannot go to both. Not surprisingly, courts have on occasion been persuaded to find that the agreement between the seller and the crook is void, because the seller was in error.

There are several possibilities:

(a) The crook may misrepresent their identity to the seller and thereby induce them other to enter into the contract.
(b) The crook may make no misrepresentation, but knows or ought reasonably to have known that the seller has mistaken the crook for someone else.
(c) The seller may erroneously make purely unilateral assumptions about the other party's identity, which may induce the seller to enter into the contract.

In the third example, there is no doubt that the seller must bear the consequences of the error. In the first example, if there has been a misrepresentation, the contract is only voidable. In the second situation, however, if the uninduced unilateral error has any effect, it will render the contract void. In the normal course of events the identity of the other party is not such an essential element: in a sale, for example, especially where the parties are dealing "face to face", the seller, such as a shopkeeper, is willing to sell to anyone offering to pay the price. The buyer's identity may be of issue only in relation to the buyer's ability to pay the price, and that is a matter which arises, normally, after the contract has been made. Ability to pay is rarely an implied term of the contract, and, therefore, error as to ability to pay, rarely a legally relevant error.

The point is clearly illustrated by the English case of *Phillips v Brooks*.[67] N, of a smart appearance, entered P's jeweller's shop and selected a pearl necklace (£2,250) and a ring (£450). N asked to take the ring as it was his wife's birthday and he wished to give her the ring that evening. P refused but when N claimed that he was "Sir George Bullough of St. James's Square" and P found the name and address in a directory, P foolishly gave the ring in return for a worthless "cheque" signed by "Sir George Bullough." When N pledged the ring with B for £50 and P subsequently discovered that the cheque was dishonoured, P could not reclaim the ring from B. P had been willing to sell to N, regardless of his identity. N's identity as Sir George Bullough was relevant only when N's ability to pay was at issue, and that had no impact upon the formation of the agreement. The contract was only voidable for fraudulent misrepresentation and, as P had not avoided at the time of resale, good title could pass to B. It will be rare to find a situation where the seller would not, ab initio, have been willing to sell to anyone; or, rarer still, would have been unwilling to sell to the crook in particular. Yet, there are instances where error as to identity has rendered the contract void.

Morrisson v Robertson 6–60

1908 S.C. 332

Court of Session, First Division: Lords McLaren, Kinnear, Pearson

At the local auction mart, Telford approached Morrisson, claiming to be the son of Wilson, whom Morrisson knew to be a dairyman and in good credit and with whom Morrisson had previously dealt on credit terms. Telford offered to buy cattle from Morrisson. Morrisson sold the cattle to Telford, who resold to Robertson. Telford never paid the price and Morrisson now sought the return of the cattle from Robertson.

The court found that there was no contract between Morrisson and Telford and that therefore the cattle still belonged to Morrisson.

"LORD KINNEAR: ... The principle is that a contract obtained by fraud is not void but voidable; and since it follows that it is valid until it is rescinded, the rescission may come too late if in the meantime third persons have acquired rights in good faith and for value. But then on the other hand if such third persons have acquired their title through a person who himself did not acquire the goods by virtue of any contract with the true owner, or to whom they were not intentionally transferred by the true owner upon any title, then the purchaser can obtain no better title than the person from whom he acquired, who *ex hypothesi* had no title at all... 6–61

Therefore I think ... that there was no contract between [Morrisson] and Telford, the fraudulent person ... If a man obtains goods by pretending to be somebody else, or by pretending that he is an agent for somebody, who has in fact given him no authority, there is no contract between the owner of the goods and him; there is no consensus which can support a contract. The owner, in this case the pursuer, does not contract with the fraudulent person who obtains the goods, because he never meant to contract with him. He thinks he is contracting with an agent for a different person altogether. He does not contract with the person with whom he in fact supposes that he is making a contract,

[67] *Phillips v Brooks* (1919) 2 P. 243.

> because that person knows nothing about it and never intended to make an agreement; therefore there is no agreement at all. I think the fallacy of the reasoning of the learned Sheriff-depute becomes quite apparent when one considers that in order to make a contract of sale you must have a certain seller and a certain buyer. The learned Sheriff says that the pursuer was willing to sell, and was in the market to sell; but then a general desire to sell to someone is not a contract to sell to any particular person, and it is as clear as evidence can make it that the pursuer never intended to sell to Telford. He knew nothing about him, he never thought of him, and never intended to deal with him. Therefore, there was no consensus which could lead to any agreement."

6–62 Was Lord Kinnear right in stating that Morrisson never intended to contract with Telford? At what point, and for what reason did Telford's identity become relevant to Morrisson?

Even so, did not the fact that Telford told a deliberate lie make it a case of inducement by fraudulent misrepresentation, rather than one of error in the substantials?

It is clear from the report that Telford approached Morrisson at the auction mart. It is also clear that, from the beginning, he represented himself to be the son of Wilson. What is less clear is whether Morrisson actually had the two cows which were the subject matter of the purported sale with him at the auction, hoping to sell them to anyone who would buy them. If so, would Lord Kinnear still be right to say that Morrisson never intended to sell to Telford? Remember, in particular, that when a contract is concluded between an agent and a third party, the resulting contract is between the third party and the principal.

There is no doubt that *Morrisson* is an unusual case. It does, however, have its English equivalent, *Cundy v Lindsay*.[68] Blenkarn, writing from 37 Wood Street, Cheapside, offered to buy handkerchiefs from C in Northern Ireland. He signed his name so that it looked like "Blenkiron & Co", a respectable firm at 123 Wood Street. C sent the goods to "Blenkiron" and Blenkarn resold to L. The House of Lords found that C intended to contract only with Blenkiron and not Blenkarn, of whom he had never heard. The contract with Blenkarn was therefore void and L acquired no title.

Both cases could be contrasted with the facts of the English case of *King's Norton Metal Co v Eldridge*.[69] X had used an entirely fictitious name in buying and paying by cheque for goods obtained from K through the post. When X resold the goods to E and the cheque was dishonoured, K could not redeem the goods since he clearly intended to deal with the person with whom he had negotiated, regardless of identity.

Far more usual, and with a far more likely result, was the following case.

6–63

Macleod v Kerr

1965 S.C. 253; 1965 S.L.T. 358

Court of Session, First Division: The Lord President (Clyde), Lords Carmont and Guthrie

A crook called Galloway, holding himself out to be L. Craig, offered to buy from Kerr a "Vauxhall Cresta" motor car which Kerr had advertised in the Edinburgh Evening News. In return for a cheque for the price, signed by "L. Craig", Kerr gave the car and its registration book to Galloway, who then drove it away. The following day, Kerr discovered that the cheque book from which the payment cheque had been issued had been stolen. Galloway resold the car to Gibson, who bought it in good faith. Galloway was arrested, tried and imprisoned, and the car traced to Gibson. Macleod, procurator fiscal, brought this action on Kerr's behalf for the recovery of the car from Gibson.

The court found that the car now belonged to Gibson.

---

68 *Cundy v Lindsay* (1878) 3 App. Cas. 459.

69 *King's Norton Metal Co v Eldridge* (1897) 14 T.L.R. 98.

"LORD PRESIDENT (CLYDE): ... The sheriff-substitute ... appears to have been misled into treating the present case as one of theft by passages in Professor T.B. Smith's *Short Commentary on the Law of Scotland* criticising the decision in *Morrisson v Robertson*, 1908 S.C. 332; 15 S.L.T. 697. But Professor Smith's criticism is erroneous. In *Morrisson's* case as in the present the seller of the article (in that case cows) was willing to convey the article for a price, and therefore no question of theft arose. But in *Morrisson's* case the party with whom he negotiated (a man Telford) fraudulently represented himself as agent of a Mr Wilson who was known to Morrisson to be a dairyman of good credit with whom Morrisson had previously had dealings, although in fact Telford was not Mr Wilson's agent and had no authority from Mr Wilson to negotiate at all. The court held that there was no sale of the cows as Morrisson had been deceived by false representation that he was selling to Wilson. The case was decided, accordingly, on the ground that there was an essential error as to the identity of the purchaser and the contract was therefore void. **6–64**

Professor T.B. Smith in his *Short Commentary on the Law of Scotland*, page 816, says in relation to this decision that: 'the case was argued and apparently decided (except possibly by Lord Maclaren) on a false premise—that this was a case of error regarding the identity of the purchaser like the English case of *Cundy v Lindsay* [1878] 3 A.C. 459. It seems self evident that this was a misconception ... Telford was in the position of a thief, and a *vitium reale* would taint any *res* handed over to him. The decision is right but the *ratio decidendi* of the majority cannot be relied on with confidence'. In reality however the alleged misconception was a correct inference from the facts and was the basis of the opinions of all the Judges in the Division. The case truly was a case of error regarding the identity of the purchaser, and the learned author was quite wrong in suggesting that Telford was in the position of a thief for Morrisson voluntarily and intentionally delivered the cows to Telford. As Lord Maclaren says at page 336: 'the pursuer believed he was selling his cows to Wilson whom he knew to be a person of reasonably good credit and to whom he was content to give credit for the payment of the price'. In my opinion the decision in *Morrisson's* case is a sound one, and the *ratio decidendi* (namely error as to the identity of the purchaser) was the correct *ratio*.

In the present case, however, the true position is that there was a complete contract of sale of the car by Mr Kerr to Galloway for there was no dubiety in the present case as to the identity of the purchaser, namely, the man who came in answer to the advertisement. But the seller Mr Kerr was induced to enter into the contract by false and fraudulent misrepresentations on the part of Galloway. In law the result is that there was a contract of sale, but it was voidable at the instance of Mr Kerr. As Lord Kinnear says in *Morrisson's* case at page 338: 'the principle is that a contract obtained by fraud is not void but voidable and since it follows that it is valid until it is rescinded and rescission may come too late if in the meantime third parties have acquired rights in good faith and for value.' (Compare Gloag on *Contract*, page 534, note 1). In the present case in my opinion although this contract with Mr Kerr was voidable, it was not rescinded before Mr Gibson had acquired the car in question from Galloway in perfect good faith and for value. For Mr Gibson knew nothing of Galloway's fraudulent operations. In my opinion therefore the car now belongs to Mr Gibson."

Was the Lord President right to classify the error in *Morrisson* as "an essential error as to the identity of the purchaser" and the contract as "void"? Would it have been more accurate to describe the error as arising from a misrepresentation and therefore making the contract "voidable"?

It is not clear from the report at which point Galloway misrepresented his identity. Nor it is clear whether Kerr had regarded Galloway's identity as in any way material before he produced the cheque book. That being so, if the contract—as is likely—was made before the cheque book was produced and "payment" was made, how could the misrepresentation have been material in inducing Kerr to sell and, therefore, how could the contract be "voidable"? If the contract was indeed valid, would Kerr's remedies against Galloway lie in fraud, or for breach of the contract?

Errors of intention and gratuitous obligations

6–65 In *Stewart v Kennedy* and in several cases since the courts have been at pains to point out that, where the obligation in question is a unilateral obligation, there is no need for the party undertaking the obligation to prove that their error was induced by the other party in order to resile from the obligation.

6–66 **Bathgate v Rosie**

1976 S.L.T. (Sh.Ct.) 16

Sheriff Court of Lothian and Borders at Edinburgh: Sheriff Neil MacVicar QC

Mr and Mrs Rosie had a son and daughter, aged 10 and seven respectively, who, it was alleged, had broken the window of Mr and Mrs Bathgate's baker's shop. Mrs Bathgate gave chase, caught the children and took them to their home. Mrs Rosie, believing wrongly that she was legally liable, agreed to pay for the cost of replacing the window. The cost, £65.69, was much more than Mrs Rosie thought it would be and much more than she felt she could pay. She, and subsequently Mr Rosie, refused to pay and the bill was finally paid by Mr Bathgate, who now sought to recover the amount from the Rosies, on the basis of Mrs Rosie's agreement to pay.

The sheriff found that Mrs Rosie could rely on her error.

6–67 "SHERIFF (NEIL MACVICAR, QC): . . . The error upon which the defenders rely is Mrs Rosie's belief, at the time, that she could be made legally liable for her son's actings . . .

It is clear that such an error is not a pure error of fact, but rather one of law, and also that it was not induced by anything which was said by Mrs Bathgate. However, where an obligation is entered into gratuitously under error, the obligant wishing to resile does not need to prove that the error was induced by the other party (*McCaig v Glasgow University Court* (1904) 6 F. 918). Further, I am of opinion that Mrs Rosie is not debarred from founding upon her error, notwithstanding that it was legal rather than factual, because it was an error not about the general law of the land, but about the legal results flowing from an application of the law to the particular circumstances of the case. (See *British Hydro-Carbon Chemicals Ltd* and *BTC, Petitioners*, 1961 S.L.T. 280). I accordingly consider that if Mrs Rosie had given her undertaking to Mrs Bathgate because of her mistaken belief about her legal obligations, she would have been entitled to withdraw it on discovering the true position."

6–68 This case is an unusual example of an error resulting from a unilateral obligation. Had Mr and Mrs Rosie been liable for their children's breaking the window, would the obligation have been gratuitous? Was the obligation only gratuitous because of the error?

The distinction drawn by the sheriff between errors of law and fact is now to be doubted. Although the sheriff allowed the pursuer's case even though founded on an error of law, this was only because it was an error about specific legal results, rather than the general law itself. In 1995, a Full Bench of the Inner House (five judges) in *Morgan Guarantee Trust of New York v Lothian Regional Council* 1995 S.L.T. 299 recognised that for the purposes of the *condictio indebiti* (a form of unjustified enrichment action), the error of law rule had no place in the law of

Scotland. Although concerning unjustified enrichment and not contract, Lord Cullen stated: "I would add that the recognition that the error of law rule has no place in the law of Scotland will put an end to the difficulty, if not impracticability, of distinguishing between an error of fact and an error of law in the construction of contracts and other writings."

There are also indications in other Inner House opinions that the error of law rule may not exist in other areas of Scots law. The following extract strengthens this view by suggesting that equitable considerations, similar to those involved with the *condictio indebiti*, may be relevant in error cases.

Security Pacific Finance Ltd v T & I Filshie's Trustee 6–69
1995 S.C.L.R. 1171
Court of Session, Extra Division: Lord McCluskey, Lords Weir and Cameron

A firm, F, owed money to Security Pacific Finance, which was secured by a standard security over a public house. F arranged re-financing with T & I Filshie's trustee. A new security was to be created over the property in favour of T & I Filshie and the security, which Standard Pacific held was to be discharged. The solicitors who acted for both T & I Filshie and Security Pacific misunderstood the instructions and discharged the security held by T & I Filshie. T & I Filshie sought reduction of the discharge and argued that it was gratuitous (as the loan had not been repaid) and was in error.

The court allowed proof of essential error.

"LORD MCCLUSKEY: We are . . . satisfied that the pursuers' averments are such that, 6–70
if they are proved, the pursuers will not necessarily fail to establish that the document was created and ultimately recorded as a result of essential error, being an error of such a grave character that had the pursuer been aware of the true situation the document would not have been brought into existence, sent to the agents for the Filshies and recorded by them. We are not persuaded that we can say at this stage that the document is plainly mutual and plainly onerous. The terms of the document are curious indeed and there is room for argument that they do not disclose consideration or onerosity. We are not persuaded that the pursuers and respondents are really seeking to use extrinsic evidence to contradict the terms of the document so as to give it a meaning that it does not ex facie bear. The case relates to error preceding the sending of the discharge to the agents for the Filshies, not to error in the drafting of its terms. Furthermore, many of the cases rest upon the application of equitable principles similar to those applicable to the condictio indebiti and we should be reluctant to make any attempt to apply or to exclude the application of equitable principles in advance of the ascertainment of the facts in a rather complicated and confused situation such as is condescended upon in the present case. In all the circumstances we consider that the proper course is to allow the case to proceed to proof before answer."

Defective expression: the relationship between error and "error in expression"

We have already seen that most cases in which uninduced unilateral error has been raised are 6–71
instances where the parties have reduced their agreement into writing. The party wishing to resile from the agreement will aver that the document does not accurately express their agreement and should be reduced since the terms of a deed cannot be altered by rectification of the court using their power in the Law Reform (Miscellaneous Provisions) (Scotland) Act 1985. The temptation, again, will be to establish that the contract was entered into under an uninduced (usually) unilateral error and can therefore be reduced. This has helped further to confuse the

status of error in the law of Scotland and to exert pressure for the creation of a remedy of rectification.

In English law, the problem may be overcome through the operation of equity. This may come about in one of two ways, neither of which has any status in the law of Scotland. First, it is always possible for a party who has mistakenly signed a document to plead *non est factum* ("it is not my deed") by showing that the document signed was fundamentally different from that which that party reasonably believed they were signing.[70] Secondly, because "equity looks on that as done which ought to be done," the court has the power to rectify the document, so that it may accurately reflect the intentions of the parties.

The relationship between "error in expression" and error proper is therefore highly vexed. It is probably inaccurate to speak of "error in expression". A more accurate term is "defective expression".[71] We are here dealing with questions of the construction of documents, not error which vitiates consent. Professor McBryde considers the topic in a chapter on interpretation of contracts, rather than a chapter on contractual errors.[72] Nevertheless, as the case of *Angus v Bryden* considered below indicates, the confusion between the two categories of "error" persists, and for that reason alone "error" in expression and the relevant provisions of the Law Reform (Miscellaneous Provisions (Scotland) Act 1985 are considered here.

6–72 **Angus v Bryden**

1992 S.L.T. 884

Court of Session, Outer House: Lord Cameron of Lochbroom

Angus owned river fishing rights and sea fishing rights on and at the mouth of the River Ayr. The Annbank Angling Club, of which the defenders were the officers, were tenants of those fishing rights. After lengthy discussions, the parties agreed that Angus would sell the river fishings to the club for £30,000. A formal offer from the club to purchase the river fishings at a price of £30,000 followed. The offer included the following:

> "We hereby offer to purchase from your client . . . all and whole sole and exclusive right to fish for salmon, sea trout and brown trout over the lands and water presently enjoyed by your client, together with the whole other fishings."

The club maintained that this was intended to include all the fishings owned by Angus, including the sea fishings.

Angus sent a qualified acceptance which, Angus averred, was intended to be an acceptance of the club's offer to purchase the river fishings. The acceptance included the following:

> "[W]e hereby accept your offer . . . to purchase all the whole certain fishings rights in the River Ayr and that at the price of £30,000 and on the terms and conditions set forth in your said offer."

The missives were concluded by a formal acceptance by the club's solicitors dated 3 November 1986. Thereafter a disposition dated 8 December 1986 was executed by the pursuer and recorded in the General Register of Sasines for the county of Ayr on 17 December 1986. The disposition specifically disponed the sea fishing as well as the river fishings.

In this action, the Lord Ordinary concluded that, on construction, only the river fishings

[70] *Saunders v Anglia Building Society* [1971] A.C. 1044.

[71] *Report on Rectification in Contracts and Other Documents* Scot. Law Com. No.79 (1983) para.2.1.

[72] WW McBryde, *The Law of Contract in Scotland*, 3rd edn (Edinburgh: W. Green, 2007), paras 8–98 onwards.

had been conveyed. Angus had further argued that, if this were not the case, the club knew that the sea fishings, were included by mistake and had taken advantage of it.

"LORD CAMERON OF LOCHBROOM: ... Counsel for the defenders [argued that this was] ... a case of uninduced unilateral error which gave no ground for reduction (*Stewart v Kennedy*; *Bennie's Trs v Couper*). In my opinion the short answer to this point is that the court is entitled in certain circumstances to go behind a disposition and consider the circumstances in which the missives came to be concluded (*Anderson v Lambie*). The question therefore which properly falls to be considered is whether the pursuer is well founded in asserting that he is entitled to a remedy where there is no inducement to error on the part of the pursuer by the defenders but rather bad faith on the part of the defenders in the sense of taking advantage of that which they know to be an unintended error by the pursuer or, as here, on the part of the pursuer's agents. 6–73

In the end of the day the issue resolved itself into two questions. The first was whether the error here averred was of the nature of the error illustrated in *Steuart's Trs v Hart* and the second was whether *Steuart's Trs v Hart* was still sound law and thus whether a remedy was available in the circumstances averred. It is appropriate to consider the second question first. Counsel for the defenders contended that the decision in *Steuart's Trs v Hart* should not be followed in the light of the line of authority which begins with *Stewart v Kennedy*. In particular he founded upon the case of *Spook Erection v Kaye*. In that case the Lord Ordinary declined to accept the decision of *Steuart's Trs v Hart* as binding upon him after a consideration of the ratio in that case in the light of later authority, including House of Lords authority in *Stewart v Kennedy*. In my opinion, the ratio of *Steuart's Trs v Hart* is that an unintentional error being an error of expression by one party to a contract known to and taken advantage of by the other party is a wrong for which our law provides a remedy, the error being of the nature of essential error, that is, one but for which the party making the error would not have contracted (*Menzies v Menzies*). In my opinion that ground of judgment clearly appears from the opinion of Lord President Inglis. At p.199 he said: 'But the pursuers allege that during the whole of the communings they had it in view to impose on this subject a feu-duty of £9, 15s, then payable to them, not in respect of this subject only, but of another also. Their object was to relieve the other subject altogether, and they say that they believed that that would be the effect of the transaction, and that the disposition was granted on that footing. They allege, farther, that the defender and his agent were aware of their intention and belief. In short, the allegation is, that the sellers were acting under essential error and that the purchaser knew that and took advantage of it. That case certainly presents an appearance of relevancy, and I think it is fairly established by the evidence.'

Subsequently he makes clear his opinion that such was a wrong which the court was entitled to right. The other opinions also appear to me to proceed upon that same ground. I refer in particular to the opinion of Lord Deas. Furthermore, as the Lord Ordinary in *Spook Erection v Kaye* pointed out, the case has been referred to with approval either explicitly or by implication in judicial opinion since the case of *Stewart v Kennedy*. More particularly that ground of judgment is specifically referred to in the speech of Lord Keith of Avonholm in *Anderson v Lambie*. The law makes a distinction between error of expression and error of intention. The latter error is that with which the cases of *Stewart v Kennedy* and *Menzies v Menzies* were concerned. See also Gloag on *Contract* (2nd ed.), pp. 440 and following. It is now clearly determined that error in intention, even if essential, but not induced by the other party, cannot ground an action of reduction. Such error affecting intention arises where it is present in the contract and the party founding on the error is ignorant of the true facts. (See Gloag on *Contract*, p.

440.) It is perhaps pertinent to observe that such would be the error which would exist in the case where a rare and valuable book was bought from a bookstall by a knowledgeable and eagle eyed book collector at its stated price, one far below what it would otherwise fetch at auction or be priced by an antiquarian book seller. In such a case the book seller intends to sell the book and has fixed the price accordingly. In such an event if he sells too cheap, he is not by reason of his mistake protected from his loss. In that context the error arises because he did not know the true facts and on the general principle stated in *Stewart v Kennedy* he cannot recover. On the other hand if one party offers to sell A and the other party in accepting the offer makes clear that he intends to do so but by mistake appears to accept B, so that the error is made in transmitting the acceptance of A, then the offeror knowing that the purpose of the acceptance is related to A, cannot deliberately proceed to acceptance as though it was an offer of B.

Such an approach seems to me to fall within the dictum of Lord Reid in *Anderson v Lambie*, 1954 S.L.T. where at p. 78 he said this: 'In my judgment, if the two parties both intend their contract to deal with one thing and by mistake the contract or conveyance is so written out that it deals with another, then as a general rule the written document cannot stand if either party attacks it. That appears to me to be supported both by authority and by principle.'

I observe that Lord Reid then goes on to express his agreement with the speech of Lord Keith of Avonholm in which explicit reference is made to the case of *Steuart's Trs v Hart* and to the ground of decision in that case. It is not without note that in the same speech Lord Reid without any disapproval examined *Krupp v Menzies*. There the defenders averred that the pursuer and her husband well knew of the clerical error as to the rate of bonus arranged for between the parties. *Steuart's Trs v Hart* was cited in argument and appears consistent with the decision that the court reached. As Lord McLaren observed, 'It is a condition of the pursuer's case that neither party was under error as to the terms of the contract intended.'

In the present case the pursuer seeks to prove that neither party was under error as to the terms of the contract intended to be constituted by the offer and qualified acceptance. The formal acceptance of the defenders did not suggest that they were extending their original offer or regarding the qualified acceptance as one which included subjects not originally included within the offer by the defenders. Differing from the Lord Ordinary in *Spook Erection v Kaye*, and in agreement with the opinion of Lord Dunpark in *Steel v. Bradley Homes*, I consider that *Steuart's Trs v Hart* is still good law and is therefore binding upon me. I would only add that counsel for the pursuer also referred me to *Rodger (Builders) Ltd v Fawdry* for the proposition that good faith was a necessary concomitant to a binding contract and as a decision providing an elegant rationalisation of the nature of the wrong which was the basis of the decision in *Steuart's Trs v Hart*. This proposition would appear to be consistent with what was said by Lord Dunpark in *Steel v Bradley Homes*, 1974 S.L.T. at p.136. There he demurs to a suggestion that *Steuart's Trs v Hart* and another case were wrongly decided. He continues: 'In neither of these cases did the court reduce the contract on the ground of "pure" uninduced unilateral error. The former may reasonably be regarded as an application of the doctrine of personal bar.' In the whole circumstances, I would have been against the defenders' argument on this branch of the case and would have allowed a proof before answer in the matter."

Look again at the *Spook Erections* case. Is there anything in Lord Marnoch's judgment to suggest that *Steuart's Trustees* "has been referred to with approval"? Did Lord Dunpark in *Steel v Bradley Homes* hold that *Steuart's Trustees* "is still good law"? 6–74

For a different interpretation of the effects of *Angus v Bryden* see JM Thomson, "Error Revised".[73] Essentially, there are two main problems with errors of expression:

(a) Where the error is latent (i.e. not obvious from the written document), parties have found it hard to satisfy the court that the document contains a mistake at all. This is due to the general disfavour with which courts view the use of extrinsic (often mis-labelled "parole") evidence—that is, evidence of acts, words or documents beyond the terms of the contract itself.
(b) Even if the pursuer is able to establish that there is a mistake, there is some doubt whether the Scottish courts have an inherent power to rectify documents. The rectification provisions contained in the Law Reform (Miscellaneous Provisions) (Scotland) Act 1985 are limited. Thus, it is often necessary to try to have the document reduced—a remedy often akin to taking a sledgehammer to crack a nut.

Errors of expression: problems of proof

The following extract is from the leading case on the question of extrinsic evidence being used to establish a latent error. 6–75

Krupp v John Menzies Ltd 6–76

1907 S.C. 903

Court of Session, First Division: Lord President (Dunedin), Lords McLaren, Kinnear and Pearson

The defenders owned the Station Hotel, Mallaig. A formal, written agreement, dated 31 October 1900, appointed Mr and Mrs Krupp managers of the hotel. Mrs Krupp's salary was to be "£148 sterling yearly" and in addition she was to receive "one fifth part of the net annual profits of the business". The employment under the agreement extended from 1 November 1900 to 31 October 1905.

Mrs Krupp claimed that the defenders should pay her one-fifth of the profits of the business during the five-year period. The defender claimed that the pursuers had been told that they would receive half the 10 per cent bonus received by Mr Rusterholz, the manager of the Palace Hotel, Inverness, also owned by the defenders. That bonus was expressed as "one-tenth part of the net annual profits" in Rusterholz's agreement. In drafting the contract, the defenders' solicitor's clerk was instructed to use Rusterholz's agreement as an example, but to halve the amount of the bonus. Instead of expressing the amount as "one-twentieth part" the clerk, by an erroneous miscalculation, expressed half of "one-tenth part" as "one-fifth part".

"LORD PRESIDENT (DUNEDIN): ... I quite agree with the words of Lord President Boyle in the case of *Carricks v Saunders* [12 D. 812] ... that it is a very delicate matter to interfere with a written contract expressed in clear terms, and that parole proof should not be rashly allowed in such a case. But there are cases in which it would be truly a disgrace to any system of jurisprudence if there was no way available of rectifying what would otherwise be a gross injustice ... This case seems to me to have nothing to do with the avoidance or re-formation of the contract. The only question is whether proof is 6–77

[73] JM Thomson, "Error Revised", 1992 S.L.T. (News) 215 (extracted above, para.6–51).

admissible that a document which in ordinary circumstances would be held to express the intentions of the parties does not in fact do so.

...

6–78 LORD MCLAREN: ... Neither party was under error as to the terms of the contract intended. That being so, we are not at all in the region of rescinding or re-forming a written contract where one of the parties has been led into error by the fault or negligence of the other party.

What it is proposed to prove is that the fraction, one-fifth, was inserted in the agreement in place of 5 per cent, the true quantity. This was either a clerical or an arithmetical error, and is *prima facie* subject to correction. We know, for example, that a misnomer is always subject to correction, for on proof of the true name of the person or thing effect is always given to that proof. Then in deeds of conveyance arithmetical errors are subject to correction when it appears on the face of the deed that they are arithmetical errors. In such cases we do not vary the terms of the contract at all, but merely seek to give expression to the true contract as agreed to by the parties.

While I have a strong opinion that such a power of correction is inherent in the Supreme Court, the first step in the operation evidently is to ascertain the facts of the case and the considerations raised by these facts."

The extrinsic evidence rule also had a role in questions of interpretation. So far as interpretation is concerned, the rule was abolished by the Contract Law (Scotland) Act 1997 s.1. This may herald a change in attitudes to how extrinsic evidence is perceived more generally.

Questions concerning errors of expression generally arise in cases concerning the sale of land. Such situations are rare because the missives normally give clear guidance as to the agreement upon which the disposition is based. However in *McClymont v McCubbin*,[74] the party alleged that the agreement was contained not only in the missives, but in a separate oral agreement which, when read with the missives, evidenced an error of expression in the disposition. The Second Division found that it was able to look to this other agreement.

6–79 **Anderson v Lambie**

1954 S.C. (H.L.) 43; 1954 S.L.T. 73

House of Lords: Lords Morton of Henryton, MacDermott, Reid and Keith of Avonholm

Blairmuckhill consisted of a 197-acre farm occupied by the Millers, tenant farmers, and 34 acres leased to the National Coal Board. The proprietor, Anderson, advertised for sale "the farm and lands of Blairmuckhill extending to 197 acres or thereby". The missives of sale referred to the farm Blairmuckhill "as presently occupied by [the Millers]". A disposition in favour of the purchaser, Lambie, and his wife was executed and recorded in the Register of Sasines. The disposition included not only the 197 acres occupied by the Millers, but also the 34 acres occupied by the National Coal Board. Both parties (through their respective solicitors) mistakenly supposed that the area of land disponed under the disposition was coextensive with the area described in the missives.

Anderson raised an action for reduction of the disposition founding on alleged "error in expression" in the disposition and offered, on record, to substitute for the original disposition a new disposition limited to the farm of Blairmuckhill alone. The purchasers pleaded that the action was irrelevant.

[74] *McClymont v McCubbin*, 1995 S.L.T. 1248.

"LORD REID: ... There is no doubt that the appellant never intended to convey more than the farm, and his solicitors did not realise that more than the farm was in fact being conveyed, but the case made for the appellant is based on essential error on the part of both parties and the respondent denies that there was any error on his part or at least any such error as would entitle the appellant to a remedy ... **6–80**

In my judgment, if the two parties both intend their contract to deal with one thing and by mistake the contract or conveyance is so written out that it deals with another, then as a general rule the written document cannot stand if either party attacks it. That appears to me to be supported both by authority and by principle ... The two cases which I propose to examine are *Krupp v Menzies*, 1907 S.C. 903, 1907, 15 S.L.T. 36, and *Glasgow Feuing and Building Co Ltd v Watson's Trs*, 14 R. 610.

I wish to make it clear at the outset that I regard cases of this kind as essentially different from cases where the question at issue is the meaning of words in the deed; where the words are those which the parties agreed to put in but the Court attaches to those words a meaning other than that which the parties or one of them intended. In that case the parties are held to their words; it is for the Court to construe the document and determine the meaning of those words; and neither party can attack the deed on the ground of error. But in the present case the error only arose after the parties had reached agreement ...

There are two matters arising from these cases which it may be convenient to deal with at this point. In the first place, in both of these cases, some importance is attached to the error being of the nature of a clerical error. The phrase 'clerical error' is generally used to mean a slip of the pen where the writer means to write one thing but by mistake writes another. But I cannot see how it can matter whether the error was the error of the person who drafted or copied the deed or the error of the person who instructed him ...

The real distinction is between cases in which it is apparent from the deed itself that there has been an error, and cases where error can only be proved by going behind the deed. If the error is apparent it can be corrected by construing the deed: for example, in *Glen's Trs v Lancashire & Yorkshire Accident Insurance Co*, 8 F. 915, a clause in an insurance policy was meaningless as it stood, but reading the document as a whole the First Division held that the word 'not' had evidently been inserted by mistake and therefore held as a matter of construction that the clause should be read as if the word 'not' was deleted. Such an error can often but not always be properly called a clerical error and there is no need to reduce the document in whole or in part to correct it. Erskine says with regard to cases of that kind (III. 3. 87): 'Where a clause in a contract obliges one of the parties to a fact which appears impossible and where the alteration of a simple word or two will bring it to a meaning which was obviously the intention of the contractors, our Supreme Court have presumed that the mistake proceeded from the inaccuracy of the writer and have therefore exercised their pretorial power of correcting the clause accordingly'. Erskine's statement that the Court have presumed that such mistake proceeded from the inaccuracy of the writer may perhaps have led to rather loose use of the phrase 'clerical error' in some cases.

With cases of apparent error I would include cases where the error becomes apparent on leading such extrinsic evidence as is ordinarily permissible for the purpose of construing a document or identifying persons or things ... [I]n the present case and cases like *Krupp v Menzies* and the *Glasgow Feuing Company* case no error is disclosed either by the terms of the deed or by any extrinsic evidence which would be competent for the purpose of construing the deed and therefore the error cannot be corrected by construing the deed. So long as the deed stands the error cannot be corrected. In such cases the error may sometimes be a clerical error and sometimes an error caused in some other way but that distinction will not by itself determine whether or not there is a remedy ...

Partial reduction of a deed may perhaps be competent where it is proposed to reduce a part of the deed which is clearly severable from the rest, but it is quite clear that it is beyond the power of a Court to make a new bargain for the parties, and if partial reduction would have that result it would plainly be incompetent: and I think that it is equally clear that a Scots Court has no power to rectify a disposition or other deed in the sense of altering its terms so as to make them conform to some earlier contract or to the real intention of the parties. In *Steuart's Trs v Hart*, 3 R. 192, Lord President Inglis said: 'It is not in the power of any Court to alter the contract of parties, or the terms of a conveyance in implement of a contract of sale'. I am not aware that this has ever been questioned, so it can only be in rare cases that partial reduction of a deed is competent . . .

Counsel for the appellant submitted as his main argument that it was enough for him to show that owing to a mistake the disposition was framed in such terms that it included subjects not included in the missives, and that it was not competent to go behind the missives to see what the parties did or said or really agreed to. In effect, the remedy which he sought was rectification of the disposition so as to make it conform to the missives. He did not argue that it is competent for a Scots Court to rectify a deed in the sense of granting a decree for deletion of part of the deed and substitution of something else, but he did argue that the same result can and should be achieved in Scotland by granting a decree for the reduction of the whole deed coupled with a condition that the pursuer should grant a new disposition to conform to the missives. This argument appears to have been accepted by the Lord Ordinary, who said: 'In my view the contract constituted by the missives is conclusive and final evidence that what the pursuer agreed to sell and the first defender agreed to buy was the farm of Blairmuckhill which was occupied by the Millers at the date of the missives whatever the area and extent of that farm might be shown to be such extrinsic evidence as was necessary to identify it on the ground'.

Although I agree with the Lord Ordinary in the result at which he arrived I agree with the Lord President that this ground of judgment cannot be supported. It makes the missives the ruling document and the disposition merely a means of giving effect to the contract contained in the missives. In my judgment that has never been the law in Scotland. The disposition has always been held to be the ruling document. A conveyance in implement of a contract of sale is not just a piece of machinery for giving effect to the contract. It has been said again and again that a disposition supersedes the earlier contract: for example, in *Edinburgh United Breweries v Molleson*, 21 R. (H.L.) 10, Lord Watson said: By the ordinary rule of law, the moment a conveyance is accepted as in implement of the obligations of a contract, the original contract is at an end, and the conveyance constitutes the only contract between the parties'. *Young v M'Kellar*, 1909 S.C. 1340 1909, 2 S.L.T. 196, an unusual case, might appear to be an exception, but otherwise the rule stands undisputed. As Lord Watson said in *Lee v Alexander*, 10 R. (H.L.) 91: 'According to the law of Scotland the execution of a formal conveyance, even when it expressly bears to be in implement of a previous contract, supersedes that contract *in toto*, and the conveyance thenceforth becomes the sole measure of the rights and liabilities of the contracting parties'.

But when it is sought to reduce a deed it is necessary to go behind the deed and discover the real facts. The fact that the parties agreed to the missives is important evidence but it is not the only competent evidence. The question is not what the missives mean: if that were the question the ordinary rule would apply that the meaning of a document must be found from its terms. The question is whether the real facts are such that the disposition must be reduced and the existence of the missives does not alter the nature of the inquiry. There is a heavy onus on a party who seeks to reduce a probative deed, but in my opinion the appellant has proved his case beyond reasonable doubt and he is entitled to succeed.

The appellant has properly undertaken that on the reduction of the existing disposition he will grant a new disposition of the farm. He is bound to do that. The missives are superseded so long, but only so long, as the disposition exists. There is no attempt to reduce the missives and when the disposition is reduced the missives will remain as an enforceable contract for the sale of the farm."

In *Aberdeen Rubber Ltd v Knowles and Sons (Fruiterers) Ltd*,[75] the House of Lords had cause to return to the question of how to deal with a disposition that did not accurately reflect the intention of the parties. The case concerned the sale of four areas of land in Aberdeen. By mistake, a fifth area of land was included in the disposition. Lord Keith of Kinkel restated that a heavy onus was placed on a party alleging that the disposition did not reflect the true intention of the parties. However, when Lord Keith looked to the admitted facts, the only "rational explanation" was that the fifth piece of land had been disponed in error. **6–81**

A great deal of the debate in *Anderson v Lambie* proceeded on a discussion concerning the role of the missives in the sale of land. At the time *Anderson* was decided, the law still was that a later contract superseded an earlier contract so that, in a conveyance, the missives were always superseded by the disposition. This was known as the rule in *Winston v Patrick*.[76] This meant that the missives fell away and could no longer be considered. This rule caused many problems and much hardship. Thus, the Contract Law (Scotland) Act 1997 s.2 abolished the rule. The fact that the missives now remain legally significant even after the disposition has been granted may result in it being easier to prove an error of expression in the disposition.

Law Reform (Miscellaneous Provisions) (Scotland) Act 1985 **6–82**

Provisions relating to other contracts and obligations

"*Rectification of defectively expressed documents*

8.—(1) Subject to section 9 of this Act, where the court is satisfied on an application made to it, that—

(a) a document intended to express or to give effect to an agreement fails to express accurately the common intention of the parties to the agreement at the date when it was made; or
(b) a document intended to create, transfer, vary or renounce a right, not being a document falling within paragraph (a) above, fails to express accurately the intention of the grantor of the document at the date when the document was executed, it may order the document to be rectified in any manner that it may specify in order to give effect to that intention.

(2) For the purposes of subsection (1) above, the court shall be entitled to have regard to all relevant evidence, whether written or oral.

(3) Subject to section 9 of this Act, in ordering the rectification of a document under subsection (1) above (in this subsection referred to as 'the original document'), the court may, at its own instance or on an application made to it, order the rectification of any other document intended for any purposes mentioned in paragraph (a) or (b) of subsection (1) above which is defectively expressed by reason of the defect in the original document.

---

[75] *Aberdeen Rubber Ltd v Knowles and Sons (Fruiterers) Ltd*, 1995 S.L.T. 870.
[76] *Winston v Patrick*, 1980 S.C. 246.

(4) Subject to section 9(4) of this Act, a document ordered to be rectified under this section shall have effect as if it had always been so rectified.

(5) Subject to section 9(4) of this Act, where a document registered in the Register of Sasines is ordered to be rectified under this section and the order is likewise recorded, the document shall be treated as having been always so recorded and rectified.

. . .

Provisions supplementary to section 8: protection of other interest

9.—(1) The court shall order a document to tie rectified under section 8 of this Act only where it is satisfied—

(a) that the interests of a person to whom this section applies would not be adversely affected to a material extent by the rectification; or
(b) that the person has consented to the proposed rectification."

The limits and function of s.8 were discussed in *Angus v Bryden*.[77]

Induced error/misrepresentation

6–83 The development of this topic in Scots law is confused. We have already seen that, in Scots law, a contract could be vitiated either by a true error in the substantials by the parties, or where one party was induced to enter into the contract by the fraud of the other. We have seen that, where the error was unilateral, but nevertheless in the substantials, Scots law gives no clear answer, except where there was evidence that the contract was induced by the fraud of the other party.

The situation for which Scots law prior to 1890 did not cater was where one party was induced to enter into the contract by the innocently made representations of the other party.

Unlike English common law and equity, Scots law had not clearly developed a separate concept of misrepresentation. Instead, the notion of misrepresentation was tacked on to the concept of error in the substantials by the House of Lords towards the turn of this century. In Scots law, therefore, there is a genus of four closely related—and often confused—vitiating factors:

(a) uninduced essential error;
(b) error induced by fraud;
(c) error induced by innocent misrepresentation; and
(d) error induced by negligent misrepresentation.

We have already considered the first category in the previous chapter. In this chapter we shall consider the remaining three categories.

The elements of misrepresentation

6–84 So far, we have considered the consequences of errors which arise from the general circumstances surrounding the agreement. What if the error is induced by a false statement or misrepresentation—made by one of the parties? Scots law will, in such cases of misrepresentation, normally permit the person to whom the misrepresentation was made to rescind the contract or have it reduced. Misrepresentation will therefore render a contract voidable or nullable whereas, as we have seen, only in certain circumstances will induce error have adverse effects upon agreement, and then generally it renders the contract void, or a nullity. It is possible, therefore,

[77] *Angus v Bryden*, 1992 S.L.T. 884. See above, paras 6–72—6–74.

that a misrepresentation creates error in the substantiality which renders the contract void, but normally it renders the contract voidable.

Professor Walker[78] describes misrepresentation as

> "an inaccurate statement of past or present fact made by or on behalf of one party to, or to an agent for, the other in the course of negotiations leading to the contract".

The following matters are essential in establishing a misrepresentation.

There must be an inaccurate statement of fact

A false statement of law cannot amount to misrepresentation, since everyone is presumed to **6–85** know the law. It is, however, very difficult to distinguish a statement of law from one of fact, especially where the two elements are mixed. In such cases, the statement will be regarded as one of fact rather than law: e.g. the statement that a flat was new (which it was not) and therefore outwith rent control legislation (which it was not); or the statement that X is married.

A statement of opinion cannot amount to a misrepresentation

This is particularly true of exaggerated or eulogistic statements made in advertisements— **6–86** note, for example, the careful terminology of estate agents' advertisements, such as "desirable residence" or "quiet residential area". Once, however, the statement purports to be a verifiable fact, or to be backed by verifiable evidence ("statistics show that" or "test after test") then it amounts to a misrepresentation if false. In *Hamilton v Duke of Montrose*[79] an advertisement in a newspaper of "a hill grazing capable of keeping about 2,000 black faced sheep and summering 100 cattle" was not a misrepresentation; and similarly in *Bissett v Wilkinson*[80] a statement in the course of negotiations that the land supported 2,000 sheep was not a misrepresentation. However, a statement that a lessee was "a most desirable tenant" was a misrepresentation, since the person making the statement knew that the tenant persistently failed to pay his rent.[81] This was more than an opinion—it was a false statement of fact that the representor knew to be untrue. Similarly, a mere statement of future intention or expectation cannot be a statement of fact. For example, to state that the value of a particular painting will increase, or that the intention is to make a company profitable, may be no more than pious aspiration. To state, however, that the proceeds of a loan would be used to expand a business when the intention had always been to pay off current debts[82]; or that a seat would be available to the ticket-holder on a particular flight that could be over-booked,[83] is to make a misrepresentation of fact, not merely a statement of intention.

The Property Misdescriptions Act 1991 now makes it a criminal offence (s.1) to make a false or misleading statement in the course of an estate agency or property development business, in relation to certain prescribed matters. Statements made in the course of the provision of conveyancing services are exempted (s.1(1) and (5)(g)). The prescribed matters are specified in the Property Misdescriptions (Specified Matters) Order 1992.[84]

---

[78] DM Walker, *The Law of Contracts and Related Obligations in Scotland*, 3rd edn (Edinburgh: T& T Clarke, 1995), para.14–51.

[79] *Hamilton v Duke of Montrose* (1906) 8 F. 1026.

[80] *Bissett v Wilkinson* [1927] A.C. 177.

[81] *Smith v Land & House Property Corporation* (1885) 28 Ch. D. 7.

[82] *Edgington v Fitzmaurice* (1885) 29 Ch. D. 495.

[83] *British Airways Board v Taylor* [1976] 1 All E.R. 65.

[84] Property Misdescriptions (Specified Matters) Order 1992 (SI 1992/2834).

The misrepresentation must have been material in inducing an error which leads the other party into the contract

6–87 Clearly a misrepresentation upon a matter inconsequential to the contract would be disregarded: the legal maxim is *de minimis non curat lex* ("the law does not notice small matters"). Furthermore, the person to whom it is made must be aware of the misrepresentation, but not aware that it was false; and must have allowed it to affect his or her judgment. This will be considered in more detail below.

Error induced by fraud: fraudulent misrepresentation

6–88 In Scots law, as in Roman law, fraud is a separate factor which may vitiate a contract. If error is induced by fraud, and the error is in the substantials, the contract is, as we saw in the preceding chapter, void. If the error is induced by a fraudulent misrepresentation, the contract is voidable on the grounds of fraud. In addition, the innocent party may recover damages in delict. Fraud, in all its manifestations, is a wrong which entitles the victim to reparation.

The central issue is: what is meant by "fraud" in this context? As the following extracts show, the question is not clearly settled in Scots law. The issue has been severely affected by the revolutionary effects of the House of Lords decisions in *Stewart v Kennedy* and *Menzies v Menzies*.[85] Those decisions, as we shall see later, introduced the concept of innocent misrepresentation into Scots law. That being so, a distinction would have to be drawn between statements innocently made and statements made fraudulently. The traditional, civilian definition of fraud in Scotland would have to be redefined in its application to misrepresentation. The concept as hitherto applied in Scotland would have been wide enough to cover circumstances which would now be regarded as innocent misrepresentations—and would almost certainly now fall in part within the definition of negligent misstatement as defined in *Hedley Byrne v Heller* (below). There would be nothing new in this. The concept of fraud is highly flexible and conveys different meanings in different circumstances. In *Derry v Peek*[86] the English House of Lords adopted a restrictive definition of fraud in the context of a case where a misrepresentation had been made to investors in a company and the remedy being sought was damages for the tort of deceit. In Scotland, the equivalent claim would have been delictual damages in reparation. In his judgment, Lord Herschell clearly differentiated fraudulent statements from those innocently made. At the very least, to be fraudulent, the statement would have to be made without an honest belief that it was true.

6–89 *Scottish Law Commission Defective Consent and Consequential Matters*

Memo. No.42 (1 June 1978)

"1.41. In the Scots law of voluntary obligations fraud ... is by no means limited to the making of false statements or to concealing of facts in circumstances in which there ought to have been disclosure. Erskine's definition Inst. III.1.16) of fraud as a 'machination or contrivance to deceive' is perhaps as good as any that can be devised and is sufficiently broad to comprehend the many cases in which fraud has been held by Scottish courts to be established even in the absence of false statements or concealments ...

1.43. The Scottish authorities, both institutional and judicial, clearly demonstrate that fraud in our law of voluntary obligations is constituted by any successful attempt to deceive, no matter the method of deceit resorted to. It is not restricted to making a false statement 'knowingly or without belief in its truth, or recklessly, careless whether it be true or false.' However, some Scottish legal authors seem to have accepted that narrow

[85] See above, paras 6–07—6–10.

[86] *Derry v Peek* (1889) 14 App. Cas. 337.

definition of fraud, derived from the speeches in the House of Lords in the English case of *Derry v Peek* (1889) 14 App. Cas. 337, as relevant in the context of the annulment of obligations for fraud in Scots law. This is all the more surprising since the case itself was not concerned with fraud as a ground for annulment or rescission of contracts, but with fraud as a ground for obtaining damages in tort. And in English law it is clearly recognised that fraud for the purposes of the common law tort of deceit is a very much narrower concept than the fraudulent misrepresentation which may entitle a party to the equitable remedy of rescission of contract . . . In view of the fact that in *Derry v Peek* it was the narrow species of common law fraud, relevant only in the law of tort, that was in issue, we think it unlikely that a Scottish court would today accept the definition of fraud there laid down as of any relevance in Scotland in relation to fraud as a ground for annulment of voluntary obligations."

The same approach to the topic can be seen in McBryde's *The Law of Contract in Scotland.*[87] It is difficult to see how the decision in *Derry v Peek* can be ignored in this way, without ignoring also the following case, which is expressly founded upon it and in which the Scottish members of the House of Lords appear to have concurred.

Boyd & Forrest v Glasgow & South-Western Railway Co **6–90**

1912 S.C. (H.L.) 93

House of Lords: The Lord Chancellor, Lords Atkinson, Shaw of Dunfermline and McNaghten

The railway company invited tenders for the construction of a new line. They produced a "journal of bores", which indicated the results of bores which were taken at intervals along the projected course of the track. The data which the borers had provided had been altered in the journal of bores by Melville, an employee of the railway company, because he did not believe that some of those data were correct. As a result, some of the rock through which the line would go was in fact harder than the journal indicated.

Relying on the journal, Boyd and Forrest submitted a tender, which was accepted. The work was carried out, but at vastly greater expense to Boyd and Forrest than would have been the case had the journal of bores stated the unamended results of the borers. They claimed that the railway company had fraudulently induced them to enter into the contract.

"LORD ATKINSON: . . . The well-known passage from Lord Herschell's judgment in *Derry v Peek* was cited by Lord Ardwall. It runs thus: 'First, in order to sustain an action for deceit there must be proof of fraud, and nothing short of that will suffice. Secondly, fraud is proved where it is shown that a false representation has been made (1) knowingly, or (2) without belief in its truth, or (3) recklessly, careless whether it be true or false. Although I have treated the second and third as distinct cases, I think the third is but an instance of the second, for one who makes a statement under such circumstances can have no real belief in the truth of what he states. To prevent a false statement being fraudulent, there must, I think, always be an honest belief in its truth. And this probably covers the whole ground, for one who knowingly alleges that which is false has obviously no such honest belief. Thirdly, if fraud be proved, the motive of the person guilty of it is **6–91**

[87] Ch.2, particularly paras 14–11—14–16. Professor McBryde appears to have formulated those views in his PhD thesis, which also greatly influenced the drafting of the Law Commission Memorandum No.42; see Pt II, paras 3.86–3.95.

immaterial. It matters not that there was no intention to cheat or injure the person to whom the statement was made.'...

Lord Johnston, the Lord Justice-Clerk, and Lord Dundas, appear to acquit Mr Melville of intentional deceit or fraud. The first named of these learned Judges states his view that the compilation of the journal of the bores was false in fact and made with a recklessness which amounts to fraud, the absence of intentional dishonesty being supplied by the presence of a reckless disregard of the interests of the opposite contracting party where these interests must have been or must be held to have been known to be materially affected by the act in question.

The Lord Justice-Clerk states the conclusion to which he has come in these words: 'I come to the conclusion, on this part of the case, that the defenders acted with culpable recklessness; that they deceived the pursuers into accepting as properly obtained data from bores data obtained from persons known to them to be incompetent, and that they further deceived the pursuers by putting before them as facts representations as to bores which they did not receive from the borers, presenting their own inferences of what they thought the borers should have said in describing strata ... I agree with the Lord Ordinary in not imputing direct mala fides to Mr Melville. But most unfortunately, he did what he had no right to do, ordered to be written down as being the facts ascertained by the borer something essentially different from what the borer reported. I have no doubt that he was drawing a sound inference, but he must have known that he was putting forward his inference and passing it off as ascertained fact stated by the borer, which it was not. I cannot acquit him of legal fraud in doing so.' Well, if Melville thought he was 'drawing a sound inference' it is difficult to see how he was guilty of recklessly asserting as true that of which he did not know whether it was true or false, but that is the very essence of what the learned Judge meant to designate as legal fraud.

I am not quite sure whether Lord Ardwall was of opinion that Mr Melville was guilty of deliberate fraud or not. From the following passage in his judgment it would appear to me somewhat doubtful. He expresses himself thus: 'I am of opinion that a false and fraudulent representation was made to the pursuers, inasmuch as it was represented to them that the schedule of quantities, the plans, and the sections were founded on a genuine and honest journal of bores, whereas they were not. That this representation was knowingly made does not admit of a moment's doubt. I have already examined the evidence on the point, and need not go into it again. Mr Melville's own evidence, which I have already referred to, is sufficient to show that he knew perfectly well that the so-called journal of bores was not a genuine journal of bores in any sense of the term, and that it was not made by responsible or competent borers. It goes without saying that the false representations were made without belief in their truth.'

With the greatest respect for each of those learned Judges, I find myself wholly unable to take their view of the result of the evidence. To my mind it appears clear that Mr Melville honestly thought he was stating in the journal of bores the information in fact conveyed to him by the borers, and that the change he made in the entry was made for the very purpose of correcting what he honestly believed to be their misdescription of the substance actually found, so that the journal should set forth the absolute truth. For the reason that I have already given, I think that, so far from not knowing or caring whether the statements contained in the journal were true or false, he was anxious to state the truth, and took such means as he honestly considered sufficient for the very purpose of ascertaining what the truth was so that he might set it forth with accuracy.

It would be a strange way of showing good faith to state the information he received as if he believed it to be true when he, in fact, thought the borers were in error, and yet abstain from correcting their error. I do not think that Mr Melville acted recklessly in any reasonable sense of the word; and am therefore of opinion that the respondents failed to prove that he was guilty of fraud of any kind."

It is clear from Lord Atkinson's judgment that he did not consider fraud, in the context of a fraudulent representation inducing a contract to have a wider meaning in Scots law than the definition in *Derry v Peek*. There is no doubt, however, that that definition has met with widespread resistance in subsequent cases. The cases which follow show how judges have attempted to reconcile these different messages with the outcome that, whether or not *Derry v Peek* is expressly being followed, the definition being applied restricts fraud to statements made in the circumstances countenanced by Lord Herschell in that case. **6–92**

Fraudulent concealment and the duty to disclose information

There will be instances where the conduct, rather than the statements of one of the parties will be seen as fraudulent. The problem is that, as Professor McBryde points out,[88] there is a difference between fraudulent concealment—that is, a failure to disclose information—and concealment in the sense of disguising of facts, through words or conduct. The latter although fraudulent, is really a false representation and, therefore if it induces the contract, a misrepresentation. Thus, to supply reconditioned cash registers without disclosing that they were not new, amounts to fraud.[89] The former suggests that, contrary to the general rule that there is no duty to volunteer information, there will be circumstances in which a party must disclose certain types of information. **6–93**

The general rule is that there is no duty to disclose information in circumstances which do not amount to fraudulent concealment. In a contract for the sale of goods, for example, the principle is caveat emptor ("buyer beware"). The exceptions to this rule are limited. There is a duty to disclose if the contract is uberrimae fidei, i.e. of the utmost good faith. The most important classes of contract in this category are contracts of insurance (a duty to disclose all information in the proposer's possession which might affect the assessment of risk); contracts of partnership on the part of those entering into the partnership and of existing partners; and contracts to take shares in a company (note particularly the requirements of the Companies Act 2006 in relation to information contained in company prospectuses). There is also a duty to disclose where the contract is between parties who are in a fiduciary relationship (relationship of trust). The category of fiduciary relationships is narrow and includes parent and child, trustee and beneficiary, agent and principal and partners inter se.

Beyond accepted categories, it is difficult to establish that there is a duty to disclose, or "duty to speak". **6–94**

Hamilton v Allied Domecq Plc
[2007] UKHL 33; 2007 S.C. (H.L.) 142
House of Lords: Lords Hoffmann, Rodger, Walker, Neuberger

Gleneagles Maltings Co Ltd (Gleneagles) was a private company that had potentially valuable for the rights to extract water from springs on the Gleneagles and sold small quantities of water under the Gleneagles brand name. Hamilton, a shareholder in Gleneagles, believed that Gleneagles water should be marketed as a high-quality brand, and should be properly marketed to hotels, restaurants and catering sector, or "on-trade". Discussions between Hamilton on behalf of existing Gleneagles shareholders and Mr Beatty on behalf of Allied Domecq Plc (Allied) led in November 1992 to a subscription agreement under which a wholly-owned Allied subsidiary became the majority shareholder in Gleneagles with the existing shareholders retaining the remaining shares. Gleneagles did not prosper and in February 1998 it was put into administration, by which time the pursuers' shareholding was virtually worthless.

[88] WW McBryde, *The Law of Contract in Scotland*, 3rd edn (Edinburgh: W. Green, 2007), paras 14–13—14–18.

[89] *Gibson v National Cash Register Co Ltd*, 1925 S.C. 500.

Hamilton and the other minority shareholders brought an action for damages on the grounds of negligent misrepresentation. This was based on Mr Beatty's statements to Hamilton during the negotiations to the effect that if they entered into the subscription agreement, Allied would assist Gleneagles, from the outset, to distribute their product to the on-trade through Britvic, an Allied subsidiary.

The Lord Ordinary (Abernethy) granted decree for £3 million against Allied. The Second Division allowed the reclaiming motion and assoilzied the defenders, on the grounds that the Lord Ordinary had erred in holding that, on the evidence, the pursuers had proved the misrepresentation. The pursuers appealed to the House of Lords. They argued that Mr Beatty was under a duty to take reasonable care not to misrepresent the strategy that would be followed, or alternatively that Mr Beatty was under a "duty to speak", namely to make it clear to the first pursuer that the active use of facilities to penetrate the on-trade must await, and perhaps be contingent upon, the successful development of the brand in the off-trade.

The House of Lords unanimously dismissed the appeal.

6–95 LORD RODGER OF EARLSFERRY—

...

[18] Both in the appellants' written case and in his helpful submissions at the hearing, counsel sought to argue that, not only was Mr Beatty under a duty to take reasonable care not to misrepresent the strategy that would be followed, but he was, alternatively, under a duty to take reasonable care to make clear to Mr Hamilton that the active use of facilities to penetrate the on-trade must await, and perhaps be contingent upon, the successful development of the brand in the off-trade. Counsel referred to this alternative formulation as a 'duty to speak'. It is convenient to address it first.

[19] ... [A subscription] agreement was not a contract *uberrimae fidei* and so no duty of disclosure would normally arise. But, even assuming that Mr Beatty knew or ought to have known that Mr Hamilton regarded access to the on-trade from the outset as essential, was he under a duty of care to make clear that the first stage would be for distribution to the off-trade, with distribution to the on-trade only following later?

[20] Doubtless, if Mr Beatty knew that this was Mr Hamilton's position, a failure on the part of Mr Beatty to speak might be regarded as morally questionable. But that is different from saying that he was under a legal duty to speak.

[21] In *Peek v Gurney* a prospectus for an intended company was issued by promoters who were aware of the disastrous liabilities of the business of Overend & Gurney which the company was to purchase. The prospectus made no mention of a deed of arrangement under which those liabilities were, in effect, to be transferred to the company. The appellant bought shares in the company and, when it was wound up, he was declared liable as a contributory and had to pay almost £100,000. He sought an indemnity against the directors, alleging misrepresentation and concealment of facts by the directors in the prospectus. His action failed because he had not in fact relied on the prospectus but had purchased the shares in the market. In the course of his speech, however, Lord Cairns expressed his agreement with the observations of Lord Chelmsford and Lord Colonsay that mere silence could not be a sufficient foundation for the proceedings. He continued (p 403):

'Mere non-disclosure of material facts, however morally censurable, however that non-disclosure might be a ground in a proper proceeding at a proper time for setting aside an allotment or a purchase of share, would in my opinion form no ground for an action in the nature of an action for misrepresentation. There must, in my opinion, be some active misstatement of fact, or, at all events, such a partial and fragmentary statement of fact, as that the withholding of that which is not stated makes that which is stated absolutely false.'

[22] Counsel for the appellants accepted that something more than mere silence would usually be required to found a delictual claim for damages, but he argued that in certain circumstances a duty to speak would arise. In such cases a failure to speak would be negligent in law and a claim for damages could arise. For support, he pointed to the passage in the decision of the Court of Appeal in *Banque Keyser Ullmann SA v Skandia (UK) Insurance Co Ltd* (pp 794H–795A) where Slade LJ said:

'We can see no sufficient reason on principle or authority why a failure to speak should not be capable of giving rise to liability in negligence under *Hedley Byrne* principles, provided that the two essential conditions are satisfied.'

Slade LJ had already identified the two essential conditions as being 'that there has been on the facts a voluntary assumption of responsibility in the relevant sense and reliance on that assumption.' He added (p 794E–F): 'These features may be much more difficult to infer in a case of mere silence than in a case of misrepresentation.'

23 [23] My Lords, the simple truth is that counsel for the appellants was unable to point to anything in the facts or evidence to show that, in this particular commercial negotiation, there had been any voluntary assumption of responsibility on the part of Mr Beatty. Nor have I been able to find any. In these circumstances the *Banque Keyser* decision does not provide a basis for holding that Mr Beatty was under a duty of care to tell Mr Hamilton about the defenders' distribution strategy if it differed from the one favoured by Mr Hamilton. Counsel for the appellants did not suggest that such a duty could be founded on anything other than a voluntary assumption of responsibility. The alternative way of putting the pursuers' case must therefore be rejected. So, if they are to succeed, it can only be on the basis that there was a negligent misrepresentation by Mr Beatty.

. . ."

This decision was recently followed by Lord Tyre in *University of Saint Andrews v Headon Holdings Ltd*[90] in holding that there was no duty to disclose in a relationship founded on a prospective joint venture.

Life Association of Scotland v Foster 6–96

(1873) 11 M. 351

Court of Session, First Division: The Lord President (Inglis), Lords Deas, Ardmillan and Jerviswoode

Mrs Foster completed a life assurance proposal form which included a declaration that she was "in good health, not being afflicted with any disorder, external or internal". During a medical examination by the association's medical officer, she stated that she did not have a rupture. At the time of the examination, she had a small swelling in her groin which, unknown to her, was a symptom of rupture. She did not think it important and did not disclose it. Subsequently, the hernia became strangulated. She underwent an operation, but gangrene set in and Mrs Foster died. The association now sought to reduce the contract, inter alia on the ground that Mrs Foster had "concealed facts highly material to the contract of assurance upon her life". There was no allegation of fraudulent concealment.

A unanimous First Division found for the defenders.

[90] *University of Saint Andrews v Headon Holdings Ltd* [2015] CSOH 113.

6–97 "LORD PRESIDENT (INGLIS): ... Concealment, or non-disclosure of material facts by a person entering into a contract is, generally speaking, either fraudulent or innocent, and in the case of most contracts where parties are dealing at arm's length, that which is not fraudulent is innocent. But contracts of insurance are in this, among other particulars, exceptional, that they require on both sides *uberrima fides*. Hence, without any fraudulent intent, and even in *bona fide*, the insured may fail in the duty of disclosure. His duty is carefully and diligently to review all the facts known to himself bearing on the risk proposed to the insurers, and to state every circumstance which any reasonable man might suppose could in any way influence the insurers in considering and deciding whether they will enter into the contract. Any negligence or want of fair consideration for the interests of the insurers on the part of the insured leading to the nondisclosure of material facts, though there be no dishonesty, may therefore constitute a failure in the duty of disclosure which will lead to the voidance of the contract. The fact undisclosed may not have appeared to the insured at the time to be material, and yet if it turns out to be material ... its non-disclosure will constitute such negligence on the part of the insured as to void the contract.

The only question therefore is, whether the existence of the swelling in Mrs Foster's groin was such a fact ... My opinion is... that the swelling which is proved to have existed at the date of the contract of insurance has not been shewn to be such a fact as a reasonable and cautious person, unskilled in medical science and with no special knowledge of the law and practice of insurance, would believe to be of any materiality or in any way calculated to influence the insurers in considering and deciding on the risk."

Although the Lord President states that concealment will void the contract, the general view is that the contract is voidable.

Innocent misrepresentation

6–98 Prior to *Stewart v Kennedy* (above, para.6–07 onwards), there was no right to annulment in Scots law where the contract was induced by a false statement innocently made. As we saw in the previous chapter, there would have had to be evidence of fraud.

This case introduced the concept of error by one party induced (and therefore unilateral) by a misrepresentation made by the other party. Note that the effect was to confer a "right to rescind" rather than to render the contract void. Note also that Lord Watson limited his comments to "onerous contracts reduced to writing". He did not, however, explain whether "essential" here has the same meaning as in "error in the essentials". In *Menzies v Menzies* (above, para.6–09), Lord Watson stated that: "[e]rror becomes essential whenever it is shewn that but for it one of the parties would have declined the contract".

The following case is an illustration of "essential error" in the context of misrepresentation.

6–99

Ritchie v Glass
1936 S.L.T. 591
Court of Session, Outer House: Lord Carmont

Glass, an architect, entered into missives with Ritchie, a licensed grocer, to purchase from Ritchie two shop premises with a frontage onto Cow Wynd, Falkirk. Glass was acting for Grant & Co Ltd, a chain of furniture stores. Festus Moffat, a Falkirk accountant who acted as Ritchie's selling agent, advertised the premises for sale. The schedule of particulars on the shops, prepared by Moffat, stated that one shop had a frontage of 30 feet and the second had a frontage of 15 feet. Mr Oppenheim, the managing director of Grants, then visited the premises. His company needed a frontage of at least 45 feet.

Mr Oppenheim instructed Glass to proceed with the purchase. The missives that were drawn up did not mention the frontage.

Preliminary work at the premises revealed that the combined frontage of the two shops was only 21 feet 7 3/4 inches. Glass was instructed by Mr Oppenheim not to proceed with the purchase. Ritchie brought this action for specific implement. Glass raised, as a defence, the alleged misrepresentation of the frontage in Moffat's particulars.

"LORD CARMONT: ... It has apparently been assumed by some that error, if induced by misrepresentation of the other party to the contract, must also be in regard to an essential—or in substantials—before the contract can be set aside. There seems to me to be no justification for that view ... **6–100**

It appears clear that Scots law recognises, as indicated by Bell, that when misrepresentation by a party is alleged inducing error in the other in regard to some matter, that matter need not be an essential of the contract, but it must be material and of such a nature that not only the contracting party but any reasonable man might be moved to enter into the contract; or, put the other way, if the misrepresentation had not been made, would have refrained from entering into the contract ...

It is still possible to represent that Mr Oppenheim's inspection was careless or casual, and it is said that once the representation is made it does not lie in the mouth of the pursuer to say that the defender's client had the means of finding out the error and didn't do so. It is said that the pursuer cannot found on Mr Oppenheim's careless or casual examination, and *Redgrave v Hurd* (1881) 20 Ch. D. 1 was relied on. I do not think that *Redgrave's* case can be applied in the circumstances of the present case. There, in order to sell a house, the seller made representations as to the amount of business carried on by himself from it. In answer to a direct question by an intending purchaser he misrepresented figures and referred to bundles of papers for verification. If these had been examined they would have been found, not to support, but to negative the representation. The purchaser did not examine the papers, and the Court held that the representer could not shelter behind that failure fully to examine what he might. But in the present case neither the pursuer nor his agent had attention drawn to what had been said about frontage, nor did they know that it was of any more than general importance to one who was buying the block. Inspection was invited by the seller, and inspection was made. The point about frontage is that it is fairly obvious to anyone, even one not vitally interested in it, as Mr Oppenheim says he was. In *Redgrave v Hurd* the Master of the Rolls (Jessel) points out that if misrepresentations are made calculated to induce a man to enter into a contract, 'it is an inference in law that he was induced by the representation to enter into it.' He says that 'in order to take away his title to be relieved from the contract on the ground that the representation was untrue it must be shewn that he had knowledge of the facts contrary to the representation, or that he stated in terms, or shewed clearly by his conduct, that he did not rely on the representation.' In my opinion it would be unjust to allow a person to pick out of a schedule of particulars some misrepresented datum, albeit one of some importance, and on the bare allegation that this error induced a contract put the burden upon the representer of shewing that the party did not rely upon the representation. On the contrary, in the present case I think the burden was on the defender, not only to prove the materiality of the representation, but plainly to prove that his client relied upon it in making the contract, notwithstanding the inspection of the shop."

Restitutio in integrum

6–101 The primary remedy for misrepresentation is that the innocent party may rescind the contract; but may do so only if it is possible to restore the parties to their original positions.

The following case is an authoritative statement of what the pursuer needs to show in order to establish that restitutio in integrum is possible.

6–102 **Boyd & Forrest v Glasgow and South-Western Railway Co**
1915 S.C. (H.L.) 21
House of Lords: Earl Loreburn, Lords Atkinson, Shaw of Dunfermline, Parmoor

Boyd & Forrest brought this action following the dismissal of their original action by the House of Lords (above, paras 6–90—6–91). They now sought to recover the extra cost of constructing the railway on the basis of innocent misrepresentation. They argued that, by the adjustment of accounts, both parties could be restored to their original positions.

The court found that restitutio in integrum was no longer possible.

6–103 "LORD SHAW OF DUNFERMLINE: ... As a ground of rescinding the contract, error and misrepresentation must be *in essentialibus*. The true essentials here were the nature of the strata themselves. And when we turn to the proof it is discovered that to this point practically no evidence was addressed. The contrast desired, and relevant, was between the strata as they were found in the bores and the denominations and measurements which the journal gave the bores. The truth is that this issue was probably obscured, for two reasons, viz., that the respondents were in the course of attempting to prove fraud, and, secondly, that they mistook one contrast for another, namely, the contrast between the journals and the borer's letters, and the contrast between the journals and the natural facts. Upon the last, which in the stage the case has now reached would have been the really valuable portion, substantially no proof was led on the evidence as it appears...

I do not find myself able fully to comprehend that view of the case which would treat the situation as one equivalent to possible restitution by a process of adjustment of accounts. The railway is there, the bridges are built, the excavations are made, the rails are laid, and the railway itself was in complete working two years before this action was brought. Accounts cannot obliterate it, and unless the railway is obliterated *restitutio in integrum* is impossible ...

In the present case *restitutio in integrum* being impossible, I think the law is very well settled, too well and too long settled to be disturbed, as expressed, for instance, by Lord Cranworth in *Western Bank of Scotland v Addie* [(1867) 5 M. (H.L.) 80, at p. 89, 'Relief under the first head [i.e., repudiation or rescission], which is what in Scotland is designated *restitutio in integrum*, can only be had where the party seeking it is able to put those against whom it is asked in the same situation in which they stood when the contract was entered into. Indeed, this is necessarily to be inferred from the very expression *restitutio in integrum*, and the same doctrine is well understood and constantly acted on in England.' I may add ... that this principle of law is ... a recognised and established doctrine of the law of contract in general ...

Nor do I think that there is a remedy in damages for an innocent misrepresentation. Such a representation is not an actionable wrong. The error under which the parties labour is common to both, and the material for a case of damages is wanting because the *injuria* is not there. I should willingly investigate this topic further were it not that I find the language of Lord M'Laren so apt in the case of *Manners v Whitehead* [(1898) 1 F. 171, at p. 176], that I do not desire to add anything which would weaken or presume to improve upon the exposition contained in these sentences, 'Where a pursuer only desires to set aside a contract of sale on the ground of innocent misrepresentations he may obtain relief, but only on condition of making *restitutio in integrum*. While the other party may thus be deprived of the benefit of a bargain which he considers advantageous to him, and is desirous of retaining, yet he receives compensation in the shape of restitution. But when we are in the region of damages it does not appear to be consistent with equity, or with any sound principle of law, that in respect of a mistake for which neither party is responsible, the seller shall pay to the purchaser a sum of damages, the purchaser retaining such benefit as the contract has given to him. The remedy of damages, according to all the light which our decisions throw on the question perhaps there is not very much light to be got from them—that remedy is confined to the case of proved fraudulent misrepresentations, and the damages are given as compensation for the loss sustained through fraud.' The same principle has been frequently enunciated in England, and I refer to the judgment of Farwell, L.J., in *Whittington v Seale-Hayne* [(1900) 16 T. L. R.181].

The subject of whether the representations went to the root of this contract may have been sufficiently adverted to in my treatment of the other steps in the case. On the facts I would simply observe, firstly, that if this were so in the present case, it would seem to me impossible to prevent almost any large contract being similarly attacked because of dissatisfaction as to one or two relatively small items; and, secondly, that I do not think it to be proved that this contract would not have been entered into if the journal had been in terms of the borer's letter, or that even its lump sum would have been different on that account."

Negligent misrepresentation

If a statement is not fraudulent, it may nevertheless be negligent. Here, as with fraud, the innocent party has the right to rescind (within the limits noted above). The issue is whether in addition, they may claim damages in delict on the basis of negligence. **6–104**

The right to recover damages for negligence in delict, as with fraud, is not dependent upon a contract between the parties. *Donoghue v Stevenson*[91] suggests that what is important is the existence of a duty of care owed by one party to the other, and a breach of that duty by failing to act as a reasonable man might do in the circumstances. Until 1964, however, no duty of care would have been owed by a person making a negligent statement (as opposed to committing a negligent act) that the other party relied upon to their detriment—unless that statement was made fraudulently or in a fiduciary relationship. In *Hedley Byrne & Co v Heller & Partners Ltd*,[92] the House of Lords established that, so long as a duty to take care existed, a statement negligently made by one party would entitle the party to whom the duty of care was owed to claim damages in negligence, if that party relied upon that statement to their detriment. Thus, if a statement is negligently made, and that statement is also a misrepresentation, the innocent party is entitled to rescind the contract; the question is whether that party is also entitled to damages for negligence. The principle is of far reaching significance in business, particularly where statements are made by persons acting in a professional advisory capacity, for example accountants, auditors, estate agents, surveyors and architects.

In England, the courts have been willing to accept that the victim of a negligent misrepresentation has a right to rescind the contract and to claim damages in negligence. In Scotland, the issue has been fraught with difficulties and has had to be resolved by legislation. In

[91] *Donoghue v Stevenson*, 1932 S.C. (H.L.) 31.
[92] *Hedley Byrne & Co v Heller & Partners Ltd* [1964] A.C. 465.

Esso Petroleum Co Ltd v Mardon,[93] Lord Denning MR stated the position in English law in the following terms:

> "It seems to me that *Hedley Byrne* ... [1964] A.C. 465, properly understood, covers this particular proposition: if a man, who has or professes to have special knowledge or skill, makes a representation by virtue thereof to another—be it advice, information or opinion—with the intention of inducing him to enter into a contract with him, he is under a duty to use reasonable care to see that the representation is correct, and that the advice, information or opinion is reliable. If he negligently gives unsound advice or misleading information or expresses an erroneous opinion, and thereby induces the other side to enter into a contract with him, he is liable in damages. This proposition is in line with what I said in *Candler v. Crane, Christmas & Co.* [1951] 2 K.B.164,179-180, which was approved by the majority of the Privy Council in *Mutual Life and Citizens' Assurance Co. Ltd. v. Evatt* (1971] A.C. 793. And the judges of the Commonwealth have shown themselves quite ready to apply *Hedley Byrne*... between contracting parties: see, in [Canada], *Sealand of the Pacific Ltd. v. Ocean Cement Ltd.* (1973) 33 D.L.R. (3d) 625; and in New Zealand *Capital Motors Ltd. v. Beecham* [1975] 1 N.Z.L.R. 576."

It proved difficult to apply the reasoning in *Esso* in Scottish courts. Several Outer House decisions indicate that the decision of the Inner House in *Manners v Whitehead*, as applied by the House of Lords in *Boyd & Forrest* was an insuperable obstacle to the development of damages for negligent misrepresentation. In that case, Lord McLaren's statement of the principle was unequivocal:

> "It does not appear to be consistent with equity or with any sound principle of law, that in respect of a mistake for which neither party is responsible the seller should pay to the purchaser a sum of damages."[94]

6–105 *Obligations: Report on Negligent Misrepresentation*

Scottish Law Commission Report No.92 (1985)

> "2.1 ... Several Scottish courts of first instance, whilst accepting the general authority of *Hedley Byrne v Heller* as a part of Scots law, have recently stated that they remained bound by *Manners v Whitehead*, though, by analogy with the facts of that case, only in so far as one party has been induced to enter a contract through the misrepresentation of another contracting party. Thus an anomaly has arisen. If a negligent misrepresentation has induced a contract with a party other than the misrepresentor, and in circumstances where all the relevant criteria for delictual liability have been satisfied, the misrepresentor can be sued for his negligence but that remedy is excluded, following *Manners v Whitehead*, if the contract is made with the misrepresentor himself, for in those circumstances only his fraudulent statements will render him liable in delict. Fraud, however, may not only be more difficult to prove than negligence, but also less frequently encountered in practice ...

[93] *Esso Petroleum Co Ltd v Mardon* [1976] Q.B. 801.

[94] *Manners v Whitehead* (1898) 1 F. 171, 177. In *John Kenway Ltd v Orcantic Ltd*, 1979 S.C. 422; 1980 S.L.T. 46, Lord Dunpark adopted the reasoning in *Esso v Mardon*. In *Eastern Marine Services (and Supplies) Ltd v Dickson Motors Ltd*, 1981 S.C. 355, Lord Grieve reluctantly found that *Manners v Whitehead* was binding upon him; whereas Lord Stewart in *Twomax Ltd v Dickson McFarlane & Robinson*, 1983 S.L.T. 98 and Lord Wylie in *Ferguson v Mackay*, 1983 S.C. 115; 1985 S.L.T. 94 distinguished that decision on its facts.

It is clear from [those first instance decisions] that it was with reluctance that their Lordships found *Manners v Whitehead* to be binding. Indeed the legal outcome of that finding in most cases effectively denies the important remedy of damages in delict in circumstances where its availability would seem fully justified. If a duty of care is owed by the provider of information to the recipient when it is reasonably foreseeable that he may rely on that information when entering a contract with a third party, it seems neither logical nor just that the duty of care should not also be owed when the party [whom] the recipient intends to contract with happens also to be the provider of the information in question (It is here assumed that there is a 'special relationship' between the parties . . . for a duty of care to be owed). In those circumstances the proximity of the relationship between the parties and the knowledge of the representor of the reliance that might be placed on his statements are particularly apparent and, we think, subject to such qualifications as the general law has already established, justify the imposition of a legal duty of care which if breached should result in delictual liability for negligence. Accordingly, we consider that the rule in *Manners v Whitehead* should be abolished."

The result of this report was the Law Reform (Miscellaneous Provisions) (Scotland) Act 1985. Section 10 of that 1985 Act provides:

"(1) A party to a contract who has been induced to enter into it by negligent misrepresentation made by or on behalf of another party to the contract shall not be disentitled, by reason only that the misrepresentation is not fraudulent, from recovering damages from the other party in respect of any loss or damage he has suffered as a result of the misrepresentation; and any rule of law that such damages cannot be recovered unless fraud is proved shall cease to have effect.

(2) Subsection (1) applies to any proceedings commenced on or after the date on which it comes into force, whether or not the negligent misrepresentation was made before or after that date, but does not apply to any proceedings commenced before that date."

Note that the provision does not affect purely innocent misrepersentation. Unlike the position in English law, the principle stated in *Manners v Whitehead* precludes the recovery of damages for purely innocent misrepresentation.

The case which follows is an application of s.10 of the 1985 Act.

Bank of Scotland v 3i Plc 6–106
1990 S.C. 215, OH
Court of Session, Outer House: Lord Cameron of Lochbroom

The facts are as stated in the opinion of Lord Cameron of Lochbroom.

"LORD CAMERON OF LOCHBROOM: In the course of negotiations for the provision by 3i plc of funding in the form of convertible loan stock for a company called IPS. Mr Wesley, a senior employee of 3i and a director of IPS, stated that 'Funds to provide a substantial proportion of the said convertible loan stock were committed and that any balance would be underwritten by the defenders.' Relying on this statement, the bank allowed overdraft facilities to be increased to IPS. IPS was put into receivership before any agreement had been reached between the parties on provision of the convertible loan stock, but the bank could not recover the additional funds made available by them to IPS . . . I turn now to the pursuers' case of reckless or negligent misrepresentation . . . 6–107

The present case is one in which there was direct contact between the allegedly negligent provider of information on the one hand and the pursuers on the other. It thus falls precisely within the category of case which is exemplified in *Hedley, Byrne & Co Ltd*. In that case in his speech at page 482, Lord Reid said: 'I shall therefore treat this as if it were a case where a negligent misrepresentation is made directly to the person seeking information, opinion or advice, and I shall not attempt to decide what kind or degree of proximity is necessary before there can be a duty owed by the defendant to the plaintiff.'

. . .

In the present case, the pursuers' averments plainly import that on 1 September 1987 the pursuers were seeking information from the defenders who were the party from whom it was reasonable to expect such information to be obtained. Counsel for the defenders argued that the fact that both parties had a common interest in the affairs of IPS was not of significance. I disagree. It seems to me that the fact that each party in its separate way was concerned to secure finance to enable IPS to continue in business is an important circumstance, not least because the pursuers plainly did not have available to them the same sources of information with regard to the arrangements to support the convertible loan stock issue as had the defenders, who had undertaken for a fee the responsibility of making those arrangements. Accordingly in my opinion the pursuers have averred sufficient by way of background circumstances as to suggest that it was reasonable for the pursuers to seek information or advice from the defenders trusting in the defenders to exercise such a degree of care as the circumstances required.

I also consider, contrary to counsel for the defenders' submissions, that there is sufficient in the background circumstances to substantiate the pursuers' averments that the defenders knew or ought to have known that the pursuers were relying on the defenders' information or advice . . .

In my opinion these circumstances, if established, would suffice to allow the court to hold that in choosing to make the statement of fact that he did, the defenders' employee on behalf of the defenders must be held to have accepted a relationship with the pursuers which required him to exercise care in giving a truthful answer, he knowing that the pursuers were likely to act upon it by extending overdraft facilities to IPS. Furthermore the averments about parties' subsequent actings, not least the defenders' attitude at the meeting on or about 23 September 1987, may also be relevant to cast light upon the extent to which such a relationship could be said to have existed on 1 September 1987. In my opinion the circumstances averred by the pursuers are such that if established by proof the court would be entitled to hold that the law deemed the defenders to have assumed responsibility to the pursuers who acted upon that advice and information. While the pursuers do not aver in terms that they were induced to provide additional bridging finance by virtue of what was said, they do say that in giving the commitment in the statement which was not expressed as qualified or conditional, the defenders knew or ought to have known that the pursuers would rely on and act on it. In my submission that averment is sufficient specification as to reliance upon the commitment in the circumstances averred."

If anything is clear about the law of error, in all its manifestations, it is that much is unclear. Judicial efforts, such as Lord Malcolm's in *Wills* and academic analysis are a boon, but the historic sparseness of worthy comment and the unfortunate conflation of the law of error with English conceptions of "misrepresentation" makes error ripe for clarification. It is a prime candidate for the Scottish Law Commission and, hopefully, for some kind of statutory reform. A possible—if not probable—form is that provided by the Draft Common Frame of Reference (DCFR).

"DCFR II.–7:201: Mistake 6–108

(1) A party may avoid a contract for mistake of fact or law existing when the contract was concluded if:

(a) the party, but for the mistake, would not have concluded the contract or would have done so only on fundamentally different terms and the other party knew or could reasonably be expected to have known this; and
(b) the other party:

(i) caused the mistake;
(ii) caused the contract to be concluded in mistake by leaving the mistaken party in error, contrary to good faith and fair dealing, when the other party knew or could reasonably be expected to have known of the mistake;
(iii) caused the contract to be concluded in mistake by failing to comply with a pre-contractual information duty or a duty to make available a means of correcting input errors; or
(iv) made the same mistake.

(2) However a party may not avoid the contract for mistake if:

(a) the mistake was inexcusable in the circumstances; or
(b) the risk of the mistake was assumed, or in the circumstances should be borne, by that party.

II.–7:202: Inaccuracy in communication may be treated as mistake 6–109

An inaccuracy in the expression or transmission of a statement is treated as a mistake of the person who made or sent the statement.

II.–7:203: Adaptation of contract in case of mistake 6–110

(1) If a party is entitled to avoid the contract for mistake but the other party performs, or indicates a willingness to perform, the obligations under the contract as it was understood by the party entitled to avoid it, the contract is treated as having been concluded as that party understood it. This applies only if the other party performs, or indicates a willingness to perform, without undue delay after being informed of the manner in which the party entitled to avoid it understood the contract and before that party acts in reliance on any notice of avoidance.

(2) After such performance or indication the right to avoid is lost and any earlier notice of avoidance is ineffective.

(3) Where both parties have made the same mistake, the court may at the request of either party bring the contract into accordance with what might reasonably have been agreed had the mistake not occurred.

II.–7:204: Liability for loss caused by reliance on incorrect information 6–111

(1) A party who has concluded a contract in reasonable reliance on incorrect information given by the other party in the course of negotiations has a right to damages for loss suffered as a result if the provider of the information:

(a) believed the information to be incorrect or had no reasonable grounds for believing it to be correct; and
(b) knew or could reasonably be expected to have known that the recipient would rely on the information in deciding whether or not to conclude the contract on the agreed terms.

(2) This Article applies even if there is no right to avoid the contract.

6–112 **II.–7:205: Fraud**

(1) A party may avoid a contract when the other party has induced the conclusion of the contract by fraudulent misrepresentation, whether by words or conduct, or fraudulent non-disclosure of any information which good faith and fair dealing, or any pre-contractual information duty, required that party to disclose.

(2) A misrepresentation is fraudulent if it is made with knowledge or belief that the representation is false and is intended to induce the recipient to make a mistake. A non-disclosure is fraudulent if it is intended to induce the person from whom the information is withheld to make a mistake.

(3) In determining whether good faith and fair dealing required a party to disclose particular information, regard should be had to all the circumstances, including:

(a) whether the party had special expertise;
(b) the cost to the party of acquiring the relevant information;
(c) whether the other party could reasonably acquire the information by other means; and
(d) the apparent importance of the information to the other party.

6–113 Several features of these provisions resonate in Scots law, despite the terminology ("avoid"; "mistake"): a party in bad faith will not be allowed to "snatch at a bargain"[95]; there is no consideration in this provision of so-called mutual errors, or errors based on lack of consent: they are rightly seen as aspects of agreement, or the intention to create a contract; and damages are available for negligent, but not for innocent misrepresentation.[96]

There are, however, points of difference: error (or "inaccuracy") of expression or transmission is regarded as a mistake by the person making it[97]; the limits to the general right to avoid contract for error appear to be wider than where restitutio in integrum is impossible[98]; performance or willingness to perform by the party not in error may deprive the party in error of the right to avoid contract[99]; in cases of common error either or both parties may seek rectification of the contract[100]; fraud is more narrowly defined.[101]

---

[95] DCFR II–7:201(1)(b)(ii).
[96] DCFR II–7:204(1)(b).
[97] DCFR II–7:202.
[98] DCFR II–7:201(2).
[99] DCFR II–7:203(1).
[100] DCFR II–7:203(3).
[101] DCFR II–7:205(2).

CHAPTER 7
ILLEGALITY

Although it is common to speak of "*pacta illicita*", there is little in the institutional writings on illegality of contracts. Stair merely states: **7–01**

> "In the matter of contracts it is requisite, that it be of things in our power in their kind; and so contracts of absolute impossibilities are void. And contracts in things unlawful are also void. But though the particular thing be not in our power, and yet be not manifestly impossible, the contract is obligatory; and albeit it cannot obtain its effect upon that thing, it is effectual for the equivalent, as damage and interest."[1]

The passage shows reluctance to condemn otherwise valid contracts as unworthy of legal recognition on the grounds of illegality or public policy.[2] The law is generally supportive of contract. Rarely will the law expressly prohibit a contract; but various categories of contract are *turpis causa*, that is, tainted with turpitude.

According to Professor McBryde,[3] "The category of 'illegal contracts' is the most difficult to explain and understand". In general terms, a contract may be "illegal" either because it is expressly or impliedly prohibited by statute or because it is contrary to public policy. Most modern writers, in common with English writers, suggest a third category of contracts illegal at common law.[4] Some categories of contract or contractual terms may simply be unenforceable because they offend public policy, such as covenants in restraint of trade, although they are not illegal in the strict sense of the word.

It is not practical within the confines of this book to provide a detailed exposition of material on the wide diversity of contracts tainted with illegality. The following material has been selected to provide guidance on the fundamental principles, rather than to illustrate the numerous categories of potential illegality. Because of limited Scottish material, appropriate reference is made to English authority, mostly of the House of Lords.

Non-statutory illegality

Not many categories of contract are illegal at common law or on grounds of public policy, but the examples show the variable effects which such illegality may have on the contract. **7–02**

---

1 Stair, *Institutions*, I, x, 13.

2 For the development of judicial changes in attitude, see WW McBryde, *The Law of Contract in Scotland*, 3rd edn (Edinburgh: W. Green, 2007), Ch.13, paras 29–40, "Illegal Contracts"; Ch.19 "Public Policy"; and L MacGregor, "Pacta Illicita", in Reid and Zimmerman (eds), *A History of Private Law in Scotland* (Oxford: Oxford University Press, 2000), Vol.2, pp.129 onwards.

3 WW McBryde, *The Law of Contract in Scotland*, 3rd edn (Edinburgh: W. Green, 2007), paras 13–29.

4 Gloag, *Contract Law in Scotland*, 2nd edn (Edinburgh: W. Green, 1929), pp.560–564) places within this category contracts tainted with crime, fraud, breach of trust, bankruptcy, illicit sexual intercourse, interference with the liberty of marriage, interference with parental relations, and promotion of immorality. DM Walker, *The Law of Contracts and Related Obligations in Scotland*, 3rd edn (Edinburgh: T& T Clarke, 1995) p.156) states that "Common law illegality tends to overlap with contrariety to public policy and some cases may be explicable on either ground". He includes in the category a far wider range than Gloag. WW McBryde *The Law of Contract in Scotland*, 3rd edn (Edinburgh: W. Green, 2007), Chs 13 and 19 appears not to recognise common law illegality as a category separate from contract illegal on grounds of public policy or by reason of being *contra bonos mores*.

7–03

Regazzoni v KC Sethia (1944) Ltd
[1958] A.C. 301
House of Lords: Viscount Simonds, Lords Reid, Cohen, Keith and Somervell

Indian regulations prohibited the export from India of goods to or via South Africa. Sethia agreed to sell to the appellant jute bags c.i.f. Genoa. Both parties knew that the bags would be resold to South Africa. The contract was governed by English law. The bags were not delivered and Regazzoni brought an action for damages for breach of contract.

The House held that the contract was not enforceable: it was the common intent of the parties to violate the law of India and it was contrary to public policy to enforce such an agreement.

7–04 "LORD REID: . . . To my mind, the question whether this contract is enforceable by English courts is not, properly speaking, a question of international law. The real question is one of public policy in English law; but, in considering this question, we must have in mind the background of international law and international relationships often referred to as the comity of nations. This is not a case of a contract being made in good faith but one party thereafter finding that he cannot perform his part of the contract without committing a breach of foreign law in the territory of the foreign country. If this contract is held to be unenforceable it should, in my opinion, be because from the beginning the contract was tainted so that the courts of this country will not assist either party to enforce it. I do not wish to express any opinion about a case where parties agree to deal with goods which they both know have already been smuggled out of a foreign country, or about a case where the seller knows that the buyer intends to use the goods for an illegal, purpose or to smuggle them into a foreign country. Such cases may raise difficult questions. The crucial fact in this case appears to me to be that both parties knew that the contract could not be performed without the respondents' procuring a breach of the law of India within the territory of that country. On that question I do not get very much assistance from the older cases. Most of them do not deal with that point and, further, it must, I think, be borne in mind that they date from the time when international relationships were somewhat different and when theories of political economy now outmoded were generally accepted. Many dealt with revenue laws or penal laws which have always been regarded as being in a special position, and I do not wish on this occasion to say more than that probably some re-examination of some of these cases may in future be necessary. The Indian law prohibiting exports to South Africa does not appear to me to be a revenue or penal law . . . Further, this case does not, in my view, involve the enforcement of Indian law in England. In fact, no breach of Indian law in the execution of this contract was ever committed or attempted because the contract came to an end by its repudiation by the respondents within a few days after it was made . . .

7–05 LORD SOMERVELL: . . . In the present case, for reasons which have been stated by your Lordships, the performance of the contract to the knowledge, and intention of both parties involved a breach of Indian law. Prima facie that is sufficient to make it unenforceable in our courts. Your Lordships were invited to make an exception to the principle on the ground that the law in question was directed against the Union of South Africa arising out of a dispute between the two states. I do not think this would justify taking the case out of the rule.

The statements that in this field one country takes no notice of the revenue laws of another seems to have been based on the principle that smuggling and freedom 'gang the gither' . . . but in any event I myself think that the courts of this country should not today enforce a contract to smuggle goods into or out of a foreign and friendly state. There may, of course, be laws the enforcement of which would be against 'morals.' In such a case an exception might be made to the general principle. The point can be dealt with if it arises.

In conclusion, I would like to say a word as to the scope of the word 'involves' in my statement of the question raised in the present appeal. One has at one end of the scale a contract which, on its face, necessitates a breach of the foreign law: a contract to deliver prohibited goods in the territory. At the other end one may have a contract of sale legal on its face at a normal market price, the vendor suspecting or knowing that the buyer intends to use the goods for an illegal purpose in a foreign country. The same problem arises when a contract is said to be unenforceable as immoral or illegal under our own law (*Pearce v Brooks* (1866), L.R. 1 Exch. 213). In *Foster v Driscoll*, the majority found that the evidence established a joint enterprise to import whisky into the United States. 'It is not a case' said Sankey, L.J. ([1929] 1 K.B. at p. 515), 'where one or other of them merely knew that the whisky was going to the States.' I am never very clear as to the effect of 'mere' and 'merely' though I may have used one or other myself. If the question is one of illegality under our law the contract is unenforceable if the defendant knew that the goods or money or other consideration were to be used for a purpose immoral or illegal under our law. It would be convenient if the same principle was applied, but it does not arise directly in this case.

I would dismiss the appeal."

LORDS COHEN, KEITH and SIMONDS concurred.

The law here was passed to prevent trade with South Africa, which discriminated against people **7–06** of Indian descent on grounds of colour and race. Would the House have decided differently had the law infringed been a revenue or tax law? Would it be different still if the law in question was that of a state which prohibited trade with another state as an act of racial or other discrimination?

Would the House have decided differently if the contract were not, as in this case, partly performed in India? What if the contract was to ship the goods to the UK and there was a subcontract to resell to South Africa: bearing in mind that there was no boycott of South Africa in this country at the time, would the House have decided differently?

There is here a public international law[5] element—notice, for example, the consistent references by the judges to the concept of "comity". This suggests that if it wants its laws to be respected internationally, a state ought to respect the laws of other states. There is also an element of private international law, or conflict of laws: in a dispute between private individuals, it is not only the law which governs the contract which determines whether the contract is valid, or "legal". In *Lemenda Trading Co Ltd v African Middle East Petroleum Co Ltd*,[6] in dealing with a contract governed by English law but performed in Qatar (involving reliance on personal influence), the English court held, inter alia, that the fact that the object of the contract was contrary to the public policy of Qatar was not of itself a bar to the enforcement of the agreement. It may, however, be a relevant factor when considering whether the court ought to refuse to enforce the agreement.

The extent of public policy

It is clear from all the speeches that in the above case public policy was the basis of illegality. **7–07** How extensive is the concept of public policy?

---

[5] Contrast the view expressed by Lord Reid.

[6] *Lemenda Trading Co Ltd v African Middle East Petroleum Co Ltd*, 1988 Q.B. 448.

What amounts to public policy cannot be rigidly defined.[7] As a doctrine, it has been compared to a very unruly horse, and when once you get astride it, you never know where it will carry you.[8] Judges resort to it with caution.[9] This is especially so in contract, where the overriding policy is the maintenance of freedom of contract. This was expressed with force by Jessel MR in *Printing & Numerical Registering Co v Sampson*[10] at 465:

> "It must not be forgotten that you are not to extend arbitrarily those rules which say that a given contract is void as being against public policy, because if there is one thing more than another public policy requires it is that men of full age and competent understanding shall have the utmost liberty of contracting, and that their contracts when entered into freely and voluntarily shall be held sacred and shall be enforced by courts of justice."

If, however, this aspect of public policy conflicts with another, the contract may be unenforceable. The cases which follow are illustrative of the categories of public policy.

7–08 **Pearce v Brooks**

(1866) L.R. 1 Exch. 213

English Court of Exchequer: Pollock CB, Bramwell, Martin and Piggott BB

Pearce and Countze, coachbuilders, agreed to sell for 135 guineas a new miniature brougham carriage to Mrs Brooks, on hire terms, with an option to purchase after payment of the final instalment. Mrs Brooks, a prostitute, took the carriage, which she used as part of her display in attracting custom. She paid one instalment and then returned the carriage in a damaged condition, but refused to pay the agreed penalty of 15 guineas for the damage. The coachbuilders sought the penalty. The contract was held to be unenforceable, as it indirectly promoted sexual immorality.

> "BRAMWELL B: ... There is no doubt that the woman was a prostitute; no doubt to my mind that the plaintiffs knew it ... The only fact really in dispute is for what purpose was the brougham hired, and if for an immoral purpose, did the plaintiffs know it? ... I think ... that it was hired for the purpose of display, that is, for the purposes of enabling the defendant to pursue her calling, and that the plaintiffs knew it.
>
> That being made out, my difficulty was, whether, though the defendant hired the brougham for that purpose, it could be said that the plaintiffs let it for the same purpose In one sense, it was not for the same purpose. If a man were to ask for duelling pistols; and to say: 'I think I shall fight a duel tomorrow', might not the seller answer: 'I do not want to know your purpose; I have nothing to do with it; that is your business; mine is to sell the pistols, and I look only to the profit of trade.' No doubt the act would be immoral, but I have felt doubt whether the act would be illegal; and I should still feel it, but for the authority of *Cannan v Bryce* [and] *McKinnell v Robinson* concludes the matter. This Court ... decided that it need not be part of the bargain that the subject of the contract should be used unlawfully, but that it is enough that it is handed over for the purpose that the borrower shall so apply it."

[7] WW McBryde, *The Law of Contract in Scotland*, 3rd edn (Edinburgh: W. Green, 2007), paras 19–01—19–16.
[8] *Richardson v Mellish* (1824) 2 Bing. 229 at 252, per Burough J.
[9] Some judges use more caution than others. "With a good man in the saddle, the unruly horse can be kept in control. It can jump over obstacles": *Enderby Town EC Ltd v Football Association Ltd* [1971] Ch. 591 at 606, per Lord Denning MR.
[10] *Printing & Numerical Registering Co v Sampson* (1875) L.R.19 Eq. 462.

How far would the courts be prepared to inquire into the motivation behind the contract and into the purposes to which the subject-matter of the contract are subsequently put? **7–09**

The above case can be contrasted with the Scottish decision of *Hamilton v Main*.[11] The pursuer succeeded in having set aside a charge on a promissory note he had issued to the defender. Hamilton brought a suspension of a charge on his promissory note of £60, granted to Main, on the grounds that it had been obtained by fraud and circumvention, while he was intoxicated, and *ob turpem causam*. In evidence of these allegations, he referred to a judicial declaration emitted by Main, in a complaint against him by the procurator-fiscal relative to this transaction. Main there stated that he was the keeper of a public house in the High Street of Glasgow, but had no licence; that Hamilton had resided there for seven days and six nights and—along with a prostitute—had, during that time, consumed 113 bottles of port and madeira, besides a large quantity of spirituous and malt liquors, the value of which, together with food and lodging, amounted to £52 6s.; that Hamilton frequently wandered through the house drunk and naked, and was always in a state of intoxication; and that, before departing, and while sober, he granted his promissory note for £60, in payment of his account, and as a reward to the prostitute. It was contended by Main that he was entitled to be repaid for the articles consumed. The court holding, that as the bill was utterly vitiated, the diligence of the law could not be allowed to proceed on it, refused the reference, reserving to him to raise an ordinary action. Main argued that he was entitled to be paid for his outgoings by enforcement of the promissory note. The court allowed Hamilton to escape liability for the debt, though the reasons are unclear from the judgment. Commentators suggest that the contract was unenforceable because enforcing it would allow the promotion of sexually immoral behaviour.[12]

McBryde[13] observes that:

> "Public policy implies a consideration of the circumstances surrounding a contract, and these have to be considered in the light of the changing attitudes of society."

This may be most obvious in terms of societal views of sexual morality. In *Armhouse Lee Ltd v Chapell*,[14] the Court of Appeal rejected the argument that it should decline to enforce a contract to advertise telephone sex lines. Simon Brown, LJ quoted Sir Nicholas Browne-Wilkinson in *Stephens v Avery*[15]:

> "Only in a case where there is still a generally accepted moral code can the court refuse to enforce rights in such a way as to offend that generally accepted code."

The appellants—who had argued that their own promotional material was so immoral that they ought not to have to pay for it—were also condemned for their "brazen cynicism".

The next case is an example of a contract illegal on grounds of public policy because of its tendency to corrupt public life.

---

[11] *Hamilton v Main* (1823) 2 S. 356.

[12] WW McBryde, *The Law of Contract in Scotland*, 3rd edn (Edinburgh: W. Green, 2007), para.19–43; J Thomson & HL MacQueen, *Contract Law in Scotland*, 3rd edn (London: Bloomsbury, 2012), para 4.75; S Woolman, *Contract* (3rd ed., 2001), para.12.4.

[13] WW McBryde, *The Law of Contract in Scotland*, 3rd edn (Edinburgh: W. Green, 2007), para.19–04.

[14] *Armhouse Lee Ltd v Chapell*, *The Times* 7 August 1996.

[15] *Stephens v Avery* [1988] 2 All E.R. 477.

7–10 **Parkinson v College of Ambulance Ltd**
[1925] 2 K.B. 1
English High Court, King's Bench: Lush J

Colonel Parkinson made a substantial contribution to the funds of the College of Ambulance, a charity. In return for the contribution the secretary of the college gave assurances that college officials would have the means to secure for him a knighthood. The knighthood never materialised, so the colonel sued for the return of his "donation".[16]

A contract for the purchase of an honour was contrary to public policy and illegal. The parties were *in pari delicto*, and neither the donation nor damages could be recovered by the colonel.

"LUSH J: . . . [A] contract to guarantee or undertake that an honour will be conferred by the Sovereign if a certain contribution is made to a public charity, or if some other service is rendered, is against public policy, and, therefore, an unlawful contract to make. Apart from being derogatory to the dignity of the Sovereign who bestows the honour, it would produce, or might produce, more mischievous consequences. It would tend to induce the person who was to procure the title to use improper means to obtain it, because he had his own interests to consider. It would make him tend to conceal facts as to the fitness of the proposed recipient. Moreover, if the contract was lawful, an action could be brought if the stipulated title was not obtained or if the money was not paid. A person in the position of this plaintiff could claim and be awarded damages for the loss of a title or of obtaining one of a less degree than that for which he had bargained; a person in the position of these defendants could claim and be awarded damages for not receiving the promised contribution, although the title had been obtained. No court could try such an action and allow such damages to be awarded with any propriety or decency."

7–11 The policy objective being enforced in this case was clear to see: such a contract would corrupt public life to the detriment of general interests of the public. In many cases it is more difficult to define the public policy element.

Sponsiones ludicrae[17]—gambling or gaming agreements—were unenforceable in Scots law on grounds of public policy,[18] despite the mass popularisation of gambling via football pools and the National Lottery itself established by statute. The Gambling Act 2005 s.335 (enforceability of gambling contracts) now provides:

"(1) The fact that a contract relates to gambling shall not prevent its enforcement.

(2) Subsection (1) is without prejudice to any rule of law preventing the enforcement of a contract on the grounds of unlawfulness (other than a rule relating specifically to gambling)."

---

[16] This particular form of corruption was, partly as a result of this case, made a criminal offence under the Honours (Prevention of Abuses) Act 1925.

[17] For an historical definition and review, see WW McBryde, *The Law of Contract in Scotland*, 3rd edn (Edinburgh: W. Green, 2007), paras 19–50—19–67.

[18] *Ferguson v Littlewoods Pools Ltd*, 1997 S.L.T. 30; but note *Knight & Co v Stott* (1892) 19 R. 959, *Robertson v Anderson*, 2003 S.L.T. 235.

> "Gambling" is defined in section 3 as gaming, betting and taking part in a lottery. "Gaming" is defined in section 6(1) as "playing a game of chance for a prize" and "game of chance" is defined in section 6(2).[19] "Betting" is defined in Section 9(1)[20] as "making or accepting a bet on (a) the outcome of a race, competition or other event or process, (b) the likelihood of anything occurring or not occurring, or (c) whether anything is or is not true." "Lottery" is widely defined in section 14."[21]

Express statutory illegality

Statutes have varying effects on contracts. Some contracts are expressly declared illegal and the parties subjected to specified penalties. Some contracts are merely expressed to be void, or unenforceable, without the imposition of criminal sanction, whereas others are merely expressed to be illegal. As Professor McBryde states[22]: **7–12**

> "The phrases 'shall be void' or 'is void' appear to be the most common statutory expressions of nullity in current use. Where the whole of the contract is not void, but only a provision of the contract and then only if that contravenes certain rules, the phrase is a variation of: 'An agreement is void, if and to the extent that'. Examples are so numerous that it is pointless to list them. There are many other styles. One Scottish Statute used 'null' instead of 'void' [Prescription and Limitation (Scotland) Act 1973, s.13), and another statute 'null and void' [Agricultural Holdings (Scotland) Act 1991, s.5(4)]. Some use the phrase 'void and unenforceable' [Agricultural Marketing Act1958, s.17(3); Conveyancing and Feudal Reform (Scotland) Act 1970 s.11(4)(b); *cf.* s.7] and there are examples of 'shall be of no effect' [Road Traffic Act 1988, s.148(1)], "ineffective" [Housing, Grants Construction and Regeneration Act 1996, s.113(1)] and of 'shall be invalid' [Films Act 1960, s.35]. An instance of a reverse phrasing is: 'the provisions of this Act shall have effect notwithstanding any contract to the contrary' [War Damage to Land (Scotland) Act 1939, s. 8. See also the Agricultural Holdings (Scotland) Act 1991, ss.3 and 21(1)]. There can be more oblique ways of invalidating an obligation as in the case of insurance on the lives of foster children in which there is deemed to be a lack of insurable interest [Foster Children (Scotland) Act 1984, s.18]. Examples of a contract being declared voidable are the irregular allotment of shares [Companies Act 1985, s.85] and the Auctions (Bidding Agreements) Act 1969 which in certain circumstances allows the seller to avoid the contract. A contractual provision may be rendered unenforceable, but not void, either by express use of 'unenforceable' or 'not enforceable' [as in the now repealed Registration of Business Names Act 1916, s.8(1)] or by equivalents such as 'shall not bind' [Merchant Shipping Act 1995, s.34(1)] or 'shall not be liable to make any payment' [Unsolicited Goods and Services Act 1971, s.3(1)]. The fee of a person who acts as a solicitor or notary public without being duly qualified to do so is not 'recoverable' [Solicitors (Scotland) Act 1980, s. 33]."

In addition the Consumer Credit Act 1974 s.127(3) and (4) prohibits a court from enforcing a regulated agreement in circumstances where there is an irregularity in the execution of the agreement. **7–13**

It is nevertheless rare that the law makes it a criminal offence to enter into particular forms of

---

19 Available at: *http://www.legislation.gov.uk/ukpga/2005/19/section/6* [Accessed 27 August 2015].

20 Available at: *http://www.legislation.gov.uk/ukpga/2005/19/section/9* [Accessed 27 August 2015].

21 Available at: *http://www.legislation.gov.uk/ukpga/2005/19/section/14* [Accessed 27 August 2015].

22 WW McBryde, *The Law of Contract in Scotland*, 3rd edn (Edinburgh: W. Green, 2007), paras 19–28—19–30.

contract. It is far more common that the making of certain contracts must comply with statutory requirements—e.g. weights and measures or food and drugs legislation, or made under licence—e.g. sales of alcohol, drugs or tobacco, or carriage for reward. In such cases failure to comply may expose one or both parties to penalties, but the contract is not directly affected—indeed, some statutes specifically state that the validity of contracts will not be affected.[23] In such cases, the effect of the statute on the contract will depend upon its purpose. If the purpose of the statute is, for example, merely to enrich the revenue, as with the use of excise licences, then validity of the contract will not be affected.

The following cases provide illustrations of the consequences of express statutory illegality.

7–14

Cuthbertson v Lowes

(1870) 8 M. 1073

Court of Session, First Division: The Lord President (Inglis), Lords Deas, Ardmillan, Kinloch

Cuthbertson sold and delivered to Lowes two fields of potatoes for £24 per Scots acre. Under the Weights & Measures Acts then in force, the sale in Scots acres was null and void. Lowes, who had paid £600 on account, now disputed what was owed and refused to pay the full purchase price. Cuthbertson brought this action for the balance.

The court held that the seller was allowed to recover the purchase price.

"LORD PRESIDENT (INGLIS): ... In the first place, where the Legislature has imposed the penalty of forfeiture of goods which are the subject of a prohibited contract, there can be no doubt that the loss falls upon one of the parties only, but then the other is not allowed to retain or resume possession of the goods forfeited, for in such a case they belong to the Crown.

Again, it is quite clear that whatever may be the result as affecting the parties, a court of law cannot entertain an action for implement of a contract which the Legislature has expressly declared to be illegal, for the court can do nothing contrary to the clear terms or necessary implication of an Act of Parliament.

There is another class of cases, those in which statutory enactments have been formed for the protection of purchasers against the fraud of traders, and in these cases the statutory penalty being directed against one of the parties only for the protection of the other, he alone must suffer the consequences of a breach of the enactment.

In the present instance, however, the statutes founded upon by the defender are directed against both of the parties—the buyer is equally prohibited with the seller; and the prohibition, or statutory nullity of the agreement is obviously not designed for the protection of either of them, but to enforce a measure of public policy.

But, my Lords, if the defender's contention were well founded, one of the parties would make a gain at the expense of the other, upon whom the whole loss would fall. The defender seeks to retain the pursuer's potatoes without paying anything for them, on the ground that the Court cannot take cognisance of an agreement which by the statutes is declared to be null and void. I cannot readily yield consent to a proposition which would be productive of a result so inequitable, and I am of the opinion that we are not constrained to do so. No doubt the Court cannot enforce performance of an illegal contract, and *in turpi causa melior est conditio possidentis*, but there is no turpitude in a man selling his potatoes by the Scotch and not by the imperial acre; and although he cannot sue for implement of such a contract, I know of no authority in the absence of *turpi causa*, to prevent the pursuer from recovering the market value of the potatoes, at

[23] For example, Trade Descriptions Act 1968 s.35; Consumer Protection Act 1987 s.41(3).

the date when they were delivered to the defender. That is not suing upon the contract; and I am of opinion, therefore, that we should adhere to the Lord Ordinary's interlocutor."

In turpi causa melior est conditio possidentis means that in an illegal situation, the person in possession is in a better position. Was the Lord President applying a principle of equity? If so, what was it? Why was the sale of potatoes by Scots acres not an act of turpitude?

Implied statutory illegality

This decision was not followed by the Inner House and received critical consideration (especially from Lord Mackay) in *Jamieson v Watt's Trustee*, considered below. In *Jamieson*, the court was faced with a statute that required a licence for the carrying out of certain work, but did not expressly prohibit the making of contracts to do such work. Many English authorities suggest that if the purpose of the statute is to protect the public, or to further some aspect of public policy, breach of the statute may render the contract illegal; but the position in Scotland, especially in terms of the consequences of such implied illegality, is far less clear.[24] **7–15**

Jamieson v Watt's Trustees **7–16**
1950 S.C. 265; 1950 S.L.T. 232
Court of Session, Second Division: The Lord Justice-Clerk (Thomson), Lords Mackay, Jamieson and Patrick

Regulation 56A of the Defence Regulations 1939 declared construction work unlawful unless under licence. Watt instructed Jamieson to execute joinery work on a cottage in Banff. Jamieson obtained a licence to carry out work to value of £40. The final bill was for £114 8s. 6d. Watt refused to pay more than £40. The court refused to enforce the contract beyond the amount authorised by the licence.

"LORD JUSTICE-CLERK (THOMSON): ... [T]he pursuer in incurring the items in respect of which he sues was in breach of the Regulation. That being so, is he to be permitted to invoke the aid of the Courts to enforce his claim for payment? **7–17**

To this question the law of England ... on the ground of public policy replies in an unequivocal negative. I am satisfied that in Scotland the answer is the same. The decision of the House of Lords in *Stewart v Gibson* (1840, 1 Robb. App. 260), puts the matter beyond doubt. If a pursuer cannot maintain his cause of action without establishing that he acted in breach of a statute, the Courts will not listen to him ... The case advanced for the pursuer invoked the doctrine of recompense and it was argued that as he had enriched the late Mr Watt's property ... equity demanded that the defender should reimburse him. It was submitted that in the interests of commercial morality the Court was bound to intervene to prevent the defender obtaining an advantage to which he was not entitled. It is obvious that if these arguments were given full effect to, the general principle that the Courts will not assist the party in breach of a statute should be completely undermined. The only logical result of the refusal of the Courts to assist him is that the opposite party who has gained an advantage is entitled to keep it. The appellant's argument at its highest involves that the Courts should be prepared to assist

[24] See WW McBryde, *The Law of Contract in Scotland*, 3rd edn (Edinburgh: W. Green, 2007), paras 19–32—19–37.

the party in breach to the whole extent of his claim and at its lowest to the extent of allowing him to recover his out-of-pocket expenditure.

The appellant's argument at its highest involves that the Courts should be prepared to assist the party in breach to the whole extent of his claim and at its lowest to the extent of allowing him to recover his out-of pocket expenditure. The appellant's argument in the end of the day came to rely on *Cuthbertson v Lowes* ((1870) 8 M. 1073) . . . I regard this as a special case turning on its own circumstances. The effect of the statute was to make the contract void and as Gloag points out (*Contract*, p. 550) a distinction can be drawn between agreements which the law will not allow to operate as contracts and contracts which are contrary to law. The position in *Cuthbertson* was that there never was a contract at all and, as a result, there was nothing to prevent the Courts from regulating the rights of parties. It is different where, as in the present case, one party comes forward to seek relief in respect of his own breach of a regulation . . .

7–18 LORD MACKAY: . . . What then is the true place and effect of *Cuthbertson v Lowes*? . . . I have come to think there are not one but many ways of refusal to give it any effect contrary to the sixty years of law stretching out on either side of it. The real embarrassment of riches is to sever out any one ground of distinction sufficient for *Cuthbertson* but which saves the general proposition, as unshaken in our law.

Firstly, I feel for myself that here is one case where a faulty headnote in a rubric has contributed to decades of misunderstanding. The first among the headlines is 'Sale—Pactum Illicitum.' Now I find that the statutes concerned, two of the Weights and Measures Acts, do not in fact pronounce the words 'illicit' or 'illegal'—they merely made certain bargains 'null and of no effect.' And further, anything struck at under the ban of old measures must necessarily have been two-sided bargains of sale. (Here of course it is not the *bargain* of Watt and Jamieson that is attacked at all. It is the unlicensed man going on to 'carry out.') The leading judgment, that of the Lord President, who commenced by saying 'it is necessary to distinguish it' (i.e. from the several decisions cited), uses only the words 'which are the subject of a prohibited contract'—a phrase that might strike a sort of mean between 'void and of no effect' and 'illegal'; but does not in my opinion amount to a statement of illegality in the full sense.

Secondly, [respondent's counsel] sought in his early address to content himself with a statement that there is a difference between a *malum prohibitum*, or an out-and-out illegality, and a mere statutory pronouncement that a bargain, if attempted will be 'null.' It may be that this alone would do to set such a narrow judgment to one side, but I dislike to found on a possibly over-forced distinction, if at least other courses are open. For, indeed, since the Lord Ordinary in that very case had . . . allowed a proof, it is true now that all the First Division did, after discussing the argued alternatives was to 'adhere,' and so to send the matter to proof. What resulted we do not know. It is quite conceivable that by the time the proof was heard Counsel had fortified their views with higher authority.

But (thirdly) I find it much more illuminating to consider what was in fact the matter their Lordships were dealing with; and particularly to observe that they neither overruled *Alexander v M'Gregor* nor *Handyside v Pringle*, nor commented on the force of the four English decisions to which the Lord Ordinary was referred. I have looked with care into the actual provisions of the two Weights and Measures Acts. They wished to discourage or disallow the use of old 'Scots' measures, or any other 'local' measures; and instituted 'imperial' ones, and in particular 'acres.' They did not ban or pronounce illegal any sale; but they definitely rendered any sale *by the seller* employing old measures nonenforceable by *him*. No provision and no ban was directed to the buyer—the taker takes such measures. And accordingly, I am, for my part, clear that, of the four classes into which Lord President Inglis placed irregular bargains of sale this one in truth fell into the third special class outlined, to wit, where the nullity was pronounced against one party, and in order to protect the other party, to the bargain. The thing *prohibitum* was forbidden only to the seller, who it was plainly conceived was in the position, for all the 'gill', 'bushel' container cases and so forth, of the provider and user of all such old containers from which goods were dispensed. The buyers did not possess or use such, in at least the typical case. It seems possible to me to say without undue disrespect that the Lord President, by a slight error treated the facts as if they fell into his fourth category, that of both partakers in a sale being *in pari casu* as regards forbiddance. The authority which has not ever, so far as known, been followed, seems thus to be a precedent of that kind that it can only now be held authoritative for its very own case—a sale 'by the Scotch acre.' Moreover, the whole statutory basis of such limited decision has since 1878 and 1897 been repealed, so that the exact case can probably not recur.

There is, then, a call upon us for a decision now, that, according to our Scots law, in any case of proper and full illegality, whether it is pronounced in a matter of contract or in the matter of operation, there is no room for avoiding the bar to a Court's aid by reason of the illicit character, by applying a *quantum meruit* or (better) a *quantum lucratus est* method of affording some relief to the person *versans in illicito*. I do so give my decision.

...

LORD PATRICK: ... Th[e] claim is not founded upon contract but upon recompense. It is a principle of equity by no means universally applied in Scots law. Considerations other than the mere fact that one party has benefited by the other's loss may prevent its application to a particular case. Where the transaction in relation to which the claim arises is prohibited by law, the enforcement of equitable adjustment as between two individuals may be outwith the province of the Courts. Gloag puts the matter thus: 'Illegality in contract admits of degrees. It may range from a statutory prohibition of a particular method of entering into a contract which may be lawfully completed in other ways, at the one end of the scale, to contracts intended to secure the commission of a crime, of some act generally recognised as immoral, or subversive of the interests of the state, at the other. And, as the degree of illegality varies, so do the legal results. On the one side are cases where, though a contract cannot be enforced, the incidental rights of parties arising under it may be subject of action; on the other, cases where a party may be entirely deprived of legal redress on the ground that to give it would involve the recognition of acts of which the law will not take cognisance except to visit them with penalties'—Gloag on *Contract*, (2nd ed.), p. 549, 550. It will be noticed that Gloag attributes the highest degree of illegality to acts 'subversive of the interests of the state.' These are acts of which the Courts cannot take cognisance except to visit them with penalties, and indeed it seems monstrous to suggest that the Courts of the State should be asked to adjust accounts as between parties in respect of claims which arose out of their being jointly engaged in acts subversive of the interests of the State. **7–19**

The Regulations which were broken in this case were made under the Emergency Powers (Defence) Act 1939. The Act and Regulations were originally passed and made, *inter alia*, to conserve the nation's resources for the prosecution of war in a time of great national danger. They were continued in being by Parliament, *inter alia*, to control the disposal of goods and services during a crisis in the national economy. The prohibited acts were declared to be involving heavy penalties. I cannot regard breach of such regulations as other than acts subversive of the interests of the State, acts of which the law will not take cognisance except to visit them with penalties. In my opinion the Courts cannot be invoked to compel recompense to a person whose claim to recompense arises out of his diverting goods and services to projects which, *ex hypothesi*, Parliament has declared to be against the national interest."

LORD JAMIESON delivered a concurring judgment.

In this case it may, however, have been possible to seek the quasi-contractual remedy of recompense—although given Lord Patrick's remarks that these were acts "subversive of the interests of the state", the pursuer's chance of success may not have been any the greater.[25]

The question of remoteness of the connection between the object of the statute and the contract is relevant here. If allowing the contract to be enforced will defeat the purpose of the statute, then the court is unlikely to intervene.[26] However, as the following case demonstrates, because of the potentially severe consequences of such a finding, courts have been reluctant to draw an inference of illegality.

7–20 **St John Shipping Corporation v Joseph Rank Ltd**

[1957] 1 Q.B. 267

English High Court, Queen's Bench: Devlin J

The "St John" loaded wheat at Mobile, Alabama. By the time she arrived at Liverpool in November, she was laden beyond her winter zone load line ("Plimsoll line") limits. By s.44 of the Merchant Shipping (Safety and Load Line Conventions) Act 1932, a British load line ship

> "shall not be so loaded as to submerge ... the load line indicating or purporting to indicate the maximum depth to which the ship is for the time being entitled under the load line rules to be loaded".

The master was prosecuted, but as the fines imposed were substantially less than the extra freight earned from overloading the ship, the cargo owners withheld an equivalent amount of freight due.

The unpaid sums were held recoverable, because it was not the purpose of the statute to prohibit contracts for the carriage of goods.

7–21 "DEVLIN J: ... [T]he question always is whether the statute meant to prohibit the contract which is sued on. One of the tests commonly used ... to ascertain the true meaning of the statute is to inquire whether or not the object of the statute was to protect the public or a class of persons, that is, to protect the public from claims for services by unqualified persons or to protect licensed persons from competition ... If in considering the effect of the statute the only inquiry that has to be made is whether an act is illegal, it cannot matter for whose benefit the statute was passed; the fact that the statute makes the act illegal is of itself enough. But if one is considering whether a contract not expressly prohibited by the Act is impliedly prohibited, such considerations are relevant in order to determine the scope of the statute ...

[T]he determining factor is the true effect and meaning of the statute ... I have already indicated the basis of this argument, namely, that the statute being one which according to its preamble is passed to give effect to a convention for promoting the safety of life and property at sea, it is therefore passed for the benefit of cargo owners among others. That this is an important consideration is certainly established by the authorities. But ... it is one only of the tests. The fundamental question is whether the statute means to prohibit the contract. The statute is to be construed in the ordinary way; one must have regard to all relevant considerations and no single consideration, however important, is conclusive.

---

[25] See LJ Macgregor, *Illegal Contracts and Unjustified Enrichment*, 2000, 4 E.L.R. 19 "[the judgments] disclose a disinclination to provide the unlucky joiner with any aid whatsoever".

[26] See, for example, *Anderson Ltd v Daniel* [1924] 1 K.B. 138.

Two questions are involved. The first—and the one which hitherto has usually settled the matter—is: does the statute mean to prohibit contracts at all. If this be answered in the affirmative, then one must ask: does this contract belong to the class which the statute intends to prohibit? For example, a person is forbidden by statute from using an unlicensed vehicle on the highway. If one asks oneself whether there is in such an enactment an implied prohibition of all contracts for the use of unlicensed vehicles, the answer may well be that there is, and that contracts of hire would be unenforceable. But if one asks oneself whether there is an implied prohibition of contracts for the carriage of goods by unlicensed vehicles or for the repairing of unlicensed vehicles or for the garaging of unlicensed vehicles, the answer may well be different. The answer may be that collateral contracts of this sort are not within the ambit of the statute.

The relevant section, s. 44(1) of the Merchant Shipping (Safety and Load Line Conventions) Act 1932, provides that the ship 'shall not be so loaded as to submerge' the appropriate load line. It may be that a contract for the loading of the ship which necessarily has this effect would be unenforceable. It might be, for example, that the contract for bunkering at Port Everglades which had the effect of submerging the load line, if governed by English law, would have been unenforceable. But an implied prohibition of contracts of loading does not necessarily extend to contracts for the carnage of goods by improperly loaded vessels. Of course if the parties knowingly agree to ship goods by an overloaded vessel, such a contract would be illegal; but its illegality does not depend on whether it is impliedly prohibited by the statute, since it falls within the first of the two general heads of illegality I noted above where there is an intent to break the law. The way to test the question whether a particular class of contract is prohibited by the statute is to test it in relation to a contract made in ignorance of its effect.

In my judgment contracts for the carriage of goods are not within the ambit of this statute at all. A court should not hold that any contract or class of contracts is prohibited by statute unless there is a clear implication, or 'necessary inference,' as Parke, B., put it, that the statute so intended. If a contract has as its whole object the doing of the very act which the statute prohibits, it can be argued that you can hardly make sense of a statute which forbids an act and yet permits to be made a contract to do it; that is a clear implication. But unless you get a clear implication of that sort, I think that a court ought to be very slow to hold that a statute intends to interfere with the rights and remedies given by the ordinary law of contract. Caution in this respect is, I think, especially necessary in these times when so much of commercial life is governed by regulations of one sort or another which may easily be broken without wicked intent. Persons who deliberately set out to break the law cannot expect to be aided in a court of justice, but it is a different matter when the law is unwittingly broken. To nullify a bargain in such circumstances frequently means that in a case— perhaps of such triviality that no authority would have felt it worth while to prosecute—a seller, because he cannot enforce his civil rights, may forfeit a sum vastly in excess of any penalty that a criminal court would impose; and the sum forfeited will not go into the public purse but into the pockets of someone who is lucky enough to pick up the windfall or astute enough to have contrived to get it. It is questionable how far this contributes to public morality ... It may be questionable also whether public policy is well served by driving from the seat of judgment everyone who has been guilty of a minor transgression. Commercial men who have unwittingly offended against one of a multiplicity of regulations may nevertheless feel that they have not thereby forfeited all right to justice, and may go elsewhere for it if courts of law will not give it to them. In the last resort they will, if necessary, set up their own machinery for dealing with their own disputes in the way that those whom the law puts beyond the pale, such as gamblers, have done. I have said enough, and perhaps more than enough, to show how important it is that the courts should be slow to imply the statutory prohibition of the contracts and should do so only when the implication is quite clear."

7–22 Note Devlin J's clear statement that a contract knowingly made in breach of the statute would be automatically illegal, which he contrasted with laws being "unwittingly broken".

This English case needs careful treatment. Although only a first instance decision, Devlin J's judgment is generally recognised as an authoritative statement of the relevant law, here as in England. Nevertheless, the remedy of withholding payment in this way would in Scotland be covered by the principle of mutuality, so that *retention* could be exercised. If, however, the owner of the wheat were allowed to withhold the freight, would they not have been unjustly enriched?

The English Court of Appeal approved Devlin J's view in the case of *Archbolds (Freightage) Ltd v Spanglett Ltd.*[27] Archbold subcontracted with Spanglett for the carriage of some whisky owned by a third party. Such carriage was only lawful by holders of an "A" type licence—a type held by Archbold, and that Archbold believed Spanglett also held. In fact, Spanglett did not. Due to a Spanglett employee's negligence, the whisky was stolen. When Archbold sued for breach of contract, Spanglett argued that the contract was impliedly illegal, since they did not in fact hold the requisite licence lawfully to carry the goods. The court held that Archbolds—who did not know about the contravention—could recover the cost of the whisky: breach of the statute regarding the subcarrier's licence did not of itself render the contract illegal, but only its method of performance.

The distinction in treatment between contracts illegal in their formation on one hand, and contracts which are legal in construction but which are performed illegally on the other, was expounded in the following Scottish case.

7–23 **Dowling & Rutter v Abacus Frozen Foods (No.2) Ltd**

2002 S.L.T. 491

Outer House: Lord Johnston

In the course of their business as an employment agency, the pursuers supplied workers to the defenders' fish processing factory. It transpired after some months that the workers were illegal immigrants, who were subsequently repatriated. The pursuers claimed fees due to them from the defenders up to the point where the illegal immigrants ceased to work. The defenders refused to pay, on the grounds that the pursuer had performed the contract in breach of immigration legislation, thus rendering the contract illegal and unenforceable. On the evidence, there was no question of either party being aware of the unlawful status of the workers.

The court held that the pursuers were allowed to claim for payment.

7–24 "LORD JOHNSTON: ... The issue of statutory illegality to my mind raises a separate issue from what might be described as simple, common law criminality or illegality either with regard to the purpose of a particular contract, or the way in which it has been performed. It is necessary to analyse in each case the extent to which the contract in question is affected by, or governed by, the illegal act, and obviously, if a party is seeking to rely upon his own illegal act, the court will not assist. This is perfectly apparent from the case of *Jamieson*, where the builder knowingly exceeded the licence and was thus performing work which was in fact unauthorised by statute and therefore illegal. On the other side of this spectrum, however, it is clear that just because illegality enters into a contract, that does not necessarily make it unenforceable. Again ... there has to be some

[27] *Archbolds (Freightage) Ltd v Spanglett Ltd* [1961] 1 Q.B. 374.

> scope for considerations of inadvertence, irrelevance, immateriality, innocence and so on to mitigate significantly or even exclude the issue.
>
> In my opinion, the most important consideration in this context in this case, relating to the issue of illegality, as a starting point is that the contract itself was perfectly legal for a legal purpose with legal aims, that is to say the provision of labour for value. If illegality supervened or entered upon the scene, it was purely by reason of the status of the workers in question in relation to the Immigration Act. This seems to me to be in a direct parallel with the position to be found in the *St John Shipping Corporation* case where the fact that the ship was overloaded did not in any way affect the performance of the contract of freight for which payment was being claimed. It was at worst or at least a parallel issue of illegality separate from the actual performance of the contract itself. It is not entirely clear to me in the *St John* case whether or not the master of the ship knew he was overloaded, but that does not appear to have affected the reasoning of the court who looked at the matter surely as an issue of connection between the performance of the contract and the so called illegality. If there is a distinction to be drawn between the present case and the *St John* case it may be that, in relation to s 8, the purpose of the statute is to prevent immigrant workers working illegally . . . Be that as it may, it does not seem to me that prevents me from looking at the role of the pursuers in this case to assess the extent to which they might be guilty of "turpitude". This is not an easy branch of the law but I have come to the view that, at the end of the day, the issue is essentially one of equitable remedy in the sense that a person who is seeking to rely knowingly on his own illegal act cannot gain by it but equally should not lose by it if the illegal act is committed by somebody else completely outwith his own knowledge, actual or constructive. This proposition seems to me to apply equally whether one is concerned with issues of public policy or statutory prohibition."

This decision has been welcomed for the fact that Lord Johnston characterised the question as being ultimately one of equity.[28]

Consequences of illegality

Apart from any criminal penalty that may result from illegality, what are the consequences of illegality upon the rights and obligations of the parties under a contract, whether the contract is void or merely unenforceable? The consequences will depend not only on the nature of the illegality, but also on whether property or money has already changed hands; on whether the contract was designed to achieve an illegal purpose; on whether the contract was legal but the intended purpose was not; and on whether the contract was legal but the method in which it was performed was not.[29] **7–25**

The contours of illegality, public policy and unenforceability are necessarily blurred and a contract need not be tainted with moral turpitude for courts to refuse to enforce it.

The general principle is *ex turpi causa non oritur actio* (no action arises from an act of turpitude). Thus, a contract tainted with illegality cannot be enforced by either party. Furthermore, in such circumstances, the person in possession of property or money transferred is in a better position (*in turpi causa melior est conditio possidentis*), in that the property may be

---

[28] J Thomson, "Illegal Contracts in Scots Law", 2002 S.L.T. 18, 153. However, the same writer also respectfully criticises the judgment as confusing the issues: whether a contract is illegal or not is not a question of equitable remedy; whether the parties to an illegal contract should be allowed to rely on the doctrine of unjustified enrichment to redress their losses is.

[29] Ultimately, it is a matter of construction of the facts whether or not the contract has an illegal purpose—a construction that is often difficult to establish. See *Neilson v Stewart*, 1991 S.L.T. 523 at 525 for a brief discussion of this point.

retained, although it may not be possible to transfer title if the contract was void ab initio as a result of illegality.

7–26 The major exception to the general principle arises where the parties are not *in pari delicto*, i.e. are not equally blameworthy. In English law, the concept is extended to introduce *locus poenitentiae*, that is room for repentance. In *Bigos v Bousted*,[30] a contract to supply lire in Italy in return for payment in sterling in England contravened UK currency regulations. The person who was to supply the currency failed to do so and the other party, in belated repentance, sought to recover payment on the basis that he was no longer *in pari delicto*. The court found that, since both parties were equally to blame, neither could enforce the contract.

Where, however, one party is subjected to fraud or oppression from that party is not *in pari delicto*; nor legally blameworthy, where the contract is illegal because it fails to comply with a statute the purpose of which is to protect a class of persons (such as hire-purchasers, or tenants) to which that party belongs.

Similarly, if one of the parties has no part in the illegality, they are not tainted by it and may still sue under the contract. If, for example, X hires a vehicle to Y and, without X's knowledge or consent, Y uses the vehicle to commit a robbery, X may nevertheless sue Y under the contract of hire.

7–27

Barr v Crawford
1983 S.L.T. 481
Outer House; Lord Mayfield

Mr and Mrs Barr owned a bar in Falkirk. Due to Mr Barr's ill health, they put the bar up for sale. The bar licence was up for renewal by the local licensing board.

The first defender (the then provost of Falkirk) and another defender indicated to Mrs Barr that the licence would be refused for a year. She was alarmed, as a sale of the bar was imminent. According to Mrs Barr, Crawford indicated that 10 people would have to be "bought" and that £10,000 would be needed. Mrs Barr averred that she initially handed over £8,000 in bank notes to the defenders.

Mrs Barr claimed the return of the alleged payments. The defenders claimed that the relationship between the parties was tainted with illegality and that the action was therefore irrelevant.

In the absence of evidence that she was not *in pari delicto*, the action was dismissed.

7–28 "LORD MAYFIELD: ... [Crawford] has averred that he had no knowledge of the £8,000 allegedly handed over to O'Connor. He avers: 'In the circumstances averred by the pursuer (which is denied) it was handed over pursuant to an agreement which constituted a *pacta illicita* [*sic*] and is accordingly not recoverable by the pursuers.' A similar averment is made in respect of the defender O'Connor. Additionally it is averred that the payment was a bribe to a public servant to act contrary to his duty. Reference is made to s.1(2) of the Public Bodies Corrupt Practices Act 1889.

As I have indicated the record is not in a satisfactory state. The pursuer has not answered or even formally denied certain averments made by both defenders. On the above averments I am satisfied that the pursuer's actings must be regarded as having been tainted with illegality. On her own averments she has stated that she handed over initially £8,000 following a meeting on 13 January 1980 with both defenders where she asked what she should do in relation to a threatened withdrawal of her husband's public house licence and was told that £10,000 would be required. It is clear on the averments that the sum was to be supplied in order, as she thought, to save the licence. The sum of

---

[30] *Bigos v Bousted* [1951] 1 All E.R. 92.

£10,000 accordingly was supplied by Mrs Barr to achieve that purpose and was in fact a bribe. Senior counsel for Mrs Barr stated at the hearing that Mrs Barr's husband was at the time seriously ill in hospital, that after she had paid the sum of £8,000 she consulted him about the matter and as a result the police were on hand when the £2,000 was later handed over. That is not clearly stated on record, however, and, in any event, in my view it would not remove the taint of illegality from Mrs Barr's earlier actings in relation to the handing over of £8,000. There was in my view illegality because the payment made by Mrs Barr was a bribe made in the course of a dishonest intention thus tainting the transaction. It can also be described more simply, perhaps, as a corrupt agreement. In my view, the averments of the pursuer indicate a corrupt intention that prevents the court from taking cognisance of the ground of action. I have reached the above conclusion on the facts and having been referred to Bell's *Principles*, s. 35, and Gloag on *Contract* in the chapter '*Pacta Illicita*' beginning at p. 549. I was not able to accept the contention of senior counsel for the pursuer that on the averments there was sufficient to indicate that Mrs Barr was not in *pari delicto*.

It appeared to me on the averments that she reached an agreement to provide the sum of £10,000 and to make payment initially of £8,000. That she did. In my view positive and clear averments would have to be made before it would be possible to draw a conclusion, warranting an inquiry, that Mrs Barr was not in *pari delicto* if, indeed, such a doctrine applies to the present circumstances. Counsel was not able to indicate to me that he could satisfactorily amend. I accordingly dismiss the action."

The effect of illegality on contracts in Scots law, despite its long history, remains uncertain and, to some extent controversial. This is in part due to a relative paucity of modern case law, and uncertainty remains in key areas like the availability of restitutionary remedies. The following extract attempts find some order in the authorities.

[31]*Pacta Illicita* 7–29

Laura J Macgregor
Reid and Zimmerman (eds), *A History of Private Law in Scotland*
(Oxford: Oxford University Press, 2000), Vol.II, p.129

"2. Restitutionary remedies

(a) *Institutional writers*

... [T]he unenforceable/void debate has less relevance to restitutionary remedies. This is because illegal contracts have unique rules governing the application of such remedies. If a contract is illegal by statute[32] or common law, then Scots law, in common with many other systems,[33] denies the contracting parties recourse to restitutionary remedies. This denial results from the application of two Latin maxims. The first, *ex turpi causa non oritur actio*, states that no action may be founded on an immoral cause.[34] Bell explains its

---

[31] Laura Macgregor, "Pacta Illicita", in Reid and Zimmerman, *A History of Private Law in Scotland* (© Oxford: Oxford University Press, 2000).

[32] A.D.M. Forte, "Pacta Illicita", in *The Laws of Scotland: Stair Memorial Encyclopaedia*, Vol.15 (1992), §765; Smith (n.22), 797.

[33] §817 BGB, Art.66 Swiss OR; Arts. 1305, 1306 Spanish Codigo Civil; art. 2035 Italian Codice Civile.

[34] Erskine, I, 3, 3; Trayner, *Latin Maxims and Phrases* (3rd ed., 1883), p.201: "No right of action arises from a disgraceful or immoral consideration-that is, no action can be maintained on a contract or obligation, the consideration of which was disgraceful or immoral".

effect (not surprisingly) by reference to Lord Mansfield's judgment in *Holman v Johnston*.[35]

The second maxim is in *pari causa potior est conditio possidentis*, translated as 'in an equal case (i.e., where the claimants are in a similar position), the possessor is in the better position'[36] or 'where the guilt is shared the defendant's position is the stronger'.[37] The maxim is sometimes stated as in *pari delicto potior est conditio possidentis* (*defendentis*) meaning that in a situation of equal wrongdoing, the position of the possessor (or the defender) is the stronger.[38]

A wealth of discussion of these maxims is found in the institutional writers. Stair's discussion (quoted above) appears in his section on restitution:[39] He distinguishes the case where something is given for an unjust cause from the situation where the parties are both in culpa. In the first case the transaction is void, but only because 'positive law . . . makes them void'. Restitutionary remedies are available as with other void contracts. If both parties are in culpa, the maxim applies and the possessor is preferred. Bankton makes the same distinction:

[W]here the unlawfulness was in the giver, and not in the receiver, in such a case the thing is not to be returned, even tho' the fact for which it was given was not performed; but if the unlawfulness was in the party receiver, and not in the giver, then the thing must be restored, even tho' the cause of giving was performed; if the turpitude was both in the party giver and receiver, then he that is in possession has the advantage by the rule *in pari casu potior est conditio possidentis*; so that the bond given on such consideration is void, but if payment is made, it is not to be repaid.[40]

In the first section he refers to 'unlawful cause' in either the giver or receiver (but not both). In the second section he considers the situation where both are affected by 'turpitude'.

It is possible to conclude from this that if only one party is involved in an unlawful cause then restitutionary remedies are available. There is no consideration of only one party being involved in turpitude, although logically the maxim should not apply, dealing as it does with mutual turpitude, and therefore restitutionary remedies should be available. If both parties are involved in unlawful conduct there is no authority. If both are involved in turpitude, the possessor is preferred.

---

[35] (1775) I Cowp 341 at 343: J.K. Grodecki in his article 'In pari delicto potior est conditio defendentis' (1955) 71 L.Q.R. 254, suggests at 257 that Lord Mansfield "took the maxim either directly from the *Digest* or indirectly from the writings of Grotius, Pufendorf or Pothier, or perhaps even from the *Liber Sextus* of Boniface VIII which contains an important collection of legal rules".

[36] Trayner, *op. cit.*, p.262.

[37] P.H.B. Birks, *An Introduction to the Law of Restitution* (1988), p.301.

[38] Trayner, *op. cit.*, p.262 explains: "When one is in possession of a subject, he is not bound to cede possession to anyone showing as good a title to it as that on which he possesses. The claimant or challenger must show a better title than the possessor, for the law presumes right to possess where possession is held." The cumulative effect of the maxims is consistent with R.I. Pothier, *A Treatise on the Law of Obligations or Contracts* (tr. w: D. Evans, 1806), Vol.I, para.43.

[39] Stair, I, 7, 8. 238.

[40] Bankton, I, 8, 22.

Kames[41] considers only the case of mutual turpitude and Erskine does not differentiate illegality and turpitude.[42] Bell states in *Principles* (but does not cover the point specifically in *Commentaries*[43]):

Illegality or immorality in the obligation itself, as in the consideration or counterpart, makes the whole agreement void; . . .When the obligation, though not illegal or immoral in itself, is entered into with an unlawful purpose or intention, it is void if that purpose was common to both parties, or even if it was known to both. If one of them was ignorant of the unlawful purpose of the other, and discovers it, *he may and ought to refuse performance; and if the contract has already been executed, he may probably obtain restitution or repetition on equitable grounds.* The maxim, 'in pari casu potior est conditio defendentis' (also '*ex turpi causa non oritur actio*'), rests on the principle that 'no court will lend its aid to a man who founds his cause on an immoral or illegal act'; and it further follows from that principle, not only that there is no repetition of money paid or property handed over in furtherance of an unlawful contract or agreement, but that a completed transfer of property or of an interest in property for an unlawful consideration cannot be set aside.[44]

This suggests:

(a) If there is illegality or immorality in the actual obligation, the consideration or counter-performance makes the contract void. This does not tell us whether restitutionary remedies will be available in this situation.
(b) If the contract is for an unlawful purpose of which only one party is aware, restitutionary remedies are available to the innocent party only.
(c) The maxim has the following effects where parties seek to rely on their own immoral or illegal acts: (aa) restitutionary remedies are not available to recover money or property transferred under an 'unlawful contract'; (bb) if the consideration under a contract is 'unlawful', the transaction once executed cannot be set aside. Title would therefore pass in this case. In (c) Bell makes no distinction between unlawful and illegal/immoral conduct.[45] This does not accord with the approach of Stair and Bankton. Bell's approach may be the result of confusing the two maxims. The first (one cannot rely on one's own wrongdoing) contains no requirement of turpitude, while the second, historically, rested on turpitude. Hume provides little assistance, dealing only with mutual *culpa* in the context of smuggling, where the possessor prevails.[46]

(b) *Development of the rules on restitutionary remedies in the cases* Discussion of restitutionary remedies tends to revolve around two cases: *Cuthbertson v Lowes*,[47] and

[41] Kames, 262.
[42] Erskine, III, I, 10. It is only later in Lord Ivory's notes that mutual turpitude is considered. Erskine, III, I, 10, n.3. He refers to the specific *condictio* available in Roman law in situations of turpitude, the *condictio ob turpem vel injustam causam*. The use of this *condictio* has however died out in Scots law, see R. Evans-Jones and D. McKenzie, "Towards a Profile of the *Condictio ob turpem vel injustam causam* in Scots Law", 1994 J.R. 60.
[43] Bell, *Commentaries*, I, 326.
[44] Bell, *Principles*, § 35.
[45] McBryde, *Contract*, 614 does not recognize this distinction.
[46] Hume, *Lectures*, II. 31. See also Kames . . ., art. 23. 151.
[47] (1870) 8 M. 1073. South African law followed the approach in *Cuthbertson* in *Jajbhay v Cassim*, 1939 A.D. 537.

Jamieson v Watt's Trs.[48] However, there are numerous examples of the operation of the maxims in the case law already examined, for example, in the context of bribes,[49] immoral contracts,[50] the sale of offices,[51] *pacta de quota litis*,[52] smuggling,[53] and *sponsiones ludicrae*.[54]

Usually the maxim *in pari causa potior est conditio possidentis* is applied without permitting either party to use a restitutionary remedy. However, in *Palmer v Hutton*, the case of a captured ship, the ship was recovered by the owner and the other party was entitled to recompense[55] for bringing the ship back. This was a contract with the enemy, a classic *pactum illicitum*. This case is difficult to explain given that both parties were undoubtedly involved in turpitude. Similarly, in *Johnston v Rome*,[56] notwithstanding the recognition that the agreement was a *pacta de quota litis*, the agent's right to remuneration was reserved.

In *Cuthbertson*, a contract for the sale of potatoes had been carried out by reference to the Scots rather than the Imperial acre, in contravention of the Weights and Measures Acts. The case pre-dates the Sale of Goods Act 1893, and therefore is not relevant to the changes made by the Act discussed above. The buyer took delivery of the potatoes but refused to pay the price, pleading the illegal nature of the contract. The court did not enforce the contract, but held that the seller was entitled to recover market value for the potatoes, which exceeded the contract price. The Lord President (Inglis) observed that: The defender seeks to retain the pursuer's potatoes without paying anything for them, on the ground that the Court cannot take cognizance of an agreement which by the statutes is declared to be null and void. I cannot readily assent to a proposition which would be productive of a result so inequitable, that I am of the opinion that we are not constrained to do so. No doubt the Court cannot enforce performance of an illegal contract, and *in turpi causa melior est conditio possidentis*, but there is no turpitude in a man selling his potatoes by the Scotch and not by the imperial acre, and although he cannot sue for implement of such a contract, I know of no authority, in the absence of *turpi causa*, to prevent the pursuer from recovering the market value of the potatoes, at the date when they were delivered to the defender.[57]

A previous case on similar facts, *Alexander v McGregor*,[58] had treated the contract as void, not illegal.[59] The Lord President used an approach which was consistent with Stair and Bankton: because no turpitude was involved a restitutionary remedy was available. The Lord President was not specific about which remedy was appropriate, although it is suggested that it was recompense.

---

[48] *Campbell v Scotland* (1778) Mor 9530; *Barr v Crawford*, 1983 S.L.T. 481.
[49] 1950 S.C. 265.
[50] *Sir William Hamilton of Westport v Mary de Gares* (1765) Mor. 9471; *Provan v Calder* (1742) Mor. 9511.
[51] *Carmichael v Erskine* (1823) 2 S. 530; *Bruce v Grant* (1839) I D. 583.
[52] *Bolden v Foggo* (1850) 12 D. 798.
[53] See Bell, *Commentaries*, I, 326.
[54] *Wordsworth v Pettigrew* (1799) Mor. 9524; *County Properties and Developments Limited v Harper*, 1989 S.C.L.R. 597.
[55] The level of recompense was the legal salvage premium ascertained by statute together with expense laid out on the vessel.
[56] (1830) 9 S. 364.
[57] (1870) 8 M .1073 at 1074–1075.
[58] (1845) 7 D. 915.
[59] See *ibid.* Lord Brougham at 917 to 918.

Cuthbertson is difficult to reconcile with *Jamieson v Watt's Trustees*, in which work had been carried out which exceeded the sum authorized under the Defence Regulations 1939. The pursuer sued for payment of the balance of the unauthorized work. using recompense on the basis of *Cuthbertson*, but was unsuccessful.

There is little evidence in the judgments of a distinction between turpitude and illegality, although both Lord Jamieson and Lord Patrick approve a passage from Gloag: 'Illegality in contract admits of degrees ...'[60] The passage from Gloag is an unusual one and does not specifically advocate a turpitude/illegality distinction. Lord Mackay, referring to this distinction, states 'I dislike to found on a possibly over-forced distinction if other courses are open'.[61]

Whether the judges considered that the actual conduct involved turpitude or illegality is not clear. Viewed in a historical context, the regulations in post-war Britain were no doubt important, and breach of the same could have been a very serious matter.

The loss of the turpitude/illegality distinction can be traced to a reliance on English rather than Scottish authorities. There is almost no reference to the works of the institutional writers, and there is a clear desire not to foster differences between English and Scots law.

Therefore, although historically the maxim applied only in cases of turpitude (as opposed to unlawful conduct), this distinction was not made by Bell and was destroyed altogether by *Jamieson v Watt's Trs.*

V. CONCLUSION 7–30

McBryde identified a movement from tolerance towards a refusal to enforce contracts in the twelve-year period following 1774. There is evidence that this was the case.[62] However, since early sources such as Roman law, the *Regiam Majestatem*, and Hope and Balfour's *Practicks* state clearly that *pacta illicita* cannot be enforced, the early eighteenth century could equally be described as a temporary period of enforcement of such contracts, before the courts began to follow the approach espoused in the early sources and particularly in the works of the institutional writers.

As to whether *pacta illicita* moved from being treated as void to unenforceable, it is clear that, historically, they were void. Whether, through the influence of English law or otherwise, such contracts begin to be treated as unenforceable is a difficult question to answer. Judgments tend to describe cases as 'irrelevant', and contracts as null or as having no effect, or the court may simply refuse to enforce the contract without further comment. To treat such contracts as unenforceable would be to follow English law but not the rest of Europe.

Although this analysis has been historical, the issues examined are live ones. Many reasons have been used to justify the non-enforcement of *pacta illicita*. Where the justification is not obvious, new cases must be decided on an incremental basis. Transfer of title is in an ambiguous and unsatisfactory state. The unresolved void/unenforceable debate surrounding illegal contracts has a real effect on this issue. Finally, although the principles governing the availability of restitutionary remedies are clear, a look at their

---

[60] Gloag (n.21), 549.

[61] 1950 S.C. 265 at 276.

[62] Particularly in *sponsiones ludicrae* and smuggling. However, in the sale of offices it was not until *Gardner v Grant* in 1835 that such contracts were not upheld, and *pacta de quota litis* have always been treated as void.

historical development shows that Scots law turned away from Stair to deny recovery in cases of illegality, whether turpitude was present or not. This approach casts the net wider, denying more parties recourse to remedies. There is evidence in other jurisdictions of a move away from this approach.[63] These issues require clarification, and this chapter has attempted to provide an historical backdrop for future developments in the law."

Contracts and contractual terms in restraint of trade

7–31 "There can be no doubt that, according to the law of Scotland, a paction against the liberty of trade is illegal; and that agreements, by which a man binds himself that he will not carry on a trade of any kind though limited in space, or a particular trade if unlimited in space, are both equally bad in law."[64]

This may have been an accurate statement of the law in 1863 in England, but whether it was also the law in Scotland is open to doubt.[65] The general principle in Scotland is, following the canon law, "every paction produceth action". The role of the courts is to enforce contracts, not otherwise. That one could contractually bind oneself through a "perpetual indenture"—effectively sell oneself into bondage—was a common feature of Scottish society until the end of the 19th century and courts were even reluctant to deny interdict to a pursuer seeking to enforce such a contract until relatively recent times.[66] Indeed, even involuntary, or forced bondage was common in Scotland until the end of the 18th century.[67]

As markets, and in particular labour markets opened up during the industrial revolution, courts increasingly came across covenants, or stipulations in contracts restricting a party's freedom to carry on business after the termination of a contract, for example of employment, of partnership or for the sale of a business. The courts were confronted with two conflicting interests: the interests of an employer, for example, to protect the business from future

---

[63] See the numerous exceptions to the non-recovery rule in English Law: G.H. Treitel, *The Law of Contract* (9th ed., 1995), 448. See also: Art.1131 French CC; Art.904 Greek Civil Code; American Law Institute, *Second Restatement of Contracts* (1991), §197; s.6 and s.7 New Zealand Contracts Act 1970; Art.1422 Quebec Civil Code; Israeli General Contracts (General Part) Law, ss.21, 31.

[64] Lord Justice-Clerk Inglis in *Watson v Neuffert* (1863) 1 M. 1110 at 1112.

[65] See WW McBryde, *The Law of Contracts in Scotland*, 3rd edn (Edinburgh: W.Green, 2007) paras 19–80—19–84; and see PJ Sutherland, "Contractual Restrictive Covenants", K Reid and R Zimmermann (eds), *A History of Private Law in Scotland* (Oxford: Oxford University Press, 2000).

[66] The new approach began with the *Nordenfelt* case, para.7–33 onwards.

[67] Writing in 1773, Erskine could state: "It has been said by some writers, that one cannot bind one's self to perpetual service; such obligation being contrary to liberty, which is an unalienable right. But it is hard to conceive, how an engagement of that sort, which is to last for life, is more inconsistent with liberty, than one which is to expire after twenty or thirty years. And there appears nothing repugnant, either to reason, or to the peculiar doctrines of Christianity, in a contract by which one binds himself to perpetual service under a master, who, on his part, is obliged to maintain the other in all the necessities of life ... This however is certain, that excepting the case either of Turks or Moors, or of negroes bought for the use of the European settlements in the Indies, the power claimed masters, of selling their servants, is not allowed in any Christian country", *Institute*, I vii 62. Despite the famous decision of Lord Kames in *Wedderburn v Knight* 1778, in which the Inner House held that "the dominion assumed over this Negro, under the law of Jamaica, being unjust, could not be supported in this country to any extent", forced labour, or "perpetual servitude" in mining and salt panning under pre-1707 Scottish statutes, and under the Scottish Poor Laws of 1579 and 1597, persisted until the end of the eighteenth century (see BF Duckham, "Serfdom in Eighteenth Century Scotland", *History* (1969) 178–197). The deportation of Scottish indentured servants to the West Indies throughout the eighteenth century is now notorious (see SP Newman, *A New World of Labor: the Development of Plantation Slavery in the British Atlantic* (Philadelphia: University of Pennsylvania Press, 2013); D Dobson, *Scottish Emigration to Colonial America, 1607–1785* (Athens: University of Georgia Press, 1994).

competition from a former employee; against the interests of a former employee to continue to earn a living. Underlying this conflict of interests were two conflicting principles of public policy: the freedom of the parties to contract; and the freedom of the parties to trade. To what extent should the parties be free, by means of a contract, to restrain their freedom to trade? In a modern economy, such issues are tackled by what are generally referred to as competition laws. In the absence of legislative intervention, redress was sought in the courts and at common law. The courts saw the issue as a matter of public policy and, on that basis, determined that covenants in restraint of trade were prima facie unenforceable.

General effect of restraints on trade

The general principles governing restraints on trade have been heavily influenced by English law. The English House of Lords decision in *Nordenfelt v Maxim Nordenfelt Gun and Ammunition Co*[68] is generally regarded as the modern restatement of the rules. **7–32**

Nordenfelt v Maxim Nordenfelt Guns and Ammunition Co **7–33**

[1894] A.C. 535

English House of Lords: Lord Herschell LC, Lords Ashbourne, Macnaghten, Morris and Watson

Nordenfelt sold his guns and ammunition business to the Nordenfelt Company (which he set up) and agreed, in writing, that he would not compete with the Nordenfelt Company. Under the agreement, Nordenfelt received £237,000 in cash, £50,000 in paid-up shares in the company and remained managing director of the company for seven years at a remuneration of £2,000 per annum and a share in the profits.

Two years later, the Nordenfelt Company combined with the Maxim Gun and Ammunition Company. The new company, Maxim Nordenfelt entered into a new covenant with the plaintiff which provided that he

> "shall not, during the term of twenty-five years . . . engage except on behalf of [Maxim Nordenfelt] either directly or indirectly in the trade or business of a manufacturer of guns, gun mountings or carriages, gunpowder explosives or ammunition, or in any business competing or liable to compete in any way with that for the time being carried on by [Maxim Nordenfelt]".

Nordenfelt subsequently entered into an agreement with other manufacturers of guns and ammunition and Maxim Nordenfelt successfully sought an injunction to restrain him.

> "LORD MACNAUGHTEN: . . . The true view at the present time, I think, is this: the public have an interest in every person's carrying on his trade freely: so has the individual. All interference with individual liberty of action in trading, and all restraints of trade of themselves, if there is nothing more, are contrary to public policy, and therefore void. That is the general rule. But there are exceptions: restraints of trade and interference with individual liberty of action may be justified by the special circumstances of a particular case. It is a sufficient justification, and indeed it is the only justification, if the restriction is reasonable—reasonable, that is, in reference to the interests of the parties concerned and reasonable in reference to the interests of the public, so framed and so guarded as to afford adequate protection to the party in whose favour it is imposed, while at the same time it is in no way injurious to the public . . .

[68] *Nordenfelt v Maxim Nordenfelt Gun and Ammunition Co* [1894] A.C. 535.

To a certain extent, different considerations must apply in cases of apprenticeship and cases of that sort, on the other hand, and cases of the sale of a business or dissolution of a partnership on the other. A man is bound an apprentice because he wishes to learn a trade and to practise it. A man may sell because he is getting too old for the strain and worry of business, or because he wishes for some other reason to retire from business altogether. Then there is obviously more freedom of contract between buyer and seller than between master and servant or between an employer and a person seeking employment.

When the question is how far interference with the liberty of an individual in a particular trade offends against the interest of the public, there is not much difficulty in measuring the offence and coming to a judgment on the question. The difficulty is much greater when the question of public policy is considered at large and without direct reference to the interests of the individual under restraint. It is a principle of law and of public policy that trading should be encouraged and that trade should be free; but a fetter is placed and trading is discouraged if a man who has built up a valuable business is not to be permitted to dispose of the fruits of his labours to the best advantage. It has been said that if the restraint be general 'the whole of the public is restrained' —a phrase not, I think, particularly accurate, or perhaps particularly intelligible. It has been said that when a person is debarred from carrying on his trade within a certain limit of space he will carry it on elsewhere, and thus the public outside the area of restriction will gain an advantage which may be set off, as it were, against the disadvantage resulting to the public within the limited area. That is, perhaps, a justified observation in a case of apprenticeship and cases of that sort; but it is, I think, rather a fanciful way of looking at the matter in the case of the sale of goodwill. Applied to that sort of case, it seems to me to be just one of those unrealities which tend to confuse this question. What has the public to hope in this question. What has the public to hope in the way of future service from a man who sells his business meaning to trade no more? Is it likely that he will begin the struggle of life again working at his old trade or profession in some remote place where he has no interest and no connections? Is the possibility that he may do so a factor to be taken into consideration? Now, when all trades and businesses are open to everybody alike, it is not very easy to appreciate the injury to the public resulting from the withdrawal of one individual . . .

Now, in the present case it was hardly disputed that the restraint was reasonable, having regard to the interests of the parties at the time when the restraint was entered into. It enabled Mr Nordenfelt to obtain the full value of what he had to sell; without it the purchasers could not have been protected in the possession of what they wished to buy. Was it reasonable in the interests of the public? It can hardly be injurious to the public, that is the British public, to prevent a person from carrying on a trade in weapons of war abroad. But apart from that present feature in the present case, how can the public be injured by the transfer of a business from one hand to another? If a business is profitable there will be no lack of persons ready to carry it on. In this particular case, the purchasers brought in fresh capital, and had at least the opportunity of retaining Mr Nordenfelt's services. But then it was said there is another way in which the public may be injured. Mr Nordenfelt has 'committed industrial suicide,' and he can no longer earn his living at the trade which he has made peculiarly his own, he may be brought to want and become a burden to the public. My Lords, this seems to me to be very far-fetched. Mr Nordenfelt received over £200,000 for what he sold. He may have got rid of the money. I do not know how that is. But even so, I would answer the argument in the words of Tindal C.J.: 'If the contract is a reasonable one at the time it is entered into we are not bound to look out for improbable or extravagant contingencies in order to make it void'."

The events described here were critical to the development of the UK arms industry. They helped establish the basis of re-armament in the period leading up to the Great War.

Reference was made earlier in this chapter to the concept of public policy and its effects on the legality of contracts. Lord Macnaughten, and in particular the Scottish judge, Lord Watson, stressed that public policy continues to lie behind the restraint of trade doctrine. Prior to this decision, the position in English law was that covenants in restraint of trade were unenforceable, on the grounds of public policy. It is doubtful whether this was the position at common law in Scotland, where

> "contracts were enforced except in the case of severe restraint on personal liberty ... Scots law mitigated the harshness of 'every paction produceth action', not the opposite".[69]

However, public policy no longer determined that restraints on trade were illegal, but merely presumed to be illegal, unless proved to be "reasonable", under Lord Macnaughten's test, in the interests of the parties and of the public. Is there any significant difference between "public policy" and "public interest" (the second limb of Lord Macnaughten's test)?

The extent of the doctrine

At about the same time, the House of Lords decided *Mogul Steamship Co v Macgregor*[70] **7–34** (referred to by Lord Reid in the following case). That case effectively allowed a cartel to drive a competitor out of business through anti-competitive practices, something that would be illegal today under the Competition Act 1998. At what was the high-water mark of laissez faire economics in Britain, *Nordenfelt* and *Mogul Steamship* both show a great reluctance by the judiciary to interfere with the "free" market. By contrast, the United States Congress in 1890 passed the Sherman Antitrust Act, 1890, making "monopolisation" (s.1) and "every contract, combination ... or conspiracy in restraint of trade or commerce' crimes to which severe penalties attached". Whereas the United States developed a panoply of antitrust, or competition laws over the next half century, it was not until 1948 that the first UK anti-monopoly laws were enacted. Instead, monopolies, cartels and restrictive practices of all sorts thrived in this country's economies.

So pervasive was the judiciary's abstention from this area, that until the 1960s it was generally assumed that even Lord Macnaughten's limited judicial constraint on anti-competitive behaviour applied only to contracts of employment (generally, courts are most strict in applying this test of reasonableness to restraints in contracts of employment); to a lesser extent partnership contracts and contracts for the sale of a business; and, to a much more limited degree, to trade association agreements.[71]

The general view was that the doctrine would have no application to any other areas of business, for example exclusive distribution and supply agreements, leases tying public houses to specific breweries and so on, even although these might impose severe restraints by a dominant supplier on the other party. In *Esso Petroleum v Harper's Garage*,[72] the House of Lords applied the doctrine to "solus" or exclusive supply agreements, thereby indicating that the categories covered by the doctrine are not closed.

---

[69] WW McBryde, *The Law of Contract in Scotland*, 3rd edn (Edinburgh: W. Green, 2007), para.19–83.
[70] *Mogul Steamship Co v Macgregor* [1892] A.C. 25.
[71] The few cases where a party asked the court to extend the doctrine were rare and unsuccessful.
[72] *Esso Petroleum v Harper's Garage* [1968] A.C. 269.

7–35 **Esso Petroleum Co Ltd v Harper's Garage (Stourport) Ltd**

[1968] A.C. 269

English House of Lords: Lords Reid, Morris of Borth-y-Gest, Hodson, Pearce and Wilberforce

Harper's owned two garages: the Corner Garage (C) and the Mustow Green Garage (M). Esso entered into "solus", or exclusive supply agreements with Harper's in relation to both sites.

In return for an advance from Esso, secured by a mortgage over C, repayable over 21 years, Harper's covenanted to keep C open during normal working hours, to purchase their total requirements of petrol from Esso for the duration of the mortgage, and not to buy or sell other than Esso's petrol and lubricants.

Harper's entered into a similar exclusive supply agreement over M, but without a mortgage, the contract to run for four years and five months, with the additional covenant by Harper's to impose a similar restraint on any purchaser of M garage.

In 1961, Jet petrol came on the market at significant discounts. Harper's began to sell it. Esso sought injunctions to restrain them.

The House applied Lord Macnaughten's test in *Nordenfelt* and found the restraint on C unreasonable and therefore void, but the restraint on M reasonable and valid.

7–36 "LORD REID: ... One must always bear in mind that an agreement in restraint of trade is not generally unlawful if the parties choose to abide by it: it is only unenforceable if a party chooses not to abide by it.

It is true that it would be an innovation to hold that ordinary negative covenants preventing the use of a particular site for trading of all kinds or of a particular kind are within the scope of the doctrine of restraint of trade. I do not think that they are. Restraint of trade appears to me to imply that a man contracts to give up some freedom which otherwise he would have had. A person buying or leasing land had no previous right to be there at all, let alone to trade there, and, when he takes possession of that land subject to a negative restrictive covenant, he gives up no right or freedom which he previously had ... In the present case the respondents, before they made this agreement, were entitled to use this land in any lawful way that they choose, and by making this agreement they agreed to restrict their right by giving up their right to sell there petrol not supplied by the appellants ...

Where two experienced traders are bargaining on equal terms and one has agreed to a restraint for reasons which seem good to him, the court is in grave danger of stultifying itself if it says that it knows that trader's interest better than he does himself. There may well be cases, however, where, although the party to be restrained has deliberately accepted the main terms of the contract, he has been at a disadvantage as regards other terms: for example, where a set of conditions has been incorporated which has not been the subject of negotiation—there the court may have greater freedom to hold them unreasonable.

I think that in some cases where the court has held that a restraint was not in the interests of the parties it would have been more correct to hold that the restraint was against the public interest. For example, in *Kores Manufacturing Co Ltd v Kolok Manufacturing Co Ltd* the parties had agreed that neither would employ any man who had left the service of the other. From their own points of view there was probably very good reason for that; but it could well be held to be against the public interest to interfere in this way with the freedom of their employees. If the parties chose to abide by their agreement an employee would have no more right to complain than the Mogul company had in the *Mogul* case [[1891-94] All E.R.Rep. 263; [1892] A.C. 25.); but the law would not countenance their agreement by enforcing it. Moreover in cases where a party, who is in no way at a disadvantage in bargaining, chooses to take a calculated risk, I see no reason why the court should say that he acted against his own interests: but it can say that the restraint might well produce a situation which would be contrary to the public interest ...

In my view there is sufficient material to justify a decision that ties of less than five years were insufficient, in the circumstances of the trade when these agreements were made to afford adequate protection to the appellants' legitimate interests. If that is so, I cannot find anything in the details of the Mustow Green agreement which would indicate that it is unreasonable. It is true that, if some of the provisions were operated by the appellants in a manner which would be commercially unreasonable, they might put the respondents in difficulties. I think, however, that a court must have regard to the fact that the appellants must act in such a way that they will be able to obtain renewals of the great majority of their very numerous ties, some of which will come to an end almost every week. If in such circumstances a garage owner chooses to rely on the commercial probity and good sense of the producer, I do not think that a court should hold his agreement unreasonable because it is legally capable of some misuse. I would therefore allow the appeal as regards the Mustow Green agreement.

...

LORD MORRIS OF BORTH-Y-GEST: ... I take the test to be as laid down by Lord **7–37**
Macnaghten in his speech in *Nordenfelt v Maxim Nordenfelt Guns and Ammunition Co Ltd* [1894) A.C. at p. 565.

If the agreements are regarded, as I think that they must be, as being prima facie in restraint of trade then the question arises whether there is validity in the contention that the restriction was merely of the trading use to be made of a particular piece of land and that, as a consequence, there was exclusion of the applicability of the doctrine of restraint of trade ... There is a considerable difference between the covenants in the present case and covenants of the kind which might be entered into by a purchaser or by a lessee. If one who seeks to take a lease of land knows that the only lease which is available to him is a lease with a restriction, then he must either take what is offered (on the appropriate financial terms) or he must seek a lease elsewhere. No feature of public policy requires that, if he freely contracted, he should be excused from honouring his contract. In no rational sense could it be said that, if he took a lease with a restriction as to trading, he was entering into a contract that interfered with the free exercise of his trade or his business or with his 'individual liberty of action in trading.' His freedom to pursue his trade or earn his living is not impaired merely because there is some land belonging to someone else on which he cannot enter for the purposes of his trade or business. In such a situation (i.e. that of voluntarily taking a lease of land with a restrictive covenant) it would not seem sensible to regard the doctrine of restraint of trade as having application. There would be nothing which could be described as interference with individual liberty of action in trading. There is a clear difference between the case where someone fetters his future by parting with a freedom than that which he possesses, and the case where someone seeks to claim a greater freedom than that which he possesses or has arranged to acquire. So, also, if someone seeks to buy a part of the land of a vendor and can only buy on the terms that he will covenant with the vendor not to put the land to some particular use, there would seem in principle to be no reason why the contract should not be honoured.

...

LORD HODSON: ... Having rejected, as I do, the argument that there is a special **7–38**
class of contract relating to land which is outside the scope of the doctrine of restraint of trade, I come now to the question whether the covenants in question here are reasonable either in the private interests of the contracting parties or in the public interest. There

might be thought to be some risk of proceedings being taken in certain cases of a nuisance character where the restraint of trade is readily justifiable on the basis of long-established practice in a particular sphere, such as the brewery cases on which the appellants rely, but I cannot see any practical way of hedging about the right of a party to a contract to attack it on the ground that it has been entered into in unreasonable restraint of trade. After all a man, who freely enters into a bargain will, normally, expect to be held bound by it, and I do not anticipate a spate of litigation in which contracts of, say, 'sole agency' will be assailed. In the case of agreements between commercial companies for regulating their trade relations the parties are usually the best judges of what is reasonable. In such a case, as Viscount Haldane L.C. said in *North-Western Salt Co Ltd v Electrolytic Alkali Co Ltd.* [1914] A.C. 461 at p. 471: 'the law ... still looks carefully to the interests of the public, but it regards the parties as the best judges of what is reasonable as between themselves ...'

I would rest my decision on the public interest rather than on that of the parties, public interest being a surer foundation than the interest of private persons or corporations when widespread commercial activities such as these are concerned.

...

7–39 LORD PEARCE: ... Where there are no circumstances of oppression, the court should tread warily in substituting its own views for those of current commerce generally and the contracting parties in particular. For that reason, I consider that the courts require on such a matter full guidance from evidence of all the surrounding circumstances and of relevant commercial practice ...

... [W]hen free and competent parties agree and the background provides some commercial justification on both sides for their bargain, and there in no injury to the community, I think that the onus should be easily discharged. Public policy, like other unruly horses, is apt to change its stance; and public policy is the ultimate basis of the courts' reluctance to enforce restraints. Although the decided cases are almost invariably based on unreasonableness between the parties, it is ultimately on the ground of public policy that the court will decline to enforce a restraint as being unreasonable between the parties; and a doctrine based on the general commercial good must always bear in mind the changing face of commerce. There is not, as some cases seem to suggest, a separation between what is reasonable on grounds of public policy and what is reasonable as between the parties. There is one broad question: is it in the interests of the community that this restraint should as between the parties, be held to be reasonable and enforceable? ...

Somewhere there must be a line between those contracts which are in restraint of trade and whose reasonableness can, therefore, be considered by the courts, and those contracts which merely regulate the normal commercial relations between the parties and are, therefore, free from the doctrine ...

One of the mischiefs at which the doctrine was aimed originally was the mischief of monopolies; but this was dealt with by legislation and the executive has from time to time taken efficient steps to prevent it. Indeed, in the case of petrol ties there has now been exacted (we are told) from the petrol producers an undertaking which in practice limits these ties to five years.

... It was the sterilising of a man's capacity for work and not its absorption that underlay the objection to restraint of trade. This is the *rationale* of *Young v Timmins* (1831) 1 Cr. & J. 331, where a brass foundry was during the contract sterilised so that it could work only for a party who might choose not to absorb its output at all but to go to other foundries, with the result that the foundry was completely at the mercy of the other party and might remain idle and unsupported.

The doctrine does not apply to ordinary commercial contracts for the regulation and promotion of trade during the existence of the contract, provided that any prevention of work outside the contract viewed as a whole is directed towards the absorption of the parties' services and not their sterilisation. Sole agencies are a normal and necessary incident of commerce, and those who desire the benefits of a sole agency must deny themselves the opportunities of other agencies. So, too, in the case of a film-star who may tie herself to a company in order to obtain from them the benefits of stardom (*Gaumont-British Picture Corpn Ltd v Alexander* [1936] 2 All E.R. 1686; see, too, *Warner Bros Pictures Inc v Nelson* [1937] 1 K.B. 209). Moreover, partners habitually fetter themselves to one another.

When a contract ties the parties only during the continuance of the contract, and the negative ties are only those which are incidental and normal to the positive commercial arrangements at which the contract aims, even though those ties exclude all dealings with others, there is no restraint of trade within the meaning of the doctrine and no question of reasonableness arises. If, however, the contract ties the trading activities of either party after its determination, it is a restraint of trade, and the question of reasonableness arises. So, too, if during the contract one of the parties is too unilaterally fettered, so that the contract loses its character of a contract for the regulation and promotion of trade and acquires the predominant character of a contract in restraint of trade. In that case the *rationale* of *Young v Timmins* comes into play and the question whether it is reasonable arises ...

Since the tie for a period of four years and five months was in the circumstances reasonable, I would allow the appeal in respect of the Mustow Green garage. Since the tie for a period of 21 years was not in the circumstances reasonable, I would dismiss the appeal in respect of the Corner garage.

...

LORD WILBERFORCE: ... The doctrine of restraint of trade is one to be applied to factual situations with a broad and flexible rule of reason. **7–40**

The use of this expression justifies restatement of its classic exposition by White C.J. in *U.S. v Standard Oil* (1911), 221 U.S. 1 at p. 63. Speaking of the statutory words 'every contract in restraint of trade' (Sherman Act, 1890), admittedly taken from the common law, almost contemporaneous with Lord Macnaghten's formula and just as wide, he said:

'As the acts which may come under the classes stated in the first section and the restraint of trade to which that section applies are not specifically enumerated or defined, it is obvious that judgment must in every case be called into play in order to determine whether a particular act is embraced within the statutory classes, and whether if the act is within such classes its nature or effect causes it to be are straint of trade within the intendment of the Act ... '

Moreover, he goes on to say that to hold to the contrary would involve either holding that the statute would be destructive of all right to contract or agree or combine in any respect whatsoever, or that, the 'light of reason' being excluded, enforcement of the statute was impossible because of its uncertainty. The right course was to leave it to be determined by the light of reason whether any particular act or contract was within the contemplation of the statute. One still finds much enlightenment in these words.

This does not mean that the question whether a given agreement is in restraint of trade, in either sense of these words, is nothing more than a question of fact to be individually decided in each case. It is not to be supposed, or encouraged, that a bare allegation that a contract limits a trader's freedom of action exposes a party suing on it to the burden of justification. There will always be certain general categories of contracts as to which it can be said, with some degree of certainty, that the 'doctrine' does or does not apply to them. Positively, there are likely to be certain sensitive areas as to which the law will require in every case the test of reasonableness to be passed: such an area has long been and still is that of contracts between employer and employee as regards the period after the employment has ceased. Negatively, and it is this that concerns us here, there will be types of contract as to which the law should be prepared to say with some confidence that they do not enter into the field of restraint of trade at all.

How, then, can such contracts be defined or at least identified? No exhaustive test can be stated—probably no precise, non-exhaustive test. The development of the law does seem to show, however, that judges have been able to dispense from the necessity of justification under a public policy test of reasonableness such contracts or provisions of contracts as, under contemporary conditions, may be found to have passed into the accepted and normal currency of commercial or contractual or conveyancing relations. That such contracts have done so may betaken to show with at least strong *prima facie* force that, moulded under the pressures of negotiation, competition and public opinion, they have assumed a form which satisfies the test of public policy as understood by the courts at the time, or, regarding the matter from the point of view of the trade, that the trade in question has assumed such a form that for its health or expansion it requires a degree of regulation. Absolute exemption restriction or regulation is never obtained: circumstances, social or economic, may have altered, since they obtained acceptance, in such a way as to call for a fresh examination: there may be some exorbitant or special feature in the individual contract which takes it out of the accepted category: but the court must be persuaded of this before it calls on the relevant party to justify a contract of this kind . . .

I turn now to the agreements. In my opinion, on balance, they enter into the category of agreements in restraint of trade which require justification. They directly bear upon, and in some measure restrain, the exercise of the respondent's trade, so the question is whether they are to be treated as falling within some category excluded from the 'doctrine' of restraint of trade. The broad test, or rather approach, which I have suggested, is capable of answering this. This is not a mere transaction in property, nor a mere transaction between owners of property: it is essentially a trade agreement between traders. It is not a mere agreement for exclusive purchase of a commodity, though it contains this element: if it were nothing more, there would be a strong case for treating it as a normal commercial agreement of an accepted type. There is the tie for a fixed period with no provision for determination by notice ... Finally the agreement is not of a character which by the pressure of negotiation or competition, has passed into acceptance or into a balance of interest between the parties or between the parties and their customers; the solus system is both too recent and too variable for this to be said."

7–41 Note that Lord Reid suggested that the doctrine applies equally while the relation subsists as well as when the contract is finished.

Lord Reid suggested that for the restraint to be valid, there must be some compensating advantage to the restrained party. What could this cover, or is it merely a statement of the English view that there can be no contract without consideration; that is, a quantifiable benefit or detriment for both parties?

Compare Lord Hodson's conception of the public interest with that of Lord Macnaughten in *Nordenfelt*.

Note that the "rule of reason" approach adopted by Chief Justice White in the United States, although it is a key element of US antitrust law, is by no means universally applied. In fact, more like the position in England (though not in Scotland) before *Nordenfelt*, US courts often regard restraints as per se illegal. Is Lord Wilberforce's approach practical, unless the courts are willing to take into account evidence of the economic consequences of particular restraints on trade?

7–42 The guiding test emerging from *Esso* appears to be whether the restraint clause or covenant fetters or restricts an existing freedom. Thus, the doctrine applied because the owner was restricting his right, as owner, to sell whichever make of petrol he wished. The doctrine would not, however, apply to the licensee of a tied public house who is restricted to selling only the brewery's products, because as tenant he would have no right to sell anything were it not for the lease and conditions granted by the brewery/landlord.

In *Alec Lobb (Garages) Ltd v Total Oil GB Ltd*,[73] the English Court of Appeal applied the restraint doctrine to a solus supply arrangement in a lease.

Following *Esso*, could the doctrine apply to other categories—franchising agreements, or agency contracts, for example—to curtail unreasonable reliance upon them? In *Agma Chemical Co Ltd v Hart*,[74] for example, Lord Hunter, without any explanation, applied the doctrine to what was clearly an agency contract, not a contract of employment, finding nevertheless that the restraint was not unreasonable. He stated (at 248):

> "The law does not say that a former employee or *agent* must be free to entice away customers of his employers or *principals*. Employers and *principals* have a legitimate interest to preserve their business connection ..." [emphasis added],

even though there are no cases in Scots law—or English law, for that matter—where the court has applied the doctrine to a commercial agency agreement. It is arguable that, following *Esso*, it was incumbent on the pursuer to show, not merely that the restraint was reasonable, but that the doctrine applied in the first place.

For a time, there was a discernible trend in the English decisions towards the development of a general restriction on "abuse of bargaining power" or "exploitation of economic inequality". In contracts normally associated with the application of the restraint of trade doctrine, this approach reached a zenith in the House of Lords in the following English decision.

Schroeder Music Publishing Co Ltd v Macaulay 7–43

[1974] 1 W.L.R. 1308

House of Lords: Lord Reid, Viscount Dilhorne, Lords Diplock, Simon of Glaisdale and Kilbrandon

A song writer, aged 21 and unknown, entered into an agreement with music publishers in their "standard form" whereby the publishers engaged his exclusive services during the term of the agreement. By cl.1 the agreement was subject as thereinafter provided, to remain in force for five years. By cl.3(a) the song writer assigned to the publishers the full copyright for the whole world in all his musical compositions during the term. Clauses 5–8 dealt with the song writer's remuneration, which was to be by royalties on works published. By cl.9(a) if the total royalties during the term exceeded £5,000 the agreement was automatically extended for a further five years. By cl.9(b) the publishers could determine the agreement at any time by one month's written notice. No such right was given to the song writer. By cl.16(a) the publishers had the right to assign the agreement. By cl.16(b) the song writer agreed not to assign his rights under the agreement without the publishers' prior written consent. The song writer brought an action claiming, inter alia, a declaration that the agreement was contrary to public policy and void. Plowman J so held and made the declaration sought and his judgment was affirmed by the Court of Appeal. The House of Lords rejected Schroeder's appeal against the decision of the Court of Appeal.

[73] *Alec Lobb (Garages) Ltd v Total Oil GB Ltd* [1985] 1 W.L.R. 173.

[74] *Agma Chemical Co Ltd v Hart*, 1984 S.L.T. 246.

7–44 "LORD REID ... The public interest requires in the interests both of the public and of the individual that everyone should be free so far as practicable to earn a livelihood and to give to the public the fruits of his particular abilities ... Any contract by which a person engages to give his exclusive services to another for a period necessarily involves extensive restriction during that period of the common law right to exercise any lawful activity he chooses in such manner as he thinks best. Normally the doctrine of restraint of trade has no application to such restrictions; they require no justification. But if contractual restrictions appear to be unnecessary or to be reasonably capable of enforcement in an oppressive manner, then they must be justified before they can be enforced.

....

7–45 LORD DIPLOCK ... It is, in my view, salutary to acknowledge that in refusing to enforce provisions of a contract whereby one party agrees for the benefit of the other party to exploit or to refrain from exploiting his own earning-power, the public policy which the court is implementing is not some 19th century economic theory about the benefit to the general public of freedom of trade, but the protection of those whose bargaining power is weak against being forced by those whose bargaining power is stronger to enter into bargains that are unconscionable. Under the influence of Bentham and of laissez-faire the courts in the nineteenth century abandoned the practice of applying the public policy against unconscionable bargains to contracts generally, as they had formerly done to any contact considered to be usurious; but the policy survived in its application to penalty clauses and to relief against forfeiture and also to the special category of contracts in restraint of trade. If one looks at the reasoning of 19th century judges in cases about contracts in restraint of trade one finds lip-service paid to current economic theories but if one looks at what they said in the light of what they did, one finds that they struck down a bargain if they thought it was unconscionable as between the parties to it, and upheld it if they thought it was not.

...

I will accordingly content myself with adding some observations directed to the argument that because the contract was in a 'standard form' in common use between music publishers and song-writers, the restraints that it imposes on the song-writer's liberty to exploit his talents must be presumed to be fair and reasonable.

Standard forms of contracts are of two kinds. The first, of very ancient origin, are those which set out the terms on which mercantile transactions of common occurrence are to be carried out. Examples are bills of lading, charterparties, policies of insurance, contracts of sale in the commodity markets. The standard clauses in these contracts have been settled over the years by negotiation by representatives of the commercial interests involved and have been widely adopted because experience has shown that they facilitate the conduct of trade. Contracts of these kinds affect not only the actual parties to them but also others who may have a commercial interest in the transactions to which they relate, as buyers or sellers, charterers or shipowners, insurers or bankers. If fairness or reasonableness were relevant to their enforceability the fact that they are widely used by parties whose bargaining power is fairly matched would raise a strong presumption that their terms are fair and reasonable.

The same presumption, however, does not apply to the other kind of standard form of contract. This is of comparatively modern origin. It is the result of the concentration of particular kinds of business in relatively few hands. The ticket cases in the 19th century provide what are probably the first examples. The terms of this kind of standard form of contract have not been the subject of negotiation between the parties to it, or approved by any organisation representing the interests of the weaker party. They have been dictated by that party whose bargaining power, either exercised alone or in conjunction with other providing similar goods or services, enables him to say: 'If you want these goods or services at all, these are the only terms on which they are obtainable. Take it or leave it.'

To be in a position to adopt this attitude towards a party desirous of entering into a contract to obtain goods or services provides a classic instance of superior bargaining power. It is not without significance that on the evidence in the present case, music publishers in negotiating with song-writers whose success has been already established do not insist on adhering to a contract in the standard form they offered to the respondent. The fact that the appellants' bargaining power vis-a-vis the respondent was strong enough to enable them to adopt this take-it-or-leave it attitude raises no presumption that they used it to drive an unconscionable bargain with him, but in the field of restraint of trade it calls for vigilance on the part of the court to see that they did not."

This radical approach has since not been followed in the House of Lords, nor in the Scottish courts. Nevertheless, in at least one recent case a Scottish court has appeared to rely on general public policy grounds (this time to enforce a restraint covenant). In *George Walker & Co v Jann*,[75] Walker, a firm of messengers-at-arms and sheriff officers entered into an agreement with Jann and his wife for the sale to the firm of a business of messengers-at-arms and sheriff officers carried on in Kirkcaldy, including the goodwill of that business. In terms of the sale agreement Jann undertook not to "carry on the business of Messenger-at-Arms or Sheriff Officer . . . within the Sheriffdom of Kirkcaldy, Dunfermline and Cupar for a period of 3 years" commencing 4 September 1989. After the sale of his business Jann opened premises in Cupar from where he carried on the business of messenger-at-arms and sheriff officer. The work he undertook included business within one or more of the three sheriff court districts referred to in the undertaking. Walker sought to interdict him from carrying on the new businesses. Jann argued that the restriction was unenforceable in respect that it was contrary to the public interest, on the ground that it would be contrary to public policy for a public officer to give an undertaking which would entail that he would fail to carry out his duty. Lord Cullen (at 773) was **7–46**

> "prepared to accept that it would be against public policy for a public officer to give an undertaking which would entail that he would fail to carry out his duty".

Interests of the parties

Where the doctrine applies, the pursuer must show that the agreement was reasonable between the parties. This will be far more difficult to show in an employment contract, where a party's freedom to earn a living is at stake, than in, say, a contract for the sale of a business. **7–47**

There are three aspects of any restraint which must be considered to establish if it is reasonable between the parties:

(1) *The duration of the restraint must be reasonable.* This is a matter of fact depending on the circumstances of the case. In *Solus* petrol supply agreements, for example, restraints of more than five years are generally unreasonable. In the *Esso* case, a mortgage over one garage tying the owner to *Esso* for 21 years was unreasonable and therefore unenforceable, whereas a restraint of four years and five months over a second garage was valid.

However, even a life restraint may be held reasonable if it's geographical or commercial extent is appropriately narrow—see, for example, *Fitch v Dewes*.[76]

[75] *George Walker & Co v Jann*, 1991 S.L.T. 771.
[76] *Fitch v Dewes* [1921] 2 A.C. 158.

(2) *The geographical extent of the restraint must be no greater than is necessary to protect legitimate interests.* In *Mason v Provident Clothing & Supply Co Ltd*,[77] M was employed as a local canvasser in Islington by the company that had branches throughout England. He was restrained from working in a similar business within 25 miles of London for a period of three years. The restraint was unreasonably wide, since the company's interests in a small part of London, Islington, were the only interests that could be legitimately protected from Mason. Consider also *Dumbarton Steamboat Co Ltd v MacFarlane*,[78] where the seller of a ferry enterprise operating in the Dumbarton area agreed not to carry on a similar business anywhere in the UK for a period of 10 years. Since the clause covered a wider geographical area than that necessary to protect the business sold it was unenforceable against the seller, who had set up in a similar business in the Dumbarton area.

(3) *The restraint must not be a general constraint on competition; it must protect a legitimate proprietary interest.* An employer, for example, may protect his trade secrets only from those employees who might be in a position to exploit them. A graphic illustration of this is the case of *Bluebell Apparel Ltd v Dickinson*,[79] below.

Similarly, in *British Concrete Co v Shelff*,[80] the seller of a business producing "loop" road reinforcements agreed not to manufacture or sell any road reinforcements, the purchaser being a large undertaking involved in the manufacture and sale of all road reinforcements. The clause was invalid, since it was not restricted to the proprietary interest which the purchaser was entitled to protect, i.e. "loop" reinforcements, the product of the business sold.

Lists of customers, business systems and investments could be similarly protected.

The public interest

7–48 Although it is a prerequisite that the restriction be in the public interest, it has been of issue in only a few cases. The courts generally equate the public interest with the need for employees to be free to work, or of traders to trade. Furthermore, courts are unwilling to accept general, or economic evidence as to what comprises the public interest. In *Texaco v Mulberry Filling Station*,[81] the owner of a garage under a *solus* agreement for the exclusive sale of Texaco petrol, broke the agreement during a tanker drivers' strike by obtaining and selling Jet petrol. Since the duration and extent of the *solus* agreement were reasonable, Texaco were entitled to enforce the agreement. The court would not accept that the agreement was contrary to the public interest on the basis of evidence that such agreements had a general adverse effect on consumer prices, the number of retail outlets, consumer choice and so on.

Issues of construction

7–49 If a clause in a contract is found to be in restraint of trade, the clause is unenforceable, but the remainder of the contract is valid. Furthermore, if it is possible to sever the offending element from the remainder of the clause, without altering or distorting its meaning, that remainder will survive.

The cases which follow establish and illustrate some of these key issues. No attempt has been made to differentiate categories of contract; rather to state generic principles which apply regardless of the category of contract.

Lord Macnaghten indicated that the question of reasonableness between the parties must be determined on the basis of their interests at the time when the contract was entered into.

---

[77] *Mason v Provident Clothing & Supply Co Ltd* [1913] A.C. 724.
[78] *Dumbarton Steamboat Co Ltd v MacFarlane* (1899) 1 F. 993.
[79] *Bluebell Apparel Ltd v Dickinson*, 1980 S.L.T. 157.
[80] *British Concrete Co v Shelff* [1921] 2 Ch. 563.
[81] *Texaco v Mulberry Filling Station* [1972] 1 All E.R. 513.

Proactive Sports Management Ltd v Wayne Rooney 7–50
[2011] EWCA Civ. 1444; 2011 W.L. 5902986
English Court of Appeal: Lady Justice Arden Lord Justice Sullivan and Lord Justice Gross

Wayne Rooney (WR), aged 17, was relatively new to football, but with the prospect of a long and lucrative career. He set up a company, Stoneygate, to which he assigned, among other matters, his "image rights"; that is his rights in his own personality and the right to exploit his name and image. In 2003, by means of an "image rights representation agreement (IRRA)", Stoneygate appointed Proactive as sole agents to exploit those image rights, for example through "endorsement contracts that used his image to advertise sportswear".

WR and his parents were not advised to and did not take independent legal advice before he signed the IRRA on behalf of Stoneygate. The IRRA contained the following terms:

"3 **Obligations of the Company**

The Company undertakes and agrees . . . that it shall . . . diligently and faithfully serve the Client and, in particular, that it shall:

3.1 use its best endeavours and work diligently to represent the Client in all areas of image rights exploitation, licensing and personality management . . .

4 **Obligations of the Client**

The Client . . . shall. . .:

. . .

4.4. not during the term of this Agreement negotiate or enter into contracts (nor permit the Player to enter into contracts) with any other . . . agents or . . . competitors of the Company, except with the prior written consent of the Company;

. . .

6 **Remuneration**

6.1 . . .[T]he Company shall pay to the Client (upon the Player's confirmation of these terms and conditions having attained 18 years of age pursuant to Clause 5.3) the sum of £25,000.

6.2 In consideration for the performance of the Services, the Client shall pay to the Company . . . a commission calculated on a percentage of all sums payable to the Client as follows:

- 20% of the gross sum payable under any contract or arrangements for the promotion, endorsement or advertisement of the Client and/or the exploitation of the Intellectual Property and/or products, goods or services to which the Client is a party.

. . .

7 **Duration and Termination**

. . .

7.2 Either the Company or the Client may terminate this Agreement immediately by giving notice in writing upon the occurrence of a material breach of this Agreement by the other party which is not remedied with 28 days of a written request, or upon the bankruptcy or insolvency (as appropriate) of the other party.

8 **Consequences of Termination**

8.1 In the event that the Client terminates this Agreement prior to the expiry of the term set out in clause 7.1, other than in accordance with clause 7.2, the Client and/or the Player shall forthwith pay to the Company:

8.1.1 £25,000.

8.1.2 a further sum payable to the Company as liquidated damages calculated as follows:

a sum equal to £37,000 multiplied by the number of complete years of the unexpired term of this Agreement (with years to commence from the date of this Agreement and anniversaries thereof).

8.1.3 a sum equivalent to the Company's total costs and expenses properly incurred in relation to its performance in the Services from the date hereof until the date of termination notice

. . .

21 **Survivorship**

This Agreement shall, as to any of its provisions remaining to be performed in whole or in part or capable of having following termination, remain in full force and effect despite termination."

The relationship was highly successful and lucrative for seven years, with a dedicated group of Proactive staff (Team Rooney), until, in 2009, following disagreements, Stoneygate and WR purported to terminate the IRRA and entered into a contract with another agency, Trile S, for a similar commission. Proactive elected to treat this as a repudiatory breach of contract. Stoneygate made no further payments to Proactive for its commission.

Proactive claimed commission at the rate of 20 per cent on all sums payable to Stoneygate under any contracts with third parties which Proactive had procured for WR during the subsistence of the IRRA, whenever they might fall due, whether before or after the expiration of the eight-year term of the IRRA. Stoneygate contended, inter alia that the IRRA was unenforceable on the grounds of restraint of trade.

At first instance the judge held that the IRRA was unenforceable on the grounds of restraint of trade.

7–51 "LADY ARDEN

. . .

Issues on this appeal

25 The five issues on this appeal are:

(1) whether, on the true construction of clause 6.2 of the IRRA, Proactive is entitled to commission on payments made by third parties after termination of the IRRA in respect of contracts negotiated by Proactive prior to termination;
(2) whether the judge's conclusion that the IRRA was unenforceable on the grounds that it was in unreasonable restraint of trade was wrong in law for any of the three grounds advanced on this appeal by Proactive;
(3) whether, if Proactive fails on Issue (2), Proactive is nonetheless contractually entitled under the IRRA to commission on sums which were actually received by or after the date of termination in respect of contracts negotiated by Proactive at the rate of 20% as set out in clause 6.2;

(4) whether, if the IRRA is held to be unenforceable under Issue (2), and Proactive fails on Issue (3), the judge should simply have applied the rate at which commission would have been payable under clause 6.2; and

(5) whether the judge was wrong to conclude that there was no implied contract between Speed and Proactive having the terms as to commission contained in the IRRA.

. . .

Issue (2): was the judge's conclusion that the IRRA was unenforceable on the grounds that it was in unreasonable restraint of trade wrong in law for any of the three grounds advanced on this appeal by Proactive? 7–52

Introduction

53 Public policy has been described as an unruly horse. It is an important but amorphous concept which the courts must keep within its proper limits. However, the courts have repeatedly held that it is against the public interest and the policy of the common law for there to be restraints on trade unless there are special circumstances.

54 There are numerous examples in the decided cases of contracts which have been held to be contrary to public policy as being in restraint of trade. The most common situation is where an employment contract seeks to impose an unreasonable restriction on an employee's activities after he has ceased to be an employee. The present case does not fall into that precise category because the alleged restraint affects activities both during and after the termination of the contract.

55 The boundary between contracts that are contrary to public policy as being in restraint of trade and that will not be enforced, and contracts that contain acceptable restrictions is an uncertain and porous one. As the leading case of *Esso Petroleum Ltd v Harper's Garage (Stourport) Ltd* [1968] AC 269 demonstrates, opinions can differ to whether and if so on what basis a particular kind of restriction is within the doctrine but can be justified, or whether it is to be regarded as outside the doctrine altogether (see, for example, per Lord Morris at page 306G, per Lord Pearce at page 327F and per Lord Wilberforce at 333F). Some contracts are treated as moulded by normal commercial experience and thus outside the doctrine even though they contain restrictions on trade (see per Lord Wilberforce at pages 332–3). These include restrictive covenants in commercial leases against user save for particular trading purposes.

56 The House of Lords sought to identify circumstances in which a contract would be held to be in restraint of trade, but eschewed the impossible task of defining those circumstances comprehensively. Thus, for example (and without trying to summarise the lengthy speeches in *Esso*), Lord Reid took the view that the doctrine could apply to any contract that restricted a person's capacity to trade that was out of the norm. Lord Pearce considered that the doctrine was directed to any contract which in substance sterilised a person's capacity to trade. Lord Wilberforce acknowledged in terms that there was no precise test for when the doctrine of restraint of trade applied. The categories were not closed. Ordinary commercial contracts, however, would be outside the doctrine.

57 I propose pragmatically to start with the approach of Jonathan Parker J in *Panayiocou* (sic) *v Sony Music Entertainment Ltd* [1994] EMLR 229 at 321, under which there are two stages involved in reaching the conclusion that a contract is in restraint of trade. At the first stage, the court has to address the question of whether the doctrine of restraint of trade is engaged, i.e. whether the contract is one to which the doctrine of restraint of trade applies at all, and, at the second stage of the process, if the party

seeking to rely on the covenant raises this as a defence, the court will have to determine whether the restraint on trade is reasonable.

...

59 However, in practice, I find that the line between the two stages identified by Jonathan Parker J is not clear cut, and that the analysis has to be an iterative one between them. In particular, the matters that might be raised under the second stage might also be relevant to the question whether the doctrine of restraint of trade is engaged at all.

60 In the present case, the contract was one for the appointment of Proactive as Stoneygate's sole and exclusive agent, and thus it restricted the whole activity of exploiting WR's image rights. The leading case on covenants for exclusivity and restraint of trade is *Esso*. In that case, the owners of two garages entered into 'solus agreements' with Esso to buy only Esso's fuel and to sell it at Esso's retail prices. The doctrine of restraint of trade was held to apply as the contract restricted the garage owners from buying petrol from other persons. In the case of one agreement, the restraint was for five years and this was held on the facts (which I need not go into) to be reasonable and enforceable. But Esso failed to discharge the onus on it of showing a restraint for twenty-one years contained in another solus agreement was justified.

61 The doctrine is clearly engaged by contracts that restrict the whole of a person's services and which are oppressive. Thus, in *A. Schroeder Music Publishing Co Ltd v Macaulay* [1974] 1 WLR 1308 a young song writer agreed to assign the copyright in all his compositions for five years and, if the royalties in that period exceeded £5,000, for a further five years. There was no obligation on the publisher to publish any of his work. There was no provision for termination of the agreement by the song writer. However, the publisher could determine the agreement at any time. The House of Lords held that the agreement was in restraint of trade and unenforceable because it was unreasonable. The leading speeches were given by Lord Reid and Lord Diplock.

62 Lord Reid principally analysed the doctrine as one based on oppression. He held:

'Any contract by which a person engages to give his exclusive services to another for a period necessarily involves extensive restriction during that period of the common law right to exercise any lawful activity he chooses in such manner as he thinks best. Normally the doctrine of restraint of trade has no application to such restrictions: they require no justification. But *if contractual restrictions appear to be unnecessary or to be reasonably capable of enforcement in an oppressive manner*, then they must be justified before they can be enforced.' [page 1314, emphasis added])

63 Lord Diplock expressed the matter differently. He concluded that the right question to be asked was whether the contract was unfair:

'So I would hold that the question to be answered as respects a contract in restraint of trade of the kind with which this appeal is concerned is:"Was the bargain fair?" The test of fairness is, no doubt, whether the restrictions are both reasonably necessary for the protection of the legitimate interests of the promisee and commensurate with the benefits secured to the promisor under the contract. For the purpose of this test all the provisions of the contract must be taken into consideration.' (page 1315–1316)

64 The other members of the House of Lords, other than Viscount Dilhorne who agreed only with Lord Reid, agreed with both speeches. In those circumstances I proceed, again as Mr Jeans invited us to do, on the basis that there is no real difference in approaches of Lord Reid and Lord Diplock.

65 Lord Reid did not seek to define the term 'oppressive'. According to its ordinary dictionary meaning, it means 'unreasonably harsh'. Astbury J at first instance in the *Hepworth* case (page 13 of the report), referred to below, used the words 'tyrannous and oppressive' to describe the agreement in that case, which emphasises the one-sided nature of oppressive restrictions. However, once the conclusion is reached that the

agreement in question is oppressive, there is no need to find that it is egregiously oppressive. Moreover, under the second stage it is always open to the other contracting party to seek to justify the restriction as no more than reasonable if he wishes to enforce the agreement. That party should have nothing to fear if the agreement is one that ought to be enforced.

The judge's reasoning 7–53

66 The judge dealt with the application of the law on this issue to the facts as found by him at paragraphs 620 to 663 of his judgment. In the course of this part of his judgment, the judge held:

'643 The particular features of the Image Rights Representation Agreement which, in Stoneygate's contention, render it unenforceable as being in unreasonable restraint of trade are set out at paragraph 37 of its Re-Re-Amended Defence. Leaving aside the initial imbalance arising out of the commercial inexperience of WR and his family and the lack of any independent advice, the particular matters picked out in the pleading relate primarily to the length of the exclusive tie, having regard to the absence of any effective right on Stoneygate's part to terminate the Agreement prior to the end of the eight-year term. Reference is also made to the fact that commission was payable at the rate of 20% during the term of the Agreement, and to the right asserted by Proactive to receive post-termination commission at the same rate notwithstanding the cessation of any obligation on its part to provide the contracted services. The latter point, of course, no longer arises, in view of my interpretation of the relevant contractual provisions.

. . .

649 The terms of the Agreement were effectively dictated by Proactive. There was no meaningful negotiation whatever, save perhaps in relation to the signing-on fee. WR and his family had no commercial experience and were utterly unsophisticated in financial and contractual matters. I am quite satisfied that they never, in fact, took independent legal advice as to the terms of the Image Rights Representation Agreement itself or, for that matter, any other Agreement between the parties; and I think it is unlikely that it was ever seriously suggested to them that they should take such independent legal advice. It is quite clear that, having decided that Proactive and, in particular, Mr Stretford were the people they wished to act for WR, they were willing to accept whatever terms Proactive put before them. It may well be the case that there were many other agents who were interested in signing up this young and exciting talent; but, in reality, there was no serious competition to Proactive. In my judgment, there was a very substantial imbalance in bargaining power between the parties.'

Submissions

67 Mr Jeans submits that this case should never have got past the first stage in this two-stage test. He makes three points, as he puts it, separately and inter-connectedly: 7–54

(a) WR's trade is as a footballer. The IRRA is a means of obtaining extra income but it is not his trade.
(b) The IRRA does not restrict his earning potential. The IRRA capitalises that potential in a particular respect.
(c) There is no feature that renders the IRRA unfair or oppressive in the sense of Schroeder. On that basis, there is nothing to bring the doctrine into play.

. . .

Discussion and conclusions on Issue (2):

. . .

7–55 92 The first challenge focuses on the ancillary nature of image rights exploitation to Stoneygate and WR. WR's primary occupation is that of a footballer: I proceed on the basis that his salary as such is paid to Stoneygate, but even if it is not Stoneygate would be equally concerned to see that WR preserves and develops his footballing skills as any image rights are dependent on his doing so. The business of image rights exploitation is, therefore, merely ancillary to the primary occupation of being a footballer. Mr Jeans submits that in these circumstances the doctrine of restraint of trade does not apply.

93 In my judgment, a person's ancillary activity of exploiting his image rights is just as capable of protection under the doctrine of restraint of trade as any other occupation. Public policy is concerned with the manner in which a person may properly realise his potential, not only for the good of that individual but for the economic benefit of society generally. It cannot logically matter whether the realisation is a person's primary activity or not. The protection for the other party to the contract is that the restriction is not a bar to enforcement of a contract if it is capable of justification as being reasonable. Moreover, the endorsement of goods encourages the purchase and consumption of goods, and the court is entitled to assume that it is in the interests of the public that image rights should be fully realisable for this economic purpose.

94 In addition, the exploitation of image rights is almost always going to be an activity which is ancillary to another occupation (saving and excepting cases such as the display of Katisha's miraculous shoulder-blade in *The Mikado*). The fact that the activity is ancillary may be such as to make the restriction on trading insubstantial and thus justifiable under the doctrine of restraint of trade. But the fact that the activity is an ancillary one is not a reason for disapplying the doctrine altogether, any more than it would be right to say that Harper's Garage would have had no claim at all in the *Esso* case if the contract had merely restricted the sort of motor accessory they could sell in the garage shop.

95 Mr Jeans' first challenge seems to me to confuse two types of (to coin a phrase) 'ancillacrity', or ancillary-ness. The first sort of ancillary feature in contracts, which fall within the doctrine is the one that appears in this case, namely an ancillary occupation. The second sort of ancillary feature in the context of restraint of trade is that of an ancillary restraint exacted on, say, the sale of business from the vendor not to compete with the business being sold. But these restraints are generally outside the doctrine of restraint of trade, or its application, because they are ancillary to the real business of the contract. The object of the covenant is to protect the value of the property being sold. That is an entirely different situation from one of exclusive agency.

96 Mr Jeans' second challenge to the judge's conclusion that the IRRA engaged the restraint of trade doctrine is that the IRRA is not about sterilising WR's ability to carry on any trade; it is a means of realising it. In his speech in *Esso*, Lord Pearce speaks of the objectionable feature of a covenant in restraint of trade being the sterilisation of the ability of the person sought to be restrained to provide services (page 328D). In other words, the doctrine of restraint of trade is about contracts which lead to the sterilisation of trade on their face or in substance.

97 The short answer to Mr Jeans' second challenge is that, as the *Schroeder* case demonstrates, it is possible for a single activity on appropriate facts to be both creative and yet 'sterilised', indeed that is perhaps the reason why the doctrine is invoked in such a situation. It was no answer to the respondent song-writer in *Schroeder* to say that the publishing contract might have been a means of bringing his creative talent to the attention of the world. The provisions of the contract allowed insufficient scope for the song-writer to ensure that this was done. So the court is inevitably driven back to the

contract in a case, such as this, where it is said that its real effect is to sterilise trading activity.

. . .

99 The judge combed through the facts with meticulous care and explained in detail the steps in his reasoning. The very unusual length of the contract term of the IRRA, the circumstances surrounding its execution, the practical difficulties of termination, and the other factors referred to by the judge have to be seen in combination. They take the IRRA out of the range of a normal commercial contract imposing restrictions on a contracting party's ability to carry on a business activity. **7–56**

100 It will be recalled that the Rooneys had no legal advice at the time of execution. This is all the more important in the light of the judge's finding that, on Proactive's side, a longer term than usual was demanded for the IRRA because it was known that WR was 'hot property'. The absence of independent legal advice in my judgment deprives the fact that the Rooneys were content with the terms of the IRRA of probative weight on the restraint of trade issue. It underscores the inequality of bargaining power between the parties. Moreover, it predisposes the agreement to a finding that it was one-sided, unfair or oppressive.

101 Furthermore, Proactive had itself had warning from different sources of the fact that the Rooneys should have independent legal advice and that the contract might be unforceable as being in restraint of trade. It appears to have brushed that advice to one side. It is a relevant part of the picture that Proactive entered into the IRRA knowing that there was a risk it could be held to be enforceable on the grounds of the doctrine of restraint of trade.

102 The term of the IRRA was much longer than the norm, and its length has to be contrasted with the likely length of a normal career in professional football. The judge found that Proactive wished to have a long contract because of the stellar potential of WR. This desire constituted a wish to restrict him from going elsewhere, not a desire justifiably to protect some legitimate interest of its own, to create stability and facilitate continuity and better planning.

103 Mr Jeans placed no reliance in his submissions on clause 8 of the IRRA, set out in paragraph 4 above. In the usual case, the fact that the party said to be oppressed can terminate the contract ought to be a good answer to a claim that the contract was oppressive and in restraint of trade. But in this case it was common ground at trial that as a matter of law and construction clause 8 did not confer a right of early termination but was an ineffective attempt to stipulate the damages payable in the event of breach.

104 It is no answer to say that there have been substantial financial rewards on all sides from the exploitation of WR's image rights. The question of restraint of trade has to be considered by reference to the terms of the IRRA. The IRRA had, moreover, two years to run at the date of its termination. Lord Diplock made this point in *Schroeder*:

'In order to determine whether this case is one in which [the power to relieve the promisor of his legal duty to fulfil his contractual promises] or exercise, what your Lordships have in fact been doing has been to assess the relative bargaining power of publisher and the song writer at the time the contract was made to decide whether the publisher had used his superior bargaining power to exact from the song writer promises that were unfairly onerous to him. Your Lordships have not been concerned to enquire whether the public have been deprived of the fruit of the song writer's talents by reason of the restrictions, nor to assess the likelihood that they would be so deprived in the future if the contract were permitted to run its full course.' (page 1315)

105 The question whether a contract is oppressive involves an evaluation of all the factors on which evidence was given at the trial in the light of the judge's findings, and an exercise of judgment by the trial judge. In such cases, an appellate court does not interfere unless it is satisfied that the trial judge is clearly wrong. In my judgment, the

judge was not clearly wrong. On the contrary, on the evidence before him, he was in my judgment entitled to come to the conclusion to which he came.

106 For these reasons I would dismiss the appeal on this issue.

...

7–57 LORD JUSTICE SULLIVAN:

138 I agree.

LORD JUSTICE GROSS:

...

140 With regard to issue (2) (*restraint of trade*), as already indicated, I have come to the same conclusion as Arden LJ and for essentially the same reasons but wish to add some observations of my own.

(I) Introduction:

7–58 141 After a careful review of the authorities, the Judge concluded, first, that the IRRA was an agreement which could properly be regarded as in restraint of trade: see, so far as relevant to this appeal, judgment at [620]–[654]. Secondly, that Proactive failed to discharge the burden resting upon it of showing that the restraints embodied in the IRRA, in particular its duration, were reasonable: judgment, at [714]–[731]. Accordingly, the Judge held that the IRRA was in unreasonable restraint of trade.

142 Before proceeding further, it is important to underline the parameters of the debate on this appeal. Proactive did not seek to challenge the Judge's second conclusion, namely, that the restraints embodied in the IRRA had not been shown to be reasonable. It followed that the appeal was solely concerned with the Judge's first conclusion, namely, that the IRRA was in restraint of trade; if that conclusion is upheld, as no attempt was made before us to justify the restraints, the appeal on this issue must fail. In his oral submissions, Mr. Jeans, for Proactive, sought to explain this stance; as he put it, either the restraint of trade doctrine was inapplicable to the IRRA in that there was nothing oppressive about the agreement – but if the agreement was oppressive, it could not be defended as reasonable. So be it. For completeness, it may be noted that no question of severance arose below (judgment, at [623]) or was raised on appeal.

7–59 **(II) The legal framework:**

143 For the purposes of this appeal, the relevant legal principles, distilled from the authorities, may be summarised as follows.

144 *First*, the doctrine of restraint of trade is one of public policy, the underlying consideration being that of freedom of trade: see the helpful discussion in *Panayiotou v Sony Music Entertainment* [1994] EMLR 229, at pp. 317 *et seq* , *per* Jonathan Parker J (as he then was).

145 *Secondly*, however, the doctrine of restraint of trade and the protection of freedom of trade do not stand alone; there is also the public interest in freedom of contract to be considered—parties are, in general, free to enter into any lawful contract they wish and it is not for the Court to rewrite their bargains. The classic expression of these two public interests is found in the speech of Lord Shaw in *Morris v Saxelby* [1916] 1 AC 688, at p.716, quoted by Lord Morris of Borth-y-Gest, in *Esso Petroleum Co Ltd v Harper's Garage (Stourport) Ltd.* [1968] AC 269, at p.306 C-D:

'The delicacy of the operation of law in settling the bounds of either freedom has been long familiar. In these cases ... there are two freedoms to be considered—one the freedom of trade and the other the freedom of contract; and to that I will now again venture to add that it is a mistake to think that public interest is only concerned with one; it is concerned with both.'

Self evidently, the doctrine of restraint of trade itself serves to limit the individual's freedom of contract. There is, accordingly, obvious scope for tension between these two public interests, involving the need for compromise. The Court should be slow to substitute its (objective) view as to the interests of the parties for the (subjective) views of the parties themselves in deciding to enter into the contract: *Panayiotou*, at pp. 330 *et seq*. But in some circumstances the doctrine of restraint of trade will prevail – where it is held that a contract is in restraint of trade and that to be enforceable it must pass a test of reasonableness: Lord Morris, in *Esso*, at p.305 B–D.

146 *Thirdly*, although all contracts in restraint of trade involve a derogation from an individual's right to trade freely, not all contracts involving such derogations are contracts in restraint of trade: Lord Reid, in *Esso*, at pp. 293–294; *Panayiotou*, at pp. 321–322.

147 *Fourthly*, the doctrine of restraint of trade is best understood as involving two separate questions, or a "two-stage approach" (*Panayiotou*, at pp. 321 *et seq*):

(i) Whether the contract in question is in restraint of trade (or, which amounts to the same thing, whether the contract attracts the doctrine of restraint of trade)?
(ii) Whether, if so, it is reasonable?

See: Lord Wilberforce, in *Esso*, at p. 331 D–E. As already underlined, this appeal is solely concerned with question i). If, of course, question i) is answered in the negative, question (ii) is not reached. It should, however, be appreciated (see below) that these questions, though analytically separate, cannot be viewed as existing in wholly watertight compartments.

148 *Fifthly*, the question of which contracts attract the doctrine of restraint of trade (question i) above) cannot be answered in a mechanistic or formalistic way: *Panayiotou*, at p.327. There is no single, exhaustive or precise test: Lord Wilberforce, in *Esso*, at p.332. A practical and flexible approach is instead to be adopted. In *Esso*, Lord Reid said this (at p.298 A–B):

'As the whole doctrine of restraint of trade is based on public policy its application ought to depend less on legal niceties or theoretical possibilities than on the practical effect of a restraint in hampering that freedom which it is the policy of the law to protect.'

In his speech in *Esso* (at p.331), Lord Wilberforce observed that the doctrine has been expressed 'with considerable generality, if not ambiguity'; this was not a reason for regret, Lord Wilberforce continued (at p.331 F–G):

'The common law has often (if sometimes unconsciously) thrived on ambiguity and it would be mistaken, even if it were possible to try to crystallise the rules of this, or any, aspect of public policy into neat propositions.'

The doctrine of restraint of trade was to be applied to factual situations with a 'broad and flexible rule of reason' (*ibid*). Thus it is important to distinguish between contracts which promote or absorb economic activity and those which restrain or sterilise it; likewise, it is or may be important to distinguish between restrictions which tie parties during the currency of the contract and those which purport to bind a party after its determination: Lord Pearce, in *Esso*, at p.328.

149 *Sixthly*, when addressing the question of whether a contract attracts the doctrine of restraint of trade, the contract must be considered when it is made: *Macaulay v Schroeder Publishing* [1974] 1 WLR 1308, at p. 1309, *per* Lord Reid. As it seems to me, how the contract has subsequently turned out is only relevant for these purposes insofar as it furnishes evidence of the nature of the contract in question when made.

150 *Seventhly*, in general, sole agency agreements will not attract the restraint of trade doctrine, at least provided they contain no restrictions other than those necessary or incidental to the inherent nature of a sole agency; the benefits of a sole agency inevitably

require giving up the opportunities of other agencies: Lord Pearce, in *Esso*, at pp. 328–329. Such agreements may be seen as promoting rather than restricting trade; in Lord Wilberforce's words, they ' ... may be found to have passed into the accepted and normal currency of commercial or contractual ... relations': *Esso*, at p.333. That said, there is, importantly, no absolute exemption from the doctrine. Two authoritative passages make this clear:

(i) The first is again from the speech of Lord Wilberforce in *Esso*, at p.333: ' ... there may be some exorbitance or special feature in the individual contract which takes it out of the accepted category: but the court must be persuaded of this before it calls upon the relevant party to justify a contract of this kind'.
(ii) The second is from the speech of Lord Reid in *Schroeder*, at p.1314: 'Any contract by which a person engages to give his exclusive services to another for a period necessarily involves extensive restriction during that period of the common law right to exercise any lawful activity he chooses in such manner as he thinks best. Normally the doctrine of restraint of trade has no application to such restrictions: they require no justification. But if contractual restrictions appear to be unnecessary or to be reasonably capable of enforcement in an oppressive manner, then they must be justified before they can be enforced.'

(III) Applying the law to the facts:

...

7–60 152 ... I am not persuaded that Proactive's case is well-founded, so that I would dismiss the appeal on this issue. I do so, however, with a measure of reluctance, as I shall explain. My reasons follow.

153 *First*, I cannot accept the distinction Mr. Jeans sought to draw between Mr. Rooney's trade as a footballer and the exploitation of his image rights. As it seems to me, both his on-field and off-field activities were part of a single trade. If, *per contra* , the two are to be separated then I can see no answer to Sir Richard Buxton's observation (when refusing permission to appeal on paper):

'It is no consolation to someone who is capable of making a good living doing A and also a good living doing B to tell him, as the applicant would, that he can be restrained from doing A because he still has B left to him.'

154 *Secondly*, I acknowledge the force in the submission that the IRRA was a very different contract from the contract in *Schroeder*, understandably disapproved of by the Courts. Amongst the positive features of the IRRA were the provision (cl. 3.3) giving Stoneygate a measure of control over negotiations conducted and contracts entered into by Proactive, the fact that Proactive was only paid by results (there was no retainer) and that Proactive was obliged to use its 'best endeavours' (cl. 3.1) to represent Stoneygate in promoting the image rights. Even if Mr. Jeans put it too high in suggesting a major distinction between an obligation to use 'best' endeavours as distinct from an obligation to use 'reasonable' endeavours, it remained the case that Proactive was under an obligation of this nature in its work on behalf of Stoneygate/Mr. Rooney. Furthermore, as to the 20% rate of commission—at first blush, on the high side—it was not in dispute that it was widespread in the market (judgment, at [430]–[433] and [760]) and that the same rate was charged on Stoneygate's subsequent contract with Triple S. There is, accordingly, to my mind, no ready analogy between the outcome in *Schroeder* and the present case.

155 *Thirdly*, nonetheless and despite the fact that sole agency agreements generally do not attract the restraint of trade doctrine (as discussed above), I think that the IRRA does do so. In my judgment, the IRRA has features which on a broad, practical, rule of

reason approach do attract the doctrine—as special or exorbitant, reasonably capable of enforcement in an oppressive manner. In summary, those features are as follows:

(i) By far the single-most important was the 8 year duration of the IRRA. Other than by accepting a possibly significant liability and unless Proactive went into liquidation or was in breach of the IRRA, Stoneygate had no means of terminating the IRRA before the expiry of the 8 year term. On any view, 8 years must amount to a very significant proportion of Mr. Rooney's football career; the Judge held that it would probably cover about half of his career (judgment, at [647]). Although there was some suggestion in the submissions of Mr. Jeans that a significant duration was necessary for purposes of stability and to match the lengthy terms of contracts with sponsors, the reality, on the facts found by the Judge, is that an 8 year term was 'unique': judgment, at [471]–[476]. The length of the IRRA contrasts starkly with the maximum term of 2 years under FIFA regulations for an on-field representation agreement (judgment, at [473]). The Judge's conclusion (admittedly in the section of the judgment dealing with the suggested justification for the restriction) was expressed in strong terms (at [723]): ' . . . I would have little difficulty in accepting that a two-year tie, running in synchrony with an on-field agency agreement, would be entirely reasonable, provided, no doubt, that the agreement did not contain any other particularly onerous terms. Indeed, I might well have been persuaded that a four or even five-year term might be regarded as reasonable. That appears to have been the sort of timescale initially envisaged within Proactive for the development of the brand . . . But I can see no justification . . . for an exclusive tie lasting for a full eight years . . . '
Interestingly, if in no way decisive, solicitors advising Proactive prior to the conclusion of the IRRA were concerned that it might be in restraint of trade and warned Proactive accordingly: judgment, at [651].

(ii) The circumstances surrounding the conclusion of the IRRA, as found by the Judge, are themselves worthy of note. Mr. Rooney was 17 at the time of entry into the IRRA: judgment, at [647]. The terms of the IRRA were effectively dictated by Proactive, with no or very limited meaningful negotiation: judgment, at [649]. Mr. Rooney and his family had no commercial experience and were unsophisticated in financial and contractual matters; they took no independent legal advice: *ibid.* Mr. Jeans submitted that the focus (or principal focus) of the doctrine of restraint of trade is on the substance of what was agreed, rather than on the circumstances in which the agreement was entered into. While there may well be a degree of force in this submission, I cannot agree that it goes so far as to preclude the Court from taking into account circumstances surrounding the conclusion of a contract when deciding whether to require a party to justify restrictions. Whereas a Court may be wise to proceed with great reserve where it appears that an agreement was negotiated between experienced commercial parties—for fear of presuming to know better than the parties what was in their own best interests—the position may be different where the facts of the individual case suggest the absence of commercial negotiations and an imbalance of power. All the more so, where, as the Judge found here (judgment, at [650]): 'The Agreement itself was not in any sense a standard form which had been tried and tested in this particular field of commerce. On the contrary, it was unusual in many respects and unique in its duration . . . '

(iii) While, for reasons already canvassed, no complaint could be made of the 20% rate of commission *per se*, the fact that it was payable throughout the agreement at a flat rate and without any tapering was regarded by the Judge as a matter of

> concern: judgment, at [650]. On the facts, the Judge 'very much' doubted (*ibid*) that a flat rate—without any provision for tapering—would have been the outcome: '... [if] there had been free and equal negotiations, with proper independent legal advice on each side and, it may be, real competition from other prospective agents ... '

Earlier (judgment, at [648]), the Judge had highlighted the consequences of this flat rate of commission: ' ... during the entirety of the eight-year term, Proactive was entitled to be paid at the rate of 20% on all income-producing opportunities which it introduced to Stoneygate and WR, without any attempt to limit or reduce the rate at which commission was payable by reference to the total income generated for Stoneygate. The same flat rate was payable whether Stoneygate's income from the exploitation of the image rights was £10,000 or £10m.'

These are conclusions of fact and I can see no proper basis for interfering with them.

156 For completeness, I am unable to accept the submission advanced by Mr. Jeans that the *duration* of the IRRA was relevant only to reasonableness and not to whether the IRRA attracted the doctrine of restraint of trade. It would be curious if (to take a hypothetical example) the term of the contract under consideration was so lengthy as to be patently unreasonable yet that factor was irrelevant to a consideration of whether the agreement attracted the doctrine of restraint of trade. As it seems to me, such a proposition is inconsistent with the authorities discussed earlier. The fallacy, with respect, is that it seeks to treat the two-stage approach as if the two questions are contained in watertight compartments. I do not think that can be right. The two-stage approach *is* to be followed but that does not mean that questions of reasonableness are necessarily irrelevant to the first question; if exorbitance and the reasonable capability for oppression are relevant to the first question (as determined by authority), then some overlap between the two questions may be unavoidable. These observations apply equally to the various circumstances surrounding the conclusion of the IRRA to which the Judge had regard.

157 *Fourthly*, pulling the threads together and despite the matters urged on behalf of Proactive, I am not at all persuaded that the Judge erred in holding that the IRRA attracted the restraint of trade doctrine. No error of law can be detected in the Judge's approach and his key findings of fact were unchallenged on this appeal. As it seems to me, an agreement which, when entered into, stood to restrict the exploitation of Mr. Rooney's/Stoneygate's image rights for so significant a part of his playing career was one which called for justification—*a fortiori* given the Judge's fact findings that the length of the term was unique, the circumstances in which it came to be concluded and the absence of any tapering provision. The nature of my conclusion should be underlined: it is and is no more than that in agreement with the Judge the restrictions in the IRRA called for justification. Before this Court, however, Proactive has made no attempt to argue that the restrictions in the IRRA were reasonable.

158 *Fifthly,* I have already confessed to a measure of reluctance in reaching this conclusion. Such reluctance is attributable (1) to the awareness that the IRRA proved extremely lucrative to Mr. Rooney; (2) the absence of evidence of any dissatisfaction on Mr. Rooney's part as to the working of the IRRA, other than that arising, collaterally, from the parting of the ways between Proactive and Mr. Stretford, the director who had been in charge of 'Team Rooney' (see Arden LJ's judgment, at [5] above); (3) the recognition, as the Judge effectively held, that as a matter of 'commercial reality' (judgment, at [22]) this is a dispute between Proactive and Mr. Stretford over the right to represent Mr. Rooney. These considerations suggested the need for careful reflection before deciding this issue adversely to Proactive. However, as a matter of law they go to post-contractual events, whereas (as discussed) the question of whether the IRRA attracts the restraint of trade doctrine must be decided at the time when it was made.

Moreover, the governing consideration is not whether Proactive has conducted itself in some morally reprehensible fashion but whether it is in the public interest that an agreement in the terms of the IRRA should require justification. For the reasons already given, I think that it does and I would dismiss the appeal on issue (2) accordingly.

Protection of a legitimate trade interest

The categories of interest which can be protected by use of a restrictive covenant were tersely expounded by Pearson LJ (as he then was) in the following case. **7–61**

Commercial Plastics Ltd v Vincent **7–62**
[1965] 1 Q.B. 623
English Court of Appeal: Sellers, Pearson and Salmon, LJJ

Commercial manufactured thin PVC calendered sheeting, holding about 20 per cent of the UK market for that product. They specialised in such sheeting for adhesive tape, where they had about 80 per cent of the market. Their pre-eminence in the field was partly due to secret processes.

Vincent, who had previously worked in PVC calendering, was employed by Commercial to work mainly on production of PVC calendered sheeting for adhesive tape. A written term of his contract of employment provided that

> "in view of the highly technical and confidential nature of this appointment you have agreed not to seek employment with any of our competitors in the PVC calendering field for at least one year after leaving our employ".

Commercial sought, but failed to obtain an injunction to restrain Vincent from working for a competitor in the PVC calendering field in breach of the term.

"PEARSON LJ: ... The restriction has to be justified in this case as being reasonably required for the protection of the plaintiffs' trade secrets by preventing the defendant from disclosing confidential information imparted to him by the plaintiffs in the course of his employment ... **7–63**

In applying the law in this case, the first question that arises is whether the plaintiffs had any trade secrets or confidential information which the defendant would be likely to divulge if he entered the employment of a competitor. They do not claim any trade secrets or confidential information in the general field of PVC calendering, or even in respect of PVC calendered sheeting as a whole, but only in the special field of such sheeting for adhesive tape. It is not easy to see what is the relevant confidential information in this case. (a) The defendant has, no doubt, gained much skill and aptitude and general technical knowledge with regard to the production of PVC calendered sheeting in general, and particularly for the production of such sheeting for adhesive tape. But such things have become part of himself, and he cannot be restrained from taking them away and using them. (b) The defendant had access to the mixing specifications recorded in code and the confidential test reports and other confidential documents. It is not contended, however, that the defendant would be able to carry away in his memory the many details recorded in such documents. If he took away, or copied, the documents, other remedies would be available. (c) The plaintiffs' scheme or organisation and methods of business are not to be counted as trade secrets, but fall into the same class as the general technical knowledge referred to in (a) above ...

... Is there some other element of confidential information which the defendant might divulge and make use of in other employment, and for which the plaintiffs can reasonably claim protection? ... The question is difficult, but, on the whole, we would agree with the view of the learned judge that there is some confidential information for which protection is required and can be claimed. The defendant would not remember the minute details recorded in the mixing specifications, but he would be likely to remember in general terms what was the problem and what was the solution, what experiments were made and whether the results were positive or negative, and so on. In the vivid phrase used by the learned judge, the defendant would be likely, when the need arose, to dredge up from the recesses of his memory the particular secret which, while he was in the plaintiffs' employ, he had found appropriate to deal with the customer's requirement. In this case, the distinctive feature, distinguishing it from *Herbert Morris Ltd. v Saxelby*, is the element of continuing new discovery of further advantageous methods or devices for producing the sheeting for adhesive tape...

The other main question which arises, on the application of the law to this case, is whether the plaintiffs have shown that the restriction is no wider than is necessary for their protection in respect of the confidential information imparted to, or gained by, the defendant, whilst in their employment, with regard to the production of sheeting for adhesive tape. Counsel for the defendant has contended that the provision is very wide in three respects: (i) it would bar the defendant from entering the employment of a competitor anywhere in the world; (ii) it is not limited to those who compete in the field of sheeting for adhesive tape, but extends to anyone who competes in any part of the PVC calendering field; (iii) it is not limited to working in some department or activity connected with the production of sheeting for adhesive tape. Counsel has also contended that these three points can be taken together and have a cumulative effect. In our judgment, those contentions are correct, and they show that the plaintiffs' burden of proving that the restrictive provision is reasonable in the interests of both parties is a heavy one.

... [A]lthough the plaintiffs required protection only for their trade secrets or confidential information relating to the production of sheeting for tape, they took protection in their restrictive provision for the whole PVC calendering field ...

In our view, the plaintiffs failed to show that it was necessary for the restrictive provision to apply to the whole of the PVC calendering field. The learned judge was inclined at any rate to decide this point against the plaintiffs.

... [T]here was in this restrictive provision no limitation in respect of the nature or scope of the employment. The defendant was barred from entering the employment of a competitor of the plaintiffs in the PVC calendering field, even if he was going to be employed in some department or activity remote from the production of sheeting for adhesive tape, and even perhaps remote from PVC calendering altogether. This point was not made a ground of decision by the learned judge, and we do not think that it is necessary to examine the evidence and arguments bearing on it, as the first two points are sufficient for upholding the decision of the learned judge ...

The decision of this case against the plaintiffs is inevitable, but it is in a way regrettable, because the plaintiffs' case has underlying merits. They do seem to have important confidential information, for which they might reasonably claim protection by a suitably limited restrictive provision. The actual provision in this case can be described as 'home-made,' that is to say, not professionally drafted. It is unfortunate that a home-made provision, offered and accepted in good faith between commercial men and not in the least intended to be oppressive, has to be ruled out and declared void in a court of law for lack of the necessary limiting words. It would seem that a good deal of legal 'know-how' is required for the successful drafting of a restrictive covenant."

It is clear that not only must there be a legitimate trade interest, in the form of a trade secret, confidential information or goodwill, for example; but also that the restraint must go no further than protecting that interest. How widely, therefore, do such legitimate trade interests extend?

Bluebell Apparel Ltd v Dickinson 7–64

1978 S.C. 16; 1980 S.L.T. 157

Court of Session, First Division: Lord President (Emslie), Lords Johnston, Avonside

Bluebell manufactured "Wrangler" jeans. They operated throughout the world selling their products in some 120 countries. "Wrangler" jeans were sold in some 25 of these countries in Europe and Asia. There were said to be only two other companies that dominated the world market in jeans.

Dickinson trained with Bluebell and became a manager at one of their factories. While there he acquired knowledge of cutting and sewing machines that enabled Bluebell (as they claimed) to manufacture jeans more speedily, less expensively and with a better finish than their trade rivals. Bluebell also claimed they had devised new methods of working and of maximum utilisation of cloth about which Dickinson had learned. All these were trade secrets unknown to their competitors in the trade. Dickinson's employment contract included conditions that: (1) he would not disclose to any unauthorised person or use any of Bluebell's trade secrets; and (2) he would not for a period of two years after the end of his employment perform any services for any person or business entity in competition with Bluebell.

Some six months after joining, Dickinson left his employment with Bluebell. He indicated to them his intention to take up employment with a competitor that manufactured "Levi" jeans.

"LORD PRESIDENT (EMSLIE): ... In our opinion the submissions for the petitioners are to be preferred. We accept that the restriction when it is properly understood, having regard to its context and the objectives of the agreement, means that the respondent must not be employed by a competitor anywhere or in any capacity for the limited period of two years after August 31, 1977. Is such a restriction too wide having regard to the legitimate interest of the petitioners to prevent their trade secrets from coming to the knowledge of any competitor of theirs? If it is accepted, as it must be at this stage, that the respondent is an employee in the possession of trade secrets which would be of value to any competitor of the petitioners in the world's jeans market and that the respondent has properly been interdicted *ad interim* from disclosing these secrets, the restriction, as we have construed it, is not *prima facie* unreasonable at all. The risk of trade secrets of the petitioners coming into the knowledge of rivals obviously arises whenever an employee in possession of these secrets joins the ranks of a competitor, for in the service of that competitor, in any capacity, anywhere in the world, the employee may deliberately or unwittingly enable the competitor to acquire the benefit of these trade secrets in the trade in which he is in competition with the petitioners. There is no doubt in this case, according to the averments, that Levi Strauss are among the most important competitors of the petitioners in the world market in jeans and, having regard to the real interest of the petitioners to prevent even unintentional disclosure of their trade secrets to a competitor by a former employee, we can see nothing unreasonable in a restriction designed not only to prevent the respondent from working for such a competitor in any of their jeans factories or departments, but also to prevent him from becoming employed by that competitor at all during the short period of the restriction. 7–65

If, as we have held, the restriction is not *prima facie* unreasonable, ought it to be enforced by interim interdict? We have no doubt that it should be, for the balance of convenience strongly favours that enforcement. The risk of serious and, it may be, irreparable damage to the petitioners' business and interests if no interim interdict is pronounced far outweighs the consequences to the respondent of restoring the order which was recalled in the vacation court. He will, no doubt, lose for two years, or until the petition is disposed of on its merits, whichever is the earlier, the opportunity of working for Levi Strauss & Co., but it cannot be left out of account that the petitioners are willing to continue to pay his salary while the litigation continues and to assist him to find other employment in the garment manufacturing industry in any capacity which does not involve direct competition with the petitioners' product nor the risk of disclosure of their secrets to their trade rivals."

Both the *Bluebell* and the *Commercial Plastics* cases were concerned with proprietary interests in trade secrets and commercial information. In the sate of a business or of an interest in a partnership, what is encompassed by the notion of "goodwill" and, therefore what can legitimately be protected?

7–66 **Deacons (a firm) v Bridge**

[1984] 1 A.C. 705

Privy Council: Lord Fraser of Tullybelton, Lords Wilberforce, Scarman, Roskill and Templeman

Deacons is a large Hong Kong firm of solicitors. Bridge was the partner in charge of the term's intellectual property and trademark department. He dealt only with clients who used his department. The partnership agreement provided that if Bridge ceased to be a partner, he would not act as a solicitor in Hong Kong for a period of five years for any client of the firm or any person who had been a client of the firm in the three years preceding Bridge's departure from the firm. Bridge resigned from the firm, set up in business on his own and acted for former clients of Deacons.

Deacons successfully sought injunctions to restrain Bridge.

7–67 "LORD FRASER OF TULLYBELTON: ... Their Lordships are of opinion that a decision on whether the restrictions in this agreement are enforceable or not cannot be reached by attempting to place the agreement in any particular category, or by seeking for the category to which it is most closely analogous. The proper approach is that adopted by Lord Reid, in the *Esso Petroleum* case [1967] 1 All E.R. 699 at 709, [1968] A.C. 269 at 301, where he said:

'I think it better to ascertain what were the legitimate interests of the appellants which they were entitled to protect, and then to see whether these restraints were more than adequate for that purpose.'

What were the plaintiff's legitimate interests will depend largely on the nature of its business, and on the position of the defendant in the firm ...

An important feature of the case, which distinguishes it from any of the reported cases on partnership agreements that were brought to their Lordship's attention, and which was strongly relied on by counsel for the defendant, is that the plaintiff's office is divided into a number of departments, largely separate from each other. This division has occurred as a result of the great expansion in the plaintiff's practice over approximately the last 20 years. The division is emphasised by the fact that each file in their office is specifically assigned to the partner who remains ultimately responsible for it and who reads all incoming correspondence and signs all outgoing correspondence relating to it.

> Consequently, each partner's knowledge of the firm's business tends to be concentrated on his own department.
>
> So far as the defendant personally was concerned, the industrial property department was moved about July 1981 to a separate suite of offices on a different floor, and served by different lifts, from the firm's other departments. He was thus physically, to some extent, cut off from the other departments, The evidence was that he had only acted for those clients of the firm who made use of the intellectual and industrial property department.
>
> In 1981 the total of delivered bills of the plaintiff was approximately $HK 132m of which only about $HK 6m was attributable to that department, that is, about 4.5 per cent. The number of files in the office as a whole was disputed but it seems that something of the order of 10 per cent of the total was marked as being the responsibility of the defendant. Thus the defendant had no connection or dealings with the great majority (over 90 per cent) of the plaintiff's clients, and, as he claimed, he had no advantage over any other solicitor in seeking to attract their business.
>
> [Counsel for the defendant] maintained that, in these circumstances, the plaintiff was not entitled to protection against the defendant's acting for clients of the firm for whom he had never acted while he was a partner. The plaintiff was only entitled to protect such part of its goodwill as would be threatened by the defendant if he were to set up practice on his own account, and that part, on the evidence which was filed, consisted only of the business which he was advantageously placed to attract because it came from clients for whom he had acted and to whom he was known.
>
> Their Lordships do not accept that submission. In their view it is necessary to recall that the partners in the plaintiff firm, as constituted from time to time, are the owners of the firm's whole assets, including its most valuable asset, goodwill. The defendant had owned a share of the assets while he was a partner, but he transferred this share to the continuing partners when he ceased to be a partner. Thereafter the continuing partners owned the whole of the assets: see 8(a) of the agreement which provides:
>
> 'The assets of the partnership including goodwill and all furniture, safes, boxes, equipment, fittings, fixtures, stores and books held or used for or in connection with the practice ... belong to the partners in proportion to their respective shares.'"

In this case the Privy Council clearly identified the legitimate interest to be protected as the general goodwill—including clients with whom the leaving partner had had no dealings. In *Dallas McMillan & Sinclair v Simpson*,[82] a partner in a firm of solicitors was prohibited from competing with the firm upon leaving the partnership, for three years within 20 miles of Glasgow Cross. The covenant added: "it being agreed by all parties hereto that this time and distance are reasonable for the protection of the parties hereto". This did not prevent Lord Mayfield in the Outer House from determining that, unlike the *Deacons* decision, the clause here was far wider than was necessary to protect the firm's legitimate interest. It meant, for example that Simpson could not work, in any capacity, in sizeable towns like Hamilton, Motherwell or Airdrie. **7–68**

In *Group 4 Total Security Ltd v Ferrier*[83] the Second Division was invited to extend the legitimate interests that an employer (rather than a partner) could protect to cover the interests of other companies with which the employer was connected, but with which the employee being restrained had no direct association. Although he did not find the restriction in the case unreasonable, Lord Ross stated:

---

[82] *Dallas McMillan & Sinclair v Simpson*, 1989 S.L.T. 454.

[83] *Group 4 Total Security Ltd v Ferrier*, 1985 S.L.T. 287.

> "Although that definition is expressed to be for the purposes of the particular chapter of the Act, it is an indication of what is meant by 'associated company'. In the circumstances of the present case it appears to me reasonable to regard the petitioners together with their subsidiaries and associated companies as a single group with business interests to protect."

The decision potentially extends the legitimate trade interests which a corporate employer, or even the purchaser of a corporate business, might legitimately protect. In *Hinton & Higgs (UK) Ltd v Murphy*[84] Lord Dervaird clearly found it permissible that an employer's entire goodwill, as that of a partnership (as in *Deacons v Bridge*), is capable of protection; but it is not enough merely to declare, in the contract, that the restriction is reasonable. More particularly, he was not prepared to accept that the *Group 4* case had established that the interests of associated companies could legitimately be protected "in the absence of some special circumstances".

[84] *Hinton & Higgs (UK) Ltd v Murphy*, 1989 S.L.T. 450.

PART 4

THE SUBSTANCE OF A CONTRACT

CHAPTER 8
THE TERMS OF A CONTRACT

Introduction

So far we have considered how contractual agreements are created and what might prevent this. Having established that a contract has come into existence, how will the parties know the extent of their obligations? What does their contract comprise? **8–01**

The starting point is to consider the evidence—what the parties said, and what they wrote or did. The value given to any particular statement will depend on the rules of evidence: whether the statement is written, whether it is signed, the point in the negotiations when the statement was made are all evidential issues that will determine what the parties have agreed. The parties may have tried to provide for contingencies in their agreement in a single document, as they might do when buying and selling a house. At the other extreme, as in the purchase of a single item in a supermarket, the contract might be made and performed with nothing being said or written by either party. Most contracts fall somewhere between such extremes, and the contract is to be found in what the parties said, and what they wrote or did.

Although it is more accurate to speak of the stipulations in a contract, the word "term" has gained general acceptance. The terms define both what the parties are obliged to do, and what they are entitled to expect under the contract. When those obligations are not performed, or performed wrongly—in other words when those terms are breached, or broken—the contract itself has been breached, or broken. In this and the following two chapters we will consider the rules for establishing the terms of the contract.

Terms and terminology

The obligations arising from a contract, like all voluntary obligations in Scots law may be classified as follows: **8–02**

(a) *pure* or *simple* obligations are those which are to be performed immediately upon formation of the obligation, or at least within a reasonable time;
(b) *future* obligations are those which arise only upon the happening of a specified, future event;
(c) *conditional* or *contingent* obligations are those subject to a condition which, unless purified, or fulfilled, precludes enforcement of the obligation. Conditions may be:
   (i) *suspensive*,[1] so that performance of the obligation does not arise until the happening of a particular event;
   (ii) *resolutive* (subsequent),[2] so that the performance of the obligation terminates upon the happening of the specified event;
   (iii) *potestative*,[3] so that the specified event may be fulfilled by one of, the parties to the contract;
   (iv) *casual*, so that the event is fulfilled by an act of a third party; or
   (v) *mixed*, containing an element of potestative and casual condition.

---

[1] Not to be confused with the term "condition precedent" in English law. See also the effect of suspensive conditions on contract formation, above, para.3–30.
[2] Not to be confused with the term "condition subsequent" in English law.
[3] See J Murray, "Potestative Conditions", 1991 S.L.T. (News) 185–188 and AF Rodger, "Potestative Conditions", 1991 S.L.T. (News) 253.

It is more accurate to speak of stipulations in a contract, but the word "term" is current usage.

The terms or stipulations of the contract define the obligations which the parties have undertaken—the subject matter, the duration of the contract and so on. Not all stipulations have equal consequences if broken.

A useful analysis is provided in the following extract.

8–03 *Review of Contract Law: Third Party Rights in Scotland*

Scottish Law Commission Discussion Paper No.157 (March 2014)

Future and conditional obligations

[2.6] Voluntary obligations may be dependent in various ways upon the occurrence or non-occurrence of external events.[15] First, an obligation may be *future* in nature: that is to say, it becomes enforceable on a fixed date (*dies*) or upon the occurrence of some event which is certain to happen but the date of which is uncertain (eg the death of some person). Here the obligation exists but cannot be enforced until the date in question arrives (*dies statim cedit, sed non venit*).

[2.7] Second, an obligation may be *contingent* or *conditional*, meaning that its existence or enforceability is dependent upon the occurrence of some uncertain event (the contingency or condition). The contingency may be *potestative*; that is, the event is one which it is in the power of one or other of the parties to the obligation to bring about. The condition may, however, be an event beyond the control of the parties.

[2.8] Contingencies or conditions may be categorised as either *suspensive* or *resolutive*. The effect of a suspensive condition may be either to prevent the obligation coming into existence at all (as for example with a provision in an oral agreement that there will be no contract between the parties until the agreement is reduced to formal writing[16]), or, more commonly, to prevent an obligation which has come into existence being enforceable until the condition is fulfilled (as for example a sale of land being subject to the purchaser obtaining satisfactory planning permission for development of the site[17]). Where the effect of the condition is to suspend the very existence of the obligation, the parties are free to resile or withdraw from the arrangement during the period of suspension.[18] But where it is merely enforceability that is suspended, the obligation exists but neither party may act in such a way as to frustrate the fulfilment of the condition by the other where it is potestative. Thus if party B's car is on party A's land and A promises B £100 if the latter removes the car by 1 June, A remains liable if he prevents B gaining access to the land for the purpose before the relevant date. But if B promises to pay A £100 if the car is still there on 1 June, and then removes the car on 31 May, B is not liable to A for frustrating the fulfilment of the suspensive condition.[19] The law on conditions is not a way of converting discretionary powers into absolute duties. It may be implied that the obligation is discharged if the suspensive condition is not fulfilled within a reasonable time.[20]

[2.9] The effect of a resolutive condition, on the other hand, is that an obligation comes into existence but may be brought to an end upon the fulfilment of the condition (as for example in provision for the termination of an agency agreement in the event that a certain level of turnover is not achieved[21]). Here, clearly, a party may perform lawful acts in order to prevent the fulfilment of the condition. But in the agency case just mentioned, it was held that the principal was personally barred from terminating the contract where the agent's failure to achieve the turnover levels required was due to the principal's failure to furnish the agent with sufficient goods to fulfil orders. An obligation of good faith may underlie the operation of the law in the whole area of potestative conditions.[22]

[2.10] Further illustrations of both types of conditions in the context of third party rights in contract will be given in what follows, as the concept plays a vital role in this area.

---

[9] See *Regus (Maxim) Ltd v Bank of Scotland plc* [2013] CSIH 12, paras 33-34 (Lord President Gill).
[10] *Cawdor v Cawdor* [2007] CSIH 3, para 15.
[11] RoW(S)A s 1(2).
[12] RoW(S)A s 2(2).
[13] RoW(S)A s 1(2). It is submitted that "in the course of business" means both a promise by one business to another and a promise made by a business to its consumer customers and to any other non-business party (eg to repair damage caused by business operations to a neighbouring private home).
[14] For statutory *rei interventus* see RoW(S)A s 1(3), (4).
[15] See generally J M Thomson, "Suspensive and Resolutive Conditions in the Scots Law of Contract" in A J Gamble (ed), *Obligations in Context: Essays in Honour of Professor D M Walker* (1990), pp 126-140; McBryde, *Contract*, paras 5.35-5.40. We have also been much helped by advance sight of a draft discussion of this subject by Professor Martin Hogg forthcoming in *SME* Reissue Obligations.
[16] As in *WS Karoulias SA v The Drambuie Liqueur Co Ltd* 2005 SLT 813.
[17] As in *Ellis Properties Ltd v Pringle* 1974 SC 200. This condition may also be seen in at least some circumstances as resolutive, which is discussed in para 2.9 below.
[18] Thomson, "Suspensive and Resolutive conditions", pp 126-129; *cf* McBryde, *Contract*, paras 5.35-5.40 who suggests a threefold distinction of suspensive conditions: those which prevent any contract at all until fulfilment, with the parties free to resile meantime; those under which a contract comes into existence but while none of it is enforceable the parties cannot resile; and those under which the contract comes into existence but only some part or parts of it are suspended.
[19] The examples elaborate one found in A F Rodger QC, "Potestative Conditions" 1991 SLT (News) 253 (part of a response to J Murray QC, "Potestative Conditions" 1991 SLT (News) 185). The leading case is *Mackay v Dick and Stephenson* (1881) 8 R (HL) 37.
[20] See *T Boland & Co Ltd v Dundas's Trs* 1975 SLT (Notes) 80.
[21] As in *Dowling v Methven & Sons & Co* 1921 SC 948.
[22] MacQueen and Thomson, *Contract*, paras 3.34 and 3.68.

Obligations arising other than from the express terms of the contract

Imagine the simplest and most common of transactions—a purchase of groceries at a local supermarket. Pleasantries were exchanged at the check-out; but nothing was said about the goods being purchased. A contract has arisen for the sale (and purchase) of goods—a contract that creates contractual rights and obligations for both parties—the buyer and the seller (the supermarket). There may be no express terms (written or oral) to define those obligations; but rights and obligations will nevertheless arise from that contract. **8–04**

Where do such obligations come from? If a dispute arises, where would a court look to find those obligations? After reviewing major judicial pronouncements on the subject, McBryde concludes:

> "It is thought that these dicta, although varying in their expression, support the proposition that implied terms are normally of two types: a term implied as a matter of general law, and a term implied in the circumstances of a particular contract."

Terms implied as a matter of general law into particular categories of contracts[4]

8–05 Throughout his discourse on contracts, Stair in his *Institutions* makes no reference to terms, express or implied.[5] Similarly Erskine in his *Institute*; but he frequently refers to "obligations".[6] They both looked to the Roman law, under which the various forms of contract are merely vehicles for establishing voluntary obligations. For example, the obligations that a contract of *depositum* (deposit) would place on the parties would be different from the obligations created by a contract of *pignus* (pledge). We have already come across the term "incidents" in describing what the essential obligations are in any particular category of contract.[7]

Strictly speaking, particular categories of contract and their incidents create particular obligations. Through the influence of English case law and, most particularly through the application of the Sale of Goods Act 1893 to Scotland, Scottish judges and commentators almost exclusively now use the expression "terms" to cover what would formerly have been referred to as the obligations arising from a contract. Similarly, whereas Stair and Erskine might use *stipulation* for an obligation created orally or in writing by the parties to a contract, the modern usage is to refer to an oral or written term. Subject to express agreement to the contrary, courts today will imply into recognised categories of nominate contract—employment, agency, partnership, carriage and so on—standard terms that have been established by precedent or by institutional writers as normal in such categories.

8–06 *The Law of Contract in Scotland*

WW McBryde, 3rd edn (Edinburgh: W. Green/SULI, 2007)

"9–02 For certain of the nominate contracts, such as sale of hire, the source of terms which may be implied is case and statute law. For innominate contracts there must be other considerations, which suggests that for a particular contract in dispute and perhaps for that contract only, a term will be implied. Implication of terms thus arises at two levels-as a matter of general law and in the case of a particular contract. There are, therefore, two types of implied terms. In other legal systems implied terms are also recognised, but in some civilian systems the concept is rather elusive. It may be that in legal systems with a general concept of good faith in the performance of contracts, implied terms can be of less importance than in Scots law (or English law). The Principles of European Contract Law mention implied terms which arise from (a) the intention of the parties, (b) the mature and purpose of the contract, and (c) good faith and fair dealing. The first two concepts bear some resemblance to Scots and English law. But the absence of a generalised concept of good faith means that the reluctance to imply terms which are strongly in favour of one party must be explained in other ways. In practice in so far as Scots law looks outside its own system of implied terms it is likely to be English las, and systems based on English law.

. . .

9–11 ... Implied terms arising from the general law are created or recognised on grounds of legal policy or precedent. Terms implied in the circumstances of a particular contract, which need not be unique, exist because of the presumed intention of the

---

[4] Please note that, in relation to consumer contracts, the Consumer Rights Act 2015 Chs 2, 3 and 4 have fundamentally revised the terms implied into virtually all forms of consumer supply contracts: see generally WCH Ervine, *Consumer Law in Scotland*, 5th edn (Edinburgh: W. Green, 2015), Chs 3 and 4.

[5] Stair, *Institutions*, I x–xviii.

[6] Erskine, *Institute*, III i 16–35.

[7] See above, Ch.3; cf. Lord Normand in *Mathieson Gee v Quigley*, above, para.6–25.

parties to have a contract which will work in a reasonable businesslike manner (although the courts refer to what is "necessary") . . . While it is possible for the courts to detect a hitherto unrecognised term as a legal incident of a particular type of contract . . . this is exceptional, and it will normally be easier to satisfy the business efficacy rule."

The rights and obligations of many employees, for example, are almost entirely defined in this way and the rights and obligations of the principal and agent in a contract of agency are similarly incorporated. These are aspects of the substantive law on those contracts and any further study of them should be pursued in more specialised texts.[8] They arise in many of the cases considered throughout this book.

The following case illustrates the difficulty in implying a term as a matter of general law.

GM Shepherd Ltd v North West Securities Ltd 8–07

1991 S.L.T. 499

Court of Session, Second Division: The Lord Justice-Clerk (Ross), Lords Murray and McCluskey

The pursuers (GMS), a firm of retail chemists hired from North West Securities (NWS) a compact printer processor for developing and printing films. NWS was to purchase the printer/processor from a supplier, then hire it to GMS. Shepherd, the managing director of GMS, saw a demonstration of a similar machine before GMS entered into the contract of hire. Clause 6 of the hire agreement stated:

> "The Hirer acknowledges that the Hirer has inspected and approved the equipment and that the Owners will have purchased the equipment and entered into the presents in reliance upon such inspection and approval and further declares that no presentation, warranty or condition in respect thereof which may have been made given or accepted by the Supplier to or in favour of the Hirer, nor any warranty or condition which might be implied by law, shall in any way bind the Owners and that in no circumstances shall the Hirer have or seek to make against the Owners any claims whatsoever in respect thereof or arising out of any delay or default in delivery or (if applicable) installation of the equipment."

Shepherd, for GMS, also signed an indemnity in favour of NWS which stated:

> "1. I . . . will indemnify . . . you . . . all loss or damage suffered and all claims costs and expenses made against or incurred by you in any way arising out of or consequent upon [the] . . . Agreement . . . or whether such loss or damage . . . arises out of a breach by the Hirer of any of the terms and conditions or otherwise or of the said Agreement being (for whatever reason) unenforceable against the Hirer."

GMS became dissatisfied with the performance of the printer/processor. They rejected it and rescinded the contract and sought damages in the sheriff court against NWS for their alleged breach of the contract of hire. They claimed, inter alia, that the contract was subject to an implied term that the equipment was hireworthy, even though GMS, unlike the owners in a normal contract of hire, had never had possession of the goods hired.

The court found no hireworthiness term that could be implied in every contract of hire, including one where the goods had never been in the owner's possession.

---

[8] A very useful analysis of some of the terms more generally found in many kinds of contract is provided by WW McBryde, *The Law of Contract in Scotland*, 3rd edn (Edinburgh: W. Green, 2007), paras 9–13—9–22.

8–08 "LORD JUSTICE-CLERK (ROSS): ... For the purposes of the present argument, I am prepared to accept that under a normal contract of hire, the owner or lessor is under an obligation to deliver the thing hired to the hirer in such a condition that it may serve the purpose for which it was let. It is, however, important to observe that, as is clear in Erskine [III. i. 15] and Gow [*Mercantile Law*, pp.242 to 243], the reference to the thing hired being in such a condition that it may serve the purposes for which it is hired, is linked to the obligation to deliver that thing. That, I think, emphasises that the implied obligation of hireworthiness is owed by a lessor who has had possession of the article hired, and delivers it to the hirer. That, however, was not the situation under the present equipment hiring agreement, because the owner never had possession of the compact printer processor, and he only purchased it from the supplier at the special request of the hirer who acknowledged that he, the hirer, had inspected and approved the equipment. The special features of the equipment hiring agreement appear to me to demonstrate that there is no room for importing into that agreement the implied obligation described in Erskine and Gow.

As Professor Gloag observed at p. 288, whether a particular term can be implied in a contract is a question of construction of that contract, and when one seeks to construe the equipment hire agreement I am of opinion that no such condition as to hireworthiness should be implied. When one bears in mind that the defenders purchased the equipment from the supplier at the request of the pursuers and in reliance upon the inspection and approval of the equipment by the pursuers, I am not persuaded that it can have been the presumed intention of the parties that the defenders should be under any such implied obligation in relation to the hireworthiness of the equipment. This appears to me to be a clear case where such an implied term would be contradictory of and inconsistent with the other terms of the contract.

One of the contentions of junior counsel for the pursuers was that an implied condition of hireworthiness was necessary in this case in order to give the contract business efficacy because the pursuers as hirers were bound to pay for the period of the hire, and, in the absence of such an implied term, they would still require to pay for the hire although the equipment was not in a hireworthy condition. In my judgment, however, such an implied condition is not necessary in order to give the contract business efficacy. It is quite intelligible that the pursuers as hirers should be bound to pay for the period of the hire even although the equipment should turn out not to be in a hireworthy condition because the pursuers agreed to enter into the equipment hire agreement upon the basis that they had inspected and approved the equipment and that the owners had purchased the equipment and entered into the equipment hire agreement in reliance upon such inspection and approval.

The present case appears to me to be quite different to the normal contract of hire where the owner will have had possession of the equipment himself and will have known the purpose for which the goods are required by the hirer. In the present case ... the pursuers aver that the processor was hired for the purpose of developing photographs within their premises at Cults, and that they required the processor to develop films 'to normal professional standards of colour, focus, and bordering and trimming, and to do so on the pursuers' shop premises in an average time of about 11 minutes all as described by and demonstrated by Photosystems (U.K.) Ltd. at said trade show.' It is, however, significant that the pursuers do not undertake to prove that the defenders were aware of the purpose for which the processor was hired or that the pursuers required the machine to develop films to the standard set forth above."

8–09 Was Lord Ross here dealing with the implication of a "common law" or "general" term into this particular category of contract; or with the implication of a term in the particular circumstances of the contract? Was Lord Ross suggesting merely that a general term will be implied into a contract only where the contract is "typical" of contracts into which the term is normally implied? If so, does this mean that no new "general" terms could be developed? If so, where did existing "generally" implied terms originate?

Note that the agreement was redolent of English terminology. Note also that under Pt 1A of the Supply of Goods and Services Act 1982, inserted by the Sale and Supply of Goods Act 1994, inter alia, for contracts of hire in Scotland entered into after 3 January 1995, terms are implied relating to quality or fitness of the goods.

Lord Ross also disposes of the argument from GMS's junior counsel that an "implied condition" of hireworthiness was necessary to give the contract "business efficacy". This test is examined further below.

This case may be contrasted with the earlier case of *North American and Continental Sales Inc v Bepi (Electronics) Ltd.*[9] In that case NACS entered into an exclusive distribution agreement with Bepi for a software process. The Scottish firm failed to market the product, claiming it did not work. NACS argued successfully in the Outer House for the implication of a term that Bepi were obliged to use the process in a business-like manner, such a term being necessary to give the contract business efficacy.

Perhaps the key factor in such cases is the "novelty" of the issue under consideration: see, for example, *Lothian v Jelonite.*[10]

Terms implied by statute as a matter of general law into a particular category of contract

The legislature rarely intervenes to impose terms on the parties to contracts. When it does **8–10**
intervene, it is often to protect a particular group of persons, for example employees, or consumers and, rather than implying terms into the contract, imposes obligations directly upon the parties and specify the remedies and penalties that apply to their breach.[11] A major exception is the sale and supply of goods, where many terms are implied directly by statute into the contract, often superseding their express terms. These statutory implied terms were first formulated in the Sale of Goods Act 1893. Their current form in the Sale of Goods Act 1979, as amended by the Sale and Supply of Goods Act 1994 and the Sale and Supply of Goods to Consumers Regulations 2002. They are merely a consolidation, if not a codification of the rules developed in predominantly English case law. There is little doubt that it reflects an anglicised version of the Scots law on the subject. European harmonisation of implied terms in contracts for the sale of goods was brought yet closer (at least insofar as the buyer deals as a consumer) by the EC Directive 1999/44/EC on Certain Aspects of the Sale of Consumer Goods and Associated Guarantees, which resulted in further amendments to the Sale of Goods Act 1979 from 31 March 2003. Inter alia, these amendments introduced the idea of "conformity to the contract". If adopted, the provisions of the Common European Sales Law would make available a standard law of sales available throughout the European Union which is based on the creation of contractual obligations, rather than through the device of implied terms.

These provisions can be contrasted with certain other contracts the contents of which are entirely regulated by UK statutes that implement international conventions, the most notable being international carriage of goods by sea, land and air. Instead of deploying the device of the implied term, the Acts in question merely impose the obligation on the appropriate party to the contract.

---

[9] *North American and Continental Sales Inc v Bepi (Electronics) Ltd*, 1982 S.L.T. 47.

[10] *Lothian v Jelonite*, 1969 S.C. 111. See below, para.8–22.

[11] For example, Employment Protection (Consolidation) Act 1978; Consumer Credit Act 1974 ss.56(3) and 59; Consumer Protection (Cancellation of Contracts Concluded Away from Business Premises) Regulations 1987 reg.10; Consumer Protection (Distance Selling) Regulations 2000 regs 24(3) and 25.

Terms implied by custom or usage into a particular category of contracts

8–11 Customary rules, for example in a particular locality, or in a particular trade, although rare today,[12] once featured prominently. "Some of the rules became absorbed into the general law; others disappeared into folklore."[13] Occasionally, courts may be asked to imply into a contract a custom which has neither died out, nor become incorporated into the general law. Whether it can be said that such a custom, by being implied into a contract thereby becomes part of the general law is open to debate; but if a custom in a particular trade or profession is reasonable, certain and well known, it is binding upon the parties, whether or not they knew of it. Local or regional, as well as general customs may be so implied, but not if the custom conflicts with the express terms of the contract.[14]

8–12

William Morton & Co v Muir Brothers & Co
1907 S.C. 1211
Court of Session, Extra Division: Lords Ardwall, McLaren and Pearson

Morton were lace curtain manufacturers in Newmilns in the Irvine Valley, a lace making centre. The lace was produced on "Jacquard" looms, which manufacture lace by reproducing the design or pattern perforated onto pattern cards.

Morton gave designs to Muir; who reproduced them onto perforated pattern cards and produced from them, on their looms in their factory, lace for Morton. The copyright in the pattern cards remained with Muir.

When the Muir business became bankrupt, the trustee in sequestration entered into an agreement with Messrs Heyman and Alexander, one of Morton's competitors, to manufacture for them lace, using pattern cards including those which reproduced Morton's designs.

Morton now sought to prevent Muir from so doing, claiming that it would be a breach of an implied term in their contract with Morton, based on a recognised custom of the lace-making trade in the Irvine Valley, to use the cards in question to produce lace only for Morton.

The Inner House agreed that there was such an implied term.

8–13 "LORD MCLAREN: ... In these circumstances the following are the questions which, as I think, arise for decision:

(1) Is the condition [*sic*] alleged by the respondents within the region of usage of trade, or customary implied condition, and is this customary condition proved?

On the first question, ... according to the general understanding of the trade in Scotland, a maker who works to a design supplied to him has not an unqualified right to the use of the cards which he makes from that design, but is held to have received that design for the purposes of the order given to him and any further orders from the same manufacturer or merchant. ... [T]he substance of the evidence is that the maker of cards to a design which is not his own is subject to a twofold condition (1) that the cards are to be kept unused for a reasonable time to admit of the merchant or purchaser of the goods giving repeat orders if he so desires; (2) that the cards are not to be used by the maker for his own purposes unless and until the merchant or purchaser has no further use for them ...

[12] See, however, discussion on "course of dealings" below, para.9–67.

[13] WW McBryde, *The Law of Contract in Scotland*, 3rd edn (Edinburgh: W. Green, 2007), para.9–60.

[14] WW McBryde, *The Law of Contract in Scotland*, 3rd edn (Edinburgh: W. Green, 2007), paras 9–61—9–66 and cases referred to there.

The conception of an implied condition is one with which we are familiar in relation to contracts of every description, and if we seek to trace any implied conditions to their source, it will be found that in almost every instance they are founded either on universal custom or in the nature of the contract itself. If the condition is such that every reasonable man on the one part would desire for his own to stipulate for the condition, and that no reasonable man on the other part would refuse to accede to it, then it is not unnatural that the condition should be taken for granted in all contracts for the class without the necessity of giving it formal expression ...

[W]ithout proposing to rest the decision on what is technically known as usage of trade, I think that evidence of the general understanding of the trade may very usefully be considered in determining whether there is or is not an implied condition in such contracts whereby the merchant who furnishes the design reserves to himself a certain control as to the use to be made of the cards which are prepared from his design.

If I had to consider the question without the aid which this evidence affords, I should think it a very unreasonable result of the bargain that the manufacturer, as soon as he had furnished the number of lace curtains that were ordered, should be at liberty to make use of the design and the cards prepared from the design to make an equal number of pieces for himself and so to compete in the market with his employer ... But now, when I learn from the evidence that what I should suppose to be a reasonable implication from the nature of the contract is in exact accordance with the understanding of the trade, uniformly accepted and acted on, although not hitherto brought to the test of a legal decision, I think the implication is very much strengthened. The two grounds of judgment are not distinct; they support each other. First, the condition must be one which the law will regard as reasonably arising from the nature of the contract when fully understood. But, secondly, as the Court is not conversant with the details of commercial business, we receive evidence on this subject, and the result of the evidence on my mind is that I am satisfied that such a condition is implied; in other words, that no merchant would furnish a design and give an order except on the understanding that the maker of the goods was not to make use of his design to compete with him in the market."

The judges of the Inner House were willing to imply a term into the contract, both on the basis of proven local custom and on the grounds that it was "reasonable" to do so in this category of contract. Lords Ardwall and Pearson in fact suggested that it was "necessary" because of the "confidential" nature of this category of contract.[15]

Just how difficult it is to imply custom into a contract is illustrated by the following case.

[15] *William Morton & Co v Muir Brothers & Co*, 1907 S.C. 1211 at 1228 and 1210.

8–14 **Strathlorne Steamship Co v Baird & Sons**

1916 S.C. (H.L.) 134

House of Lords: Lord Chancellor (Buckmaster), Lords Atkinson, Kinnear, Shaw of Dunfermline

"The Strathlorne" loaded a cargo of barley in sacks at a North Pacific port under a charter-party which provided for discharge at a port in the UK "according to the custom at port of discharge for steamers". She was ordered to discharge at Leith, where the consignees demanded delivery of the barley in the original sacks. The shipowners claimed the right to discharge the cargo according to an alleged custom at Leith whereby grain shipped on steamers from North Pacific ports would be bulked in the hold, from which it would be hoisted in tubs to the deck and poured into sacks of a uniform size.

In the previous 20 years some 80 such cargoes of grain had been discharged at Leith, and all but two had been discharged by the receivers bulking the cargo in the hold. In every instance, however, the ship-owners had written a formal letter protesting against being held liable for the number of sacks shipped, if that method of discharge was adopted. The evidence of two firms of receivers who had received most of these cargoes was that this method of discharge did not depend upon custom, but had merely been adopted by them to suit their convenience and to save expense.

A unanimous House of Lords held that the uniformity of the practice alone did not prove a binding custom of port.

8–15 "LORD CHANCELLOR . . . In order that a custom or, to use a more exact phrase, a commercial usage, may be binding upon parties to a contract, it is essential that it should be certain, that it should be uniform, that it should be reasonable, and that it should be notorious. To use the words of Sir George Jessel in the case of *Nelson v Dahl*, 'It . . . must have quite as much certainty as the written contract itself'.

. . . [If] . . . the practice possessed the other attributes necessary for it to be recognised as a custom, the question of its reasonableness would be almost necessarily involved in the facts which were necessary to show that it was a uniform and accepted practice . . . Notoriety in this connexion mean[s] that it must be well known at the place to which it applies, and be capable of ready ascertainment by any person who proposes to enter into a contract of which that usage would form part. It is in fact to be regarded as though it were a term so well known in connexion with the particular transaction that it was nothing but waste of time and writing to introduce it into the contract.

. . .

[T]he two people whose practice in connexion with this matter must be the practice mainly relied upon by the respondents, . . . both . . . say that their act is due to the deliberate election on their own part to accept the cargo in this particular form to suit their particular business, and that they have never regarded that they were doing it in connexion with any general practice; but that, if occasion arose and their convenience would be better suited by another method of delivery, that method of delivery they would adopt.

. . .

[T]he proof of the custom is sadly lacking; and that is a matter of considerable consequence, because an essential condition of this custom being as I have stated, that anyone engaged in this trade should be able whenever he entered into a bargain to find out if it existed, the appellants in this case would have been quite unable, if they had applied either to the two large firms of receivers or to the shipowners in this case, to have ascertained, in answer to their inquiry, that the custom which the respondents allege existed in fact at all.

LORD SHAW OF DUNFERMLINE 8–16

... I regret to have to differ from the judgment of the Second Division ... [T]he learned Judges ... considered that the custom of the Port of Leith was established by the number of instances in fact in which the practice of unloading in bulk had been adhered to. ... Lord Blackburn in ... *Postlethwaite v Freeland* ... grounded the question of custom upon what he called 'settled and established practice'. If by settled and established practice the learned Judge meant (as I am certain he did not) that all that was required to establish an obligatory custom was to tick off through a course of years a number of instances in which a certain practice had been followed, then I should certainly venture to doubt whether such an opinion was sound.

... In the first place, no number of contracts to do a thing which is expressly specified can ever establish a binding custom to do that thing without its being specified. In the second place, you cannot build up a custom of trade or of a port out of a series of protests against it. These protests may be expressly against the admission of a custom, or they may be by implication against it in respect of making demands which would have been unfounded if such a custom had already bound the parties. With regard to this case the letters founded on contain the characteristics of both of these protests.

... I think that the distinction should be made plain between a settled and established practice in the general sense of the mere occurrence of instances (many of which may have sprung from express contract), and a settled and established practice which amounts to the acceptance of a binding obligation of a custom apart from particular bargain."

The Lord Chancellor was referring to the English version of what is necessary to establish a custom; but the point is well made that the custom must be certain and capable of being stated precisely.

The *Strathlorne* was one of the ships ultimately owned by Sir William Burrell, the man who collected the artefacts that comprise the Burrell Collection in Glasgow. She was build in Dumbarton in 1909. Burrell sold the *Strathlorne* to Greek shipowners Pateras and, renamed *Aghia Eirini* she ran aground and was wrecked in December 1940.

Although the concern in *Morton v Muir* and in *The Strathlorne* was with custom and usage—that is, as a matter of general application to a category of contracts in a particular area of Scotland—much of the discussion in the judgments concerned the implication of particular terms in the circumstances of a particular contract. It is this we must now address.

Individual terms implied in the circumstances of a particular contract

In cases like *GM Shepherd Ltd v North West Securities Ltd* and "*The Strathlorne*" the courts 8–17 were dealing with contracts that were written and contained detailed, express terms. What if a dispute arises that is not addressed by those express terms? It is not the function of the courts to write the terms of a contract for the parties, especially where they have committed that contract to writing. The court, however, must deal with the problem. As we have seen, the court may find that no contract has arisen, because the parties have failed to agree the essentials of an agreement, or even because what they have agreed is too uncertain to be enforced as a contract.[16] Alternatively, the court may consider the problem as one of interpretation of the words used by the parties.[17] A further possibility is that the court will imply a term into the contract.

There is a great deal of case law, both Scottish and English, upon the implication of terms into

[16] Above, para.3–12.

[17] See below, para.8–30.

contracts. It is nevertheless difficult to discern from those cases a uniform test which is applied and the citation of previous authority can be of limited value,[18] except by way of illustration.

It is difficult to extract a basic principle underlying the decisions. This is partly because each case depends specifically on its facts; but also because the cases reveal various approaches and not all are applied with consistency or priority. To complicate matters further, although Scottish courts make frequent reference to English authority, in recent years House of Lords, and now Supreme Court decisions show a divergence north and south of the border.

What follows highlights the basic principles and how they might be applied.

The "business efficacy" test[19]

8–18 Exceptionally, courts are willing to imply a term into a contract so as to give it business efficacy. Where the contract is unworkable without such a term, it will be implied if it was the presumed intention of the parties. In *The Moorcock*,[20] Bowen LJ stated the principle:

> "I believe if one were to take all the cases, and they are many, of implied warranties or covenants in law, it will be found that in all of them the law is raising an implication from the presumed intention of the parties with the object of giving the transaction such business efficacy as both parties must have intended that at all events it should have. In business transactions such as this, what the law desires to effect by the implication is to give such efficacy to the transaction as must have been intended at all events by both parties who are business men; not to impose on one side all the perils of the transaction, or to emancipate one side from all the chances of failure, but to make each party promise in law as much, at all events, as it must have been in the contemplation of both parties that he should be responsible for in respect of those perils or chances."

The court implied a term that wharfingers would take reasonable care to ensure that the river bed would not cause injury to the ship, the *Moorcock* when she came to discharge her cargo at the wharf.

Bowen LJ limited his principle to cases where both parties "are business men". In *Crawford v Bruce*, Lord President Hope said[21]:

> "The use of the word 'business' is appropriate where the contract which is in question is one which can properly be described as a business transaction between business men. It is perhaps open to question whether the same word is applicable where the contract is a formal written lease of heritable property, even if the subjects are business premises. But the principle is not confined only to business transactions. The concept of giving such efficacy to the transaction as both parties must have intended it to have is of wide application."

In *Lothian v Jelonite*[22] the court stressed the need to restrict the implication of terms to those that are *essential* to give effect to the parties' intentions.

Business efficacy and reasonableness

8–19 Lord McLaren in *Morton v Muir* that before any term can be implied, it must be

---

[18] WW McBryde, *The Law of Contract in Scotland*, 2nd edn (Edinburgh: W. Green, 2001), para.9–76.

[19] See WW McBryde, *The Law of Contract in Scotland*, 2nd edn (Edinburgh: W. Green, 2001), paras 9–67—9–76.

[20] *The Moorcock* (1889) 14 P.D. 64.

[21] *Crawford v Bruce*, 1992 S.L.T. 524, at 531. See below, para.8–24.

[22] Below, para.8–22.

"such that every reasonable man on the one part would desire for his own to stipulate for the condition, and that no reasonable man on the other part would refuse to accede to it".[23]

The test is, in other words, an objective test, not based on the subjective intentions of the parties. In subsequent decisions, this statement has been seen as a gloss on the "business efficacy" test, so that a term will be implied into a particular contract only if it is necessary and also reasonable between the parties.

McWhirter v Longmuir 8–20

1948 S.C. 577

Inner House, Second Division: Lords MacKay, Jamieson and Stevenson

During World War II, a centrally administered scheme divided Ayrshire into zones to control the delivery of milk. M, who operated one such zone, was conscripted into the armed forces and divided his area into three shares. The recipient of one share, A, sold it to L. Some two and a half years later, M sought the return of the share operated by L. L refused, arguing that, although the agreement between M and A provided a mechanism for retransfer of the share to M, L argued that an implication of reasonable time within which M had to serve notice was necessary to give business efficacy to the contract. The agreement was silent on the point, so L sought the implications of a term to that effect, which M had failed to meet.

The court refused to imply such a term.

"LORD JAMIESON: ... [I]t was argued that some term limiting the pursuer's right to a reasonable time must be implied, and the *dicta* of Lord McLaren in *Morton v Muir Brothers*, 1907 S.C. 1211, and Bowen, L.J., in *The "Moorcock"*, 14 P.D. 64 at p.68, were founded on ... 8–21

Professor Gloag in his work on the Law of Contract has a cogent criticism on the opinion that the implication of a term depends on the presumption that the parties would have agreed to it. He points out that it raises 'the obvious difficulty that it is usually clear, either directly from his evidence or indirectly from his attitude to the case, that one of the parties would not have agreed to it had it been originally suggested.' He adds, 'The hypothetical agreement which justifies the implication of a term is not, it is submitted, that of the parties to the contract, but that of two reasonable men in the same circumstances' (Gloag on Contract, (2nd ed.) p. 288). There is force in the learned author's comment, and applying it to the circumstances of the present case the members of the association, who had full knowledge of the business, considered and rejected the proposal that any such term, as is now contended must be implied, should be added to the contract.

The Court will only hold a term or condition to be implied in a written contract if its nature is such that it must necessarily be implied to give the contract business efficacy, and in the circumstances under which this contract came into being I think a strong case of necessity would require to be made out. But I find nothing in the nature of the contract to require any such implication to give it efficacy. Its purpose was to provide that the customers in the parts of the zone transferred should receive their supplies. The occasion of the contract was the pursuer being called up for military service, but there is nothing to suggest that the period of its endurance was to coincide with his absence on service. Had that been the intention I think the agreement would have taken a very

[23] That case involved only a term implied from custom, but the judge's comment clearly applied to all implied terms (although he referred to "conditions" rather than terms throughout).

different form and not that of an out-and-out sale with a mere option to the pursuer to buy back. He was not placed under any obligation to do so if he returned from the war. It was not disputed that the right of pre-emption might be exercised before he returned, and the clause of reversion was one which might come into operation during his absence or even after his death. Further, the last clause is expressly unlimited as regards time. In terms of it the pursuer or his heirs may 'at any time' give notice that it is not his or their intention to resume the zone. I see no reason to read into that clause a limitation to any time anterior to a reasonable time after his return or his death if he should not return. If he may give notice of his intention not to resume at any time, I think it follows that no limitation falls to be read in as regards the time at which he may give notice to resume."

This combined "reasonable/business efficacy" test was applied in the following case.

8–22 **Lothian v Jenolite Ltd**

1969 S.C. 111

Court of Session, Second Division: Lords Wheatley, Walker and Milligan

Jenolite agreed to pay Lothian, its Scottish agent, commission on sales. The written contract was for four years, but Jenolite terminated it after 17 months, on the basis that Lothian had also sold products which competed with their own. Jenolite claimed that Lothian was an agent and had breached implied terms that he would not compete with his principal (Jenolite) and to use his best endeavours to market Jenolite's products in Scotland.

The court held that there were no such implied terms.

8–23 "LORD MILLIGAN: ... It is ... more difficult to imply a condition in a written contract than it is in a verbal contract: Gloag on *Contract* (2nd ed.), p. 289. The circumstances in which a condition may be implied were referred to by Lord McLaren in ... *William Morton & Co. v Muir Brothers & Co* ... This passage was considered in *McWhirter v Longmuir* (1948 S.C. 577), and in that case Lord Jamieson said (at p. 589): 'The Court will only hold a term or condition to be implied in a written contract, if its nature is such that it must necessarily be implied to give the contract business efficacy ...' In McWhirter's case the Court held that a time limit could not be implied and in doing so were admittedly to some extent influenced by the fact that the parties had considered the possibility of introducing a time limit but had not done so. I am satisfied, however, that even if there had been no previous discussion about the inclusion of a time limit, the Court would nevertheless have reached the same conclusion.

The tests proposed by Lord McLaren and Lord Jamieson are formidable tests and it is now necessary to consider whether the defenders can satisfy either of them. The test desiderated by Lord McLaren and approved by Professor Gloag involves an old friend of the Courts, the 'reasonable man,' or, to be more accurate, 'two reasonable men.' It is an objective test. In the present case, while it could no doubt be said that principals in the position of the defenders would desire the condition which the defenders seek to have introduced, it cannot be said that an agent in the position of the pursuer would be prepared, far less desire, to have such a condition. He might, I should imagine, be prepared to agree to such a condition if, for example, he were to get a higher commission. The condition upon which the defenders rely is not, in my opinion, a condition which should, in Lord McLaren's words, 'be taken for granted in all contracts of the class without the necessity of giving it formal expression.' It may be that there are certain business transactions in which it is well recognised that a condition such as the one presently under consideration falls to be implied (see, for example, *William Morton & Co v Muir Brothers & Co* (1907 S.C. 1211)) but there are no averments in this case to introduce any particular custom of trade.

The test referred to by Lord Jamieson introduces the question of 'business efficacy' ... While the contract in the present case would clearly be more advantageous to the defenders if the condition referred to were to be implied, I cannot say that the absence of such a condition makes the contract unworkable nor can I say that without the condition the contract would be so one-sided that both parties must have intended that the condition should apply. The introduction of the condition would, as the Lord Ordinary has said, make the contract a different contract altogether, and moreover it was a condition to which the parties could readily have given expression if that were their intention (see, for example, *Graham & Co v United Turkey Red Co.*,1922 S.C. 533).

... The circumstances in which a condition may be implied are, particularly where the contract has been reduced to writing, rightly very limited, and I am satisfied that they have not been shown to exist in the present case. If the defenders had wanted to restrict the activities of the pursuer, they could have asked him to agree to their proposed restriction. Not having done so, they cannot now seek to rectify the position by attempting to discover an implied condition."

Note that, again, the court was considering a written contract, in which there was no specific provision for the issues in dispute. The function of the court is not to write the contract for the parties. Nevertheless, on the facts of the case before him, Lord Milligan argued strongly that a term should not be implied unless it is objectively reasonable. He clearly also applied the *Moorcock* "efficacy" principle. Whether he decided that a term must be reasonable to be necessary; or that an unreasonable term cannot be necessary is less clear.[24] This suggested two-part efficacy test was further examined in the following case.

Crawford v Bruce 8–24

1992 S.L.T. 524

Court of Session, First Division: The Lord President (Hope), Lords Allanbridge and Mayfield

The proprietor of shop premises in Edinburgh entered into a 10-year lease with a tenant. The rent was set under the terms of the lease at £3,250 per annum, "with a review of the rent on the expiry of each three year period". At the end of the first period, the landlord gave notice that the rent was to go up to £6,500 per annum. The tenant responded that she believed the rent review provisions of the lease were so uncertain as to be unenforceable.

The landlord raised an action of declarator asking, inter alia, for the implication of a term that at each review the rent was to be set at the fair market rate set by an arbiter or court. Having failed in the Outer House, the landlord appealed and sought additional declarators in respect of subsequent three-year periods. These additional terms were required to be implied, the landlord contended, in order to give efficacy to the lease—in their absence, there was no way of knowing what amount of rent was to be paid.

The court refused to imply the terms.

[24] WW McBryde, *The Law of Contract in Scotland*, 3rd edn (Edinburgh: W. Green, 2007), para.9–70 states "the term must be both reasonable and necessary", but also points out that "the case was decided on the basis of a proven custom or trade".

8–25 "THE LORD PRESIDENT (HOPE): ... The pursuer's argument was that the additional terms must be implied, because this was necessary to give efficacy to the lease. It was submitted also that the terms set out in the conclusion for declarator were such that both parties would have agreed to them in order to give effect to the rent review. Reference was made to *McWhirter v Longmuir* at 1948 S.L.T., p. 499 where Lord Jamieson said: 'The court will only hold a term or condition to be implied in a written contract if its nature is such that it must necessarily be implied to give the contract business efficacy, and in the circumstances under which this contract came into being I think a strong case of necessity would require to be made out.'

It is clear from Lord Jamieson's opinion that the source to which he looked for the use of the phrase 'to give the contract business efficacy' was the well known dictum of Bowen L.J. in *The Moorcock* at p. 68, where he said: 'In business transactions such as this, what the law desires to give effect by the implication is to give such business efficacy to the transaction as must have been intended at all events by both parties who are business men.'

The use of the word 'business' is appropriate where the contract which is in question is one which can properly be described as a business transaction between businessmen. It is perhaps open to question whether the same word is applicable where the contract is a formal written lease of heritable property, even if the subjects are business premises. But the principle is not confined only to business transactions. The concept of giving such efficacy to the transaction as both parties must have intended it to have is of wide application ... [Lord Hope referred to Lord McLaren in *Morton v Muir Bros*. And continued.]

But, while the test which the pursuer's counsel asked us to apply was that of necessity, it is important not to lose sight of the fact that the implication arises from the presumed intention of the parties to the contract to give it such efficacy as they must both have intended it to have. As Gloag on *Contract* (2nd ed.), pp. 288-289 observes, it is always a question of the construction of each contract whether a particular term can be implied, and the term will more easily be implied in a verbal than in a written and formal contract such as we have here before us in this case.

The basis for the pursuer's argument on the point of necessity was that the lease had failed to provide for the amount of the rent which was to be paid after the expiry of the first three year period. It was contended that there had to be a review after this period had expired, because without it there would be no way of knowing what was the amount of the rent to be paid. The parties had provided that there was to be a review of the rent at this stage, which meant that a review must be carried out, and it was necessary to give effect to their intention by implying the terms which were required to arrive at the amount of the rent which was to be paid for each successive three year period ...

Since the pursuer accepts that the review clause is incomplete without the terms which she seeks to be implied in it, that really is an end of the case. It is obvious that the clause as it stands is incapable of being enforced. This is not just because it contains no convenient machinery for its enforcement, such as for the rent to be fixed by an arbiter should the parties fail to agree. That would not necessarily be fatal to the efficacy of the clause if there had been set out in it the basis upon which the reviewed rent was to be fixed. Had there been a sufficient explanation of the basis the amount of the rent could, as a last resort, have been fixed by the court in the light of the appropriate expert evidence. As it is, the clause must be regarded as void for uncertainty because it lacks the elements which would be necessary for the court to arrive at a figure which could be taken to be the result of what the parties had always intended to agree as the basis on which the rent was to be calculated.

The need for agreement on these points is all the more obvious when we examine the terms of the declarator which is set out in the conclusion. The hypothesis on which we are asked to say the rent should be fixed is that the rent should be a market rent, and that the duration on the expiry of each three year period is to be the same as the initial duration in the lease. But both points could be said to be likely to operate to the disadvantage of the tenant, and it is far from clear that the hypothesis is one which satisfies the test which Lord McLaren described in *Morton v Muir Bros.*, namely that the implied condition is such that no reasonable man in the tenant's position would have refused to accede to it.

It would be both inconsistent with this provision and unfair for the tenant to be required by an implied term on a rent review to pay an open market rent which reflected the value of her own expenditure by way of improvement to the premises. The point was also recognised by Goff L.J. in *Beer v Bowden* at [1981] 1 W.L.R., p. 527F when he said that the rent should be increased to such amount as would be a fair rent for the premises excluding tenant's improvements."

It appears from these extracts that Lord Hope is equating Lord McLaren's "reasonableness" requirement with Lord Bowen's statement that the term must be "intended at all events by both the parties". Ultimately, what seems to have mattered most is that to imply the term would have been "unfair to the tenant". That could be seen both as "unreasonable" to and "unintended" by the parties. In any case the test seems to be objective—that for a condition to be implied, it should be such that no reasonable person would refuse to accede to it. In *Crawford*, the implication of such a term could have resulted in unfairness to the tenant, and so it could not meet that test. There was nothing in the terms of the lease from which could be deduced any such common intention as the landlord sought to have imputed to the contract. **8–26**

Note again Lord Hope's confirmation of the view that, while the test is commonly referred to as one of "business efficacy", the principle is not confined to business transactions. Most importantly, because these terms could not be implied into this written contract, the rent review clause—*not the entire lease*—was void for uncertainty.

Efficacy and the "officious bystander"

The suggestion in several cases is that a court will imply a term that was so obvious to the parties that it was not worth stating it expressly in the contract. Such a term will be extremely rare, but it may be argued that a term could not be necessary unless it is so obvious that it would not occur to the parties to state it. The principle was stated by MacKinnon LJ in the English case of *Shirlaw v Southern Foundries (1926) Ltd*[25]: **8–27**

> "Prima facie that which in any contract is left to be implied and need not be expressed is something so obvious that it goes without saying; so that, if, while the parties were making their bargain, an officious bystander were to suggest some express provision for it in their agreement, they would testily suppress him with a common 'Oh, of course!'"

In that case *Shirlaw*, under a written agreement, was appointed managing director of the company for a fixed term of 10 years. Article 91 of the company's articles of association stated that "if he cease to hold the office of director he shall ipso facto and immediately cease to be a managing director". Article 105 gave the company power to remove a director before the end of his period of office. Following restructuring of the company, Shirlaw was removed as a director and treated as having ceased to be managing director. Shirlaw claimed an implied term that he could not be removed as a director while in the post of managing director and that, as a consequence, his contract with the company had been wrongfully repudiated. A narrow majority found in favour of Shirlaw and implied the term.

[25] *Shirlaw v Southern Foundries (1926) Ltd* [1939] 2 K.B. 206.

The principle enunciated in this case has subsequently been applied, but there is a clear reluctance on the part of judges to write the contract for the parties. Courts must be circumspect in implying into contracts terms of which they and the parties' counsel may with hindsight be aware; but which may have meant little to the parties themselves at the tune when they made the contract. In *Spring v National Amalgamated Stevedores and Dockers Society*,[26] for example, the court was asked to imply into a contract of trade union membership a term that the contract was governed by the "Bridlington Agreement". This is an agreement between TUC-affiliated unions that they will not poach each others' members. In the course of his judgment, Sir Leonard Stone, VC, said:

> "If the [officious bystander] test were to be applied to the facts of this case and the bystander had asked the plaintiff, at the time when the plaintiff paid his Ss and signed the acceptance form, 'Won't you put into it some reference to the Bridlington Agreement?' I think (indeed, I have no doubt) that the plaintiff would have answered 'What's that?'"

Nevertheless, the two tests, that of "business efficacy" and that of the "officious bystander" are now generally applied together.[27]

8–28 **J & H Ritchie Ltd v Lloyd Ltd**
[2007] UKHL 9
2007 S.C. (H.L.) 89
House of Lords: Lords Hope of Craighead, Scott of Foscote, Rodger of Earlsferry, Brown of Eaton-under-Heywood, Mance

Ritchie, a farmer near Paisley, bought from Lloyd Ltd a modified drill and power harrow combine for £14,217.50. He noticed vibrations when using the harrow, stopped using it and immediately contacted Lloyd. They inspected the machine and removed the harrow to their premises in Kelso to investigate the cause and possibly repair the machine. They found that the vibrations had been caused by the absence of two bearings, which they obtained and fitted. Lloyd telephoned the appellants to advise that the harrow was ready for collection, but refused to disclose what had been wrong with the harrow. Ritchie discovered informally what the problem had been, but despite repeated requests Lloyd refused to disclose the defect, but said that the harrow had been repaired to "factory gate specification". Worried that operating the harrow without the two bearings might have affected other parts, Ritchie asked Lloyd for an engineer's report, which Lloyd refused to provide. Ritchie then rejected the equipment and raised an action in the sheriff court seeking declarator that they had validly rescinded the contract of sale and decree for repayment of the price. In this appeal to the House of Lords, Ritchie's claim was successful.

8–29 "LORD HOPE ... 12. The issue which lies at the heart of this case, as Lord Philip observed, is the effect of section 35(6)(a) of the Sale of Goods Act 1979, as amended, on the buyer's right to reject goods which, on delivery, are materially disconform to the contract. Section 35 as a whole is concerned with when the buyer is, and is not, deemed to have accepted the goods. Subsection (6) provides:

'(6) The buyer is not by virtue of this section deemed to have accepted the goods merely because —

---

[26] *Spring v National Amalgamated Stevedores and Dockers Society* [1956] 1 W.L.R. 585.
[27] See for example *Express Newspapers Plc v Silverstone Circuits Ltd*, Independent, 16 June 1989; *The Times*, 20 June 1989.

(a) he asks for, or agrees to, their repair by or under an arrangement with the seller, or
(b) the goods are delivered to another under a sub-sale or other disposition.'

...

13 .... In the absence of express agreement, the answer to it must depend on what terms, if any, are to be implied into the contract at this stage, bearing in mind that the seller was in breach at the time of delivery and that the buyer retains the right to resile because the goods were not in conformity with the contract.

14. In *William Morton & Co v Muir Brothers & Co*, 1907 SC 1211, 1224 Lord McLaren said:

'The conception of an implied condition is one with which we are familiar in relation to contracts of every description, and if we seek to trace any such implied conditions to their source, it will be found that in almost every instance they are founded either on universal custom or in the nature of the contract itself. If the condition is such that every reasonable man on the one part would desire for his own protection to stipulate for the condition, and that no reasonable man on the other part would refuse to accede to it, then it is not unnatural that the condition should be taken for granted in all contracts of the class without the necessity of giving it formal expression.'

In *Liverpool City Council v Irwin* [1977] AC 239, 258A–C Lord Cross of Chelsea pointed out that there was an important distinction between laying down by this means a prima face rule applicable to all cases of a defined type and cases where what the court was being in effect asked to do was to rectify a particular contract by inserting in it a term which the parties have not expressed. Dealing with the latter kind of case, he said at p. 258B–C:

'Here it is not enough for the court to say that the suggested term is a reasonable one the presence of which would make the contract a better or fairer one; it must be able to say that the insertion of the term is necessary to give—as it is put—"business efficacy" to the contract and that if its absence had been pointed out at the time both parties—assuming them to have been reasonable men—would have agreed without hesitation to its insertion.'

15. The present context is one where it would, in my opinion, be not at all out of place to resort to an implied term to fill the gap in the statutory code and govern the relationship between the parties when it was arranged that the harrow would be taken back to Kelso. What term, if any, it would be right to imply into the contract of sale at that stage will depend on the circumstances. There may be cases, for example, where the nature of the defect and exactly what needs to be done to correct it, and at what expense to the seller, are immediately obvious to both parties. It may then be said that a buyer who, having been equipped with all that knowledge, allows the seller to incur the expense of repair is under an implied obligation to accept and pay for the goods once the repair has been carried out. His right to resile will be lost when the repair has been completed. The buyer's protection is the reasonable opportunity to examine the goods after delivery which he is given by section 35(2) of the 1979 Act. Lord Marnoch said in para 14 that the doctrine of personal bar would provide the answer if the buyer claimed the right to reject in such circumstances. But, as we are dealing here with a statutory code and its consequences, I would prefer to find the solution in an implied term.

16. That however is not this case. The nature of the defect was not immediately obvious and it was not known what, if anything, could be done to correct it. But the underlying principles are the same. The effect of section 35(2)(a) is that, as the buyer is not deemed to have accepted the goods, he retains the right to reject them. That right will, of course, be lost if, at any time, he decides to accept the goods or is deemed to have accepted them. But it is a right of election which the buyer cannot be expected to exercise

until he has the information that he needs to make an informed choice. The seller, for his part, cannot refuse to give him the information that he needs to exercise it. ...

17. ... Should the fact that it did not occur to Mr Ritchie to obtain an express undertaking to that effect before the harrow was taken away make any difference?

18. The harrow was a complex piece of power operated agricultural machinery. Information of the kind that Mr Ritchie was asking for was obviously needed if the appellants were to make a properly informed choice between accepting and rejecting the equipment on being told that the harrow had been repaired to factory gate standard. A condition that the seller would provide this information, if it was asked for, was one which every buyer would seek for his own protection in such circumstances. It was one which no reasonable seller, who was already in breach of contract, could refuse as a condition of being given the opportunity to cure the defect and preserve the contract.

19. In these circumstances—which cannot be assumed to apply in every case—I would hold that the respondents were under an implied obligation to provide the appellants with the information that Mr Ritchie asked for. As they refused to give them that information the respondents were in breach of that obligation. The appellants were deprived of the information that they needed to make a properly informed choice. In my opinion they were entitled to reject the equipment even although, as it turned out, the respondents were able to prove afterwards that the harrow had been repaired to factory gate standard.

34. What, then, was the effect, if any, of this agreement on the appellants' right to rescind the contract of sale because of the respondents' material breach? Merely entering into the agreement did not mean that the appellants had accepted the harrow and so extinguished their right to rescind. But, equally clearly, it must have been an implied term of the inspection and repair agreement that, so long as the respondents were duly performing their obligations under it, the appellants were not to exercise their right to rescind the contract of sale. In particular, if, in accordance with the terms of that agreement, the respondents eventually repaired the equipment to the proper standard and duly made it available to the appellants, the appellants would not be entitled to rescind the contract of sale and reject the equipment because of the original breach. A term to this effect would have been necessary to give the inspection and repair agreement business efficacy.

35. If, on the other hand, when Mr Fairley took the harrow back to Kelso, the respondents had decided that repairing it was going to be too much trouble and had decided to do nothing, the appellants could have rescinded the agreement on the ground of the respondents' repudiatory breach. Being thus freed from their implied obligations under that agreement, the appellants could then have forthwith rescinded the contract of sale on the basis of the respondents' material breach in supplying the defective harrow.

36. Therefore, when Mr Elliot told Mr Ritchie that the harrow was ready for collection, he was not exercising any right, or performing any obligation, under the contract of sale: he was making the harrow available for collection under the parties' inspection and repair agreement. But, though asked repeatedly, neither he nor anyone else in an official position in the respondents' organisation would tell Mr Ritchie what had been wrong with the harrow. This eventually led to Mr Ritchie refusing to take the harrow back. So the crucial question is whether the respondents were under any obligation to tell Mr Ritchie what had been wrong with the harrow and, if so, whether their refusal to do so justified the appellants in rescinding the inspection and repair agreement and refusing to take the harrow back.

37. Naturally enough, when Mr Ritchie agreed to Mr Fairley taking the harrow away, nothing was said about the respondents providing information to the appellants. So, again, the question is whether a term obliging them to do so is to be implied into the agreement between the parties. Normally, when I put my clock in for repair, for

instance, I do not stipulate that the clockmaker must tell me what is wrong with it. But, usually, once he has inspected it, he will contact me to let me know what the problem is, how long the repair will take and what it is likely to cost, so that I can decide what to do. At the very least, I cannot be expected to pay for a repair without knowing what I am paying for. So a term about supplying such information on request would be readily implied. Here the appellants were not going to have to pay for the inspection and repair. So that basis for an implication is missing. But other circumstances are relevant. The respondents were taking the appellants' property to inspect it: an owner who surrenders his property for inspection in this way can surely insist on being told the outcome of the inspection. More particularly, in this case, the respondents were the very people who had supplied the harrow in a defective state. The appellants were surely entitled, at the very least, to insist on being told what the respondents had now discovered which they had not discovered before they originally supplied the harrow. Moreover, a refusal by the respondents' representatives to provide that information would inevitably undermine the appellants' trust and confidence in the respondents' due performance of the contract. In these circumstances I am satisfied that business efficacy required the implication of a term that, if asked, the respondents would tell the appellants what their inspection had shown to be wrong with the harrow and what they had done to put it right. The respondents' outright refusal to supply that information constituted a material breach of the inspection and repair agreement, entitling the appellants to rescind it and to refuse to collect the harrow, even though—as the sheriff principal found—it had actually been repaired to a factory gate standard.

38. In addition, once the appellants had rescinded the inspection and repair agreement, with its implied term preventing them from exercising their right to rescind the sale contract during its currency, there was nothing to prevent them from exercising that right of rescission or termination. Which is precisely what they did by their solicitors' letter of 26 May 1999."

Implying terms: a matter of reasonable interpretation?

In recent years, the courts in England have followed a different path in implying terms into a contract. Where a party challenges the meaning of words in a written contract—and invariably it is a written contract—the practice is for counsel to seek to imply a term into the contract that would make it make sense. Too frequently, such a request is bound to fail. As MacKinnon LJ put it in *Shirlaw v Northern Foundries*: **8–30**

> "I recognise that the right or duty of a Court to find the existence of an implied term or implied terms in a written contract is a matter to be exercised with care; and a Court is too often invited to do so upon vague and uncertain grounds. Too often also such an invitation is backed by the citation of a sentence or two from the judgment of Bowen LJ in *The Moorcock* ... I fancy that he would be rather surprised if he could have foreseen that these general remarks of his would come to be a favourite citation of a supposed principle of law, and I think that he might sympathise with the occasional impatience of his successors when *The Moorcock* is so often flushed for them in that guise."

The alternative, of course, is that the defective wording might, as in *Crawford v Bruce*, will be seen as simply meaningless. Rather than see it as a duty to seek to imply a term into such a contract, some judges have seen it as their duty to persevere in interpreting the meaning of the words the parties actually used, and to give them the interpretation that most accurately reflects the parties' intentions. The following decision of the House of Lords might be seen as the origin of this approach.

8–31 **Liverpool City Council v Irwin**

1977 A.C. 239

English House of Lords: Lords Wilberforce, Cross of Chelsea, Salmon, Edmund-Davies and Fraser of Tullybelton

Irwin, a tenant in a council block of flats, acting in common with other tenants, withheld rent in protest against conditions in the building. The lifts were out of action, the staircases unlit and conditions were generally appalling as a result of vandalism that the council had in vain, and at great expense, tried to control. There were even defects in the flats themselves: every time a toilet was used, the cistern flooded.

All tenants had received the "conditions of tenancy" and had signed a form stating that they accepted the tenancy on those conditions. The conditions dealt solely with the obligations of the tenant and not of the landlord.

The House of Lords found that there was no implied term imposing a duty on landlords to keep common parts in repair and properly lighted.

8–32 "LORD WILBERFORCE: ... Where there is, on the face of it, a complete, bilateral contract, the courts are sometimes willing to add terms to it, as implied terms; this is very common in mercantile contracts where there is an established usage; in that case the courts are spelling out what both parties know and would, if asked, unhesitatingly agree to be part of the bargain. In other cases, where there is an apparently complete bargain, the courts are willing to add a term on the ground that without it the contract will not work—this is ... the doctrine of *The Moorcock* as usually applied ... There is a third variety of implication ... and that is the implication of reasonable terms ...

The present case, in my opinion, represents a fourth category or, I would rather say, a fourth shade on a continuous spectrum. The court here is simply concerned to establish what the contract is, the parties not having themselves fully stated the terms. In this sense the court is searching for what must be implied ...

[I]t is necessary to define what test is to be applied, and I do not find this difficult. In my opinion such obligation should be read into the contract as the nature of the contract itself implicitly requires, no more, no less; a test in other words of necessity. The relationship accepted by the corporation is that of landlord and tenant; the tenant accepts obligations accordingly, in relation, inter alia, to the stairs, the lifts and the chutes. All these are not just facilities, or conveniences provided at discretion; they are essentials of the tenancy without which life in the dwellings, as a tenant, is not possible. To leave the landlord free of contractual obligation as regards these matters, and subject only to administrative or political pressure, is, in my opinion, totally inconsistent with the nature of this relationship. The subject matter of the lease (high-rise blocks) and the relationship created by the tenancy demands, of its nature, some contractual obligation on the landlord.

I do not think that this approach involves any innovation as regards the law of contract. The necessity to have regard to the inherent nature of a contract and of the relationship thereby established was stated in this House in *Lister v Romford Ice & Cold Storage Co Ltd* [1957] A.C. 555. That was a case between master and servant and of a search for an 'implied term'. Viscount Simonds made a clear distinction between a search for an implied term such as might be necessary to give 'business efficacy' to the particular contract and a search, based on wider considerations, for such a term as the nature of the contract might call for, or as a legal incident of this kind of contract. If the search were for the former, he said '... I should lose myself in the attempt to formulate it with the necessary precision' [p. 576.] We see an echo of this in the present case, when the majority in the Court of Appeal, considering a 'business efficacy term', that is, a

'Moorcock' term, found themselves faced with five alternative terms and therefore rejected all of them. But that is not, in my opinion, the end, or indeed the object, of the search ...

It remains to define the standard. My Lords, if, as I think, the test of the existence of the term is necessity the standard must surely not exceed what is necessary having regard to the circumstances. To imply an absolute obligation to repair would go beyond what is a necessary legal incident and would indeed be unreasonable. An obligation to take reasonable care to keep in reasonable repair and usability is what fits the requirements of the case. Such a definition involves—and I think rightly—recognition that the tenants themselves have their responsibilities. What it is reasonable to expect of a landlord has a clear relation to what a reasonable set of tenants should do for themselves ...

I would hold therefore that the corporation's obligation is as I have described. And in agreement, I believe, with your Lordships, I would hold that it has not been shown in this case that there was any breach of that obligation. On the main point therefore I would hold that the appeal fails ... "

Note that the contract here was partly in writing. Would the principles under which terms might have been implied be different if the contract was entirely in writing and, more specifically, if it had been on a single document signed by the tenant? **8–33**

This decision has been extensively cited in the Court of Session. Nevertheless, Lord Wilberforce's speech contains two embryonic notions that run against the grain of the then existing case law. First, there is the "interpretative", or "contextualising" approach to the problem; and secondly, the notion that a term would be implied if reasonable in the circumstances. Thus McBryde,[28] referring in part to Lord Wilberforce in *Liverpool City Council v Irwin* merely states:

> "It is thought that these dicta, although varying in their expression, support the proposition that implied terms are normally of two types—a term implied as a matter of general law, and a term implied in the circumstances of a particular contract. Custom or usage might on one view be treated as a form of implication somewhat between those two categories."

Alternatively, Lord Wilberforce's pronouncements on the "fourth shade on a continuous spectrum" might be seen as a new development. The court, in seeking to

> "establish what the contract is, the parties not having themselves fully stated the terms ... such obligation should be read into the contract as the nature of the contract itself implicitly requires, no more, no less; a test in other words of necessity".

Lord Hoffmann, in the following case, took this "interpretative" approach to a new level.

[28] WW McBryde, *The Law of Contract in Scotland*, 3rd edn (Edinburgh: W. Green, 2007), para.9–07.

8–34 **Attorney General of Belize v Belize Telecom Ltd (Belize)**
[2009] UKPC 10; [2009] W.L.R. 1988
Privy Council: Lords Brown, Carswell, Hoffmann, Rodger, Baroness Hale

The Government of Belize privatised the publicly owned telecommunications corporation by transferring its assets to a newly created company. The Government retained a degree of control over the industry through the company's articles of association, which created two classes of ordinary shares, B and C, and one special share, which would be issued to the Government and which could only be held by a party authorised by the Government; that there were to be eight directors, two appointed by, and removable by, a majority of the B shareholders and four appointed by, and removable by, a majority of the C shareholders, and two appointed by, and removable by, the holder of the special share. If the holder of the special share also owned 37.5 per cent of the issued share capital in C shares, the articles provided that the special shareholder would be entitled to appoint two of the four directors allocated to the C shareholders, regardless of the wishes of the majority of C shareholders, and that those directors could only be removed by the special shareholder holding the additional 37.5 per cent in C shares.

Belize Telecom Ltd purchased the special share and 37.5 per cent in C shares and appointed two directors in its capacity as special shareholder holding 37.5 per cent in C shares. Within a year Belize Telecom Ltd no longer held 37.5 per cent in C shares, but retained the special share. The articles of association made no provision for the removal of directors appointed by a party acting in its capacity as special shareholder holding 37.5 per cent in C shares in circumstances where such a party no longer existed.

The claimants sought to imply a term into the articles that, in such circumstances, the directors concerned would vacate office.

The court found, as a matter of construction of the instrument, that there was such an implied term.

8–35 "16. LORD HOFFMANN ... The court has no power to improve upon the instrument which it is called upon to construe, whether it be a contract, a statute or articles of association. It cannot introduce terms to make it fairer or more reasonable. It is concerned only to discover what the instrument means. However, that meaning is not necessarily or always what the authors or parties to the document would have intended. It is the meaning which the instrument would convey to a reasonable person having all the background knowledge which would reasonably be available to the audience to whom the instrument is addressed: see *Investors Compensation Scheme Ltd v West Bromwich Building Society* [1998] 1 WLR 896, 912-913. It is this objective meaning which is conventionally called the intention of the parties, or the intention of Parliament, or the intention of whatever person or body was or is deemed to have been the author of the instrument.

17. The question of implication arises when the instrument does not expressly provide for what is to happen when some event occurs. The most usual inference in such a case is that nothing is to happen. If the parties had intended something to happen, the instrument would have said so. Otherwise, the express provisions of the instrument are to continue to operate undisturbed. If the event has caused loss to one or other of the parties, the loss lies where it falls.

18. In some cases, however, the reasonable addressee would understand the instrument to mean something else. He would consider that the only meaning consistent with the other provisions of the instrument, read against the relevant background, is that something is to happen. The event in question is to affect the rights of the parties. The instrument may not have expressly said so, but this is what it must mean. In such a case,

it is said that the court implies a term as to what will happen if the event in question occurs. But the implication of the term is not an addition to the instrument. It only spells out what the instrument means.

19. The proposition that the implication of a term is an exercise in the construction of the instrument as a whole is not only a matter of logic (since a court has no power to alter what the instrument means) but also well supported by authority. In *Trollope & Colls Ltd v North West Metropolitan Regional Hospital Board* [1973] 1 WLR 601, 609 Lord Pearson, with whom Lord Guest and Lord Diplock agreed, said:

'[T]he court does not make a contract for the parties. The court will not even improve the contract which the parties have made for themselves, however desirable the improvement might be. The court's function is to interpret and apply the contract which the parties have made for themselves. If the express terms are perfectly clear and free from ambiguity, there is no choice to be made between different possible meanings: the clear terms must be applied even if the court thinks some other terms would have been more suitable. An unexpressed term can be implied if and only if the court finds that the parties must have intended that term to form part of their contract: it is not enough for the court to find that such a term would have been adopted by the parties as reasonable men if it had been suggested to them: it must have been a term that went without saying, a term necessary to give business efficacy to the contract, a term which, though tacit, formed part of the contract which the parties made for themselves.'

20. More recently, in *Equitable Life Assurance Society v Hyman* [2002] 1 AC 408, 459, Lord Steyn said:

'If a term is to be implied, it could only be a term implied from the language of [the instrument] read in its commercial setting.'

21. It follows that in every case in which it is said that some provision ought to be implied in an instrument, the question for the court is whether such a provision would spell out in express words what the instrument, read against the relevant background, would reasonably be understood to mean. It will be noticed from Lord Pearson's speech that this question can be reformulated in various ways which a court may find helpful in providing an answer – the implied term must 'go without saying', it must be 'necessary to give business efficacy to the contract' and so on—but these are not in the Board's opinion to be treated as different or additional tests. There is only one question: is that what the instrument, read as a whole against the relevant background, would reasonably be understood to mean?

22. There are dangers in treating these alternative formulations of the question as if they had a life of their own. Take, for example, the question of whether the implied term is 'necessary to give business efficacy' to the contract. That formulation serves to underline two important points. The first, conveyed by the use of the word 'business', is that in considering what the instrument would have meant to a reasonable person who had knowledge of the relevant background, one assumes the notional reader will take into account the practical consequences of deciding that it means one thing or the other. In the case of an instrument such as a commercial contract, he will consider whether a different construction would frustrate the apparent business purpose of the parties. That was the basis upon which *Equitable Life Assurance Society v Hyman* [2002] 1 AC 408 was decided. The second, conveyed by the use of the word "necessary", is that it is not enough for a court to consider that the implied term expresses what it would have been reasonable for the parties to agree to. It must be satisfied that it is what the contract actually means.

23. The danger lies, however, in detaching the phrase 'necessary to give business efficacy' from the basic process of construction of the instrument. It is frequently the case that a contract may work perfectly well in the sense that both parties can perform their express obligations, but the consequences would contradict what a reasonable person

would understand the contract to mean. Lord Steyn made this point in the *Equitable Life* case (at p. 459) when he said that in that case an implication was necessary 'to give effect to the reasonable expectations of the parties'.

24. The same point had been made many years earlier by Bowen LJ in his well known formulation in *The Moorcock* (1889) 14 PD 64, 68:

'In business transactions such as this, what the law desires to effect by the implication is to give such business efficacy to the transaction as must have been intended at all events by both parties who are business men.'

25. Likewise, the requirement that the implied term must 'go without saying' is no more than another way of saying that, although the instrument does not expressly say so, that is what a reasonable person would understand it to mean. Any attempt to make more of this requirement runs the risk of diverting attention from the objectivity which informs the whole process of construction into speculation about what the actual parties to the contract or authors (or supposed authors) of the instrument would have thought about the proposed implication. The imaginary conversation with an officious bystander in *Shirlaw v Southern Foundries (1926) Ltd* [1939] 2 KB 206, 227 is celebrated throughout the common law world. Like the phrase 'necessary to give business efficacy', it vividly emphasises the need for the court to be satisfied that the proposed implication spells out what the contact would reasonably be understood to mean. But it carries the danger of barren argument over how the actual parties would have reacted to the proposed amendment. That, in the Board's opinion, is irrelevant. Likewise, it is not necessary that the need for the implied term should be obvious in the sense of being immediately apparent, even upon a superficial consideration of the terms of the contract and the relevant background. The need for an implied term not infrequently arises when the draftsman of a complicated instrument has omitted to make express provision for some event because he has not fully thought through the contingencies which might arise, even though it is obvious after a careful consideration of the express terms and the background that only one answer would be consistent with the rest of the instrument. In such circumstances, the fact that the actual parties might have said to the officious bystander 'Could you please explain that again?' does not matter.

26. In *BP Refinery (Westernport) Pty Ltd v Shire of Hastings* (1977) 180 CLR 266, 282-283 Lord Simon of Glaisdale, giving the advice of the majority of the Board, said that it was 'not . . . necessary to review exhaustively the authorities on the implication of a term in a contract' but that the following conditions ('which may overlap') must be satisfied:

'(1) it must be reasonable and equitable; (2) it must be necessary to give business efficacy to the contract, so that no term will be implied if the contract is effective without it; (3) it must be so obvious that "it goes without saying" (4) it must be capable of clear expression; (5) it must not contradict any express term of the contract.'

27. The Board considers that this list is best regarded, not as series of independent tests which must each be surmounted, but rather as a collection of different ways in which judges have tried to express the central idea that the proposed implied term must spell out what the contract actually means, or in which they have explained why they did not think that it did so. The Board has already discussed the significance of 'necessary to give business efficacy' and 'goes without saying'. As for the other formulations, the fact that the proposed implied term would be inequitable or unreasonable, or contradict what the parties have expressly said, or is incapable of clear expression, are all good reasons for saying that a reasonable man would not have understood that to be what the instrument meant.

28. The Board therefore turns to consider the question raised by the articles of association. Two things are immediately apparent. The first is that the board has been constructed so that its membership will reflect the interests of the various participants in

the company: the political interest of the Government, represented through its special share; the economic interest (if any) of the Government, represented by its holding of C shares; the economic interests of the ordinary B and C shareholders. The second is that the powers which the articles confer upon the Government ... are carefully graduated according to its economic interest in the company at the relevant time. Thus, ... the power to appoint and remove special C directors is exercisable 'at any time' when the special shareholder has a 37.5% or more holding.

...

32. ... If implication is necessary to prevent what would otherwise be absurd consequences following from redemption of the special share, the Board considers that there is no difficulty about applying the same principle to the case in which the special shareholder continues to exist but no longer has the 37.5% holding which would entitle him to appoint and remove special C directors. In such a case too, the implication is required to avoid defeating what appears to have been the overriding purpose of the machinery of appointment and removal of directors, namely to ensure that the board reflects the appropriate shareholder interests in accordance with the scheme laid out in the articles."

Lord Hoffmann's approach effectively conflates the implication of terms and the interpretation of the instrument (contract). As one recent commentator, put it: **8–36**

"Following Lord Hoffmann's approach, it seems that the implication of terms in fact is no longer to be regarded as a separate process with its own rules and restrictions, which have traditionally been associated with the application of the 'business efficacy' and 'officious bystander' tests. After *Belize,* there is only one question for the court to answer: 'is that what the instrument, read as a whole against the relevant background, would reasonably be understood to mean?'"[29]

The approach has been considered extensively in the English courts, there is little consistency of application.[30] There has also been extensive criticism of the approach, both judicial and academic,[31] and at least one jurisdiction has said that the "interpretative" approach is wrong.[32] In support of the approach, Hooley draws the following conclusions:[33]

"There is a clear linkage between interpretation and implication. Whether you are interpreting the express words of a contract, or whether you are interpreting the gaps between the words of the contract as a whole, you are, in both cases, seeking to identify and give effect to the meaning or intention of the parties. Interpretation is the process by which the court identifies the common intention of the parties. This is an objective process. Interpretation is a necessary prerequisite before implication can take place. Implication of terms is a means (but not the only means) by which effect is given to the parties' intention once identified by the court. The basic principle that runs through interpretation and implication is the same: the need to identify and give effect to the meaning or intention of the parties. There is then the question whether it remains necessary, or even helpful, to continue to make reference to tests based on 'business efficacy' or the 'official [*sic*] bystander'. It is

---

[29] R Hooley, "Case Comment: Implied terms after *Belize Telecom*" 2014 C.L.J. 315–349, 316.
[30] R Hooley, "Case Comment: Implied terms after *Belize Telecom*" 2014 C.L.J. 315–349, 317.
[31] See particularly PS Davies, "Recent Developments in the Law of Implied Terms" [2010] L.M.C.L.Q. 140, 144.
[32] *Foo Jong Peng v Phua Kiah Mai* [2012] S.G.C.A. 55; [2012] 4 S.L.R. 1267, per Andrew Phang JA, Singapore Court of Appeal.
[33] R Hooley, "Case Comment: Implied terms after *Belize Telecom*" 2014 C.L.J., 315–349, 317–318.

argued that continued reference to these tests distracts from the central idea advanced by Lord Hoffmann and has led to uncertainty as to its application."

The truth remains that the Hoffmann approach has generated a degree of uncertainty in an area where certainty is of paramount importance. Contractual parties need to know that judges will not readily alter the wording or meaning of what they have written. The suspicion, valid or not, is that they might. Lord Hoffman's pronouncements on interpretation generally have not found favour in Scotland.[34] Whether his pronouncements in *Belize* will be more favourably viewed remains to be seen; but Lord Hoffman's approach was expressly applied in the Outer House, albeit, as in the *Belize Telecom* case itself, to an instrument other than a contractual document.[35] In the contract dispute that arose in the following case Lord Reed, although making no reference to *Belize Telecom*, took a similar approach.

8–37

Credential Bath Street Ltd v Venture Investment Placement Ltd
Outer House, Court of Session
[2007] CSOH 208

In 2001 the pursuer, Credential, leased premises to Callpoint Europe, the tenant, a subsidiary of Venture, the defender. The rent was £328,320 per annum and the term was 25 years. At the same time the tenant, under an "amortisation agreement", agreed to pay the pursuer £103,680 per annum, as reimbursement for work carried out by the pursuer at the tenant's request. Service charges were an additional £100,000 per annum. In 2003, the defender granted the pursuer a guarantee, under cl.3 of which, if the tenant failed to perform its obligations, the pursuer would do so "on demand" and also take over the lease as tenant for the remaining terms of the lease (the "step-in" obligation).

Under cl.3.4, the defender would be released from the guarantee "on 1 January 2005, save in respect of any antecedent breach of the guarantee occurring prior to 1 January 2005".

In April 2004, the pursuer sent a letter to the tenant and the defender with a schedule of dilapidations, but no repairs were carried out by the tenant, although that was their obligation as tenants. In July 2004, the pursuer presented a petition for the winding up of the tenant, Callpoint Europe. The tenant opposed the petition, but it was granted in April 2007.

In this action, Credential sought to recover the cost of the repairs from Venture as guarantors, arguing, inter alia, that it was an implied term of the guarantee that the defenders would not cause the tenants to oppose any petition for their winding up when they knew or ought reasonably to have known that the opposition was unjustified in law or in fact. The defenders, they argued, had broken that implied term by opposing the winding-up petition without justification, as the tenant was unable to pay its debts because the value of its liabilities exceeded its assets.

The court found that the test of necessity of the implied term was not met, the term seemed neither reasonable nor equitable and it was not capable of clear expression.

8–38 "LORD REED: ... [53] The nature of the implication of a contractual term, and the basis upon which such a term can be implied, were authoritatively considered by the House of Lords in *Equitable Life Assurance Society v Hyman* [2002] 1 A.C. 408. In a speech with which the other members of the House expressed their agreement, Lord Steyn said (at pages 458-459):

---

[34] Above, para.8–34.

[35] *Joint Liquidators of Direct Sharedeal Ltd, Petitioners* [2013] CSOH 45, per Lord Hodge, [19].

'The critical question is whether a relevant restriction may be implied in [the provision in question]. It is certainly not a case in which a term can be implied by law in the sense of incidents impliedly annexed to particular forms of contracts. Such standardised implied terms operate as general default rules: see *Scally v Southern Health and Social Services Board* [1992] 1 A.C. 294. If a term is to be implied, it could only be a term implied from the language of [the provision in question] read in its particular commercial setting. Such implied terms operate as ad hoc gap fillers. In *Luxor (Eastbourne) Ltd v Cooper* [1941] A.C.108, 137 Lord Wright explained this distinction as follows:

'The expression "implied term" is used in different senses. Sometimes it denotes some term which does not depend on the actual intention of the parties but on a rule of law, such as the terms, warranties or conditions which, if not expressly excluded, the law imports, as for instance under the Sale of Goods Act and the Marine Insurance Act ... But a case like the present is different because what it is sought to imply is based on an intention imputed to the parties from their actual circumstances.'

It is only an individualised term of the second kind which can arguably arise in the present case. Such a term may be imputed to parties: it is not critically dependent on proof of an actual intention of the parties. The process 'is one of construction of the agreement as a whole in its commercial setting': *Banque Bruxelles Lambert SA v Eagle Star Insurance Co Ltd* [1997] A.C. 191, 212E, per Lord Hoffmann. This principle is sparingly and cautiously used and may never be employed to imply a term in conflict with the express terms of the text. The legal test for the implication of such a term is a standard of strict necessity ...

The enquiry is entirely constructional in nature: proceeding from the express terms of [the provision in question], viewed against its objective setting, the question is whether the implication is strictly necessary.'

[54] As Lord Steyn made clear in that passage, and as Lord Hoffmann had earlier emphasised in the *Banque Bruxelles Lambert* (or *SAAMCO*) case, there is a close affinity between the interpretation of express terms of a contract and the implication of terms which have not been expressed. At the same time, the implication of a term is a more far-reaching exercise in construction than the interpretation of the express terms of a contract, as Sir Thomas Bingham M.R. explained in *Philips Electronique Grand Public SA v British Sky Broadcasting Ltd* [1995] E.M.L.R. 472 at pages 481-482:

'The courts' usual role in contractual interpretation is, by resolving ambiguities or reconciling apparent inconsistencies, to attribute the true meaning to the language in which the parties themselves have expressed their contract. The implication of contract terms involves a different and altogether more ambitious undertaking: the interpolation of terms to deal with matters for which, *ex hypothesi*, the parties themselves have made no provision. It is because the implication of terms is so potentially intrusive that the law imposes strict constraints on the exercise of this extraordinary power.

There are of course contracts into which terms are routinely and unquestioningly implied. If a surgeon undertakes to operate on a patient a term will be implied into the contract that he exercise reasonable care and skill in doing so. It is inconceivable that any patient would in any imaginable circumstance commit his bodily well-being to the ministrations of a surgeon who did not undertake that obligation, or that a surgeon could hope to remain in practice without professing to discharge it. Again, quite apart from statute, the courts would not ordinarily hesitate to imply into a contract for the sale of unseen goods that they should be of merchantable quality and answer to their description and conform with sample. It is hard to imagine trade conducted, in the absence of express agreement, on any other terms.

But the difficulties increase the further one moves away from these paradigm examples. In the first case, it is probably unlikely that any terms will have been expressly agreed, except perhaps the nature of the operation, the fee, and the time and the place of operation. In the second case, the need for implication usually arises where the contract terms have not been spelled out in detail or by reference to written conditions. It is much more difficult to infer with confidence what the parties must have intended when they have entered into a lengthy and carefully-drafted contract but have omitted to make provision for the matter in issue. Given the rules which restrict evidence of the parties' intention when negotiating a contract, it may well be doubtful whether the omission was the result of the parties' oversight or of their deliberate decision; if the parties appreciate that they are unlikely to agree on what is to happen in a certain not impossible eventuality, they may well choose to leave the matter uncovered in their contract in the hope that the eventuality will not occur.'

[55] Like the interpretation of express terms, the implication of a term is an objective exercise. It involves asking what the reasonable person (who sometimes appears, in this context, in the dubious guise of the officious bystander) would understand the parties to have intended to be the terms of their contract. That process of construction is based, as Lord Steyn explained in *Equitable Life*, on the express terms of the contract, viewed against their objective setting.

[56] As with the interpretation of express terms so as to 'correct' mistakes in expression, as discussed above, it is the objective approach to intention which fundamentally distinguishes this aspect of the construction of a contract, so as to insert into it a term which the parties have not expressed, from the process of rectification of a document. As Mason J. observed in *Codelfa Construction Prop. Ltd v State Rail Authority of New South Wales* (1982) 149 C.L.R. 337 at page 346:

'The implication of a term is to be compared, and at the same time contrasted, with rectification of the contract. In each case the problem is caused by a deficiency in the expression of the consensual agreement. A term which should have been included has been omitted. The difference is that with rectification the term which has been omitted and should have been included was actually agreed upon; with implication the term is one which it is presumed that the parties would have agreed upon had they turned their minds to it—it is not a term that they have actually agreed upon. Thus, in the case of the implied term the deficiency in the expression of the consensual agreement is caused by the failure of the parties to direct their minds to a particular eventuality and to make explicit provision for it. Rectification ensures that the contract gives effect to the parties' actual intention; the implication of a term is designed to give effect to the parties' presumed intention.'

[57] In some cases, particularly in a commercial context, the objective setting of the contract may include an established usage which a reasonable person would understand the parties to the contract as having intended to apply (*Liverpool City Council v Irwin* [1977] A.C. 239 at page 253 per Lord Wilberforce). In the present case, however, there was no established usage which went without saying. In such a case, the test which has to be satisfied, before the reasonable person will presume the parties to have intended that their contract should be understood as including a term which they did not express, is one of necessity. A classic statement of the test is that contained in the speech of *Lord Wright in Luxor (Eastbourne) Ltd v Cooper* at page 137:

'But it is well recognised that there may be cases where obviously some term must be implied if the intention of the parties is not to be defeated, some term of which it can be predicated that 'it goes without saying', some term not expressed but necessary to give to the transaction such business efficacy as the parties must have intended. This does not mean that the court can embark on a reconstruction of the agreement on equitable principles, or on a view of what the parties should, in the opinion of the court, reasonably have contemplated. The implication must arise inevitably to give effect to the intention of the parties.'

As appears from that passage, necessity is to be understood in this context in a practical rather than a logical sense. That is consistent with the underlying basis of the implication of a term, namely to give the contract the effect which the parties would reasonably be understood as having intended. The test of necessity was reaffirmed in *Equitable Life*, following the earlier decision of the House of Lords in *Liverpool City Council v Irwin*.

[58] The term sought to be implied must therefore be one which is necessary, in addition to the express terms, in order to make the contract work as the parties can be taken to have intended. Putting the matter differently, a term will not be implied if the contract is effective without it. Furthermore, it follows from the criterion of necessity that a term cannot be implied where there are a number of different terms to which the parties might have agreed: *Trollope & Colls Ltd v North West Metropolitan Regional Hospital Board* [1973] 1 W.L.R. 601; *Philips Electronique Grand Public SA v British Sky Broadcasting Ltd* at page 482 per Sir Thomas Bingham M.R.

[59] The test of necessity is not of course the only condition which must be satisfied before a term can be implied into a contract. A clear statement of the relevant criteria is contained in the judgment of the majority of the Judicial Committee of the Privy Council in *BP Refinery (Westernport) Pty Ltd v Hastings Shire Council* (1978) 52 A.J.L.R. 20, in which Lord Simon of Glaisdale said (at page 26):

'In their [Lordships'] view, for a term to be implied, the following conditions (which may overlap) must be satisfied: (1) it must be reasonable and equitable; (2) it must be necessary to give business efficacy to the contract, so that no term will be implied if the contract is effective without it; (3) it must be so obvious that it goes without saying; (4) it must be capable of clear expression; (5) it must not contradict any express term of the contract.'

The requirement that the term must be capable of clear expression is illustrated by *Shell UK Ltd v Lostock Garage Ltd* [1976] 1 W.L.R. 1187, where the Court of Appeal rejected an implied term that a supplier of petrol under a solus agreement would not discriminate abnormally against the buyer. Ormrod L.J. said (at page 1201):

'The second obstacle is the difficulty in formulating the proposed terms, as demonstrated by the vagueness and ambiguity inherent in such words as "discriminate" and "abnormality".'

[60] In the present case, it appears to me that the first, second, third and fourth of the conditions listed by Lord Simon of Glaisdale in the *BP Refinery* case are not satisfied. Considering first the question whether the proposed term is necessary to give business efficacy to the contract, it was argued on behalf of the pursuers that ... without such an implied term the guarantor would be free to take deliberate steps to cause liquidation to be postponed beyond the expiry of the guarantee, even on grounds which the guarantor knew were unjustified in fact and law. The result would be that the step-in obligation would be evaded.

...

[65] ... I am inclined to doubt whether a reasonable person would have envisaged that the pursuers would have sought to place the tenant in liquidation under section 123(2) of the 1986 Act for the purpose of enforcing the guarantor's step-in obligation. In the event that the pursuers elected to do so, however, it does not appear to me that clause 3.3 of the guarantee could only work if there was some implicit contractual restriction on the ability of the guarantor to support the tenant's opposition to the application for its winding up.

...

[67] If, notwithstanding the court's control of the procedure and the professional responsibilities of those acting on behalf of the tenant, an application for its winding up was nevertheless delayed by unmeritorious opposition beyond the point in time at which

the guarantee expired, that would not demonstrate that the contract was unworkable. It would merely be one of several circumstances in which the pursuers would be unable to enforce the step-in obligation: the guarantee might, for example, expire during the period allowed for answers to be lodged or, in the event that answers were lodged, during the further period which would then elapse before a hearing. It was open to the parties to eliminate the risk of such circumstances, and thereby strengthen the pursuers' position: for example, by making the step-in obligation conditional solely on the lodging, or service, of an application for winding up. They did not do so.

[69] The most obvious difficulty with the proposed implied term, however, is its lack of clarity. As I have explained, the implied term for which the pursuers' counsel finally contended in argument was materially different from the implied term set out in the pursuers' pleadings (and would, as counsel acknowledged, necessitate an amendment of the pleadings): something which in itself indicates the lack of obviousness of the proposed term. In its final form, it reads:

'that the defender would not cause Callpoint Europe to oppose any motion for its winding up when it knew or ought reasonably to have known that the opposition was unjustified either in law or in fact (or in both)'.

[70] The lack of clarity of such a term is apparent. In the first place, whose knowledge is relevant? Counsel for the pursuers argued that 'it' meant the defenders (rather than Callpoint Europe), but that the knowledge (actual or imputed) of the defenders' legal advisers could also be attributed to the defenders. Thus the implied term would apply, it was argued, if the defenders' legal advisers made an 'undergraduate error' as to the law. That is one possible interpretation, but it is not the only one. Secondly, what is meant by the word 'unjustified'? I understood the argument of counsel for the pursuers to be that opposition is 'unjustified' in every case in which the defender or respondent is ultimately unsuccessful. That is one possible interpretation, but not in my opinion the only one. One might hesitate, for example, to describe Mr Stevenson's defence of Mrs Donoghue's action as 'unjustified', merely because a majority of the House of Lords ultimately found in her favour. Equally, the lodging of answers to a petition for winding up in order to preserve the position, while detailed consideration was given to the matter, might not in all circumstances be regarded as unjustified, even if the answers were subsequently withdrawn. If, however, one adopts that interpretation, how does one then decide whether the party in question 'knew or ought reasonably to have known' that the opposition would be ultimately unsuccessful? The prospects of success in any litigation can rarely, if ever, be predicted with certainty. Counsel generally resort to some such formula as 'reasonable prospects of success', without attempting to quantify more precisely the probability of success or failure. Would the test be satisfied if the prospects of success were (or ought to have been) known to be nil, or 49 per cent, or somewhere in between?

[71] In short, it appears to me that the proposed implied term is not clearly expressed, and on that ground fails to meet the fourth of the conditions listed by Lord Simon of Glaisdale in the *BP Refinery* case. If the implied term were to be made more specific, so as to reflect the submissions of counsel for the pursuers, it might be re-formulated along the following lines:

'that the defenders will not cause Callpoint Europe to oppose any motion for their winding up when the defenders, or the solicitors or counsel acting on their behalf, know or ought reasonably to know that, on a balance of probabilities, the opposition is unlikely to be successful'.

The fact that that is only one of the possible terms which might be devised demonstrates that the test of necessity is not met. In addition, such a term could not be said to be 'so obvious that it goes without saying'. Furthermore, such a term would not appear to me to be reasonable or equitable: it would be liable to prevent a winding up petition

> from being opposed in circumstances in which opposition would otherwise have been appropriate in professional and commercial terms; and it would be difficult to apply in practice, both by the defenders as a party to the contract, and by any court which required to enforce the term."

Although only a model framework and therefore not part of the law of Scotland, the provisions of Ch.9 (Contents and effects of contracts) of the Draft Common Frame of Reference (DCFR) attempts to provide a common framework for determining the terms of a contract. **8–39**

> "**DCFR. II.–9:101: Terms of a contract**
>
> (1) The terms of a contract may be derived from the express or tacit agreement of the parties, from rules of law or from practices established between the parties or usages.
> (2) Where it is necessary to provide for a matter which the parties have not foreseen or provided for, a court may imply an additional term, having regard in particular to:
>
> (a) the nature and purpose of the contract;
> (b) the circumstances in which the contract was concluded; and
> (c) the requirements of good faith and fair dealing.
>
> (3) Any term implied under paragraph (2) should, where possible, be such as to give effect to what the parties, had they provided for the matter, would probably have agreed.
> (4) Paragraph (2) does not apply if the parties have deliberately left a matter unprovided for, accepting the consequences of so doing."

Obligations arising from the express terms of the contract: interpretation

Wherever possible, it is advantageous to document contracts, preferably in a single document, often drawn up by the parties' legal advisers. A good example is the contract for the sale of a house or flat. If the parties write down, or otherwise document terms, such as in an email or a text message, then if they later disagree on the meaning or extent of their obligations, this will be evidence of what was agreed. Where there is no such evidence, what the parties said—their oral communications, or "communings"—and their actions, or "actings" must be considered. This is an expensive and often painful process in a dispute, requiring the court to hear the evidence of the parties and of other witnesses. This is why in many of the cases in this book, the decision has gone to the Court of Session for proof before answer. **8–40**

Although the terms have been put down in permanent form, specifically in a single document, it may be possible for terms to be implied into the contract, and to a limited extent terms can be incorporated into a written contract is considered in the next chapter.[36] However, even where the terms are in writing, and even where they are contained in a single document, the very words used will be open to interpretation.

Aids to interpretation: rules of construction/preference

To interpret the words in a document is to explain their meaning; to construe them is to interpret them in a particular way. Although the words are frequently used interchangeably by judges and commentators, it is worth bearing the distinction in mind. Over time, a host of *rules of construction* have developed to aid judges in interpreting documents, of which contracts are one example. Deeds, wills, even statutes have to be construed, so it is also important to bear in mind that rules of construction are rules of evidence that are of far wider application than contractual documents. For example, the Scottish Law Commission's "Report on **8–41**

---

[36] Below, Ch.10.

Interpretation in Private Law",[37] (RIPL), although dealing extensively with contracts, is concerned with the law of evidence as it applies to all documents in all fields of private law or, to use the term coined by the RIPL, "juridical acts".[38] For that reason, and because this is not a place to deal with the law of evidence extensively, reference is made to rules of construction throughout as and when appropriate as, for example, the *contra proferentem* rule.[39]

The express terms of the contract are what the parties have stipulated—whether by what they said, or what they put into writing—they will undertake.

8–42 *Report on Interpretation in Private Law*

Scottish Law Com. No.160 (1997)

"Part VI Canons of construction

Introduction

6.1 In this part we deal with certain canons of construction, or rules of preference, which relate, not to the interpretation of particular expressions, but rather to the construction of a juridical act as a whole. Similar rules are found in many legal systems. Many of them are derived from texts in Justinian's Digest.

6.2 ... They are largely a matter of simple common sense ... some of these canons of construction are regularly referred to and are found useful. They are not in fact empty of content. They can provide solutions in difficult cases. The more important ones feature in international instruments. They have been part of the European legal tradition since at least the time of Justinian's Digest ...

6.6 The canons of construction can be classified according to whether they relate to the terms or to the result. Some of them express a preference for looking at the terms in a certain way, or giving effect to terms of one type rather than another. These are result-neutral: they can operate in favour of either party and nothing turns overtly on the fairness or reasonableness of the result to which the process of interpretation leads.[5] The other canons are result-related. They express a preference for a construction which leads to a certain result—such as freedom from a burden—or away from a certain result—such as donation.

8–43 *Term-related preferences*

6.7 *Give effect to the whole terms.* There is a well-established rule that a construction of a juridical act which enables it to take effect is preferred to one which does not (*ut res magis valeat quam pereat*). In relation to contracts, Gloag expresses the rule as follows.[6]

'Again, if one of two constructions will make the contract valid, the other deprive it of any operative effect, the former is generally to be preferred.'

...

6.8 A closely related rule is that a construction of a juridical act which gives effect to all its terms is preferred to one which gives effect to only some of them. Gloag expressed this rule of preference as follows.

[37] Scottish Law Commission's "Report on Interpretation in Private Law" (Scot Law Com. No.160, 1997).

[38] "A juridical act will include a contract; a grant, assignation or renunciation of a right; a discharge of an obligation; a conveyance of property; a declaration of trust; a will or other testamentary deed; a grant of consent to what would otherwise be an invasion of a legal right; a notice required by law for any purpose; and an acceptance of office as an arbiter, trustee or guardian." Scottish Law Commission's "Report on Interpretation in Private Law" (Scot Law Com. No.160, 1997), para.1.11.

[39] Below, para.10–08. The clearest exposition of the "Canons of Construction" is Ch.VI of RIPL. See also WW McBryde, *The Law of Contract in Scotland*, 3rd edn (Edinburgh: W. Green, 2007), Ch.8; J Thomson & HL MacQueen, *Contract Law in Scotland*, 3rd edn (London: Bloomsbury 2012), paras 3–40—3–50.

. . .

'It is an argument not without weight, though far from conclusive, that the construction is to be preferred which gives a meaning to every word and clause of the contract . . . '[8]

The Unidroit Principles of International Commercial Contracts provide that contract terms are to be interpreted so as to give effect to all the terms rather than to deprive some of them of effect.[9] This way of formulating the rule embraces both the rule in favour of giving effect to the juridical act as a whole and the rule in favour of giving effect to all its terms.

. . .

6.10 *Give effect to precise terms, rather than vague terms.* If in the same juridical act parties have used precise terms and vague general language, and if there is a conflict between the two, it is reasonable to prefer the construction which gives effect to the precise terms rather than one which gives effect to the general language or to any implication which might be drawn from it (*specialia generalibus derogant*).[11] . . .

6.11 A particular example of the preference for the specific is that in appropriate cases the expression of one thing may be held to imply the exclusion of another (*expressio unius est exclusio alterius*).[14] This should not, however, in our view, be elevated into a separate rule of preference. There are many cases where it would be unreasonable to conclude that an express reference to one thing excluded others. Indeed, the French and Italian civil codes provide that a reference to one illustrative example is presumed not to exclude other cases.[15]

6.12 *The eiusdem generis rule.* This rule has been described as follows.

'Where a list of things of the same class is followed by general words, the general words may be construed as limited to members of that class.'[16]

'Where a list of things is given, to which some provision of the contract applies, and that list concludes with wide general words, the meaning of these general words is so far controlled by the context that they apply only to things of the same class (*ejusdem generis*) as those in the preceding list.'[17]

Although the *eiusdem generis* rule could be regarded as simply an example of the importance of construing terms in their context it is such a specific rule, and such a familiar rule, that it should perhaps feature in its own right in the proposed list of canons of construction . . . It is clear from the rule itself that there must be a class or *genus* before the rule comes into operation.[18] And it can only come into operation where there is room for doubt. If the general words make it clear that they are intended to be absolutely general, the rule cannot apply.[19]

6.13 *Prefer a construction against the party who supplied the term.* A canon of construction which is frequently called in aid in the Scottish courts is the rule that, where any terms which have not been separately negotiated have been supplied by one party, there is a preference for their interpretation against that party (*contra proferentem*).[20] The rule comes into operation only in the event of doubt or ambiguity.[21] It is based on the consideration that the party who supplied the term had the opportunity to make it clear and has only himself to blame if, in a case of doubt, it is construed against him.[22] There is some doubt in the existing law as to the precise circumstances in which the rule applies and as to the way in which it should be formulated.[23] The formulation at the beginning of this paragraph is limited to terms which have not been individually negotiated. In this respect it differs from the formulation in the Unidroit *Principles of International Commercial Contracts*[24] but is similar to the formulation in the proposed new *Principles of European Contract Law*.[25] The question would be whether an individual term had been separately negotiated, not whether the juridical act as a whole had been. It seems to us that it would be difficult and rather artificial to seek to identify which party had 'supplied' a term which had been inserted as a result of negotiation between the parties.[26] We accept, however, that it could also be difficult in some cases to decide whether a term had been separately negotiated.

. . .

6.15 *Give effect to more important terms, rather than less important terms.* If it is not possible to give effect to all the terms of a juridical act by construing them together,[27] and a conflict remains between an essential term and an incidental term, it is reasonable to attach more weight to the essential term than to the incidental term . . .

In South Africa there have been several cases in which it has been held that operative clauses prevailed over preambles and similar narrative clauses.[31] The reasoning is that the decision by the parties to put something into a mere narrative clause indicates a deliberate choice to refrain from incorporating it in the operative clauses.[32]

6.16 *Give effect to separately negotiated terms, rather than standard terms.* It very often happens that a contract or similar juridical act consists partly of standard terms and partly of terms which have been separately negotiated. In such cases the separately negotiated terms are more likely to express the intentions of the parties and, in case of any conflict which cannot otherwise be resolved, it is reasonable to give the preference to them.[33] A rule to this effect appears in the proposed new *Principles of European Contract Law*.[34]

6.17 *Prefer original language.* The *Unidroit Principles of International Commercial Contracts* contain a rule that

'Where a contract is drawn up in two or more language versions which are equally authoritative there is, in case of discrepancy between the versions, a preference for the interpretation according to a version in which the contract was originally drawn up.'[35]

. . .

8–44 **Summary**

6.28 We would be grateful for views on the following proposal.

5.(1) In construing a juridical act, the following canons of construction may be applied where appropriate in order to resolve any doubt or conflict.

(a) A construction of the juridical act which gives effect to all its terms is preferred to one which does not.
(b) A construction which gives effect to precise terms is preferred to one which gives effect to general language.
(c) Where a list of items, all of which are members of the same class is followed by a general term, there is a preference for interpreting the general term as applying only to items of the same class as those in the specific list.
(d) Where, in an onerous juridical act, any terms which have not been separately negotiated have been supplied by one party, there is a preference for their interpretation against that party.
(e) A construction which gives effect to operative or essential terms is preferred to one which is in accordance with narrative or incidental terms.
(f) A construction which gives effect to separately negotiated terms is preferred to one which gives effect to standard terms not separately negotiated.
(g) Where a juridical act is drawn up in two or more linguistic versions which are equally authoritative, there is, in case of discrepancy, a preference for construction according to the version in which it was originally drawn up.
(h) There is a preference for a construction which favours a result other than donation and which, in the case of a gratuitous unilateral act, favours the result least burdensome to the granter.
(i) There is a preference for a construction in favour of freedom from burdens or restrictions.

(j) There is a preference for a construction which leads to results which are lawful, fair and reasonable.

5.(2) The above list is without prejudice to any other rule of preference which would be applied by any reasonable person in interpreting a juridical act.

---

[5] We say 'overtly' because in reality an interpreter in applying a rule which expresses a preference for a construction which gives effect to one type of term rather than another will have some regard to the nature of the 'effect'. The rules would not, and should not, be read as requiring a construction to be preferred if it gave a totally fanciful and unreasonable effect to the preferred type of term.

[6] *Contract* 402. See also McBryde, *Contract* 429. For a recent application, see *Scottish Wholefoods Collective Warehouse Ltd v Raye Investments Ltd* 1993 GWD 36-2346.

...

[8] Gloag, *Contract* 399. See e.g. *Bank of Scotland v Secretary of State for Scotland* 1996 GWD 9-470.

[9] Art. 4.5.

...

[11] See the American Law Institute's *Restatement of the Law (Second), Contracts 2d* s 203(c) and comment. See also *Earl of Kintore v Lord Inverury* (1863) 4 Macq 522.

...

[14] See Gloag, 404-406. We have said "in appropriate cases" and "may be held to imply" because the *expressio unius* maxim cannot be applied rigidly. "It is often a valuable servant, but a dangerous master to follow in the construction of statutes or documents. The *exclusio* is often the result of inadvertence or accident...": *Colquhoun v Brooks* (1888) 21 QBD 52 at 65. See also *Stevenson v Hunter* (1903) 5F 761 at 765.

[15] French Civil Code art. 1164; Italian Civil Code art. 1365.

[16] McBryde, *Contract* 431. See eg *Abchurch SS Co Ltd v Stinnes* 1911 SC 1010. The rule is not always described in the way which has become standard in Scotland. It is sometimes regarded as relating to the whole subject matter of the contract - so that, for example, in a contract about gold mining a general assignation of all claims or rights might be read as being limited to claims or rights relating to gold and as not extending, for example, to grazing rights. See Christie, *The Law of Contract in South Africa* (2d edn 1991) 255-256.

[17] Gloag, *Contract* (2d ed 1929) 403.

[18] *The Admiralty v Burns*, 1910 SC 531.

[19] *Glasgow Corporation v Glasgow Tramway and Omnibus Co Ltd* (1898) 25R (HL) 77 (words "free from all expenses whatever" could not be cut down by the *eiusdem generis* rule without denying effect to "all" and "whatever").

[20] See Gloag, *Contract* (2d ed 1929) 400; McBryde, *Contract* 19-26 to 19-31; Rankine, *The Law of Leases in Scotland* (3d ed, 1916) 98; *Aitken's Trs v Bank of Scotland* 1944 SC 270; *Carrick Furniture House Ltd v General Accident* 1977 SC 308. Recent cases where the rule has been considered include:- *G A Estates Ltd v Caviapen Trs Ltd* 1993 GWD 24-1482; *Shanks & McEwan (Contractors) Ltd v Strathclyde Regional Council* 1994 GWD 10-576; *Eurocopy Rentals Ltd v McCann Fordyce* 1994 GWD 19-1155; *Huewind Ltd v Clydesdale Bank plc* 1995 GWD 25-1345. It is doubtful whether the rule applies where the parties contract on the basis of standard terms drawn up by a trade or professional organisation: in such a case neither party can properly be said to have supplied any particular term. See *SSHA v Wimpey Construction (UK) Ltd* 1986 SC (HL) 57.

[21] See *MW Wilson (Lace) Ltd v Eagle Star Insurance Co Ltd* 1993 SLT 938, where the *contra proferentem* rule did not apply because there was no ambiguity.

[22] See D.45, 1, 99 (*Deverb.oblig.*) (Celsus); Bankton, *Institute*, I.11.62 (Rule1); Erskine, *Institute*, III.3.87.

[23] See McBryde, *Contract* 19-26 to 19-31.

[24] Article 4.6 provides that "If contract terms supplied by one party are unclear, an interpretation against that party is preferred". The comment on the article states that "the less the contract term in question was the subject of further negotiations between the parties, the greater the justification for interpreting it against the party who included it in the contract".

[25] Article 5:103 of the draft of April 1996 provides that "Where there is doubt about the meaning of a contract terms not individually negotiated, an interpretation of the term against the party who supplied it is to be preferred."
[26] See *Birrell v Dryer* (1884) 11R (HL) 41 at 47 where it was said that the *contra proferentem* rule did not apply to a term when "in substance, its authorship is attributable to both parties alike".
[27] For example, an essential term of a deed in apparently general terms may be read as qualified by a later term. See eg *Sutherland v Sinclairs and Baillie* (1801) M App voce Tailzie No 8; *Dick-Lauder v Leather-Cully* 1920 SC 48 in both of which the dispositive clause was read as qualified by a later clause, it being possible to read the two together.
...
[31] See Christie, *The Law of Contract in South Africa* (2d edn 1991) 244-245.
[32] *Ex parte Johannesburg City Council* 1975 1 SA 816 (W) at 819.
[33] See Gloag, *Contract* (2d ed 1929) 399 ("It is a general rule that if the record of the contract consists of a printed form with alterations or additions in writing, the written portion is to rule in the event of any discrepancy."); *Barry D Trentham Ltd v McNeil* 1996 SLT 202 at 207 ("it is necessary on general principle to have regard to the rule that typewritten elements of the documents have priority over standard printed conditions"). And see the American Law Institute's *Restatement of the Law (Second), Contracts 2d* s 203(d) in Appendix A.
[34] Article 5:104 of the draft of April 1996 provides that "Terms which have been individually negotiated take preference over those which are not."
[35] Article 4.7. There is a similar provision in article 5:107 of the proposed new *Principles of European Contract Law* (draft of April 1996)."

A court will give ambiguous words such meaning as will give effect to the contract. Generally, courts do not expect the same precision from commercial documents that they would expect from legally drafted documents. Nevertheless, a court will not enforce a contract which is so vague as to be uncertain[40]; nor will they give effect to a meaningless term. These issues are closely connected with the issue of whether a contract is inchoate or incomplete. Contracts which inhibit or restrict freedom are strictly construed. This means that, for example, a restriction on the use of land, or on a person's subsequent employment or trade must be expressed with the utmost clarity, otherwise it will have no effect.

Interpretation of contracts: the meaning of words and the circumstances that define them

8–45 Even where the actual words of the express terms of the contract have been established, the question remains: how are those words to be interpreted? What do they actually mean? The words themselves have a dictionary meaning, which is relatively easy to establish. The meaning they convey will depend on their context and will be determined "by considering the whole express terms of the contract and any admissible surrounding circumstances".[41] McBryde regards this as "the one principle of construction to which all other rules are subsidiary".[42] Although it can be seen as a "rule" of construction, interpretation is essentially an aspect of the law of evidence: what evidence is permissible to interpret the words of the document? This itself raises several questions.

Is it the meaning as understood by the parties? If so, is it the meaning as understood subjectively by either, or is it the meaning understood objectively by both parties?

Is it the meaning as it would be understood by a reasonable, impartial observer?

If the meaning is not ambiguous, if it makes sense on the face of it, can the "surrounding circumstances" be considered to give them a different meaning?

What does the phrase "admissible surrounding circumstances" cover? Does it include evidence

---

[40] See *Crawford v Bruce*, 1992 S.L.T. 524, above paras 8–24—8–27.
[41] WW McBryde, *The Law of Contract in Scotland*, 3rd edn (Edinburgh: W. Green, 2007), para.8–08.
[42] WW McBryde, *The Law of Contract in Scotland*, 3rd edn (Edinburgh: W. Green, 2007), para.8–08.

of what was said and done during negotiations, or even after the contract is formed; or is evidence restricted to the circumstances surrounding the making of the contract?

Mot controversially, if the meaning is on the face of it unambiguous, can a different meaning be deduced from the "surrounding circumstances"?

The cases that follow provide answers to most of those questions, but some remain unclear. **8–46**
The need to establish clarity is emphasised by the Law Commission's Impact Statement in its recent Discussion Paper, *Review of Contract Law: Interpretation of Contract*.[43]

> "Interpretation is currently a matter of common law not statute, and the rules must be gleaned from an analysis of court decisions. At present, the Scottish courts are not clearly agreed on the correct basic approach to the interpretation of contracts, and there is uncertainty on such issues as whether ambiguity is required before a court may consider extrinsic evidence from which guidance may be sought as to the meaning of a written contract. The rules on admissibility also involve some fine distinctions between the types of use to which extrinsic evidence may be put: for example, it may be used to assess the parties' shared understanding of the commercial purpose of their contract, but not as a guide to what they meant by expressions used in the contract. Thus in disputes about the interpretation of contracts, advisers must first consider all the potentially relevant evidence in order to determine what to submit to the judge or arbitrator, who then in turn must take time to decide on the admissibility or not of the material put before them ... It has been suggested to us by some on our Advisory Groups that extra costs will arise inasmuch as advisers in any dispute will have to investigate all the potentially relevant evidential material; but we think ... that this may already be the case. We also think that the corresponding risk of the courts being deluged with evidential material whenever there is a dispute about a contract's meaning can be minimised by legal rules specifying, not the evidence to be excluded, but rather what evidence is relevant, i.e. that which, objectively assessed from the perspective of a reasonable person, shows the parties' common intention. With clearer, simpler rules there may anyway be less need for disputes about a contract's meaning to have to go before a court or arbitrator, which would save costs generally. It would also cease to be necessary to use the back door of rectification when one was unable to go through the front door of interpretation as a result of the rules of evidence."

In that same Discussion Paper, the Commission commented:

> "The leading modern case on how to interpret contracts in Scotland is usually taken to be *Bank of Scotland v Dunedin Property Investment Co Ltd*, starting with the words used but avoiding interpretations in conflict with business reality or producing an absurd result. In that process the court is entitled to be placed in the same position as the parties were themselves at the time the contract was concluded, 'not in order to provide a gloss on the terms of the contract, but rather to establish the parties' knowledge of the circumstances with reference to which they used the words in the contract [Ibid at 665 per LP Rodger]'."

---

[43] Scottish Law Commission, *Review of Contract Law: Interpretation of Contract* (Scottish Law Com. No.147, 2011), paras 1.16–1.18.

8–47 **Bank of Scotland v Dunedin Property Investment Co Ltd**

1998 S.C. 657

Court of Session, First Division: The Lord President (Rodger), Lords Kirkwood and Caplan

Dunedin (D) consolidated several loans from the bank into a single loan of £10 million, secured by a debenture over D's stock, repayable over 10 years at a fixed rate of interest. The bank entered into an interest rate swap agreement with another lending institution, to protect itself against interest rate fluctuations. In pre-contractual discussions with D, the bank explained that it intended to enter into an interest rate swap agreement, and that early redemption of the loan by D would create knock-on costs to the bank for early termination of the swap agreement, which it would expect D to pay. The bank also explained that it could not guarantee the amount of such knock-on costs, but that it would attempt to minimize them.

By condition 3 of the loan agreement, in the event of early redemption by D repurchasing the debenture loan stock from the Bank, the repurchase would be "subject to the Bank being fully reimbursed for all costs, charges and expenses incurred by it in connection with the Stock". D gave notice of its intention to repurchase the loan stock. The Bank claimed the consequential costs it would incur by terminating its interest rate swap agreement early—costs in the region of £1.25 million—as such costs were incurred "in connection with the Stock". D argued that the bank's rate swap agreement was independent of the loan agreement with D, having been taken out by the bank for its own purposes, and D was therefore not liable for the termination costs.

The question for the First Division was whether the phrase "in connection with the Stock" properly was interpreted as including the knock on costs to the bank of terminating the interest rate swap agreement.

The court held that it was legitimate to examine the surrounding circumstances to ascertain the parties' intentions, and that when the condition was examined in the light of the background facts known to both parties, the costs were incurred "in connection with the Stock". The phrase "in connection with" did not mean only a direct connection—establishing a substantial relationship in a practical business sense was sufficient. The Bank accordingly was entitled to claim the knock on costs of the early redemption.

8–48 "THE LORD PRESIDENT (RODGER): ... [T]here remains only one issue in the case, viz whether the cost of breaking the swap contract was incurred by the bank 'in connection with the Stock'. It is this phrase which the court requires to interpret.

During the hearing before this court we were referred to a number of authorities on the approach which should be taken to the interpretation of a contract. In particular counsel analysed the five principles enunciated by Lord Hoffmann in a speech in which both Lord Hope of Craighead and Lord Clyde concurred in *Investors Compensation Scheme Ltd v West Bromwich Building Society* at [1998] 1 All ER, pp 114–115. For my part, however, in the present case I am content to follow Lord Steyn's general guidance that in interpreting a commercial document of this kind the court should apply the 'commercially sensible construction' of the condition in question: *Mannai Investment v Eagle Star* [1997] AC, p 771A. I also find it helpful to start where Lord Mustill began when interpreting the reinsurance contracts in *Charter Reinsurance Co Ltd v Fagan* [1997] AC, p 384B–C: 'I believe that most expressions do have a natural meaning, in the sense of their primary meaning in ordinary speech. Certainly, there are occasions where direct recourse to such a meaning is inappropriate. Thus, the word may come from a specialist vocabulary and have no significance in ordinary speech. Or it may have one meaning in common speech and another in a specialist vocabulary; and the content may show that the author of the document in which it appears intended it to be understood in the latter sense. Subject to this, however, the inquiry will start, and usually finish, by asking what is the ordinary meaning of the words used.'

I begin therefore, not by inquiring into the state of knowledge of the parties to the contract, but by asking myself what is the ordinary meaning of the words 'in connection with' in condition 3.

...

The Lord Ordinary, on the other hand, held that the phrase 'in connection with the Stock' imposed a limitation to costs 'directly connected with the stock' and he instanced drafting costs in connection with the loan agreement, the costs of any necessary registration or any administrative costs that might be incurred. I can, however, find no justification in the wording of Condition 3 for inserting the adverb 'directly' to describe the manner in which the costs are to be connected with the Stock.

...

Since the phrase 'in connection with' is an ordinary English phrase, rather than a technical legal phrase, there is probably little to be gained from scrutinising too closely the interpretations which have been placed on it in different contexts in other cases.

...

I have reached this view as to the construction of Condition 3 by asking what is the ordinary meaning of the words used by the parties and without considering the background of the matrix of facts, known to the parties, in which the loan stock agreement was set. It is, however, trite that in interpreting a provision in a contract the court may 'enquire beyond the language and see what the circumstances were with reference to which the words were used, and the object, appearing from those circumstances, which the person using them had in view': *Prenn v Simmonds* at p 1384 *per* Lord Wilberforce, citing the speech of Lord Blackburn in *Macdonald v Longbottom*. See also *Inglis v Buttery & Co* at pp 102–103 and *Bovis Construction (Scotland) Ltd v Whatlings Construction Ltd* at p 357 *per* Lord President Hope. It would therefore be open to the court to consider the surrounding circumstances in which the words of Condition 3 were used; indeed we were urged to do so by counsel for the Bank.

...

As these authorities demonstrate, the rule which excludes evidence of prior communings as an aid to interpretation of a concluded contract is well-established and salutary. The rationale of the rule shows, however, that it has no application when the evidence of the parties' discussions is being considered, not in order to provide a gloss on the terms of the contract, but rather to establish the parties' knowledge of the circumstances with reference to which they used the words in the contract. For that reason I am satisfied that it was proper for the Lord Ordinary to take account of the evidence about what was said at the meeting on 8 June in order to establish the relevant circumstances in which the words of Condition 3 were used.

LORD KIRKWOOD: ... If our task had been to construe condition 3 *in vacuo*, **8–49**
without reference to any of the surrounding circumstances established by the evidence, then it would, in my view, have been difficult to draw the conclusion that the cost of breaking the interest rate swap agreement was a cost, charge or expense incurred by the bank 'in connection with the Stock'. So, if condition 3 had to be construed in isolation, I would have been inclined to agree with the Lord Ordinary that the condition would not have entitled the bank to recover the cost of breaking the swap transaction. However, as Lord Wilberforce observed in *Reardon Smith Line Ltd v Yngvar Hansen-Tangen* at [1976] 1 WLR, p 995H: 'No contracts are made in a vacuum; there is always a setting in which they have to be placed. The nature of what is legitimate to have regard to is usually described as "the surrounding circumstances" but this phrase is imprecise: it can be illustrated but hardly defined. In a commercial contract it is certainly right that the court

should know the commercial purpose of the contract and this in turn presupposes knowledge of the genesis of the transaction, the background, the context, the market in which the parties are operating.'

In *Bank of Scotland v Stewart* Lord President Inglis observed at (1891) 18 R, p 960: 'In a question of this kind, arising upon the construction of a contract, the Court are quite entitled to avail themselves of any light they may derive from such evidence as will place them in the same state of knowledge as was possessed by the parties at the time that the contract was entered into.'

In *Scottish Power plc v Britoil (Exploration) Ltd* Staughton LJ observed as follows: 'It has been established law for the greater part of this century that contracts are not construed in a vacuum. The court is entitled to know the surrounding circumstances which prevailed when the contract was made'.

Further, in *Investors Compensation Scheme Ltd v West Bromwich Building Society* Lord Hoffmann (at [1998] 1 All ER, p 114h) summarised the principles by which contractual documents are nowadays construed and he observed *inter alias* as follows:

'Interpretation is the ascertainment of the meaning which the document would convey to a reasonable person having all the background knowledge which would reasonably have been available to the parties in the situation in which they were at the time of the contract ... The meaning which a document (or any other utterance) would convey to a reasonable man is not the same thing as the meaning of its words. The meaning of words is a matter of dictionaries and grammars; the meaning of the document is what the parties using those words against the relevant background would reasonably have been understood to mean.'

So it is legitimate to look at the surrounding circumstances in order to ascertain what was the intention of the parties 'expressed in the words used as they were with regard to the particular circumstances and facts with regard to which they were used' (*Inglis v Buttery & Co* per Lord Blackburn at p 103).

The question then arises as to the nature of the surrounding circumstances which the court is entitled to take into account. It is clear, on the authorities, that evidence of prior negotiations and evidence of the subjective intention of either of the parties will not be admissible. However, the court can have regard to 'facts which both parties would have had in mind and known that the other had in mind at the time when the contract was made' (*Scottish Power plc v Britoil (Exploration) Ltd*, per Staughton LJ). The limits to be placed on the evidence of surrounding circumstances which will be admissible in any particular case may be difficult to define and in the present case it seems to me that certain of the evidence led by the bank at the proof went rather beyond what was properly admissible as evidence of the surrounding circumstances.

...

For my part I am prepared to accept that the words 'in connection with' are capable of a wide construction and in a case of this nature I would be prepared to accept that it would be sufficient if it was demonstrated that there was a substantial relationship in a practical business sense.

8–50 LORD CAPLAN: ... [R]ecent authority has given important guidance on the interpretation of commercial contracts (of which this is plainly one). The emphasis of these authorities is placed on the desirability of arriving at a common sense practical construction likely to reflect what the parties must be taken to have meant. Formal language is less important than an attempt to extract from the language what parties must in all the circumstances have intended. I am certainly not suggesting that plain words should be ignored but equally it is not useful or sensible to struggle with contorted semantic exercises if it is perfectly obvious what reasonable and informed business people must have meant if they were hoping to achieve a workable and intelligent result.

In *Prenn v Simmonds*, in a passage since much quoted, Lord Wilberforce said: 'In order for the agreement of July 6, 1960, to be understood it must be placed in context. The time has long passed when agreements, even those under seal, were isolated from the matrix of facts in which they were set and interpreted purely on linguistic considerations.'

Certainly Lord Wilberforce proceeds to explain how the substance of negotiations must be excluded from questions of construction. However I do not think his Lordship meant this to be applied too rigidly. As he states (p 1385): 'It may be said that previous documents may be looked at to explain the aims of the parties. In a limited sense this is true: the commercial, or business object, of the transaction, objectively ascertained, may be a surrounding fact.'

More recent enlightenment is given in *Investors Compensation Scheme Ltd v West Bromwich Building Society*. At p 1257 Lord Hoffmann observed: 'I do not think that the fundamental change which has overtaken this branch of the law, particularly as a result of the speeches of Lord Wilberforce in *Prenn v Simmonds* and *Reardon Smith Line Ltd v Yngvar Hansen-Tangen*, is always sufficiently appreciated. The result has been, subject to one important exception, to assimilate the way in which documents are interpreted by judges to the common sense principles by which any serious utterance would be interpreted in ordinary life. Almost all the old intellectual baggage of legal interpretation has been discarded. The principles may be summarised as follows: (1) Interpretation is the ascertainment of the meaning which the document would convey to a reasonable person having all the background knowledge which would reasonably have been available to the parties in the situation in which they were at the time of the contract; (2) The background was famously referred to by Lord Wilberforce as the "matrix of fact", but this phrase is, if anything, an understated description of what the background may include. Subject to the requirement that it should have been reasonably available to the parties and to the exception to be mentioned next, it includes absolutely anything which would have affected the way in which the language of the document would have been understood by a reasonable man.'

Lord Hoffmann then proceeds to exclude from the admissible background the previous negotiations of the parties and their declarations of subjective intent.

Another case that was referred to in connection with contractual interpretation was *Mannia (sic) Investment Co Ltd v Eagle Star Life Assurance Co Ltd*. At p 372 Lord Steyn observed: 'In determining the meaning of the language of a commercial contract, and of unilateral contractual notices, the law generally favours a commercially sensible construction. The reason for this approach is that commercial construction is more likely to give effect to the intention of the parties. Words are therefore interpreted in the way in which a reasonable commercial person would construe them.'

In the same case Lord Hoffmann gives a very expansive and detailed analysis of the topic I am considering. However some of his *obiter* observations have attracted comment in other recent cases and I do not think that I need to become entrapped in such issues for I have all the guidance I need from Lord Hoffmann and others in the passages I have already quoted.

...

The defenders argued that the court could not derive any help in construction from the pre-contract discussions. These were of the nature of negotiations and were superseded by the final Loan Stock Agreement. An attempt was made to gain support for this from the analyses of Lord Wilberforce and Lord Hoffman which I have already referred to. However I do not think that their Lordships were trying to exclude from the construction process communications which themselves bear on the factual matrix against which the parties were contracting. What, of course, cannot be prayed in aid are pre-contract communications which reflect the parties' aspirations and intentions at the time when they were made. In *Bovis Construction (Scotland) v Whatlings Construction* before the First Division it was made clear that the correspondence preceding the contract could be looked at to determine the circumstances in which a provision in the contract was intended to apply. This is consistent with long established Scottish authority. Thus in *Mackenzie v Liddell* it was held that telegrams preceding the contract could be looked at as proof of surrounding circumstances although not as proof of the parties' meaning itself.

...

Construing Clause 3 against the whole background circumstances I think it would not have made much sense if the parties had merely been attempting to provide for the relatively minor expenses that may have resulted from administering the repurchase of the loan stock. During discussions there does not appear to have been any mention of the administrative costs.

...

Construing Clause 3 against the whole background circumstances I think it would not have made much sense if the parties had merely been attempting to provide for the relatively minor expenses that may have resulted from administering the repurchase of the loan stock. During discussions there does not appear to have been any mention of the administrative costs."

From this and other recent Scottish decisions the Commission has suggested a list of "principles of interpretation".

8–51 *Review of Contract Law: Interpretation of Contract*

Scottish Law Commission Discussion Paper No.147 (February 2011)

"Principles of interpretation?

5.13 Several judges (mostly in the Outer House) have attempted to formulate lists of the principles to be applied to the interpretation of contracts. While no one of these lists was intended to be comprehensive or definite, and they therefore sometimes differ in content and emphasis, a compilation on which there would probably be fairly general agreement can be put together as follows:

1. The words used by the parties must generally be given their ordinary meaning.[43]
2. A contractual provision must be construed in the context of the contractual document or documents as a whole.[44]
3. In construing a contract drafted by lawyers, the words may be expected to have been chosen with care and to be intended to convey the meaning which the words chosen would convey to a reasonable person.[45]
4. The process of construction is objective, according to the standards of a reasonable third party aware of the commercial context.[46]
5. Regard is to be had to the circumstances in which the contract came to be concluded to discover the facts to which the contract refers and its commercial purposes objectively considered, although this is limited to matters known or reasonably to be known by both parties.[47]
6. Where more than one construction is possible, the commercially sensible construction is taken to be what the parties intended.[48]
7. The court must not substitute a different bargain from that made by the parties.[49]"

---

[43] *City Wall Properties (Scotland) Ltd v Pearl Assurance plc* [2003] CSOH 211; 2004 SC 214;

Middlebank Ltd v University of Dundee [2006] CSOH 202; *Macdonald Estates plc v Regenesis (2005) Dunfermline Ltd* [2007] CSOH 123; 2007 SLT 791; *Autolink Concessionaires (M6) plc v Amey Construction Ltd* [2009] CSIH 14; 2009 GWD 9-146.
[44] *MRS Distribution Ltd v DS Smith (UK) Ltd* 2004 SLT 631; *Emcor Drake & Scull Ltd* [2005] CSOH 139; 2005 SLT 1233; *Forbo-Nairn Ltd v Murrayfield Properties Ltd* [2009] CSIH 94; 2009 GWD 16-251.
[45] *City Wall Properties* (fn 43); *Credential Bath Street Ltd v Venture Investment Placement Ltd* [2007] CSOH 208; 2008 GWD 9-168; *Forbo-Nairn* (fn 44).
[46] *Emcor Drake & Scull Ltd* (fn 44); *Middlebank Ltd* (fn 43); *Forbo-Nairn* (fn 44).
[47] *MRS Distribution Ltd* (fn 44); *Emcor Drake & Scull Ltd* (fn 44); *Middlebank Ltd* (fn 43); *Autolink Concessionaires* (fn 43); *Forbo-Nairn* (fn 44).
[48] *MRS Distribution Ltd* (fn 44); *Emcor Drake & Scull Ltd* (fn 44); *Autolink Concessionaires* (fn 43); *Forbo-Nairn* (fn 44); *Forbo-Nairn* (fn 44).
[49] *City Wall Properties* (fn 43); *Emcor Drake & Scull Ltd* (fn 44); *Middlebank Ltd* (fn 43); *Macdonald Estates* (fn 43); *Credential Bath Street* (fn 45); *Forbo-Nairn* (fn 44)."

The judgments in *BoS v Dunedin* are also notable because although all three judges referred to *Investors Compensation Scheme Ltd v West Bromwich Building Society (No.1)*, none relied upon it in his judgment. That decision has had a major impact on the approach it interpretation in England and throughout the common law world and continues to influence Scottish jurisprudence.

Lord Hoffmann and the "contextual" approach to interpretation

There is no doubt that, for English law, Lord Hoffmann's speech in the *ICS* decision[44] was a radical departure from previous practice on interpretation. Until 1997, the "parole evidence" rule was strictly applied, so that **8–52**

> "where a contract was reduced to writing a court was not supposed to go outside the document for any further terms or material that would contradict what had been written (the parole evidence rule). Reference to external material was allowed only where the document was ambiguous or unclear".[45]

By extending the "matrix of facts" on which the court could rely in interpreting the words of a contract, he was bringing English law closer to the position in Scotland; but a careful reading of the principles he enunciated shows that he had gone much further.

[44] Below, para.8–53 onwards. See also *Charter Reinsurance Co Ltd (In liquidation) v Fagan* [1996] 1 All E.R. 406; and *Mannai Investment Co Ltd v Eagle Star Life Assurance Co Ltd* [1997] A.C. 749.
[45] Scottish Law Commission, *Review of Contract Law: Interpretation of Contract* (Scot Law Com. Discussion Paper No.147 (February 2011)), para.4.3.

8–53 **Investors Compensation Scheme Ltd v West Bromwich Building Society (No.1)**
[1998] 1 W.L.R. 896
House of Lords: Lords Goff of Chieveley, Lloyd of Berwick, Hoffmann, Hope of Craighead, Clyde

In the 1980s, a number of homeowners (acting on financial advice) entered into home income plans that involved mortgaging their homes with West Bromwich Building Society (WBBS). This realised money for the homeowners, which was then invested in stock market equity bonds. When interest rates rose and share prices did not, the homeowners suffered tremendous losses. The homeowners claimed compensation under the Investors Compensation Scheme, a statutory body set up under the Financial Services Act 1986.

ICS then brought proceedings against WBBS and numerous law firms involved in the mortgages, while some of the investors commenced separate actions against W for rescission of the mortgages and damages. The claim form, which formed the contract between each homeowner and ICS, stated that the homeowner had assigned absolutely to ICS all third party claims except, in s.3(b):

> "Any claim (whether sounding in rescission for undue influence or otherwise) that you have against the [WBBS] in which you claim an abatement of sums which you would otherwise have to pay to that Society."

Dispute arose as to the meaning of s.3(b). WBBS argued successfully at the Court of Appeal that on proper construction of this the investors had not validly assigned their right to sue WBBS in damages to ICS. ICS appealed to the House of Lords.

The court held that on the proper construction of the claim form, particularly in the light of the accompanying explanatory note (which did not form part of the contract), it was clear that all claims for damages and compensation by the homeowners had been validly assigned to ICS, so that the homeowners were not entitled to maintain their claims against WBBS, but ICS could validly maintain such claims. The homeowners did, however, retain the right to claim rescission of their mortgage contracts.

8–54 "LORD HOFFMANN: ... I think I should preface my explanation of my reasons with some general remarks about the principles by which contractual documents are nowadays construed. I do not think that the fundamental change which has overtaken this branch of the law, particularly as a result of the speeches of Lord Wilberforce in *Prenn v Simmonds* [1971] 1 W.L.R. 1381, 1384–1386 and *Reardon Smith Line Ltd v Yngvar Hansen-Tangen* [1976] 1 W.L.R. 989, is always sufficiently appreciated. The result has been, subject to one important exception, to assimilate the way in which such documents are interpreted by judges to the common sense principles by which any serious utterance would be interpreted in ordinary life. Almost all the old intellectual baggage of 'legal' interpretation has been discarded. The principles may be summarised as follows:

(1) Interpretation is the ascertainment of the meaning which the document would convey to a reasonable person having all the background knowledge which would reasonably have been available to the parties in the situation in which they were at the time of the contract.

(2) The background was famously referred to by Lord Wilberforce as the 'matrix of fact', but this phrase is, if anything, an understated description of what the background may include. Subject to the requirement that it should have been reasonably available to the parties and to the exception to be mentioned next, it

includes absolutely anything which would have affected the way in which the language of the document would have been understood by a reasonable man.

(3) The law excludes from the admissible background the previous negotiations of the parties and their declarations of subjective intent. They are admissible only in an action for rectification. The law makes this distinction for reasons of practical policy and, in this respect only, legal interpretation differs from the way we would interpret utterances in ordinary life. The boundaries of this exception are in some respects unclear. But this is not the occasion on which to explore them.

(4) The meaning which a document (or any other utterance) would convey to a reasonable man is not the same thing as the meaning of its words. The meaning of words is a matter of dictionaries and grammars; the meaning of the document is what the parties using those words against the relevant background would reasonably have been understood to mean. The background may not merely enable the reasonable man to choose between the possible meanings of words which are ambiguous but even (as occasionally happens in ordinary life) to conclude that the parties must, for whatever reason, have used the wrong words or syntax. (see *Mannai Investments Co Ltd v Eagle Star Life Assurance Co Ltd* [1997] 2 W.L.R. 945)

(5) The 'rule' that words should be given their 'natural and ordinary meaning' reflects the common sense proposition that we do not easily accept that people have made linguistic mistakes, particularly in formal documents. On the other hand, if one would nevertheless conclude from the background that something must have gone wrong with the language, the law does not require judges to attribute to the parties an intention which they plainly could not have had. Lord Diplock made this point more vigorously when he said in *The Antaios Compania Neviera SA v Salen Rederierna AB* 1985 1 A.C. 191, 201: '[I]f detailed semantic and syntactical analysis of words in a commercial contract is going to lead to a conclusion that flouts business commonsense, it must be made to yield to business commonsense.'

If one applies these principles, it seems to me that the judge must be right and, as we are dealing with one badly drafted clause which is happily no longer in use, there is little advantage in my repeating his reasons at greater length. The only remark of his which I would respectfully question is when he said that he was 'doing violence' to the natural meaning of the words. This is an over-energetic way to describe the process of interpretation. Many people, including politicians, celebrities and Mrs. Malaprop, mangle meanings and syntax but nevertheless communicate tolerably clearly what they are using the words to mean. If anyone is doing violence to natural meanings, it is they rather than their listeners.

...

[In] the Court of Appeal. Leggatt L.J. said that his construction was 'the natural and ordinary meaning of the words used.' I do not think that the concept of natural and ordinary meaning is very helpful when, on any view, the words have not been used in a natural and ordinary way. In a case like this, the court is inevitably engaged in choosing between competing unnatural meanings. Secondly, Leggatt L.J. said that the judge's construction was not an 'available meaning' of the words. If this means that judges cannot, short of rectification, decide that the parties must have made mistakes of meaning or syntax, I respectfully think he was wrong. The proposition is not, I would suggest, borne out by his citation from *Alice Through the Looking Glass*. Alice and Humpty Dumpty were agreed that the word 'glory' did not mean 'a nice knock-down argument'. Anyone with a dictionary could see that. Humpty Dumpty's point was that 'a nice knock-down argument' was what *he* meant by using the word 'glory'. He very

> fairly acknowledged that Alice, as a reasonable young woman, could not have realised this until he told her, but once he had told her, or if, without being expressly told, she could have inferred it from the background, she would have had no difficulty in understanding what he meant."

8–55 Lord Hoffman's remarks have been seen as the high water mark (thus far) of his "radically contextual" approach to interpretation, wherein the relevant "matrix of fact" surrounding the contract is both wider and more central than previously envisaged.[46]

> "This ... was a genuine shift in approach to contractual interpretation. Ambiguity is not a pre-requisite of an investigation of the factual matrix in which a contract had been concluded. Such an investigation is an indispensable part of the process of understanding what a contract means in all cases. The background enables the reader, above all the judge, to determine the intended meaning of the expressions actually used in the contract. Even more radically, however, the actual words used do not necessarily govern the meaning to be given to the contractual; the background can let the judge decide that the parties used the wrong words, or mis-ordered their words, and he or she may read them in such a way as to give the parties' expressions the meanings they must have intended, in the light of the background."[47]

Lord Hoffmann's approach seems to go even further than broadening the "factual matrix" and the circumstances in which it may be investigated. His statement that "[a]lmost all the old intellectual baggage of 'legal' interpretation has been discarded" suggests that even the long-established rules or canons of construction must also give way to the new approach.[48] Given the controversy aroused by his remarks, Lord Hoffmann was perhaps grateful for the chance to clarify matters in *Bank of Credit and Commerce International SA v Ali*[49]:

> "The background is however very important. I should in passing say that when, in *Investors Compensation Scheme Ltd v West Bromwich Building Society* [1998] 1 WLR 896, 913, I said that the admissible background included 'absolutely anything which would have affected the way in which the language of the document would have been understood by a reasonable man', I did not think it necessary to emphasise that I meant anything which a reasonable man would have regarded as relevant. I was merely saying that there is no conceptual limit to what can be regarded as background. It is not, for example, confined to the factual background but can include the state of the law (as in cases in which one takes into account that the parties are unlikely to have intended to agree to something unlawful or legally ineffective) or proved common assumptions which were in fact quite mistaken. But the primary source for understanding what the parties meant is their language interpreted in accordance with conventional usage: 'we do not easily accept that people have made linguistic mistakes, particularly in formal documents'. I was certainly not encouraging a trawl through 'background' which could not have made a reasonable person think that the parties must have departed from conventional usage."

---

[46] See SC Smith, "Making Sense of Contracts", 1999 S.L.T. (News) 307. For an English perspective, see J Chuah, "The Factual Matrix in the Construction of Commercial Contracts—The House of Lords Clarifies", I.C.C.L.R. 2001, 12(12), 294–299.

[47] Scottish Law Commission, *Review of Contract Law: Interpretation of Contract,* Discussion Paper No.147 (February 2011), para.4.4.

[48] See also Lord Reed's comments in *Bath Street Ltd v Venture Investment Placement Ltd* [2007] CSOH 208; 2008 G.W.D. 9-168, [38].

[49] *Bank of Credit and Commerce International SA v Ali* [2002] 1 A.C. 251 at 269, [39].

Even this, however left unclear how extensive the search for "surrounding circumstances" might be. In particular, could a court take into consideration any pre-contractual negotiations between the parties? This was emphatically rejected in the following case.

Chartbrook Ltd v Persimmon Homes Ltd 8–56
House of Lords
[2009] UKHL 38; [2009] 1 A.C. 1101
Baroness Hale, Lords Hoffmann, Hope, Rodger, Walker,

Persimmon contracted to obtain planning permission for a plot of land owned by Chartbrook and then to construct a mixed residential and commercial development and sell the properties on long leases. Chartbrook would grant the leases at the direction of Persimmon, who would receive the proceeds and pay Chartbrook an agreed price for the land. Planning permission was granted and the development was built. A dispute arose between the parties regarding a term of the contract which provided for an "additional residential payment", which was a term defined in the contract. The dispute related to the calculation of the amount payable under that term. Persimmon calculated the sum due as £897,051 whereas Chartbrook claimed to be entitled to £4,484,862. In support of their construction of the term of the contract Chartbrook sought to rely on documents which were part of the pre-contractual negotiations. Persimmon counterclaimed for rectification of the contract to accord with what they claimed to be the parties' common agreement. The judge held that evidence of the pre-contractual negotiations was not admissible, particularly when an express definition was contained within the contract. The Court of Appeal, by a majority, upheld the judge's decision.

The House of Lords held that the definition of "additional residential payment" in the contract was ambiguous and obviously defective as a piece of drafting; that there was always a commercial context to a contract negotiated between businessmen, and to interpret the definition in accordance with the ordinary rules of syntax made no commercial sense; and that, accordingly, taking into consideration the background and context but not the pre-contractual negotiations and applying the established principles of construction, the claimants' construction could not be upheld, and the construction put forward by the defendants was more appropriate.

"LORD HOPE OF CRAIGHEAD 8–57

. . .

[2] I agree that Persimmon's argument that the House should take account of the pre-contractual negotiations raises an important issue. Every so often the rule that prior negotiations are inadmissible comes under scrutiny. That is as it should be. One of the strengths of the common law is that it can take a fresh look at itself so that it can keep pace with changing circumstances. But for the reasons that have been set out by Lord Hoffmann I think that the arguments for retaining the rule have lost none of their force since *Prenn v Simmonds* [1971] 1 WLR 1381 demonstrated, as Lord Wilberforce put it at p 1384, the disadvantages and danger of departing from established doctrine.

. . .

LORD HOFFMANN 8–58

. . .

[28] The rule that pre-contractual negotiations are inadmissible was clearly reaffirmed by this House in *Prenn v Simmonds* [1971] 1 WLR 1381, 1384 where Lord Wilberforce said that earlier authorities 'contain little to encourage, and much to discourage, evidence of negotiation or of the parties' subjective intentions'. It is clear that the rule of inadmissibility has been established for a very long time. In *A & J Inglis v John Buttery &*

Co (1878) 3 App Cas 552, 577 Lord Blackburn said that Lord Justice Clerk Moncreiff, at (1877) 5 R 58, 64, had laid down a principle which was nearly accurate but not quite when he said that in all mercantile contracts 'whether they be clear and distinct or the reverse, the court [is] entitled to be placed in the position in which the parties stood before they signed' ...

...

[30] To allow evidence of pre-contractual negotiations to be used in aid of construction would therefore require the House to depart from a long and consistent line of authority, the binding force of which has frequently been acknowledged: see *Bank of Scotland v Dunedin Property Investment Co Ltd* 1998 SC 657, 665 ('well established and salutary', per Lord President Rodger; *Alexiou v Campbell* [2007] UKPC 11 at [15] ('vouched by ... compelling authorities', per Lord Bingham of Cornhill). The House is nevertheless invited to do so, on the ground that the rule is illogical and prevents a court from, as the Lord Justice Clerk in *A & J Inglis v John Buttery & Co* 3 App Cas 552 said, putting itself in the position of the parties and ascertaining their true intent.

[31] In *Prenn v Simmonds* [1971] 1 WLR 1381, 1384–1385 Lord Wilberforce said by way of justification of the rule:

'The reason for not admitting evidence of these exchanges is not a technical one or even mainly one of convenience, (though the attempt to admit it did greatly prolong the case and add to its expense). It is simply that such evidence is unhelpful. By the nature of things, where negotiations are difficult, the parties' positions, with each passing letter, are changing and until the final agreement, though converging, still divergent. It is only the final document which records a consensus. If the previous documents use different expressions, how does construction of those expressions, itself a doubtful process, help on the construction of the contractual words? If the same expressions are used, nothing is gained by looking back: indeed, something may be lost since the relevant surrounding circumstances may be different. And at this stage there is no consensus of the parties to appeal to. It may be said that previous documents may be looked at to explain the aims of the parties. In a limited sense this is true: the commercial, or business object, of the transaction, objectively ascertained, may be a surrounding fact. Cardozo J thought so in the *Utica Bank* case [*Utica City National Bank v Gunn* (1918) 118 NE 607]. And if it can be shown that one interpretation completely frustrates that object, to the extent of rendering the contract futile, that may be a strong argument for an alternative interpretation, if that can reasonably be found. But beyond that it may be difficult to go: it may be a matter of degree, or of judgment, how far one interpretation, or another, gives effect to a common intention: the parties, indeed, may be pursuing that intention with differing emphasis, and hoping to achieve it to an extent which may differ, and in different ways. The words used may, and often do, represent a formula which means different things to each side, yet may be accepted because that is the only way to get 'agreement' and in the hope that disputes will not arise. The only course then can be to try to ascertain the 'natural' meaning. Far more, and indeed totally, dangerous is it to admit evidence of one party's objective-even if this is known to the other party. However strongly pursued this may be, the other party may only be willing to give it partial recognition, and in a world of give and take, men often have to be satisfied with less than they want. So, again, it would be a matter of speculation how far the common intention was that the particular objective should be realised.'

... [After consideration of several criticisms of the rule, Lord Hoffmann continued]

[33] I do however accept that it would not be inconsistent with the English objective theory of contractual interpretation to admit evidence of previous communications between the parties as part of the background which may throw light upon what they meant by the language they used. The general rule, as I said in *Bank of Credit and Commerce International SA v Ali* [2002] 1 AC 251, 269, is that there are no conceptual

limits to what can properly be regarded as background. Prima facie, therefore, the negotiations are potentially relevant background. They may be inadmissible simply because they are irrelevant to the question which the court has to decide, namely, what the parties would reasonably be taken to have meant by the language which they finally adopted to express their agreement. For the reasons given by Lord Wilberforce, that will usually be the case. But not always. In exceptional cases, as Lord Nicholls has forcibly argued, a rule that prior negotiations are always inadmissible will prevent the court from giving effect to what a reasonable man in the position of the parties would have taken them to have meant ...

[34] It therefore follows that while it is true that, as Lord Wilberforce said, inadmissibility is normally based in irrelevance, there will be cases in which it can be justified only on pragmatic grounds ...

[35] The first is that the admission of pre-contractual negotiations would create greater uncertainty of outcome in disputes over interpretation and add to the cost of advice, litigation or arbitration. Everyone engaged in the exercise would have to read the correspondence and statements would have to be taken from those who took part in oral negotiations ...

[36] There is certainly a view in the profession that the less one has to resort to any form of background in aid of interpretation, the better ...

[37] I do not think that these opinions can be dismissed as merely based upon the fallacy that words have inherent or 'available' meanings, rather than being used by people to express meanings, although some of the arguments advanced in support might suggest this. It reflects what may be a sound practical intuition that the law of contract is an institution designed to enforce promises with a high degree of predictability and that the more one allows conventional meanings or syntax to be displaced by inferences drawn from background, the less predictable the outcome is likely to be ...

[38] ... I rather doubt whether the *ICS* case produced a dramatic increase in the amount of material produced by way of background for the purposes of contractual interpretation. But pre-contractual negotiations seem to me capable of raising practical questions different from those created by other forms of background. Whereas the surrounding circumstances are, by definition, objective facts, which will usually be uncontroversial, statements in the course of pre-contractual negotiations will be drenched in subjectivity and may, if oral, be very much in dispute. It is often not easy to distinguish between those statements which (if they were made at all) merely reflect the aspirations of one or other of the parties and those which embody at least a provisional consensus which may throw light on the meaning of the contract which was eventually concluded. But the imprecision of the line between negotiation and provisional agreement is the very reason why in every case of dispute over interpretation, one or other of the parties is likely to require a court or arbitrator to take the course of negotiations into account. Your Lordships' experience in the analogous case of resort to statements in Hansard under the rule in *Pepper v Hart* [1993] AC 593 suggests that such evidence will be produced in any case in which there is the remotest chance that it may be accepted and that even these cases will be only the tip of a mountain of discarded but expensive investigation. *Pepper v Hart* has also encouraged ministers and others to make statements in the hope of influencing the construction which the courts will give to a statute and it is possible that negotiating parties will be encouraged to improve the bundle of correspondence with similar statements.

[39] Supporters of the admissibility of pre-contractual negotiations draw attention to the fact that continental legal systems seem to have little difficulty in taking them into account. Both the *Unidroit Principles of International Commercial Contracts* (1994 and 2004 revision) and the *Principles of European Contract Law* (1999) provide that in ascertaining the 'common intention of the parties', regard shall be had to prior

negotiations: articles 4(3) and 5(102) respectively. The same is true of the *United Nations Convention on Contracts for the International Sale of Goods* (1980) ...

[40] In his judgment in the present case [2007] 1 All ER (Comm) 1083, Briggs J thought that the most powerful argument against admitting evidence of pre-contractual negotiations was that it would be unfair to a third party who took an assignment of the contract or advanced money on its security. Such a person would not have been privy to the negotiations and may have taken the terms of the contract at face value. There is clearly strength in this argument ...

[41] The conclusion I would reach is that there is no clearly established case for departing from the exclusionary rule. The rule may well mean, as Lord Nicholls has argued, that parties are sometimes held bound by a contract in terms which, upon a full investigation of the course of negotiations, a reasonable observer would not have taken them to have intended. But a system which sometimes allows this to happen may be justified in the more general interest of economy and predictability in obtaining advice and adjudicating disputes. It is, after all, usually possible to avoid surprises by carefully reading the documents before signing them and there are the safety nets of rectification and estoppel by convention. Your Lordships do not have the material on which to form a view. It is possible that empirical study (for example, by the Law Commission) may show that the alleged disadvantages of admissibility are not in practice very significant or that they are outweighed by the advantages of doing more precise justice in exceptional cases or falling into line with international conventions. But the determination of where the balance of advantage lies is not in my opinion suitable for judicial decision. Your Lordships are being asked to depart from a rule which has been in existence for many years and several times affirmed by the House. There is power to do so under the *Practice Statement (Judicial Precedent)* [1966] 1 WLR 1234. But that power was intended, as Lord Reid said in *R v National Insurance Comrs, Ex p Hudson* [1972] AC 944, 966, to be applied only in a small number of cases in which previous decisions of the House were 'thought to be impeding the proper development of the law or to have led to results which were unjust or contrary to public policy'. I do not think that anyone can be confident that this is true of the exclusionary rule.

[42] The rule excludes evidence of what was said or done during the course of negotiating the agreement for the purpose of drawing inferences about what the contract meant. It does not exclude the use of such evidence for other purposes: for example, to establish that a fact which may be relevant as background was known to the parties, or to support a claim for rectification or estoppel. These are not exceptions to the rule. They operate outside it.

...

8–59 LORD RODGER OF EARLSFERRY

...

[69] Like Lord Hoffmann, I would decline counsel's elegant but, in the event, unnecessary invitation to revisit the rule in *Prenn v Simmonds* [1971] 1 WLR 1381. No one could possibly say that the rule is based on some error of law or misconception. On the contrary, the main pros and cons of having regard to prior negotiations when interpreting a formal contract have been known and discussed for centuries. The present law represents a choice which was already second nature to the Earl of Eldon LC as long ago as *Miller v Miller* (1822) 1 Sh App 308. When interpreting a clause in a marriage contract which had been preceded by 'a vast deal of correspondence', the Earl of Eldon LC assured the House that he did not recollect a case to which he had given more earnest attention, but still gave the correspondence short shrift, at p 317:

'My Lords, all the previous correspondence I lay entirely out of the case, because I cannot conceive that any thing can be more dangerous than the construing deeds by the effect of letters and correspondence previous to the execution of them.'

Subsequently, at p 319, he described the possibility of looking at the effect of the correspondence as 'a very singular thing'. Some 60 years later, with rather more deliberation, the House affirmed that approach in *A & J Inglis v John Buttery & Co* (1878) 3 App Cas 552 and, a century after that, reaffirmed it in *Prenn v Simmonds* [1971] 1 WLR 1381. The rule could scarcely be more firmly embedded in our law.

[70] ... [T]he rule about prior negotiations forms part of the law of evidence and there are no particular pressing circumstances which call for a change. The House is simply being asked to make a fresh policy decision and, in effect, to legislate to provide for a different rule. The wisdom of the proposed change is, however, debatable. So, if there is to be a change, it should be on the basis of a fully informed debate in a forum where the competing policies can be properly investigated and evaluated. Although counsel presented the rival arguments with conspicuous skill, your Lordships' House in its judicial capacity is not that forum.

...

LORD WALKER OF GESTINGTHORPE **8–60**

...

[97] I have also read with interest and admiration Lord Hoffmann's observations, in the remaining part of his opinion, on the important questions that we do not have to decide. I would not differ from any of these views ...

BARONESS HALE OF RICHMOND **8–61**

[98] My Lords, I too have had the privilege of reading in draft the opinions of my noble and learned friends, Lord Hoffmann and Lord Walker of Gestingthorpe. For the reasons they give, together with those of Lawrence Collins LJ in the Court of Appeal, I agree that Persimmon's construction of this contract is correct and that this appeal should be allowed.

[99] ... My experience at the Law Commission has shown me how difficult it is to achieve flexible and nuanced reform to a rule of the common law by way of legislation. In the end abolition may be the only workable legislative solution ... Even that can prove difficult if, on analysis, the view is taken that the rule has no real content, as with the parol evidence rule (the Law Commission's Report on The Parol Evidence Rule (1986) (Law Com No 154) (Cmnd 9700)). The courts, on the other hand, are able to achieve step-by-step changes which can distinguish cases in which such evidence is 'helpful' from cases in which it is not.

[100] ... It is perhaps surprising that questions of such practical and theoretical importance in the law of contract should still be open to debate and development. But that is also the great strength of the common law."

Although the House of Lords unanimously rejected the general admissibility of pre-contractual negotiations into the "matrix of facts", Lord Hoffmann allowed the possibility that it will be admissible where the issue is rectification of a mistake in a document, or where "estoppel by convention" (an English form of personal bar) is raised.[50] **8–62**

Even more significantly, he concedes that it may be admissible "to establish that a fact which may be relevant as background was known to the parties" (at [42]).

The speeches are also significant in recognising that the approach they adopted differs from that adopted by various international conventions and that this may be a matter for the Law Commission (for England and Wales) to consider. The Scottish Law Commission took up that challenge in Discussion Paper 147 and is considered below.[51]

The House, however, did not consider whether the court could the trawl for "circumstances"

[50] See above, para.8–58.

[51] See para.6–07 onwards.

extend to the words and conduct of the parties after the contract was made. The position still appears to be as described in the following English case.

8–63 **L Schuler AG v Wickman Machine Tool Sales Ltd.**

[1974] A.C. 235

House of Lords: Lords Reid, Morris of Borth-Y-Gest, Wilberforce, Simon of Glaisdale, Kilbrandon

S were manufacturers of industrial panel presses that could be used in motor car production. S entered into a sole distributor agreement with W in the UK. The agreement contained the following:

> "7(b) It shall be [a] condition of this agreement that (i) [W] shall send its representatives to visit the [UK's six largest car makers] at least once in every week for the purpose of soliciting orders for panel presses."

The word "condition" was not used elsewhere in the contract.

W failed to make the required visits, although these breaches were allowed to be remedied within 60 days, as per cl.11(a)(i). However, following a further failure to make a visit, S claimed the right to terminate the agreement forthwith as W had breached a "condition". W claimed damages for wrongful repudiation. Dispute arose as to the meaning of the word "condition". S contended that the word was used deliberately and in the strict technical and legal sense, such that its slightest breach was fundamental and entitled repudiation. W argued that the word had a popular meaning, was not a technical term but was capable of different meanings to the lawyer or the layperson. Given the ambiguity, W argued, the subsequent actions of S (i.e. allowing remediation of similar breaches) should be referred to in construing the meaning of "condition".

The court rejected S's argument: to allow such a construction was so unreasonable that the parties could not have intended it. However, in doing so, it was neither necessary nor permissible to have regard to the subsequent actions of the parties.

8–64 "LORD REID: ... Schuler maintains that the word 'condition' has now acquired a precise legal meaning; that, particularly since the enactment of the Sale of Goods Act 1893, its recognised meaning in English law is a term of a contract any breach of which by one party gives to the other party an immediate right to rescind the whole contract. Undoubtedly the word is frequently used in that sense. There may, indeed, be some presumption that in a formal legal document it has that meaning. But it is frequently used with a less stringent meaning. One is familiar with printed 'conditions of sale' incorporated into a contract and with the words 'for conditions see back' printed on a ticket. There it simply means that the 'conditions' are terms of the contract.

In the ordinary use of the English language 'condition' has many meanings, some of which have nothing to do with agreements. In connection with an agreement it may mean a pre-condition: something which must happen or be done before the agreement can take effect. Or it may mean some state of affairs which must continue to exist if the agreement is to remain in force. The legal meaning on which Schuler relies is, I think, one which would not occur to a layman; a condition in that sense is not something which has an automatic effect. It is a term the breach of which by one party gives to the other an option either to terminate the contract or to let the contract proceed and, if he so desires, sue for damages for the breach.

Sometimes a breach of a term gives that option to the aggrieved party because it is of a fundamental character going to the root of the contract, sometimes it gives that option because the parties have chosen to stipulate that it shall have that effect. Blackburn J said in *Bettini v Gye* (1876) 1 Q.B.D. 183, 187: 'Parties may think some matter, apparently of very little importance, essential; and if they sufficiently express an intention to make the literal fulfillment of such a thing a condition precedent, it will be one; ...'

In the present case it is not contended that Wickman's failures to make visits amounted in themselves to fundamental breaches. What is contended is that the terms of clause 7 'sufficiently express an intention' to make any breach, however small, of the obligation to make visits a condition so that any breach shall entitle Schuler to rescind the whole contract if they so desire.

Schuler maintains that the use of the word 'condition' is in itself enough to establish this intention. No doubt some words used by lawyers do have a rigid inflexible meaning. But we must remember that we are seeking to discover intention as disclosed by the contract as a whole. Use of the word 'condition' is an indication—even a strong indication—of such an intention but it is by no means conclusive.

The fact that a particular construction leads to a very unreasonable result must be a relevant consideration. The more unreasonable the result the more unlikely it is that the parties can have intended it, and if they do intend it the more necessary it is that they shall make that intention abundantly clear.

Clause 7 (b) requires that over a long period each of the six firms shall be visited every week by one or other of two named representatives. It makes no provision for Wickman being entitled to substitute others even on the death or retirement of one of the named representatives. Even if one could imply some right to do this, it makes no provision for both representatives being ill during a particular week, and it makes no provision for the possibility that one or other of the firms may tell Wickman that they cannot receive Wickman's representative during a particular week. So if the parties gave any thought to the matter at all they must have realised the probability that in a few cases out of the 1,400 required visits a visit as stipulated would be impossible. But if Schuler's contention is right, failure to make even one visit entitle them to terminate the contract however blameless Wickman might be.

This is so unreasonable that it must make me search for some other possible meaning of the contract. If none can be found then Wickman must suffer the consequences. But only if that is the only possible interpretation.

If I have to construe clause 7 standing by itself then I do find difficulty in reaching any other interpretation. But if clause 7 must be read with clause 11 the difficulty disappears. The word 'condition' would make any breach of clause 7 (b), however excusable, a material breach. That would then entitle Schuler to give notice under clause 11 (a) (i) requiring the breach to be remedied. There would be no point in giving such a notice if Wickman were clearly not in fault but if it were given Wickman would have no difficulty in showing that the breach had been remedied. If Wickman were at fault then on receiving such a notice they would have to amend their system so that they could show that the breach had been remedied. If they did not do that within the period of the notice then Schuler would be entitled to rescind.

In my view, that is a possible and reasonable construction of the contract and I would therefore adopt it. The contract is so obscure that I can have no confidence that this is its true meaning but for the reasons which I have given I think that it is the preferable construction. It follows that Schuler was not entitled to rescind the contract as it purported to do. So I would dismiss this appeal.

I must add some observations about a matter which was fully argued before your Lordships. The majority of the Court of Appeal were influenced by a consideration of actings subsequent to the making of the contract. In my view, this was inconsistent with the decision of this House in *Whitworth Street Estates (Manchester) Ltd v James Miller & Partners Ltd* [1970] A.C. 583. We were asked by the respondent to reconsider that decision on this point and I have done so. As a result I see no reason to change the view which I expressed in that case. It was decided in *Watcham v Attorney-General of East Africa Protectorate* [1919] A.C. 533 that in deciding the scope of an ambiguous title to land it was proper to have regard to subsequent actings and there are other authorities for that view. There may be special reasons for construing a title to land in light of subsequent possession had under it but I find it unnecessary to consider that question. Otherwise I find no substantial support in the authorities for any general principle permitting subsequent actings of the parties to a contract to be used as throwing light on its meaning. I would therefore reserve my opinion with regard to Watcham's case but repeat my view expressed in *Whitworth* with regard to the general principle.

8–65 LORD WILBERFORCE: ... The first qualification involves the legal question whether this agreement may be construed in the light of certain allegedly relevant subsequent actions by the parties. Consideration of such actions undoubtedly influenced the majority of the Court of Appeal to decide, as they did, in the respondent's favour: and it is suggested, with much force, that, but for this, Edmund Davies L.J. would have decided the case the other way. In my opinion, subsequent actions ought not to have been taken into account. The general rule is that extrinsic evidence is not admissible for the construction of a written contract; the parties' intentions must be ascertained, on legal principles of construction, from the words they have used. It is one and the same principle which excludes evidence of statements, or actions, during negotiations, at the time of the contract, or subsequent to the contract, any of which to the lay mind might at first sight seem to be proper to receive. As to statements during negotiations this House has affirmed the rule of exclusion in *Prenn v Simmonds* [1971] 1 W.L.R. 1381 as to subsequent actions (unless evidencing a new agreement or as the basis of an estoppel) in *Whitworth Street Estates (Manchester) Ltd v James Miller & Partners Ltd.* [1970] A.C. 583.

There are of course exceptions. I attempt no exhaustive list of them. In the case of ancient documents, contemporaneous or subsequent action may be adduced in order to explain words whose contemporary meaning may have become obscure, and evidence may be admitted of surrounding circumstances or in order to explain technical expressions or to identify the subject matter of an agreement: or (an overlapping exception), to resolve a latent ambiguity. But ambiguity in this context is not to be equated with difficulty of construction, even difficulty to a point where judicial opinion as to meaning has differed. This is, I venture to think, elementary law. On this test there is certainly no ambiguity here.

The arguments used in order to induce us to depart from these settled rules and to admit evidence of subsequent conduct generally in aid of construction, were fragile. They were based first on the *Privy Council judgment in Watcham v Attorney-General of East African Protectorate* [1919] A.C. 533 not, it was pointed out, cited in Whitworth's case. But there was no negligence by counsel or *in curia* by their Lordships in omitting to refer to a precedent which I had thought had long been recognised to be nothing but the refuge of the desperate. Whether, in its own field, namely, that of interpretation of deeds relating to real property by reference to acts of possession, it retains any credibility in the face of powerful judicial criticism is not before us. But in relation to the interpretation of contracts or written documents generally I must deprecate its future citation in English courts as an authority. It should be unnecessary to add that the well-known words of Sir Edward Sugden (later Lord St. Leonards) (*Attorney-General v Drummond* (1842) 1 Dr. & War. 353, 368) '... tell me what you have done under *such* a deed, and I will tell you what that deed means' relate to ancient instruments and it is an abuse of them to cite them in other applications. Secondly, there were other authorities cited, *Hillas & Co Ltd v Arcos Ltd* (1932) 43 Ll.L.R. 359 and *Foley v Classique Coaches Ltd* [1934] 2 K.B. 1. But, with respect, these are not in any way relevant to the present discussion, and the judgment of Lawrence J. in *Radio Pictures Ltd v Inland Revenue Commissioners* (1938) 22 T.C. 106, so far as it bears on this point was disapproved in the Court of Appeal and in my opinion was not correct in law.

In my opinion, therefore, the subsequent actings relied upon should have been left entirely out of account: in saying this I must not be taken to agree that the particular actings relied on are of any assistance whatever towards one or other construction of the contract. Indeed if one were to pursue the matter, the facts of the present case would be found to illustrate, rather vividly, the dangers inherent in entertaining this class of evidence at all."

The court's considered view in *Schuler*, deprecating the use of subsequent conduct to aid construction, is reflected in the following Scottish Law Commission Report.

Report on Interpretation in Private Law **8–66**

Scottish Law Commission Report No.160 (28 October 1997)

"2.24 *Subsequent conduct*. One of the few questions to give rise to a difference of view on consultation was the relevance of subsequent conduct in the interpretation of juridical acts.

2.25 It seems clear on principle that subsequent conduct of the granter of, or parties to, a juridical act should not be regarded as part of the surrounding circumstances. That expression refers to the circumstances surrounding the act at the time when it was done. Later conduct cannot be part of the factual matrix within which the juridical act was done.

2.26 That, however, is not the end of the question. It would be possible to provide specifically that in interpreting an expression in a juridical act, regard could be had to subsequent conduct as well as to the circumstances surrounding the juridical act at the time when it was entered into. One objection to such a course is that subsequent conduct cannot affect the view which would reasonably have been taken as to the meaning of an expression immediately after the juridical act. To allow subsequent conduct to be taken into account in the application of the general rule would mean that an expression which was supposed to be objectively construed would have a meaning which varied over time. Another objection is that to allow reference to subsequent conduct would lead to uncertainty and expense.

2.27 The existing Scottish law on this point is not clear. The many Scottish cases allowing reference to subsequent conduct to establish the common intention of the parties at the time of the contract now have to be read in the light of observations in more recent English House of Lords cases, which cast doubt on them. In the discussion paper we provisionally suggested that, for the purposes of a new rule on the interpretation of juridical acts in general, subsequent conduct should be left out of account.

2.28 Two consultees expressed doubts on the question of subsequent conduct. They referred to two types of case. One was the case where a term such as 'the development' was used in a contract and where the question later arose whether this meant the development as at the time of the contract or the development as it was in fact from time to time. The other was the case where the parties to a contract proceeded over a prolonged period on the basis that a particular term was to be interpreted in a particular way. The consultees suggested that in such cases justice might not be done between the parties unless the interpreter looked at what happened after the contract.

2.29 We have found this a difficult question. However, we think that, unless it is varied, the meaning of a juridical act ought to be consistent over time. We remain therefore of the view that subsequent conduct ought not in general to affect interpretation where an objective test is applied. It may, however, be relevant in the interpretation of certain contracts where it is claimed that one party (or each party) used an expression in a particular sense, which was known to the other. Subsequent conduct may cast a light backwards for this purpose."

The Report went on (para.2.36) to recommend, as part of a general rule on interpretation of juridical acts, that conduct subsequent to the juridical act be excluded from the surrounding circumstances which should be regarded in interpreting such acts. This, however, no longer appears to be a universally accepted view and, to some extent, might not reflect the position in Scotland.

8–67 *Review of Contract Law: Interpretation of Contract*

Scottish Law Commission Discussion Paper No.147 (February 2011)

"Conduct of the parties subsequent to the contract's formation as admissible background

4.17 Although the rule excluding evidence of parties' conduct after contract formation has been the subject of critical discussion in the periodical literature,[66] there has been no high-level judicial discussion or review of the law, comparable with that in *Chartbrook*, in England. Such material continues to be excluded from the interpretative process following decisions of the House of Lords in the 1970s.[67] Lord Hoffmann's statement of the principles of interpretation in the *ICS* case did not specifically mention subsequent conduct, but it can probably be inferred that he accepted its established exclusion from the admissible background in the following passage of his speech:

'Interpretation is the ascertainment of the meaning which the document would convey to a reasonable person having all the background *knowledge which would reasonably have been available to the parties in the situation in which they were at the time of the contract*.'[68]

4.18 In New Zealand, however, the Supreme Court has departed from this exclusionary rule in a pre-*Chartbrook* decision,[69] while the South African courts have admitted subsequent conduct as an evidentiary guide where contracts are found to be ambiguous.[70] Likewise, the Canadian courts have adopted the view that subsequent conduct evidence can assist with determinations on the interpretation of written contracts.[71] The USA's Uniform Commercial Code and Restatement (Second) of Contracts provides that:

'Where [a contract] involves repeated occasions for performance by either party with knowledge of the nature of the performance and opportunity for objection to it by the other, any course of performance accepted or acquiesced in without objection *shall be relevant to determine the meaning of the agreement*.'[72]

4.19 Writing extra-judicially at a time when he was still a Lord of Appeal in Ordinary, Lord Nicholls criticised the justification for the subsequent conduct rule stated by Lord Reid in 1970,[73] that it might lead to contracts meaning one thing one day and another the next:

'This is puzzling. Evidence of the parties' subsequent conduct is sought to be used as a means of identifying the meaning borne by the language of the contract from its inception. The fact that this evidence only came into being after the contract was made can hardly be a good reason for declining to admit it.'[74]

Lord Nicholls' article was influential in the New Zealand decision to make evidence of subsequent conduct admissible for purposes of interpretation.

...

The exclusionary rule on evidence of subsequent conduct 8–68

5.21 There have also been a number of cases since the publication of RIPL in 1997 in which examination of the parties' subsequent conduct as an aid to the interpretation of their contract was refused.[77] RIPL itself stated that 'the existing Scottish law on this point is not clear', citing numerous cases in which reference to subsequent conduct to establish the common intention of the parties at the time of the contract was allowed, but observing that these had now to be read in the light of observations in more recent English House of Lords decisions going the other way.[78] But the position recommended in RIPL, on the grounds that admitting evidence of subsequent conduct might mean that the meaning of a juridical act could vary over time, now seems firmly crystallised in the courts. The decisions have, however, been criticised by commentators, the exclusionary rule being regarded as 'unfortunate' by Professor McBryde.[79] In *Wincanton Group Ltd v Reid Furniture plc*[80] Lord Glennie suggested that, as with pre-contractual negotiations, evidence about parties' subsequent conduct might be relevant in establishing surrounding circumstances and the parties' knowledge before and at the time of the contract. But this raises again the reality of a distinction between the different uses to which particular kinds of evidence may be put.[81]

. . .

Exception to the exclusionary rule on pre-contractual negotiations? 8–69

5.23 RIPL suggested that existing Scottish authority allowed the court to give a word the particular meaning it had for one of the parties if every other party at the time of contracting knew, or could reasonably have been assumed to know, that it was being used in this sense. In particular, it cited the House of Lords decision in *Houldsworth v Gordon Cumming*.[86] A question arises, however, as to the impact of the *Chartbrook* judgment on the authority of *Houldsworth*. *Chartbrook*, it will be recalled, over-ruled *The Karen Oltmann*,[87] a case very similar to *Houldsworth* and also referred to in RIPL on the present point,[88] because in allowing the judge to consider the meaning attached to a word by parties during their negotiations to determine the meaning of the word in their eventual contract, it was thought to have the effect of destroying the exclusionary rule on pre-contractual negotiations. *Houldsworth* was, however, not cited in *Chartbrook*. The House of Lords' unanimous judgement in 1910 does not seem to have involved any specifically Scottish considerations, and the two English judges involved, the Lord Chancellor (Loreburn) and the Earl of Halsbury, had no doubt, in the words of the former, that 'these negotiations are crucial, and all that passed, either orally or in writing, is admissible in evidence to prove what was in fact the subject of sale; not to alter the contract, but to identify its subject'.[89] *Chartbrook* is notable for cautionary remarks from Lords Hoffmann and Rodger on when to use the 1966 Practice Statement to over-rule previous decisions of the House.[90] In any event, as a matter of the formal doctrine of precedent, the four-judge House of 1910 in a Scottish appeal cannot be over-ruled by even a five-judge one of 2009 in an English appeal, however persuasive the latter might seem to a subsequent Scottish court. Indeed, it might be questioned whether, perhaps, the later English decision loses something of its own authority by virtue of having been determined without a full view of all the relevant precedents.

5.24 A further discussion point may be whether *BoS v Dunedin* is in fact another illustration of this exception to the exclusionary rule about pre-contractual negotiations . . . While therefore *BoS v Dunedin* is indeed authority for an exclusionary rule in Scots law in relation to the admissibility of pre-contractual negotiations, that authority is limited, not only by the extent to which pre-contractual negotiations were admitted as evidence of surrounding circumstances, but also as an implicit reaffirmation of the exception to the rule in *Houldsworth v Gordon Cumming*.

---

[66] See e.g. Gerard McMeel, "Prior negotiations and subsequent conduct – the next step forward for contractual interpretation?" (2003) 119 LQR 272 at 290-293; Donald Nicholls, article cited at fn 50 above, at 588-589.
[67] *James Miller & Partners Ltd v Whitworth Estates (Manchester) Ltd* [1970] AC 583; *Schuler v Wickman Machine Tool Sales Ltd* [1974] AC 235.
[68] [1998] 1 WLR 896 at 912 (with added emphasis).
[69] *Wholesale Distributors Ltd* v *Gibbons Holdings Ltd* [2008] 1 NZLR 277.
[70] See e.g. *Breed v Van den Berg* 1932 AD 283 and also the cases cited at fn 65 above.
[71] See *Manitoba Development Corporation v Columbia Forest Products Ltd* [1974] 2 WWR 237 (Man CA), followed in *Palansky v Palansky* (1993) 89 Man R (2d) 1 (Man QB) and *Montreal Trust Co of Canada v Birmingham Lodge Ltd* (1995) 24 OR (3d) 97 (Ont CA) and, in Alberta, in *Beller Carreau Lucyshyn Ltd v Cenalta Oilwell Servicing Ltd* (1997) 211 AR 1 (Alta QB).
[72] UCC art 2-208(1); Restatement, Section 202(4). In the UCC the words in square brackets are replaced by "a contract of sale", and in the Restatement by "an agreement". The italicised words are found in the UCC but replaced in the Restatement by "is given great weight in the interpretation of the agreement".
[73] *James Miller & Partners Ltd v Whitworth Estates (Manchester) Ltd* [1970] AC 583 at 603: "I must say that I had thought that it is now well settled that it is not legitimate to use as an aid in the construction of the contract anything which the parties said or did after it was made. Otherwise one might have the result that a contract meant one thing the day it was signed, but by reason of subsequent events meant something different a month or a year later."
[74] Donald Nicholls, ["My kingdom for a horse: the meaning of words" (2005) 121 LQR 577], at 589.
[86] 1910 SC (HL) 49. See para 2.8 for a summary of this case.
[87] See para 4.12.
[88] RIPL, para 3.5.
[89] 1910 SC (HL) 49 at 51. The parties were agreed that there was a valid contract between them (as indeed there was from an objective point of view), so the court could not consider whether a lack of actual consensus meant there never had been a contract. The case is distinguishable in this way from *Mathieson Gee (Ayrshire) Ltd v Quigley* 1952 SC (HL) 38, where objectively there was no contract (although there may have been a subjective consensus).
[90] [2009] UKHL 38; [2009] 1 AC 1101, paras 41 and 70. It is unclear to what extent the Supreme Court can over rule HL decisions, or indeed its own decisions, as the 1966 Practice Statement has not been carried over into the new dispensation."

The contextual approach in the Scottish courts

8–70 Reaction to the contextual approach outlined by Lord Hoffmann in England and throughout the common law world was mixed.

8–71 *Review of Contract Law: Interpretation of Contract*

Scottish Law Commission Discussion Paper No.147 (February 2011)

"4.6 The precise scope of the Hoffmann approach has continued to be controversial in England, although the general approach, sometimes labelled 'contextual' (in contrast with 'literalist') interpretation,[16] is now widely accepted in the courts[17] and amongst academic lawyers,[18] while it is also the starting point of a standard practitioners' textbook on the subject written by a serving High Court judge[19] . . . The Hoffmann approach has also been the subject of severe and continuing criticism from contract draftsmen, understandably concerned that their carefully crafted documents may not completely tie the creative hands of the judges or be a wholly self- contained statement of the content of the parties' legal relationship.[28]

> 4.7 The present general position in English law has been systematised as follows by the leading academic commentator on the subject, Professor Gerard McMeel:[29]
>
> '1. The aim of the exercise of the construction of a contract is to ascertain the meaning it would convey to a reasonable business person.
> 2. An objective approach is to be taken, concerned with a person's expressed rather than actual intentions.
> 3. The exercise is a holistic one, based on the whole contract, rather than excessive focus on particular words, phrases, sentences or clauses.
> 4. The exercise is informed by the surrounding circumstances or external context, with it being permissible to have regard to the legal, regulatory and factual matrix constituting the background to the making of the expression being interpreted.
> 5. Within this framework due consideration is given to the commercial purpose of the transaction or provision.'
>
> ---
>
> [16] The use of the adjective "contextual" is awkward in relation to RIPL, where "context" refers only to the juridical act itself, and "surrounding circumstances" to the external fact matrix thereof: see para 2.7 above.
> [17] See Lord Bingham, "A new thing under the sun? The interpretation of contract and the *ICS* decision" (2008) 12 Edin LR 374.
> [18] See e.g. McMeel, *Construction*; Catherine Mitchell, *Interpretation of Contracts: Current Controversies in the Law* (2007); Burrows and Peel, chs 3-5. An influential New Zealand proponent of the Hoffmann approach is Professor David McLauchlan: see e.g. "Contract interpretation: what is it about?" (2009) 31 Sydney LR 5. Other recent articles by Professor McLauchlan are cited later in this Chapter.
> [19] Kim Lewison, *The Interpretation of Contracts* (4th ed, 2007). See in particular ch 1. The author is a Justice of the High Court of England and Wales.
> . . .
> [28] See e.g. Alan Berg, "Thrashing through the undergrowth" (2006) 122 LQR 354; Richard Calnan, "Construction of commercial contracts: a practitioner's perspective", in Burrows and Peel, pp 17-24; James J Spigelman, "From text to context: contemporary contractual interpretation" (2007) 81 ALJ 322.
> [29] Gerard McMeel, "The principles and policies of contractual construction", in Burrows and Peel, pp 27-51 at pp 50-51. Professor McMeel offers five further propositions, which are versions of the main "rules of preference" (see paras 3.20 and 7.36-7.38). The approach informs the structure of his book on the subject (above, fn 18)."

Early reaction in Scotland to the contextual approach was muted,[52] or even critical.[53] The approach is not binding in Scotland, but here too in some quarters there was a suggestion that the established rules of interpretation were unduly restrictive. The Scottish Law Commission proposed (previously to the *ICS* decision) a general rule that an expression in a juridical act[54] is given the meaning that would reasonably given to it in its context, having regard where **8–72**

---

[52] In *Bank of Scotland v Dunedin Property Investment Co Ltd*, 1998 S.C. 657 (see above) Lord President Rodger and Lords Kirkwood and Caplan all referred to Lord Hoffmann's five principles while nimbly avoiding becoming "entrapped" in discussion of the wider implications.

[53] In *Partnership of MFV Ocean Quest v Finning Ltd*, 2000 S.L.T. (Sh. Ct.) 157, Sheriff Principal DJ Risk QC said at 161, [G], of Lord Hoffmann's statement: "As a traditionalist, I am respectfully taken aback by the principles enunciated in that passage, which seem to me to come perilously close to permitting a court to rewrite the terms of a contract".

[54] Scottish Law Commission, *Report on Interpretation in Private Law* (Scot Law Com. No.160). See discussion of "juridical acts" above, paras 8–41—8–43.

appropriate to surrounding circumstances and the nature and purpose of the juridical act, insofar as the latter can be objectively ascertained. The Commission also recommended[55] that "surrounding circumstances" should not include statements of intention, prior communings, instructions or negotiations preparatory to the juridical act, nor conduct subsequent to the juridical act. McBryde too concedes that "we have moved a long way from the historic approach of the pleader stating the parole evidence rule and insisting that nothing other than the terms of the contract can be examined" but elaborates the negative consequences of extending the matrix of fact to all background material.[56]

> "The old references to 'admissible' surrounding circumstances, nevertheless, implied that there were limits to the examinable circumstances. How these limits were to be expressed was not entirely clear, but it was the general setting of the contract and the aim of the parties that were important. An extension to background material (irrespective of any ambiguity) has the following potential consequences: (1) it makes the discussion and settlement of disputes involving the meaning of contracts more expensive and time consuming; the parties may have to produce evidence of their knowledge, of communications between them and also background information; advice on the meaning of the contract may have to consider much more than the words of the contract; (2) given the time which may have lapsed since the contract was entered into the evidence may be incomplete or unreliable; (3) although prior negotiations are inadmissible to explain the words used, lawyers will have to see the relevant information to decide what is admissible and what is not, which will not always be easy because in reality the negotiations are part of the background; (4) if the dispute proceeds to litigation some may be tempted to have pleadings and evidence which examine in detail every communication, and every matter of knowledge, expectation and commercial practice; all with great expense; (5) as the case law shows, often the result will not be helpful, and the court will be left with the terms of the contract which were not drafted with the event which as occurred in mind; and (6) uncertainty is caused for draftsmen, and parties, who cannot be sure whether or not the express terms of their contract will be overridden by reference to facts outside the contract; this will encourage prolixity in drafting. One reaction has been to consider drafting a clause which contracts out of the Hoffmann approach. Even if it is feasible to alter this rule of law, it may be dangerous to attempt to do so; the background circumstances may have some relevance to make sense of the contract. It may be better to rely on the common sense of judges who may take the view ... that the words of the contract are paramount."

The only Scottish decision that deals at length with the Hoffmann approach is on Outer House decision by Lord Reed before he was elevated to the Supreme Court. A key feature of the Hoffmann approach that Lord Reed considers is whether the words must be ambiguous before surrounding circumstances can be considered and, if they are, whether they must be considered objectively from the perspective of both parties, or the perspective of the reasonable observer and, indeed, whether there is a difference between the two perspectives.

8–73 **Credential Bath Street Ltd v Venture Investment Placement Ltd**
Outer House, Court of Session
[2007] CSOH 208; 2008 G.W.D. 9-168

The facts are stated above, para.8–37.

[55] Scottish Law Commission, *Report on Interpretation in Private Law* (Scot Law Com. No.160), para.2.36.
[56] WW McBryde, *The Law of Contract in Scotland*, 3rd edn (Edinburgh: W. Green, 2007), para.8–27.

"LORD REED ...

The first issue: the construction of clause 3.4

[14] The first issue raises a question as to the permissible limits of the construction of contracts. Clause 3.4 provides that the guarantor is released from its obligations under the guarantee on 1 January 2005 'save in respect of any antecedent breach of the Guarantee'. It might be thought that the meaning of those words is clear and unambiguous: they have only one tenable construction, and they cannot mean 'save in respect of any antecedent breach of the Lease or the Amortised Payment Agreements' or, what amounts to the same thing, 'save in respect of any antecedent breach by the Tenant for which the Guarantor is liable under the Guarantee'. In those circumstances, it might be thought that there is no legally permissible technique, other than rectification, by which a different meaning can be ascribed to clause 3.4. That would however be a mistaken view.

[15] The meaning of a document (or any other utterance) is not the same thing as the meaning of its words. As Lord Nicholls of Birkenhead has written extra-judicially:

'Words used as a medium of communication do not have a "meaning" of their own. They do not have a "meaning" independently of the person who utters them or the person who hears them'

('My Kingdom for a Horse: the Meaning of Words' (2005) 121 L.Q.R. 577). The point can be illustrated by the examples used by Lord Hoffmann in *Mannai Investment Co Ltd v Eagle Star Life Assurance Co Ltd* [1997] A.C. 749 at pages 774–775:

'I propose to begin by examining the way we interpret utterances in everyday life. It is a matter of constant experience that people can convey their meaning unambiguously although they have used the wrong words. We start with an assumption that people will use words and grammar in a conventional way but quite often it becomes obvious that, for one reason or another, they are not doing so and we adjust our interpretation of what they are saying accordingly. We do so in order to make sense of their utterance: so that the different parts of the sentence fit together in a coherent way and also to enable the sentence to fit the background of facts which plays an indispensable part in the way we interpret what anyone is saying. No one, for example, has any difficulty in understanding Mrs Malaprop. When she says "She is as obstinate as an allegory on the banks of the Nile", we reject the conventional or literal meaning of allegory as making nonsense of the sentence and substitute "alligator" by using our background knowledge of the things likely to be found on the banks of the Nile and choosing one which sounds rather like "allegory".'

Mrs Malaprop's problem was an imperfect understanding of the conventional meanings of English words. But the reason for the mistake does not really matter. We use the same process of adjustment when people have made mistakes about names or descriptions or days or times because they have forgotten or become mixed up. If one meets an acquaintance and he says 'And how is Mary?' it may be obvious that he is referring to one's wife, even if she is in fact called Jane. One may even, to avoid embarrassment, answer 'Very well, thank you' without drawing attention to his mistake. The message has been unambiguously received and understood.

...

It is of course true that the law is not concerned with the speaker's subjective intentions. But the notion that the law's concern is therefore with the 'meaning of his words' conceals an important ambiguity. The ambiguity lies in a failure to distinguish between the meanings of words and the question of what would be understood as the meaning of a person who uses words. The meaning of words, as they would appear in a dictionary, and the effect of their syntactical arrangement, as it would appear in a grammar, is part of the material which we use to understand a speaker's utterance. But it is only a part;

another part is our knowledge of the background against which the utterance was made. It is that background which enables us, not only to choose the intended meaning when a word has more than one dictionary meaning but also, in the ways I have explained, to understand a speaker's meaning, often without ambiguity, when he has used the wrong words."

[16] The principles by which contractual documents are construed, as explained by Lord Hoffmann in *Investors Compensation Scheme Ltd* v *West Bromwich Building Society* [1998] 1 W.L.R. 896 at pages 912-913, reflect that approach:

[Lord Reid quoted Rules 1, 4 and 5 in Lord Hoffmann's speech and his comments on Leggatt LJ's judgment in the Court of Appeal and continued]

[17] In the present case, a number of Scottish judgments were cited to me (including *City Wall Properties (Scotland) Ltd* v *Pearl Assurance plc* 2004 S.C. 214 and *Middlebank Ltd* v *University of Dundee* [2006] CSOH 202) in which, it appeared to be suggested, a different approach had been adopted, generally under reference to the *dictum* of Lord Mustill in *Charter Reinsurance Co Ltd* v *Fagan* [1997] A.C. 313 at page 384 that "the inquiry will start, and usually finish, by asking what is the ordinary meaning of the words used". That dictum might be contrasted with an observation made by Lord Hoffmann in the same case at page 391:

"I think that in some cases the notion of words having a natural meaning is not a very helpful one. Because the meaning of words is so sensitive to syntax and content, the natural meaning of words in one sentence may be quite unnatural in another".

Consistently with that approach, whereas Lord Mustill based his conclusion in that case solely on an analysis of the provisions of the contract, Lord Hoffmann reinforced the same conclusion by reference to such external matters as the history of reinsurance clauses and the regulatory regime for insurers. That contextual approach appears to me to have been followed in the subsequent decisions of the House of Lords. I refer in particular to *Mannai Investments*, the *Investors Compensation Scheme* case itself (in which the other members of the majority in the House of Lords concurred in Lord Hoffmann's speech), *Bank of Credit and Commerce International SA* v *Ali* [2002] 1 A.C. 251 and *Hombourg Houtimport BV* v *Agrosin Private Ltd* (*The Starsin*) [2004] 1 A.C. 715.

[18] It is clear from the passages which I have quoted that, as part of the process of construction, the court can ascribe to a document the meaning which it would convey to a reasonable person aware of the context, notwithstanding mistakes in the written expression of the parties' intention: "allegory" may reasonably be understood to mean "alligator", "Mary" may reasonably be understood as referring to Jane, and so forth. It is also clear that the court will not readily construe a document on the basis that there has been a mistake in expression. In the fifth of the principles stated by Lord Hoffmann in the *Investors Compensation Scheme* case, his Lordship observed that "we do not easily accept that people have made linguistic mistakes, particularly in formal documents", and said that the court might nevertheless conclude that "something *must* have gone wrong with the language" and therefore refrain from attributing to the parties "an intention which they *plainly* could not have had" (emphasis added). The high standard set by Lord Diplock, in the *dictum* which Lord Hoffmann quoted ("flouts business commonsense"), reinforces the point. His Lordship has emphasised the point again in subsequent cases, including *BCCI* v *Ali* (at para.39) and *Jumbo King Ltd* v *Faithful Properties Ltd* (1999) 2 HKCFAR 279 at para.59:

"The construction of a document is not a game with words. It is an attempt to discover what a reasonable person would have understood the parties to mean. And this involves having regard, not merely to the individual words they have used, but to the agreement as a whole, the factual and legal background against which it was concluded and the practical objects which it was intended to achieve. Quite often this exercise will lead to the conclusion that although there is no reasonable doubt about what the parties meant, they have not expressed themselves very well. Their language may sometimes be careless and they may have said things which, if taken literally, mean something different from what they obviously intended. In ordinary life people often express themselves infelicitously without leaving any doubt about what they meant. Of course in serious utterances such as legal documents, in which people may be supposed to have chosen their words with care, one does not readily accept that they have used the wrong words. If the ordinary meaning of the words makes sense in relation to the rest of the document and the factual background, then the court will give effect to that language, even though the consequences may appear hard for one side or the other".

[19] Although the approach to construction laid down in the *Investors Compensation Scheme* case represents a significant development in the law, reflecting developments in philosophy associated with Wittgenstein and Austin, there is nothing new about the construction of documents so as, in effect, to correct mistakes in expression. . . .

. . .

[21] As well as construing a document in such a way that a word may be understood as if another word had been used, or in such a way that words which are plainly inept are disregarded, the court can also construe a document as if it contained words which have been omitted from it. Scottish examples can readily be found in the law relating to wills. In *McLaren on Wills and Succession*, 3rd ed., for example, it is said at para. 654:

"Where it is apparent from the language of a will that the testator has not accurately or completely expressed his meaning by the words he has used, and it is also apparent what are the words that have been omitted, the necessary words may be supplied by construction in order to effectuate the intention as collected from the context".

[22] What the court is doing when it construes a document as if it contained words which are not there—just as when it construes "John" as meaning "Mary" (*Wilson* v *Wilson* (1854) 5 H.L.Cas 40, 10 E.R. 811)—is properly described as construction, and is to be distinguished from rectification. The court cannot, as a matter of construction, alter, add to or subtract from the words of a written instrument: as Romer L.J. said in *Re Sassoon* [1933] Ch. 858 at page 890, that can be done only by rectification. When the court construes a document as if it contained words which are not to be found there, it is performing the same exercise as is involved in any other aspect of the construction of a document: it is "ascertaining the meaning which the document would convey to a reasonable person having all the background knowledge which is reasonably available to the person or class of persons to whom the document is addressed" (*The Starsin* at para.73 *per* Lord Hoffmann). We all from time to time read letters, emails, and other documents in which a word or a phrase has been omitted; but we do not throw up our hands and say "I can make nothing of this", if the context enables us to infer what was meant. It is also to be noted that, just as in everyday life, the construction of documents so as to correct mistakes is not confined to mistakes which are apparent from the terms of the utterance itself. It is inherent in the contextual approach to interpretation that mistakes in a document which are apparent in the light of the surrounding circumstances can be corrected through the process of construction in the same way as mistakes which are apparent on the face of the document: the classification of mistakes as "patent" or "latent" is no longer determinative of the court's power to cure mistakes by construction.

[23] The technique of correcting mistakes by construction (if it may loosely be so described) has been vigorously applied by the House of Lords in the recent decisions which I have mentioned. In *Charter Reinsurance* a term referring to sums "actually paid" was construed as meaning sums "actually payable". In *Mannai Investments* a tenant who had served notice under the lease purporting to bring it to an end on 12 January, when the lease permitted termination only on 13 January, was held to have successfully

communicated his intention to terminate. In the *Investors Compensation Scheme* case itself, the syntax of the provision in question was altered, so that "Any claim (whether sounding in rescission for undue influence or otherwise)" was construed as meaning "Any claim sounding in rescission (whether for undue influence or otherwise)". The decision in *The Starsin* is discussed below.

[24] The court will not, of course, interpolate words or substitute one word for another merely because the result might appear to be fairer or more commercially sensible. One of the parties may simply have made a bad bargain; and the court is not entitled to impose on the parties some other bargain, under the guise of construction, on the basis that it might be thought to be fairer or more sensible. It is also necessary to heed the warnings which have been given, not least by judges with commercial experience (e.g. *The World Symphony* [1992] 2 Lloyd's Rep.115, 117 *per* Lord Donaldson M.R.; *Capital Land Holdings Ltd* v *Secretary of State for the Environment*, 16 May 1995, *per* Lord Penrose, cited in *Ben Cleuch Estates Ltd* v *Scottish Enterprise* [2006] CSOH 35 at para.139), against excessive confidence that a judge's view as to what might be commercially sensible necessarily coincides with the views of those actually involved in commercial contracts. As Lord Mustill said in *Torvald Klaveness A/S* v *Arni Maritime Corp (The Gregos)* [1994] 1 W.L.R. 1465 at page 1473:

"Naturally no judge will favour an interpretation which produces an obviously absurd result unless the words drive him to it, since it is unlikely that this is what the parties intended. But where there is no obvious absurdity, and simply assertions by either side that its own interpretation yields the more sensible result, there is room for error".

[25] Equally, in attempting to ascertain what the parties must be taken to have meant, it is necessary to have regard to the positions of both parties. As the Court of Appeal said in *Bank of Nova Scotia* v *Hellenic Mutual War Risks Association (Bermuda) Ltd* [1990] 1 Q.B. 818 at page 870:

"It is nonetheless important, in attributing a purpose to a commercial transaction, to be sure that it is the purpose of both parties and not just one. If the purpose of the transaction is seen through the eyes of one party only an unbalanced view of the transaction may result. Many contracts represent a compromise between what one party wishes to obtain and the other is willing to give".

[26] In the discussion in the present case, attention focused on three recent decisions in which words were interpolated into a document as a matter of construction. The first was *Folkes Group plc* v *Alexander* [2002] 2 B.C.L.C. 254, where an amendment to a company's articles which referred to shares "owned by a member of the Folkes Family Company" was construed as meaning "owned by a member of the Folkes Family *or by a Folkes Family* Company". The decision was an application of the fifth principle of interpretation set out by Lord Hoffmann in the *Investors Compensation Scheme* case. A literal interpretation of the amendment led, in the view of the judge, to "an absurd result". Comparing the amendment with the unamended version of the articles, the interpolated words had "obviously been mistakenly omitted". In those circumstances, the amendment could be construed with the addition of those words.

[27] In the second case, *The Starsin*, one of the issues concerned an apparent omission in a Himalaya clause. The House of Lords accepted that the missing words were to be found in a standard form of bill of lading, on which the clause in question had been modelled, and that the form had been inaccurately copied. Lord Bingham of Cornhill said (at para.23):

'I take it to be clear in principle that the court should not interpolate words into a written instrument, of whatever nature, unless it is clear both that words have been omitted and what those omitted words were ... In the present case there is agreed to be an omission. It is also plain, in my opinion, for the reasons which Mr Gee gave, what words were omitted and how they came to be omitted. I would accordingly construe the clause as if the words "acting as aforesaid and for the purpose of all the foregoing provisions of this clause the carrier" appeared in place of the square brackets I have inserted'.

Lord Millett did not consider it essential that the court be certain of the precise words which were missing, observing (at para.194) that it was impossible to identify the particular precedent from which the clause had been taken, but that all the relevant precedents contained a similar provision in identical or nearly identical words. His Lordship said (at para.192):

'It is not necessary that the court should be certain precisely what words have been omitted; it is sufficient that it knows their gist. The process is one of construction, not rectification; this is evident from the fact that the Court of Chancery not infrequently supplied omissions in wills at a time when it had no jurisdiction to rectify them.'

In Scots law, also, it appears to me that it is sufficient to know the substance of the missing words. I also observe that the process in Scots law is equally one of construction, not rectification: Lord Millett's observation about the Court of Chancery is also true of the Court of Session, as the discussion in *McLaren on Wills and Succession* (at paras 654 ff, 'of supplying words necessary to complete the sense') demonstrates.

[28] The third case, *KPMG LLP v Network Rail Infrastructure Ltd* [2007] Bus. L.R. 1336, concerned an apparent omission in a commercial lease. Read literally, the clause did not make sense. By comparison with an earlier agreement, it could be seen that a number of words had been omitted. The omission had been noticed by one party to the lease, who had assumed (mistakenly) that it was deliberate, and had contracted on that basis. In those circumstances, the lease could not be rectified under English law, since there was no common intention that the omitted words should be included, and the party who had noticed the omission had been acting in good faith. The Court of Appeal however held that the omitted words could be inserted as a matter of construction, so as to give the lease the meaning which it would convey to a reasonable person aware of the background circumstances. It was not argued that there was no contract. The decision is a striking illustration of the distinction between the parties' actual intentions and the common intention, objectively ascertained, which the process of construction assumes to exist. The case was cited in the present case for a passage in the judgment of Carnwath L.J., in which the other members of the court concurred, in which his Lordship considered (at para.64) what had been said in *The Starsin* by Lord Bingham and Lord Millett:

'I think it would be wrong to apply too literally Lord Bingham's reference to the need for clarity both as to the omission of words and "what those relevant words were". As Lord Millett said, it is sufficient if the court is able to ascertain "the gist" of what has been omitted.'

I respectfully agree with that view.

...

[36] It appears to me that the commercial considerations on which the pursuers rely come nowhere near the standard set by the authorities. This is not a case in which it can be said, in the language used by Lord Hoffmann in the *Investors Compensation Scheme* case, that 'something must have gone wrong with the language', or that the natural reading of clause 3.4 would 'attribute to the parties an intention which they plainly could not have had'. If the pursuers are not protected against disrepair which was latent when the guarantee expired, that is not, in Lord Diplock's words in *The Antaios*, 'a conclusion that flouts business commonsense'. Nor is this a case where 'it is clear ... that words have been omitted' (*The Starsin* at para.23 *per* Lord Bingham). A passage in Lord Hoffmann's judgment in the *Jumbo King* case appears to me to be apposite (at para.59):

'If the ordinary meaning of the words makes sense in relation to the rest of the document and the factual background, then the court will give effect to that language, even though the consequences may appear hard for one side or the other. The court is not privy to the negotiation of the agreement—evidence of such negotiations is inadmissible—and has no way of knowing whether a clause which appears to have an onerous effect was a *quid quo pro* for some other concession. Or one of the parties may simply have made a bad bargain.'

[37] In these circumstances, the commercial background does not lead me away from the starting point: that one would ordinarily expect the parties to a formal document to have chosen their words with care, and to have intended to convey the meaning which the words they chose would convey to a reasonable person.

[38] I have reached that conclusion without referring to the various traditional canons of construction to which counsel for the defenders referred, such as the *contra proferentem* principle and the principle that guarantees should be narrowly construed. Canons of that kind require in my opinion to be reconsidered, and in some cases reformulated or discarded, in the light of the modern approach to the construction of contracts. As Lord Hoffmann observed in the *Investors Compensation Scheme* case at page 912,

'Almost all the old intellectual baggage of "legal" interpretation has been discarded.'

I note what was said by Arden L.J. in *Egan* v *Static Control Components (Europe) Ltd* [2004] 2 Lloyd's Rep.429, rejecting (at para.37) a submission that a guarantee should be construed *contra proferentem:*

'There is no reason of public policy why guarantees should not in general be construed in accordance with the principles enunciated in *Prenn* v *Simmonds* [1971] 1 W.L.R. 1381 and the *ICS* case.'

[39] My conclusion on the first issue is therefore that the pursuers' contention should be rejected. It follows that their action, so far as based on clause 3.1 of the guarantee, depends on establishing that a 'demand' was made on the defenders prior to 1 January 2005. That takes me to the second issue.

The second issue: was the letter of 30 April 2004 a demand?

. . .

[46] In that regard, counsel for both parties referred to *Mannai Investments*, where the construction of notices (in that case, a break notice under a lease) was considered by the House of Lords. The objective nature of such construction was made clear in the speeches. Lord Steyn, for example, said (at page 767):

'The question is not how the landlord understood the notices. The construction of the notices must be approached objectively. The issue is how a reasonable recipient would have understood the notices. And in considering this question the notices must be construed taking into account the relevant objective contextual scene.'

. . .

[47] Applying that approach, counsel were in agreement that the relevant question was whether the letter of 30 April 2004 brought home to any reasonable recipient that the landlord was demanding performance under the guarantee. In other words, the question is whether the reasonable recipient of the letter would have said to himself, 'I am being called on to do the work specified in the schedule'.

[48] In my opinion that question must be answered in the negative . . . "

8–74 Despite his apparent adoption of Lord Hoffmann's "contextual" approach, Lord Reed eventually found it unnecessary to apply it in reaching his conclusion, because he saw the approach as one applicable to errors in expression (at [18] and [19]). There was no error of expression here that suggested "something must have gone wrong with the language" used, or that would "flout commercial common sense" ([36], [37]). More striking is Lord Reed's suggestion that canons of construction, such as *contra proferentem* should be "reformulated or discarded" ([38]). His extensive, albeit obiter review of the contextual approach was not referred to in the two Scottish appeals on interpretation heard since 2007/2008.

A "re-working" of the words?

Chartbrook went some way to explain why matters like pre-contractual negotiations might be excluded from the "surrounding circumstances" or "matrix of facts"; but it also considered when an *English* court might alter, or "re-work" the words of the contract after consideration of the surrounding circumstances. This, after all, is the central—and most contentious—aspect of the contextual approach. **8–75**

Chartbrook Ltd v Persimmon Homes Ltd **8–76**
House of Lords
[2009] UKHL 38; [2009] 1 A.C. 1101
Lords Hope, Hoffmann, Rodger, Walker, Baroness Hale

The facts are stated above, para.8–56.

"LORD HOPE OF CRAIGHEAD **8–77**

[1] My Lords, I have had the privilege of reading in draft the opinion of my noble and learned friend, Lord Hoffmann. Like my noble and learned friend, Lord Walker of Gestingthorpe, whose opinion I have also had the privilege of reading, I agree with all his reasoning and I share Lord Walker's admiration for the way it has been expressed. For the reasons they give I would allow the appeal.

LORD HOFFMANN **8–78**

...

[14] There is no dispute that the principles on which a contract (or any other instrument or utterance) should be interpreted are those summarised by the House of Lords in *Investors Compensation Scheme Ltd v West Bromwich Building Society* [1998] 1 WLR 896, 912–913 ... [T]he question is what a reasonable person having all the background knowledge which would have been available to the parties would have understood them to be using the language in the contract to mean. The House emphasised that 'we do not easily accept that people have made linguistic mistakes, particularly in formal documents' (similar statements will be found in *Bank of Credit and Commerce International SA v Ali* [2002] 1 AC 251 , 269; *Kirin-Amgen Inc v Hoechst Marion Roussel Ltd* [2005] 1 All ER 667, 681–682 and *Jumbo King Ltd v Faithful Properties Ltd* (1999) 2 HKCFAR 279 , 296) but said that in some cases the context and background drove a court to the conclusion that 'something must have gone wrong with the language'. In such a case, the law did not require a court to attribute to the parties an intention which a reasonable person would not have understood them to have had.

[15] It clearly requires a strong case to persuade the court that something must have gone wrong with the language and the judge and the majority of the Court of Appeal did not think that such a case had been made out ... The subtleties of language are such that no judicial guidelines or statements of principle can prevent it from sometimes happening. It is fortunately rare because most draftsmen of formal documents think about what they are saying and use language with care. But this appears to be an exceptional case in which the drafting was careless and no one noticed.

[16] I agree with the dissenting opinion of Lawrence Collins LJ because I think that to interpret the definition of ARP in accordance with ordinary rules of syntax makes no commercial sense. The term 'minimum guaranteed residential unit value', defined by reference to total residential land value, strongly suggests that this was to be a

guaranteed minimum payment for the land value in respect of an individual flat. A guaranteed minimum payment connotes the possibility of a larger payment which, depending upon some contingency, may or may not fall due. Hence the term 'additional residential payment'. The element of contingency is reinforced by para 3.3 of the sixth schedule, which speaks of the 'date of payment *if any* of the balancing payment' (my emphasis).

...

[20] It is of course true that the fact that a contract may appear to be unduly favourable to one of the parties is not a sufficient reason for supposing that it does not mean what it says. The reasonable addressee of the instrument has not been privy to the negotiations and cannot tell whether a provision favourable to one side was not in exchange for some concession elsewhere or simply a bad bargain ...

[21] ... When the language used in an instrument gives rise to difficulties of construction, the process of interpretation does not require one to formulate some alternative form of words which approximates as closely as possible to that of the parties. It is to decide what a reasonable person would have understood the parties to have meant by using the language which they did. The fact that the court might have to express that meaning in language quite different from that used by the parties ('12 January' instead of '13 January' in *Mannai Investment Co Ltd v Eagle Star Life Assurance Co Ltd* [1997] AC 749; 'any claim sounding in rescission (whether for undue influence or otherwise)' instead of 'any claim (whether sounding in rescission for undue influence or otherwise)' in *Investors Compensation Scheme Ltd v West Bromwich Building Society* [1998] 1 WLR 896) is no reason for not giving effect to what they appear to have meant.

[22] In *East v Pantiles (Plant Hire) Ltd* (1981) 263 EG 61 Brightman LJ stated the conditions for what he called 'correction of mistakes by construction':

'Two conditions must be satisfied: first, there must be a clear mistake on the face of the instrument; secondly, it must be clear what correction ought to be made in order to cure the mistake. If those conditions are satisfied, then the correction is made as a matter of construction.'

[23] Subject to two qualifications, both of which are explained by Carnwath LJ in his admirable judgment in *KPMG LLP v Network Rail Infrastructure Ltd* [2007] Bus LR 1336, I would accept this statement, which is in my opinion no more than an expression of the common sense view that we do not readily accept that people have made mistakes in formal documents. The first qualification is that 'correction of mistakes by construction' is not a separate branch of the law, a summary version of an action for rectification. As Carnwath LJ said, at p 1351, para 50:

'Both in the judgment, and in the arguments before us, there was a tendency to deal separately with correction of mistakes and construing the paragraph "as it stands", as though they were distinct exercises. In my view, they are simply aspects of the single task of interpreting the agreement in its context, in order to get as close as possible to the meaning which the parties intended.'

[24] The second qualification concerns the words 'on the face of the instrument'. I agree with Carnwath LJ, paras 44–50, that in deciding whether there is a clear mistake, the court is not confined to reading the document without regard to its background or context. As the exercise is part of the single task of interpretation, the background and context must always be taken into consideration.

[25] What is clear from these cases is that there is not, so to speak, a limit to the amount of red ink or verbal rearrangement or correction which the court is allowed. All that is required is that it should be clear that something has gone wrong with the language and that it should be clear what a reasonable person would have understood the parties to have meant. In my opinion, both of these requirements are satisfied."

This approach was confirmed by the Supreme Court in the following case.

Rainy Sky SA v Kookmin Bank 8–79
Supreme Court: Lord Phillips PSC, Lords Mance, Kerr, Clarke, Wilson JJSC
[2011] UKSC 50; [2011] 1 W.L.R. 2900

A shipbuilder entered into six contracts to build and sell a vessel to each of the first six claimants. The purchase price of each vessel was payable in five equal instalments at specified times with the final instalment being paid on delivery. It was a term of the contract that as a condition precedent to the payment of the first instalment the shipbuilder would give the buyers refund guarantees relating to the instalments. In accordance with that term the defendant bank issued each claimant with advance payment bonds. After the six claimants had paid the first instalment and the first claimant had paid the second instalment, the shipbuilder experienced financial difficulties and became the subject of a debt work-out procedure. The shipbuilder refused to refund the instalments paid. The first six claimants together with the seventh claimant who was the assignee of the benefit of the bonds, brought proceedings against the bank claiming repayment under para.3 of the bonds of the instalments paid to the shipbuilder, and issued an application for Pt 24 summary judgment. The bank refused to pay on the grounds that para.3 had to be read with para.2 and on its true construction para.3 did not cover the refunds which the six claimants sought, but covered pre-delivery instalments prior to the termination of the contract or a total loss of the vessel ...

The Supreme Court held that, having regard to "considerations of commercial common sense" the claimants' construction of the bonds was more consistent with their commercial purpose.

"LORD CLARKE JSC (with whom LORD PHILLIPS PSC, LORDS MANCE, KERR and WILSON JJSC agreed). 8–80

The correct approach to construction

[14] For the most part, the correct approach to construction of the bonds, as in the case of any contract, was not in dispute. The principles have been discussed in many cases, notably of course, as Lord Neuberger of Abbotsbury MR said in *Pink Floyd Music Ltd v EMI Records Ltd* [2010] EWCA Civ 1429, para 17, by Lord Hoffmann in *Mannai Investment Co Ltd v Eagle Star Life Assurance Co Ltd* [1997] AC 749, *passim*, in *Investors Compensation Scheme Ltd v West Bromwich Building Society* [1998] 1 WLR 896, 912 f–913 g and in *Chartbrook Ltd v Persimmon Homes Ltd (Chartbrook Ltd Part 20 defendants)* [2009] AC 1101, paras 21–26. I agree with Lord Neuberger (also at para 17) that those cases show that the ultimate aim of interpreting a provision in a contract, especially a commercial contract, is to determine what the parties meant by the language used, which involves ascertaining what a reasonable person would have understood the parties to have meant. As Lord Hoffmann made clear in the first of the principles he summarised in the *Investors Compensation Scheme case* [1998] 1 WLR 896, 912h, the relevant reasonable person is one who has all the background knowledge which would reasonably have been available to the parties in the situation in which they were at the time of the contract.

[15] The issue between the parties in this appeal is the role to be played by considerations of business common sense in determining what the parties meant ...

...

[20] It is not in my judgment necessary to conclude that, unless the most natural meaning of the words produces a result so extreme as to suggest that it was unintended, the court must give effect to that meaning.

[21] The language used by the parties will often have more than one potential meaning ... [T]he exercise of construction is essentially one unitary exercise in which the court must consider the language used and ascertain what a reasonable person, that is a person who has all the background knowledge which would reasonably have been available to the parties in the situation in which they were at the time of the contract, would have understood the parties to have meant. In doing so, the court must have regard to all the relevant surrounding circumstances. If there are two possible constructions, the court is entitled to prefer the construction which is consistent with business common sense and to reject the other.

[22] This conclusion appears to me to be supported by Lord Reid's approach in *Wickman Machine Tool Sales Ltd v L Schuler AG* [1974] AC 235 ...

[23] Where the parties have used unambiguous language, the court must apply it. This can be seen from the decision of the Court of Appeal in *Co-operative Wholesale Society Ltd v National Westminster Bank plc* [1995] 1 EGLR 97 ...

...

[25] In 1997, writing extra-judicially in 'Contract law: Fulfilling the reasonable expectations of honest men' 113 *LQR* 433, 441, Lord Steyn expressed the principle thus:

'Often there is no obvious or ordinary meaning of the language under consideration. There are competing interpretations to be considered. In choosing between alternatives a court should primarily be guided by the contextual scene in which the stipulation in question appears. And speaking generally commercially minded judges would regard the commercial purpose of the contract as more important than niceties of language. And, in the event of doubt, the working assumption will be that a fair construction best matches the reasonable expectations of the parties.'

I agree. He said much the same judicially in *Society of Lloyd's v Robinson* [1999] WLR 756, 763:

'Loyalty to the text of a commercial contract, instrument, or document read in its contextual setting is the paramount principle of interpretation. But in the process of interpreting the meaning of the language of a commercial document the court ought generally to favour a commercially sensible construction. The reason for this approach is that a commercial construction is likely to give effect to the intention of the parties. Words ought therefore to be interpreted in the way in which a reasonable commercial person would construe them. And the reasonable commercial person can safely be assumed to be unimpressed with technical interpretations and undue emphasis on niceties of language.'

26 Similar assistance is at hand nearer at home. In *Gan Insurance Co Ltd v Tai Ping Insurance Co Ltd (No 2)* [2001] 2 All ER (Comm) 299, Mance LJ said:

'Construction, as Sir Thomas Bingham MR said in *Arbuthnott v Fagan* [1995] CLC 1396, 1400 is thus "a composite exercise, neither uncompromisingly literal nor unswervingly purposive". To para 5, one may add as a coda words of Lord Bridge of Harwich in *Mitsui Construction Co Ltd v Attorney General of Hong Kong* (1986) 10 Con LR 1, cited in my judgment in *Sinochem International Oil (London) Co Ltd v Mobil Sales and Supply Corpn (Sinochem International Oil Co Ltd, Third Party)* [2000] 1 All ER (Comm) 474, 482. Speaking of a poorly drafted and ambiguous contract, Lord Bridge said that poor drafting itself provides: "no reason to depart from the fundamental rule of construction of contractual documents that the intention of the parties must be ascertained from the language that they have used interpreted in the light of the relevant factual situation in which the contract was made. But the poorer the quality of the drafting, the less willing the court should be to be driven by semantic niceties to attribute to the parties an improbable and unbusinesslike intention, if the language used, whatever it may lack in precision, is reasonably capable of an interpretation which attributes to the parties an intention to make provision for contingencies inherent in the work contracted for on a sensible and businesslike basis".'

'16 . . . in my judgment the subclause has no very natural meaning and is, at the least, open to two possible meanings or interpretations—one the judge's, the other that it addresses two separate subject matters. In these circumstances, it is especially important to undertake the exercise on which the judge declined to embark, that is to consider the implications of each interpretation. In my opinion, a court when construing any document should always have an eye to the consequences of a particular construction, even if they often only serve as a check on an obvious meaning or a restraint upon adoption of a conceivable but unbusinesslike meaning. In intermediate situations, as Professor Guest wisely observes in *Chitty on Contracts* (28th ed) (1999), vol 1, para 12–049, a "balance has to be struck" through the exercise of sound judicial discretion.'

[27] More generally, in *Homburg Houtimport BV v Agrosin Private Ltd (The Starsin)* [2004] 1 AC 715, para 10, Lord Bingham referred to

'the rule to which Lord Halsbury LC alluded in *Glynn v Margetson & Co* [1893] AC 351, 359, "that a business sense will be given to business documents". The business sense is that which businessmen, in the course of their ordinary dealings, would give the document'.

[28] Three other cases merit brief reference. The same approach was adopted by Arden LJ in *In re Golden Key Ltd* [2009] EWCA Civ 636 at [29] and [42] and by this court in *In re Sigma Finance Corpn* [2010] 1 All ER 571, para 12, where Lord Mance said that the resolution of an issue of interpretation in a case like the present was an iterative process, involving checking each of the rival meanings against other provisions of the document and investigating its commercial consequences.

[29] Finally, it is worth setting out two extracts from the judgment of Longmore LJ in *Barclays Bank plc v HHY Luxembourg SARL* [2011] 1 BCLC 336, paras 25 and 26:

'25. The matter does not of course rest there because when alternative constructions are available one has to consider which is the more commercially sensible. On this aspect of the matter Mr Zacaroli has all the cards . . .

26. The judge said that it did not flout common sense to say that the clause provided for a very limited level of release, but that, with respect, is not quite the way to look at the matter. If a clause is capable of two meanings, as on any view this clause is, it is quite possible that neither meaning will flout common sense. In such circumstances, it is much more appropriate to adopt the more, rather than the less, commercial construction.'

[30] In my opinion Longmore LJ has there neatly summarised the correct approach to the problem. That approach is now supported by a significant body of authority. As stated in a little more detail in para 21 above, it is in essence that, where a term of a contract is open to more than one interpretation, it is generally appropriate to adopt the interpretation which is most consistent with business common sense . . .

. . .

[45] In these circumstances I would, if necessary, go so far as to say that the omission of the obligation to make such re-payments from the bonds would flout common sense but it is not necessary to go so far. I agree with the judge and Sir Simon Tuckey that, of the two arguable constructions of paragraph 3 of the bonds, the buyers' construction is to be preferred because it is consistent with the commercial purpose of the bonds in a way in which the bank's construction is not."

When a Scottish case came to the Supreme Court for consideration that raised similar issues to those considered in the long line of English decisions leading up to *Rainy Sky*, the response of the two Scottish judges showed a degree of variance and a reluctance wholly to endorse the approach.

8–81

Multi-Link Leisure Developments Ltd v North Lanarkshire Council
Supreme Court
[2010] UKSC 47; 2011 S.C. (U.K.S.C.) 53
Lord Hope DPSC, Lord Rodger, Baroness Hale, Lord Clarke, Sir John Dyson SCJ

Multi-Link developed a pay and play golf course at Cumbernauld on land they leased from the Council in 1999 on a 50 year term. The lease granted Multi-Link an option to purchase the land. The lease also provided that the option price

> "shall be equal to the full market value of the subjects hereby let as at the date of entry for the proposed purchase (as determined by the landlords) of agricultural land or open space suitable for development as a golf course".

In 2005 Multi-Link expressed an interest in exercising the option. In 2006 the land in which the golf course lay was marked for development and by 2008 the Council's draft local plan had earmarked the area as potential housing-led urban expansion.

In 2007 Multi-Link gave notice that they would exercise their option and asked the Council for their view on what would be the full market value of the subjects as defined in the option clause. The Council fixed the price at £5.3 million. Multi-Link refused to pay more than £500,000, which they claimed was the full market value of the subjects as agricultural land or open space suitable for a golf course, without reference to any increase in value that might be attributable to planning permission for housing development. The Council claimed that failure to pay the £5.3 million was a breach of the option so that it was thereby rescinded and no longer available during the remaining term of the lease.

Multi-Link sought declarator that the price payable under the option was no more than £500,000. The Lord Ordinary (Glennie) held that the full market value was to be assessed by reference only to the use of the subjects as a golf course. An Extra Division allowed the landlords' reclaiming motion. The Council appealed to the Supreme Court, which held that the option price was to be determined by the full market value of the land.

8–82 "LORD HOPE DPSC—

. . .

[2] . . . The parties are agreed that, if the tenants are right, the contract remains in force and the landlords will require to value the subjects anew on the basis of the construction of the clause contended for by the tenants. They are also agreed that, if the landlords are right, the option is spent and can no longer be exercised during the remaining term of the lease.

. . . .

8–83 *Option clause*

. . .

[21] It has, of course, long been recognised that the commercial or business object of the provision in question may be relevant (*Prenn v Simmonds*, Lord Wilberforce, p 1385; see also *Aberdeen City Council v Stewart Milne Group Ltd*, para 11, although I think that the way this issue should be approached is less clearly explained in the nineteenth century Scottish cases referred to by the Extra Division in that paragraph: *Mackenzie v Liddell*; *Bank of Scotland v Stewart*; *Jacobs v Scott & Co*). In *Antaios Compania Naviera SA v Salen Rederierna AB* (p 201) Lord Diplock said that if detailed and syntactical analysis of words in a commercial contract is going to lead to a conclusion that flouts business commonsense, it must yield to business commonsense (see also *Investors*

Compensation Scheme Ltd v West Bromwich Building Society (No 1), p 913, where Lord Hoffmann included this as the fifth of his commonsense principles). In *Mannai Investment Co Ltd v Eagle Star Life Assurance Co Ltd* (p 771) Lord Steyn, making the same point, said that words are to be interpreted in the way in which a reasonable commercial person would construe them, and that the standard of the reasonable commercial person is hostile to technical interpretations and undue emphasis on niceties of language (see also *Bank of Scotland v Dunedin Property Investment Co Ltd (No 1)*, Lord President Rodger, p 661). In *Deutsche Genossenschaftsbank v Burnhope* (p 1587), however, Lord Steyn reminded us that our law of construction is based on an objective theory, and he emphasised the objective nature of the exercise of searching for meaning of language in its contractual setting:

'The court must not try to [divine] the purpose of the contract by speculating about the real intention of the parties. It may only be inferred from the language used by the parties, judged against the objective contextual background.'

[22] What then of the objective commercial background in this case? The landlords are a local authority. They were under a statutory duty not to dispose of land for a consideration less than the best that could reasonably be obtained (Local Government (Scotland) Act 1973 (cap 65)). The tenants are a commercial organisation. They are in business to make money. They undertook to use the subjects during the period of the lease for the development of a pay and play golf course and for no other purpose without the prior express written consent of the landlords. But a successful exercise of the option would transfer to them all the rights of ownership, which they could be expected to turn to their financial advantage if the opportunity of doing so were to present itself. The land itself was in use as grazing land when the lease was entered into. It was situated about a mile from the town centre and the lease was entered into for a period of 50 years. It can be inferred from the price that was agreed for the exercise of the option within the first 12 months that at that stage there was no evidence that it had any hope value and that it was thought to be suitable only for recreational activities. But much can change within a period of 50 years, and there has been no indication that there were any planning constraints such as a designation of the land as part of a green belt that would inhibit its potential for development.

[23] The land has now been identified as lying within a potential area for housing-led urban expansion. If the tenants are right, acquiring the land at a price which ignores its potential for development will provide them with a very substantial windfall at the expense of the landlords. This was something that the wording of the option clause might have been expected to guard against. The tenants, on the other hand, did not ensure that the opportunity to obtain a windfall in circumstances such as have now arisen was expressly provided for. I do not think that the assumptions and disregards at the end of the option clause, which sit uneasily with the clause when read as a whole, carry sufficient weight to overcome the message conveyed by its opening words by attributing to them the meaning that the tenants contend for. They indicate that the parties were agreed that the option price was to be determined by the full market value of the land as described, taking full account of its potential, if any, for development. That is what reasonable commercial men would have agreed to when the lease was entered into, if they had applied their minds to the benefits that would accrue to the tenants if they were to exercise the option to purchase. I would hold that it must be taken to be what the parties agreed to in this case.

Conclusion **8–84**

[24] Although I prefer not to endorse the Extra Division's reasoning, I consider that it arrived at the right result. I would dismiss the appeal and affirm the Extra Division's interlocutor.

8–85 LORD RODGER

[25] Lord Hope has set out the background and the wording of the clause which the court has to interpret. I can accordingly explain my approach very briefly.

[26] ... This was a commercial venture: the course was to be a pay and play course. In these circumstances it is appropriate to treat the lease as a commercial agreement which is to be construed accordingly. It is therefore noteworthy that Multi-Link's interpretation of the disputed clause of the lease produces a result—whether or not appropriately described as "a windfall"—which it seems unlikely that the parties to a commercial agreement would ever have intended: that Multi-Link should be able to buy the land for a sum that takes no account of its (substantial) hope value. That result is even more surprising when the clause provides that, in the circumstances which have occurred, the price is to be 'the full market value' of the subjects.

[27] Nevertheless, something has gone wrong with the drafting of the relevant clause, cl 18.2. So no construction is ever going to produce perfect harmony among all its elements ...

[28] When translating a document written in a foreign language, it often makes sense to start with the parts whose meaning is clear and then to use those parts to unravel the meaning of the parts which are more difficult to understand. The same applies to interpreting contracts or statutes. Here, since their meaning is not really in doubt, I find it helpful to start with the assumptions and disregards that the landlords are to apply when determining the full market value.

[29] First, the landlords are to assume that the subjects are in good and substantial order and repair and that all the obligations of the landlords and tenants under the lease have been complied with. Since more than five years have passed, this means, in particular, that the landlords are to proceed on the basis that the golf course, which the tenants were obliged to construct in terms of cl 9, has indeed been constructed and is in good order and repair. In fact, the golf course has been duly created. So Multi-Link are to pay for the golf course on the assumption that it is in good condition.

[30] The Extra Division, who did not refer to this part of cl 18.2, proceeded on the basis that, in assessing the full market value, the landlords were to ignore anything done by the tenants to develop the golf course ([2009] CSIH 96, para 26). This was understandable, since, curiously enough, it was the basis upon which both parties proceeded in the Inner House and—in the face of some resistance—in this court. Nevertheless, I am quite unable to approach the interpretation of the clause on that basis since it is inconsistent with the specific direction in the later part of the clause.

[31] The suggestion seemed to be that the words 'of agricultural land or open space suitable for development as a golf course' meant that the landlords were to value the subjects as if the golf course had not been developed and that this was justified because, otherwise, Multi-Link would be paying twice over for the development of the course. But that approach is utterly inconsistent with the assumption that is spelled out in the later part of the clause. And that assumption itself is entirely consistent with cl 21, which provides that, at the expiry or termination of the lease, the tenants are to yield up the subjects 'with any buildings and others thereon well and substantially maintained in accordance with the obligations hereinbefore specified and that without any compensation being paid therefor'. Since, on its expiry or termination, Multi-Link are not to be paid for the buildings etc which they may have constructed in accordance with their obligations under the lease, it would make no sense whatever if they could buy the subjects under the option without paying for the same buildings etc. In effect, the cost of constructing the golf course in terms of cl 9 is treated as part of the consideration which Multi-Link provide in return for the lease of the land. Therefore, as the assumption makes clear, if Multi-Link want to buy a completed golf course, they have to pay for it.

[32] On the other hand, the landlords are to disregard any improvements which the tenants may have carried out 'otherwise than in pursuance of an obligation [to] the landlords'. Again, this makes sense, since those improvements form no part of the consideration for the lease. So, having paid to make these improvements which they were not obliged to make, the tenants should not have to pay again if they buy the land.

[33] In my view the problematical words 'of agricultural land or open space suitable for development as a golf course' cannot be construed in a manner that is inconsistent with the clear directions as to the assumptions which the landlords are to adopt in assessing the full market value. In the circumstances of this case they have to value the golf course which has been laid out and they have to do so on the basis that it is in good and substantial order and repair. If Multi-Link have carried out other improvements which they were not obliged to carry out, these are to be ignored.

[34] If the landlords proceed in this way, they will comply with the instructions in the clause. And, if there were no other elements in the picture, no doubt they would be able to assess what someone wanting to buy a golf course would pay for this course in this area. But the instructions in the clause do not tell the landlords to ignore any other factor which might be relevant to the value of the golf course. And there is indeed a further, very significant, factor: in 2006 the Glasgow and Clyde Valley joint structure plan identified the area where the land lies as a community growth area for an indicative capacity of 2,000 houses. In addition, in 2008 the final draft of the relevant local plan identified that community growth area as a suitable location for medium-term housing development.

[35] Obviously, these changes mean that the possible purchasers of the golf course would now include developers who were interested in acquiring the land, not as a golf course, but as a site for a possible housing development. So the potential value of the golf course on the open market will have increased accordingly.

[36] Multi-Link contend, however, that the words 'of agricultural land or open space suitable for development as a golf course' show that this factor and this increase in value are to be ignored. The valuation is to proceed on the basis that the land is to be used as a golf course and nothing else. Given that—apart from planning considerations—there is no limit on the use to which the land could be put if Multi-Link successfully exercised their option to purchase it, that would be a highly unusual and artificial approach to valuation—far less to determining 'the full market value' of the land. Construing cl 18.2 as a whole and as part of a commercial agreement, I am satisfied that the words in question are not to be interpreted as requiring the landlords to adopt this unusual approach and to ignore the hope value. Had the parties intended the landlords to assume that the land was to be used only as a golf course, I would have expected to find that assumption included among the others at the end of the clause. For these reasons the landlords are entitled to have regard to the hope value of the golf course when assessing its full market value.

[37] Although my reasoning is different, I agree with the result reached by the Extra Division. I would accordingly dismiss the appeal. It will be up to the parties to work out how, if at all, they are to arrange for the lease to be terminated and the hope value to be unlocked.

LADY HALE **8–86**

...

[41] I do not regard the tenants' position as quite as fanciful as others might. Local authorities are not commercial organisations. They are there to serve the local population, not to make money. ...

...

[44] Thus, by a route mapped out by Lord Rodger, I too arrive at the conclusion that this appeal should be dismissed.

8–87 LORD CLARKE

[45] I agree that this appeal should be dismissed. I detect no difference between the principles applicable to the construction of a lease in Scotland and in England. The true construction of cl 18.2 of the lease depends upon the language of the clause construed in the context of the lease as a whole, which must in turn be considered having regard to its surrounding circumstances or factual matrix. I do not think that the parties can have given express consideration to the question that has arisen in this case. If they had, they would surely have expressly provided that, if the tenants exercised the option to purchase in cl 18 of the lease, they must pay the full market value of the land as described, taking full account of its potential, if any, for development. Any other conclusion would flout business commonsense because it would give the tenants an unwarranted windfall. Applying the principles stated by Lord Hope in his para 20, I would construe the reference to 'full market value' in cl 18.2 of the lease as meaning the full market value of the land, including its potential development value.

8–88 SIR JOHN DYSON SCJ

[46] I agree that this appeal should be dismissed. To the extent that there is any difference between the reasoning of Lord Hope and Lord Rodger, I prefer that of Lord Rodger."

In the following case, the Inner House of the Court of Session had the opportunity again to consider the extent to which surrounding circumstances and, more specifically, prior negotiations could be taken into account in interpreting the words of a contractual document.

8–89 **Luminar Lava Ignite Ltd v Mama Group Plc**

Court of Session: Inner House, First Division
Court of Session, Outer House
[2010] CSIH 1; 2010 S.C. 310
Lord President (Hamilton), Lords Eassie, Hodge and Glennie

Luminar operated a discotheque called "Lava Ignite" (formerly "The Cavendish") in Tollcross, Edinburgh. Luminar also owned, through an associated company, "The Picture House" on Lothian Road, which until 2006 they had operated as a discotheque, but subsequently as a live music venue.

In 2007, Luminar advertised "The Picture House" for sale, indicating that they would not sell to a nightclub or pub operator. In 2008 Luminar contracted to sell the Lothian Road premises to Mama, who intended to operate the premises as a "Mean Fiddler" live music venue.

In accordance with the missives of sale, the parties entered into a "Non Compete Agreement". Clause 2.1 of that agreement provided that Mama would not use the premises "for late night entertainment in direct competition on a like for like basis" with the discotheque business operated by Luminar at Tollcross.

Mama initially operated "The Picture House" as a live music venue, but then advertised their intention to operate the premises as a nightclub/discotheque on Friday and Saturday evenings.

Luminar sought interdict against the use of the premises as a discotheque on the days and times they operated their Tollcross premises. On appeal to the Inner House, the principal issue was the proper construction of the contractual restriction which the contract of sale imposed on Mama and Mean Fiddler. In support of their interpretation of the agreement, Luminar sought to rely on two pre-contractual statements by Mama.

Following a proof, the Lord Ordinary assoilzied the defenders. The pursuers reclaimed. The Inner House (the Lord President dissenting in part) allowed the reclaiming motion.

"LORD PRESIDENT (HAMILTON) 8–90

[1] I have had the opportunity of reading Lord Hodge's opinion in draft. I agree with him that, for the reasons he gives, the two items of evidence sought to be relied on from the parties' pre-contractual communings ought to be excluded from consideration when construing the contract. . . .

[2] I am also in agreement with Lord Hodge that the most difficult issue is the correct construction of the critical phrase in cl 2.1, in the context of the clause as a whole and in the light of the surrounding circumstances. I have not found that issue easy to resolve.

[3] . . . The issue remains the objective construction of the words used, according to the standards of a reasonable third party who is aware of the commercial context in which the contract occurred (*Emcor Drake and Skull Ltd v Edinburgh Royal Joint Venture*, per Lord Drummond Young, p 1237I; see also *Reardon Smith Line Ltd v Yvgvar Hansen-Tangen (t/a HE Hansen-Tangen)*, per Lord Wilberforce, p 996; *Investors Compensation Scheme Ltd v West Bromwich Building Society*, per Lord Hoffmann, p 912).

. . .

[7] I find nothing in the admissible evidence of the circumstances surrounding the making of the contract which is of material assistance in resolving the issue of its construction. I am not persuaded that any difficulties in policing performance of the contract are such as to render the reclaimers' construction the only sensible result.

[8] Although I regard this as a narrow issue, I am of opinion that the Lord Ordinary's construction of the contract was correct. In these circumstances I would have refused the reclaiming motion. However, as I understand that both your Lordships are in favour of allowing it, I merely with diffidence record my dissent.

. . .

LORD EASSIE 8–91

[10] I have had the opportunity of reading in draft both the opinion of your Lordship in the chair and the opinion of Lord Hodge.

. . .

[17] . . . I join with Lord Hodge in his motion that the reclaiming motion be allowed and that interdict be granted in the terms amended on the motion of counsel for the reclaimers made at the Bar.

LORD HODGE 8–92

. . .

Discussion

[38] In relation to the first ground of challenge [that the Lord Ordinary erred in holding that the restriction was unambiguous] . . . I do not consider that the words 'late night entertainment in direct competition on a like for like basis with the discotheque business of Luminar as carried out . . . as at 1st March 2008' have a clear meaning when considered in isolation . . . But I see no error in law in the Lord Ordinary's approach of considering first the words in question and then reassessing his view of them after having regard to the relevant background circumstances. It is not part of our law of contract that the court can have regard to relevant background circumstances only if there is ambiguity in the words of an agreement. The Lord Ordinary is supported by Lord Mustill's view, which he quotes, that in most cases 'the enquiry will start, and usually finish, by asking what is the ordinary meaning of the words used' (*Charter Reinsurance Co Ltd v Fagan*, p 384B–C).

[39] The second ground of challenge [that the Lord Ordinary also erred in rejecting as inadmissible all of the evidence of the parties' prior communings] relates to the admissibility of the two selected statements in the course of the prior negotiations. While there may be uncertainties as to the boundaries of the rule excluding the use of parties' negotiations as an aid to construction, as Lord Kingarth observed in *City Wall*

Properties (Scotland) Ltd v Pearl Assurance plc (para 38), the law on this matter is well established and the House of Lords recently upheld the general exclusionary rule in *Chartbrook Ltd v Persimmon Homes Ltd.* The general rule is that the court will not have regard to statements of parties or their agents in the course of the negotiation of a contract as an aid to the construction of the words which the parties use in the final version of the contract which alone expresses their consensus.

[40] That rule is justified on two grounds. First, the consideration and interpretation of previous formulations of what one or other party was seeking in the negotiations may be irrelevant to the construction of the words which they eventually adopt to express their consensus. Secondly, even if the words which parties used in the negotiations are not irrelevant, they are excluded on pragmatic grounds. In *Prenn v Simmonds* Lord Wilberforce (pp 1384G–1385A) discussed the basis of the exclusionary rule and stated that the reason for excluding evidence of the exchanges in negotiations was that such evidence was 'unhelpful'. He stated:

'[W]here negotiations are difficult, the parties' positions, with each passing letter, are changing and until the final agreement, though converging, still divergent. It is only the final document which records a consensus. If the previous documents use different expressions, how does construction of those expressions, itself a doubtful process, help on the construction of the contractual words? If the same expressions are used, nothing is gained by looking back; indeed something may be lost since the relevant surrounding circumstances may be different.'

The pragmatism, which underlies the exclusionary rule, is concerned with predictability and economy. There is considerable scope for dispute about the meaning of the statements, whether oral or in writing, which parties make in their negotiations. This may distract attention from the construction of the words which parties eventually used to express their consensus and cause greater uncertainty of outcome in contractual disputes. Admission of evidence of the negotiations will in any event, as Lord Hoffmann observed in *Chartbrook Ltd v Persimmon Homes Ltd* (para 35), 'add to the cost of advice, litigation or arbitration'.

[41] But the exclusion of evidence of the prior negotiations is not absolute. The court's task in construing a contract is to ascertain what a reasonable person, having all the background knowledge which would have been available to the parties, would have understood them to be using the words in the contract to mean (*Chartbrook Ltd v Persimmon Homes Ltd*, Lord Hoffmann, para 14). As a result the court has for a long time looked at what Lord Ormidale called 'the surrounding circumstances' when construing the words of the contract (*Inglis v Buttery & Co*, Lord Ormidale, pp 67, 68, Lord Blackburn (HL), pp 102, 103). In some cases things said and done in the process of negotiation may be part of 'the surrounding circumstances'.

[42] Evidence of the factual background to the contract is relevant where the facts are known to both parties and those facts can cast light on either (i) the commercial purpose or purposes of the transaction objectively considered or (ii) the meaning of the words which the parties used in their contract. The two cases very often overlap as the ascertained commercial purpose gives meaning to particular words or phrases.

[43] In the former case, the surrounding circumstances may disclose the commercial object of the intended transaction. If an interpretation of the contract frustrated that object, the court would prefer an alternative interpretation. The contract should make commercial sense. In order to understand the commercial purpose of the contract the court may need to know 'the genesis of the transaction, the background, the context, the market in which the parties are operating' (*Reardon Smith Line Ltd v Yvgvar Hansen-Tangen*, Lord Wilberforce, p 995H).

[44] In the latter case the court is looking for the meaning of particular words or phrases. The context may give the words a formal or a popular and looser meaning. The

surrounding facts are relevant 'to establish the parties' knowledge of the circumstances with reference to which they used the words in the contract' (*Bank of Scotland v Dunedin Property Investment Co Ltd*, Lord President (Rodger), p 665G). Thus in that case the court, in interpreting the meaning of the phrase, 'costs . . . incurred . . . in connection with the stock', looked to the fact that Dunedin was aware (a) that the bank would borrow money to fund the purchase of its long-term fixed-interest loan stock and would hedge the transaction and (b) that the bank would incur costs in relation to the hedging if Dunedin repaid the loan and purchased the loan stock early. It was in this context that Cardozo J used the phrase 'genesis and aim' on which counsel for Luminar relied (*Utica City National Bank v Gunn*, p 308).

[45] Facts which are known only to one party are not admissible as part of the surrounding circumstances. For such circumstances to be available to the court in its task of ascertaining how a reasonable person would interpret the words of the contract, the circumstances must have been known to both parties or at least such knowledge must have been reasonably available to both of them (*Howgate Shopping Centre Ltd v Catercraft Services Ltd*, Lord Macfadyen, para 36). In that case he referred to the judgment of Lord Wilberforce in *Reardon Smith Line Ltd v Yvgvar Hansen-Tangen*, in which he stated (p 996E–F):

'It is often said that, in order to be admissible in aid of construction, these extrinsic facts must be within the knowledge of both parties to the contract, but this requirement must not be stated in too narrow a sense. When one speaks of the intention of the parties to the contract, one is speaking objectively—the parties cannot themselves give direct evidence of what their intention was—and what must be ascertained is what is to be taken as the intention which reasonable people would have had if placed in the situation of the parties. Similarly when one is speaking of aim, or object, or commercial purpose, one is speaking objectively of what reasonable persons would have in mind in the situation of the parties. It is in this sense and not in the sense of constructive notice or of estopping fact that judges are found using words like "knew or must be taken to have known" (see for example, the well-known judgment of Brett L.J. in *Lewis v Great Western Railway Co.*'

Knowledge which was reasonably available only to one party would not form part of the factual matrix which could assist the court in the construction of the contract (see also *Emcor Drake and Skull Ltd v Edinburgh Royal Joint Venture*, Lord Drummond Young, para 14). Facts of which both parties were aware but which were not at the forefront of their minds may still form part of the objective setting of the contract or, in Lord Drummond Young's words, 'the commercial context in which the contract occurs' (para 13). In most cases involving the construction of a contract there is no need for a detailed enquiry into which of the parties knew what. Most background facts which are relevant to the written contract in a particular case are, in Brett LJ's words in *Lewis v Great Western Rly* (p 208), 'things which must be taken to have been known by both parties to the contract.' But there is, as Lord Macfadyen stated in the paragraph referred to above, a need for particular care where the respective parties to a contract had differing degrees of knowledge about certain of the background circumstances.

. . .

[50] It is not necessary to dwell on the third ground of challenge [that the Lord Ordinary had misapplied his findings of fact in his construction of the contractual restriction]. The market research evidence which Luminar presented suggested that between 30 and 65 per cent of their customers who were shown Mama's flyers might visit the Picture House to dance to recorded music. Unsurprisingly, the Lord Ordinary concluded that there was a significant body of potential customers who might be attracted to different types of nightclub. But he interpreted this as simply competition for the leisure pound, which, on his construction, the clause did not prevent.

. . .

[54] Luminar's fourth ground of challenge [that the construction which the Lord Ordinary favoured was not commercially sensible] rested on the well-established proposition that a contract should if possible be given a commercially sensible construction (*Bank of Scotland v Dunedin Property Investment Co Ltd*, p 661D–F)

. . .

[56] I consider therefore that it would be more difficult for parties to know where they stood in relation to the restriction on the respondents' construction than on the reclaimers' and that delicate questions of subjective judgment would arise . . .

[57] The most difficult issue, in my opinion, is raised to [*sic*] in Luminar's first and fifth ground of challenge: what is the correct construction of the phrase in the context of the clause as a whole and in the light of the surrounding circumstances? The phrase which the parties used seems to me to be a recipe for litigation. As I consider that those words of restriction, taken by themselves, are capable of bearing the meaning which each party suggests, it is only after some hesitation that I have reached a concluded view.

[58] I have respectfully found myself differing from the Lord Ordinary in the construction of the provision. I have reached the view that Luminar are correct in their assertion that the provision prohibited Mama from putting on any discotheque at which recorded music was played for dancing at the times when Luminar were providing such entertainment at their Tollcross venue

. . .

[69] I conclude that the restriction entitles Luminar to the interdict which it has sought. I would therefore allow the reclaiming motion, sustain the reclaimers' first plea in law and repel the respondents' pleas in law. I would also reserve all questions of expenses."

As the following extract shows, the status and extent of the contextual approach in Scotland since *BoS v Dunedin*, remained unclear. The extract is a clear analysis of the status in Scotland of the contextual approach to interpretation in contract.

8–93 *Review of Contract Law: Interpretation of Contract*

Scottish Law Commission Discussion Paper No.147 (February 2011)

"The Scottish response to Lord Hoffmann's approach[1]

5.1 In the *ICS* case the then Scottish Law Lords, Lord Hope of Craighead and Lord Clyde, agreed with Lord Hoffmann's speech, while Lord Hope and Lord Rodger of Earlsferry (the other then Scottish Law Lord) concurred with Lord Hoffmann in the *Chartbrook* case. Lord Hope has also cited the Hoffmann approach, albeit in a qualified way . . . in the recent Supreme Court decision, *Multi-Link Leisure Developments Ltd v North Lanarkshire Council.*[3] This may be seen as a reasonably clear lead that the Hoffmann approach is to be followed by other Scottish courts; and it has indeed been cited with approval several times at Inner House level in the Court of Session.[4] There is even a perception that the Hoffmann approach has fore-runners amongst nineteenth and early twentieth century Scottish judges in so far as, in the words of Gloag on *Contract* published in 1929, 'it is always competent to lead evidence of the circumstances surrounding the parties at the time the contract was made'.[5] But on the whole the Scottish courts have confined themselves to what is usually called a commercial or purposive approach to interpretation, seeking to give effect to the actual words used in the light of the circumstances surrounding the parties at the time they entered their contract.[6] The approach is in line as much with Lord Wilberforce's earlier speeches as with Lord

Hoffmann's, and sometimes tends to downplay any innovation the latter might be thought to involve with regard to re-working the text.[7] The Hoffmann approach has also been strongly criticised in the leading modern text on contract law, especially in so far as it might involve over-riding the express terms of the contract;[8] and an Extra Division has recently expressed its "considerable sympathy" for such criticism.[9]

...

Re-working the words 8–94

5.5 [T]here have not in fact been any recent Scottish cases in which re working of the words used has taken place on the scale seen in the *ICS* case or *The Starsin*. Perhaps the nearest the courts have come to such an approach is *Multi-Link* ...

5.6 ... [T]he Lord Ordinary (Glennie) made no reference at all to the Hoffmann approach and was provided with no evidence outside the contractual documents, but held in reaching his conclusion that 'certain parts of the wording within [clause 18] can safely be disregarded'.[20] Without commenting on the legitimacy of this approach (but rejecting the Hoffmann approach in general terms, at least as applicable to leases), an Extra Division reversed the decision of the Lord Ordinary, holding that in a lease due to last for 50 years the words 'full market value' should be given a wide meaning unless there were express words to the contrary.[21] The court noted that 'the critical sentence of clause 18.2 shows all the signs of having been modified in the course of negotiations without taking full account of the effect on the text read as a whole'.[22] However, the court found it clear that the parties' method of valuation involved considering the land at two points in time. The land was to be valued as at the date of the purchaser's entry, but as though it were in the state it was in when the lease began (i.e. agricultural land). The Division observed: 'We understood the parties to agree that this is the proper starting pointing for assessment.'[23]

5.7 The Supreme Court upheld the decision of the Extra Division but applied different reasoning. Lord Hope (with whom Lord Clarke agreed) criticised the Lord Ordinary for departing from the words used by the parties,[24] and the Extra Division for paying no heed to the words in the clause following the phrase 'full market value'.[25] He thought that the part of the clause dealing with the 'assumptions and disregards' to be carried out by the Council 'looks as if it had been borrowed from a different lease without regard to the context',[26] and was 'designed to settle the basis for a purchase of subjects in their existing use', whereas the earlier part was 'designed to settle the price for the purchase of subjects that will have a value in the open market that takes account of their potential for development'.[27] While normally the words used were the starting point, in cases of such poor quality drafting and ambiguity as the present one, it was legitimate to try and give a sensible meaning to the clause as a whole. Account should be taken of the factual background known to both parties at the time of contracting and the aim should be to achieve a result consistent with business commonsense. It was in this context of the pursuit of business commonsense, but almost in passing, that Lord Hope made reference to Lord Hoffmann's speech in the *ICS* case. Approached in this way, the 'assumptions and disregards' could not outweigh the words pointing to the commercially sensible meaning contended for by the Council.

5.8 Lord Rodger (with whom Lady Hale and Sir John Dyson SCJ[28] agreed) made no reference to the Hoffmann approach, however, although he recognised that 'something has gone wrong with the drafting of the relevant clause'.[29] Like Lord Hope, his focus was on the words used in the contract viewed in the light of what would make commercial sense. But his point of departure was different from Lord Hope's. Lord Rodger said that one should 'start with the parts whose meaning is clear and then [...] use those parts to unravel the meaning of the parts which are more difficult to understand'.[30] The meaning of the 'assumptions and disregards' was clear, in his view. The contract required the

Council to take account of what Multi-Link had done to develop the golf course, meaning that the course had to be valued as such on the basis it was in good order and repair. Lord Rodger acknowledged that neither party had supported this position in argument (as we have seen,[31] the parties were agreed that the land's value as a golf course was to be completely ignored, and that the land was to be valued on the basis that it was still agricultural land). But, Lord Rodger continued, there was nothing in the contract to require the Council to ignore other factors in value, such as the land's suitability for a possible housing development. To use the words 'of agricultural land or open space suitable for development as a golf course' to eliminate that element would lead to 'a highly unusual and artificial approach to valuation'.[32] An assumption for the purposes of valuation that the land would only be used as a golf course required clearer words than that. Accordingly the Council was entitled to have regard to the housing development value in fixing the sale price of the land.

5.9 It will be apparent from this summary that the approaches of the two Justices are not only different from each other but also, to varying degrees, far from pure applications of the Hoffmann approach as expounded in the *ICS* and, indeed, the *Chartbrook* case. Other than a reference to a prior requirement of ambiguity, Lord Hope's is much the more Hoffmannesque of the two judgments. Some glancing references to commercial sense possibly apart, Lord Rodger ignores the Hoffmann approach altogether. Even although both Justices recognise that the case is one of bungled drafting, neither feels free to cut away from the words actually used and proceed on the basis of what the parties must be taken to have intended. In part this was probably because they did not have any extrinsic evidence upon which to be reasonably certain of what that intention might have been. While reference is made to business commonsense and the unlikelihood of a commercial agreement taking the form contended for by Multi-Link, some unease must have been caused by Lady Hale's observation that the Council, not being a commercial organisation but one set up to serve the local population rather than make money, might have had only the objective of providing recreational facilities for that population at the time the lease was entered upon, and that it was now the one seeking the benefit of a windfall brought about by subsequent changes to the local structural plan.[33] It is, finally, hard to avoid the impression that actually both Justices are engaging in a degree of re-working what was said in the contract to get it to make some sort of sense: Lord Hope by setting aside express words (despite his criticisms of the courts below for doing exactly the same thing), Lord Rodger first by refusing to accept the common position of the parties that the value of the golf course was not to be brought into account, and then stressing the significance of the absence of certain words from the document. In his construction of clause 18.2, Lord Rodger also appears to take as a relevant circumstance the fact that five years had passed and the course had been completed. But this was only one of the possible scenarios for which the parties provided when the lease was entered in 2000. The price could also have been required to be fixed at a point between the first and fifth anniversaries of the date of entry when, consistently with their obligations, the tenants still might not have developed a course. Whether it was right in any way to set aside the parties' common position on not taking account of the golf course value is therefore doubtful.

5.10 Where adjustments have been explicitly made to a written text by a Scottish court in the process of interpretation, they have been of a modest nature. Indeed arguably they could have been made under the long-established but much more limited rule allowing correction of 'patent errors' in a document as a matter of its construction.[34] In *Hardie Polymers Ltd v Polymerland Ltd*[35] consideration of the surrounding circumstances relating to a commercial agency contract led Lord Macfadyen to conclude that the parties had used the word 'compensation' when what they meant to say was 'indemnity', and he read the contract accordingly. In *Macdonald Estates plc v Regenesis (2005) Dunfermline Ltd*[36] Lord Reed concluded of a particular contractual provision:

'The words "it" and "its" must be a mistake: the defenders could not sensibly be undertaking to relieve the pursuers of outlays which the defenders had themselves made. Those words must be understood as meaning "you" and "your". So understood, clause 4.5 entitles the pursuers to be relieved of the outlays reasonably required to be made by them as an incident of the performance of their obligations under the contract.'[37]

5.11 Lord Reed also discussed the approach to correction of contracts by way of interpretation in *Credential Bath Street Ltd v Venture Investment Placement Ltd*.[38] Although the court would not readily construe a document as having been mistakenly expressed, especially one that had been formally drawn up, it would do so to ascribe to the document the meaning it would convey to a reasonable person aware of the context. The right word might be supplied for a wrong one, or inapt ones disregarded, or missing words inserted. It was not necessary, however, to know more than the substance of what was to be supplied; exactitude was the province of rectification rather than interpretation. This process of correction was, critically, not confined to mistakes apparent from the document itself, but included those which were apparent in the light of the surrounding circumstances: 'the classification of mistakes as "patent" or "latent" is no longer determinative of the court's power to cure mistakes by construction'.[39] But in the actual decision of the case Lord Reed found that the commercial background did 'not lead me away from the starting point: that one would ordinarily expect the parties to a formal document to have chosen their words with care, and to have intended to convey the meaning which the words they chose would convey to a reasonable person'.[40]

5.12 This discussion of the court's power to correct mistakes by interpretation brings us to an initial consideration of the relationship between this branch of the law and the remedy of rectification of a contract document under sections 8 and 9 of the Law Reform (Miscellaneous Provisions) (Scotland) Act 1985. In the *Credential Bath Street* case Lord Reed says that altering, adding to or subtracting from the words of a written instrument is a matter for rectification rather than interpretation, and, as already noted,[41] states that with interpretation only the substance of the correction, rather than exact wording, is needed. Although the basis of the distinction between interpretation and rectification is not further elaborated, it may be that in interpretation words are supplied (or perhaps corrected or omitted) to 'complete the sense' of a document, whereas in rectification the document is recast to reflect accurately the common intention of the parties to it. Putting it in another way, the interpreter with the document and evidence of admissible surrounding circumstances can determine what must have been meant, whereas in rectification such is the mis-writing of the document that even with the aid of admissible surrounding circumstances the court will be unable to find the parties' common intention correctly. This seems broadly to anticipate and be in line with Lord Hoffmann's discussion of the same subject in English law in the *Chartbrook* case.[42]

---

[3] [2010] UKSC 47, paras 19-23 (hereafter "*Multi-Link*").

[4] *Bank of Scotland v Dunedin Property Investment Co Ltd* 1998 SC 557; *Project Fishing International v CEPO Ltd* 2002 GWD 16-125; *Simmers v Innes* [2007] CSIH 12; 2007 GWD 9-159. This last case went on to the House of Lords ([2008] UKHL 24; 2008 SC (HL) 137), but there was no discussion of the Hoffmann approach in their Lordships' speeches.

[5] See Gloag, *Contract* (2nd ed, 1929), pp 373-375 (quotation in the text at p 373), and the cases there cited; also, e.g., the speeches of Lord Kinnear and Lord Dunedin in *Charrington & Co Ltd v Wooder* [1914] AC 71, cited by Lord Wilberforce in *Reardon Smith Line Ltd v Yngvar Hansen-Tangen* [1976] 1 WLR 989 (HL) at 996-997. See also *Aberdeen City Council v Stewart Milne Ltd* [2010] CSIH 81, para 11 per Lord Drummond Young; but note the comment by Lord Hope in *Multi-Link* [2010] UKSC 47, para 2.

[6] ... See further for general discussion Laura Macgregor and Carole Lewis, "Interpretation of

contract", in Reinhard Zimmermann, Daniel Visser and Kenneth Reid (eds), *Mixed Legal Systems in Comparative Perspective: Property and Obligations in Comparative Perspective* (2004), pp 66-93; Lord Bingham, "A new thing under the sun? The interpretation of contract and the *ICS* decision" (2008) 12 Edin LR 374 at 385; David Cabrelli, "Interpretation of contracts, objectivity and the elision of consent reached through consent and compromise" 2011 JR (forthcoming).

[7] See e.g. *City Wall Properties (Scotland) Ltd v Pearl Assurance plc* [2003] CSOH 211; 2004 SC 214.

[8] McBryde, *Contract*, paras 8.25-8.27.

[9] *Multi-Link Leisure Developments Ltd v North Lanarkshire Council* [2009] CSIH 96; 2010 SC 302, paras 23-25. The Division's suggestion that Lord Hoffmann's observations were more relevant to commercial contracts than to leases of heritable property (the subject matter of the case before the court) was implicitly rejected in the Supreme Court: see [2010] UKSC 47, para 26 per Lord Rodger ("it is appropriate to treat the lease as a commercial agreement which is to be construed accordingly") and para 45 (Lord Clarke). Lord Hope clearly sees the lease concerned as a commercial contract.

. . .

[20] [2009] CSOH 114, para 5.

[21] [2009] CSIH 96; 2010 SC 302.

[22] Ibid, para 26.

[23] Ibid.

[24] [2010] UKSC 47, para 14.

[25] Ibid, para 15.

[26] Ibid, para 17.

[27] Ibid.

[28] Now Lord Dyson, Supreme Court Justices appointed since the Court's establishment in October 2009 having been given the courtesy title of "Lord" or "Lady" (as required) from 13 December 2010: see the Court's press release of that date, available at *http://www.supremecourt.gov.uk/docs/pr_1013.pdf*.

[29] [2010] UKSC 47, para 27.

[30] Ibid, para 28.

[31] At para 5.6.

[32] [2010] UKSC 47, para 36.

[33] Ibid, para 41.

[34] Gloag, *Contract* (2nd ed, 1929), p 435; McBryde, *Contract*, para 8.99. Such errors are evident on the face of the document and do not need reference to the background to become apparent. Nonetheless the doctrine is one which might have been developed in the direction of the Hoffmann approach. See e.g., the addition of "to" to the lease in *Multi-Link* "to make good an obvious omission": [2010] UKSC 47, para 12 per Lord Hope.

[35] 2002 SCLR 64.

[36] [2007] CSOH 123; 2007 SLT 791.

[37] Ibid, para 114

[38] [2007] CSOH 208; 2008 GWD 9-168, paras 18-24.

[39] Ibid, para 22.

[40] Ibid, para 37.

[41] See para 5.11.

[42] See para 4.23.

The latest decisions from the Supreme Court on interpretation suggests that, in the words of Lord Mance, "the proper approach is contextual and purposive" and "there is no need to appeal here to any modern, anti-literal, tendencies".

Lloyds TSB Foundation for Scotland v Lloyds Banking Group Plc 8–95
[2013] UKSC 3; 2013 S.C. (U.K.S.C.) 169
Supreme Court: Lord Hope (DPSC), Lords Mance, Clarke, Reed; Carnwath

In 1997, Lloyds and the Foundation entered into a contract by deed, which replaced an earlier deeds of 1986 and 1993, under cl.2 of which Lloyds would pay the Foundation the greater of "(a) an amount equal to one-third of 0.1946 per cent of the Pre-Tax Profits (after deducting Pre-Tax Losses)" for the relevant accounting reference periods and "(b) the sum of £38,920".

Clause 1 defined "pre-tax profit" and "pre-tax loss" as meaning

> "in relation to any Accounting Reference Period ... respectively the 'group profit before taxation' and the 'group loss before taxation' (as the case may be) shown in the Audited Accounts for such period adjusted to exclude therefrom any amounts attributable to minority interests and any profits or losses arising on the sale or termination of an operation, such adjustment to be determined by the Auditors on such basis as they shall consider reasonable, which determination shall be conclusive and binding on the parties hereto".

The legal and accounting principles that applied to the 1997 deed and its predecessors were that: (a) a profit and loss account was concerned with ordinary activities before taxation; and (b) only profits realised at the balance sheet date could lawfully be included in the profit and loss account.

Article 4 of EU Regulation 1606/2002, adopted on 19 July 2002 required listed company consolidated accounts to conform with International Financial Reporting Standards (IFRS). Paragraph 34 of IFRS 3 required that any negative goodwill[57] arising from a bargain purchase should be recognised in the profit and loss account as from the acquisition date. The effect is that such a gain on acquisition is recognised immediately in the consolidated income statement, notwithstanding that it reflects an unrealised gain. The regulation did not require negative goodwill to be shown in the profit and loss accounts of the individual companies that contributed to the consolidated accounts as a pre-tax profit.

In the financial crisis of 2008 Lloyds Bank rescued HBOS Plc, acquiring it at half book value in anticipation of the likely losses in HBOS's assets. Lloyds audited consolidated income statement for 2009 included a gain on acquisition of over £11 billion reflecting the difference between the book value of HBOS's assets and the price paid. This negative goodwill converted a Lloyds loss of over £10 billion into a profit before taxation of over £1 billion.

The Foundation raised an action in the Court of Session seeking payment of £3,543,333 under cl.2(a) of the 1997 deed, based on profits that included the negative goodwill from the purchase of HBOS.

In this appeal to the Supreme Court the Bank successfully argued inter alia that, on construction of the terms of the deed, the gain on acquisition should be left out of account, so that the amount due to the Foundation would be restricted to £38,920 under cl.2(b) of the 1997 deed.

The Foundation argued that the phrase "group profit before taxation ... shown in the Audited Accounts" in cl.1 should be given its ordinary meaning.

---

[57] Negative goodwill arises when the price paid for an acquisition is lower than the true value of the acquisition's tangible assets, i.e. a bargain purchase.

8–96 "LORD MANCE (with whom Lord Reed and Lord Carnwath agree)—

[1] The issue on this appeal is how a covenant should be construed and understood as applying in a novel legal and accounting context, which was not foreseen or foreseeable—or was, according to uncontradicted expert evidence, 'unthinkable'—when the covenant was entered into.

...

[17] The parties did not discuss or agree any further exclusion following the 2002 Regulation, and the change only became relevant as a result of the well-publicised rescue of HBOS undertaken at short notice by Lloyds TSB Group as the financial crisis threatened mortgage lenders in September 2008. If the 1997 deed does not require an unrecognised gain on acquisition of this nature to be taken into account in identifying the 'group profit before taxation', it is circular to try to draw any inference from the fact that the parties did not renegotiate or amend the deed. It would also be illegitimate to try to do so, since parties' subsequent conduct cannot, in Scots or English law, construe an earlier contract. In any event, it is clear that neither party actually foresaw the present issue until it arose after the acquisition of HBOS.

...

[21] The Dean of Faculty forcefully advocated the Foundation's case as reflecting an appropriately mechanical application of the combination of cll 1 and 3. The description mechanical is appropriate, but the value of machinery depends upon its being correctly directed towards the right end. In this respect, the proper approach is contextual and purposive. That this is so needs today relatively little citation of authority. As Lord Wilberforce said in *Prenn v Simmonds* (pp 1383H–1384B):

'The time has long passed when agreements, even those under seal, isolated from the matrix of facts in which they were set and interpreted purely on internal linguistic considerations There is no need to appeal here to any modern, anti-literal, tendencies for Lord Blackburn's well-known judgment in *River Wear Commissioners v Adamson* (1877) App Cas 743, 763 provides ample warrant for liberal approach. We must, as he said, inquire beyond the language and see what the circumstances were with reference to which the words were used, and the object, appearing from those circumstances, which the person using them had in view.'

Construing the words 'actually paid' in *Charter Reinsurance Co Ltd v Fagan* (p 384C–D), Lord Mustill stated that, in cases not involving a specialist vocabulary, 'the inquiry will start, and usually finish, by asking what is the ordinary meaning of the words used' and that he had (p 384F–G):

'initially thought that the meaning of the words ["actually paid"] was quite clear, and that the complexities and mysteries of this specialist market had hidden the obvious solution, and had led the courts below to abjure the simple and right answer and to force on the words meaning which they could not possibly bear'.

But he went on (p 384G–H):

'This is, however, an occasion when a first impression and a simple answer no longer seem the best, for I recognise now that the focus of the argument is too narrow. The words must be set in the landscape of the instrument as whole'.

[22] Here, the landscape, matrix and aim of the 1997 deed as well as its predecessors could not be clearer. They were, when made, and could only have been, concerned with and aimed at realised profits or losses before the taxation which would fall on group companies. The change occurring in 2005 was to introduce negative goodwill into the profit and loss account as a 'gain on acquisition', which would not appear in Lloyds Bank's individual company accounts (since the HBOS transaction was there accounted for on a cost basis) and which could never attract taxation. In the light of the legal position of the 1980s and 1990s and the Lord Ordinary's findings on the accountancy

evidence (para 19), the change was wholly outside the parties' original contemplation, and something which they would not have accepted, had they foreseen it.

[23] No one suggests or could suggest that the change meant that the 1997 deed was frustrated, so the question is how its language best operates in the fundamentally changed and entirely unforeseen circumstances in the light of the parties' original intentions and purposes (*Bank of Credit and Commerce International SA v Ali (No 1)*; *Bromarin AB v IMD Investments Ltd*; *Debenhams Retail plc v Sun Alliance and London Assurance Co Ltd*). The answer is evident. It operates best, and quite naturally, by ignoring in the 2009 accounts the unrealised gain on acquisition and treating the loss which exists apart from that as the relevant figure for the purposes of cl 2.

[24] No principle of construction insists that the words 'group profit [or loss] before taxation . . . shown in the Audited Accounts' can only be satisfied by reference to a single line entry in accounts, however great and unforeseen the changes in law and accounting practice which have in the meantime occurred and whatever the consequences. On the contrary, it is not at all difficult to imagine that, if (as might have occurred between 1986 and 1991: see para 10) no single line could plausibly be identified as the 'group profit before taxation' and it was necessary to refer to two or more lines to achieve a result marrying with the parties' originally contemplated scheme, the Foundation itself would then be urging that approach.

[25] The proper approach as a matter of construction is to identify and use the figures in the consolidated income statement which show the group profit or loss before taxation in the sense intended by the deed. That means realised profit or loss before taxation, and it excludes a wholly novel element which was included in the income statement by a change which was neither foreseen nor foreseeable and which, had it been foreseen when the deeds were executed, would not have been accepted as part of the computation of profit or loss. The unrealised 'gain on acquisition' thus falls out of account and the balance is the relevant group profit or (on the facts of this case) loss before taxation. In respect of the accounting reference period to which the 2009 accounts relates, it follows that the Foundation receives only the minimum sum of £38,920, rather than the £3,543,333 which on their case results from the unrealised gain (after taking into account £135 million attributable to minority interests in the group).

. . .

Conclusion

[30] The Lord Ordinary thought that the words 'shown in the Audited Accounts' in cl 1 could simply be disregarded. The Inner House was correct to reject that approach. In some contractual contexts, words may have to be disregarded. But so radical an approach is both inappropriate and unnecessary to give effect to the intention of the 1997 deed, when understood in its context and properly construed. As demonstrated above, the words 'shown in the Audited Accounts' are well capable of catering for the present situation, and must on any view be understood as flexible enough to cover situations in which there is no single identifiable line in audited accounts describing 'group profit [or loss] before taxation' or anything like it. **8–97**

[31] The Inner House itself failed properly to identify what the parties had in mind by 'group profit [or loss] before taxation', at the times when the 1997 deed and its predecessors were executed. It did not appreciate the significance of the legal and accounting context in which the deeds were made, and it in effect assumed, contrary to all the indications and regardless of the consequences, that the contract must operate on an entirely literal basis by reference to a single line in whatever accounts might in future be produced in circumstances and under legal and accounting conventions entirely different from those in and for which it was conceived. As a result the Inner House thought that Lloyds Bank's construction would involve 're-writing' the deed, when in

fact it reflects the proper approach, of giving effect to the parties' original intentions in the radically different legal and accounting context which existed by 2009. The Inner House further failed to recognise the incongruity of the result for which the Foundation contends.

[32] The issue has been extremely well argued on both sides. For the reasons I have given, I would allow the appeal, and restore the decision of the Lord Ordinary to grant decree of absolvitor, albeit for reasons different to those he gave.

8–98 LORD HOPE DPSC (with whom Lord Reed and Lord Carnwath agree)—

[33] Like Lord Clarke, I was inclined at the end of the argument to accept the Dean of Faculty's submission that the phrase 'group profit before taxation ... shown in the audited accounts' in cl 1 of the 1997 deed should be given its ordinary meaning. It was, as he said, a simple and straightforward point of reference, which left no doubt as to what was to be taken to be the pre-tax profits for the relevant accounting reference period.

[34] But I have been persuaded by Lord Mance's judgment that these words must be read in the light of what a reasonable person would have taken them to mean, having regard to what was known in 1997 when the idea of introducing negative goodwill into the profit and loss account was unthinkable. Read in that context, the words do not have the weight that the Dean's argument would give to them. That would be to give them a meaning which no reasonable person would have dreamed of at that time. The words used are capable of meaning realised profit or loss before taxation, and of excluding elements which would not have been contemplated as having anything to do with the computation of profit or loss when the deed was executed. On that reading I am left in no doubt that the argument for Lloyds Bank, which accords with the landscape at the time when the words were written, must prevail over that for the Foundation.

[35] For the reasons that Lord Mance gives, therefore, I too would allow the appeal. I would recall the Inner House's interlocutor and restore the interlocutor of the Lord Ordinary ... "

This approach appears to be reinforced by the majority in the following Supreme Court decision.

8–99

Arnold v Britton

[2015] UKSC 36; [2015] 2 W.L.R. 1593

Supreme Court: Lord Neuberger of Abbotsbury PSC, Lord Sumption, Lord Carnwath, Lord Hughes, Lord Hodge JJSC

From 1974 the then owners of the Oxwich Leisure Park in the Gower Peninsula, Wales, granted a number of 99-year leases of plots on which holiday chalets were to be built. The preamble to each lease stated that it would be granted "upon terms similar in all respects" to the other leases. The introductory words of cl.3 provided that each lessee's (tenant's) covenants as to use and repair of chalets were for the benefit of other tenants. Clause 4(8) contained a covenant by the lessor (landlord) that the covenants imposed on other tenants were to like effect.

Clause 3 of the first group of leases included, in cl.3(2), a tenant's covenant "to pay ... a proportionate part of the expenses and outgoings incurred by the lessor in the repair, maintenance, renewal and the provision of services [as set out in the lease] in the yearly sum of £90", increasing thereafter triennially (that is, every three years) at a compound rate of 10 per cent.

Subsequent leases of further chalets were granted in which cl.3(2) provided for an *annual* 10 per cent compound increase. In 2011 the tenants of those chalets, whose annual service charge had risen to over £2,700 as opposed to £282 for the chalets subject to the earlier leases. They claimed that an interpretation of the clause that required a fixed sum payment resulted in such a high annual service charge was absurd. Clause 3(2) should be read as requiring them to pay a variable sum, being a fair proportion of the cost of providing the services, with the specified sum being no more than a cap on the maximum sum payable.

The current landlord, Mrs. Arnold sought a declaration (declarator) that cl.3(2) required the payment of the fixed sum and not any lesser variable amount. The judge dismissed the claim. On appeal by the landlord the High Court judge held that, on a natural reading of the clause, the object of the verb "to pay" was the fixed sum of £90 as escalated, whereas the construction contended for by the tenants would involve rewriting the bargain which the parties had made, which, given the high levels of inflation in the UK when those leases had been granted, could not be said at that time to have lacked commercial purpose. Dismissing the tenants' appeal, the Court of Appeal affirmed the High Court judge's reasoning and held, additionally, that the words "a proportionate part" were not inconsistent with a fixed service charge in circumstances where other lessees were contributing to the overall service charge, which in consequence was to be apportioned between them.

The Supreme Court dismissed the tenants' further appeal (Lord Carnwath JSC dissenting).

"LORD NEUBERGER OF ABBOTSBURY PSC (with whom LORD SUMPTION and LORD HUGHES JJSC agreed) **8–100**

...

Interpretation of contractual provisions

[14] Over the past 45 years, the House of Lords and Supreme Court have discussed the correct approach to be adopted to the interpretation, or construction, of contracts in a number of cases starting with *Prenn v Simmonds* [1971] 1 WLR 1381 and culminating in *Rainy Sky SA v Kookmin Bank* [2011] 1 WLR 2900.

[15] When interpreting a written contract, the court is concerned to identify the intention of the parties by reference to "what a reasonable person having all the background knowledge which would have been available to the parties would have understood them to be using the language in the contract to mean", to quote Lord Hoffmann in *Chartbrook Ltd v Persimmon Homes Ltd* [2009] AC 1101, para 14. And it does so by focussing on the meaning of the relevant words, in this case clause 3(2) of each of the 25 leases, in their documentary, factual and commercial context. That meaning has to be assessed in the light of (i) the natural and ordinary meaning of the clause, (ii) any other relevant provisions of the lease, (iii) the overall purpose of the clause and the lease, (iv) the facts and circumstances known or assumed by the parties at the time that the document was executed, and (v) commercial common sense, but (vi) disregarding subjective evidence of any party's intentions. In this connection, see *Prenn* [1971] 1 WLR 1381, 1384-1386; *Reardon Smith Line Ltd v Yngvar Hansen-Tangen (trading as HE Hansen-Tangen)* [1976] 1 WLR 98, 995-997 per Lord Wilberforce; *Bank of Credit and Commerce International SA v Ali* [2002] 1 AC 251, para 8, per Lord Bingham of Cornhill; and the survey of more recent authorities in *Rainy Sky* [2011] 1 WLR 2900, paras 21-30, per Lord Clarke of Stone-cum-Ebony JSC.

[16] For present purposes, I think it is important to emphasise seven factors.

[17] First, the reliance placed in some cases on commercial common sense and surrounding circumstances (eg in *Chartbrook* [2009] AC 1101 , paras 16-26) should not be

invoked to undervalue the importance of the language of the provision which is to be construed. The exercise of interpreting a provision involves identifying what the parties meant through the eyes of a reasonable reader, and, save perhaps in a very unusual case, that meaning is most obviously to be gleaned from the language of the provision. Unlike commercial common sense and the surrounding circumstances, the parties have control over the language they use in a contract. And, again save perhaps in a very unusual case, the parties must have been specifically focussing on the issue covered by the provision when agreeing the wording of that provision.

[18] Secondly, when it comes to considering the centrally relevant words to be interpreted, I accept that the less clear they are, or, to put it another way, the worse their drafting, the more ready the court can properly be to depart from their natural meaning. That is simply the obverse of the sensible proposition that the clearer the natural meaning the more difficult it is to justify departing from it. However, that does not justify the court embarking on an exercise of searching for, let alone constructing, drafting infelicities in order to facilitate a departure from the natural meaning. If there is a specific error in the drafting, it may often have no relevance to the issue of interpretation which the court has to resolve.

[19] The third point I should mention is that commercial common sense is not to be invoked retrospectively. The mere fact that a contractual arrangement, if interpreted according to its natural language, has worked out badly, or even disastrously, for one of the parties is not a reason for departing from the natural language. Commercial common sense is only relevant to the extent of how matters would or could have been perceived by the parties, or by reasonable people in the position of the parties, as at the date that the contract was made. Judicial observations such as those of Lord Reid in *Wickman Machine Tools Sales Ltd v L Schuler AG* [1974] AC 235, 251 and Lord Diplock in *Antaios Cia Naviera SA v Salen Rederierna AB (The Antaios)* [1985] AC 191, 201, quoted by Lord Carnwath JSC at para 110, have to be read and applied bearing that important point in mind.

[20] Fourthly, while commercial common sense is a very important factor to take into account when interpreting a contract, a court should be very slow to reject the natural meaning of a provision as correct simply because it appears to be a very imprudent term for one of the parties to have agreed, even ignoring the benefit of wisdom of hindsight. The purpose of interpretation is to identify what the parties have agreed, not what the court thinks that they should have agreed. Experience shows that it is by no means unknown for people to enter into arrangements which are ill-advised, even ignoring the benefit of wisdom of hindsight, and it is not the function of a court when interpreting an agreement to relieve a party from the consequences of his imprudence or poor advice. Accordingly, when interpreting a contract a judge should avoid re-writing it in an attempt to assist an unwise party or to penalise an astute party.

[21] The fifth point concerns the facts known to the parties. When interpreting a contractual provision, one can only take into account facts or circumstances which existed at the time that the contract was made, and which were known or reasonably available to both parties. Given that a contract is a bilateral, or synallagmatic, arrangement involving both parties, it cannot be right, when interpreting a contractual provision, to take into account a fact or circumstance known only to one of the parties.

[22] Sixthly, in some cases, an event subsequently occurs which was plainly not intended or contemplated by the parties, judging from the language of their contract. In such a case, if it is clear what the parties would have intended, the court will give effect to that intention. An example of such a case is *Aberdeen City Council v Stewart Milne Group Ltd* 2012 SCLR 114, where the court concluded that "any . . . approach" other than that which was adopted "would defeat the parties' clear objectives", but the

conclusion was based on what the parties "had in mind when they entered into" the contract: see paras 21 and 22.

[23] Seventhly, reference was made in argument to service charge clauses being construed "restrictively". I am unconvinced by the notion that service charge clauses are to be subject to any special rule of interpretation. Even if (which it is unnecessary to decide) a landlord may have simpler remedies than a tenant to enforce service charge provisions, that is not relevant to the issue of how one interprets the contractual machinery for assessing the tenant's contribution. The origin of the adverb was in a judgment of Rix LJ in *McHale v Earl Cadogan* [2010] HLR 412, para 17. What he was saying, quite correctly, was that the court should not "bring within the general words of a service charge clause anything which does not clearly belong there". However, that does not help resolve the sort of issue of interpretation raised in this case.

...

[41] I do not think that this is a case where the approach adopted by this court in *Aberdeen City Council* 2012 SCLR 114 can assist the appellants. Unlike that case, this is not a case where one of the parties has done something which was not contemplated by the contract. It is clear that the 10% per annum increase in clause 3(2) was included to allow for a factor which was out of the control of either party, namely inflation. In my judgment, there is no principle of interpretation which entitles a court to re-write a contractual provision simply because the factor which the parties catered for does not seem to be developing in the way in which the parties may well have expected.

...

Conclusion

[60] Accordingly, in agreement with the reasons given by Lord Hodge JSC in this **8–101**
court, Davis LJ in the Court of Appeal and Morgan J in the High Court, I would dismiss this appeal, and I do not consider that the appellants are assisted by the additional argument raised in this court. I should, however, make five final points.

[61] First, the Court of Appeal suggested that the only way the lessees under the 25 leases could escape from their problems would be by surrendering or suffering forfeiture. In case this is misinterpreted, it is right to point out that surrender is consensual between lessee and lessor, and forfeiture involves unilateral action by a lessor, and so neither course can be forced on the lessor.

[62] Secondly, I have considerable sympathy with Lord Carnwath JSC's conclusion that the appeal should be allowed (not least because it is a much more satisfactory outcome in common sense terms, particularly viewed as at today), and I acknowledge that his reasons are as powerful as his conclusion allows. However, for the reasons I have given, I cannot agree with him.

[63] Thirdly, the fact that four leases were granted to associates of the lessor with the proviso described in para 8 above, and that three of the deeds of variation described in para 9 above were entered into with a lessee who was a close relation of the lessor, is worthy of comment. It suggests that the lessor or her advisers may have appreciated the potential disadvantages of the clause now contained in the 25 leases. However, I do not see how it can assist the lessees on the issue in these proceedings, namely the interpretation of the clause in the 25 leases.

[64] Fourthly, as Lord Carnwath JSC records in para 155 below, it appears that the respondent realistically recognises the unsatisfactory situation in which the lessees under the 25 leases find themselves, and is prepared to agree appropriate amendments to their leases. I hope that a fair and just amendment can be agreed.

[65] Finally, as Lord Carnwath JSC also points out in paras 90-93 below, there are various statutory provisions which protect tenants against unreasonable service charges, but none of them applies here. The present case suggests that there may be a strong case

for extending such provisions to cases such as the present, even though they involve a fixed sum payable by way of service charge. But that is a policy issue for Parliament, and there may be arguments either way.

8–102 LORD HODGE JSC

[66] I agree that the appeal must be dismissed for the reasons which Lord Neuberger of Abbotsbury PSC sets out. But it is a highly unsatisfactory outcome for the chalet tenants who are affected by the annual escalator of the service charge. It is not clear whether there are many long leases containing fixed service charges with escalators which are beyond the reach of statutory regulation. If there are, there may be a case for Parliament to consider extending the provisions that protect tenants against unreasonable service charges.

[67] Mr Morshead QC for the appellants submitted in his written case that what was important was "(a) that the risk [of inflation falling and remaining substantially below 10%] would have been obvious to the officious, reasonable bystander who must be imagined interrogating the actual parties and (b) that no reasonable person in the position of the parties, looking at the leases in their entirety and in context, would understand them to have intended that the tenants should assume that risk". He envisaged that in a hypothetical dialogue the officious bystander would warn the parties of the risks of their proposed contract and they would make it clear that that was not their intention.

[68] In the course of the debate we were referred directly or by reference to several cases concerning the remediation of a mistake by construction or the implication of a term. In my view they do not give the support that Mr Morshead needs.

[69] In *Homburg Houtimport BV v Agrosin Private Ltd (The Starsin)* [2004] 1 AC 715 the mistaken omission of words in a clause was apparent because the bill of lading had been modelled on a standard clause. The person who had transposed the standard clause into the bill of lading had omitted a phrase in the standard clause in which the same word had appeared at the end of two consecutive phrases. The mistake was clear and it was apparent what correction was called for: paras 22 and 23 per Lord Bingham of Cornhill.

[70] In *Chartbrook Ltd v Persimmon Homes Ltd* [2009] AC 1101 a definition, which contained a grammatical ambiguity, made no commercial sense if interpreted in accordance with the ordinary rules of syntax. The background to the deal and the internal context of the contract showed that there was a linguistic mistake in the definition, which the court was able to remove by means of construction. In his speech Lord Hoffmann, at p 1114, referred with approval to the judgment of Carnwath LJ in *KPMG LLP v Network Rail Infrastructure Ltd* [2007] Bus LR 1336. In that case, which concerned a rent review clause in a lease, it was clear from the terms of the clause that its wording did not make sense. The court was assisted by an earlier agreement which set out the then intended clause containing a parenthesis, of which only part had remained in the final lease. It was not clear whether the parties had mistakenly deleted words from the parenthesis, which they had intended to include, or had failed to delete the parenthesis in its entirety. But that uncertainty as to the nature of the mistake, unusually, did not matter as the outcome was the same on either basis.

[71] In *Aberdeen City Council v Stewart Milne Group Ltd* 2012 SCLR 114 the internal context of the contract provided the answer. The sale contract provided for the payment to the vendor of a further sum on disposal of the land by the purchaser. Two of the methods of disposal required the parties to ascertain the market value of the property on disposal in calculating the additional payment and the other used the "gross sales proceeds" in calculating that payment. The purchaser sold the site at an under-value to an associated company, a circumstance which on the face of the contract the parties had not contemplated. The courts at each level interpreted the provision, which used the

gross sales proceeds in the calculation, as requiring a market valuation where there was a sale which was not at arm's length. They inferred the intention of the parties at the time of the agreement from the contract as a whole and in particular from the fact that the other two methods of disposal required such a valuation. While this line of reasoning was criticised by Professor Martin Hogg "Fundamental Issues for Reform of the Law of Contractual Interpretation" (2011) 15 Edin LR 406 on the ground that it protected a party from its commercial fecklessness, it seems to me to be the correct approach in that case as the internal context of the contract pointed towards the commercially sensible interpretation.

[72] The context, whether internal to the contract or otherwise, provides little assistance in this case. Beyond the words of the relevant clauses, there is the context of the other provisions of each of the 25 individual leases which are at issue. They are long leases, having a term of 99 years. The court in interpreting the leases can and should take into account the great difficulty in predicting economic circumstances in the distant future and ask itself whether the parties really intended to do so.

[73] The court also can and should take into account the economic circumstances which prevailed at the time each lease was entered into. It is clear from the table which Lord Carnwath JSC has set out in para 100 of his judgment that between 1974 and 1988 the use of a 10% annual escalator achieved a result which was not far off the diminution of the value of money in the difficult economic circumstances that then prevailed. The future was and is unknown.

[74] Little else is known and I do not think that it is appropriate to speculate about the extent to which lessees would have known the terms of earlier leases. In my view there is much to be said for the practice, which Lord Drummond Young and other judges have encouraged in Scotland, of requiring parties to give notice in their written pleadings both of the nature of the surrounding circumstances on which they rely and of their assertions as to the effect of those facts on the construction of the disputed words: *MRS Distribution Ltd v DS Smith (UK) Ltd* 2004 SLT 631, para 14. Such notice of relevant facts, which are either admitted or proved at trial, would avoid disputes on appeal such as whether the affected lessees were aware of the earlier leases.

[75] While there are infelicities in the language of the relevant clauses in some of the leases and no clear explanation of minor changes in drafting, I am not persuaded that the meaning of the language is open to question when full weight is given to the very limited factual matrix with which the courts have been presented in this case. We are invited to construe that which reads on a first consideration as a fixed service charge with an escalator to deal with future inflation, as a variable service charge which is subject to a cap to which the escalator applies. I find that very difficult. In my view there is nothing in the relevant context to support the construction of the clause as creating a cap, other than the view, which events have fully justified, that it was unwise of the lessees to agree to a fixed service charge with an escalator based on an assumption that the value of money would diminish by 10% per year.

[76] This conclusion is not a matter of reaching a clear view on the natural meaning of the words and then seeing if there are circumstances which displace that meaning. I accept Lord Clarke of Stone-cum-Ebony JSC's formulation of the unitary process of construction, in *Rainy Sky SA v Kookmin Bank* [2011] 1 WLR 2900, para 21:

'the exercise of construction is essentially one unitary exercise in which the court must consider the language used and ascertain what a reasonable person, that is a person who has all the background knowledge which would reasonably have been available to the parties in the situation in which they were at the time of the contract, would have understood the parties to have meant. In doing so, the court must have regard to all the relevant surrounding circumstances. If there are two possible constructions, the court is entitled to prefer the construction which is consistent with business common sense and to reject the other.'

[77] This unitary exercise involves an iterative process by which each of the rival meanings is checked against the provisions of the contract and its commercial consequences are investigated: *In re Sigma Finance Corpn* [2010] 1 All ER 571, para 12, per Lord Mance JSC. But there must be a basis in the words used and the factual matrix for identifying a rival meaning. The role of the construct, the reasonable person, is to ascertain objectively, and with the benefit of the relevant background knowledge, the meaning of the words which the parties used. The construct is not there to re-write the parties' agreement because it was unwise to gamble on future economic circumstances in a long term contract or because subsequent events have shown that the natural meaning of the words has produced a bad bargain for one side. The question for the court is not whether a reasonable and properly informed tenant would enter into such an undertaking. That would involve the possibility of re-writing the parties' bargain in the name of commercial good sense. In my view, Mr Morshead's formulation (para 67 above), on which his case depends, asks the court to re-write the parties' leases on this illegitimate basis.

[78] Nor is this a case in which the courts can identify and remedy a mistake by construction. Even if, contrary to my view, one concluded that there was a clear mistake in the parties' use of language, it is not clear what correction ought to be made. The court must be satisfied as to both the mistake and the nature of the correction: *Pink Floyd Music Ltd v EMI Records Ltd* [2010] EWCA Civ 1429 at [21], per Lord Neuberger of Abbotsbury MR. This is not an unusual case, such as *KPMG* [2007] Bus LR 1336 in which a mistake was obvious on the face of the contract and the precise nature of the correction had no effect on the outcome.

[79] My conclusion that the court does not have power to remedy these long term contracts so as to preserve the essential nature of the service charge in changed economic circumstances does not mean that the lessees' predicament is acceptable. If the parties cannot agree an amendment of the leases on a fair basis, the lessees will have to seek parliamentary intervention.

8–103 LORD CARNWATH JSC

Preliminary comments

[80] The contractual provisions in this case pose unusual interpretative challenges, which may call for unusual solutions. The leases with which we are concerned are of 25 chalets within Oxwich Leisure Park, in south Wales. It is an estate of 91 such chalets first developed in 1974. It is in an attractive holiday location close to Oxwich Beach on the Gower peninsular. The challenges arise from a combination of factors. The intention, stated in the preamble to each lease, was that they should be 'upon terms similar in all respects ...'. Yet we are faced with five forms of service charge provision, agreed over a period of some 20 years, the variations in which at first sight defy rational analysis. As interpreted by the Court of Appeal, they would lead over the course of the leases to supposedly 'proportionate' service charges becoming wholly disproportionate to the costs of the relevant services, to extreme and arbitrary differences between the treatment of different groups of leases within the estate, and to the prospect in the foreseeable future of potentially catastrophic financial consequences for the lessees directly concerned.

[81] It does not help that, remarkably, the case has come to us with minimal evidence to explain the circumstances, or "factual matrix", in which these variations were agreed at different times, or even simply to add some context or colour to the bare legal and statistical analysis. That applies even to the most recent, and most surprising, of the transactions, effected as recently as 2000, and to which Mrs Arnold the present

respondent was herself a party. Nor have we been told anything about how the clauses have been operated in practice at any time: for example how the estate has been managed and what costs incurred by the lessor, what service charge payments have been demanded of the various categories of lessee, and what has happened to any surplus.

[82] It is to be borne in mind also that in the early 1970s (when this clause was first devised) variable service charge provisions were a relatively 'new and modern' addition to the law, prompted in part by rapidly increasing prices: see Mark Wonnacott, *The History of the Law of Landlord and Tenant in England and Wales* (2012), p 105 and *Hyams v Titan Properties Ltd* (1972) 24 P & CR 359. Since then, it is said in the same history (p 106), service charges have caused 'more trouble between landlord and tenant than anything else', but they have in turn been regulated by statute to such an extent as to make it 'all but impossible for an amateur landlord to recover [a service charge] in the event of a dispute'. Whether or not that extreme view is justifiable, the need for special measures to safeguard the interests of lessees has been acknowledged by the legislature, which has thus for the most part relieved the courts of responsibility for developing a common law response to the problems.

[83] As I shall explain, these leases are a rare example of a category of residential lease which has slipped through the statutory net. That is of no direct relevance to the legal issues before us, save that it may help to explain why no ready solutions are to be found in the authorities. Furthermore, in so far as policy has a part to play in the development of the common law, it may be legitimate to seek guidance in the approaches adopted by the legislature in analogous contexts: see *Johnson v Unisys Ltd* [2003] 1 AC 518, para 37, per Lord Hoffmann.

. . .

The statutory provisions

[90] By sections 18 and 19 of the Landlord and Tenant Act 1985, a 'service charge' (as defined) payable by a tenant of a 'dwelling', is limited to an amount which reflects the costs 'reasonably incurred' in the provision of services. The controls originally applied only to 'flats' but were extended by amendment in 1987 to include 'dwellings' as defined: see sections 41 and 60 of, and paragraph 1 of Schedule 2 to, the Landlord and Tenant Act 1987. It is not in dispute, in these proceedings at least, that the chalets are 'dwellings' for this purpose. The issue is whether the charges are 'service charges' as defined by section 18(1): **8–104**

' "service charge" means an amount payable by the tenant of a dwelling as part of or in addition to the rent—(a) which is payable, directly or indirectly, for services, repairs, maintenance, improvements or insurance or the landlord's costs of management, and (b) the whole or part of which varies or may vary according to the relevant costs.'

[91] The lessees submit that properly interpreted the clause imposes an obligation to pay a 'proportionate part' of the costs incurred, subject only to an upper limit or cap determined by reference to the formula in the second part of the clause. On this footing it is an amount which 'varies or may vary according to the relevant costs': section 18(1)(b). The respondent submits that charge is outside the statutory definition because the annual amount is fixed by that formula, without any reference to the costs actually incurred by the lessor. If the lessees are right, the amount of the charge is limited to the amounts reasonably incurred. If the lessor is right, there is no statutory limit or other control.

[92] Other safeguards for lessees were introduced by the 1987 Act, but none covers the present situation. Thus it introduced a new right for any party to a long lease (not only the lessee) of a 'flat' to apply to the court (now the First-tier Tribunal) for an order varying a lease on the grounds that it 'fails to make satisfactory provision' in respect of various matters, one being the computation of service charges, but this did not apply to

other forms of dwelling such as in this case. There is a more general provision, for application by 'a majority of parties' for variation of a number of leases under a single lessor (section 37), but again it applies only to flats. On the other hand, section 40, which allows similar applications for variation of insurance provisions, applies to 'dwellings' in general. It is difficult to detect any legislative purposes for these distinctions. The present case illustrates the potentially unfortunate consequences for parties to those rare forms of residential lease which for no apparent reason fall outside any of the protections given by the legislative scheme.

[93] For completeness, I note also that no issue arises in the present proceedings as to the possible application of other more general protections relating to unfair contractual terms. Sections 2 to 4 of the Unfair Contract Terms Act 1977 do not in any event apply to contracts relating to the creation or transfer of interests in land: paragraph 1(b) of Schedule 1. No such limitation appears in the Unfair Terms in Consumer Contracts Regulations 1999 (SI 1999/2083), which give effect in this country to Council Directive 93/13/EEC of 5 April 1993 on unfair terms in consumer contracts. The Directive was first transposed in 1994 Regulations (SI 1994/3159) which were later replaced by the 1999 Regulations. The 1994 Regulations came into effect on 1 July 1995, and therefore would not it seems apply to contracts concluded before that date: regulation 1; *Chitty on Contracts*, 31st ed (2014), para 37-087. Accordingly, it could be relevant if at all only to version 5 (2000).

. . .

Approach to interpretation

8–105 [108] In an unusual case such as this, little direct help is to be gained from authorities on other contracts in other contexts. As Tolstoy said of unhappy families, every ill-drafted contract is ill-drafted 'in its own way'. However, the authorities provide guidance as to the interpretative tools available for the task. The general principles are now authoritatively drawn together in an important passage in the judgment of Lord Clarke of Stone-cum-Ebony JSC in *Rainy Sky SA v Kookmin Bank* [2011] 1 WLR 2900, paras 14-30. As that passage shows, there is often a tension between, on the one hand, the principle that the parties' common intentions should be derived from the words they used, and on the other the need if possible to avoid a nonsensical result.

[109] The former is evident, as Lord Clarke JSC emphasised, in the rule that 'where the parties have used unambiguous language, the court must apply it': para 23. However, in view of the importance attached by others to the so-called 'natural meaning' of clause 3(2), it is important to note that Lord Clarke JSC (paras 20–23) specifically rejected Patten LJ's proposition that 'unless the most natural meaning of the words produces a result so extreme as to suggest that it was unintended, the court must give effect to that meaning.' In Lord Clarke JSC's view it was only if the words used by the parties were 'unambiguous' that the court had no choice in the matter.

[110] He illustrated the other side of the coin by quotations from Lord Reid in *Wickman Machine Tools Sales Ltd v L Schuler AG* [1974] AC 235, 251:

'The fact that a particular construction leads to a very unreasonable result must be a relevant consideration. The more unreasonable the result, the more unlikely it is that the parties can have intended it, and if they do intend it the more necessary it is that they shall make that intention abundantly clear.'

and Lord Diplock in *Antaios Cia Naviera SA v Salen Rederierna AB (The Antaios)* [1985] AC 191, 201:

'if detailed and syntactical analysis of words in a commercial contract is going to lead to a conclusion that flouts business common sense, it must yield to business common sense.'

As a rider to the last quotation, Lord Clarke JSC cited the cautionary words of Hoffmann LJ (*Co-operative Wholesale Society Ltd v National Westminster Bank plc* [1995] 1 EGLR 97, 99):

'This robust declaration does not, however, mean that one can rewrite the language which the parties have used in order to make the contract conform to business common sense. But language is a very flexible instrument and, if it is capable of more than one construction, one chooses that which seems most likely to give effect to the commercial purpose of the agreement.'

[111] I agree with Mr Morshead (questioning in this respect the approach of Davis LJ (para 35)) that it may be unnecessary and unhelpful to draw sharp distinctions between problems of ambiguity and of mistake, or between the different techniques available to resolve them. In *Chartbrook Ltd v Persimmon Homes Ltd* [2009] AC 1101, para 23, Lord Hoffmann cited with approval a passage of my own (in *KPMG LLP v Network Rail Infrastructure Ltd* [2007] Bus LR 1336, para 50) where I discussed the role of what is sometimes called 'interpretation by construction'. I criticised the tendency to deal separately with 'correction of mistakes' and 'construing the paragraph "as it stands"', as though they were distinct exercises, rather than as 'aspects of the single task of interpreting the agreement in its context, in order to get as close as possible to the meaning which the parties intended'. Lord Hoffmann added, at para 25:

'What is clear from these cases is that there is not, so to speak, a limit to the amount of red ink or verbal rearrangement or correction which the court is allowed. All that is required is that it should be clear that something has gone wrong with the language and that it should be clear what a reasonable person would have understood the parties to have meant.'

[112] Another permissible route to the same end is by the implication of terms 'necessary to give business efficacy to the contract'. I refer again to Lord Hoffmann's words, this time in *Attorney General of Belize v Belize Telecom Ltd* [2009] 1 WLR 1988, para 22, explaining the 'two important points' underlined by that formulation:

'The first, conveyed by the use of the word 'business', is that in considering what the instrument would have meant to a reasonable person who had knowledge of the relevant background, one assumes the notional reader will take into account the practical consequences of deciding that it means one thing or the other. In the case of an instrument such as a commercial contract, he will consider whether a different construction would frustrate the apparent business purpose of the parties ... The second, conveyed by the use of the word "necessary", is that it is not enough for a court to consider that the implied term expresses what it would have been reasonable for the parties to agree to. It must be satisfied that it is what the contract actually means.'

[113] *Aberdeen City Council v Stewart Milne Group Ltd* 2012 SCLR 114 is a useful recent illustration in this court of how these various principles may be deployed, to enable the court to achieve a commercially sensible result in the face of apparently intractable language. A contract for the sale of development land gave the council the right to an uplift (described as 'the profit share') in certain defined circumstances, one being the sale of the property by the purchaser. The issue was the calculation of the profit share, which the contract defined as a specified percentage of the 'estimated profit' (defined by reference to 'open market value') or 'the gross sale proceeds'. The issue was how the definition should be applied in the case of a sale by the purchaser to an associated party at an undervalue. The court held in agreement with the lower courts that, in that event, notwithstanding the apparently unqualified reference to gross sale proceeds, the calculation should be based on open market value.

[114] In a concurring judgment, with which all the members of the court agreed, Lord Clarke JSC, at para 28, referred to his own judgment in Rainy Sky as indicating the 'ultimate aim', that is:

'to determine what the parties meant by the language used, which involves ascertaining what a reasonable person would have understood the parties to have meant; the relevant reasonable person being one who has all the background knowledge which would reasonably have been available to the parties in the situation in which they were at the time of the contract.'

As he pointed out, 'on the face of it' the reference in the contract to the gross sale proceeds was a reference to the 'actual sale proceeds' received by the appellants. It was not easy to conclude 'as a matter of language' that the parties meant, not the actual sale proceeds, but the amount the appellants would have received on an arm's length sale at market value of the property; nor was it easy to conclude that the parties 'must have intended' the language to have that meaning. He referred, at para 31, to the comment of Baroness Hale of Richmond JSC in the course of the argument that:

'unlike *Rainy Sky*, this is not a case in where there are two alternative available constructions of the language used. It is rather a case in which, notwithstanding the language used, the parties must have intended that, in the event of an on sale, the appellants would pay the respondents the appropriate share of the proceeds of sale on the assumption that the on sale was at a market price.'

He thought the problem should be solved by implying a term to the effect that, in the event of a sale which was not at arm's length in the open market, an open market valuation should be used. As he explained, at para 33:

'If the officious bystander had been asked whether such a term should be implied, he or she would have said "of course". Put another way, such a term is necessary to make the contract work or to give it business efficacy.'

He preferred the use of an implied term to 'a process of interpretation', although 'the result is of course the same': paras 30–33.

[115] As Mr Morshead observes, the result in the Aberdeen case could probably have been explained equally as a case of correction by interpretation. In any event, this example provides support for his proposition that, where an ordinary reading of the contractual words produces commercial nonsense, the court will do its utmost to find a way to substitute a more likely alternative, using whichever interpretative technique is most appropriate to the particular task.

. . .

Conclusion

8–106 [155] The true explanation for these wretchedly conceived clauses may be lost in history, but the problems for the parties are all too present and deeply regrettable. No doubt in recognition of such considerations, Mr Daiches, on behalf of Mrs Arnold, indicated that his client 'fully understands the appellants' predicament and is sympathetic to it', and that if the appeal fails there would have to be a re-negotiation of the leases 'for pragmatic if not for legal reasons'. She wished it to be stated openly that:

'she is willing for the appellants' leases to be renegotiated on terms that would, among other things, involve the leases being varied by substituting an adjustment linked to the Consumer Price Inflation index instead of the current fixed adjustment of 10% per annum.'

[156] Although on its face this indication seems helpful and realistic, it is not clear what it would mean in practical terms. It rightly acknowledges that the problems may well be incapable of truly satisfactory resolution by conventional legal analysis. The main obstacle may be that hinted at in Mr Daiches' post-hearing submission. That is the need to find some way of making good the shortfall resulting from the unrealistically low contributions required from more than two-thirds of the lessees under the pre-1980 leases. Even if the lessees' interpretation prevails, it will still leave an unhappy imbalance

between these lessees, and the version 1 lessees, who will be left paying substantially less than their proportionate share.

[157] Whatever the strict legal position, the other lessees may perhaps be persuaded that they have a common interest in the good management of the estate, and at least a moral obligation to contribute their fair share of its costs. A long-running dispute of this kind can hardly be conducive to the atmosphere appropriate to a holiday location, even for those not directly involved. It is to be hoped that some way can be found of bringing them into the discussions. On any view, the case seems to cry out for expert mediation, if it has not been attempted before, preferably not confined to the present parties. If thought appropriate, one possibility might be an application by consent to the President of the First-Tier Tribunal (Property Chamber—Residential Property) to appoint as mediator a senior judge of that tribunal, with the benefit of that tribunal's experience of dealing with service charge issues under statute. However, that must be a matter for the parties not this court.

[158] It is necessary therefore to return to the essential question: what in the view of a reasonable observer did clause 3(2) mean? It will be apparent from my detailed analysis that I regard the consequences of the lessor's interpretation as so commercially improbable that only the clearest words would justify the court in adopting it. I agree with Judge Jarman QC that the limited addition proposed by the lessees does not do such violence to the contractual language as to justify a result which is commercial nonsense.

[159] For these reasons, in respectful disagreement with the majority, I would have allowed the appeal and restored the order of Judge Jarman QC."

Although only a model framework and therefore not part of the law of Scotland, the DCFR attempts to provide a common framework for the interpretation of contracts. The DCFR was a major consideration in the Scottish Law Commission's Discussion Paper No.147 on *Interpretation of Contracts* and the relevant sections from Ch.8 (Interpretation) s.1 (Interpretation of contracts) are reproduced here.

"DCFR II.–8:101: General rules 8–107

(1) A contract is to be interpreted according to the common intention of the parties even if this differs from the literal meaning of the words.

(2) If one party intended the contract, or a term or expression used in it, to have a particular meaning, and at the time of the conclusion of the contract the other party was aware, or could reasonably be expected to have been aware, of the first party's intention, the contract is to be interpreted in the way intended by the first party.

(3) The contract is, however, to be interpreted according to the meaning which a reasonable person would give to it:

(a) if an intention cannot be established under the preceding paragraphs; or
(b) if the question arises with a person, not being a party to the contract or a person who by law has no better rights than such a party, who has reasonably and in good faith relied on the contract's apparent meaning.

II.–8:102: Relevant matters 8–108

(1) In interpreting the contract, regard may be had, in particular, to:

(a) the circumstances in which it was concluded, including the preliminary negotiations;
(b) the conduct of the parties, even subsequent to the conclusion of the contract;

(c) the interpretation which has already been given by the parties to terms or expressions which are the same as, or similar to, those used in the contract and the practices they have established between themselves;
(d) the meaning commonly given to such terms or expressions in the branch of activity concerned and the interpretation such terms or expressions may already have received;
(e) the nature and purpose of the contract;
(f) usages; and
(g) good faith and fair dealing.

(2) In a question with a person, not being a party to the contract or a person such as an assignee who by law has no better rights than such a party, who has reasonably and in good faith relied on the contract's apparent meaning, regard may be had to the circumstances mentioned in sub-paragraphs (a) to (c) above only to the extent that those circumstances were known to, or could reasonably be expected to have been known to, that person.

8–109 **II.–8:103: Interpretation against supplier of term or dominant party**

(1) Where there is doubt about the meaning of a term not individually negotiated, an interpretation of the term against the party who supplied it is to be preferred.
(2) Where there is doubt about the meaning of any other term, and that term has been established under the dominant influence of one party, an interpretation of the term against that party is to be preferred.

8–110 **II.–8:104: Preference for negotiated terms**

Terms which have been individually negotiated take preference over those which have not.

8–111 **II.–8:105: Reference to contract as a whole**

Terms and expressions are to be interpreted in the light of the whole contract in which they appear.

8–112 **II.–8:106: Preference for interpretation which gives terms effect**

An interpretation which renders the terms of the contract lawful, or effective, is to be preferred to one which would not.

8–113 **II.–8:107: Linguistic discrepancies**

Where a contract document is in two or more language versions none of which is stated to be authoritative, there is, in case of discrepancy between the versions, a preference for the interpretation according to the version in which the contract was originally drawn up.

Section 2: Interpretation of other juridical acts

8–114 **II.–8:201: General rules**

(1) A unilateral juridical act is to be interpreted in the way in which it could reasonably be expected to be understood by the person to whom it is addressed.
(2) If the person making the juridical act intended the act, or a term or expression used in it, to have a particular meaning, and at the time of the act the person to whom it was

addressed was aware, or could reasonably be expected to have been aware, of the first person's intention, the act is to be interpreted in the way intended by the first person.

(3) The act is, however, to be interpreted according to the meaning which a reasonable person would give to it:

(a) if neither paragraph (1) nor paragraph (2) applies; or
(b) if the question arises with a person, not being the addressee or a person who by law has no better rights than the addressee, who has reasonably and in good faith relied on the contract's apparent meaning.

II.–8:202: Application of other rules by analogy **8–115**

The provisions of Section 1, apart from its first Article, apply with appropriate adaptations to the interpretation of a juridical act other than a contract."

More recently, the principles enunciated in *Rainy Sky* have been extensively applied in the Scottish courts,[58] and by the Supreme Court[59] in a Scottish appeal.[60] In *Vernon v Crown Aerosols UK Ltd*[61] Lord Tyre summarised the current approach:

> "[12] The lease requires to be read as a whole and given the interpretation that a reasonable person with background knowledge reasonably available to the parties at the time of the contract would have understood them to have meant."

[58] See above, para.8–79.
[59] *Global Port Services (Scotland) Ltd v Global Energy (Holdings) Ltd* [2015] CSIH 42; *Gyle Shopping Centre General Partners Ltd v Marks and Spencer Plc* [2015] CSOH 14; *PDF GP Ltd v Santander UK Plc* [2015] CSOH 40; *NHS24 v Capgemini UK Plc* [2015] CSOH 54.
[60] *L Barley Pet Products Ltd v North Lanarkshire Council* [2014] UKSC 27; 2014 S.C. (UKSC) 174.
[61] *Vernon v Crown Aerosols UK Ltd* [2015] CSOH 58.

Chapter 9

IMPORTATION OF TERMS

Importation of terms from prior negotiations

The previous chapter considered the extent to which terms might be *implied* into a contract from other sources, such as custom, statute, etc. This chapter will deal with the extent to which terms may be *incorporated* into the contract from sources other than the contract itself. Often that source will be a written document, but even in an unwritten contract terms might be incorporated from other sources, written or otherwise. 9–01

The incorporation of terms into a written contract from other sources, such as pre-contractual negotiations

The inadmissibility of pre-contractual negotiations in the interpretation of contracts was considered in the preceding chapter. The status of such negotiations as a source of terms to be incorporated into a written contract is a different matter. The rule before 1997—the "parole evidence" rule[1]—was that where a contract appeared to be embodied entirely in writing, extrinsic evidence, whether written or oral, was not admissible for the purpose of proving additional terms. The rule was abolished by the Contract (Scotland) Act 1997 and replaced by a rebuttable presumption that a contract document which appears to contain all the express terms does, in fact, do so. 9–02

Contract (Scotland) Act 1997 9–03
Ch.341

"(1) Where a document appears (or two or more documents appear) to comprise all the express terms of a contract or unilateral voluntary obligation, it shall be presumed, unless the contrary is proved, that the document does (or the documents do) comprise all the express terms of the contract or unilateral voluntary obligation.

(2) Extrinsic oral or documentary evidence shall be admissible to prove, for the purposes of subsection (1) above, that the contract or unilateral voluntary obligation includes additional express terms (whether or not written terms).

(3) Notwithstanding the foregoing provisions of this section, where one of the terms in the document (or in the documents) is to the effect that the document does (or the documents do) comprise all the express terms of the contract or unilateral voluntary obligation, that term shall be conclusive in the matter.

(4) This section is without prejudice to any enactment which makes provision as respects the constitution, or formalities of execution, of a contract or unilateral voluntary obligation."

As stated above, the effect of this section is to replace the "parole evidence" rule with the rebuttable presumption stated in s.1. The Contract (Scotland) Act 1997 (the 1997 Act) was based directly on the recommendations in and the attached draft bill attached to the Scottish Law Commission's *Report on Three Bad Rules in Contract* (Scot Law Com No.152 (10 January 1996)). The fact that additional terms can now be proved does not mean that they are formally

[1] The rule still applies in England.

valid (for instance, a term creating, varying or extinguishing an interest in land would have to comply with the provisions of the Requirements of Writing (Scotland) Act 1995).[2] Similarly, the fact that an additional term may now more easily be proved does not alter its effect once proved.[3]

It should also be noted that s.1 of the 1997 Act refers to "express terms". The position relating to *implied* terms, therefore, remains unaffected.

9–04 *Three Bad Rules in Contract*
Scottish Law Commission No.152 (January 10, 1996)

"**Assessment and recommendation**

2.34 We would not wish to underestimate in any way the advantages of having contracts reduced to final written form or the advantages of being able to rely on such contractual documents as the sole source of the terms of the contract where that is what the parties have intended. Where the parties take the trouble to prepare an apparently complete contractual document we think that it is reasonable to suppose that in most cases their intention will have been to regard that document as containing all the express contractual terms agreed up to that point, even if the document does not contain a clause making this clear. The defect in the existing law is not that it proceeds on this basis but that it does so in a rigid way which leaves no room for exceptional cases, and which is therefore liable to produce manifest injustice. For this reason we think that the most appropriate reform would be the replacement of the present rule on proof of additional contract terms—which is in effect, in those cases where no exception applies, an irrefutable presumption that a document which looks like a complete contract is the complete contract—with a rebuttable presumption to the same effect. Outright abolition of the rule would not contain the same overt recognition of the useful role of contractual documents and it would look like a more violent break with the existing law. Two separate consultations, in 1980 and again in 1994, produced majority support for a rebuttable presumption rather than outright abolition of the rule on proof of additional terms."

The incorporation of pre-contractual representations and warranties into a contract

9–05 There will also be cases where the parties have said or done things which do not conform with what they eventually reduced to writing. There may be things said in the course of negotiations leading up to the contract; are they merely representations which, if they turn out to be false, will amount to misrepresentations; or are they actually terms of the contract? The substance of a contract will always depend upon evidence of what the parties agreed. In many ordinary contracts, all but the simplest terms of an agreement may be implied, either by common law or, as is often the case today, by statute.

How is it determined whether a particular statement is part of the contract, rather than a mere representation leading up to the contract? The basic rule is that a statement is a stipulation of the contract if it was intended by the parties to be so. This intention is sometimes expressly stated. Insurance proposal forms, for example, clearly state that answers to questions will form the basis of the contract. Where there is no such express intention, it may be inferred from surrounding facts. In so doing, courts are guided by various factors. There is relatively little Scottish case law on the subject, but the following questions might relevantly be asked:

---

[2] Scottish Law Commission, *Report on Three Bad Rules in Contract* (Scot Law Com. No.152 (10 January 1996)), para.2.30.

[3] Scottish Law Commission, *Report on Three Bad Rules in Contract* (Scot Law Com No.152 (10 January 1996)), para.2.31.

Question 1: At what stage of the transaction was the statement made? A statement is not a contractual stipulation if it is part of preliminary negotiations leading up to the contract. The longer the time lapse between the making of the statement and the making of the contract, the less likely that the statement is a term. It is not necessary that the statement be made at the time of making the contract, but it must be operative at that time. In *Bannerman v White*,[4] a prospective buyer of hops said he was not interested if the hops had been treated with sulphur. The seller said they had not and negotiations resulted in a sale. When he subsequently discovered that only some of the hops had been sulphur treated, the buyer was held entitled to treat the seller's statement as a term of the contract that had been broken. In *Routledge v McKay*,[5] however, a statement by a seller (relying on information in the vehicle's registration book), on 23 October, that a motor cycle was a 1942 model was not a term in a written contract of sale made on 30 October. (The motor cycle turned out to be a 1930 model!) The following two cases provide a useful contrast on whether a representation or warranty has been incorporated. **9–06**

Scott v Steel **9–07**

Court of Session, Inner House, Second Division: Lord Justice-Clerk (Hope); Lords Murray, Wood and Cowan.

(1857) 20 D. 253

Scott, a farmer in Craiglockhart, brought this action against Steel, a horse-dealer, for repetition "of the sum of £65 sterling, being the price of a bay horse" sold to him by Steel. At the time of sale Steel warranted the horse "to be quiet to ride and steady in harness". That same afternoon the horse proved restive and refractory" when ridden by Scott and a few days later,

> "when yoked in a car, he ran backwards, and brought the wheel of the car on a wall, and that this was done twice, and that, on another occasion, about a week afterwards, the said horse also shewed a restive disposition, and that for a considerable time".

"LORD JUSTICE-CLERK (HOPE): ... I have no doubt that the horse was bought on representation. **9–08**

The pursuer tried him, and thereafter put the question, "Is the horse steady in harness, and quiet to ride?" and the defender said he was. On that representation the horse was bought. It is quite true he did not use the words, 'I warrant'; but he did make such a representation as the purchaser showed was essential in his mind to make him buy the horse. There was an assurance given in order to induce him to complete the sale; and the representation is all the stronger, that the question put showed that the purchase was to be made for Scott's own use, not for resale. Much stress was laid upon the pursuer's trial of the horse. That seems to me here of little moment ...

LORD WOOD: On the evidence I think it clear that a representation was made on which the purchaser was entitled to rely, and did rely—the representation so made, according to the law of Scotland, amounting to a warranty. Then I do not think that the trial at the time of the sale took off the effect of it, and threw it on the purchaser to satisfy himself as to the qualities of the horse. For after the trial, and while writing out the cheque, he said, 'Are you sure the horse is steady in harness, and quiet to ride?' and thus the sale did not come to depend on the trial, but rested on the representation. Well, if there was warranty, assuredly the horse did not come up to it ... **9–09**

---

[4] *Bannerman v White* (1861) 10 C.B.N.S. 844.

[5] *Routledge v McKay* [1954] 1 All E.R. 855.

9–10 LORD COWAN: I have no doubt upon the first point. There was express warrandice; and this is the foundation of the pursuer's claim. The words 'I warrant' are not required. It is quite enough that the purchaser says he wishes a horse for a particular purpose; and that the seller says the horse will suit for that purpose. That is quite as good as the use of express words of warrandice.

The doubtful part of the case is in the evidence as to the alleged unfitness of the horse for the purpose warranted . . . I have the greatest hesitation in holding the evidence of the purchaser and his groom sufficient to establish that the horse did not come up to the warranty . . .

On the whole, I have great doubt as to the result on the proof to which your Lordships have come."

Note the use by Lord Cowan of "warrandice" rather than warranty. The use of the expression "warrandice" in modern usage is restricted to a clause, usually in a disposition of land, guaranteeing that the land being sold is, in fact, owned by the seller.

9–11 **Paul & Co v Corporation of Glasgow**

Court of Session, Inner House, Second Division: Lord Justice-Clerk (Lord Kingsburgh), Lords Kincairney, Young Trayner and Moncreiff

(1900) 3 F. 119

Paul & Co were the sole licencees and makers of an apparatus known in the trade as "Patterson's Smoke-Prevention Suction Draught for Land and Marine Boilers".

In March 1897 Paul & Company wrote to the engineer of the Corporation of Glasgow calling his attention to their apparatus as a means of both increasing boiler capacity and largely reducing or entirely preventing smoke; and also enclosing a circular, in which it was stated that "The smoke prevention is absolute, and is attained by a proper arrangement of . . . ", etc.

In March 1898 the Corporation by letter accepted a written offer by Paul & Company to install their apparatus at a price stated. Neither the offer nor the acceptance contained any reference to the circular.

The apparatus having been erected, and the Corporation having thereafter rejected it as disconform to contract, Paul & Company brought an action against the Corporation for the price.

The defenders denied that the pursuers had implemented their contract, and stated—that they, the defenders, had ordered the installation, "relying on the statements and warranty contained in the said circular", and—that the apparatus erected did not prevent smoke. They pleaded that the apparatus supplied being disconform to warranty and having been rejected they ought to be assoilzied.

9–12 "LORD JUSTICE-CLERK [LORD KINGSBURGH].

. . . The order and the supply of the article ordered not being denied, the question is narrowed down to this point, whether the defenders have upon record any statements relevant to be remitted to probation for the purpose of proving that the pursuers gave a warranty which they have failed to make good. Now, the only warranty alleged is that already referred to, namely, the trade circular containing the statement above quoted. But the fact is stated, and not denied, that that circular was sent to the defenders, not at the time of the bargain of sale, but many months before any negotiations for a sale took place between the parties. It was sent on 9th March 1897, and no communication took place between the parties until 27th of December of the same year. It is thus plain that the circular was sent as an advertising circular only, stating that the pursuers had an article to sell of which they expressed a high opinion as to its efficiency for the purpose for which it was intended. I am unable to see how the sending of that circular in the spring of 1897 can be held to be a warranty in regard to a sale of a specific article which did not take place till January 1898 by offer and acceptance, and in which no allusion is made to any statements regarding the efficiency of the apparatus contained in the trade circular. It was frankly admitted by Mr Lees in his argument that if the letters of contract did not embody the circular, there was no warranty upon which he could support his case. Being of opinion, as I have already said, that the circular cannot be connected with the letters so as to make it part of the contract, even assuming that what was contained in the circular might constitute a warranty, I must hold that the defenders have no relevant defence to the demand that, having purchased a specified article, they should pay the price. I see no ground for allowing the defenders a proof. I do not see any averment by them, which, if they could prove it, would be an answer to the pursuers' case, and, therefore, I move your Lordships to recall the Lord Ordinary's interlocutor, and to grant decree.

LORD YOUNG. **9–13**

—I differ from the opinion which your Lordship has expressed, and agree with the Lord Ordinary, that we cannot decide this case without evidence ...

LORD TRAYNER. **9–14**

... The only question therefore is, did the pursuers warrant the apparatus as the defenders allege? There is here no case for implied warranty, for according to the provisions of the Sale of Goods Act, 1893 (sec. 14, subsec. 1), when an article is sold by its patent or trade-name (as this apparatus was), there is no implied condition as to its fitness for any particular purpose. The warranty therefore, must be express; and as the contract was in writing, it is to the contract we must look for the warranty, if it exists.

... But we are not called on to consider whether the terms of the circular amounted to warranty, or merely to the laudation of his goods by a seller, which the buyer must check for himself, because neither the circular nor the letter of 9th March 1897 are made part of or even referred to in the contract, which was not made until March 1898. The contract then made contains no allusion to the results which the apparatus is calculated or expected to produce. Its smoke-preventing capacity or quality is not mentioned. The only defence to this action, however, is that the pursuers warranted that the apparatus would prevent smoke, and that this warranty had not been fulfilled. I think it plain, on the terms of the contract, that there was no warranty, and that therefore there could not be the breach of warranty on which the defenders alone rely. The defence accordingly, in my opinion, fails, and the pursuers are entitled to decree.

LORD MONCREIFF. **9–15**

...

The question remains whether there was an express warranty. The letters which constitute the contract do not contain one. The circular, which was sent a year before, is not imported. But if we can look at the circular it does not contain a warranty. What is contained in the circular is, at most, an undue laudation of the pursuers' patent."

The difference in this case was the great lapse of time between the making of the statement and the making of the contract.

There is a suggestion, in English law at least, that the time at which the statement was made is not the only relevant factor.

Question 2: Does the person making the statement have or profess to have special skill or knowledge? If so, their statement is more likely to be regarded as a term. It is by no means clear **9–16** whether this principle would be applied by a Scottish court,[6] since its application can only be illustrated by reference to some of the English decisions which must be considered with great caution.

Oscar Chess Ltd v Williams
[1957] 1 All E.R. 325
English Court of Appeal: Denning, Hodson and Morris, LJJ

Williams offered his "Morris 10 saloon" in part-exchange for a "Hillman Minx". After consulting the registration book, Williams stated that the Morris was a 1948 model. Chess agreed to allow £290 part exchange. The Morris turned out to be a 1939 model, with a trade-in price of £175. The appearance of the Morris 10 saloon had not changed between 1939 and 1948. A majority of the court found that Chess was not entitled to recover from Williams the difference between the two trade-in prices. In the course of his judgment Denning LJ made the following comments.

9–17 "DENNING LJ: ... It seems to me clear that the plaintiffs, the motor dealers who bought the car, relied on the year stated in the log-book. If they had wished to make sure of it, they could have checked it then and there, by taking the engine number and chassis number and writing to the makers. They did not do so at the time, but only eight months later. They are experts, and, as they did not make that check at the time, I do not think that they should now be allowed to recover against the innocent seller who produced to them all the evidence which he had, namely, the registration book. I agree that it is hard on the plaintiffs to have paid more than the car is worth, but it would be equally hard on the seller to make him pay the difference. He would never have bought the Hillman car unless he had received the allowance of £290 for the Morris car. The best course in all these cases would be to 'shunt' the difference down the train of innocent sellers until one reached the rogue who perpetrated the fraud; but he can rarely be traced, or if he can, he rarely has the money to pay the damages. Therefore, one is left to decide between a number of innocent people who is to bear the loss. That can only be done by applying the law about representations and warranties as we know it, and that is what I have tried to do. If the rogue can be traced, he can be sued by whomsoever has suffered the loss: but, if he cannot be traced, the loss must lie where it falls. It should not be inflicted on innocent sellers, who sold the car many months, perhaps many years before, and have forgotten all about it and have conducted their affairs on the basis that the transaction was concluded. Such a seller would not be able to recollect after all this length of time the exact words which he used, such as whether he said 'I believe it is a 1948 model', or 'I warrant it is a 1948 model.' The right course is to let the buyer set aside the transaction if he finds out the mistake quickly and comes promptly before other interests have irretrievably intervened, otherwise the loss must lie where it falls: and that is, I think, the course prescribed by law. I would allow this appeal accordingly."

Lord Denning was dealing with what would be an innocent misrepresentation, if the statement could not be incorporated into the contract as a term. At that time, as is still the law in Scotland, no damages were available for innocent misrepresentation in England. By holding that the statement was not incorporated into the contract because the maker of the statement did not have relatively superior knowledge, the statement would be treated as an innocent

[6] WW McBryde, *The Law of Contract in Scotland*, 3rd edn (Edinburgh: W. Green, 2007), paras 5–48—5–53.

misrepresentation, so that no damages could be recovered. Although Lord Denning would have been unwilling to imply the terms partly on the basis of the relative expertise of the garage, neither Hodson LJ nor Morris LJ (who, in his dissenting judgment, was prepared to incorporate the statement as a term on other grounds) even considered doing so. Furthermore, Lord Denning himself distinguished the case in the following judgment.

Dick Bentley Productions Ltd v Harold Smith (Motors) Ltd 9–18
[1965] 1 W.L.R. 623
English Court of Appeal: Lord Denning MR, Danckwerts and Salmon LJJ

Bentley, a well-known U.S. entertainer, was seeking a well-vetted British car. Smith said he had a "Bentley drop-head coupé" owned only by a German baron and had only done 20,000 miles since being fitted with a new engine and gearbox. Bentley bought the car for £1,850, but found it unsatisfactory and the stated mileage untrue. Smith's erroneous statement regarding the mileage was held to be a term of the contract, more than a mere misrepresentation.

"LORD DENNING, MR: ... In the *Oscar Chess* case ... a man had bought a second-hand car and received with it a log-book, which stated the year of the car; 1948. He afterwards resold the car. When he resold it he simply repeated what was in the log-book and passed it on to the buyer. He honestly believed on reasonable grounds that it was true. He was completely innocent of any fault. There was no warranty by him but only an innocent misrepresentation. Whereas in the present case it is very different. The inference is not rebutted. Here we have a dealer, Mr. Smith, who was in a position to know, or at least to find out, the history of the car. He could get it by writing to the makers. He did not do so. Indeed it was done later. When the history of this car was examined, his statement turned out to be quite wrong. He ought to have known better. There was no reasonable foundation for it."

The statement here was made not by the consumer/purchaser, but by the garage. It was relatively easy to show that the garage had superior skill and knowledge and thereby to incorporate the statement into the contract. Would a Scots court merely regard them as misrepresentations?

The Misrepresentation Act 1967 s.2(a), created a limited right to claim damages, in England, for innocent misrepresentation. This has limited the need to show that the statement was a term in the contract (but see *Esso Petroleum v Mardon*[7]). Would it be possible, in Scotland, where no damages can be recovered for an innocent misrepresentation, to seek damages on the basis that the statement was incorporated into the contract?

A statement prior to the agreement, made in the course of negotiations, will not normally be a term, although it may be a representation, as was made clear in Ch.6. If so, the remedies for misrepresentation will apply if it turns out to be false. If, however, a statement is made after agreement has been reached, it can never be incorporated into the contract. As Lord Justice-Clerk Wheatley stated in *CEA Airexchangers Ltd v James Howden & Co Ltd*[8]:

> "I would regard reference to communings between parties subsequent to the conclusion of a contract as being irrelevant to the definition of the terms of the contract if such communings are not averred to have constituted an agreement to have the contract modified in a certain way as a result thereof."

[7] See above, para.6–102.
[8] *CEA Airexchangers Ltd v James Howden & Co Ltd*, 1984 S.L.T. 264.

Collateral contracts

9–19 Even if a statement does not amount to a misrepresentation or a term of the contract, it may be considered a collateral contract which exists independently of the main contract, but is collateral to it. Prior to the Contract (Scotland) Act 1997, the "parole evidence" rule meant that proving such agreements was difficult (since, for instance, an agreement in writing could not be contradicted or added to by oral terms). Cases such as that below are therefore very unusual.

9–20 **McKillop v Mutual Securities Ltd**
1945 S.C. 166
Court of Session, First Division: The Lord President (Normand), Lords Moncrieff and Stevenson

By an exchange of letters with the defenders, Mrs McKillop purchased in 1935 a shop which was being erected at 59–85 Kilmarnock Road, Glasgow. In one of their letters forming the contract, the defenders undertook to "complete the frontage of the shop according to the description thereof ... in ... the plan and specification".

Mrs McKillop came into occupancy of the shop in 1936. In 1942 the premises became dangerous because of a latent structural defect.

Mrs McKillop now claimed, inter alia, the cost of repairs from the defenders, on the ground that, if the contract was for the sale of the shop, they had breached a collateral obligation to ensure that the building would be erected with proper skill and materials.

Recalling the judgment of the sheriff, the Inner House held that Mrs McKillop's averments were relevant to infer such an obligation on the part of the defenders, and allowed a proof before answer.

9–21 "LORD MONCRIEFF: ... (The defenders' offer can be construed) as an offer of a twofold nature: an offer on the one hand upon completion of the shop to convey it to the pursuer in return for the price, and a further offer immediately to undertake and complete the erection of the shop as being a shop which the seller had become bound to erect for the purchaser. The ... offer makes this even more clear, because it bears that the sellers will complete the frontage of the shop according to a certain description and plan. I can imagine no undertaking more habile to indicate that the sellers were charging themselves at the call of the purchaser with the duty of completing the erection of the shop and of carrying to a conclusion the work of erection ... I cannot conceive that the sellers would have undertaken this work of construction had they not recognised that they were bound to do so under the obligations which they had assumed ...

No doubt when the parties are at issue as to the purport of certain matters regulated *ad interim* by the missives, as for example as regards the subjects of sale, a formal document which also purports to deal with the same matter will displace the less formal writings which had preceded it. But if in the missives there be not only an agreement for the purchase and sale but be also, as I have suggested there is here, a second independent but collateral agreement for the doing of supplementary work and the doing of that work skilfully, such an independent agreement will not be discharged by the taking of a formal disposition, seeing that the formal disposition does not enter into the area of that particular separate agreement."

LORD PRESIDENT (NORMAND) and LORD STEVENSON agreed with LORD MONCRIEFF.

In English law, a statement could be regarded as a collateral warranty, that is, a common law obligation which exists apart from the contract, but is collateral to it. In *Brown v Sheen & Richmond Car Sales Ltd*,[9] the salesman stated that the car would give "thousands of trouble-free miles". The customer entered into a hire-purchase contract with a finance company on the strength of the statement, which turned out expensively false. Nevertheless the statement was a contract with the garage, collateral to the hire-purchase contract, and the customer was entitled to damages: similarly in *Andrews v Hopkinson*,[10] where the dealer maladroitly said: "she's a good little bus; I would stake my life on it", he was liable when the car turned out to be unroadworthy. The following case indicates that collateral warranty, or indeed collateral contract is not readily recognisable in Scots law and certainly does not have the meaning and import (if it has any import at all) that it has in English law.

Royal Bank of Scotland Plc v Carlyle 9–22

[2013] CSIH 75; 2013 W.L. 5328729

Court of Session, Inner House, Second Division: Lord Justice Clerk (Lord Carloway), Lady Dorrian, Lord Bracadale

Mr. Carlyle was a property developer specialising in private housing, who would buy land with the assistance of loans from RBS, build a new house on it, live in it for a limited period and then sell it at a profit.

In April 2007 Mr. Carlyle's tenders (one on his own behalf at £1,350,000 and one on behalf of Carlyco, a company that he owned and controlled, at £995,000) to purchase two plots of land at Gleneagles were accepted. In the negotiations and eventually in the missives of sale the sellers reserved a right to re-purchase (buy-back) the land if the building was not completed by March 2011.

Before completing missives, Mr Carlyle approached RBS, with whom he had dealt before in building development transactions. He sought funding for the deposit to purchase the properties and for the cost of building the properties in the land. Mr Carlyle also indicated that, as on previous occasions when he had dealt with RBS, he would require the necessary funding to carry out the development of the land purchased. He also pointed out that the sale would be subject to a buy-back clause.

After lengthy consultations between Mr Carlyle and staff at the RBS Hamilton branch, Ms Hamilton from that branch telephone Mr Carlyle on 14 June 2007 stating: "You'll be pleased to know it's all approved. Edinburgh [RBS head office] are going for it for both houses".

On that basis Mr Carlyle instructed his solicitor to pay the deposits on the plots and, at that point, he became "committed to the project". On 21 June 2007 he signed a document entitled "Credit Approved Indicative Terms for Carlyco Limited" for an advance of £2,587,000 for the purchase of both plots at £2,350,000. The agreement was secured against both plots and some property in Bothwell belonging to Mr Carlyle. It contained no reference to funding for building.

On 24 July 2007 Mr Carlyle signed two documents, dated 24 and 25 June 2007 and headed "Bridging Finance Agreement", which took the form of an offer and acceptance, for the advancement of £845,000 and £560,000 "to assist with the purchase of" the plot; with repayment 12 months from the draw down of the monies; security over the Bothwell properties and the plot, with interest.

In about November 2007, when RBS began to ask when building funding would be required, Mr Carlyle advised that this would not be until March 2008. In August 2008, the defender was told that no further funding would be made available.

[9] *Brown v Sheen & Richmond Car Sales Ltd* [1950] 1 A11 E.R. 1102.
[10] *Andrews v Hopkinson* [1957] 1 Q.B. 229.

In this action, RBS claimed repayment of £845,000 and £560,000, with interest, which they lent for use in the purchase of the land at Gleneagles. Mr Carlyle counterclaimed damages of £1,500,000 for a material breach by RBS of a "collateral warranty" given by RBS in advance of the signing of the agreements, notably in the telephone conversation with Ms Hutchison, on 21 June 2007 that RBS would, in addition to the sums lent to buy the land, advance further "funding for the development".

9–23 "LORD JUSTICE CLERK (LORD CARLOWAY): ...

The commercial judge's consideration of the law and his conclusions

26 At the proof, the pursuers were content to accept (para [38]) that there existed in Scots law a legal concept called a 'collateral warranty' which could be created if a party to a contract provided antecedent assurances to the other about matters not covered by the contract. The commercial judge was referred by the defender to a number of cases, all under English law, and notably to *dicta* of Lord Denning MR in *Dick Bentley Productions v Harold Smith (Motors)* [1965] 1 WLR 623, (at 627) and *J Evans & Son (Portsmouth) v Andrea Merzario* [1976] 1 WLR 1078 (at 1081). However, it is worth observing *in limine* that the commercial judge may have been uneasy with this concept as he refers almost immediately in his analysis not just to a collateral *warranty*, which is what is pled on record, but to a collateral *contract*, misrepresentation inducing contract and promise, none of which is pled. He expands on this as follows:

'[37] There is no magic in a collateral warranty or contract. It is simply a contract, usually oral, which is collateral or ancillary to another contract (the principal contract) between the same parties. Its existence, formation and interpretation are governed by the same rules as apply to similar questions in relation to other contracts. Its peculiarity, if it can be called that, lies in its relationship to another (the principal) contract between the parties. Classically, a collateral contract is derived from a representation or promise made by one party to the other in the course of the negotiations for the principal contract, which representation or promise is intended to have binding effect (notwithstanding that it is not included in the terms of the principal contract), on the strength of which the person to whom the representation or promise is made agrees to enter into the principal contract.'

27 The commercial judge did note the words of caution delivered by Lord Moulton in *Heilbut, Symons & Co v Buckleton* [1913] AC 30 (at 47) upon the rarity of collateral contracts. He went on to quote the five propositions which Lightman J identified in *Inntrepreneur Pub Co (GL) v East Crown* [2000] 2 Lloyd's Rep 611 (at para 10) as pertaining to 'pre-contractual promises or assurances as collateral warranties' and continued:

'[40] I have already found that in the telephone conversation of 14 June 2007, Ms Hutchison made a statement which, viewed objectively in the context of what had gone on before, meant that the [pursuers were] committing [themselves] to providing the development funding ... The defender was entitled ... to take the view that the state of his indebtedness was a matter which the [pursuers] had already taken into account. The [pursuers] knew from what the defender had said on more than one occasion, that the defender was not going to go ahead with the purchase unless he had an assurance that he would get the development funding. In those circumstances I have no doubt that, viewed objectively, the [pursuers'] statement (which was reasonably interpreted to be such an assurance) was intended to be binding or, as it is sometimes put, to have contractual effect; and was reasonably understood as such ...

[41] . . . the defender has made good his case that the [pursuers] gave him an assurance that funding would be made available for the development . . . in an amount of up to £700,000. [The pursuers] did so in circumstances where [the pursuers] knew (or ought to have known) that he was waiting for such an assurance before committing himself to the purchase. [They] knew, therefore, that he would rely on that assurance in going ahead with the purchase and entering into loan agreements with the [pursuers]. He did rely on it in the manner anticipated. The case for collateral warranty had (*sic*) been made out.'

Under reference to *R & J Dempster v Motherwell Bridge and Engineering Co* 1964 SC 308 (LP (Clyde) at 328), the commercial judge did not consider that the absence of an express agreement on the amount of the loan, the term of that loan or the rate of interest rendered the 'promise or assurance' (para [42]) too vague.

28 In his subsequent Note (*supra*), the commercial judge addressed the issue raised by the pursuers of whether what the pursuers had undertaken was a unilateral promise or a bilateral agreement. He responded (para [9]):

'I had decided that the [pursuers] had given an *unconditional commitment* (*emphasis added*), and although I had put it in terms of a bilateral agreement it did not seem to me to make any difference if it were put in terms of a unilateral promise in circumstances where the defender had proceeded with the transaction on the strength of the promise.'

. . .

Decision

[50] It is of the essence of the law of voluntary obligations that a party who seeks to enforce, what he maintains is, an obligation upon another is able to identify both the source and nature of that obligation. He must be able to point to words and deeds on the part of the other party which are said to have created the obligation and to specify the extent of the obligation thus arising. It will not do for a party to say simply that an obligation has somehow been created, if he cannot demonstrate where it came from and what it obliges the other party to do. Where, after a contested proof, the court considers that an obligation has been breached, it is equally important that the court specify the source and nature of that obligation. If the obligation arises from contract, it will normally be necessary also for the party and the court to identify the essential terms of that contract. **9–24**

51 A voluntary obligation can arise, and generally only arise, in two different ways (see eg Black: *"Obligations"*; Stair Memorial Encyclopaedia vol 15, para 611). It can be created by a contract between two parties; in which case there are usually, but not always, obligations on both parties. It can also be created by one party making a promise to the other; in which case the obligation will be a unilateral one, albeit that it may be the subject of conditions which must be purified by the other party. The creation of a voluntary obligation falls to be distinguished from the existence of a representation made by a party in advance of contracting which may not form part of a later contract, but which may have induced the party to enter into that contract.

52 It may be, as the commercial judge put it, that there is no 'magic' in a 'collateral warranty'. However, when two such words are used in legal pleading, they each have a well known meaning. First, a warranty in Scots Law is a term of a contract (see McBryde: *Contract* (3rd ed) para 20-93; and notably Smith: *Short Commentary* at 766). It is not something which exists as a free standing legal entity outwith a contract. It is not the same as an 'assurance', which may or may not be a term of a contract. Secondly, if something is to be regarded as 'collateral', it must be linked to a principal item. If something is described as a collateral warranty, it must be taken to relate to a term of an existing contract which is collateral to another, different, contract (cf a collateral undertaking in *British Workman's and General Assurance Co v Wilkinson* (1900) 8 SLT 67).

53 A representation may amount to a warranty, in the sense of being a term of a contract, when, at or about the time of contracting, what is said relates to the subject matter of the contract. Thus, classically, in a contract of sale, where the representation concerns the conformity of the item for sale with a given description, that conformity will be taken to be a term of the contract, if that is what can be deduced as being what the parties intended (*Hyslop v Shirlaw* (1905) 7 F 875, Lord Kyllachy at 881; *McInally v Esso Petroleum Co* 1965 SLT (Notes) 13; cf the approach in England in *Dick Bentley Productions v Harold Smith (Motors)* [1965] 1 WLR 623 and *Inntrepreneur Pub Co (GL) v East Crown* [2000] 2 Lloyd's Rep 611, which will often achieve a similar practical result). That exercise in deduction is an objective one. As the Lord President (Dunedin) said in *Muirhead & Turnbull v Dickson* (1905) 7 F 686 (at 694): 'commercial contracts cannot be arranged by what people think in their inmost minds. Commercial contracts are made according to what people say'.

54 For an obligation to arise, the words (and deeds) must objectively convey that a party is thereby committing himself to be legally bound to do something. In the case of a contract, there must be agreement on all the essentials of the particular contract; a sound test for whether that has occurred being whether the obligation said to have arisen can be enforced in practical terms (*McArthur v Lawson* (1877) 4 R 1134, LP (Inglis) at 1135–6). Equally, if it is said that a party has promised to enter into a contract (eg of loan), the essentials of that contract must be readily capable of ascertainment. An agreement or a promise to enter into a contract, where the essentials are not ascertainable, cannot be regarded as legally binding. It is always a matter of fact whether a particular feature is an essential element and the court will be anxious to give validity to agreements or promises in the commercial sector (*R & J Dempster v Motherwell Bridge and Engineering Co* 1964 SC 301, LP (Clyde) at 328, Lord Guthrie at 332). There will be situations where essential elements will be capable of agreement or ascertainment after a concluded bargain or an unconditional promise has been made, especially where there has been a course of prior dealing.

55 As indicated above, the obligation arising may involve a unilateral obligation created by promise or a unilateral or mutual one created by contract. However, if the import of the circumstances is that the party or parties did not intend to be bound until the obligation was enshrined in a formal, or at least written, contract, then no legal obligation will arise until that is done (McBryde (*supra*) at para 5-41 under reference to *Stobo v Morrisons (Gowns)* 1949 SC 184, LP (Cooper) at 192 and *Van Laun & Co v Neilson Reid & Co* (1904) 6 F 644, LP (Kinross) at 650 and see eg *WS Karoulias v Drambuie Liqueur Co* 2005 SLT 813. Furthermore, if, after a course of dealing, the parties do reduce their bargain to writing, it will normally be presumed that the writing contains the terms of that bargain (Contract (Scotland) Act, s 1). It will be difficult to argue that the terms are different by reason of an earlier statement by one of the parties in relation to a matter specifically provided for, and hence expressly agreed upon, in the writing (*Norval v Abbey* 1939 SC 724, cf an additional term or clarification in *McInally v Esso Petroleum Co* (*supra*); see also *Hanoman v Southwark LBC (No. 2)* [2009] 1 WLR 374, Arden LJ at para 48). The defender's position founders both in relation to the words and deeds said to have created an obligation and, in any event, upon when such an obligation was to become legally binding.

56 The defender maintains that an obligation on the pursuers arose on (or before) 14 June 2007, during the course of a telephone conversation when, after a course of dealings between the parties, the pursuers' employee stated 'It's all approved. Edinburgh are going for it for both houses'. The defender's position is that this created a 'collateral warranty' to the effect that the pursuers would provide funding for his (and his company's) development at Gleneagles, including finance for the building of a house(s) on the plot(s). The commercial judge has sustained the defender's plea to the effect that the

pursuers have breached this 'collateral warranty', albeit that he seems unable to characterise the obligation as arising from contract or promise. He has pronounced a declarator that, in effect, the pursuers are in breach of an obligation to provide development funding of £700,000 by way of a 'loan', albeit that none of the terms of that prospective loan, other than its amount, are specified and where that amount is expressly contradicted by the subsequent written agreements.

57 The court disagrees with the commercial judge's conclusion. On a proper analysis of the parties' dealings, and in particular what was said in the telephone conversation, at most all that the pursuers' employee was doing was advising the defender of an internal decision of the pursuers, which amounted to approval in principle of the proposal to lend the defender (and his company) funding for the development(s). She was not, in so communicating to the defender, creating a legal obligation on the pursuers to lend to the defender (and his company) several million pounds. In this regard, applying the test of the objective observer, such an observer, if informed of the background of dealings between the parties and the defender's knowledge of how the pursuers, like most other banks, operate, would not have regarded what was said as creating such an obligation. Standing the parties' prior dealings and what had happened prior to the telephone conversation, such an obligation could arise only in the event of the parties entering into a written contract to that effect. That is what had happened in the past between the parties. It is what was clear from what was happening in the lead up to the telephone conversation. It is evident from what actually happened after the telephone conversation and, in particular, the production of the Indicative Terms, which the defender signed and which identified in clear written form, the state of the parties' negotiations as acknowledged by the defender's signature at the time. It is clear from the written agreements which the defender in fact entered into.

58 The defender, and to a degree the commercial judge, seek to dismiss the Indicative Terms and the written agreements as mere 'paperwork'; as if they amounted to no more than the written expression of what the parties had already orally agreed. However, since whatever had been said in the telephone conversation made no reference to any of the necessary elements which required to be agreed before any draw down (loan) would be permitted, it is clear that this is not what the writings were intended to be. Rather, in accordance with what the informed observer would expect, it is these documents, and effectively these documents alone, which create, define and express the mutual obligations of the parties in relation to the provision of banking facilities. Without specification of the essential elements of that provision (including the maximum draw down, interest rates, time of drawn down, method and time of repayment and securities), there could be no concluded agreement capable of enforcement. In this context, it is of some significance to note that the defender is a businessman, acting with advice from both an accountant and a solicitor. He has had a course of dealing with the pursuers and he is aware that, whatever oral discussions there may be between himself and the pursuers' local staff, no draw down of funds (ie actual lending) would be permitted unless and until a written contract was entered into between the parties which set out, in detail, the parties' obligations in relation to the funds to be drawn down.

59 One thing is clear, this is not a case of 'collateral warranty'. If the defender were correct to say that the pursuers had "assured" him that full funding for the whole development would be made available, such an assurance could conceivably, in certain circumstances (notably specification of all essential terms), amount to a promise on the pursuers' part in relation to the provision of that entire funding. That is not, of course, the defender's case on record. But even if it were, it can be seen that such an assurance could not be 'collateral' to any other bargain. No other bargain then existed. It cannot be regarded as 'collateral' to the later agreements, which themselves defined different levels of funding and different purposes for that funding. If it existed at all, it would

effectively be an entire obligation in itself stipulating, in particular, the level of funding to be provided. However, it would then be an obligation which would, in due course, be in direct conflict with that to which it is said to be collateral (ie the written agreements). This in itself would be a sufficient basis upon which to reject the defender's counterclaim, since it is not based upon the existence of such an entire or overarching obligation, of which the written agreements constituted only part implement. The defender has not proved his case upon record concerning the existence of a 'collateral warranty' as those terms might be properly understood (see *supra*). Nevertheless, the court would be reluctant to decide the case purely on that basis. Rather, it will set out its view on the import of the telephone conversation as the vehicle for the creation of an obligation.

60 It is no doubt true that the defender had told the pursuers that he required funding for the whole project to be successful and that he would lose money, were his development not to proceed to a conclusion. The commercial judge has found that to be the position and this court has no cause to interfere with his findings of primary fact. He has also found that, in the telephone conversation, Ms Hutchison had said the words which the defender attributed to her. The court proceeds upon the basis that this finding (that 'it's all approved') is sound. It is the import of these words that must be considered. Again, despite the arguments to the contrary by the pursuers, the court will proceed on the basis that what was meant was that approval had been given by 'Edinburgh' for the whole development and not just the purchase funding, even if this does seem to this court to be somewhat improbable. However, quite apart from the generality that major banks do not normally lend private individuals (or companies) millions of pounds (in this case some £3.745M) without setting out the terms and conditions of such a facility in writing, the defender himself knew that, whatever had been said in oral discussions, the parties' obligations would have to be formulated in writing. The defender would have to sign a formal written agreement before he was given access to any funding (see *supra* under reference to Transcript at II, 181). Until that was done, the matter was, as the defender himself put it, a matter of 'trust'.

61 In such circumstances, looked at objectively, all that took place on the telephone was that Ms Hutchison had told the defender of what was effectively approval of funding for the development in principle in accordance with the pursuers' internal procedures. Such a communication could not of itself create a binding legal obligation with the other party and would not be seen by the informed observer to do so. It amounted only to a statement of future intention. Legally binding obligations would, and could, only occur once the appropriate official of the pursuers signed the appropriate offer letter and this was accepted by the defender. Legal obligations thus would only arise by means of a written mutual contract. They would not be created by an expression that the pursuers intended to proceed with the funding (ie by unilateral obligation created by oral promise). They would be created by that later stage (ie by mutual written contract).

62 The first stage in the progress towards the creation of binding legal relations occurred a week after the telephone conversation and was the production of the Indicative Terms. Whatever might have been said before then, the defender signed those terms as representing the state of relations then pertaining between the parties. It will not do to dismiss these Terms as 'paperwork' which would not raise 'alarm bells'. Whether alarm bells ought to have rung is entirely irrelevant as is what the defender thought might happen thereafter. The reality is that the parties signed 'Indicative Heads of Terms'. They may have been inaccurate in their exclusive reference to Carlyco, but what is important is that they refer only to purchase funding and to such funding being made available in terms of a 'Facility Letter' to be produced by the pursuers. It states that 'representations and warranties' would be the 'usual' ones. It would presumably not be usual for a Facility Letter to warrant funding beyond that which was actually offered.

The binding element of this document is simply, as it says, that the pursuers have made a 'formal offer of facilities' to the extent of the purchase funding only and that a period of 'exclusivity' would follow, during which the defender would produce the required documentation to enable the pursuers to 'conclude diligence and proceed to draw down'. As at 21 June, therefore, both parties having signed the Indicative Terms, the informed observer would understand that, whatever had occurred before, the parties' legal relationship was henceforth defined by those Terms. There is no other possible objective interpretation of the factual circumstances.

63 It is an interesting feature of the defender's position that he maintains that it was as a result of the pursuers' collateral warranty that he entered into the written agreement(s). However, it was not the entering into these agreements that caused him any loss. After all, these agreements did not oblige him to do anything unless and until he wished to draw down funds. It was entering into missives with the sellers binding himself to purchase the plot on the strength of what he had been told by Ms Hutchison that may have resulted in such losses as he avers. Be that as it may, the fact that he entered into the written agreements, in the terms which he did, provides further confirmation that it was those agreements, and only those agreements, that thereafter defined the mutual obligations between the parties in relation to borrowing facilities and set the limit of those facilities, in relation to the defender's own plot, at £1.405M. The agreements, which were presumably similar to those which the parties had used previously, take the form of an offer (and acceptance) of borrowing facilities on detailed terms and conditions. The agreements make it clear that no obligations would arise unless and until the defender had signed and returned the acceptance part of the offer, which had already been signed by the pursuers. The agreements make it equally clear that the facility for draw down was subject to the written terms of the offer and acceptance and not any earlier assurance. Again, no matter what had been said in the past, the signing of those agreements meant that each party acknowledged these as defining the state of their legal relations. If the defender considered that they did not properly reflect what he understood was to be agreed, or had been agreed orally, then he ought not to have signed the agreements. At all events, whatever the defender thought was the position, the informed observer would understand the written agreements to cover all matters agreed to date. It may well be that, at that time, the pursuers fully intended to enter into a further bargain with the defender to advance additional funding for the building works. However, they had not done so and did not do so. That may have been contrary to the spirit of the negotiations prior to the signing of the written agreements, but that spirit, or its moral content, cannot be taken as creating a legally binding voluntary obligation.

64 In these circumstances, the court will: allow the reclaiming motion ... "

Although only a model framework and therefore not part of the law of Scotland, the Draft Common Frame of Reference (DCFR) attempts to provide a common framework for the incorporation of pre-contractual statements. **9–25**

"DCFR. II–9:102: Certain pre-contractual statements regarded as contract terms

(1) A statement made by one party before a contract is concluded is regarded as a term of the contract if the other party reasonably understood it as being made on the basis that it would form part of the contract terms if a contract were concluded. In assessing whether the other party was reasonable in understanding the statement in that way account may be taken of:

(a) the apparent importance of the statement to the other party;
(b) whether the party was making the statement in the course of business; and

> (c) the relative expertise of the parties.
>
> (2) If one of the parties to a contract is a business and before the contract is concluded makes a statement, either to the other party or publicly, about the specific characteristics of what is to be supplied by that business under the contract, the statement is regarded as a term of the contract unless:
>
> (a) the other party was aware when the contract was concluded, or could reasonably be expected to have been so aware, that the statement was incorrect or could not otherwise be relied on as such a term; or
> (b) the other party's decision to conclude the contract was not influenced by the statement.
>
> For the purposes of paragraph (2), a statement made by a person engaged in advertising or marketing on behalf of the business is treated as being made by the business.
>
> Where the other party is a consumer then, for the purposes of paragraph (2), a public statement made by or on behalf of a producer or other person in earlier links of the business chain between the producer and the consumer is treated as being made by the business unless the business, at the time of conclusion of the contract, did not know and could not reasonably be expected to have known of it.
>
> In the circumstances covered by paragraph (4) a business which at the time of conclusion of the contract did not know and could not reasonably be expected to have known that the statement was incorrect has a right to be indemnified by the person making the statement for any liability incurred as a result of that paragraph.
>
> In relations between a business and a consumer the parties may not, to the detriment of the consumer, exclude the application of this Article or derogate from or vary its effects."

The incorporation of terms from pre-contractual documents

9–26 The express, written terms of a contract are not always on a single document. The intention may be to state them in a variety of sources, such as public notices, timetables, tickets, standard terms and conditions, etc. This is common business practice. A party may attempt to incorporate express terms from such sources by actually handing over the document to the other party, or by orally notifying him or her of its existence, or by referring to it elsewhere (for example, by stating on a notice that the contract is made subject to standard terms and conditions which are available from a particular person or place). There are severe limits placed upon the use of such methods to import terms into a contract.

A document or statement containing express terms must be a contractual document capable of importing terms into a contract. Advertisements, for example, would not normally be regarded as contractual documents; nor would a ticket or a receipt. Such documents cannot import terms into the contract.

9–27

Taylor v Glasgow Corporation

1952 S.C. 440; 1952 S.L.T. 399

Court of Session, Second Division: The Lord Justice-Clerk (Thomson), Lords Mackay and Patrick

Mrs Taylor went to the Woodside Public Baths, Glasgow, to take a hot bath, as she had regularly done on a weekly basis for about two years. It was a Saturday morning. She paid her sixpence at the window just inside the entrance and was given a ticket. She knew that the ticket had writing on it, but not that it contained conditions.

On one side, the ticket contained the legible words: "For conditions see other side". On the other side of the ticket were printed the legible words:

> "The Corporation of Glasgow are NOT responsible for any loss injury or damage sustained by persons entering or using this establishment or its equipment".

Mrs Taylor had to wait in a well-lit corridor for half an hour before a bath became available. She had ample opportunity to read the ticket, but did not do so. When a bath was available, she handed her ticket to an attendant and took her bath. She alleged that she suffered serious injury, when she was allowed to fall down an internal stair as a result of the negligence of the bath attendant. The court held that the defenders had not given Mrs Taylor adequate notice of the condition, and that she was entitled to treat the ticket merely as a voucher.

"LORD JUSTICE-CLERK (THOMSON): ... As the party seeking to maintain the condition is doing so with a view to restricting his liability, the onus is broadly on him. Further, in certain well-known types of case, in particular those relating to carriage and deposit, it is now settled that a reference to conditions, legibly printed on the face of the ticket, is sufficient notice of conditions. The person who buys a railway ticket or a cloakroom ticket is doing a thing which is now recognised by the public in general as entering into a contract which may contain special conditions. This is a situation which is now regarded as notorious and customary. The real question is how far this now established rule is to be extended. It was submitted to us that all the elements obtaining in the carriage and deposit cases were present in the pursuer's case. There was a contract; that contract was embodied in a ticket; that ticket contained on the face of it a clear statement that there were conditions on the back; when one turned the ticket over there were the conditions; and there was time and opportunity for any ordinary person to read the ticket. **9–28**

I agree that, if these elements are present in the usual carriage and deposit case, the defenders must succeed. But the argument lays too much emphasis on the ticket itself. It assumes that because in carriage and deposit cases the 'ticket' has been given a definite function, as embodying the conditions binding both parties to the contract, all pieces of paper popularly called tickets are to be similarly regarded. In fact, 'tickets' may perform different functions. The ticket in the present case was a domestic check on the defenders' running of their establishment, the register and the ticket having taken the place of the old-fashioned receipt. Further, as the defenders were affording a variety of services, some sort of voucher was necessary in order to ensure that the pursuer got what she paid for and only what she paid for. This latter was the significance of the 'ticket' which would strike the pursuer. She wanted a hot bath, she paid for a hot bath. She got a voucher for a hot bath, and unless she produced the voucher to the hot bath attendant, she would not get a hot bath. If she wanted something extra for the enjoyment of her hot bath, that extra would be stamped on her ticket and would be her warrant for being supplied with it. It was therefore a convenient, practical method, both from her point of view and the defenders', of passing her into the establishment and thereafter passing her on to the particular facility which she was to be afforded. My view of the evidence is that this voucher aspect of this 'ticket' was the significant aspect, and that if the pursuer regarded it as a pass or voucher or as a receipt for sixpence which entitled her to be given a hot bath, she was entitled so to regard it. There was no evidence that the public regarded it in any other way.

No doubt a railway ticket has these elements also; it is a domestic check, a receipt and a pass to the train, but I am not satisfied on the evidence in the present case that a 'ticket' for a hot bath in the Woodside Public Baths has yet acquired the special contractual feature which the law now ascribes to a railway ticket.

If that be so, the sheriff was right to regard this 'ticket' as in substance a voucher. If so, the pursuer could not be reasonably expected to study it for conditions, and it follows that in the absence of some other method of calling her attention to its 'conditional' function the defenders cannot be said to have done what was reasonably sufficient to give the pursuer notice of the condition.

In my opinion the appeal should be refused."

Did Lord Thomson regard the contract as already made at the time when the ticket was issued?

The "ticket" cases

9–29 The major exceptions to the rule that the document importing terms must be a contractual document appear to be tickets issued for carriage by railway and other forms of transport and similar contracts. The limits to this historical exception have been established by the following cases.

9–30

Parker v South Eastern Railway Co
(1877) 2 C.P.D. 416
English Court of Appeal: Mellish, Baggallay and Bramwell LJJ

Parker deposited a bag in the railway's station cloakroom. He paid 2d and was given a ticket which, on the face of it, contained the words "see back". On the reverse were the words: "The company will not be responsible for any package exceeding the value of £10". Conditions on a notice in the cloakroom were to the same effect.

Parker claimed £24 l0s, being the value of the bag and contents which he had deposited and which had been lost.

The court found in favour of the defendants.

9–31 "MELLISH LJ: ... In an ordinary case, where an action is brought on a written agreement which is signed by the defendant, the agreement is proved by proving his signature, and in the absence of fraud, it is wholly immaterial that he has not read the agreement and does not know its contents. The parties may, however, reduce their agreement into writing, so that the writing constitutes the sole evidence of the agreement, without signing it; but in that case there must be evidence independently of the agreement itself to prove that the defendant has assented to it. In that case, also, if it is proved that the defendant has assented to the writing constituting the agreement between the parties it is, in the absence of fraud, immaterial that the defendant had not read the agreement and did not know its contents. Now if in the course of making a contract one party delivers to the other a paper containing writing, and the party receiving the paper knows that the paper contains conditions which the party delivering it intends to constitute the contract, I have no doubt that the party receiving the paper does, by receiving and keeping it, assent to the conditions contained in it, although he does not read them, and does not know what they are ...

I think there may be cases in which a paper containing writing is delivered by one party to another in the course of a business transaction, where it would be quite reasonable that the party receiving it should assume that the writing contained in it no condition, and should put it in his pocket unread. For instance, if a person driving through a turnpike-gate received a ticket upon paying the toll, he might reasonably assume that the object of the ticket was that by producing it he might be free from paying toll at some other turnpike-gate, and might put it in his pocket unread. On the other hand, if a person who ships goods to be carried on a voyage by sea receives a bill of lading signed by the master, he would plainly be bound by it, although afterwards in an action against the shipowner for the loss of the goods, he might swear that he had never read the bill of lading, and that he did not know that it contained the terms of the contract of carriage; and the shipowner was protected by the exceptions contained in it. Now the reason why the person receiving the bill of lading would be bound seems to me to be that in the great majority of cases persons shipping goods do know that the bill of lading contains the terms of the contract of carriage; and the shipowner, or the master delivering the bill of lading, is entitled to assume that the person shipping goods has that knowledge. It is, however, quite possible to suppose that a person who is neither a man of business nor a lawyer might on some particular occasion ship goods without the least knowledge of what a bill of lading was, but in my opinion such a person must bear the consequences of his own exceptional ignorance, it being plainly impossible that business could be carried on if every person who delivers a bill of lading had to stop and explain what a bill of lading was.

BRAMWELL LJ: ... Has not the giver of the [ticket] a right to suppose that the receiver is content to deal on the terms in the [ticket]? What more must be done? Must he say, 'Read that'? As I have said, he does so in effect when he puts it into the other's hands. The truth is, people are content to take these things on trust. They know that there is a form which is always used—they are satisfied it is not unreasonable, because people do not usually put unreasonable terms into their contracts. If they did, then dealing would soon be stopped. Besides, unreasonable practices would be known. The very fact of not looking at the [ticket] shews that this confidence exists ... I think there is an implied understanding that there is no condition unreasonable to the knowledge of the party tendering the document and not insisting on its being read— no condition not relevant to the matter in hand. I am of opinion, therefore, that the plaintiffs, having notice of the printing, were in the same situation as if the porter had said, 'Read that, it concerns the matter in hand'; that if the plaintiffs did not read it, they were as much bound as if they had read it and had not objected." **9–32**

Note that Mellish LJ refers to "the course of a business transaction". What do you think he meant by that phrase in the context of this case?

Was Mellish LJ suggesting that a reasonable person should expect to find contract terms on certain types of documents? If so, what test should be applied in defining them? Alternatively, was he suggesting a test of reasonable practicability: i.e. that a party should not, in certain circumstances, be expected expressly to draw the attention of the other party to such terms? Contrast his comments with those of Lord Denning in *Thornton v Shoe Lane Parking*, below, para.9–38.

Was Bramwell LJ correct to assume that "people do not usually put unreasonable terms into their contracts"?

9–33 **Hood v Anchor Line (Henderson Brothers) Ltd**

1918 S.C (H.L.) 143

House of Lords: Lord Chancellor (Finlay), Viscount Haldane, Lords Dunedin and Parmoor

Hood was a passenger on *The SS California*, owned by the Anchor Line, on a voyage from New York to Glasgow. He was injured when, the vessel having run aground off the Irish coast, he was being hoisted from a lifeboat on board *The Cassandra* to continue his journey to Glasgow.

Anchor Line claimed that, under a condition in the contract of carriage, they were not liable in damages for more than £10. The condition was one of several contained on a portion of the ticket retained by the passenger. The conditions were prefaced: "NOTICE This ticket is issued to and accepted by the passenger subject to the following conditions".

At the foot of the document, in capital letters, were the words: "PASSENGERS ARE PARTICULARLY REQUESTED TO CAREFULLY READ THE ABOVE CONTRACT."

The ticket had been handed over to Hood's clerk in return for the price in an unsealed white envelope. The face of the envelope contained details of the voyage and a printed hand at the top pointed to the following words printed in capitals at the top of the envelope: "PLEASE READ THE CONDITIONS OF THE ENCLOSED CONTRACT".

Neither Hood, who had travelled on the Anchor Line's steamers on previous occasions, nor his agent, had looked at the ticket or the conditions; nor did they know that conditions were attached.

The court held that the defenders had taken all reasonable steps to bring to the knowledge of the pursuer the conditions, and accordingly the pursuer was bound by them.

9–34 "VISCOUNT HALDANE: … [T]he real question is not whether they did read [the contract], but whether they can be heard to say that they did not read it. If it had been merely a case of inviting people to put a penny into an automatic machine and get a ticket for a brief journey, I might think differently. In such a transaction men can not be expected to pause to look whether they are obtaining all the rights which the law gives them in the absence of a special stipulation. But when it is a case of taking a ticket for a voyage of some days, with arrangements to be made, among other things as to cabins and luggage, I think ordinary people do look to see what bargain they are getting, and should be taken as bound to have done so and as precluded from saying that they did not know.

The question is not whether the appellant actually knew of the condition. I have no doubt that he did not. The real question is whether he deliberately took the risk of there being conditions, in the face of a warning sufficiently conveyed that some conditions were made and would bind him. If he had signed the contract, he certainly could not have been heard to say that he was not bound to look. The common sense of mankind which the law expresses here would not permit him to maintain such a position. And when he accepted a document that told him on its face that it contained conditions on which alone he would be permitted to make a long journey across the Atlantic on board the steamer, and then proceeded on that journey, I think he must be treated according to the standards of ordinary life applicable to those who make arrangements under analogous circumstances, and be held as bound by the document as clearly as if he had signed it.

9–35 LORD DUNEDIN: … Contracts of carriage are not usually made by parole, nor are they usually embodied in signed writings. In so saying I am proceeding on common knowledge as to railways, stage-conches, and steamers. But what is unusual is in truth a question of fact. Accordingly, it is in each case a question of circumstances whether the sort of restriction that is expressed in any writing (which, of course, includes printed matter) is a thing that is usual, and whether, being usual, it has been fairly brought before the notice of the accepting party ... How that question is to be answered depends not only on the circumstances of that particular case, but also on the circumstances of the class of cases of which it is one. It is vain to attempt to lay down general rules."

Viscount Haldane appears to differentiate automatic vending machine tickets. Look at the case of *Thornton v Shoe Lane Parking*, below, para.9–38, and consider, for example, the next case.

Not only must the document be contractual, but it must be issued, or brought to the other party's notice prior to completion of the agreement.

Chapelton v Barry Urban District Council 9–36

[1940] 1 K.B. 532

English Court of Appeal: Slesser, Mackinnon and Goddard, LJJ

Chapelton took a deck chair from a pile of chairs on Barry beach. A notice near the pile stated: "Barry Urban District Council. Cold Knap. Hire of chairs, 2d. per session of 3 hours". The notice also stated that a ticket would be issued by an attendant and that the ticket should be retained for inspection. Chapelton took two chairs and an employee of the district council issued him with two tickets, in return for the price. The tickets, at which Chapelton briefly glanced, stated that "the council will not be liable for any accident or damage arising from the hire of the chair".

While Chapelton was sitting on the chair, the canvas came away from the top of the wooden frame. The deck chair collapsed and Chapelton was injured. He sued (with eventual success) the council for their negligence.

Held that the ticket was a mere voucher or receipt—the conditions of the contract were those on the notice, which did not refer to limitation of liability.

"SLESSER LJ: ... In the class of case where it is said that there is a term in the contract freeing railway companies, or other providers of facilities, from liabilities which they would otherwise incur at common law, it is a question of how far that condition has been made a term of the contract and whether it has been sufficiently brought to the notice of the person entering into the contract with the railway company, or other body, and there is a large number of authorities on that point. In my view, however, the present case does not come within that category at all. 9–37

The local authority offered to hire chairs to persons to sit upon on the beach, and there was a pile of chairs there standing ready for use by anyone who wished to use them, and the conditions on which they offered persons the use of those chairs were stated in the notice which was put up by the pile of chairs, namely, that the sum charged for the hire of a chair was 2d. per session of three hours. I think that was the whole of the offer which the local authority made in this case. They said, in effect: 'We offer to provide you with a chair, and if you accept that offer and sit on the chair, you will have to pay for that privilege 2d. per session of three hours.'

I think that Mr Chapelton, in common with other persons who used these chairs, when he took the chair from the pile (which happened to be handed to him by an attendant, but which, I suppose, he might have taken from the pile of chairs himself if the attendant had been going on his rounds collecting money, or was otherwise away) simply thought that he was liable to pay 2d. for the use of the chair. No suggestion of any restriction of the council's liability appeared in the notice which was near the pile of chairs. That, I think, is the proper view to take of the nature of the contract in this case ... It is wrong, I think, to look at the circumstance that the plaintiff obtained his receipt at the same time that he took his chair as being in any way a modification of the contract which I have indicated. This was a general offer to the general public, and I think it is right to say that one must take into account here that there was no reason why anybody taking one of these chairs should necessarily obtain a receipt at the moment he took his chair—and, indeed, the notice is inconsistent with that, because it 'respectfully requests' the public to obtain receipts for the money. It may be that somebody might sit in one of those chairs for one hour, or two hours, or, if the holiday resort was a very popular one, for a longer time, before the attendant came round for his money, or it may be that the attendant would not come to him at all for payment for the chair, in which case I take it that there would be an obligation upon the person who used the chair to search out the attendant, like a debtor searching for his creditor, in order to pay him the sum of 2d. for the use of the chair and to obtain a receipt for the 2d. paid ...

I do not think that the notice excluding liability was a term of the contract at all ... the object of the giving and the taking of this ticket was that the person taking it might have evidence at hand by which he could show that the obligation he was under to pay 2d. for the use of the chair for three hours had been duly discharged, and I think it is altogether inconsistent, in the absence of any qualification of liability in the notice put up near the pile of chairs, to attempt to read into it the qualification contended for. In my opinion, this ticket is no more than a receipt, and is quite different from a railway ticket which contains upon it the terms upon which a railway company agrees to carry the passenger."

It is clear from this case that a standard "offer/acceptance" analysis of the transaction may prevent the incorporation of terms from a document which is issued after the offer has been accepted. There are many instances where the analysis was applied with similar results: see above, Ch.4.

9–38

Thornton v Shoe Lane Parking Ltd
[1971] 2 Q.B. 163
English Court of Appeal: Lord Denning MR, Megaw LJ, Sir Gordon Willmer

A notice outside the Shoe Lane Car Park in London stated: "All Cars Parked at Owner's Risk". Thornton, who had not parked there before, drove his car to the entrance, where a traffic light showed red. As he drove in, the light turned to green and then a ticket was produced by a machine. Thornton took the ticket (which he did not read) and parked his car. The ticket stated, in small print in the corner: "This ticket is issued subject to the conditions of issue as displayed on the premises".

The conditions, which were not visible at the time when the ticket was issued, were printed on a notice on a pillar opposite the ticket machine and in the paying office. These stated:

> "The company shall not be responsible or liable for ... injury to the customer ... occurring when the customer's motor vehicle is in the parking building, howsoever that ... injury shall be caused."

Thornton was injured in an accident in the car park when he returned to collect his car. The court held that the defendants had not done enough to draw the condition to the notice of the plaintiff.

"LORD DENNING MR: ... We have been referred to the ticket cases of former times from *Parker v South Eastern Railway Co* (1877) 2 C.P.D. 416 to *McCutcheon v David MacBrayne Ltd* [1964] 1 W.L.R. 125. In those cases the issue of the ticket was regarded as the offer by the company. If the customer took it and retained in without objection, his act was regarded as an acceptance of the offer ... These cases were based on the theory that the customer, on being handed the ticket, could refuse it and decline to enter into a contract on those terms. He could ask for his money back. That theory was, of course, a fiction. No customer in a thousand ever read the conditions. If he had stopped to do so, he would have missed the train or the boat. 9–39

None of those cases has any application to a ticket which is issued by an automatic machine. The customer pays his money and he gets a ticket. He cannot refuse it. He cannot get his money back. He may protest to the machine, even swear at it. But it will remain unmoved. He is committed beyond recall. He was committed at the very moment when he put his money into the machine. The contract was concluded at that time. It can be translated into an offer and acceptance in this way: the offer is made when the proprietor of the machine holds it out as being ready to receive the money. The acceptance takes place when the customer puts his money into the slot. The terms of the offer are contained in the notice placed on or near the machine stating what is offered for the money. The customer is bound by those terms as long as they are sufficiently brought to his notice beforehand, but not otherwise. He is not bound by the terms printed on the ticket if they differ from the notice, because the ticket comes too late. The contract has already been made: see *Olley v Marlborough Court Ltd* [1949] 1 K.B. 532. The ticket is no more than a voucher or receipt for the money that has been paid (as in the deck chair case, *Chapelton v Barry Urban District Council* [1940] 1 K.B. 532), on terms which have been offered and accepted before the ticket is issued.

In the present case the offer was contained in the notice at the entrance giving the charges for garaging and saying 'at owner's risk', i. e. at the risk of the owner so far as damage to the car was concerned. The offer was accepted when the plaintiff drove up to the entrance and, by the movement of his car, turned the light from red to green, and the ticket was thrust at him. The contract was then concluded, and it could not be altered by any words printed on the ticket itself. In particular, it could not be altered so as to exempt the company from liability for personal injury due to their negligence.

SIR GORDON WILLMER: ... [T]he really distinguishing feature of this case is the fact that the ticket on which reliance is placed was issued out of an automatic machine ... in all the previous so-called 'ticket' cases the ticket has been proffered by a human hand, and there has always been at least the notional opportunity for the customer to say—if he did not like the conditions—'I do not like your conditions: I will not have this ticket.' But in the case of a ticket which is proffered by an automatic machine there is something quite irrevocable about the process. There can be no *locus poenitentiae*. I do not propose to say any more upon the difficult question which has been raised as to the precise moment when a contract was concluded in this case; but at least it seems to me that any attempt to introduce conditions after the irrevocable step has been taken of causing the machine to operate must be doomed to failure." 9–40

Was Lord Denning right in saying that, in *Parker*, the ticket was an offer? Note that neither Willmer nor Megaw LJJ adopted Lord Denning's strict "offer/acceptance" analysis of the facts.

Incorporation by "reasonable notice"

A document containing terms, even if it is covered by the "ticket" cases or is otherwise a contractual document, can only incorporate those terms if it is either notified to the other party before the contract is made, or handed over to them, or reasonable steps taken to bring the 9–41 document to the other party's notice. It is not necessary that the other party knows, or has read the terms (although both would be sufficient notice); merely that reasonable steps were taken to bring them to their notice. The basic principles were outlined by Mellish LJ in the following case.

9–42 **Parker v South Eastern Railway Co**
(1877) 2 C.P.D. 416
English Court of Appeal: Mellish, Baggallay and Bramwell LJJ

The facts are as stated above, paras 9–30—9–32.

9–43 "MELLISH, LJ: ... Now the question we have to consider is whether the railway company were entitled to assume that a person depositing luggage, and receiving a ticket in such a way that he could see that some writing was printed on it, would understand that the writing contained the conditions of contract, and this seems to me to depend upon whether people in general would in fact, and naturally, draw that inference. The railway company, as it seems to me, must be entitled to make some assumptions respecting the person who deposits luggage with them: I think they are entitled to assume that he can read, and that he understands the English language, and that he pays such attention to what he is about as may be reasonably expected from a person in such a transaction as that of depositing luggage in a cloakroom. The railway company must, however, take mankind as they find them, and if what they do is sufficient to inform people in general that the ticket contains conditions, I think that a particular plaintiff ought not to be in a better position than other persons on account of his exceptional ignorance or stupidity or carelessness. But if what the railway company do is not sufficient to convey to the minds of people in general that the ticket contains conditions, then they have received goods on deposit without obtaining the consent of the persons depositing them to the conditions limiting their liability ... [I]f the person receiving the ticket did not see or know that there was any writing on the ticket, he is not bound by the conditions; that if he knew there was writing, and knew or believed that the writing contained conditions, then he is bound by the conditions; that if he knew there was writing on the ticket, but did not know or believe that the writing contained conditions, nevertheless he would be bound, if the delivering of the ticket to him in such a manner that he could see there was writing upon it, was, in the opinion of the jury, reasonable notice that the writing contained conditions."

This statement by Mellish LJ is of a rule that has been consistently applied. Nevertheless, there are instances where the courts have refused to incorporate terms from a document of which there was inadequate notice. In *Richardson v Rowntree*,[11] for example, Mrs Rowntree was not bound by conditions on a ticket handed to her, but folded so that no writing was visible until unfolded and, even then, was in microscopic print and obscured by a messy red stamp. The onus, however, is on the party denying notice to show that there was no reasonable notice. The following case illustrates how difficult that may be.

---

[11] *Richardson v Rowntree* [1894] A.C. 217.

Thompson v London, Midland and Scottish Railway Co 9–44
[1930] 1 K.B. 41
English Court of Appeal: Lord Hanworth M.R., Lawrence and Sankey LJJ

Thompson, who was elderly and could not read, was bought a ticket by Alcroft, her niece's father. The ticket stated: "Excursion: For conditions see back".

The reverse of the ticket stated: "Issued subject to the conditions and regulations in the company's timetables and notices and excursion and other bills".

The excursion bill stated: "Excursion tickets are issued subject to the notices and conditions shown in the company's current time tables".

The timetable contained the words:

> "Excursion tickets . . . are issued subject to the . . . condition that neither the holders or [*sic*] any other person shall have any right of action against the company . . . in respect of . . . injury (whether fatal or otherwise)."

Thompson was seriously injured while on a journey covered by her ticket as a result of the company's negligence.

Held that Thompson's illiteracy did not alter the legal position, and that the references to the conditions constituted sufficient notice.

"LORD HANWORTH MR: . . . The plaintiff in this case cannot read; but, having regard to the authorities, and the condition of education in this country, I do not think that avails her in any degree. The ticket was taken for her by her agent. The time of the train was ascertained for her by Miss Alcroft's father, and he had made the specific inquiry in order to see at what time and under what circumstances there was an excursion train available for intending travellers. He ascertained, therefore, and he had the notice put before him before ever the ticket was taken, that there were conditions on the issue of excursion and other reduced-fare tickets . . . 9–45

The railway company is to be treated as having made an offer to intending passengers that if they will accept the conditions on which the railway company make the offer they can be taken at suitable times, in suitable days and by indicated trains from Darwen to Manchester and back at a price largely reduced from the common price; but upon certain conditions which can be ascertained, and of the existence of which there can be no doubt, for they are indicated clearly upon the ticket which is issued.

Whether or not the father of Miss Alcroft took the trouble to search out the conditions, or to con them over or not, it appears to me that when that ticket was taken it was taken with the knowledge that the conditions applied, and that the person who took the ticket was bound by those conditions. .

Now there is the present case. It was quite clear, and everybody understood and knew that there would have to be a ticket issued. Without such ticket, which is the voucher showing the money has been paid, it would not be possible for the lady to go on the platform to take her train, or on reaching the end of her transit to leave the platform without giving up a ticket. It is quite clear, therefore, that it was intended there should be a ticket issued; and on that ticket plainly on its face is a reference made to the conditions under which it is issued."

This case should be contrasted with the *Thornton* decision on this point. Note that exclusion of the company's liability was comprehensive and even covered the company's negligence. The punitive harshness of this decision and the devastating effect it could have on the lives of victims and their families was not mitigated until the Passenger Charges Scheme 1952, promulgated under powers contained in the Transport Act 1947 s.78. Until 1952, the railways remained free to exclude liability for death and personal injury to passengers caused by their negligence. This they consistently did in the case of holders of free passes and excursion tickets. Operators of passenger road transport were prohibited from excluding such liability by the Road Traffic Act 1930 s.97 (now the Road Traffic Act 1988 s.149).

The above case, and many other of the "ticket cases", may well have been argued and decided differently had their facts arisen after the enactment of the Unfair Contract Terms Act 1977 and subsequent consumer protection legislation (see para.10–25 onwards).

Must there be reasonable notice of conditions in general, or of the condition in question in particular?

9–46 **Thornton v Shoe Lane Parking Ltd**

[1971] 2 Q.B. 163

English Court of Appeal: Lord Denning MR, Megaw LJ, Sir Gordon Willmer

The facts are as stated above, para.9–38.

9–47 "LORD DENNING MR: ... Assuming, however, that an automatic machine is a booking clerk in disguise, so that the old-fashioned ticket cases still apply to it, we then have to go back to the three questions put by Mellish LJ in *Parker v South Eastern Railway Co* (1877) 2 C.P.D. 416, 423, subject to this qualification: Mellish LJ used the word 'conditions' in the plural, whereas it would be more apt to use the word 'condition' in the singular, as indeed Mellish LJ himself did on the next page. After all, the only condition that matters for this purpose is the exempting condition. It is no use telling the customer that the ticket is issued subject to some 'conditions' or other, without more; for he may reasonably regard 'conditions' in general as merely regulatory, and not as taking away his rights, unless the exempting condition is drawn specifically to his attention. (Alternatively, if the plural 'conditions' is used, it would be better prefaced with the word 'exempting,' because the exempting conditions are the only conditions that matter for this purpose.) Telescoping the three questions, they come to this: the customer is bound by the exempting condition if he knows that the ticket is issued subject to it; or, if the company did what was reasonably sufficient to give him notice of it ... [T]he defendants did not do what was reasonably sufficient to give the plaintiff notice of the exempting condition. That admission was properly made. I do not pause to inquire whether the exempting condition is void for unreasonableness. All I say is that it is so wide and so destructive of rights that the court should not hold any man bound by it unless it is drawn to his attention in the most explicit way. It is an instance of what I had in mind in *J. Spurling Ltd v Bradshaw* [1956] 1 W.L.R. 461, 466. In order to give sufficient notice, it would need to be printed in red ink with a red hand pointing to it, or something equally startling.

But, although reasonable notice of it was not given, counsel for the defendants said that this case came within the second question propounded by Mellish L.J., namely that the plaintiff 'knew or believed that the writing contained conditions.' There was no finding to that effect. The burden was on the defendants to prove it, and they did not do so. Certainly there was no evidence that the plaintiff knew of this exempting condition. He is not, therefore, bound by it. Counsel for the defendants relied on a case in this court last year—*Mendelssohn v Normand Ltd.* [1970] 1 Q.B. 177. Mr Mendelssohn parked his car in the Cumberland Garage at Marble Arch and was given a ticket which contained an exempting condition. There was no discussion as to whether the condition formed part of the contract. It was conceded that it did ... Yet the garage company were not entitled to rely on the exempting condition for the reasons there given.

That case does not touch the present, where the whole question is whether the exempting condition formed part of the contract. I do not think it did. The plaintiff did not know of the condition, and the defendants did not do what was reasonably sufficient to give him notice of it.

I do not think the defendants can escape liability by reason of the exempting condition. I would, therefore, dismiss the appeal.

MEGAW LJ: For myself, I would reserve a final view on the question at what precise moment of time the contract was concluded . . . [T]he appropriate questions for the jury in a ticket case were: (1) Did the passenger know that there was printing on the railway ticket? (2) Did he know that the ticket contained or referred to conditions? and (3) Did the railway company do what was reasonable in the way of notifying prospective passengers of the existence of conditions and where their terms might be considered? . . . **9–48**

So I come to the third of the three questions . . . I agree with Lord Denning M.R. that the question here is of the particular condition on which the defendants seek to rely, and not of the conditions in general . . .

In my view the learned judge was wholly right on the evidence in the conclusion which he reached that the defendants have not taken proper or adequate steps fairly to bring to the notice of the plaintiff at or before the time when the contract was made that any special conditions were sought to be imposed.

I think it is a highly relevant factor in considering whether proper steps were taken fairly to bring that matter to the notice of the plaintiff that the first attempt to bring to his notice the intended inclusion of those conditions was at a time when as a matter of hard reality it would have been practically impossible for him to withdraw from his intended entry on the premises for the purpose of leaving his car there. It does not take much imagination to picture the indignation of the defendants if their potential customers, having taken their tickets and observed the reference therein to contractual conditions which, they said, could be seen in notices on the premises, were one after the other to get out of their cars, leaving the cars blocking the entrances to the garage, in order to search for, find and peruse the notices! Yet, unless the defendants genuinely intended the potential customers should do just that, it would be fiction, if not farce, to treat those customers as persons who have been given a fair opportunity, before the contracts are made, of discovering the conditions by which they are to be bound.

I agree that this appeal should be dismissed."

What is encompassed by the expression, used by Megaw LJ, "a matter of general knowledge, custom and practice"? Note that all three judges agreed that notice must be give of the particular condition, not of the conditions generally.

Onerous or unusual terms

It will be recalled that Lord Denning, in *Thornton*, thought that an "exempting condition" may be **9–49**

> "so wide and so destructive of rights that the court should not hold any man bound by it unless it is drawn to his attention in the most explicit way".

He added that

> "to give sufficient notice, it would need to be printed in red ink with a red hand pointing to it, or something equally startling".

These dicta have subsequently been applied: see, for example, *Hollier v Rambler Motors*, below, para.9–72. More recently, they were considered by the English Court of Appeal in the following case.

9–50 **Interfoto Picture Library Ltd v Stilletto Visual Programmes Ltd**
[1988] 1 All E.R. 348
English Court of Appeal: Bingham and Dillon LJJ

Stilletto needed photographs from the 1950s for an advertising presentation to a client. As was normal in the trade, they sought these from a picture library, in this case, Interfoto. Forty-seven transparencies were delivered, packed in a jiffy bag which also contained a delivery note. This clearly stated the date by which the transparencies had to be returned. The delivery note also contained writing prominently headed "CONDITIONS" and which stated: "A holding fee of £5.00 plus VAT will be charged for each transparency which is detained by you longer than ... 14 days".

Stilletto did not use the transparencies and, having forgotten about them, did not return them until well after 14 days from the day they were delivered. Interfoto now claimed a charge of £3,783.50 under the clause in the conditions.

Held that, in light of the extortionate nature of the condition, it had not been sufficiently drawn to the attention of the defendant.

9–51 "DILLON LJ: ... Condition 2 of these plaintiffs' conditions is in my judgment a very onerous clause. The defendants could not conceivably have known, if their attention was not drawn to the clause, that the plaintiffs were proposing to charge a 'holding fee' for the retention of the transparencies at such a very high and exorbitant rate.

At the time of the ticket cases in the last century it was notorious that people hardly ever troubled to read printed conditions on a ticket or delivery note or similar document. That remains the case now. In the intervening years the printed conditions have tended to become more and more complicated and more and more one-sided in favour of the party who is imposing them, but the other parties, if they notice that there are printed conditions at all, generally still tend to assume that such conditions are only concerned with ancillary matters of form and are not of importance. In the ticket cases the courts held that the common law required that reasonable steps be taken to draw the other parties' attention to the printed conditions or they would not be part of the contract. It is, in my judgment, a logical development of the common law into modern conditions that it should be held, as it was in *Thornton v Shoe Lane Parking Ltd.* [1971] 2 Q.B. 163, that, if one condition in a set of printed conditions is particularly onerous or unusual, the party seeking to enforce it must show that that particular condition was fairly brought to the attention of the other party.

In the present case, nothing whatever was done by the plaintiffs to draw the defendants' attention particularly to condition 2; it was merely one of four columns' width of conditions printed across the foot of the delivery note. Consequently condition 2 never, in my judgment, became part of the contract between the parties ...

9–52 BINGHAM LJ: ... In many civil law systems, and perhaps in most legal systems outside the common law world, the law of obligations recognises and enforces an overriding principle that in making and carrying out contracts parties should act in good faith. This does not simply mean that they should not deceive each other, a principle which any legal system must recognise; its effect is perhaps most aptly conveyed by such metaphorical colloquialisms as 'playing fair,' 'coming clean' or 'putting one's cards face upwards on the table.' It is in essence a principle of fair and open dealing. In such a forum it might, I think, be held on the facts of this case that the plaintiffs were under a

> duty in all fairness to draw the defendants' attention specifically to the high price payable if the transparencies were not returned in time and, when the 14 days had expired, to point out to the defendants the high cost of continued failure to return them ...
>
> The common law also has made its contribution, by holding that certain classes of contract require the utmost good faith, by treating as irrecoverable what purport to be agreed estimates of damage but are in truth a disguised penalty for breach, and in many other ways.
>
> The well-known cases on sufficiency of notice are in my view properly to be read in this context. At one level they are concerned with a question of pure contractual analysis, whether one party has done enough to give the other notice of the incorporation of a term in the contract. At another level they are concerned with a somewhat different question, whether it would in all the circumstances be fair (or reasonable) to hold a party bound by any conditions or by a particular condition of an unusual and stringent nature ...
>
> Turning to the present case, I am satisfied for reasons that Dillon LJ has given that no **9–53** contract was made on the telephone when the defendants made their initial request. I am equally satisfied that no contract was made on delivery of the transparencies to the defendants before the opening of the jiffy bag in which they were contained. Once the jiffy bag was opened and the transparencies taken out with the delivery note, it is in my judgment an inescapable inference that the defendants would have recognised the delivery note as a document of a kind likely to contain contractual terms and would have seen that there were conditions printed in small but visible lettering on the face of the document. To the extent that the conditions so displayed were common form or usual terms regularly encountered in this business, I do not think the defendants could successfully contend that they were not incorporated into the contract.
>
> The crucial question in the case is whether the plaintiffs can be said fairly and reasonably to have brought condition 2 to the notice of the defendants ... In my opinion the plaintiffs did not do so. They delivered 47 transparencies, which was a number the defendants had not specifically asked for. Condition 2 contained a daily rate per transparency after the initial period of 14 days many times greater than was usual or (so far as the evidence shows) heard of. For these 47 transparencies there was to be a charge for each day of delay of £235 plus value added tax. The result would be that a venial period of delay, as here, would lead to an inordinate liability. The defendants are not to be relieved of that liability because they did not read the condition, although doubtless they did not; but in my judgment they are to be relieved because the plaintiffs did not do what was necessary to draw this unreasonable and extortionate clause fairly to their attention. I would accordingly allow the defendants' appeal and substitute for the judge's award the sum which he assessed upon the alternative basis of quantum meruit."

Note that in this case the clause in question was not an exclusion clause in the strictest sense. Should that matter? Is it true that the general perception today is that "such conditions are only concerned with ancillary matters of form and are not of importance"? If so, is that a popular misconception, or a verifiable fact?

Note that Bingham LJ framed his comments in the light of a document which had not been **9–54** read. Reference should be made to the comments of Blackburn J in *Harris v Great Western Railway*[12] and those of Lord Devlin in *McCutcheon v David MacBrayne Ltd.* These are considered below, para.9–68.

A further feature of the facts is that the delivery note was not visible until the jiffy bag had been opened. Was it not therefore a post-contractual document which could not in any

---

[12] *Harris v Great Western Railway* (1876) 1 Q.B.D. 515, 530, para.9–60 below.

circumstances impose conditions? Contrast the practice in the supply of consumer software on disks. Here, the terms and conditions of any licence are clearly printed on the *outside* of the envelope containing the disks, with words and instructions clearly drawing attention to them. Contrast sales online, where the purchaser, before the contract is made, must tick the box stating that the suppliers terms and conditions are available, have been accessed by and accepted by the purchaser.

Are Bingham LJ's comments about "civil law systems" an accurate description of the role of "good faith" in Scots law as a civil law system? Can it be said that, in Scots law, a failure to draw attention to such an "onerous or unusual term" would be a breach of faith similar to that which led the Inner House in *Steuart's Trustees v Hart*[13] to conclude that the seller's silence "induced" the buyer to enter into the contract? If so, what is the true position of contracts uberrimae fidei in Scots law: are they a separate category borrowed from English law, or are they merely another aspect of this rule of "good faith"?

The *Interfoto* decision was recently considered by Lord Glennie in the following case.

9–55 **Langstane Housing Association Ltd v Riverside Construction (Aberdeen) Ltd, Ramsay & Chalmers**

[2009] CSOH 52 (OH); [2010] Const LJ, 566
Court of Session, Outer House: Lord Glennie

Langstane contracted with Riverside to carry out renovation of their flats. Ramsay (one of the defenders) were employed as engineers following a letter from Ramsay dated March 2001, which in turn was followed by Langstane allocating the work to Ramsay. During the renovation, the building partially collapsed after a fire. It was unclear which of the defenders' actions had caused the collapse, or in what proportion they had contributed to it.

Ramsay had been appointed to the Panel by a letter dated March 1985 "on the basis of the current ACE Conditions of Service". This was a reference to the Association of Consulting Engineers Conditions of Engagement, of which there are several versions.

In a preliminary proof, Ramsay claimed that the 1998 conditions had been incorporated into the contract with Ramsay. Clause B8.2 of this version was an innovation that incorporated a net contribution clause to the effect that the consulting engineer's liability for any claim should be limited to such sum as they ought reasonably to pay having regard to their responsibility for the loss or damage suffered.

Langstane argued that the 1985 letter did not incorporate the later 1998 ACE Conditions. Even if the 1998 version had been incorporated, Langstane claimed that the clause would be invalidated by s.17 of the Unfair Contract Terms Act 1977, which excludes a term that is objectively unreasonable, where the pursuer is a customer.

The court found that the net contribution clause was valid, and exempted the second defender from joint and several liability. The clause could not be subject to UCTA since the pursuer was not a customer and, even if it had been, since the clause sought not to restrict the second defendant's liability for its own fault but to prevent it from becoming liable for damage caused by co-defendants, it was not unreasonable within the meaning of s.17(1).

[13] *Steuart's Trustees v Hart* (1875) 3 R. 192.

"LORD GLENNIE: 9–56

. . .

Discussion

[33] In considering whether any and if so what terms are incorporated into a contract between the parties, the starting point is to look at the language that the parties have used in any written document forming part of the contract. In the present case, it is agreed between the parties that the second defenders' engagement as Consulting Engineers for the project at 411/2 Union Street came into being by virtue of the second defenders' letter of 15 March 2001 and the pursuers' conduct thereafter in instructing the work to be done and paying for it against the second defenders' invoice. This is not, therefore, a written contract in the ordinary meaning of that expression. Nonetheless, the effect of the pursuers' conduct was, to put it in conventional terms, to accept the offer made in the second defenders' letter. The correct approach, therefore, is to look to that letter to see what terms were proposed and, by conduct, accepted.

[34] The letter of 15 March 2001 set out the Basis of Engagement in the following terms:

'Basis of Engagement—ACE Conditions of Engagement Agreement—B1'

There is no doubt that the second defenders were proposing, and the pursuers were accepting, that the ACE Conditions of Engagement should apply to the contract. I consider that the obvious construction of the document is that the current up-to-date version of those Conditions should apply. I accept the evidence of Mr Barter that that would be the understanding of those involved in the industry, not only of consulting engineers but of those who regularly deal with and contract with them.

. . .

[38] Having decided that the terms on which the second defenders undertook to provide services for the project at 411/2 Union Street bore to include the Form of Agreement B1 of the 1995 ACE Conditions of Engagement (2nd edition 1998), I next have to consider whether the whole of those terms was incorporated into the contract and, in particular, whether clause B8.2 applied.

[39] The starting point, so it seems to me, must be that the contract specifically refers to those Conditions. In those circumstances it is difficult to see on what principle clause B8.2 might fall to be excluded. The only argument put forward is based upon the decision of the Court of Appeal in *Interfoto*. In my opinion that case does not bear the weight sought to be placed upon it by the pursuers in the present circumstances.

[40] It is necessary to consider the *Interfoto* case in some detail. [After summarising the facts of the case, Lord Glennie continued] . . . Dillon LJ relied upon the ticket cases, and in particular *Parker* v *South Eastern Railway Co* (1877) 2 CPD 416 and *Thornton* v *Shoe Lane Parking Ltd* [1971] 2 QB 163, to hold that, because the defendants had not had their attention drawn to what was, on any view, a particularly onerous and unusual clause, that clause had not been effectively incorporated into the contract. His reasoning is summarised in the following passage taken from pp.438-9 [which are reproduced in the extract from Dillon LJ's judgment, above. Lord Glennie then continued] . . .

Bingham LJ began his judgment by remarking that in many, perhaps most, legal systems outside the common law world, the law of obligations recognises and enforces an overriding principle that parties should act in good faith. He described that as, 'in essence a principle of fair and open dealing'. Noting that English law had committed itself to no such overriding principle, he cited the cases on sufficiency of notice as an example of the kind of response which the courts had developed on a piecemeal basis to demonstrated problems of unfairness. He referred in detail to *Parker* v *South Eastern Railway Co*, *Hood* v *Anchor Line (Henderson Brothers) Ltd* [1918] AC 837, *J Spurling Ltd* v *Bradshaw* [1956] 1 WLR 461 and *Thornton* v *Shoe Lane Parking Ltd*. He went on to say this [Lord Glennie quoted the last two paragraphs in the extract from Bingham LJ's judgment in *Interfoto* reproduced above and continued] . . .

It has been suggested in some of the cases decided subsequently that Bingham LJ decided the case on a different basis from that adopted by Dillon LJ, in that whereas Dillon LJ proceeded on the basis that, if the clause was incorporated, that was the end of the matter, Bingham LJ dealt with it on the basis that, even if it was incorporated, it could not be relied upon by the pursuers because they had not done enough to draw this 'unreasonable and extortionate clause' fairly to the attention of the defenders. For my part, although I do not think it really matters, I do not read the judgements in that way. It seems to me that Bingham LJ also decided the case on the basis that the failure sufficiently to draw the clause to the attention of the defenders meant that it was not incorporated into the contract. This seems to me to follow from the last sentence of the first of the two paragraphs quoted above, in which he says that if the conditions were common form or usual terms, the defendants could not contend that they were not incorporated into the contract; *per contra*, the discussion in the following paragraph about the term being unreasonable and extortionate and it not having been brought adequately to the attention of the defendants, appears to lead to the conclusion that it was not effectively incorporated into the contract.

[41] The *Interfoto* case was not concerned with a written contract. The terms upon which the plaintiffs sought to rely where set out on a document sent to the defendants when the transparencies were delivered to them. The first question that arose, therefore, was whether the defendants had been given sufficient notice that the document contained terms which it was intended should be binding on the parties under the contract. That question was answered in the affirmative. The reason that the question has to be asked at all is because, as Dillon LJ noted in the passage quoted above, it was and still is the case that people hardly ever trouble to read printed conditions on a ticket or delivery note or similar document. Therefore it is necessary, if the terms are to be incorporated into a contract between the parties, that the recipient should have had it brought to his attention that the document contains contractual terms. But, as Dillon LJ goes on to say, even if people notice that there are printed conditions, they tend to assume that they are not of any great importance. If there is some condition which is of particular importance, in the sense of departing in a material way from the terms usually incorporated into that type of contract, then, by a parity of reasoning, the recipient of the document should not only be made aware that the document contains contractual terms but should have his attention drawn to that condition. This has been described in the cases as applying to unusual, onerous, exorbitant or draconian conditions, but I do not think that anything turns on the epithet. The important characteristic is that the condition departs in a material way from the terms which would reasonably be expected to apply to that type of contract.

[42] All of this arises in the context of the conditions upon which one party seeks to rely having being given to the other party by means of a ticket or receipt or some other similar document, in circumstances where the recipient might not know that the document was intended to affect the legal relationship between the parties and, even if he did, would probably assume that it was not intended to import a set of terms that required to be thought about carefully before being accepted. *Interfoto* is therefore a case in the direct line of ticket cases dating back to the nineteenth century. More particularly, it confirms the line of authority in cases such as *Spurling* v *Bradshaw* and *Thornton* v *Shoe Lane Parking* to the effect that it is not necessarily sufficient to draw attention to the set of conditions as a whole if amongst those conditions there is one that is particularly onerous or unusual. However, I share the doubts, which have been expressed in the cases to which the Dean of Faculty referred (see para.[30] above), as to whether that principle can have any application to the case of a written agreement, between commercial parties,

and where the parties have had the opportunity of considering the proffered terms before deciding whether or not to proceed. Although, as I have said, the present case is not one of a wholly written agreement, it shares the important characteristics of a written agreement in that the terms proposed by the second defenders were identified in the second defenders' letter of 15 March 2001 and were the terms upon the basis of which the pursuers instructed the work to proceed.

[43] In the present case, therefore, I consider that the enquiry begins and ends with the question of whether, on a proper construction of the letter of 15 March 2001, the terms of that letter having been accepted by the pursuers by conduct, the parties are to be taken as having intended the 1995 ACE Conditions of Engagement (2nd Edition 1998) to govern the engagement of the second defenders as Consulting Engineers. I have held that they are to be taken as having intended those conditions to apply. In those circumstances, I consider that the whole of those conditions should apply save where the parties by act or omission have indicated that a particular condition should not.

...

[46] I should, however, deal with the parties' submissions on the basis that the principles set out in *Interfoto* apply to this case. Even on that basis, I do not think that the pursuers can successfully contend that the Net Contribution Clause was not incorporated into the contract. I say this for two reasons. First, I do not consider that this is a case where the second defenders can properly be said to be putting forward the ACE Conditions so as to place the onus on them to show that they had drawn attention to any unusual term. Rather it is a case of two contracting parties, who have dealt with each other over a period of over 20 years, entering into a new agreement in respect of a particular project on the same or substantially the same terms as they had applied to their contracts over the course of their relationship. As far as the evidence shows, they had always dealt on the basis that the second defenders would carry out work and be paid for it according to the ACE Conditions. Both parties would have known that those Conditions might be altered from time to time by the Association of Consulting Engineers. Both parties had the opportunity over the years to make themselves familiar with the ACE Conditions of Engagement. Each would be entitled to assume that the other had made itself as familiar as it wanted to make itself with the terms. Without going so far as to say that the pursuers were the *proferentes* of the ACE Conditions—the evidence does not show enough of the background to enable me to reach that conclusion—it is enough to say that both parties had always worked on the basis of those conditions and that there was no need for either to bring to the attention of the other any particular term, whether unusual, onerous or otherwise. Secondly, it does not seem to me that the Net Contribution Clause can properly be categorised as either unusual or onerous. Certainly it is a term which places a burden on the pursuers if they wish to litigate. Further, it clearly transfers to the pursuers the risk that one of its contracting parties might become insolvent. But, as was submitted by the Dean of Faculty (see para.[29] above), it is the pursuers who choose their contracting parties and it is the pursuers who can, no doubt at a price, insist that their contracting parties carry appropriate insurance. Further, as became clear in the evidence of Mr Barter, it is a term which has become the subject of argument amongst parties using the ACE Conditions and, possibly, amongst parties using other forms as well. The clause was first introduced, as I understand it, into the 1984 Conditions (1988 revision) by Amendment Sheet No 6 in September 1993. Accordingly, by the time that the second defenders submitted their proposal for the project at 411/2 Union Street in March 2001, the clause had been in circulation for over seven years. Anyone who contracted on the basis of the ACE Conditions, and was interested in what they said, would have been well aware of the existence of the Net Contribution Clause and, if not aware of its introduction in 1993 by way of that Amendment Sheet, would have been aware of its inclusion in the 1995 Conditions and in

the 1998 revision. Accordingly, I see no basis upon which it can plausibly be argued that the second defenders ought to have drawn the pursuers' attention specifically to the clause or that, because they did not, that clause was not incorporated into the contract between the parties."

Signed documents

9–57 If a party signs a document containing terms, they will, as a rule, be bound by it, whether or not they have read or understood it. The person signing will not, of course, be bound if they signed as a result of fraud or misrepresentation by the other party. The general position is as stated in the following case, however a potentially significant development in the Scottish case of *Montgomery Litho* (below) should also be borne in mind.

9–58 **L'Estrange v F Graucob Ltd**

[1934] 2 K.B. 394

English High Court, King's Bench: Scrutton and Maugham LJJ

L'Estrange owned and ran a cafe in Llandudno. She decided to buy one of Graucob's cigarette-vending machines. One of Graucob's representatives produced a form which was headed "Sales Agreement". He inserted on the form details of L'Estrange's sale and she signed it. The document stated that the agreement was "on the terms stated below". One of those terms, in small print, stated:

> "This agreement contains all the terms and conditions under which I agree to purchase the machine specified above, and any express or implied conditions, statement, or warranty, statutory or otherwise not stated herein is hereby excluded."

The machine was delivered and installed but within a few days it became jammed and unworkable. After a month, L'Estrange sought to terminate the contract, to have the machine removed and for her payment to be returned. Graucob refused.

L'Estrange was bound by signing of the contract, notwithstanding her ignorance of its contents.

9–59 "SCRUTTON LJ: . . . The present case is not a ticket case, and it is distinguishable from the ticket cases. In *Parker v South Eastern Ry Co* (1877) 2 C.P.D. 416 Mellish L.J. laid down in a few sentences the law applicable to this case. He there said (at p. 421):

'In an ordinary case, where an action is brought in a written agreement which is signed by the defendant, the agreement is proved by proving his signature, and, in the absence of fraud, it is wholly immaterial that he has not read the agreement and does not know its contents.'

Having said that, he goes on to deal with the ticket cases, where there is no signature to the contractual document, the document being simply handed by one party to the other:

'The parties may, however, reduce their agreement into writing, so that the writing constitutes the sole evidence of the agreement, without signing it; but in that case there must be evidence independently of the agreement itself to prove that the defendant had assented to it. In that case, also, if it is proved that the defendant has assented to the writing constituting the agreement between the parties, it is, in the absence of fraud, immaterial that the defendant had not read the agreement and did not know its contents.'

In cases in which the contract is contained in a railway ticket or other unsigned document, it is necessary to prove that an alleged party was aware, or ought to have been aware, of its terms and conditions. These cases have no application when the document has been signed. When a document containing contractual terms is signed, then, in the absence of fraud, or, I will add, misrepresentation, the party signing is bound, and it is wholly immaterial whether he has read the document or not."

This decision, although English, is a useful illustration. It is generally accepted as expressing the Scottish rule: see particularly Lord Devlin's speech in *McCutcheon v David MacBrayne Ltd*, below. **9–60**

In *Harris v Great Western Railway*,[14] Blackburn J stated (at 530):

> "And it is clear law that where there is a writing, into which the terms of any agreement are reduced, the terms are to be regulated by that writing. And though one of the parties may not have read the writing, yet, in general, he is bound to the other by those terms; and that, I apprehend, is on the ground that, by assenting to the contract thus reduced to writing, he represents to the other side that he has made himself acquainted with the contents of that writing and assents to them, and so induces the other side to act upon that representation by entering into the contract with him, and is consequently precluded from denying that he did make himself acquainted with those terms."

Lord Devlin, in *McCutcheon v David MacBrayne Ltd*, thought that "this is a dictum which some day [the Supreme Court] may have to examine more closely". His comments are reproduced below, para.9–70.

Could it be argued that, in Scots law, failure to draw attention to the exclusion clause before the other party signs the document amounts to fraud? If so, what would be the effects on the contract?

The following decision did not consider fraud, but robustly applied the principle that a particularly onerous condition may only be founded on if it is fairly drawn to the other party's attention—notwithstanding the fact that the contract document in this case had been signed by the defender.

Montgomery Litho Ltd v Maxwell **9–61**
2000 S.C. 56
Court of Session, Extra Division: Lords Sutherland, Prosser and Hamilton

Maxwell was a former director of a company that had gone into liquidation with a bill for printing services provided by Montgomery outstanding. Montgomery sued Maxwell personally, founding on the defender's signature on a credit application. The credit form included a statement that the debtor had read and agreed to the pursuer's standard terms and conditions.

Condition 7(e) of the standard terms and conditions provided:

> "In the case of a limited company the director responsible for opening a credit account with the printer and who signs the application shall be jointly and severally liable for any and all payments that become due to the printer."

The court rejected the appeal on the grounds that the condition was of a particularly onerous nature and that it had not been specifically drawn to Maxwell's attention.

[14] *Harris v Great Western Railway* (1876) 1 Q.B.D. 515.

9–62 "OPINION OF THE COURT (per LORD SUTHERLAND): ... The second submission was based on the proposition that there was nothing in the credit application form to indicate that the person signing it was doing anything other than applying for credit on behalf of Newtext, and nothing to indicate that there was anything special or unusual in the terms and conditions referable to that contract. Whatever terms and conditions there might be in a contract between two companies, the acceptance by a third party of a personal cautionary obligation is not such a term or condition. In such circumstances it is not sufficient to draw attention generally to standard terms and conditions, but it is necessary to draw specific attention to any unusual or special condition which might be regarded as something more than the normal ancillary terms of a contract. In *Interfoto Picture Library Ltd v Stiletto Visual Programmes Ltd* it was held that where clauses incorporated into a contract contained a particularly onerous or unusual condition, the party seeking to enforce that condition had to show that it had been brought fairly and reasonably to the attention of the other party. It was pointed out that it was notorious that people hardly ever troubled to read printed conditions on a ticket or delivery note or similar document. In the older ticket cases the courts held that the common law required that reasonable steps be taken to draw the other party's attention to the printed conditions or they would not be part of the contract. Dillon LJ said that a logical development of the common law into modern conditions is that it should be held that if one condition in a set of printed conditions is particularly onerous or unusual the party seeking to enforce it must show that that particular condition was brought fairly to the attention of the other party. Bingham LJ, as he then was, said that the well known cases on sufficiency of notice are concerned, at one level, with a question of pure contractual analysis, but at another level are concerned with a somewhat different question, namely whether it would in all the circumstances be fair or reasonable to hold a party bound by any conditions or by a particular condition of an unusual and stringent nature.

Having reviewed some of the authorities he came to the conclusion that on the facts of that particular case the condition in question was of a particularly onerous nature which should specifically have been drawn to the attention of the other party and that the failure to do so relieved the defendants from liability under that condition. Amongst the authorities founded on by Bingham LJ were two Scottish cases, *Hood v Anchor Line Ltd* and *McCutcheon v David MacBrayne Ltd.* Although the analysis of Dillon LJ appears to show some differences inter se, we see no reason to doubt that the general principle upon which they both proceeded, *viz* that the failure by the *proferens* fairly to draw attention to a particularly onerous and unusual provision may disable him from effectually founding on it, represents also the law of Scotland.

Counsel for the respondents maintained that cases such as *Interfoto* and other ticket cases were not in point because in the present case the defender had signed the application form which contained the statement 'I have read and accepted the company's standard terms and conditions'. In our view, however, the addition of this statement adds nothing to what is normally found in offers or acceptances, namely a statement that the offer or acceptance is to be governed by the standard terms and conditions of the proferens. The point is not whether the standard terms and conditions, which may be voluminous, have been read in whole or in part by one of the parties. The question really is whether a particular condition is of such an unusual nature that it should specifically be drawn to the attention of the other party rather than being left simply as part of a large collection of other terms and conditions which are of a fairly standard nature. We are quite satisfied that in the present case the imposition of a personal obligation of guarantee on a director of a company is something which is unusual, to say the least of it, to be found in terms and conditions which purport to regulate the contract as between the two companies. It is certainly not unusual for a director to be asked to sign an obligation guaranteeing the company's liability, particularly in the case of a small limited liability company. It is, however, distinctly unusual for this to be done under the guise of terms and conditions relating to the contract between the two companies. We accept that there is no reason in principle why a credit application form of this kind could not incorporate both an application for credit on behalf of the company and a personal guarantee by an individual of the company's obligations. The latter provision would, however, require in our view to be so expressed as to give fair notice that it concerned the individual as such and that it imported an obligation by him personally. In the present case there is nothing to indicate that the defender signed the form in any capacity other than as a director of Newtext. There is nothing to indicate that he signed it in a personal capacity, giving a personal guarantee for the company's obligations. It follows that there is no legal basis for the pursuers' assertion of joint and several liability and accordingly the sheriff principal's interlocutor must be recalled and the action dismissed."

Woolman points out that the case could have been analysed by the court in terms of offer and acceptance—that Maxwell had signed the contract document in his capacity as company director, and not in any personal capacity (and therefore had not personally accepted the offer). It may be significant that the court did not choose this path. As Woolman remarks:

> "Time will tell whether the avenue opened up by the judges in *Montgomery Litho* leads somewhere interesting or turns out to have been a wrong turning and a dead end."[15]

Montgomery Litho was recently considered and applied in:

Brandon Hire Plc v Russell 9–63
Extra Division, Inner House, Court of Session
[2010] CSIH 76; 2010 W.L. 3257460
Lord Carloway Lord Clarke Lord Bonomy
24 June 2010

Brandon Hire Plc (Brandon) obtained an English judgment for a debt of £23,647.61 against LMG Projects Services Ltd (LMG).

Russell, a director of LMG had signed, on behalf of LMG the plant hire contract from which the debt arose. The contract document stated, under the heading "E. GUARANTEE":

> "Please read and sign the following declaration.
>
> I (the undersigned) agree that all transactions of hire or sale entered into by my company (known as 'the Customer') shall be subject to Brandon Hire Plc's 'Conditions of Hire or Sale', as the case may be, operative at the time of any contract of hire or sale. I will make full settlement of all monies due within one month from the date of Brandon Hire's invoice and I have answered all questions on this application form truly and fully. I hereby, personally guarantee payment in respect of all sums due from my company ('the Customer') to Brandon Hire Plc, together with all ancillary costs incurred. I have retained a copy of this form for my records."

---

[15] It may be arguable that *Montgomery Litho* hints at an implicit doctrine of good faith in Scots private law, at least insofar as a failure to disclose facts (or draw attention to them) in circumstances which could indicate bad faith. Cases such as *Steuart's Trustees v Hart* (1875) 3 R. 192 may support such a notion.

Russell's signature appeared at the foot of Section E in a space headed "Signature of Director", followed by his name in block capitals. Against the words "Position within company" he had written "Director".

Brandon claimed that this amounted to a personal guarantee by Russell, which they were entitled to enforce against him.

9–64 "LORD CARLOWAY: ...

6 Before the sheriff, and before this court, the appellant relied heavily on the decision of the Extra Division in the case of *Montgomery Litho Limited v Maxwell* 2000 SC 56. In that case, the pursuers entered into a contract with a company of which the defender was the managing director, for the supply, to the company, of printing services. The contract for the printing services, itself, was never reduced to writing. An application had been presented to the pursuers for a credit account. It was held that that application formed part of the contract between the company and the pursuers. The application provided 'I have read and accepted the company's Standard Terms and Conditions ... all transactions are subject to the company's Standard Terms and Conditions'. The defender had signed the application. The defender, however, had at no time requested to see the Standard Terms and Conditions. Standard condition 7 of the pursuers' Terms and Conditions provided as follows:

'In the case of a Limited Company the Director responsible for opening a credit account with the printer and who signs the application shall be jointly and severally liable for any and all payments that become due to the printer.'

The Standard Terms and Conditions defined the 'printer' as the pursuers. The pursuers sought to recover from the defender payment of the company's debts, due to them, for printing services on the footing that he had guaranteed these. The Extra Division dismissed the action. It is clear to us that the Extra Division reached the decision, in that case, on the basis that the terms of the personal guarantee had not been made the subject of any contract between the pursuers and the defender. The mere reference to the standard terms and conditions of the pursuers was not sufficient for that purpose, particularly where the defender had never actually seen those terms and conditions. The principal reasoning of the court is to be found at page 59F to page 60A, in the Opinion of the Court delivered by Lord Sutherland where he said:

'The question really is whether a particular condition is of such an unusual nature that it should specifically be drawn to the attention of the other party rather than being left simply as part of a large collection of other terms and conditions which are of a fairly standard nature. We are quite satisfied that in the present case the imposition of a personal obligation of guarantee on a director of a company is something which is unusual, to say the least of it, to be found in terms and conditions which purport to regulate the contract as between the two companies. It is certainly not unusual for a director to be asked to sign an obligation guaranteeing the company's liability, particularly in the case of a small limited liability company. It is, however, distinctly unusual for this to be done under the guise of terms and conditions relating to the contract between the two companies. We accept that there is no reason in principle why a credit application form of this kind could not incorporate both an application for credit on behalf of the company and a personal guarantee by an individual of the company's obligations. The latter provision would, however, require in our view to be so expressed as to give fair notice that it concerned the individual as such and that it imported an obligation by him personally. In the present case there is nothing to indicate that the defender signed the form in any capacity other than as a director of Newtext. There is nothing to indicate that he signed it in a personal capacity, giving a personal guarantee for the company's obligations. It follows that there is no legal basis for the pursuers' assertion of joint and several liability ... '

That that decision is one which arises from the approach of the law as to what is required to bring adequately to the notice of a person, a contractual obligation of an unusual or unduly onerous nature if he is to be bound by it, can be seen from the discussion in the court's opinion at page 58F to page 59E and the authorities referred to, in particular the decision of the Court of Appeal in *Interfoto Picture Library Ltd v Stiletto Visual Programmes Ltd* [1989] 1 QB 433 which the Extra Division followed. It should be noted that, in the passage cited from the judgment of the court in *Montgomery Litho Limited*, the court expressly recognised that there was nothing unusual for a director to be asked to sign an obligation guaranteeing the company's liability, particularly in the case of a small limited liability company. The problem in that case was that the obligation in question had not been brought adequately to the attention of the defender so as to produce an implied assent thereto by him.

7 In the present case, as has been noted, it was not contended that it was not insufficient notice given to the appellant of the terms in question to render them as being of no contractual effect at all. That concession, in our view, was not surprising having regard to the bold heading of Section E. The argument rather was that, as a matter of construction, the provision should not be found to have imposed any personal liability on the appellant. We cannot agree with that submission. The wording 'I will make full settlement of all monies due within one month from the date of Brandon Hire's invoice' and 'I hereby, personally guarantee payment in respect of all sums due from my company' can, in our opinion, only be read as amounting to an agreement by the appellant to undertake personal liability for the company's obligations. To accept the approach advanced on behalf of the appellant, would mean that Section E had added virtually nothing to the contractual arrangements that would otherwise subsist in the circumstances. The present case is, in our judgment, clearly distinguishable from the circumstances in the case of *Montgomery Litho Limited, supra* because in that case the director had never adhibited his signature underneath words which provided for joint and several liability between himself and his company. He had, in fact, never seen the wording of any such a provision. A mere reference to the company's Standard Terms and Conditions, in which the provision was to be found, was held not to provide sufficient notice to the director that not only was his company bound to pay for the printing charges, but that he too was jointly and severally liable therefor.

8 It follows that we agree with the reasoning of the sheriff, in the passage from his Note cited above, for refusing to allow the appellant's averments relating to the defence on the merits to be admitted to probation. For the foregoing reasons the appeal fell to be refused."

The following case is an English decision and a difficult case to place in a Scottish context. The case is clearly founded on English conceptions of misrepresentation. It may well be that a case such as this would come within the Scottish notion of error or of fraud; but this as we have seen is a troublesome area, particularly when, as here, we are dealing with a failure to disclose information. It is far more likely that facts such as these would raise a personal bar in Scots law.

9–65

Curtis v Chemical Cleaning and Dyeing Co Ltd
[1951] 1 K.B. 805
English Court of Appeal: Somervell, Singleton and Denning LJJ

Curtis took to the defendants, a firm of dyers and cleaners, a white satin wedding dress for cleaning. She was asked to sign a "receipt" that contained the following clause: "[t]his article is accepted on condition that the company is not liable for any damage howsoever arising".

Before signing she asked why she had to sign it. An assistant told her that the company would not accept any liability for damage done to beads or sequins on the dress. Curtis then signed the "receipt" without having read all of it. When the dress was returned, there was a stain on it.

Held that there had been a misrepresentation, and as a result the condition did not form part of the contract between the parties.

9–66 "DENNING LJ: ... In my opinion, any behaviour by words or conduct is sufficient to be a misrepresentation if it is such as to mislead the other party about the existence or extent of the exemption. If it conveys a false impression, that is enough. If the false impression is created knowingly, it is a fraudulent misrepresentation; if it is created unwittingly, it is an innocent misrepresentation. But either is sufficient to disentitle the creator of it to the benefit of the exemption. It was held in *R v Kylsant (Lord)* [1932] 1 K.B. 442 that a representation might be literally true but practically false, not because of what it said, but because of what it left unsaid: in short, because of what it implied. This is as true of an innocent misrepresentation as it is of a fraudulent misrepresentation. When one party puts forward a printed form for signature, failure by him to draw attention to the existence or extent of the exemption clause may in some circumstances convey the impression that there is no exemption at all, or, at any rate, not so wide an exemption as that which is in fact contained in the document. The present case is a good illustration. The customer said in evidence: 'When I was asked to sign the document I asked why. The assistant said I was to accept responsibility for damage to beads and sequins. I did not read it all before I signed it.' In those circumstances, by failing to draw attention to the width of the exemption clause, the assistant created the false impression that the exemption related to the beads and sequins only, and that it did not extend to the material of which the dress was made ... a sufficient misrepresentation to disentitle the cleaners from relying on the exemption, except in regard to the beads and sequins. In the present case the misrepresentation was as to the extent of the exemption. In other cases it may be as to its existence. For instance, if nothing was said by the assistant, this document might reasonably be understood to be, like a boot repairer's receipt, only a voucher for the customer to produce when collecting the goods, and not to contain conditions exempting the cleaners from their common law liability for negligence, in which case it would not protect the cleaners: see *Chapelton v Barry Urban District Council*. I say this because I do not wish it to be supposed that the cleaners would have been better off if the assistant had simply handed over the document to the customer without asking her to sign it, or if the customer was not so inquiring as the plaintiff, but was an unsuspecting person who signed whatever she was asked without question. In those circumstances the conduct of the cleaners might well be such that it conveyed the impression that the document contained no conditions, or at any rate, no condition exempting them from their common law liability, in which case they could not rely on it ... In my opinion, when a condition, purporting to exempt a person from his common law liabilities, is obtained by an innocent misrepresentation, the party who has made that misrepresentation is disentitled to rely on the exemption."

SINGLETON and SOMERVELL LJJ concurred.

Previous course of dealings between the parties

A court may infer notice from a previous course of dealings between the parties, into which the documents or terms in question had been regularly imported. Even a document that was given after the contract was made may thus become binding. The limits of this "course of dealings" rule are illustrated by the next case. 9–67

McCutcheon v David MacBrayne Ltd 9–68
1964 S.C. (H.L.) 28
House of Lords: Lords Reid, Hodgson, Guest, Devlin, Pearce

McCutcheon, a farm grieve on Islay, had crossed to the mainland. He wanted to use his car, so he contacted his brother-in-law, McSporran, a farmer on Islay, to send it over by MacBrayne's ferry. McSporran drove the car to the pier at Port Askaig and, at MacBrayne's office, booked the car on to a ferry for West Loch Tarbert on the mainland. The car was shipped on the MV "Lochiel". The ferry sank due to negligent navigation and the car was lost. The value of the car was £480. MacBrayne claimed that the contract of carriage excluded their liability for the loss.

When booking goods for shipment, MacBrayne's normal practice was to issue a receipt for the freight and a "risk note", which would be signed by the shipper. The risk note comprised MacBrayne's conditions of carriage and a docket signed by the shipper agreeing that the goods were shipped "on the conditions stated above". Normal practice was that the docket would be signed by the shipper.

On previous occasions when McCutcheon and McSporran had shipped goods, they had received the receipt and the risk note and had signed the docket. On this particular occasion, McSporran was not asked to sign, and he did not sign.

Held that the conditions had not been imported into the contract.

"LORD REID: ... The question is, what was the contract between the parties? The contract was an oral one. No document was signed or changed hands until after the contract was completed. I agree with the unanimous view of the learned judges of the Court of Session that the terms of the receipt which was made out by the pursuer and handed to Mr McSporran after he had paid the freight cannot be regarded as terms of the contract. So the case is not one of the familiar ticket cases where the question is whether conditions endorsed on, or referred to in, a ticket or other document handed to the consignor in making the contract are binding on the consignor. If conditions not mentioned when this contract was made are to be added to, or regarded as part of, this contract, it must be for some reason different from those principles which are now well settled in ticket cases. If this oral contract stands unqualified, there can be no doubt that the respondents are liable for the damage caused by the negligence of their servants ... 9–69

The respondents contend that, by reason of knowledge ... gained by the appellant and his agent in ... previous transactions, the appellant is bound by their conditions. But this case differs essentially from the ticket cases. There the carrier in making the contract hands over a document containing or referring to conditions which he intends to be part of the contract ... But here, in making the contract, neither party referred to, or indeed had in mind, any additional terms, and the contract was complete and fully effective without any additional terms. If it could be said that, when making the contract, Mr McSporran knew that the respondents always required a risk note to be signed and knew that the pursuer was simply forgetting to put it before him for signature, then it might be said that neither he nor his principal could take advantage of the error of the other party of which he was aware ...

The only other ground on which it would seem possible to import these conditions is that based on a course of dealing. If two parties have made a series of similar contracts each containing certain conditions, and then they made another without expressly referring to those conditions, it may be that those conditions ought to be implied. If the officious bystander had asked them whether they had intended to leave out the conditions this time, both must, as honest men, have said 'Of course not'. But again here the facts will not support that ground. According to Mr McSporran, there had been no consistent course of dealing; sometimes he was asked to sign and sometimes not. And, moreover, he did not know what the conditions were. This time he was offered an oral contract without any reference to conditions, and he accepted the offer in good faith.

9–70 LORD DEVLIN: ... If it were possible for your Lordships to escape from the world of make-believe which the law has created into the real world in which transactions of this sort are actually done, the answer would be short and simple. It should make no difference whatever. This sort of document is not meant to be read, still less to be understood. Its signature is in truth about as significant as a handshake that marks the formal conclusion of a bargain ...

The fact that a man has made a contract in the same form ninety-nine times (let alone three or four times which are here alleged) will not of itself affect the hundredth contract, in which the form is not used. Previous dealings are relevant only if they prove knowledge of the terms, actual and not constructive, and assent to them. If a term is not expressed in a contract, there is only one other way in which it can come into it and that is by implication. No implication can be made against a party of a term which was unknown to him. If previous dealings show that a man knew of and agreed to a term on ninety-nine occasions, there is a basis for saying that it can be imported into the hundredth contract without an express statement. It may or may not be sufficient to justify the importation—that depends on the circumstances; but at least by proving knowledge the essential beginning is made. Without knowledge there is nothing ...

If a man is given a blank ticket without conditions or any reference to them, even if he knows in detail what the conditions usually exacted are, he is not, in the absence of any allegation of fraud or of that sort of mistake for which the law gives relief, bound by such conditions. It may seem a narrow and artificial line that divides a ticket that is blank on the back from one that says 'For conditions see time-tables,' or something of that sort, that has been held to be enough notice. I agree that it is an artificial line and one that has little relevance to everyday conditions. It may be beyond your lordships' power to make the artificial line more natural: but at least you can see that it is drawn fairly for both sides, and that there is not one law for individuals and another for organisations that can issue printed documents. If the respondents had remembered to issue a risk note in this case, they would have invited your lordships to give a curt answer to any complaint by the appellant. He might say that the terms were unfair and unreasonable, that he had never voluntarily agreed to them, that it was impossible to read or understand them and that anyway, if he had tried to negotiate any change, the respondents would not have listened to him. The respondents would expect him to be told that he had made his contract and must abide by it. Now the boot is on the other foot. It is just as legitimate, but also just as vain, for the respondents to say that it was only a slip on their part, that it is unfair and unreasonable of the appellant to take advantage of it and that he knew perfectly well that they never carried goods except on conditions. The law must give the same answer: they must abide by the contract which they made. What is sauce for the goose is sauce for the gander. It will remain unpalatable sauce for both animals until the legislature, if the courts cannot do it, intervenes to secure that when contracts are made in circumstances in which there is no scope for free negotiation of the terms, they are made on terms that are clear, fair and reasonable and settled independently as such. That is what Parliament has done in the case of carriage of goods by rail and on the high seas."

LORDS GUEST, HODSON AND PEARCE delivered similar speeches.

Was Lord Reid here applying the "officious bystander" test? Which did Lord Reid regard as fatal to MacBrayne's claim: the lack of consistency in the course of dealing, or their failure to refer to the conditions on this particular occasion? 9–71

Note that Lord Devlin goes to great pains to distinguish the ticket cases, on the basis that such tickets were "contractual documents". Is that true? In any case, was Lord Devlin saying that the only reason why the terms in question here were not incorporated into the contract by a course of dealings was because they were not given to Mr MacSporran on this occasion?

Lord Devlin went much further than the other judges by suggesting that the failure to refer to the document in the particular instance was fatal to the carrier's case. This approach has been resisted in subsequent decisions.

Note too Lord Devlin's advance call for legislation in the area of contracts with no scope for free negotiation of the terms, to ensure fairness, clarity and independent settlement.

Hollier v Rambler Motors (AMC) Ltd 9–72
[1972] 2 Q.B. 71
English Court of Appeal, Civil Division, Salmon and Stamp LJJ and Latey J

Hollier owned an American Rambler motor car which developed an oil leak. He telephoned the manager of Rambler Motors to book the car in. It was agreed that if he had the car towed to the garage the work would be done in due course. Hollier had frequently bought spare parts for his car from Rambler Motors during the previous five years. On three or four occasions during those five years he had had repairs or servicing carried out there. When doing repairs or servicing to a car, but not when merely supplying spare parts, the customer was required to sign an "invoice". The form contained a description of the work to be carried out and the price for doing it. Underneath the customer's signature was the clause: "The Company is not responsible for damage caused by fire to customer's cars on the premises".

Hollier had signed this form on at least two previous occasions.

While the car was in the garage a fire broke out as a result of the negligence of garage staff. It caused substantial damage to the car. In an action for damages for negligence, Rambler Motors contended that, although on this occasion Hollier had not signed their "invoice" form, the clause therein had been incorporated in the oral contract between the parties by a course of dealing and that its effect was to exclude their liability for negligently causing a tire while the car was in their care.

Held in favour of Hollier that the defendants had not established a course of dealing, and so the clause had not been incorporated into the contract.

"SALMON LJ: ... I will deal first of all with the point whether the clause relied on by the defendants can properly be implied into this oral contract by reason of the course of dealing between the parties ... 9–73

It seems to me that if it was impossible to rely on a course of dealing in *McCutcheon v David MacBrayne Ltd* [1964] 1 W.L.R. 125, still less would it be possible to do so in this case, when the so-called course of dealing consisted only of three or four transactions in the course of five years. As I read the speeches of Lord Reid, Lord Guest and Lord Pearce, one, but only one amongst many, of the facts to be taken into account in considering whether there had been a course of dealing from which a term was to be implied into the contract was whether the consignor actually knew what were the terms written on the back of the risk note. Lord Devlin said that this was a critical factor. Even on the assumption that Lord Devlin's dictum went further than was necessary for the decision in that case, and was wrong—which I think is the effect of *Henry Kendall & Sons (a firm) v William Lillico & Sons Ltd* [1969] 2 A.C. 31—I do not see how that can help the defendants here. The speeches of the other members of the House and the decision itself in *McCutcheon's* case make it plain that the clause on which the defendants seek to rely cannot in law be imported into the oral contract they made in March 1970."

It appears from Salmon LJ's judgment that the mere fact that the other party knew that terms and conditions were included on the document will not be enough to import the term into the contract. A previous course of dealings implies also that the parties have dealt with each other in a series of transactions that can properly be described as a "course". Here, "three or four transactions in the course of five years" would not be enough.

The following case suggests that what may be decisive in establishing a course of dealings is whether the parties are of equal bargaining power.

9–74 **British Crane Hire Corporation Ltd v Ipswich Plant Hire Ltd**

1975 Q.B. 303

English Court of Appeal: Lord Denning MR, Megaw LJ and Sir Eric Sachs

IPC, who had contracted to carry out construction work in marshy ground near the river Stour in Essex, hired a crane from BCH. The crane was delivered and BCH subsequently sent IPC a printed form setting out the conditions of hire. The form contained conditions that the hirer would be responsible for the recovery of the crane from soft ground and that IPC should be responsible for, and indemnify BCH against, all expenses arising from the use of the crane. IPC neither signed nor returned the form to BCH.

IPC instructed the driver (an employee of BCH) of the crane to drive on to the marsh using "navimats", or timber baulks, over which the crane could be driven without sinking. The driver did not use the "navimats" and the crane sank and had to be recovered. On the second day, the driver did use the "navimats", but the crane nevertheless sank.

BCH, relying on the conditions, sought to recover from IPC the costs of the second recovery of the crane; IPC sought to recover from BCH the cost of the first.

BCH were successful: the parties were both in the trade, of equal bargaining power, and the evidence showed that IPC were aware of the conditions of hire.

9–75 "LORD DENNING MR: ... In support of the course of dealing, the plaintiffs relied on two previous transactions in which the defendants had hired cranes from the plaintiffs. One was 20th February 1969; and the other 6th October 1969. Each was on a printed form which set out the hiring of a crane, the price, the site, and so forth; and also the setting out the conditions the same as those here. There were thus only two transactions many months before and they were not known to the defendants' manager who ordered this crane. In the circumstances I doubt whether those two would be sufficient to show a course of dealing.

In *Hollier v Rambler Motors (AMC) Ltd* [1972] 2 Q.B. 71, 76, Salmon L.J. said he knew of no case 'in which it has been decided or even argued that a term could be implied into an oral contract on the strength of a course of dealing (if it can be so called) which consisted at the most of three or four transactions over a period of five years.'

That was a case of a private individual who had had his car repaired by the defendants and had signed forms with conditions on three or four occasions. The plaintiff there was not of equal bargaining power with the garage company which repaired the car. The conditions were not incorporated.

But here the parties were both in the trade and were of equal bargaining power. Each was a firm of plant hirers who hired out plant. The defendants themselves knew that firms in the plant-hiring trade always imposed conditions in regard to the hiring of plant; and that their conditions were on much the same lines. The defendants' manager, Mr Turner (who knew the crane), was asked about it. He agreed that he had seen these conditions or similar ones in regard to the hiring of plant. He said that most of them were, to one extent or another, variations of a form which he called 'the Contractors' Plant Associations form.' The defendants themselves (when they let out cranes) used the conditions of that form. The conditions on the plaintiffs' form were in rather different words, but nevertheless to much the same effect ...

From that evidence it is clear that both parties knew quite well that conditions were habitually imposed by the supplier of these machines: and both parties knew the substance of those conditions. In particular that, if the crane sank in soft ground, it was the hirer's job to recover it; and that there was an indemnity clause. In these circumstances, I think the conditions on the form should be regarded as incorporated into the contract. I would not put it so much on the course of dealing, but rather on the common understanding which is to be derived from the conduct of the parties, namely, that the hiring was to be on the terms of the plaintiffs' usual conditions.

As Lord Reid said in *McCutcheon v David MacBrayne Ltd.* [1964] 1 W.L.R. 125,128, quoting from the Scottish textbook, *Gloag on Contract*, 2nd ed. (1929), p. 7: 'The judicial task is not to discover the actual intentions of each party; it is to decide what each was reasonably entitled to conclude from the attitude of the other.'

It seems to me that, in view of the relationship of the parties, when the defendants requested this crane urgently and it was supplied at once—before the usual form was received—the plaintiffs were entitled to conclude that the defendants were accepting it on the terms of the plaintiffs' own printed conditions—which would follow in a day or two. It is just as if the plaintiffs had said, 'We will supply it on our usual conditions,' and the defendants said, 'Of course, that is quite understood.'

Applying the conditions, it is quite clear that conditions 6 and 8 cover the second mishap. The defendants are liable for the cost of recovering the crane from the soft ground.

But, so far as the first mishap is concerned, neither condition 6 or condition 8 (the indemnity clause) is wide enough to cover it; because that mishap was due to the negligence of their own driver. It requires very clear words to exempt a person from responsibility for his own negligence: see *Gillespie Brothers & Co Ltd v Roy Bowles Transport Ltd.* [1973] Q.B. 400, 415. There are no such words here."

Lord Denning was here objectively attempting to assess whether a course of dealing had arisen. He relied strongly on the evidence that the parties were in the same line of business and should have been aware of the normal conditions of trade. The case can be contrasted with the following Scottish decision.

9–76

Continental Tyre & Rubber Co Ltd v Trunk Trailer Co Ltd
1987 S.L.T. 58
Court of Session, First Division: The Lord President (Lord Emslie), Lords Dunpark and Ross

Trunk Trailer ordered tyres from Continental, using their printed purchase order form. Trunk Trailer's standard conditions of purchase were printed on the back of the order. There was no written acceptance of the order, but Continental supply the tyres in batches, each accompanied by a delivery note followed by an invoice, both of which referred to Continental's standard conditions of sale. The parties' respective conditions of purchase and conditions of sale were mutually inconsistent.

In a dispute about the quality and fitness for purpose under s.14 of the Sale of Goods Act 1979 of the tyres supplied, Continental sought to rely on one of their standard conditions which specifically excluded liability under s.14. Trunk Trailer argued that the condition was neither fair nor reasonable in the circumstances.

The court found in favour of the Trunk Trailer.

9–77 "LORD PRESIDENT (LORD EMSLIE): ... [D]id the parties, by word, writing, deed, and silence, so conduct themselves as to justify the inference that it was their mutual intention that the pursuers' conditions of sale should be part of the particular contract which is in dispute? ...

It could not in all the circumstances reasonably be concluded that the defenders must be taken to have assented to the incorporation of these conditions of sale in this particular contract. My reasons for this opinion can be briefly stated. The documents in which it is stated that 'all offers and sales are subject to Company's current terms and Conditions of Sale' was, in every case, a non-contractual document. It was a document, the only purpose of which was to record performance of a particular transaction with a view to payment. Such a document might be expected to be directed to a part of the defenders' organisation not concerned with the making of contracts and since there are no averments that it was on any prior occasion brought to the attention of any of those officers of the defenders who placed orders with the pursuers, I cannot regard it as an apt vehicle for intimating to the defenders any policy which the pursuers proposed to follow in relation to future contracts. However that may be, it cannot be held that the defenders so conducted themselves that they must be taken to have assented to the incorporation of the pursuers' conditions of sale in the contract with which we are concerned. Condition 1 of the pursuers' conditions of sale is in these terms: 'General: Unless otherwise agreed by the Company in writing, all goods are supplied on the following conditions to the exclusion of any terms or conditions stipulated by the buyer and of any previous communications, representations or warranties not expressly incorporated herein. No order shall result in a binding contract of sale unless and until the Company has accepted it in writing.' Examination of the defenders' purchase order which was used in each transaction stated prominently on its face: 'Your attention is directed to the General Conditions printed overleaf.' The conditions of purchase on the reverse side of the purchase order begin with this declaration: 'This order is subject to any Special Conditions or instructions on the face thereof and to the following General Conditions of Purchase so far as not altered or modified by or inconsistent with such special Conditions or instructions. In event of conditions of this Order conflicting with any standard conditions of the Supplier, our condition shall prevail.' The short point is that, notwithstanding the receipt of invoices relating to prior transactions, the defenders continued to order goods in terms of their own conditions of purchase and the pursuers continued, without question or objection, to deliver goods in response to the defenders' orders. It appears to me to be impossible, therefore, to hold that the defenders, in placing their order, PO 9503, on 3 May 1979, must be taken to have assented to that exclusion of all their own conditions of purchase."

LORD DUNPARK and LORD ROSS concurred.

This case may usefully be compared with *McCrone v Boots Farm Sales Ltd*[16] (see paras 10–23—10–24 below), which again involved the exclusion of statutory implied terms in a contract for the sale of goods. **9–78**

Although only a model framework and therefore not part of the law of Scotland, the DCFR attempts to provide a common framework for such terms.

"DCFR. II–9:103: Terms not individually negotiated

(1) Terms supplied by one party and not individually negotiated may be invoked against the other party only if the other party was aware of them, or if the party supplying the terms took reasonable steps to draw the other party's attention to them, before or when the contract was concluded.

(2) If a contract is to be concluded by electronic means, the party supplying any terms which have not been individually negotiated may invoke them against the other party only if they are made available to the other party in textual form.

(3) For the purposes of this Article

(a) 'not individually negotiated' has the meaning given by II.–1:110 (Terms 'not individually negotiated'); and
(b) terms are not sufficiently brought to the other party's attention by a mere reference to them in a contract document, even if that party signs the document.'"

[16] *McCrone v Boots Farm Sales Ltd* 1981 S.L.T. (O.H.) 103.

CHAPTER 10

EXCLUSION AND SIMILAR CLAUSES

Most cases in the previous chapter concern clauses that in some way exclude or restrict the liabilities of the parties to the contract. Such clauses, generally referred to as "exclusion" clauses, are common in business contract documents, especially standard form contracts (increasingly referred to as "boilerplate"[1] contracts). In a business context, such clauses are attempts by the parties to define the extent—and limits—of their obligations to each other. They are useful in clarifying who bears the risks in the transaction and by implication who should insure. Parties to a commercial contract should be free to negotiate their terms without interference. **10–01**

What if the parties are not of equal bargaining power and one party can impose terms upon the other? The resultant contract is potentially a one-sided, or "leonine" bargain or "contract of adhesion". Commuters do not freely negotiate terms every time they board the train, but travels subject to the rail company's standard terms and conditions of which they have probably never heard, let alone read. In recent decades, the courts have been much concerned with the balance between the need to permit the incorporation of such clauses into contracts and the need to protect those perceived to be the weaker parties, normally consumers. Despite such efforts, the redress of this imbalance has been achieved largely by statute. The result is a great deal of protective legislation that is now so detailed and complex that it forms a distinct aspect of consumer law,[2] most of which is now consolidated in and extended by the Consumer Rights Act 2015 Pt 2, Unfair Terms.[3] In its explanatory notes to the Consumer Rights Act 1915[4] the UK Government states:

Advice and Consultations **10–02**

...

Part 1

...

"14. The Government has also implemented the majority of the recommendations made by the Law Commission and Scottish Law Commission ('the Law Commissions') following their findings that the law surrounding consumer rights to redress following misleading or aggressive practices by traders is fragmented, complex and unclear[2]

...

---

[1] An Americanism, arising from the use of boiler plate steel for the casting of widely distributed printing plates among newspaper printers in 19th century United States.

[2] For that reason, and because of the need to make the most sensible use of space available, unfair terms in consumer contracts are no longer considered in this text. Readers are referred to Cowan Irvine's *Consumer Law in Scotland*, 5th edn (Edinburgh: W. Green, 2015). Reference should also be made to relevant sections in WW McBryde, *The Law of Contract in Scotland*, 3rd edn (Edinburgh: W. Green, 2007) and HL MacQueen & J Thomson, *Contract Law in Scotland*, 3rd edn (London: Bloomsbury, 2012).

[3] Available at: *http://www.legislation.gov.uk/ukpga/2015/15/part/2* [Accessed 2 September 2015]. The Act received the Royal Assent on 26 March 2014, but the bulk of its provisions, including those on unfair terms, will be brought into force by statutory instrument at a date yet to be specified.

[4] Available at: *http://www.legislation.gov.uk/ukpga/2015/15/pdfs/ukpgaen_20150015_en.pdf* [Accessed 2 September 2015].

> *Part 2*
>
> 18. Legislation on unfair contract terms is contained in the [Unfair Contract Terms Act], which currently applies to contracts between businesses and between consumers but contains some particular rules about business to consumer contracts. It makes some terms in contracts automatically non-binding and subjects others to a test of reasonableness. The Unfair Terms in Consumer Contract Regulations 1999 ('UTCCRs') enable consumers to challenge most non-negotiated terms of a contract on the grounds that they are unfair. There are certain terms that cannot be assessed for fairness: terms that relate to the definition of the main subject matter of the contract and those that relate to the adequacy of the price or remuneration as against the goods or services supplied in exchange. These are known as "exempt terms". In August 2002 the Law Commissions issued a consultation proposing a unified law on unfair contracts terms and, in February 2005, they issued a report setting out detailed recommendations, which was published alongside a draft Bill[13]. These recommendations were not taken forward at the time. However, in May 2012 the [government] asked the Law Commissions to look again at unifying a regime on unfair terms in consumer contracts, focusing on the exempt terms. From July to October 2012 the Law Commissions sought views on a discussion paper on revised proposals for the exempt terms and made recommendations to BIS in March 2013[14] concerning terms in consumer contracts.
>
> [2] The Law Commission No.332/The Scottish Law Commission No.226, March 2012.
> [13] The Law Commission No.292/The Scottish Law Commission No.199, 2005.
> [14] Unfair terms in consumer contracts – advice to BIS, The Law Commission & The Scottish Law Commission, 2013."

The new Act, when fully implemented, will draw a clear distinction between unfair terms in business to consumer (B2C) contracts, on the one hand, and unfair terms in business to business (B2B) and consumer to consumer (C2C) contracts on the other.[5] For business to consumer contracts the existing law is to be replaced by the provisions of the Consumer Rights Act 2015 Pt 2; for all other contracts, the existing law will remain, but amended to indicate that it applies only to B2B and C2C contracts. For that reason, the remainder of this chapter will deal first with exclusion and similar clauses at common law, and second with the statutory provisions that apply to such clauses in B2B and C2C contracts.

The categories of clauses

10–03 Exclusion clauses are one of several devices which circumscribe liability. The major categories are:

10–04 *Exclusion clauses*: these attempt to exclude an obligation otherwise imposed by law or to exclude remedies available for breach: for example, a clause excluding the liability of one party for the acts of their employees, for which they would normally be responsible; or a clause excluding liability for terms implied by the Sale of Goods Act 1979 (as amended). Such clauses are strictly interpreted by the courts and great care must be taken in drafting them.

10–05 *Exemption or exception clauses*: here, liability is not excluded, but is exempted in certain circumstances. Such clauses are common in all forms of contracts of carriage and include, for example, exemption for losses resulting from act of God, or force majeure, or inherent vice. Such clauses, like exclusion clauses, may be void as a result of legislative provision (for which see below).

---

[5] See explanatory notes to the Consumer Rights Act 1915, para.22.

Limitation clauses: where liability is not excluded or exempted, these limit the extent of that liability, normally in cash terms: for example, a clause stating that damages recoverable will be limited to a stated sum. Such clauses are better referred to as "liquidate damages" clauses (on which see para.12–69 below). They are particularly common practice in hire and construction contracts. A clause may also limit liability in time: for example, a clause which states that claims must be notified to the party in breach within seven days of commission of the breach. Limitation clauses tend to be less strictly construed than exclusion or exemption clauses. **10–06**

Indemnity clauses: such clauses normally stipulate that if one party incurs a loss in performing the contract, the other must indemnify them for such loss. Again, such clauses are common and courts regard them with the same severity as exclusion clauses. **10–07**

As is clear from the case of *Interfoto Picture Library Ltd v Stiletto Visual Programmes Ltd*,[6] it is not possible to arrive at a strict classification of such clauses and to delineate precisely the categories covered by the following rules of construction.

The construction of exclusion and similar clauses

In construing all such clauses, courts apply the rules outlined in the previous chapter[7] and, in particular, they construe such clauses strictly and *contra proferentem*, i.e. against the party seeking to rely upon the clause for whose benefit the clause was inserted. **10–08**

The contra proferentem *rule and liability for negligence*

The *contra proferentem* rule is applied with particular stringency to clauses which attempt to exclude liability in negligence. This must be done with clear, unambiguous language. The case that follows is a modern restatement of that position. **10–09**

Smith v UMB Chrysler and South Wales Switchgear Ltd **10–10**

1978 S.L.T. 21

House of Lords: Lords Wilberforce, Dilhorne, Salmon, Fraser of Tullybelton and Keith of Kinkel

For some years Chrysler had engaged SWS to carry out an annual overhaul of electrical equipment at Linwood. Chrysler requested SWS to overhaul the equipment during July 1970. SWS replied that they were able to do so. Chrysler sent SWS a purchase note requesting them to overhaul the equipment, "subject to ... our General Conditions Contract 24001, obtainable on request". SWS wrote informing Chrysler that they had given instructions for the work to be carried out. SWS did not request a copy of the general conditions, although a copy was sent to them. The general conditions contained an indemnity clause which provided:

> "In the event of [the] order involving the carrying out of work by the Supplier and its sub-contractors on land and/or premises of the [respondents], the Supplier will keep the [respondents] indemnified against ... Any liability, loss, claim or proceedings, whatsoever under Statute or Common Law (i) in respect of personal injury to, or death of, any person whomsoever, (ii) in respect of any injury or damage whatsoever to any property, real or personal, [*sic*] arising out of or in the course of ... the execution of [the] order."

---

[6] See above, para.9–50.

[7] See above, para.9–26 onward.

Smith, an employee of SWS who was engaged on the overhaul at Linwood was seriously injured in an accident at the factory. He brought an action for damages against Chrysler in the Court of Session alleging negligence and breach of statutory duty. Chrysler served a third party notice on SWS claiming indemnity in respect of the claim under the indemnity clause. The court held that the accident was wholly caused by Chrysler's negligence and breach of statutory duty and awarded Smith damages against them. In this appeal to the House of Lords, SWS contended, inter alia, that on its proper construction the indemnity clause did not require them to indemnify Chrysler against liability for Chrysler's own negligence or that of their employees.

The decision of the House was that express words would have been required to include within the indemnity clause liability for the respondents' own negligence.

10–11 "LORD FRASER OF TULLYBELTON: ... I come now to the question of construction ... The principles which are applicable to clauses which purport to exempt one party to a contract from liability were stated by Lord Greene M.R. in *Alderslade v Hendon Laundry Ltd.* [1945] K.B. 189 at 192 and were quoted with approval by Lord Morton of Henryton in the Privy Council in *Canada Steamship Lines Ltd v Regem* [1952] A.C. 192 at 208 where he summarised them as follows:

'(i) If the clause contains language which expressly exempts the person in whose favour it is made (hereafter called "the proferens") from the consequence of the negligence of his own servants, effect must be given to that provision ...

(ii) If there is no express reference to negligence, the court must consider whether the words used are wide enough, in their ordinary meaning, to cover negligence on the part of the servants of the proferens. If a doubt arises at this point, it must be resolved against the proferens ... (iii) If the words used are wide enough for the above purpose, the court must then consider whether "the head of damage may be based on some ground other than that of negligence", to quote again Lord Greene, M.R., in the *Alderslade* case. The "other ground" must not be so fanciful or remote that the proferens cannot be supposed to have desired protection against it, but subject to this qualification, which is, no doubt, to be implied from Lord Greene's words, the existence of a possible head of damage other than that of negligence is fatal to the proferens even if the words used are, *prima facie*, wide enough to cover negligence on the part of his servants.'

These rules were stated in relation to clauses of exemption, but they are in my opinion equally applicable to a clause of indemnity which in many cases, including *Canada Steamship Lines Ltd v Regem*, is merely the obverse of the exemption. The statement has been accepted as authoritative in the law of Scotland: see *North of Scotland Hydro-Electric Board v D & R Taylor*, 1956 S.C. 1, which was concerned with a clause of indemnity and it was accepted by both parties, rightly in my opinion, as being applicable to the present appeal.

The argument based on the first of Lord Morton of Henryton's tests can be disposed of quickly. Counsel for the respondents argued that para. (b) in the present indemnity clause contained language which 'expressly' entitled the respondents to indemnity against the consequence of their own negligence and that the first test was satisfied. The argument was that the words 'any liability, loss, claim or proceedings whatsoever' amounted to an express reference to such negligence because they covered any liability however caused ... I do not see how a clause can 'expressly' exempt or indemnify the proferens against his negligence unless it contains the word 'negligence' or some synonym for it and I think that is what Lord Morton of Henryton must have intended as appears from the opening words of his second test ('If there is no express reference to negligence') ...

I pass then to consider the second test. The words 'Any liability ... whatsoever under ... Common Law ... in respect of personal injury' which occur near the beginning of cl. 23(b), if read in isolation, are of course wide enough to cover liability arising from negligence of the respondents or their servants. But they cannot properly be read in isolation from their context in cl. 23 and in the general conditions. I have reached the opinion that cl. 23(b), read as a whole, does not apply to liability arising from negligence by the respondents or their servants. The general conditions are evidently intended to apply to many contracts where the respondents are 'the Purchaser' and some other party is the supplier of goods or services to them. But cl. 23 applies only 'in the event of (the particular contract) involving the carrying out of work by the supplier and its sub-contractors on' the respondents' premise ... The clause is thus looking to cases where the employees of the supplier will be working on the respondents' premises and it very naturally provides for an indemnity against the consequences of negligence by those employees while working there. But the employees of the respondents would not require to do any work in carrying out the contract and it seems unlikely that the parties intended that the respondents were to be indemnified by the appellants against liability as occupiers of the factory, especially as the indemnity is against claims in respect of injury to any person whomsoever and is not limited to servants of the suppliers or sub-contractors. Moreover, the indemnity is, in the final words of para. (b), in respect of injuries etc. 'arising out of or in the course of or caused by the execution of this order' and the only parties who will be concerned in 'execution' of the order are the appellants and any sub-contractors. 'In the course of' must convey some connection with execution of the order beyond the merely temporal; and thus they appropriately apply to activities of the party who is carrying out work under the order ...

That is enough for the decision of the appeal, but if it were necessary to go on to consider the third test I would hold that the head of damage under liability at common law for personal injury may be based on some ground other than the respondents' own negligence. The possibility of common law liability falling on the respondents, as occupiers of the premises, through the fault of the suppliers' servants is in my opinion not fanciful or remote. Nor is the possibility of claims for nuisance or for breach of contract caused by defective work by the suppliers. No doubt the respondents would have a right of relief against the supplier in most if not all of these cases, but that is not a sufficient answer as they might well prefer to rely on the protection of an express right of indemnity rather than on their right to raise an action of relief with all its inevitable hazards. See *North of Scotland Hydro-Electric Board v D & R Taylor*, per the Lord Justice-Clerk (Thomson) and Lord Patrick, 1956 S.C. 1 at 8, 10.

The conclusion that I have reached is in harmony with several recent decisions both in Scotland and in England to which we were referred, particularly *North of Scotland Hydro-Electric Board v D & R Taylor* and *Gillespie Brothers & Co Ltd v Roy Bowles Transport Ltd*, and *Walters v Whessoe Ltd*."

The applicable test, which was approved by the House of Lords in *Smith* appears to be:

(a) express language excluding liability for negligence must be given effect to;
(b) if there is no express reference to negligence, the words must be considered, in their ordinary meaning, to establish if they are wide enough to cover negligence;
(c) if the words are wide enough to cover negligence, liability will not be excluded if liability on some ground other than negligence can also be established.

Contra proferentem and indemnity clauses

10–12 Lord Fraser in *Smith* regarded an indemnity clause as "the obverse" of an exemption clause and therefore covered by the same rules.

Smith, like the case of *North of Scotland Hydro-Electric Board v Taylor* to which Lord Fraser referred in *Smith*, involved the construction of indemnity clauses: should limitation clauses be treated more favourably than exclusion clauses? In the following case Lord Fraser stressed that clauses which limit liability should not "be judged by the specially exacting standards which are applied to exclusion and indemnity clauses".

10–13 **Ailsa Craig Fishing Co v Malvern Fishing Co**

1982 S.C. (H.L.) 14; 1982 S.L.T. 377

House of Lords: Lords Wilberforce, Elwyn-Jones, Salmon, Fraser of Tullybelton and Lowry

The *George Craig* and the *Strathallan* both sank in Aberdeen harbour as the bow of the *Strathallan* became caught under the dock of the quay where the two vessels were berthed. Securicor, who were responsible for supervising vessels in the harbour, were convened as third parties to the action between the owners of the two vessels. Their contract contained a clause limiting Securicor's liability to £1,000

> "for any loss or damage of whatever nature arising out of or connected with the provision of, or purported provision of, or failure in provision of the services provided".

Securicor contended that the clause, as drafted, limited their liability regardless of the negligence of their employees.

The court held, dismissing AC's appeal, that on the true construction of the contract, the clause was effective to limit liability even where there had been no performance at all by the offending party.

"LORD FRASER OF TULLYBELTON: ... The question whether Securicor's liability has been limited falls to be answered by construing the terms of the contract in accordance with the ordinary principles applicable to contracts of this kind. The argument for limitation depends upon certain special conditions attached to the contract prepared on behalf of Securicor and put forward in their interest. There is no doubt that such conditions must be construed strictly against the *proferens*, in this case Securicor, and that in order to be effective they must be 'most clearly and unambiguously expressed'—see *Pollock & Co v Macrae*, 1922 S.L.T. at p. 512 per Lord Dunedin. *Pollock* was a decision on an exclusion clause but insofar as it emphasised the need for clarity in clauses to be construed *contra proferentem* it is in my opinion relevant to the present case also.

There are later authorities which lay down very strict principles to be applied when considering the effect of clauses of exclusion or of indemnity—see particularly the Privy Council case of *Canada Steamship Lines Ltd v R.* at p. 208, where Lord Morton of Henryton, delivering the advice of the Board, summarised the principles in terms which have recently been applied by this House in *Smith v UMB Chrysler (Scotland) Ltd.* In my opinion these principles are not applicable in their full rigour when considering the effect of clauses merely limiting liability. Such clauses will of course be read *contra proferentem* and must be clearly expressed, but there is no reason why they should be judged by the specially exacting standards which are applied to exclusion and indemnity clauses. The reason for imposing such standards on these clauses is the inherent improbability that the other party to a contract including such a clause intended to release the *proferens* from a liability that would otherwise fall upon him. But there is no such high degree of improbability that he would agree to a limitation of the liability of the *proferens*, especially when, as explained in cl. 4(i) of the present contract, the potential losses that might be caused by the negligence of the *proferens* or its servants are so great in proportion to the sums that can reasonably be charged for the services contracted for. It is enough in the present case that the clause must be clear and unambiguous."

The House of Lords determined that the clause was wide enough to limit liability to negligence; yet the language of the clause is similar to that in *Smith*. Would the House have decided differently had the clause attempted to "limit" liability to, say, £10? (Note that the £1,000 actually recoverable was a tiny fraction of the loss incurred by the shipowners.)

The relationship between indemnity and the obligation to insure

It is common in standard form contracts to provide that the party who is to indemnify must also carry insurance. How far should that obligation to insure be taken into account when construing the extent of liability under the indemnity clause? **10–14**

Scottish Special Housing Association v Wimpey Construction UK Ltd **10–15**
1986 S.L.T. 559
House of Lords: Lords Keith of Kinkel, Brandon of Oakbrook, Brightman, Mackay of Clashfern and Ackner

The Scottish Special Housing Association (SSHA) entered into a contract with Wimpey for the modernisation of houses which it owned. The works were to be carried out in accordance with a Standard Form of Building Contract. Clause 18(2) provided:

> "Except for such loss or damage as is at the risk of the employer under clause 20[C] of these conditions, the contractor shall be liable for, and shall indemnify the employer against, any liability . . . in respect of any . . . damage whatsoever to any property . . . due to any negligence, omission or default of the contractor."

Clause 19(1)(a) provided:

> "The contractor shall maintain . . . such insurance as is necessary to cover the liability of the contractor . . . in respect of injury or damage to property . . . caused by any omission or default of the contractor."

Clause 20[C] stated:

> "The existing structures . . . shall be at the sole risk of the employer as regards loss or damage by fire . . . and the employer shall maintain adequate insurance against those risks."

One of the houses being modernised was damaged by fire. In an action to establish liability, Wimpey claimed that they were exempted from liability in respect of any damage caused to the property by fire, even although it was due to their own negligence.

Held, that on the true construction of cll.18(2) and 20[C] the employer bore the whole risk of damage by fire, even where caused by the contractors' negligence.

10–16 "LORD KEITH OF KINKEL: ... The opening words of cl. 18(2) make it clear that the liability of the contractor for damage to property caused by his negligence or that of a sub-contractor or of anyone for whom either of them is responsible is subject to an exception. The ambit of the exception is to be found in cl. 20[C]. Clause 19(1)(a), dealing with the contractor's obligation to insure against inter alia damage to property, does not shed any light on that matter, since the insurance is to cover only the contractor's liability for such damage, whatever that liability may be. Clause 20[C] provides that the existing structures and contents owned by the employer are to be at his sole risk as regards damage by inter alia fire. No differentiation is made between fire due to the negligence of the contractor and that due to other causes. The remainder of the catalogue of perils includes some which could not possibly be caused by the negligence of the contractor, such as storm, tempest and earthquake, but others which might be, such as explosion, flood and the bursting or overflowing of water pipes. There is imposed upon the employer an obligation to insure against loss or damage by all these perils, in quite general terms. I have found it impossible to resist the conclusion that it is intended that the employer shall bear the whole risk of damage by fire, including fire caused by the negligence of the contractor or that of sub-contractors. The exception introduced by the opening words of cl. 18(2) must have the effect that certain damage caused by the negligence of the contractor or of sub-contractors, for which in the absence of these words the contractor would be liable, is not to result in liability on his part. The nature of such damage is to be found in cl. 20[C], which refers in general terms to damage by fire to the existing structures. No sensible content can be found for the words of exception in cl. 18(2) if they are not read as referring to damage of the nature described in cl. 20[C]. Counsel for the association strove valiantly to indicate some such alternative content but was unable, in my view, to do so convincingly.

A similar conclusion was arrived at by the Court of Appeal in England in *James Archdale & Co Ltd v Comservices Ltd* [1954] 1 W.L.R. 459 upon the construction of similarly but not identically worded corresponding clauses in a predecessor of the standard form. I consider that case to have been correctly decided and to be indistinguishable from the present one.

The judges of the First Division were much impressed by what Lord Cameron described as a bizarre consequence of the construction contended for by Wimpey, namely, that if correct it would result in their being remunerated, assuming the contract was not terminated under cl. 20[C](b), for putting right damage caused by their own negligence. The result, however, does not appear bizarre when it is kept in view that the association would have received policy moneys representing the cost of putting right the damage under the insurance which cl. 20[C] required them to effect. In substance, the question at issue comes to be one as to which party had the obligation to insure against damage to existing structures due to fire caused by the negligence of the contractors or of sub-contractors."

The exclusion of liability for fundamental breach

10–17 A particular rule of construction of special significance for exclusion clauses is that general words will not be sufficient to exclude liability for a fundamental, or "total" breach of the contract. For some time judges, particularly Lord Denning in the English Court of Appeal, regarded this as a rule of law rather than of construction: an exclusion clause could never protect a party for a fundamental breach [or breach of a "fundamental term"[8]] of the contract.

[8] Note that matters are confused by the peculiarly English notion of classifying particular terms as "fundamental", whereas the Scottish approach, as the next case indicates, has always been to regard certain *breaches* of contractual obligation as fundamental.

This was particularly useful in protecting consumers against the most serious abuses of exclusion clauses in standard form contracts prior to the enactment of the Unfair Contract Terms Act 1977, but the origins of this approach go much further.

W & S Pollock & Co v Macrae 10–18
1922 S.C. (H.L) 192
House of Lords: Viscounts Haldane and Cave, Lords Dunedin, Parmoor and Wrenbury

Pollock & Co manufactured engines for fishing boats. Following a meeting between Pollock (one of the partners in Pollock & Co) and Macrae, Macrae ordered from Pollock & Co "a twin screw set of model 'K' Clyde 35/40 B.H.P. marine paraffin motors". Pollock & Co acknowledged the order in a letter which also contained Macrae's order for the goods, conditions of tender and guarantee, and the specification, which contained the technical specifications of the engines, the price, the terms of payment and the conditions of installation, delivery and guarantee.

The conditions of tender stated:

> "All goods are supplied on the condition that we shall not be liable for any direct or consequential damages arising from defective material or workmanship, even when such goods are supplied under the usual form of guarantee."

The guarantee in the specification added:

> "Apart from the above guarantee the works sell their engines under the condition that they are free from any claims arising through the breakdown of any parts or stoppages of the engines, or from any consequential damages arising from same, direct or indirect."

The engines had been installed by the end of October. On 1 November, Macrae telegraphed that the port engine leaked badly. Pollock & Co agreed to put it right, but pressed for payment of the final instalment. Pollock brought an action against Macrae for unpaid sums under the contract and Macrae claimed damages for losses arising from the engines being disconform to the contract.

On appeal by Pollock, the House of Lords rejected their claim and allowed Macrae to claim damages.

"LORD DUNEDIN: ... It is necessary first to determine what was the contract ... the letter of the 24th of December clearly showed that the respondent did not consider the matter as settled until he had approved of the specification ... This being so, it follows, I think, that the conditions of tender and guarantee were embodied in the contract. They were all obviously sent together, and I have no doubt they were attached so as to form one document ... 10–19

Taking it, however, that the documents form part of the contract, it is necessary to settle what they effectuate. The usual function of a specification is, as its name denotes, to specify exactly what the seller is to deliver to the buyer. It is also usual that it should contain clauses protecting the seller from the effect of causes over which he has no control, and which may hinder or render impossible the performance of the contract. Such are strike clauses, clauses as to the supply of material from other sources, clauses as to the effect of weather, such as frost, etc. But it is not usual that it should in addition contain conditions which amount to a counter-stipulation on the part of the buyer that he will forgo the ordinary remedies which the law gives him in the event of breach of contract. Such conditions to be effectual will be most clearly and unambiguously expressed, as is always necessary in cases where a well-known common law liability is sought to be avoided. Illustrations of the necessity may be found in numerous cases where carriers have sought to limit or avoid their liability, and a particular instance may be given in the case decided a short time ago by your Lordships of *London and North-Western Railway Co v Neilson* [1922] A.C. 263. Reading the clauses in this light, I am of opinion that, although they excuse from damage flowing from the insufficiency of a part or parts of the machinery, they have no application to damage arising when there has been a total breach of contract by failing to supply the article truly contracted for."

10–20 Lord Dunedin's language is ambiguous, but suggests a rule of construction rather than a rule of law. This was made clear by Lord Fraser of Tullybelton in the *Ailsa Craig* case, where he said of the decision in *Pollock*:

> "It has sometimes apparently been regarded as laying down, as a proposition of law, that a clause excluding liability can never have any application where there has been a total breach of contract, but I respectfully agree with the Lord President who said in his opinion in the present case that that was a misunderstanding of *Pollock*. *Pollock* was followed by the Second Division in *Mechans Ltd v Highland Marine Charters Ltd* and there are passages in the judgments in that case which might seem to treat *Pollock* as having laid down some such general proposition of law, although it is not clear that they were so intended. If they were I would regard them as being erroneous."[9]

The issue of fundamental or total breach does, nevertheless, create specific problems for Scots law. Most of the leading cases on the subject are English decisions of the House of Lords. As such, they fail to make a distinction, if there is one, between such a breach and what in Scotland would be regarded as a "material" breach. It is clear from the judgment of Lord Dunedin in *Pollock* that it was a "material" breach with which he was concerned.

In *Suisse Atlantique Société d'Armement Maritime SA v NV Rotterdamische Kolen Centrale*,[10] the House of Lords, albeit obiter, firmly stated that a fundamental breach, *as a rule of construction*, might or might not be covered by a particular exclusion clause. More particularly, Lord Reid, at 397, found

> "nothing to indicate that [fundamental breach] means either more or less than the well-known type of breach which entitled the innocent party to treat it as repudiatory and to rescind the contract".

It is hardly surprising that, following *Suisse Atlantique*, the drafters of contracts began expressly to exclude liability for fundamental breach. In addition, resistance to the new, tougher line of the House of Lords emerged in the Court of Appeal in England in Lord Denning's judgment in *Harbutt's Plasticine Ltd v Wayne Tank and Pump Co Ltd*.[11] The essence of Lord Denning's argument there was that some breaches are so fundamental in their consequences that they destroy not only the obligations of the parties, but also the contract itself and the exclusion clauses with it, even if, on construction, such clauses excluded liability for fundamental breach. Both of these issues were considered in *Alexander Stephen (Forth) Ltd v JJ Riley (UK) Ltd*.[12] This decision confirmed that, in Scotland, the rule that an exclusion clause will not cover a *material* breach is one of construction, so that if the clause is wide enough in its terminology, it

---

[9] *Ailsa Craig Fishing Co Ltd v Malvern Fishing Co Ltd*, 1982 S.L.T. 377, 381–382.

[10] *Suisse Atlantique Société d'Armement Maritime SA v NV Rotterdamische Kolen Centrale* [1966] 2 W.L.R. 944.

[11] *Harbutt's Plasticine Ltd v Wayne Tank and Pump Co Ltd* [1970] 1 Q.B. 447.

[12] *Alexander Stephen (Forth) Ltd v J.J. Riley (UK) Ltd*, 1976 S.L.T. 269.

may exclude liability for such a breach. This the House of Lords reaffirmed in the following English decision which has not been challenged as representing also the position in Scotland.

Photo Production Ltd v Securicor Transport Ltd 10–21
[1980] A.C. 827
English House of Lords: Lords Wilberforce, Diplock, Salmon, Scarman and Keith of Kinkel

Securicor provided their "night patrol service" as security for Photo Production's premises under a contract which stated:

> "Under no circumstances shall [Securicor] be responsible for any injurious act or default of any employee . . . unless such act or default could have been foreseen and avoided by the exercise of due diligence on the part of [Securicor] as his employer; nor, in any event, shall the company be held responsible for . . . any lose suffered by the customer through . . . fire . . . except insofar as such loss is solely attributable to the negligence of [Securicor's] employees acting within the course of their employment."

On the night of Sunday, 18 October 1970, Musgrove, one of Securicor's employees, was on duty at Photo Production's card factory. For reasons unclear at the time of the action, Musgrove started a fire by throwing a lighted match on to a cardboard box. Damage amounting to £615,000 was caused to the factory. Securicor claimed that the contract excluded their liability for Musgrove's actions. Eventually this argument proved successful in the House of Lords.

"LORD WILBERFORCE: . . . I am convinced that, with the possible exception of Lord Upjohn whose critical passage, when read in full, is somewhat ambiguous, their Lordships [in *Suisse Atlantique*], fairly read, can only be taken to have rejected those suggestions for a rule of law which had appeared in the Court of Appeal and to have firmly stated that the question is one of construction, not merely of course of the exclusion clause alone, but of the whole contract . . . 10–22

1. The doctrine of 'fundamental breach' in spite of its imperfections and doubtful parentage has served a useful purpose. There were a large number of problems, productive of injustice, in which it was worse than unsatisfactory to leave exception clauses to operate. Lord Reid referred to these in the *Suisse Atlantique* case [[1967] 1 A.C. 361, 406], pointing out at the same time that the doctrine of fundamental breach was a dubious specific. But since then Parliament has taken a hand: it has passed the Unfair Contract Terms Act 1977. This Act applies to consumer contracts and those based on standard terms and enables exception clauses to be applied with regard to what is just and reasonable. It is significant that Parliament refrained from legislating over the whole field of contract. After this Act, in commercial matters generally, when the parties are not of unequal bargaining power, and when risks are normally borne by insurance, not only is the case for judicial intervention undemonstrated, but there is everything to be said, and this seems to have been Parliament's intention, for leaving the parties free to apportion the risks as they think fit and for respecting their decisions.

   At the stage of negotiation as to the consequences of a breach, there is everything to be said for allowing the parties to estimate their respective claims according to the contractual provisions they have themselves made, rather than for facing them with a legal complex so uncertain as the doctrine of fundamental breach must be. What, for example, would have been the position of Photo Productions' factory if instead of being destroyed it had been damaged, slightly or moderately or severely? At what point does the doctrine (with what logical justification I have not understood) decide *ex post facto* that the breach was (factually) fundamental before going on to ask whether legally it is to be regarded as fundamental? How is the date of 'termination' to be fixed? Is it the date of the incident causing the damage, or the date of the innocent party's election, or some other date? All these difficulties arise from the doctrine and are left unsolved by it.

At the judicial stage there is still more to be said for leaving cases to be decided straightforwardly on what the parties have bargained for rather than on analysis, which becomes progressively more refined, of decisions in other cases leading to inevitable appeals. The learned judge was able to decide this case on normal principles of contractual law with minimal citation of authority. I am sure that most commercial judges have wished to be able to do the same: see *Trade and Transport Inc v Iino Kaiun Kaisha Ltd* [1973] 1 W.L.R. 210, 232, *per* Kerr J. In my opinion they can and should.

2. The case of *Harbutt* [[1970] 1 Q.B. 447] must clearly be overruled. It would be enough to put that on its radical inconsistency with the *Suisse Atlantique* case [1967] 1 A.C. 361]. But even if the matter were *res integra* I would find the decision to be based on unsatisfactory reasoning as to the 'termination' of the contract and the effect of 'termination' on the plaintiffs' claim for damage. I have, indeed, been unable to understand how the doctrine can be reconciled with the well-accepted principle of law, stated by the highest modern authority, that when in the context of a breach of contract one speaks of 'termination' what is meant is no more than that the innocent party or, in some cases, both parties are excused from further performance. Damages, in such cases, are then claimed under the contract, so what reason in principle can there be for disregarding what the contract itself says about damages, whether it 'liquidates' them, or limits them, or excludes them? These difficulties arise in part from uncertain or inconsistent terminology. A vast number of expressions are used to describe situations where a breach has been committed by one party of such character as to entitle the other party to refuse further performance: discharge, rescission, termination, the contract is at an end, or dead, or displaced; clauses cannot survive, or simply go. I have come to think that some of these difficulties can be avoided; in particular the use of 'rescission,' even if distinguished from rescission *ab initio*, as an equivalent for discharge, though justifiable in some contexts (see *Johnson v Agnew* [[1980] A.C. 367]) may lead to confusion in others. To plead for complete uniformity may be to cry for the moon. But what can and ought to be avoided is to make use of these confusions in order to produce a concealed and unreasoned legal innovation: to pass, for example, from saying that a party, victim of a breach of contract, is entitled to refuse further performance, to saying that he may treat the contract as at an end, or as rescinded, and to draw from this the proposition, which is not analytical but one of policy, that all or (arbitrarily) some of the clauses of the contract lose automatically, their force, regardless of intention.

... [T]he whole foundation of *Harbutt's* case is unsound. *A fortiori*, in addition to *Harbutt's* case there must be overruled *Wathes (Western) Ltd v Austins (Menswear) Ltd* [[1976] 1 Lloyd's Rep. 14] which sought to apply the doctrine of fundamental breach to a case where, by election of the innocent party, the contract had not been terminated, an impossible acrobatic, yet necessarily engendered by the doctrine. Similarly, *Charterhouse*

Credit Co Ltd v Tolly [[1963] 2 Q.B. 683] must be overruled, though the result might have been reached on construction of the contract ...

In this situation the present case has to be decided. As a preliminary, the nature of the contract has to be understood. Securicor undertook to provide a service of periodical visits for a very modest charge which works out at 26p per visit. It did not agree to provide equipment. It would have no knowledge of the value of Photo Productions' factory; that, and the efficacy of their fire precautions, would be known to Photo Productions. In these circumstances nobody could consider it unreasonable that as between these two equal parties the risk assumed by Securicor should be a modest one, and that Photo Productions should carry the substantial risk of damage or destruction.

The duty of Securicor was, as stated, to provide a service. There must be implied an obligation to use care in selecting their patrolmen, to take care of the keys and, I would think, to operate the service with due and proper regard to the safety and security of the premises. The breach of duty committed by Securicor lay in a failure to discharge this latter obligation. Alternatively it could be put on a vicarious responsibility for the wrongful act of Musgrove, *viz.* starting a fire on the premises; Securicor would be responsible for this on the principle stated in *Morris v CW Martin & Sons Ltd* [[1966] 1 Q.B. 716, 739.] This being the breach, does condition 1 apply? It is drafted in strong terms: 'Under no circumstances' ... 'any injurious act or default by any employee.' These words have to be approached with the aid of the cardinal rules of construction that they must be read *contra proferentem* and that in order to escape from the consequences of one's own wrongdoing, or that of one's servant, clear words are necessary. I think that these words are clear. Photo Productions in fact relied on them for an argument that since they exempted from negligence they must be taken as not exempting from the consequence of deliberate acts. But this is a perversion of the rule that if a clause can cover something other than negligence it will not be applied to negligence. Whether, in addition to negligence, it covers other, e.g. deliberate, acts, remains a matter of construction requiring, of course, clear words. I am of opinion that it does and, being free to construe and apply the clause, I must hold that liability is excluded. On this part of the case I agree with the judge and adopt his reasons for judgement. I would allow the appeal."

LORD KEITH OF KINKEL and LORD SCARMAN agreed with Lord Wilberforce's speech. LORD SALMON delivered a speech in terms similar to those of Lord Wilberforce. LORD DIPLOCK also allowed the appeal, but for different reasons.

The rejection by the House of Lords of *Harbutt's Plasticine* was unequivocal. It is also clear **10–23**
from Lord Wilberforce's speech—with which the majority concurred—that courts are more willing to construe a clause as covering fundamental breach where the parties are bargaining on equal terms in apportioning risk as they think fit. In the *Photo Production* case itself, on construction, the terms of the contract were wide enough to exclude deliberate acts as well as negligence; but the question remains: when is a breach to be regarded as "fundamental"?

Whether a term is fundamental depends on how central it is to the objects of the contract. The classic illustration is contracting to deliver peas, but delivering beans instead, i.e. something fundamentally different from that stated in the terms. Similarly, supplying a car in a totally unroadworthy condition would be a fundamental breach; but supplying the wrong type of cabbage seed, as in *Mitchell v Finney Lock Seed* (below, para.10–46), would not be a fundamental breach. In long-established categories of contract, like contracts for carriage of goods by sea, certain terms, such as the duty not to deviate, are regarded as fundamental. Furthermore, as *Stephen v Riley* recognises, the parties may expressly state in the contract which terms are fundamental.

A breach is fundamental if it renders performance totally different from that originally contemplated. It is the effect of the breach which is significant, so that in *Pollock v Macrae* a series of defects in machinery supplied which rendered it totally unserviceable was not covered by a general exclusion of liability clause. Each case will necessarily depend on its facts.

Sometimes, it is the manner of the breach which is important—for example, where the breach is committed wilfully—though this, as Lord Wilberforce makes clear both in *Suisse Atlantique* and in *Photo Production*, would not itself be decisive.

Statutory control of exclusion clauses

10–24 It is clear from the preceding pages that a consumer may easily be disadvantaged by carefully constructed clauses in standard forms. In some cases, even liability for death or personal injury could be excluded. Although for some time protection was conferred on passengers in most forms of transport against such devices,[13] it was not until the Supply of Goods (Implied Terms) Act 1973 that protection was given in relation to the supply of goods, and not until 1977 that unfair or excessive exclusion clauses (primarily, although not exclusively in consumer contracts) were constrained by the Unfair Contract Terms Act 1977.

This 1977 Act is in three parts: Pt I amends English law on exclusion clauses; Pt II amends Scots law on exclusion clauses; and Pt III is of general application. Significant subsequent amendments to the 1977 Act, often abbreviated to UCTA, extended the application of Pt II of the Act to non-contractual notice (a matter which is not therefore directly within the scope of this book).

10–25 European efforts to harmonise the law in this area began with EC Council Directive on Unfair Terms in Consumer Contracts.[14] This was implemented in the UK by the Unfair Terms in Consumer Contracts Regulations 1999.[15] Lord Steyn, in *Director General of Fair Trading v First National Bank*[16] summarised the purpose and effect of the Directive:

> "The purpose of the Directive is twofold, viz. the promotion of fair standard contract forms to improve the functioning of the European market place and the protection of consumers throughout the European Community. The Directive is aimed at contracts of adhesion, viz. 'take it or leave it' contacts. It treats consumers as presumptively weaker parties and therefore fit for protection from abuses by stronger contracting parties. This is an objective which must throughout guide the interpretation of the Directive as well as the implementing Regulations. If contracting parties were able to avoid the application of the Directive and Regulations by exclusionary stipulations the regulatory scheme would be ineffective. The conclusion that the Directive and Regulations are mandatory is inescapable."

The Law Commissions produced a Joint Consultation Paper[17] recommending, inter alia, unification and simplification of the regime. The paper referred to the 1977 Act as

> "a complex piece of legislation. As we know from our own experience, it is hard to understand without very careful reading. [The Act] is structured in a way which, given its complexity, is economical but which is not easy to grasp".[18]

---

[13] See, for example, para.9–45 above.

[14] EC Council Directive on Unfair Terms in Consumer Contracts (Council Directive 93/13/EEC, OJ L95 21.4.93, p.29).

[15] Unfair Terms in Consumer Contracts Regulations 1999 (SI 1999/203), which replaced the original implementing Regulations of 1994 (SI 1994/3159).

[16] *Director General of Fair Trading v First National Bank* [2002] A.C. 481.

[17] The Law Commissions, *Unfair Terms in Contracts* (Law Commission Consultation Paper No.166; Scot. Law Com. Discussion Paper No.119, 7 August 2002).

[18] The Law Commissions, *Unfair Terms in Contracts* (Law Commission Consultation Paper No.166; Scot. Law Com. Discussion Paper No.119, 7 August 2002), p.3, para.1.6.

The Law Commissions' consultation paper included a comprehensive analysis of both the Unfair Contract Terms Act 1977 and the 1999 Regulations. The analysis includes a concise summary of the principal differences between the Act and the Regulations, which it is useful to reproduce.

Unfair Terms in Contracts 10–26

Scottish Law Commission Consultation Paper No.166, Discussion Paper No.119 (7 August 2002)

"A summary of the principal differences between UCTA and UTCCR
2.17.1 . . .
2.18 UCTA:

- applies to both consumer and business to business contracts, and also to terms and notices excluding certain liabilities in tort [delict];
- applies only to exclusion and limitation of liability clauses (and indemnity clauses in consumer contracts);
- makes certain exclusions or restrictions of no effect at all;
- subjects others to a reasonableness test;
- contains guidelines for the application of the reasonableness test;
- puts the burden of proving that a term within its scope is reasonable on the party seeking to rely on the clause;
- applies for the most part whether the terms were negotiated or were in a 'standard form';
- does not apply to certain types of contract, even when the are consumer contracts;
- has effect only between the immediate parties; and
- has separate provisions for Scotland.

2.19 In contrast, UTCCR:

- apply only to consumer contracts;
- apply to any kind of term other than the definition of the main subject matter of the contract and the price;
- do not make any particular type of term of no effect at all;
- subject the terms to a 'fairness' test;
- do not contain detailed guidelines as to how that test should be applied, but contain a so-called 'grey list' of terms which 'may be regarded' as unfair;
- leave the burden of proof that the clause is unfair on the consumer;
- apply only to 'non-negotiated' terms;
- apply to consumer contracts of all kinds;
- are not only effective between the parties but empower various bodies to take action to prevent the use of unfair terms; and
- apply to the UK as a whole."

One of the Commissions' concerns was that the 1977 Act both overlaps with and yet is distinct from the other main statutory control, the Unfair Terms in Consumer Contracts Regulations 1999. This led to complicated differences in the interpretation arising from differences in terminology and concepts that often overlapped and sometimes conflicted.

The unsatisfactory dual system for controlling unfair contract terms in *consumer* contracts was further complicated by the fact that the regulatory regime in the 1977 Act applied in part to *non*-consumer contracts. This was confusing and potentially costly, both for business and for consumers.

In 2012, the Department for Business, Innovation and Skills (BIS) asked the Commissions to update its 2005 Report in so far as it affects contracts made between businesses and consumers. The Commissions' report, published in 2013,[19] made numerous recommendations that were largely implemented as Pt 2 of the Consumer Rights Act 2015, a UK Act that consolidates the law on consumer rights generally.

The result is that there are now two distinct regimes for the regulation of unfair contract terms. The Unfair Contract Terms Act 1977, as amended by the Consumer Rights Act 2015, covers contracts between one business[20] and another and Pt 2 of the Consumer Rights Act 2015, covers contracts between a trader[21] and a consumer.[22] The legislation does not at present cover private transactions where neither party is acting as a business, trader or consumer, for example a private sale of a motor car.

Unfair contract terms in non-consumer contracts

10–27 The Unfair Contract Terms, in its truncated form following amendment by the Consumer Rights Act, is limited in scope. It is a regulatory regime completely separate from that governing contracts with consumes in Pt 2 of the Consumer Rights Act 2015.

Contracts covered by the Act

10–28 The 1977 Act, in s.15, contains several important exclusions and other provisions in the Act further limit its scope. The section is specific about the kinds of contract covered by the Act.

Unfair Contract Terms Act 1977: Pt II

AMENDMENT OF LAW FOR SCOTLAND

"15.—. . .[23]

(2) Subject to subsection (3) below, sections 16 and 17 of this Act apply to any contract only to the extent that the contract—

(a) relates to the transfer of the ownership or possession of goods from one person to another (with or without work having been done on them);

(b) constitutes a contract of service or apprenticeship;

---

[19] The Law Commissions, *Unfair Terms in Consumer Contracts: Advice to the Department for Business, Innovation and Skills* available at: *http://www.scotlawcom.gov.uk/files/3113/6361/9437/Unfair_Terms_in_-Consumer_Contracts_Advice.pdf* [Accessed 25 October 2015].

[20] The term "business" includes a profession and the activities of any government department or local or public authority: Unfair Contract Terms Act 1977 s.25(1).

[21] "'Trader' means a person acting for purposes relating to that person's trade, business, craft or profession, whether acting personally or through another person acting in the trader's name or on the trader's behalf": Consumer Rights Act 2015 s.2(2). "Business" is given the same definition in s.1(7) of the Consumer Rights Act 2015 as in Unfair Contract Terms Act 1977 s.25(1).

[22] "'Consumer' means an individual acting for purposes that are wholly or mainly outside that individual's trade, business, craft or profession": Consumer Rights Act 2015 s.2(3), amending Unfair Contract Terms Act 1977 s.25(1).

[23] Unfair Contract Terms Act 1977 s.15(1) limited the substantive sections of Pt II (ss.16, 17 and 18) to contracts. This was fundamentally different from the English provisions which, under s.2, extended to non-contractual notices. Section 15(1) was repealed by the Law Reform (Miscellaneous Provisions) (Scotland) Act 1990.

(c) relates to services of whatever kind, including (without prejudice to the foregoing generality) carriage, deposit and pledge, care and custody, mandate, agency, loan and services relating to the use of land;
(d) relates to the liability of an occupier of land to persons entering upon or using that land;
(e) relates to a grant of any right or permission to enter upon or use land not amounting to an estate or interest in land.

(3) Notwithstanding anything in subsection (2) above, sections 16 and 17—

(a) do not apply to any contract to the extent that the contract—

(i) is a contract of insurance (including a contract to apply an annuity on human life);
(ii) relates to the formation, constitution or dissolution of any body corporate, unincorporated association or partnership;

(b) apply to—
a contract of marine salvage or towage; a charter party of a ship or hovercraft; a contract for the carriage of goods by ship or hovercraft; or a contract to which subsection (4) below relates,
only to the extent that both parties deal or hold themselves out as dealing in the course of a business (and then only in so far as the contract purports to exclude or restrict liability for breach of duty in respect of death or personal injury).

(4) This subsection relates to a contract in pursuance of which goods are carried by ship or hovercraft and which either—

(a) specifies ship or hovercraft as the means of carriage over part of the journey to be covered; or
(b) makes no provision as to the means of carriage and does not exclude ship or hovercraft as that means, in so far as the contract operates for and in relation to the carriage of the goods by that means."

This extensive list of exceptions reflects the fact that many such contracts recovered by specific statutory regimes of their own.[24] What is more important is that the Scottish provision in s.15, unlike its equivalent in England, specifically includes contracts of service (or employment) and apprenticeship which, being usually standard form contracts, are given the same protection against unfair contract terms that are not "fair and reasonable". The removal of references to consumers in the 1977 Act and the specific exclusion of such contracts from the consumer provisions in Pt 2 of the Consumer Rights Act 2015, following the recommendations of the Law Commissions, make Scotland unique in affording employees and apprentices such protection although there seems to be no litigation specifically on these provisions.[25]

---

[24] See also the exclusion of contracts in Pt 2 of the Consumer Rights Act 2015, below, para.10–54.

[25] See D Brodie, "The employment contract and unfair contracts legislation" (2007) 27(1) Legal Studies 95; D Brodie, *The Contract of Employment* (Edinburgh: W. Green, 2008), Ch.17. See particularly the discussion of such contracts in The Law Commissions, *Unfair Terms in Consumer Contracts: Advice to the Department for Business, Innovation and Skills* available at: *http://www.scotlawcom.gov.uk/files/3113/6361/9437/Unfair_Terms_in_Consumer_Contracts_Advice.pdf*, paras 7.117–7.227 [Accessed 25 October 2015].

Section 15(2)(e) could also be of significance in commercial contracts where land is used for commercial purposes, such as a venue for an event or a conference, but is not the subject of a lease. Also, the removal of all references to consumers in the 1977 Act, following the Law Commissions' recommendation,[26] means that businesses can no longer rely on the protection of the 1977 Act by claiming that in contracting they were not acting in their capacity as a business, but as a consumer.[27]

10–29 "**Liability for breach of duty**

16.—(1) Subject to subsection (1A) below, where a term of a contract or a provision of a notice given to persons generally or to particular persons purports to exclude or restrict liability for breach of duty arising in the course of any business or from the occupation of any premises used for business purposes of the occupier, that term or provision—

(a) shall be void in any case where such exclusion or restriction is in respect of death or personal injury;
(b) shall, in any other case, have no effect if it was not fair and reasonable to incorporate the term in the contract or,as the case may be, if it is not fair and reasonable to allow reliance on the provision.

(1A) Nothing in paragraph (b) of subsection (1) above shall be taken as implying that a provision of a notice has effect in circumstances where, apart from that paragraph, it would not have effect . . .

(3) Where under subsection (1) above a term of a contract or a provision of a notice is void or has no effect, the fact that a person agreed to, or was aware of, the term or provision shall not of itself be sufficient evidence that he knowingly and voluntarily assumed any risk."

(4) This section does not apply to—

(a) a term in a consumer contract, or
(b) a notice to the extent that it is a consumer notice,

(but see the provision made about such contracts and notices in sections 62 and 65 of the Consumer Rights Act 2015)."

There has been no litigation in Scotland directly on this provision. The limited exclusion of contracts in subss.3 and 4 reflects the primary intention of the Act as it was passed in 1977, namely to eliminate the exclusion of liability for causing death or personal injury. Such clauses would always be void under s.16(1)(a). However, all other attempts to "exclude or restrict" liability for breach of statutory duty are subjected to a "fair and reasonable" test. The definition of "breach of duty" is wide in its scope:

[26] "Recommendation 32: Following the new legislation, the Unfair Contract Terms Act 1977 should no longer regulate business to consumer contracts. Nor should it continue to provide additional protection to a business that deals as a consumer." The Law Commissions, *Unfair Terms in Consumer Contracts: Advice to the Department for Business, Innovation and Skills* available at: *http://www.scotlawcom.gov.uk/files/3113/6361/9437/Unfair_Terms_in_Consumer_Contracts_Advice.pdf* [Accessed 25 October 2015].

[27] The new definition of "consumer", being limited to an "individual", reinforces the point. See below, para.10–56.

Unfair Contract Terms Act 1977: Pt II 10–30

> "25(1): In this part of this Act—
> 'breach of duty' means the breach—
>
> (a) of any obligation, arising from the express or implied terms of a contract, to take reasonable care or exercise reasonable skill in the performance of the contract;
> (b) of any common law duty to take reasonable care or exercise reasonable skill;
> (c) of the duty of reasonable care imposed by section 2(1) of the Occupiers' Liability (Scotland) Act 1960."

Furthermore, the words "exclude or restrict" in s.16(1) are also narrowly defined:

Unfair Contract Terms Act 1977: Pt II 10–31

> "25(3) In this Part of this Act, any reference to excluding or restricting any liability includes—
>
> (a) making the liability or its enforcement subject to any restrictive or onerous conditions;
> (b) excluding or restricting any remedy in respect of the liability, or subjecting a person to any prejudice in consequence of his pursuing any such right or remedy;
> (c) excluding or restricting any rule of evidence or procedure;
>
> but does not include any agreement to submit any question to arbitration."

Thirdly, under s.16(3), agreeing to, or being aware of a term is not sufficient evidence of knowingly and voluntarily assuming a risk.

The most significant limit to the "fair and reasonable" regime is that it is limited to terms in "standard form contracts".

Unfair Contract Terms Act 1977: Pt II 10–32

Control of unreasonable exemptions in standard form contracts

> "17.—(1) Any term of a contract which is a standard form contract shall have no effect for the purpose of enabling a party to the contract—
>
> (a) who is in breach of a contractual obligation, to exclude or restrict any liability of his to the customer in respect of the breach;
> (b) in respect of a contractual obligation, to render no performance, or to render a performance substantially different from that which the customer reasonably expected from the contract;
>
> if it was not fair and reasonable to incorporate the term in the contract.
>
> (2) In this section 'customer' means a party to a standard form contract who deals on the basis of written standard terms of business of the other party to the contract who himself deals in the course of a business.
>
> (3) This section does not apply to a term in a consumer contract (but see the provision made about such contracts in section 62 of the Consumer Rights Act 2015)."

Several points arise in relation to the 1977 Act s.17. The "fair and reasonable" test is applied by this section to the vast majority of exclusion clauses, so that it supersedes, in all but a few cases, the need to rely upon the fundamental breach doctrine, although the rules of construction continue to apply (the "fair and reasonable" test is analysed in more detail below).

Secondly, the combined effect of the two prohibitions in s.17 is such that even a clause which allows substituted performance would be covered. In *Elliot v Sunshine Coast International*,[28] a consumer who booked a trip on a coach with a toilet was unable to go on holiday as the company had sent a bus with no toilet. The company attempted to rely on a contractual term allowing alteration to the form of transport. It was held that the substitute transport was contrary to the consumer's reasonable expectation, and thus would not be covered by the term allowing transport alterations.

Thirdly, s.17 does not prohibit clauses that define what constitutes a breach, i.e. clauses that establish the limits of the parties' obligations; it prohibits terms that attempt to limit the consequences flowing from a breach, and this is clearly a matter of construction.

Definition of "standard form contract"

10–33 The term "standard form contract" is not defined by the 1977 Act, although s.17(2) defines a "customer" in terms of a standard form contract. Not surprisingly, this provision has given rise to some litigation.

10–34

McCrone v Boots Farm Sales Ltd

1981 S.L.T. (O.H.) 103 Court of Session, Outer House: Lord Dunpark

McCrone bought weedkiller from Boots. Boots' general conditions of sale, which were not expressly included in the contract nor specifically brought to McCrone's notice, included a condition excluding liability under s.14(3) of the Sale of Goods Act 1979 (fitness for purpose).

McCrone alleged that the weedkiller was not fit for the purpose for which Boots knew that McCrone had purchased it and claimed damages. Boots argued that their conditions of sale were part of a course of dealings with McCrone and that the contract was not a "consumer contract" or "standard form contract" within the meaning of s.17 of the Unfair Contract Terms Act 1977, so that the Act did not apply to it or its terms.

The court rejected Boots' argument—s.17 was wide enough to include any contract which included a set of fixed terms applied by their proponer to the contracts in question.

10–35 "LORD DUNPARK: ...

(2) *Standard form contract* Notwithstanding the defenders' averment that their general conditions of sale were part of their contract with the pursuer, they nevertheless aver that the contract 'was not a standard form contract within the meaning of the Unfair Contract Terms Act 1977' and that s.17 of that Act has no application to said contract.

...

The Act does not define 'standard form contract,' but its meaning is not difficult to comprehend. In some cases there may be difficulty in deciding whether the phrase properly applies to a particular contract. I have no difficulty in deciding that, upon the assumption that the defenders prove that their general conditions of sale were set out in all their invoices and that they were incorporated by implication in their contract with the pursuer, the contract was a standard form contract within the meaning of the said s.17.

[28] *Elliot v Sunshine Coast International*, 1989 G.W.D. 28-1252.

> Since Parliament saw fit to leave the phrase to speak for itself, far be it from me to attempt to formulate a comprehensive definition of it. However, the terms of s.17 in the context of this Act make it plain to me that the section is designed to prevent one party to a contract from having his contractual rights, against a party who is in breach of contract, excluded or restricted by a term or condition, which is one of a number of fixed terms or conditions invariably incorporated in contracts of the kind in question by the party in breach, and which have been incorporated in the particular contract in circumstances in which it would be unfair and unreasonable for the other party to have his rights so excluded or restricted. If the section is to achieve its purpose, the phrase 'standard form contract' cannot be confined to written contracts in which both parties use standard forms. It is, in my opinion, wide enough to include any contract, whether wholly written or partly oral, which includes a set of fixed terms or conditions which the proponer applies, without material variation, to contracts of the kind in question. It would, therefore, include this contract if the defenders' general conditions of sale are proved to have been incorporated in it. In that event, it would be for the defenders to prove that it was fair and reasonable for their cond. 6 to be incorporated in this contract.
>
> Counsel for the defenders referred to s. 24(1) of the 1977 Act which limits the circumstances relevant to the 'reasonableness' test to those which were, or ought reasonably to have been, known to or in contemplation of the parties at the same time when the contract was made. So he argued, ingeniously but fallaciously, this contract was concluded as an oral contract and it could not be transformed into a standard form contract by the addition of the defenders' written general conditions. The fallacy, in my opinion, is that these general conditions were added to the contract after its conclusion. Not so. The basis of the defenders' case that these conditions were incorporated in this particular contract is that the pursuer knew that the defenders always inserted these conditions in their contracts of sale and that the reasonable inference from this knowledge is that the pursuer impliedly accepted them as included in this particular contract at the time it was concluded. The defenders have no averments which even suggest that their contract was modified after its conclusion by the addition of their general conditions. Accordingly, it follows from the assumption that the general conditions were part of this contract, that it was a standard form contract."

The definition adopted by Lord Dunpark is broad and inclusive. It has the potential to bring a very wide variety of non-consumer contracts within the scope of an act designed primarily to deal with consumer issues. In *Border Harvesters Ltd v Edwards Engineering (Perth) Ltd*,[29] Lord Kincraig referred to Lord Dunpark's view of s.17, but was unable to apply it to the facts of that case.

Border Harvesters Ltd v Edwards Engineering (Perth) Ltd 10–36
1985 S.L.T. 128
Court of Session, Outer House: Lord Kincraig

Edwards contracted with Harvesters to supply and install a dryer capable of drying grain at a specified rate. The contract document stated:

> "Customers are advised to note that the company's Product and Public Liability Insurance Cover in respect of goods and services provided by them is limited to £500,000. In the event of injury, damage or loss being sustained for which the company may be responsible resulting in the claims in excess of said sum, the

[29] *Border Harvesters Ltd v Edwards Engineering (Perth) Ltd*, 1985 S.L.T. 128.

> company will not be liable for such excess. For other Conditions of Sale, see reverse."

On the reverse side of the last page of the document were printed "conditions of sale", including the following:

> "Condition 20—General Liability. The sellers' liability under the contract shall be limited to the obligations imposed by . . . these conditions, and the sellers shall not be liable further or otherwise than therein mentioned, and shall not be liable for any loss due to stoppage ... or for any consequential damage direct or indirect however caused. Notwithstanding anything contained in these conditions the sellers shall have no liability of any kind in respect of or arising from defective material supplied or defects or omissions in work carried out by anyone other than the sellers and any claim in respect of such materials or workmanship shall be settled between the purchaser and such third parties and the sellers shall have no concern therewith."

Edwards began installation in May 1980. The equipment was not operational by August 1980.

Harvesters brought an action for breach of contract claiming damages. Edwards claimed payment of the balance of the contract price, £87,912.39. Harvesters claimed that Edwards were in material breach of contract, but Edwards claimed that this was excluded by the conditions of the contract and that in any event their liability was limited to £500,000 under the conditions.

The court held that the sale was not one by description, that there was no breach of any implied term as to quality, and thus the Unfair Contract Terms Act 1977 s.20 was irrelevant to the case.

10–37 "LORD KINCRAIG: . . . [D]oes condition 20 exclude claims for consequential loss? In my judgment it does. The condition is not an 'excluding' condition, merely a 'limiting' one, and is therefore not subject to strict construction. (See the speech of Lord Fraser in *Ailsa Craig Fishing Co v Malvern Fishing Co Ltd.*) Even, however, on a strict construction it is clear to me that the words at the end of the first sentence of condition 20 mean that the seller shall not be liable for any consequential damage direct or indirect, however caused. I do not think that these words are qualified by what comes before as was submitted by counsel for Harvesters. Accordingly the pursuers' claims being excluded by condition 20, the action should be dismissed.

Harvesters, however, invoke the provisions of the Unfair Contract Terms 1977, Pt. II whereof is applicable to Scotland, and they contend that by that Act Edwards are unable to found on the conditions, especially condition 20. The sections relied on are ss.17, 20 and 24.

I shall deal with s. 17 first . . . [I]t is necessary to consider what is meant by a standard form contract. I think it is a pity that no guidance has been given by the Act to the courts as to what Parliament meant by a standard form contract. The phrase has no ordinary meaning in the English language and so far as I was informed is not a term used in textbooks on the law of contract. It may be that 'its meaning is not difficult to comprehend' (per Lord Dunpark in *McCrone v Boots Farm Sales Ltd* at p.105). His Lordship was able to hold in that case that the contract in question was a standard form contract, if the defenders proved that their general conditions of sale were set out in all their invoices and that they were incorporated by implication into the contract with the pursuers, i.e. that the defenders' regular practice was to impose a set of conditions which were suitably phrased to apply to all their contracts—a standard set of contractual conditions. There are no similar averments in this case by either party.

> I do not find myself able to decide on the averments in this case, including the incorporation of the written part of the contract into the pleadings, whether this contract was one to which s.17 applies. The written part of the contract does not appear to be on a 'pro forma.' The conditions, though they appear to be printed, are incorporated into the contract by a typed reference which may or may not always be done in Edwards' contracts. The written estimate produced is very detailed in its terms, all of which have a special reference to the equipment being supplied, that is to say, they are more consistent with an ad hoc situation rather than one where this contract is merely one of numerous contracts entered into regularly by Edwards. Certainly there are indications in the conditions themselves which suggest that they are standard to the contracting practice of Edwards concerning all kinds of machinery which it is their business to supply."

Lord Kincraig places great stress on the fact that a "pro forma" set of conditions was not used. It is worth noting that the equivalent provision in England, s.3(1) of the 1977 Act, uses the expression "written standard terms of business". It has been held that the expression does not generally cover specially negotiated contracts,[30] but does cover terms which, although subjected to negotiation, "remained effectively untouched by those negotiations".[31]

Unfair contract terms concerning statutory implied terms

The validity of contract terms that restrict or exclude statutory implied terms in sale and hire contracts are subject to the following provisions. **10–38**

> *Obligations implied by law in sale and hire-purchase contracts*
>
> 20.—(1) Any term of a contract which purports to exclude or restrict liability for breach of the obligations arising from—
>
> (a) section 12 of the Sale of Goods Act 1979 (seller's implied undertakings as to title etc.);
> (b) section 8 of the Supply of Goods (Implied Terms) Act 1973 (implied terms as to title in hire-purchase agreements), shall be void.
>
> (1A) Any term of a contract which purports to exclude or restrict liability for breach of the obligations arising from—
>
> (a) section 13, 14 or 15 of the 1979 Act (seller's implied undertakings as to conformity of goods with description or sample, or as to their quality or fitness for a particular purpose);
> (b) section 9, 10 or 11 of the 1973 Act (the corresponding things in relation to hire purchase),
>
> shall have effect only if it was fair and reasonable to incorporate the term in the contract.
> (1B) This section does not apply to a consumer contract (but see the provision made about such contracts in section 31 of the Consumer Rights Act 2015).
>
> *Obligations implied by law in other contracts for the supply of goods*
>
> 21.(1) Any term of a contract to which this section applies purporting to exclude or restrict liability for breach of an obligation such as is referred to in subsection (3) below

[30] *The Flammar Pride* [1990] 1 Lloyd's Rep. 434.
[31] *The Flammar Pride* [1990] 1 Lloyd's Rep. 434.

shall have no effect if it was not fair and reasonable to incorporate the term in the contract.

(2) This section applies to any contract to the extent that it relates to any such matter as is referred to in section 15(2)(a) of this Act, but does not apply to—

(a) a contract of sale of goods or a hire-purchase agreement; or
(b) a charterparty of a ship or hovercraft.

(3) An obligation referred to in this subsection is an obligation incurred under a contract in the course of a business and arising by implication of law from the nature of the contract which relates—

(a) to the correspondence of goods with description or sample, or to the quality or fitness of goods for any particular purpose; or
(b) to any right to transfer ownership or possession of goods, or to the enjoyment of quiet possession of goods.

...

Evasion by means of secondary contract

23. Any term of any contract shall be void which purports to exclude or restrict, or has the effect of excluding or restricting—

(a) the exercise, by a party to any other contract, of any right or remedy which arises in respect of that other contract in consequence of breach of duty, or of obligation, liability for which could not by virtue of the provisions of this Part of this Act be excluded or restricted by a term of that other contract;
(b) the application of the provisions of this Part of this Act in respect of that or any other contract."

A person cannot, by reference to a contract term, be made to indemnify another person (whether a party to the contract or not), in respect of liability incurred by such other person, in the course of business, for breach of duty or of contract. So, for example, a consumer hiring caterers who poison the guests at their party may not be made to indemnify the caterer for damages payable to the injured guests. Note that such terms are, however, subject to the "fair and reasonable" test (for which see below).

Limits on the exclusion of statutory implied terms in non-consumer contracts.

10–39 We have already seen[32] that certain terms are implied into certain categories of contract, notably contract for the sale or supply of goods and contracts of hire purchase. A seller, or hire-purchase company, for example, would be free at common law to exclude or limit liability under such implied terms. The 1977 Act was in part an attempt to limit abuse of this freedom of contract and placed limits on it, which are embodied in ss.20 and 21.

10–40 **Unfair Contract Terms Act 1977**

"20 Obligations implied by law in sale and hire purchase contracts

(1) Any term of a contract which purports to exclude or restrict liability for breach of the obligations arising from—

(a) section 12 of the Sale of Goods Act 1979 (seller's implied undertakings as to title etc.);

[32] Above, para.8–05 onwards.

> (b) section 8 of the Supply of Goods (Implied Terms) Act 1973 (implied terms as to title in hire-purchase agreements),
>
> shall be void.
>
> (1A) Any term of a contract which purports to exclude or restrict liability for breach of the obligations arising from—
>
> (a) section 13, 14 or 15 of the 1979 Act (seller's implied undertakings as to conformity of goods with description or sample, or as to their quality or fitness for a particular purpose);
> (b) section 9, 10 or 11 of the 1973 Act (the corresponding things in relation to hire purchase),
>
> shall have effect only if it was fair and reasonable to incorporate the term in the contract.
>
> (1B) This section does not apply to a consumer contract (but see the provision made about such contracts in section 31 of the Consumer Rights Act 2015).
>
> **21 Obligations implied by law in other contracts for the supply of goods.**
>
> (1) Any term of a contract to which this section applies purporting to exclude or restrict liability for breach of an obligation such as is referred to in subsection (3) below shall have no effect if it was not fair and reasonable to incorporate the term in the contract.
>
> (2) This section applies to any contract to the extent that it relates to any such matter as is referred to in section 15(2)(*a*) of this Act, but does not apply to—
>
> (a) a contract of sale of goods or a hire-purchase agreement; or
> (b) a charterparty of a ship or hovercraft.
>
> (3) An obligation referred to in this subsection is an obligation incurred under a contract in the course of a business and arising by implication of law from the nature of the contract which relates—
>
> (a) to the correspondence of goods with description or sample, or to the quality or fitness of goods for any particular purpose; or
> (b) to any right to transfer ownership or possession of goods, or to the enjoyment of quiet possession of goods.
>
> (3A) Notwithstanding anything in the foregoing provisions of this section, any term of a contract which purports to exclude or restrict liability for breach of the obligations arising under section 11B of the Supply of Goods and Services Act 1982 (implied terms about title, freedom from encumbrances and quiet possession in certain contracts for the transfer of property in goods) shall be void.
>
> (3B) This section does not apply to a consumer contract (but see the provision made about such contracts in section 31 of the Consumer Rights Act 2015)."

Section 20(1)(a), like s.20(2) of the 1977 Act, which it replaced, cannot be invoked unless one of the statutory provisions referred to in that section has been breached.

In *Knight Machinery (Holdings) Ltd v Rennie*,[33] an Extra Division of the Court of Session held that the least that could be expected of a term excluding liability for breach of the Sale of Goods Act 1979 s.14, was that it should be clear and unambiguous. Otherwise, given that it was

---

[33] *Knight Machinery (Holdings) Ltd v Rennie*, 1995 S.L.T. 166.

conceived wholly in the interests of its author at the expense of the other party's rights, it could not pass the reasonableness test. Giving the opinion of the court, Lord McCluskey said:

> "The intention of s 20 (2) of the Unfair Contract Terms Act 1977 is to prevent a party to a contract from contracting out of liability for breach of obligations arising from certain terms and undertakings implied by statute, unless he is able to establish that when the contract was entered into it was fair and reasonable to incorporate in the contract the term limiting his liability for such breach. The onus rests upon the party who seeks to found upon such a term. The reasonableness judgment is one to be made objectively by the court having regard to the circumstances of the particular case and to the guidelines prescribed by s 24 (2) of and Schedule 2 to the Act. The very width of the matters listed in Sched 2 appears to us to be indicative of the court's responsibility to look critically at any provision which is conceived wholly in the interests of the author of the words of the contract and at the expense of the other party's rights derived from statute. The least that can be expected of such a term before it can pass the reasonableness test is that the meaning of the term should be clear and unambiguous."

10–41 Section 20 limits the exclusion or limitation of liability in contracts for sale or hire-purchase, and is a restatement of provisions originally introduced by the Supply of Goods (Implied Terms) Act 1973. As was explained earlier, in every contract for the sale of goods, certain terms are implied concerning the seller's rights to sell; the merchantable quality of the goods; their fitness for their purpose; and their correspondence to any sample or description attached to them. Similar terms are implied into every contract of hire-purchase.

Under s.55 of the Sale of Goods Act 1979, it is possible to negative or exclude any or all of the implied terms, subject to the provisions of the 1977 Act. The effects of s.20 are that the implied terms as to the seller's title cannot be excluded; that all the other implied terms, namely the implied terms as to merchantable quality, fitness for purpose and correspondence with description or sample cannot be excluded in a consumer contract; and that the implied terms (other than the implied terms as to seller's title) cannot be excluded in other contracts unless the exclusion or restriction is fair and reasonable.

The section has a similar impact in contracts of hire-purchase.

Under the Consumer Transactions (Restrictions on Statements) Order 1976,[34] the furnishing of such terms in writing to a consumer by a person acting in the course of a business may also constitute a criminal offence.

Section 21 applies almost identical provisions to contracts for the supply of goods other than those covered by s.20 and to charterparties. The major difference is that, under s.21, terms as to title may also be excluded if it is fair and reasonable to do so.

A person is not bound by a contract term which attempts to limit or exclude that person's rights against another person under some other contract if such rights could not have been excluded or limited under that other contract by virtue of the 1977 Act's provisions.

The "fair and reasonable" test

10–42 The "fair and reasonable" test set out in the 1977 Act s.24 may well have been in the minds of the Law Commissioners when they described the Act as "a complex piece of legislation".[35] There are in fact three slightly different tests of what constitutes reasonableness. As the Scottish Law Commission Discussion Paper No.119 explains[36]:

---

[34] Consumer Transactions (Restrictions on Statements) Order 1976 (SI 1976/1813).

[35] The Law Commissions, *Unfair Terms in Contracts* (Law Commission Consultation Paper No.166, Scot. Law Com. Discussion Paper No.119, 7 August 2002), p.3, para.1.6.

[36] The Law Commissions, *Unfair Terms in Contracts* (Law Commission Consultation Paper No.166, Scot. Law Com. Discussion Paper No.119, 7 August 2002), p.41, para.3.50.

"Technically there appear to be no fewer than three slightly different tests of reasonableness under these provisions. The general test is that set out in s.24(1). Secondly, for cases falling within ss.20 and 21 only, the court is required to have regard to a list of 'guidelines' specified in Sch.2. Thirdly, where the clause restricts liability to a specified sum, s.24 (3) requires the court to have regard in particular to questions of the resources available to the party and insurance."

Unfair Contract Terms Act 1977: Pt II **10–43**

"24.—(1) In determining for the purposes of this Part of this Act whether it was fair and reasonable to incorporate a term in a contract, regard shall be had only to the circumstances which were or ought reasonably to have been, known to or in contemplation of the parties to the contract at the time when the contract was made.

(2) In determining for the purposes of section 20 or 21 of this Act whether it was fair and reasonable to incorporate a term in a contract, regard shall be had in particular to the matters specified in Schedule 2 to this Act; but this subsection shall not prevent a court or arbiter from holding, in accordance with any rule of law, that a term which purports to exclude or restrict any relevant liability is not a term of the contract.

(2A) In determining for the purposes of this Part of this Act whether it is fair and reasonable to allow reliance on a provision of a notice (not being a notice having contractual effect), regard shall be had to all the circumstances obtaining when the liability arose or (but for the provision) would have arisen.

(3) Where a term of a contract or a provision of a notice purports to restrict liability to a specified sum of money, and the question arises for the purposes of this Part of this Act whether it was fair and reasonable to incorporate the term in the contract or whether it was fair and reasonable to allow reliance on the provision, then, without prejudice to subsection (2) above in the case of a term in a contract, regard shall be had in particular to—

(a) the resources which the party seeking to rely on that term or provision could expect to be available to him for the purpose of meeting the liability should it arise;
(b) how far it was open to that party to cover himself by insurance.

(4) The onus of proving that it was fair and reasonable to incorporate a term in a contract or that it is fair and reasonable to allow reliance on a provision of a notice shall lie on the party so contending.

...

SCHEDULE 2: 'GUIDELINES' FOR APPLICATION OF REASONABLENESS TEST **10–44**

The matters to which regard is to be had in particular for the purposes of sections 6(3), 7(3) and (4), 20 and 21 are any of the following which appear to be relevant—

(a) the strength of the bargaining positions of the parties relative to each other, taking into account (among other things) alternative means by which the customer's requirements could have been met;
(b) whether the customer received an inducement to agree to the term, or in accepting it had an opportunity of entering into a similar contract with other persons, but without having to accept a similar term;
(c) whether the customer knew or ought reasonably to have known of the existence and extent of the term (having regard, among other things, to any custom of the trade and any previous course of dealing between the parties);

> (d) where the term excludes or restricts any relevant liability if some condition is not complied with, whether it was reasonable at the time of the contract to expect that compliance with that condition would be practicable;
> (e) whether the goods were manufactured, processed or adapted to the special order of the customer."

10–45 Although there are three distinct tests in these provisions, in practice there is but a single reasonableness test. The courts have indicated that they will take the factors referred to by the guidelines into account in all cases in which they appear relevant, and questions of insurance are also treated as highly relevant in cases in which the 1977 Act s.24(3) does not strictly apply.[37] In, for example, *Stewart Gill Ltd v Horatio Myer & Co Ltd*,[38] a contract term preventing a payment or credit from being set off against the price claimed was held unreasonable after consideration of the whole term.[39] In *Phillips Products v Hyland*,[40] the availability or not of insurance was considered among other factors to be relevant in construing the reasonableness of an exclusion clause.[41]

In *Stag Line Ltd v Tyne Ship Repair Group Ltd (The Zinnia)*,[42] the court took into account the equal bargaining position of the parties to a commercial contract in determining that a clause excluding liability for breach of duty was neither unfair nor unreasonable. The decision of the House of Lords in *George Mitchell (Chesterhall) Ltd v Finney Lock Seeds Ltd*[43] is examined below.

While the above cases are English, it is submitted that the test is the same in substance as in Scotland.[44] In *Knight Machinery (Holdings) Ltd v Rennie*,[45] (above), the court discussed the guidelines set out in Sch.2, paras (c) and (d).

10–46

George Mitchell (Chesterhall) Ltd v Finney Lock Seeds Ltd
[1983] 2 A.C. 803
English House of Lords: Lords Diplock, Roskill, Scarman, Brightman and Bridge of Harwich

Mitchell farmed in East Lothian. Over several years they had purchased seed from Finney's catalogue that was supplied to them annually and that contained Finney's conditions of contract. Mitchell ordered from Finney 30lbs of "Finney's Late Dutch Special" cabbage seed, which both parties knew could withstand the rigours of the East Lothian winter.

The seed was supplied with an invoice which stated:

"1. . . . we will, at our option, replace . . . defective seals or plants . . .

[37] See also WCH Ervine, *Consumer Law in Scotland*, 2nd edn (Edinburgh: W. Green, 2000), p.225, paras 10–55—10–59; WW McBryde, *The Law of Contract in Scotland*, 3rd edn (Edinburgh: W. Green, 2007) paras 18–27—18–38; and WJ Stewart, "15 Years of Fair Contracts in Scotland?", 1993 S.L.T. (News) 15.

[38] *Stewart Gill Ltd v Horatio Myer & Co Ltd* [1992] Q.B. 600.

[39] See also *Horace Holman Group Ltd v Sherwood International Group Ltd*, 2000 W.L. 491372.

[40] *Phillips Products v Hyland* [1987] 2 All E.R. 620.

[41] In *Woodman v Photo Trade Processing Ltd* unreported 3 April 1981 Exeter County Court, discussed in WCH Ervine, *Consumer Law in Scotland*, 2nd edn (Edinburgh: W. Green, 2000) p.226, para.10–56), the availability of indemnity insurance to the proponer of the limitation clause was relevant in determining the clause unreasonable.

[42] *Stag Line Ltd v Tyne Ship Repair Group Ltd (The Zinnia)* [1984] 2 Lloyd's Rep. 211.

[43] *George Mitchell (Chesterhall) Ltd v Finney Lock Seeds Ltd* [1983] 2 A.C. 803.

[44] The Law Commissions, *Unfair Terms in Contracts* (Law Commission Consultation Paper No.166; Scot. Law Com. Discussion Paper No.119, 7 August 2002), p.41, para.3.49.

[45] *Knight Machinery (Holdings) Ltd v Rennie*, 1995 S.L.T. 166.

> We hereby exclude all liability for any loss or damage arising from the use of any seeds or plants supplied by us ... or for any other loss or damage whatsoever save for, at our option, liability for any such replacement or refund as aforesaid.
> In accordance with the accepted custom of the seed trade any express or implied condition, statement or warranty, statutory or otherwise, not stated in these conditions is hereby excluded."

The seed was planted. It turned out to be autumn cabbage so that although it germinated and grew it was commercially useless and had to be ploughed in at a loss of £61,000. The cost of replacing the seed or refunding the price was £101.60.

In this action by Mitchell to recover their actual losses, Mitchell successfully claimed that Finney could not rely on the exclusion of liability, because to do so would not be "fair and reasonable" as defined by s.55(5) of the Sale of Goods Act 1979 (a provision similar to Sch.2 to the Unfair Contract Terms Act 1977 which replaced it).

"LORD BRIDGE OF HARWICH: ... [I]t is common ground that the onus was on the respondents to show that it would not be fair or reasonable to allow the appellants to rely on the relevant condition as limiting their liability. It was argued for the appellants that the court must have regard to the circumstances as at the date of the contract, not after the breach ... The question whether it is fair or reasonable to allow reliance on a term excluding or limiting liability for a breach of contract can only arise after the breach. The nature of the breach and the circumstances in which it occurred cannot possibly be excluded from 'all the circumstances of the case' to which regard must be had ... **10–47**

My Lords, at long last I turn to the application of the statutory language to the circumstances of the case. Of the particular matters to which attention is directed by paragraphs (*a*) to (*e*) of section 55(5), only those in (*a*) to (*c*) are relevant. As to paragraph (*c*), the respondents admittedly knew of the relevant condition (they had dealt with the appellants for many years) and, if they had read it, particularly clause 2, they would, I think, as laymen rather than lawyers, have had no difficulty in understanding what it said. This and the magnitude of the damages claimed in proportion to the price of the seeds sold are factors which weigh in the scales in the appellants' favour.

The question of relative bargaining strength under paragraph (*a*) and of the opportunity to buy seeds without a limitation of the seedman's liability under paragraph (*b*) were interrelated. The evidence was that a similar limitation of liability was universally embodied in the terms of trade between seedsmen and farmers and had been so for very many years. The limitation had never been negotiated between representative bodies but, on the other hand, had not been the subject of any protest by the National Farmers' Union. These factors, if considered in isolation, might have been equivocal. The decisive factor, however, appears from the evidence of four witnesses called for the appellants, two independent seedsmen, the chairman of the appellant company, and a director of a sister company (both being wholly-owned subsidiaries of the same parent). They said that it had always been their practice, unsuccessfully attempted in the instant case, to negotiate settlements of farmers' claims for damages in excess of the price of the seeds, if they thought that the claims were 'genuine' and 'justified.' This evidence indicated a clear recognition by seedsmen in general, and the appellants in particular, that reliance on the limitation of liability imposed by the relevant condition would not be fair or reasonable.

Two further factors, if more were needed, weigh the scales in favour of the respondents. The supply of autumn, instead of winter, cabbage seed was due to the negligence of the appellants' sister company. Irrespective of its quality, the autumn variety supplied could not, according to the appellants' own evidence, be grown commercially in East

Lothian. Finally, as the trial judge found, seedsmen could insure against the risk of crop failure caused by supply of the wrong variety of seeds without materially increasing the price of seeds.

My Lords, even if I felt doubts about the statutory issue, I should not, for the reasons explained earlier, think it right to interfere with the unanimous original decision of that issue by the Court of Appeal. As it is, I feel no such doubts. If I were making the original decision, I should conclude without hesitation that it would not be fair or reasonable to allow the appellants to rely on the contractual limitation of their liability.

I would dismiss the appeal."

LORDS DIPLOCK, ROSKILL, SCARMAN AND BRIGHTMAN agreed with the speech of Lord Bridge.

The court was influenced by the fact that the suppliers normally negotiated settlements rather than attempt to rely on the clause; that the suppliers could have insured against such risks without substantial increase in cost; and that the breach was due to the suppliers' negligence. Other factors that might be relevant are considered in the next case.

10–48 **Border Harvesters Ltd v Edwards Engineering (Perth) Ltd**

1985 S.L.T. 128

Court of Session, Outer House: Lord Kincraig

The facts are as stated above at para.10–34.

10–49 "LORD KINCRAIG: ... Harvesters' argument based upon the applicability of s. 20(2) now falls to be considered ... Two points arise here. First of all, whether this was a sale by description within the meaning of s.13 of the Sale of Goods Act and secondly, whether it was a contract to which s.14 of the same Act applies. As to whether this contract was a sale by description within the meaning of s.13 the argument was that the equipment was described as having a certain performance capacity and was therefore a sale by description within the meaning of s. 13 of the Sale of Goods Act 1979. I disagree. What was contracted for in this case was described as a Kamas dryer; what was supplied was a Kamas dryer. What the dryer was capable of doing was in my judgment not part of the description of the goods supplied ... The pursuers are not entitled to invoke s. 20 of the 1977 Act on the ground that this was a sale by description and that there is an implied obligation that the goods should correspond with the description.

So far as s.14 of the Sale of Goods Act 1979 is concerned ... s. 20 cannot apply where such an obligation arises from the express terms of the contract as it does here, where Edwards expressly obliged themselves to supply a dryer of a stated quality. If the condition as to quality or fitness is expressed in the contract there is in my judgment no need for the protecting provisions of the 1977 Act. I accordingly would reject Harvesters' contention that Edwards require to prove that it was fair and reasonable to incorporate into the contract the clause limiting their liability for breach of the express term as to fitness."

Denholm Fishselling Ltd v Anderson 10–50
1991 S.L.T. (Sh. Ct.) 24
Sheriff Court of Grampian, Highlands and Islands at Peterhead: Sheriff Principal RD Ireland, QC

Denholm sold 11 boxes of cod to Anderson in the fish market at Peterhead under terms and conditions printed on a document headed "Peterhead Fishsalesmen's Association Conditions of Sale". Clause 6 of the document reads:

> "Buyers shall be afforded reasonable opportunity to examine all fish exposed for sale and shall be held to have satisfied themselves, before completion of the transaction, as to their condition, weight and quantity, and in every other respect."

Some time after the sale the 11 boxes were examined by an environmental health officer and found to be unfit for human consumption. Anderson refused to pay for them on the ground that they were not of merchantable quality, in breach of the obligation implied by s.14 of the Sale of Goods Act 1979. Denholm claimed that liability was excluded by cl.6. Anderson claimed that the clause was not "fair and reasonable" under ss.20(2), 24(2), 24(4) of and Sch.2 to the Unfair Contract Terms Act 1977.

On appeal, the sheriff principal agreed that given the commercial realities of the fish market, a finding that cl.6 was fair and reasonable was a justifiable one.

"SHERIFF PRINCIPAL (RD IRELAND, QC): ... It was agreed on behalf of the defenders that in considering the strength of the bargaining positions of the parties the sheriff had failed to have regard to the fact that the fishsellers of Peterhead have what was described as a monopoly, in the sense that they all contract on the standard conditions of sale, so that anyone who wants to buy fish at Peterhead has to do so on these terms. Since similar standard conditions apply at neighbouring ports, the intending buyer must buy fish on the standard conditions or go without. In such circumstances all the bargaining strength is on the side of the sellers, and it is unfair to allow them to take advantage of that by forcing buyers to give up the protection which they enjoy under the Sale of Goods Act. The argument is at first sight attractive, but I have come to the conclusion that it is unsound. The objection to a monopoly is not that all sales are subject to the same contractual terms, but that buyers are compelled to buy from the same seller. If that were the case at Peterhead, it might well be that buyers were in a disadvantageous bargaining position. But the fishsellers of Peterhead have no monopoly in that sense. The fact that one party tenders to the other a set of non-negotiable contractual terms is not in itself evidence of inequality of bargaining power or that the terms themselves are unfair and unreasonable. The buyer may not be able to buy fish except on the standard conditions, but he is not forced to purchase fish from a single fish salesman or prevented from discriminating between one vessel and another when deciding whether or not to buy from a particular catch. It is implicit in the 1977 Act that there can be non-negotiable contractual terms which are fair and reasonable. In the present case both buyers and sellers are substantial organisations, employing skilled and experienced staff who are capable of looking after the interests of their employers when deciding whether or not to enter into contractual relations. The fact that when they have decided to enter into a contract the terms of that contract are not negotiable does not show that there is a preponderance of bargaining power in favour of the seller or that the conditions are unfair or unreasonable. 10–51

The other ground of the defenders' attack on the standard conditions was that because it was impracticable to make an exhaustive examination of the fish before the sale it was unfair to deprive the buyer of his remedy against defects which he could discover only when the sale had been completed and the fish had come into his possession. This argument does not however take account of the commercial realities of the fish market, which are well known to those who do business there, whether as buyers or as sellers. Because of the nature of the business and the speed with which the transactions have to be put through it is impracticable for a buyer to examine every single box of fish thoroughly before purchase. The buyer is however given some protection by the provision in cl. 6 for reasonable opportunity to examine the fish exposed for sale. The clause recognises the practical limitations of the business by the use of the word 'reasonable' rather than 'complete' or 'exhaustive.' Moreover fish are perishable; they have to be removed from the market shortly after the sale, sometimes to a destination many miles away. If after the consignment has been removed the buyer disputes his liability for the price on the ground of defects in the goods, it may be very difficult to prove either that the defects existed at the time of the sale, or even that the consignment in question was bought in a particular transaction.

The sheriff had in my opinion material on which he was entitled to hold that it was fair and reasonable to incorporate cl. 6 into the contract between the parties. Its purpose is to eliminate difficult and costly disputes which in the end would benefit neither party. It takes account of the commercial situation as it exists in the fish market at Peterhead and strikes an equitable balance between the interests of buyer and seller. It therefore has the effect of excluding the buyers' remedy under s.14 of the Sale of Goods Act. The defenders were therefore not entitled to withhold payment of the balance of the price, and the pursuers are entitled to decree. The appeal is accordingly refused."

The 1977 Act (s.24(4)) places the burden of proving fairness and reasonableness upon the party relying on the clause. Lord Bridge's comments in *Mitchell* (above, para.10–46) confirm this.

Despite the drafting of s.24(4) and the dicta in *Mitchell*, the next case suggests that it will always be necessary for the party seeking to avoid the effects of the exclusion clause initially to raise the issue of fairness and reasonableness.[46]

10–52 **William Teacher & Sons Ltd v Bell Lines Ltd**

1991 S.L.T. 876

Court of Session, Outer House Lord Marnoch

Teachers employed Bell Lines to carry a consignment of whisky. Bell subcontracted the work to Slaters Transport. The whisky went missing whilst in the hands of Slaters. Teachers sued both Bell and Slaters. Bell claimed a right of relief from Slaters. Slaters claimed that their contract was subject to the conditions of carriage of the Road Haulage Association, condition 11 of which limited their liability to £800 per ton, and which had been referred to in pro forma receipts that had been given to Bell on previous occasions. Bell argued that only in exceptional circumstances could a mere reference to conditions contained in non-contractual documents provide a basis for their inclusion in a contract. Furthermore, the conditions limiting liability were in standard form and it was for the party

[46] This is to be contrasted with the apparent position under the Council Directive 93/13/EEC on unfair terms in consumer contracts (OJ 1993 L 95, p.29). The ECJ ruled in the joined cases of *Oceano Grupo Editorial SA v Quintero* (ECJ C-240/98 to C-244/98) that consumer protection under the Directive involves the national court being able to recognise of its own volition whether a term of a contract is unfair. M Hogg, in *Scottish Law and Unfair Contract Terms*, E.R.P.L. 2002, 10(1), 160–162, comments that whatever the previous position in Scots courts, the decision requires them now actively to consider the unfairness of contract terms whether pleaded by a party or not.

seeking to rely on them to prove that they were fair and reasonable under the Unfair Contract Terms Act 1977, but that no such averment had been made. The court held that Slaters would have to do so by reference to Sch.2 of the 1977 Act, only once the issue had been raised by Bell.

"LORD MARNOCH: . . . I agree with counsel for the second defenders that it is for the party wishing to found on the substantive statutory provision to 'raise the issue,' as counsel put it, in the first instance. This it seems to me, is in accordance with at least the spirit, if not the letter, of the maxim omnia rite acta praesumuntur. It also appears to have been the view of Lord Davidson in *Landcatch Ltd v Marine Harvest Ltd.* That was a case in which the customer averred that the condition in question was '*not* fair and reasonable' (my emphasis), and the suppliers submitted that this averment was lacking in specification. Lord Davidson had little hesitation in repelling that submission and in the course of his judgment said this (at p. 481): 'In my opinion a supplier seeking to discharge the onus imposed upon him by s. 24(4) is obliged to aver which of the matters detailed in Sched. 2 he relies upon, and to specify the facts which he proposes to prove in relation to these matters. On the other hand once the issue of "fair and reasonable" is raised the customer is not bound to make any averments. He may find it prudent to shelter behind a general denial of the defenders' averments.' **10–53**

While Lord Davidson was dealing with a rather different argument, it is, I think, reasonably clear that he envisaged the 'issue' being raised by the customer rather than by the supplier. In this connection it is perhaps important to remember that the 'fair and reasonable provision is not one which applies to every commercial contract. On the contrary, in terms of s.17 of the 1977 Act, it is only applicable where the contract in question is a 'customer [*sic*] contract' or 'standard form contract.' There may be real doubt as regards the existence of either of these prerequisites and the former, in particular, seems to me to raise issues of fact which in the majority of cases will be more within the knowledge of the customer than of the supplier. This again suggests that it should be for the customer, if so advised to raise the issue of fairness in the first instance."

Unfair contract terms in consumer contracts

According to the Explanatory Notes to the Consumer Rights Act 2015, Pt 2 of the Act: **10–54**

- "Consolidates the legislation governing unfair contract terms in relation to consumer contracts, which currently is found in two separate pieces of legislation, into one place, removes anomalies and overlapping provisions in relation to consumer contracts.
- Makes clearer the circumstances when the price or subject matter of the contract cannot be considered for fairness and in particular makes clear that to avoid being considered for fairness those terms must be transparent and prominent.
- Clarifies the role of and extends the indicative list of terms which may be regarded as unfair (the so-called 'grey list')."[47]

[47] Consumer Rights Act 2015, Explanatory Notes: Summary of Part 2, *http://www.legislation.gov.uk/ukpga/2015/15/notes/division/2* [Accessed 26 October 2015].

The two pieces of legislation in question are the Unfair Contract Terms Act and the Unfair Terms in Consumer Contracts Regulations 1999 (UTCCR).[48] Although the Law Commissions recommended that the Unfair Terms in Consumer Contracts Directive (Council Directive 93/13/EEC) (UTCCD) be written into UK legislation,[49] Pt 2 of the 2015 Act is a consolidation Act only. Although Pt 2 deals with unfair terms, it also deals with terms that exclude or limit liability for negligence that causes death or personal injury (s.65) and Pt 1 of the 2015 Act establishes a new regime for implied statutory terms in consumer contracts.

Unfair terms in consumer contracts: scope of the Consumer Rights Act 2015 Pt 2

10–55 The scope of Pt 2 is defined in ss.61 and 76 (the interpretation section for Pt 2).

10–56 **Consumer Rights Act 2015**

PART 2

Unfair terms

What contracts and notices are covered by this Part?

"61 Contracts and notices covered by this Part

(1) This Part applies to a contract between a trader and a consumer.
(2) This does not include a contract of employment or apprenticeship.
(3) A contract to which this Part applies is referred to in this Part as a "consumer contract".
(4) This Part applies to a notice to the extent that it—

(a) relates to rights or obligations as between a trader and a consumer, or
(b) purports to exclude or restrict a trader's liability to a consumer.

(5) This does not include a notice relating to rights, obligations or liabilities as between an employer and an employee.
(6) It does not matter for the purposes of subsection (4) whether the notice is expressed to apply to a consumer, as long as it is reasonable to assume it is intended to be seen or heard by a consumer.
(7) A notice to which this Part applies is referred to in this Part as a "consumer notice".
(8) In this section "notice" includes an announcement, whether or not in writing, and any other communication or purported communication."

"Trader" is defined as

> "a person acting for purposes relating to that person's trade, business, craft or profession, whether acting personally or through another person acting in the trader's name or on the trader's behalf".[50]

"Business" includes the activities of any government department or local or public authority.[51] However "consumer" is "an individual acting for purposes that are wholly or mainly outside

[48] See above, para.10–25.
[49] Recommendation 21, The Law Commissions, *Unfair Terms in Consumer Contracts: Advice to the Department for Business, Innovation and Skills* available at: *http://www.scotlawcom.gov.uk/files/3113/6361/9437/Unfair_Terms_in_Consumer_Contracts_Advice.pdf*, paras 7.117–7.227 [Accessed 25 October 2015].
[50] Consumer Rights Act 2015 s.2(2).
[51] Consumer Rights Act 2015 s.2(7).

that individual's trade, business, craft or profession".[52] A corporate body, such as a company, a charity or public body—indeed any entity that is not an individual, is not a consumer under the 2015 Act and would have to rely on the protection of the 1977 Act where the contract is not a consumer contract.[53]

The definition of "consumer", which was transposed from the Directive, therefore excludes all non-natural persons. This point of definition was considered by the European Court of Justice in *Cape SNC v Idealservice*[54] and *Idealservice v OMAI*.[55] The companies contracted with Idealservice for supply of automatic drink dispensers installed on company premises for sole use by the company staff. In a dispute, a question arose over the fairness of a jurisdiction clause in Idealservice's standard form contract. The companies asked whether the undertaking, not relating or conducive to their business, could be regarded as that of a consumer, and whether a company could be regarded as a consumer. The court held that it could not. This may be contrasted with *R & B Customs Brokers Co Ltd v United Dominions Trust*,[56] when a firm of shipping brokers was held to have been dealing as a consumer for purposes of the 1977 Act s.12.

The expression "relating to" in the definition of "business", however, is wide enough to bring the business activities of most corporate and public bodies within the definition of "trader". A contract by such a body with a consumer (for example, a one-off business transaction, or even a regular transaction that relates to that body's main activities) would be covered by the 2015 Act.[57]

The broad definition of a consumer notice in s.61(8) extends Pt 2 to any non-contractual notice that affects consumer rights. The provisions in s.61 and throughout the 2015 Act are founded on the Law Commissions' recommendation[58] and, although primarily aimed at non-contractual liability, such as liability in negligence or libel, is intended also to cover potentially unfair terms in end user licence agreements (EULAs) frequently attached to contracts for software and other digital products. The problem with EULAs was highlighted by the Law Commissions in their Report to BIS[59]:

> "7.20 ... For a term to be reviewable for fairness, it must be part of a contract. The internet includes many sites which state that by downloading material the consumer will be taken to have agreed to the owner's terms and conditions, but there is no box or icon to click. These so called "browse wrap licences" probably do not have the status of contract terms, so the UTCCR would not apply to them.
>
> ...
>
> 7.26 ... Having considered the problems which arise over EULAs, we now think that protection should extend more widely than negligence. Many exclusions in EULAs refer to other forms of liability, including liability for defamation or breach of privacy. Some exclusions are written in such vague, general terms that it is difficult to pin-point what liability is intended to be excluded.

---

[52] Consumer Rights Act 2015 s.2(3).

[53] Above, para.10–26 onward.

[54] *Cape SNC v Idealservice* (C541/99).

[55] See *Idealservice v OMAI* (C-542/99), judgment available on *http://www.curia.eu.int/en/content/juris/index.htm* [Accessed 2 September 2015].

[56] *R & B Customs Brokers Co Ltd v United Dominions Trust* [1988] 1 All E.R. 847.

[57] Above, para.10–25. See also WCH Ervine, *Consumer Law in Scotland*, 5th edn (Edinburgh: W. Green, 2015), para.9–25 and the cases referred there.

[58] Recommendation 26 and paras 7.18–7.37, The Law Commissions, *Unfair Terms in Consumer Contracts: Advice to the Department for Business, Innovation and Skills* available at: *http://www.scotlawcom.gov.uk/files/3113/6361/9437/Unfair_Terms_in_Consumer_Contracts_Advice.pdf* [Accessed 25 October 2015].

[59] The Law Commissions, *Unfair Terms in Consumer Contracts: Advice to the Department for Business, Innovation and Skills* available at: *http://www.scotlawcom.gov.uk/files/3113/6361/9437/Unfair_Terms_in_-Consumer_Contracts_Advice.pdf* [Accessed 25 October 2015].

7.27 We have therefore been persuaded to extend the provisions on notices to include any notice which purports to exclude any legal liability which the trader would have to the consumer in the absence of the notice."

"Core terms" not covered by the Regulations

10–57 Certain "core terms" are excluded from the Regulations.

Consumer Right Act 2015 Part 2

"64 Exclusion from assessment of fairness

(1) A term of a consumer contract may not be assessed for fairness under section 62 to the extent that—

(a) it specifies the main subject matter of the contract, or
(b) the assessment is of the appropriateness of the price payable under the contract by comparison with the goods, digital content or services supplied under it.

(2) Subsection (1) excludes a term from an assessment under section 62 only if it is transparent and prominent.
(3) A term is transparent for the purposes of this Part if it is expressed in plain and intelligible language and (in the case of a written term) is legible.
(4) A term is prominent for the purposes of this section if it is brought to the consumer's attention in such a way that an average consumer would be aware of the term.
(5) In subsection (4) 'average consumer' means a consumer who is reasonably well-informed, observant and circumspect.
(6) This section does not apply to a term of a contract listed in Part 1 of Schedule 2."

The exclusion of such core terms in what was formerly reg.6(2) of UCTCCR 1999 (and before that reg.3(2) of the 1994 Regulations) and now s.64(1) above, and in particular terms relating to price and remuneration, was considered in *Director General of Fair Trading v First National Bank*.[60]

10–58 **Director General of Fair Trading v First National Bank**
[2002] A.C. 481 House of Lords

First National Bank (FNB) carried on a consumer credit business, making agreements using printed forms containing a number of standard terms. The Director General, under their powers in the Regulations, sought a court order to restrain the use of or reliance on condition 8 of the standard form. That condition stated:

"Interest on the amount which becomes payable shall be charged in accordance with condition 4, at the rate specified in paragraph D overleaf (subject to variation) until payment after as well as before any judgment (such obligation to be independent of and not to merge with the judgment)."

[60] See *Director General of Fair Trading v First National Bank* [2002] A.C. 481. The applicable law was the 1994 version of the Regulations. The injunctive power of the Director General previously embodied in reg.8 of the 1994 Regulations was now contained in reg.12 of the 1999 Regulations. The fairness test of reg.5 of the 1999 Regulations replaced the fairness test in reg.4 of the 1994 Regulations, which was the subject matter of the decision.

The purpose of condition 8 was to ensure that if the debtor defaulted and judgment was given against them, interest would nonetheless continue to accrue on the sums outstanding, whatever installment provision a court might order for repayment of such sums. Accordingly debtors paying off all installments nonetheless would find themselves still in debt at the end. FNB resisted the Director General's application on the grounds that the term was within the exception laid down in reg.3(2) of the Unfair Terms in Consumer Contract 1994, and that in any event the term was not unfair.

The House found that the term did not fall within the "main subject matter" provision of reg.3(2), and its fairness or otherwise fell to be assessed under reg.4 of the 1994 Regulations.

"LORD BINGHAM OF CORNHILL: ... **10–59**

[12]. In agreement with the judge and the Court of Appeal, I do not accept the bank's submission on this issue. The Regulations, as Professor Sir Guenter Treitel QC has aptly observed (Treitel *The Law of Contract*, 10th ed (1999), p 248), 'are not intended to operate as a mechanism of quality or price control' and regulation 3(2) is of 'crucial importance in recognising the parties' freedom of contract with respect to the essential features of their bargain': p 249. But there is an important 'distinction between the term or terms which express the substance of the bargain and "incidental" (if important) terms which surround them': *Chitty on Contracts*, 28th ed (1999), vol 1, ch 15 'Unfair Terms in Consumer Contracts', p 747, para 15-025. The object of the Regulations and the Directive is to protect consumers against the inclusion of unfair and prejudicial terms in standard-form contracts into which they enter, and that object would plainly be frustrated if regulation 3(2)(b) were so broadly interpreted as to cover any terms other than those falling squarely within [regulation 3(2)(b)]. In my opinion the term, as part of a provision prescribing the consequences of default, plainly does not fall within [regulation 3(2)(b)]. It does not concern the adequacy of the interest earned by the bank as its remuneration but is designed to ensure that the bank's entitlement to interest does not come to an end on the entry of judgment. I do not think the bank's argument on merger advances its case. It appears that some judges in the past have been readier than I would be to infer that a borrower's covenant to pay interest was not intended to extend beyond the entry of judgment. But even if a borrower's obligation were ordinarily understood to extend beyond judgment even in the absence of an independent covenant, it would not alter my view of the term as an ancillary provision and not one concerned with the adequacy of the bank's remuneration as against the services supplied."

The decision was applied in several English decisions,[61] but it was distinguished by the Supreme Court decision in *OFT v Abbey National*.

Office of Fair Trading v Abbey National Plc **10–60**

[2009] EWCA Civ. 116; [2010] 1 A.C. 696

Supreme Court: Lord Phillips of Worth Matravers PSC, Lord Walker of Gestingthorpe, Baroness Hale of Richmond, Lord Mance JJSC, Lord Neuberger of Abbotsbury MR

The Office of Fair Trading investigated the fairness of certain overdraft charges on current accounts levied by banks. It issued proceedings against the defendants, seven banks and one mutual building society, for a declaration that the standard terms and charges in

[61] See, e.g. *Virstow Eves London Central Ltd v Smith* [2004] EWHC 263.

question were not excluded from an assessment for fairness under the Unfair Terms in Consumer Contracts Regulations 1999 (the 1999 Regulations) by reg.6(2)(b) of those Regulations.

Andrew Smith J found that the relevant terms and charges were not covered by reg.6(2)(b) and the Court of Appeal dismissed an appeal by the defendants, because the relevant terms were ancillary rather than essential terms relating to price or remuneration.

The Supreme Court allowed an appeal by the banks, holding that any monetary price or remuneration payable under a contract fell within reg.6(2)(b) and distinguished *General of Fair Trading v First National Bank Plc.*[62]

10–61 "LORD WALKER OF GESTINGTHORPE JSC

The limited nature of the issue

[1] The members of the court are well aware of the limited nature of the issue which we have to decide in this appeal. But many of the general public (who are understandably taking a close interest in the matter) are not so well aware of its limited scope. It is therefore appropriate to spell out at the outset that the court does not have the task of deciding whether the system of charging personal current account customers adopted by United Kingdom banks is fair. The appellants are seven of the largest banks in the United Kingdom and one building society (but I shall for convenience refer to them all as 'the banks'). The banks accept that the system of 'free-if-in-credit' banking prevalent in this country involves a significant cross-subsidy (amounting to about 30% of the banks' total revenue stream from current account customers) provided by those customers who regularly incur charges for unauthorised overdrafts (a cohort, we were told, of the order of 12 million people) to those customers (a cohort of about 42 million people) who are in the fortunate position of never (or very rarely) incurring such charges. Banks in other European countries adopt different forms of cross-subsidy; French banks, for instance, concentrate their charges on processing standing orders and debit card transactions.

. . .

[3] The question for the court is much more limited, and more technical. It is whether as a matter of law the fairness of bank charges levied on personal current account customers in respect of unauthorised overdrafts (including unpaid item charges and other related charges as described below) can be challenged by the respondent, the Office of Fair Trading ('OFT'), as excessive in relation to the services supplied to the customers.

[4] That issue depends on the correct interpretation (in its European context) and application of regulation 6(2) of the Unfair Terms in Consumer Contracts Regulations 1999. Regulation 6(2) provides:

'In so far as it is in plain intelligible language, the assessment of fairness of a term shall not relate—(a) to the definition of the main subject matter of the contract, or (b) to the adequacy of the price or remuneration, as against the goods or services supplied in exchange.'

The context requires 'adequacy' to be read in the sense of 'appropriateness', as Lord Rodger of Earlsferry pointed out in *Director General of Fair Trading v First National Bank plc* [2002] 1 AC 481, para 64.

. . .

[62] *General of Fair Trading v First National Bank Plc* [2002] 1 A.C. 481.

The meaning of regulation 6(2) 10–62

. . .

[39] I start with the language of article 4(2) and regulation 6(2) (I can see no significant difference between them, although for no obvious reason article 4(2) refers to assessing the unfair nature of a term whereas regulation 6(2) refers to assessment of fairness of a term). Paragraphs (a) and (b) are, as I have said, concerned with the two sides of the quid pro quo inherent in any consumer contract. The main subject matter may be goods or services. If it is goods, it may be a single item (a car or a dishwasher) or a multiplicity of items. If for instance a consumer orders a variety of goods from a mail-order catalogue—say clothing, blinds, kitchen utensils and toys—there is no possible basis on which the court can decide that some items are more essential to the contract than others. The main subject matter is simply consumer goods ordered from a catalogue . . .

[40] Similarly, a supply of services may be simple (an entertainer booked to perform for an hour at a children's party) or composite (a week's stay at a five-star hotel offering a wide variety of services). Again, there is no principled basis on which the court could decide that some services are more essential to the contract than others and again the main subject matter must be described in general terms—hotel services. The services that banks offer to their current account customers are a comparable package of services. These include the collection and payment of cheques, other money transmission services, facilities for cash distribution (mainly by ATM machines either at manned branches or elsewhere) and the provision of statements in printed or electronic form.

[41] When one turns to the other part of the quid pro quo of a consumer contract, the price or remuneration, the difficulty of deciding which prices are essential is just the same, and regulation 6(2)(b) contains no indication that only an 'essential' price or remuneration is relevant. Any monetary price or remuneration payable under the contract would naturally fall within the language of paragraph (b) (I discount the absence of a reference to part of the price or remuneration for reasons already mentioned).

[42] In the case of banking services supplied to a current account customer under the 'free-if-in-credit' regime, the principal monetary consideration received by the bank consists of interest and charges on authorised and unauthorised overdrafts, and specific charges for particular non-routine services (such as expedited or foreign money transmission services). The most important element of the consideration, however, consists of the interest foregone by customers whose current accounts are in credit, since whether their credit balance is large or small they will be receiving a relatively low rate of interest on it (sometimes a very low rate or no interest at all) . . . [I]t is clear that just as banking services to current account customers can aptly be described as a package, so can the consideration that moves from the customer to the bank. Interest foregone is an important part of that package for customers whose accounts are in credit, and overdraft interest and charges are the most important element for those customers who are not in credit. Lawyers are very used to speaking of a package (or bundle) of rights and obligations, and in that sense every obligation which a consumer undertakes by a consumer contract could be seen as part of the price or remuneration received by the supplier. But non-monetary obligations undertaken by a consumer contract (for instance, to take proper care of goods on hire-purchase, or to treat material supplied for a distance-learning course as available only to the customer personally) are not part of the 'price or remuneration' within the regulation. That is the point of Lord Steyn's observation in the *First National Bank* case [2002] 1 AC 481, para 34, that 'in a broad sense all terms of the contract are in some way related to the price or remuneration'.

[43] The House of Lords' decision in the *First National Bank* case shows that not every term that is in some way linked to monetary consideration falls within regulation 6(2)(b). Paragraphs (d), (e), (f) and (l) of the 'grey list' in Schedule 2 to the 1999 Regulations are an illustration of that. But the relevant term in the *First National Bank* case was a default

provision. Traders ought not to be able to outflank consumers by 'drafting themselves' into a position where they can take advantage of a default provision. But *Bairstow Eves London Central Ltd v Smith* [2004] 2 EGLR 25 shows that the court can and will be astute to prevent that. In the First National Bank case Lord Steyn, at para 34, indicated that what is now regulation 6(2) should be construed restrictively, and Lord Bingham said, at para 12, that it should be limited to terms 'falling squarely within it'. I respectfully agree. But in my opinion the relevant terms and the relevant charges do fall squarely within regulation 6(2)(b).

[44] That conclusion is not to my mind at variance with the message to be derived from the travaux. It is a fairly complex message, reflecting not only a compromise between the opposing aims of consumer protection and freedom of contract, but also the contrast between consumer protection and consumer choice (the latter being more central, perhaps, to basic Community principles). This point was explored and explained in an article (not mentioned by the Court of Appeal) to which Mr Sumption referred, that is, "Good Faith in European Contract Law" by Professor Hugh Collins (1994) 14 *OJLS* 229. Mr Sumption placed particular emphasis on the following passage, at p 238:

'The history of the EC Directive on Unfair Terms in Consumer Contracts reveals the struggle between these two interpretations of the economic interests of consumers. Even at a late stage in the negotiations, the draft Directive proposed by the commission envisaged the introduction of a general principle against substantive unfairness in consumer contracts. It invalidated terms in standard form consumer contracts which caused "the performance of the contract to be significantly different from what the consumer could legitimately expect", or which caused "the performance of the contract to be unduly detrimental to the consumer". But in the battle between the advocates of consumer rights and the supporters of free competition, eventually the latter emerged victorious in the Council of Ministers. The fairness of the transaction in the sense of the price paid for the goods or services should not be subjected to review or control. This is the meaning of the obscure article 4(2) [which is then set out]. The final reservation in this provision ["plain intelligible language"] is significant. The Directive does not require consumer contracts to be substantively fair, but it does require them to be clear. Clarity is essential for effective market competition between terms. What matters primarily for EC contract law is consumer choice, not consumer rights.'

...

10–63 **The application of regulation 6(2)**

[47] I can state my opinion much more briefly on the second main issue in the appeal, that is the application of regulation 6(2), properly construed, to the facts. Charges for unauthorised overdrafts are monetary consideration for the package of banking services supplied to personal current account customers. They are an important part of the banks' charging structure, amounting to over 30% of their revenue stream from all personal current account customers. The facts that the charges are contingent, and that the majority of customers do not incur them, are irrelevant. On the view that I take of the construction of regulation 6(2), the fairness of the charges would be exempt from review in point of appropriateness under regulation 6(2)(b) even if fewer customers paid them and they formed a smaller part of the banks' revenue stream. Even if the Court of Appeal's interpretation had been correct, I do not see how it could have come to the conclusion, ante, p 738, para 111, that charges amounting to over 30% of the revenue stream were 'not part of the core or essential bargain'.

...

[51] For these reasons I would allow the appeal ... I would declare that the bank charges levied on personal current account customers in respect of unauthorised overdrafts (including unpaid item charges and other related charges) constitute part of the

price or remuneration for the banking services provided and, in so far as the terms giving rise to the charges are in plain intelligible language, no assessment under the Unfair Terms in Consumer Contracts Regulations 1999 of the fairness of those terms may relate to their adequacy as against the services supplied.

[52] If the court allows this appeal the outcome may cause great disappointment and indeed dismay to a very large number of bank customers who feel that they have been subjected to unfairly high charges in respect of unauthorised overdrafts. But this decision is not the end of the matter, as Lord Phillips PSC explains in his judgment. Moreover ministers and Parliament may wish to consider the matter further. They decided, in an era of so-called 'light-touch' regulation, to transpose the Directive as it stood rather than to confer the higher degree of consumer protection afforded by the national laws of some other member states. Parliament may wish to consider whether to revisit that decision.

LORD PHILLIPS OF WORTH MATRAVERS PSC

...

Conclusions 10–64

[78] I can see no justification for excluding from the application of regulation 6(2) price or remuneration on the ground that it is 'ancillary or incidental price or remuneration'. If it is possible to identify such price or remuneration as being paid in exchange for services, even if the services are fringe or optional extras, regulation 6(2) will preclude an attack on the price or remuneration in question if it is based on the contention that it was excessive by comparison with the services for which it was exchanged. If, on analysis, the charges are not given in exchange for individual services but are part of a package of different ways of charging for a package of varied services, this does not mean that they are not price or remuneration for the purpose of regulation 6(2). As I observed earlier, an assessment of the fairness of the charges will be precluded if the basis of the attack is that, by reason of their inclusion in the pricing package, those who pay them are being charged an excessive amount in exchange for the overall package.

[79] The Court of Appeal accepted the following argument advanced by the OFT. The object of regulation 6(2) is to exclude from assessment for fairness that part of the bargain that will be the focus of a customer's attention when entering into a contract, that is to say the goods or services that he wishes to acquire and the price he will have to pay for doing so. Market forces could and should be relied upon to control the fairness of this part of the bargain. Contingencies that the customer does not expect to involve him will not be of concern to him. He will not focus on these when entering into the bargain. The relevant charges fall into this category. Free-if-in-credit current accounts are opened by customers who expect to be in credit. Customers who go into debit without making a prior agreement for an overdraft normally do so because of an unforeseen contingency. Customers do not have regard to the consequences of such a contingency when opening a current account. Accordingly, the relevant charges that are then levied do not fall within regulation 6(2).

[80] It seems to me that this reasoning is relevant not to the question of whether the relevant charges form part of the price or remuneration for the package of services provided but to whether the method of pricing is fair. It may be open to question whether it is fair to subsidise some customers by levies on others who experience contingencies that they did not foresee when entering into their contracts. If it is not it may then be open to question whether the relevant terms fall within regulation 5(1). These questions do not, however, bear on the question of whether the relevant charges form part of the price or remuneration that is paid in exchange for the services provided to the holder of a current account. In agreement with Lord Walker JSC, and for the additional

reasons that he gives, I am not persuaded by the Court of Appeal's reasons for excluding the relevant charges from the 'price or remuneration' in regulation 6(2).

. . .

10–65 BARONESS HALE OF RICHMOND JSC

[92] For the reasons given by Lord Walker of Gestingthorpe and Lord Mance JJSC, I too would allow this appeal and make the declaration proposed by Lord Walker JSC.

[93] I would only add that, should this or any other Parliament be minded to take up the invitation given in the last paragraph of Lord Walker JSC's judgment, it may not be easy to find a satisfactory solution. The banks may not be the most popular institutions in the country at present, but that does not mean that their methods of charging for retail banking services are necessarily unfair when viewed as a whole. As a very general proposition, consumer law in this country aims to give the consumer an informed choice rather than to protect the consumer from making an unwise choice. We buy all sorts of products which a sensible person might not buy and some of which are not good value for the money. We do so with our eyes open because we want the product in question more than we want the money. Should financial services be treated differently from other goods and services? Or is the real problem that we do not have a real choice because the suppliers all offer much the same product and do not compete on some of their terms? This is the situation here. But it is not clear to me whether the proper solution is to find some way of forcing the suppliers to compete with one another in the terms they offer or whether the solution is to condemn one particular model of charging for those services. Fortunately, however, that is for Parliament and not for this court.

10–66 LORD MANCE JSC

. . .

[102] In the *First National Bank* case, the House of Lords was concerned with a provision in a regulated credit agreement for interest to continue at the credit agreement rate as against a borrower who had defaulted and against whom judgment had been entered for the principal and interest outstanding to judgment. The County Courts (Interest on Judgment Debts) Order 1991 (SI 1991/1184) meant that there was no statutory claim for or right to post-judgment interest. Hence, the rationale for including a continuing interest provision in the credit agreement. The case arose under regulation 3(2) of the Unfair Terms in Consumer Contracts Regulations 1994, which provided that 'no assessment shall be made of the fairness of any term which … (b) concerns the adequacy of the price or remuneration, as against the goods or services sold or supplied'. (This is slightly, though possibly materially, different wording to that of regulation 6(2) of the 1999 Regulations which replaced it.) The House held that regulation 3(2) did not apply, but went on to hold the term to have been fair. Passages from the speeches of Lord Bingham of Cornhill, at para 12, and Lord Steyn, at para 34, have been set out by Lord Walker of Gestingthorpe JSC. Both considered that clause 8 fell outside regulation 3(2)(b), as a provision prescribing the consequences of default. Lord Bingham added in a sentence drawing on the particular wording of regulation 3(2)(b) that

'It does not concern the adequacy of the interest earned by the bank as its remuneration but is designed to ensure that the bank's entitlement to interest does not come to an end on the entry of judgment.'

Lord Hope of Craighead's explanation is also relevant. He said, at para 43, that:

'Condition 8 is a default provision. The last sentence of it is designed to enable interest to be recovered on the whole of the amount due on default. That amount includes legal and other costs, charges and expenses, so it is not confined to the outstanding balance due by the borrower. I do not think that it can be said to be directly related to the price charged for the loan or to its adequacy. It is concerned instead with the consequences of the borrower's breach of contract. It sets out what is to happen if he fails to make the repayments to the bank as they fall due. I agree that regulation 3(2)(b) does not apply to it, and that its fairness as defined in regulation 4(1) of the 1994 Regulations must be assessed.'

This underlines the distinction between payments due in exchange for the original loan and the financial payments (including those relating to 'costs, charges and expenses') due on default under the clause. The decision of Gross J in *Bairstow Eves London Central Ltd v Smith* [2004] 2 EGLR 25 provides another example of the same distinction.

[103] The contracts made by customers for an overall package of banking facilities have been described as on a 'free-if-in-credit' basis. The OFT submits that this indicates or suggests that the agreement to pay relevant charges cannot be regarded as the or a part of the price or remuneration in exchange for which banking facilities are supplied. The banks submit, on the contrary, that the clear corollary of 'free-if-in-credit' is that the services provided will not be free if the customer is not in credit. They ask rhetorically what other price or remuneration there is, if not the relevant charges. The OFT's response is that it is conceptually possible to have a contract for services without anything in exchange that counts in terms of regulation 6(2)(b) as either price or remuneration. That I would accept. The bank might (especially under a basic banking contract which did not allow any overdraft in any circumstances) be content to operate on the basis that its profit would come solely from its power to use money which customers deposited with or arranged to have transferred to it. That power follows from the bank's ownership of money deposited with or transferred to it. (Further, since the deposit with or transfer to a bank of money is the main or part of the main subject matter of a banking contract, any assessment of the fairness of it or its legal consequences would appear to be excluded under regulation 6(2)(a), rather than (b).) Alternatively, the OFT suggests, without committing itself, that, if there is any price or remuneration under a free-if-in-credit banking contract, it is more easily found in the customer's agreement to pay overdraft interest.

[104] In accordance with general European legal principle, article 4(2) and regulation 6(2) are as exceptions to be construed narrowly. Nevertheless, the concepts of 'price or remuneration' must, I think, be capable in principle of covering, under a banking contract, an agreement to make a payment in a particular event. The language of regulation 6(2)(b) is on its face therefore capable of covering a customer's commitment, under the package contracts put before the House, to pay the relevant charges in the specified events. There is no reason why a customer should not be given free services in some circumstances, but, as a quid pro quo, be expected to pay for them in others.

[105] At various points the submissions before the House addressed the policy underlying the free-if-in-credit system of charging. It is clear from the description 'free-if-in-credit' itself that the system is likely to involve significant elements of cross-subsidy. Some customers (those remaining always or largely in credit) pay no or few charges, while others pay charges more regularly. Overall, around 30% of the banks' income from their customers is derived from the relevant charges. According to the OFT's own market study of July 2008, 77% of customers surveyed who had incurred a relevant charge in the past 12 months had heard of such charges before they incurred one. The relevant charges levied on any particular customer greatly exceed the actual net cost to the bank of complying with the request(s) impliedly made by the customer leading to the incurring of such charges. But it is obvious on reading the charging structure that charges cannot be directly related to the actual costs of providing any particular service triggering them. There are of course other obvious elements of cross-subsidy, even between customers who remain in credit. Customers who maintain large current accounts and receive no or limited interest on them subsidise in a sense customers who manage consistently to keep just in credit. Mr Jonathan Crow QC for the OFT made clear that the OFT does not contend that the element of cross-subsidy provided by the relevant charges affects the question whether regulation 6(2)(b) applies. Regulation

6(2)(b) would apply if the banks simply decided to charge more for particular services in order to pay their directors more or to earn more for their shareholders. It cannot make any difference to its application if the banks decide to adopt a business model which charges more for one type of transaction in order to subsidise another.

[106] The OFT's case, essentially accepted by the Court of Appeal, is that the agreement to pay the relevant charges is not price or remuneration, because regulation 6(2)(b) is confined in scope to payments in exchange for sales or supplies on which payments the consumer can be taken to have focused and to which he can be taken truly to have consented. The Court of Appeal, ante, p 730, para 86 encapsulated this conclusion as 'import[ing] the notion of essential bargain into the construction of article 4(2) and into both paragraphs (a) and (b) of regulation 6(2)'. It added that 'the concept of the essential bargain flows naturally' from the structure and purpose of the Directive because not every payment that a consumer makes falls within regulation 6(2)(b), and such a construction 'prevents regulation 6(2)(b) from being construed too widely'. It considered that its conclusion reflected 'the reasoning both in the travaux préparatoires and in the First National Bank case', which it interpreted as indicating that ancillary or incidental payment terms were not intended to be exempt from assessment for their 'adequacy' under regulation 6(2) (paras 64, 69 and 86).

. . .

[113] In my opinion, the identification of the price or remuneration for the purposes of article 4(2) and regulation 6(2) is a matter of objective interpretation for the court. The court should no doubt read and interpret the contract in the usual manner, that is, having regard to the view which the hypothetical reasonable person would take of its nature and terms. But there is no basis for requiring it to do so by attempting to identify a 'typical consumer' or by confining the focus to matters on which it might conjecture that he or she would be likely to focus. The consumer's protection under the Directive and Regulations is the requirement of transparency on which both insist. That being present, the consumer is to be assumed to be capable of reading the relevant terms and identifying whatever is objectively the price and remuneration under the contract into which he or she enters. A contract may of course require ancillary payments to be made which are not part of the price or remuneration for goods or services to be supplied under its terms. The First National Bank case and *Bairstow Eves London Central Ltd v Smith* [2004] 2 EGLR 25 illustrate the distinction by reference to default terms.

. . .

[118] I would therefore allow the appeal and grant the relief proposed by Lord Walker JSC in para 51. I would also endorse Lord Walker JSC's final paragraph.

10–65

LORD NEUBERGER OF ABBOTSBURY MR

[119] I also would allow this appeal for the reasons given by Lord Walker of Gestingthorpe and Lord Mance JJSC, and would grant the relief proposed by Lord Walker JSC in para 51.

. . ."

The decision, in refusing to treat the charges in dispute as ancillary to the core terms of the contract in question caused much controversy and not a little uncertainty. It undoubtedly gave impetus to the drafting of the Consumer Rights Bill and was a major reason for referring unfair contract terms in consumer contracts again to the Law Commissions.

The "core terms" exemption: the new test of "transparency and prominence"

The recommendations in the Commissions' Report to BIS guided the drafting of what are now s.64(2)–(6) of the 2015 Act. A term in a consumer contract is a core term only if its transparent and prominent. The Commissions' detailed report is extensively included here. **10–67**

Unfair Terms in Consumer Contracts: Advice to the Department for Business, Innovation and Skills **10–68**

The Law Commissions (March 2013)

PART 2

"THE EXEMPTION: THE NEED FOR REFORM

THE EXEMPTION

2.1 The exemption for main subject matter and price is currently set out in Regulation 6(2) of the Unfair Terms in Consumer Contracts Regulations 1999 (UTCCR), which states:

In so far as it is in plain intelligible language, the assessment of fairness of a term shall not relate—

(1) to the definition of the main subject matter of the contract, or

(2) to the adequacy of the price or remuneration, as against the goods or services supplied in exchange.

2.2 This reflects the exclusion set out in article 4(2) of the Unfair Terms Directive (UTD):

Assessment of the unfair nature of the terms shall relate neither to the definition of the main subject matter of the contract nor to the adequacy of the price and remuneration, on the one hand, as against the services or goods supplied in exchange, on the other, in so far as these terms are in plain intelligible language.

2.3 Article 4(2) was inserted into the text at a late stage in the negotiations. Originally, the European Commission had sought to subject every term in a consumer contract to a standard of fairness, whether or not it was individually negotiated.[1] However, two influential German academics, Professors Brandner and Ulmer, argued that in a free market, 'the relationship between the price and the goods or services provided is determined not according to some legal formula but by the mechanisms of the market':

The consumer would no longer need to shop around for the most favourable offer, but rather could pay any price in view of the possibility of subsequent control of its reasonableness.[2]

2.4 The exemption has generated considerable litigation. In the Issues Paper we concluded that its scope was fundamentally uncertain and proposed that the exemption should be rewritten.

THE BANK CHARGES LITIGATION **10–69**

2.5 The scope of the exemption came to prominence during the bank charges litigation, culminating in the 2009 Supreme Court decision, *Office of Fair Trading v Abbey National plc*.[3]

2.6 This was a test case brought by the Office of Fair Trading (OFT) against seven banks and one building society. The issue before the court was whether charges for unauthorised overdrafts were exempt from an assessment for fairness because they were price terms within the meaning of Regulation 6(2). The High Court and Court of Appeal found that the terms were not exempt, because they were not part of the essential bargain between the parties, and a typical consumer would not recognise the charges as part of the price. Conversely, the Supreme Court rejected the idea that price terms could be divided into those which formed the essential bargain and those which were ancillary. It said that the price should be determined 'objectively', rather than from the viewpoint of a typical consumer. The overdraft charges, therefore, fell within the exemption and could not be assessed for fairness.

10–70 WHAT THE ISSUES PAPER SAID ABOUT THE NEED FOR REFORM

Uncertainty in the law

2.7 In the Issues Paper, we reviewed the law in some detail, taking account of the purpose of the Directive, UK litigation, decisions of the Court of Justice of the European Union (CJEU) and the approach of other Member States.[4]

2.8 We concluded that the Supreme Court decision can be interpreted in several ways, and the courts could use it to justify a variety of approaches:

(1) Some judicial statements in the case say that price terms in plain, intelligible language are exempt from review – and suggest that any term requiring the consumer to pay money may constitute the price if it forms part of the trader's revenue stream.

(2) Other statements suggest that not all payments constitute the 'price or remuneration' of goods or services supplied in exchange. In particular, terms on the grey list, including default payments and price escalation charges are not exempt from review.

(3) Some statements say that even price terms can be challenged as unfair, provided the challenge is on grounds which do not relate to the appropriateness of their amount.

2.9 These various statements are not easy to reconcile, which allows for differing interpretations of the decision. This can be seen in subsequent decisions and in the various ways the case has been interpreted by enforcement bodies and business groups.

2.10 Furthermore, academics have suggested that the Supreme Court decision may be overturned by the CJEU. The exemption has been approached differently in other Member States. For example, the German Federal Supreme Court (*Bundesgerichtshof*) has consistently assessed ancillary bank charges for fairness.5 We commented that this may be 'a background factor influencing the approach of the CJEU in a future case'.[6]

2.11 The Supreme Court itself, aware of the significance and controversy of the decision, explicitly invited Parliament to legislate on the issue. Lord Walker, for example, stated: 'Ministers and Parliament may wish to consider the matter further'.[7]

10–71 Problems in practice

2.12 Our preliminary discussions with stakeholders revealed a concern about the complexity of the law.[8] This was said to cause real problems in practice. The law requires significant legal expertise to navigate, and even then the outcome is unpredictable. This disadvantages smaller traders and individual consumers who do not have access to sophisticated legal resources and do not want to take the risk of litigation.

2.13 We thought that larger traders may also suffer from the current uncertainty. The CJEU may take a narrower approach to interpreting the exemption than the Supreme Court. If this were to happen, traders who have built their business model on a wide interpretation of exempt terms may be faced with expensive litigation and not be able to enforce terms in their contracts.

2.14 Consumer groups told us that the bank charges case has rendered the law so unclear that it is difficult to advise consumers. Furthermore, it was suggested that enforcement bodies have to dedicate significant legal resources to interpret the law. Consequently, some Trading Standards Services and consumer advisers have become wary of using the UTCCR, which could undermine consumer protection.

CONCLUSION 10–71

2.38 There is widespread agreement that the scope of the exemption in Regulation 6(2) is uncertain. We think that all parties suffer through this uncertainty. It increases legal costs for all concerned. It also discourages regulators from bringing action against any terms relating to price.

2.39 There are particular problems where traders use hidden price terms, which undermine the competitiveness of the market. It is too easy for traders to gain market share by offering low headline prices, and then adding hidden extras. This causes detriment to consumers and disadvantages honest traders who are upfront about their charges.

2.40 The current state of the law also poses risks for traders using hidden price terms. We can understand why HSBC has formed the view that, following the Supreme Court's decision, 'any monetary price or remuneration payable under the contract' would naturally fall within the exemption. We think, however, that the words of the Supreme Court may be lulling businesses into a false sense of security. As we explored in the Issues Paper, there are several other interpretations of the judgment – and it is quite possible that the judgment may be overturned by the CJEU. In particular, the CJEU may be influenced by the very different interpretation taken by the German Federal Supreme Court.[11]

2.41 A business would be ill-advised to build its business model on the basis that plainly expressed price terms are automatically exempt, no matter how hidden they might be. If a business does use a hidden price term to subsidise a low headline price, the business is put at risk if the term is later found to be unfair. It faces the substantial costs of litigation; the reputational damage to its business; and the cost of repaying consumers for up to six years in England and Wales and five years in Scotland.[12] The amount could be substantial. In the bank charges litigation, the banks had raised £2.56 billion from unauthorised overdraft charges in 2006 alone.

2.42 We have reached the conclusion that the exemption for main subject matter and price set out in Regulation 6(2) of the UTCCR should be reformed. We have been encouraged by the overwhelming support for reform from stakeholders. We have received consistent feedback throughout this project that those involved in this area of law welcome this review, and agree that there is a need for clarification and simplification, for the benefit of traders and consumers alike.

2.43 Recommendation 1: The exemption for main subject matter and price set out in Regulation 6(2) of the Unfair Terms in Consumer Contracts Regulations 1999 should be reformed.

---

[1] See M Schillig, "Directive 93/13 and the 'price term exemption': a comparative analysis in the light of the 'market for lemons rationale'" (2011) International & Comparative Law Quarterly 933, p 937.

[2] Contracts: Some Critical Remarks on the Proposal Submitted by the EC Commission" E Brandner and P Ulmer, "The Community Directive on Unfair Terms in Consumer (1991) 28 Common Market Law Review 647, p 656.

[3] [2009] UKSC 6, [2010] 1 AC 696.

[4] For a full legal review, see Parts 4 to 7 of the Issues Paper.

5 See Issues Paper, paras 7.56 to 7.86.

6 Issues Paper, para 7.61.

7 [2009] UKSC 6, [2010] 1 AC 696 at [52] by Lord Walker.

. . .

[11] See Issues Paper, paras 7.56 to 7.86.

[12] These are the lengths of the limitation period (England and Wales) and prescriptive period (Scotland) respectively.

10–72 **PART 3**

THE EXEMPTION: A NEW APPROACH BASED ON TRANSPARENCY AND PROMINENCE

3.1 In the Issues Paper we proposed that price and main subject matter terms should only be exempt if they were transparent and prominent. By transparent we meant that a term must be in plain, intelligible language; legible and readily available. By prominent we meant that the term was presented in such a way that a reasonably circumspect consumer would be aware of it.

. . .

10–73 **THE ISSUES PAPER PROPOSALS**

Is the exemption needed at all?

3.7 The UTD is a minimum harmonisation measure, which means that the United Kingdom may provide more protection to consumers than is required by the Directive, but may not provide less protection.

3.8 One possibility would be to omit the exemption altogether and make all terms of consumer contracts reviewable for fairness. In 2000, the European Commission observed that many countries had not introduced the exemption, including Denmark, Greece, Finland, Portugal and Spain. The Commission commented that:

> 'The courts of these Member States have not taken it upon themselves to revise prices or to meddle with the main subject matter of contracts in a massive or indiscriminate way, as has been feared by the proponents of certain doctrines and in certain professional circles.[1]'

3.9 Despite this experience, however, we accepted the principle put forward by Professors Brandner and Ulmer that the relationship between the price and the goods or services should be determined by 'the mechanisms of the market' rather than the courts.[2] We thought that businesses needed the reassurance that if a term was subject to competition, it would not need to be justified before a court. We therefore proposed that the exemption should be retained, but rewritten.

10–74 **The problems of small print**

3.10 In view of the uncertainty surrounding the way the exemption is currently drafted, the Issues Paper looked again at the purpose underlying the Directive.

3.11 We argued that one rationale of the exemption is to distinguish between terms which are subject to competition and those which are buried in 'small print'. Where consumers know about the terms proffered by traders, they are able to take them into account in their choices: in other words, the traders' terms are subject to competition. If the information is available, the law should not seek to protect consumers from the consequences of their own decisions.

3.12 By contrast, consumers rarely read 'small print'. 'Small print' is a concept instantly understood by consumers in their daily lives, though it is difficult to pin down in legal terms. It is not just about font size. It is also marked by poor layout, many and densely phrased paragraphs, legal jargon, and inadequate sign- posting around the text. Often simply labelling a hyperlink as 'terms and conditions' is sufficient to ensure that most consumers do not read the document.

Transparency and prominence 10–75

3.13 Our 2005 draft Bill included a clause to state that the price exemption did not include payments which would be 'incidental or ancillary to the main purpose of the contract'. In *Abbey National*,[3] the Supreme Court rejected this approach, on the ground that in many contracts it was impossible to distinguish between main and ancillary charges. Some business groups also considered these words to be too uncertain.

3.14 In the Issues Paper we responded to these concerns by shifting the focus from whether a term is incidental or ancillary to whether a term is *transparent and prominent*. We argued that if a term is transparent and prominent, it will be subject to competitive pressures, and should not be assessed for fairness.

3.15 By 'transparent' we meant that the term should be in plain, intelligible language; legible and readily available to the consumer. By 'prominent' we meant that the term should be presented in such a way that a 'reasonably well informed, reasonably observant and circumspect' consumer would be aware of it.

3.16 We explained that a test which focused on whether a term is transparent and prominent would often produce much the same effect as a test which focused on whether it is ancillary or incidental. Both approaches seek to distinguish between terms which consumers take into account in their decision to buy the product and those which become lost in small print. The emphasis on prominence, however, offers a practical way of distinguishing between a headline price and what are commonly thought of as incidental and ancillary terms. It also emphasises that whether a term is exempt is within the control of the trader. A trader may ensure that a price term is exempt from review by making it prominent.

3.17 We thought that all terms in a consumer contract should be transparent. In a lengthy contract, not all terms can be prominent, but terms which an observant and circumspect consumer is unlikely to read should not contain unfair surprises. They should therefore be reviewable for fairness. By contrast, where a trader ensures that a price or main subject matter term is sufficiently transparent and prominent, we thought that the term should be exempt from review. The trader should not have to justify the fairness of the term to a regulator or court.

PRICE TERMS: TRANSPARENCY AND PROMINENCE 10–76

. . .

Discussion: transparent and prominent price terms

3.46 The responses we received show a divergence of views on this issue. Some businesses argue that all price terms should be exempt from review. Meanwhile consumer groups and regulators were concerned that consumers may ignore charges which may arise on some future contingent event, even if those charges are reasonably prominent in the documentation.

3.47 Nevertheless, most consultees accepted that confining the price exemption to terms which were transparent and prominent represented a reasonable and practical solution to the difficulties encountered in the bank charges litigation and other cases.

The concerns of business groups 10–77

3.48 We accept the argument put forward by business groups that for some services it may not be possible for the trader to make all charges prominent. There is often too much information for consumers to take in, which is why we need unfair terms legislation. Businesses may well include charges which are not prominent, and which are therefore assessable for fairness. Simply because a term is not prominent does not make it unfair; nor does it even raise a presumption that it may be unfair.

3.49 ... We think, however, that if a business wishes an unusual or onerous charge to be exempt from review, it should make it prominent.

3.50 We also acknowledge the concern that businesses should have clarity about what they need to do to bring charges to the attention of consumers. It is also important that the practicalities of making price charges prominent should fit in with other regulations, particularly for financial services. As we explore in Part 4, we recommend that guidance on transparency and prominence should be available to assist businesses. Businesses should have the reassurance of knowing that if they have complied with a regulator's guidance, the regulator will not take action against them.

10–78 ***Behavioural biases***

3.51 Many regulators and consumer groups thought that the emphasis on what an average consumer knows does not take sufficient account of behavioural biases.

3.52 In the Issues Paper we explained that unfair terms legislation assumes that consumers are rational but too busy to read the many complex standard terms presented to them. The problem is therefore one of information asymmetry. Classic economic theory assumes that when consumers are presented with the right information in a way they can understand, they make good decisions.

3.53 Recent economic literature, however, suggests that consumers are only rational up to a point.[7] Consumers approach products with several behavioural biases: they are more concerned with present costs than future costs; they do not pay attention to things that are unlikely to happen; and they are often over-confident. For example, people think that they will go to the gym more often than they do, and that they will become overdrawn less often than actually occurs.[8] Several regulators thought that our test should draw more directly on this literature to allow all terms which are not subject to competition in fact to be assessed, even if a hypothetical 'average consumer' would be aware of them.

3.54 It has been pointed out that many of these behavioural biases are irrational but predictable.[9] It is therefore possible to foresee how they will be exploited by traders. Many of the most common forms of exploitation are reflected in Schedule 2 paragraph 1 of the Unfair Terms in Consumer Contracts Regulations 1999 (UTCCR), which is an 'indicative and non-exhaustive' list of terms which may be unfair (referred to as "the grey list"). ...

3.55 The Directive therefore represents a compromise between classical and behavioural economic approaches. The exemption in article 4(2) seeks to exempt terms which consumers know about, while some paragraphs of the grey list protect consumers against common terms which are known to exploit their behavioural biases.

3.56 Our recommendations seek to preserve this compromise. In general, we think that the courts should not assess the price or main subject matter where the terms were made clear to consumers before they entered into the contract. On the other hand, the legislation is right to recognise well-known ways in which consumers' biases can be exploited.

3.57 In Part 5 we argue that any term on the grey list does not fall within the exemption. We recommend that this should be made explicit in the legislation. We also propose some limited expansion of the grey list to cover terms known to cause particular problems, such as early termination clauses and terms granting traders unilateral discretion.

3.58 We think that the test of prominence and transparency, when coupled with the extensions to the grey list,[10] will enable the courts to assess the fairness of terms which are not subject to market pressure. It will, however, provide traders with some certainty that if the term is not a grey list term, and if it is made transparent and prominent, they will not be required to justify it to a court or a regulator.

3.59 Recommendation 2: The price exemption should be reformulated, to apply only to terms which are transparent and prominent. 10–79

MAIN SUBJECT MATTER TERMS: TRANSPARENCY AND PROMINENCE

3.60 The 2005 draft Bill provided that a term should only be exempt if it was transparent and 'substantially the same as the definition the consumer reasonably expected'. In the Issues Paper, we explained that we proposed to replace the reasonable expectation test with one based on transparency and prominence.

3.61 We did not think that this was a substantive difference. A reasonable consumer's expectations are formed by the deal that is presented – that is by prominent terms.[11] Business groups, however, were concerned that the 2005 test was too vague. We thought that the point would be clearer if one focuses on how the deal was presented rather than on what a reasonable consumer may have expected. Thus, we proposed that terms relating to the main subject matter of the contract should be exempt if they are transparent and prominent, rather than transparent and 'reasonably expected'.

. . .

3.79 Recommendation 3: The main subject matter exemption should be reformulated to apply only to terms which are transparent and prominent. 10–80

PRICE TERMS: EXCLUDED TERM OR EXCLUDED ASSESSMENT?

The Issues Paper proposal

3.80 In the Issues Paper our proposal focused on the nature of the term. We thought that a price term should be excluded from the fairness review if it was transparent and prominent.

3.81 The words of the Directive are slightly different. They do not refer to the nature of the term, but to the nature of the assessment. Article 4(2) states that an 'assessment of the unfair nature of the terms' shall not relate to 'the adequacy of the price and remuneration, on the one hand, as against the services or goods supplied in exchange, on the other, in so far as these terms are in plain intelligible language'.

3.82 In *Abbey National*, the Supreme Court held that price terms may be assessed for fairness, provided that the assessment does not relate to the appropriateness of the price in relation to the goods or services supplied in exchange.

3.83 A similar approach has been taken in European case law. In *Caja de Ahorros*,[16] the Advocate General explained that 'it is only the assessment of the terms that is limited', not the term itself. She went on to explain that 'even contractual terms relating to the main subject-matter or the price/quality ratio may sometimes certainly be unfair'.[17]

3.84 Furthermore, the European Commission report on the implementation of the UTD appears to suggest that the excluded assessment approach is the correct approach:

> Terms concerning the price do indeed fall within the remit of the Directive, since the exclusion concerns the adequacy of the price and remuneration as against the services or goods supplied in exchange and nothing else. The terms laying down the manner of calculation and the procedures for altering the price remain entirely subject to the Directive.[18]

3.85 If one takes an excluded assessment approach, it is open to a court to consider aspects of a price term which do not relate to the adequacy of the price. The court would be entitled to consider the fairness of other aspects, such as timing of payment, method of payment or the procedures for altering the price. In *Foxtons v O'Reardon*,[19] for example, the court applied the excluded assessment approach to state that a commission payable to Foxtons under a sole agency agreement could be challenged on the basis of its timing, but not the amount. In this case the commission payable to the real estate agent became payable on exchange of contracts for sale rather than on completion of the transaction.[20]

3.86 In the Issues Paper we favoured the excluded term approach. We thought that it was simpler. We pointed out that it could be difficult to distinguish between the amount of the price and other aspects of a price term, and artificial to look at some aspects of price without considering the amount.

3.87 We noted, however, that there was an argument that the excluded term approach was not compatible with European law. As we have seen, the UTD is a minimum harmonisation measure. Member States may give more protection to consumers, but they may not give less. Applied literally, the Directive appears to say that the court must be entitled to assess any aspect of the term apart from 'the adequacy of the price or remuneration, as against the services or goods supplied in exchange'. If this is the right way to read the Directive, then it is not open to Member States to widen the exemption to all aspects of a price term, even if the term is transparent or prominent.

3.88 We therefore asked consultees whether, in order to implement the Unfair Terms Directive fully, it was necessary to specify that even transparent, prominent price terms may be assessed for matters other than 'the adequacy of the price as against the goods or services supplied in exchange'.[21]

Consultation responses

3.89 The responses to this difficult question were evenly split. Generally, consumer organisations and public bodies favoured the excluded assessment approach, while businesses favoured the excluded term approach. Members of the judiciary, legal profession and academics were divided.

. . .

10–81 **Discussion**

The need to ensure minimum harmonisation

3.99 Our terms of reference specifically require us to ensure that the UK meets its minimum harmonisation obligations. The UK may narrow the price exemption, but is not entitled to expand it.

3.100 After considering the responses carefully, we have been persuaded that in order to implement the Directive fully, it is necessary to take the excluded assessment approach to price. Thus the new legislation should use a simplified version of the words of article 4(2) by stating that if a price term is transparent and prominent, the court may not assess the amount of the price as against the services or goods supplied in exchange.

3.101 In practice, we do not think that this will make much difference to the decisions which courts reach. If a price term is transparent and prominent, a court would be unlikely to find that any aspect of the term is unfair.

3.102 Furthermore, many transparent and prominent price terms will form the main subject matter of the contract. As we discuss below, the excluded assessment approach does not apply to the exclusion for main subject matter. We recommend that all transparent and prominent terms which form the main subject matter should be excluded from review; and price terms may also be the main subject matter. For example, in a monthly phone contract, the obligation to pay monthly may be excluded from review – not because the assessment relates to the amount of the price, but because the obligation forms the main subject matter of the contract.[22]

3.103 We understand the concerns of some business groups that the excluded assessment approach is less clear cut than the excluded term approach. We would point out, however, that in the Abbey National litigation the banks accepted that this was the correct interpretation of the Directive. The alternative excluded term approach carries a risk that UK legislation may be found to be incompatible with European law, which introduces its own uncertainty.

"Adequacy" or "amount"?

3.104 It seems odd that the Directive should refer to the 'adequacy' of the price. In most consumer contracts, the consumer pays the price – and in these circumstances, no consumer would argue that the price is too low (or 'inadequate'). A consumer's objection will usually be that the price is too high. As the late Lord Rodger of Earlsferry noted in Director General of Fair Trading v First National Bank, the language used is 'somewhat strange'.[23] The Supreme Court referred to 'the appropriateness' of the price.[24]

3.105 We have considered different language versions of the Directive to gain a better understanding of what is meant by 'adequacy'.

3.106 Analysis revealed that most versions follow the English version and use an equivalent of the word adequacy. However, there are some exceptions. For example, both the Polish and Swedish versions use the word 'relationship' ('relacja' and 'förhållandet' respectively). The Danish version phrases it as 'correlation' between price and goods or between services and payment for them ('overensstemmelsen mellem pris og varer eller mellem tjenesteydelser og betalingen herfor').

3.107 The use of these different formulations shows that there is no particular importance to the word 'adequacy'. We think that it is simpler to refer instead to 'the amount' of the price.

3.108 We discuss the definition of 'price' in Part 4 and conclude that price means a monetary obligation. It must therefore be quantifiable. We do not think the reference to 'remuneration' adds anything in this context and we recommend that it is removed.[25]

3.109 Recommendation 4. Provided that a price term is transparent and prominent, the court may not assess the amount of the price as against the services or goods supplied in exchange. 10–82

THE MAIN SUBJECT MATTER: AN EXCLUDED TERM CONSTRUCTION

3.110 As currently drafted, Regulation 6(2) of the UTCCR states that the assessment of fairness of a term shall not relate to 'the definition' of the main subject matter of the contract. This follows the words of article 4(2) of the UTD, which states that 'assessment of the unfair nature of the terms' shall not relate to 'the definition of the main subject matter of the contract'.

3.111 There are two ways of interpreting this provision. The first is to apply an excluded term construction. In other words, any transparent and prominent term which specifies the main subject matter of the contract is wholly excluded from review. The court may not assess the fairness of any aspect of such a term.

3.112 The other approach would be to treat main subject matter terms in the same way as price terms and to apply an excluded assessment construction. On this basis, the court could look at any aspect of the main subject matter except the way that it had been defined. For example, in a contract for gym membership, the court could consider the fairness of any aspect of the main subject matter, except the way that 'gym' or 'membership' had been defined.

3.113 We have concluded that, unlike the exemption for price, the exemption for main subject matter applies to the whole term – not just to the way the term has been defined. We say this for two reasons. First, on the policy level, it makes little sense to separate the fairness of the definition from the fairness of other aspects of the main subject matter. In the Issues Paper we thought that this distinction was particularly confusing. It encouraged the courts to assess main subject matter terms on the ground that the unfair aspect did not relate to 'the definition of the term' but to some other unfair feature.[26] An excluded assessment approach appears to undermine the purpose of the exemption, as consumers will know more about the overall nature of the subject matter than about the details of how terms have been defined.

3.114 Secondly, we do not think that the inclusion of the word 'definition' in article 4(2) should be accorded any particular weight. To explore this issue further, we analysed the words of the Directive in 18 different languages. This analysis strongly suggests that the reference to 'definition' is not a key aspect of the Directive. The German version of the Directive omits the word 'definition' altogether. Other language versions contain a word that comes closer to being synonymous with 'description' or 'determination' rather than 'definition'. Examples are 'beskrivningen' and 'bepaling' in Swedish and Dutch respectively.

3.115 The original proposal for the Consumer Rights Directive, which covered unfair terms, also omitted a reference to 'definition' when dealing with the exemption for the main subject matter of the contract. It appears that the word 'definition' was simply considered unimportant, rather than there being a substantive policy reason for this change. This provides further support for the argument that the word 'definition' is not a key aspect of the exemption. The exemption for main subject matter relates to all aspects of main subject matter terms, not just the way that those terms have been defined.

3.116 We have concluded that the UTD deals with main subject matter and price terms in different ways. Whereas the exclusion relating to price only applies to the adequacy or amount of the price, the exclusion for main subject matter applies to all aspects of the main subject matter.

3.117 We think that the reference to 'definition' within Regulation 6(2)(a) is confusing. If taken literally, it seems to suggest that a court can assess main subject matter terms for aspects of fairness that do not relate to their definitional qualities. We think this method of interpreting the Directive is mistaken. The word definition in this context merely refers to a term which describes or determines the main subject matter. We recommend following the German language version of the Directive, by omitting the word 'definition' altogether.

3.118 We appreciate, however, that an exemption for any terms which relate to the main subject matter of the contract could be interpreted very widely. Despite the fact that this phrase is used in the UTD, we think that it would be better to express it as terms which 'specify' or 'embody' the main subject matter of the contract.

10–83 **3.119 Recommendation 5. The exemption for main subject matter should apply to any term which specifies the main subject matter, and not simply to the way that the main subject matter has been defined.**

. . .

---

[1] April 1993 on Unfair Terms in Consumer Contracts, COM(2000) 248 final, p 15. Report from the Commission on the implementation of Council Directive 93/13/EEC of 5

[2] E Brandner and P Ulmer, "The Community Directive on Unfair Terms in Consumer Contracts: Some Critical Remarks on the Proposal Submitted by the EC Commission" (1991) 28 *Common Market Law Review* 647, p 656. See also para 2.3 above.

[3] [2009] UKSC 6, [2010] 1 AC 696.

. . .

[7] The literature is summarised in a report for the OFT: S Huck, J Zhou and C Duke, *Consumer Behavioural Biases in Competition* (OFT1324) (May 2011). See also the discussion in Part 3 of the Issues Paper.

[8] See Issues Paper, paras 3.27 to 3.28.

[9] D Ariely, *Predictably Irrational: The Hidden Forces That Shape Our Decisions* (2008). For further literature on this issue see D Kahneman, *Thinking Fast and Slow* (2011); and R Thaler and C Sunstein, *Nudge: Improving Decisions about Health, Wealth, and Happiness* (2008).
[10] See Part 5.
[11] In *Zockoll Group Ltd v Mercury Communications Ltd* (No 2) [1999] EMLR 385, p 395, Lord Bingham MR pointed out that what was reasonably expected seems to refer to the other party's reasonable expectations derived from all the circumstances, including the way the contract was presented to them.
. . .
[16] Case C-484/08 *Caja de Ahorros y Monte de Piedad de Madrid v Asociación de Usuarios de Servicios Bancarios (Ausbanc)* [2010] ECR I-04785.
[17] Opinion of Advocate General Trstenjak Case C-484/08 [2010] ECR I-04785 at [65].
[18] Report from the Commission on the implementation of Council Directive 93/13/EEC of 5 April 1993 on Unfair Terms in Consumer Contracts, COM(2000) 248 final, p 15.
[19] [2011] EWHC 2946 (QB).
[20] The court did not consider this to be unfair and in any event it decided that the term was exempt as a result of the operation of the first limb of the exemption (Regulation 6(2)(a)).
. . .
[22] See also *Foxtons v O'Reardon* [2011] EWHC 2946 (QB) discussed at para 3.85 for another example of a price term which was deemed to form the main subject matter of a contract and was thus exempted from assessment of fairness.
[23] [2001] UKHL 52, [2002] 1 AC 481 at [64].
[24] Above.
[25] Paras 4.49 to 4.66.
[26] See in particular the discussion of *OFT v Ashbourne Management Services* [2011] EWHC 1237 (Ch), at paras 5.74 to 5.83 of the Issues Paper.

PART 4 10–84

DEFINING 'TRANSPARENT', 'PROMINENT' AND 'PRICE'

4.1 In this Part we look in more detail at the definition of 'transparent', 'prominent' and 'price'. Finally, we consider the role of guidance.

THE DEFINITION OF "TRANSPARENT" 10–85

The Issues Paper proposal

4.2 The Unfair Terms Directive (UTD) requires that where written terms are offered to the consumer, 'these terms must always be drafted in plain, intelligible language'.[1] Recital 20 explains this and goes slightly further by stating that 'the consumer should actually be given an opportunity to examine all the terms'.

4.3 In 2005 we thought that Recital 20 would only be satisfied if the term was legible and readily available to the consumer.[2] An early example of a case where terms were not available is *Thompson v LM&S Railway*.[3] There the ticket referred the customer to the railway's standard terms and conditions in a separate document which the customer had to buy for 6d at another railway station. We thought that where terms were in writing, they should be available free of charge at the point of sale. Therefore, clause 14(3) of the 2005 draft Bill spelt out that terms should also be legible, presented clearly and readily available to the consumer.

4.4 In the Issues Paper we argued that all written terms of a consumer contract should be transparent. We said that this must mean more than that the language would be intelligible if the words were reproduced in another document. The term must also be legible and readily available.

4.5 Given that this transparency requirement applies to all terms, even unimportant terms, we kept it simple. We asked whether consultees agreed that transparent should be defined as:

(1) in plain, intelligible language;
(2) legible; and
(3) readily available to the consumer.[4]

---

[1] Art 5.
[2] Unfair Terms in Contracts (2005) Law Com No 292; Scot Law Com No 199, Appendix A, Explanatory notes, para 13.

. . .

10–86 **Discussion**

4.16 We have considered the definition of 'transparent' in detail following the consultation responses.

4.17 We do not think that our definition 'gold plates' the Directive. The articles of the Directive must be interpreted in line with the recitals, and Recital 20 is clear that 'the consumer should actually be given an opportunity to examine all the terms'. We think that this principle is already part of the Directive and should appear on the face of the legislation.

10–87 ***Legibility***

4.18 We accept that the requirement of legibility can only apply if the term is in writing. We think this should be specified in the legislation.

4.19 We note the suggestion from the Bar Council and the Law Society that the requirement should be changed to 'easily legible'. The FLA pointed out, however, that legibility is subjective: it expressed concern that too high a test could be exploited by claims management companies. We wish to keep this requirement simple, and think that it would be sufficient to state that if a term is in writing it must be legible. By this we mean legible to most consumers of the product.

10–88 ***Readily available***

4.20 We have been asked to explain the concept of 'readily available'. We think that it is implicit within the Directive that terms should be available to consumers before they become bound by the contract. Furthermore, the terms should be provided free of charge, without requiring the consumer to travel or to incur other costs: hence the reference to 'readily available' rather than just 'available'.

4.21 It is, however, a relatively low test. The intention is that consumers should have the opportunity to examine the terms – not necessarily that most consumers will examine them. The issue of how far an average consumer would actually be aware of the term goes to 'prominence' rather than 'availability', which we consider below.

10–89 ***The fit with FSA rules***

4.22 The BBA asked how the requirement for terms to be 'readily available' ties in with Financial Services Authority requirements. It drew our attention to the requirement in BCOBS 4.1.1 that a bank must make available appropriate information to retail customers:

(1) in good time;

(2) in an appropriate medium;
(3) in easily understandable language and in a clear and comprehensible form.[6]

4.23 This is a very similar concept to 'transparent'. If the information met this test, we think that it would also meet our test of transparency. The guidance in BCOBS 4.1.2 is, however, more detailed. It specifies, for example, that the terms and conditions must be on paper or in another durable medium. Our test is less prescriptive: it would be possible for a purely oral price term to meet our test if the consumer was told about it before becoming bound. Given that unfair terms legislation applies to all consumer contracts across the board, we would not wish to be as prescriptive as the FSA rules.

Telephone contracts 10–90

4.24 HSBC asked whether terms would be considered 'readily available' if a consumer purchased a product over the phone, and was then sent the full Terms and Conditions in an email after the phone conversation has finished. We think this must depend on what was said during the phone call, and when the consumer became bound by the contract.[7] We have identified four scenarios:

(1) *The consumer is told about the term during the phone conversation.* In this case, the term is available to the consumer as they have been told about it. If the term is in plain intelligible language and sufficiently prominent, it would be exempt from review.
(2) *The consumer is not told about the term during the phone call, but may cancel the order after receiving the email.* In this case, we think that the terms are available to the consumer before they are bound by the contract. The term meets the criterion of availability. Whether the term is prominent is a different question.
(3) *The consumer is told that the sale is 'subject to our standard terms and conditions' but becomes bound by the terms without having an opportunity to examine them.* In this case, the terms might be incorporated within the contract by strict application of contract law, but they must be fair. It would be incompatible with the Directive to state that such terms were exempt from review, given the explicit statement in Recital 20 that the consumer must be given an opportunity to examine all the terms.
(4) *No mention is made of the terms during the phone call.* The consumer is bound by the contract before receiving the email and has no opportunity to cancel or withdraw thereafter. In this case, it is highly doubtful that the terms and conditions are part of the contract at all. A court may well find that the terms have no effect as they have not been incorporated into the contract.

Conclusion 10–91

4.25 We have reached the conclusion that price terms should only be exempt from review if they are transparent. By this we mean that they must be in plain, intelligible language, legible (if in writing) and readily available.

4.26 Recommendation 6. To be 'transparent' a term must be

(1) in plain, intelligible language;
(2) readily available to the consumer;
(3) and, if in writing, it must be legible.

10–92 **THE DEFINITION OF "PROMINENT"**

The Issues Paper proposal

4.27 In the Issues Paper we argued that a term should only be exempt from review if it is prominent. By this we meant that it is presented during the sales process in such a way that a reasonable consumer would be aware of the term even if they did not read the full contractual document.

4.28 European law relies on the concept of 'the average consumer'. This hypothetical person is 'reasonably well informed, reasonably observant and circumspect',[8] but their 'level of attention is likely to vary according to the category of goods and services in question'.[9] In the Issues Paper, we asked whether it would it be helpful to adopt this test. We suggested that a term should be considered prominent if it was presented in a way that the average consumer would be aware of the term.[10]

4.29 We said that in an individual challenge, the court should consider evidence of how the term was actually presented, including the material the consumer was sent, and what the salesperson said. In a general challenge, the court would need to look at the firm's general business practices. This might include evidence about the advertising material used, the structure of the firm's website, any key fact documents or information leaflets provided and the instructions given to sales staff. Often it will involve more than just looking at the structure of the written contract document, though this may also be important.

4.30 In the Issues Paper we commented that the more unusual or onerous the term, the more prominent it needs to be. This is in line with the policy behind the general common law rule that a party should take steps to bring particularly unusual or onerous terms to the other party's attention. The leading case is *Interfoto*,[11] which approved an earlier statement from Lord Denning that some clauses 'would need to be printed in red ink on the face of the document with a red hand pointing to it before the notice could be held to be sufficient' to bind the other party.[12] The question before the court in that case was whether a term was sufficiently brought to the defendants' attention to make it part of the contract. The wider principle at stake, however, is the same – whether the term is fairly brought to the other party's attention.

. . .

10–93 **Discussion**

4.41 There was a good level of support for our test of prominence. It is right that the issue of prominence should be assessed from the point of view of a consumer, but we think that the standard should be objective and reasonably high. The concept of a 'reasonably well informed, observant and circumspect' consumer is well-established in European law, and we think that it can be useful in this context.

4.42 The legislation needs to use a general test that can be applied across all sectors. We understand businesses' desire for more detail, but think that this is best addressed through guidance.

4.43 The OFT feared that the 'average consumer' would spread across different tests in unfair terms litigation, so as to prevent the court from looking at all the circumstances of the case. We stress that under our recommendations the fairness test will continue to operate in the same way and 'all the circumstances attending to the conclusion of the contract' will still have to be taken into account by the courts. If a consumer's vulnerability is a relevant circumstance, then the court must take it into account.

4.44 The average consumer standard we recommend is to be applied to the prominence test for the purposes of establishing whether or not a term can be exempt. We do not believe that this particular test should be subjective, or else it would be too difficult to apply in practice.

4.45 After considering the OFT's concerns, we think it would be useful to state in the legislation that the more unusual or onerous the term, the more prominent it needs to be. This clarifies that there is an element of relativity to the definition of 'prominent'. Some terms may need to be more prominent than others. As we have seen, this is not a novel concept; it reflects Lord Denning's 'red hand rule' as endorsed in *Interfoto*.[14]

4.46 Recommendation 7. To be 'prominent' a term must be presented in such a way that the average consumer would be aware of the term. The more unusual or onerous the term, the more prominent it needs to be. 10–94

THE RELATIONSHIP BETWEEN TRANSPARENCY AND PROMINENCE

4.47 There is considerable overlap between the concepts of transparency and prominence. Although transparent terms will not always be prominent, prominent terms will usually be available and legible. Even prominent terms, however, may not necessarily be in plain and intelligible language, and we need to preserve this important element of the UTD. We think that a term should only be exempt when both tests are satisfied.

4.48 The difference between the two concepts is that while all terms should be transparent, not all terms need to be prominent. As we explore in Part 6,[15] we think that all terms in a consumer contract should be transparent. Regulators should have power to ensure that terms are rewritten in plain intelligible language or produced in a more legible and available form if they are not. Unlike the transparency requirement, however, the issue of prominence is only relevant to the exemption.

THE DEFINITION OF "PRICE" 10–95

The Issues Paper proposal

4.49 In the Issues Paper we explained that in English and Scots law, price is defined as 'money consideration'.[16] This is also the approach taken in the Draft Common Frame of Reference, which defines price as the 'monetary obligation' in exchange for what is being supplied or provided.[17] The price may include a variety of payment methods (such as cash or cheque) and may be paid through a third party, as where a consumer tenders a credit card and the finance company pays on the consumer's behalf. A price term, however, must be expressed in terms of money.

4.50 Article 4(2) refers to 'price and remuneration'. 'Remuneration' has no particular legal meaning, and we doubted that it extended more widely than price.

4.51 We argued that the article 4(2) exemption should not apply to terms which were not expressed in money. An example of a non-money term would be the term in the Facebook t&cs which grants Facebook a worldwide licence to use any photographs which the consumer posts.[18] Although in common speech this might be considered 'the price' which the consumer pays for joining Facebook, we do not think that this corresponds to the legal meaning of either price or remuneration. Terms which impose non-money obligations on consumers can be particularly problematic and we did not think that they should fall within the price exemption.

4.52 In some cases, where the consumer is selling goods to a trader, the 'price' may be paid by the trader. We thought that article 4(2) was intended to apply to money paid by the trader in these circumstances.

4.53 We concluded that where the consumer buys goods or services, a price term means an obligation on the consumer to pay money; and where the consumer sells or supplies goods or services, it means an obligation on the trader to pay money. We asked whether consultees agreed.[19]

. . .

10–96 **Discussion**

4.61 As we discussed earlier,[21] our proposals do not distinguish between main price and ancillary price. In *Abbey National*,[22] the Supreme Court rejected this approach, on the ground that it was often impossible to make such a distinction. Price is therefore intended to be a broad concept which includes ancillary and contingent charges. We agree with the OFT that some terms, such as early termination charges, may be particularly problematic, which is why they are dealt with by our recommendation to extend the grey list, as discussed in Part 5.

4.62 As we discussed in Part 3, we recommend that the price exemption would apply not to the whole term but to an assessment of the amount of the price as against the services or goods supplied in exchange. Given this approach, relatively little turns on the definition of 'price' as such. We do not think that it is necessary to include our original definition within the legislation. We accept that the Issues Paper formulation was imprecise when it referred to a consumer 'buying' goods or services, and we do not propose to proceed with it.

4.63 The only significant aspect of the definition of price is that it refers to 'money consideration'. This definition is already included in section 2(1) of the Sale of Goods Act 1979, and we think that the same definition should apply to price in this context.

4.64 As we explained in the Issues Paper, we do not think that the reference to 'remuneration' adds anything and we think it could cause confusion. It is unlikely that remuneration includes non-monetary obligations (such as terms requiring consumers to grant traders intellectual property rights). Even if such terms are included with the definition of remuneration, however, we do not think that it is right in policy terms for them to be exempted. Non-monetary obligations on the consumer which do not form the main subject matter are unlikely to be subject to competition. We therefore recommend that the word 'remuneration' should be omitted from the new legislation.

10–97 **4.65 Recommendation 8. Price should be defined as 'money consideration', in line with the definition currently found within section 2(1) of the Sale of Goods Act 1979.**

10–98 **4.66 Recommendation 9. The reference to 'remuneration' within article 4(2) of the Unfair Terms Directive should be omitted from the new legislation.**

NEED FOR GUIDANCE

The Issues Paper proposal

4.67 In the Issues Paper we asked whether the court should have regard to statutory guidance when deciding whether a term is transparent and prominent.[23]

4.68 We noted that for distance and off-premises contracts, Member States cannot introduce specific requirements for how information is presented, as this would be inconsistent with the Consumer Rights Directive (CRD).[24] This does not, however, prohibit the provision of guidance by bodies such as the OFT and the Financial Conduct Authority. Nor did we suggest that terms which do not comply with the guidance would be void or unfair – simply that they would be reviewable for fairness, like most terms in consumer contracts.

Consultees strongly supported guidance

. . .

10–99 **Discussion**

4.78 There was strong support for guidance. We think that it would give businesses greater clarity over how to make terms transparent and prominent and how this ties with other sector-specific regulation. This will inform businesses about the regulators' approach to enforcement and provide some reassurance on the question of compliance. Guidance should not, however, prevent other parties from bringing proceedings alleging unfairness of a term.

4.79 Unfair terms legislation is one-size-fits-all. It affects a wide range of consumer contracts. That includes contracts in complex sectors, many of which are highly regulated (such as banking, insurance, utilities or telecommunications). We believe that it would be helpful for businesses operating in these sectors to have sector-specific guidance on the meaning of transparent and prominent and how these tests overlap with other legislative requirements.

4.80 Any guidance produced by regulators would not be intended to supplement the law or constrain the courts in any way, but only to assist businesses in understanding the tests in the specific context in which they operate. The guidance we recommend would not be binding on the court or amount to a code of practice leading to specific outcomes. Thus, there would be no potential for gold plating the Directive. The courts should, however, be able to have regard to guidance as opinion evidence if they consider it helpful.

4.81 Recommendation 10: The Department for Business, Innovation and Skills should hold discussions with the Office of Fair Trading and other regulators about the mechanics of preparing guidance. Subject to these discussions, it should ensure that in deciding whether a term is transparent or prominent, the courts may have regard to guidance. **10–100**

---

[3] [1930] 1 KB 41.

[4] Issues Paper, para 8.67(3).

. . .

[6] BCOBS stands for "Banking: Conduct of Business sourcebook" and is part of the Financial-Services Authority rule book.

[7] The Consumer Protection (Distance Selling) Regulations 2000 (SI 2000 No 2334) might also be of relevance here. Regs 11 and 12 give the consumers a period of seven working days to cancel a contract (or three months plus seven working days where the supplier has not complied with the information requirements in Reg 8). This will be extended to 14 days once the Consumer Rights Directive (Directive 2011/83/EU) is transposed into UK law.

[8] Reg 2(2) Consumer Protection from Unfair Trading Regulations 2008 (SI 2008 No 1277), mirroring the European Court of Justice's approach in Case C-210/96 *Gut Springenheide GmbH and Rudolf Tusky v Oberkreisdirektor des Kreises Steinfurt-Amt für Lebensmittelüberwachung* [1998] ECR I-4657.

[9] See Joined Cases T-183/02 and T184/02 *El Corte Inglés v Office for Harmonisation in the Internal Market (Trade Marks and Designs)* [2004] ECR II-00965 at [68].

[10] Issues Paper, para 8.68(1).

[11] *Interfoto Picture Library Ltd v Stiletto Visual Programmes Ltd* [1989] 1 QB 433, [1988] 2 WLR 615. It was applied in Scotland in *Montgomery Litho Ltd v Maxwell* 2000 SC 56.

[12] The quote comes from *J. Spurling v Bradshaw* [1956] 1 WLR 461 at p 466.

. . .

[14] *Interfoto Picture Library Ltd v Stiletto Visual Programmes Ltd* [1989] 1 QB 433. [1988] 2 WLR 615.

[15] Paras 6.47 to 6.64.

[16] Sale of Goods Act 1979, s 2(1).

[17] C Von Bar and E Clive (ed), *Principles, Definitions & Model Rules of European PrivateLaw, Draft Common Frame of Reference (DCFR)*, Vol 1 (Full edition, 2010), p 77.

[18] The June 2012 version of Facebook contract includes the following term: For content that is covered by intellectual property rights, like photos and videos (IP content), you specifically give us the following permission, subject to your privacy and application settings: you grant us a non-exclusive, transferable, sub-licensable, royalty-free, worldwide license to use any IP content that

you post on or in connection with Facebook (IP License). This IP License ends when you delete your IP content or your account unless your content has been shared with others, and they have not deleted it. See *http://www.facebook.com/legal/terms*.

[19] Issues Paper, para 8.67(2).

. . .

[21] Paras 3.13 to 3.59.

[22] [2009] UKSC 6, [2010] 1 AC 696.

[23] Issues Paper, para 8.68(2).

[24] Directive 2011/83/EU of 25 October 2011, OJ 2011 L 304/64. The CRD requires price terms to be clear and comprehensible (arts 5(1) and 6(1)). As the CRD is a maximum harmonisation measure (art 4), the UK is not able to impose any additional formal requirements about the way information is presented for distance or off-premises contracts (art 6). Financial services, however, are excluded from the provisions of the CRD (art 3(3)(d)."

The test of unfairness in consumer contracts

10–101 The unfairness test is set out in s.62(4) of the 2015 Act. This is based on the definition in art.3 of the Unfair Terms in Consumer Contracts Directive 1993, which previously was incorporated in UK law as reg.5 of Unfair Terms in Consumer Contracts Regulations 1999 (and before that as reg.4 in the 1994 Regulations).

10–102 **Consumer Rights Act 2015**
Part 2

"*What are the general rules about fairness of contract terms and notices?*

62 Requirement for contract terms and notices to be fair

(1) An unfair term of a consumer contract is not binding on the consumer.

(2) An unfair consumer notice is not binding on the consumer.

(3) This does not prevent the consumer from relying on the term or notice if the consumer chooses to do so.

(4) A term is unfair if, contrary to the requirement of good faith, it causes a significant imbalance in the parties' rights and obligations under the contract to the detriment of the consumer.

(5) Whether a term is fair is to be determined—

(a) taking into account the nature of the subject matter of the contract, and
(b) by reference to all the circumstances existing when the term was agreed and to all of the other terms of the contract or of any other contract on which it depends.

(6) A notice is unfair if, contrary to the requirement of good faith, it causes a significant imbalance in the parties' rights and obligations to the detriment of the consumer.

(7) Whether a notice is fair is to be determined—

(a) taking into account the nature of the subject matter of the notice, and
(b) by reference to all the circumstances existing when the rights or obligations to which it relates arose and to the terms of any contract on which it depends.

(8) This section does not affect the operation of—

(a) section 31 (exclusion of liability: goods contracts),
(b) section 47 (exclusion of liability: digital content contracts),
(c) section 57 (exclusion of liability: services contracts), or
(d) section 65 (exclusion of negligence liability)."

The Unfair Contract Terms Directive is a European Union instrument of minimum harmonisation. The definition of "unfair terms" in s.62(4) goes beyond the Directive's minimum requirements. Concerns over the economic consequences of allowing individually negotiated terms to be challenged as unfair led the European Commission to limit the protection against unfair terms to those that had "not been individually negotiated". That limitation was copied into the 1994 and 1999 Regulations. On the Law Commissions' recommendation, that limitation was removed in s.62.[63] The definition of what is unfair in art.3(2) of the Directive is replicated in s.62(4).

The Law Commissions also recommended that, following the jurisprudence of the Court of Justice of the European Union,[64] that courts are under a duty to consider the fairness of a term, whether or not the parties raise the issue. They concluded that it was unnecessary to place the burden of proving fairness upon the trader.[65] This recommendation was implemented by s.71 of the 2015 Act.

71 Duty of court to consider fairness of term **10–103**

(1) Subsection (2) applies to proceedings before a court which relate to a term of a consumer contract.

(2) The court must consider whether the term is fair even if none of the parties to the proceedings has raised that issue or indicated that it intends to raise it.

(3) But subsection (2) does not apply unless the court considers that it has before it sufficient legal and factual material to enable it to consider the fairness of the term.

The primary test for fairness in s.62(4) is the requirement of good faith.[66] The Commissions' **10–104** original suggestion was that it might be replaced in new legislation with a "fair and reasonable" test, but ultimately recommended retaining the test in the Directive without additions.[67] However, the 2015 Act includes various provisions to assist in the assessment of fairness, not least of which is the requirement that written terms must be transparent.

---

[63] "Recommendation 28: Any term, with the exception of exempted terms, should be subject to the fairness assessment, whether negotiated or not." The Law Commissions, *Unfair Terms in Consumer Contracts: Advice to the Department for Business, Innovation and Skills* available at: *http://www.scotlawcom.gov.uk/files/3113/6361/9437/Unfair_Terms_in_Consumer_Contracts_Advice.pdf* [Accessed 25 October 2015].

[64] "The nature and importance of the public interest underlying the protection which the Directive confers on consumers justify, moreover, the national court being required to assess of its own motion whether a contractual term is unfair, compensating in this way for the imbalance which exists between the consumer and the seller and supplier." Case C-168/05, *Elisa María Mostaza Claro v Centro Móvil Milenium SL* [2006] ECR I-10421 at [38]. In 23 Case C-243/08 *Pannon GSM Zrt v Erzsébet Sustikné Győrfi* [2009] ECR I-04713 at [35] the court added: "The national court is required to examine, of its own motion, the unfairness of a contractual term where it has available to it the legal and factual elements necessary for that task".

[65] Recommendation 29. See also paras 7.67–7.95, the Law Commissions, *Unfair Terms in Consumer Contracts: Advice to the Department for Business, Innovation and Skills* available at: *http://www.scotlawcom.gov.uk/files/3113/6361/9437/Unfair_Terms_in_Consumer_Contracts_Advice.pdf* [Accessed 25 October 2015].

[66] Above, para.10–102

[67] The Law Commissions,*Unfair Terms in Consumer Contracts: Advice to the Department for Business, Innovation and Skills* available at: *http://www.scotlawcom.gov.uk/files/3113/6361/9437/Unfair_Terms_in_Consumer_Contracts_Advice.pdf* [Accessed 25 October 2015], para.6.33 and Recommendation 22.

10–105

Consumer Rights Act 2015

"68 Requirement for transparency

(1) A trader must ensure that a written term of a consumer contract, or a consumer notice in writing, is transparent.

(2) A consumer notice is transparent for the purposes of subsection (1) if it is expressed in plain and intelligible language and it is legible.

69 Contract terms that may have different meanings

(1) If a term in a consumer contract, or a consumer notice, could have different meanings, the meaning that is most favourable to the consumer is to prevail.

. . ."

10–106 Finally, there is the "grey list". This was introduced as "an indicative and non-exhaustive list of terms that might be regarded as unfair" in an Annex to the Unfair Contract Terms Directive in 1983 and was reproduced verbatim as a schedule to the implementing regulation. After exhaustive analysis, the Law Commissions recommended that the list should be retained, extended and made capable of further extension, but that all the terms on it should be assessable for fairness.[68]

10–107

Consumer Rights Act 2015

"63 Contract terms which may or must be regarded as unfair

(1) Part 1 of Schedule 2 contains an indicative and non-exhaustive list of terms of consumer contracts that may be regarded as unfair for the purposes of this Part.

(2) Part 1 of Schedule 2 is subject to Part 2 of that Schedule; but a term listed in Part 2 of that Schedule may nevertheless be assessed for fairness under section 62 unless section 64 or 73 applies to it.

(3) The Secretary of State may by order made by statutory instrument amend Schedule 2 so as to add, modify or remove an entry in Part 1 or Part 2 of that Schedule.

. . .

(6) A term of a consumer contract must be regarded as unfair if it has the effect that the consumer bears the burden of proof with respect to compliance by a distance supplier or an intermediary with an obligation under any enactment or rule implementing the Distance Marketing Directive.

. . .

[68] The Law Commissions, *Unfair Terms in Consumer Contracts: Advice to the Department for Business, Innovation and Skills* available at: *http://www.scotlawcom.gov.uk/files/3113/6361/9437/Unfair_Terms_in_Consumer_Contracts_Advice.pdf* [Accessed 25 October 2015], Recommendations 8.11–8.20 and paras 5.1–5.28.

SCHEDULE 2

Consumer contract terms which may be regarded as unfair

PART 1

List of terms

1 A term which has the object or effect of excluding or limiting the trader's liability in the event of the death of or personal injury to the consumer resulting from an act or omission of the trader.

2 A term which has the object or effect of inappropriately excluding or limiting the legal rights of the consumer in relation to the trader or another party in the event of total or partial non-performance or inadequate performance by the trader of any of the contractual obligations, including the option of offsetting a debt owed to the trader against any claim which the consumer may have against the trader.

3 A term which has the object or effect of making an agreement binding on the consumer in a case where the provision of services by the trader is subject to a condition whose realisation depends on the trader's will alone.

4 A term which has the object or effect of permitting the trader to retain sums paid by the consumer where the consumer decides not to conclude or perform the contract, without providing for the consumer to receive compensation of an equivalent amount from the trader where the trader is the party cancelling the contract.

5 A term which has the object or effect of requiring that, where the consumer decides not to conclude or perform the contract, the consumer must pay the trader a disproportionately high sum in compensation or for services which have not been supplied.

6 A term which has the object or effect of requiring a consumer who fails to fulfil his obligations under the contract to pay a disproportionately high sum in compensation.

7 A term which has the object or effect of authorising the trader to dissolve the contract on a discretionary basis where the same facility is not granted to the consumer, or permitting the trader to retain the sums paid for services not yet supplied by the trader where it is the trader who dissolves the contract.

8 A term which has the object or effect of enabling the trader to terminate a contract of indeterminate duration without reasonable notice except where there are serious grounds for doing so.

9 A term which has the object or effect of automatically extending a contract of fixed duration where the consumer does not indicate otherwise, when the deadline fixed for the consumer to express a desire not to extend the contract is unreasonably early.

10 A term which has the object or effect of irrevocably binding the consumer to terms with which the consumer has had no real opportunity of becoming acquainted before the conclusion of the contract.

11 A term which has the object or effect of enabling the trader to alter the terms of the contract unilaterally without a valid reason which is specified in the contract.

12 A term which has the object or effect of permitting the trader to determine the characteristics of the subject matter of the contract after the consumer has become bound by it.

13 A term which has the object or effect of enabling the trader to alter unilaterally without a valid reason any characteristics of the goods, digital content or services to be provided.

14 A term which has the object or effect of giving the trader the discretion to decide the price payable under the contract after the consumer has become bound by it, where no price or method of determining the price is agreed when the consumer becomes bound.

15 A term which has the object or effect of permitting a trader to increase the price of goods, digital content or services without giving the consumer the right to cancel the contract if the final price is too high in relation to the price agreed when the contract was concluded.

16 A term which has the object or effect of giving the trader the right to determine whether the goods, digital content or services supplied are in conformity with the contract, or giving the trader the exclusive right to interpret any term of the contract.

17 A term which has the object or effect of limiting the trader's obligation to respect commitments undertaken by the trader's agents or making the trader's commitments subject to compliance with a particular formality.

18 A term which has the object or effect of obliging the consumer to fulfil all of the consumer's obligations where the trader does not perform the trader's obligations.

19 A term which has the object or effect of allowing the trader to transfer the trader's rights and obligations under the contract, where this may reduce the guarantees for the consumer, without the consumer's agreement.

20 A term which has the object or effect of excluding or hindering the consumer's right to take legal action or exercise any other legal remedy, in particular by—

(a) requiring the consumer to take disputes exclusively to arbitration not covered by legal provisions,
(b) unduly restricting the evidence available to the consumer, or
(c) imposing on the consumer a burden of proof which, according to the applicable law, should lie with another party to the contract."

The meaning of "good faith" and its relationship with the "grey list" arose in *First National Bank*.

10–108

Director General of Fair Trading v First National Bank
[2002] A.C. 481

The facts are as stated above at para.10–58.

"LORD BINGHAM OF CORNHILL: ...

17. The test laid down by regulation 4(1), deriving as it does from article 3(1) of the Directive, has understandably attracted much discussion in academic and professional circles and helpful submissions were made to the House on it. It is plain from the recitals to the Directive that one of its objectives was partially to harmonise the law in this important field among all member states of the European Union. The member states have no common concept of fairness or good faith, and the Directive does not purport to state the law of any single member state. It lays down a test to be applied, whatever their pre-existing law, by all member states. If the meaning of the test were doubtful, or vulnerable to the possibility of differing interpretations in differing member states, it might be desirable or necessary to seek a ruling from the European Court of Justice on its interpretation. But the language used in expressing the test, so far as applicable in this case, is in my opinion clear and not reasonably capable of differing interpretations. A term falling within the scope of the Regulations is unfair if it causes a significant imbalance in the parties' rights and obligations under the contract to the detriment of the consumer in a manner or to an extent which is contrary to the requirement of good faith. The requirement of significant imbalance is met if a term is so weighted in favour of the supplier as to tilt the parties' rights and obligations under the contract

significantly in his favour. This may be by the granting to the supplier of a beneficial option or discretion or power, or by the imposing on the consumer of a disadvantageous burden or risk or duty. The illustrative terms set out in Schedule 3 to the Regulations provide very good examples of terms which may be regarded as unfair; whether a given term is or is not to be so regarded depends on whether it causes a significant imbalance in the parties' rights and obligations under the contract. This involves looking at the contract as a whole. But the imbalance must be to the detriment of the consumer; a significant imbalance to the detriment of the supplier, assumed to be the stronger party, is not a mischief which the Regulations seek to address. The requirement of good faith in this context is one of fair and open dealing. Openness requires that the terms should be expressed fully, clearly and legibly, containing no concealed pitfalls or traps. Appropriate prominence should be given to terms which might operate disadvantageously to the customer. Fair dealing requires that a supplier should not, whether deliberately or unconsciously, take advantage of the consumer's necessity, indigence, lack of experience, unfamiliarity with the subject matter of the contract, weak bargaining position or any other factor listed in or analogous to those listed in Schedule 2 to the Regulations. Good faith in this context is not an artificial or technical concept; nor, since Lord Mansfield was its champion, is it a concept wholly unfamiliar to British lawyers. It looks to good standards of commercial morality and practice. Regulation 4(1) lays down a composite test, covering both the making and the substance of the contract, and must be applied bearing clearly in mind the objective which the Regulations are designed to promote.

LORD STEYN: ... **10–109**

36. It is now necessary to refer to the provisions which prescribe how it should be determined whether a term is unfair. Implementing article 3(1) of the Directive regulation 4(1) provides:

'unfair term' means any term which contrary to the requirement of good faith causes a significant imbalance in the parties' rights and obligations under the contract to the detriment of the consumer.

There are three independent requirements. But the element of detriment to the consumer may not add much. But it serves to make clear that the Directive is aimed at significant imbalance against the consumer, rather than the seller or supplier. The twin requirements of good faith and significant imbalance will in practice be determinative. Schedule 2 to the Regulations, which explains the concept of good faith, provides that regard must be had, amongst other things, to the extent to which the seller or supplier has dealt fairly and equitably with the consumer. It is an objective criterion. Good faith imports, as Lord Bingham of Cornhill has observed in his opinion, the notion of open and fair dealing: see also *Interfoto Picture Library Ltd v Stiletto Visual Programmes Ltd* [1989] QB 433. And helpfully the commentary to *Lando & Beale, Principles of European Contract Law, Parts I and II* (combined and revised 2000), p 113 prepared by the Commission of European Contract Law, explains that the purpose of the provision of good faith and fair dealing is 'to enforce community standards of decency, fairness and reasonableness in commercial transactions'; *a fortiori* that is true of consumer transactions. Schedule 3 to the Regulations (which corresponds to the annex to the Directive) is best regarded as a check list of terms which must be regarded as potentially vulnerable. The examples given in Schedule 3 convincingly demonstrate that the argument of the bank that good faith is predominantly concerned with procedural defects in negotiating procedures cannot be sustained. Any purely procedural or even predominantly procedural interpretation of the requirement of good faith must be rejected.

37. That brings me to the element of significant imbalance. It has been pointed out by Hugh Collins that the test 'of a significant imbalance of the obligations obviously directs attention to the substantive unfairness of the contract': 'Good Faith in European Contract Law' (1994) 14 Oxford Journal of Legal Studies 229, 249. It is however, also

right to say that there is a large area of overlap between the concepts of good faith and significant imbalance.

10–110 LORD MILLETT: ...

54. A contractual term in a consumer contract is unfair if 'contrary to the requirement of good faith [it] causes a significant imbalance in the parties' rights and obligations under the contract to the detriment of the consumer'. There can be no one single test of this. It is obviously useful to assess the impact of an impugned term on the parties' rights and obligations by comparing the effect of the contract with the term and the effect it would have without it. But the inquiry cannot stop there. It may also be necessary to consider the effect of the inclusion of the term on the substance or core of the transaction; whether if it were drawn to his attention the consumer would be likely to be surprised by it; whether the term is a standard term, not merely in similar non-negotiable consumer contracts, but in commercial contracts freely negotiated between parties acting on level terms and at arms' length; and whether, in such cases, the party adversely affected by the inclusion of the term or his lawyer might reasonably be expected to object to its inclusion and press for its deletion. The list is not necessarily exhaustive; other approaches may sometimes be more appropriate."

10–111 At first glance, the decision in *First National* is a surprisingly poor one for consumers, given the origin and purpose of the Regulations. Lord Millett conceded that default debtors, on discovering the extra sums owed despite having paid off the amount of the judgment, must suffer a "nasty shock", and do in his view "have a legitimate grievance".[69] Even so, the decision of the court was unanimous. However, it was noted by Lords Millet and Hope of Craighead that the "real source of the problem"[70] thrown up by the case remains untackled: that is, the lack of obligation to make debtors aware of the court's powers to relieve hardship. The inadequacies may lie, therefore, in the Consumer Credit Act 1974. It should also be noted that post-judgment interest has been lawful in Scotland for many years.[71] An alternative view (not followed by the court) is that while the substantive term was not unfair, the manner of its presentation could have rendered it so—in other words, that the term was procedurally unfair.[72] Given the onerous effects of condition 8, might there be a case for Lord Denning's famous "red ink with a red hand pointing" to be invoked?[73]

More generally, the decision has been welcomed as a clear exposition of the law. C MacMillan, in *Evolution or Revolution? Unfair Terms in Consumer Contracts*,[74] identifies three reasons to welcome the decision: first, the judgments attempt to construe the Regulations and case law so as to provide a system of substantive fairness to borrowers independent of the Directive; secondly, the emphasis that the doctrine of good faith is a requirement of European Union law, rather than that of a Member State; and thirdly (and of more relevance to English lawyers), the

---

[69] *Director General of Fair Trading v First National Bank* [2002] A.C. 481, at 506.

[70] *Director General of Fair Trading v First National Bank* [2002] A.C. 481, at 501.

[71] *Bank of Scotland v Davis*, 1982 S.L.T. 20.

[72] For a discussion of the relationship between substantive and procedural unfairness in the context of the Regulations, see the Law Commissions, *Unfair Terms in Contracts* (Law Commission Consultation Paper No.166; Scot. Law Com. Discussion Paper No.119, 7 August 2002), pp.45–48, paras 3.63–3.69, and references therein.

[73] *Thornton v Shoe Lane Parking Ltd* [1971] 2 Q.B. 163, and see Ch.9. At the same time as FNB were appealing to the Lords, Paragon Group of Companies Plc, another lender, undertook to the Director General of Fair Trading not to enforce a similar term unless it had informed consumers and the court of the consumer's right to ask the court to reduce or stop the interest.

[74] C MacMillan, in *Evolution or Revolution? Unfair Terms in Consumer Contracts*, C.L.J. 2002, 61(1), 22–24.

acknowledgment that this concept is not alien to the common law, but is present therein in various forms.

Limits on the exclusion of statutory implied terms in a consumer contract **10–112**

Part 1 of the 2015 Act is a fundamental revision of statutory implied terms in consumer contracts. Whereas in non-consumer contracts the implied terms are those in existing legislation,[75] Pt 1 redefines and extends the implied terms in various ways. The detailed provisions of Pt 1 are beyond the scope of this book, but some explanation of its main features is essential.

Part 1 differentiates three major categories of consumer contract: a contract for the trader to supply goods[76]; a contract for the trader to supply digital content[77]; and a contract for the trader to supply a service.[78] Contracts for the supply of goods[79] include a sales contract[80]; a contract for the hire of goods[81]; a hire-purchase agreement[82]; and a contract for the transfer of goods[83]; and mixed contracts.[84]

Sections 9–18 in Ch.2 of Pt 1 define the consumer's rights in supply of goods contracts; ss.34–41 define the consumer's rights in supply of digital content contracts; and ss.49–53 define the consumer's rights in supply of services contracts. Unlike previous legislation, the rights are not referred to as "implied terms", but as terms that are treated as included in the contract. Rather than stating that such "implied terms" are "void" as in previous legislation, the 2015 Act provides that any term excluding or restricting the trader's liability arising under these provisions is not binding on the consumer.

The terms that cannot be excluded in a contract for the supply of goods are:

"31 Liability that cannot be excluded or restricted **10–113**

(1) A term of a contract to supply goods is not binding on the consumer to the extent that it would exclude or restrict the trader's liability arising under any of these provisions—

(a) section 9 (goods to be of satisfactory quality);
(b) section 10 (goods to be fit for particular purpose);
(c) section 11 (goods to be as described);
(d) section 12 (other pre-contract information included in contract);
(e) section 13 (goods to match a sample);
(f) section 14 (goods to match a model seen or examined);
(g) section 15 (installation as part of conformity of the goods with the contract);
(h) section 16 (goods not conforming to contract if digital content does not conform);

---

[75] Above, paras 10–37—10–39.
[76] Consumer Rights Act 2014 s.1(3)(a). "Goods" means any tangible moveable items, but that includes water, gas and electricity if and only if they are put up for supply in a limited volume or set quantity: s.2(8).
[77] Consumer Rights Act 2015 s.1(3)(b). "Digital content" means data which are produced and supplied in digital form.
[78] Consumer Rights Act 2015 s.1(3)(c). Contracts of employment and apprenticeship (s.48(2)) and gratuitous contracts (s.48(3) are excluded.
[79] Gratuitous contracts for the supply of goods are not included: Consumer Rights Act 2014 s.3(3)(e).
[80] Consumer Rights Act 2014 s.3(2)(a).
[81] Consumer Rights Act 2014 s.3(2)(b). Secondhand goods bought at auction by a person who had the opportunity of attending the sale in person are deemed not to have been bought by a consumer and are therefore mostly not covered by these provisions: ss.2(5) and 2(6).
[82] Consumer Rights Act 2014 s.3(2)(c).
[83] Consumer Rights Act 2014 s.3(2)(d).
[84] Consumer Rights Act 2014 ss.1(5)–(7) and 3(7).

> (i) section 17 (trader to have right to supply the goods etc);
> (j) section 28 (delivery of goods);
> (k) section 29 (passing of risk).
>
> . . ."

This list is far more extensive than that in the Sale of Goods Act, but the impact of the provision is similar to that previously in the 1977 Act: these terms are always binding on the trader.

The terms that cannot be excluded in a contract for the supply of digital content are:

10–114

> **"47 Liability that cannot be excluded or restricted**
>
> (1) A term of a contract to supply digital content is not binding on the consumer to the extent that it would exclude or restrict the trader's liability arising under any of these provisions—
>
> (a) section 34 (digital content to be of satisfactory quality),
> (b) section 35 (digital content to be fit for particular purpose),
> (c) section 36 (digital content to be as described),
> (d) section 37 (other pre-contract information included in contract), or
> (e) section 41 (trader's right to supply digital content).
>
> . . ."

This is an innovation. The fact that digital content ("data which are produced or supplied in digital form": s.1(3)(b)) cannot be included in the definition of "goods"[85] necessitated specific provision for it.

The terms that cannot be excluded in a contract for the supply of services are:

10–115

> **"57 Liability that cannot be excluded or restricted**
>
> (1) A term of a contract to supply services is not binding on the consumer to the extent that it would exclude the trader's liability arising under section 49 (service to be performed with reasonable care and skill).
>
> (2) Subject to section 50(2), a term of a contract to supply services is not binding on the consumer to the extent that it would exclude the trader's liability arising under section 50 (information about trader or service to be binding).
>
> (3) A term of a contract to supply services is not binding on the consumer to the extent that it would restrict the trader's liability arising under any of sections 49 and 50 and, where they apply, sections 51 and 52 (reasonable price and reasonable time), if it would prevent the consumer in an appropriate case from recovering the price paid or the value of any other consideration. (If it would not prevent the consumer from doing so, Part 2 (unfair terms) may apply.)
>
> . . ."

[85] Consumer Rights Act 2014 s.2(8). "Services" are not defined in the Act, but clearly would not cover digital content per se.

These provisions are supplemented as follows:

"31 Liability that cannot be excluded or restricted 10–116

...

(2) That also means that a term of a contract to supply goods is not binding on the consumer to the extent that it would—

(a) exclude or restrict a right or remedy in respect of a liability under a provision listed in subsection (1),
(b) make such a right or remedy or its enforcement subject to a restrictive or onerous condition,
(c) allow a trader to put a person at a disadvantage as a result of pursuing such a right or remedy, or
(d) exclude or restrict rules of evidence or procedure.

(3) The reference in subsection (1) to excluding or restricting a liability also includes preventing an obligation or duty arising or limiting its extent.

(4) An agreement in writing to submit present or future differences to arbitration is not to be regarded as excluding or restricting any liability for the purposes of this section.

..."

Identical provision is made for digital content supply contracts (ss.47(2), 47(3) and 47(4)) and service supply contracts (ss.57(4), 57(5) and 57(6)). They effectively prevent the trader from avoiding liability by inhibiting the consumer's access to remedies or rules of evidence and procedure.

Finally, s.65 re-enacts the ban on exclusion of liability for death or personal injury caused by negligence.

"65 Bar on exclusion or restriction of negligence liability 10–117

(1) A trader cannot by a term of a consumer contract or by a consumer notice exclude or restrict liability for death or personal injury resulting from negligence.

(2) Where a term of a consumer contract, or a consumer notice, purports to exclude or restrict a trader's liability for negligence, a person is not to be taken to have voluntarily accepted any risk merely because the person agreed to or knew about the term or notice.

(3) In this section "personal injury" includes any disease and any impairment of physical or mental condition.

(4) In this section "negligence" means the breach of—

(a) any obligation to take reasonable care or exercise reasonable skill in the performance of a contract where the obligation arises from an express or implied term of the contract,
(b) a common law duty to take reasonable care or exercise reasonable skill,

...

(d) the duty of reasonable care imposed by section 2(1) of the Occupiers' Liability (Scotland) Act 1960.

(5) It is immaterial for the purposes of subsection (4)—

(a) whether a breach of duty or obligation was inadvertent or intentional, or
(b) whether liability for it arises directly or vicariously.
(6) This section is subject to section 66 (which makes provision about the scope of this section).

66 Scope of section 65

(1) Section 65 does not apply to—

(a) any contract so far as it is a contract of insurance, including a contract to pay an annuity on human life, or
(b) any contract so far as it relates to the creation or transfer of an interest in land.

(2) Section 65 does not affect the validity of any discharge or indemnity given by a person in consideration of the receipt by that person of compensation in settlement of any claim the person has.

(3) Section 65 does not—

(a) apply to liability which is excluded or discharged as mentioned in section 4(2)(a) (exception to liability to pay damages to relatives) of the Damages (Scotland) Act 2011, or
(b) affect the operation of section 5 (discharge of liability to pay damages: exception for mesothelioma) of that Act.

(4) Section 65 does not apply to the liability of an occupier of premises to a person who obtains access to the premises for recreational purposes if—

(a) the person suffers loss or damage because of the dangerous state of the premises, and
(b) allowing the person access for those purposes is not within the purposes of the occupier's trade, business, craft or profession."

PART 5

PERFORMANCE AND ITS CONSEQUENCES

CHAPTER 11

THE TERMINATION OF CONTRACTUAL OBLIGATIONS

Having established what the obligations of the parties are, by defining the terms of the contract, it is essential to know when the parties' obligations terminate—when the parties are liberated, or discharged from those obligations. 11–01

Termination by contractual stipulation

The cases on exclusion clauses and similar express terms in the previous chapter show that the parties may expressly stipulate circumstances that will extinguish their obligations. They show also that the parties can stipulate what will happen when things go wrong. The contract may stipulate, for example, that specified payments would have to be made by a party who breaks, or breaches the contract to the other party. Such *liquidate damages* are considered in the next chapter. Only a material breach entitles the party not in breach to terminate the contract; but the contract may itself stipulate that a contract will come to an end, even if a breach is not material. Alternatively, regardless of breach, the contract may come to an end by a resolutive condition. A common example of discharge by contractual stipulation is a term that the contract will subsist for a specified period of time, or until the happening of a specified event (such as the sale of a house by an estate agent). Thus, a contract of employment ends on the expiry of a period of notice given in accordance with the terms of the contract. Similarly, it is common to insert into a contract an "excepted perils" clause, or a force majeure clause, the effect of which would be to excuse non-performance. What if the parties make no stipulation as to discharge—might the contract last indefinitely? Courts are willing to imply a term of reasonable notice into a contract. This would be common, for example, in a contract of employment, but might even occur where without the implication of such a term, changing economic realities, like inflation, would render the contract unworkable. In *Staffordshire Area Health Authority v South Staffordshire Waterworks Co*,[1] for example, a 1909 Private Act of Parliament authorised the defendants to appropriate underground waters in their area for the water mains. Section 23 of the 1909 Act gave certain rights to water supply to a hospital that was then under the control of the county council (now under the control of the plaintiffs). The defendants had taken a water supply from a well situated on the hospital's grounds. By 1929, the well had been abandoned and the hospital took its water supply from the mains. The defendants and the plaintiffs entered into a formal agreement under which the hospital would "at all times hereafter" be supplied with 5,000 gallons per day free of charge and that "at all times hereafter" the hospital could take from the mains any further quantity it needed at 7d. for every 1,000 gallons. There was no express provision for termination, but, due to great increases in water rates, in 1975 the defendants gave the plaintiffs six months' notice of termination of the agreement. The English Court of Appeal was prepared to imply a term that the contract could be terminated on reasonable notice. In Scotland, the position is described by McBryde[2]: 11–02

> **9–14** Where a contract lacks an express term on duration three problems arise: (1) Is it possible to imply a term on duration? (2) If the contract is of indefinite duration, may it be ended by notice given by one party? (3) If the contract may be ended by notice must there be a period of reasonable notice or does notice take effect immediately? This issue 11–03

[1] *Staffordshire Area Health Authority v South Staffordshire Waterworks Co* [1978] 1 W.L.R. 1387.

[2] WW McBryde, *The Law of Contract in Scotland*, 3rd edn (Edinburgh: W. Green, 2007), paras 9–14—9–21.

involves both implications which apply to all contracts and also those arising from the circumstances of a particular contract.

...

9–19 [I]n *Fifeshire Road Trustees v Cowdenbeath Coal Co*[63] in a dispute about a level crossing Lord President Inglis, with the concurrence or agreement of the other judges, referred to a general rule that either party may put an end to a contract, 'not on reasonable cause shewn, but on reasonable notice'.[64] There is also an obiter dictum of Lord Young to the same effect.[65] ...

9–20 There is an attraction in the concept of 'reasonable notice' because it seems fair, at least if a large part of a person's energy or enterprise is devoted to the one contract,[67] although that does not explain the law on ... contracts of limited application such as that for use of the level crossing in *Fifeshire Road Trustees*. The probability is that Scots law has evolved without full consideration of all the authorities and consistent principle may be elusive, but the issue is also one of construction of the express terms of the particular contract and the effect of any relevant implied terms.

---

[63] (1883) 11 R 18.
[64] (1883) 11 R 18 at 21.
[65] *Dowling ve Henderson & Son* (1890) 17 R 921.
...
[67] Which was, more or less, Gloag's way of trying to explain the two lines of authorities; *Contract* p. 731; see also at pp. 301 & 302.

Termination by lapse of time

11–04 Although parties to a contract for a specific transaction, e.g. the sale of a specific article, are discharged by exchange of the article for the price, parties to a contract of indeterminate duration (such as one of employment, or partnership) have a contract at will. Such contracts may be determined by either party, usually, at common law, by giving reasonable notice, although the minimum length of notice to discharge a contract of employment is closely regulated by statute. If a contract is for a definite term, and the parties continue their relationship beyond the expiry of such term, there is "tacit relocation", and courts will infer from the parties' conduct the intention to renew the contract for a similar term.

Termination by performance

11–05 The obvious—and most common—way to end contractual obligations is to perform them. Refusal or failure to perform is a breach of contract and the other party is entitled to appropriate remedies. Performance or tender of performance by one party entitles that party to demand performance by the other party.

But what amounts to performance? The precise extent of a party's obligations to perform depends on the terms of the contract.

What if a party's performance is incomplete? Subject to the principle de minimis non curat lex, performance must be in strict compliance with the terms of the contract. Partial performance is no performance, and confers no right to demand performance by the other party: for example, a builder who partly completes a house, has no claim for the purchase price.[3] The standard of performance may also vary with the obligation in question. If the obligation is to make payment, what amounts to payment is a matter for the contract, but generally payment, or the tender of payment, discharges the debtor. Specific rules apply to payment by money in legal tender, payment by cheque and other forms of credit transfer, and specific rules apply to

---

[3] The builder may of course be able to recover any unjustified enrichment from the other party.

the *appropriation*, or *ascription* of payments made to the contract.[4] Some obligations, such as those of a common carrier of goods, are strict, whereas others need only be performed with reasonable care or reasonable diligence. If there are several stipulations in the contract and they are divisible, in the sense that they can be separately performed, such as an instalment contract, failure to perform one stipulation will not amount to failure to perform the entire contract.

What if performance is slow, or late? Unless a specific time is prescribed in the contract, or the circumstances indicate that it is of the essence (for example, in a contract involving perishable goods), time will not be of the essence and the parties must fulfil their obligations within a reasonable time.

Time may become of the essence if one party unduly delays in performance and the aggrieved party gives notice of a new time for performance.

What if a party performs badly; or not at all; or refuses; or indicates a refusal to perform? The answers to these questions will depend on whether the contract has been *broken*, or *breached* by any of these failures to perform. Only if the contract is broken can the party not in breach take remedial action. That may involve, as a last resort, seeking remedies that can only be granted by a court. In most cases, the parties will seek solutions that do not involve legal action. Litigation is usually a last resort.

Nor is there a right, unless specifically granted in the contract, to give equivalent performance **11–06** or, where there is *delectus personae* (performance by a specific person), to permit substituted performance. If, however, the other party accepts part-performance, there is a duty to pay a *quantum lucratus* for that part-performance. The general rule is that only a person who is a party to a contract derives benefits or undertakes obligations under that contract: only a party to a contract may seek performance, and only a party to a contract may and must perform. This general rule is subject to several exceptions. A contract made by an agent on the principal's behalf with a third party is a contract between the principal and that third party. The agent, although in an agency contract with the principal, has no contractual relationship with the third party (although the agent is bound by the contract of *agency* with the principal). Certain contracts to pay money are embodied in documents called "negotiable instruments", including cheques, bills of exchange and promissory notes are another exception. It is possible to transfer rights to payment under such documents by *negotiation*, i.e. by physical transfer of the document or, where required, by endorsement, without the need for a contractual relationship to be created between the holder of the document, or instrument, and the person who drew up the document, the drawer. The essence of negotiation, and what distinguishes it from assignation, is that the transferee, if they take the instrument in good faith, for value and without notice of any defects in the title of the transferor, takes it free from such defects.[5] Also, by *transmission,* rights and obligations of a party to a contract, upon death of that party, pass to that party's executor, unless there was an element of *delectus personae*. Similarly, insolvency and bankruptcy will affect contract already made with the insolvent or bankrupted person, as well as contracts made after insolvency or bankruptcy.[6]

It is also possible to "assign" or "cede" rights or obligations to a third party, or "assignee". Rights to performance by the other party are generally assignable where, for example, the performance outstanding is payment of money, or transfer of goods. Where, however, there is *delectus personae creditoris* (selection of the person seeking performance), the right to demand performance cannot be assigned. An employer, for example, cannot assign the right to an employee's labour to a third party without that employee's permission. Even if a right to performance is assignable, assignation may be expressly prohibited. Obligations to perform are

---

[4] See generally WW McBryde, *The Law of Contract in Scotland*, 3rd edn (Edinburgh: W. Green, 2007), Ch.24.

[5] Agency and bills of exchange are beyond the scope of this work and should be explored in commercial law texts.

[6] See generally WW McBryde, *The Law of Contract in Scotland*, 3rd edn (Edinburgh: W. Green, 2007), Ch.26.

similarly assignable, unless there is *delectus personae debitoris* (selection of the person performing). Where the performance is to be personal, as with a contract of employment, or for personal services, the duty to perform cannot be assigned. If, however, the contract can be equally well performed by others, there is no *delectus personae*. Unlike the *jus quaesitum tertio*, an assignation, to be valid, must be intimated to the other party to the contract. When duly effected, assignation puts the assignee in the cedent's position as regards rights and obligations under the contract. The assignee takes the cedent's rights under the contract subject to any existing defects, such as defects of title.[7]

A contract may also directly confer a right upon a third party.

Third party rights: the *jus quaesitum tertio*

11–07 A third party may acquire a *jus* (alternatively *ius*), or right or benefit under a contract, although not a party to it, where that contract specifically confers upon them such a *jus quaesitum tertio* (a right accruing to a third party). The third party can enforce the right, although not a party to the contract, but does not thereby become entitled to any other rights under the contract, nor liable to any other obligations. Although the doctrine is firmly established in the law of Scotland and the laws of many European jurisdictions, it remains vague in its scope and application. There is much academic comment (much of it recent) on the topic,[8] but there are few recent detailed judicial expositions of the doctrine and judges apply it narrowly and seem reluctant to expand it.[9] There is even much controversy about the origins and nature of the rule. Professor McBryde states:

> "The precise nature of [the third party's] right is uncertain. The temptation is to treat it as analogous to the rights of a donee or promisee. It is questionable whether it is wise to rely on the law of donations or promises whose specialities may be inapplicable to *jus quaesitum tertio*, as for example the strong presumption against donation, or the method of proof of a

---

[7] See generally WW McBryde, *The Law of Contract in Scotland*, 3rd edn (Edinburgh: W. Green, 2007), Ch.12.

[8] See the Scottish Law Commission's *Discussion Paper on Third Party Rights in Scotland* (fn 13 below); AF Rodger, "Molina, Stair and the *Jus Quaesitum Tertio*" 1969 J.R. 34, 128 (two parts); EM Clive, "*Jus Quaesitum Tertio* and the Carriage of Goods by Sea" in C Miller and Meyers (eds), *Comparative and Historical Essays in Scots Law* (Edinburgh: Bloomsbury, 1992); HL MacQueen, "Third Party Rights in Contract: Jus Quaesitum Tertio" in KGC Reid and R Zimmermann, *A History of Private Law in Scotland, Volume II: Obligations* (Oxford: Oxford University Press, 2000); JAK Huntley and AK Dedouli, "Third Party Rights, Promises and the Classification of Obligations" 2004 J.R. 303; P Sutherland and D Johnston, "Contracts for the Benefit of Third Parties" in R Zimmermann, D Visser and KGC Reid (eds), *Mixed Legal Systems in Comparative Perspective: Property and Obligations in Scotland and South Africa* (Oxford: Oxford University Press, 2004), pp.208–239; P Sutherland, "Third-Party Contracts" in HL MacQueen and R Zimmermann (eds), *European Contract Law; Scots and South African Perspectives* (Edinburgh: Edinburgh University Press, 2006), pp.203–229; S Vogenauer, "Contracts in Favour of a Third Party" in J Basedow, KJ Hopt, R Zimmermann and A Stier (eds), *The Max Planck Encyclopaedia of European Private Law* (Oxford: Oxford University Press, 2012); HL MacQueen, "Third Party Rights in Contract: A Case Study on Codifying and not Codifying" in L Chen and CH (Remco) van Rhee (eds), *Towards a Chinese Civil Code: Comparative and Historical Perspectives* (Leidan: Martinus Nijhoff Publisher, 2012).

[9] See, however, Lord Penrose's suggestions in *Beta computers v Adobe Systems*, 1996 S.L.T. 604 and comments by HL MacQueen, "Third Party Rights in Contract: *Jus Quaesitun Tertio*" in KGC Reid and R Zimmerman, *A History of Private Law in Scotland* (Oxford: Oxford University Press, 2000), pp.220, 248; but note, more recently, *Marquess of Aberdeen and Temair v Turcan Connell* [2008] CSOH 183; 2009 S.C.L.R. 336; 2009 G.W.D. 1-18; *Kenneil v Kenneil*, 2006 S.L.T. 449; *Smith v Stuart* [2010] CSIH 29; 2010 S.C. 490; 2010 S.L.T. 1249; 2010 G.W.D. 14-270.

promise. It may be better to treat *jus quaesitum tertio* as an independent right, which shares some of the characteristics of other contractual rights but also has special features."[10]

There is no doubt that Stair regarded the right as arising out of unilateral promise.[11]

Clarification of the definition, meaning and extent of the *jus quaesitum tertio* is needed. English law, following the Law Commission's extensive review of the law of privity,[12] put the right of the third party into statutory form, the Contracts (Rights of Third Parties) Act 1999. That right is entirely derivative (in the sense that it is only enforceable as a term of the contract) and can be expressly excluded by the parties to the contract.[13]

Further impetus for action in Scotland comes from several restatements principles of contract law in Europe.[14] These pressures have led the Scottish Law Commission to include the topic in its Review of Contract Law, initiated in 2009 following the publication of the Draft Common Frame of Reference: Principles, Definitions and Model Rules of European Private Law (DCFR). The Scottish Law Commission has published a *Discussion Paper on Third Party Rights in Scotland*[15] that, following the consultation, may lead to a report with legislative proposals for reform. The discussion paper is the most thorough review of third party rights in contract in Scotland and provides the student with a wealth of useful detail and a comprehensive survey of the issues and controversies surrounding this subject. For the present, the discussion paper contains a succinct, but comprehensive review on the topic.

---

[10] WW McBryde, *The Law of Contract in Scotland*, 3rd edn (Edinburgh: W. Green, 2007), para.10–07. Donations and promises are not, of course, contractual rights.

[11] "It is likewise the opinion of Molina, cap. 263 and it quadrates to our customs, that when parties contract, if there be any article in favours of a third party, at any time, *est jus quaesitum tertio*, which cannot be recalled by both the contractors, but he may compel either of them to exhibit the contract, and thereupon the obliged may be compelled to perform. So a promise, though gratuitous, made in favour of a third party, that party, albeit not present, nor accepting, was found to have right thereby, Had. November 25, 1609, Auchinmutie *contra* Hay [*Sub nom. Auchmouty v Mayne*, Haddington, *fol. Dict.* 11, 200; M. 12126]." Stair, *Institutions*, I.x.5. This statement suggests that, unlike Roman law, Scottish law, influenced by canon law, recognises the right of the third party. Stair appears to regard the *jus quaesitum tertio* as a development of unilateral promise. This has led to much debate and the following extract shows the complexity of the issues involved. See TB Smith, *Studies Critical and Comparative* (Edinburgh: W. Green, 1962), p.183; AF Rodger, "Molina, Stair and the *Jus Quaesitum Tertio*", 1969 J.R. 128; HL MacQueen, "Third Party Rights in contract: *Jus Quaesitum Tertio*" in KGC Reid and R Zimmerman (eds), *A History of Private Law in Scotland* (Oxford: Oxford University Press, 2000), Vol.II, p.220; HL MacQueen, "*Jus Quaesitum Tertio*" in *Stair Memorial Encyclopaedia*, Vol.15.

[12] Low Commission, *Privity of Contract: Contracts for the Benefit of Third Parties* (Law Com. No. 242, 1996).

[13] H Beale, "A Review of the Contracts (Rights of Third Parties) Act 1999" in A Burrow sand E Peel (eds), Contract Formation and Parties (Oxford: Oxford University Press, 2010).

[14] Notably Proposal for a Regulation on a Common European Sales Law (CESL), COM(2011) 635 final, available at: *http://eur-lex.europa.eu/LexUriServ/LexUriServ.do?uri=COM:2011:0635:FIN:en:PDF* [Accessed 3 September 2015]; and C von Bar and E Clive (eds), *Principles, Definitions and Model Rules of European Private Law: Draft Common Frame of Reference* (DCFR) (2010) (available as Outline Edition at: *http://ec.europa.eu/justice/policies/civil/docs/dcfr_outline_edition_en.pdf* [Accessed 3 September 2015]).

[15] Scottish Law Commission, *Review of Contract Law: Discussion Paper on Third Party Rights in Contract*, Discussion Paper No.157 (March 2014) available at: *http://www.scotlawcom.gov.uk/files/8913/9599/7785/DP_formatted_for_web.pdf* [Accessed 3 September 2015].

11–08 *Third Party Rights in Scotland*

Scottish Law Commission Discussion Paper No.157 (March 2014)

Chapter 2 Third Party Rights in Scots Law

"Origins

2.1 Scots contract law has long recognised rights in favour of third parties. In 1591, for example, it was held in *Wood v Moncur*[1] that a provision in favour of a third party in a contract of excambion[2] could be invoked by that party ('albeit [he] was no contractor, yet there was a provision made in the same in his favours').[3] In the first half of the seventeenth century Sir Thomas Hope recognised third party rights in his *Major Practicks*,[4] and the cases of *Renton v Ayton*[5] and *Supplicants v Nimmo*[6] provide further authority for the existence of such rights before 1650.

2.2 These cases and writings constitute the background to the first general statement of the Scots law on third party rights (termed the *jus quaesitum tertio*) by Stair in his *Institutions*, first published in 1681.[7] Stair recognised that a contract might create a *jus quaesitum tertio* if it included clauses conceived in the third party's (or *tertius'*) favour. The third party might compel either of the contracting parties to 'exhibit' the contract and then seek performance of the 'article' in its favour from whichever of them was bound to make it.[8]

2.3 The term *jus quaesitum tertio* ('JQT') is still used in Scots law today. This Commission's Consultative Memorandum published in 1977 refers to the parties to the contract conferring the right on the third party as the debtor (the party bound to make a payment or other performance to the third party) and the stipulator (the other party to the contract, who requires the debtor to perform) ...

11–09 **Principles of voluntary obligations**

...

Privity of contract and third party rights

2.13 Third party rights in contracts between two or more others raise special issues because in general a contract creates enforceable rights and duties only between those who are party to its formation. Third parties are typically unaffected by the contract, whether in terms of acquiring rights or being subject to duties. The idea that a contract is a relationship exclusive to, or private between, the parties who made it which they alone can enforce is sometimes known as the principle of privity of contract.

2.14 Privity applies even if the third party's interests are affected in some way by the contract. Merely having an interest in a contract is not sufficient to give a third party any right in relation to it.[28] In a recent example of the application of this principle, a contract between solicitors and a client under which the former were to draw up a trust deed of which a known third party was to be a beneficiary, and then to advise on its administration, was held not to confer a contractual JQT upon that third party such that he could sue for damages for loss caused the solicitor's negligent failure to give appropriate advice. '[T]he contract ... was not one which directly conferred a right to any benefit upon [the third party]. At best, he was entitled to have the trustees have regard to him as being a possible recipient of the trust assets but nothing further than that.'[29]

2.15 Privity is an important principle of the law of contract, but it yields to one even more fundamental, *viz* giving effect to the intention of the contracting parties. If upon interpretation of the contract it appears that the parties intended to confer rights upon a third person, then, subject to certain further requirements, the law will give effect to that intention and allow the third person to make claims under the contract. The intention may be implied as well as express.[30] It is not enough, however, as already pointed out, that a third party benefits as the result of a contract; the contracting parties must *intend* that the third party have a right in the sense of an entitlement to claim or enforce the benefit in question.

2.16 A JQT can only arise when two or more parties *contract to* confer a benefit on a third. A unilateral promise cannot confer a *third* party right on anyone, there being only one party to the creation of the obligation in question, namely the promisor.[31] The promisee or promisees are, if anything, *second* parties, and their right or rights arise directly against the promisor. But, since the third party's acceptance of the right is not required for a JQT, it is possible to analyse it as a promise or set of promises made to the third party by the contracting parties within the framework of their contract. This was the approach of Stair, and it has been followed by several (although not all) modern commentators, including our predecessors in the mid-1970s.[32]

2.17 One consequence of the promissory analysis in Stair's thinking was that a JQT, once created, is irrevocable. For other commentators, however, the fact that JQT can only spring from a contract, and not from a unilateral promise, means that analysing the right in terms of promise is inapt, and they prefer to see it as a separate legal institution with its own unique character (*sui generis*).[33] We will return below to the possible significance of this debate. But it is worth noting here that the third party is not a contracting party, and the third party's right is thus not a contractual right, at least in a narrow sense.

2.18 The significance of allowing the creation of a JQT within a contract may be seen by contrasting it with some of the other legal institutions which enable third parties to acquire rights in relation to contracts made between others. ...

[The discussion paper goes on to consider assignation, agency, trusts and donation in this context.]

...

2.22 A final observation is that the law of JQT has often become clouded by its close functional links with the other areas of law just described, with insufficient attention being given to the different significance of such concepts as delivery, intimation and irrevocability in different legal contexts. In particular, where they arise in the law of assignation, trusts and donation, they may have more to do with real rights—or at least the claims to the same thing—whereas in JQT we are typically concerned only with the existence of personal rights in the third party. It is necessary to keep this point in mind in what follows as an account of the current Scots law of JQT, although that is not to say that the JQT may never come into conflict with other rights, especially those of the contracting parties.

Rights, not Duties **11–10**

2.23 Contracting parties can only confer *rights* upon a third party. Contracts cannot impose *duties* upon third parties without that party's consent.[42] If such consent is given, the result again seems to be the making of a second contract between the parties to the original arrangement and the third party, not a JQT. The essence of JQT is the third party's acquisition of a right under a single contract between two (or more) others.

Immunities as rights?

2.24 But it does also seem possible to confer immunity from liability upon a third party by way of contract.[43] Contracts often contain clauses restricting not only the liability of a contracting party but also that of others connected with him such as employees, agents, independent contractors, and subsidiary, parent or other associated companies. The courts have sometimes given effect to such clauses by way of a JQT in favour of the third party. In the early case of *Renton v Ayton*, Lady Ayton's claim of immunity from liability on the basis of an agreement between the pursuer and other parties was upheld.[44] Another case of the conferral of a third party immunity is *Magistrates of Dunbar v Mackersy*, in which the defender, as present owner of a property for which the magistrates now sought the payment of rates, successfully relied on a letter in which the pursuers' predecessors entered a commitment to the then-owner of the property, to 'free you and your successors in the said tenement and garden of all cess, feuduty and other publick taxations payable for the same to the Town from the date hereof for ever'.[45] In the more recent decision of *Melrose v Davidson and Robertson* it was accepted that a disclaimer contained in a mortgage application form with contractual effect between a building society and prospective borrowers could, on the principle of JQT, be invoked by the property valuer whom it was designed to protect.[46]

11–11 **Identification of the third party**

2.26 For a third party right to arise, the contract must identify the third party in some way. Identification may be of a particular individual or through membership of a class of persons. In *Rose, Murison and Thomson v Wingate, Birrell & Co's Trustee*, for example, guarantors of an association of underwriters were held liable to persons assured by a member of the association. The relevant clause read: 'We guarantee the liabilities arising on the account of JB [the underwriter] underwritten by us in his name'. The persons assured were therefore not individually identified in the guarantees and in turn their assurance policies made no reference to the guarantees. The third parties could be identified, however, as members of a class—the persons insured by JB—and it was held that the purpose of the guarantees was to ensure the protection of their interests.[49] In *Thomson v Thomson* a contract of partnership provided that either partner might by will or otherwise nominate his widow, son or daughter to his share in the partnership. Lord Reid observed: 'It appears to me that the original partners agreed that a nominee should have a right, by way of *ius quaesitum tertio*, to become a partner with the survivor on the same terms, *mutatis mutandis*, as those contained in their own contract of partnership.'[50] Here again there is a group, albeit limited to three individuals, the enforcement of whose right is contingent upon the nomination of the original partner.[51]

11–12 *Third party as person fulfilling specified conditions*

2.27 There may be a JQT if the provision in favour of a third party is expressed in a form such that *any* person fulfilling certain conditions would acquire a right against the contracting parties. An example may be found in *Kelly v Cornhill Insurance Company Ltd.*[52] A motor insurance policy insured any person driving the motor car on the order of or with the permission of the owner. Here the suspensive condition was the owner's order or permission to drive the car, which could be given to any person in the world. Provided that the other conditions for a JQT were satisfied, it could be argued that, although the third party might be anybody, the fulfilment of the conditions would identify the person (or perhaps persons) who would ultimately have the right under the relevant contract provision. The case of *Thomson v Thomson*, referred to in the previous paragraph, suggests another possible example, namely that the third party be a person nominated as such by one of the contracting parties, by will or otherwise, without, however, any limit to widows, sons or daughters.[53]

2.28 We think that this issue may be especially important when a third party right is expressed in favour of a class of persons the membership of which may vary over time, depending on whether and when persons satisfy the conditions for joining the class. Indeed, a set of conditions may be a way of describing a class: for example, all those injured by the negligent driving of a car are entitled to recover from the driver's insurer under his insurance policy . . .

Third party not in existence when the contract is formed 11–13

2.29 As recognised by all the early Institutional Writers, the third party need not be in existence at the time the contract is made.[54] The leading case on the creation of a right for a third party yet to come into existence is *Morton's Trustees v Aged Christian Friend Society of Scotland*.[55] There M wrote to a committee offering financial support for a charitable society which it was seeking to set up. The committee accepted the offer and the society was duly brought into existence. It was held that the society had a right as a third party to the original contract which could be enforced against M's estate, even though it was not in existence when that contract was formed.[56]

. . .

Must the third party always be expressly identified in, or identifiable from, the contract? 11–14

2.35 Professor McBryde asks whether it is always necessary that the third party be expressly identified in the contract for a JQT to arise. He figures the case of a person buying goods and services for a third person who as the ultimate consumer is the person 'most directly affected by inadequate performance of the contract' and the only one to suffer loss. Was *Donoghue v Stevenson* actually a case of JQT rather than delict?[71] Would it have been more clearly so had Mrs Donoghue's unknown friend[72] told the café owner at the time of purchase that the ginger beer was being purchased for another (whether or not she was named)? Suppose again that Mrs Donoghue had not consumed the contaminated drink but had merely observed the presence in it of the snail: then, while she would certainly have had no claim in delict, since she suffered no physical injury, might she have had a third party claim under her friend's contract in respect of the defects in the goods, perhaps for the shock or disgust inflicted upon her by an arrangement intended to give her pleasure?[73]

2.36 Other examples of the kind can be readily imagined: for example, an arrangement by which the parents of a bride contract with a wedding photographer for the supply of multiple albums to be presented to various friends and relatives around the world unable to travel to the nuptials, but the photographer fails to turn up or to produce images of the anticipated quality.[74] A more complex example is the scaffolding sub-contractor whose scaffolding around a tenement building to enable a main contractor to carry out repair and renovation work collapses, damaging the building. Even if the flat owners within the tenement building were not named or mentioned as a class in the scaffolding sub-contract, it seems clear that their existence and exposure to risk of loss must have been at least a consideration for the contracting parties."

---

[1] *Wood v Moncur* (1591) Mor 7719.

[2] 'Excambion' is an exchange of heritable property: G Watson (ed), *Bell's Dictionary and Digest of the Law of Scotland* (7th edn, 1890, reprinted 2012), pp 422-423.

[3] *Wood v Moncur* (1591) Mor 7719, 7719

[4] Sir T Hope, *Major Practicks* (1608-33), II, 1, 30 (1616); II, 3, 37 (1612).

[5] *Renton v Ayton* (1634) Mor 7721.

[6] *Supplicants v Nimmo* (1627) Mor 7740.

[7] MacQueen, "Third Party Rights in Contract: Jus Quaesitum Tertio", pp 221-223.

[8] Stair, *Institutions* I, 10, 5.

. . .

[28] *Finnie v Glasgow and South-Western Railway Co* (1857) 20 D (HL) 2.

[29] *Marquess of Aberdeen and Temair v Turcan Connell* [2008] CSOH 183, para 47 (Lady Smith).

[30] See further at para 2.39 below.

[31] See *Smith v Stuart* 2010 SC 490, para 15; also *Cawdor v Cawdor* 2007 SC 285, paras 13-14 and *Regus (Maxim) Ltd v Bank of Scotland plc* [2011] CSOH 129, paras 54-55 (point not discussed on appeal: [2013] CSIH 12). In *Smith v Stuart* the defender promised certain benefits to the pursuer in the event of the former making a contract for the sale of certain land. Even if the defender had made such a contract, the basis for any claim by the pursuer would still have been the promise, which was clearly quite separate from any such contract. It might have been possible, of course, for the contract to give effect to the promise by way of a provision for performance to the pursuer, in which case the latter's claim might have become one based on JQT rather than the earlier promise.
[32] T B Smith, A *Short Commentary on the Law of Scotland* (1962), pp 746-747; SLC Memo No 38, 1977; *SME* Vol 15, para 827; M Hogg, *Promises and Contract Law: Comparative Perspectives* (2011), pp 305-307; Huntley and Dedouli, "Third Party Rights" 307-321.
[33] Rodger, 143, 144; McBryde, *Contract*, para 10.07; Sutherland and Johnston, "Contracts for the Benefit of Third Parties", pp 216-217; Sutherland, "Third-Party Contracts", pp 209-210.

. . .

[42] See, eg, *Howgate Shopping Centre Ltd v GLS 164 Ltd* 2002 SLT 820.
[43] McBryde, *Contract*, paras 8.80-8.82, explores some of the possible difficulties.
[44] *Renton v Ayton* (1634) Mor 7721.
[45] *Magistrates of Dunbar v Mackersy* 1931 SC 180.
[46] *Melrose v Davidson and Robertson* 1993 SC 288 (Lord President Hope). Section 16 of the Unfair Contract Terms Act 1977, regulating non-contractual notices excluding or limiting liability for breaches of a duty of care, could then be applied. See further *SME* Vol 15, para 846; *British Telecommunications Plc v James Thomson & Sons (Engineers) Ltd* 1999 SC (HL) 9; and, in relation to this case, J Convery "Contractual Structures and the Duty of Care" 1997 SLT (News) 113; H L MacQueen, "Concrete Solutions to Liability: Changing Perspectives in Contract and Delict" (1998) 64 Arbitration: Journal of the Chartered Institute of Arbitrators 285, 288-289; and Hogg, *Obligations*, paras 3.97-3.100.

. . .

[49] *Rose, Murison and Thomson v Wingate, Birrell & Co's Tr* (1889) 16 R 1132.
[50] *Thomson v Thomson* 1962 SC (HL) 28, 32.
[51] It was held that the condition was not satisfied by a universal bequest in a will of one of the partners. 52 1964 SC (HL) 46.

. . .

[71] McBryde, *Contract*, para 10.15. See also W W McBryde, "Contract Law – a Solution to Delictual Problems?", 2012 SLT (News) 45. In *Donoghue v Stevenson* 1932 SC (HL) 31 the House of Lords held relevant Mrs Donoghue's delictual claim of negligence against the manufacturer of a bottle of ginger beer the contents of which she had partly consumed before discovering that they included the decomposing remains of a dead snail. She thereafter suffered from gastro-enteritis. The bottle had been purchased for Mrs Donoghue by a friend.
[72] For the most recent discussion of the gender of Mrs Donoghue's unidentified companion in Minghella's Paisley café on 26 August 1928, see J Conn, "Gingerlore: The Legends of *Donoghue v Stevenson*" 2013 JR 265, 272- 274.
[73] Damages can be awarded for distress caused by breach of contract: see McBryde, *Contract*, paras 22.104–22.105. It is undecided whether such a claim might be open to a third party upon whom the contracting parties intended to confer a right.
[74] *Cf Diesen v Samson* 1971 SLT (Sh Ct) 49."

11–15 The cases referred to in this extract clearly illustrate that to establish such a right, two things are essential: the contract must name or refer to the third party or the class to which they belong; and the parties must have intended to benefit the third party.

The *jus quaesitum tertio* has arisen occasionally in insurance contracts and other family dealings. This does not obscure its potential commercial significance, as is again illustrated by the cases referred to in the extract.[16]

In a modern context, the rights of third parties are most likely to arise in a commercial environment where subcontracting and multiparty contracting are a common feature, for example in the construction industry. Clauses may be inserted at one level in the contracting chain with the intention of benefiting contractors at another level. Similarly a transaction, for example the development of a piece of land, may involve companies that are separate legal entities, but otherwise interrelated. This matter will be considered again in the context of claims for damages,[17] but the following extract illustrates the complex issues involved.

Third Party Rights in Scotland 11–16

Scottish Law Commission Discussion Paper No.157 (March 2014)

"Contracting parties' intention to create third party rights

2.38 It is not enough for a JQT that a contract simply refers to a third party since, as already noted, there must also be manifest an intention to confer an enforceable right upon that third party.[78] Thus for A and B to contract that A shall pay B's debts does not without more confer any right upon B's creditors as third parties.[79]

2.39 The intention to confer a third party right may be express or implied in the contract. As Gloag remarked, 'The most unequivocable indication of an intention that a third party should have a *jus quaesitum* under a contract is an express provision that he should have a title to enforce it, and it is conceived that there is no principle of the law of Scotland which should prevent a stipulation of this kind having the effect intended'.[80] But, as Professor McBryde also observes, 'Full express terms have probably been uncommon, although not unknown when the draftsman deliberately sets out to create a right which may be enforced by a third party.'[81]

2.40 The difficulty on this subject in the cases has thus been over when, in the absence of such an express and deliberate provision but where the contract nonetheless identifies a party or class of parties to be benefited by its performance, it can be held that the contracting parties intended these third parties to have a *right* to that benefit. The question has to be taken with the rule that the mere existence of a third party benefit from, or interest in, the contract is insufficient for the creation of a right.

2.41 Gloag proposed a rule that a third party right could be implied 'where A by contract obliges B to do something for C, when his own interest in the fulfilment of these obligations is non-existent or negligible.'[82] Gloag gives several examples, starting with a case in which, when Mr A sold his hotel to B in a contract including an undertaking by B to pay Mrs A £100 'as some compensation for the annoyance and worry of the past few days and for kindness and attention to me on my several visits to Crieff', it was held that Mrs A had a direct claim for the £100 even though her husband's interest in the contract had been discharged by the successful completion of the sale of the hotel.[83] Professor McBryde does not state an equivalent rule, although he gives this and further examples

---

[16] It is probably the case that an indorsee of a bill of lading relating to goods being carried by sea acquires rights against the carrier even though he was not a party to the initial contract. It has been doubted, at least by Lord Trayner in *Delaurier v Wylie* (1889) 17 R. 167, whether the special rights conferred on the indorsee by the Bills of Lading Act 1955, now replaced by the Carriage by Sea Act 1992, are necessary in Scots law (they are necessary in English law because of the operation of the doctrine of privity). See EM Clive, "*Jus Quaesitum Tertio* and the Carriage of Goods by Sea" in C Miller and Meyers (eds), *Comparative and Historical Essays in Scots Law* (Edinburgh: Bloomsbury, 1992).

[17] The issue of the so-called "black hole", consider below para.12–24 onwards.

of similar cases (many of which have already been cited in this Chapter) in discussing implied intention.[84]

2.42 The fact that the contracting parties have ongoing obligations between themselves as well as in relation to the third party does not, however, prevent the latter having an enforceable right. This can be illustrated by the case of *Mercedes-Benz Finance Ltd v Clydesdale Bank plc*.[85] Mercedes-Benz (MB) supplied cars to Glen Henderson (Stuttgart) Ltd (GH) for re-sale to customers in Scotland. When GH sold a car, the proceeds were lodged in an account held with the Clydesdale Bank (CB). GH and CB had agreed that appropriate transfers should then be made to MB by CB. GH went into receivership indebted to both CB and MB but with funds sitting in GH's account with CB which had been due to be transferred to MB. Lord Penrose found that the agreement between GH and CB could give a JQT to MB; he rejected CB's argument that a JQT could only arise where the third party alone had a substantial interest in the performance whereas, in this case, CB clearly also had an interest in ensuring the payment to themselves of the debt which they were owed by GH.

. . .

2.48 The requirement of intention to confer a right probably explains why, as is noted in the *SME*, there is often not a JQT in cases where there are a contract and a dependent sub-contract, or a series of connected sub-contracts and sub-sub-contracts.[96] Although the performances of the sub-contractors and the sub-sub-contractors may be ultimately for the benefit of the employer of the principal contractor, the purpose of such contractual arrangements is 'usually . . . to distance parties from each other rather than to bring them into a direct legal relationship. Thus the employer has only to pay, and can only sue, the main contractor; equally, the sub-contractor can only look to the main contractor.'[97]

2.49 It is not impossible, however, for a JQT to arise between parties linked through a chain of contracts and sub-contracts, albeit not directly.[98] In *Scott Lithgow Ltd v GEC Electrical Projects Ltd*,[99] an employer claimed a JQT in a sub-contract to which it was not a party on the basis that it was named in the sub-contract and that the sub-contractor's work was for the advancement of the employer's interests. Although there were no averments about the actual terms of the sub-contract, Lord Clyde allowed the case to go to proof on the basis that the evidence at the proof might show that the intention to confer a third party right indeed existed.

11–17 **No requirement of third party acceptance**

2.50 There is no need for any acceptance or equivalent by the third party before its right can come into existence. Thus for Stair a third party right could be created in favour of an absent person, as well as for someone lacking the active capacity to carry out a legally effective act of acceptance.[100] Stair's position was consistent with his espousal of a 'declaration of will' theory under which obligations could be constituted by a seriously intended and objectively verifiable undertaking without any need for communication thereof to the other party . . .

. . .

2.52 In Scots law it is clearly not a JQT when two parties contract and provide that a third party is to have a right only upon its acceptance by the third party. There is, however, nothing to prevent parties setting up such an arrangement if they wish.[105] In that case, the third party's right does not exist until acceptance of what is in effect an offer made by either or both of the contracting parties. Thus, as Stair pointed out: '[I]f a promise be made by one to another in favour of a third, importing the acceptance of that third, it is pendent and revocable by these contractors, til the third accept.'[106] The third party's right then rests entirely upon a further contract between that party and one or more of the originally contracting parties. There is no need in such circumstances to make the third party's right dependent in any way upon the first-made contract, the legal significance of which is confined to the relationship of the original contracting parties. It would also be possible with this mechanism to subject the third party to enforceable duties.[107]

...

Third party remedies and exclusion clauses 11–18

2.84 A person with a JQT may raise an action for payment or performance of the benefit due by the debtor under the contract. But some doubt exists about whether or not the third party can claim damages for the debtor's breach, whether through non-performance, partial or defective performance, or delay. The view that a damages claim is competent, however, is the direction which the law is apparently taking.[172] The most significant judicial discussion is by Lord Clyde in the Outer House, when he reviewed the cases and writings upon the subject and concluded that there was:

'... no reason why a third party should not be entitled to sue for damages for negligent performance of a contract under the principle of *jus quaesitum tertio*, but whether he is so entitled must be a matter of the intention of the contracting parties.'[173]

Lord Clyde thus laid more stress upon the intention of the parties than upon any general right to claim damages for breach of a voluntary obligation, and left open the question of liability not based on negligence—for example, in respect of the quality of goods or services supplied to the third party. The overall position accordingly remains in a state of some uncertainty.

2.85 The contract may seek to exclude or limit any third party's claim of damages. It is a moot point whether or not the controls of the Unfair Contract Terms Act 1977 apply to such an exclusion.[174] It has been suggested that, because the controls generally apply expressly in favour of contracting parties only, they cannot help third parties. Some of the controls can, however, apply to non-contractual notices,[175] and exclusion clauses against third parties might fall into that category. If so, the controls come in where the third party's claim is in respect of a contractual duty of care: for example, where a parent buys tickets to enable the whole family to have a ride on the negligently maintained or operated Ferris wheel and they, having suffered injury as a result of the negligence, are then confronted with a widely-drawn clause purporting to exclude liability in damages to any user of the device.[176] But where the breach is something other than failure to take care—supplying safe but shoddy goods, services defective without negligence, other forms of inflicting economic loss irrecoverable in delict—then the exclusion clause will apply according to its terms.

---

[78] McBryde, *Contract*, para 10.17.

[79] *Henderson v Stubbs Ltd* (1894) 22 R 51.

[80] Gloag, *Contract*, p 236.

[81] McBryde, *Contract*, para 10.12 (citing *Denny's Trs v Dumbarton Magistrates* 1945 SC 147, and also giving as an example "a takeover agreement or sale of a business where it is expressly provided that the workforce or pension trustees may enforce rights against the buyer, or a building contract which gives rights to an ultimate buyer or tenant").

[82] Gloag, *Contract*, p 236.

[83] *Lamont v Burnett* (1901) 3 F 797. Gloag's other cases are *Wood v Moncur* 1591 Mor 7719; *Rose Murison & Thomson v Wingate Birrell & Co's Trs* (1889) 16 R 1132; *Clan Steam Trawling Co v Aberdeen Steam Trawling Co* 1908 SC 651; *Dryburgh v Fife Coal Co* (1905) 7 F 1083.

[84] McBryde, *Contract*, para 10.14 (citing *Thomson v Thomson* 1962 SC (HL) 28; *Wallace v Simmers* 1960 SC 255; *Beta Computers (Europe) Ltd v Adobe Systems (Europe) Ltd* 1996 SLT 604; and *Kelly v Cornhill Insurance Co* 1964 SC (HL) 46).

[85] *Mercedes-Benz Finance Ltd v Clydesdale Bank plc* 1997 SLT 905.

...

[96] *SME* Vol 15, para 836, and authorities cited therein. See also *Sears Properties Netherlands BV v Coal Pension Properties Ltd* 2001 SLT 761 (OH).
[97] *SME* Vol 15, para 836. There may, however, be claims between the distant parties in other areas of the law such as delict or unjustified enrichment.
[98] Note on third party rights in 'contract chains': Beale, "Review", pp 226-228.
[99] 1989 SC 412 (OH).
[100] Stair, *Institutions*, I, 10, 4-5.
. . .
[105] An example may, we think, be provided by the Master Policy for Professional Indemnity Insurance provided through the Law Society of Scotland: see further at para 3.32 below.
[106] Stair, *Institutions*, I, 10, 6.
[107] Sutherland and Johnston, "Contracts for the Benefit of Third Parties", p 219; Sutherland, "Third-Party Contracts", p 212.
. . .
[172] *SME* Vol 15, para 837; McBryde, *Contract*, paras 10.23-10.24; Sutherland, "Third-Party Contracts", pp 221- 225. The assumption that the third party may claim damages for breach of its right underlies the discussion of the applicability of JQT in the 'black hole' or 'transferred loss' cases . . .
[173] *Scott Lithgow Ltd v GEC Electrical Projects Ltd* 1989 SC 412, 438-439.
[174] The Unfair Terms in Consumer Contracts Regulations 1999 do not apply in this situation. The question is not discussed in our joint advice with the English Law Commission on Unfair Terms in Consumer Contracts (2013) and no change in the position can be expected when that advice is implemented in the Consumer Rights Bill which is currently before Parliament.
[175] Unfair Contract Terms Act 1977 s 16."

Even if it can be shown that an intended benefit was bestowed, the question of form may be an issue. If, as some authorities and commentators contend, the right is founded on promise, the right must be in a form that complies with the Requirements of Writing (Scotland) Act 1995. As the following extract shows, this aspect of third party rights remains unclear.

11–19 *Third Party Rights in Scotland*

Scottish Law Commission Discussion Paper No.157 (March 2014)

"Formalities

2.53 There has been little consideration of whether the JQT is subject to any requirements of writing, although our predecessors observed in 1988: 'In all of the reported cases on *jus quaesitum tertio* the contracts have in fact been in writing.'[108] One of the possible implications of the promissory analysis of JQT, however, is that third party rights would be required to adhere to the Requirements of Writing (Scotland) Act 1995 rules on the formation of promises; that is, they would have to be in formally valid writing unless made in the course of business or if there had been appropriate actings upon the faith of the promise such as to bar the promising parties from withdrawing it.[109] This should of course present no barrier to the recognition of third party rights in commercial transactions like those to be discussed in the next chapter.[110] Further, the current rules on actings upon informal undertakings barring withdrawal therefrom despite the absence of writing (statutory *rei interventus*) are more liberal than the previous law requiring proof of promises by the promisor's writ or oath.[111] This can be shown by considering how the pre-1995 Act case of *Smith v Oliver*[112] would be dealt with today: the church, far from failing (because unable, in the absence of the deceased Mrs Oliver's writ or oath) to prove her promise to pay for the construction of its building, would now succeed in its claim against her estate, because it acted in reliance upon Mrs Oliver's proved oral statements, was affected to a material extent by laying out funds and other resources on the project, and would also be adversely affected to a material extent if the estate was allowed to withdraw from performance of Mrs Oliver's undertakings because they were not in formal writing.[113]

2.54 An alternative possibility is that if the underlying contract is not one that required to be in formal writing (ie is not one dealing with a real right in land), then nor should any third party right which that contract may also confer. Under the law before the 1995 Act, the rule limiting proof of gratuitous obligations to the writ or oath of the promisor was not applicable where the obligation in question was added to others contained in a mutual or onerous contract. In the leading case on the subject, parties reached a compromise in which one who was relieved of a possible claim of damages for failure to implement a lease also undertook to endorse a grocer's licence which had been granted in his name. At first instance it was held that this undertaking could be proved parole, ie did not require reference to the undertaker's writ or oath.[114] Lord Kyllachy said:

'A promise or undertaking is not in the eyes of the law gratuitous—that is to say, it is not a mere *nudum pactum*, if it be part of a transaction which includes *hinc inde* onerous elements, such, for example, as a waiver or discharge of claims, or objection to claims—claims or objections which, whether good or bad, it is desired to extinguish. In such a case the whole transaction—unless heritable rights are affected—may, I think it is clear, be the subject of parole proof.'[115]

2.55 It is not settled, however, whether this broad permissive approach outside transactions involving real rights in land continues to apply under the more formal regime of the 1995 Act. Professor Hogg opines:

'As the Act contains no provision exempting ... a unilateral promise from the requirement of writing merely because of its containment within a contract, it is to be presumed that the promise at least would require to be subscribed (which, in practice, would mean the whole contract would be subscribed).'[116]

The need for such a rule may well have been thought limited, given that promises made in the course of business are exempted from the requirement of formal writing.[117] But there may still be difficult situations needing to be dealt with. Professor Hogg gives the example of 'a contract between two parties not undertaken in the course of business containing a gratuitous option in favour of one of the parties to purchase property'.[118] In a discussion of third party rights, this example might be elaborated to consider the possibility that the contract is, say, a short-term residential letting between an uncle and a student niece or nephew when the latter's university career begins, with the option to buy the let property provided to the student's parents if one or more of their other younger children later go to the same university. The letting does not need to be in formal writing; but does the grant of the option?

2.56 The Requirements of Writing (Scotland) Act 1995 imposes the requirement of formal writing on unilateral *gratuitous* obligations. There is currently no consensus in Scots law regarding whether a promise is always gratuitous, or whether it may be either gratuitous or onerous.[119] Whilst Professor MacQueen, Professor Black, David Sellar, Professor Huntley and Dr Dedouli, and Professor Hogg are all of the opinion that a promise is always gratuitous,[120] Professor Thomson and Professor McBryde think otherwise.[121] If Professor Thomson and Professor McBryde are right, then whenever a promisee has to fulfil some onerous condition before becoming fully entitled to the benefit of the promise, there is no need for that particular promise to be in writing. Since unconditional promises are perhaps rare, the requirement of formal writing thus would not have much practical bite. If a JQT is characterised as a promise, this analytical debate about what is meant by 'gratuitous' will apply in that context too, with uncertainty of outcome continuing until the courts have an opportunity to provide a definitive ruling on the matter.[122] In our example of the student let with a third party's option to buy, does the fact that the third parties will have to raise finance in order to make any purchase mean that the uncle's obligation is not gratuitous and can therefore escape the requirement of formal writing after all?[123]

---

[108] Report on Requirements of Writing (SLC No 112, 1988), para 2.26.
[109] See discussion in Huntley and Dedouli, "Third Party Rights" 332-336.
[110] See Chapter 3.
[111] RoW(S)A ss 1(3), (4). See para 2.5 above.
[112] 1911 SC 103.
[113] HL MacQueen and M Hogg, "Donation in Scots Law" 2012 JR 1, 13-14.
[114] *Hawick Heritable Investment Bank v Hoggan* (1902) 5 F 75.
[115] At 79.
[116] Hogg, *Obligations*, para 2.22.
[117] RoW(S)A s 1(2)(a)(ii).
[118] Hogg, *Obligations*, para 2.22.
[119] Hogg, *Obligations*, para 2.06.
[120] See HL MacQueen, "Constitution and Proof of Gratuitous Obligations" 1986 SLT (News) 1, 2; *SME* Vol 15, para 613; W D H Sellar, "Promise" in K G C Reid and R Zimmermann (eds), *History of Private Law in Scotland* , Vol 2, pp 252, 279-282; Huntley and Dedouli "Third Party Rights" 318-321; Hogg, *Obligations*, paras 2.06-2.11.
[121] J Thomson, "Promises and the Requirement of Writing" 1997 SLT (News) 284; W W McBryde, "Promises in Scots Law" (1993) 42 International and Comparative Law Quarterly 48. McBryde, *Contract*, para 2.03, is less definite on the point.
[122] The 1995 Act does not support any idea that all unilateral obligations are *ipso facto* gratuitous: see s 1(2)(a)(i) referring to "unilateral obligation" whereas s 1(2)(a)(ii) refers to "gratuitous unilateral obligation". See the *obiter* comments of Lord President Gill on this topic in *Regus (Maxim) Ltd v Bank of Scotland plc* [2013] CSIH 12, paras 40, 41. On when a cautionary obligation is not gratuitous (because the transaction also involved co-extensive cautionary obligations of the debtor in favour of the first cautioner), see *Royal Bank of Scotland plc v Wilson* 2004 SC 153.
[123] On the characterisation of options see MacQueen and Thomson, *Contract*, para 2.61(6) and authorities cited therein."

Even if the third party can establish that they are an intended beneficiary and that formal requirements have been complied with, there is yet another, often insuperable hurdle to overcome. The right must be irrevocable.

11–20

Carmichael v Carmichael's Executrix
1920 S.C. (H.L.) 195
House of Lords: Viscounts Haldane, Finlay and Cave, Lords Dunedin and Shaw of Dunfermline

Hugh Carmichael took out a policy of assurance on the life of his son, Ian, when Ian was nine years old. Under the policy, the father undertook to pay the premiums, was entitled to the surrender value of the policy and was entitled to repayment of the premiums should the son die before majority (then 21 years). If, after majority, the son continued paying the premiums, he was entitled to exercise various options and upon his death the sum insured was payable to his estate. Ian knew of the existence of the policy.

Ian, while on active service, died in an air accident in July 1916, aged 21 years. By his will, he conveyed all his property to his aunt, Miss McColl who, as the executrix of Ian's will, now contested with the father the proceeds of the assurance policy. The issue was whether Ian had derived a *jus quaesitum tertio* under his father's contract with the life assurance company which he could then convey to his aunt.

The court found that he had.

"LORD DUNEDIN: ... I think it necessary to begin by pointing out that the expression '*jus quaesitum tertio*' is, in different cases and different circumstances, used in a varying sense ... The one sense is meant when the question being considered is simply whether the *tertius* C has any right to sue A in respect of a contract made between A and B to which contract C is no party. The controversy then arises between C, who wishes to sue, and A, who denies his title to do so. It is here that there is a sharp technical diversity between the laws of England and Scotland. In England, no matter how much the contract contained provisions for the behoof of C, C could never sue at law. In equity he could sue, but he could only sue if, by the terms of the contract, he could successfully maintain that A was constituted a trustee in his favour. In Scotland, if the provision is expressed in favour of C, he can sue, and this is often designated by saying 'he has a *jus quaesitum tertio*.' Probably the reason of the difference indicated lies in the simple fact that in Scotland law and equity were never separate ... Examples of this first class of controversy may be found in such cases as *Finnie v Glasgow and South-Western Railway Co* (1857) Macq. 75, *Henderson v Stubbs* 22 R. 51, and *Love v Amalgamated Society of Lithographic Printers*, 1912 S.C. 1078. The other sense of the expression is when the emphasis is, so to speak, on the *quaesitum*, and when the controversy arises not between C and A but between C and B. In such a case A is willing to perform his contract, and the contract in form provides that A will do something for C, but B, or those who represent B's estate, interfere and say that B and not C is the true creditor in the stipulation. Of this second class are the deposit-receipt cases such as *Jamieson v McLeod* (1880) 7 R. 1131 ... and insurance policy cases such as *Hadden v Bryden* (1899) 1 F. 710 and *Jarvie's Trustee v Jarvie's Trustees* (1887) 14 R. 411 ... **11–21**

Using the letters above, A is here willing to pay: the controversy is as to whether B or C is entitled to receive. It may therefore thus be stated—Has C a *jus* acknowledged by A which is *quaesitum* to him in a question with B? ... The ... method of approaching the present question is to ask oneself whether under all the circumstances, and in view of the terms of the document, there was created a *jus quaesitum* in the second sense in the person of the *tertius*, in this case the son.

[I]rrevocability is the test; but the mere execution of the document will not constitute irrevocability. It is obvious that if A and B contract and nothing else follows, and no one is informed of the contract, A and B can agree to cancel the contract ...

There must therefore be something more than the form of the document forming the contract and conceived in favour of the *tertius* to effectuate irrevocability. This something may be provided in different ways, for, after all, it is a question of evidence. Now the most obvious evidence is the delivery of the document to the *tertius* himself. The delivery of a deposit-receipt taken to the *tertius*, or the endorsement of a deposit-receipt taken to the depositor and the handing of the receipt to the *tertius*, are familiar examples. In place of delivery of the document to the *tertius* there may be a dealing with the document in such a way as to put it out of the power of the original contractors to deal with it. This may be effected by a registration ...

This, however, does not exhaust the ways in which irrevocability may be shown. Intimation to the *tertius* may be quite sufficient ...

There is also the class of cases where the *tertius* comes under the onerous engagements on the faith of his having a *jus quaesitum*, though the actual contract has not been intimated to him. This is at the root of a feuar being able to enforce building restrictions against a co-feuar; the conditions under which such a *jus quaesitum* may be inferred being set forth with great detail in the well-known judgment of Lord Watson in *Hislop's Trustees v MacRitchie* (1881) 8 R. (H.L.) 95.

I have gone through these various ways in which the intention that a vested *jus tertio* should be created can be shown, but, after all, they are only examples and not an exhaustive list, for in the end it is a question of evidence, and the only real rule to be deduced is that the mere expression of the obligation as giving a *jus tertio* is not sufficient ...

I find a contract which makes a marked distinction between the period up to the majority of the life assured and the period thereafter. Up to the majority it is [the father] who engages to pay the premiums. After majority ... [the father] no longer engages to pay the premiums, but [the son] is given several options. These options ... are strangely inconsistent with the idea of there being no vested interest in [the son]. Then comes the fact that the son undoubtedly knew of the assurance ... though the proof falls short of direct communication ... Taking all the circumstances together, I come to the conclusion that we have here the evidence necessary, when taken along with the terms of the document, to show that an irrevocable *jus quaesitum* was constituted in favour of Ian Carmichael."

This judgment is a fundamental reinterpretation of Stair, *Institutions*, I.x.5, and has attracted severe academic criticism,[18] in particular that Lord Dunedin went further than Stair by suggesting that irrevocability is a precondition for the creation of the *jus*, rather than a consequence of it. As the following extract suggests, this remains an issue.

11–22 *Third Party Rights in Scotland*

Scottish Law Commission Discussion Paper No.157 (March 2014)

"The requirement of irrevocability

2.57 A key issue is whether, in order to enable a third party right to come into existence, it is sufficient that there is a term in a contract which purports to do so or whether a further step is required of the parties. At the heart of this issue is the freedom which contracting parties normally enjoy to change the contents of the contract by agreement between themselves or to cancel it altogether. Just as a contract is made by the parties' agreement, so it can be unmade and remade by the same process. But if the parties succeed in creating a right for a third party, it would seem elementary that that right cannot be undone merely by the agreement of the contracting parties; in addition, the consent of the third party should also be necessary.[124]

2.58 The courts have tended to provide that before contracting parties can be held to have deprived themselves of their ordinary freedom to adjust their relations as they wish, there must be something more than just a term in favour of a third party. It must be clear that the contracting parties intended not only to confer a benefit upon a third party but also to give up the freedom to change their minds. In the technical language used by the courts, the contracting parties must have taken additional steps to make the term irrevocable; the term alone being insufficient for this purpose.

2.59 Some issues about the meaning of 'irrevocability' seem never to have been addressed by the courts, and have received limited attention from commentators. 'Revocation' would generally be taken as meaning 'termination' or 'cancellation'; but does it also cover 'variation' or 'alteration' or 'modification' of the third party's right short of outright cancellation? It does not seem to be necessary, however, that the whole contract be irrevocable: variation of their agreement by the contracting parties not affecting the rights of the third party is permissible.[125]

---

[18] See WW McBryde, *The Law of Contract in Scotland*, 3rd edn (Edinburgh: W. Green, 2007), pp.412–416, paras 18–11—18–19. It is tempting to agree with Professor McBryde that the case is better considered as one concerned with delivery, rather than *jus quaesitum tertio*.

2.60 The leading case is *Carmichael v Carmichael's Executrix*.[126] Late in July 1916, Ian Neil Carmichael, who had joined the Royal Naval Air Service (precursor of the RAF) the previous October, was killed in an air accident. He was 21 years of age. There was in force a policy of assurance upon Ian's life, worth £1,000. It had been taken out with the English and Scottish Law Life Assurance Association in 1903 by Ian's father, a consulting engineer in Hong Kong called Hugh Fletcher Carmichael.[127] The policy provided that Hugh should pay the annual premiums each 22 October during Ian's minority and be entitled to repayment thereof should the assured die before attaining majority. But once Ian attained majority, and if he took over payment of the premiums, then the sum assured was to be paid on his death to his executors. The object of this 'deferred assurance on the life of a child' was 'to encourage thrift in the young by giving the child on attaining majority an inducement to continue the assurance at a low rate of premium, and on the footing that there would be no liability to extra premium on account of family history or personal delicacy or on the ground of his being engaged in some hazardous occupation or residing in some unhealthy climate'.[128] Hugh paid all the premiums due up to Ian's twenty-first birthday on 29 October 1915, and retained custody of the relevant documentation throughout this period and up to Ian's death. Immediately after his birthday in 1915, Ian inquired of the insurance company whether his entry upon active service would affect the policy; having been told that it would not, and having declared his willingness to take over payment of the premiums, he executed a holograph will on 11 November 1915 in which he bequeathed to his aunt, Miss Catherine M'Coll, his whole estate, and appointed her as his executrix. Ian never paid a premium before his death, since the next one would have fallen due to be paid on 22 October 1916. On 7 October 1916, the insurance company, confronted with the competing claims of Hugh Carmichael and Catherine M'Coll to the £1,000 payable under the policy, raised an action of multiplepoinding in the Court of Session. The action proceeded to the House of Lords which, reversing a Court of Seven Judges split 5:2 below, eventually held in favour of Ian's executrix, i.e. that there was in existence an enforceable third party right under an irrevocable contract.

2.61 In *Carmichael* Lord Dunedin explained that irrevocability can be achieved in various ways: (1) delivery or intimation of the contract to the third party; (2) otherwise putting the contract out of the power of the contracting parties; (3) registration of the contract, for example in the Books of Council and Session; (4) third party's knowledge of the contract term in its favour; and (5) third party's reliance upon the contract term in its favour. The basis for the finding that a third party right existed in *Carmichael's* case was (4).

2.62 Lord Dunedin did not explore any underlying policy rationale for these rules on how to make a contract irrevocable, but the first three at least can be explained upon the basis that if these events occur it is objectively manifest that the contracting parties have moved beyond the stage of thinking about the creation of a right for the third party to a concluded intention that such a right should exist. There may, in other words, be some link with the implication of intention to create a right. The fourth and fifth rules, however, seem to be driven more by considerations of fairness and justice to the third party when other objective manifestations of the contracting parties' intention have not taken place.

2.63 With regard to the relevance of the contract terms, Lord Dunedin said:

'[T]he only real rule to be deduced is that the mere expression of the obligation as giving a *jus tertio* is not sufficient. … Now, in examining the evidence, while, as I have already said more than once, the terms of the document are not conclusive, that does not mean that they are not to be considered. On the contrary, they form a very important piece of evidence.'[129]

2.64 This view of the law, and Lord Dunedin's speech in general, has long been the subject of academic criticism,[130] which some thought gained support from Lord Reid when he commented in a 1971 case before the House of Lords: 'I do not think that Lord Dunedin meant to say that this intention to make the provision in favour of the third party irrevocable can never be established by the terms of the contract itself. Generally it cannot, and then other evidence of intention is required.'[131] The suggestion that Lord Reid's use of the word 'generally' here left open the possibility that exceptionally the terms of the contract might be enough to constitute a third party right without delivery or an equivalent has been doubted;[132] but it seems to be at least implicit in his preceding sentence, whether or not it is a correct interpretation of the meaning that Lord Dunedin had intended to convey in *Carmichael.*

2.65 Professor McBryde argues, however, that, as a result of the principle requiring delivery of documents to give them obligatory force,[133] for a third party right to come into existence there must indeed be delivery to that third party, or some equivalent, of any document embodying a JQT.[134] The relevant equivalents to delivery laid down in *Carmichael v Carmichael's Executrix* are very wide in scope.[135] They include intimation to the third party, the third party's knowledge of the provision in its favour, and the third party's detrimental reliance on that provision, as well as registration of the contract. In *Carmichael*, the House of Lords held it to be enough that the third party knew of the provision in his favour albeit not as a result of any formal intimation or direct communication by either of the contracting parties. It may have been relevant to that result that the third party was a young man who had just attained majority, and so full capacity; this, rather than lack of obligatory intention, could explain why his father, as the 'natural custodier' for an under-age son, had retained possession of the insurance policy which was the contract in the case, rather than deliver it to the son. Nor was any creditor of the father prejudiced by the son's right.[136]

...

2.69 A final observation on the requirement of delivery in the context of third party rights is that it cannot apply at all where the obligation—unilateral, bilateral or multilateral—is not in writing. In that case, as between specific parties at least, the key seems to be communication between the parties or at least some objectively verifiable manifestation of a party's intention to be bound in an obligation to the third party. Although there are no examples in the case law of a JQT springing from an unwritten contract, it has not been suggested until recently that a JQT can arise only from a written one.[141]

Revocation of a third party right: conditionality

11–23 2.70 Professor McBryde distinguishes between what is needed to create a third party right in the first place, and the power or possibility that a right once created may come to an end before it is enforced, either in whole or in part, by the right-holder. ...

2.71 Professor McBryde explains: '[A] right once created may be revoked. There are many instances of revocable rights in Scots law, eg rights under some contracts of mandate or deposit, the contract created between a company and its members by ... s.33 of the Companies Act 2006, or the revocable promise to keep an offer open.[143] In Stair's time donations between man and wife, *stante matrimonio*, were revocable by the giver during life. Nor should we be surprised if a legal system recognises revocable rights. Many contractual rights are only exercisable if certain conditions are satisfied, and there is no reason why one of these conditions could not be the absence of prior revocation. Similarly, a law which recognises resolutive conditions or irritancies, surely recognises the concept of a right which may vest, but which can in certain circumstances be revoked.'[144]

2.72 Professor McBryde points to the JQT case of *Love v Amalgamated Society of Lithographic Printers of Great Britain and Ireland*,[145] as an illustration of a right that was held to have been created although revocable by the parties who created it. The society operated a scheme which provided certain benefits for the relatives of sick members but which also provided that the rules of the scheme could be changed. In other words, the scheme which was constituted by the contract amongst all the members of the society was revocable. But when a particular relative claimed a benefit under the scheme, the court found a JQT in her favour since the rules had not in fact been changed or revoked at the time the claim was made.[146]

2.73 Another example which seems not to have been noticed in this context in the previous literature is the more recent case of *Kelly v Cornhill Insurance Company Ltd.*[147] A motor insurance policy insured any person driving the motor car on the order of or with the permission of the owner. The owner gave his son unlimited permission to drive the insured vehicle, but clearly had the right to withdraw that permission. The question in the case was whether the permission was terminated by the death of the owner, the son having continued to drive the car after that event and having had an accident while the policy remained in force. The House of Lords held by a narrow majority that the son could enforce the policy. Although his right could have been revoked by his father, it had not been; on construction, the policy (and the father's permission to drive the car) continued in force despite the father's death, and for as long as the car continued to be an asset in the father's estate.

2.74 We think that the distinction between the rules on creation and termination of rights drawn by Professor McBryde is correct and amply borne out by authority as well as by principle. In particular, we agree that it is possible for parties to draw up a contract providing for a third party right subject to a resolutive condition under which upon the occurrence of an event the right ceases to exist. As the *Love* case demonstrates, the resolutive condition may also be a potestative one; that is, one under the control of the contracting parties themselves. It was for the members of the society to determine what its rules were and these could be changed by appropriate action, including the rules on the provision of benefits to third parties.[148] So long as the power of a party to resolve the contract under the potestative condition is exercised in good faith, there should be no difficulty in recognising this possibility.[149]

2.75 There seems to have been no suggestion in *Love* that the very third party right itself did not come into existence at all until the suspensive condition of the member's sickness was fulfilled. Rather, the enforceability of the right under the contract as it stood was what was subject to the suspensive condition; and that right could also be terminated during its period in suspense provided that the resolutive condition—a proper procedure under the society's rules to change the rule on dependant benefits—was followed. That would not have been a case of the contracting parties frustrating the fulfilment of the suspensive condition but rather one of them exercising a contractual entitlement in good faith.[150]

2.76 A third party right may also be future in nature, that is, subject to some time limit which is certain to occur, such as some given future date (the right becomes enforceable on 25 December 2014), or an event such as the death of a contracting party who is a natural person (even although that date is uncertain, it will occur some time). The obligation exists, but is not enforceable until the date or event in question occurs.[151] An example of the latter might be a donation of money to the third party to take effect on the death of a party who has contracted with another to make the payment required.[152] There may also be a provision about the death of the third party at a point before the right could be claimed. For example, in *Carmichael* the son's right became enforceable on his reaching the age of 21 (i.e. it was suspended rather than future, because it was not certain at the time of contracting that the son would reach the age of 21). The contract also provided that the son's death before the age of 21 would bring this suspended right to an end. If the son had died before, rather than after, he reached his majority, that resolutive condition would have prevented any right from being transmitted to his estate, which would instead have reverted to his father.

2.77 It must be recognised, however, that if the contracting parties reserve to themselves the power to change or remove altogether the third party's right in a more absolute way than is apparent in *Love*, or indeed in *Kelly* or *Carmichael*, there may well be a question as to whether they ever intended to give the third party a right at all. In his discussion of promises, Professor Hogg observes:

'[A] condition which undermines the very idea that a binding commitment was being undertaken in the first place would seem to be impermissible in the sense that it would prevent fulfilment of the requirement that a speaker must commit to a future act. Thus if the condition stipulated related to whether or not the person making the commitment still wished to perform the commitment at a future date, this would bring in to question whether any commitment was seriously being undertaken to begin with. So, for instance, the statement "I promise to pay you £100 next Monday, if I have not changed my mind by then" would not seem capable of being considered a promise because the condition attached undermines the very notion that any definite commitment has been undertaken to begin with. On the other hand, a condition which permits the promisor to revoke the promise at some future point, but is not so sweeping as to be suggestive of a lack of an original intention to be bound at all, might be argued to be a permissible condition. Thus a promise of the type "I promise to pay you £1,000 on 1st January, but I retain the power to revoke this promise should I deem the changed nature of our relationship so to warrant" might fall within the category of valid promises, albeit that a fairly wide power of revocation is retained by the promisor.'[153]

We think however that the *Love* and *Kelly* cases clearly fall within the second category of conditional promise identified by Professor Hogg. It is also arguable, we would suggest, that his first example is actually a suspended promise, ie one where the right does not exist until the Monday when the promisor has not in fact changed his mind. But the matter strikes us as above all a question of construing what is said in the contract, in order to determine whether or not a third party right is intended and to what conditions, suspensive or resolutive, the existence and enforceability of that right has been subjected by the contracting parties.

2.78 We should note finally that the authority of *Love* was questioned by the late Professor David Walker on the grounds of its inconsistency with *Carmichael* (although it ought to have been noted that the earlier decision was cited in the later without any suggestion of disapproval).[154] But Gloag, a predecessor of Professor Walker in Glasgow's Regius Chair of Law, had no difficulty with the decision,[155] and as already noted it is accepted in all the modern literature on third party rights.[156] The case has also been occasionally cited or referred to in subsequent Scottish decisions, without any suggestion of disapproval, although without any real discussion of its third party right aspects.[157] It—and *Kelly v Cornhill Insurance Company Ltd*[158]—are perhaps simply not well enough known to the legal profession in Scotland in this context.

. . .

---

[124] In the case of the incapable third party the consent may be given by the guardian or other responsible person. Note that in the case of the non-existent third party there is no right at all until the third party comes into existence or is recognised by the law as having done so.

[125] McBryde, *Contract*, para 10.06.

[126] *Carmichael v Carmichael's Ex* 1920 SC (HL) 195.

[127] Today there would be a question whether, on policy grounds, parents have an insurable interest in the life of their child: see *Insurance Contract Law: Post Contract Duties and other Issues* (Joint Consultation Paper LC CP 201; SLC DP No 152, 2011), paras 11.76-11.78 and 13.77–13.86.

[128] *Carmichael v Carmichael's Ex* 1919 SC 636 (Seven Judges), 648 (Lord Salvesen).

[129] *Carmichael v Carmichael's Ex* 1920 SC (HL) 195, 203.

[130] See MacQueen, "Third Party Rights in Contract: *Jus Quaesitum Tertio*", pp 245-250, for references. The late Lord Rodger of Earlsferry went so far as to say that Lord Dunedin had "taken leave of his senses" in his speech in *Carmichael*: see "Law for all times: the work and contribution of David Daube" [2004] 2 Roman Legal Tradition 3, 16. More charitable views of the speech are taken in McBryde, *Contract*, para 4.43 ("the substance of Lord Dunedin's approach may be more accurate than his critics have allowed") and MacQueen, "Third Party Rights in Contract: Jus Quaesitum Tertio", p 244 ("a remarkable endeavour to reconcile two seemingly irreconcilable branches of the law").
[131] *Allan's Trs v Lord Advocate* 1971 SC (HL) 45, 54.
[132] McBryde, *Contract*, para 4.36, note 82.
[133] See paras 2.11-2.12 above.
[134] McBryde, *Contract*, paras 4.34-4.38.
[135] As pointed out by McBryde, *Contract*, para 4.38; MacQueen, "Third Party Rights in Contract: Jus Quaesitum Tertio", p 245.
[136] See McBryde, *Contract*, paras 4.50-4.56 for "deeds to the family" as one of the exceptions to the requirement of delivery. The first example of "writs effectual without delivery" in Stair, *Institutions*, I, 7, 14, is "writs granted by parents in favours of their children" (although he goes on to note that for policy reasons delivery is not presumed in such cases in competition with creditors of the parents, "otherwise creditors would be most insecure by parents making large bonds of provision, which they ordinarily keep by them"). The family would of course provide one very significant context for the creation of rights in favour of the absent, the unborn and *incapaces*.

...

[141] McBryde, *Contract*, para 4.35; Huntley and Dedouli, "Third Party Rights" 332-336. See further paras 2.53-2.56 above.

...

[143] The observation here about the promise to keep an offer open is slightly puzzling. Such a promise is usually seen as making the offer irrevocable (McBryde, *Contract*, para 6.57). The offer lapses upon expiry of the period for which it was stated to be open rather than being revoked, ie it is obligatory only until a given day and time. McBryde also notes, however, that "an offer made on condition that it is accepted within three days may be withdrawn prior to the expiry of the three days" (*ibid*), citing *Heys v Kimball & Morton* (1890) 17 R 381 and *Effold Properties v Sprot* 1979 SLT (Notes) 84. It may be this to which he is referring in the quoted phrase. But the offer in such a case is not any sort of promise at all, at least according to the cited decisions.
[144] McBryde, *Contract*, paras 10.27-10.28.
[145] 1912 SC 1078, discussed by McBryde, *Contract*, para 10.31. See also *SME* Vol 15, para 830; MacQueen & Thomson, *Contract*, para 2.78.
[146] Gloag, *Contract*, p 242 notes, in contrast to *Love*, that the rule in the co-feuar cases already referred to, namely that the reservation by the feudal superior of a right to dispense with the building restrictions imposed in the feu-contracts he has granted (ie alter or revoke the contract), prevents there being any right in the co-feuars to enforce the restrictions in their own right as third parties.
[147] 1964 SC (HL) 46. Also discussed at para 2.27 above.
[148] For an example of such a revocation of a benefit provided for employees of local authorities, see *Cadoux v Central Regional Council* 1986 SLT 117.
[149] See para 2.9 above.
[150] See para 2.8 above.
[151] See para 2.6 above.
[152] See also *Fox v British Airways plc* [2013] EWCA Civ 972, in which, under a contract of employment, upon the death in service of an employee a lump sum became payable at the discretion of the employer's pension fund trustees to any member or members of one or more of various classes of beneficiary, namely: the employee's family; his dependants; any individual or individuals, charity, society or club nominated by the employee during his lifetime; and his personal representatives. These third party benefits were all contingent on the employee's death while still in the employer's service. The interposition of the trust between the contract and the third party benefit probably means that this would not have been a case of JQT in Scots law (see *Allan's Trs v Lord Advocate* 1971 SC (HL) 45), while in England & Wales the 1999 Act does not apply to contracts of employment ...

[153] M Hogg, *Promises and Contract* Law, pp 33-34.
[154] D M Walker, *The Law of Contracts and Related Obligations in Scotland* (3rd edn, 1995), para 29.14; *Carmichael v Carmichael's Ex* 1920 SC (HL) 195, 197.
[155] Gloag, *Contract*, pp 242-243.
[156] See para 2.72 above.
[157] See also *McDowall v McGhee* 1913 2 SLT 238; *Muir v Associated Iron Moulders of Scotland* 1914 2 SLT 463 (Glasgow Sheriff Court); *Alderwick v Craig* 1916 2 SLT 161; *McLaren v National Union of Dock Labourers & Riverside Workers in Great Britain & Ireland* 1918 SC 834; *Aberdeen, Banff, and Moray Master Slaters' Association v Dickie & Son* 1925 SLT (Sh Ct) 59; *Mercedes-Benz Finance Ltd v Clydesdale Bank Plc* 1997 SLT 905. In several of these cases *Love* was cited only in argument and not by the court itself; and most of the early references are in connection with the then law relating to trade unions.
[158] 1964 SC (HL) 46. Also discussed at paras 2.27 and 2.73 above.

11–24 These extracts show that the law on third party rights in contract is in several respects unclear and in some instances confused. The more recent cases referred to in the extracts from the Commission's Discussion Paper suggest that this is a matter of commercial concern and therefore ripe for reform. One possibility would be to adopt a scheme such as that proposed in the DCFR, which provides:

11–25 **"Effect of stipulation in favour of a third party**

II.–9:301: Basic rules

(1) The parties to a contract may, by the contract, confer a right or other benefit on a third party. The third party need not be in existence or identified at the time the contract is concluded.
(2) The nature and content of the third party's right or benefit are determined by the contract and are subject to any conditions or other limitations under the contract.
(3) The benefit conferred may take the form of an exclusion or limitation of the third party's liability to one of the contracting parties.

II.–9:302: Rights, remedies and defences

Where one of the contracting parties is bound to render a performance to the third party under the contract, then, in the absence of provision to the contrary in the contract:

(a) the third party has the same rights to performance and remedies for non-performance as if the contracting party was bound to render the performance under a binding unilateral undertaking in favour of the third party; and
(b) the contracting party may assert against the third party all defences which the contracting party could assert against the other party to the contract."

The Scottish Law Commission, however, has outlined a detailed scheme for reform and indicates an initial preference for a statutory restatement like the English Contracts (Rights of Third Parties) Act 1999.

Third Party Rights in Scotland 11–26

Scottish Law Commission Discussion Paper No.157 (March 2014)

"Chapter 9 Overview of Suggestions for Reform

9.1 In this concluding Chapter we offer a brief overview of the model of third party rights in contract which would be produced if the provisional proposals made in the preceding chapters were implemented. We also seek views on the best general approach to take.

9.2 As at present, it would be possible for contracting parties to create by way of their contract a right (but not a duty)[1] for a third party or parties. The third party would have to be identified in or identifiable from the express terms of the contract,[2] but need not be in existence at the time the contract is formed.[3] There is no requirement that the third party accept the right,[4] or that the contract be in writing.[5]

9.3 The intention of the contracting parties to confer a right, as distinct from the third party having an interest in or being benefited by the performance of the contract, may be expressed in or implied from the contract.[6] The third party right may co-exist with the rights of the contracting parties between themselves.[7] The contracting parties may make clear by express provision that they intend no third party right to arise from their contract,[8] or exclude or limit liabilities to the third party which might otherwise arise, the latter always being subject to the applicability of the unfair contract terms legislation.[9]

9.4 The third party's right may be to claim payment or other performance from one or more of the contracting parties, but can also take the form of an immunity against a claim by one or more of the contracting parties.[10] The right may be future in nature (that is, dependent upon the occurrence of an event that is certain to happen) or conditional (that is, dependent for its existence or enforceability upon an uncertain future event, which may also be one within the power of the parties to bring about).[11]

9.5 The third party can be a particular person, or a person meeting certain conditions laid down in the contract such as coming into existence, some other event in the person's life (e.g. attainment of majority, marriage, entry into university), membership of a class of persons, or later nomination or authorisation by one or more of the contracting parties.[12]

9.6 We leave open as a question for consultees the possibility that a third party may be identified or identifiable from sources other than the contract and that an intention to confer a right upon the third party might be implied in all the circumstances;[13] but we suggest that this could take the law of third party rights in contract into the territory of delict, with possible uncertainty then resulting.[14]

9.7 Contrary to the standard view of the present law,[15] it would not be necessary for contracting parties wishing to create a third party right to take steps to make the third party right irrevocable from the outset.[16] They would instead be free to make provision in their contract for the cancellation or variation of the third party's right, and to exercise those powers at any time prior to the crystallisation of the third party's right.[17]

9.8 Contracting parties are also free to make the third party right irrevocable or unmodifiable by provision in their contract should they so wish. They will be bound by that contractual provision at least where there has been delivery, intimation or other communication of the contract to the third party.[18]

9.9 If the third party's right is dependent upon the fulfilment of conditions,[19] and this happens before any cancellation or alteration is made to it by the contracting parties, then the latter lose their freedom to revoke or vary the right.[20] The same result follows if the contracting parties subsequently promise not to exercise their entitlements under the contract,[21] or if they make representations to the third party that they will not do so, upon which the third party then acts in detrimental reliance.[22]

9.10 An open question for consultees is whether the law should go further than this in protecting the third party from the contracting parties' power to revoke or alter its right when the contract makes no provision on the matter one way or another. The following specific possibilities on when the right might become unalterable are canvassed:

- delivery of the contract or its relevant terms to the third party (subject to an entitlement of the contracting parties to reserve the power to change or cancel the right);[23]
- intimation of the contract or its relevant terms to the third party (subject to an entitlement of the contracting parties to reserve the power to change or cancel the right);[24]
- registration of the contract, whether for preservation only or also for execution;[25]
- detrimental reliance of the third party based upon informally acquired knowledge of its right, the form of reliance required being perhaps modelled upon the statutory *rei interventus* familiar from section 1(3) and (4) of the Requirements of Writing (Scotland) Act 1995;[26]
- death of the third party;[27]
- assignation of its right by the third party;[28]
- formation of a trust over its right by the third party.[29]

9.11 We do not think, however, that the third party's informally acquired knowledge of the existence of a contractual provision purporting to create a right for it should be enough to deprive the contracting parties of the power to change their minds on either the existence or the content of that right.[30]

. . .

9.13 Whether or not it has crystallised . . . , the third party right may be renounced or rejected by the third party expressly or impliedly. Since no acceptance by the third party is required in the constitution of the right,[31] mere passivity by the third party in response to the prospect or tender of a benefit from or by the contracting parties is not enough for such renunciation to be implied.[32]

9.14 The third party has available in principle all the usual remedies by means of which any personal right can be enforced,[33] and also the remedy of rectification of the contract.[34] Where one of the contracting parties has the primary duty of performance to the third party, but is disabled from fulfilling it through a default by the other contracting party, the third party might perhaps have an appropriate remedy against the defaulter;[35] this however is a question which we regard as an open one for consultees' advice. Otherwise there is no need for the third party to involve in the enforcement process any party other than those with the primary responsibility to perform under the right in question.

9.15 The defences available to the contracting parties against the third party include those which may arise from the invalidity, illegality or frustration of the contract insofar as these may impact upon the third party right.[36] Compensation (or 'set off') may be available to the contracting parties against the third party's claim.[37] The third party's right is in general subject to the short negative prescription of five years, although in some cases it may be subject to the long negative prescription.[38]

9.16 We think that this scheme of reform would produce a law of third party rights in contract very much in line with the international standards described in the quotation from Professor Vogenauer given in the first chapter.[39] It would meet what we have identified as the needs of business in this area, while also providing a means by which private individuals may choose to do good and confer legally enforceable benefits upon others, especially those in need of the support of others such as minors or adults with incapacity. Moreover, it might provide a means by which the courts could find just solutions in complex situations.

9.17 As a final issue, we would be grateful for views on what we see as two alternative methods of enacting whatever policy goals are recommended after consultation. In broad terms, the legislation could either set out a comprehensive statement of the new law on third party rights, which would entirely replace the common law, or alternatively it could leave the common law in place except for certain specific reforms, such as the removal of the requirement of irrevocability.[40] The first approach is, in essence, that adopted by the 1999 Act.[41] It is at present our favoured option in this exercise, on the grounds that it is better to set out a reasonably clear overall statement of the law rather than wait for it to be filled in by decisions of the courts. This should provide the sort of certainty which practitioners in particular look for from the law in preparing transactions and drafting their documentation. We think however that it might not be necessary to go into full detail on every point, especially those referred to in Chapter 7, and in particular those dealing with the topics of remedies and defences ... "

---

[1] See para 2.23.
[2] See paras 2.26, 2.35-2.37, 3.11-3.18, 5.3-5.8.
[3] See paras 2.29-2.32, 3.9, 5.9-5.10.
[4] See paras 2.16, 2.50-2.52, 6.20.
[5] See paras 2.53-2.56, 4.14-4.15.
[6] See paras 2.38-2.49, 3.11-3.18, 3.37-3.47, 5.16-5.21.
[7] See paras 2.80,7.34-7.35.
[8] See para 3.32, 7.28-7.30.
[9] See paras 2.85, 7.28-7.30.
[10] See paras 2.24-2.25, 4.6, 5.22-5.25.
[11] See paras 2.6-2.9, 4.19-4.20
[12] See paras 2.26-2.32, 3.11-3.18, 5.3-5.15.
[13] See paras 2.35-2.36, 2.43-2.47, 3.37-3.47, 5.12-5.15. 14 See paras 2.37.
[15] See paras 2.57-2.78, paras 3.1-3.5.
[16] See paras 6.1-6.6.
[17] See paras 6.6-6.9.
[18] See paras 6.10-6.11.
[19] See paras 2.6-2.9, 4.19-4.20.
[20] See paras 6.7-6.9.
[21] See para 6.18.
[22] See paras 6.16-6.17.
[23] See paras 2.61, 6.21.
[24] See paras 2.61, 6.21.
[25] See paras 2.61, 6.23.
[26] See paras 2.61, 6.24-6.27.
[27] See para 6.31.
[28] See paras 2.81, 6.32-6.37.
[29] See para 6.38.
[30] See paras 2.61, 6.28-6.30.
[31] See paras 2.16, 2.50-2.52, 6.20.
[32] See paras 2.79, 7.2-7.8.
[33] See paras 2.84-2.85, 7.9-7.13.
[34] See para 7.14.
[35] See para 7.27.
[36] See paras 2.82-2.83, 7.15-7.19.
[37] See paras 7.20-7.24.
[38] See paras 2.86-2.89, 7.26.
[39] See para 1.17 above.
[40] See paras 2.57-2.78 and ch 6 above.

[41] Though the comparison cannot be pushed too far, as it was enacted against the background of common law rules on privity of contract, which differs fundamentally from the current Scots common law of JQT."

Termination by frustration

11–27 In certain circumstances, events subsequent to the making of the contract may affect it so that performance is impossible. The contract is then deemed to be "frustrated"; and the parties are discharged from performing their obligations. It is important to differentiate here cases of error about the existence of the subject matter, and of existing illegality upon a contract. Such events are not supervening or frustrating events as they precede the making of the contract. We are here dealing with situations where a contract has arisen, but is rendered impossible to perform by an event beyond the parties' control and contemplation. If, for example, the goods which are the subject matter of the contract should perish before it was made, or if the contract was to commit an illegal act, no valid or enforceable contract arises. If, however, the subject matter should perish after the contract is made, but before performance, or if the performance of the contract should subsequently become illegal, the contract may be frustrated.

What, then, is the theoretical basis of the concept?[19]

11–28 **Davis Contractors Ltd v Fareham Urban District Council**
[1956] A.C. 696
House of Lords: Viscount Simonds, Lords Morton of Henryton, Reid, Radcliffe and Somervell of Harrow

In March 1946, Davis tendered to build 78 houses for the council within a period of eight months. The tender was "subject to adequate supplies of material and labour being available as and when required to carry out the work within the time specified". In July 1946, a formal contract was entered into to build the house at a fixed price subject to certain adjustments. The phrase about "adequate supplies of material and labour" was not included. Primarily because of the lack of skilled labour, the work took 22 months. Davis was paid the contract price together with stipulated increases and adjustments. They claimed a quantum meruit for the extra expenditure during the remaining 14 months, partly on the ground that owing to the long delay due to the scarcity of labour the contract had been frustrated.

The House rejected the claim.

11–29 "LORD REID: ... I think it is necessary to consider what is the true basis of the law of frustration. Generally, this has not been necessary; for example, Lord Porter said in *Denny, Mott & Dickson Ltd v James B Fraser & Co Ltd* [1944] 1 All E.R. 678 (at p. 678): 'Whether this result follows from a true construction of the contract or whether it is necessary to imply a term or whether again it is more accurate to say that the result follows because the basis of the contract is overthrown, it is not necessary to decide ... ' These are the three grounds of frustration which have been suggested from time to time, and I think that it may make a difference in two respects which is chosen. Construction of a contract and the implication of a term are questions of law, whereas the question whether the basis of a contract is overthrown, if not dependent on the construction of

[19] For analysis of the contending theories, see WW McBryde, *The Law of Contract in Scotland*, 3rd edn (Edinburgh: W. Green, 2007), paras 21–05—21–08. For the implied resolutive condition as the basis of frustration, see HL MacQueen and J Thomson, *Contract Law in Scotland*, 3rd edn (London: Bloomsbury, 2012), para.4.71.

the contract, might seem to be largely a matter for the judgment of a skilled man comparing what was contemplated with what has happened. And, if the question is truly one of construction, I find it difficult to see why we should not apply the ordinary rules regarding the admissibility of extrinsic evidence whereas, if it is only a matter of comparing the contemplated with the actual position, evidence might be admissible on a wider basis. Further, I am not satisfied that the result is necessarily the same whether frustration is regarded as depending on the addition to the contract of an implied term or as depending on the construction of the contract as it stands.

Frustration has often been said to depend on adding a term to the contract by implication: for example, Earl Loreburn in *FA Tamplin SS Co Ltd v Anglo-Mexican Petroleum Products Co Ltd* [1916] 2 A.C. 397, 404, after quoting language of Lord Blackburn, said:

'That seems to me another way of saying that from the nature of the contract it cannot be supposed the parties, as reasonable men, intended it to be binding on them under such altered conditions. Were the altered conditions such that, had they thought of them, they would have taken their chance of them, or such that as sensible men they would have said "if that happens, of course, it is all over between us"? What, in fact, was the true meaning of the contract? Since the parties have not provided for the contingency, ought a court to say it is obvious they would have treated the thing as at an end?'

I find great difficulty in accepting this as the correct approach, because it seems to me hard to account for certain decisions of this House in this way. I cannot think that a reasonable man in the position of the seaman in *Horlock v Beal* [1916] 1 A.C. 486 would readily have agreed that the wages payable to his wife should stop if his ship was caught in Germany at the outbreak of war, and I doubt whether the charterers in *Bank Line Ltd v A Capel & Co* [1919] A.C 435 could have been said to be unreasonable if they had refused to agree to a term that the contract was to come to an end in the circumstances which occurred. These are not the only cases where I think it would be difficult to say that a reasonable man in the position of the party who opposes unsuccessfully a finding of frustration would certainly have agreed to an implied term bringing it about.

I may be allowed to note an example of the artificiality of the theory of an implied term given by Lord Sands in *Scott & Sons v Del Sel*, 1922 S.C. 592, 597:

'A tiger has escaped from a travelling menagerie. The milkgirl fails to deliver the milk. Possibly the milkman may be exonerated from any breach of contract; but, even so, it would seem hardly reasonable to base that exoneration on the ground that "tiger days excepted" must be held as if written into the milk contract.'

I think that there is much force in Lord Wright's criticism in *Denny, Mott & Dickson* at p. 683:

'The parties did not anticipate fully and completely, if at all, or provide for what actually happened. It is not possible to my mind to say that, if they had thought of it, they would have said, "Well, if that happens, all is over between us." On the contrary, they would almost certainly on the one side or the other have sought to introduce reservations or qualifications or compensations.'

It appears to me that frustration depends, at least in most cases, not on adding any implied term but on the true construction of the terms which are, in the contract, read in light of the nature of the contract and of the relevant surrounding circumstances when the contract was made. There is much authority for this view ... On this view, there is no need to consider what the parties thought, or how they or reasonable men in their shoes would have dealt with the new situation if they had foreseen it. The question is whether the contract which they did make is, on its true construction, wide enough to apply to the new situation: if it is not, then it is at an end ...

In a contract of this kind, the contractor undertakes to do the work for a definite sum, and he takes the risk of the cost being greater or less than he expected. If delays occur through no one's fault, that may be in the contemplation of the contract and there may be provision for extra time being given. To that extent, the other party takes the risk of delay. But he does not take the risk of the cost being increased by such delay. It may be that delay could be of a character so different from anything contemplated that the contract was at an end, but in this case, in my opinion, the most that could be said is that the delay was greater in degree than was to be expected. It was not caused by any new and unforeseeable factor or event; the job proved to be more onerous but it never became a job of a different kind from that contemplated in the contract.

11–30 LORD RADCLIFFE: ... By this time it might seem that the parties themselves have become so far disembodied spirits that their actual persons should be allowed to rest in peace. In their place there rises the figure of the fair and reasonable man. And the spokesman of the fair and reasonable man, who represents after all no more than the anthropomorphic conception of justice, is and must be the court itself. So perhaps it would be simpler to say at the outset that frustration occurs whenever the law recognises that without default of either party a contractual obligation has become incapable of being performed because the circumstances in which performance is called for would render it a thing radically different from that which was undertaken by the contract. *Non haec in foedera veni.* It was not this that I promised to do ...

The court must act upon a general impression of what its rule requires. It is for that reason that special importance is necessarily attached to the occurrence of any unexpected event that, as it were, changes the face of things. But, even so, it is not hardship or inconvenience or material loss itself which call the principle of frustration into play. There must be as well such a change in the significance of the obligation that the thing undertaken would, if performed, be a different thing from that contracted for ...

Two things seem to me to prevent the application of the principle of frustration to this case. One is that the cause of the delay was not any new state of things which the parties could not reasonably be thought to have foreseen. On the contrary, the possibility of enough labour and materials not being available was before their eyes and could have been the subject of special contractual stipulation. It was not made so. The other thing is that, though timely completion was, no doubt, important to both sides, it is not right to treat the possibility of delay as having the same significance for each. The owner draws up his conditions in detail, specifies the time within which he requires completion, protects himself both by a penalty clause for time exceeded and by calling for the deposit of a guarantee bond, and offers a certain measure of security to a contractor by his escalator clause with regard to wages and prices. In the light of these conditions the contractor makes his tender, and the tender must necessarily take into account the margin of profit that he hopes to obtain on his adventure, and in that any appropriate allowance for the obvious risks of delay. To my mind, it is useless to pretend that the contractor is not at risk if delay does occur, even serious delay. And I think it a misuse of legal terms to call in frustration to get him out of his unfortunate predicament."

What emerges from the speeches is that merely because a contract has become more onerous to perform, it has not been frustrated. The key issue is *impossibility*. In *Tsakiroglou & Co Ltd v Noblee & Thorl GmbH*,[20] sellers of groundnuts in Sudan failed to ship the consignment for Hamburg as agreed because of the sudden closure of the Suez Canal during the Suez Crisis in November 1956. This, the House of Lords held, was a breach of the contract. Performance had become more onerous, in that the goods would have to be shipped via the Cape of Good Hope, leading only to some four weeks' delay and slightly greater expense.

It may become impossible to perform the contract because of a supervening event. For

[20] *Tsakiroglou & Co Ltd v Noblee & Thorl GmbH* [1962] A.C. 93.

example, the subject matter of the contract may have perished before performance is due. Such are cases of *rei interitus* (destruction of the subject matter). It is often difficult to establish when, or if such subject-matter "perished".

Tay Salmon Fisheries Co Ltd v Speedie 11–31
1929 S.C. 593
Court of Session, First Division: The Lord President (Clyde), Lords Blackburn, Morrison and Sands

Tay were tenants of salmon fishings under a 1916 lease for 19 seasons. In 1925 and 1928, under bye-laws made under statutory powers, the Air Force took over—for target practice—the land on which the fishings were situated. Observance of the bye-laws would render the fishings incapable of possession for the purposes of the lease, even though target practice was only sporadically carried out.

Tay successfully sought declarator that they were entitled to abandon the lease.

"LORD PRESIDENT (CLYDE): ... The case resembles that of *rei interitus*—as when lands, the subject of an agricultural lease, are overblown with sand so as to prevent the exercise of the arts of cultivation on them—*Lindsay v Home* (1612) Mor. 10120; or when a house is rendered incapable of being used for habitation by fire—*Duff v Fleming* (1870) 8 M. 768; or by vermin which cannot be easily exterminated—*Kippen v Oppenheim* (1847) 10 D. 242. But the difficulty of applying the principle of *rei interitus* to the present case is that the trouble arises, not from any defect in the subject itself, but from the interference of a third party, under statutory powers, with the possession of the subject. 11–32

It was sought to bring the case under the principle on which the decision in *Metropolitan Water Board v Dick, Kerr & Co* proceeded, namely that the interference resulting from the bye-laws was such as to make the contract of lease a different contract from what it originally was, and so to bring it to an end. But I doubt if that principle, which is highly appropriate to the application of an executory contract, is germane to a grant of land (and in law a salmon fishery is land) in lease. The point in the present case is not that the original lease has become a different lease, but that the possession secured by the lease cannot any longer be enjoyed.

Nor do I think it would be accurate to say that the tenants are entitled to abandon their lease merely on the general principle of mutual contract, whereby performance of the obligations of one party (the lessees) cannot be insisted on when the obligations of the other (the lessor) are not performed. For, although no doubt a lease is a mutual contract with obligations on both sides, the rights of a dispossessed tenant truly depend on the special character of the lessor's obligation of warrandice ...

The argument was pressed upon us that, if the eviction is the result of supervenient legislation, no recourse is possible against the lessor under his warrandice—*Holliday v Scott* (1830) 8 S. 831, *Goldie v Williamson Hume's Dec.*

793. It is undoubtedly the case that the bye-laws, and also the Act giving the Air Force power to make them, were subsequent to the date of the lease in the present case. But I do not think this principle is capable of application by circumstances in which the effect of the supervening legislation is to create a complete eviction from the subject let. Neither by Stair (Inst., II.iii.46), nor by Erskine (Inst., II.iii.29), is the principle applied to complete evictions, but only to burdens imposed on the subject by supervenient legislation. So long as the eviction which results from the supervenient legislation is partial, and not such as completely to destroy the tenants possession, it may well be that it infers no recourse against the lessor under the warrandice, and both parties may justly

be said to have taken their chance. But if it is such as totally to destroy the tenant's enjoyment of the subject beyond any reasonable immediate possibility of restoration, the obligations of warrandice cannot but result in a liberation of the tenant from the bonds of the lease; for, as it turns out, the lessor has warranted the tenant in a possession in which he is unable to maintain him in any extent."

11–33 Similarly, if a contract involves *delectus personae*, the contract may be frustrated by the illness of one of the parties. The illness must be such that it prevents performance. A throat infection lasting but a few days may frustrate an opera singer's performance,[21] whereas even prolonged illness, involving several operations, would not frustrate a shipyard fitter's contract of employment.[22]

Other supervening events, if they have serious effects on performance, may frustrate a contract with *delectus personae*, e.g. conscription into the army,[23] or imprisonment.[24]

Changes in the law may render performance of the contract illegal; e.g. refusal of an export licence. A common occurrence is the requisition of merchant vessels in time of war. Whether the illegality frustrates the contract depends upon the duration of the illegality and the amount of the contract yet to be performed.

11–34

Denny, Mott & Dickson Ltd v Fraser & Co Ltd

1944 S.C. (H.L.) 35

House of Lords: Viscount Simon L.C., Lords Macmillan, Thankerton, Porter and Wright

Under a contract made in 1929, Fraser agreed to buy all their timber from Denny and to lease to them a timber yard, together with an option to buy or take a long lease on the timber yard. The contract provided for termination by notice. By an Order made in 1939 under emergency statutory war powers, it became illegal for the parties to continue trading in timber. In 1941, Denny purported to terminate the agreement and gave notice of their intention to exercise their option to buy the yard. Fraser successfully contended that this was no longer possible, since the contract had already been frustrated.

11–35 "LORD MACMILLAN: . . . The principle of contract law which has come to be known as the doctrine of frustration and which has recently in England been accorded statutory recognition, is common to the jurisprudence alike of Scotland and of England, although the leading cases are to be found in the English reports. It is a principle so inherently just as inevitably to find a place in any civilised system of law. The manner in which it has developed in order to meet problems arising from the disturbance of business due to world wars is a tribute to the progressive adaptability of the common law . . . The earlier cases both in England and in Scotland are mostly concerned with the consequences of the perishing of the thing on whose continued existence the contract depended for its fulfilment, but many of the recent cases have arisen from the supervention of emergency legislation rendering the implement of the contract illegal. It is plain that a contract to do what has become illegal to do cannot be legally enforceable. There cannot be default in not doing what the law forbids to be done.

The present case belongs to the latter category. It seems to me to be a very clear one for the application of the principle I have just enunciated. Here is an agreement between

---

[21] *Poussard v Spiers* (1876) 1 Q.B.D. 410.

[22] *Marshall v Harland & Wolff Ltd* (1972) 1 W.L.R. 899.

[23] *Morgan v Manser* [1948] 1 K.B. 84.

[24] *Hare v Murphy Bros* [1974] 3 All E.R. 940.

two parties for carrying on dealings in imported timber. By emergency legislation the importation of timber has been rendered illegal. Neither party can be said to be in default. The further fulfilment of their mutual obligations has been brought to an abrupt stop by an irresistible extraneous cause for which neither party is responsible. But it has been suggested, and the Lord Ordinary and Lord Jamieson have taken the view, that one of the stipulations of the contract is severable from the rest and remains enforceable, inasmuch as its fulfilment would involve no illegality. This contention is, in my opinion, untenable. It is true that the respondents could, without infringing the emergency legislation, sell or let their Grangemouth timber yard to the appellants on the terms stated in the agreement, but the right to require such a sale or lease is conferred on the appellants only as a consequence of one or other of the parties having voluntarily taken advantage of the right to terminate the agreement on notice. The operation of the agreement having been compulsorily terminated, neither party can thereafter terminate it voluntarily. You cannot slay the slain.

I would only add that, in judging whether a contract has been frustrated, the contract must be looked at as a whole. The question is whether its purpose as gathered from its terms has been defeated. A contract whose purpose has been defeated may contain subsidiary stipulations which it would still be possible and lawful to fulfil, but to segregate and enforce such a stipulation would be to do something which the parties never intended."

As with supervening impossibility, if the change in law merely makes the contract more onerous to perform, there is no frustration.

Where the event which is the object of contract has not occurred

There are many cases, beyond supervening impossibility or illegality as described above, **11–36** where the courts have found the contract frustrated by an external event which renders performance fundamentally different from that originally contemplated. Two contrasting English cases resulting from the postponement due to illness of Edward VII's coronation illustrate the point. In *Krell v Henry*,[25] a contract to hire a room along the coronation procession route was frustrated, as the purpose of the hire (to view the procession) was destroyed; but in *Herne Bay Steamboat Co v Hutton*,[26] a contract to hire a steamer to view the Royal Naval Fleet was not frustrated merely because the royal party would not be present: the contractual purpose, to see the fleet, was still possible. It is doubtful whether the doctrine applies to long-term leases. The reasoning behind this is best illustrated by the following case which, although founded on English property law, is nevertheless relevant to the position in Scotland.

[25] *Krell v Henry* [1903] 2 K.B. 740.

[26] *Herne Bay Steamboat Co v Hutton* [1903] 2 K.B. 683.

11–37

National Carriers Ltd v Panalpina (Northern) Ltd
[1981] A.C. 675
English House of Lords: Lord Hailsham of Marylebone LC, Lords Roskill, Russell, Simon and Wilberforce

National leased a warehouse from Panalpina for 10 years from 1 January 1974 at an annual rent of £6,500 for the first five years and £13,300 for the second five years. In May 1979 the local authority closed the street giving the only access to the warehouse because of the dangerous condition of a building opposite the warehouse. As a "listed" building of special architectural or historical interest the local authority required the consent of the Secretary of State to demolish it. The Secretary of State gave his consent in March 1980, and it was envisaged by the local authority that the demolition would be completed and the street reopened in January 1981. The closure of the street prevented National from using the premises as a warehouse—the only purpose contemplated by the lease—and from May 1979 they stopped paying rent. In July 1979 Panalpina brought an action against National claiming payment of two quarterly instalments due under the lease.

The House found that although the doctrine of frustration applied to the contract, the contract was not frustrated on its facts.

11–38 "LORD SIMON OF GLAISDALE: . . . Frustration of a contract takes place when there supervenes an event (without default of either party and for which the contract makes no sufficient provision) which so significantly changes the nature (not merely the expense or onerousness) of the outstanding contractual rights and/or obligations from what the parties could reasonably have contemplated at the time of its execution that it would be unjust to hold them to the literal sense of its stipulations in the new circumstances; in such case the law declares both parties to be discharged from further performance.

Whether the doctrine can apply to a lease is of more than academic interest, considerable though that is. In the *Cricklewood Property* case [1945] A.C. 221, 229 Viscount Simon L.C., who favoured the extension of the doctrine to leaseholds, nevertheless considered it likely to be limited to cases where 'some vast convulsion of nature swallowed up the property altogether, or buried it in the depths of the sea.' But I think this puts the matter too catastrophically, even in the case of a long lease. There are several places on the coast of England where sea erosion has undermined a cliff causing property on the top of the cliff to be totally lost for occupation; obviously occupation of a dwelling-house is something significantly different in nature from its aqualung contemplation after it has suffered a sea-change. And in the case of a short lease something other than such natural disaster (the sort of occurrence, for example, that has been held to be the frustrating event in a charterparty) might in practice have a similar effect on parties to a lease. Take the case of a demise-chartered oil tanker lying alongside an oil storage tank leased for a similar term, and an explosion destroying both together.

The question is entirely open in your Lordships' House, as was recognised in the *Cricklewood Property* case. In my view a lease is not inherently unsusceptible to the application of the doctrine of frustration.

In the first place, the doctrine has been developed by the law as an expedient to escape from injustice where such would result from enforcement of a contract in its literal terms after a significant change in circumstances. As Lord Sumner said, giving the opinion of a strong Privy Council in *Hirji Mulji v Cheong Yue Steamship Co Ltd* [1926] A.C. 497, 510: 'It is really a device, by which the rules as to absolute contracts are reconciled with a special exception which justice demands.' Justice might make a similar demand as to the absolute terms of a lease.

Secondly, in the words of Lord Wright in the *Cricklewood Property* case, at p. 241: 'The doctrine of frustration is modern and flexible and is not subject to being constricted by an arbitrary formula.' It is therefore on the face of it apt to vindicate justice wherever owing to relevant supervening circumstances the enforcement of any contractual arrangement in its literal terms would produce injustice.

Thirdly, the law should if possible be founded on comprehensive principles: compartmentalism, particularly if producing anomaly, leads to the injustice of different results in fundamentally analogous circumstances. To deny the extension of the doctrine of frustration to leaseholds produces a number of undesirable anomalies.

Fourthly, a number of theories have been advanced to clothe the doctrine of frustration in juristic respectability, the two most in favour being the 'implied term theory' (which was potent in the development of the doctrine and which still provides a satisfactory explanation of many cases) and the 'theory of a radical change in obligation' or 'construction theory' (which appears to be the one most generally accepted today) ... Of all the theories put forward the only one, I think, incompatible with the application of the doctrine to a lease is that which explains it as based on a total failure of consideration. Though such may be a feature of some cases of frustration, it is plainly inadequate as an exhaustive explanation: there are many cases of frustration where the contract has been partly executed...

Fifthly, a lease may be prematurely determined in a considerable variety of circumstances. I can see no reason why a rule of law should not ... declare that a lease is automatically discharged on the happening of a frustrating event.

Sixthly, it seems that authorities in some other common law jurisdictions have felt no inherent difficulty in applying the doctrine of frustration to a lease. This appears especially in the American cases on the frustration of leases of premises to sell liquor by the advent of constitutional Prohibition (see *Corbin, Contracts*, Vol. 6, pp. 336 *et seq.* for a general discussion and pp. 388–390 for a discussion of the prohibition cases in particular). *Corbin's* summary at p. 391 has relevance to such a lease as is under your Lordships' instant consideration:

'If there was one principal use contemplated by the lessee, known to the lessor, and one that played a large part in fixing rental value, a governmental prohibition or prevention of that use has been held to discharge the lessee from his duty to pay the rent. It is otherwise if other substantial uses, permitted by the lease and in the contemplation of the parties, remain possible to the lessee.' I therefore turn to consider the arguments to the contrary ... The arguments are, I think, fourfold.

1. The lease itself is the 'venture' or 'undertaking' on which the parties have embarked. In so far as the lease is contractual, the 'foundation' of the contract is the transfer of the landlord's possession of the demised property for a term of years in return for rent; that happens once and for all on the execution of the lease; so that its contractual 'foundation' is never destroyed.
2. The lease is more than a contract: it creates a legal estate or interest in land; and, added counsel for the respondents, it operates *in rem*.
3. The contractual obligations in a lease are merely incidental to the relationship of landlord and tenant.
4. On the conveyance the 'risk' of unforeseen events passes to the lessee, as it does to the purchaser of land.

I presume to think that the third proposition adds nothing to the first two, from which it necessarily follows if they are valid. As for the lease itself being the 'venture' or 'undertaking' the same might be said of a licence or of a demise charter. So, too, it may be said that the 'foundation' of a demise charter is that the shipowner parts with his possession of the demised property for a term of years in return for hire. In truth, 'venture', 'undertaking' and 'foundation' are picturesque or metaphorical terms; though useful in illuminating the doctrine, they are too vague to be safe for juristic analysis. The real questions, in my respectful submission, are the second and fourth, namely, whether the fact that a legal estate or interest in land has been created makes a lease inherently unsusceptible of the application of the doctrine of frustration, and that the risk of what might otherwise be a frustrating event passes irrevocably to the lessee on execution of the lease.

As for the significance of the creation of a legal estate or interest in land ... I cite *Denny, Mott & Dickson Ltd v James B Fraser & Co Ltd* [1944] A.C. 265 with some hesitation, since your Lordships did not have the benefit of adversary argument on it. But it was a case where both a contract to grant a lease (which may have operated as a lease) and an option to purchase land were held to be frustrated. It is true that they were part of a larger agreement including trading arrangements which had been frustrated; but I do not think that this can affect the force of the decision as regards the frustration of the contract for a lease (or the lease) and of the option. It is also true that it was a Scottish appeal; but Lord Macmillan stated that the incidence of the Scots doctrine of frustration was the same as the English (though the consequences might be different); and none of their Lordships indicated that the decision depended on any peculiar rule of Scots land law ...

In a lease, as in a licence or a demise charter, the length of the unexpired term will be a potent factor. So too, as the American cases show, will be any stipulations about, particularly restrictions on, user. In the instant case the lease was for a short term, and had only about four and a half years to run at the time of the alleged frustrating event, the closure of Kingston Street. The demised premises were a purpose-built warehouse, and both parties contemplated its use as a warehouse throughout the term. This use, in Corbin's words (*Contracts*, Vol. 6, p. 391), 'played a large part in fixing rental value,' as the rent review clause shows. After the closure of Kingston Street it could no longer be used as a warehouse. No 'other substantial use, permitted by the lease and in the contemplation of the parties,' remained possible to the lessee.

Therefore, although I do not think that there is any definable class of lease which is specifically susceptible of frustration, the facts of the case as I have summarised them in the previous paragraph indicates that this lease is very much the sort that might be frustrated in the circumstances that have occurred.

The question therefore arises whether the appellants have demonstrated a triable issue that the lease has been frustrated. The matter must be considered as it appeared at the time when the frustrating event is alleged to have happened. Commercial men must be entitled to act on reasonable commercial probabilities at the time when they are called on to make up their minds (Scrutton J. in *Embiricos v Sydney Reid & Co* [1914] 3 K.B. 45, 54). What we know has in fact happened is, however, available as an aid to determine the reasonable probabilities at the time when decision was called for (Lord Wright in *Denny, Mott & Dickson Ltd v James B Fraser & Co Ltd.* [1944] A.C. 265, 277, 278) ...

Weighing all the relevant factors, I do not think that the appellants have demonstrated a triable issue that the closure of the road so significantly changed the nature of the outstanding rights and obligation under the lease from what the parties could reasonably have contemplated at the time of its execution that it would he unjust to hold them to the literal sense of its stipulations."

11–39 An event that frustrates a contract, must be external to that contract. In this case, the potentially frustrating event was that of the local authority. If the event was brought about by the act of one party, i.e. if it was "self-induced," the contract is not frustrated. What if, for example, a developer contracts to carry out works for a landowner, but fails to complete them because planning permission was refused, because the developer failed to apply in time for the necessary planning consents? In *Maritime National Fish Ltd v Ocean Trawlers Ltd*,[27] Ocean Trawlers Ltd chartered five vessels from MNF, but were only granted three trawling licences. They allotted the licences to other trawlers in their fleet and claimed frustration. This was rejected by the Privy Council, because the so-called frustrating event (the failure to obtain licences) was not external to the contract (the act of a government agency), but the result of Ocean Trawlers Ltd's voluntary act.

Not every act of volition may be considered "self-induced". In *Constantine Steamship Line Ltd v Imperial Smelting Corporation Ltd*,[28] a boiler explosion aboard ship frustrated the contract, although allegedly caused by the shipowner's negligence. As Lord Russell of Killowen said in that case:

> "The possible varieties [of fault] are infinite, and can range from the criminality of the scuttler who opens the sea-cocks and sinks his ship, to the thoughtlessness of the prima donna who sits in a draught and loses her voice."[29]

It is also possible that the parties may both have foreseen the frustrating event and made express provision for its effects in the contract.

Effects of frustration

As a rule, frustration terminates the contract and discharges the parties upon the happening of the frustrating event. Until then, the contract subsists, and rights and obligations arise under it. From that point, neither party is under obligation to perform and no action for breach of contract arises. **11–40**

If payment has been made by one party to the contract, but performance by the other party is precluded by frustration, it may be recovered in quasi-contract by an action for repetition. Similarly, a party who has partly performed the contract before the frustrating event, but has not yet received payment, may claim partial payment on the basis of recompense.

Cantiere San Rocco SA v Clyde Shipbuilding & Engineering Co Ltd **11–41**
1923 S.L.T. 624
House of Lords: Earl of Birkenhead, Viscount Finlay, Lords Dunedin, Atkinson and Shaw of Dunfermline

Cantiere, an Austrian shipbuilding company based in Trieste (then part of the Austro-Hungarian Empire) contracted to buy from Clyde Shipbuilding three engines, f.o.b. Port Glasgow. The contract price was £11,550, payable in instalments. The first instalment was paid on 20 May 1914. War was declared on 12 August 1914 and the contract could no longer legally be fulfilled. Cantiere now claimed the return of the first instalment.

The House decided that, even though the contract had been frustrated, Cantiere was entitled to restitution of the moneys paid.

> "LORD SHAW OF DUNFERMLINE: ... [T]he law of Scotland ... for over half a century [has] stood expounded with unquestioned authority by Lord President Inglis in *Watson & Co v Shankland* (1871) 10 M.142 at p.152 ... Until this case occurred the principle laid down by that most distinguished judge has never been doubted, if it has **11–42**

[27] *Maritime National Fish Ltd v Ocean Trawlers Ltd* [1935] A.C. 524.
[28] *Steamship Line Ltd v Imperial Smelting Corporation Ltd* [1942] A.C. 154.
[29] See also *London and Edinburgh Shipping Co Ltd v The Admiralty*, 1920 S.C. 309.

been doubted now ... [H]e explained that although the particular question arose under a charter-party, its settlement depended on principles with a much wider range:

'The general principles of law applicable to the contract of affreightment are not essentially different from those applicable to other similar contracts, such as contracts of land carriage, or building contracts, or any others, in which one party agrees to pay a certain price as the return for materials furnished or work done, or services rendered by the other party ...

'There is no rule of the civil law, as adopted into all modern municipal codes and systems, better understood than this—that if money is advanced by one party to a mutual contract, on the condition and stipulation that something shall be afterwards paid or performed by the other party, and the latter party fails in performing his part of the contract, the former is entitled to repayment of his advance on the ground of failure of consideration. In the Roman system the demand for repayment took the form of a *condictio causa data causa non secuta*, or a *condictio sine causa*, or a *condictio indebiti*, according to the particular circumstances. In our own practice these remedies are represented by the action of restitution and the action of repetition. And in all systems of jurisprudence there must be similar remedies, for the rule which they are intended to enforce is one of universal application in mutual contracts.'

It is true that since that judgment was pronounced a good deal has happened in England to make or to widen the breach between the English practice and that of Scotland and other nations. The particular instance of divergence in regard to this principle was as to advance of freight, on which subject the Lord President referred to the practice of 'all the nations of the trading world with the exception of England.'

The divergence of law may be said to have culminated in what are known as the Coronation cases ... No doubt the occasion will arise when that chapter of English law will have to be considered in this House ...

Upon the facts of this case only 20 per cent of the purchase price was paid as part of the consideration for delivery of the engines to be supplied. But suppose the whole purchase price—£11,550—had been paid at the signing of the contract; then the war breaks out; and the engines are neither supplied nor even begun to be made. In that situation, ... on the English cases, the very same result should and would follow. The builder would retain as his own the whole price of an article which he never supplied and would never supply ... This result under other systems of jurisprudence would be viewed as monstrous: but in England, it was contended, this is the law; and the principle is worthy of acceptance in Scotland: such is the argument ... [T]he rule, admitted to be arbitrary, is adopted because of the difficulty, nay the apparent impossibility, of reaching a solution of perfection ... [U]nder this application innocent loss may and must be endured by the one party, and the unearned aggrandisement may and must be secured at his expense to the other party. That is part of the law of England.

I am not able to affirm that this is any part, or even was any part, of the law of Scotland.

No doubt the adjustment of rights after the occurrence of disturbances, interruptions or calamities is in many cases a difficult task. Under [the law of Scotland] restitution against calamity or mischance which produces a failure of consideration is one thing that the law must and will do its best to accomplish ...

To apply these principles to the case in hand, there can be no doubt that the person who received £2,310 in part payment of engines which were built and supplied, must restore money in the event of the engines not having been supplied, and not even having been built. Both the law of Rome and the law of Scotland, not to speak of the equity of the situation, would have been clear on the subject.

I have not adverted to the puzzle that was attempted in argument as to whether the remedy of restoration sought was under the contract or not under the contract, and that

> but for the single reason which is thus put unanswerably by Lord Mackenzie [in the Inner House]: 'The pursuers sue for repetition of the part of the price which they paid. Their case involves construction of the contract, more particularly Article 9, but it is not an action on the contract. It is a claim for restitution; and unless the contract contains express terms to the contrary, the law of Scotland will give the remedy asked.' To which I venture to add this further remark, that suppose the contract of sale referred to is entirely out of the case, there is another contract so simple and elementary as *do ut des*, enrolled by the civil law in its list of innominate contracts, and that would amply justify in itself, and even on the grounds of contract and its recognised consequences, the restitution sought."

It is clear from this decision that relief is available only where there is unjustified enrichment. In England, where that remedy was not available at common law and the loss would have to lie where it fell,[30] statute provides detailed rules for the return of money paid, that money payable ceases to be payable, and that benefits obtained must be paid for.[31] It has been suggested that a legislative regime to provide "equitable readjustment" is similarly needed in Scotland.[32] The same writers further suggest that "frustration is a restrictively applied doctrine" and "an all-or-nothing solution to the problem of change".[33] One possibility is the adoption of a rule like that in DCFR, which provides: **11–43**

> **III.–1:110: Variation or termination by court on a change of circumstances** **11–44**
>
> (1) An obligation must be performed even if performance has become more onerous, whether because the cost of performance has increased or because the value of what is to be received in return has diminished.
>
> (2) If, however, performance of a contractual obligation or of an obligation arising from a unilateral juridical act becomes so onerous because of an exceptional change of circumstances that it would be manifestly unjust to hold the debtor to the obligation a court may:
>
> (a) vary the obligation in order to make it reasonable and equitable in the new circumstances; or
> (b) terminate the obligation at a date and on terms to be determined by the court.
>
> (3) Paragraph (2) applies only if:
>
> (a) the change of circumstances occurred after the time when the obligation was incurred;
> (b) the debtor did not at that time take into account, and could not reasonably be expected to have taken into account, the possibility or scale of that change of circumstances;
> (c) the debtor did not assume, and cannot reasonably be regarded as having assumed, the risk of that change of circumstances; and

[30] *Fibrosa Spolka Akcyjna v Fairbairn Lawson Combe Barber Ltd* [1943] A.C. 32.
[31] Law Reform (Frustrated Contracts) Act 1943, enacted in response to the House of Lords decision in *Fibrosa*.
[32] HL MacQueen and J Thomson, *Contract Law in Scotland*, 3rd edn (London: Bloomsbury, 2012), para.4.85.
[33] HL MacQueen and J Thomson, *Contract Law in Scotland*, 3rd edn (London: Bloomsbury, 2012), para.4.88.

(d) the debtor has attempted, reasonably and in good faith, to achieve by negotiation a reasonable and equitable adjustment of the terms regulating the obligation.

Because the provision extends to circumstances where performance has merely become more onerous or more costly, it clearly goes well beyond providing remedies in circumstances that would be recognised as frustration.

At all stages in the *Lloyds TSB Foundation* litigation, the courts were invited to apply the principle of 'equitable readjustment'. In particular, the courts were referred to what became *Article 89: Change of Circumstances* in the *Draft Regulation on a Common European Sales Law*.[34] This provides:

'1. A party must perform its obligations even if performance has become more onerous, whether because the cost of performance has increased or because the value of what is to be received in return has diminished.

Where performance becomes excessively onerous because of an exceptional change of circumstances, the parties have a duty to enter into negotiations with a view to adapting or terminating the contract.

2. If the parties fail to reach an agreement within a reasonable time, then, upon request by either party a court may:

(a) adapt the contract in order to bring it into accordance with what the parties would reasonably have agreed at the time of contracting if they had taken the change of circumstances into account; or
(b) terminate the contract within the meaning of Article 8 at a date and on terms to be determined by the court.

3. Paragraphs 1 and 2 apply only if:

(a) the change of circumstances occurred after the time when the contract was concluded;
(b) the party relying on the change of circumstances did not at that time take into account, and could not be expected to have taken into account, the possibility or scale of that change of circumstances; and
(c) the aggrieved party did not assume, and cannot reasonably be regarded as having assumed, the risk of that change of circumstances.

4. For the purpose of paragraphs 2 and 3 a 'court' includes an arbitral tribunal.'"

This principle would also provide "remedies" where performance has merely become "excessively onerous" rather than impossible, or frustrated. In *TSB Foundation for Scotland v Lloyds Banking Group Plc*,[35] the Inner House refused to do so in the following terms:

11–45 "THE LORD PRESIDENT (LORD HAMILTON):

[23] Before us, as before the Lord Ordinary, the respondent advanced an alternative contention. That was that, in the event of the court being against it on the issue of construction, it should, by applying a concept referred to as 'equitable adjustment', exclude from the calculation of profit before taxation the sum brought in for negative

[34] COM(2011) 635 final; available at: *http://ec.europa.eu/justice/contract/files/common_sales_law/regulation_sales_law_en.pdf* [Accessed 3 September 2015].

[35] *TSB Foundation for Scotland v Lloyds Banking Group Plc* [2011] CSIH 87. The facts are stated above, para.8–95.

goodwill, thus in effect holding that the respondent had for 2009 no liability to the reclaimer under clause 2(1)(a); the amount due would accordingly be restricted to £38,920.

[24] The Lord Ordinary rejected this contention. Before us Mr Wolffe relied primarily on two authorities in Scots law—though he maintained that a consideration of comparative materials and certain European proposals provided at least a reassurance that what was contended for was not incompatible with a modern legal system. The two Scots authorities were *Muir* v *McIntyres* (1887) 14 R 470 and *Wilkie* v *Bethune* (1848) 11 D 132.

[25] *Muir* v *McIntyres* was concerned with an issue between an agricultural landlord and his tenant. The subjects had in the course of the lease been badly affected by fire. The landlord sued for the contractual rent; the tenant responded by claiming an abatement by reason of the reduced value of the subjects. The issue before the court was a technical one of whether the tenant's claim was truly one for abatement of rent or rather one of an illiquid claim for damages (which was not pleadable in answer to a demand for rent). Lord President Inglis observed at page 472:

'... it is quite settled in law that an abatement is to be allowed if a tenant loses the beneficial enjoyment of any part of the subject let to him either through the fault of the landlord or through some unforeseen calamity which the tenant was not able to prevent. There are many examples of this in the books.'"

He then goes on to illustrate that proposition. He accordingly held that there was a good claim for abatement and that it was competent to plead that claim as a defence to the action for the full rent. The other judges agreed.

"[26] As the Lord President noticed, there was a long tradition in the Scots law of landlord and tenant of an entitlement in the tenant to an abatement of the contractual rent in the event of the subjects of lease being partially destroyed. Although neither the judges in *Muir* v *McIntyres* nor the earlier authorities cited explain the jurisprudential foundation of that entitlement, it is no doubt, as Lord Cooper observed in an article entitled "Frustration of Contract in Scots Law" (1946) 28th Journal of Comparative Legislation 1 at page 4, related to the concept of *rei interitus*. That concept, however, as its Latin expression imports, is concerned with the destruction (partial or total) of property. There is nothing in the authorities to suggest that the concept of abatement extends more widely.

[27] *Wilkie* v *Bethune* is an extraordinary case. Its background was the failure of the potato crop in 1846. The pursuer was a farm servant who had been engaged under an agreement which entitled him, in addition to money wages, to certain allowances, part of which were 'nine bolls of potatoes laid down at his door'. As a result of the failure of the crop, the market price of potatoes rose dramatically. No potatoes having been delivered, the servant sued his master for their market price. Lord Jeffrey, who delivered the fullest opinion in the First Division, described the contract as one '*inter rusticos*', construing its nature, in relation to the potatoes, as being 'an undertaking by the master to furnish a certain amount of aliment. The price of provisions may rise, but the master is bound, at whatever cost, to supply aliment in one shape or another' (page 139). Lord Mackenzie had observed that the servant, and his fellow servants, were 'entitled to an equivalent amount of sustentation' (page 137). A doctrine expounded in *Chitty* on Contracts (3rd ed) at page 735 was distinguished, having regard to the peculiar nature of the contract under discussion (see Lord Jeffrey at page 139). A 'very equitable adjustment' between

the respective figures contended for by the parties was settled upon by the court. *Bell's Principles* (Guthrie's edition) at para 29, footnote (i), describes this as a 'remarkable and exceptional case of supervening difficulty'. *Gloag on Contract* (2nd ed) page 339 describes it as 'a very special case'. Both these descriptions are well justified. All that can be taken from *Wilkie* v *Bethune* is that, in a very unusual case where the parties had contracted for an alimentary provision, the court was able to settle the dispute by fixing upon a sum which was regarded equitably as the money equivalent of the obligation. No general principle can be derived from it.

[28] *McBryde on Contract* (3rd ed) at para 21.21 refers to *Wilkie* v *Bethune* in the context of a discussion of frustration of contract. But it is not suggested that the present contract has been frustrated. We are unable to find in Scots law any general doctrine of 'equitable adjustment' which would allow the court to moderate the obligation contractually owed by the respondent to the reclaimer under clause 2(1)(a).

[29] We were referred to the decision of the Court of Appeal in *Pole Properties* v *Feinberg* (1982) 43 P & CR 121, another case of landlord and tenant. In a situation where there had been a radical change in the way in which heating was provided to residential flats and where it was accepted on both sides that the provisions in respect of payment for that service were no longer operable, the court fixed an equitable charge. But this does not help in establishing any broad principle which could apply in the present case. We were referred to a Feasibility Study (dated 3 May 2011) by the Commission Expert Group on European Contract Law on a possible Future Instrument in European Contract Law. This includes an article (Article 92)[36] on obligations and remedies of the parties to a sales contract which provides for a situation in which performance of an obligation under such a contract has become excessively onerous because of an exceptional change of circumstances. This proposal, which appears to relate only to contracts of sale, is not uncontroversial. The Scottish Law Commission has responded with the observation that it is 'not convinced of the utility of Article 92'. The Commission noted that, 'there is no doctrine of equitable adjustment in Scots law to deal with change of circumstances, as distinct from the law of frustration'. While it appears that certain European jurisdictions do have some form of equitable adjustment of contracts, there is, as yet, no foundation for it, as a generality, in Scots law. It would be beyond the proper scope of judicial power to develop it in any way which would assist the respondent in this case."

In the Supreme Court, Lord Hope DPSC (with whom Lord Reed agreed) went even further in his reasoning in refusing to extend "equitable readjustment" beyond its present limits:

11–46 "LORD HOPE DPSC:

...

[36] Junior counsel for the bank submitted that, should it fail on the issue of construction, the court should adjust the 1997 deed by applying to it a doctrine referred to as equitable adjustment. The effect of applying that doctrine, he submitted, would be to exclude the sum brought in for negative goodwill from the calculation of the group's profit or loss before taxation. This would create a loss in the 2009 audited accounts, so the amount due to the Foundation for 2009 under cl 3 of the deed would be restricted to £38,920.

[37] The Lord Ordinary recognised, when this argument was before him in the Outer House, that the bank's success on the issue of construction made it unnecessary for him to deal with it. He had held that the Foundation must fail in its claim against the bank in

---

36 This became article 89 of the Draft Regulation on a Common European Sales Law—see above.

any event. But he dealt with the argument nevertheless and, having examined the authorities, he concluded that there was no such doctrine in Scots law ([2011] CSOH 105, para 89). The point was raised in the Inner House by way of a cross-appeal. As the First Division decided to reverse the Lord Ordinary on the issue of construction, it had to deal with it ([2011] CSIH 87, para 22). In its view however there was no foundation for the equitable adjustment of contracts, as a generality, in Scots law. Lord President Hamilton recognised the existence of the doctrine, but he said it would be beyond the judicial power to develop it in a way that would assist the bank in this case (para 29).

[38] We are in the same position as the Lord Ordinary. The bank's success on the main issue makes it unnecessary for us to decide whether a remedy by way of equitable adjustment is available. But the point was dealt with fully in the parties' written cases as well as in oral argument, and it is of some general interest. So I should like to say a word or two about it. Despite junior counsel for the bank's able submissions to the contrary, I have reached the same conclusion as the judges in the Court of Session. I add these few words to explain why.

[39] The proposition for which junior counsel contended was that the doctrine was available where, as a result of supervening events, performance of a contract no longer bears any realistic resemblance to that which was originally contemplated. He made it clear in his written case that it was not his position that it would be impossible to implement the deed if it were to be construed in the manner argued for by the Foundation. The contract had not been frustrated. Nor was it his case that the court had any general power to adjust or alter contracts to achieve what one or other of the parties might regard as an equitable result. His proposition was a narrow one, confined to a case where the alteration in the circumstances in which the contract came to be performed was affected in a material way by supervening events for which neither party was responsible. There had to be a supervening event which was not foreseen and was not foreseeable when the contract was made, and that event must affect the substance of the contract.

[40] The Foundation, for its part, made it clear in its written case that it did not suggest that there was no concept of equitable adjustment in Scots law. It is to be found, for example, where the future performance of a contract is frustrated. The rule in Scots law is that the loss does not lie where it falls on the frustration of a contract. There must be, as McBryde, *The Law of Contract in Scotland* (para 21.47), puts it, an equitable adjustment. That was what was done in *Cantiere San Rocco SA v Clyde Shipbuilding and Engineering Co Ltd* where it was held that the buyer was entitled to repetition of the instalment of the price that was paid on signature of the contract as, owing to the war, further performance of the contract had become impossible. As Lord Dunedin explained (p 126 (SC); pp 248, 249 (AC)) the remedy for frustration of the contract was given 'not under the contract or because of breach of the contract inferring damages, but in respect of the equitable (of course I am not using the words in the technical English sense) doctrine of *condictio causa data causa non secuta*.' It should be noted that the term *causa data causa non secuta* is used today not to describe a remedy as such, but rather to describe one particular group of situations in which the law may provide a remedy because one party is unjustifiably enriched at the expense of the other (*Shilliday v Smith*, per Lord President Rodger, p 728).

[41] The situation that was discussed in *Cantiere San Rocco SA v Clyde Shipbuilding and Engineering Co Ltd* is not the situation in this case, as it was not part of the bank's argument that if the Foundation were to succeed on the interpretation argument its obligations under the deed could not be implemented. But Lord President Cooper, '*Frustration of Contract in Scots Law*' (p 1), saw frustration of the contract as a byproduct of a wider question:

'[H]ow the relations of two parties should be equitably readjusted by the Court when the one has been unintentionally enriched at the expense of the other.'

He made it clear (pp 4, 5) that in his opinion the principle of frustration was capable of being expanded in the future into other areas. In *James B Fraser & Co Ltd v Denny, Mott and Dickson Ltd* (p 41 (SC); p 272 (AC)), Lord Macmillan (who was counsel for the unsuccessful shipbuilding company in *Cantiere San Rocco*) said that the doctrine of frustration was so inherently just as inevitably to find a place in any civilised system of law:

'The manner in which it has developed in order to meet the problems arising from the disturbances of business due to world wars is a tribute to the progressive adaptability of the common law.'

In *Muir v McIntyre* it was held that a tenant was not bound to pay the full rent where, due to no fault of his own, almost the whole of the accommodation on the farm was destroyed by a fire. Lord Shand said (p 473) that the principle on which the tenant was entitled to an abatement of his rent was 'founded on the highest equity'.

[42] These observations provide the background to junior counsel for the bank's submission that, while the concept of equitable adjustment overlapped with unjustified enrichment, it was broader in its application. It was a matter of degree, he said, whether the contract was discharged or was equitably adjusted. It all depended on the extent or nature of the change. Cases such as *Muir v McIntyre* and *Sharp v Thomson*, where the tenant was held to be entitled to an abatement of his rent upon the partial destruction of the subjects, showed how equitable principles could operate where the contract was not frustrated. It could continue on terms which were adjusted to reflect the changed circumstances. Rankine, *A Treatise on the Law of Leases in Scotland* (p 227), said that the court will not be confined in adjusting the rights of the parties by any artificial rule that the loss must either be total or at least *plus quam tolerabile*. In *Wilkie v Bethune*, due to the failure of the potato crop, the farm servant's employer was unable to deliver the potatoes to which the servant was entitled in addition to his money wages. The court fixed a sum which was regarded equitably as the money equivalent of the employer's obligation. The contract had not been frustrated, but the court applied an equitable construction and held the servant entitled, not to his potatoes, but to a sum which would purchase the equivalent of other food (McBryde, *The Law of Contract in Scotland*, para 21.21).

[43] This is not the occasion to cast doubt on the ability of Scots law to find equitable solutions to unforeseen problems. Adaptability has a part to play in any civilised system of law, as Lord Macmillan recognised in *James B Fraser & Co Ltd v Denny, Mott and Dickson Ltd* (p 41 (SC); p 272 (AC)). The way that use has been made of civilian principles to develop the law of frustration of contract in Scots law is a powerful demonstration of that fact. So too is Zimmermann's observation that the doctrine of *Wegfall der Geschäftsgrundlage* (collapse of the underlying basis of the transaction), which was formulated in response to the problems posed by the consequences of the First World War, has become part and parcel of the modern German law of contract (*The Law of Obligations*, p 582). It can also be seen in the way strict rules for the interpretation of contracts have been discarded in favour of giving effect to what a reasonable person would have understood the parties to have meant by the language used (see *Rainy Sky SA v Kookmin Bank Co Ltd*, per Lord Clarke, para 14).

[44] That development as to how contracts are to be interpreted is very much in point in this case. It would have created a very real problem for the bank, had it been necessary for it to rely on an equitable adjustment. The assumption must be that it had to resort to this argument because it had lost on the issue of construction. In other words, the 1997 deed had been held, by applying that principle of construction, to mean what the Foundation contends it means. The obligation that, so construed, it sets out is not

impossible of performance. Can it really be said that it would be appropriate to resort to an equitable doctrine in order that the deed should mean something else? None of the examples of equitable adjustment that are to be found in the reported cases go that far. And it is hard to see how this, the enrichment, can be regarded as unjustified, if including the sum for negative goodwill results from the meaning that must be given to the covenant.

[45] In *Bank of Credit and Commerce International SA v Ali (No 1)* (paras 55, 56), Lord Hoffmann drew attention to the way that eighteenth and nineteenth century English judges, when faced with rigid rules of construction which were productive of injustice, resorted to solutions based on what was referred to as an equitable doctrine. But, as he went on to say (para 60), judicial creativity of that kind was to be invoked only if it was necessary to remedy a widespread injustice. Otherwise there was much to be said for giving effect to what on ordinary principles of construction the parties agreed. Those are the principles that have been applied in this case. There surely is no need, if that approach is adopted, to strive to find a basis in equity for arriving at a different result. On the contrary, to do that would be to look for a result which was different from that which the parties must be taken, by placing the words used in their legal and accounting context at the date when the deed was executed, to have agreed to.

[46] There is a place for such a result where the contract has become impossible of performance or something essential to its performance has been totally or partially destroyed, as in the case of leases. But not, as the Lord Ordinary put it (para 92), where a contract is nearly frustrated but not quite. Moreover it could hardly be said that there is anything in this case that could reasonably be described as inequitable if the result were to come down in favour of the Foundation. As the Dean of Faculty pointed out, the unrealised gain on acquisition was due to Lloyds TSB Group's decision to acquire HBOS in January 2009 by which date *IFRS 3* had already been issued. The situation which has resulted from this was described by the bank's expert Mr Simmonds as 'unthinkable' when the covenant was entered into. But the acquisition was a voluntary act. It was not something that was beyond the control of either party.

[47] For all these reasons I would hold that the proposition that the court can equitably adjust a contract on the basis that its performance, while not frustrated, is no longer that which was originally contemplated is not part of Scots law. To hold otherwise would be to undermine the principle enshrined in the maxim *pacta sunt servanda* which lies at the root of the whole of the law of contract. I see no need for this and, as there is no need for it, I would reject the suggestion that the court should assume that function.

. . ."

Termination following breach

A breach of obligation by one party to the contract does not itself terminate the contract or discharge either party, but the party not in breach is entitled to several remedies. One possibility is that the breach is a repudiation of the contract, which entitles the party not in breach to rescind, or terminate the contract. **11–47**

Terminology of breach

Professor McBryde states[37]: **11–48**

[37] WW McBryde, *The Law of Contract in Scotland*, 3rd edn (Edinburgh: W. Green, 2007), paras 20–02—20–05.

> "One of the most confusing aspects of the Scots law on breach is the terminology. It has become common to say that a party can 'breach' a contract, with 'breach' being a verb and not a noun ... More problems arise with the difference between the three 'r's—repudiation, resiling and rescission ... Repudiation is sometimes used to mean anticipatory breach and, in other cases, a party in material breach is said to have repudiated the contract ... The term 'repudiatory breach' is also confusing ... Resiling can also be used as a general expression meaning to withdraw lawfully from a contract but not in response to an anticipatory or other breach ... Rescission is correctly used in the context of a material breach but, confusingly, can be used in the context of reduction of a voidable contract where *restitutio in integrum* is not possible. Rescission in cases where the contract is affected by invalidities of consent is an act of the court; following material breach rescission is the act of the innocent party (and *restitutio in integrum* is not required)."

Although it is common to do so, it is not always accurate to speak of a party in breach as "guilty" and the other party as "innocent". Contractual obligations are *strict*, so that they can be broken without even where the party in breach is not at "fault". The manager in *Blyth v Scottish Liberal Club* (considered below, para.11–81) honestly believed he was in the right in refusing to perform certain duties; but he was still in breach of contract by doing so. Some contractual obligations, however, are based on duty to take reasonable care or duty to exercise reasonable skill—see, for example, the discussion in Ch.10 on s.16 of the Unfair Contract Terms Act 1977.

To avoid confusion and ensure a degree of consistency to facilitate understanding, references to rescission and resiling will be avoided. Repudiation will be used to describe the effects of a material breach, which the party not in breach is entitled to accept or reject. The expression "innocent party" will not be used to describe the party not in breach.

What constitutes a breach?

11–49 Professor Walker, in *Law of Contracts and Related Obligations in Scotland*, states:

> "Breach of contract takes place when either party to a valid and binding contract refuses or fails, without legal justification, to perform in an acceptable manner any of the things which he is required by the contract to do."[38]

A refusal or failure to perform may therefore relate to a fundamental aspect of the contract, or, at the other extreme to a trifling matter. The law looks to the *effects*, or *materiality* of a breach.[39] The innocent party is entitled to terminate the contract only if there has been a material breach of the contract. That, in turn will depend on what each party had undertaken in the contract, which will in turn depend on what the contract stipulates—on the stipulations, or terms of the

[38] DM Walker, *The Law of Contracts and Related Obligations in Scotland*, 3rd edn (Edinburgh: W. Green, 1995).

[39] This can be contrasted with the position in English law, where terms are normally classified as "*conditions*" or "*warranties*". Only breach of the former giving the right to the innocent party to terminate the contract. This has created serious definitional problems in that jurisdiction which Scots law has generally avoided. English case law in this area must be treated with more than usual caution. At all costs, the word "condition" must be avoided in describing terms. WW McBryde's reference to Stair *Institutions,* I, iii 8 (*The Law of Contract in Scotland*, 3rd edn (Edinburgh: W. Green, 2007), para.9–01) must be seen in context, i.e. Stair was dealing with implied conditions that render the obligation (not necessarily a contractual obligation) conditional, not implied conditions in the English law sense of implied terms.

contract.[40] If the party not in breach decides to terminate, but it transpires that the breach was not material, that is a failure to perform and entitles the other party to redress.

Wade v Waldon 11–50

1909 S.C. 571

Court of Session, First Division: Lord President (Dunedin), Lords Kinnear, McLaren and Pearson

George Robey (real name George Wade) was a very popular music-hall comedian. He contracted with Waldon to perform at the Palace and Pavilion Theatres in Glasgow, at £350 per week, for the week beginning Monday, 16 March 1908. Rule 6 of the written contract stated: "All parties engaged ... must give fourteen days' notice prior to such engagement, such notice to be accompanied with bill matter".

On 13 March, having noticed that his name did not appear on advertisements for the theatre for the week beginning 16 March, he sent the following telegram: "name not in call for Monday, presume mistake". He received the following telegraphed replies: "you never sent bill matter or notification, consequently contract broken, see rule six, contract" and "call in order. Your name does not appear. Will not play you owing to breach of contract".

Wade claimed £300 damages for Waldon's breach of contract by not allowing him to play; Waldon claimed £500 damages for breach of contract by Wade.

The court held that Wade's failure to forward confirmation and materials was not a material breach of contract entitling Waldon to terminate the contract. By not allowing Wade to play, Waldon was in breach of contract and liable in damages.

"LORD PRESIDENT (DUNEDIN): ... The whole point then is, is this stipulation one of such a kind that a breach of it would entitle the defender without more ado to declare the contract at an end? It is familiar law, and quite well settled by decision, that in any contract which contains multifarious stipulations there are some which go so to the root of the contract that a breach of those stipulations entitles the party pleading the breach to declare that the contract is at an end. There are others which do not go to the root of the contract, but which are part of the contract, and which would give rise, if broken, to an action of damages. I need not cite authority on what is trite and very well settled law. 11–51

The only other point to which I should allude is this, that, as was pointed out by Lord Watson in the case of the *London Guarantee Company* (1880) 5 A.C. 911, quoting a sentence from Lord [sic] Blackburn's judgment in *Bettini v. Gye* (1876) 1 Q.B.D. 183, that it is quite in the power of the parties to stipulate that some particular matters, however trivial they may be, yet shall, as between them, form conditions precedent. If they have said so, then their agreement in the matter will be given effect to, but where they have not said so in terms, as is the case here, then the court must determine, looking to the nature of the stipulation, whether it goes to the essence of the contract or not ...

I am very clearly of opinion that this is a stipulation which does not go to the root of the contract. This case is scarcely distinguishable from the case of Bettini, and I think that the Lord Ordinary has come to a right conclusion. He has found that there was an undoubted breach of contract by the defender here in not allowing the pursuer to play, and that that breach was unjustified, inasmuch as the defender had no right to treat the non-fulfilment of this article 6 as a breach entitling him to put an end to the contract altogether."

[40] See above, paras 8–01—8–08. Materiality is considered more fully later in this chapter, at para.11–80 onwards.

11–52 In *Bettini v Gye*, to which the Lord President refers, Bettini, a singer, was required by his contract to be present for rehearsals six days before the week in which he was due to perform. He arrived three days late.

The Lord President spoke of terms which do not go to the root of the contract "but which are part of the contract". Can there be "terms" which are not part of the contract? If so, what would be their effects?

His Lordship also refers to "conditions precedent". This is one example of the importation of English terminology to describe a concept which is better described by traditional Scottish terms.

The parties may *expressly stipulate* the consequence of a particular breach in the contract, thereby avoiding at least some of the uncertainty in cases like *Wade v Waldon*. In particular, the parties may agree the compensation payable to the party not in breach—a matter considered more fully below, para.11–69 onwards.

A breach may occur at the most embarrassing and inconvenient moments, but that alone does not make it material. Consider, for example, the difference between an opera singer giving advance notice that they would be unable to perform as planned, or who merely forgets the odd line of the libretto; and the prima donna who walks off stage, half way through the opening night! Clearly, not all breaches will entitle the innocent party to the same remedies.

Principle of mutuality

11–53 It is a long-established rule of Scots law, with roots in Roman law, that a party to a contract must have performed, or be in a position to perform, before demanding performance from the other party. According to professor McBryde[41]:

> "The concept of mutuality involves at least five ideas:
>
> (1) A party who is in breach of obligations cannot enforce performance by the other party.
> (2) The party who is not in breach may withhold performance until the other has performed or is seen to be willing to perform the counter stipulations. Once the breach ends, so does the right to suspend performance.
> (3) The mutuality concept only applies if the obligations of the parties are the causes of one another or are reciprocal undertakings.
> (4) The operation of the principle can be affected by the express terms of the contract.
> (5) It may not be for every trifling breach, or every breach, that a party can withhold performance of part of the contract."

The application of the principle is illustrated in the two decisions that follow.

---

[41] WW McBryde, *The Law of Contract in Scotland*, 3rd edn (Edinburgh: W. Green, 2007), para.20–47. For a recent application of the principle of mutuality, see *Glen Clyde Whisky Ltd v Campbell Meyer & Co Ltd* [2015] CSOH 97.

Bank of East Asia Ltd v Scottish Enterprise 11–54
1997 S.L.T. 1213 (H.L.)
House of Lords: Lords Jauncey, Browne-Wilkinson, Mustill, Slynn and Woolf

In 1989 Scottish Enterprise (then the Scottish Development Agency, or SDA) contracted with Stanley Miller (SM) for the erection of factory units on an industrial site in Hamilton. The contract was governed by Scottish law. Payment was by monthly instalments, but this was changed later by agreement to monthly valuations of work, with the first instalment payable on 15 May 1990. SM agreed their own interim funding with the Bank of East Asia (BEA), secured by an assignation of all sums due to SM under the contract with the SDA. On 16 May 1990 it was agreed that a sum of £416,964.72 was due, but the SDA claimed £168,512.40 for loss and damage that resulted from some negligent construction work by SM. Within weeks SM became insolvent and was in the hands of receivers and work on site ceased. The SDA became entitled to liquidated and ascertained damages under the terms of the contract and refused to make payment to BEA. BEA accepted that the SDA were entitled to retain £168,512.40 but claimed the balance (approximately £250,000). BEA sought payment in the English High Court and the judge held that the SDA were only entitled to withhold payment of sums related to breaches of contract occurring prior to the payment date, relying on *Redpath Dorman Long Ltd v Cummins Engine Co Ltd*. Scottish Enterprise appealed to the Court of Appeal which held that both the judge at first instance and the Court of Appeal were bound to apply Scots law as a matter of fact and had no jurisdiction to consider whether the Scottish court had reached a wrong conclusion on a point of Scots law in *Redpath Dorman Long Ltd*.

Scottish Enterprise appealed to the House of Lords, arguing that retention was an example of the principle of mutuality and that it operated as a defence from the time that payment became due until at least the date of raising proceedings, if not until decree. BEA argued that retention was merely a self-help remedy the exercise of which had to be contemporaneous with the obligation.

The House dismissed the appeal.

"LORD JAUNCEY OF TULLICHETTLE: This appeal is entirely concerned with a question of Scots law. . . . 11–55

In *Redpath Dorman Long Ltd* building contractors sued their employers for payment of sums due under interim certificates issued by the architect. The employers sought to retain these sums against illiquid claims for damages resulting from the contractors' breach of contract. It was held inter alia that any retention by the employers could only be in respect of a claim for breach of contract which was in existence at the time when payment fell due under the certificate. The Lord Justice Clerk (Wheatley) at 1981 SC, p 375; 1982 SLT, p 491, after citing a dictum of Lord Benholme in *Johnston v Robertson* to which I shall refer later and in which he referred to satisfaction by one party of the corresponding and contemporaneous claims of the other, said:

'Applying that dictum to the facts of this case and the instant argument we turn to consider in the first place the point of time at which the test of the existence of a contemporaneous counter claim, even if illiquid, has to be determined. Counsel for the pursuers maintained that it was the time when payment fell due, namely 21 days after the issue of the certificate. Counsel for the defenders submitted *per contra* that it was the time at which the pursuers sought to enforce payment, e.g., by raising an action. In our view the submission by the pursuers is the correct one. At the expiry of the 21 days, the pursuers had an unqualified legal right to the sum of money specified in the certificate and the defenders had an unqualified legal obligation to pay that money forthwith, unless there was in existence at that time, even if illiquid, a counter claim under the contract. That, in our opinion, is what the word 'contemporaneous' means and involves. Moreover, this is a test which has to be applied in respect of each certificate as it fell due to be implemented.'

It was this passage which the courts below felt bound to accept as an authoritative statement of the law of Scotland . . . [Lord Jauncey referred to *Johnston v Robertson* and quoted this extract from Lord Benholme's judgment at (1861) 23 D, p 652]

'. . .The plea of the defender is based mainly on the rule of the law of Scotland, that one party to a mutual contract, in which there are mutual stipulations, cannot insist on having his claim under the contract satisfied, unless he is prepared to satisfy the corresponding and contemporaneous claims of the other party to the contract. I think the rule of law, that an illiquid claim cannot be set off against a liquid claim, does not apply to such a case; and that, at all events, if the one claim be liquid, and the other partly illiquid, yet contemporaneous, the rule should suffer some qualification or relaxation if the claims arose under one contract. The counter claims must be contemporaneous, for, if not, the rule would apply.' . . .

Much argument in this House was directed to Lord Benholme's use of the word 'contemporaneous'. Did it refer to the time when the claims arose or merely to the time when the withholder was sued or tabled the defence as in the case of compensation for liquid debts?

In seeking to answer this question I propose to look at a number of authorities dealing with the enforceability of stipulations in mutual contracts. I start with Erskine at III iii 86, who said:

'No party in a mutual contract, where the obligations on the parties are the causes of one another, can demand performance from the other, if he himself either cannot or will not perform the counter-part; for the mutual obligations are considered as conditional.' . . . Counsel for SE argued that retention was merely an example of the principle of mutuality and that it operated as a defence from the time that payment became due until at least the date of raising of an action if not until decree. This, it was submitted, appeared from the foregoing authorities which also made plain that a party in breach such as SM was alleged to be could not enforce SE's obligation to make payment without taking account of the counterclaim for damages. Counsel for the bank submitted that the retention was no more than a remedy of self help and that contemporaneity of obligations had to be looked at when retention was first operated and not at the later stage when an action was raised.

My Lords, I do not consider that the authorities warrant so broad a proposition as that any material breach by one party to a contract necessarily disentitles him from enforcing any and every obligation due by the other party.

[Lord Jauncey reviewed several authorities on the matter and continued] . . .

In the light of these cases I turn to consider in a little more detail the three principles enunciated in *Turnbull v McLean*. The first one is readily applicable to a case where the obligation by A to pay the price is the counterpart of the obligation by B to complete the works or deliver the goods. I do not, however, consider that the Lord Justice Clerk intended to state that each and every obligation by one party to a mutual contract was necessarily and invariably the counterpart of each and every obligation by the other. It must be a matter of circumstances. Thus in a contract to be performed by both sides in stages, the counter obligation and consideration for payment of stage one is the completion of the work for that stage conform to contract. The second principle must, having regard to the first principle, be construed as referring to performance by the other in relation to the part of the contract which the one party has failed to perform, rather than to the whole contract, although in many cases the part will amount to the whole. The third plainly has in contemplation the material part of a contract which the one party has refused to perform and which may be the subject of specific implement. So analysed it becomes apparent that these principles do not produce the result that any claim under a mutual contract can be set against any other claim thereunder howsoever or whensoever such claim may arise.

Turnbull v McLean arose out of an unsuccessful challenge to a supplier's right to withhold performance of a current obligation on account of non-payment of a prior completed obligation. If a supplier who had made two monthly deliveries conform to contract for which payment was due at the end of each month, had then made a third delivery disconform to contract, the consignee, who had failed to pay, would have no right to retain the payment for the first two deliveries. Breach of contract in relation to the third delivery could not give rise ex post facto to a right of retention in respect of obligations which had been duly performed. The only counter obligation to payment at the end of the month would be delivery conform to contract at that time."

Lord Jauncey attempted to set limits on the operation of mutuality. First, he disposed of the notion that a party is unable to enforce any claims if the other party has any claims outstanding. He affirmed that the obligations must be "contemporaneous", but that whether or not obligations are contemporaneous depends on the circumstances of the case. What kinds of circumstances did he have in mind?

It will also be noticed that Lord Jauncey referred to the need for the obligation of one party to be the "counterpart" of the obligation by the other party. The next case provided the Inner House with a more recent opportunity to review that issue in establishing the mutuality of obligations.

Macari v Celtic Football and Athletic Co Ltd 11–56

2000 S.L.T. 80

First Division: The Lord President (Rodger), Lords Caplan and Marnoch

Macari was dismissed as manager of Celtic and raised an action of damages for wrongful dismissal. Celtic's defence was that Macari had been in material and repudiatory breach of contract by failing to obey instructions of the managing director, McCann (particularly a requirement that Macari report to him on a weekly basis and attend more regularly at Celtic Park), and by not residing within a radius of 45 miles from Glasgow's George Square, as required by his contract. In his appeal against refusal of his claim, Macari argued that the instructions of the managing director had been given in bad faith with the intention of putting the manager in a situation where he could be dismissed; or that the club were in breach of the implied obligation of trust and confidence, which entitled Macari to withhold performance of his obligations as an employee of the club.

The court found that Macari's dismissal was justified.

"THE LORD PRESIDENT (RODGER): ... The whole picture is of the pursuer refusing to acknowledge the need to comply with an important term of his contract and so repudiating the contract. Unless the particular circumstances are such as to take the case outside the normal application of the law of contract, on this basis alone the defenders were entitled to accept that repudiation and to dismiss the pursuer, as they did. 11–57

The contention for the pursuer is that there are indeed circumstances which make the case special. Counsel expressed the point in two ways: either Mr McCann was acting in bad faith in giving instructions to the pursuer or else the defenders were in breach of an implied term of their contract with the pursuer since his conduct, as their managing director, was calculated and likely to destroy or seriously damage the relationship of confidence between the defenders and the pursuer (*Malik v Bank of Credit and Commerce International*, per Lord Steyn at [1998] AC, p 45). These two aspects underlie the pursuer's case that his failure to comply with various instructions given to him did not amount to a breach of contract on his part.

. . .

So far as the implied obligation of an employer is concerned, the formulation approved by their Lordships [in *Malik*] is that the employer shall not 'without reasonable and proper cause, conduct itself in a manner calculated and likely to destroy or seriously damage the relationship of confidence and trust between employer and employee' (p 45).

. . .

Viewed as a whole, the deliberate exclusion of the pursuer from board meetings and this conduct of the managing director do indeed appear to me to have been calculated and likely to cause serious damage to the relationship of confidence and trust between the pursuer, as manager, and the defenders, as his employers. The defenders were therefore in breach of the implied term of trust and confidence.

The contention for the pursuer was that this breach by the defenders went to the heart of the parties' contractual relationship and in effect meant that the defenders were not entitled to insist on the pursuer performing his corresponding duty of loyalty or fidelity to the defenders. The effect of this was said to be that the defenders could not insist on the pursuer obeying the instructions given to him on their behalf and he could choose not to obey such instructions and to do the manager's job in his own way, while receiving his salary and other benefits under the contract.

Where, as here, an employee continues to work despite a breach of the implied term, depending on the circumstances, this may entitle a court to infer that he has waived all or some of his rights against the employer arising out of the breach. The issue of waiver was not explored in the court below and in the circumstances I proceed on the basis, most favourable to the pursuer, that the defenders' was a continuing breach and that the pursuer had not waived his rights arising out of it.

Unquestionably, our law recognises that in certain circumstances a party is entitled to withhold performance of an obligation under a contract when the other party has failed to perform his obligation. The rule is found in many systems, sometimes being referred to as the *exceptio non adimpleti contractus*. The development and scope of the rule are surveyed by Jansen JA by way of background to the decision of the Appellate Division in *BK Tooling v Scope Precision Engineering* at 1979 (1) SA, pp 415–419. Although there is therefore no doubt about the existence of the rule, it is considerably harder to define its scope in our law.

The starting point for the rule is the idea, hardly novel or controversial in itself, that in a contract containing mutual obligations, the obligations of the one party can be seen as counterbalancing the obligations of the other. It is but a short step to say that the one party undertakes to perform his obligations *on condition that* the other party does so too. This in turn leads to the conclusion that one party does not need to perform his obligations where the other party is not performing the obligations on him. Some very general statements to this effect are found in our books—for example, in Erskine's *Institute,* III iii 86: 'No party in a mutual contract, where the obligations on the parties are the causes of one another, can demand performance from the other, if he himself either cannot or will not perform the counterpart, for the mutual obligations are considered as conditional.'

A similar rather sweeping approach is to be found in the opinion of Lord Justice Clerk Moncreiff in *Turnbull v McLean* at (1874) 1 R, p 738: 'I understand the law of Scotland, in regard to mutual contracts, to be quite clear—1st, that the stipulations on either side are the counterparts and the consideration given for each other; 2d, that a failure to perform any material or substantial part of the contract on the part of one will prevent him from suing the other for performance; and, 3d, that where one party has refused or failed to perform his part of the contract in any material respect the other is entitled either to insist for implement, claiming damages for the breach, or to rescind the contract altogether,—except so far as it has been performed.'

This statement is in turn used by Gloag, *Contract* (2nd ed), p 592 as authority for his own statement to the effect that the normal construction of a contract containing mutual obligations is that one party 'obliges himself subject to the implied condition that performance cannot be required from him unless it is given or tendered on the other side'.

Such general statements may give rise to few problems in the case of simple contracts involving only a limited number of obligations on either side. They can, however, be difficult to apply in practice to situations arising out of complex contracts containing a wide spread of obligations. This was recognised, in the context of a contract for performance in stages, in *Bank of East Asia Ltd v Scottish Enterprise*, where the House of Lords re-examined the scope of the rule. General statements, such as those which I have quoted, must now be studied in the light of the qualifications introduced by that decision. An indication of the overall approach adopted by the House is to be found in the comment of Lord Jauncey at 1997 SLT, p 1216: [The Lord President quoted extensively from the speech of Lord Jauncey and continued]:

This authoritative gloss by Lord Jauncey confirms that the law does not regard each and every obligation by one party as being necessarily and invariably the counterpart of every obligation by the other. One has to have regard to the circumstances. Lord Jauncey deduces from this that a material breach by one party of a particular term of a contract does not of itself mean that he cannot require the other party to perform *any* of his obligations under the contract. Rather, the party in breach cannot insist on the other party performing his obligations in relation to the part of the contract of which the first party is in breach. It is perhaps worth making the point that equally the party not in breach is entitled to withhold performance only for so long as the other party is in breach . . .

Lord Jauncey does not spell out the circumstances in which one obligation will fall to be regarded as the counterpart of another. Sometimes, of course, the express terms of the contract will regulate the matter. In other cases it depends on the intention of the parties as gleaned from the terms of the contract. Lord McLaren said as much long ago in *Sivright v Lightbourne* at (1890) 17 R, p 920: 'The question whether the two obligations are conditional with respect to one another, so that nonperformance by the one party entitles the other party to withhold performance of his obligation, is always a question of intention to be determined by the terms of the contract itself, and the surrounding circumstances, which often point to implied terms.'

. . .

In the present case I have approached the matter on the basis of the *Bank of East Asia*. In my view the argument for the pursuer is unsound.

The defenders' breach of the trust and confidence term was a material breach of contract on their part which the pursuer would have been entitled to accept by leaving his employment and suing them for damages. In fact he did not do so: he remained and drew his salary under his contract but failed to comply with the instructions given to him by the managing director. Of course, as the defenders pointed out, the pursuer did not refuse to obey these instructions because he had lost trust or confidence in the defenders. Rather, he deliberately chose not to comply with them, believing that he knew best what was involved in managing a football club and being determined to do it in his own way. In itself that point would not assist the defenders: whatever his reasons, the pursuer would not have been in breach of contract if any breach of the implied term by the defenders meant that they were not entitled to insist on him complying with their instructions.

As his counsel acknowledged, if sound, the argument for the pursuer would have potentially far reaching consequences. If it were the case that a breach of the implied term of trust and confidence meant that an employee was entitled to ignore his employer's instructions, then it would mean, for instance, that he could continue working and draw his salary but refuse to obey instructions relating to matters of health and safety. The true position seems to me to be that, if an employee is faced with a breach of the trust and confidence term by his employer but chooses to continue to work and draw his salary, he must do the work in accordance with the terms of his contract. That in turn means that, as regards his work, he must obey any lawful and legitimate instructions which his employer gives him. It is in return for such work in conformity with the contract that the employer is obliged to pay the employee his salary under the contract. On the other hand, in no relevant sense can it be said that an employee's obligation to do his work in accordance with the lawful and legitimate instructions of his employer is, in the words of Lord Jauncey, 'the counterpart' of his employer's obligation under the implied term. . . .

In the present case the pursuer continued to work as manager of the club and to draw the salary for that work. The defenders' managing director gave him instructions about residence, attendance and reporting, all of which were lawful and legitimate and related to his work under the contract. For the reasons which I have given, the pursuer was obliged to comply with those instructions and his persistent failures to do so were not only breaches but material breaches of his contract with the defenders.

In any event, the pursuer had an obligation under a specific term of his contract, rather than by virtue of any instruction, to reside within 45 miles of George Square. When asked what obligation the defenders had breached which was the counterpart of this obligation, counsel for the pursuer could refer only to the general implied obligation of trust and confidence. But there is nothing in the residence obligation which relates to that implied obligation, or makes it the counterpart of that obligation. Therefore any breach of the implied term would not disable the defenders from insisting that the pursuer should comply with the residence clause.

For all these reasons in June 1994 the pursuer was in material breach of contract by reason of his failure to comply with the residence clause, by reason of his failure to comply with the instruction to attend more regularly at Celtic Park and by reason of his failure to comply with his undertaking to report to Mr McCann on a weekly basis . . .

Conclusion

For these reasons the defenders did not breach their contract with the pursuer in dismissing him and the pursuer's action must fail. It is accordingly, unnecessary to deal with the separate issue about the quantum of damages which would fall to be awarded if the defenders were in breach. I simply invite your Lordships to refuse the reclaiming motion."

In addition to the obligations being contemporaneous, Lord Rodger stressed that the obligations of the parties, to be mutual, must also be counterparts. He placed important limits on the power of one party to claim the right to refuse performance on the ground that the other party has failed to perform.

Anticipatory breach[42]

In a contract between A and B, A may indicate to B that although A's performance is not yet due, A will not be in a position to perform when it does fall due. This is not uncommon in executory contracts and raises a question similar to that just examined: what are the rights of the party not in breach? **11–58**

Such a breach may take several forms. For example, a party is in breach by intimating an unwillingness or inability to perform at the time when performance is due and indicating thereby repudiation of the contract. In *Hoechster v De la Tour*,[43] the English case often regarded as the origin of the modern rule, an indication by a courier in May that he would not be willing to take charge of a tour of the Alps in June, as agreed in a contract made in April, was anticipatory breach, entitling the party not in breach to immediate remedies. Examples are, however, relatively rare in the Scottish reports. The following Outer House decision provides a more recent illustration and a review of the current law.

Edinburgh Grain Ltd (in liquidation) v Marshall Food Group Ltd **11–59**
1999 S.L.T. 15
Outer House: Lord Hamilton

P supplied D with grain and barley under regular contracts made orally between P's managing director and the managing director of one of D's subsidiaries. P went into liquidation and sued D for sums outstanding on past deliveries. In the week commencing Monday 13 November 1995, P failed to deliver to D all of the grain for which they had contracted. On Friday of the same week P's managing director, after taking advice, decided to liquidate P and advised D that, due to their financial situation, P would be unable to make deliveries under the outstanding contracts with D. He also later confirmed that P did not have any grain for onward delivery and on Thursday, 23 November, D's managing director was advised that a provisional liquidator had been appointed the previous Tuesday. D told P that P had already repudiated the contracts on 23 November and that this had been accepted by D, so that D were entitled to withhold payment of invoices sought by the liquidator pending ascertainment of their claim against P for breach of contract. P argued that there was no conduct in relation to repudiation which clearly demonstrated an intention not to fulfil the series of contracts as a whole.

The Lord Ordinary found that P had repudiated the contract.

"LORD HAMILTON: ... The principal matter for determination was whether, in the period referred to, Edinburgh Grain had repudiated these contracts as a whole. **11–60**

In Scotland there has been limited judicial discussion of what is commonly referred to as 'anticipatory breach' of contract. In *Monklands District Council v Ravenstone Securities* Lord Dunpark, in discussing the legal effect of repudiation of an onerous consensual contract, said at 1980 SLT (Notes), p 31: 'The concept of such a contract is that the undertaking of a duty (i.e. the promise of performance) by an obligant creates a corresponding right of the obligee to demand performance when that becomes due; but

[42] For a discussion of the definition of anticipatory breach, see WW McBryde, *The Law of Contract in Scotland*, 3rd edn (Edinburgh: W. Green, 2007) paras 20–23—20–31. As he points out (at para.20–23), "[t]he whole concept has been the subject of much hostile academic comment". Even the expression itself is a matter of debate, although the Scottish Law Commission had no problem with it in its *Report on Remedies on Remedies for Breach of Contract* (1999), para.7.3 onwards. HL MacQueen and J Thomson, *Contract Law in Scotland*, 3rd edn (London: Bloomsbury, 2012) avoid the term altogether, preferring instead "Refusal to perform (repudiation)" (at para.5.28 onwards but see also para.5.31).

[43] *Hoechster v De la Tour* (1853) 2 E.B. 678.

that is not all. In my opinion, the undertaking to perform at the due date binds the obligant not only to perform at the due date, but also to adhere to that undertaking from the conclusion of the contract until performance. Accordingly, if at any time during that period the obligant informs the obligee that he will not perform his contractual duty when the time comes, that, in my opinion, is a breach of contract. Indeed, it is so material a breach that the law entitles the obligee to treat that statement as a repudiation by the obligant of his contractual obligations and at once to declare the contract terminated and to claim damages, without waiting for the date when performance is due. The fact that the law allows the obligee this option demonstrates that intimation of refusal or inability to perform given before the due date is per se a breach of contract; if it were not, the obligee would have no rightful claim for damages in advance of non-performance at the due date'.

He later described such a breach as 'an inchoate breach'.

Lord Dunpark speaks in the context of that case of the obligant informing the obligee that he will not perform his contractual duty and of intimation of refusal or inability to perform; but it is plain on authority that action to the same effect may also constitute anticipatory breach (*Forslind*). Moreover, silence or inaction may, when taken along with other conduct, be as eloquent of repudiation as express statements or positive action alone. As Lord Steyn said in a slightly different context in *Vitol SA v Norelf Ltd* at [1996] AC, p 812: 'Sometimes in the practical world of businessmen an omission to act may be as pregnant with meaning as a positive declaration'.

What, in my view, is required for repudiation is conduct demonstrative of an intention not to perform fundamental contractual obligations as and when they fall due. That intention may have its origin in a choice by the obligant not to fulfil his contract or in an inability on his part to do so.

Both counsel cited English authority and neither suggested that there was any material difference between Scots and English law in this field. It is accordingly useful to examine the approach adopted by the English courts.

In *Heyman v Darwins Ltd* at [1942] AC, p 397 Lord Porter, having referred to Anson on Contracts, stated: 'The three sets of circumstances giving rise to a discharge of contract are tabulated by Anson as: (i) renunciation by a party of his liabilities under it; (ii) impossibility created by his own act; and (iii) total or partial failure of performance. In the case of the first two the renunciation may occur or impossibility be created either before or at the time for performance. In the case of the third, it can occur only at the time or during the course of performance.'

All these acts, he added, might compendiously be described as repudiation, though that expression was more particularly used of renunciation before the time of performance had arrived.

In *Universal Cargo Carriers Corporation v Citati* at [1957] 2 QB, p 436, having quoted the above words from Lord Porter, Devlin J continued:

'The third of these is the ordinary case of actual breach, and the first two state the two modes of anticipatory breach. In order that the arguments which I have heard from either side can be rightly considered, it is necessary that I should develop rather more fully what is meant by each of these two modes.

'A renunciation can be made either by words or by conduct, provided it is clearly made. It is often put that the party renunciating must "evince an intention" not to go on with the contract. The intention can be evinced either by words or by conduct. The test of whether an intention is sufficiently evinced by conduct is whether the party renunciating has acted in such a way as to lead a reasonable person to the conclusion that he does not intend to fulfil his part of the contract'.

In later discussion of renunciation Devlin J said at pp 437–438: 'Since a man must be both ready and willing to perform, a profession by words or conduct of inability is by itself enough to constitute renunciation. But unwillingness and inability are often difficult to disentangle, and it is rarely necessary to make the attempt. Inability often lies at the root of unwillingness to perform. Willingness in this context does not mean cheerfulness; it means simply an intent to perform. To say: "I would like to but I cannot" negatives intent just as much as "I will not."'

At a later point in his judgment Devlin J discussed various aspects of the second mode of anticipatory breach (namely impossibility created by his own act).

I adopt the quoted passages from Devlin J's judgment as an accurate analysis of the first mode of anticipatory breach and as consistent with Scots law. In particular, profession by words or conduct either of unwillingness or of inability to perform is, in my view, enough to constitute renunciation.

Counsel for the defender submitted that a contracting party, for his own good reasons, might be unwilling to give or might not give intimation of his intention in an unequivocal form. However, the question, he argued, had to be viewed objectively, it being sufficient if the contracting party by his conduct led a reasonable person to conclude that there was an absence of intention to fulfil his basic contractual obligations (*Forslind*, especially per Lord Shaw of Dunfermline at 1922 SC (HL), p 191; 1922 SLT, pp 508–509).

I accept that intention in this context requires to be viewed objectively (*Woodar Investment v Wimpey Construction*, per Lord Keith at p 586) and that the party's words, if inconsistent with his actings, need not necessarily be accepted at face value (*Forslind*, especially per Viscount Haldane at p 179 (p 502) and Lord Shaw of Dunfermline at p 191 (pp 508–509)).

The conduct viewed objectively as a whole must, in my view, clearly indicate that the contracting party has adopted an attitude that he will not or cannot perform.

In my view, the attitude adopted by Edinburgh Grain towards the defender in the period between Friday 17 and Thursday 23 November 1995 in respect of its outstanding contracts, viewed objectively as at the end of that period, clearly indicated that Edinburgh Grain had by its conduct renounced its obligations of delivery of grain under those contracts. The implicit basis of that renunciation was an acknowledged inability, prospective to the respective dates of performance, so to perform."

The unilateral cancellation of a contract before the due date of performance is in that sense a repudiatory breach. Nevertheless, to avoid confusion with the consequences of material breach, the expression anticipatory breach is to be preferred, since it emphasises that it precedes the time due for performance. In this case, the breach was anticipatory to the extent that it related to those contracts that had yet to be performed. Because P had already gone into liquidation, D had little choice but to accept P's anticipatory breach. There will be circumstances where, as in the following case the party not in breach has an apparent choice: to accept the repudiation, bring the contract to an end and recover any losses; or reject the breach, continue with the contract and, if the other party fails to perform on the date due for performance, bring the contract to an end and seek to recover any losses. **11–61**

11–62

White and Carter (Councils) Ltd v McGregor

1962 S.C. (H.L.) 1

House of Lords: Lords Hodson, Keith of Avonholm, Morton of Henryton, Reid and Tucker

In 1954 McGregor, who owned a garage in Clydebank, contracted with White and Carter, a firm of advertising contractors, that they would display advertisements of the garage on litter bins which White and Carter supplied to local authorities. In 1957 Ward, McGregor's sales manager, entered into a further contract with White and Carter that they would continue advertising the garage in this way for a period of three years from the date of the first advertisement. Ward had no authority to enter into the contract. The same day, McGregor wrote cancelling the contract. White and Carter refused to accept the cancellation and exhibited the advertisements in accordance with the contract. They now claimed payment under the contract for three years' advertising.

A majority of the House (Lords Reid, Hodson and Tucker) found for White and Carter. Lords Morton and Keith delivered dissenting judgments.

11–63 "LORD REID: ... The general rule cannot be in doubt. It was settled in Scotland at least as early as 1848, and it has been authoritatively stated time and again both in Scotland and England. If one party to the contract repudiates it in the sense of making it clear to the other party that he refuses or will refuse to carry out his part of the contract, the other party, the innocent party, has an option. He may accept that repudiation and sue for damages for breach of contract, whether or not the time of performance has come; or he may, if he chooses, disregard or refuse to accept it and then the contract remains in full effect ...

[I]t never has been the law that a person is only entitled to enforce his contractual rights in a reasonable way, and that a court will not support an attempt to enforce them in an unreasonable way. One reason why that is not the law is, no doubt, because it was thought that it would create too much uncertainty to require the Court to decide whether it is reasonable or equitable to allow a party to enforce his full rights under a contract ...

It may well be that, if it can be shown that a person has no legitimate interest, financial or otherwise, in performing the contract rather than claiming damages, he ought not to be allowed to saddle the other party with an additional burden with no benefit to himself. If a party has no interest to enforce a stipulation, he cannot in general enforce it: so it might be said that, if a party has no interest to insist on a particular remedy, he ought not to be allowed to insist on it. And, just as a party is not allowed to enforce a penalty, so he ought not to be allowed to penalise the other party by taking one course when another is equally advantageous to him. If I may revert to the example which I gave of a company engaging an expert to prepare an elaborate report and then repudiating before anything was done, it might be that the company could show that the expert had no substantial or legitimate interest in carrying out the work rather than accepting damages: I would think that the *de minimis* principle would apply in determining whether his interest was substantial, and that he might have a legitimate interest other than an immediate financial interest. But if the expert has no such interest, then that might be regarded as a proper case for the exercise of the general equitable jurisdiction of the Court. But that is not the case. Here, the respondent did not set out to prove that the appellants had no legitimate interest in completing the contract and claiming the contract price rather than claiming damages; there is nothing in the findings of fact to support such a case, and it seems improbable that any such case could have been proved. It is, in my judgment, impossible to say that the appellants should be deprived of their right to claim the contract price merely because the benefit to them, as against claiming damages and reletting their advertising space, might be small in comparison with the loss to the respondent: that is the most that could be said in favour of the respondent. Parliament has on many occasions relieved parties from certain kinds of improvident or oppressive contracts, but the common law can only do that in very limited circumstances.

LORD MORTON OF HENRYTON: ... It is well established that repudiation by one party does not put an end to a contract. The other party can say: 'I hold you to your contract, which still remains in force.' What then is his remedy if the repudiating party persists in his repudiation and refuses to carry out his part of the contract? The contract has been broken. The innocent party is entitled to be compensated by damages for any loss which he has suffered by reason of the breach, and in a limited class of cases the Court will decree specific implement. The law of Scotland provides no other remedy for breach of contract, and there is no reported case which decides that the innocent party may act as the appellants have acted. The present case is one in which specific implement could not be decreed, since the only obligation of the respondent under the contract was to pay a sum of money for services rendered by the appellants. Yet the appellants are claiming a kind of inverted specific implement of the contract. They first insist on performing their part of the contract, against the will of the other party, and then claim that he must perform his part and pay the contract price for unwanted services. In my opinion, the appellants' only remedy was damages, and they were bound to take steps to minimise their loss, according to a well-established rule of law. Far from doing this, having incurred no expense at the date of repudiation, they made no attempt to procure another advertiser, but deliberately went on to incur expense and perform unwanted services with the intention of creating a money debt which did not exist at the date of the repudiation." 11–64

Lord Morton's speech dissented from the decision of the majority.

The case restates the principle that acts that will prevent a party from performing when performance is due, amount to repudiation. The "innocent" party may accept the breach and seek remedies immediately; or reject the breach, wait until the due day for performance, and if performance is not forthcoming, seek remedies. The important fact in this case was that the breach did not terminate the contract; it merely entitled the party not in breach to do so. If that party chooses not to do so, the contract, and the rights under it, continue. The decision could allow a party to seek payment for a totally unwanted performance.

Salaried Staff London Loan Co Ltd v Swears and Wells Ltd 11–65

1985 S.L.T. 326

Court of Session, First Division: The Lord President (Emslie), Lords Cameron and Ross

Swears and Wells were tenants of Salaried under a commercial lease which was expressly stated to last until 2011. In March 1982, Swears and Wells purported to renounce the lease and vacated the premises by the end of the month. Salaried refused to accept this repudiation and successfully sought recovery of the rent.

"LORD PRESIDENT (EMSLIE): ... The common law which is applicable in the events which have happened in this case is not in doubt. In *Stewart v Kennedy*, Lord Watson at pp. 9–10 said this: 'I do not think that upon this matter any assistance can be derived from English decisions; because the laws of the two countries regard the right to specific performance from different standpoints. In England the only legal right arising 11–66 from a breach of contract is a claim of damages; specific performance is not a matter of legal right, but a purely equitable remedy, which the Court can withhold when there are sufficient reasons of conscience or expediency against it. But in Scotland the breach of a contract for the sale of a specific subject such as landed estate gives the party aggrieved the legal right to sue for implement, and although he may elect to do so, he cannot be compelled to resort to the alternative of an action of damages unless implement is shown to be impossible, in which case *loco facti subit damnum et interesse*. Even where implement is possible, I do not doubt that the Court of Session has inherent power to refuse the legal remedy upon equitable grounds, although I know of no instance in which it has done so. It is quite conceivable that circumstances might occur which would make it inconvenient and unjust to enforce specific performance of a contract of sale, but I do not think that any such case is presented in this appeal.'

That these observations are of general application in all cases of breach of contract is clear enough and I cannot do better than to quote from the speech of Lord Reid in *White and Carter (Councils) Ltd*, 1962 S.L.T. at p.10: 'The general rule cannot be in doubt, It was settled in Scotland at least as early as 1848, and it has been authoritatively stated time and again in both Scotland and England. If one party to a contract repudiates it in the sense of making it clear to the other party that he refuses or will refuse to carry out his part of the contract, the other party, the innocent party, has an option. He may accept that repudiation and sue for damages for breach of contract whether or not the time for performance has come; or he may if he chooses disregard or refuse to accept it and then the contract remains in full effect.'

The only question which remains is as to the circumstances in which the Court of Session may deny to the victim of a breach of contract the exercise of his undoubted legal right to sue for implement of all or any of the obligations incumbent upon the party in breach. It has already been noted that the court may only do this on equitable grounds and in this connection the case of *Grahame v Magistrates of Kirkcaldy* offers authoritative guidance. In that case Lord Watson, in a passage quoted by Lord Reid in his speech in *White and Carter (Councils) Ltd* at p.11, expressed himself thus: 'It appears to me that a superior Court, having equitable jurisdiction, must also have a discretion, in certain exceptional cases, to withhold from parties applying for it that remedy to which, in ordinary circumstances, they would be entitled as a matter of course ... In order to justify the exercise of such a discretionary power there must be some very cogent reason for depriving litigants of the ordinary means of enforcing their legal rights. There are, so far as I know, only three decided cases in which the Court of Session, there being no facts sufficient to raise a plea in bar of the action, have nevertheless denied to the pursuer the remedy to which, in strict law, he was entitled. These authorities seem to establish, if that were necessary, the proposition that the Court has the power of declining, upon equitable grounds, to enforce an admittedly legal right, but they also show that the power has been very rarely exercised.'

As the speeches of Lords Reid and Hodson in *White and Carter (Councils) Ltd* show, the court is not concerned at all with the question whether it is reasonable for a pursuer to enforce his contractual rights in a particular way. From this brief examination of the authorities it will be seen that the court will only decline to allow a pursuer to enforce an admittedly legal right in exceptional circumstances and must find some very cogent reason for exercising the particular power which has been rarely used. Considerations of what is or is not reasonable are quite irrelevant. I have only to add that Lord Reid in *White and Carter (Councils) Ltd*, in examining the possibility that there is some general equitable principle or element of public policy which requires some limitation of the contractual rights of an innocent party, expressed the view that the court might not allow such a party to enforce a legal right if he has no legitimate interest, financial or otherwise, in performing the contract rather than claiming damages.

In this settled state of our law I have not the slightest doubt that the pursuers in this action do not require to make averments in justification of their claim. They sue for payment of a contractual debt, in the exercise of a legal right to do so. They are not seeking an equitable remedy at the hands of the court. It is not for the pursuers to show that there are no circumstances which might lead the court to decline to enforce their legal right. If there are exceptional circumstances and cogent reasons which might persuade the court on equitable grounds to refuse to the pursuers their legal remedy it is for the defenders to make the appropriate averments in defence to the action. They have not done so in this case. In the result there is no room for the view that the pursuers' averments are irrelevant or lacking in specification. The reclaiming motion for the pursuers must, accordingly, in my opinion, be allowed.

In expressing this opinion I should say that I consider that in this action, which is concerned only with rents which have accrued unpaid in the relatively short period between the repudiation of the lease by the defenders and 31 December 1982, it would be extremely difficult to envisage the existence of cogent reasons to support the suggestion that it is somehow inconvenient and unjust for the pursuers to maintain the contract instead of accepting the repudiation and suing for damages. If the pursuers continue to maintain the contract and continue to sue for payment of unpaid rent in subsequent actions it may well be that different considerations will then arise. These, no doubt, will be focused in the defenders' pleadings. Lest it may be thought that I may have overlooked the matter I should add that in the single action which we are considering in this reclaiming motion, it is impossible to support the suggestion that the pursuers have no legitimate interest, financial or otherwise, to insist at least meantime, in maintaining the lease instead of accepting the repudiation and claiming damages."

It is clear from this decision—and from Lord Reid's speech in *White and Carter*—that the right to continue with the contract is hedged with limitations: notably, that the party not in breach must be able to perform without co-operation from the other party and must have a legitimate interest, financial or otherwise, in performing. The English courts have avoided this interpretation. Lord Reid's suggested limitations were raised directly in the next case.

AMA (New Town) Ltd v Law 11–67

Court of Session, Inner House: Lady Dorrian, Lords Menzies, Philip

[2013] CSIH 61; 2013 S.C. 608

Law, one of several defenders to this action, had entered into missives to buy off-plan flats in a housing development being undertaken by AMA. The price was £212,000. Under cl.3 of the missives, the outstanding balance of £201,400 was payable "in full before 2.00 p.m. on the date of entry". The clause also provided that the date of entry was to be 14 days from the later of: (a) the date on which the plot was passed by the local authority as habitable and fit for occupation; and (b) the date on which a cover note was issued by the National House Building Council and Zurich Insurance confirming that a new home warranty would be issued for the plot. In each case the date of entry was 23 December 2009. Clause 3 also provided:

> "Entry and vacant possession will be given and the keys released to the Purchaser only on payment of the full purchase price (including the price of any extra items not previously paid for) and any interest due on the purchase price. Consignation of the price will not be accepted."

At the date of entry, agents for Law and other defenders indicated to agents for AMA that their clients were not in a position to proceed with their respective purchases. AMA made a formal demand for payment on 24 December 2009 and, when no payment was forthcoming, they sued for payment of the balance of the purchase price. Law and the other defenders counterclaimed that AMA were in breach of the missives because some the flats had been let as serviced apartments and therefore the use had changed from residential to commercial, and in respect of a planning requirement.

The sheriff dismissed the counterclaim and all parties appealed to the Court of Session. The Inner House decided that the sheriff was correct to dismiss the counterclaim and allowed the appeal in favour of AMA.

11–68 "LORD MENZIES—

[1] I have had the advantage of reading in draft the opinion of Lady Dorrian, and I am in complete agreement with her reasoning and with the result produced by it. The submissions advanced on behalf of the defenders and respondents would have the effect of inverting the well-established rule of Scots law that if one party to a contract repudiates it, the innocent party has an option to accept the repudiation and sue for damages for breach of contract, or to seek enforcement of the contract. That this option rests with the innocent party cannot be in doubt—it has been stated repeatedly in the most authoritative terms in the several authorities referred to by Lady Dorrian. If the submissions for the defenders and respondents were well founded, this option could be negated simply by the repudiating party declining to pay the sum due in terms of the contract, in which case the innocent party would be confined to seeking damages for breach of contract. That is not our law.

...

LADY DORRIAN—

...

11–69 **Discussion and decision**

[46] It is clear from the speech of Lord Reid in *White and Carter (Councils) Ltd v McGregor* that in a situation such as the present, the innocent party has the choice either of accepting the repudiation and seeking damages or of refusing to accept it, in which case the contract remains in full force and may be implemented. That this is the basic principle is emphasised by the Lord President in the passage from *Salaried Staff London Loan Co Ltd v Swears and Wells Ltd* quoted above. He approved the words of the Lord Ordinary that the innocent party 'cannot in the normal case be compelled to seek the alternative remedy if he does not wish to do so.' The matter was put very succinctly by Lord Cameron in *Salaried Staff*, thus (p 195):

'The freedom of the innocent party's choice of remedy is uncontrolled by the party in breach; it is for the innocent party primarily to select that course which to him seems appropriate, subject, however, to a very limited discretionary power in the court which may be invoked in certain exceptional circumstances, to control and direct the remedy which the innocent party will be held entitled to exercise.'

[47] In the Inner House in *White and Carter* , the Lord President rejected the pursuers' claim on the basis that the court could not force the defenders to accept advertisements which they did not want. This reasoning was not endorsed in the House of Lords, where the innocent party's right to a choice of remedy was emphasised. The exception recognised by Lord Reid was not based on any equitable considerations of not forcing a party to accept that which they no longer want. It was limited to the situation where the innocent party was unable to earn the contract price without the assent or co-operation of the other. That is echoed, in my view, by the Lord President in *Salaried Staff* when he said that an innocent party 'cannot be compelled to resort to the alternative of an action

of damages unless implement is shown to be impossible'. That is not the position in the present case. The terms of the contract are clear: payment was triggered by the date of entry and nothing else. Clearly, once payment had been made the appellants would be obliged to grant a valid disposition granting a valid title, and to give vacant possession of the property. They aver that they are ready, willing and able to do so. It is not averred for the respondents that there is any impediment to the appellants' being able to do so. They rely entirely on their own unwillingness to meet their obligations under the contract. Indeed, they admit that the appellants are willing and able to perform their side of the bargain. In my view this is far from the sort of situation envisaged by Lord Reid, and I agree that the examples given by counsel for the appellants are more apposite to reflect those exceptions.

[48] With respect to the sheriff principal in *AMA (New Town) Ltd v McKenna*, I do not agree that the extent to which an innocent party may be able to enforce a repudiated contract is 'restricted'. In my view the opposite is the case: the innocent party will be able to do so unless circumstances render it impossible, or in exceptional circumstances, wholly unjust.

[49] The sheriff principal referred to the usual practice of raising an action for implement, failing which damages—what is referred to by *McBryde and Gretton* ['Sale of Heritable Property and Failure to Pay' 2012 SLT (News) 17–21)] as the judicial ultimatum. No doubt it may be the more usual practice to follow such a course, and no doubt that is why the stylebooks give this form of action as the appropriate style in the circumstances, but it seems to me that this is in all likelihood a practice which has sprung up for practical considerations. In the vast majority of cases the reason for default on the part of the purchaser will be impecuniosity. In the vast majority of such cases there would be little to be gained for a seller in obtaining a decree for payment, and the more sensible and practical step would be to resell the property and seek damages, a course which would probably also lead to a quicker resolution of the problem, at least if he is able to resell the property. That is however only in 'most cases'. The respondent in the principal case and the company which he controls are said to be property developers themselves. The appellants clearly believe that the alleged impecuniosity is rather an unwillingness to proceed further because it is now not convenient. They clearly believe that they will be able to recover the funds they seek. They may be right about that; they may be wrong; but the risk is one for them to choose to take. It is not something about which they should be dictated to by the party in default.

[50] The same practical considerations in my view underlie the practice that payment of the price and delivery of the disposition with vacant possession are treated in practice as contemporaneous events. The practice seems to be that the disposition is provided in advance to the purchaser's agents on condition that it is held to be undelivered until payment is made, thus achieving contemporaneity. Again, this is a sensible practical step for parties to take. On the one hand a seller would not wish to part with the title until he is sure of payment; a purchaser would be unwilling to hand over his money until he is sure of the title. However this again is a matter of convenience and not any formal requirement or condition of a contract for the sale of heritage. Counsel for the respondents referred to the obligation under the missives as concurrent and reciprocal. They are certainly reciprocal, and by common practice they may usually be concurrent but in the present case they are not and there is no fundamental requirement that they require to be so. Parties are free to agree that the money will be handed over in advance of the title; or that the title will be transferred in advance of payment. The risks which they run by so doing are risks which they are entitled to take. In this case handing over the disposition in advance is not a prerequisite for payment of the purchase price.

[51] The submission for the respondents was that 'since it would be necessary for the respondents to co-operate before the contract could be completed', the only available

remedy was damages. In the course of discussion, the court sought to clarify exactly what was the nature of the required co-operation upon which the respondents relied. It seems to me that there was a certain inconsistency in the position adopted. He submitted that in order for the contract to be completed the respondents had to 'accept' the disposition. However, he rejected the suggestion that there was any obligation on them to do so, and in so far as the sheriff principal in *AMA (New Town) Ltd v McKenna* had appeared to think otherwise, counsel did not support that reasoning. Accordingly, what it amounted to was that he agreed that there was no contractual requirement on them to accept the disposition, but argued that nevertheless their practical cooperation was required to enable the contract to be completed. As far as I can see the only cooperation, either contractually or in practical terms, was to pay the price, which they refused to do. Effectively his submission amounted to saying that a party who had no further obligation under a contract but to pay the price, could prevent performance or enforcement of the contract by the willing party by simply refusing to do so. He submitted that the matter would not even be improved were the appellants to deliver the disposition and keys to the defenders' agents, or lodge them in court, because although 'the pursuer had done all in his power, he could not complete the contract without assistance from defender'. Having rejected the notion that there was any obligation to accept the disposition he went on to say that the purchaser had to accept vacant possession, but again said that there was no contractual obligation to do so. Nevertheless he sought to rely on cl 3 but that only refers to the obligation to give vacant possession. Counsel specifically submitted that 'there is no contractual obligation to accept the keys'. 'The concurrent and reciprocal obligations are payment of price and vacant possession being given'.

[52] The absolute nature of the respondents' position can be seen from this submission:

'The respondents' case is whether they can fall within the exception of *White & Carter*: it is not necessary for there to be a positive obligation to bring themselves under that exception, because by refusing to co-operate they make it impossible for the pursuers to complete the contract.'

The contract would not be complete, not because the respondents had failed to honour an obligation but simply because they failed to co-operate.

[53] It is important to note that the argument proceeded on an absolute rejection of any suggestion that there was an obligation on the defenders to accept the disposition, despite a passing reference in the *McBryde and Gretton* article thus:

'But what if (as is likely) the defender is not willing to take delivery of the disposition—one of the simultaneous and reciprocal obligations under the missives? The court could be asked to ordain the defender to accept delivery (see *Harvey v Smith* [(1904) 6 F 511], following a 19th century style we cannot here examine). But how would such a decree be enforced against an unwilling defender?'

Given the position adopted for the respondents we were not therefore addressed on this issue and proceed on the basis that there is in current practice no such obligation, and that even if there were, it is not relied upon. Certainly, while formerly it could be argued that there might have been an implied obligation to register the title, for reasons of obligations to feudal superiors, which would I suppose have implied a need to take delivery of the disposition in the first place, it is difficult to see why such an implied obligation should in the majority of cases survive in a post-feudal world.

[54] It is also worth noting that in their article the professors note that '[i]f the price were to be payable without the conditions for payment being met, the court would be rewriting the contract.' In many cases that would be correct: it is not the case here since the conditions for payment have all been met. The exact nature of the missives entered into was not apparent from the report in *AMA (New Town) Ltd v McKenna* so would not have been available to them, but we have been assured on behalf of the appellants

who were of course parties to the case that they were to all intents and purposes identical with those under consideration in the present litigation.

. . .

[56] I accept that in certain circumstances it would be open to the court, for reasons of equity, to refuse to grant implement but in my view those circumstances would require to be highly unusual—'wholly exceptional' as it was put by Lord President Rodger in *Highland and Universal Properties Ltd v Safeway Properties Ltd (No 2)*—circumstances in which implement would impose a burden on the repudiating party completely out of proportion to the remainder of the contract; where the circumstances fell short of frustration but where implement of the contract would be so unreasonable as to be manifestly unjust. Here, the burden is simply payment of the price which has been contractually agreed.

[57] If the boot were on the other foot, the court would not refuse implement to a purchaser just because there would be inconvenience to the seller in granting a marketable title, for example, where the purchaser required to purchase a ransom strip. Only if the price demanded were exorbitant would the court contemplate refusing implement to the purchaser.

[58] Of course, I acknowledge that if the respondent is in truth so impecunious as to be unable to pay the price, complications can arise. However, there are ways in which such complications can be resolved. Moreover, it is not the case that no complications might follow were the appellants to accept repudiation and claim damages. They might not be able to resell the property; the impecuniosity of the respondents might mean that they would not be able to pay the award of damages. Many different situations could be envisaged. The mere fact that there might be awkward consequences, which require further legal steps to resolve, is not a reason for refusing the appellants their remedy.

. . .

LORD PHILIP— 11–70

[61] I too am in complete agreement with your Ladyship's opinion, with the conclusions reached, and the reasons for those conclusions.

[62] I would only add one point. Your Ladyship referred to the article by Profs McBryde and Gretton relied on by counsel for the respondent, in which they express concerns about the perceived difficulties which may arise if a seller of heritable property were to be granted decree for the unpaid price. What they appeared to me to be saying was that the 'judicial ultimatum' approach was the only reasonable one for the court to take in any such action by an unpaid seller. That, it seems to me, is at odds with a passage in Lord Reid's speech in *White and Carter (Councils) Ltd v McGregor* (p 14) cited by your Ladyship. His Lordship said:

'It might be, but it never has been, the law that a person is only entitled to enforce his contractual rights in a reasonable way, and that a court will not support an attempt to enforce them in an unreasonable way. One reason why that is not the law is, no doubt, because it was thought that it would create too much uncertainty to require the court to decide whether it is reasonable or equitable to allow a party to enforce his full rights under a contract. The Lord President cannot have meant that.'

[63] It follows from that that if the seller is entitled to decree for the unpaid price, it is not for the court to speculate about the possible consequences of granting such a decree."

This is a case of repudiation only, where one party is merely refusing to perform at the time when performance is due. It is not an anticipatory breach, such as that in *White and Carter v McGregor*. Nevertheless, the applicable principles are clearly the same. The Scottish Law Commission as long ago as 1999 considered the matter and made proposals for reform.[44]

11–71 *Report on Remedies for Breach of Contract*

Scottish Law Commission Report No.174 (December 1999)
Pt 1, Introduction

"**Part 2 Unreasonably Proceeding with Unwanted Performance**

Existing law

2.1 The leading case in this area is *White & Carter (Councils) Ltd v McGregor*.[1] The case involved a contract for the display, for three years, of advertisements of the business of a Clydebank garage. In 1954 there had been an agreement to display the advertisements. In 1957 there was a further three year contract, which became the subject of the dispute. The second contract was made by the sales manager of the garage but on the day it was made the owner of the garage wrote to the pursuers to cancel the contract. The pursuers refused to accept this cancellation and the advertisements were displayed. The pursuers successfully brought an action for the price due under the contract.

2.2 Because *White & Carter (Councils) Ltd* involved a party who did not claim damages, but instead the price due under the contract, the rules on mitigation of loss did not apply. The result was wasted and unwanted performance.[2] Lord Keith, dissenting, gave the example of an expert who goes to Hong Kong and prepares a report for a fee of £10,000, knowing from the beginning that the report is no longer wanted.[3] Many similar examples could be given.

2.3 A possible qualification of the rule affirmed in *White & Carter (Councils) Ltd* may be recognised if the pursuer had no 'legitimate interest' in performing. Lord Reid left this possibility open when he said:[4]

'It may well be that, if it can be shown that a person has no legitimate interest, financial or otherwise, in performing the contract rather than claiming damages, he ought not to be allowed to saddle the other party with an additional burden with no benefit to himself.'

This has enabled *White & Carter (Councils) Ltd* to be distinguished in England when it has appeared that full performance of the contract was wasteful.[5]

2.4 The problems were illustrated again in *Salaried Staff London Loan Company Ltd v Swears and Wells Ltd*.[6] Tenants under a 35 year lease repudiated the lease after 5 years. The landlords refused to accept the repudiation and held the tenants to their contract. The tenants were sued for rent and service charges for a period of nearly a year subsequent

the repudiation. The landlords' action succeeded. On the question whether the landlords could have sued each year for the next 29 years Lord President Emslie said:[7]

'If the pursuers continue to maintain the contract and continue to sue for payment of unpaid rent in subsequent actions it may well be that different considerations will then arise.'

[44] The proposals are based on what is now DCFR III.–3:301(2): "Where the creditor has not yet performed the reciprocal obligation for which payment will be due and it is clear that the debtor in the monetary obligation will be unwilling to receive performance, the creditor may nonetheless proceed with performance and may recover payment unless: (a) the creditor could have made a reasonable substitute transaction without significant effort or expense; or (b) performance would be unreasonable in the circumstances".

Similar reservations were expressed by Lord Cameron[8] and Lord Ross,[9] who referred to the possibility that

'it might be inferred that it would be manifestly unjust or unreasonable to allow the pursuers to continue suing for rent'.

These remarks recognised that there is a problem but do not provide a solution.

2.5 The rule in *White & Carter (Councils) Ltd* operates only when, as in that case, one party could perform without the co-operation of the other party. The advertisements were placed on litter bins. The pursuers could perform without the assistance of the garage. It would presumably have been a different matter if it had been the first contract between the parties and the garage had been required to provide the material for the advertisement. The pursuers would have had no option but to seek damages. It is difficult to defend a principle which turns on the distinction between contracts which require the co-operation of the other party for performance, and those which do not.[10]

Criticism of existing law

2.6 There is nothing unreasonable in a general rule that contracts must be performed and that a party is entitled to perform and claim payment in accordance with the agreed terms. What is unreasonable is to push that general rule to absurd lengths. Most people, we believe, would consider it absurd to allow a party who has been clearly told that performance is unwanted, who has no special interest in tendering performance, and for whom damages would be an adequate remedy, to proceed to perform simply in order to increase the burden on the other party. And yet that appears to be the existing law, although it is true that the courts might yet be able to recognise exceptions to it. Almost all the consultees who responded on this issue considered that reform was desirable. 11–72

Recommendation

2.7 Our recommendation is based on the solution to this problem contained in the *Principles of European Contract Law*. The *Principles* have the following provision.[11] 11–73

'Where the creditor has not yet performed its obligation and it is clear that the debtor will be unwilling to receive performance, the creditor may nonetheless proceed with its performance and may recover any sum due under the contract unless:

(a) it could have made a reasonable substitute transaction without significant effort or expense; or
(b) performance would be unreasonable in the circumstances.'

The starting point is that, notwithstanding intimation that performance is no longer wanted, a contracting party is entitled to perform in accordance with the contract and to sue for the contract price, but there are exceptions for the cases where there is no legitimate interest in performing or where performance would be unreasonable. In such cases the pursuer's remedy is to rescind the contract and claim damages. The rules on mitigation of loss would then apply.

2.8 The reference to a 'substitute transaction' is to a transaction by which the creditor obtains a satisfactory substitute performance. A common example would be that of a commercial manufacturer of standard goods with a ready market who is able to obtain another buyer without difficulty. The manufacturer could not force unwanted goods on a purchaser and sue for the price. Another example would be that of a landlord whose tenant repudiates a lease which has still many years to run. The landlord could not go on claiming rent for the whole duration of the lease if the subjects could easily be re-let to another tenant on reasonable terms. The landlord would, of course, be able to rescind and claim damages for the difference between the rent obtainable from the new tenant (if less) and the rent due under the repudiated contract.

2.9 Cases where a reasonable substitute transaction could easily have been obtained are examples of cases where it would have been unreasonable to proceed with unwanted performance. Paragraph (b) deals with the situation where performance would be unreasonable for some other reason.[12] A typical example would be a case like *White and Carter (Councils)* where, before the performance has begun, the party entitled to it says that it is no longer required and where the performing party has no legitimate interest in continuing with performance rather than claiming damages for the repudiation.

2.10 We recommend that

11–74 **1. There should be legislation, designed to solve the problem revealed by *White & Carter (Councils) Ltd v McGregor*, to the effect that a party to a contract who has been told that performance under the contract is no longer wanted but who, being in a position to give performance without the co-operation of the other party, has proceeded to perform, is not entitled to recover payment for performance occurring after intimation that further performance is unwanted if (a) that party could have entered into a reasonable substitute transaction without unreasonable effort or expense or (b) it was unreasonable for that party to proceed with the performance.**

---

[1] 1962 SC(HL)1.
[2] Treitel, *The Law of Contract* (9th ed, 1995) 915-918; Burrows, *Remedies for Torts and Breach of Contract* (2nd ed, 1994) 318-322.
[3] 1962 SC(HL)1 at 24.
[4] 1962 SC(HL)1 at 14.
[5] *Attica Sea Carriers Corp v Ferrostaal Poseidon Bulk Reederei GMBH* [1976] 1 Lloyds Rep 250; *Clea Shipping Corp v Bulk Oil International Ltd (The Alaskan Trader)* [1984] 1 All ER 129.
[6] 1985 SC 189.
[7] At 194.
[8] At 197.
[9] At 199.
[10] Scott, "Contract-Repudiation-Performance by InnocentParty" [1962] Cambridge Law Journal 12 at 14.
[11] Art 9:101(2).
[12] See also *Clea Shipping Corp v Bulk Oil International Ltd (The Alaskan Trader)* [1984] 1 All ER 129, where the court held that the question was simply whether continued performance by one party against the wishes of the other was reasonable in the circumstances.

Draft Contract (Scotland) Bill ...

11–75 1. **Restriction of right to payment for unwanted performance**

(1) Where—

(a) a party to a contract or the beneficiary under a conditional unilateral voluntary obligation (the 'performing party') is, before completion of performance, informed by another party to the contract or the person undertaking the obligation that performance is no longer required;

(b) the performing party is able to proceed or continue with performance without the co-operation of that other party or that person; and

(c) either—

(i) the performing party can, without unreasonable effort or expense, secure a reasonable substitute transaction; or

(ii) it is unreasonable for the performing party to proceed or continue with performance, then the performing party is not entitled, on so proceeding or continuing, to recover the consideration due under the contract or benefit due under the obligation in respect of performance occurring after the performing party has been so informed.

(2) Subsection (1) above does not affect any right of the performing party to recover damages for breach of contract or conditional unilateral voluntary obligation.

Explanatory notes **11–76**

Section 1

Section 1 is designed to modify the law resulting from the case of *White & Carter (Councils) Ltd v McGregor* 1962 SC (HL) 1 . . . The section prevents payment for unwanted performance from being recovered in cases where it is unreasonable to proceed with the unwanted performance. See Part 2 of the report.

In such cases damages could still be recovered. The section applies to conditional unilateral voluntary obligations, such as a promise to pay a reward for doing something, in the same way as to contracts. See para 6.2 of the report.

Example. A company contracts with a botanist to go to Brazil, spend six months on **11–77** field research and produce a report. The day after the contract has been completed the company discovers that it no longer needs the research. It tells the botanist that it no longer wants the report, that the contract is cancelled and that it will pay full compensation, including compensation for any non-patrimonial loss or harm suffered by the loss of the contract. As the botanist could readily obtain other suitable work, compensation would be much less than the full contract fee. The botanist rejects this offer, proceeds to Brazil, produces an unwanted report and claims the full contractual fee. Under the existing law it seems that the botanist will succeed, although some judges have indicated that exceptions to the normal rule may have to be recognised. The new section would prevent the contractual fee from being recovered but would not prevent damages from being recovered.

Subsection (1) **11–78**

This subsection restricts the right of the performing party to recover the consideration or benefit due for the unwanted performance. Paragraphs (a) to (c) set out the conditions which have to be met before the statutory restriction of the right to recover comes into effect. The party who is entitled to render the performance must have been told that the performance is no longer wanted. That party must have been able to proceed to perform without the cooperation of the other party or person. (If such co-operation was needed and was not provided then the result sought by the section is achieved automatically without legislation because the performing party, being unable to perform, is thrown back on the remedy of damages.) The performing party must have been in a position to secure a reasonable substitute transaction without unreasonable effort or expense or it must have been, for some other reason, unreasonable for the performing party to proceed with performance. If these conditions are met, the concluding lines of the subsection prevent the performing party from recovering the consideration or benefit due for any performance given after intimation that performance was no longer wanted.

Subsection (2) **11–79**

This makes it clear that the performing party is not prevented from claiming damages."

Material breach

If a breach occurs either on the due date for performance or during performance itself, it is **11–80** important to know whether it is so material that it implies repudiation of the contract by the party in breach. Only then can the party not in breach rescind the contract.

The notion of materiality is sometimes expressed as breach which "goes to the root of the contract" or which is "of the essence of the contract". In all cases, except where parties have expressly stipulated the consequence of a particular breach, whether a breach is material is a matter of construction of the contract. "The question is the nature of the breach rather than its consequences, although these may illustrate materiality."[45] Certainly the consequence of material breach is to entitle party not in breach to a range of remedies beyond seeking damages.

Refusal to perform is normally material, but delay, deviations from agreed performance, or defective performance are not always material.

One way of looking at material breach is as a breach which amounts to a failure to perform and therefore a repudiation. In any case, a material breach does not itself terminate the contract; it entitles, but does not compel the innocent party to rescind—to accept the breach (to accept the repudiation of the contract by the party in breach) and terminate the contract. The party not in breach would have no further obligation to perform, but the contract would otherwise subsist—for example, clauses relating to matters like arbitration "liquidate damages" exclusion of liability and so on. In the English case of *Woodar Investment Development Ltd v Wimpey Construction Ltd*[46] a majority in the House of Lords decided that for conduct to amount to repudiation, it must show an intention to abandon and refuse performance of the contract. This would place a restraint on the other party in exercising the right to accept the breach that, in Scots law, is not a discretionary right dependant on assessment by the court. It suggests that a subjective, rather than an objective assessment would be made of the conduct alleged to be a breach. The matter might be complicated by the fact that the party in breach does not believe that the conduct amounts to a breach. The following decision considered these matters and the standing of the *Woodar* decision in Scotland.

11–81 **Blyth v Scottish Liberal Club**

1982 S.C. 13; 1983 S.L.T. 260

Court of Session, Second Division: Lord Justice-Clerk (Wheatley), Lords Dunpark and Wylie

Blyth was employed by the club as managing secretary under a contract which terminated on Blyth's 65th birthday. When the contract had about five years to run, the club premises on Princes Street were closed and the contents sold. Blyth's managerial duties ended, but he was told that his contract would be continued "for at least twelve months" and continued to be paid his full salary for some months. During this period, the parties had been "maneuvering for position" in terms of compensation. Blyth was asked by the club to attend a committee meeting and provide administrative back-up; and to take the minutes of a management committee meeting in the absence of the honorary secretary of the club. On both occasions he refused, having misunderstood his legal position, whereupon the club terminated his contract. Blyth claimed damages for wrongful dismissal. The Lord Ordinary (Lord Ross) found that both refusals were repudiatory breaches, the materiality of which was not affected by Blyth's genuine belief that he was entitled to refuse.

Blyth appealed to the Inner House, but his reclaiming motion was refused.

11–82 "LORD DUNPARK: ... [Blyth's] submission was that a breach of contract could not be material unless the act or conduct giving rise to the breach amounted to a repudiation of the contract by the party in breach. [M]y own view of the law of Scotland [is] as stated by Lord President Dunedin in *Wade v Waldon*, 1909 1 S.L.T. at p. 219: 'It is familiar law,

[45] WW McBryde, *The Law of Contract in Scotland*, 3rd edn (Edinburgh: W. Green, 2007), para.20–94.

[46] *Woodar Investment Development Ltd v Wimpey Construction Ltd* [1980] 1 W.L.R. 277.

and quite well settled by decision, that in any contract which contains multifarious stipulations there are some which go so to the root of the contract that a breach of those stipulations entitles the party pleading the breach to declare that the contract is at an end. There are others which do not go to the root of the contract, but which are part of the contract, and which would give rise, if broken, to an action of damages.' In every case the question of whether a breach of contract is material is one of fact and degree. Having regard to ... the fact that [Blyth] deliberately, wilfully if you like, refused to obey two reasonable orders relating to his participation in the business of the club, which it is now conceded that he was contractually bound to obey, these were breaches of a contractual duty which went to the root of the contract.

[Blyth contended] that the only proper test of materiality of a breach of contract was that stated by Lord Coleridge C.J. in *Freeth v Burr* (1874) L.R. 9 C.P. 208 at p. 213: 'The true question is whether the acts and conduct of the party evince an intention no longer to be bound by the contract.' That statement, in my opinion, is an accurate statement of the law as applied to the facts of that case, where the defendants wrongfully treated the temporary refusal of the plaintiffs to pay for the first instalment of goods in a contract of sale as an abandonment of the contract by the plaintiffs. While it was an appropriate test to apply in that case, it is certainly not the only test of the materiality of a breach of contract. There are any number of cases in which one party has fulfilled, or been willing to fulfil, all of his contractual obligations except one, and that one failure has been held to be a material breach of contract ...

If by words or deed one party to a contract demonstrates that he will no longer be bound by his contract that is actual repudiation which entitles the other party at once to cancel or rescind the contract. But the remedy of cancellation is also given to a party who is not in breach of contract whenever the other party is in breach of an essential condition going to the root of the contract, even if the party in breach is willing to fulfil all his other contractual obligations. In such a case the innocent party may treat the breach of one essential condition as if the party in breach has repudiated all his unperformed contractual duties. He has not actually repudiated these but he is deemed to have done so because he is in breach of one material term or condition of his contract.

It is difficult to treat this case as one of actual repudiation because [Blyth] seems to have been waiting for the [club] to terminate his contract so that he could pursue his compensation claim; but, assuming that [Blyth] was prepared to continue, pending termination of his contract, to perform such routine duties as he had been performing since the closure of the club premises, his refusal to obey the two lawful and reasonable instructions which he was given was, in my opinion, a breach of one of the essential conditions of his contract, namely, that as managing secretary of the club he should carry out such duties as the club might reasonably request its managing secretary to perform in the interests of the club.

(2) Did the reclaimer's apparent genuine belief that his contract of employment did not bind him to comply with these instructions have the effect of depriving the respondents of their right to terminate his contract on the ground of his failure to obey them? **11–83**

Like the Lord Ordinary, I find it to be 'a startling proposition that a person in breach of contract can avoid the consequences of his breach by contending that he has formed an erroneous view of his legal rights under the contract.' It is, in my opinion, a proposition without legal foundation. It is based upon two fallacies. The first is the fallacy that a party cannot be in material breach of contract unless his conduct is such as to evince an intention no longer to be bound by the contract. If that were the only test of materiality, there may be a certain logicality in submitting that the failure to obey an order to perform a task which the employee genuinely believes to be outwith the scope of his employment cannot *per se* be construed as evincing an intention to throw up the whole contract. But, as I have pointed out, this argument fails because the test of Lord Coleridge is not the only test of the materiality of a breach of contract . . .

At this stage I pause to observe that the word 'repudiation' may be used in two senses. The first meaning is that one party to a contract has been held by his conduct to have cancelled or terminated continuing obligations in the course of their performance. The other meaning is that used in cases of what is often called 'anticipatory breach,' where one party indicates to the other before the date when performance is due that he will not perform his contractual obligations when performance becomes due. The next case to which counsel for the reclaimer attached great weight is a case of 'anticipatory breach.' . . . *Woodar Investment Development Ltd v Wimpey Construction UK Ltd* ([1980] 1 W.L.R. 277) . . .

[Blyth's] attempt to apply the *ratio* of *Woodar* to the facts of this case illustrated what, in my opinion, is the second fallacy in their submission, namely their failure to distinguish between conduct which demonstrates a refusal to fulfil contractual obligations before the time for performance has arrived and a refusal to perform a contractual duty which the contract requires to be performed at the time of refusal. Counsel referred to a passage from the speech of Lord Keith of Kinkel which, in my opinion, demonstrates the falsity of the submission that the erroneous belief of [Blyth] that the two tasks which he was instructed to perform were outwith the scope of his employment in some way deprives the [club] of the right, which they would otherwise have had, to treat [Blyth's] refusal to perform these tasks as a material breach of contract. At p. 296 Lord Keith said this: 'I would accept without hesitation the statement of Lord Denning M.R. in *Federal Commerce & Navigation Co Ltd v Molena Alpha Inc* [1978] 1 Q.B. 927, 979 that a party who breaks a contract cannot excuse himself by saying that he did it on the advice of his lawyers, or that he was under an honest misapprehension. If in the present case the time for performance had passed while the appellants were still maintaining their position based on the erroneous interpretation of special condition E(a)(iii), they would have been in breach of contract and liable in damages accordingly. Lord Denning goes on to say: 'Nor can he excuse himself on those grounds from the consequences of a repudiation.' That may be so, but it is first necessary to determine whether or not there has been a repudiation.

Now in *Woodar* it was necessary for their Lordships to decide whether the conduct of Wimpey evinced a positive refusal to complete the purchase when the date for completion fell due. In this case the reclaimer failed on two specific occasions to fulfil his existing contractual obligation to comply with the reasonable requests of the management. Whether or not [Blyth) intended to repudiate his contract is not to the point. He had broken his contract and, as Lord Denning said, he 'cannot excuse himself by saying that he did it on the advice of his lawyers, or that he was under an honest misapprehension.' So . . . this reclaiming motion should be refused . . . [Blyth] accepted the Lord Ordinary's assessment of damages except for his exclusion of the sum of £1,250 incurred by [Blyth] as expenses in his application to the industrial tribunal and the [club's] appeal to the employment appeal tribunal. I refer to this only out of courtesy to the new ground founded on by [Blyth] as a reason for the inclusion of this sum in the assessment of the damages which would have been due to [Blyth] if he had been successful in this action. He submitted that this sum was covered by the second branch of the rule in *Hadley v Baxendale*, namely that the expenses incurred by [Blyth] before these tribunals were 'such as may reasonably be supposed to have been in the contemplation of both parties at the time they made the contract as the probable result of the breach of it' by the [club]. I reject this submission because on my interpretation of the facts the only loss which the [club] could reasonably have contemplated as resulting from a premature termination of [Blyth's] contract of employment was that found by the Lord Ordinary. I do not consider that the decision of [Blyth] to pursue a claim before an industrial tribunal should reasonably be supposed to have been in the contemplation of both parties at the time the contract was made. That was [Blyth's] own decision. As the Lord Ordinary says, [Blyth] could have recovered his whole loss by way of ordinary action, if necessary. In the event of such an action being necessary and successful, [Blyth] would have recovered his judicial expenses from the [club] as expenses, not as damages.

LORD WYLIE: ... Termination of a contract following on the repudiation of the **11–84** contract by one party only arises however if this is accepted by the other, exercising the right to rescind. This is a right which he may elect to exercise, but he is not bound to do so (Gloag on *Contract* (2nd ed.), pp. 598–660). See also *Heyman v Darwins Ltd* [[1942] A.C. 356], per Lord Wright at pp. 378–379: 'perhaps the commonest application of the word "repudiation" is to what is often called the anticipatory breach of a contract where the party by words or conduct evinces an intention no longer to be bound and the other party accepts the repudiation and rescinds the contract.'

The present case however does not turn on repudiation or anticipatory breach followed by rescission. The contract remained afoot until the time for performance had arrived and dismissal followed after actual breach of contract had taken place. It is in these circumstances that the dicta drawn from the case of *Woodar Investment Development Ltd* and other cases cited have no bearing on the present case, where actual breach of contract at the time of performance has arisen.

The issue in this case narrows down to the question as to whether the pursuer's acts of disobedience, now conceded as constituting breach of contract, can properly be regarded as material. In this context the alleged genuine misunderstanding of the true legal position cannot avail the pursuer. 'I have yet to learn that a party who breaks a contract can excuse himself by saying that he did it on the advice of his lawyers: or that he was under an honest misapprehension' (per Lord Denning M.R. in *Federal Commerce & Navigation Co Ltd v Molena Alpha Inc*, at p. 979). This statement of the law was expressly accepted by Lord Keith in *Woodar Investment Development Ltd* at p. 296, where his Lordship went on to add: 'If in the present case the time for performance had passed while the appellants were still maintaining their position based on the erroneous interpretation of special condition E(a)(iii), they would have been in breach of contract and liable in damages accordingly.' The wording of this passage fits precisely the circumstances of the present case and the only question which arises relates to the materiality of the breach.

From the very nature of the contract of service the obligation on the servant to carry out the legitimate and reasonable orders of the master is fundamental. It must always of course be a question of fact and degree in each case as to whether or not the refusal was sufficiently serious to justify dismissal. '[I]t follows that the question must be—if summary dismissal is claimed to be justifiable—whether the conduct complained of is such as to show the servant to have disregarded the essential conditions of the contract of service. It is, no doubt, therefore, generally true that ... wilful disobedience of a lawful and reasonable order shows a disregard—a complete disregard—of a condition essential to the contract of service, namely, the condition that the servant must obey the proper orders of the master, and that unless he does so the relationship is, so to speak, struck at fundamentally' (per Lord Evershed M. R. in *Laws v London Chronicle (Indicator Newspapers) Ltd* [[1959] 1 W.L.R. 698], at p. 700). I readily accept that statement of the law as applicable to this case and in all the circumstances as disclosed by the evidence in the case I consider that the Lord Ordinary was fully justified in holding material breach of contract established. On each occasion the pursuer's refusal to carry out his instructions was quite deliberate. He was fully aware that his employers regarded any refusal to do so as of significance.

> He likewise knew that by refusing to carry out these duties he was declining to perform about the only significant functions left open to him, when the other work content of his employment had become minimal, albeit through no fault of his own."

11–85 Did Lord Dunpark mean that the duty was material, or that the breach was?

The question arises: is the breach so material that it precludes the party in breach from any right to the opportunity to remedy the breach? In *Lindley Catering Investments Ltd v Hibernian Football Club Ltd*,[47] under an agreement between Lindley and Hibernian, Lindley was granted the exclusive licence "to manage and control the public catering rights" at Easter Road football ground. The club terminated the contract because of complaints of slow service, supplies running out and failure to clean up properly after matches. Such food and drink, when provided, was cold or lukewarm. Lindley sued Hibernian for breach of contract. Lord Thomson held that the defenders had failed to prove such a breach of contract on the part of the pursuers as would justify a rescission of the contract by the defenders without giving the pursuers a reasonable opportunity to remedy the breach. In the course of his judgment he said:

> "In my opinion the legal position in a case like the present can be broadly stated thus: if one party so breaches a material stipulation in the contract as to preclude the other from fulfilling his part of the contract, the innocent party is entitled to regard himself as absolved from further performance of his obligations and to rescind the contract. But if the breach is such, by degree or circumstances, that it can be remedied so that the contract as a whole can thereafter be implemented, the innocent party is not entitled to treat the contract as rescinded without giving to the other party an opportunity so to remedy the breach. This seems to me to be in substance the view of Lord President Dunedin in ... *Municipal Council of Johannesburg v D Stewart & Co* (1902) Ltd. [1909 S.C. 860] when he says: 'You have so broken the contract that I am entitled to say that it is at an end through your fault, I shall not perform any more of my stipulations, because you have precluded me.' I find support also for the view I have expressed in *Barclay & Co v Anderston Foundry Co* (1856) 18 D. 1190, per Lord Cowan, at p.1198, and in *McKimmie's Trustees v Armour* (1899) 2 F. 156 (a case of landlord and tenant), per Lord McLaren, at pp.161–162 and Lord Kinnear, at p.162."

---

[47] *Lindley Catering Investments Ltd v Hibernian Football Club Ltd*, 1975 S.L.T. (Notes) 56.

CHAPTER 12

DAMAGES FOR BREACH OF CONTRACT

Introduction

Once it is established, or even anticipated, that a party is in breach, it is possible for the other party to seek remedies. Most of these are beyond the limited scope of this book and are best explored in the standard texts. Some remedies are defensive, or precautionary, to ensure, as far as possible, that performance, or payment, is eventually made. They are "self-help" measures that can be implemented by the party seeking them. They include the right of rescission[1] and the right of retention, lien, hypothec and compensation of debts[2]; but some remedies may only be exercised by the intervention of the courts, such as the claim to damages, but also the enforcement of the contract by specific implement and interdict.[3] The most common of these is the claim for damages, and that is the focus of this chapter. **12–01**

The right to damages, like any other right to enforce an obligation, may be extinguished in a variety of circumstances. The lapse of time may prevent enforcement of obligations so that delay may extinguish remedies for breach of contract, including the right to claim damages. The contract itself may provide such time limits; but the law in general provides time limits for claims, generally known as *prescription*.[4] The right to claim damages may also be extinguished, or otherwise affected by death and insolvency,[5] or it may be varied or extinguished by the actions of the parties.[6]

In all other cases, the standard and major remedy for breach of contract is the action for damages, or pecuniary compensation for loss sustained in consequence of the breach, regardless of whether the breach is a material breach entitling the party not in breach to terminate the contract. The pursuer must prove:

(1) breach of contract;
(2) loss or damage attributable to that breach;
(3) mitigation of such loss or damage;
(4) the extent, or measure of damage. Since the circumstances amounting to breach have already been considered, the other elements in the action of damages must now be analysed.

Causation of loss by the breach

A party in breach is liable only for losses directly caused by the breach. There must be a direct causal link between breach and loss. **12–02**

---

1 See above, paras 11–47—11–57.

2 See WW McBryde, *The Law of Contract in Scotland*, 3rd edn (Edinburgh: W. Green, 2007), paras 20–62—20–87 (retention and compensation) and Ch.24 (Payment); HL MacQueen and J Thomson, *Contract Law in Scotland*, 3rd edn (London: Bloomsbury, 2012), paras 5.7–5.23 (self-help remedies), paras 5.40–5.55 (restitution).

3 See WW McBryde, *The Law of Contract in Scotland*, 3rd edn (Edinburgh: W. Green, 2007), Ch.23; HL MacQueen and J Thomson, *Contract Law in Scotland*, 3rd edn (London: Bloomsbury, 2012), paras 13—6.15.

4 See WW McBryde, *The Law of Contract in Scotland*, 3rd edn (Edinburgh: W. Green, 2007), paras 25–74—25–101.

5 See WW McBryde, *The Law of Contract in Scotland*, 3rd edn (Edinburgh: W. Green, 2007), Ch.26.

6 See WW McBryde, *The Law of Contract in Scotland*, 3rd edn (Edinburgh: W. Green, 2007), paras 25–01—25–73.

12–03

Monarch Steamship Co Ltd v Karlshamns Oljefabriker (A/B)
1949 S.C. (H.L.) 1
House of Lords: Lords Porter, Wright, Uthwatt, du Parcq and Morton of Henryton

Monarch Steamship (MS), Glasgow shipowners, owned the SS *British Monarch*. In April, 1939 they chartered the ship to Mitsui, a Japanese company. KO, a Swedish company, bought a quantity of soya beans from Mitsui in May. MS issued bills of lading in May 1939, in favour of KO, as purchasers under a cif contract for a cargo of 8,200 tons of Manchurian soya beans "to be shipped from . . . Rashin . . . *per* S.S. *British Monarch*". The voyage charterparty provided that upon loading, the ship would "proceed [to] one or two ports at charterers' option". Because the parties were aware of the worsening international situation and of the likelihood of war, the charterparty also included a "war risks" clause that exonerated the owners of the vessel in the event of compliance with any orders given by the government of the nation under whose flag she sailed, as to destination, delivery or otherwise. The charterparty also included a standard condition that the ship would be in a seaworthy condition.

The vessel loaded the cargo and sailed on 12 May 1939. Karlshamn in Sweden was nominated on 7 June 1939, as the sole port of discharge. The voyage should normally have taken about 60 days. The ship was expected to arrive in July, but her speed was slow due to defective boilers, caused by using bad coal on her previous voyage. She reached Aden on 4 August, undertook further boiler repairs, left on 16 August, reached Port Said on 30 August and was there detained for further repairs until 24 September.

War between Great Britain and Germany broke out on 3 September and the British Admiralty prohibited the vessel from proceeding to Karlshamn. She was ordered to proceed to and discharge at Glasgow, which she reached on 21 October. In Glasgow the boilers were renewed. On 23 October KO's agents took delivery upon payment of freight.

KO urgently needed the beans for their production process and expected them to arrive at Karlshamn before the end of July. No other soya beans being available there, they had bought the shortfall from the Swedish Government on the terms of being paid an equivalent quantity on the vessel's arrival. KO were then granted permission by the British Government to charter three smaller Swedish vessels to proceed with the beans to Karlshamn, where they were eventually delivered. The cost of transhipment was £22,134, 7s. 4d.

MS, in their defence, claimed that the loss was caused by the British Government's action, which was excluded under the war risks clause.

The House of Lords found that the delay in the voyage caused by the vessel's unseaworthiness was the effective cause of the requisitioning and KO were entitled to recover from MS the costs of transhipment that were the direct and natural consequence of their failure to deliver at Karlshamn.

12–04 "LORD WRIGHT: . . . At the conclusion of the arguments Sir William McNair admitted that the appellants had broken their contract, but claimed that the damages were only nominal. I agree, however, with the unanimous decision of all the judges below that the claim for the damages is justified. It in truth gives effect to the broad general rule of the law of damages that a party injured by the other party's breach of contract is entitled to such money compensation as will put him in the position in which he would have been but for the breach. In that respect this case is singularly clear, because the contract entitled the respondents to have the beans delivered at Karlshamn and the damages claimed and awarded represent simply the sum necessary to effect that result, namely the cost of transhipment from Glasgow to Karlshamn . . .

> But a question of remoteness in another connexion and in another sense has been raised. That is in reference to remoteness in the sense of causal connexion. The claim here is for damages for unseaworthiness, which, it is said, caused delay on the voyage, and the delay exposed the vessel to being diverted by order of the Admiralty. This, it was said, may properly be regarded as coming within the exception of restraints of princes, though, indeed, it was for the benefit of the appellants, because, if it could be invoked by the appellants, it gave them a right to the bill of lading freight in full as on performance of the contract by a delivery short of the bill of lading destination. In my opinion, this objection, which would treat restraints of princes as the immediate or dominant cause of the delay, fails ...
>
> There is, however, in this case a contention of a more general nature, which is that the delay which resulted from the defective boilers did not in any legal sense cause the diversion of the vessel. It is said that the relation of cause and effect cannot be postulated here between the unseaworthiness and the restraints of princes or the delay. As to such a contention it may be said at once that all the judges below have rejected it. As I have pointed out, if the vessel had arrived at Karlshamn in July she could not have been exposed to the risk of the restraint of princes, but she did not arrive until October, and thereby (in the historic phrase) 'missed the bus'. If a man is too late to catch a train, because his car broke down on the way to the station, we should all naturally say, that he lost the train because of the car breaking down. We recognize that the two things or events are causally connected. Causation is a mental concept, generally based on inference or induction from uniformity of sequence as between two events that there is a causal connexion between them. This is the customary result of an education which starts with our earliest experience the burnt child dreads the fire. I am not entering upon or discussing any theory of causation. Those interested in philosophy will find modern philosophic views on causation explained in Russell's History of Western Philosophy in the chapter on Hume, Book 3, ch. xvii. The common law however is not concerned with philosophic speculation, but is only concerned with ordinary everyday life and thoughts and expressions, and would not hesitate to think and say that, because it caused the delay, unseaworthiness caused the Admiralty order diverting the vessel. I think the common law would be right in picking out unseaworthiness from the whole complex of circumstances as the dominant cause. I have assumed that the bills of lading and charterparty exceptions which are expressed to be conditional on the vessel being seaworthy, use 'seaworthy' in the sense that the breach of warranty was a breach which caused the loss. This is assumed in *Paterson Steamships Ltd v Canadian Co-operative Wheat Producers Ltd* [1934] A. C. 539, in respect of a similar provision in the Water Carriage of Canada Act, and in other cases."

Important in this decision was that all parties were aware, at the time when the various contracts were made, that war was imminent. The contract terms indicated this. The loss was therefore not too remote.[7] Also, the duty of the shipowner was to provide a seaworthy ship at the commencement of the voyage. The ship continued to be unseaworthy throughout the voyage and was therefore operative throughout performance of the contract up to the requisitioning of the ship and probably beyond that.

Remoteness of damage

Even if it is established that loss was a consequence of the breach, the party in breach will only be responsible: **12–05**

[7] See para.12–05 onwards.

(a) for such damage as, in ordinary circumstances, flows naturally from the breach; or
(b) for such damage as could reasonably be in the contemplation of the parties when making the contract—i.e. where the party in breach was aware of special circumstances.

These rules were established by and applied in *Hadley v Baxendale*,[8] the details of which are explained in Lord Reid's speech in *Koufos v Czarnikow*.[9] The party not in breach may only recover for a loss if it can be shown that effort was made to mitigate that loss. For example, where goods delivered are defective, and the purchaser delays unduly in replacing them, with the result that the price has risen, the purchaser may be unable to recover the loss consequential upon the delay.

12–06 **Victoria Laundry (Windsor) Ltd v Newman Industries Ltd**
[1949] 2 K.B. 528
English Court of Appeal: Asquith, Singleton and Tucker LJJ

Victoria, wishing to expand their business with a view to procuring further profitable contracts, contracted with Newman for the purchase of a new boiler for £2,150, to be installed on Victoria's premises, delivery by 6 June. Delivery was delayed until 8 November. Newman knew the nature of Victoria's business and had been asked to instal the boiler as quickly as possible.

A unanimous Court of Appeal found Newman liable for the loss of profits caused by the loss of prospective lucrative contracts by Victoria, as a direct result of the late installation of the boiler.

12–07 "ASQUITH LJ: ... What propositions applicable to the present case emerge from the authorities as a whole ... ? We think they include the following:

(1) It is well settled that the governing purpose of damages is to put the party whose rights have been violated in the same position, so far as money can do so, as if his rights had been observed (*Wertheim v Chicoutimi Pulp Co* [1911] A.C. 301). This purpose, if relentlessly pursued, would provide him with a complete indemnity for all loss *de facto* resulting from a particular breach, however improbable, however unpredictable. This, in contract at least, is recognised as too harsh a rule. Hence
(2) In cases of breach of contract the aggrieved party is only entitled to recover such part of the loss actually resulting as was at the time of the contract reasonably foreseeable as liable to result from the breach.
(3) What was at that time reasonably so foreseeable depends on the knowledge then possessed by the parties or, at all events, by the party who later commits the breach.
(4) For this purpose, knowledge 'possessed' is of two kinds; one imputed, the other actual. Everyone, as a reasonable person, is taken to know the 'ordinary course of things' and consequently what loss is liable to result from a breach of contract in that ordinary course. This is the subject-matter of the 'first rule' in *Hadley v Baxendale*. But to this knowledge, which a contract-breaker is assumed to possess whether he actually possesses it or not, there may have to be added in a particular case knowledge which he actually possesses, of special circumstances outside the 'ordinary course of things,' of such a kind that a

[8] *Hadley v Baxendale* (1854) 9 Ex. 341.
[9] Below, para.12–08.

breach in those special circumstances would be liable to cause more loss. Such a case attracts the operation of the 'second rule' so as to make additional loss also recoverable.

(5) In order to make the contract-breaker liable under either rule it is not necessary that he should actually have asked himself what loss is liable to result from a breach. As has often been pointed out, parties at the time of contracting contemplate not the breach of the contract, but its performance. It suffices that, if he had considered the question, he would as a reasonable man have concluded that the loss in question was liable to result (see certain observations of Lord du Parcq in the recent case of *A/B Karlshamns Oljefabriker v Monarch Steamship Co Ltd* [1949] A.C. 486).

(6) Nor, finally, to make a particular loss recoverable, need it be proved that upon a given state of knowledge the defendant could, as a reasonable man, foresee that a breach must necessarily result in that loss. It is enough if he can foresee that it was likely so to result. It is indeed enough, to borrow from the language of Lord du Parcq in the same case, at page 158, if the loss (or some factor without which it would not have occurred) is a 'serious possibility' or a 'real danger.' For short, we have used the word 'liable' to result. Possibly, the colloquialism 'on the cards' indicates the shade of meaning with some approach to accuracy."

These comments received general acceptance, but the term "reasonably foreseeable" over the years, came to resemble closely the test applied to remoteness of damage in cases of negligence in delict, rather than contract.

Koufos v C Czarnikow Ltd; The Heron II 12–08
[1969] 1 A.C. 350
English House of Lords: Lords Hodson, Morris of Borth-y-Gest, Pearce, Reid and Upjohn

Koufos chartered his ship, the *Heron II*, to Czarnikow. She was to proceed from Piraeus to Constanza, and from there to carry a consignment of sugar owned by Czarnikow, to Basrah. The charter gave the charterer the option to discharge the cargo at Jeddah.

Koufos knew that Czarnikow were sugar merchants and that there was a sugar market in Basrah but did not know that Czarnikow intended to sell the sugar promptly upon arrival at Basrah. In breach of the charterparty, the *Heron II* deviated from the voyage and called at other ports so that the ship was delayed by about 10 days in arriving at Basrah. As was normal for that time of year, the price for sugar fell at Basrah. Czarnikow sought to recover from Koufos the difference between the price at which the sugar was sold and the price at which it would have been sold had the ship arrived at Basrah on time.

The House dismissed Koufos's appeal against the decision that the difference in price was not too remote and was therefore recoverable.

"LORD REID: ... For over a century everyone has agreed that remoteness of damage in contract must be determined by applying the rule (or rules) laid down by a court including Lord Wensleydale (then Parke B.), Martin B. and Alderson B. in *Hadley v Baxendale*, 9 Ex. 341; but many different interpretations of that rule have been adopted by judges at different times. So I think that one ought first to see just what was decided in that case, because it would seem wrong to attribute to that rule a meaning which, if it had been adopted in that case, would have resulted in a contrary decision of that case. 12–09

In *Hadley v Baxendale* the owners of a flour mill at Gloucester, which was driven by a steam engine, delivered to common carriers, Pickford & Co., a broken crank shaft to be sent to engineers in Greenwich. A delay of five days in delivery there was held to be in breach of contract, and the question at issue was the proper measure of damages. In fact the shaft was sent as a pattern for a new shaft and until it arrived the mill could not operate. So the owners claimed £300 as loss of profit for the five days by which resumption of work was delayed by this breach of contract; but the carriers did not know that delay would cause loss of this kind.

Alderson B., delivering the judgment of the court said (at pp. 355–6):

'. . . we find that the only circumstances here communicated by the plaintiffs to the defendants at the time the contract was made were that the article to be carried was the broken shaft of a mill and that the plaintiffs were the millers of that mill. But how do these circumstances shew reasonably that the profits of the mill must be stopped by an unreasonable delay in the delivery of the broken shaft by the carrier to the third person? Suppose the plaintiffs had another shaft in their possession put up or putting up at the time, and that they only wished to send back the broken shaft to the engineer who made it; it is clear that this would be quite consistent with the above circumstances, and yet the unreasonable delay in the delivery would have no effect upon the intermediate profits of the mill. Or, again, suppose that at the time of the delivery to the carrier the machinery of the mill had been in other respects defective, then, also the same results would follow.'

Then having said that in fact the loss of profit was caused by the delay, he continued:

'But it is obvious that, in the great multitude of cases of millers sending off broken shafts to third persons by a carrier under ordinary circumstances, such consequences would not, in all probability, have occurred . . .'

Alderson B. clearly did not and could not mean that it was not reasonably foreseeable that delay might stop the resumption of work in the mill. He merely said that in the great multitude—which I take to mean the great majority—of cases this would not happen. He was not distinguishing between results which were foreseeable or unforeseeable, but between results which were likely because they would happen in the great majority of cases, and results which were unlikely because they would only happen in a small minority of cases. He continued:

'It follows, therefore, that the loss of profits here cannot reasonably be considered such a consequence of the breach of contract as could have been fairly and reasonably contemplated by both the parties when they made this contract.'

He clearly meant that a result which will happen in the great majority of cases should fairly and reasonably be regarded as having been in the contemplation of the parties, but that a result which, though foreseeable as a substantial possibility, would happen only in a small minority of cases should not be regarded as having been in their contemplation. He was referring to such a result when he continued:

'For such loss would neither have flowed naturally from the breach of this contract in the great multitude of such cases occurring under ordinary circumstances, nor were the special circumstances, which perhaps, would have made it a reasonable and natural consequence of such breach of contract, communicated to or known by the defendants.'

. . . The rule is (9 Ex. at p. 354) that the damages '. . . should be such as may fairly and reasonably be considered either arising naturally, *i.e.* according to the usual course of things, from such breach of contract itself, or such as may reasonably be supposed to have been in the contemplation of both parties at the time they made the contract as the probable result of the breach of it.' I do not think that it was intended that there were to be two rules or that two different standards or tests were to be applied . . . I am satisfied that the court did not intend that every type of damage which was reasonably foreseeable by the parties when the contract was made should either be considered as arising naturally, *i.e.* in the usual course of things, or be supposed to have been in the contemplation of the parties. Indeed the decision makes it clear that a type of damage which was plainly foreseeable as a real possibility but which would only occur in a small minority of cases cannot be regarded as arising in the usual course of things or be supposed to have been in the contemplation of the parties: the parties are not supposed to contemplate as grounds for the recovery of damage any type of loss or damage which, on the knowledge available to the defendant, would appear to him as only likely to occur in a small minority of cases. In cases like *Hadley v Baxendale* or the present case it is not enough that in fact the plaintiff's loss was directly caused by the defendant's breach of contract. It clearly was so caused in both. The crucial question is whether, on the information available to the defendant when the contract was made, he should, or the reasonable man in his position would, have realised that such loss was sufficiently likely to result from the breach of contract to make it proper to hold that the loss flowed naturally from the breach or that loss of that kind should have been within his contemplation.

The modern rule in tort is quite different and it imposes a much wider liability. The defendant will be liable for any type of damage which is reasonably foreseeable as liable to happen even in the most unusual case, unless the risk is so small that a reasonable man would in the whole circumstances feel justified in neglecting it; and there is good reason for the difference. In contract, if one party wishes to protect himself against a risk which to the other party would appear unusual, he can direct the other party's attention to it before the contract is made, and I need not stop to consider in what circumstances the other party will then be held to have accepted responsibility in that event. In tort, however, there is no opportunity for the injured party to protect himself in that way, and the tortfeasor cannot reasonably complain if he has to pay for some very unusual but nevertheless foreseeable damage which results from his wrongdoing. I have no doubt that today a tortfeasor would be held liable for a type of damage as unlikely as was the stoppage of Hadley's Mill for lack of a crank shaft: to any one with the knowledge the carrier had that may have seemed unlikely, but the chance of it happening would have been seen to be far from negligible. But it does not at all follow that *Hadley v Baxendale* would today be differently decided.

... I do not think it useful to review the authorities in detail, but I do attach importance to what was said in this House in *Re R & H Hall Ltd v WH Pim (Junior) & Co Ltd* [1928] 33 Com. Cas. 324 ...

Hall's case must be taken to have established that damages are not to be regarded as too remote merely because, on the knowledge available to the defendant when the contract was made, the chance of the occurrence of the event which caused the damage would have appeared to him to be rather less than an even chance. I would agree with Lord Shaw that it is generally sufficient that that event would have appeared to the defendant as not unlikely to occur. It is hardly ever possible in this matter to assess probabilities with any degree of mathematical accuracy. But I do not find in that case, or in cases which preceded it, any warrant for regarding as within the contemplation of the parties any event which would not have appeared to the defendant, had he thought about it, to have a very substantial degree of probability.

But then it has been said that the liability of defendants has been further extended by *Victoria Laundry (Windsor) Ltd v Newman Industries Ltd* [1949] 2 K.B. 528. I do not think so ... what is said to create a 'landmark' is the statement of principles by Asquith L.J. This does to some extent go beyond the older authorities and in so far as it does so, I do not agree with it. In paragraph (2) (*Ibid.* 539) it is said that the plaintiff is entitled to recover 'such part of the loss actually resulting as was at the time of the contract reasonably foreseeable as liable to result from the breach.' To bring in reasonable foreseeability appears to me to be confusing measure of damages in contract with measure of damages in tort. A great many extremely unlikely results are reasonably foreseeable: it is true that Asquith L.J. may have meant foreseeable as a likely result, and if that is all he meant I would not object farther than to say that I think that the phrase is liable to be misunderstood. For the same reason I would take exception to the phrase (*Ibid.* 540) 'liable to result' in paragraph (5). Liable is a very vague word, but I think that one would usually say that when a person foresees a very improbable result he foresees that it is liable to happen.

. . . It has never been held to be sufficient in contract that the loss was foreseeable as 'a serious possibility' or 'a real danger' or as being 'on the cards.' It is on the cards that one can win £100,000 or more for a stake of a few pence—several people have done that; and anyone who backs a hundred to one chance regards a win as a serious possibility—many people have won on such a chance. Moreover the *Wagon Mound (No. 2)* [1967] 1 A.C. 617 could not have been decided as it was unless the extremely unlikely fire should have been foreseen by the ship's officer as a real danger. It appears to me that in the ordinary use of language there is a wide gulf between saying that some event is not unlikely or quite likely to happen and saying merely that it is a serious possibility, a real danger, or on the cards. Suppose one takes a well-shuffled pack of cards, it is quite likely or not unlikely that the top card will prove to be a diamond: the odds are only three to one against; but most people would not say that it is quite likely to be the nine of diamonds for the odds are then 51 to one against. On the other hand I think that most people would say that there is a serious possibility or a real danger of its being turned up first and, of course, it is on the cards. If the tests of 'real danger' or 'serious possibility' are in future to be authoritative, then the *Victoria Laundry* case [1949] 2 K.B. 528 would indeed be a landmark because it would mean that *Hadley v Baxendale* would be differently decided today. I certainly could not understand any court deciding that, on the information available to the carrier in that case, the stoppage of the mill was neither a serious possibility nor a real danger. If those tests are to prevail in future, then let us cease to pay lip service to the rule in *Hadley v Baxendale*. But in my judgment to adopt these tests would extend liability for breach of contract beyond what is reasonable or desirable. From the limited knowledge which I have of commercial affairs I would not expect such an extension to be welcomed by the business community; and from the legal point of view I can find little or nothing to recommend it.

Lord Asquith took the phrases 'real danger' and 'serious possibility' from the speech of Lord du Parcq in *Monarch Steamship Co Ltd v AB Karlshamns Oljefabriker* [1949] A.C. 196, 233 [where the pursuer's action depended on] whether the outbreak of war and consequent embargo were or ought to have been within the contemplation of the contracting parties in April, 1939. By that time war was much more than merely a serious possibility. Lord Porter said [1949] A.C. 196, 219: 'Accepting, then, the view that the appellants ought to have foreseen the likelihood of war occurring . . .' Lord Wright said at p. 222: 'There was, indeed, in 1939 the general fear that there might be a war . . . The possibility must have been in the minds of both parties.' Lord Uthwatt said at p. 232 that a reasonable shipowner 'would regard the chance of war, not as a possibility of academic interest to the venture, but as furnishing matter which commercially ought to be taken into account.' Finally Lord Morton of Henryton said at p. 235 that the shipowner 'would feel that there was a grave risk of war breaking out in Europe . . .' On these assessments of the situation holding that the damage which flowed from the outbreak of war was not too remote to be recoverable was well within the existing law. I do not think that Lord du Parcq intended to say that his view was materially different. Indeed he quoted from Sir Winston Churchill, *The Second World War*, Vol. 1, p. 270: 'No one who understood the situation could doubt that it meant in all human probability a major war in which we should be involved.' So there was no need for him to go farther than the existing law and I do not think that he intended to do so. It is only by taking these two phrases put out of their context that any such intention could be inferred.

It appears to me that, without relying in any way on the *Victoria Laundry* case [1949] 2 K.B. 528, and taking the principle that had already been established, the loss of profit claimed in this case was not too remote to be recoverable as damages ...

For the reasons which I have given I would dismiss this appeal."

Comment

Why "the nine of diamonds?" Lord Reid's views did not receive universal approval in that decision. In particular, the view has been again expressed that there need not be material difference between the test applied in contract and that applied in negligence. **12–10**

H Parsons (Livestock) Ltd v Uttley Ingham & Co **12–11**

[1978] Q.B. 791

English Court of Appeal: Lord Denning MR, Orr and Scarman LJJ

Parsons ordered a bulk food storage hopper from Uttley Ingham, who knew that Parsons intended to use it to store pignuts for feeding to their pig herd. Having installed the hopper, Uttley Ingham failed to open the ventilator, so that the pignuts stored in the hopper turned mouldy. Some of the pigs ate of the mouldy nuts and contracted E. coli, a highly contagious intestinal infection that soon spread through the herd. As a result, 254 pigs died. Parsons sought substantial damages, including their loss of profit. Scarman LJ, with whose judgment Orr LJ concurred, found for Parsons. Lord Denning also found for Parsons, but for different reasons.

"SCARMAN LJ: ... Two problems are left unresolved by *C Czarnikow Ltd v Koufos*: (1) the law's reconciliation of the remoteness principle in contract with that in tort where, as, for instance, in some product liability cases, there arises the danger of differing awards, the lesser award going to the party who had a contract, even though the contract is silent as to the measure of damages and all parties are, or must be deemed to be, burdened with the same knowledge, or enjoying the same state of ignorance; and (2) what is meant by 'serious possibility' or its synonyms: is it a reference to the type of consequence which the parties might be supposed to contemplate as possible though unlikely, or must the chance of it happening appear to be likely? (See the way Lord Pearce puts it, at pp. 416–417.) **12–12**

As to the first problem, I agree with Lord Denning M.R. in thinking that the law must be such that, in a factual situation where all have the same actual or imputed knowledge and the contract contains no term limiting the damages recoverable for breach, the amount of damages recoverable does not depend upon whether, as a matter of legal classification, the plaintiff's cause of action is breach of contract or tort. It may be that the necessary reconciliation is to be found, notwithstanding the strictures of Lord Reid at pp. 389–390, in holding that the difference between 'reasonably foreseeable' (the test in tort) and 'reasonably contemplated' (the test in contract) is semantic, not substantial. Certainly Asquith L.J. in *Victoria Laundry (Windsor) Ltd v Newman Industries Ltd* [1949] 2 K.B. 528, 539 and Lord Pearce in *C Czarnikow Ltd v Koufos* (at p. 414) thought so; and I confess I think so too. The second problem—what is meant by a 'serious possibility'—is, in my judgment, ultimately a question of fact ... The court's task, therefore, is to decide what loss to the plaintiffs it is reasonable to suppose would have been in the contemplation of the parties as a serious possibility had they had in mind the breach when they made their contract ...

I would agree with *McGregor on Damages*, 13th Ed. (1972) pp. 131–132 that '... in contract as in tort, it should suffice that, if physical injury or damage is within the contemplation of the parties, recovery is not to be limited because the degree of physical injury or damage could not have been anticipated.'

This is so, in my judgment, not because there is, or ought to be, a specific rule of law governing cases of physical injury but because it would be absurd to regulate damages in such cases on the necessity of supposing the parties had a prophetic foresight as to the exact nature of the injury that does in fact arise. It is enough if on the hypothesis predicated physical injury must have been a serious possibility. Though in loss of market or loss of profit cases the factual analysis will be very different from cases of physical injury, the same principles, in my judgment, apply. Given the situation of the parties at the time of contract, was the loss of profit, or market, a serious possibility, something that would have been in their minds had they contemplated breach?

It does not matter, in my judgment, if they thought that the chance of physical injury loss of profit, loss of market, or other loss as the case may be, was slight or that the odds were against it provided they contemplated as a serious possibility the type of consequence, not necessarily the specific consequence, that ensued on breach. Making the assumption as to the breach that the judge did, no more than common sense was needed for them to appreciate that food affected by bad storage conditions might well cause illness in the pigs fed on it.

As I read the judgment under appeal, this was how the judge, whose handling of the issues at trial was such that none save one survives for our consideration, reached this decision. In my judgment, he was right, on the facts as found, to apply the first rule in *Hadley v Baxendale* (1854) 9 Ex. 341 or, if the case be one of breach of warranty, as I think it is, the rule in s. 53(2) of the Sale of Goods Act 1893 without inquiring whether, on a juridical analysis, the rule is based on a presumed contemplation. At the end of a long and complex dispute the judge allowed common sense to prevail. I would dismiss the appeal."

The case leaves open the question of whether the party in breach might have in contemplation the other party's business activities. The issue arose in:

12–13

Balfour Beatty Construction (Scotland) Ltd v Scottish Power Plc

1994 S.L.T. 807

House of Lords, Lords Keith, Bridge, Jauncey, Browne-Wilkinson and Nolan

Balfour Beatty were building a roadway and associated structures, including an aqueduct. They contracted with Scottish Power for the supply of electricity to operate a concrete batching plant. During the construction of the aqueduct, which required a continuous pour operation, the batching plant stopped working.

In an action for damages for breach of contract brought by Balfour Beatty against Scottish Power, it was established that the electricity supply had been interrupted and that the interruption was a breach of contract by Scottish Power. Balfour Beatty claimed the cost of demolishing and rebuilding a substantial part of the works resulting from the interruption of the electricity supply and the consequent interruption of the required continuous pour.

After proof, the Lord Ordinary found that Scottish Power had not known of the need for a continuous pour, nor that it would not be possible simply to cut back part of the hardened concrete to a face against which fresh concrete could be poured to form a joint. He therefore concluded that the need to condemn the whole operation had not been within Scottish Power's reasonable contemplation, and assoilzied them. Balfour Beatty successfully reclaimed in the Inner House.

The House of Lords allowed Balfour Beatty's appeal and reversed the judgment of the Second Division.

"LORD JAUNCEY OF TULLICHETTLE: ... My Lords, in my view the Second Division were in error in imputing to the board, at the time of entering into the contract, technical knowledge of the details of concrete construction with which they had not been furnished by Balfour Beatty. I am prepared to accept that as a matter of general knowledge the board would have appreciated that concrete poured would ultimately harden. I do not, however, consider that the board had any reason to be aware of the importance of the time involved in the hardening process, nor of the consequences of adding freshly poured concrete to that which had already hardened. Indeed, the board had no reason to expect that concrete would be required for the construction of a watertight aqueduct. **12–14**

There are two passages in the speech of Lord Wright in *A/B Karlshamns Oljefabriker v Monarch Steamship Co* which were relied upon by Balfour Beatty before your Lordships and which must, I believe, have influenced the reasoning of the Lord Justice Clerk. At 1949 S.C. (H.L.), p. 19; 1949 S.L.T., p. 57 Lord Wright, after referring to the celebrated dictum of Alderson B in *Hadley v Baxendale* and to what would have been the position if the pursuers in the appeal before him had claimed special and particular loss, said: 'The Court will, however, assume that the parties as business men have all reasonable acquaintance with the ordinary course of business'.

He expressed similar views in the following terms at p 21 (p 58): 'but the question in a case like the present must always be what reasonable business men must be taken to have contemplated as the natural or probable result if the contract was broken. As reasonable business men each must be taken to understand the ordinary practices and exigencies of the other's trade or business'.

My Lords, *A/B Karlshamns Oljefabriker v Monarch Steamship Co* was a case concerning the extra cost of transhipment of a cargo of Soya beans due to the delay in contemplation of the voyage caused by the unseaworthiness of the ship. The facts were simple and the consequences of delay were in the circumstances within the reasonable contemplation of the shipowners. I do not, however, understand that Lord Wright was laying down a general rule to the effect that in all circumstances contracting parties are presumed to have reasonable knowledge of the course of business conducted by each other. I find support for this view in the following passage in the speech of Lord Upjohn in *Czarnikow* at [1969] 1 AC, p 424C: 'Lord Wright pointed out in *The Monarch* that each must be taken to understand the ordinary practices and exigencies of the other's trade but it must be remembered when dealing with the case of a carrier of goods by land, sea or air, he is not carrying on the same trade as the consignor of the goods and his knowledge of the practices and exigencies of the other's trade may be limited and less than between buyer and seller of goods who probably know far more about one another's business.'

It must always be a question of circumstances what one contracting party is presumed to know about the business activities of the other. No doubt the simpler the activity of the one, the more readily can it be inferred that the other would have reasonable knowledge thereof. However, when the activity of A involves complicated construction or manufacturing techniques, I see no reason why B who supplies a commodity that A intends to use in the course of those techniques should be assumed, merely because of the order for the commodity, to be aware of the details of all the techniques undertaken by

A and the effect thereupon of any failure or of deficiency in that commodity. Even if the Lord Ordinary had made a positive finding that continuous pour was a regular part of industrial practice it would not follow that in the absence of any other evidence suppliers of electricity such as the board should have been aware of that practice. I consider that the Lord Ordinary correctly interpreted Lord Wright's statements in the *A/B Karlshamns* case.

My Lords, at the end of the day it is a question of fact what must have been within the reasonable contemplation of the board at the date of the contract. The Lord Ordinary in a carefully reasoned judgment has found that the demolition and reconstruction of the aqueduct consequent upon failure of the power supply was not within that contemplation. Their Lordships were referred to no evidence from which it could be said that it should have appeared to the board that these consequences of the rupturing of the fuses would have had a very substantial degree of probability, from which it follows that the Second Division were not justified in differing from those findings.

Balfour Beatty argued that since the board should have contemplated that some remedial work to the concrete already poured would be rendered necessary by an interruption of continuous pouring, they must therefore be held to have contemplated demolition and reconstruction which differed only in degree from other remedial work such as the insertion of a construction joint involving cutting back the concrete. In support of this proposition a number of cases were cited including *Parsons (H) (Livestock) Ltd v Uttley Ingham & Co Ltd.* In view of the conclusion which I have already arrived at, I do not find it necessary to deal with this argument nor to determine whether *Parsons* correctly stated the law in relation to this matter.

For the foregoing reasons I would allow the appeal, recall the interlocutor of the Second Division and restore that of the Lord Ordinary subject only to the question of expenses ..."

The measure of damages

12–15 Once the court has established a breach, that loss has occurred as a consequence of that breach and that the loss is not too remote, it must measure that loss. The general measure is that damages should, so far as possible, put the party suffering loss in the position they should have been had the breach not occurred and the contract performed. The rule has been variously expressed: "a party injured by the other party's breach is entitled to such money compensation as will put him in the position in which he would have been *but for* the breach"[10]; "where a party sustains a loss by reason of a breach of contract, he is, *so far as money can do it*, to be placed *in the same situation*, with respect to damages, as if the contract had been performed"[11]; "as far as possible, he who has proved a breach ... is to be placed, *as far as money can do it*, in *as good a situation* as if the contract had been performed"[12] [emphasis added]. Generally, this is often referred to as the *expectation* or *performance* interest—awarding in money to the injured party the difference between what they expected to get from performance of the contract and what they actually received. This is a far more complex calculation than at first appears. Does it mean the difference in terms of market value; or the difference in terms of the personal expectations of the particular injured party? More particularly, must the party in breach bear the cost of fulfilling the original terms of the contract, even where that cost is out of all proportion to the true loss suffered by the other party? This issue arose in stark terms in:

---

[10] *A/B Karlshamns Oljefabriker v Monarch Steamship Co*, 1949 S.C. (H.L.) 1, at 18, per Lord Wright.

[11] *Robinson v Harman*, 1 Exch. 850, at 855, per Parke B.

[12] *BritishWestinghouse Electric and Manufacturing Co Ltd v Underground Electric Railways Co of London Ltd* [1912] A.C. 673, at 689, per Viscount Haldane LC.

Ruxley Electronics and Construction Ltd v Forsyth 12–16
[1996] A.C. 344
House of Lords: Lords Keith, Bridge, Jauncey, Mustill and Lloyd

Ruxley contracted to build a swimming pool for Forsyth in his garden. The contract specified that the pool should have a diving area seven feet and six inches deep. On completion the diving area was only six feet deep. This had no adverse effect on the value of the property.

Forsyth refused to pay the outstanding balance of the contract price, which Ruxley brought an action to recover. Forsyth claimed breach of contract and the cost of rebuilding the pool to the specified depth (estimated at the trial as £21,560).

The trial judge found in favour of Ruxley, held that the cost of reinstatement was an unreasonable claim by Forsyth and awarded Forsyth only £2,500 for loss of amenity.

The Court of Appeal (by a majority) allowed Forsyth's appeal holding that the defendant's loss as a result of the breach of contract was the amount required to place him in the same position as he would have been in if the contract had been performed, which in the circumstances, was the cost of rebuilding the pool.

The House allowed an appeal by Ruxley on the basis that the appropriate measure of damages was not the cost of reinstatement, but the diminution in the value of the work occasioned by the breach even if that would result in a nominal award; and that, accordingly, since there was no dispute over the amount awarded by way of general damages, the judgment of the trial judge should be restored.

"LORD JAUNCEY OF TULLICHETTLE: Damages are designed to compensate for an established loss and not to provide a gratuitous benefit to the aggrieved party from which it follows that the reasonableness of an award of damages is to be linked directly to the loss sustained. If it is unreasonable in a particular case to award the cost of reinstatement it must be because the loss sustained does not extend to the need to reinstate. A failure to achieve the precise contractual objective does not necessarily result in the loss which is occasioned by a total failure ... 12–17

... A man contracts for the building of a house and specifies that one of the lower courses of brick should be blue. The builder uses yellow brick instead. In all other respects the house conforms to the contractual specification. To replace the yellow bricks with blue would involve extensive demolition and reconstruction at a very large cost. It would clearly be unreasonable to award to the owner the cost of reconstructing because his loss was not the necessary cost of reconstruction of his house, which was entirely adequate for its design purpose, but merely the lack of aesthetic pleasure which he might have derived from the sight of blue bricks. Thus in the present appeal the respondent has acquired a perfectly serviceable swimming pool, albeit one lacking the specified depth. His loss is thus not the lack of a useable pool with consequent need to construct a new one. Indeed were he to receive the cost of building a new one and retain the existing one he would have recovered not compensation for loss but a very substantial gratuitous benefit, something which damages are not intended to provide.

What constitutes the aggrieved party's loss is in every case a question of fact and degree. Where the contract breaker has entirely failed to achieve the contractual objective it may not be difficult to conclude that the loss is the necessary cost of achieving that objective. Thus if a building is constructed so defectively that it is of no use for its designed purpose the owner may have little difficulty in establishing that his loss is the necessary cost of reconstructing. Furthermore in taking reasonableness into account in determining the extent of loss it is reasonableness in relation to the particular contract and not at large. Accordingly if I contracted for the erection of a folly in my garden which shortly thereafter suffered a total collapse it would be irrelevant to the determination of my loss to argue that the erection of such a folly which contributed nothing to the value of my house was a crazy thing to do. As Oliver J. said in *Radford v De Froberville* [1977] 1 W.L.R. 1262, 1270:

'If he contracts for the supply of that which he thinks serves his interests—be they commercial, aesthetic or merely eccentric—then if that which is contracted for is not supplied by the other contracting party I do not see why, in principle, he should not be compensated by being provided with the cost of supplying it through someone else or in a different way, subject to the proviso, of course, that he is seeking compensation for a genuine loss and not merely using a technical breach to secure an uncovenanted profit.'

However where the contractual objective has been achieved to a substantial extent the position may be very different.

It was submitted that where the objective of a building contract involved satisfaction of a personal preference the only measure of damages available for a breach involving failure to achieve such satisfaction was the cost of reinstatement. In my view this is not the case. Personal preference may well be a factor in reasonableness and hence in determining what loss has been suffered but it cannot per se be determinative of what that loss is.

My Lords, the trial judge found that it would be unreasonable to incur the cost of demolishing the existing pool and building a new and deeper one. In so doing he implicitly recognised that the respondent's loss did not extend to the cost of reinstatement. He was, in my view, entirely justified in reaching that conclusion. It therefore follows that the appeal must be allowed.

... The appellant argued that the cost of reinstatement should only be allowed as damages where there was shown to be an intention on the part of the aggrieved party to carry out the work. Having already decided that the appeal should be allowed I no longer find it necessary to reach a conclusion on this matter. However I should emphasise that in the normal case the court has no concern with the use to which a plaintiff puts an award of damages for a loss which has been established. Thus irreparable damage to an article as a result of a breach of contract will entitle the owner to recover the value of the article irrespective of whether he intends to replace it with a similar one or to spend the money on something else. Intention, or lack of it, to reinstate can have relevance only to reasonableness and hence to the extent of the loss which has been sustained. Once that loss has been established intention as to the subsequent use of the damages ceases to be relevant.

...

12–18 LORD LLOYD OF BEWICK. *Reasonableness* ... In building cases, the pecuniary loss is almost always measured in one of two ways; either the difference in value of the work done or the cost of reinstatement. Where the cost of reinstatement is less than the difference in value, the measure of damages will invariably be the cost of reinstatement. By claiming the difference in value the plaintiff would be failing to take reasonable steps to mitigate his loss. In many ordinary cases, too, where reinstatement presents no special problem, the cost of reinstatement will be the obvious measure of damages, even where there is little or no difference in value, or where the difference in value is hard to assess. This is why it is often said that the cost of reinstatement is the ordinary measure of damages for defective performance under a building contract.

But it is not the only measure of damages. Sometimes it is the other way round. This was first made clear in the celebrated judgment of Cardozo J. giving the majority opinion in the Court of Appeals of New York in *Jacob & Youngs v Kent*, 129 N.E. 889. In that case the building owner specified that the plumbing should be carried out with galvanized piping of 'Reading manufacture.' By an oversight, the builder used piping of a different manufacture. The plaintiff builder sued for the balance of his account. The defendant, as in the instant case, counter-claimed the cost of replacing the pipe work even though it would have meant demolishing a substantial part of the completed structure, at great expense. Cardozo J. pointed out, at p. 891, that there is 'no general license [*sic*] to install whatever, in the builder's judgment, may be regarded as 'just as good.' But he went on to consider the measure of damages [and his] judgment is important, because it establishes two principles, which I believe to be correct, and which are directly relevant to the present case; first, the cost of reinstatement is not the appropriate measure of damages if the expenditure would be out of all proportion to the benefit to be obtained, and, secondly, the appropriate measure of damages in such a case is the difference in value, even though it would result in a nominal award.

The first of these principles is contrary to Staughton L.J.'s view that the plaintiff is entitled to reinstatement, however expensive, if there is no cheaper way of providing what the contract requires. The second principle is contrary to the whole thrust of Mr. Jacob's argument that the judge had no alternative but to award the cost of reinstatement, once it became apparent that the difference in value produced a nil result.

...

If the court takes the view that it would be unreasonable for the plaintiff to insist on reinstatement, as where, for example, the expense of the work involved would be out of all proportion to the benefit to be obtained, then the plaintiff will be confined to the difference in value. If the judge had assessed the difference in value in the present case at, say, £5,000, I have little doubt that the Court of Appeal would have taken that figure rather than £21,560. The difficulty arises because the judge has, in the light of the expert evidence, assessed the difference in value as nil. But that cannot make reasonable what he has found to be unreasonable.

So I cannot accept that reasonableness is confined to the doctrine of mitigation ...

I am far from saying that personal preferences are irrelevant when choosing the appropriate measure of damages ('predilections' was the word used by Ackner L.J. in *GW Atkins Ltd v Scott*, 7 Const.L.J. 215, 221, adopting the language of Oliver J. in *Radford v De Froberville* [1977] 1 W.L.R. 1262). But such cases should not be elevated into a separate category with special rules. If, to take an example mentioned in the course of argument, a landowner wishes to build a folly in his grounds, it is no answer to a claim for defective workmanship that many people might regard the presence of a well built folly as reducing the value of the estate. The eccentric landowner is entitled to his whim, provided the cost of reinstatement is not unreasonable. But the difficulty of that line of argument in the present case is that the judge, as is clear from his judgment, took Mr. Forsyth's personal preferences and predilections into account. Nevertheless, he found as a fact that the cost of reinstatement was unreasonable in the circumstances. The Court of Appeal ought not to have disturbed that finding.

...

Intention

I fully accept that the courts are not normally concerned with what a plaintiff does with his damages. But it does not follow that intention is not relevant to reasonableness, at least in those cases where the plaintiff does not intend to reinstate. Suppose in the present case Mr. Forsyth had died, and the action had been continued by his executors. Is it to be supposed that they would be able to recover the cost of reinstatement, even though they intended to put the property on the market without delay? **12–19**

...

In the present case the judge found as a fact that Mr. Forsyth's stated intention of rebuilding the pool would not persist for long after the litigation had been concluded. In these circumstances it would be 'mere pretence' to say that the cost of rebuilding the pool is the loss which he has in fact suffered. This is the critical distinction between the present

> case, and the example given by Staughton L.J. of a man who has had his watch stolen. In the latter case, the plaintiff is entitled to recover the value of the watch, because that is the true measure of his loss. He can do what he wants with the damages. But if, as the judge found, Mr. Forsyth had no intention of rebuilding the pool, he has lost nothing except the difference in value, if any."

12–20 This decision is in many ways a departure from the traditional calculation of the measure of damages. What further complicates matters is that there is no single judgment of the court, but various speeches from their lordships, each arriving at similar conclusions, but via very different routes. This was, of course, not remarkably unusual in the House of Lords, but it makes it extremely difficult to search for the ratio decidendi. First, Lord Jauncey clearly places great stress on the requirement of reasonableness, in deciding whether the cost of reinstatement was recoverable. The suggestion is, therefore, that it would be a matter of "reasonable" assessment in each case, of the cost of reinstatement against the loss sustained. What if the pool was built with a "deep end" when none was required by the owner? What if the owner wanted an "Olympic standard" swimming pool and the depth was 18 inches too short?

Implicit in the decision is that the aggrieved party will be entitled to some compensation for unfulfilled expectations, even though not entitled to substantive damages. Nominal, or non-pecuniary damages were awarded to Mr Forsyth and this is a matter considered below.[13] Note also the references in Lord Lloyd's speech to the need for the party claiming damages to mitigate loss.

Does the decision signal a move away from the expectation test traditionally applied to measuring damages and is this likely to find favour in the Scottish courts? The problem was defined by the Scottish Law Commission in the following terms in its *Discussion Paper on Remedies for Breach of Contract*[14]:

12–21

> "8.37 the problem is that it would be grossly unreasonable to base damages, in accordance with the normal rule, on the amount required to make the aggrieved party's position as nearly as possible what it would have been if the contract had been duly performed. In the case of defective work on property which is not intended for resale the best way of giving effect to the normal rule is usually to award the costs of rectification. However, that method sometimes produces absurd and unacceptable results.
>
> . . .
>
> 8.41 Cases of the *Ruxley* type demonstrate that there is a need to recognise an exception to the normal rule for damages where the normal rule would suggest using the cost of rectification but where using the cost of rectification would be unreasonable . . . It is clear that it would be wrong to regard the difference in the value of the property as the only alternative . . . People can contract for a performance which decreases the value of their property if they wish. They ought still to be entitled to damages for breach of contract. A clear recognition that damages can be awarded for non-patrimonial loss of any kind, including the loss of the satisfaction of receiving what was contracted for, would help in this type of case . . . Beyond that, what might be useful in Scotland would be a provision to the effect that the cost of rectification need not be used as the basis of assessing damages in any case where to do so would be unreasonable and that in such a case damages should be based on an assessment of the aggrieved party's loss, including non-partimonial loss, in the absence of rectification. That would enable diminution of

[13] Below, at paras 12–44—12–47.

[14] Scottish Law Commission, *Discussion Paper on Remedies for Breach of Contract* (Discussion Paper No.109, April 1999).

value to be taken into account, where appropriate, but would not limit damages to loss of value."

The following decision suggests that such an approach is making some headway in Scotland.

McLaren Murdoch & Hamilton Ltd v Abercromby Motor Group Ltd 12–22
2002 G.W.D. 38-1242
Court of Session, Outer House: Lord Drummond Young

P were architects who agreed to construct four car dealership showrooms and associated workshops at Kerse Road, Stirling for D, who own and operate car dealerships in a number of places in Scotland.

A dispute arose between the parties and at about the same time ownership in the showrooms and workshops was transferred to another company within the same group as D.

P claimed unpaid fees for the works at Kerse Road. D counterclaimed alleging breach of contract and negligence by P in the design of the heating system for the showrooms and workshops. P accepted that they were at fault in the design of the heating system, but denied that P had suffered any loss or damage consequential upon P's fault.

The court found that D were entitled to the cost of replacing the heating system.

"LORD DRUMMOND YOUNG: ... 12–23

Loss established by defenders in consequence of pursuers' negligent design of heating system ...

[29] In my opinion the defenders are entitled to damages based on the cost of installing a completely new heating system. The relevant principles are as follows. First, following a breach of contract the innocent party is entitled, generally speaking, to be placed in as good a situation financially as he would have been in had the contract been properly performed. Second, where the obligation incumbent upon the party in breach of contract is a duty to exercise reasonable care, rather than a duty to achieve a particular result, the result is the same; in this case the innocent party is entitled to be placed in the position that he would have been in had the party in breach exercised due care: *Farley* v *Skinner*, [2001] 4 All E.R. 801, at 812 per Lord Steyn, 818 per Lord Clyde, 822-823 per Lord Hutton. Third, in cases involving construction contracts, including claims based on the professional negligence of an architect or engineer, the pursuer's loss is normally measured in one of two ways, either the cost of making the works conform to contract or the difference between the value of the works as built and the value of the works as they ought to have been built: *Ruxley Electronics Limited* v *Forsyth*, [1996] AC 344, at 366 per Lord Lloyd of Berwick; the same approach is taken by the other members of the House of Lords. If the cost of making the works conform to contract is less than the difference in value, that will be the measure of damages. Even in other cases, however, the cost of making the works conform to contract may be the natural and obvious measure of damages. That is so even where there is little or no difference in value, or where, as will often happen, the difference in value is hard to assess: *ibid.* For these reasons the cost of making the works conform to contract is regarded as the ordinary measure of damages for defective performance under building and similar contracts. Fourth, in some cases the cost of making the works conform to contract, by reinstating what ought to have

> been built, will not be the appropriate measure of loss. The relevant principle has been expressed as follows:
>
> 'First, the cost of reinstatement is not the appropriate measure of damages if the expenditure would be out of all proportion to the benefit to be obtained, and, secondly, the appropriate measure of damages in such a case is the difference in value, even though it would result in a nominal award': *ibid,* at 367 per Lord Lloyd of Berwick.
>
> [30] It is in my opinion important to notice the relationship between the third and fourth principles discussed in the last paragraph. In effect, they amount to this: a pursuer will be entitled to the cost of making building works conform to contract unless that cost is significantly disproportionate to the benefit that is obtained from it. That appears from Lord Lloyd's formulation in *Ruxley Electronics* v *Forsyth,* and also from the original formulation of the principle in question. That appears in the opinion of Cardozo J., sitting in the Court of Appeals of New York, in *Jacob & Youngs* v *Kent* ... Cardozo J. stated
>
> 'In the circumstances of this case, we think the measure of the allowance is not the cost of replacement, which would be great, but the difference in value, which would be either nominal or nothing ... It is true that in most cases the cost of replacement is the measure ... The owner is entitled to the money which will permit him to complete, unless the cost of completion is grossly and unfairly out of proportion to the good to be obtained. When that is true, the measure is the difference in value'.
>
> The emphasis in this passage is on the cost of replacement as the norm, subject to an exception where that cost is seriously disproportionate to the good to be obtained. In other words, the reasonableness of the pursuer's remedial works is not to be weighed in fine scales. That seems only fair. The pursuer is the victim of a breach of contract, and it should not be open to the party responsible for that breach to place unreasonable obstacles in the way of the pursuer's recovery of damages. In my opinion the proper relationship between the third and fourth principles discussed in the last paragraph is this, that a pursuer will be entitled to the cost of making the works conform to contract except in two situations: firstly, where the cost involved is manifestly disproportionate to any benefit that will be obtained from it, in which case the court should take notice of the disproportion; and, secondly, where the defender leads evidence to show that there is a significant disproportion between the cost and the benefit. Even in the latter category of case, I consider that the balance between cost and benefit should not be weighed too finely. Nevertheless, where the defender leads such evidence, the court will be entitled to take a more critical view of the pursuer's actions."

Although reinstatement was the appropriate remedy in this case, the judge's approach was that outlined in *Ruxley*. The cost of reinstatement would be the less expensive and less disruptive measure for damages. Furthermore, the decision reaffirms the emphasis on the restitutive purpose of damages, ultimately to restore the parties to their original positions in the most reasonable way. For a recent application of the principles, see *Forrest v Fleming Buildings Ltd.*[15]

Damages for loss or harm to third parties

12–24 The general principle is that a person can only recover damages for patrimonial losses that the pursuer has actually suffered. We have already seen that in certain circumstances damages might be recoverable for certain types of non-patrimonial losses; but the rule has been that the loss must be suffered by the pursuer, not by another party with whom the pursuer may or may not be connected. That third party may have a *jus quaesitum tertio* on which to base a claim against the party in breach, or an action in delict may be possible. In reality, such an action may be difficult or impossible, or the third party may not be willing to bring such an action. In such cases, a loss

[15] *Forrest v Fleming Buildings Ltd* [2015] CSOH 90.

may be suffered, but unless the pursuer can make a claim, that loss will be irrecoverable and will disappear into a "legal black hole". The matter was considered by the Scottish Law Commission in 1999 and the Commission put forward proposals for legislative change.

Discussion Paper on Remedies for Breach of Contract **12–25**

Scottish Law Commission Discussion Paper No.109 (April 1999)

"Damages for loss or harm to third parties

8.43 The question for consideration under this head is whether there should be any further[87] exception to the normal, and understandable, rule that the aggrieved party cannot recover damages for a loss suffered by someone else.

The problem

8.44 The problem is that cases arise where it seems that the party who breaches a contract and thereby causes loss escapes all liability because the other contracting party does not suffer the loss and the party who suffers the loss is not a party to the contract. The contract breaker's liability appears to vanish 'into some legal black hole'.[88] Here are some examples.

1. A, a whisky manufacturer, sells some casks of whisky to C. Property passes immediately. A enters into a contract with a carrier, B, for the transport of the whisky to C. Due to a breach of contract by B, the whisky is lost.[89]
2. A, a sugar merchant, enters into a contract with a carrier, B, for the transport of a cargo of sugar to Scotland. The cargo is to be delivered to A. Due to a breach of contract by B some of the sugar fails to arrive. The sugar at all times belongs to C.[90]
3. A, a firm of shipbuilders, contracts with B, a firm of engineers, for the construction of engines for a ship. A sells the ship to C while it is still unfinished. C is caused loss by a subsequent breach of contract on the part of B.[91]
4. A, who run a fish farm, contract with B, who operate a neighbouring sawmill, that B will not engage in certain activities which might affect the purity of the water used by A. A sell the fish farm to C. B breaches the contract and causes loss to C.
5. A, wishing to give a present to C, enters into a contract with B for the construction of a greenhouse on C's property. There is a material breach of contract by B. The greenhouse is shoddily constructed and unacceptable.
6. A contracts with a tour operator, B, for a holiday for herself and her friend C. The tour operator repudiates the contract. A wishes to recover damages not only for her own loss but also for C's.[92]
7. A, a firm of property developers, enter into a contract with B, a firm of builders, for the construction of buildings on A's property. A transfer the property to an associated company, C. They attempt to assign their rights under the contract but the assignation turns out to be ineffective. B, in breach of the contract, does defective work which has to be rectified by C.[93]

In all of these cases A has the contractual rights, B is in breach of contract but C suffers the loss. Other similar cases can easily be imagined. The problem sometimes presents itself as one where A has title to sue, but no interest, and C has an interest to sue but no title; but this is not the real nature of the problem. A may well have some interest to sue. That will depend on the facts. The real problem is that A cannot normally recover damages for a loss suffered by C, and C does not normally have rights under a contract between A and B.

Some possible solutions under the existing law

12–26 8.45 This problem has been known for a long time and there are various possible solutions to it under the existing law.

Agency. It may be possible to show that A was acting as C's agent in entering into the contract with B.[94]

Assignation. A may be able to assign A's rights under the contract to C.[95] B's obligations under the contract would, from then on, be owed to C instead of to A.[96]

Jus quaesitum tertio. In some cases C may have rights under the contract as a third party under the doctrine of *jus quaesitum tertio*. It is perfectly possible in Scotland for a contract between A and B to confer rights on C. However, the intention to confer rights on C must be clear and there must be at least intimation to C.[97]

Delict. In some cases, for example where B has by negligent acts caused damage to C's property, C may be able to recover damages from B on the basis of delict rather than contract.[98]

Claim by A for consequential loss to A. In some cases, for example where B's breach causes A to incur liability to C under a separate contract between A and C, A may be able to claim the amount of this liability from B as a consequential loss arising from B's breach of contract.[99]

Ordinary claim by A for primary loss to A. In some cases A may be able to claim full damages on normal principles. For example, if A has contracted with B for a greenhouse to be built on C's ground and there is a material breach of contract by B, there would be nothing to stop A claiming damages from B based on the cost of rectification. A's primary loss is the loss of the contractual performance. A normal way of measuring that is by reference to the cost of rectification.[100]

Real burden. If the parties exercise sufficient foresight it may be possible to constitute the obligation owed by B as a real burden on the land owned by B in favour of the land owned by A. The obligation would then run with the land. However the requirements for the constitution of a real burden are strict.[101]

Assessment

12–27 8.46 The first question is whether it necessarily matters that work to be done under a contract between A and B is to be done on property belonging to C. It seems clear on principle that it does not. It would be fallacious to suppose that only owners of property, or indeed only those with real rights in property, can suffer loss as a result of a breach of contract to do work on the property. A tenant can with the landlord's agreement have work carried out on the property for the improvement of the tenant's comfort. It cannot be doubted that the tenant, however short the tenancy, can recover damages for breach of the contract if the work is not done to the required standard.[102] The cost of rectification is the normal, but not the only possible, way of measuring the loss.[103] The same argument applies where the contracting party does not even have a tenancy. The fundamental point is that a person who has contracted for a certain performance is entitled to damages if it is not provided in accordance with the contract. There is no obvious need for reform here, at least if our earlier suggestion on non-patrimonial loss is accepted.

8.47 The second question is whether the law on assignation of contractual rights is adequate to enable rights to be transferred when the property or enterprise to which they relate is transferred. We can see no reason to suppose that it is not, at least in most situations.[104] There may be cases where A and B agree that A's rights under the contract cannot be assigned. In such a case it would seem to be wrong on principle to override this agreement. C should simply pay less for property that does not have useful contractual rights assigned with it. There may also be cases where an attempted assignation turns out to be defective. In such a case the remedy ought to be sought against whoever was responsible for bungling the assignation. There may also be cases where A and C do not arrange an assignation until it is too late—that is, until after the loss or damage has been sustained by C.[105] It is not obvious, however, that special rules, contrary to normal principles and likely to be productive of difficulty, are required merely because parties do not assign rights or bungle the attempt to assign rights.

8.48 There might also be questions as to whether the rules on the other possible solutions under the existing law—and, in particular, on delict and the *jus quaesitum tertio*—are adequate. However, an examination of these questions would take us far beyond the reasonable limits of this paper. The important point is that there is no reason on principle why these other rules of law, as they are or as they might be developed, should not provide acceptable solutions in a wide range of cases where a breach of contract causes loss or harm to a person who is not an original party to the contract.

Request for views

8.49 Our preliminary view is that it would be unnecessary and contrary to principle to introduce a special rule allowing the party aggrieved by a breach of contract to recover damages for losses suffered by third parties. We would welcome views on the following provisional proposition. **12–28**

29. No new special rule is necessary to enable a party to a contract to recover damages for losses suffered by a third party.

---

[87] There is already a limited exception for some contracts for the carriage of goods by sea. See the Carriage of Goods by Sea Act 1992 s 2 (4). The effect is to enable, for example, the lawful holder of a bill of lading to sue the carrier for breach of contract causing damage to goods belonging to someone else. The holder sues for the benefit of the owner.

[88] *GUS Property Management v Littlewoods* 1982 SC (HL) 157 at 177.

[89] *Dunlop & Co v Lambert* (1839) 1 Macl & Rob 663.

[90] *Campbell v Tyson* (1840) 2 D 1215.

[91] *Blumer & Co v Scott & Sons* (1874) 1 R 379.

[92] Example suggested by *Jackson v Horizon Holidays Ltd* [1975] 1 WLR 1468.

[93] Example suggested by *Linden Gardens Trust Ltd v Lenesta Sludge Disposals Ltd* [1994] 1 AC 85.

[94] A case like example 2 (sugar merchants shipping sugar belonging to a third party) might well lend itself to decision on this basis. Cases like example 6 (holiday booked for friend) might also lend themselves, depending on the exact facts, to decision on this basis.

[95] See MacQueen, "Assignation and Breach of Contract" 1997 SLPQ 114.

[96] In relation to a loss sustained after the assignation it would not matter that A would not have suffered any loss if the contract had not been assigned. A's losses are by that time irrelevant. C has stepped into A's place as the other party to the contract. C could not, for example, recover for a loss suffered by A after the date of the assignation. There may be less difficulty here for Scottish law than for English law because Scottish law concentrates on the transfer of substantive rights rather than rights of suit or rights to damages. On the English law see *Darlington Borough Council v Wiltshier Northern Ltd* [1995] 1 WLR 68 at 73 - 74.

[97] *Carmichael v Carmichael's Exrx* 1920 SC (HL) 195; *Cullen v McMenamin* 1928 SLT (Sh Ct) 2; *Scott Lithgow Ltd v GEC Electrical Projects Ltd* 1992 SLT 244. The Law Commission for England and Wales have recommended the introduction of rules to allow third parties to acquire rights under contracts in certain situations (*Privity of Contract: Contracts for the Benefit of Third Parties*, Law Com No 242, 1996) and a Bill has now been introduced to implement these recommendations. One of the reasons for the reform is to deal with problems of the type under discussion here.

[98] See the analysis in *Scott Lithgow Ltd v GEC Electrical Projects Ltd* 1992 SLT 244 where, on the facts of that case, it was held that there was no liability in delict. The law on liability for delict in this type of situation has shown a remarkable tendency to fluctuate. See eg *Anns v Merton London Borough Council* [1978] AC 728; *D & F Estates Ltd v Church Commissioners for England* [1989] AC

177; *Murphy v Brentwood District Council* [1991] 1 AC 398; *Department of the Environment v Thomas Bates and Son Ltd* [1991] 1 AC 499. It does not matter for the purposes of this paper where the precise boundaries are at any given time. The point is simply that in certain cases the law of delict may provide a solution.

[99] This was the basis of the decision in *Dunlop & Co v Lambert* (1839) 1 Macl & Rob 663 where the key point was that, although property had passed, the risk of loss of the whisky casks had remained with A who had in fact reimbursed C. See Clive, "Jus Quaesitum Tertio and Carriage of Goods by Sea" in *Comparative and Historical Essays in Scots Law* (Carey Miller and Meyers, eds, 1992) 47.

[100] This was the basis of Lord Griffiths' decision in *St Martins Property Corporation Ltd v Sir Robert McAlpine Ltd* [1994] 1 AC 85. The other judges saw much force in the analysis but, as it had not been fully explored in argument, preferred to decide the case on a more narrow and technical ground. See also the comments in *Darlington Borough Council v Wiltshier Northern Ltd* [1995] 1 WLR 68. English cases in this area are not, however, a reliable guide in so far as they found on the special rule of English law developed in *The Albazero* [1977] AC 774 or on doctrines of constructive trust. It is possible that English law has been distorted because of the absence of a doctrine allowing rights to be conferred directly on third parties under contracts.

[101] The leading case is *Tailors of Aberdeen v Coutts* (1840) 1 Rob 296. We have recently consulted on reform of the law relating to real burdens. See our discussion paper on *Real Burdens* (Scot Law Com DP No 106, 1998) .

[102] In *Steel Aviation Services Ltd v Allan & Son Ltd* 1996 GWD 28-1699 A claimed damages for breach of contract by B to do work, on C's land, in connection with a concession held by A to operate certain services on B's land. It was held that A had averred a sufficient interest as sub-tenants or licensees to entitle them to sue. A were suing for their own primary loss, not for any loss alleged to be sustained by C.

[103] See paras 8.37–8.42.

[104] One of the reasons for the Carriage of Goods by Sea Act 1992 was that assignation is not a satisfactory solution in contracts for the carriage of goods by sea where ownership may pass frequently during a voyage and where foreign parties may be involved. See the joint report of the English and Scottish Law Commission on *Rights of Suit in Respect of Carriage of Goods by Sea* (Law Com No 196; Scot Law Com No 130, 1991) at para 2.13.

[105] The time when the loss or harm occurs is crucial in this type of case."

In its *Report on Remedies for Breach of Contract* (Scot. Law Com. No. 174),[16] the outcome of the Discussion Paper and also published in 1999, the Scottish Law Commission confirmed the preliminary view:

12–29 **"Losses suffered by a third party**

7.35 We expressed the provisional view in the discussion paper that no new special rule was necessary to enable a party to a contract to recover damages for losses suffered by a third party. [Para 8.49, Proposition 29.] Almost all consultees agreed. We do not therefore recommend any legislation on this matter."

12–30 The vision outlined in Discussion Paper No.109 has since been clouded by events in England. The paper makes passing reference to *The Albazero* (an English House of Lords decision, but based on the Scottish case of *Dunlop v Lambert*[17]) which established that, in a contract for the carriage of goods by sea, a person who contracted with the carrier for the carriage of the goods may sue the carrier, even if the ownership of the goods has passed to another. That person must account to the owner of the goods for any damages recovered. As the discussion paper points out, the application of this special rule of English law has been extended to construction

[16] Scottish Law Commission, *Report on Remedies for Breach of Contract* (Scot. Law Com. No.174).

[17] *Dunlop v Lambert*, 1839 Macl. & Rob 663.

contracts, where a developer has been allowed to claim damages from the builder/contractor, even though the property/land on which the work was carried out by the contractor was owned by a third party.[18] In *St Martins*, Lord Griffiths suggested a second, "wider" ground for recovery by the developer. Even though he did not own the property being developed, the developer had an interest in the performance of the contract and an expectation that it would be performed and should therefore recover the losses incurred.[19] *The Albazero* and *St Martins* are two distinct methods for dealing with the problem of the "legal black hole" that is likely to arise in building contract especially where the person contracting for work to be done on premises is not necessarily the owner. Similar problems could arise, for example in a domestic environment where the partner who contracts for the work might not be the person who owns the domestic property; or in a tenancy where the tenant who contracts for the work does not own the property.

In *Alfred McAlpine Construction Ltd v Panatown Ltd*[20] the House of Lords reviewed the right to recover damages for losses suffered by third parties in English law. The case itself is highly complex and raises many technical aspects of English law. The facts were that, in 1989, McAlpine contracted to construct an office block and car park in Cambridge on a site owned by UIPL. For tax reasons, the construction contract was made not with UIPL, but with Panatown, a company in the same group of companies (the Unex group) as UIPL. On the same day, McAlpine entered into a "duty of care deed" (the DCD) with UIPL, under which UIPL acquired a direct remedy against McAlpine in respect of failure to exercise reasonable skill, care and attention to any matter concerning McAlpine's responsibilities under their contract with Panatown. The deed was expressly assignable by UIPL. Serious defects were found in the building and the Unex Group decided that Panatown should initiate arbitration proceedings against McAlpine to recover costs that, by the time of the House of Lords hearing, Panatown alleged stood at £40 million.

In the House of Lords, McAlpine sought to set aside the Arbitrator's award (that Panatown were entitled to substantial, rather than nominal damages) because Panatown had suffered no loss and therefore had no claim for damages. The House (Lords Goff and Millett dissenting) allowed McAlpine's appeal, finding that the duty of care deed provided UIPL with a direct remedy against McAlpine and that Panatown, having suffered no financial loss, was entitled to nominal damages.

In the course of their speeches, the majority redefined the scope of the exception in *The Albazero*, but refused to apply the *St Martins* exception.

The issues addressed by the House of Lords in *Panatown* came before Lord Drummond Young in the following case. In the course of a detailed judgment, he reviewed thoroughly both *The Albazero* and the *St Martins* exceptions to the rule that damages are not recoverable for losses suffered by third parties.

McLaren Murdoch & Hamilton Ltd v Abercromby Motor Group Ltd **12–31**
2002 G.W.D. 38-1242
Court of Session, Outer House: Lord Drummond Young

The facts are as stated above, para.12–22.

---

[18] *Linden Gardens Trust Ltd v Lenesta Sludge Disposals Ltd* [1994] 1 A.C. 85; *St Martin's Property Corporation Ltd v Sir Robert McAlpine Ltd* [1994] 1 A.C. 85 (generally referred to as the *St Martins* case).
[19] See also, in Scotland, LJ Macgregor "The Expectation, Reliance and Restitution Interests in Contract Damages", 1996 J.R. 227.
[20] *Alfred McAlpine Construction Ltd v Panatown Ltd* [2001] 1 A.C. 518.

12–32 "LORD DRUMMOND YOUNG: ... [32] The second submission for the pursuers in relation to the counterclaim was that the defenders had failed, in respect of certain heads of the damages claimed by them, to establish that the loss had been sustained by them as against other companies in the Abercromby group. The first of these heads was the claim to the cost of replacing the heating system ... The relevant invoices ... were all in the name of a company known as Carden Investments Ltd. [which was] in the same group of companies as the defenders, and was a wholly owned subsidiary of the same holding company ... It followed, counsel argued, that the defenders could not establish any loss in respect of that property ...

[33] This argument raises the issue of the legal 'black hole', a phrase originally used by Lord Stewart in *GUS Property Management Ltd* v *Littlewoods Mail Order Stores Ltd*, 1982 S.C. (H.L.) 157, at 166. That expression is normally used to refer to the situation where a breach of contract has occurred, and loss has resulted from the breach, but that loss has been sustained, wholly or partly, by a person other than a party to the contract. That occurs typically in two categories of case: where one family member has concluded a contract on behalf of himself or herself and other members of the family, and where a contract has been concluded by a company forming part of a group and the subject matter of the contract belongs to or has been transferred to another member of the group. In such cases, the argument for the person responsible for the breach is typically that the other party to the contract has suffered no loss, and thus is not entitled to damages, whereas the party who has sustained the loss is not a party to the contract, and accordingly has no title to sue. The claim for breach of contract accordingly disappears, it is said, into a black hole. That result is clearly undesirable; in a well-regulated legal universe black holes should not exist. Nevertheless, the basis in principle on which recovery can be achieved in such cases has been the subject of some disagreement. The matter has been considered at length by the House of Lords in a number of English cases ... While those cases turned to some extent on specialties of English law, they provide some guidance as to the manner in which Scots law might approach the problem of the black hole. That is particularly true of the speech of Lord Clyde in the most recent case, *Alfred McAlpine Construction Ltd* v *Panatown Ltd*, which considers the underlying principles in detail and indeed makes reference to Scots law.

[34] In any such case, however, the initial task is to identify the precise loss that has been sustained, and consequently the person who has sustained that loss. That is because the problem of a 'black hole' truly arises only if loss has been sustained by a person other than a party to the contract. In identifying the loss, it is of critical importance to bear in mind that the loss resulting from a breach of contract is not the same thing as the quantification of that loss. Nor is it the same as the remedial measures necessary to put right the loss. The loss is rather the actual physical or economic damage sustained in consequence of the breach of contract. In the present case, the loss sustained in consequence of the pursuers' breach of contract in respect of the Fiat showroom and workshop is that that building had an inadequate heating system. That loss was sustained as soon as the building was completed. No doubt it took some time for the inadequacy of the system to be noticed, and a considerably longer time for remedial measures to be taken. Nevertheless, the loss itself existed independently of those remedial measures, and indeed before it was even noticed. At a time when the loss was sustained, the building was the property of the present defenders; it was not until May 2000 that it was transferred to Carden Investments Ltd. It follows, accordingly, that the defenders were the party who initially sustained the loss. That in my opinion of itself entitles them to sue in respect of that loss ... If I am wrong in that conclusion, however, I

am of opinion that the defenders are still entitled to recover the cost of the necessary remedial works from the pursuers, for the reasons stated in the following paragraphs.

[35] The starting point in the English cases has been the formulation, by Lord Diplock in *The Albazero*, of the special rule applicable to contracts of carriage. That rule is generally attributed to the Scottish case of *Dunlop* v *Lambert*, 1839, Macl & Rob 663, but precisely what that case decided was a matter of some confusion until it was fully analysed by Lord Clyde in *Alfred McAlpine Construction Ltd* v *Panatown Ltd.*, and it is probably not authority for the formulation of the rule in *The Albazero*. The latter rule is regarded as an exception to the general principle that a person cannot recover substantial damages for breach of contract where he himself has suffered no loss by reason of the breach. The exception applicable to contracts of carriage has been stated as follows (per Lord Diplock at [1977] AC 847):

'In a commercial contract concerning goods where it is in the contemplation of the parties that the proprietary interests in the goods may be transferred from one owner to another after the contract has been entered into and before the breach which causes loss or damage to the goods, an original party to the contract, if such be the intention of them both, is to be treated in law as having entered into the contract for the benefit of all persons who have or may acquire an interest in the goods before they are lost or damaged, and is entitled to recover by way of damages for breach of contract the actual loss sustained by those for whose benefit the contract is entered into'.

In such cases, however, the party who sues on the contract is accountable to the true owner of the goods for the proceeds of any decree that he obtains: *ibid* at 844. In subsequent cases there has been discussion of the question whether the foregoing rule is better regarded as a rule of law or a rule of implication based on the intention of the parties. In *Alfred McAlpine Construction Ltd* v *Panatown Ltd,* Lord Clyde preferred the former view, as the parties may in reality not have applied their minds to the point: [2001] 1 A.C. 530.

[36] A similar rule was applied to building contracts in *Linden Gardens Trust Ltd* v *Lenesta Sludge Disposals Ltd; St Martins Property Corporation Ltd* v *Sir Robert McAlpine Ltd*, although the basis in principle for the extension of the rule is not entirely clear, beyond a desire to ensure that damages could be recovered for a breach of contract. The result was that the employer under a building contract could, on the facts of the case, sue the contractor for breach of contract even though the loss resulting from the breach had been sustained by a third party to whom the employer had sold the building while it was under construction. In *Alfred McAlpine Construction Ltd* v *Panatown Ltd*, Lord Clyde commented on the *St Martins* case as follows (at [2001] 1 A.C. 530):

'In that case the point was made that the contractor and the employer were both aware that the property was going to be occupied and possibly purchased by third parties so that it could be foreseen that a breach of the contract might cause loss to others than the employer. But such foresight may be an unnecessary factor in the applicability of the exception. So also an intention of the parties to benefit a third person may be unnecessary . . . If the exception is founded primarily upon a principle of law, and not upon the particular knowledge of the parties to the contract, then it is not easy to see why the necessity for the contemplation of the parties that there will be potential losses by third parties is essential'.

The principle applicable in cases such as *St Martins* was summarised by Lord Clyde in the following terms (at [2001] 1 AC 532):

'The approach under *The Albazero* exception has been one of recognising an entitlement to sue by the innocent party to a contract which has been breached, where the innocent party is treated as suing on behalf of or for the benefit of some other person or persons, not parties to the contract, who have sustained loss as a result of the breach. In such a case the innocent party to the contract is bound to account to the person suffering the loss for the damages which the former has recovered for the benefit of the latter'.

In *Alfred McAlpine Construction Ltd* v *Panatown Ltd*, the majority of the House of Lords held that the exception described in *The Albazero* could not apply on the facts of the case. A building contractor entered into a contract with an employer for the construction of an office block. The site, and consequently the building when it was constructed, were the property of another company in the same group as the employer. The contractor entered into an agreement with the owner of the site under which it undertook a duty of care in favour of the owner. That agreement conferred a direct remedy against the contractor by the owner. In those circumstances it was held that the arrangements between the parties did not require that the employer should be able to sue under the building contract on the owner's behalf; the owner had its own direct right of action.

[37] Apart from the argument based on the rule formulated in *The Albazero*, the employer in *Alfred McAlpine Construction Ltd* v *Panatown Ltd* argued that it should be entitled to sue the contractor on a wider ground. This was that the innocent party to the contract should be entitled to recover damages because he had not received the performance that he was entitled under the building contract to receive from the contractor. This has been described by academic writers as a contracting party's 'performance interest', that is to say, a party's interest in having the contract performed by the other party. If there is a failure to perform, the innocent party is entitled to recover damages for himself as compensation for what is seen as his own loss, with no obligation to account to anyone else for the amount recovered. This approach, which had been supported by a substantial number of distinguished academic writers, found favour with Lord Goff of Chieveley and Lord Millett. They accordingly dissented, and would have found the contractor liable to the employer in substantial damages. The majority of the House of Lords, however, rejected this approach. Their reasons for doing so were summarised by Lord Clyde at [2001] 1 A.C. 533–534:

'First, if the loss is the disappointment at there not being provided what was contracted for, it seems to me difficult to measure that loss by consideration of the cost of repair. A more apt assessment of the compensation for the loss of what was expected it[21] should rather be the difference in value between what was contracted for and what was supplied. Secondly, the loss constituted by the supposed disappointment may well not include all the loss which the breach of contract has caused. It may not be able to embrace consequential losses, or losses falling within the second head of *Hadley* v *Baxendale* (1854) 9 Exch 341 . . . Thirdly, there is no obligation on the successful plaintiff to account to anyone who may have sustained actual loss as a result of the faulty performance. Some further mechanism would then be required for the court to achieve the proper disposal of the monies awarded to avoid a double jeopardy. Alternatively, in order to achieve the effective solution, it would seem to be necessary to add an obligation to account on the part of the person recovering the damages. But once that step is taken the approach begins to approximate to *The Albazero* exception. Fourthly, the "loss" constituted by a breach of contract has usually been recognised as calling for an award of nominal damages, not substantial damages'.

Lord Clyde continued:

[21] This is a misquotation: the word "it" does not appear in this extract from Lord Clyde's speech, which reads: " . . . what was expected should rather be . . . ".

'The loss of an expectation which is here referred to seems to me to be coming very close to a way of describing a breach of contract. A breach of contract may cause a loss, but is not in itself a loss in any meaningful sense. When one refers to a loss in the context of a breach of contract, one is in my view referring to the incidence of some personal or patrimonial damage'.

[38] Lord Clyde went on to discuss the significance of the doctrine of privity of contract to the problem of the legal black hole. He suggested, at [2001] 1 A.C. 534–535, that the solution to the problem might lie in the *jus quaesitum tertio*, particularly in cases where a husband instructs repairs to the roof of his wife's house, or orders and pays for a holiday which results in disappointment to all the members of the family. By using the *jus quaesitum tertio*, compensation might be paid to those who actually suffer the loss. Such a solution is available in German law, and Lord Clyde suggested that it might also be available in Scotland. It was not, however, available in England, where the *jus quaesitum tertio* was not recognised at common law. In the absence of any remedy using the *jus quaesitum tertio*, Lord Clyde concluded, in a passage that sums up the views of the majority of the House of Lords, that the best solution was

'to permit the contracting party to recover damages for the loss which he and a third party has suffered, being duly accountable to them in respect of their actual loss . . . The solution is required for the law will not tolerate a loss caused by a breach of contract to go uncompensated through an absence of privity between the party suffering the loss and the party causing it. In such a case, to avoid the legal black hole, the law will deem the innocent party to be claiming on behalf of himself and any others who have suffered loss. It does not matter that he is not the owner of the property affected, nor that he has not himself suffered any economic loss. He sues for all the loss which has been sustained and is accountable to the others to the extent of their particular losses . . . If there is an anxiety lest the exception would permit an employer to receive excessive damages, that should be set at rest by the recognition of the basic requirement for reasonableness which underlies the quantification of an award of damages' ([2001] 1 A.C. 535).

[39] In Scots law, the *jus quaesitum tertio* may clearly provide a remedy in a significant number of cases. If, for example, a man concludes a contract for a holiday on behalf of himself, his wife and his children, the requirements of the *jus quaesitum* will almost certainly be met, and the individual members of the family will then be able to sue for their own losses. The *jus quaesitum tertio* is of limited utility, however, owing to certain of the restrictions that have been built into its application. In the first place, the parties to the contract must intend to benefit the third party: *Peddie* v *Brown*, (1857) 3 Macq 65; and *Finnie* v *Glasgow & South Western Railway*, (1857) 3 Macq 75. In the second place, the third party who is to benefit must be identified in the contract: *ibid; Kelly* v *Cornhill Insurance Company*, 1964 S.C. (H.L.) 46. These restrictions would exclude from the application of the *jus quaesitum tertio* any case in which one party to a contract was unaware that the other intended to benefit a third party, such as a member of his family or a company in the same group. They would also exclude any case where the contract was for work on a particular property which was thereafter transferred to a third party. For these reasons the *jus quaesitum tertio* in its present form is of relatively limited utility in dealing with the problem of the legal black hole. No doubt the applicability of the principle might be extended by removing the two restrictions referred to above, but that is clearly beyond the competence of the Outer House. In any event, while it is always tempting to develop solutions to legal problems by extending the existing institutions of Scots law, it is not obvious that the *jus quaesitum tertio* is appropriate for such extension by removing the two restrictions referred to above. Both restrictions are founded on the fundamental principle that the terms of a contract must be based on the parties' agreement; that is why the parties must intend to benefit the third party and identify him sufficiently in their agreement. Consequently it does not seem appropriate that a contract

should confer a direct benefit on any person who was not contemplated by the parties as a beneficiary at the time when they entered into their agreement. For these reasons I am of opinion that the *jus quaesitum tertio*, at least as it has developed in Scots law, is incapable of providing a general solution to the problem of the legal black hole.

[40] I am equally of opinion that the solution favoured by the minority of the House of Lords in *Alfred McAlpine Construction Ltd* v *Panatown Ltd* is not in accordance with the underlying principles of the Scots law of contract. That solution is based on two propositions, that a party who enters into a contract has an interest in having the contract performed, and that that interest is sufficient to entitle him to claim substantial damages if there is any failure in performance. In my opinion the second of these propositions does not follow from the first; indeed, the distinction between them is emphasised by the traditional approach of Scots law to contractual remedies. The first proposition, that a party to a contract has an interest in enforcing the contract, merely by virtue of his position as a party to it, clearly accords with Scots law. Thus a party to a contract has title and interest to sue on the contract merely because he is a party. Equally, a party to a contract will, merely because he is a party, be entitled to enforce the contract by compelling the other party to implement his obligations, whether by specific implement or interdict; that assumes, obviously, that the other necessary conditions exist for the remedies of specific implement or interdict. Similarly, a party to a contract will be entitled to obtain a declarator of his rights under the contract merely because he is a party.

[41] It does not follow, however, that a party to a contract should be entitled to recover substantial damages merely because he is a party to the contract. The remedy of damages is fundamentally different from implement. Implement involves the direct enforcement of the contract, and can thus be regarded as the primary remedy for a failure to perform. Damages, by contrast, is a secondary, substitutionary remedy. The purpose of damages is to provide financial redress for the loss caused by a breach of contract. That result is achieved by ordering the party in breach of contract to pay a sum sufficient to place the other party in the same position as he would have been in had the contract had been performed. Thus the notions of loss and financial redress for that loss are central to the remedy. That indicates that a loss itself must be substantial, capable of being measured in financial terms. The mere existence of a breach of contract does not of itself create a loss of that nature; the loss is rather something flowing from and independent of the breach, and must be substantial in the sense that it can be measured in financial terms. That is the point made by Lord Clyde in the second of the passages quoted in paragraph [37] above. If damages requires a loss capable of measurement in financial terms, it is obvious that the loss must be that of a particular person. In a case where, for example, a husband has contracted for repairs to a house that belongs to his wife, or a company has contracted for building works on land belonging to another company in the same group, it cannot be said that the person who is a party to the contract is the person who has suffered loss in the sense described above. The person who suffers that loss is rather the person who owns the property on which the work is performed. I am accordingly of opinion that in Scots law a party to a contract should not be entitled to recover substantial damages for breach of contract merely by virtue of that breach, although he may be entitled to specific implement or interdict in that situation. It seems to me that the difficulty that confronts English law is that damages is regarded as the primary remedy for breach of contract. Consequently the minority of the House of Lords in *Alfred McAlpine Construction Ltd* v *Panatown Ltd,* together with a number of distinguished academic writers, took the view that that primary remedy should be available whenever there is a breach of contract. In Scots law, by contrast, while damages is undoubtedly the commonest remedy for breach of contract, the primary remedy is implement. It is that remedy that is available merely by virtue of the

breach of contract. Damages requires more, and thus is not a remedy available on the mere occurrence of a breach of contract.

[42] It is clear in my opinion that the existence of legal 'black holes' is undesirable; if a breach of contract has caused loss, it should be possible to obtain redress for that loss from the party in breach. The same is true of delict, although somewhat different considerations apply there. That has been recognised in a series of cases in the House of Lords, including *GUS Property Management Ltd* v *Littlewoods Mail Order Stores Ltd*, 1982 S.C. (H.L.) 157, *Linden Gardens Trust Ltd* v *Lenesta Sludge Disposals Ltd; St Martin's Property Corporation Ltd* v *Sir Robert McAlpine Ltd, supra,* and *Alfred McAlpine Construction Ltd* v *Panatown Ltd, supra.* Although the approach of the majority of the House of Lords in the latter case was based on a series of English authorities (apart from *Dunlop* v *Lambert*, which is restricted in its ambit to contracts of carriage by sea), the result is in my opinion wholly consistent with the principles of Scots law. I am accordingly of opinion that Scots law should adopt the same general rule as that applied by the majority of the House of Lords in that case, as described by Lord Clyde in the passage quoted above at paragraph [38]. In effect the rule comes to this: if a breach of contract occurs, causing loss that can be measured in financial terms, the party who is not in breach may recover substantial damages even if that loss has been sustained by another person; if a loss has been sustained by a person other than the contracting party, however, the contracting party must sue on behalf of that other, and must accordingly account to that other for the damages recovered. The right to raise an action in this way is deemed by law to exist in any case where the loss resulting from the breach of contract occurs to a person other than the correcting party. It should not in my view be based on the intention of the parties; the right is rather conferred as a matter of general legal policy, to ensure that if a loss results from a breach of contract damages can be recovered from the party responsible for the breach; that was Lord Clyde's conclusion at [2001] 1 A.C. 530-531. Nevertheless, if the third party who suffers loss has a direct right of action against the party in breach of contract, for example under a duty of care warranty, there is no need for the contracting party to have a right of action on the third party's behalf, and the law will not deem such a right to exist. That was critical to the decision of the majority in *Alfred McAlpine Construction Ltd* v *Panatown Ltd.* While the contracting party is obliged to account for the damages recovered, he will in my opinion be entitled to the expenses that he has incurred in conducting the litigation, so far as he has been unable to recover those from the person in breach of contract. Such an approach has a number of advantages. In the first place, it provides a solution to the problem of the legal black hole that is capable of almost universal application. In the second place, it permits recovery even in the case of contracts that are incapable of assignation, since it is the original party to the contract who is responsible for raising any action. That is particularly important in relation to the standard forms of building contract, as it was held in *Linden Gardens Trust Ltd* v *Lenesta Sludge Disposals Ltd; St Martin's Property Corporation Ltd* v *Sir Robert McAlpine Ltd, supra,* that the employer's rights under the J.C.T. standard form could not be assigned to a third party. In the third place, it maintains the fundamental principle that the remedy of substantial damages can only be available if there exists a loss capable of being measured in financial terms. That means that the usual rules on remoteness of damage will continue to apply.

[43] On the foregoing analysis, I am of opinion that the defenders would be entitled to raise proceedings against the pursuers for substantial damages even in respect of a loss that had been suffered by another company such as Carden Investments Ltd. The defenders would be subject to an obligation to account for any damages recovered to such third party, but that is not a matter that concerns me in the present proceedings."

12–33 Three matters of particular importance in Lord Drummond Young's approach to the problem of the "black hole" deserve further comment. First, he stressed that the majority of the House of Lords in *Panatown* (the leading English case) had rejected the "performance interest" approach advocated by Lord Goff (and to a lesser extent Lord Millett).[22] Secondly, he emphatically stressed that, unlike English law, interdict or specific performance, not damages, are the primary remedy in Scots law,[23] and that a breach does not automatically create a substantial, measurable loss capable of being assessed as pecuniary damages. Thirdly, he adopted and applied the *Albazero* exception developed in the English courts and approved by Lord Clyde in *Panatown*,[24] the so-called "piggy back" claim.

Perhaps the last—but not the final—word on the subject should be Professor MacBryde's.

12–34 *The Law of Contract in Scotland*

WW McBryde, 3rd edn (Edinburgh: W. Green/SULI, 2007)

"**22–28** ... The difficulty with this as a general approach could be that it breaches the principle that the claimant can only recover loss actually suffered by the claimant. This is, however, a way in which contract law may be developing following academic discussion of disappointment of an expectation interest [see Lord Goff, dissenting in *Panatown* at 546, 547] ...

22–29 Assume another set of facts. A seller of a building is aware that there is a defect in the building that will hinder a sale. He engages a builder to remedy the defect. The builder is not told about the impending sale. After the work is done the seller sells the building for a high price. Three years after taking entry the purchaser discovers that the building work was defective and there are now serious structural problems with the building. There is no doubt that the builder was in breach of contract. But who sues him and why? *Jus quaesitum tertio* cannot be used, because the builder was unaware of the identity of the purchaser ... The seller has not sustained any loss. If there is to be an action based on the builder's breach of contract, it would have to be by the seller seeking the damages which must be accounted for to the purchaser. This is *The Albazero* exception and involves determining that there is a 'black hole'. *The Albazero* exception, as explained by Lord Clyde in *Panatown* [at 530], ... does not depend on the foresight, knowledge or intention of the seller and the builder. It is a rule of law. The real problem is not the absence of the *jus quaesitum tertio*, but the lack of a satisfactory remedy for recovery of economic loss in delict ... Also the law of delict might provide a more sensible solution in that the builder would be liable to the purchaser only for loss caused by negligence, and not for every failure to comply with the terms of the contract, including the detailed specification some of which might be of little interest to the purchaser. Nevertheless, the law of contract is changing with a solution which it is admitted 'may carry with it some element of artificiality and may not be supportable on any clear or single principle' [Lord Clyde in *Panatown* at 535] ...

[22] See particularly Lord Drummond Young's comments at [37] and [40]. On "reliance interest" in damages, see below, para.12–44 onwards.

[23] *McLaren Murdoch & Hamilton Ltd v Abercromby Motor Group Ltd*, 2002 G.W.D. 38-1242, para.41. In England the reverse is true—damages is the primary remedy for breach of contract. The reason is that English contract law developed in the common law courts, where the only remedy was damages, a person seeking specific performance (implement) or an injunction (interdict) would have to pursue the claim in the court of Chancery.

[24] *McLaren Murdoch & Hamilton Ltd v Abercromby Motor Group Ltd*, 2002 G.W.D. 38-1242, [42], [43]. Note, however, that the claimant in *Panatown* could not rely on this exception, because of the duty of care clause in the original contract giving it a direct claim against the contractor. For a recent decision rejecting a claim based both on *Panatown* and *Albazero*, see *Axon Well Intervention Products Holdings AS v Craig* [2015] CSOH 4.

...

22–31 ... In any event, the way the law has developed will lead to many problems and discussion about what contracts should contain. As Lord Clyde stated [*Panatown* at 530] ... :

The terms and provisions of the contract will then require to be studied to see if the parties have excluded the operation of the exception."'

The recovery of non-patrimonial loss

Cases like *Forsyth v Ruxley* and *McLaren Murdoch & Hamilton v Abercromby Motor Group Ltd* highlight that unless the pursuer's patrimonial interest—an interest in property, injury to the person, etc.—has been injured by the breach, the pursuer may have difficulty in recovering damages. For example, merely because a breach has resulted in a benefit or gain to the party in breach, the pursuer cannot claim that gain as damages. **12–35**

Teacher v Calder **12–36**
(1898) 25 R. 661
Court of Session, 1st Division: Lord President (Low), Lords Adam, M'Laren.

In 1889 Adam Teacher, the whisky distiller advanced £15,000 to Calder, to be used in Calder's timber merchant business for five years. The agreement did not make Teacher a partner, but gave him a 37.5 per cent share of the profits, in addition to 5 per cent interest on the loan. It also provided that Calder should always keep at least £15,000 of his own capital in the business. In breach of the agreement, Calder reduced his capital in the business much below £15,000 by withdrawing large sums which he invested in a distillery business, where he earned large profits.

In 1894 differences arose between the parties as to items in the balance sheet for the last year of the agreement, and the trustees for Mr Teacher (now deceased) raised an action.

In this appeal against the decision of the Outer House, the trustees claimed, in addition to Teacher's contractual right to interest and a share of the profits, damages based on the profits gained by Calder diverting £15,000 of his own capital from the business.

The Inner House rejected the appeal.

"LORD PRESIDENT (LOW):— **12–37**

...

I turn now to the conclusion for damages. It was allowed by both parties that the defender was under obligation to keep the £15,000 of capital of his own in the business, and it was admitted by the defender that he did not do so. ...

That this withdrawal of capital was a breach of contract the defender admits, and the Lord Ordinary pronounces; and there can be no doubt about it. ...

The claim of damages is therefore not met by any defence. Yet the Lord Ordinary has dismissed the conclusion for damages on the ground that, while there was a technical breach of the agreement, it is not proved that the pursuer has sustained any actual damage.

This judgment cannot stand, because, even if no substantial damage had been proved, the mere fact of the breach of contract entitles the pursuer to damages, even were they merely nominal— *Webster* v *Cramond Iron Company* [2 R. 752] ... When the pursuer lent the defender his £15,000 it was on the representation, expressed in the contract, that it was to work an extended timber business, which should have a constant capital of

£30,000, backed by a bank credit of £20,000. Having got the money for an extended timber business, the defender made, so far as appears, no attempt whatever to extend the business, having promptly and gladly withdrawn the bulk of his own capital into the more lucrative business of distilling, the profits of which he was not obliged to share with the pursuer. With the money of the timber business much more lucratively employed in distilling, it is not difficult for the defender to say, with a tolerably good conscience, that the timber business, which he himself managed, really did not need the money. But I decline to content myself with such excuses, for what I think was a material and not a technical breach of contract.

The question as to the remedy has been left by the pursuer in a somewhat unsatisfactory position. The pursuer has been attracted by the large gains of the distilling business; he has sought to capture these by the misapplication of rules of trust law and of partnership law; and less attention has, in consequence, been bestowed on his true claim of damages.

In my opinion, it is impossible for the pursuer to claim the profits made in the distillery with the defender's capital, which ought to have been in the timber business. The money traded with in the distillery was not the pursuer's but the defender's; and the defender was neither a trustee, nor (in relation to the pursuer) a partner. The fact that the pursuer was entitled to a share of profits did not under this agreement make him a partner; and his relation to the defender was simply that of creditor in a contract obligation.

The question then is, what damage has the pursuer sustained? or, to put it otherwise, what would he have gained more than he has done through the five per cent return had the defender kept the stipulated capital in the timber business? ... There is adequate evidence that the timber market admitted of the remunerative employment of capital during the period of the agreement, and that 8 per cent was being earned ... We sit as a jury; and the sum which I propose is, in my judgment, a very moderate estimate of the damage caused by the defender's breach of contract during the five years. I am for giving the pursuer decree for £250, in name of damages.

12–38 LORD ADAM.—

...

In the view your Lordship has taken of the case, I agree in the amount of damages proposed to be awarded.

12–39 LORD M'LAREN.—

...

... [T]he only question before the Court is, whether the damage shall be assessed at the minimum sum of £250 proposed by the Lord President, and my answer is in the affirmative."

Comment

12–40 On further appeal, the House of Lords (Lords Blackburn, Shand and Davey) upheld the decision of the Inner House.[25] Lord Davey commented[26]:

"The learned Dean of Faculty claimed to follow these sums, and sought to make the respondent account to the appellants for the profits derived by the use of them. The contention was a novelty unsupported by either authority or principle. The money withdrawn was not Mr Teacher's in any sense, and he had no interest in it except to have it employed in the respondent's timber business. But his representatives are entitled to

[25] *Teacher v Calder* (1899) 1 F. (H.L.) 39.
[26] *Teacher v Calder* (1899) 1 F. (H.L.) 39, 50.

> damages for the loss he sustained by the respondent's breach of the agreement so to employ it. There is evidence that money could at that time he profitably employed, say at 8 per cent per annum, in the timber business. But there is no evidence of any business being lost by the respondent, or of his being unable to tender for any contract from want of capital, and there is some affirmative evidence to the contrary . . . On the whole, taking all the circumstances into consideration, I am unable to say that the appellants, Mr Teacher's trustees, have made out to my satisfaction that Mr Teacher suffered any larger damages by the respondent's breach of his agreement than the sum which has been awarded to them by the Court of Session."

There is English authority[27] that in exceptional circumstances where no other remedy is available, gains from a breach of contract may be recoverable as damages, but so far this has not been applied in Scotland.[28] Note also the question whether restitution is possible for any unjustified enrichment.[29]

Damages for "non-pecuniary" loss

Even where a right to damages is established, the amount recoverable for such a "non-pecuniary" loss is likely to be nominal. The decision of the House of Lords in *Addis v Gramophone Co*[30] (although an English decision) has generally been regarded as precluding the recovery of damages for injury to feelings or general mental distress. In the English case of *Johnson v Gore Wood Ltd*[31] the House of Lords affirmed *Addis*. It refused damages for injury to feelings and distress caused by the manner in which the employee was wrongfully dismissed. More recently, the exceptions to rule in *Addis* has been extended. In appropriate circumstances, courts will, for example award damages for injury to feelings. The joint claimants in *Eastwood v Magnox Electric Plc* and *McCabe v Cornwall County Council*[32] were successful in recovering damages for stress-related illness and inability to work, not because of the manner of their dismissal, but because of the behaviour of their employers towards them *in the period leading up to their dismissal*. That behaviour amounted to breach of their duty of trust and confidence as employers and their duty to provide a safe system of work. In *Jarvis v Swans Tours*[33] Mr Jarvis, a solicitor, booked a fortnight's skiing package holiday in Switzerland through Swans Tours. The Swans Tours brochure described the "houseparty centre" at which Mr Jarvis and his family were to stay in very favourable terms. Mr Jarvis discovered that only 13 people constituted the "houseparty" at the centre where he was booked; the hotel owner spoke no English, contrary to statements in the brochure; by the second week he was the only person in the "houseparty"; the skiing was inadequate; and the facilities poor. In addition to recovery of the cost of the holiday, Mr Jarvis successfully claimed damages in compensation for the disappointment, distress and loss of enjoyment which the breaches of contract had caused. In the course of his judgment in the English Court of Appeal Lord Denning MR, said[34]: **12–41**

---

[27] *Attorney-General v Blake* [2001] 1 AC 268, the "Spycatcher" litigation.

[28] See discussion in WW McBryde, *The Law of Contract in Scotland*, 3rd edn (Edinburgh: W. Green, 2007), para.22–94. MacQueen and Thomson, *Contract Law in Scotland*, 6.17 and the references therein.

[29] See generally WW McBryde, *The Law of Contract in Scotland*, 3rd edn (Edinburgh: W. Green, 2007), paras 20–142, 22–94 and more generally 20–132 to 20–147; and note HL MacQueen, "Unjustified Enrichment and Breach of Contract," 1994 JR 137.

[30] *Addis v Gramophone Co* [1909] A.C. 488.

[31] *Johnson v Gore Wood Ltd* [2002] 2 A.C. 1.

[32] *Eastwood v Magnox Electric Plc* and *McCabe v Cornwall County Council* [2004] UKHL 35; [2005] 1 A.C. 503.

[33] *Jarvis v Swans Tours Ltd* [1973] 1 Q.B. 233.

[34] *Jarvis v Swans Tours Ltd* [1973] 1 Q.B. 233 at 237–238.

"In a proper case damages for mental distress can be recovered in contract, just as damages for shock can be recovered in tort. One such case is a contract for a holiday, or any other contract to provide entertainment and enjoyment. If the contracting party breaks his contract, damages can be given for the disappointment, the distress, the upset and frustration caused by the breach. I know that it is difficult to assess in terms of money, but it is no more difficult than the assessment which the courts have to make every day in personal injury cases for loss of amenities. Take the present case. Mr Jarvis has only a fortnight's holiday in the year. He books it far ahead, and looks forward to it all that time. He ought to be compensated for the loss of it."

12–42 **Diesen v Samson**

1971 S.L.T. (Sh. Ct.) 49

Sheriff Court of Lanark at Glasgow: Sheriff-Substitute JM Peterson

Mrs Diesen married her Norwegian husband in Langside Parish Church in Glasgow. She employed Mr Samson to take the wedding photographs, both at the church and at the reception afterwards. Because there would be several wedding guests in Norwegian national costume, the *Scottish Daily Express* also sent their photographer, Mr Beltrami, to the wedding. Mr Samson forgot to turn up to the wedding. Fortunately, Mr Beltrami took photographs at the church and was persuaded to take the photographs at the reception. Unfortunately the photographs at the reception failed to come out, so that Mrs Diesen's only photographs of her wedding were those which Mr Beltrami had taken at the church. She successfully claimed damages from Mr Samson for the loss and disappointment that had been caused by his breach of contract.

12–43 "SHERIFF-SUBSTITUTE (JM PETERSON): . . . [Samson claimed] that the absence of any photographs was due to the failure of Mr Beltrami's photographic equipment, and the defender could not be held responsible for that. This contention also is devoid of merit. It was only the defender's breach of contract which made it necessary for the pursuer to attempt to diminish her loss by invoking the assistance of Mr Beltrami, and the fact that it proved unavailing is no excuse for the defender.

The real issue in the case is whether it can ever be proper for a court to award damages for injury to feelings resulting from breach of contract. It is quite clear that the pursuer's claim is of this nature. I was referred by the defender's solicitor to Gloag on *Contract* (2nd ed.), p. 686, where *Addis v Gramophone Co.* [1909] A.C. 488 is cited for the proposition that—'it is conceived that injury to the feelings of the party whose contract has been broken, either from the fact or the manner of the breach, are not elements to be taken into account in estimating damages.'

Since *Addis* (supra) was an English appeal and other Scottish text-writers cite it also (Walker on *Damages*, p.123, *Principles of Scottish Private Law*, Vol. I, p. 728, Gloag and Henderson, *Introduction to the Law of Scotland* (7th ed.), p.135, Green, *Encyclopaedia of the Laws of Scotland*, Vol. V, pp. 390, 405), it would seem that the law of Scotland is the same as the law of England on the subject, and that English textbooks may be of assistance. Mayne and McGregor (12th ed.), suggest that there may be room for exceptions. I quote the passage in full as I adopt it as the ratio decidendi in this case. Mayne and McGregor, at p. 43, state the general rule—'No damages may be recovered in contract for injury to feelings'—and they go on to cite various authorities, including *Addis*, in support of it, but at p. 44 they write: 'It may, however, be respectfully suggested that there is no reason why there could not be exceptions in proper cases to this sound general rule. Just as failure to pay money will generally attract no damages, at least beyond interest, because no more is in the parties' contemplation, mental distress likewise does not form a head of damages for the same reason. But the basic criterion is the parties' contemplation and the scope of the contract, and just as the Court of Appeal has spoken cautiously about whether the rule as to non-payment of money is without exception, one may justifiably be equally cautious as to a dogmatic rule in the case of mental suffering. The reason for the general rule is that contracts normally concern commercial matters and that mental suffering on breach is not in the contemplation of the parties as part of the business risk of the transaction. If, however, the contract is not primarily a commercial one, in the sense that it affects not the plaintiffs business interests but his personal, social and family interests, the door is not closed to awarding damages for mental suffering should the court think that in the particular circumstances the parties to the contract had such damage in their contemplation. The types of contract where these considerations could apply would be contracts giving the plaintiff a right to come on the defendant's property from which he is then forcibly removed by the defendant, as from a theatre, racecourse, train or hotel, and also contracts connected with the ill-health or death of the plaintiff or members of his family, such as lack of attention by a doctor, hospital or undertaker, or a failure or delay in delivery of a telegram announcing illness or death to a family member...'

'It is true that in the case of forcible removal or expulsion from premises in breach of contract the plaintiff has always framed his action in tort for assault and not always successfully, which suggests that the contract action would not have satisfied his purpose. But the matter has never been tested, and all that is suggested here is that the rule against recovery for mental suffering in contract should not be regarded as rigid, so as to debar recovery if ever a deserving case should arise.'

The contract in the present case would seem to be one of the kind envisaged by these authors, because it was not commercial in that sense and was exclusively concerned with the pursuer's personal, social, and family interests and with her feelings. Wedding photographs generally are of no interest to anyone except the bride and bridegroom and their relatives and friends, and then only because they serve to stimulate recollection of a happy occasion and so give pleasure. What both the parties obviously had in their contemplation was that the pursuer would be enabled to enjoy such pleasure in the years ahead. This has been permanently denied her by the defender's breach of contract and, in my opinion, it is as fitting a case for the award of damages as the examples cited.

The assessment of damages is a matter of great difficulty. The loss which the pursuer has sustained is of the kind which might affect one individual very much more than another, and there can be little corroboration for the pursuer's testimony as to how much it means to her, since the matter is so largely subjective. Also, while every bride may be presumed to look happily forward to the future of her wedding day, the future cannot be foretold. If a marriage is happy, there will be in it satisfactions which will help to make up for the loss, and if it is not the recollection of the ceremony with which it began may be the less cherished. In either case the persons concerned will have other things to think about as time goes by. The defender has done nothing to impair the pursuer's marriage itself. It is only the pictorial record of the initial ceremony which has been lost. The court is required to preserve a sense of proportion and to exercise moderation where the quantification of the loss is so difficult. In my opinion an award of £30 is as much as can be justified."

There is no doubt that courts are willing to award nominal damages in instances of serious injury to feelings[35] and more recently they have shown a willingness to extend the exceptions to

[35] WW McBryde, *The Law of Contract in Scotland*, 3rd edn (Edinburgh: W. Green, 2007), paras 22–100, 22–101; WW McBryde, "Remedies for breach of contract" (1996) 1 E.L.R. 43.

Addis to the recovery of damages for the personal disappointment occasioned by the convenience of the contract not being properly performed. The personal preferences of the pursuer, it would appear, are a factor to be taken into account.

12–44 **Ruxley Electronics and Construction Ltd v Forsyth**
[1996] A.C. 344
House of Lords: Lords Keith, Bridge, Jauncey, Mustill and Lloyd

The facts are as stated above, para.12–16.

12–45 "LORD JAUNCEY OF TULLICHETTLE: . . . The second matter relates to the award of £2,500 for loss of amenity made by the trial judge. The respondent argued that he erred in law in making such award. However as the appellant did not challenge it, I find it unnecessary to express any opinion on the matter.

12–46 LORD MUSTILL: . . .

There are not two alternative measures of damage, at opposite poles, but only one; namely, the loss truly suffered by the promisee. In some cases the loss cannot be fairly measured except by reference to the full cost of repairing the deficiency in performance. In others, and in particular those where the contract is designed to fulfil a purely commercial purpose, the loss will very often consist only of the monetary detriment brought about by the breach of contract. But these remedies are not exhaustive, for the law must cater for those occasions where the value of the promise to the promisee exceeds the financial enhancement of his position which full performance will secure. This excess, often referred to in the literature as the 'consumer surplus' (see for example the valuable discussion by Harris, Ogus and Philips (1979) 95 L.Q.R. 581) is usually incapable of precise valuation in terms of money, exactly because it represents a personal, subjective and non-monetary gain. Nevertheless where it exists the law should recognise it and compensate the promisee if the misperformance takes it away. The lurid bathroom tiles, or the grotesque folly instanced in argument by my noble and learned friend, Lord Keith of Kinkel, may be so discordant with general taste that in purely economic terms the builder may be said to do the employer a favour by failing to install them. But this is too narrow and materialistic a view of the transaction. Neither the contractor nor the court has the right to substitute for the employer's individual expectation of performance a criterion derived from what ordinary people would regard as sensible. As my Lords have shown, the test of reasonableness plays a central part in determining the basis of recovery, and will indeed be decisive in a case such as the present when the cost of reinstatement would be wholly disproportionate to the non-monetary loss suffered by the employer. But it would be equally unreasonable to deny all recovery for such a loss. The amount may be small, and since it cannot be quantified directly there may be room for difference of opinion about what it should be. But in several fields the judges are well accustomed to putting figures to intangibles, and I see no reason why the imprecision of the exercise should be a barrier, if that is what fairness demands.

My Lords, once this is recognised the puzzling and paradoxical feature of this case, that it seems to involve a contest of absurdities, simply falls away. There is no need to remedy the injustice of awarding too little, by unjustly awarding far too much. The judgment of the trial judge acknowledges that the employer has suffered a true loss and expresses it in terms of money. Since there is no longer any issue about the amount of the award, as distinct from the principle, I would simply restore his judgment by allowing the appeal.

12–47 LORD LLOYD OF BEWICK: . . .

Loss of amenity

I turn last to the head of damages under which the judge awarded £2,500 ... Mr. Jacob was contending that the judge's award of £2,500 was without precedent in the field of damages, and was fundamentally inconsistent with the decision of this House in *Addis v Gramophone Co Ltd* [1909] A.C. 488 ...

Addis v Gramophone Co Ltd established the general rule that in claims for breach of contract, the plaintiff cannot recover damages for his injured feelings. But the rule, like most rules, is subject to exceptions. One of the well established exceptions is when the object of the contract is to afford pleasure, as, for example, where the plaintiff has booked a holiday with a tour operator. If the tour operator is in breach of contract by failing to provide what the contract called for, the plaintiff may recover damages for his disappointment: see *Jarvis v Swans Tours Ltd* [1973] Q.B. 233 and *Jackson v Horizon Holidays Ltd* [1975] 1 W.L.R. 1468.

[The trial judge] took the view that the contract was one 'for the provision of a pleasurable amenity.' In the event, Mr. Forsyth's pleasure was not so great as it would have been if the swimming pool had been 7 feet 6 inches deep. This was a view which the judge was entitled to take. If it involves a further inroad on the rule in *Addis v Gramophone Co Ltd* [1909] A.C. 488, then so be it. But I prefer to regard it as a logical application or adaptation of the existing exception to a new situation. I should, however, add this note of warning. Mr. Forsyth was, I think, lucky to have obtained so large an award for his disappointed expectations. But as there was no criticism from any quarter as to the quantum of the award as distinct from the underlying principle, it would not be right for your Lordships to interfere with the judge's figure.

That leaves one last question for consideration. I have expressed agreement with the judge's approach to damages based on loss of amenity on the facts of the present case. But in most cases such an approach would not be available. What is then to be the position where, in the case of a new house, the building does not conform in some minor respect to the contract, as, for example, where there is a difference in level between two rooms, necessitating a step. Suppose there is no measurable difference in value of the complete house, and the cost of reinstatement would be prohibitive. Is there any reason why the court should not award by way of damages for breach of contract some modest sum, not based on difference in value, but solely to compensate the buyer for his disappointed expectations? Is the law of damages so inflexible, as I asked earlier, that it cannot find some middle ground in such a case? I do not give a final answer to that question in the present case. But it may be that it would have afforded an alternative ground for justifying the judge's award of damages and if the judge had wanted a precedent, he could have found it in Sir David Cairns's judgment in *GW Atkins Ltd v Scott*, 7 Const. L.J. 215, where, it will be remembered, the Court of Appeal upheld the judge's award of £250 for defective tiling. Sir David Cairns said, at p. 221:

'There are many circumstances where a judge has nothing but his common sense to guide him in fixing the quantum of damages, for instance, for pain and suffering, for loss of pleasurable activities or for inconvenience of one kind or another.'

If it is accepted that the award of £2,500 should be upheld, then that at once disposes of Mr. Jacob's argument that Mr. Forsyth is entitled to the cost of reinstatement, because he must be entitled to something. But even if he were entitled to nothing for loss of amenity, or for difference in value, it would not follow as Mr. Jacob argued that he was entitled to the cost of reinstatement. There is no escape from the judge's finding of fact that to insist on the cost of reinstatement in the circumstances of the present case was unreasonable."

The decision of the House of Lords in *Ruxley* led the Scottish Law Commission to reconsider the recovery of patrimonial interest and to seek views on whether change to the rule in *Addis* was appropriate. The outcome of that consultation process was a suggestion for legislative change.

12–48 *Report on Remedies for Breach of Contract*

Scottish Law Commission Report No.174 (December 1999)

"Part 3 Recovery of Non-patrimonial Loss Introduction

3.1 The question for consideration here is whether it should be made clear that there is no bar, other than the normal rule disallowing damages for losses which are too remote,[1] to the recovery of damages for non-patrimonial[2] loss or harm caused by a breach of contract.

Non-patrimonial loss may take the form, for example, of loss of reputation[3] or loss of amenity or loss of the satisfaction of obtaining performance precisely in accordance with the contract. Non-patrimonial harm may take the form, for example, of physical illness or injury, pain or suffering, distress or more severe psychological harm, or trouble and inconvenience.

3.2 Compensation for loss of the satisfaction of obtaining the due performance, sometimes called disappointed expectations, may be particularly important in cases where there is no other obvious loss or harm. If damages for this type of loss cannot be awarded there may be cases where no damages at all can be awarded even if the aggrieved party has been deprived of the agreed performance.[4]

Example. For nostalgic reasons A wishes to have the lower parts of the walls of a new house constructed from granite from the part of the country where he was born and brought up. He contracts for this specifically and informs the builder, B, of the importance he attaches to the source of the stone. B uses local granite which costs the same but is of a superior quality for building. One of B's employees tells A where the stone came from but by this time the house is completed. The court would not order specific implement because that would be too harsh and unreasonable.[5] It would not order damages based on the cost of tearing the house down and rebuilding it because that would be equally unreasonable.[6] The house is no less valuable than it would have been with the other granite. So no damages could be obtained on the basis of diminution in value. Yet most people would probably consider that A should receive some damages for B's breach of contract.[7]

12–49 **Existing law**

3.3 Under the existing law it is clear that damages can be recovered for physical illness or injury caused by a breach of contract,[8] although often there will be an overlapping claim in delict which may mask the contractual claim. Damages can also be recovered for trouble and inconvenience cause by a breach of contract.[9] It is not clear whether damages can be recovered for loss of reputation caused by a breach of contract.[10] It was for a long time considered that, following the decision of the House of Lords in the English case of *Addis v Gramophone Co*,[11] damages could not be recovered for mental distress or injured feelings caused by a breach of contract.[12] More recently, exceptions have been recognised in cases where, because of the nature of the contract, the likelihood of distress was or ought to have been in the contemplation of the defender at the time of the contract. For example, damages were awarded when a photographer was in breach of a contract to take photographs at a wedding[13] and a proof was allowed on a claim for damages for 'upset and distress' when a caravan site proprietor was in breach of a contract to provide a site 'of the highest amenity' for a residential caravan.[14] There have also been cases in England where the nature of the contract has meant that the likelihood of distress or injured feelings being caused by a breach was reasonably foreseeable at the time of the conclusion of the contract.[15] There have been suggestions in some of these cases that a distinction falls to be drawn between commercial and 'social' contracts but the soundness and practicability of that distinction is doubtful. The true distinction seems to be between those cases where the likelihood of distress or injured feelings is foreseen or reasonably foreseeable at the time of the contract and cases where it is not. Mental distress or injury to feelings cannot be suffered by a company or other legal entity, although such an entity can be put to trouble and inconvenience,[16] and that in itself serves to rule out this head of damages in many commercial contracts.

3.4 Some of the judges in the English case of *Ruxley Electronics Ltd v Forsyth*[17] clearly favoured the allowance of damages for non-patrimonial loss caused by a breach of contract, including loss of the personal value to the aggrieved party in receiving the performance contracted for, but the statement on this point in the House of Lords were on a matter which did not fall to be decided at that stage.

Criticism of existing law 12–50

3.5 The courts have shown signs of breaking free from the restrictions once thought to be imposed by the *Addis* case. The law, however, is not clear. *Addis* has never been overruled.

It creates an unnecessary difficulty and a temptation to resort to unsound distinctions. It would not, in our view, make any sense to perpetuate an arbitrary distinction between inconvenience and distress or to introduce an arbitrary distinction between commercial and social contracts. The normal test for remoteness, which disallows damages for any loss which the defender could not reasonably have contemplated at the time of the contract, would be adequate in this area.

3.6 The Scottish law in this area is out of line with recent international models. The Unidroit *Principles* have the following rule on the types of loss for which damages may be obtained.[18]

> '(1) The aggrieved party is entitled to full compensation for harm sustained as a result of the non-performance. Such harm includes both any loss which is suffered and any gain of which it was deprived, taking into account any gain to the aggrieved party resulting from its avoidance of cost or harm. (2) Such harm may be non-pecuniary and includes, for instance, physical suffering or emotional distress.'

The European *Principles* also expressly allow damages for non-pecuniary loss of any kind.[19]

3.7 Almost all consultees supported reform to allow damages to be recovered for nonpatrimonial loss or harm caused by a breach of contract. The Faculty of Advocates, however, expressed doubts. It said that contract law was about economic relations,[20] noted that damages for non-patrimonial loss caused by a breach of contract could already be recovered in a number of defined instances, and suggested that the law should be left to develop on an incremental, case by case basis. We accept that that would be a possible course of action but, given the long-standing difficulties in this area, we consider that a more rapid and reliable method of achieving reform is by legislation.

Recommendation

3.8 We recommend that:

2. It should be made clear that, subject to the normal remoteness rule, the loss or harm for which damages may be recovered for breach of contract includes non-patrimonial

loss or harm of any kind, and in particular includes loss of the satisfaction of obtaining what was contracted for and harm in the form of pain, suffering or mental distress.

12–51 **Draft Contract (Scotland) Bill 2 Non patrimonial loss recoverable on breach**

(1) Non-patrimonial loss or harm is included within the heads of damages which may be awarded for breach of contract or for breach of a unilateral voluntary obligation.

(2) The following are examples of the kinds of loss or harm referred to in subsection (1) above: injury to feelings, loss of reputation, loss of amenity, loss of satisfaction in obtaining performance of the contract or obligation, grief and distress.

12–52 **Explanatory notes**

Section 2

This section makes it clear that damages for breach of a contract or unilateral voluntary obligation can be recovered for non-patrimonial loss or harm—that is, for loss or harm not consisting of monetary or economic loss, or damage to property—caused by the breach. The existing law allows such damages to be recovered in some types of cases but not generally. See paras 3.3–3.5 of the report.

Subsection (1)

This sets out the general rule.

Subsection (2)

This subsection gives some examples of the types of non-patrimonial loss or harm which could be recovered.

The type described as loss of satisfaction in obtaining performance of the contract or obligation (sometimes called 'disappointed expectations') is particularly important for the future development of the law. See para 3.2 of the report and *Ruxley Electronics Ltd v Forsyth* [1996] AC 344."

---

[1] Under this normal rule damages will be limited to the loss which the defender might reasonably have contemplated at the time of the contract, taking into account any special circumstances made known to the defender by the pursuer. See *Balfour Beatty Construction (Scotland) Ltd v Scottish Power plc*, 1994 S.L.T. 807 and the discussion paper, paras 8.15–8.22.

[2] Patrimonial loss covers financial or economic loss, such as loss of profit or the cost of rectification or replacement, or the loss caused by a diminution in the value of property. Non-patrimonial loss is all other loss.

[3] Loss of reputation may in turn lead to financial loss. For example, loss of an employee's reputation for honesty may lead to a loss of employment opportunities. There is no reason why such financial loss should not be recovered in appropriate cases. See *Mahmud v BCCI* [1998] A.C. 20; *Johnson v Unisys Ltd* [1999] 1 All E.R. 854 at 860.

[4] See *Ruxley Electronics Ltd v Forsyth* [1996] A.C. 344 at 374.

[5] See the discussion paper, para.6.7.

[6] See the discussion paper, paras 8.37–8.42 and *Ruxley Electronics Ltd v Forsyth* [1996] A.C. 344.

[7] A similar case was first mentioned by Cardozo J. in *Jacob & Youngs Inc v Kent* (1921) 129 N.E. 889. Other examples of the same kind were given in *Ruxley Electronics Ltd v Forsyth* [1996] A.C. 344.

[8] See, *e.g.* *Cameron v Young*, 1907 S.C. 475; *Dickie v Amicable Property Investment Building Society*, 1911 S.C. 1079; *Fitzpatrick v Barr*, 1948 S.L.T. (Sh.Ct) 5.

[9] *Webster & Co v Cramond Iron Co* (1875) 2 R. 752; *McArdle v City of Glasgow D.C.*, 1989 S.C.L.R. 19; *Hardwick v Gebbie*, 1991 S.L.T. 258; *Mills v Findlay*, 1994 S.C.L.R. 397.

10 The question was raised but not settled in any satisfactory way in *Millar v Bellvale Chemical Co*

(1898) 1 F. 297 and *Dodwell v Highland Industrial Caterers Ltd*, 1952 S.L.T. (Notes) 57. In English law, the statements in *Mahmud v BCCI* [1998] A.C. 20 are rather against recoverability of damages for non-financial aspects of loss of reputation.

[11] [1909] A.C. 488.

[12] See Gloag, *Contract* (2nd ed., 1929), p.686. It is by no means certain that, properly read, *Addis* justifies any such general conclusion. There was earlier Scottish authority to the contrary effect. See *Cameron v Fletcher* (1872) 10 M. 301; *Campbell v MacLachlan* (1896) 4 S.L.T. 143.

[13] *Diesen v Samson*, 1971 S.L.T. (Sh.Ct) 49.

[14] *Colston v Marshall*, 1993 S.C.L.R. 43.

[15] *Jarvis v Swans Tours Ltd* [1973] Q.B. 233 (contract to provide holiday); *Jackson v Horizon Holidays Ltd* [1975] 3 All E.R. 92 (contract to provide holiday); *Heywood v Wellers* [1976] Q.B. 446 (solicitor failed, in breach of contract, to obtain injunction against molestation); *Calabar Properties Ltd v Stitcher* [1984] 1 W.L.R. 287 (contract for occupation of house as a home); *Ruxley Electronics Ltd v Forsyth* [1996] A.C. 344 (contract for construction of swimming pool).

[16] *Webster & Co v Cramond Iron Co* (1875) 2 R. 752.

[17] [1996] A.C. 344. See in particular Lord Bridge of Harwich at 354; Lord Mustill at 360–361 and Lord Lloyd of Berwick at 373–374.

[18] Art.7.4.2.

[19] Art.9:501(2).

[20] This is perhaps not wholly true. Certainly, people often contract for non-economic benefits or for a mixture of economic and noneconomic benefits."

The report does at least indicate that consensus is emerging on the need for and definition of non-patrimonial loss, especially in circumstances that amount to disappointed expectations following from non-performance of the contract. The following decision suggests that it is a matter likely to be litigated in the absence of legislative reform. It results from the attempt by Bingham LJ in *Watts v Morrow*[36] to define the limits to damages for distress and inconvenience. Thus, in addition to the call for change in the Scottish Law Commission Report, English case law is developing this area in a way that will prove difficult to resist in Scotland.

Farley v Skinner 12–53

[2002] 2 A.C. 732

House of Lords: Lords Steyn, Browne-Wilkinson, Clyde, Hutton and Scott

Mr Farley, a successful businessman was seeking a home for his retirement. He found one that offered the peace and tranquility he sought, but it was located some 15 miles from Gatwick Airport. He employed Mr Skinner, a surveyor, specifically to investigate whether the property would be affected by aircraft noise, telling him that he did not want to be on a flight path. On this matter, Mr Skinner reported that he thought it "unlikely that it would suffer greatly from such noise". Mr Farley bought the house for £420,000 and spent £125,000 on modernisation and refurbishment.

After moving in, Mr Farley discovered that the property was located close to the "Mayfield Stack" navigation beacon and therefore substantially affected by aircraft noise, especially at peak times in early morning (a time when Mr Farley, an early riser, often wished to be in the gardens) and early evening (a time when Mr Farley often enjoyed pre-dinner drinks on the terrace). He sought damages based on breach of contract arising from Mr Skinner's failure to take reasonable care in advising Mr Farley on aircraft noise.

The trial judge found that Mr Skinner had been negligent and that if he had carried out his instructions properly Mr Farley would not have bought the property. Since the price Farley had paid for the property coincided with its market value taking account of aircraft noise, no loss had been suffered; but since the noise was a "confounded nuisance" to

[36] *Watts v Morrow* [1991] 1 W.L.R. 1421.

Farley, he should not be penalised for not selling up and moving and awarded him £10,000 for discomfort. The House, reversing the Court of Appeal found that, although general damages could not in principle be awarded, non-pecuniary damages could be awarded for his disappointment at loss of a pleasurable amenity that was of no economic value, but was of importance to him in ensuring his pleasure, relaxation or peace of mind, and the amenity need not be physical inconvenience or discomfort.

12–54 "LORD STEYN: ...

V. Recovery of non-pecuniary damages

16 ... In contract law distinctions are made about the kind of harm which resulted from the breach of contract. The general principle is that compensation is only awarded for financial loss resulting from the breach of contract: *Livingstone v Rawyards Coal Co* (1880) 5 App Cas 25, 39, per Lord Blackburn. In the words of Bingham LJ in *Watts v Morrow* [1991] 1 WLR 1421, 1443 as a matter of legal policy 'a contract-breaker is not *in general* liable for any distress, frustration, anxiety, displeasure, vexation, tension or aggravation which his breach of contract may cause to the innocent party' (my emphasis). There are, however, limited exceptions to this rule. One such exception is damages for pain, suffering and loss of amenities caused to an individual by a breach of contract: see *McGregor on Damages*, 16th ed (1997), pp 56-57, para 96. It is not material in the present case. But the two exceptions mentioned by Bingham LJ, namely where the very object of the contract is to provide pleasure ... and recovery for physical inconvenience caused by the breach ... are pertinent. The scope of these exceptions is in issue in the present case. It is, however, correct, as counsel for the surveyor submitted, that the entitlement to damages for mental distress caused by a breach of contract is not established by mere foreseeability: the right to recovery is dependent on the case falling fairly within the principles governing the special exceptions. So far there is no real disagreement between the parties.

VI. The very object of the contract: the framework

...

18 It is necessary to examine the case on a correct characterisation of the plaintiff's claim ... The plaintiff made it crystal-clear to the surveyor that the impact of aircraft noise was a matter of importance to him. Unless he obtained reassuring information from the surveyor he would not have bought the property. That is the tenor of the evidence. It is also what the judge found. The case must be approached on the basis that the surveyor's obligation to investigate aircraft noise was a major or important part of the contract between him and the plaintiff. It is also important to note that, unlike in *Addis v Gramophone Co Ltd* [1909] AC 488, the plaintiff's claim is not for injured feelings caused by the breach of contract. Rather it is a claim for damages flowing from the surveyor's failure to investigate and report, thereby depriving the buyer of the chance of making an informed choice whether or not to buy resulting in mental distress and disappointment.

19 The broader legal context of *Watts v Morrow* [1991] 1 WLR 1421 must be borne in mind. The exceptional category of cases where the very object of a contract is to provide pleasure, relaxation, peace of mind or freedom from molestation is not the product of Victorian contract theory but the result of evolutionary developments in case law from the 1970s. [Lord Steyn referred to several decisions including *Diesen v Samson* and *Jarvis v Swans Tours Ltd* and continued]

. . .

VII. The very object of the contract: the arguments against the plaintiff's claim

22 Counsel for the surveyor advanced three separate arguments each of which he said was sufficient to defeat the plaintiff's claim. First, he submitted that even if a major or important part of the contract was to give pleasure, relaxation and peace of mind, that was not enough. It is an indispensable requirement that the object of the entire contract must be of this type . . . **12–55**

24 There is no reason in principle or policy why the scope of recovery in the exceptional category should depend on the object of the contract as ascertained from all its constituent parts. It is sufficient if a major or important object of the contract is to give pleasure, relaxation or peace of mind. In my view *Knott v Bolton* 11 Const LJ 375 was wrongly decided and should be overruled. To the extent that the majority in the Court of Appeal relied on *Knott v Bolton* their decision was wrong.

25 That brings me to the second issue, namely whether the plaintiff's claim is barred by reason of the fact that the surveyor undertook an obligation to exercise reasonable care and did not guarantee the achievement of a result . . . As far as I am aware the distinction was first articulated in the present case. In any event, I would reject it. I fully accept, of course, that contractual guarantees of performance and promises to exercise reasonable care are fundamentally different . . . But why should this difference between an absolute and relative contractual promise require a distinction in respect of the recovery of non-pecuniary damages? Take the example of a travel agent who is consulted by a couple who are looking for a golfing holiday in France. Why should it make a difference in respect of the recoverability of nonpecuniary damages for a spoiled holiday whether the travel agent gives a guarantee that there is a golf course very near the hotel, represents that to be the case, or negligently advises that all hotels of the particular chain of hotels are situated next to golf courses? If the nearest golf course is in fact 50 miles away a breach may be established. It may spoil the holiday of the couple. It is difficult to see why in principle only those plaintiffs who negotiate guarantees may recover non-pecuniary damages for a breach of contract. It is a singularly unattractive result that a professional man, who undertakes a specific obligation to exercise reasonable care to investigate a matter judged and communicated to be important by his customer, can in Lord Mustill's words in *Ruxley Electronics and Construction Ltd v Forsyth* [1996] AC 344, 360 'please himself whether or not to comply with the wishes of the promise which, as embodied in the contract, formed part of the consideration for the price'. If that were the law it would be seriously deficient. I am satisfied that it is not the law. In my view the distinction drawn by Hale LJ and by the majority in the Court of Appeal between contractual guarantees and obligations of reasonable care is unsound.

LORD CLYDE . . . **12–56**

34 . . . In the ordinary case accordingly damages may be awarded for inconvenience, but not for mere distress; but where the contract is aimed at procuring peace or pleasure, then, if as a result of the breach of contract that expected pleasure is not realised, the party suffering that loss may be entitled to an award of damages for the distress.

35 . . . The expression 'physical inconvenience' may be traced back at least to the judgments in *Hobbs v London and South Western Railway Co* (1875) LR 10 QB 111, where damages were awarded for the inconvenience suffered by the plaintiffs for having to walk between four and five miles home as a result of the train on which they had taken tickets to Hampton Court travelling instead to Esher. They had tried to obtain a conveyance but found that there was none to be had . . . As a matter of terminology I should have thought that 'inconvenience' by itself sufficiently covered the kinds of difficulty and discomfort which are more than mere matters of sentimentality, and that 'disappointment' would serve as a sufficient label for those mental reactions which in general the policy of the law will exclude.

36 In *Hobbs's* case the defendants were prepared to compensate the plaintiffs for the cost of a conveyance, even although they had not been able to find any. In the present case the defendant would be prepared to pay for the costs of sale and removal if the plaintiff had decided to sell because of the noise. It is said by the respondent that since he has decided to keep the house he is not entitled to any damages at all. But in *Hobbs* the plaintiffs were entitled to damages in respect of the inconvenience. It is hard to understand why a corresponding result should not follow here. That an award may be made in such circumstances is to my mind in line with the thinking of this House in *Ruxley Electronics and Construction Ltd v Forsyth* ... So also here, where the plaintiff has decided to remain in the property despite its disadvantage, he should not be altogether deprived by the law of any compensation for the breach of contract. It may be noticed in passing that in *Hobbs's* case the damages awarded for the inconvenience were substantially more than the cost of the conveyance. In the present case it seems that the cost of removal, for which at an earlier stage the plaintiff was claiming, far exceeded the sum awarded for inconvenience. But those differences do not affect the principle.

39 But it is possible to approach the case as one of the exceptional kind in which the claim would be for damages for disappointment. If that approach was adopted so as to seek damages for disappointment, I consider that it should also succeed.

40 It should be observed at the outset that damages should not be awarded, unless perhaps nominally, for the fact of a breach of contract as distinct from the consequences of the breach. That was a point which I sought to stress in *Alfred McAlpine Construction Ltd v Panatown Ltd* [2001] 1 AC 518. For an award to be made a loss or injury has to be identified which is a consequence of the breach but not too remote from it, and which somehow or other can be expressed and quantified in terms of a sum of money. So disappointment merely at the fact that the contract has been breached is not a proper ground for an award. The mere fact of the loss of a bargain should not be the subject of compensation. But that is not the kind of claim which the plaintiff is making here. What he is seeking is damages for the inconvenience of the noise, the invasion of the peace and quiet which he expected the property to possess and the diminution in his use and enjoyment of the property on account of the aircraft noise.

...

42 ... The present case is not an 'ordinary surveyor's contract'. The request for the report on aircraft noise was additional to the usual matters expected of a surveyor in the survey of a property and could properly have attracted a extra fee if he had spent extra time researching that issue. It is the specific provision relating to the peacefulness of the property in respect of aircraft noise which makes the present case out of the ordinary. The criterion is not some general characteristic of the contract, as, for example, that it is or is not a 'commercial' contract. The critical factor is the object of the particular agreement.

LORD HUTTON: ...

54 ... [I]n order to preserve the fundamental principle that general damages are not recoverable for anxiety and aggravation and similar states of mind caused by a breach of contract and to prevent the exception expanding to swallow up, ... I consider that as a general approach it would be appropriate to treat as cases falling within the exception and calling for an award of damages those where: (1) the matter in respect of which the individual claimant seeks damages is of importance to him, and (2) the individual claimant has made clear to the other party that the matter is of importance to him, and (3) the action to be taken in relation to the matter is made a specific term of the contract. If these three conditions are satisfied, as they are in the present case, then I consider that the claim for damages should not be rejected on the ground that the fulfilment of that obligation is not the principal object of the contract or on the ground that the other party does not receive special and specific remuneration in respect of the performance of that obligation.

LORD SCOTT OF FOSCOTE: . . . 12–57

75 In my opinion, the issue can and should be resolved by applying the well known principles laid down in *Hadley v Baxendale* (1854) 9 Exch 341 (as restated in *Victoria Laundry (Windsor) Ltd v Newman Industries Ltd* [1949] 2 KB 528) in the light of the recent guidance provided by Bingham LJ in *Watts v Morrow* [1991] 1 WLR 1421 and by this House in *Ruxley Electronics and Construction Ltd v Forsyth* [1996] AC 344.

76 The basic principle of damages for breach of contract is that the injured party is entitled, so far as money can do it, to be put in the position he would have been in if the contractual obligation had been properly performed. He is entitled, that is to say, to the benefit of his bargain: see *Robinson v Harman* (1848) 1 Exch 850, 855.

. . .

79 *Ruxley's case* establishes, in my opinion, that if a party's contractual performance has failed to provide to the other contracting party something to which that other was, under the contract, entitled, and which, if provided, would have been of value to that party, then, if there is no other way of compensating the injured party, the injured party should be compensated in damages to the extent of that value. Quantification of that value will in many cases be difficult and may often seem arbitrary. In *Ruxley's case* the value placed on the amenity value of which the pool owner had been deprived was £2,500. By that award, the pool owner was placed, so far as money could do it, in the position he would have been in if the diving area of the pool had been constructed to the specified depth.

80 In *Ruxley's case* the breach of contract by the builders had not caused any consequential loss to the pool owner. He had simply been deprived of the benefit of a pool built to the depth specified in the contract. It was not a case where the recovery of damages for consequential loss consisting of vexation, anxiety or other species of mental distress had to be considered . . .

85 Second, the adjective 'physical', in the phrase 'physical inconvenience and discomfort', requires, I think, some explanation or definition. The distinction between the 'physical' and the 'non-physical' is not always clear and may depend on the context. Is being awoken at night by aircraft noise 'physical'? If it is, is being unable to sleep because of worry and anxiety 'physical'? What about a reduction in light caused by the erection of a building under a planning permission that an errant surveyor ought to have warned his purchaser-client about but had failed to do so? In my opinion, the critical distinction to be drawn is not a distinction between the different types of inconvenience or discomfort of which complaint may be made but a distinction based on the cause of the inconvenience or discomfort. If the cause is no more than disappointment that the contractual obligation has been broken, damages are not recoverable even if the disappointment has led to a complete mental breakdown. But, if the cause of the inconvenience or discomfort is a sensory (sight, touch, hearing, smell etc) experience, damages can, subject to the remoteness rules, be recovered.

. . .

[Lord Scott reviewed the case law and continued] . . .

105 . . . In my judgment, Mr Farley is entitled to be compensated for the 'real discomfort' that the judge found he suffered. He is so entitled on either of two alternative bases.

106 First, he was deprived of the contractual benefit to which he was entitled. He was entitled to information about the aircraft noise from Gatwick-bound aircraft that Mr Skinner, through negligence, had failed to supply him with. If Mr Farley had, in the event, decided not to purchase Riverside House, the value to him of the contractual benefit of which he had been deprived would have been nil. But he did buy the property. And he took his decision to do so without the advantage of being able to take into account the information to which he was contractually entitled. If he had had that information he would not have bought. So the information clearly would have had a value to him. Prima facie, in my opinion, he is entitled to be compensated accordingly.

107 In these circumstances, it seems to me, it is open to the court to adopt a *Ruxley Electronics and Construction Ltd v Forsyth* [1996] AC 344 approach and place a value on the contractual benefit of which Mr Farley has been deprived. In deciding on the amount, the discomfort experienced by Mr Farley can, in my view, properly be taken into account. If he had had the aircraft noise information he would not have bought Riverside House and would not have had that discomfort.

108 Alternatively, Mr Farley can, in my opinion, claim compensation for the discomfort as consequential loss. Had it not been for the breach of contract, he would not have suffered the discomfort. It was caused by the breach of contract in a *causa sine qua non* sense. Was the discomfort a consequence that should reasonably have been contemplated by the parties at the time of contract as liable to result from the breach? In my opinion, it was. It was obviously within the reasonable contemplation of the parties that, deprived of the information about aircraft noise that he ought to have had, Mr Farley would make a decision to purchase that he would not otherwise have made. Having purchased, he would, having become aware of the noise, either sell in which case at least the expenses of the resale would have been recoverable as damages or he would keep the property and put up with the noise. In the latter event, it was within the reasonable contemplation of the parties that he would experience discomfort from the noise of the aircraft. And the discomfort was 'physical' in the sense that Bingham LJ in *Watts v Morrow* [1991] 1 WLR 1421, 1445 had in mind. In my opinion, the application of *Watts v Morrow* principles entitles Mr Farley to damages for discomfort caused by the aircraft noise.

109 I would add that if there had been an appreciable reduction in the market value of the property caused by the aircraft noise, Mr Farley could not have recovered both that difference in value and damages for discomfort. To allow both would allow double recovery for the same item."

Contributory negligence

12–58 Unlike many civil law systems, but like most common law systems, the negligence or fault of the pursuer in an action for damages for breach of contract is generally irrelevant in assessing the quantum of damages. This principle is different from the pursuer's obligation to mitigate loss, which arises only after the occurrence of the breach of contract. Once a breach has occurred, the party not in breach is under a duty to mitigate the loss, for example by seeking alternative employment upon being wrongly dismissed. Failure to mitigate loss will always lead to a reduction in damages and may totally eliminate a substantive claim.

The English Law Commission in its memorandum[37] endorsed the possibility that damages recoverable for breach of contract might be reduced by the contributory negligence of the person claiming. The following case suggested that this might be a possibility in Scots law.

[37] Law Commission, *Contributory Negligence as a Defence in Contract* (Law Com. No.219, 1993).

Lancashire Textiles (Jersey) Ltd v Thomson, Shepherd & Co Ltd 12–59
1985 S.C. 135; 1986 S.L.T. 41
Court of Session, Outer House: Lord Davidson

Lancashire bought carpeting from Thomson Shepherd, a carpet manufacturer, and installed it in the premises of Coopers & Lybrand in St Helier, Jersey. Coopers & Lybrand complained about its quality. Replacement and additional carpeting supplied to Lancashire by Thomson Shepherd was installed. This was also rejected by Coopers & Lybrand, who obtained replacement carpeting from other suppliers. Lancashire sought damages from Thomson Shepherd on the grounds that the carpet supplied was not reasonably fit for its purpose. Thomson claimed that the problem was the defective laying of the carpet and, in their defence, claimed contributory negligence by Lancashire.

The Lord Ordinary rejected the claim for contributory negligence.

"LORD DAVIDSON: ... I turn now to consider the pursuers' attack on the defenders' averments relating to the allegedly defective laying of the carpet. In my opinion these averments are relevant in so far as they form a basis for the defenders' contention that the pursuers' customers had no ground for complaining about the quality of the carpet itself, but that any trouble experienced over rucking is attributable to faulty laying. I therefore consider that for that purpose the defenders' averments on this matter can be allowed to go to proof. 12–60

I am however of opinion that the same averments form no relevant basis for a plea of contributory negligence. A plea of contributory negligence can come into play, if at all, only if the defenders were in breach of their contract. But once it is established that the carpeting was defective in quality, I see no room for an argument that the carpet was incompetently laid. The pursuers aver that the carpeting was rejected by Coopers & Lybrand. If that is right, then the defenders' difficulty is that their plea of contributory negligence has to be considered against the background of an assumed breach of contract on their part which entitled the customer forthwith to reject the goods. Since the pursuers aver that the carpeting was in fact rejected, I do not consider that on any view the allegedly faulty laying of the carpet can become a relevant defence to their assumed breach of contract.

In addition I am not satisfied that the defenders' plea to contributory negligence is covered by s. 1 of the Law Reform (Contributory Negligence) Act 1945. That section cannot be invoked unless 'any person suffers damage as the result partly of his own fault and partly of the fault of any other person or persons.' Section 5 provides that in the application of the Act to Scotland 'fault' means 'wrongful act, breach of statutory duty or negligent act or omission which gives rise to liability in damages.' In the present case the defenders are sued on the basis that the carpeting was not of merchantable quality and that it was not reasonably fit for the purpose for which it was bought. There is no averment that the defenders were guilty of any wrongful act towards the pursuers. The pursuers rely upon s. 14 of the Sale of Goods Act 1979, but that does not mean that they sue in respect of a breach of statutory duty in the sense in which that expression is used in s. 5. In my opinion a breach of contract may form the basis of a plea of contributory negligence, but only if that breach can also be described as constituting a wrongful act, breach of statutory duty or negligent act or omission within the meaning of s. 5. The breaches of contract relied upon by the pursuers in the present action do not satisfy these requirements. Accordingly in my opinion the defenders' eighth plea-in-law is unsound and should be repelled. I note that a similar conclusion was reached in relation to the definition of fault contained in s. 4 of the 1945 Act by Judge Newey, Q.C., in *Basildon District Council v JE Lesser (Properties) Ltd*."

The decision at least opened up the possibility of contributory negligence impacted directly on the damages recoverable in a contract action. The matter was recently considered by the Scottish Law Commission, which has produced proposals for legislative change.

12–61 *Report on Remedies for Breach of Contract*

Scottish Law Commission Report No.174 (December 1999)

"Part 4 Loss Partly Attributable to Aggrieved Party

Existing law

4.1 A plea of contributory negligence[1] is not generally available in claims based on breach of contract.[2] At least according to the prevailing view, a person aggrieved by a breach of contract can often recover full damages for any foreseeable loss or harm caused by the breach, without any possibility of a deduction to take account of the extent to which that person may have contributed to the loss or harm suffered. This forces questions of causation into an unnatural framework. It obliges courts to reach all or nothing conclusions.

Earlier proposals for reform

12–62 4.2 In 1988 this Commission published a report[34] with the following key recommendations.

Report on *Civil Liability—Contribution*, Scot. Law Com. No. 115 (1988).

'20. Where the defender's liability for breach of a contractual duty of care is the same as his liability in delict for negligence, the plea of contributory negligence should be available as a defence whether the action is framed in delict or in contract.

- The plea of contributory negligence should be available to the defender where he is in breach of a contractual duty of care but is under no corresponding common law duty to take reasonable care.
- The plea of contributory negligence should not be available where the defender's breach of a contractual obligation does not depend on his having been negligent.
- In so far as contributory negligence is relevant in actions founded on breach of contract, parties should be entitled to exclude the plea in their contract.
- The plea of contributory negligence should not be available in answer to any action founded on ... liability for an intentional breach of a contractual duty of care.'[3]

These recommendations have not been implemented. The first one may have been overtaken by case law.[4]

4.3 In 1993 the English Law Commission came to very similar conclusions.[5] Like the Scottish Law Commission it drew short of recommending that contributory negligence should be generally available in breach of contract cases. It did recommend that it should be available whenever a plaintiff suffered damage as the result partly of the breach of a contractual duty to take reasonable care or exercise reasonable skill and partly of the plaintiff's own contributory negligence. These recommendations have not been implemented either.

International models

4.4 The European *Principles* have an article headed 'Loss Attributable to Aggrieved Party' which provides as follows.[6] 'The non-performing party is not liable for loss suffered by the aggrieved party to the extent that the aggrieved party contributed to the non-performance or its effects.' 12–63

One criticism of this rule is that it is too mechanistic. It takes no account of degree of fault. The aggrieved party may have contributed accidentally or blamelessly to the nonperformance or its effects. The Unidroit *Principles* are more subtle. They provide that[7]

'Where the harm is due in part to an act or omission of the aggrieved party or to another event as to which that party bears the risk, the amount of damages shall be reduced to the extent that these factors have contributed to the harm, having regard to the conduct of each of the parties.'

Assessment 12–64

4.5 We regard the earlier Commission recommendation as the minimum reform which should be considered in this area. The question for consideration now is whether it would be desirable to go beyond the Commission's earlier recommendation and introduce a wider provision.

4.6 The main reason for this Commission's recommendation that contributory negligence should not be available to the defender where the defender's breach did not consist of negligence was that where the defender's fault was irrelevant to the breach, the pursuer's fault should also be irrelevant.[8] This, however, does not necessarily follow. The fact that the party in breach is liable notwithstanding absence of fault does not necessarily mean that liability should extend to loss or damage which was partly caused by the aggrieved party. In any event it could be provided, as in the Unidroit *Principles*, that the conduct of both parties can be taken into consideration where both have contributed to the loss or harm.

4.7 There was also an argument that the parties should be free to contract for extensive liability, regardless of contributory fault, if they so wished.[9] However, there is no reason why legislation on contributory fault should prevent them from doing this.

4.8 It was also said that to allow contributory negligence to operate in all contractual cases would weaken the position of consumers and give rise to unacceptable uncertainty in commercial dealings.[10] Neither argument now seems convincing.

The present law does not prevent arguments about who caused loss or harm. It just forces the arguments into an unrealistic framework where only extreme solutions are possible and whether there is no room for fair and reasonable results, based on an apportionment of blame.[11] It is difficult to believe that that is in the interests of either consumers or commercial contracting parties.

4.9 In making its modest and limited recommendations in 1988 the Scottish Law Commission was adopting a cautious approach. A similar approach had been adopted in many common law jurisdictions and, as we have seen, was adopted, for substantially the same reasons, by the English Law Commission five years later. Nonetheless it is clear that there were, and are, arguments for going further.

4.10 On principle it would seem to be desirable to take into account the conduct of the aggrieved party in contributing to the loss or harm. This is just an extension of the policy underlying the well-established rules on mitigation of loss. In cases where loss or damage is sustained as a result of breach of contract it will often be the case that the aggrieved party is partly to blame for the loss or harm. To force courts into an all or nothing choice is likely to produce unreasonable results.

12–65 *Example*. A contractor contracts with an electricity supply company for a continuous supply of electricity. The company, in breach of the contract, allows an interruption in the supply. This is one of the causes of a loss to the contractor who has to re-lay a large volume of concrete. Another casual factor was that the contractor failed to take reasonable steps to see that a back-up system was available before beginning a task for which a continuous supply of concrete was indispensable.[12]

In a case like this, awarding the contractor full damages or no damages may be equally unattractive. The reasonable course may be to apportion the liability, taking the conduct of both parties into account.[13] Other, more commonplace, examples could easily be imagined. For example, a party to a contract for the carriage of goods gives the carrier a wrong address and then, when the carrier fails to take all reasonable steps to ascertain the correct address in time, claims damages for late delivery. Or a person who has bought sophisticated electronic equipment which is not in all respects conform to contract causes damage to it by ignoring the clear instructions supplied with it and taking foolish and unreasonable steps to remedy the small defect. Or a woman injures herself in foolishly and unreasonably attempting to climb over a high gate which ought, in terms of a contract, to have been left open.[14] In some such cases the effect of the existing law may be that the aggrieved party recovers nothing. A court, faced with arguments that there is no room for apportioning liability, may feel obliged to hold that the aggrieved party's conduct was the sole cause, or the sole effective cause, of the loss.[15]

4.11 It is not, in our view, justifiable to draw a distinction between contracts involving the exercise of care or skill and other contracts. The above examples are all ones where it would seem reasonable to take contributory fault into account but none of them involves a contract to exercise care or skill. It may be a matter of chance whether an obligation is expressed as an obligation to achieve a result or to use all reasonable care and skill to achieve a result.

4.12 On consultation almost all of the consultees who responded on this issue favoured reform along the lines suggested in the discussion paper.

Recommendation

12–66 4.13 We recommend that

3. It should be provided that, where loss or harm is caused partly by a breach of contract and partly by the act or omission of the aggrieved party, the amount of damages should be reducible to take account of the extent to which the aggrieved party's conduct contributed to the loss or harm, the conduct of both parties being taken into account.

Draft Contract (Scotland) Bill

3 Damages where losses etc. caused also by party not in breach

12–67 (1) Where loss or harm is caused to a party to a contract or a beneficiary of a unilateral voluntary obligation—

(a) partly by breach of the contract by another party to it or breach of the obligation by the person undertaking it; and
(b) partly by an act or omission of the first mentioned party or the beneficiary, the damages recoverable in respect of the breach may be reduced proportionately to the extent that the loss or harm was caused by that act or omission.

(2) In considering whether to reduce damages under subsection (1) above and the extent to which loss or harm was caused by a person's act or omission, a court shall have regard to the whole circumstances of the case, including the conduct of both or all persons concerned.

Explanatory notes

Section 3

This section allows damages to be reduced to take account of the fact that both parties to a contract or unilateral voluntary obligation may have contributed to the loss or harm. At present, under the Law Reform (Contributory Negligence) Act 1945, it is possible to apportion damages in this way in cases based on delict and probably also in cases based on contract where a delict claim would have been possible on the same facts. Apportionment is not, however, possible in other cases based on breach of a contract or unilateral voluntary obligation. See *Lancashire Textiles (Jersey) Ltd v Thomson Shepherd & Co Ltd* 1986 SLT 41 at 45; *Forsikringsaktieselskapet Vesta v Butcher* [1989] AC 852 at 860–867 and 875. The existing law forces questions of causation into an artificial framework. In some cases the courts may be forced to deny any claim for damages because the claimant had the last chance to avoid the loss or harm complained of. See Part 4 of the report. **12–68**

Subsection (1)

This gives the courts a discretion to reduce the damages proportionately to take account of the fact that both parties were partly responsible for the loss or harm.

Subsection (2)

This subsection requires the court to have regard to the whole circumstances of the case, including the conduct of both or all parties to the contract or obligation.

---

[1] The term "contributory negligence" is commonly used in this context but is inappropriate. The important question is whether the aggrieved party contributed to the loss or its exacerbation. It does not matter whether that was done intentionally or negligently. Indeed there is a stronger argument for taking account of intentional conduct than there is for taking account of negligent conduct in this area.

[2] The Law Reform (Contributory Negligence) Act 1945 allowed damages to be apportioned to take account of the pursuer's contributory negligence. Its wording, using terms like "fault" and "damage", is such that it might be applicable in certain cases of breach of contract but it was intended for delict cases and, in practice, has not been used in contract cases except where there is, or could be, a delict claim on the same facts. The point is considered in *Lancashire Textiles (Jersey) Ltd v Thomson Shepherd & Co Ltd*, 1986 S.L.T. 41 at 45. See also *Forsikringsaktieselskapet Vesta v Butcher* [1989] A.C. 852 at 860–867 and 875.

3 Page 57 of Report. See also paras 4.15–4.26 of Report.

[4] This depends on whether the reasoning of the majority of the English Court of Appeal in *Forsikringsaktieselskapet Vesta v Butcher* [1989] A.C. 852 would be followed in Scotland.

[5] Report on *Contributory Negligence as a Defence in Contract*, Law Com. No.219 (1993).

[6] Art.9:504.

[7] Art.7.4.7.

[8] Scot. Law Com. No.115 (1988), para 4.18—"The fault of the defender is irrelevant to liability: therefore any fault on the part of the pursuer should also be irrelevant."

[9] Scot. Law Com. No.115 (1988), para.4.19—"If [a person] agrees to be bound by the contract in all circumstances, even those involving carelessness by the other contracting party, he should not, as a matter of general law, be able to plead that party's conduct in answer to a claim for breach of contract."

[10] Scot. Law Com. No. 115 (1988), para.4.20.

[11] "In cases of shared responsibility for damage it is as unjust that the person suffering the damage should recover 100 per cent. as it is that he should recover nothing." O'Connor L.J. in *Forsikringsaktieselskapet Vesta v Butcher* [1989] A.C. 852 at 862.

[12] This is a hypothetical example suggested by the case of *Balfour Beatty Construction v Scottish Power*, 1994 S.L.T. 807.
[13] If the electricity company had caused the loss intentionally, having been warned, for example, that the operation was beginning and that there were no back-up arrangements, then the deliberate nature of their conduct would no doubt be taken fully into account.
[14] This is a less colourful version of the facts in *Sayers v Harlow UDC* [1958] 1 W.L.R. 623, where the plaintiff injured herself in attempting to climb out of a locked toilet cubicle.
[15] See, *e.g. Quinn v Burch Bros (Builders) Ltd* [1966] 2 Q.B. 370; *Lambert v Lewis* [1982] A.C. 225 at 277B; *Young v Purdy* [1996] 2 F.L.R. 795."

Liquidate damages

12–69 Where the contract stipulates the amount recoverable for *breach*, the innocent party may recover only such *liquidate amount*, unless the breach was a fundamental breach not covered by the clause; or the clause by the amounted to a *penalty*. It is difficult to distinguish a penalty from a liquidate damages clause. The test for establishing whether clause is a penalty generally applied is that postulated by Lord Dunedin in *Dunlop v Selfridge*.[38] The essential elements of Lord Dunedin's test are:

(a) The terminology used by the parties is not conclusive;
(b) A clause is a penalty if it is there as a threat or punishment, whereas liquidate damages are "genuine pre-estimate of loss";
(c) whether a clause is a penalty must be decided on circumstances when the contract was made;
(d) relevant factors in making that decision are:
    (i) whether the sum is "extravagant or unconscionable";
    (ii) whether a single sum is payable for events some of which are serious, other trifling; and
    (iii) a sum is not penal merely because the consequences of breach cannot easily be estimated.

There are great advantages to the parties, especially in certain types of contracts where uncertainty can be particularly costly, such as construction contracts or ship charterparties (where the payment of demurrage for delay in loading or unloading the ship is quite common). To enforce such a clause, Scottish courts had to overcome a deep rooted dislike of usury (unscrupulously high interest), "because all sic panis are in ane maner usaris, and unhonest, maid for lucre or gane".[39] It is nevertheless surprising that it was not until the end of the 19th century that the House of Lords began to lay down the main principles governing the enforcement of such clauses.

[38] *Dunlop v Selfridge* [1915] A.C. 79.
[39] *Home v Hepburn* (1549) Mor. 10033; quoted WW McBryde, *The Law of Contract in Scotland*, 3rd edn (Edinburgh: W. Green, 2007), para.22–146.

Clydebank Engineering and Shipbuilding Co Ltd v Don Jose Ramos Yzquierdo Y Castaneda 12–70

(1904) 7 F. (H.L.) 77

House of Lords: Earl of Halsbury LC, Lords Davey and Robertson

The Spanish Government entered into contracts with Clydebank to build four torpedo boats and deliver each within specified periods from the date of the contracts. The contracts provided: "The penalty for later delivery shall be at the rate of £500 per week for each vessel". This was a large amount.

The boats were delivered many months late and the Spanish Government, having paid the price, claimed from Clydebank £500 for each week of late delivery. Clydebank claimed that this amounted to a penalty and was therefore not payable.

The House found that the Spanish Government were entitled to recover.

"EARL OF HALSBURY LC: . . . Two objections have been made to the enforcement of [the] payment. The first objection is one which appears upon the face of the instrument itself, namely, that it is a penalty, and not, therefore, recoverable as a pactional arrangement of the amount of damages resulting from the breach of contract. It cannot, I think, be denied indeed, I think it has been frankly admitted by the learned counsel—that not much reliance can be placed upon the mere use of certain words. Both in England and in Scotland it has been pointed out that the Court must proceed according to what is the real nature of the transaction, and that the mere use of the word 'penalty' on the one side, or 'damages' on the other, would not be conclusive as to the rights of the parties . . . 12–71

We come then to the question, What is the agreement here? and whether this sum of money is one which can be recovered as an agreed sum as damages, or whether, as has been contended, it is simply a penalty to be held over the other party *in terrorem*—whether it is, what I think gave the jurisdiction to the Courts in both countries to interfere at all in an agreement between the parties, unconscionable and extravagant, and one which no Court ought to allow to be enforced.

My Lords, it is impossible to lay down any abstract rule as to what it may or it may not be extravagant or unconscionable to insist upon without reference to the particular facts and circumstances which are established in the individual case . . . The parties may agree beforehand to say, 'Such and such a sum shall be damages if I break my agreement.' The very reason why the parties do in fact agree to such a stipulation is that sometimes, although undoubtedly there is damage and undoubtedly damages ought to be recovered, the nature of the damage is such that proof of it is extremely complex, difficult, and expensive. If I wanted an example of what might or might not be said and done in controversies upon damages, unless the parties had agreed beforehand, I could not have a better example than that which the learned counsel has been entertaining us with for the last half-hour in respect of the damage resulting to the Spanish Government by the withholding of these vessels beyond the stipulated period. Supposing there was no such bargain, and supposing the Spanish Government had to prove damages in the ordinary way without insisting upon the stipulated amount of them, just imagine what would have to be the cross-examination of every person connected with the Spanish Administration such as is suggested by the commentaries of the learned counsel:

'You have so many thousand miles of coast-line to defend by your torpedo-boat destroyers; what would four torpedo-boat destroyers do for that purpose? How could you say you are damaged by their non-delivery? How many filibustering expeditions could you have stopped by the use of four torpedo-boat destroyers?'

My Lords, I need not pursue that topic. It is obvious on the face of it that the very thing intended to be provided against by this pactional amount of damages is to avoid that kind of minute and somewhat difficult and complex system of examination which would be necessary if you were to attempt to prove the damage. As I pointed out to the learned counsel during the course of his argument, in order to do that properly and to have any real effect upon any tribunal determining that question, one ought to have before one's mind the whole administration of the Spanish Navy—how they were going to use their torpedo-boat destroyers in one place rather than another, and what would be the relative speed of all the boats they possessed in relation to those which they were getting by this agreement. It would be absolutely idle and impossible to enter into a question of that sort unless you had some kind of agreement between the parties as to what was the real measure of damages which ought to be applied.

Then the other learned counsel suggests that you cannot have damages of this character, because really in the case of a warship it has no value at all. That is a strange and somewhat bold assertion. If it was an ordinary commercial vessel capable of being used for obtaining profits, I suppose there would not be very much difficulty in finding out what the ordinary use of a vessel of this size and capacity and so forth would be, what would be the hire of such a vessel, and what would therefore be the equivalent in money of not obtaining the use of that vessel according to the agreement during the period which had elapsed between the time of proper delivery and the time at which it was delivered in fact. But, says the learned counsel, you cannot apply that principle to the case of a warship because a warship does not earn money. It is certainly a somewhat bold contention. I should have thought that the fact that a warship is a warship, her very existence as a warship capable of use for such and such a time, would prove the fact of damage if the party was deprived of it, although the actual amount to be earned by it, and in that sense to be obtained by the payment of the price for it, might not be very easily ascertained—not so easily ascertained as if the vessel were used for commercial purposes and where its hire as a commercial vessel is ascertainable in money. But, my Lords, is that a reason for saying that you are not to have damages at all? It seems to me it is hopeless to make such a contention, and although that would not in itself be a very cogent argument because the law might be so absurd, yet it would be a very startling proposition to say that you never could have agreed damages for the non-delivery of a ship of war although, under the very same words with exactly the same phraseology in the particular contract, you might have damages if it was a vessel used for commercial purposes; so that you would have to give a different construction to the very same words according to whether the thing agreed to be built was a warship or a ship intended for commercial purposes. My Lords, I think it is only necessary to state the contention to shew that it is utterly unsound.

Then there comes another argument which, to my mind, is more startling still: the vessel was to be delivered at such and such a time; it was not delivered, but the fleet the Spanish Government had was sent out at such a time and the greater part of it was sunk, and, says the learned counsel, 'If we had kept our contract and delivered these vessels they would have shared the fate of the other vessels belonging to the Spanish Government, and therefore in fact you have got your ships now, whereas if we had kept our contract they would have been at the bottom of the Atlantic.' My Lords, I confess, after some experience, I do not think I ever heard an argument of that sort before, and I do not think I shall often hear it again. Nothing could be more absurd than such a contention, which, if it were reduced to a compendious form such as one has in a marginal note, would certainly be a striking example of jurisprudence. I think I need say no more to shew how utterly absurd such a contention is. I pass on to the other question.

It seems to me, when one looks to see what was the nature of the transaction in this case, it is hopeless to contend that the parties only intended this as something in terrorem. Both parties recognised the fact of the importance of time; it is a case in which time is of the essence of the contract and so regarded by both parties, and the particular sum fixed upon as being the agreed amount of damages was suggested by the defendants themselves, and to say that that can be unconscionable or something which the parties ought not to insist upon, that it was a mere holding out something in terrorem, after looking at the correspondence between the parties is, to my mind, not a very plausible suggestion. I have, therefore, come to the conclusion that the judgments of the Courts in Scotland are perfectly right in this respect, and I think there is no ground for the contention that this is not pactional damage agreed to between the parties—and for very excellent reason agreed to between the parties—at the time the contract was entered into."

Lord Halsbury (and the rest of the bench) thus gave a green (or perhaps green and amber) light to what are perhaps better called pre-estimated damages clauses. Characteristically, he allowed a "blatant interference with freedom of contract",[40] but within limits. It was not until the following decision that those limits were more systematically proscribed.

Dunlop Pneumatic Tyre Co Ltd v New Garage and Motor Company Ltd 12–72
[1915] A.C. 79
House of Lords: Lords Dunedin, Atkinson, Parker of Waddington and Parmoor

Dunlop supplied tyres to New Garage under a provision which bound New Garage not to sell tyres to customers at less than Dunlop's current list prices, and to pay £5 as liquidated damages for every tyre sold in breach of the agreement.

Dunlop sold tyres below the current list price. In an action for breach of contract, the House of Lords held that the stipulated sum was liquidated damages.

"LORD DUNEDIN: . . . 12–73

My Lords, we had the benefit of a full and satisfactory argument, and a citation of the very numerous cases which have been decided on this branch of the law . . . In view of that fact, and of the number of the authorities available, I do not think it advisable to attempt any detailed review of the various cases, but I shall content myself with stating succinctly the various propositions which I think are deducible from the decisions which rank as authoritative:—

1. Though the parties to a contract who use the words 'penalty' or 'liquidated damages' may prima facie be supposed to mean what they say, yet the expression used is not conclusive. The Court must find out whether the payment stipulated is in truth a penalty or liquidated damages. This doctrine may be said to be found passim in nearly every case.
2. The essence of a penalty is a payment of money stipulated as in terrorem of the offending party; the essence of liquidated damages is a genuine covenanted pre-estimate of damage (*Clydebank Engineering and Shipbuilding Co v Don Jose Ramos Yzquierdo y Castaneda* [1905] A. C. 6.
3. The question whether a sum stipulated is penalty or liquidated damages is a question of construction to be decided upon the terms and inherent circumstances of each particular contract, judged of as at the time of the making of the

[40] *Elsey v Collins Insurance Agencies* (1978) 83 D.L.R. 1, 15, per Dickson J.

contract, not as at the time of the breach (*Public Works Commissioner v Hills* [1906] A. C. 368 and *Webster v Bosanquet* [1912] A. C. 394.

4. To assist this task of construction various tests have been suggested, which if applicable to the case under consideration may prove helpful, or even conclusive. Such are:

   (a) It will be held to be penalty if the sum stipulated for is extravagant and unconscionable in amount in comparison with the greatest loss that could conceivably be proved to have followed from the breach. (Illustration given by Lord Halsbury in *Clydebank* Case [1905] A. C. 6.)
   (b) It will be held to be a penalty if the breach consists only in not paying a sum of money, and the sum stipulated is a sum greater than the sum which ought to have been paid (*Kemble v Farren* 6 Bing. 1). This though one of the most ancient instances is truly a corollary to the last test. Whether it had its historical origin in the doctrine of the common law that when A. promised to pay B. a sum of money on a certain day and did not do so, B. could only recover the sum with, in certain cases, interest, but could never recover further damages for non-timeous payment, or whether it was a survival of the time when equity reformed unconscionable bargains merely because they were unconscionable—a subject which much exercised Jessel M.R.in *Wallis v Smith* 21 Ch. D. 243—is probably more interesting than material.
   (c) There is a presumption (but no more) that it is penalty when 'a single lump sum is made payable by way of compensation, on the occurrence of one or more or all of several events, some of which may occasion serious and others but trifling damage' (Lord Watson in *Lord Elphinstone v Monkland Iron and Coal Co.* 11 App. Cas. 332).

On the other hand:

   (d) It is no obstacle to the sum stipulated being a genuine pre-estimate of damage, that the consequences of the breach are such as to make precise pre-estimation almost an impossibility. On the contrary, that is just the situation when it is probable that pre-estimated damage was the true bargain between the parties (*Clydebank* Case, Lord Halsbury [1905] A. C. at p. 11; *Webster v Bosanquet* Lord Mersey [1912] A. C. at p. 398)."

12–74 This statement, although laying down clear guidelines, has raised more questions than it answers. What is a "genuine pre-estimate of damage" and when is that estimate of loss to be made? Who must establish that the clause is not a genuine pre-estimate? Must there be breach of contract for the limits in *Dunlop* to apply?

There is a general presumption of fact that the sum stated in the contract is a genuine pre-estimate and that presumption is strongest (and most difficult to rebut) where the damage is difficult to assess precisely. It is also the case that where the clause is invalid as a penalty and the loss suffered is greater than the sum stipulated in the clause, the innocent party need not rely on the clause and can claim as unliquidated damages in excess of the figure in the clause, if such were the true loss.[41] These and many other uncertainties surround such clauses, even though they form a very important part of commercial practice. The matter is further complicated by the fact that internationally the *Dunlop* test is no longer applied as widely as it was and that the

[41] See *Dingwall v Burnett*, 1912 S.C. 1097. (Contrast the position in England, where the person relying on the clause is not entitled to recover more than the sum stipulated in the penalty: *Cellulose Acetate Co v Widnes Iron Foundry Co* [1933] A.C. 20.)

UK practice is gradually diverging from prescriptions in international conventions and the like. The matter is thought so important in many quarters that the Scottish Law Commission issued a very detailed and thorough *Discussion Paper on Penalty Clauses*[42] which led to the following report and proposal for legislative change.

Report on Penalty Clauses 12–75

Scottish Law Commission Report No.171 (April 1999)

"**Part 1 Introduction**

European and international developments

1.7 There has been recent European and international activity in the area of penalty clauses ...

1.8 There has been a convergence between the formerly disparate approaches of civil and common law countries. In countries whose law was heavily influenced by the English common law, penalty clauses were once viewed as completely unenforceable. In countries whose law was heavily influenced by the Napoleonic code, however, penalty clauses were fully enforceable and were seen as an effective way to encourage performance and thus avoid litigation. However, most modern or recently revised civil codes now depart from the general principle of literal enforcement by allowing penalties to be modified where they are 'disproportionately high' or 'excessively high' or 'excessive' or 'unreasonable' or 'manifestly excessive'.[19] In common law systems the distinction between penalties and liquidated damages can be used, or deliberately blurred, to allow recovery of many sums which the parties have agreed should be payable in the event of non-performance. Thus, in many systems it seems that a degree of compromise has been accepted in order to minimise the tension between the desire to enforce what was agreed between the parties and the injustice of enforcing an excessively penal provision.

1.9 This convergence of approaches is reflected in recent international instruments on the subject. The Council of Europe's Resolution on Penalty Clauses, for example, assumes that penalty clauses are, in general enforceable, but provides that

'The sum stipulated may be reduced by the court when it is manifestly excessive.'[20]

The Principles of European Contract Law provide that

'(1) Where the contract provides that a party who fails to perform is to pay a specified sum to the aggrieved party for such non-performance, the aggrieved party shall be awarded that sum irrespective of his actual loss.

(2) However, despite any agreement to the contrary the specified sum may be reduced to a reasonable amount where it is grossly excessive in relation to the loss resulting from the non-performance and the other circumstances.'[21]

The Unidroit *Principles* have a virtually identical provision.[22]

...

---

19 Treitel, *Remedies for Breach of Contract: A Comparative Account* (1988) at p.224.
20 Art.7.
21 Art.4.508.
22 Art.7.4.13.

---

42 Scottish Law Commission, *Discussion Paper on Penalty Clauses* (Scot. Law Com. Discussion Paper No.103, 1997).

12–76 **Part 2 The existing law**

The development of the law

2.1 The early law was concerned with exorbitant sums payable by borrowers and was affected by attitudes to usury.[1] It was accepted that the court could modify exorbitant penalties in bonds for the payment of money even if they were disguised as payments to cover the expenses of recovering the debt.[2] Stair regarded the modification of exorbitant penalties in bonds and contracts as part of the *nobile officium* of the Court of Session.[3] Extortionate credit bargains are now regulated by statute.[4]

2.2 A practice which gave rise to much early litigation was miscropping by tenants under leases. It was held that the words used in the lease were not conclusive. A payment might be a penalty in reality, and subject to control by the court, even if it was described as an additional rent.[5] However, it was also held that if the lease genuinely gave the tenant an option to follow a less desirable rotation of crops on paying additional rent, then the court could not interfere.[6] Penalty clauses in leases of agricultural holdings are now controlled by statute.[7]

2.3 After the middle of the nineteenth century most of the reported cases on penalties were concerned with building contracts[8] or contracts for the supply of goods or services.[9] In one case in 1869, concerning a penalty for delay in supplying a crane to shipbuilders, the court took the view that whether a clause provided for a penalty or for liquidated damages made no difference.[10] If the amount payable on breach was, in all the circumstances, exorbitant and unreasonable it could be modified. Unfortunately these statements were later 'explained' as meaning that if a liquidated damages clause were exorbitant it must really be a penalty clause.[11]

The modern law

12–77 2.4 Two House of Lords decisions at the beginning of this century are often taken as encapsulating the present law.

2.5 In *Clydebank Engineering and Shipbuilding Co Ltd v Don Jose Ramos Yzquierdo y Castaneda*,[12] it was confirmed that the courts had to look at the substance rather than the form of the provision in deciding whether it provided for liquidated damages, in which case it would be enforceable, or a penalty, in which case it would not be enforceable. If a sum was proportionate to the rate of non-performance it was *prima facie* liquidated damages. An extravagant or unconscionable or exorbitant provision, however, would not be enforced.

2.6 In *Dunlop Pneumatic Tyre Co Ltd v New Garage and Motor Co Ltd*[13] Lord Dunedin summed up the law ...

---

[1] *Home v Hepburn* (1549) Mor 10033; McBryde, *Contract*, para.20-127.

[2] This power was given a statutory basis by the Debts Securities (Scotland) Act 1856 which provided that "it shall be in the power of the court to modify and restrict such penalties, so as not to exceed the real and necessary expenses incurred in making the debt effectual".

[3] Stair, IV.3.2; I.10.14; III.2.32; IV.5.7, and IV.51.11.

[4] Consumer Credit Act 1974, ss.137–140 (replacing earlier provisions in the Pawnbrokers Acts 1872 and 1960 and the Moneylenders Acts 1900 and 1927).

[5] *Stratton v Graham* (1789) 3 Pat. 119.

[6] *Fraser v Ewart*, February 25, 1813, F.C.

[7] The Agricultural Holdings (Scotland) Act 1991, s.48 (re-enacting earlier legislation) prevents a landlord obtaining more than actual loss in consequence of "any breach or non-fulfilment" of a term or condition of the lease.

[8] See, *e.g.* *Johnston v Robertson* (1861) 23 D. 646.

[9] See, *e.g.* *Forrest and Barr v Henderson, Coulborn & Co* (1869) 8 M. 187.

[10] *Forrest and Barr v Henderson, Coulborn & Co*, above.
[11] See *Clydebank Engineering and Shipbuilding Co Ltd v Don Jose Ramos Yzquierdo y Castaneda* (1904) 7 F. (H.L.) 77 at 82.
[12] (1904) 7 F. (H.L.) 77.
[13] [1915] A.C. 79. This was an English case but Lord Dunedin's statement of the law is accepted as describing the law of both Scotland and England.

Part 3 A more realistic test

. . .

Assessment and recommendation

3.8 We doubt whether there would be any difference in practice between 'grossly excessive' and 'manifestly excessive'. Either term would do, as indeed would various alternatives such as 'exorbitant and unreasonable'. On reflection, however, we have come down in favour of the term 'manifestly excessive' which is used in the Council of Europe's recommendation on this subject. It helps to give the impression that the court should not examine agreed sanctions too closely. The excessive nature of the penalty should be immediately obvious to anyone considering it. It should be manifest and not a matter of nice calculation. Unless the specified penalty is manifestly excessive, it should be enforceable. **12–78**

3.9 In our discussion paper,[9] we considered whether a comparison with actual loss should always be required when it was being considered whether a penalty was excessive. We provisionally decided against such a requirement.[10] We remain of this view. Penalty clauses are often used in cases where actual loss cannot, or cannot readily, be ascertained or where compensation for actual monetary loss would be an inadequate remedy. In such cases important factors to be taken into account in assessing whether a penalty is manifestly excessive might be the nature of the contract and the importance of providing an adequate incentive to due performance. However, in many ordinary cases a comparison between the amount or value of the penalty and the amount of the aggrieved party's loss will be a factor to be taken into account in deciding whether the penalty is manifestly excessive.[11]

3.10 Taking into account the comments by consultees on our earlier proposal, we now recommend that:

(1) There should continue to be judicial control over contractual penalties.

(2) The criterion for the exercise of that control should be whether the penalty is 'manifestly excessive'.

(3) Penalties which are not manifestly excessive should be enforceable even if they cannot be regarded as based on a genuine pre-estimate of loss.
(Draft Bill, clause 1)

---

[9] Para.4.9.
[10] Para.4.10.
[11] Para.4.10.

Part 4 Penalties arising otherwise than on breach

The existing law

4.1 Under the existing law the control of penalty clauses applies only where there is a breach of contract and not, for example, where one party exercises a contractual option **12–79** to perform in one way rather than another or where a contract is terminated early under its terms.[1]

4.2 The distinction has been important in hire purchase cases where the exercise of an option to terminate may result in clauses, which are in effect penal in nature, escaping all judicial control.[2]

4.3 The problem has also been illustrated by two cases involving claims arising on the appointment of a liquidator or a receiver. In the first case,[3] an agreement between the parties provided that in the event of a company going into voluntary liquidation, the owners of machinery let to the company should be entitled to retake possession of the machinery, that the agreement should terminate and that the company should pay the owners a sum of money calculated as set forth in the agreement. The court held that the law on penalty clauses did not apply other than in cases involving breach of contract. In the second case,[4] the lessees of an item of printing equipment became liable upon the appointment of a receiver (when the lessors exercised an option to terminate the agreement), for the rental payments which would have been payable during the unexpired period of the contract. The court held that the sum due under the contract was not subject to the rules on penalties, which were confined to cases of breach of contract, and was accordingly enforceable.

Criticisms of existing law

12–80 4.4 Because the law on penalty clauses applies only when there is a breach of contract, the law seems to favour the party who acts in breach rather than the party who complies with the terms of the contract. This is because the party in breach can seek judicial scrutiny of a penalty whilst the other party may not. 'The hirer who honestly admits that he cannot keep up payments and terminates his agreement may have to pay a penalty; his less responsible neighbour, who simply goes on failing to pay the instalments until the finance company is forced to take action, may escape ... I have felt myself oppressed by that consideration. But the remedy is for the legislature.'[5]

4.5 Take, for example, the instance of a contract terminated on an event such as insolvency or the appointment of an insolvency practitioner.[6] As we have seen, the rules on penalty clauses do not apply. Potentially, claims made in the insolvency may therefore be out of all proportion to any loss. Indeed, they may be extravagant or unconscionable or excessive. This could severely prejudice other creditors and might provide an incentive to draft extortionate provisions, and to have a termination without a breach.

4.6 Indeed there exists general scope for avoiding the rules on penalties by drafting contracts so that, instead of providing for one method of performance with a penalty for breach, they provide options for performing in different ways, some of which may attract heavy penal consequences.

Extension of control over penalty clauses

12–81 4.7 In our discussion paper we suggested that control over penalty clauses should not be confined to cases involving breach of contract.[7] We provisionally proposed that it should extend to cases where the penalty is due if the promisor fails to perform, or to perform in a particular way, under a contract or where there is an early termination of a contract. In expressing our proposal in this limited way, rather than just referring to penal provisions generally, we were attempting to distinguish between sanctions due on breach or some other abnormal event and any consideration due in respect of the performance of the contract in the normal way. We had no wish to subject ordinary bad bargains to judicial control.

4.8 The Council of Europe's Resolution on Penal Clauses is confined to clauses which provide that if the promisor fails to perform the principal obligation, he is to be liable to pay a sum of money by way of penalty or compensation.[8] However, it recommends governments of member states 'to consider the extent to which the principles . . . can be applied, subject to any necessary modifications, to other clauses which have the same aim or effect as penal clauses'.[9]

. . .

Recommendation

4.10 We accordingly recommend that: 12–82

2. Judicial control over contractual penalties should not be confined to cases where the penalty is due when the promisor is in breach of contract. It should extend to cases where the penalty is due if the promisor fails to perform, or to perform in a particular way, under a contract or when there is an early termination of a contract.
(Draft Bill, clause 1(3))

---

[1] *Export Credits Guarantee Department v Universal Oil Products Co* [1983] 1 W.L.R. 399; *Bell Brothers (HP) Ltd v Aitken*, 1939 S.C. 577; *Granor Finance Ltd v Liquidator of Eastore Ltd*, 1974 S.L.T. 296; *EFT Commercial Ltd v Security Change Ltd*, 1992 S.C. 414.

[2] See *e.g. United Dominions Trust (Commercial) Ltd v Bowden*, 1958 S.L.T. (Sh.Ct) 10, where the hirer of a car had to pay up to 75% of the total cost of hiring as agreed compensation for depreciation when the contract was terminated. This case was followed in *United Dominions Trust (Commercial) Ltd v Murray*, 1966 S.L.T. (Sh.Ct) 21. See also *Mercantile Credit Co Ltd v McLachlan*, 1962 S.L.T. (Sh.Ct) 58; *Eurocopy Rentals Ltd v McCann Fordyce*, 1994 S.L.T. (Sh.Ct) 63; *Common Services Agency v Purdie and Kirkpatrick Ltd*, 1995 S.L.T. (Sh.Ct) 34; *Eurocopy (Scotland) plc v Lothian Health Board*, 1995 S.L.T. (Sh.Ct) 34; 1995 S.L.T. 1356; *Eurocopy Rentals Ltd v Tayside Health Board*, 1996 S.L.T. 224; 1996 S.L.T. 1322.

[3] *Granor Finance Ltd v Liquidator of Eastore Ltd*, 1974 SLT 296.

[4] *EFT Commercial Ltd v Security Change Ltd*, 1992 S.C. 414.

[5] *Mercantile Credit Co Ltd v McLachlan*, 1962 S.L.T. (Sh.Ct) 58 at 59. Similar comments can be found in *Mercantile Credit Co Ltd v Brown*, 1960 S.L.T. (Sh.Ct) 41 at 43, and *Campbell Discount Co Ltd v Bridge* [1961] 1 QB 445 at 458.

[6] See *Granor Finance Ltd v Liquidator of Eastore Ltd*, 1974 S.L.T. 296 and *EFT Commercial Ltd v Security Change Ltd*, 1992 S.C. 414.

[7] Para.4.18. The Law Commission for England and Wales reached a similar provisional conclusion in its Working Paper on *Penalty Clauses and Forfeiture of Monies Paid* (W.P. No. 61, 1975) paras 17–26.

[8] Art.1.

[9] Para.2 of the recommendations introducing the principles.

. . .

Part 6 Court powers 12–83

. . .

Power to consider substance rather than form

Existing law

6.2 It is well established in the existing law that a court should have regard to substance rather than form in deciding whether a clause is a penalty clause.[1]

. . .

Recommendation

6.6 We therefore recommend that:

4. In deciding whether a clause comes within the scope of the new law on penalty clauses regard should be had to the substance of the clause rather than to its form.
(Draft Bill, clause 1(3))

12–84 **Power to consider all the circumstances**

Existing law

6.7 Under the current law a court puts itself, initially at least, in the position of the parties at the time of contracting.[4] What happened after the date of contracting may, however, influence the court in its decision as to whether the clause was exorbitant at the time of contracting.[5] The court may be forced to consider the events following the contract if, for example, the sum sued for is based on the number of days the defender was late in making delivery, or the changing salary of an employee under a contract of service.[6]

6.8 Currently, it is logical for the court to take the circumstances at the date of the contract as the starting point because of the application of the 'genuine pre-estimate of loss' test. If, however, the courts were to ask whether a penalty was 'manifestly excessive' in a particular case it would be inappropriate to restrict consideration to the circumstances prevailing at the time at which the contract was made. Provided that the sum payable is not extortionate in relation to the breach or other triggering event which has in fact occurred, there is no reason why the penalty should not be enforceable.

. . .

12–85 *Recommendation*

6.12 On balance, and having taking into account the views of consultees, our view remains that, if the law were to move away from the liquidated damages test, as we have recommended,[9] there would be great advantage in expressly stating that all the circumstances can be taken into account in deciding whether a penalty is manifestly excessive. The focus of attention under the new rule would not be whether the penalty clause was enforceable in the abstract but whether the penalty could be enforced in the particular circumstances which had arisen. Although not advocating the disturbance of parties' agreements merely because, with the benefit of hindsight, their predictions were incorrect, we believe that under the approach which we recommend the only realistic course is to allow courts to consider all the circumstances, including those arising after the date of the contract, in assessing whether a penalty is manifestly excessive.

6.13 We accordingly recommend that:

5. The enforceability of a penalty should be judged according to all the circumstances, including circumstances arising since the contract was entered into.
(Draft Bill, clause 1(4))

12–86 **Power to modify**

Existing law

6.14 In the earlier law it was accepted that the court could modify exorbitant penalties or irritancies. Stair, for example, pointed out that penalties in bonds which were disguised as payments for the creditor's expenses would be modified to the real expenses and damages but that the court took 'slender probation of the true expenses' and in practice allowed more than would have been allowed in the absence of the penalty clause.[10] He also saw the allowance of time to purge an irritancy as an example of the power to modify.[11] The courts regularly talked of modifying penalties.[12] Under the present law it is accepted that the power of a court which finds a provision to be a penalty clause, and hence unenforceable, is restricted to awarding provable loss.[13] The court, at present, has no power to modify the penalty by reducing the sum to a reasonable amount. By contrast, most of the modern or recently revised civil codes envisage the possibility that excessive penalties can be modified to a reasonable amount,[14] as do recent international instruments.[15]

Advantages and disadvantages of power to modify

6.15 Enabling the courts to modify penalties would facilitate the enforcement of parties' original agreements as nearly as possible. If, for example, a contract has been entered into where non-performance could not be compensated by damages to the satisfaction of one of the parties, then it is likely that an unusually high penalty may be included in the contract in order to encourage performance. The promisee may also have paid a high price under the contract to obtain the other party's agreement to the substantial penalty. If non-performance ensues, in the absence of a power to modify, the penalty may be struck down as unenforceable and the aggrieved party's only course of action would be to resort to a claim for damages—a remedy earlier rejected as inadequate. The advantage to the contract breaker is only too clear. A power to modify would thus encourage performance and, in the event of litigation, prevent the contract breaker from achieving an unfair advantage. **12–87**

6.16 Generally, a power to modify would provide the courts with the ability to enforce penalty clauses in a fair and flexible manner, thus facilitating the achievement of the objectives of penalty clauses. This might be particularly useful if it is made clear that a penalty may consist of a transfer of, or forfeiture of, property. There may be cases where a forfeiture of property would be a manifestly excessive penalty by itself but would cease to be so if the person forfeiting the property were compensated for improvements made to it. A power to modify would be particularly useful, if not essential, in those cases where a claim for damages exists[16] or where the penalty has been agreed precisely because damages would be difficult or impossible to quantify.

6.17 On the other hand, a power to modify could be criticised on the ground that it would be difficult for the courts to exercise. Deciding on what an appropriate penalty might be may not be an easy task. Another criticism might be that such a power would lead to uncertainty. In relation to penalty clauses, however, judicial control already leads to an element of uncertainty. It is not clear that such uncertainty would be greater if a power to modify existed in addition to a power to strike down the penalty totally. It could be argued that the uncertainty is greater in the absence of a power to modify, because there is more of a gamble involved.

6.18 It might be suggested that a power to modify would encourage the use of manifestly excessive penalty clauses because the party seeking to insert them would know that, at worst, the penalty might be modified and that the other party would have to litigate to obtain the modification. This argument, however, could be levelled just as easily at the present law where an aggrieved party may opt for damages in the event of a penalty being unenforceable. It must be remembered that contractual penalty clauses require the agreement of both parties. The promisor would not wish to agree to a manifestly excessive penalty clause, even if there was the possibility of judicial modification of any penalty incurred. Moreover the court would have a discretion as to modification. A court might decline to exercise its power to modify and might hold the penalty manifestly excessive and entirely unenforceable.

Recommendation

6.22 We consider that a power to modify would be in line with the approach recommended in this report and would be useful in some cases and essential in others. We therefore recommend that:

6. A court, or a tribunal or arbiter adjudicating on a penalty clause, should have power to modify a manifestly excessive penalty so as to make it enforceable—by for example, reducing its amount or attaching conditions to the exercise of the relevant right.
(Draft Bill, clause 4)

---

[1] *Stration v Graham* (1789) 3 Pat. 119; *Johnston v Robertson* (1861) 23 D. 646; *Forrest and Barr v Henderson, Coulborn and Co.* (1869) 8 M. 187.

. . .

[4] *Clydebank Engineering and Shipbuilding Co Ltd v Don Jose Ramos Yzquierdo y Castaneda* (1904) 7 F. (HL) 77 at 82.

[5] *Forrest and Barr v Henderson, Coulborn and Co* (1869) 8 M. 187; *Craig v McBeath* (1863) 1 M. 1020; *Mercantile Credit Co v Brown*, 1960 S.L.T. (Sh.Ct) 41.

[6] *Paterson v South West Scotland Electricity Board*, 1950 S.C. 582.

. . .

[9] Para.3.10.

[10] IV.3.2.

[11] IV.18.3.

[12] See, *e.g.* the statements in *Craig v McBeath* (1863) 1 M. 1020 and *Forrest and Barr v Henderson, Coulborn and Co* (1869) 8 M. 187.

[13] There is a theoretical debate as to whether the court modifies the penalty to the amount of the provable loss or holds the penalty completely unenforceable and awards damages for the provable loss as if there had been no penalty clause. See the discussion paper, paras 5.30–5.35.

[14] See the discussion paper, paras 1.10, 5.41–5.47.

[15] See the Council of Europe's Resolution on Penal Clauses, Art.7; the *Principles of European Contract Law*, Art.4.508; the Unidroit *Principles*, Art.7.4.13.

[16] *E.g.* where the penalty is not payable in respect of a breach of contract.

INDEX

extortion, 5–01, 5–36—5–41